ENCYCLOPEDIA OF
Homosexuality

EDITED BY WAYNE R. DYNES

ASSOCIATE   WARREN JOHANSSON
EDITORS   WILLIAM A. PERCY

WITH THE
ASSISTANCE OF   STEPHEN DONALDSON

St-J
St James Press
Chicago and London

VOLUME 2
M - INDEX

Published in the United Kingdom by
St. James Press
2-6 Boundary Row
London SE1 8HP
England

Originally published in the United States by
Garland Publishing, Inc., New York.

British Library Cataloguing-in-Publication Data

Encyclopedia of homosexuality.
  1. Homosexuality
  I. Dynes, Wayne 1934-
  306.766

    ISBN 1-55862-115-6 vol. 1
    ISBN 1-55862-116-4 vol. 2
    ISBN 1-55862-147-4 set

*Book and cover design by
Renata Gomes*

Printed on acid-free, 250-year-life paper.
Manufactured in the United States of America.

MABLEY, JACKIE "MOMS" (LORETTA MAY AIKEN; 1894–1975)

American **black** comedienne. Born to poverty in North Carolina, Mabley ran away at the age of 14 to join a minstrel show. After many difficult years, she gained renown and worldly success through her frank portrayals of race and sex before all-black audiences. Mabley was a favorite at **Harlem**'s legendary Cotton Club and at the Club Harlem in Atlantic City, where she performed with such headliners as Count Basie, Duke Ellington, and Cab Calloway. In her last years, she was able to achieve a "cross-over" to general audiences, appearing on television with Merv Griffin, Johnny Carson, Flip Wilson, and Bill Cosby.

Although one of her best-known personas was of a man-crazy older black woman, Mabley regarded herself as a lesbian. Her performances made fun of older men, satirizing the way they wielded authority over women as well as the fading of their sexual powers. In 1986–87, the black actress Clarice Taylor commemorated her life and work in an Off Broadway play with music entitled *Moms*, employing texts by Alice Childress and Ben Caldwell.

While she may be compared with such blues singers as Bessie Smith and Billie Holliday, Mabley's pioneering role in stand-up comedy was unique, and clearly linked to the difference in her sexual orientation.

MACDONALD, HECTOR, SIR (1853–1903)

British general. Born the son of a poor Scottish crofter (tenant farmer) on the Black Isle, Macdonald made a career in the British Army, choosing to live abroad where social barriers and conventions mattered far less and a meager officer's wages went farther than they did at home. In 1870, lying about his age, he joined the 92nd, or Gordon, Highlanders, and as the purchase of officers' commissions had been abolished, it was possible for a mere private to rise through the ranks and even become a general—which he did. He served in India and accompanied his regiment during a British incursion into Afghanistan. Sent to fight against the rebellious Transvaal colony, he was captured by the Boers in the signal defeat of the British at Majuba Hill in June 1881.

In the spring of 1884 Macdonald married in the old Scots style by pledging his troth to his bride with only heaven as their witness. The common law marriage remained a secret even to the War Office, and to the world Macdonald was a stern, somewhat forbidding figure. A son was born to the couple in 1887—an only child. The reason for the concealment was that married officers were discouraged in Victorian times; it was believed both that they were less than efficient and that it was unfair to expose them to the constant perils of disease and death on the remote periphery of the Empire. In 1884 also, Macdonald transferred to the first battalion in order to see active service in Egypt. In Cairo he met Horatio Herbert Kitchener, a young officer of the Royal Engineers, under whom he commanded the Egyptian brigade in the Nile campaign against the Dervishes. Here his bravery and resourcefulness earned him the thanks of Parliament and the appointment of aide-de-camp to Victoria, an honor continued by Edward VII. His valor on the battlefield won him the nickname of "Fighting Mac." During the Boer War of 1899–1901 he commanded the Highland Brigade and was wounded in action.

In 1902 he was appointed commander of the troops in Ceylon (Sri Lanka). However, "grave suspicions" had begun to form about him, inspired in part by the offence he had given to the closeknit society of British planters on the island. Accused of a "habitual crime of misbehavior with several schoolboys," he requested leave to return home to discuss the matter with the War Office, which directed a court of inquiry to be held in Ceylon. Macdonald set off in the hope that a session "behind closed doors" might settle the matter without embarrassment, but in Paris, on learning from the European edition of the *New York Herald* that the story had been broken to the press, he returned to his hotel room and shot himself in the head. Thus his outstanding military career ended tragically because the homosexual side of his character had been disclosed to an intolerant society.

BIBLIOGRAPHY. Trevor Royle, *Death Before Dishonour: The True Story of Fighting Mac*, Edinburgh: Mainstream Publishing Company, 1982.
Warren Johansson

MACHO

The term *macho* is simply the Spanish word for "male," but in the context of the American gay **subculture** it designates the male whose virility is ostentatious and often emphasized by conventional symbols—in a word, the tough guy as opposed to the feminine or even effeminate type of homosexual. There is a subtlety in the use of the term in English, because the Latin American norm of heterosexual manhood strikes the Anglo-Saxon as exaggerated and inappropriate. The **Hemingway** image, with its ambivalent and often overstated masculinity, played a role in the adoption of the Hispanic term.

The contrast between the "super-male" and the sensitive androgynous type has recurred at various times and places. The split within the early German homosexual rights **movement** stemmed in large part from the unwillingness of the virile man-lovers to identify with the effeminate "inverts." Benedict **Friedlaender** and Karl Franz von Leexow focused on this virile type, as did (in part) Edward **Carpenter** in England. They cited in evidence the long line of homosexual or bisexual military leaders, from **Alexander the Great** and Julius **Caesar** in antiquity to Prince **Eugene** of Savoy and Charles XII of Sweden in the eighteenth century, not to mention many figures in the medieval Islamic and Japanese annals of warfare. This phase of the pre-1933 movement was all but forgotten by the 1950s, and the homophile movement of that decade stressed the effeminate model who could pursue "real men," but would never think of becoming one. This style of behavior was almost normative in the gay subculture of that era.

In the 1960s, however, gay circles saw the emergence of a new style of manliness, influenced in part by a trend toward proletarianization in the **counterculture**: blue jeans and casual clothing, rock music, the surliness known as "attitude," beer instead of cocktails. The leather cult emerged as a distinctive minority style, making inroads even into the mainstream of the gay subculture. The emphasis on the masculine culminated in the **clone** look, with its emphasis on rugged, though neat clothing (the Hollywood/television fantasy of how men dressed in the American West of the late nineteenth century), and a body kept in good shape by regular exercise in the gymnasium.

Some observers claim that the macho aspect of the homosexual subculture is strongly conditioned by the inner anxieties that many gay men harbor on the subject of their own maleness, which is not an absolute and unalterable given but a matter of physical culture and personal grooming and dress. In other words, butchness must be maintained, its presence can never be taken for granted. There are also pressures to conform to the current notion of what is acceptable and appealing. The haircuts and informal clothing of one generation are out-of-date in the next. American culture has come to tolerate an increasing amount of exposure of the body: what was strictly beachwear forty years ago is now *de rigueur* in metropolitan areas in summertime, hence there is greater pressure on the American male to "keep his body in shape."

At the same time, the ideological currents of the late 1960s led many heterosexual men to adopt styles of dress and hairdo that would have been intolerably effeminate in earlier decades. Such shifts in the definition of masculinity have given men a greater freedom to express their maleness in symbols congruent with their self-image.

Warren Johansson

MACKAY, JOHN HENRY (1864–1933)

German poet, novelist, and anarchist writer. Mackay also campaigned for the acceptance of man/boy love.

Born in Greenock, Scotland, on February 6, 1864, Mackay was scarcely two years old when his Scottish father, a marine insurance broker, died. His mother then returned with her son to her native Germany, where she later remarried. After completing his schooling, Mackay was briefly an apprentice in a publishing house and then attended several universities, but never completed his studies. An allowance from his mother, who was of a well-off merchant family, gave him enough money to live modestly, so that he was able to choose the career of writer without worrying about eventual sales of his books. This situation changed in later years, especially after World War I when runaway inflation in Germany wiped out the value of the annuity he had purchased with money inherited from his mother. Thus his last years were spent in relative poverty. He settled in **Berlin** in 1892 and died there on May 18, 1933.

Mackay began publishing in 1885, but instant fame came in 1891 with his non-novel *Die Anarchisten* (The Anarchists), which also appeared in English that same year and was quickly translated into six other languages. He also published short stories, several volumes of lyric poetry, and in 1901 *Der Schwimme* (The Swimmer), one of the first literary sports novels. This output was then interrupted, but when his Collected Works were printed in 1911, they already filled eight volumes. In the meantime he was engaged in a literary campaign, using the pseudonym Sagitta, to promote the acceptance of man/boy love. The effort was crushed in 1909 by the state, which simply declared the Sagitta books immoral and ordered them destroyed. But Mackay completed and published underground a one-volume complete edition in 1913. In 1926, again as Sagitta, Mackay released his classic novel of man/boy love, *Der Puppenjunge* (The Hustler), which is set in the milieu of boy prostitutes in Berlin in the 1920s.

At the time, Mackay was nearly unique in not basing his argument on a biological theory of homosexuality (e.g., the theory of "sexual intermediates" of Magnus **Hirschfeld**) or on a glorification of male cultural values. As an individualist anarchist, Mackay applied his principle of "equal freedom for all" to all relations between and within the sexes. He did not exalt man/boy love above others. For Mackay, all forms of love, if truly love, were equally valid. That love between men and boys was possible he knew from his own experience; and he rejected the reformist efforts of Hirschfeld, who was willing to raise the legal "age of consent" (Hirschfeld proposed sixteen) in order to gain the legalization of adult homosexuality. Mackay basically saw his fight for "the nameless love" (as he called it) as part of the general struggle for the right of the individual to freedom from all oppression of whatever kind.

BIBLIOGRAPHY. Edward Morning, *Kunst und Anarchismus: "Innere Zusammenhänge" in den Schriften John Henry Mackay*, Freiburg im Breisgau, Germany: Verlag der Mackay Gesellschaft, 1983; Thomas A. Riley, *Germany's Poet-Anarchist John Henry Mackay*, New York: Revisionist Press, 1972; K. H. Z. Solneman, *Der Bahnbrecher John Henry Mackay: Sein Leben und sein Werk*, Freiburg im Breisgau, Germany: Verlag der Mackay Gesellschaft, 1979.

Hubert Kennedy

MAMLUKS

The Mamluk military elite, purchased anew in each generation from the steppes of Eurasia, ruled Egypt and Syria from 1249, when they defeated an invading army of Crusaders led by Louis IX, until they were overcome by the mass army of Napoleon in 1799. Their unusual social system suggests the interlinked acceptance of homosexuality, relatively high status of women, and lack of inheritance. Yet amidst the details of battles and palace intrigues in histories of the period, there is disappointingly little evidence of the everyday life even of the rulers.

Neither the wealth nor the status of Mamluk could be inherited. Upon the death of a warrior, his property, house, goods, wife, children, and slaves were sold for the benefit of the treasury. Thus, the common motivation in most social systems of passing on wealth and position to one's children was missing among the Mamluks. Their children were proscribed from becoming soldiers, as the elite of the next generation was always recruited afresh from Eurasia. Attempts were made to pass the sultanate itself through primogeniture, but time after time the throne was usurped by the strongest amir. A more successful attempt by lesser Mamluks to guarantee a place for descendants was to endow mosques and libraries tended by heirs, who could not directly receive any patrimony.

Mamluks did not much mix with the Arab populations they were bought to protect. For the most part they despised the Arab language and kept to their native Turkish dialects. They also lived apart from the existing cities in their own colonies and only rarely intermarried with local notables' daughters.

Along with many special prerogatives (notably their own courts of law), the Mamluks were distinguished from the rest of the population by being forbidden divorce (out of keeping with a fundamental tenet of Islam). Still more astonishing, their wives received a fixed salary from the state, just as did the warriors themselves. These two customs greatly enhanced the autonomy of women among the Mamluks, although they may also have discouraged marriage altogether.

The mode of homosexuality favored by the Mamluks was **pederasty**, apparently with boys recruited from the wilderness who were undergoing military training, rather than with boys raised in civilized Egypt. None of the military historians who have written about the Mamluks seem to have surmised that sexual attraction might have played some part in selecting which boys to buy.

In addition to the general pederasty with the cadets, several sultans showed marked favoritism for some of their courtiers. The most interesting case is that of an-Nasir Abu as-Sa'adat Muhammad, who scandalized his society in 1498 by the "unnatural" interest he showed in the (black) Sudanese slaves who bore firearms, and for their leader, Farajallah, in particular. The youthful Sultan attempted to raise the status of the modern weapons that only a few years later would be turned on the traditional, brave, sword-wielding Mamluk cavalry with devastating results by the Ottomans. This attempt to modernize the technology of warfare was motivated in part by the Sultan's taste for the black men who had been assigned the use of the low status weaponry. Homophobic historians are, thus, presented the dilemma that the sultan who tried to modernize the army—in precisely the way they recognize was necessary for continued military success—was a youth of "unstable character" much given to "debauchery" and that his "debauchery" was inextricably tied together with his motivation for the modernization that might have maintained Mamluk military superiority.

When the (white) Mamluks revolted and slew Farājallah, they told the Sultan, "We disapprove of these acts [of favor for the black firearm users]. If you wish to persist in these tastes, you had better ride by night and go away with your black slaves to faroff places!" (Lewis, p. 75–76). The sultan agreed to desist.

When the Mamluks began the sixteenth century with one of their traditional thirteenth century cavalry charges against the Ottoman infantry of Selim I, they met their first defeat. Several centuries later, Ottoman control began to slip, the Mamluk aristocracy regained dominance, and the venerable cavalry charge that was their only tactic—whether against Mongols, Ottomans or French armies of Louis IX or Napoleon—was mowed down by a fusillade from Napoleon's army. Rifles of 1798 proved even more deadly than the 1517 models that had first revealed the obsolescence of the Mamluk cavalry.

The Mamluks exemplify a social system not built on family aggrandizement and patrimony. Without inheritance, with a very slim likelihood of living to a peaceful old age, and with wives paid directly by the state, the usual motivation for building families was lacking. The Mamluk case shows that both a military tradition and an advanced artistic culture can be transmitted with no bonds of blood. The guardians of high Arabic civilization from barbarians (whether Mongols or Crusaders), each new unrelated generation of recruits to the elite was noted for appreciation for and patronage of the arts. The Mamluks built the mosques, palaces,

and tombs that are the glory of Cairo, and "delighted in the delicate refinement which art could afford their home life, were lavish in their endowment of pious foundations, magnificent in their mosques and palaces and fastidious in the smallest details of dress, furniture and court etiquette" (Lane-Poole, p. 97), though they were recruited from their rude surroundings not for their aestheticism or refined tastes but for their horsemanship and prowess with sword and bow.

BIBLIOGRAPHY. David Ayalon, *Gunpowder and Firearms in the Mamluk Kingdom*, second ed., Totowa, NJ: Frank Cass, 1978; John B. Glubb, *Soldiers of Fortune*, Toronto: Hodder & Stoughton, 1973; Stanley Lane-Poole, *Cairo*, London: J. S. Virtue, 1898; Bernard Lewis, *Race and Color in Islam*, New York: Harper & Row, 1971.

Stephen O. Murray

MANICHAEANISM

Manichaeanism was a religion based on the teachings of the visionary prophet Mani (ca. 216–ca. 277 A. D.), who lived and was crucified in southern Babylonia. His doctrine incorporated various aspects of the **Gnostic**, **Christian**, and **Zoroastrian** belief systems, to which he fused a neo-Platonic and **Stoic** ethical strain.

Essentially Manichaeanism was a dualistic religion in which the universe was divided into kingdoms of light and darkness which were in juxtaposition, each reaching out into infinity. Heading one force was the Prince of Darkness while the other was directed by the God of Light. Human beings were called to choose which of the forces they would follow while they were on earth, where their material body acted as a prison for the spiritual light. To gain the Kingdom of Light it was necessary to free the spirit from the material: this separation could be accomplished by avoiding sexual activities and refusing to eat foods resulting from sexual union. Light was released and grew stronger by eating bread, vegetables, or fruit, and was kept imprisoned by eating flesh, drinking wine, or having sexual intercourse—all of which reinforced the material (and evil) aspects of being human. Intercourse leading to procreation was particularly offensive because it caused other souls to be imprisoned in spiritual bodies, thus continuing the cycle of good versus evil. Such an austere religion was difficult to practice, but the Manichaeans effected a compromise for their believers by dividing all humanity into three principal groups: (1) the Elect, those believers who had renounced private property, practiced sexual abstinence, observed strict vegetarianism, and never engaged in trade; (2) the Auditors, those who believed in the teachings of Mani and who were striving to become Elect, but could not as yet adhere to all the requirements; and (3) all the rest of humanity who did not know or accept Mani's teachings and were lost in wickedness.

St. **Augustine** of Hippo, who died in 430, was a Manichaean for some eleven years. Undoubtedly the system's austerity in sexual matters left an enduring impress in his later Christian writings, and these in turn were enormously influential in imposing a standard of sex only within marriage and solely for procreation for over a thousand years in the West.

Apart from some eastern offshoots, Manichaeanism proper died out in the early **Middle Ages**. Yet a related dualistic sect called the Paulicians appeared in the Byzantine Empire, and this trend in turn contributed to the Bogomil **heresy**, documented in the Balkans by the tenth century. In its turn Bogomilism spread to the West, where it became known as Albigensianism or Catharism. The Albigensians were popularly known as *bougres*, from their Bulgarian origin. (This term eventually gave rise to the English word **bugger**.) Although the highest rank of Albigensians, the *perfecti*, were supposed to abstain from sex, in keeping with the Manichaean precept that procreation was

evil, this principle was apparently interpreted by some as allowing same-sex activity which could not lead to impregnation. One must allow, of course, for some exaggeration on the part of Catholic opponents, whose zeal to stamp out Catharism knew no bounds. Yet a detailed trial record (1323) of one Arnold of Verniolle, residing in Pamiers in the south of France, seems to provide an authentic record of the combination of sodomy and heresy.

BIBLIOGRAPHY. Peter R. L. Brown, "The Diffusion of Manichaeism in the Roman Empire," in his *Religion and Society in the Age of Saint Augustine*, London: Faber, 1977, pp. 94–118.

Vern L. Bullough

MANN, KLAUS (1906-1949)

German author and critic (prose, lyric, drama, and nonfiction). The themes of his literary works, to a greater extent than is the case with other authors, rose out of his own life: loneliness, suffering, outsider status, decadence, opposition to fascism, and homosexuality. This oldest son of Thomas **Mann**'s six children, Klaus played an important role in German letters as an author, as a critic of the younger generation of authors, as the editor of a literary/political journal, and as a forceful voice against the Third Reich while in American exile.

Mann lived an openly homosexual life and included homosexual characters or portrayals of homosexuality in many of his works. In his first collection of stories, *Vor dem Leben* (Before Life, 1925), he describes a vision of homosexuality which would change little over the years: homosexuality is normal and natural, but the status of the homosexual as outsider makes integration into any larger social unit impossible. While this stance affords a critical view, it dooms the homosexual continually to attempt to open a door forever closed to him.

In his autobiography, *The Turning Point* (1942), Mann wrote: "To be an outsider is the one unbearable humiliation." That belief shaped his portrayal of male and female homosexuality in such works as *Anja und Esther* (1925), *Der fromme Tanz* (1926), *Abenteuer* (1929), and *Treffpunkt im Unendlichen* (1932). In each, same-sex love ends or bears no hope of success, for those involved switch their affections to a heterosexual love object, literally succumb to the futility of such relationships and die, or continue to suffer a lonely existence. Often, homosexuality functions as a symbol of the decadence Mann saw within his own generation. A futile society can engender only futile love. Mann's view of homosexuality does not transcend that hopelessness as his literary works did not articulate a method of social or political change. This stands in contrast to his non-fiction works and to his involvement with the U.S. Army in working for the end of National Socialism and toward a more egalitarian future. Yet his fictional view seems to reveal the truth, for Klaus Mann chose to end the existence in which he could not overcome that hopelessness.

In exile, he turned to the past for inspiration: *Alexander* (1930), *Symphonie pathétique* (1935), and *Vergittertes Fenster* (1937). These great men from the homosexual pantheon—**Alexander the Great**, **Tchaikovsky**, and **Ludwig II**—function, however, as lonely figures whose love separates them from their societies. His most openly homosexual novel, *Windy Night, Rainy Morrow* (also called *Peter and Paul*, 1947), remained unfinished at his death.

BIBLIOGRAPHY. Wilfried Dirschauer, ed., *Klaus Mann und das Exil*, Worms: Georg Heintz, 1973; Michel Grünewald, *Klaus Mann, 1906–1949: Eine Bibliographie*, Munich: edition spangenberg im Ellermann Verlag, 1984; Fredric Kroll, ed., *Klaus-Mann-Schriften-reihe*, vols. 1–5, Wiesbaden: Edition Klaus Blahak, 1976–1986; Friedrich Kröhnke, *Propaganda für Klaus Mann*, Frankfurt am Main: Materialis Verlag, 1981; Susanne Wolfram, *Die tödliche Wunde: Über die Untrennbarkeit von Tod und Eros in Werk von Klaus Mann*, Europäische Hochschulschriften, Reihe 1, vol. 935, Frankfurt am Main: Peter Lang, 1986; Stefan Zynda, *Sexualität bei Klaus Mann*, Bonn: Bouvier Verlag Herbert Grundmann, 1986.

James W. Jones

MANN, THOMAS (1875–1955)

German novelist, critic, and essayist. One of Germany's greatest authors of this century, Mann bridged nineteenth-century realism and twentieth-century **modernist** style. For many in the German-speaking world, Mann was the epitome of the "educated burgher," that man of the upper middle class whose comfortable economic status allowed him to acquire not only possessions, but a cultural education, a spirit of refinement and good taste. Indeed, his works and his interests reflect such a status. Many of his stories and novels depict an upper middle class milieu and the concerns of family life (e.g. *Buddenbrooks*, 1901). Mann was greatly influenced by some of the nineteenth century's German cultural icons: Wagner, Nietzsche, **Schopenhauer**, as well as by the music and theories of Arnold Schoenberg.

Yet he battled against a complete identification with such a status. His major works speak in an ironic narrative voice in order to create distance between the subject matter (*Bürgertum*, family life, in short: integration into the status quo) and the author. Indeed, one of Mann's major themes throughout his work concerned the central problematic of his own life, namely how to combine the seemingly antithetic spheres of artist and everyday man without destroying the uniqueness of art in the banalities of existence. An additional, more personal struggle, but still evident in his work and related to the previous theme, is Mann's sexual desire for other males, particularly for males younger than himself. In his "essay" "Über die Ehe" ("On Marriage": actually part of a letter to a friend), Mann described his belief that homosexuality was linked to death, and, although it may play a role in the formation of states (compare the theories of **Blüher**), it undermined the family.

These two themes are woven into several of Mann's best works. *Death in Venice* (1912) depicts the downfall of the writer Gustav Aschenbach after he becomes entranced with a young Polish boy, Tadzio, whom he sees at a Venice resort. The boy embodies the spiritual beauty Aschenbach has sought but his desire and pursuit of this angelic youth led him to his death. Adolescent love between two males figures strongly in *Tonio Kröger* (1903) and in *Magic Mountain* (1924) as a factor which separates the character more strongly involved (Tonio and Hans Castorp, respectively) from his society. *Doctor Faustus* (1947), Mann's great novel about Germany's descent into fascism, also contains an artist figure who is homosexual. As in the other works, homosexuality is linked to creativity, but when it is not overcome by a move to heterosexuality, balanced by other forces, it inevitably leads to destruction.

BIBLIOGRAPHY. Gerhard Harle, *Die Gestalt des Schönen: Untersuchung zur (Homosexualitätsthematik in Thomas Manns Roman 'Der Zauberberg,'* (Hochschulschriften Literaturwissenschaft, vol. 74), Königstein: Hain Verlag bei Athenäum, 1986; C. A. M. Noble, *Krankheit, Verbrechen und künstler-isches Schaffen bei Thomas Mann* (Europäische Hochschulschriften, Reihe 1, vol. 30), Bern: Herbert Lang, 1970; T. J. Reed, *Thomas Mann: "Der Tod in Venedig": Text, Materialien, Kommentar*, Munich: Carl Hanser Verlag, 1983; Hans Wanner, *Individualität, Identität und Rolle: Das frühe Werk Heinrich Manns und Thomas Manns Erzählungen "Gladius Dei" and "Der Tod in Venedig,"* Munich: Tuduv-Verlagsgesellschaft, 1976.

James W. Jones

MANSFIELD, KATHERINE (1888–1923)

New Zealand short-story writer, who resided mainly in England and Europe. Born Katherine Mansfield Beauchamp, the writer was the daughter of a prominent New Zealand businessman. In 1908 she moved to England where she gravitated to bohemian circles, entering into a brief unhappy marriage. A year in Germany produced a volume of short stories, *In a German Pension* (1911). Returning to England, she began an important liaison with the editor and writer John Middleton Murry, whom she finally married in 1918. While personal circumstances and the state of her health denied Mansfield the stamina to attempt novels, she compensated by refining her short stories so that each made a memorable point.

Having developed tuberculosis in 1917, after World War I she moved to the country establishment of the mystic George Gurdjieff, La Prieuré near Fontainebleau south of Paris. Exuberantly heterosexual himself, Gurdjieff had a number of lesbian and male homosexual acolytes, and was at the time generally linked with "advanced thought." Unfortunately, Mansfield's guru decided to cure her tuberculosis by having her sleep in an unheated stable. She died at La Prieuré in January 1923.

When she was eighteen and still living in New Zealand, Mansfield fell in love with a painter, Edith Bendall, who was twenty-seven. However, Bendall soon married, denying that there was anything sexual in her relations with the future writer. Yet Mansfield had a lifelong relationship with Ida Constance Baker, whom she met at college in London. She referred to Baker as her "slave," her "wife," "the Monster," and "the Mountain." Despite these epithets, throughout her life Mansfield relied on her, taking her money and possessions when she needed them. Later, when her circumstances had improved, she employed Baker as a personal servant. It is possible that D. H. **Lawrence** based the lesbian episode in his novel *The Rainbow* on material gleaned indirectly from Mansfield. While some have denied any lesbian component to Mansfield's personality, the cumulative evidence makes this denial unlikely, and she is probably best regarded as bisexual.

BIBLIOGRAPHY. Claire Tomalin, *Katherine Mansfield: A Secret Life*, New York: Knopf, 1987.

Evelyn Gettone

MARDI GRAS AND MASKED BALLS

Both of pagan-Christian descent, they survive in only a few places today. Carnivalesque observances of this kind have long homosexual associations.

Historical Development. Mardi Gras and masked balls are not so very distant cousins, stemming from a union of pagan religious-theatrical festival and Christian tradition. The ancient Greek *Anthesteria,* honoring **Dionysus** with a boisterous mid-February revel in which celebrants, costumed as satyrs and maenads, drank, danced, feasted, and fornicated, later blended with the Roman *Februa* and *Lupercalia*. Held at the same time of year, the latter two rituals centered on protecting villagers and livestock from wild animal molestation and on insuring fertility. In earlier centuries, young nobles, acting as priests and called *creppi* or "he-goats," chased naked youths, representing wolves, through grain fields in a sort of reverse-molestation rite. The chase climaxed in festal drinking, feasting, and ceremonial sacrifice of dogs (wolves) and goats. Celebration of this festival continued until A.D. 494 when the church, unable to suppress it, shrouded it in religious garb as the Feast of the Purification of the Virgin. But many of the common people continued the old celebration.

Similarly, the masking associated with Greek and Roman drama, which itself had originated in music, song, and dance in honor of Dionysus, survived in medieval mystery, miracle, and morality plays, and in more altered form, in mummers' plays and morris dances. A small gilded beard instead of a full mask, for example, served in the Middle Ages to identify St. Peter. Italy's medieval **theatre** retained a particularly high degree of spectacular and magnificent display, as well as use, in street processions, of "players' wagons" from the old Roman carnival tradition.

Because medieval religious drama focused on the Easter passion, Holy Week would normally have been the time for most of that age's theatrical presentations and their associated festivities. But the forty-day pre-Easter period of Lenten fasting and abstinence imposed by the church in the seventh century precluded that possibility. Instead, Lent effectively separated the devotional elements of theatre from the festive. The devotional elements were reserved for Holy Week itself, and the feasting and festive elements were made to precede the beginning of Lent.

Thus the pre-Lenten festivities fell during the time of year still associated, in the minds of many people, with the old pagan holiday. Thus evolved the tradition of plunging into fleshly indulgence during the days immediately preceding Lent. The last day for such worldly indulgence, the Tuesday before Ash Wednesday (which begins the Lenten season, and on which Catholics go to confession and are forgiven the sins committed in days previous), became the high point of the new festival. Hence *Mardi gras*, or "Fat Tuesday" in French alludes to a fatted ox paraded through the streets on that day, before being butchered for feasting. In England the day is called Shrove, Shrift, or Confession Tuesday, and in the Germanies *Fastendienstag* or *Fastnacht* for the fasting required out of religious obligation to follow that day. Common in medieval Europe, and extravagant by the time of the Renaissance, Mardi Gras celebrations survived the sixteenth-century religious reformations only in Catholic Europe, for

Protestantism either abandoned Lent altogether or so weakened its strictures as to make any pre-Lenten fleshly indulgence pointless. In England, for example, the only remaining vestige of the festival is a now near-forgotten tradition of eating buttered pancakes on Shrove Tuesday.

On the other hand, the Reformation did not affect the tradition of masking. Renaissance princes and nobles took theatrical performances out of the hands of clerics, secularized them, and made them into court spectacles and masquerades. The anonymity afforded by masks soon made masked balls, as well as individual masking for an evening on the town, the rage of Europe. So masked, a Romeo could infiltrate the household of his love; a Turk could move unobserved; and a **Henri III** of France could accost boys in Paris dives. The practice migrated from the continent to England, beginning in 1717 when the Swiss entrepreneur John James Heidegger organized public masked balls at the Haymarket Theatre in London.

For the most part, both Mardi Gras and masked balls died with the *ancien régime* at the end of the eighteenth century. Mardi Gras survived the nineteenth century to continue into the twentieth in only a few Catholic cities, most notably in **Venice**, Munich, and Cologne; on certain Caribbean islands, where it acquired many African attributes; in Rio de Janeiro, where it was heavily influenced by both African and American Indian tradition; and in **New Orleans**, where, while incorporating a number of African and Indian elements, it preserved more of its original European form.

In Sydney, **Australia**, the local Gay Pride March was moved from wintry June to late-summer February and became the Sydney Gay Mardi Gras, which is now the city's largest annual street parade.

New Orleans. The Louisiana city was the only place where masked balls continued into modern times in an unbroken tradition. Begun as private affairs in the mid-1700s, when the city was the rough-and-tumble capital of France's frontier Louisiana colony, masked balls represented little more than stylish imitations of the mother country's social forms. But before the end of the eighteenth century, public dance halls adopted the trappings of masque and rented simple disguises to those among their patrons who failed to bring their own. After the United States purchased Louisiana from Napoleon in 1803 and began trying, largely unsuccessfully, to force its Anglo-Protestant values and racial attitudes on carefree, tolerant, French, Catholic New Orleans, the masked balls took on a new importance for the city's natives. Behind their masks and under their cloaks, rich and poor, black and white, free and slave, straight and gay could meet and mingle, safe from authorities. Along with "quadroon balls," public dance halls run by free people of color but to which white men regularly went in quest of free black mistresses, masked balls flourished until the Civil War ended slavery in the 1860s. Vestiges of the masque tradition remain today, not only in the markedly high degree of **transvestism** seen in New Orleans streets, but in the pronounced and unparalleled delight that the local population, black as well as white, takes in the inordinate number of female impersonators featured by straight nightclubs throughout the city.

New Orleans' masked balls also bore, historically, a direct relationship to the city's Mardi Gras. Celebrated since the original French colonizers landed at the mouth of the Mississippi River on Fat Tuesday of 1699, Carnival came under hostile attacks from the city's new American masters after the Louisiana Purchase. During the first half of the nineteenth century, the ballrooms, of which the "Salle de St. Louis" and the "Café de Paris" were particularly notorious for their racial and sexual mix, served as meeting and robing places for groups bent upon holding Mardi Gras masques and parades.

Unable to stamp out Mardi Gras, the ruling American elite changed its tactic, and in 1857 simply coopted the holiday. By the end of the century it had tied Carnival into the world of New Orleans high society. The Mardi Gras season became the social season; debutantes reigned, and continue to reign today, as queens of the fifty or more "krewes," the Carnival organizations that hold parades; and the spectacular masked balls to which the parades lead function as the city's debutante parties.

The pageantry and costuming, the anonymity of masking, and the freewheeling tolerance and sexual permissiveness characteristic Carnival made it a natural attraction for homosexuals. From early on, individuals as well as organized groups took part in the festival, first with greater decorum and later with greater abandon. In the nineteenth and early twentieth centuries, groups of affluent young men, still dressed in white-tie formals from balls the night before, drank, sang, and danced together in the streets on Mardi Gras day, but went little further.

Black celebrants, on the other hand, showed considerably more exuberance. A group of black transvestites calling themselves "The Million Dollar Dolls," made Carnival appearances from the 1920s through the 1940s dressed in extravagant wigs, sequined blouses, and leotards covered with hundreds of one-dollar bills. In 1931 the King of Zulu, the major black Carnival krewe, chose as his queen one of the city's most outrageous female impersonators. And the relationships of the *runners*, *spy boys*, and *flag boys*, youths who attend the needs of the *braves* of the nine famous, and curious, straight, black, all-male Carnival groups called "Indians," are reminiscent of the relationships between ancient Greek warriors and their young pages.

In 1959 a number of individuals who had been masking in groups for some years formally organized the first gay Mardi Gras krewe, Yuga-Duga. Established *ad hoc* as a mockery of straight krewes and balls, it caught on and lasted a rocky three years, including a police raid on its first ball, only to disband in 1962. But other gay krewes, intent upon establishing permanent social organizations, immediately formed. By the end of the eighties, there were twelve, including one all-female organization. The gay krewes now closely copy, and often equal in size and wealth, the straight krewes they once parodied. Each holds a series of "King Cake" parties that begin on Twelfth-night (January 6) and end at Mardi Gras; some have elaborate parades. All stage, during Carnival season, huge masked balls featuring spectacular tableaux that rival, or sometimes surpass, their straight counterparts. The gay balls fill the five weeks before Mardi Gras day. Though technically private affairs, the balls fill with invited guests, most of whom are straight, the 2,000-plus-seat civic arenas in which they are held. This popularity makes them, far and away, the largest regularly scheduled gay social events in the world.

Lucy J. Fair

MARÉES, HANS VON (1837–1887)

German painter. Marées was born into comfortable circumstances in Dessau, where his father was a jurist and poet and his mother a cultivated scion of a Jewish banking family. After study with Karl Steffeck in Berlin in 1853–54, he gravitated to Munich, then Germany's premier center of artistic culture. There he struck up a friendship with the society painter Franz von Lenbach, who in 1864 took him to Italy where Marées subsisted for a time making copies of the Old Masters. Since the time of Goethe, Italy had been the promised land of sensitive Germans, and Marées, even more loyal than the Italophile painters of the time (the "Deutsch-Römer"), was to remain there for the rest of his life—except for the period 1869–73 which he passed in Berlin and Dresden. Italian landscapes and Italian men (especially peasants and fishermen)—together with such Renaissance masters as Signorelli, Giorgione, and **Michelangelo**—were to provide unfailing sources of inspiration. These interests contributed to his mastery—unsurpassed for his time—of the theme of the male nude. Marées' frescoes in the Zoological Institute of Naples (1873) were his first monumental works—an impulse he continued in his celebrated triptychs.

Marées, who never married, maintained a lifelong pair bond with the art theorist Konrad Fiedler (1841–1895). His deepest attachment, however, was to the sculptor Adolph von Hildebrand, ten years his junior, who helped him with the Naples frescoes. For several months the two artists lived in virtual isolation in the monastery of San Francesco near Florence, where Hildebrand posed for a major Marées canvas *Three Youths among Orange Trees* (1875–80). Later, to the painter's sorrow, relations lapsed.

Marées' work is characterized by a rich coloristic chiaroscuro that creates a mysterious bond between his figures and their landscape setting. The prevailing mood is one of arcadian nostalgia, suffused with classical and medieval reminiscences—the former recalling such contemporaries as the French painters Puvis de Chavannes and Odilon Redon, and the latter the English Pre-Raphaelites. Several canvases show a man who, while embracing a woman, looks wistfully at a third figure, a man—as if pondering the choice between female and male love. Marées' last major work is an enigmatic version of *The Rape of Ganymede* (1885).

Marées had no immediate followers and was little appreciated until the twentieth century. Even today his works defy assimilation into any of the standard sequences of the history of art; they belong to a category of their own, accessible only to a select few.

BIBLIOGRAPHY. Christian Lenz, et al., *Hans von Marées*, Munich: Prestel, 1987.

Wayne R. Dynes

MARLOWE, CHRISTOPHER (1564–1593)

English playwright and poet. Born two months before Shakespeare, Marlowe was the son of an established and respectable shoemaker in Canterbury, where he attended the King's School, later going on to take both his B.A. and M.A. degrees at Corpus Christi College, **Cambridge**. One month before he was to appear for his commencement in 1587, amid rumors of his conversion to Catholicism and flight to France, the university received a letter from the Queen's Privy Council excusing his absence and assuring them of his loyal service to Elizabeth. This letter has created a great deal of speculation about the dashing and iconoclastic young man's activities, suggesting that he was probably working as a government spy.

The final six years of his short life were spent in London where "Kit" Marlowe was usually involved in something scandalous or illegal, resulting in several scrapes with the law and at least one prison confinement. During these years, he produced his slender but highly important and influential canon: *Dido Queen of Carthage* (1586), *Tamburlaine I and II* (1597), *The Jew of Malta* (1589), *The Massacre at Paris* (1590), *Edward II* (1591), *Doctor Faustus* (1592), and the unfinished narrative poem *Hero and Leander*. The first genuine poet to write for the English theatre was killed, perhaps assassinated, under highly suspicious circumstances by a knife wound to the head in a private dining room in an inn in Deptford on May 30, 1593.

Twelve days before his death, Marlowe had been arrested on charges of atheism, stemming in part from his reputation and from accusations made against him by fellow playwright Thomas Kyd, who had been charged earlier; Kyd's claim was based on documents seized during a search of the rooms both men used for writing. This sort of sensation followed Marlowe throughout his life and, seemingly, was fostered by the poet himself.

After his death, claims about him became more personal and explicit. In the proceedings of his inquest, government informer Richard Baines claimed that Marlowe had said that "all they that love not Tobacco & Boies were fooles," and in 1598, Francis Meres wrote that he "was stabbed to death by a bawdy seruing man, a riuall of his in his lewde loue." However characteristic of what we do know of Marlowe's life, these posthumous comments do little to establish his homosexuality.

However, Marlowe's work does demonstrate an understanding and compassion for mythological and historical homosexuality. His *Hero and Leander* deals directly with Jupiter's passionate infatuation for **Ganymede**, a story which is also mentioned in *Dido*, and his masterwork, *Edward II*, based on fact, can be considered the first gay play in English.

An effeminate child, **Edward** was given as a companion the orphaned son of a Gascon knight at age 14 by his royal father, who hoped that the handsome and virile 16-year-old Piers Gaveston would exert a positive and masculine influence on his son. However, Edward fell passionately in love, and the king banished Gaveston in 1307. Marlowe's play begins shortly after this point with Edward (who had become king upon his father's death) immediately recalling his love to court, much to the anger of his barons, who demand Gaveston's permanent banishment. Edward, more the lover than the ruler, will accept nothing of this and even shares his throne with Gaveston, who is eventually seized and beheaded. Enraged in his grief, Edward involves himself in a bloody civil war, eventually taking another lover, young Spenser, who also is killed by the barons. Edward himself is seized, forced to abdicate, and, in 1327, is murdered by having a heated poker inserted into his anus, "intended as just retribution for his sins." In this one play, Marlowe surpasses the achievements of many explicitly gay writers in his sensitive and complex portrayal of a doomed and passionate relationship between two men caught up in a repressive and homophobic society.

BIBLIOGRAPHY. Alan Bray, *Homosexuality in Renaissance England*, London: Gay Men's Press, 1982; Paul H. Kochner, *Christopher Marlowe: A Study of His Thought, Learning, and Character*, Durham, N.C.: University of North Carolina Press, 1946.

Rodney Simard

MARRIAGE

It has long been observed that many married men and women have sexual desires for members of their own sex. In the case of those who are primarily homosexual in orientation (Kinsey **Incidence** nos. 4 to 6), the question which follows is why they marry. Marriage may be camouflage, a response to societal or familial pressure, and the relationship unconsummated; marriages of convenience between gay men and lesbians are not unknown. Marriage may also occur because the person does not understand or is unable to accept his or her sexual makeup; some of the latter group turn to marriage with the unrealistic hope of changing themselves. The desire for children is a motive for some, as is a desire for the public commitment and legal rights only available, at present, to heterosexual couples. Some simply happen to fall in love with a member of the opposite sex and try to make the best of it, and some, while preferring sexual partners of the same sex, or the anonymity and promiscuity readily available in the gay male world, prefer a marital partner of the opposite gender. A successful union of this kind is possible if honesty and tolerance are found on both sides, or if the **bisexual** partner is able to keep any extramarital activities from the other partner. Some report that a person aware and accepting of the homosexual component within him- or herself makes a better partner in a heterosexual relationship.

In the case of married persons who are primarily heterosexual (Kinsey 1 or 2), the problem is somewhat different: how to deal with occasional erotic desires for a partner of the same gender. In theory this is equally a problem for those in homosexual relationships who desire occasional sexual interaction with members of the opposite sex, and interest in the opposite sex can be more threatening to a homosexual relationship than same-sex interest is to a heterosexual one. Because male–female sex is less freely available for men than male–male sex, however, the question comes up less often. Again, the problem is not sexual activity but how the desired activity is viewed and the extent to which it threatens or is permitted to threaten the primary relationship. Not all desires need to be satisfied through activity, and questions of commitment, maintaining sexual interest, and protection from sexually transmitted diseases come up in relationships regardless of sexual orientation.

Marriage among members of the same sex existed in ancient **Rome** but then disappeared until the present century, when it has returned as a goal for some gay people. Even for heterosexuals, marriage is becoming an emotional union and commitment rather than an arrangement to produce and protect children, and if it is that then there is no rational reason why marriages of homosexuals should not be endorsed by society. This proposal is controversial, however, even in the gay community, since marriage has long been viewed by **libertarian** thinkers as an outmoded and repressive institution, and a significant number of homosexuals, male and female, have "come out" from very unhappy marriages. Public and religious opinion is moving toward permitting same-sex unions for those desiring them. Currently they are available only in **Denmark** (in **Sweden**, while they may not marry, same-sex **couples** have more legal rights than in the U.S.). Elsewhere, ceremonies and rituals, even though they lack legal status, can serve some of the same purposes as marriage.

BIBLIOGRAPHY. Philip Blumstein and Pepper Schwartz, *American Couples*, New York: William Morrow, 1983; John Malone, *Straight Women/Gay Men*, New York: Dial, 1980; David R. Matteson, "Married and Gay," *Changing Men*, No. 19 (Spring–Summer, 1988), pp. 14–16, 45.

Daniel Eisenberg

MARTIAL, MARCUS VALERIUS (CA. 40–CA. 104)

The greatest epigrammatist in Latin literature and an inexhaustible source of information on sexual life in the **Rome** of the first century. Born in Bilbilis in Spain, he settled in Rome at the age of 24, living as a client of the Senecas, his renowned countrymen, and then of other wealthy patrons. His poems won him the favor of the court; he was honored by Titus and Domitian and awarded a knighthood. A friend of the leading intellectuals of his day, he lived in the capital until 98, when he returned to his Spanish homeland for the remaining years of his life. His major work is his twelve books of *Epigrams*, published between 85 and 103. The books were arranged and numbered by the author on the basis of smaller collections and individual pieces that he had composed over the years, with dedications to particular friends and patrons. In form and language the poems exhibit the greatest possible variety: a wide assortment of meters and speech ranging from artificial heights of literary diction to the coarsest and most vulgar slang. Martial's treatment of the sexual life of his contemporaries was so candid and unvarnished—particularly where homosexuality was concerned—that many of the epigrams could not be published in the modern languages until quite recently.

Martial knew and freely described in verse all possible varieties of sexual conduct: from heterosexual love to the bizarre practices that would later occupy **Krafft-Ebing**. He disavowed personal involvement in the sexual life that he described so piquantly: *Lasciva est mea pagina, vita proba*, "My page is wanton, but my life is pure." He seems to have known happiness and pain both, but never passionate love. The poet had some close female friends, but was deeply moved by the beauty of young boys and sings their charms in various poems. In Martial's character—bisexual by nature—the homosexual side came out very strongly. A boy with the pseudonym Dindymus figures in a number of the epigrams, and like the Greek poets before him he writes of the perfume of the boy's kiss (xi, 8), but also of the disappointments which the lad made him suffer (xi, 73).

The homosexual types disparaged by the ancients—the passive-effeminate homosexual and the active-viraginous lesbian—are mercilessly satirized in his epigrams, which flagellate the *cinaedus*, the *fellator* and the *tribas*: the master who is sodomized by his slaves, the fellator with stinking breath, and the hyper-masculine tribade. Martial acknowledged that he himself desired a male who was neither too coarse nor too effeminate—the golden mean. The aesthetic element predominated in his affection for boys, as in his brief and graceful epigrams on Domitian's cupbearer (ix, 12 and 16). Though unmarried himself, he urged married men to devote themselves to their wives, no longer to younger males. Martial's work remains as a detailed record of the sexual life of the ancient world, of Rome in its heyday, a treasury of the Latin vocabulary of sexuality, and as a model for the erotic epigram in centuries to come. The entire collection survived the medieval period and continued to amuse classical scholars, as well as to inspire poets in the vernacular languages of Europe.

BIBLIOGRAPHY. Otto Kiefer, *Sexual Life in Ancient Rome*, London: Routledge & Kegan Paul, 1934.

Warren Johansson

MARXISM

Stemming from the writings of Karl Marx (1819–1883) and Friedrich Engels (1820–1895), the political philosophy of "historical materialism" emerged in the *Communist Manifesto* to revolutionaries in 1848. Today their views, or versions of them, are official policy in the countries of "actually existing socialism"—in the Warsaw Pact nations of Eastern Europe, as well as in Yugoslavia, **Albania**, the People's Republic of **China**, Vietnam, Laos, Cambodia, Ethiopia, **Cuba**, and Nicaragua. Outside these countries vigorous schools of Marxist thought have flourished, notably late nineteenth-century revisionism, democratic evolutionary socialism, and twentieth-century Trotskyism, as well as so-called "Western Marxism" and "Euro-Communism" which had a considerable impact on academic circles in the 1960s and 70s.

Foundations. The ideas of Marx and Engels fermented from radical thought in Restoration Europe, which included positivist, empiricist, anarchist, utopian socialist, and Christian-socialist strains. Unlike the individualist utopian Charles **Fourier**, Marx and Engels showed little interest in sex and sexual orientation; indeed they were typical Victorians in this respect. There can be little doubt that, as far as they thought of the matter at all, Marx and Engels were personally homophobic, as shown by an acerbic 1869 exchange of letters on Jean-Baptiste von Schweitzer, a German socialist rival. Schweitzer had been arrested in a park on a morals charge and not only did Marx and Engels refuse to join a committee defending him, they resorted to the cheapest form of bathroom humor in their private comments about the affair. Similar lack of subtlety characterizes their views on the pioneering homophile theories of Karl Heinrich **Ulrichs**, in which they confused uranism with **pederasty** and pederasty with pedication (anal intercourse).

The only important sexual passage, however, in the corpus of work published in the lifetimes of the two founders occurs in Engels' *Origin of the Family, Private Property and the State* (1884): "Greek women found plenty of opportunity for deceiving their husbands. The men . . . amused themselves with *hetaerae*; but this degradation of women was avenged on the men and degraded them till they fell into the abominable practice of pederasty (*Knabenliebe*) and degraded alike their gods and themselves with the myth of Ganymede." Engels' tracing of the problem to heterosexual infidelities is curious in view of his own record of amorous adventurism. Of course there is no truth in the innuendo propagated by a widely reprinted modern cartoon showing Marx and Engels walking hand in hand as lovers.

Setting aside these personalia, as a general principle one may concede the possibility that flaws in the initial formulation of a theory may be eliminated in its later maturing. It remains to be seen, however, whether the "flaw" of homophobia has been, or can be excised from orthodox Marxism.

Historical Unfolding. As in Freudian **psychoanalysis**, the very question of what is orthodox in Marxism has incited an enormous debate. Marx himself ejected Mikhail Bakunin and other anarchists, all of whom by doctrine tolerated homosexuality, from the First International. Yet one is on firm ground in saying that **Social Democracy** (which also had non-Marxist roots) departed in two fundamental respects: it favored gradual reform instead of revolutionary upheaval and held that attitudes could be changed before the economy was transformed—thus eroding the basic Marxist doctrine of the dependency of the cultural superstructure on the economic base. In the 1890s, some Social Democrats like August Bebel and Eduard Bernstein in Germany sought to foster a more enlightened social attitude, advocating women's rights and the elimination of laws criminalizing homosexuals. Such efforts were largely conducted among intellectuals and bureaucrats who intuited

that the masses were not yet prepared to discard inherited prejudices. The Social Democrats were after 1918 to be violently rejected on other grounds as renegades by the more orthodox wing of Marxism under the leadership of Vladimir Il'ich Lenin. Out of this difference arose, after the Russian Revolution, a sharp antagonism between European Social Democratic and Labor parties on one hand and Communist and Trotskyist groups on the other.

Some gay leftists have projected a rosy picture of homosexual life in **Russia** in the years after the 1917 revolution. Yet the abrogation of the tsarist law against sodomy was simply part of an overall rejection of the laws of the old regime, and significantly the Soviets never undertook any campaign to reduce popular prejudice against homosexuality, as they did, for example, against the inferior status of women, Great Russian chauvinism, and anti-Semitism. Also, despite much searching, no unequivocal statement in support of homosexual rights has ever been unearthed from the prolific writings of Lenin and Trotsky, even though both had lived in Western Europe at the time of the early German homosexual rights **movement**. Under Lenin Russian homosexuals fared no better—if even as well—as they had done in the last decades of tsarist rule, when such brilliant figures as **Tchaikovsky, Kuzmin**, and Kluev came to the fore.

In the 1920s some German homosexual movement figures such as Magnus **Hirschfeld** and Richard Linsert (the latter a minor Communist Party functionary in Berlin) were favorably impressed by reports of apparently enlightened attitudes in the Soviet Union—about which they had no direct knowledge. They would appear to have been the victims of an early disinformation campaign. Not everyone was taken in. Although André **Gide** proclaimed his sympathy for the Soviet Union in 1932, four years later after visiting the country he wrote openly of his disillusionment. Aware of antihomosexual legislation passed in 1934, he attempted to bring up the matter with Stalin, though without success. On publishing his defection from the "Popular Front" line he was attacked by French and Czechoslovak party stalwarts (who had previously lauded him to the skies) as a "poor bugger" who had mixed up "revolution and pederasty."

As early as the 1920s leaders of Western Communist parties began to float the idea that the public discussion of homosexuality, and the seeming increase in homosexual activity, resulted from the **decadence** of capitalism in its death throes. Homosexuality was to disappear in the healthy new society of the future. These negative attitudes also had their parallels in cultural criticism. In 1930 in the American Communist Party journal *New Masses*, Herbert Gold and others launched a campaign against "effete, fairy literature." Thornton Wilder, a principal target of the attacks, was accused of propagating a "pastel, pastiche, dilettante religion, . . . a daydream of homosexual figures in graceful gowns moving among the lilies."

After the **Nazis** came to power in Germany in 1933, Marxist proponents of the decadence theory added a new layer to these attacks in their myth of "**fascist perversion,**" some purported affinity between homosexuality and National Socialism. Leftist propaganda of this type may have played a part in Hitler's decision to liquidate his homosexual henchman Ernst **Röhm**, thereby distancing himself from the accusation. In June 1934, for example, the exiled Marxian psychoanalyst Wilhelm **Reich** opined: "The more clearly developed the natural heterosexual inclinations of the juvenile are, the more open he will be to revolutionary idea; the stronger the homosexual tendency within him . . . the more easily he will be drawn to the right." More generally, the heterosexualism that is so salient in the Marxist tradition may be augmented by the felt link between production and *reproduction*. Most Marxists are, of course, heterosexual and, in keeping with the tendency of true-believer groups to exalt all their shared traits, subject to an unthinking bias.

Despite Gide's experience, the temptations and pleasures of political pilgrimage continued as seductive as before. Wide-eyed delegations visited the Soviet Union, China, and Cuba, as often as not being taken on excursions to Potemkin villages and being regaled with highly romanticized accounts of the happiness of the masses under "actually existing socialism." After Castro's rude suppression of homosexuals in Cuba, the favorite destination of these pilgrims, who included some gay men and lesbians, shifted in the 1980s to Nicaragua, yet even there the authorities would not recognize a gay organization. Gay visits to Third World Socialist countries tend to be emotionally tinged with sympathy for nonwhite peoples as an oppressed world proletariat, mirroring the gay sense of oppression at home, while freighted with a certain amount of guilt over sexual tourism—the descent of well-heeled western gay men on the impoverished fleshpots of the tropics. Somehow sympathetic visits to struggling, Third World countries are held to atone for this perceived exploitation—even as it continues to occur.

Communist parties outside the Soviet bloc have generally been unsympathetic to homosexual participation in their activities and indifferent to gay issues. The only significant exception seems to be the independent-minded Italian Communist Party, the promoter of "Euro-Communism," which has provided material assistance to gay groups and published sensitive discussions in party periodicals. In most western countries it has been Trotskyists, with their claustrophobic and faction-ridden experience of marginality, who have provided the few organizational havens open to gay people in the world Communist movement.

Contributions of Marxism. Despite all these negative considerations, the contribution of Marxism to the movement for gay rights and to the interpretation of homosexual behavior itself merits separate consideration. When the second gay rights **movement** emerged in the form of the **Mattachine Society** in Los Angeles in 1950, a number of its leaders, preeminently Henry Hay, had backgrounds in the Communist Party (CP) of the United States. Hay used the CP model for the cellular structure he designed for Mattachine. In an era in which homosexuality was illegal in every American state, the organizational structure of a political group that had, in many countries, been forced into clandestinity in order to survive seemed relevant. The American Communist Party had also been in the forefront of the early struggle against racial segregation, and this example also proved attractive: gay rights as a form of civil rights. When the civil rights movement entered its major phase in the 1960s, Marxist groups continued active but were less visible and dominant. At this time, however, they made a major contribution to the organizing of the protests against the Vietnam war, though this was also permeated by New Left, anarchist, and hippie elements. This amalgam made its effect felt on the new gay organizations that arose in the wake of the **Stonewall Rebellion** of 1969— especially the Gay Liberation Fronts of New York and other cities. At the same time Marxist influences were appearing in some sectors of renascent feminism, and through this channel came such organizational devices as **consciousness raising**.

By the middle seventies the Marxist influence on the gay liberation movement was receding, a decline reflecting recognition of its perennial marginality in American political life and the arcane, even scholastic character of many of its intellectual debates. Before the wave ebbed, however, Marxism had caused a reexamination of the fundamentally reformist cast of the earlier movement, which saw education of the electorate and the lifting of legal restrictions as virtually the only tasks and toleration as the goal. Ridiculing such a limited approach, Marxists insisted that deep structural changes were necessary for true sexual and personal freedom and social acceptance to become possible. To be sure, many were sceptical of the specific content of Marxist promises and visions, in view of the poor performance of countries under "actually existing socialism." The imposition of Soviet-style totalitarianism in Castro's Cuba, once the cynosure of gay radicals, dashed many hopes, and rival visions came forward: anarchist, libertarian, and communitarian. But an important lesson had been learned: that a mere subtractive approach, getting rid of oppressive laws and restrictions, would not suffice. For gay men and lesbians to flourish something more fundamental was needed: not so much a political revolution as a "change of heart."

Some of the graduate students who had been converted to Marxism in academia went on to assume tenured teaching jobs. These scholars formed what has been called the "Marxist academy," and the periodicals they created were sometimes hospitable to gay scholarship. Some who found a home in this milieu held that Marxism could make a fundamental contribution to the understanding of homosexuality itself. They argued that studies of homosexual behavior had neglected the element of **class** and class struggle, which in the standard Marxist view is the chief motor of social change. While feminists had rightly criticized this exclusive model, pointing out that gender, sexual orientation, and race are also of prime importance, there can be no doubt that class differences have been neglected even in sociological work on homosexuality. Influenced by the solidarity proclaimed by the gay movement, much empirical work tends to assume a unitary model of "the homosexual" and "the lesbian."

Some scholars influenced by Marxist dialectic advanced a more fundamental criticism of what they regarded as a mistaken notion of "unchanging gayness." Noting the anachronism that results when present-minded concepts of gay people are projected back into the past, they boldly proposed that there is no single nature of homosexuality that is stable across time. It has been shown that the broader attempt to derive this demolition of the whole idea of human nature from the writings of Marx and Engels themselves is shaky, and that it really belongs to the thought of Georg Lukacs and the "Marxist-humanist" trend of revisionism that succeeded him. Also, it proved difficult to find a "historical materialist" grounding for the changing concepts of homoerotic behavior, an accommodation to the well-known Marxist sequence of slave-owning, feudal, capitalist, and socialist societies. What caused the shifts in same-sex paradigms remained mysterious. Moreover, this attack on the unchanging nature of homosexuality—on "essentialism," as the assumption of uniformity has been called—was not restricted to Marxists. The **Social Constructionists**, as the opponents of "essentialism" styled themselves, included symbolic interactionists, pragmatists, and nominalists. Still, when all is said and done, academic Marxism deserves credit for bringing into question assumptions of the historical uniformity of homosexual identities and relationships, and for asking scholars to seek an understanding of the place which these occupy within the larger framework of social change.

Finally, Marxism has made a contribution in an unexpected quarter—in the realm of theology. The 1960s and 1970s saw the rise in Latin America of "liberation theology," strongly influenced by the Marxist critique of **oppression**. Some scholars have sought to adapt this perspective to the emerging theology of the gay **churches**, where it may well serve as a useful corrective to traditionalism and liturgical preoccupations.

As this last aspect shows, the Marxist influence on homosexuality has often been indirect, mediated by feminism, by the New Left, or by liberation theology. It seems that Marxist theories must be adapted or reformulated before they can function in the study of same-sex behavior. Moreover, Marxist concepts seem more suited to posing questions than to providing firm answers. The greatest weakness of the Marxist approach is the difficulty in correlating the changes in homosexual behavior and the attitudes toward it with the technological and economic determinism that is the very heart of Marxism, not to speak of the inability (or better refusal) of Marxian thinkers to incorporate the biological dimension of human existence into their reasoning. All the same, the Marxist contribution, whether direct or indirect, has served to broaden horizons and to strengthen the trend to supplant the present-mindedness and provincialism of the gay movement and **gay studies** on 1950s lines with a new outlook that is potentially subtle, critical, and multicultural.

BIBLIOGRAPHY. David Fernbach, *The Spiral Path: A Gay Contribution to Human Survival*, Boston: Alyson, 1981; Gay Left Collective, *Homosexuality: Power and Politics*, London: Allison and Busby, 1980; Hubert Kennedy, "J. B. von Schweitzer, the Faggot Marx Loved to Hate," *Fag Rag*, 19 (1977), 6–8.

Wayne R. Dynes

MASQUERADE
See **Mardi Gras** and **Masked Balls**.

MASTURBATION
Broadly defined, masturbation is tactile sexual stimulation obtained by means other than intercourse.

Techniques. Masturbation is harmless, legal, and carries no risk of disease. Typical masturbation, involving pleasurable stroking, caressing, or massaging of the genitals and other parts of the body, is healthy fun and cannot be overdone. Soreness or chafing heals easily if treated gently, and use of a lubricant reduces irritation. For men an oil, including household oils (Crisco, cooking oil, baby oil) and some hand lotions, will work well;

for women a water-based lubricant intended for genital lubrication, such as K-Y or Astroglide, will give better results. Through experimentation with different strokes and caresses, not just on the genitals but all over the body, each person can discover what, for him or her, is most pleasurable. Some find the use of a vibrator helpful, and a variety of gadgets, store-bought or homemade, are used to assist in providing the desired sensations. However, a good masturbation machine for male use has yet to be developed. Thoughts or pictures of stimulating scenes, whether provided by individual **fantasies** or acquired **pornography**, can increase one's excitement. If desired, masturbation can be prolonged, and the intensity of orgasm enhanced, by stopping just before orgasm, to begin again when excitement has somewhat subsided.

Masturbation with friends, a common male experience of adolescence, is becoming an adult practice as well. Pairs or groups can either masturbate separately while watching and talking to each other, or partners can masturbate each other, either simultaneously or taking turns. Masturbation while talking over the telephone (**phone sex**) has been a spreading practice in the 1980s.

Masters and Johnson reported that many find masturbation produces more intense orgasms than intercourse, and it also avoids the discomfort that anal penetration produces in many men. It is also reported that masturbation by a partner produces more intense orgasms, for some, than masturbating alone. If free of guilt, masturbation is said to have a positive effect on the personality. Masturbation, alone or with a partner, can be part of a spiritual experience.

History, Men. Masturbation in males is nearly universal. It is engaged in spontaneously by infants and children, and is found in many mammalian species, although no animal other than man masturbates to orgasm on a regular basis. Anthropological evidence suggests that masturbation rituals have been part of male coming-of-age ceremonies since prehistoric times. Temporary abstention from sexual activity, including masturbation, may be presumed to have been a common means to summon extra physical performance (as today in the advice of some athletic coaches), and abstention from and indulgence in masturbation have been part of the worship of the generative powers.

Civilizations have been indifferent or hostile to adult masturbation according to the fertility which they desired. (Masturbation by children has usually been treated more leniently.) In bellicose societies, those trying to populate new land, and those subject to heavy losses from a hostile environment, there was pressure to direct sex toward reproduction, although masturbation's simplicity no doubt made it impossible to suppress. In more urban and pacifist cultures, in which population pressures were felt, reproduction then became a problem rather than a necessity. In such settings masturbation could be tolerated, along with prostitution and homosexuality, all of which were preferable to the infanticide which was common in parts of the ancient Mediterranean world.

In classical antiquity masturbation was called a "natural sexual practice," and physicians recommended it as preferable to harmful continence, and as a treatment for impotence. Indeed to be masturbated was recognized as a delicacy, and masseurs, prostitutes, and especially slaves provided this service. Anal masturbation using fingers, dildos, and eggs is reported, as is auto-fellatio. The Greek Cynic Diogenes, and others following him, openly masturbated, saying that experience revealed masturbation to be the easiest and best sexual practice, that it was not shameful and did not need to be concealed, and that masturbation could have prevented the Trojan War. Masturbation's mythical inventor was said to have been Hermes, who taught it to his son Pan.

Among the extensive sexological literature of **Islam** is the first treatise on masturbation, by the ninth-century Al-Saymari (*Encyclopedia of Islam*, article "Djins"); it is today unavailable or lost. Classical Islamic culture was supportive of partnered sex, and masturbation, especially in solitude, was mildly condemned. In part this was because one was not supposed to touch the "unclean" genitals; handless masturbation through use of a melon, though, is widely known in Arabic folklore. In the modern Islamic world it is sometimes considered more reprehensible than sodomy and bestiality. Classical Chinese culture encouraged masturbation without orgasm; emission of semen was only supposed to take place during intercourse with a woman.

Early Christian writers paid little attention to masturbation and fantasy. In the fourth and fifth centuries, with the spread of clerical **celibacy** and **monasticism**, masturbation and nocturnal emission appear as concerns, though in the hierarchy of sexual offenses these were among the mildest. Handbooks to assist priests in hearing confessions, including a treatise of Jean Gerson (1363–1429) on taking the confession of masturbators, reveal that Catholics masturbated just like everyone else. Concern within Catholicism reached a peak after the Council of Trent (1545–63), when masturbation was seen as a more serious social problem than fornication or even adultery. Masturbation and sodomy were seen as related expressions of the same allegedly perverted sexual instinct, and the former was believed to lead to the latter.

In the eighteenth century the medical profession proclaimed loss of semen a serious threat to health, and condemned above all the voluntary and unprocreative "wasting" of semen with masturbation. During the nineteenth century concern over masturbation rose to hysteria, and it was said to cause homosexuality as well as diseases: insanity, epilepsy, heart disease, impotence, and many others. Masturbation was even called "humanity's worst vice." Means employed to control masturbation included circumcision, pharmaceuticals, mechanical devices, and foods (Graham crackers and Kellogg breakfast cereals). Inasmuch as physicians based themselves solely on anecdotal (unsystematic) observations, and emission of semen is healthful rather than a threat to health, this medical "breakthrough" may confidently be attributed to puritanism.

In the twentieth century opposition to sexuality has been deflected elsewhere, and masturbation is no longer condemned in Western culture, except by the Catholic church and a small minority of conservatives. The influential **Kinsey** surveys (1948, men; 1953, women), documented how widespread masturbation is. Physicians have admitted that masturbation is harmless, and masturbation is an important part of sex therapy. Enlightened advice books recommend to parents that they allow their children privacy to masturbate. That adolescents need to masturbate to become fully functioning sexual adults is recognized, although the point is not made, in the United States, in sex education materials directed to youth. (Masturbation is presented as harmless but optional; instruction in masturbation is only given informally, usually by peers.) There are no figures by which to check, but it seems likely that over the past generation there has been more masturbation and less guilt about it. The recent boom in pornography is itself evidence of a similar increase in masturbation. It remains a socially suspect practice, however, and is often viewed as a poor alternative to intercourse. In most of the Third World masturbation is still condemned.

History, Women. As with all aspects of women's sexuality, the history of female masturbation is much less known than is that of men; since it did not involve semen, it was seldom discussed by moralists. Furthermore, what glimpses one has of female masturbation are mostly through the eyes of male writers and artists, and it is likely that in large part they observed what women found it profitable to show them, i.e., what they wanted to see. The vagina was believed to be the focus of women's sexual pleasure, and thus masturbation was seen as focused there. Masturbation with dildos made of leather and other materials was known in both Western antiquity and the Renaissance, and evidence for its existence is found in the prohibition of it by medieval Christian writers. In Islamic culture the use of both dildos and vegetables is reported. It is very likely that such masturbation occurred in many other parts of the world. Classical Chinese culture was one of the most tolerant of female sexuality, and there are reports of masturbation with a variety of objects inserted into the vagina, including small bells; special instruments made of wood and ivory, with silk bands attached, could be used by two women together or, through use of the leg, by one alone. Female masturbation using the hand alone (i.e., clitoral stimulation) is documented in antiquity, but until the nineteenth century there is no further mention of it. To the Victorians who discussed the topic, female sexual desire was threatening, and female masturbation caused terror. Clitoridectomy (surgical removal of the clitoris) was used as a "treatment," especially in England and the United States. The operation was last performed in a western country (the United States) in 1937; as a means of forcing fidelity to husbands, however, it still survives in Africa.

Betty Dodson, Joani Blank, and other feminists, trying to help women get more and better orgasms, have taken the lead in removing the stigma from masturbation. The use of vibrators has been repeatedly recommended, and they are now sold openly; the San Francisco store Good Vibrations, which specializes in vibrators, is openly pro-masturbatory. Sex therapist Ruth Westheimer has recommended the use of a cucumber, and that this was broadcast on network television itself shows a big change in national attitude. Dodson has organized masturbation workshops and parties. In San Francisco, St. Priapus Church has made group male masturbation a worship ceremony. However, the group masturbation movement, while growing, remains surprisingly small.

Politics. As it is the only sex practice available to an unpartnered person, masturbation has often been associated with loneliness. While apparently there have always been a number of cognoscenti who preferred it, masturbation has had a stigma and been ignored as a partnered activity. Thus it has not been, historically, a practice of the rich and powerful, who could purchase or otherwise compel the service of sexual partners. It has, rather, been a practice of the powerless. This means the poor and the isolated, those with elaborate fantasy lives or specialized sexual tastes, and, in recent times especially, it has meant the young. Among men, the average age of those reaching orgasm through masturbation is much lower than those reaching it through intercourse. Some of the opposition to masturbation has been hostility to the sexuality of young people.

Masturbation, like homosexuality, has been opposed because it has been believed antithetical to human relationships. However, as writers on the topic point out, masturbation can not only be a pleasurable activity for a couple, it can be relationship-enhancing. Masturbation can discharge an imbalance of sexual desire, a hidden and destructive issue in many relationships. It can be a means of low-risk adventures outside the relationship for those who find a single sexual partner confining. Masturbation can also enhance the bonds between a group or community, and it is inherently egalitarian.

BIBLIOGRAPHY. Joani Blank, *Good Vibrations: The Complete Guide to Vibrators*; Burlingame, CA: Down There Press, 1982; Joani Blank and Honey Lee Cottrell, *I Am My Lover*, Burlingame, CA: Down There Press, 1978; Betty

Dodson, *Liberating Masturbation. A Meditation on Self Love*, New York: Betty Dodson, 1974; idem, *Sex for One*, New York: Crown, 1987; John P. Elia, "History, Etymology, and Fallacy: Attitudes Toward Male Masturbation in the Ancient Western World," *Journal of Homosexuality*, 14 (1987), 1–19; *How to Have a JO Party in Your Home*, San Francisco: JO Buddies, 1985; Werner A. Krenkel, "Masturbation in der Antike," *Wissenschaftliche Zeitschrift der Wilhelm-Pieck-Universität Rostock: Gesellschafts- und sprachwissenschaftliche Reihe*, 28 (1979), 159–78; Jack Morin, *Men Loving Themselves: Images of Male Self-Sexuality*, Burlingame, CA: Down There Press, 1980; R. P. Neuman, "Masturbation, Madness, and Modern Concepts of Childhood and Adolescence," *Journal of Social History*, 8 (1975), 1–27; René A. Spitz, "Authority and Masturbation" (1952), reprinted in *Masturbation: From Infancy to Senescence*, New York: International University Press, 1975, pp. 381–409; Margo Woods, *Masturbation, Tantra and Self Love*, San Diego: Mho and Mho, 1981.

Daniel Eisenberg

MATTACHINE SOCIETY

One of the earliest American gay **movement** organizations, the Mattachine Society began in Los Angeles in 1950–51. It received its name from the pioneer activist Harry Hay in commemoration of the French medieval and Renaissance Société Mattachine, a somewhat shadowy musical masque group of which he had learned while preparing a course on the history of popular music for a workers' education project. The name was meant to symbolize the fact that "gays were a masked people, unknown and anonymous," and the word itself, also spelled *matachin* or *matachine*, has been derived from the Arabic of Moorish Spain, in which *muta-wajjihīn*, is the masculine plural of the active participle of *tawajjaha*, "to mask oneself." Another, less probable, derivation is from Italian *matto*, "crazy." What historical reality lay behind Hays' choice of name remains uncertain, just as the members of the group never quite agreed on how the opaque name Mattachine should be pronounced. Such gnomic self-designations were typical of the **homophile** phase of the movement in which open proclamation of the purposes of the group through a revealing name was regarded as imprudent.

Political Setting. The political situation that gave rise to the Mattachine Society was the era of **McCarthyism**, which began with a speech by Senator Joseph R. McCarthy of Wisconsin at a Lincoln's Birthday dinner of a Republican League in Wheeling, West Virginia, on February 9, 1950. In it McCarthy accused the Truman Administration of harboring "loyalty and security risks" in government service. And the security risks, he told Congressional investigators, were in no small part "sex perverts." A subcommittee of the Senate was duly formed to investigate his charges, which amounted to little more than a list of government employees who had run afoul of the Washington vice squad, but such was the mentality of the time that all seven members of the subcommittee endorsed McCarthy's accusations and called for more stringent measures to "ferret out" homosexuals in government.

Formation and Structure. The organization founded by Hay and his associates was in fact modeled in part on the Communist Party, in which secrecy, hierarchical structures, and "democratic centralism" were the order of the day. Following also the example of **freemasonry**, the founders created a pyramid of five "orders" of membership, with increasing levels of responsibility as one ascended the structure, and with each order having one or two representatives from a higher order of the organization. As the membership of the Mattachine Society grew, the orders were expected to subdivide into separate cells so that each layer of the pyramid could expand horizontally. Thus members of the same order but different cells would remain unknown to one another. A single fifth order consisting of the founders would provide the centralized leadership whose decisions would radiate downward through the lower orders.

The discussions that led to the formation of the Mattachine Society began in the fall of 1950, and in July 1951 it adopted its official designation. As **Marxists** the founders of the group believed that the injustice and oppression which they suffered stemmed from relationships deeply embedded in the structure of American society. These relationships they sought to analyze in terms of the status of homosexuals as an oppressed cultural minority that accepted a "mechanically . . . superimposed heterosexual ethic" on their own situation. The result was an existence fraught with "self-deceit, **hypocrisy**, and charlatanism" and a "disturbed, inadequate, and undesirable . . . sense of value." Homosexuals collectively were thus a "social minority" unaware of its own status, a minority that needed to develop a group consciousness that would give it pride in its own identity. By promoting such a positive self-image the founders hoped to forge a unified national movement of homosexuals ready and able to fight against oppression. Given the position of the Mattachine Society in an America where the organized left was shrinking by the day, the leaders had to frame their ideas in language accessible to non-Marxists. In April 1951 they produced a one-page document setting out their goals and some of their thinking about homosexuals as a minority. By the summer of 1951 the initial crisis of the organization was surmounted as its semipublic meetings suddenly became popular and the number of groups proliferated. Hay himself had to sever his ties with the Communist Party so as not to burden it with the onus of his leadership of a group of homosexuals, though by that time the interest of the Communist movement in sexual reform had practically vanished.

Early Struggles and Accomplishments. In February 1952 the Mattachine Society confronted its first issue: police harassment in the Los Angeles area. One of the group's original members, Dale Jennings, was entrapped by a plainclothesman, and after being released on bail, he called his associates who hastily summoned a Mattachine meeting of the fifth order. As the Society was still secret, the fifth order created a front group called Citizens Committee to Outlaw Entrapment to publicize the case. Ignored by the media, they responded by distributing leaflets in areas with a high density of homosexual residents. When the trial began on June 23, Jennings forthrightly admitted that he was a homosexual but denied the charges against him. The jury, after thirty-six hours of deliberation, came out deadlocked. The district attorney's office decided to drop the charges. The contrast with the usual timidity and hypocrisy in such cases was such that the Citizens Committee justifiably called the outcome a "great victory."

With this victory Mattachine began to spread, and a network of groups soon extended throughout Southern California, and by May 1953 the fifth order estimated total participation in the society at more than 2,000. Groups formed in Berkeley, Oakland, and San Francisco, and the membership became more diverse as individual groups appealed to different segments of gay society.

Emboldened by the positive response to the Citizens Committee, Hay and his associates decided to incorporate in California as a not-for-profit educational organization. The Mattachine Foundation would be an acceptable front for interfacing with the larger society, especially with professionals and public officials. It could conduct research on homosexuality whose results could be incorporated in an educational campaign for homosexual rights. And the very existence of the Foundation would convince prospective members that there was nothing illegal about participation in an organization of this kind. The fifth order had modest success in obtaining professional support for the Foundation. Evelyn Hooker, a research psychologist from UCLA, declined to join the board of directors, but by keeping in close touch with Mattachine she obtained a large pool of gay men for her pioneering study on homosexual personality.

Crisis. The political background of Hay and the other founders, while it gave them the skills needed to build a movement in the midst of an intensely hostile society, also compromised them in the eyes of other Americans. An attack on the Mattachine Society by a Los Angeles newspaper writer named Paul Coates in March 1953 linked "sexual deviates" with "security risks" who were banding together to wield "tremendous political power." To quiet the furor, the fifth order called a two-day convention in Los Angeles in April 1953 in order to restructure the Mattachine Society as an above-ground organization. The founders pleaded with the Mattachine members to defend everyone's First Amendment rights, regardless of political affiliations, since they might easily find themselves under questioning by the dreaded House Un-American Activities Committee. Kenneth Burns, Marilyn Rieger, and Hal Call formed an alliance against the leftist leadership that was successful at a second session held in May to complete work on the society's constitution. The results of the meeting were paradoxical in that the views of the founders prevailed on every issue, yet the anti-Communist mood of the country had so peaked that the fifth-order members agreed among themselves not to seek office in the newly structured organization, and their opponents were elected instead. The convention approved a simple membership organization headed by an elected Coordinating Council with authority to establish working committees. Regional branches, called "area councils," would elect their own officers and be represented on the main council. The unit for membership participation became the task-oriented chapter. Harry Hay emerged from the fra-

cas crushed and despondent, and never again played a central role in the gay movement.

Mattachine Restructured. The new leadership changed the ideology of the Mattachine Society. Rejecting the notion of a "homosexual minority," they took the opposite view that "the sex variant is no different from anyone else except in the object of his sexual expression." They were equally opposed to the idea of a homosexual culture and a homosexual ethic. Their program was, in effect, assimilationist. Instead of militant, collective action, they wanted only collaboration with the professionals—"established and recognized scientists, clinics, research organizations and institutions"—the sources of authority in American society. The discussion groups were allowed to wither and die, while the homosexual cause was to be defended by proxy, since an organization of "upstart gays . . . would have been shattered and ridiculed." At an organization-wide convention held in Los Angeles in November 1953, the conflict between the two factions erupted in a bitter struggle in which the opponents of the original perspective failed to put through motions aimed at driving out the Communist members, but the radical, militant impulse was gone, and many of the members resigned, leaving skeleton committees that could no longer function. Over the next year and a half, the Mattachine Society continued its decline. At the annual convention in May 1954, only forty-two members were in attendance, and the presence of women fell to token representation.

An important aspect of Mattachine was the issuing of two monthly periodicals. *ONE Magazine*, the product of a Los Angeles discussion group, began in January 1953, eventually achieving a circulation of 5000 copies. Not formally part of Mattachine, in time the magazine gave rise to a completely separate organization, ONE, Inc., which still flourishes, though the periodical ceased regular publication in 1968. In January 1955 the San Francisco branch began a somewhat more scholarly journal, *Mattachine Review*, which lasted for ten years.

Helped by these periodicals, which reached many previously isolated individuals, Mattachine became better known nationally. Chapters functioned in a number of American cities through the 1960s, when they were also able to derive some strength from the halo effect of the civil rights movement. As service organizations they could counsel individuals who were in legal difficulties, needed psychotherapy, or asked for confidential referral to professionals in appropriate fields. However, they failed to adapt to the militant radicalism of the post-**Stonewall** years after 1969, and they gradually went under. The organization retains, together with its lesbian counterpart, the Daughters of **Bilitis**, its historical renown as the legendary symbol of the "homophile" phase of the American gay movement.

BIBLIOGRAPHY. John D'Emilio, *Sexual Politics, Sexual Communities: The Making of a Homosexual Minority in the United States, 1940–1970*, Chicago: Chicago University Press, 1983.

Warren Johansson

MATTHIESSEN, F[RANCIS] O[TTO] (1902–1950)

American scholar and literary critic. Having completed his undergraduate work at Yale, Matthiessen set out for European study on the ocean liner Paris in the summer of 1924. On the ship he met the American painter Russell Cheney, twenty years his senior. After an initial separation, they were to remain together as lovers for most of the ensuing years until Cheney's death in 1945.

Matthiessen's teaching career was spent chiefly at Harvard University, where he quickly became known as an energetic and devoted tutor and lecturer. He also found time to write a number of books, including monographs on Theodore Drei-

ser, T. S. **Eliot**, and Henry **James**. However, his massive *American Renaissance* (1941) ranks as his most important achievement. Concentrating on major writings of Emerson, Thoreau, Hawthorne, **Melville**, and **Whitman** from the years 1850–55, Matthiessen showed that these works reflect social reality—the reform trends of the 1840s—while standing on their own as works of art. This dual approach, external and internal, left an enduring impress on the field of American studies. For much of his life Matthiessen was involved in leftist political causes, and it is thought that political disappointments, together with the loneliness that Cheney's death caused, contributed to his decision to take his own life on April 1, 1950.

During periods when they were apart Matthiessen and Cheney wrote to each other almost daily. The selection of their 3000 surviving letters that has been edited and published by Louis Hyde allows one to observe two men who first begin to understand their homosexuality and then find increasing strength in their bond. Unfortunately all was not roses: Matthiessen had a nervous breakdown in 1938, and Cheney suffered from a chronic drinking problem. Significantly, Cheney seemed able to bring his alcoholism under control when far away from his lover, as at his sister's ranch in Texas, but when he returned to live with Matthiessen in New England it would recur. This pattern suggests that the drinking was grounded in guilt. Matthiessen, for his part, was closeted in his relations with most of his Harvard colleagues, going so far as to express disapproval when the homosexuality of someone else came up. In the *American Renaissance* he did not venture even to hint at homophile aspects in the work of Melville and Whitman. Yet Cheney and Matthiessen were figures of their time and this representative character, together with their unusual articulateness, makes the record of their relationship virtually *sui generis*.

BIBLIOGRAPHY. Louis Hyde, ed., *Rat and the Devil: Journal Letters of F. O. Matthiessen and Russell Cheney*, Hamden, CT: Archon Books, 1978.

Wayne R. Dynes

Maugham, W. Somerset (1874–1965)

English novelist, short story writer, playwright, and essayist. A descendant of English barristers, W. Somerset Maugham was born in the British embassy in Paris. French was his mother tongue; he began to master English only when he was orphaned at the age of ten and sent to live with his uncle, Henry Maugham, a clergyman in the Church of England. Maugham had his first homosexual experience in 1890 with the aesthete John Ellingham Brooks, during a stay in Germany. But Maugham was and remained an Edwardian, who insisted on keeping up appearances. He refused to admit his homosexuality until the end of his life, and then only to a trusted few. Attempts to discuss the subject in any favorable way were sure to bring instant and permanent ostracism.

Not daring to tell his uncle that he had decided to become a writer, Maugham enrolled in medical school and produced his first novel, *Liza of Lambeth*. He passed the next ten years in some desperation. He witnessed, with dismay, the trial of Oscar **Wilde**: like the Great Depression, the Wilde trial left its mark on an entire generation.

Maugham was contemplating a return to medicine when success struck. On October 26, 1907, Maugham's comedy "Lady Frederick" opened in London. The play was a smash hit; he soon had four plays running simultaneously, and began to grow rich. He abandoned the novel for the theatre, and spent the next two decades churning out product for this market.

During World War I Maugham served as a British spy in Russia—an experience which he used for his "Ashenden" stories. Just before his (unsuccessful) mission to Russia, Maugham had met and fallen in love with Gerald Haxton, a San Francisco youth of twenty-two who was serving in the same ambulance unit. It was an attraction of opposites: Haxton was a gregarious, extroverted, dashing scoundrel, while Maugham was shy and closeted. Maugham also had a daughter during the war, by Mrs. Syrie Wellcome, whom he married after she was divorced.

The marriage was not a success: Maugham spent most of his time abroad, traveling in exotic locales with Haxton, who not only supplied local boys for Maugham, but much of the raw material for his short stories. Maugham finally fled to his new villa, the famous "Mauresque," on the French Riviera, to take up life with Haxton. Mr. and Mrs. Maugham were divorced in 1928.

Maugham had returned to the novel in 1918 with *Of Human Bondage*. Others followed in succeeding years, as well as several collections of short stories. He had the knack of creating "properties" and was able to sell his work several times over—the short story could be turned into a play, which was then filmed and filmed again. The money flowed in and Maugham entertained the titled, the famous, and the intelligent at the Mauresque—as well as handsome young men, frequently procured for him by Haxton, who was rapidly slipping into alcoholism.

Between the wars, Maugham continued to turn out short stories, many of them about his travels in the Far East. He antagonized the entire British population of Malaya by staying as their honored guest, absorbing all the local gossip, and writing up the nastiest bits in flimsy disguise when he returned to Europe.

He spent much of World War II as a guest of the Doubledays in South Carolina. An estrangement between Maugham and Haxton was suddenly ended by Haxton's death in New York in 1944. For a moment, Maugham's treasured façade disappeared; he wept openly and bitterly at the funeral.

He returned to the Mauresque after the war and acquired a docile young man to replace Haxton: Alan Searle. The new man had the unpleasant chore of attending to the famous writer during his last twenty years, which were marred by paranoia and immense bitterness. He brooded particularly on his worth as an author; his wealth was obvious but his merit remained problematic. In the last years, Maugham fell victim to senile dementia, and would burst into obscenities during an otherwise friendly conversation. Many of the attacks were so severe that he had to be put to sleep with tranquilizers. He also made a bizarre attempt to disinherit his daughter and adopt Alan Searle as his son, an effort which was defeated by French law.

Maugham's place as a writer, the question which so obsessed him, is fairly secure. He is frequently referred to as a writer of the second rank, but also admitted to be of the very best second-raters. Throughout his working life, Maugham wrote for six hours in the morning, never rising without having completed at least a thousand words. Over a long career, he would have produced over ten million words of material; he was prolific through discipline.

His plays have mostly perished, although "The Circle" and "The Constant Wife" have been revived in the 1970s. Of his novels, at least four have shown staying power: *Of Human Bondage* (notable for its treatment of unrequited love, as well as its cruel portrait of his uncle Henry Maugham), *The Moon and Sixpence* (a thinly disguised fictionalization of Paul Gauguin's life), *Cakes and Ale* (Maugham's own favorite and perhaps his best, a fictionalization of the life of Thomas Hardy), and *The Razor's Edge* (a story of Eastern mysticism which strangely presaged the hippie movement of the 1960s and has been filmed several times). Maugham's short stories stand unchallenged—he made the world of the British colonials in the Far East his own territory, and he had a definite genius for telling a tale.

Maugham's influence on homosexuality in our time has been at once nonexistent and pervasive. Securely closeted, his literary work contains only a few passing mentions of the subject, from a very safe distance. Yet he was known to be homosexual, and discreetly entertained the international gay community at the Mauresque. Maugham set the style for many upper-class homosexuals of his time: they were to be Anglophile gentlemen, of urbane wit and a taste for modern art, with a strong bias toward the French as the second-most-preferred nation. They would not discuss such mundane matters as sex, using polished manners to protect their closeted existence. The pattern is certainly not extinct today.

Maugham summed up his own life bitterly in his famous remark to the effect that he had wasted his life pretending that he was three quarters heterosexual and one quarter homosexual, while the reality was the other way round.

After Somerset Maugham's death, his nephew Robin Maugham (1916–1981) recycled his "memoirs" of Uncle Willie into no less than three books. Robin, a lifelong alcoholic with a history of mental illness and sadomasochism, never had the intimate acquaintance he claimed with his celebrated uncle, and often retells stories heard from Barbara Back and Gerald Haxton. Some of these may be pure fantasy, such as the bizarre theory that Maugham sold his soul to Aleister **Crowley** in return for literary success. Robin pursued a literary career with little distinction (*The Servant* is still remembered today); his real energies were devoted to the bottle and to social climbing. A collection of dismal homosexual stories (*The Boy from Beirut*, San Francisco, 1982) did nothing to enhance his tarnished reputation.

BIBLIOGRAPHY. Ted Morgan, *Maugham*, New York: Simon & Schuster, 1980.

Geoff Puterbaugh

McALMON, ROBERT (1896–1956)

American writer and publisher. McAlmon was born in Clifton, Kansas, the son of an itinerant Presbyterian minister, the youngest of ten children. Of his mother (Bess Urquhart), he wrote: "Her love's my prison,/ and my pity is the lock." The family migrated through a number of South Dakota towns into Minneapolis and eventually California. McAlmon attended the universities of Minnesota (1916) and Southern California (1917–20), but he received more education as a Western farmhand, as a merchant mariner, and in the Army Air Force, where he was stationed at San Diego in 1918. The airmen inspired his first poems published in college and in *Poetry* (March 1919).

In 1920, McAlmon moved first to Chicago and then to New York City in search of freedom and companions. In New York he worked nude as a male model and formed a life-long friendship with artist and poet Marsden **Hartley**. With William Carlos Williams, McAlmon founded *Contact*, which in its short life published Ezra Pound, Wallace Stevens, Marianne Moore, H. D. (Hilda **Doolittle**), Kay Boyle, and Hartley.

On February 14, 1921, McAlmon married Bryher (Winifred Ellerman), heiress to a vast English fortune and H. D.'s lover. Their arrangement—"legal only, unromantic, and strictly an agreement," McAlmon wrote—served both Bryher, who received control of her inheritance, and McAlmon, who gained financial independence. (They were amicably divorced in 1927.) After a short stay in London, McAlmon made Paris his base where his Contact Press published (with Three Mountains Press) a group of then-unpublishable authors: Bryher, Mina Loy, Ernest **Hemingway**, Marsden Hartley, William Carlos Williams, Ford Madox Ford, Ezra Pound, Mary Butts, Gertrude **Stein**, H. D., Djuna **Barnes**, and **Saikaku** Ihara (*Quaint Tales of Samurais*).

In their magazine Williams and McAlmon had called for an "essential contact between words and the locality." In his own fiction, McAlmon achieved that goal. His own Contact Press issued his first volumes: *A Hasty Bunch* (1922), *A Companion Volume* (1923), *Post-Adolescence* (1923), *Village: As It Happened through a Fifteen Year Period* (1924), *Distinguished Air (Grim Fairy Tales)* (1925); while Black Sun Press published *The Indefinite Huntress and Other Stories* (Paris, 1932). In his portraits of Dakota farm life, Greenwich Village parties, and gay **Berlin**, McAlmon wrote it down just as it happened, but he did not then find and has not now found a wide audience. His four volumes of poetry found a wider range of publishers: *Explorations* (London: Egoist Press, 1921), *The Portrait of a Generation* (Paris: Contact, 1926), *North America, Continent of Conjecture* (Paris: Contact, 1929), *Not Alone Lost* (Norfolk, CT: New Directions, 1937). But his only book to find wide circulation has been his memoir of the twenties: *Being Geniuses Together* (London: Secker & Warburg, 1938). And even it has been somewhat diluted with interleaved chapters by Kay Boyle in the later (New York: Doubleday, 1968; San Francisco: North Point, 1984) editions.

McAlmon became a drinking buddy with both James Joyce and Ernest Hemingway. When a prude destroyed the only copy of the concluding erotic soliloquy in *Ulysses*, McAlmon reconstructed the text from Joyce's notes, improvising as he went along. Hemingway's relationship with McAlmon was rockier. McAlmon took him to his first bullfight and published his first two books, but Hemingway was upset by McAlmon's homosexuality. McAlmon teased Hemingway for his friendship with F. Scott Fitzgerald, whose cock Hemingway examined at a urinal. Both James Joyce and Ezra Pound declared that McAlmon was tougher, more courageous, and a better writer than Hemingway.

McAlmon kept his distance from the French homosexuals. From parties, bars, and cafés he knew Jean **Cocteau**, Raymond Radiguet, René **Crevel**, Louis Aragon, and others. While his French may not have been sufficient to follow their writings, Dada and Surrealism left him completely cold. His ties were closer with artists Francis Picabia and Constantin Brancusi, but McAlmon saw in Europe only "the rot of ripe fruit."

John Glassco, who arrived as a teenager in Paris with his best friend and who received financial favors from McAlmon, claims that he and his friend did not have to put out for the older man because "he was more vain of being seen with young men than actually covetous of their favors." McAlmon's preferences for men are not entirely clear: he found Marsden Hartley too old. McAlmon liked bullfighters who (like himself) had tight, lean bodies. A Paris bartender describes McAlmon's impassioned speech defending Plato, Michelangelo, and other creative geniuses who celebrated the masculine form. "I'm a bisexual myself," McAlmon shouted, "like Michelangelo, and I don't give a damn who knows it." (A similar speech is credited by other sources to Arthur Craven, Mina Loy's lover, who claimed to be Oscar Wilde's nephew and was a professional boxer.) In the 1950s, McAlmon wrote, "There are no real homos, male or female, but there is the bi-sex, and in more people than know it themselves." The "real abnorms" were the men who swagger "with virility."

How can one explain McAlmon's lack of success? He had little appreciation, but Fitzgerald and Hemingway were ruined by too much acclaim. He drank plenty and enjoyed drugs, but so did Joyce, Cocteau, and Crevel. Coming into money may have been corrupting, but H. D. thrived with the Ellerman wealth. Perhaps he was too far ahead of his time. When Allen Ginsberg with his poetry or Jack **Kerouac** with his prose made "first thought best thought" an axiom, McAlmon was dead. Moreover, his precise rendering of gay bar talk in *Distinguished Air* (1925) may be too advanced even now. He uses terms like "blind meat" (uncircumcised hard cock whose foreskin does not pull back), "rough trade," and "auntie."

McAlmon wrote very little after 1935; he was interested in radical politics but found little support among the expatriates. He was caught in France by the German occupation, came down with tuberculosis, and escaped through Spain to the United States, where he joined his brothers in a surgical supply house in El Paso. He died at Desert Hot Springs, California, in 1956.

BIBLIOGRAPHY. Robert E. Knoll, *McAlmon and the Lost Generation, A Self Portrait*, Lincoln: University of Nebraska, 1962; idem., *Robert McAlmon: Expatriate Publisher and Writer*, Lincoln: University of Nebraska, 1959; Robert K. Martin and Ruth L. Strikland, "Robert McAlmon," *American Writers in Paris, 1920–1939*, Karen Lane Rood, ed., Detroit: Gale Research, 1980; Sanford J. Smoller, *Adrift Among Geniuses: Robert McAlmon, Writer and Publisher of the Twenties*, University Park: Pennsylvania State University Press, 1975.

Charley Shively

McCarthyism

The political tactics of the United States Senator from Wisconsin Joseph R. McCarthy (1908–1957) have since the 1950s been labeled McCarthyism. They consisted in poorly founded but sensationally publicized charges against individuals in government service or public life whom McCarthy accused on the Senate floor of being Communists, security risks, or otherwise disloyal or untrustworthy. Senator McCarthy's campaign did not spare "sex perverts in government," and so it made homosexuality an issue in American political life for the first time since the founding of the republic.

Emergence of the Tactics. Elected in the Republican landslide of 1946, McCarthy attracted little attention as the junior Senator from Wisconsin during his first three years in office. But in a Lincoln's Birthday address delivered in Wheeling, West Virginia on February 9, 1950, he catapulted himself into national fame by claiming that he had "in his hand a list of 205" active members of the Communist Party and members of a spy ring in the State Department. With attention now focused on possible "security risks in government," Under Secretary of State John Peurifoy testified on February 28, 1950 that most of 91 employees dismissed for "moral turpitude" were homosexuals. On March 14 McCarthy himself raised the alleged case of a convicted homosexual who had resigned from the State Department in 1948 but was currently holding a "top-salaried, important position" with the Central Intelligence Agency; he would divulge the name of the accused only in executive session, but demanded his immediate dismissal: "It seems unusual to me, in that we have so many normal people . . . that we must employ so many very, very unusual men in Washington." After the head of the District of Columbia vice squad told a Senate committee that thousands of "sexual deviates" worked for the government, the Republican floor leader, Kenneth Wherry of Nebraska—a minor demagogue in his own right—demanded a full-scale investigation. In June 1950 the full Senate bowed to mounting pressure and authorized an investigation into the alleged employment of "homosexuals and other sex perverts" in government.

Apogee and Decline. The subcommittee headed by Senator Clyde Hoey of North Carolina consisted of 4 Democrats and 3 Republicans; it was to deliver its report in December 1950, thus after the mid-term Congressional elections. Hoey, a conservative on many issues, neverthe-less had stood his ground against right-wing attacks on civil liberties until then. But the Report of the subcommittee—in contrast with an earlier finding that McCarthy "had perpetrated a monstrous fraud and a hoax on the Senate"—was a bloodless victory for the senator from Wisconsin. The subcommittee found that homosexual acts were illegal and that those who committed them were "social outcasts," and more relevantly, that fear of exposure made homosexuals subject to **blackmail** for espionage purposes. The only evidence that it could present to bolster this assertion was the case of a homosexual Austrian counter-intelligence officer (Alfred **Redl**) who had committed suicide in 1913 after he was discovered to be receiving payment for information that he furnished to the intelligence service of Tsarist Russia! The far more interesting—and politically embarrassing—Harden-**Eulenburg** affair that had occurred a few years earlier in imperial Germany was never mentioned. The subcommittee discovered, moreover, that the laws against sexual perversion in the District of Columbia were inadequate—in other words, that homosexual acts in private were *not* a crime, and that individuals arrested by the vice squad were allowed to disappear after posting trivial sums of money as surety. Its recommendations were to correct these shortcomings in the law and its administration so that no one would escape identification and punishment. The vicious circle of reasoning involved in such a policy was lost on all concerned, simply because the traditional attitudes toward homosexuality precluded a rational approach to the matter. It is also noteworthy that the danger of blackmail which Magnus **Hirschfeld** and his Berlin Scientific-Humanitarian Committee had used as an argument for the repeal of **Paragraph 175** was now turned against homosexuals to deny them employment in the name of "national security." This factor and others worked so strongly in McCarthy's favor that despite bitter opposition he was reelected in 1952 in the Eisenhower landslide that brought the Republican Party back to the White House after 20 years of Democratic rule.

Once the Republicans had become the majority party for a brief time, McCarthy's tactics became a source of embarrassment to them, and in 1954 a campaign was launched against him in the Senate which included the (true) accusation that a young University of Wisconsin graduate employed in his office in 1947 to handle veterans' affairs had been arrested as a homosexual and then promptly fired, and the (probably false) accusation that McCarthy himself was a homosexual, which Senator Ralph Flanders of Vermont included in his denunciation. However, it was alleged that McCarthy's marriage in 1953 at the age of 45 was motivated by his need to squelch the rumors of his own sexual deviation; the marriage remained childless, though the couple did adopt a little girl. What is significant in retrospect is that Roy Cohn, a young attorney who was one of McCarthy's chief aides during his heyday, was a lifelong homosexual who died of AIDS in 1986. Censured by the Senate in 1954, McCarthy thereafter faded in political importance, and when he died in 1957 no great wave of emotion went through the ranks of either his friends or his enemies.

Aftermath. The policy of denying employment to homosexuals on moral grounds and as security risks, however, remained long after McCarthy himself. It was only in the 1970s that concerted efforts were begun to combat the exclusionary measures that had cost many hundreds of homosexuals and lesbians their jobs in the Federal Government—often in positions where no element of security was involved. Given the absence of any organized gay movement in the United States in 1950 and the defensive on which McCarthy's unprecedented accusations had put the Democratic administration, homosexuals were the most exposed of his targets.

Broader Perspectives. Fairness requires one to note that the left has also sometimes employed its own variety of McCarthyism. During the 1930s the young Whittaker Chambers was a clandestine member of the Communist Party of the United States who cooperated with others in securing information for the Soviet Union. By the 1950s, having become more conservative, he denounced his former companions and their ideas. His testimony was of central importance in the conviction of Alger Hiss for perjury. In their turn his erstwhile friends began a word-of-mouth campaign based on the claim that his information was tainted because he was a homosexual and therefore untrustworthy by nature. While Chambers was in fact homosexual, the way his opponents used the allegation amounted to a homophobic smear campaign. In France, after André **Gide** published his negative reflections on his trip to the Soviet Union in 1936–37, he was attacked by his former Communist associates as a *pédé* (faggot).

These recent events are in fact the newest episodes in a long history. The sexual aspect of McCarthyism has an ancestry going as far back as **Aeschines**, **Cicero**, and the **Byzantine** Emperor Justinian (r. 527–565), whose laws against sodomites forged the "crime of those to whom no crime could be imputed," a weapon for political intimidation and blackmail that even the enlightened twentieth century has not deprived of its cutting edge.

BIBLIOGRAPHY. John D'Emilio, *Sexual Politics, Sexual Communities: The Making of a Homosexual Minority in the United States, 1940–1970*, Chicago: University of Chicago, 1983; Thomas C. Reeves, *The Life and Times of Joe McCarthy: A Biography*, New York: Stein and Day, 1982.

Warren Johansson

McCULLERS, CARSON (1917–1967)

American novelist, short-story writer, and playwright. Born Carson Smith in Columbus, Georgia, the writer lived in a small town world of summer heat, drab houses, greasy-spoon cafés, and small-scale factories that provides the basic setting for her work. Her typical characters suffer alienation through loneliness, inadequate financial and psychological support, and incomprehension of their fellows. McCullers further sets her characters apart by making them freaks, oddities, and outcasts. Despite this unpromising material, her central theme is love, which though often thwarted nonetheless casts a transcendent note that cuts through the otherwise overpowering bleakness. Without love the human community could not survive the corrosive pressures of fear, violence, and racial and social injustice. As she wrote: "[L]ove is a joint experience between two persons—but the fact that it is a joint experience does not mean that it is a similar experience to the two people involved. There are the lover and the beloved, but these come from two different countries . . . . So there is one thing for the lover to do. He must house his love within himself as best he can; he must create for himself a whole new inward world—a world intense and strange, complete in himself." At the time she wrote, the pre-gay liberation years, this underlying philosophy of love struck a deep chord in many homosexual readers.

As a young woman her determination to succeed was exemplified by her siege at the door of the cottage of her idol, the established writer Katherine Anne Porter, whom she forced literally to step over her. Her relationship with her husband Reeves was unhappy, and after repeated bouts with alcoholism he committed suicide. At several points in her life she felt strong lesbian attraction, as with the aristocratic Swiss Annemarie Clarac-Schwarzenbach. McCullers had major friendships with gay male writers, including Tennessee **Williams**, Truman **Capote**, and W. H. **Auden**.

Published when she was twenty-three, the novel *The Heart is a Lonely Hunter* (1940) presents the isolation of the deaf-mute hero and the effort of the other characters to break through to some kind of communication with him. *Reflections in a Golden Eye* (1941) deals, in sometimes opaque prose, with the thwarted homosexual longings of an army officer, Captain Penderton. In the homophobic climate of the time, such themes earned her scorn from establishment critics, who adjured her to give up her "preoccupation with perversion and abnormality." She did not do so, and attained fame nonetheless. Although her last years were marred by illness, her New York funeral produced a remarkable outpouring of writer solidarity, reflecting esteem for her person and her work. Subsequently, material from *Ballad of a Sad Cafe* (1951) was adapted for the stage by the homosexual playwright Edward Albee.

BIBLIOGRAPHY. Virginia Spencer Carr, *The Lonely Hunter: A Biography of Carson McCullers*, Garden City, NY: Doubleday, 1975.

Evelyn Gettone

MEDICAL THEORIES OF HOMOSEXUALITY

Since **Greek** antiquity medical science has pondered the issue of homosexuality, seeking an explanation for behavior that seemed to contradict the evident anatomical dimorphism of the opposite sexes in human beings. Broadly speaking, the theories proposed by medical authors fall into two categories: those which explain the phenomenon as the result of innate or constitutional factors, and those which see in it a purely psychological disorder, one possibly amenable to therapy.

Classical Antiquity. The Greek **Hippocratic Corpus**, the collection of medical treatises ascribed to Hippocrates of Cos but actually written by an entire school of physicians from the sixth to the first century, touches upon the issue from the standpoint of generative secretions from the parents. If both male and female parents secrete "male bodies," the offspring are men "brilliant in soul and strong in body." If the secretion from the man is male and that from the woman is female, the former gains the upper hand, so that the offspring turn out less brilliant, but still brave. In case, however, the man's secretion is female and the woman's is male, the fusion of the two produces a "man-woman" (androgynos), which corresponds to the modern notion of effeminate homosexual. The same is true of girls: if the man's secretion is female and the woman's male, and the female gains the upper hand, the offspring will be "mannish" (andreiai). Hence by the fourth century B.C. the Hippocratic school saw characterological intersexuality as determined by factors of procreation (Peri diaites, 28–29).

Aristotle formulated his own theory of homosexuality with reference to love and friendship. When love has a boy as its object, the object of sexual desire, namely procreation, is excluded, but the wish for pleasurable intimacy remains. The wise man will either resist these desires or make of them a means to win the love of the boy. The beauty of an adolescent boy greatly resembles that of a girl, and the lover can err in the object of his desire, which can become a habit strong enough to seem a natural tendency, although it has no constitutional or pathological cause. In some pederasts the desire for boys has the quality of an animal-like ferocity that resembles epilepsy, and such individuals should be regarded as mentally ill rather than as vicious (Nicomachean Ethics, Book 7). On the other hand, the pathicus, the passive-effeminate homosexual, presents a special problem because he plays the role that should belong to the woman, and in an organ not destined for sexual pleasure. The explanation for him lies in an abnormality of the channels through which the bodily secretions flow: in the pathicus the seat of sexual pleasure is the rectum, to which his sperm flows instead of to the penis, while those in

whose bodies the flow is divided between the two organs take both the active and the passive roles. This last point occurs in Problems, Book 4, a work produced by Aristotle's school, rather than by the philosopher himself.

Still later, the school of **astrology** that flourished in **Alexandria** sought to explain homosexuality and lesbianism as determined by planetary influences, in particular the position of Venus in the subject's horoscope. Remarkably enough, the ancient mind placed the woman who was aggressive in heterosexual relations (crissatrix) in the same category as the tribade or lesbian (fricatrix), because both departed from the female norm of passivity in sexual relations. This theory, making the sexual orientation of the subject dependent upon environmental factors (the position of the planets at the moment of birth), but still anchored in the individual's constitution, was propounded by authors from Teucer of Babylon to Firmicus Maternus.

In the fourth century of our era, Caelius Aurelianus addressed himself to the problem of the passive-effeminate homosexual (malthakos, mollis), whom he regarded not as the victim of a disease, but as suffering from unrestrained libido that causes the subject to lose all shame, to behave like a woman and to use for sexual gratification the parts of the body that are not destined by nature for such enjoyment (Chronic Diseases, IV, 9). Thus for the ancients—given their strict active–passive dichotomy—the paradox was that of the passive homosexual and the active lesbian; in their thinking the active homosexual and the passive lesbian had nothing of the "abnormal."

Medieval and Renaissance Traditions. The medieval period was marked by the continuity of the ancient tradition in both medicine and astrology. The conservatism of medieval culture allowed for only a gradual shift in the direction of a new conceptual framework. Arab astrologers took considerable interest in the variety of sexual expression, assigning the determining role to the heavenly bodies. The notions formulated by Claudius Ptolemy in his *Tetrabiblos*, composed about 161–182, that divided the sky into masculine and feminine zones, with Mars and Venus occupying the crucial positions, continued to be echoed down to the end of the Middle Ages by Ali ibn Ridwan, Albubather, Ibn Ezra, Albohali, Abenragel, and Alchabitius.

For Christian authors beginning with the **Patristic writers** the notion of the "sin against nature" (*peccatum contra naturam*) little by little modified the attitudes of the ancients in regard to homosexuality. While Albertus Magnus could still quote an Arab author to the effect that inordinate itching in the posteriors caused the desires of the *pathicus* and could be relieved by a salve applied to the region in question, his contemporary Thomas **Aquinas** struck out on a new path. In citing Aristotle's *Nicomachean Ethics* in the medieval Latin translation by William of Moerbeck, he deliberately omitted the reference to innate homosexual tendencies, thus leaving medicine in the Western tradition with no function except the forensic task of examining the accused to determine whether his anatomy revealed signs of "unnatural abuse." The primacy of genital anatomy over the rest of the constitution thus being affirmed, modern medicine had painfully to rediscover the possibility that an individual could reach sexual maturity with no attraction to members of the opposite sex but only to his own.

The forensic tradition of the Renaissance begins with Paulus Zacchias (1584–1659), the physician at the papal court, who in his *Quaestiones medico-legales* (1621–50) dealt with the evidence for submission to anal sodomy. His views were parroted by a score of writers down to the last quarter of the nineteenth century in books duly illustrated with engravings of the areas of the body to be scrutinized by the medical examiner. The eighteenth century saw an extensive literature, mainly in Latin but sometimes in the vernacular, that dealt with the various sexual offenses, never challenging the assumption that the guilty party was acting out of wilful depravity and merited only the sanctions adopted by the criminal codes of the Christian states from the canon law of the Church.

Theoretical Innovations. In the first half of the nineteenth century, psychiatry introduced a number of concepts that were to prove crucial for the understanding and classification of homosexuality in the second. The French psychiatrist J. D. E. Esquirol (1772–1840) invented the concept of monomania in 1816 for a specific type of partial insanity in which only one faculty of the mind is diseased. Two subdivisions were *instinctive monomania*, in which only the will is diseased, and *affective monomania*, in which the emotions are excessive or "perverted," and therefore distort behavior; and a quite specific type of the illness was *erotic monomania*, in which the sexual appetite was diseased and abnormal. Then in 1857 Bénédict Auguste Morel (1809–1873) introduced the term degeneration as a complex of religious, anthropological, and pathological assumptions, in particular the belief that acquired defects of the organism can be transmitted to later generations. This innovation led to the psychiatric hypothesis that a whole range of abnormal mental states could be explained by "degeneration of the central nervous system." In Germany the physician and author Ernst von Feuchtersleben (1806–1849) introduced the term *psychopathy* for "illness of the mind" in general, with the implicit notion that there could be a pathological state of the mind without a lesion of the brain or central nervous system. Alongside these, the word *perversion* had come to be employed in medicine in the sense of "pathological alteration of a function for the worse." Then *deviation* had in French assumed the meaning of "a departure from the normal functioning of an organ." In England, to complete the series, James Cowles Prichard (1786–1848) coined the expression "moral **insanity**": "a morbid perversion of the natural feelings, . . . moral dispositions, and natural impulses, without any remarkable disorder or defect of the intellect or knowing and reasoning faculties, and particularly without any insane illusion or hallucination."

This was the situation on the eve of the discoveries in forensic psychiatry that were prompted by the writings of the early homosexual apologists, Karl Heinrich **Ulrichs** and Károly Mária **Kertbeny**; but crucial as their arguments were for the continuing development of "sexual psychopathology," they also had a distant background in the Greek and Latin literature which, never entirely forgotten, had preserved the tradition of a culture that had been far more tolerant of homosexual expression and certainly did not relegate it to the category of the rare and monstrous. The interplay of the ancient, medieval, and modern ideas on homosexuality thus constitutes the history of the medical theories of the period from 1869 to the present.

The Modern Period. The earliest paper that mentioned homosexuality in a psychiatric context was written in 1849 by Claude-François Michéa (1815–1882), in connection with the famous case of Sergeant Bertrand, who was charged with violation of graves for the purpose of engaging in necrophilia. Faced with the claim of the defense that Bertrand was suffering from an instinctive monomania, the court merely sentenced him to a year in prison. But Michéa had the inspiration that there could exist a whole series of "erotic monomanias," one of which was an attraction to members of one's own sex, and he mentioned the poetess **Sappho** of antiquity as having exhibited such a condition. This isolated study, however, had no impact on medical thinking at the time.

In Germany the expert in forensic medicine Johann Ludwig Casper (1796–1864) had occasion to examine individuals accused of "pederasty" (= anal intercourse) for the purpose of determining whether their persons revealed that the crime had been committed. In a note appended to a paper of 1833 by the anatomist Robert Froriep, he casually remarked that he had observed a subject in whom sexual desire for the opposite sex was absent—the first such instance in modern medical literature. Toward the close of his life he became convinced that a species of mental alienation was present in at least some of the subjects he had examined.

The medical concept of homosexuality could not, however, have arisen without the intervention of the pioneers of the movement, Karl Heinrich Ulrichs (1825–1895) and Károly Mária Kertbeny (1824–1882). All the early physicians whose papers introduced "sexual inversion" to the medical world had read the works of one or both of these authors; none arrived at the notion by his own reasoning or by pointed interrogation of a patient with the condition. If they rejected the apologetic claim that the condition was an idiosyncrasy, a normal variety of the human sexual drive, it was largely because their case material was small and atypical; it usually amounted to one or two individuals examined in prisons or insane asylums. They were confronted with an unknown and paradoxical state of mind, all the more enigmatic because Darwinian biology, which just then was becoming an issue of the day in Europe, emphasized procreation as the mechanism of the evolutionary process. The total absence of the urge to procreate one's kind, and an attraction to members of the same sex with whom coupling could only be sterile, could for the progressive psychiatrists of that era only be a pathological condition.

It was against the background of these concepts and notions that Carl Friedrich Otto Westphal (1833–1890), Richard Freiherr von **Krafft-Ebing** (1840–1902), and Arrigo Tamassia (1849–1917) introduced *die conträre Sexualempfindung* = sexual **inversion** to psychiatry in articles published between 1869 and 1878. The condition itself they defined as "absence of sexual attraction to members of the opposite sex, with a substitutive attraction to members of one's own sex." The reasoning that underlay their definition was that in normal subjects sexual contact with members of the opposite sex excites pleasure, while with members of the same sex it elicits disgust, but in the cases which they had observed the reverse was true. The condition itself was an "affective monomania," since the rest of the personality of the subject was unaffected. At first only sporadic reports of such abnormal individuals appeared in the literature, but in 1882 the Russian psychiatrist Vladimir Fiodorovich **Chizh** published an article with the insight that far from being the rare anomaly that psychiatric science had assumed, this condition was in fact the explanation of many of the cases of "pederasty" that daily came to the attention of the police; and in 1886 a book earlier published in Russian and then translated into German by Veniamin Mikhaïlovich Tarnovskiĭ, *Die krankhaften Erscheinungen des Geschlechtssinnes* (The Morbid Manifestations of the Sexual Instinct), communicated this finding to the European public. In the same year Krafft-Ebing published the first edition of his *Psychopathia sexualis*, in which sexual inversion was only one of a series of newly discovered abnormalities of the sexual drive. Although the author stressed that the sexual act itself, however monstrous it may be, is no proof of the mental abnormality of the subject who has committed it, only that some individuals commit forbidden sexual acts because they are compelled by an exclusive and involuntary urge, this caveat has been too subtle for the mass mind—and even for many so-called experts—to grasp.

A long and in some respects futile controversy has ensued over whether homosexuality is to be classified as a "disease." Often the physicians who have debated this issue have argued that they were taking a truthful middle ground between the religious attitude toward homosexuals as depraved and vicious individuals, and the claims of homosexual apologists that their condition was "normal." The medical concept of homosexuality as disease has in fact been utilized by both sides: on the one hand to deny the legitimacy of homosexual expression by labeling the condition pathological, and on the other to exculpate defendants caught in the toils of the law by claiming that they were only "sick individuals" in need of treatment rather than punishment.

In relation to the legal and political debates engendered by the issue, the psychiatric concept of homosexuality is a secondary derivative of Christian asceticism and of the condemnation of homosexual acts in Roman law by the Christian emperors, and in the canon law of the Church based in part upon it. These in turn were incorporated into European civil law between the thirteenth and sixteenth centuries. In other words, it was only because the laws stemming from the Christian Roman Empire and the late Middle Ages made homosexual acts criminal that the forensic psychiatrist had any reason to take note of them, and the homophile apologist had to argue for removing the statutes from the penal code. As an issue of private morality homosexuality would scarcely have interested the psychiatrist in modern times any more than it did in ancient Greece. And underlying the argument for legal toleration has been the (usually unstated) assumption that healthy adult human beings have a sexual drive which they need to gratify and therefore cannot be expected to practice "lifelong abstinence" as demanded by the Church of celibates. Often the debate on this issue has therefore been a kind of intellectual shadowboxing between the opponents of an ascetic morality and its defenders, who ignoring the history of its origins pretend that it is virtually coterminous with the universe.

Psychoanalysis and Its Aftermath. The **psychoanalytic** school originated by Sigmund **Freud** has largely perpetuated the belief in homosexuality as a mental illness, if only because its adherents rejected the theory of an innate and unmodifiable condition in favor of a search for its origins in the psychodynamics of the human personality. Some of the case histories published sporadically in the psychoanalytic press are accompanied by quite fanciful theories, while others show genuine insight into certain causal factors. But on the whole the patient universe into which the psychotherapist has delved has been atypical of the homosexual population in general, and consisted mainly of subjects with acute moral and legal, if not psychological, problems. Only recent studies by academic psychologists have been able to break out of this vicious circle and produce the experimental or statistical evidence such as **Kinsey**'s that homosexual subjects were, on standard tests and by a multitude of criteria, indistinguishable from heterosexual ones. However, during the more than a century in which the subject has been debated, one clear line of demarcation has emerged: those who believed in the innate and constitutional origins of homosexuality have with **rare** exceptions been friends of the movement, while conversely those who held to a psychogenic explanation have been its often vociferous enemies—Alfred **Adler**, Edmund **Bergler**, Abram Kardiner, and Charles Socarides. And the proponents of the latter view usually reinforced the Christian dogma that the homosexual character was replete with moral failings, or else maintained that the spread of homosexuality was contingent upon some malaise within society itself—an assertion that played into the hands of dogmatic **Marxists** who, echoing such fin-de-siècle authors as Max Nordau and Cesare **Lombroso**, would dub homosexuality a symptom of the "decadence" of bourgeois society.

In 1980 the American Psychiatric Association was finally persuaded to remove homosexuality per se from its nomenclature of mental illnesses, and in 1986 even the compromise **"ego-dystonic homosexuality"** was stricken from the list, though the World Health Organization continues the classification. But the issue lingers within the psychiatric profession independent of any politically motivated decision, and decades of controversy echoed in the mass media have left the general public with the ill-defined belief that "homosexuality is a disease."

BIBLIOGRAPHY. Henry Werlinder, *Psychopathy: A History of the Concepts*, Ph.D. dissertation, University of Uppsala, 1978; Georges Lantéri-Laura, *Lecture des perversions: Histoire de leur appropriation médicale*, Paris: Masson, 1979.

Warren Johansson

MEDIEVAL LATIN POETRY

The classical tradition of pederastic poetry may never have completely died out despite Christian homophobia, though no examples in Latin survive from the fifth through the eighth century. But then little was written in the so-called Dark Ages (476–1000), and less survives. If the last surviving pagan homoerotic poems in Latin by Nemesianus in his fourth Bucolic were made in the reign of Numerian (283–284), Christian Latin pederastic verses appeared about a century later, best exemplified by Ausonius (d. ca. 395). Ausonius' library contained homosexual literature that scandalized Romans and he translated from Greek into Latin Strato's riddle about three men simultaneously enjoying four sexual postures. Saint Paulinus of Nola expressed his love for Ausonius: "As long as I am held in this confining, limping body . . . , I will hold you, intermingled in my very sinews." (Stehling, p. 5). Production of pederastic poetry, as indeed of most other Latin literature, declined and almost ceased after 476. Whatever forms of sexuality the Merovingian kings (420–751) practiced—

especially the degenerate, drunken later ones, the *Rois Fainéants*, with their long golden locks—shocked observers.

Elements of Continuity. A tradition of tolerance for sodomy can be traced from Ausonius through Sidonius Apollinarius to the monks of the central Middle Ages with their taste for "particular friendships." A North Italian among poets of the ninth century who rescued classical traditions wrote: "Hard marrow from mother's bones/Created men from thrown stones;/Of which one is this young boy,/Who can ignore tearful sobs./When I am heartbroken, my mind will rejoice./I shall weep as the doe whose fawn has fled." ("O admirabile Veneris ydolum.") So much of the classical tradition had survived that poems of love or intimate friendship for other men could be written by bishops and men of learning without incurring scorn or censure as would have happened in nineteenth-century Europe. The masters of Latin literature, having written in their own spoken tongue, were revered as models by authors composing in a learned, artificial speech, not their own vernacular, and celebrated in their writing their affection for other men, and especially the passion which as adult males they felt for boys. The whole homoerotic tradition of Mediterranean culture, made this inevitable. And the contrasts and antagonisms—the boy who scorns his lovers, the lover who is interested only in a boy's looks and not his mind and character—are commonplaces in the Latin literature of pederasty.

From the Carolingians to the Later Middle Ages. In the revival of learning during the Carolingian era (late eighth and ninth centuries), a distinctly erotic element can be perceived in the circle of clerics over which Alcuin, the "friend of Charlemagne," presided. The direction of the passion, however, was largely from Alcuin to his pupils; he went so far as to bestow upon a favorite student a "pet name" from one of **Vergil**'s Eclogues. The affection of Walafrid Strabo for his friend Liutger took on more specifically Chris-

tian terms, anticipating Elizabethan love sonnets. His friend Gottschalk while in exile wrote a tender poem to a young monk, probably at Reichenau.

After the restoration of order imposed by counts and kings during the central **Middle Ages** (1000–1300) literature once again flourished in Western Europe, gushing forth in the vernaculars, as well as in Latin during the "Renaissance of the twelfth century," and pederastic poems were part of this new wave. Marbod of Rennes (ca. 1035–1123), master of the school of Chartres, who wrote mainly on religious themes, became involved in a frustrating triangle with a boy whom he loved, but who loved a very beautiful girl herself in love with Marbod. Baudri of Bourgueil (1046–1130), his disciple, exemplifies the transition to the more baldly erotic poetry of the new era. Some of his poems address the moral qualities of the addressee, others extol merely his physical charms. Hildebert of Lavardin (ca. 1055–1133) repeats standard moralizing objections to the "plague of Sodom," suggesting that the hated practices were common enough in his time. Another poem of his boldly asserts that calling male love a sin is an error and that "heaven's council" was at fault in so doing.

Medieval allegorical poetry was less favorable to love for one's own sex. **Alan of Lille** composed a didactic poem entitled *De Planctu Naturae* (On the Complaint of Nature; ca. 1170), in which mankind is indicted for having invented monstrous forms of love and perverted her laws. In his continuation of the *Roman de la Rose* (ca. 1270), Jean de Meun has nature's genius liken those engaging in nonprocreative sex to plowmen who till stony ground, and other metaphors convey the message that if such practices are not halted, the human race will die out in two more generations.

A German manuscript of the twelfth or thirteenth century contains two anonymous lesbian love letters. Anonymous likewise is the *Dispute of Ganymede and Helen* in rhyming Latin verse, which is a **contest** over the merits of love for boys against love for women, in which a not exactly unprejudiced jury opts for heterosexuality.

When homophobic repression by clerical and secular authorities mounted during the thirteenth and fourteenth centuries, pederastic verse disappeared until the Italian **Renaissance**, when interest in classical antiquity gave it a rebirth.

BIBLIOGRAPHY. John Boswell, *Christianity, Social Tolerance, and Homosexuality*, Chicago: Chicago University Press, 1980; Ramsay MacMullin, "Roman Attitudes to Greek Love," *Historia*, 31 (1982), 484–502; Thomas Stehling, trans., *Medieval Latin Poems of Male Love and Friendship*, New York: Garland Publishing, 1984.

William A. Percy

MEDITERRANEAN HOMOSEXUALITY

This term serves to designate a paradigm of homosexual behavior found in the Latin countries of Europe and the Americas, in the **Islamic** countries of the Mediterranean, as well as in the Balkans. The diffusion of the paradigm is not uniform, but for the most part coincides with areas in which industrialization is recent or has not yet begun. In countries such as **Italy** and **Spain** it is not found in industrial areas and is starting to recede in those that are industrializing.

The Mediterranean paradigm may be defined as an attempt to interpret and harmonize exclusive homosexual conduct employing the same conceptual framework as that in use for heterosexuality. Its most salient characteristic is the sharp dichotomy between the one who is considered the "homosexual" in the strict sense, that is the one who plays the insertee role, as against the one who plays the insertor role (the **"active"**).

To designate the insertee there are various terms in various countries: in Italy, *arruso* and *ricchione*—which indicate that the passive homosexual so named does not cross-dress—and *femmenella* for the transvestite; in Spain and Spanish-speaking **Latin America**, *loca* and *maricón*; in **Brazil**, *bicha* and *veado*; in **Haiti**, *masisi*; in North **Africa**, *zamel*. By contrast the insertor is not differentiated, either by concept or by a separate name, from the *maschio/macho*, "(male) heterosexual." (For clarity henceforth the southern Italian *ricchione* stands as a generic name for the passive type.)

The consequences of this system of interpreting homosexual behavior are striking. In the first place, only the *ricchione*, that is, the passive homosexual (who is often recognizable by external signs of stereotypical feminine behavior, which in the *femmenella* becomes unmistakable because of cross-dressing), feels the need to build a subculture, to create an argot, and to form peer networks. In areas where the Mediterranean paradigm is still dominant, the homosexual subculture is in reality the subculture of the *ricchioni* alone.

In the second place, the members of the **subculture** generally regard it as inconceivable to have sexual relations with one another. The idea of copulation between two *ricchioni* is satirized by referring to it as "lesbianism," meaning that actually it is nothing but intercourse between "women," since no "real male" is present. This subculture only valorizes sexual relations between a *ricchione* and a "man." Relations between two "men" or two *ricchioni* are senseless, being scarcely imaginable.

Social Advantages of the Paradigm. This system of conceiving homosexuality offers several advantages. The first is that by accommodating homosexual acts to the dichotomies male/female and active/passive their apparent illogicality is elided—that is, the anomaly that comes from the presence of a male (by definition "active") who lends himself to the passive role (by definition "feminine") disappears. By affirming that whoever has an active role in a homosexual act is *in reality* a "male," while whoever takes the passive role is *in reality* a kind of woman (*femmenella* means "little female") the integrity of the dichotomy male-active vs. female-passive is safeguarded.

Moreover, the grotesqueness of the *ricchione* status constitutes a warning to anyone who might feel homosexual tendencies and be tempted to act upon them. The alternatives are clear: on the one hand, to live one's desires exclusively and openly, while accepting that one's level be lowered to that of a caricature, a queen; on the other hand, living one's own desires but keeping the privileges connected with the male role—at the price of renouncing living them in an exclusive manner and of contracting a heterosexual marriage.

Finally, and paradoxically, the *ricchione*'s sexual activity performs a socially useful function. Relations with *ricchioni* provide a safety valve for the relief of sexual tensions, especially those of adolescents. In the peasant and patriarchal societies of the Mediterranean type women are (or were until very recently) carefully supervised and chaperoned until marriage, while the modest economic situation of adolescents usually does not suffice to gain access to prostitutes, the only women who are not off-limits. In this context it is impossible to obtain sexual relief without infringing on one of the basic social taboos: the seduction of virgins or married women. The homosexual act can be regarded as a "lesser evil," though it is not openly acknowledged as such.

Advantages of the Role for the Homosexual Individual. The homosexuals also profit from this "unwritten social pact." There is no other way of explaining why millions of them throughout the world cling to this paradigm, rejecting as absurd the figure of the "gay man" in whom they cannot recognize themselves.

First, as long as those who are "different" decline to claim for themselves a deviant identity and to construct an alternative lifestyle that might challenge the dominant one, they are granted a fairly wide margin of manoeuvre without social constraints. (Note that in most of the countries in which the Mediterranean paradigm prevails there are no laws against homosexuality; where such laws do exist, as in a few Arab countries, they were imposed long after the social pattern emerged and are rarely enforced.)

Secondly, they can count on very easy contacts with "macho men," including heterosexual ones. Inasmuch as the society assures that as long as he plays the insertor **role**, he is not a *ricchione*, the "man" (hetero- or homosexual according to the individual) is always ready for sex with the *ricchione*, for the inviolability of his role provides the needed guarantee. (To try to get him to reverse his role would risk violence.)

Moreover, although the role of *ricchione* exposes one to ridicule, as does the prostitute role for women, the folk cultures of the countries that have Mediterranean homosexuality have developed remarkable zones of tolerance for those who are viewed as "nature's mistakes," individuals who are not afflicted with guilt for what they are. Hence the social acceptance in Naples of a ritual that would elsewhere be incomprehensible—the mock marriage of *femmenelle* (one of them dressed as a man), which takes place in public. People accept it as a rightful attempt to obtain at least a surrogate of that "normality" precluded by nature's mistake.

Finally, one must not underestimate the importance of the availability of a sexual identity (personal and social) that is extremely simple, powerful, and above all not in conflict with the sexual identity of "normals." Paradoxically, many *ricchioni* refuse to recognize themselves in the image of the "homosexual" and the "gay man," because they perceive the latter as "deviant"—as roles, that is, that can find no place within the "natural" polarity of human categories (male and female) and that create an artificial third category.

All this does not mean that the *ricchione* thinks of himself as a woman. His awareness of being different both from men and from women (that is to say, of being simply a *ricchione*) is strong and clear, and it expresses itself in a very **camp** manner. Nonetheless, the absence of a clear boundary between the condition of *ricchione* and that of the woman favors in some the acquisition of a feminine identity and, as an ultimate step, of transsexuality. In fact change of sex permits one to bring to completion the process of normalization and social integration that began with the acceptance of the *ricchione* role.

Present Status and Prospects of Mediterranean Homosexuality. Today Mediterranean homosexuality is slowly retreating, at least in the industrialized countries of the West. This decline is not due to the struggles of the gay **movement** (which is always weak where homosexuals reject the figure of the "gay" as aberrant), nor does it result from the theories of physicians and psychiatrists (who have little resonance among the uneducated, who are the bulwark of this paradigm of sexual behavior). The reasons for the retreat must rather be sought in the fading of peasant patriarchal society, in the impossibility of continuing to seclude women, and in the spread of the "sexual revolution." These factors are inexorably eroding the ranks of "macho men" who are disposed to have relations with *ricchioni*.

A part is certainly played by the concept of the **homosexual** that is rooted in the culture of northern and central Europe and diffused by the mass media—a concept which melds in a single category the (homosexual) "men" and the *ricchioni*. The acceptance of this model is hampered by Catholic propaganda, which denies the existence of homosexual individuals, claiming that there exist only homosexual *acts* but no persons as such. Finally, AIDS

has had a certain impact, making the "men" shy away from contact with those known to be exclusively homosexual.

However, what is occurring is not the disappearance of the paradigm but its adaptive transformation. It is not a matter of an "old" concept simply yielding to a "new" one. What is observable today in such countries as Italy and Spain is the mingling of two different models, though the model of the "gay man" seems to be gaining the upper hand.

The lingering substratum of the Mediteranean paradigm probably accounts for the slight success in Latin countries of the **clone** subculture, the persistence of a certain camp taste in the gay movements of the countries in question, the greater difficulty experienced by homosexuals in gaining self-acceptance, reduced hostility toward transvestites, as well as a continuing gay enthusiasm for sexual contacts with "heterosexual males."

Curiously, while the transformation of Mediterranean homosexuality is taking place, one also finds its glorification in literary works of high quality, such as *The Kiss of the Spider Woman* by Manuel Puig. In the book, though not in the film, the hero is a *teresita*, the Argentine equivalent of the *ricchione*.

BIBLIOGRAPHY. Evelyn Blackwood, ed., *Anthropology and Homosexual Behavior*, New York: Haworth Press, 1986; "Mediterranée," *Masques* 18 (Summer 1983); Stephen O. Murray, *Male Homosexuality in Central and South America*, New York: Gay Academic Union, 1987 (Gai Saber Monographs, 5).
Giovanni Dall'Orto

MELANESIA
See **Pacific Cultures.**

MELVILLE, HERMAN (1819–1891)
American novelist and short story writer. Born in New York City of Boston Calvinist and New York Dutch ancestry, Melville grew up in an educated and

comfortable environment that ended when his father went bankrupt and then died insane. In 1839 Melville became a ship's cabin boy and was exposed to menial squalor and brutal vice both at sea and in Liverpool. After further adventures, first on a whaling ship in the South Pacific, then in Hawaii, he returned to Boston in 1844. Extensive reading and research reinforced his experience at sea and underlies the series of novels that he wrote, beginning with *Typee* in 1846 and followed by *Redburn* (1849) and *White Jacket* (1850). But his greatest work is *Moby-Dick* (1851), the classic novel that combines **seafaring** and allegory into one of the masterpieces of American literature. *Moby-Dick* proved too difficult for both critics and public at the time, and his next novel, *Pierre* (1852), was inaccessible because of its psychological complexity and elaborate prose. Despite the lack of appreciation of his work, Melville continued to write prose and poetry until his death. He left *Billy Budd, Sailor: An Inside Story* in manuscript. By that time his literary reputation had nearly vanished, and only in the twentieth century, beginning in the 1930s, was the greatness of his accomplishment realized.

The homoerotic component of Melville's writing is subtle, pervasive, and rich in symbolic overtones. It was Leslie **Fiedler**, in *Love and Death in the American Novel*, who first glimpsed this element in the work. The Hero, the ego-persona of the author, is caught between two opposing forces. One is the Captain, the superego authority figure, who represents the moral demands of Western civilization and the imperative of obedience; the other is the Dark Stranger—or later, the Handsome Sailor—who personifies a state of innocence or of uninhibited nature, replicating the myth of Tahiti inherited from the travel literature of the eighteenth century. As part of a primitive culture free of the restraints of Christian morality, the Dark Stranger embodies the allure of primitive sensuality and eroticism. The novels depict the hero's psycho-logical progress toward opting for the Dark Stranger and rebelling against the Captain. The fulfillment of homoerotic longing is thus contingent upon rejecting the dictates of Western civilization.

Melville's work is imbued with intense sexual awareness, but couched in terms that betrayed nothing to the prudish nineteenth-century reader. There is much phallic imagery, but also a blatant association of sexuality with **friendship** and the assumption that male friendship is subversive to the social order. The masculinity of Melville's heroes is their endearing quality; it is a celebration of male bonding in its classic form, to the exclusion of the feminine. Within the American society of his time overt male homosexuality had no place; it had to be relegated to the margin of consciousness or to an exotic setting, with partners of another race and culture. The implicit sexual politics of the novels is a rejection of the norms of nineteenth-century America and an affirmation of an erotic fraternity, an alternate style of relationship between males that takes the form of a democratic union of equals.

BIBLIOGRAPHY. Leslie Fiedler, *Love and Death in the American Novel*, New York: Criterion Books, 1960; Robert K. Martin, *Hero, Captain, and Stranger: Male Friendship, Social Critique, and Literary Form in the Sea Novels of Herman Melville*, Chapel Hill: University of North Carolina Press, 1986.
Warren Johansson

MERCHANT MARINE
See **Seafaring**.

MESOPOTAMIA
Named the "land between the two rivers," the Tigris and the Euphrates, Mesopotamia was the cradle of the earliest human civilization, where the art of writing began shortly before 3000 B.C. Here Sumer and Akkad created a culture that was already old when the golden age of **Greece** was just beginning. Its literary languages, Sumerian and Akkadian (Se-

mitic), were the medium of a vast corpus of texts of mythology and poetry, law and administration, religion and magic, written in the cuneiform script. The earlier phase of Mesopotamian history saw the rise of the Sumerian city-states, which was followed by the formation of the Babylonian and Assyrian empires. The later achievements of Judaea and Greece were heavily indebted to Mesopotamia for the enormous fund of science and technology that it had accumulated over the centuries, as well as for the legal and ethical lore that it bequeathed to their prophets and philosophers. What kept this contribution from being appreciated was the historical circumstance that the literary idioms of Mesopotamia became extinct, knowledge of the cuneiform writing was lost, and the horizon of the past limited to the fragments preserved in Hebrew and Greek sources. In modern times, the decipherment of Sumerian and Akkadian, and then of Hittite and Hurrian, revealed the millennia of cultural evolution that underlay the high civilizations of middle antiquity.

Basic Attitude toward Sexuality. The Mesopotamian attitude toward sexuality lacked the religious and philosophical inhibitions which Judaism and Hellenic thought were to develop, and it had not even begun to cultivate the ascetic ideal that came to flower in Christianity. Moreover, one of the principal divinities of Mesopotamia, Inanna/Ishtar, was the goddess of love in all the senses of the term. Nearly all of what survives in regard to homosexuality pertains specifically to relations between men, which are attested from the beginning of the third millennium. A depiction of anal intercourse shows the receptor kneeling while drinking through a straw, perhaps a scene of an orgy in a tavern. It is paralleled by a tableau in which a woman takes the passive role. There are also lead figurines from the end of the second millennium depicting amorous encounters between males.

Literary sources include oneiric texts devoted to erotic dreams in which the subject has intercourse with males: a god, a king, a notable, another man's son, a young man, a child, his own father-in-law, even a corpse. The manner in which the material is codified does not allow the modern investigator to derive much information, although several passages insist on the youth of the partner, hence on the pederastic character of their relationship. There are also divination texts in which the sexual happenings of everyday life are the basis for prognostication; a small number presuppose a male partner, who may be either an equal in social rank, a professional prostitute, or a slave belonging to the household. The homosexual activity is nowhere reproved, and does not even incur the stigma of "pollution," as may result from sexual contact with a woman.

Laws. The Middle Assyrian laws contain a provision that penalizes the active partner who has forcibly sodomized his equal by prescribing that he be anally penetrated and then castrated, in strict accordance with the *lex talionis*. The preceding article in this text deals with the false accusation of repeated passive anal intercourse, treated as analogous to the slanderous charge that one's wife has engaged in prostitution. The stigma in both cases would have attached to the passive partner trafficking in his or her body. The passive role in the homosexual relationship is assimilated to the woman's in the heterosexual one.

Prostitution. Mesopotamian society did possess its class of professional male prostitutes, the *assinnu*, the *kulu'u*, and the *kurgarru*, some specified as being young, who performed various functions in the sphere of entertainment and religious liturgy. In the former capacity, they played musical instruments, sang and danced, and may even have performed pantomimes or dramatic pieces; in the latter, they officiated at ceremonies in honor of Ishtar, sometimes in the costume of the opposite sex, sometimes in erotic rites for the pleasure of the worshipper.

They are clearly associated with female devotees of Ishtar, whose role as hierodules is abundantly attested in the cuneiform literature. In one text the *assinnu* is overpowered by a desire to be penetrated by other males, while in others the physical charm of the subject is stressed. On the other hand, the androgyne of later Greek art and mythology was unknown to the Mesopotamians. That these hierodules could be bisexual and father children emerges from passages that allude to their children, with no suggestion that these were merely adopted. However, the *assinnu* might also be a **eunuch**, a "half male" in the language of the texts, which further equate him with a "broken vessel."

The appearance and behavior of the male prostitute were markedly effeminate: one of the emblems that he carried was the spindle, the symbol par excellence of women's labor; in one cuneiform text the term *nas pilaqqi*, "spindle-bearer" immediately follows *assinnu* and *kurgarru*, an affinity that sheds light on **David's** imprecation in II Samuel 3:29 ("one holding the spindle"). Certain of them had feminine names, and the guilds of male and female prostitutes at times included persons of the opposite sex from that of virtually all the others. The male might even serve as the lover of a woman, so that no strict line of demarcation was observed. There is even an astrological text in which the outcome of a given juxtaposition of the planets is that "Men will install *kurgarrus* in their homes, and the latter will bear them children."

The attitude of contemporary Mesopotamian society toward these male prostitutes was ambivalent at best; even if they played a necessary role in its civilization, as individuals they were marginalized and subjected to intense contempt. In the Akkadian version of the Descent of Ishtar to the Nether World, Ereshkigal burdens Asushu-namir (and through him, all his imitators in the future), with a great curse that afflicts him with a pitiful existence, exposed to every mishap, and banished to the very fringe of the social space occupied by the denizens of the city. Others who shared this marginality were the "ecstatics," the eccentrics, and the insane. As "men transformed into women," male prostitutes were stigmatized even when they performed in the cult of Ishtar.

Literary Aspects. Quite different was the role of the homoerotic in the encounter of the hero **Gilgamesh** with the companion of his adventrues, Enkidu. Here the analogy with the **Achilles**–Patroclus relationship in the *Iliad* is striking. If the institutionalized pederasty of the golden age of Hellenic civilization had not yet come into being, still the homosexual element entered spontaneously into friendship between males, and was not suppressed or condemned by their peers. It could even rival a heterosexual attachment, as when Gilgamesh spurns Ishtar's advances. Male bonding was superior to marriage in a society where the sexes were rigidly segregated in private life and loyalty on the battlefield was a vital element of comradeship. Recent investigators have discovered subtle patterns of erotic double-entendre in the original texts of the epic of Gilgamesh, one of the first classics of world literature. That such effusions of sexual feeling should have been present in historical liaisons, such as between David and Jonathan, is therefore only natural.

If love in the explicit sense is but rarely mentioned in Mesopotamian texts, the same intensity of feeling that occurs today could not have been alien to the hearts of men who lived four thousand years ago. In a series of prayers to accord divine favor to amorous attachment, one is concerned with "the love of a man for a man." No religious condemnation or taboo in any way analogous to the one in Judaism and Christianity has ever been found in the sources for modern knowledge of the land between the two rivers— texts that have the advantage of being contemporary and authentic, not copies made (or censored) by scribes of later centuries who cherished a wholly different moral code.

Of lesbianism the Mesopotamian literature has virtually nothing to say: there is but a single mention of a homosexual relationship between two women in the thousands of cuneiform texts uncovered and deciphered since the mid-nineteenth century. This may be explained partly by the fact that the scribes who composed and transcribed the tablets were male, and partly by the circumstance that women's lives were private and outside the concern of male society. The lone exception is an astrological prognosis that "women will be coupled," which reveals that such practices were not unknown, and need not even have been rare.

Conclusion. Mesopotamian records attest that at the dawn of Near Eastern civilization, homosexual activity was, if not glorified, at least accepted as a part of everyday life alongside its heterosexual counterpart, and while the passive-effeminate male prostitute was stigmatized, the heroic component of male love was recognized and celebrated in literature of true verbal art. No ascetic tendencies in Mesopotamian religion cast their shadow over the erotic bond between males, and Ishtar, the goddess of love, gave her blessing to homosexual and heterosexual adorers alike.

BIBLIOGRAPHY. Jean Bottéro and H. Petschow, "Homosexualität," *Reallexikon der Assyriologie*, 4 (1975), 459–468; Harry A. Hoffner, Jr., "Incest, Sodomy and Bestiality in the Ancient Near East," *Orient and Occident: Essays Presented to Cyrus H. Gordon*, Kevelaer: Verlag Butzon & Bercker, 1973, pp. 81–90; Anne Draffkorn Kilmer, "A Note on an Overlooked Word-play in the Akkadian Gilgamesh," *Zikir Sumim: Assyriological Studies Presented to F. R. Kraus*, Leiden: E. J. Brill, 1982, pp. 128–32.

Warren Johansson

METASTASIO (ASSUMED NAME OF PIETRO TRAPASSI; 1698–1782)

Italian poet and **opera** librettist. Hearing the ten-year-old lad improvising poems to a street crowd, an aristocratic literary critic, Gian Vincenzo Gravina, adopted the son of a Roman grocer. Gravina hellenized Trapassi to Metastasio and gave his young protégé, whom he made his heir adoptive, a fine education, but when the strain of competing with the leading *improvvisatori* in Italy nearly wrecked the ambitious boy's health, he sent his beloved protégé to rest quietly by the sea in Calabria.

In 1718 Gravina died, bequeathing a fortune to Metastasio, who had become an abbé. Having squandered his legacy in a mere two years, he had to apprentice himself to a Neapolitan lawyer. In 1721 he composed a serenata, *Gli Orti Esperidi*, at the request of the viceroy, to celebrate the birthday of the Empress of Austria. The Roman prima donna Marianna Benti-Bulgarelli (known as "La Romanina" [1684–1734]), who had played the leading role in the serenata, took Metastasio into her house where he long resided (together with her husband), and eventually moved in his parents and siblings. La Romanina persuaded him to abandon the law and to devote himself to music. Through La Romanina he came to know the leading composers: Porpora, Hasse, Pergolesi, Alessandro Scarlatti, Vinci, Leo, Durante, and Marcello—all of whom later set his libretti to music, and singers, with one of whom, the castrato Carlo Broschi (better known as Farinelli; 1705–1782), he may have had an affair. His 26 somewhat conventional melodramas (1723–1771), based on heterosexual love stories from classical mythology and history influenced by the seventeenth-century French theatre, often had absurd plots and little concern for historical accuracy. Yet when set to music, particularly of the Venetian school which was then eclipsing the Neapolitan, they became masterpieces, some being adapted over seventy times.

After 1723, always encouraged by La Romanina, Metastasio produced libretti rapidly, beginning with *Didone abandonata*, which was loosely derived from Vergil. In 1729 he was appointed poet to the court at Vienna, then beginning its rise to become the world center of music, where Haydn arrived fifteen years later. He moved in with a Spanish Neapolitan, Nicolò Martinez, with whom he remained until his death and composed there his finest plays, including *Olimpiade*, *La Clemenza di Tito* (later set by Wolfgang Amadeus Mozart), *Achille in Sciro*, and *Attilio Regolo*, his own favorite. He became so close to the Countess of Althann, Marianna Pignatelli, that many believed that they had secretly married. Perhaps out of jealousy and seeking an engagement at the court theatre, La Romanina set out for Vienna, but died en route, leaving her fortune to Metastasio, who declined it.

Metastasio's later cantatas and the canzonetti he sent his friend the castrato Farinelli were produced before the Countess of Althann died in 1755. As his fame increased, the collection of his works in his own library stretched to over forty editions and were translated into all major languages, even modern Greek. With the musical changes introduced by Christoph Willibald Gluck and Mozart, the innovator who created the "modern" opera, his works came to seem old fashioned and increasingly difficult to adapt, and after 1820 were neglected. Farinelli, whom he called his "twin brother," best expounded his poetry. The decline of **castrati** combined with the popularity of *opéra bouffe* to end his domination of the operatic stage, which had lasted almost a century. Maria Theresa prohibited the huge sums expended by her predecessor Charles VI on operas.

Opera, the chief cultural export of eighteenth-century Italy to northern Europe, was often regarded with suspicion there—especially in England, where it was even blamed for the spread of homosexuality. Inasmuch as Italy was then in the throes of Counter-Reformation repression and papal obscurantism, this claim seems ironic until one remembers that the balconies of Sicilian opera houses and the standing room of the old Metropolitan in New York (to give two far-flung examples) provided not only quarry but even sexual action for homosexuals, a disproportionate number of whom are *aficionados* of this artificial but consummate art form. Yet Metastasio sailed serenely—more or less through troubled waters. With today's revival of *opera seria*, works set to his libretti are once again being performed, including his *Olimpiade* during the 1988 Olympic Games.

William A. Percy

MEXICO

The modern Mexican republic displays a fascinating duality of indigenous (Amerindian) and European-derived themes. The process of integrating the two streams is still continuing.

Pre-Columbian Societies. At the point of European contact, the area we now call Mexico (along with parts of Guatemala and Honduras) was inhabited by numerous diverse societies. But in spite of prominent regionalism exhibited by Mayas, Zapotecs, Mexicas (Aztecs), and others, it was a single culture area. When the Spaniards arrived early in the sixteenth century, some parts of Mesoamerica were in a state of urban decline—particularly the Mayan areas. Yet the central highlands of Mexico were experiencing a cultural florescence. In the Valley of Mexico, the Nahuatls or "Aztecs" of the central valley of Mexico lived in urban centers such as Texcoco, Tlatelolco, and Mexico/Tenochitlán (all now part of the federal district). These people claimed a direct heritage of urban living on a massive scale which dated back to the founding of Teotihuacán, about 300 B.C. In comparison with European cities of the time, the largest Aztec

City, Mexico/Tenochitlán, is said to have been surpassed only by Paris. From the Valley of Mexico, the Aztecs politically dominated most of Mesoamerica and extracted a heavy tribute of raw materials, finished products, slaves, and sacrificial victims. However, they usually allowed a fair degree of home rule and the continuance of local traditions within the various cultures of their empire.

The Aztecs exhibited a profound duality in their approach to sexual behavior. On one hand, they held public rituals which were at times very erotic, but on the other, they were extremely prudish in everyday life. In their pantheon, the Mexicans worshipped a deity, Xochiquetzal (feathered flower of the maguey), who was the goddess of non-procreative sexuality and love. Originally the consort of Tonacatecutli, a creator god, Xochiquetzal dwelled in the heaven of Tamaoanchan, where she gave birth to all humankind. However, subsequently she was abducted by Tezcatlipoca, a war god, and raped. This event mystically redefined her character from the goddess of procreative love to the goddess of non-reproductive activities. Aztec deities often had such multiple dualistic aspects such as male and female and good and evil. Xochiquetzal was both male and female at the same time and in her male aspect (called Xochipilli), s/he was worshipped as the deity of male homosexuality and male prostitution. In Xochiquetzal's positive aspect, s/he was the deity of loving relationships and the god/dess of artistic creativity; it was said that non-reproductive love was like a piece of art—beautiful and one-of-a-kind. But in her dualistic opposite, as the deity of sexual destruction, s/he incited lust and rape, and inflicted people with venereal disease and piles.

In a partly mythical, partly historical account of their past, the Aztecs asserted that there had been four worlds before their own and that the world immediately preceding the present was one of much homosexuality. This "world" may refer to the Toltec empire (conquered by the Aztecs around 1000 A.D.). In this "Age of the Flowers, of Xochiquetzal," the people supposedly gave up the "manly virtues of warfare, administration and wisdom," and pursued the "easy, soft life of sodomy, perversion, the Dance of the Flowers, and the worship of Xochiquetzal." It has been suggested that the "Fourth World" refers to the empire of the Toltecs because there are similar statements referring to Toltec invaders in historical records of the Maya in Yucatan, e.g., the Chilam Balam of Chumayel state. The Yucatan Maya held large private sexual parties which included homosexuality. However, according to J. Eric Thompson, they were aghast at the public sexual rites of their Toltec conquerors.

As noted, the Aztecs allowed the people they conquered to maintain their own customs. Thus, although the Aztecs were publically sexually exuberant and privately prudish, their subjects varied greatly in their sexual customs—as the Maya example illustrates; and in some Mesoamerican cultures it appears that homosexuality was quite prominent. The area that is now the state of Vera Cruz was very well known for this activity. When Bernal Díaz del Castillo reached Vera Cruz with Cortes, he wrote of the native priests: "the sons of chiefs, they did not take women, but followed the bad practices of sodomy" (Idell, p. 87). When the conquistadors reached Cempoala, near the present city of Vera Cruz, Cortes felt compelled to make a speech in which he stated, "Give up your sodomy and all your other evil practices, for so commands Our Lord God . . ." (Díaz del Castillo in Idell, p. 8). Also, Cortes wrote his king, the Emperor Charles V: "We know and have been informed without room for doubt that all (Veracruzanos) practice the abominable sin of sodomy." Most of them were sodomites and especially those who lived along the coast and in the hot lands were dressed as women; "boys went about to make money by this diabolical and abominable vice"

(Idell, p. 87). It would be folly to accept all the statements about homosexuals at face value. Spaniards of the time also claimed that homosexuality had been introduced into Spain by the Moors and attributed sodomy to new enemies as well. Nonetheless, there is an interesting legend in Mexico that says the Spaniards were more easily able to capture the Aztec emperor Montezuma because they sent a blond page to seduce the ruler; and when the emperor had fallen thoroughly in love, threatened to separate the two if the emperor did not place himself in the hands of the Spaniards. While the Spaniards' allies, the Tlaxcalans, asserted the story was true, the Spaniards denied it. However, the tale may help us to understand why the Aztecs, who were so blatant in public but puritanical in private shouted "Cuilone, Cuilone" ("queer, queer") from their canoes at the Spaniards during the "Noche Triste" when Cortes was forced to retreat from Mexico City losing many soldiers (Novo, p. 43). The warriors' epithets, of course, may only have been another example of labeling one's enemies homosexual.

To summarize the material we have at the time of the conquest, homosexuality played an important part in much of the religious life in Mexico, and was commonly accepted in private life in many Mesoamerican cultures as well; but the prevailing sentiment of the ruling Aztecs outside of ritual was one of sexual rigidity, prudishness, and heavy repression.

Colonial Mexico. In the opening years of the sixteenth century, the Spaniards discovered Mesoamerica and conquered it. One of the most dramatic social changes which occurred was the evolution of Mestizo or *ladino* culture. Miscegenation, acculturation, and the melding of beliefs created a social milieu which was neither Spanish nor Indian, but which has come to form the core features of modern Mexico. The Spaniards held a moral viewpoint toward homosexuality which (aside from ritual) paralleled that of the Aztecs.

In Mexico, after the conquest, all pagan rituals were banned and their rationale discredited. Mestizo culture came to exhibit a melding of Aztec attitudes toward private homosexuality with those of the Spaniards. Indeed, the former Aztec ritual tradition which celebrated homosexuality as communion with the gods was all but lost. In early Colonial times, when Bishop Zumarraga was the Apostolic Inquisitor of Mexico, sodomy was a prime concern for the **Inquisition**. The usual penalties for homosexuality were stiff fines, spiritual penances, public humiliation, and floggings. However, homosexuality was tried by the civil courts as well, whence people were sentenced to the galleys or put to death.

Homosexual Social Life. At present, the only records which give us a glimpse of homosexual social life during the Colonial period are the records of court proceedings when homosexual scandals occurred. Of such events, a purge which took place in Mexico City between 1656 and 1663 is the best known. Whereas heretics and Jews were burned in the Alameda, now a park near the center of Mexico City, homosexual sodomites were burned in a special burning ground in another part of the city, San Lázaro, because sodomy was not a form of heresy and thus fell into an ambiguous category of offenses. Thus, the group was marched to San Lázaro where the officials first garroted them, starting with one Cotita de la Encarnación. They "were done with strangling all of them at eight o'clock that night; . . . then they set them afire." Novo states that several hundred people came from the city to watch the event. It should be noted that strangling the victims before burning them was considered an act of mercy; for burning was such terrible agony that it was feared that the prisoners would forsake their faith in God and thus lose their immortal souls. The purge seems to have ended when the superiors in Spain wrote back to Mexico that they did not have papal authority to grant the jurisdiction the Mexican Holy Office requested, and that the Inquisitors were "not to become involved in these matters or to enter into any litigation concerning them."

Independent Mexico. Mexican independence from Spain in 1821 brought an end to the Inquisition and the kind of homosexual oppression described above. The intellectual influence of the French revolution and the brief French occupation of Mexico (1862–67) resulted in the adoption of the Napoleonic Code. This meant that sexual conduct in private between adults, whatever their gender, ceased to be a criminal matter. In matters concerning homosexuality, the Mexican government held that law should not invade the terrain of the individual moral conscience, in order to protect the precious concerns of sexual freedom and security; and that the law should limit itself "to the minimum ethics indispensable to maintaining society." In limiting itself thus, the Mexican law would seem to be obeying a certain Latin tradition of overt indifference.

This change of legal attitude was obviously a tremendous improvement for homosexuals over previous Aztec and Spanish ways of dealing with homosexuality, and was considerably more liberal than legislation in much of the United States. Yet it did not grant people the right to be overtly homosexual; for included in the "minimum ethics indispensable to maintaining society" are laws against solicitation and any public behavior which is considered socially deviant or contrary to the folkways and customs of the time. Accordingly, one is again confronted with the basic cultural structure—homosexual expression between individuals if known is considered a form of deviation which can bring serious consequences.

"The Dance of the Forty-One Maricones." On the night of November 20, 1901, Mexico City police raided an affluent drag ball, arresting 42 cross-dressed men and dragging them off to Belén Prison. One was released. The official account

was that she was a "real woman," but persistent rumors circulated that she was a very close relative of President Porfirio Díaz, and even today "número cuarenta-y-dos" (number 42, the one who got away) is used to refer to someone covertly *pasivo.* Those arrested were subjected to many humiliations in jail. Some were forced to sweep the streets in their dresses. Eventually, all 41 were inducted into the 24th Battalion of the Mexican Army and sent to the Yucatan to dig ditches and clean latrines. The ball and its aftermath were much publicized, among other places in broadsides by Guadalupe Posada (who provided the cross-dressed men with moustaches and notably upper-class dress). Although the raid on the dance of the 41 *maricones* was followed by a less-publicized raid of a lesbian bar on December 4, 1901, in Santa María, the regime was soon preoccupied by more serious threats.

The Mexican Revolution is generally dated 1901–10, but if one includes the attempted counter-revolutions of the Cristeros, armed conflict continued through the end of the 1920s. The capital city with a population of half a million before the revolution became a major metropolis with seven million residents by 1959, eighteen million or more by 1988.

Despite the international depression of the 1930s and along with the social revolution overseen by President Lázaro Cárdenas (1934–40), the growth of Mexico City was accompanied by the opening of homosexual bars and baths supplementing the traditional cruising locales of the Alameda, the Zócalo, Paseo de Reforma, and Calle Madero (formerly Plateros). Those involved in homosexual activity continued to live with their families, and there were no homophile publications. In the absence of a separate residential concentration, the lower classes tended to accept the stereotypes of the dominant society and enact them. While some of the cosmopolitan upper classes rejected the stereotypical effeminacy expected of maricones, they tended to emulate European dandies of the late nineteenth century—"clever, non-political, elegant, charming men trying to outdo everybody else in the Salon . . . the Mexican homosexuals aspired to be French decadents like **Montesquiou**" in the characterization of one interviewee. Wildean influence and the emulation of Hollywood screen goddesses followed. During World War II, ten to fifteen gay bars operated in Mexico City, with dancing permitted in at least two, El África and El Triunfo. Relative freedom from official harassment continued until 1959 when Mayor Uruchurtu closed every gay bar following a grisly triple murder. Motivated by moralistic pressure to "clean up vice," or at least to keep it invisible from the top, and by the lucrativeness of bribes from patrons threatened with arrests and from establishments seeking to operate in comparative safety, Mexico City's policemen have a reputation for zeal in persecution of homosexuals.

Some observers claim that gay life is more developed in the second-largest city, Guadalajara. In both cities there have been short-lived gay liberation groups since the early 1970s, e.g., La Frente Liberación Homosexual formed in 1971 around protesting Sears stores' firing of gay employees in 1971 in Mexico City, and La Frente Homosexual de Acción Revolucionaria which protested the 1983 roundups in Guadalajara. There are now annual gay pride marches, gay publications (e.g., *Macho Tips* which includes a nude centerfold), and gay and lesbian organizations in contact with organizations in other countries. Although there have been challenges to the dominant conception of homosexuality as necessarily related to gender-crossing, the simplistic *activo–pasivo* logic continues to channel thought and behavior in Mexico, as elsewhere in **Latin America**.

BIBLIOGRAPHY. Albert Idell, *The Bernal Díaz Chronicles*, Garden City, NY: Doubleday, 1956; Salvador Novo, *Las Locas, el sexo, los burdeles*, Mexico City: Novaro, 1972; Antonio Requena, "Noticias y consideraciones sobre las anormalidades de los aborígenes americanos: sodomía," *Acta Venozolana*, 1 (1945), 43–71 (trans. as "Sodomy Among Native American Peoples," *Gay Sunshine* 38/39 [1979], 37–39); J. Eric Thompson, *Maya History and Religion*, Norman: University of Oklahoma Press, 1970.

Stephen O. Murray and
Clark L. Taylor

MICHELANGELO BUONARROTI (1475–1564)

Italian sculptor, painter, architect, and poet. Michelangelo, who was to become the greatest artist of the **Renaissance**, was born the son of a magistrate in Caprese near Florence. Raised in **Florence**, he was apprenticed for three years to the artist Domenico Ghirlandaio. His studies of the antique sculptures in the Boboli gardens brought him into contact with the neo-Platonist thinker **Ficino**. Although there has been some dispute as to the direct effect of neo-Platonic ideas on his early work, they certainly surfaced later, shaping his self-concept as an artist and a psychosexual being.

In 1496 Michelangelo went to Rome, where he carved his first great masterpiece, the Vatican *Pietà*. This work, which solved the problem that had vexed earlier sculptors of convincingly showing a grown man reclining in the lap of his mother, made him famous, and Michelangelo triumphantly returned to Florence in 1501. Here he carved the heroic nude *David*, a traditional symbol of the city's underdog status that he endowed with a new power. He then returned to Rome to work on a vast project for the tomb of pope Julius II. This daunting task was never completed, in part because the pope diverted Michelangelo's efforts to the fresco painting of the Sistine ceiling, a work of encyclopedic scope and ubiquitous urgency. In the 1980s the cleaning of the ceiling, which had become much obscured with grime and restorations over the centuries, revealed brilliant colors, but was attacked by some critics as having damaged it in other respects.

The artist then turned to the Medici tombs in Florence, which were commissioned by the new pope, Leo X. After the expulsion of the Medici from the city in 1529, Michelangelo defected to the republicans, but was forgiven and reinstated by that powerful family not long thereafter. In 1534 he returned to Rome. In the thirty years that remained to him he painted the *Last Judgment* on the wall of the Sistine Chapel and the frescoes of the Capella Paolina. He also addressed himself to architecture, and to several unfinished sculptures.

When Michelangelo was a boy, his father had opposed his choice of profession as being fit only for a laborer. Long before the artist died, however, he was regularly hailed as *Il Divino*, an almost blasphemous title for a unique artist who exemplified the idea that the supreme genius surpasses the ordinary rules to which other artists are subject.

For fifty years Michelangelo enjoyed undisputed sway as an artist. Yet his psychosexual identity was much less secure. Throughout his life Michelangelo experienced a powerful emotive and erotic attraction to men, particularly those in their late teens and early twenties. The presence of apprentices in his studio, who were undoubtedly among the models for such sensual male nudes as the Slaves for the Julius tomb and the *ignudi* of the Sistine ceiling, exposed him to constant temptation. At least one case is recorded where a former apprentice attempted to blackmail the artist by threatening to tell tales, while in another instance the father of a potential apprentice offered the boy's services in bed. (Michelangelo indignantly refused.)

In 1532 the artist met a young Roman nobleman, Tommaso de' Cavalieri, to whom he was to be devoted for the rest of his life. To Cavalieri he sent drawings, including the famous one of an eagle (evidently himself) carrying a beautiful **Ganymede** (Cavalieri) aloft. Poems and letters also avow his passion. However, beginning in his late fifties, this love, being directed to a person whose standing placed him far above the working-class youths to whom he was accustomed, assumed a sublimated character.

Michelangelo's poems contain many fascinating hints of his self-understanding. Yet his language is difficult and his handling of philosophical ideas unsure. Revealingly, in 1623 the artist's grandnephew and editor, Michelangelo the Younger, bowdlerized them, changing many male pronouns to female ones. This act (since remedied in modern editions) shows that contemporaries were embarrassed by his love objects.

While Michelangelo's enemies (including the spiteful **Aretino**) gossiped, his friends insisted on his chaste purity. As yet we have no actual proof of genital contacts with young men. However, what evidence there is suggests that they were not lacking—though probably sparse—in his earlier years, ceasing later. Michelangelo was born into an era in which the relatively easy-going attitudes toward artists' sexual peccadillos that prevailed in the early and middle decades of the fifteenth century had yielded to more disapproving ones, a development that climaxed in the bigoted prudery of the incipient Counterreformation of the middle decades of the sixteenth century. Michelangelo witnessed such contemporaries as **Leonardo** da Vinci, Sandro **Botticelli**, and Benvenuto **Cellini** disgraced by charges of sodomy. Evidently, he was able to convince himself, and many others as well, that his "spiritual" love of beautiful young men had nothing in common with base acts of buggery.

In an as-told-to life penned by his epigone Ascanio Condivi, Michelangelo seems to have intended to attribute his attraction to men to the stars. Referring to the fact that he was born under the joint influence of Mercury and Venus, he surely knew that the ancient **astrological** tradition stemming from Ptolemy held that this conjunction caused men to be attracted more to boys than women. Thus the tendency was not the product of a whim, but was foreordained by cosmic forces. However this may be, because of his fame and the changing temper of the times in which he lived, Michelangelo experienced unique pressures on his sexual self-understanding. These pressures are linked to—though they cannot explain— the special intensity of his art, the *terribiltà* for which he is renowned.

BIBLIOGRAPHY. Giorgio Lise, *L'Altro Michelangelo*, Milan: Cordani, 1981; James M. Saslow, "'A Veil of Ice between My Heart and the Fire': Michelangelo's Sexual Identity and Early Modern Constructs of Homosexuality," *Genders*, 2 (July 1988), 77–90.

Wayne R. Dynes

MIDDLE AGES

The Middle Ages constitute the major phase of European history that stands between classical antiquity (**Greece** and **Rome**), on the one hand, and the **Renaissance**, on the other. The beginning of the Renaissance can be placed with relative precision in fifteenth-century Italy, whence the new outlook spread in the following century to the rest of Europe. The other boundary, the end of classical antiquity, cannot be pinpointed, as the change was a gradual process beginning in the third century of our era and not completed until the fifth or even later. Moreover, to understand the formation of the Middle Ages it is necessary to look back even earlier: to the origins of **Christianity**. Inspired by the teachings of **Jesus** Christ, the church did not achieve firm institutions until the latter half of the second century. At this time one can confirm the separation from Judaism, the consolidation of the canon of writings known as the **New Testament**, the crystalization of a system of governance based on bishops as presiding officers, and a growing roster of martyrs created by official persecution—in attacks which were to have the ultimate effect of strengthening rather than smothering the church.

The Patristic Period and the Official Recognition of Christianity. From this time onwards comes a large body of exegetical tracts and theological disquisitions known as the **Patristic** writings. Taken as a whole, these texts tend to confirm the ascetic morality of the New Testament. In those rare instances where they depart from rigorism, as in relaxation of the ban on visual images, there was extensive and heated controversy, with both sides strenuously maintaining their positions. In the case of sex between males, no such debate occurred, a silence signifying that the matter needed no discussion, for the negative judgment of homosexuality enshrined in the Levitical prohibitions was incorporated in the constitution of the primitive church and reinforced by New Testament passages condemning sexual activity between males in particular and all forms of sexual depravity and impurity in general. Occasionally, the Fathers do attack the corrupt morals of pagan pederasty, warning their own flock not to yield to temptation.

The transition from the toleration and indifference which the pagan ancient Mediterranean world had shown toward homosexuality to the implacable intolerance and social ostracism of the later Middle Ages could not have been effected overnight. Apologists for Christian rigorism would like to begin *in medias res*, claiming that "the Church taught, and people universally believed" that homosexual behavior was a crime against nature for which an act of divine wrath had destroyed Sodom and the neighboring cities. But this Jewish legend embellished with Hellenic moralizing was only gradually inculcated into the mass mind, particularly in countries outside the classical world and ignorant of Palestine and its geographical myths.

Constantine the Great's Edict of Milan (313) transformed Christianity from the faith of an embattled minority to what amounted to a state religion. Heretofore, the Roman empire had known no general antihomosexual legislation—the shadowy "Scantinian law" notwithstanding. In 342, however, the emperor Constantius issued a somewhat opaque decree making male homosexual conduct a capital crime. This enactment was followed in 390 by a more unambiguous antihomosexual statute, decreed by Valentinian II, Theodosius the Great, and Arcadius. It was Theodosius who consolidated the Christianization of the Roman empire by banning all competing faiths other than Judaism.

At the same time the ascetic ideal became diffused throughout Christian society, as monks took over leadership of the church, replacing the cultivated aristocracy that had earlier predominated. A key feature of asceticism was the exaltation of virginity for both men and women. Two polemical writings of St. Jerome, *Against Helvidius* (ca. 383) and *Against Jovinian* (ca. 393), advance arguments that condemn marriage altogether. Though St. Augustine and others modified this position, an aura of the less than ideal hung over even the limited acceptance of marriage for procreation only, and celibate monks and nuns became the culture heroes of the new society. Meanwhile Christian monasticism took shape.

Byzantium. The reign of Justinian (527–565) is remembered as a highwater mark of antihomosexuality. Of two novellae (new laws) referring to sodomy, one accuses the perpetrators of bringing on famines, earthquakes, and pestilences. Incorporated into the *Corpus Juris Civilis*, the great codification of Roman law undertaken at Justinian's behest, they lent official sanction to the superstitious fear of the homosexual as a Jonah figure. Justinian's court also made political use of charges of homosexual conduct to blackmail or discredit opponents, particularly of the Green circus faction. Needless to say, these measures did not stop same-sex activity in the ensuing centuries. A number of Byzantine emperors themselves are believed to have been homosexual, including Constantine V (741–775), Michael III (842–870)—who was murdered by his lover—Basil II (976–1025), Constantine VIII (1025–1028), and Constantine IX (1042–1055). Research is needed to document homosexuality in other sectors of Byzantine society. It is known to have flourished in the monasteries, and was an undoubted feature of urban life. There was also an interface, particularly in the later centuries, with Islamic homosexuality.

The So-Called "Dark Ages" in the West. In Western Europe the year 476 is the traditional date for the end of the Roman Empire, which was succeeded by barbarian kingdoms controlled by monarchs and gentry of Germanic origin. In their northern European home some Germanic tribes had prohibited certain types of homosexuality. According to a much-discussed passage in Tacitus "cowards and shirkers and the sexually infamous (*corpore infames*) are plunged in the mud of marshes with a hurdle on their heads" (*Germania*, 12), but close analysis of this passage shows that the Latin terms paraphrase Old Norse *argr* and that the text as a whole refers to cowardice in battle, not sexual conduct in private life. In apparent continuation of this tradition the medieval Scandinavians associated passive homosexuality with cowardice, subsuming both under the aforementioned epithet *argr*. In the fifth century when the Vandals took possession of Carthage in North Africa, they supposedly suppressed effeminate homosexuality with great brutality.

Despite this background, however, the barbarian kingdoms showed relatively little interest in antihomosexual legislation. The Germanic penal codes that replaced Roman law in territories detached from the Western Empire make little mention of homosexual conduct and have no term that in any way corresponds to the later notion of sodomy. Exceptionally, in seventh-century Visigothic Spain a particularly severe regime persecuted Jews and subjected homosexuals to the novel penalty of castration, clearly under the influence of inchoate **canon law**. Charlemagne (768–814), otherwise distinguished for his impressive program of administrative and cultural reform, contrived only to repeat the old prohibitions in a routine manner. The church, in the hands of manor-raised sons and brothers with little spiritual calling, was weak and ineffective.

What would appear to be the most important legal document from Western Europe in the period 500–1000 is in fact a forgery. Yet forgeries are sometimes even more revealing of the climate of opinion than authentic documents, for they express what their devisers would *like* the case to have been. A capitulary, supposedly issued by Charlemagne in 770, was actually written by one Benedict Levita about 850. The author shows interest in a number of sexual offenses, including sodomy. Apparently for the first time, he explicitly connects the penalty of burning at the stake with God's punishment of Sodom. A novel element is his ascription of the Christian defeat in Spain to the toleration of sodomy—echoing the old Germanic preoccupation with cowardice, but also anticipating the role of the sodomite as a scapegoat for all of society's ills and misfortunes, from earthquakes to reverses in battle.

More significant for the long run was the church's innovation of the **penitential** system for chastising sins according to their gravity. For the early Christians, still anticipating the imminence of the Second Coming, to commit a sin was an ineradicable blemish for which one must suffer the full dire penalty at the hour of Judgment. In time, however, the church began to modify this severity. In exchange for a specified penance the sinner could wipe his or her slate clean. This major change seems to have begun in the Celtic Church, from which we have the first main body of manuals, the Penitentials. These books assigned penalties in ascending order of severity ranging from simple kissing through mutual masturbation and interfemoral connection through oral and anal intercourse. They made due allowance for the age of the partners and occasionally mentioned lesbian behavior. The penalties vary considerably, from as little as 20 to 40 days' restriction of liberty for mutual masturbation to as much as 7 to 15 years for sodomy itself. We know little of the way these procedures worked in practice, but a certain amount of "plea bargaining" probably occurred. While the death penalties remained as part of inherited Roman law (civil as distinct from canon law), they do not seem to have been much imposed, if at all, in the early Middle Ages. With much of the countryside unconverted and unadministered, it would have been difficult to enforce draconian measures. The laws and regulations of this period are virtually the only source for the occurrence of homosexuality; no surviving documents record the disciplining or punishing of an individual or group of individuals by ecclesiastical or secular courts.

The Carolingian empire, poor and weak because Muslims controlled the Mediterranean and shut it off from world trade, collapsed when Charlemagne's grandsons warred over their portions of the legacy. Meanwhile, invaders came from all sides: Saracens by sea from the south, Magyar horsemen from the east, and, worst of all, Northmen from **Scandinavia** who, as their epics and sagas mostly written in thirteenth-century Iceland reveal, had their own form of homosexuality. Wreaking the worst devastation on Ireland and England, which like Normandy they eventually conquered and settled, the Northmen came in their long boats to ravage western Europe. The later Carolingians and their local officers, the counts, could not cope with the disintegrating empire. Consequently local strong men, barons, built wooden castles and manned them with knights, the new heavily armored horsemen developed by the Carolingians. A baron dominated the neighborhood from his rough castle, where he lived with his knights and squires, who often slept on pallets around the big center room, with the baron and his lady enjoying separate quarters. Commonly before 1000, knights did not marry, living rather like cowboys of the Old West in the one big room, occasionally seducing serving wenches, peasant girls, and inexperienced nuns. Such opportunities notwithstanding, a good deal of "situational homosexuality," especially between the knight and his squire, must have taken place. Evidence of such involvements is fragmentary, but it can be gathered among the Anglo-Norman, Northern French, and Provençal nobility, as well as among German royal families (witness **Frederick II**).

The Central Middle Ages. After 1000 an extraordinary economic advance in Western Europe spurred the growth of towns and educational institutions. Especially during "the Renaissance of the twelfth century" a remarkable body of homosexual love poetry in Latin reflects a highly sophisticated literary culture of a restricted upper crust. No evidence indicates that the text circulated generally among even the small community of the literate. Moreover, classical literary commonplaces and allusions suffuse this **medieval Latin poetry**. While it would be wrong to dismiss the texts as mere literary exercises, they cannot be regarded as direct and candid reflections of experience either. In addition, a tradition of effusive **friendship** among monks should not be confused with avowals of sexual passion. One is confronted then with what must be termed gay literature, but one that allows few conclusions about gay life in general.

Yet other less beguiling evidence survives. A passage from a late twelfth-century British historian, Richard of Devizes, gives a glimpse of a homosexual subculture that coexisted in medieval London with other marginalized elements of society, while Walter Map, an Englishman who had studied in Paris, complained of homosexuality there. In keeping with the German proverb "City air makes one free," the towns were increasingly the refuge of individuals uncomfortable living elsewhere. The migration of gay men and women to urban centers had begun. The new conditions of town life probably inspired the enactment of new sodomy legislation, beginning with that of the Council of Nablus in the Latin Kingdom of Jerusalem in 1120.

The authorities after 1000 became very interested in religious deviation or **heresy**. Perhaps the most formidable of these spiritual movements of dissidence was Albigensian dualism, which flourished particularly in the south of France. This heresy was believed, not altogether wrongly, to have come from the Balkans, from the Bulgarian Bogomils in particular. Their French persecutors applied the term *bougre* (*bulgarus*; bugger) to them, and by extension to heretics generally, from the beginning of the thirteenth century, which saw the establishment of the papal **Inquisition**. The association of heresy with sodomy, a recurring feature from this point onwards, gave *bougre* an additional meaning, that of sodomite. In English this sense has usurped the older one of "heretic," though the term is also used for heterosexual anal intercourse and for sexual relations with animals. Yet another medieval transformation gave *bougre* the meaning of **usurer**, someone who lent money at prohibited rates of interest. The attacks on the heretics are major historical exemplars of the orchestration of popular fears and prejudices by clerical and lay authority to punish actual deviation and to cow the rest of society into continued submission. The most notorious instance is Philip the Fair's repression of the **Templar** Order for heresy and sodomy in the early fourteenth century.

To the disciplining and purification of the people assured by the "two swords" of church and state corresponded a regimentation of higher knowledge, symbolized by the Scholastic movement. The best known figure in this trend is

Thomas **Aquinas**, whose *Summa Theologica* (1266–73) remains an imposing point of reference. As is well known, Aquinas created a new synthesis by weaving Aristotle together with the Patristic corpus, imparting to the whole a transcendent sense of order which compels comparison with the great Gothic cathedrals. Aquinas' classification of unnatural vice was to have resounding influence over the centuries. After a brief mention of masturbation, he divides unnatural intercourse into three kinds: with the wrong species (bestiality), the wrong gender (homosexual sodomy), and the wrong organ or vessel (heterosexual oral and anal intercourse), and declares that such sins are in gravity second only to murder.

If a certain degree of toleration or indifference to homosexuality had prevailed previously, after the end of the thirteenth century the individual known to have engaged in homosexual activity was both a criminal and an outcast, without rights or feelings that church or state needed to recognize in any way. Not to denounce and persecute him meant complicity. The penalties for homosexual activity between males (rarely between females, and then only when an artificial phallus was employed) ranged from compulsory fasting to confinement in irons, running the gauntlet, flogging with the cat o'nine tails, the pillory, branding, blinding, cutting off the ears, castration, and perpetual banishment. The death penalty prescribed by Leviticus was rarely enforced, but when it was, it took the form of hanging or burning at the stake. Some of the inhuman punishments of the Middle Ages lingered into the early nineteenth century, when the reformers of the criminal law secured their abolition by denouncing them as survivals of superstition and fanaticism.

The Later Middle Ages. In the fourteenth century the medieval synthesis began to break down, signaled by a climactic struggle between the papacy and the secular authorities. The only major innovation in official attitudes toward homosexuality was a gradual shift to enforcement by the secular authorities, beginning in such Italian cities as **Florence** and **Venice**, which had become sensitive not only through their growth and diversity, but also through greater appreciation of the literary heritage of classical antiquity, permeated with pederasty. Even king **Edward II** of England was overthrown and murdered because of his homosexuality. What effects the Black Death (1348–49), Europe's greatest epidemic, may have had on sexuality are unknown, but the Jews, already persecuted since the Crusades, were made scapegoats. Certainly a vital urban subculture of homosexuality was alive at this time, though one catches only fleeting glimpses of it in the literature. With the coming of a new secular spirit in the **Renaissance** more detailed records of the life and attitudes of homosexual men and women finally emerge.

The disapproval of homosexuality in Western Christian civilization is the last and most pertinacious survival of medieval intolerance, one for which the church would now gladly disown responsibility, even while its political supporters do everything in their power to keep the archaic statutes on the books and frustrate liberal demands for the acknowledgement of gay rights. Even the medieval attitudes have not totally lost their respectability— witness the undisguised hatred and contempt which many display without compunction in regard to homosexuals, when they would be ashamed to avow such feelings toward members of religious communities other than their own. So the homophobia of today is a part of the "living past"—of the persistence of the beliefs and superstitions of the Middle Ages in the midst of an otherwise enlightened successor civilization.

See also **Capital Crime, Homosexuality as; Common Law; Law, Feudal and Royal; Law, Germanic; Law, Municipal; Papacy.**

BIBLIOGRAPHY. John Boswell, *Christianity, Social Tolerance and Homosexuality*, Chicago: Chicago University Press, 1980; Michael Goodich, *The Unmentionable Vice: Homosexuality in the Later Medieval Period*, Santa Barbara: ABC-Clio, 1979.
Wayne R. Dynes

MILITARY

The relationship between homosexuality and the military profession is a complex and paradoxical one. The modern stereotype of the homosexual male as lacking in manliness is utterly belied by the masculine character of the traditional warrior who is also passionately attracted to his own sex. Instead of diminishing the warlike nature of the tribe, this tendency immensely strengthened its valor and endurance. The homoerotic bond fostered ideals of heroism, courage, resourcefulness, and tenacity among the warrior caste, and exalted these virtues to the apogee of public honor. Such was the case among the Dorians of ancient **Greece** in the seventh century B.C. and among the **Samurai** of feudal Japan.

Ancient Greece. The virile and warlike Hellenic tribes, migrating southward into the Peloponnesus and to the island of **Crete**, institutionalized the custom of *paiderasteia* (literally "boy-love"). This custom meant the love of an older warrior for a younger one, who corresponded to the squire or page attending the medieval knight. The attachment was always conceived as having an element of physical passion, sometimes slight, sometimes dominant and all-engrossing. If it originally designated the heroic devotion of comrades to each other, it was later extended to the more spiritual relationship that prepared a boy for intellectual life and for public service to the *polis* (city-state), and also to the unabashed sensuality recorded in the twelfth book of the **Greek Anthology**.

In **Sparta** and in Crete it was customary for every youth of good character to have his lover, and every educated and honorable adult was bound to be the lover and protector of a youth. The connection was intimate and faithful, and recognized by the state. The citizen of Sparta was a professional soldier throughout life; his landholding, cultivated by helots, assured him a sufficient income to devote himself to his obligations to the state. The Spartan form of pederasty was imprinted with virility, with male comradeship, and with fidelity; the physical aspect was secondary, though rarely absent. At home the youth was constantly under the gaze of his lover, who was to him a role model and mentor; on the battlefield they fought side by side, if need be to the death, as in the inscription commemorating the battle of Thermopylae: "O stranger, tell the Lacedaemonians that we fell here in obedience to our country's sacred laws." The pederastic spirit guarded the cradle of Western civilization against the Oriental despotism that a Persian victory would have imposed on the Hellenes.

Whether or not a formal abduction of the youth by his lover took place, the institution of military comradeship spread far and wide among the Greeks, and immense importance accrued to what was regarded as a cornerstone of public life, a recognized source of political and social initiative, an incentive to valor, an inspiration to art and literature, and a custom consecrated by religion and divine sanction. The ethos of the ruling caste was inculcated by pederasty, so that Pausanias of Athens could solemnly declare that the strongest army would be one composed entirely of pairs of male lovers. Stories of the heroic feats of such couples testify to the profound concern which the Greeks felt for the subject. The heroism of the Sacred Band of **Thebes**, organized on Pausanias' model, who perished to the last man in the battle of Chaeronea (338 B.C.) while fighting against the huge army of

Philip of Macedon, sealed the glorious tradition of comradeship-in-arms, and engraved upon it for all time an ineffaceable symbol of valor.

Japan. The Samurai of feudal **Japan** afford another example of the part played by homoerotic attachments in the military life of a nation; the Japanese knighthood dominated its country until the end of the Tokugawa era (1867). The Samurai had their own tradition of chivalry, simplicity of living, bravery, and loyalty and dedication to the service of nation and Emperor. Numbering some two million in all, the Samurai were exempted from taxation and privileged to wear two swords. The ideals of Bushido, as the Japanese code of knighthood was called, were those of a nobleman and warrior: heroism, courage, endurance, justice in dealing with others, and unflinching readiness to die in the call of duty. "To live when it is right to live, and to die only when it is right to die—that is true courage," said a Japanese author. All commercial pursuits and gainful activity were forbidden the warrior caste, but the finer arts were not neglected. The blend of the masculine and feminine that marks the homosexual personality was inherent in the Japanese character— the virile strongly pronounced but alloyed with a feminine tenderness and delicacy. The study of letters, of poetry, and of music was widespread. The intellectual and moral heritage of feudal Japan stemmed from the Samurai ethos, which like *paiderasteia* in ancient Greece, gave an impetus to every facet of national life.

To the Samurai it seemed more manly and heroic that men should love other males and consort sexually with them than with women. Almost every knight sought out a youth who could be worthy of him, and formed a close blood brotherhood. The attachment could provoke jealousy or even lead to a duel, as the stories told by **Saikaku** Ihara in *Nanshoku Okagami* (Tales of Manly Love; 1687) attest. The passionate love of a knight for his page—*kosho* in Japanese—could at times end in the heroic death of both partners on the battlefield. Such relationships were characteristic of the southern rather than the northern provinces. The region of Satsuma is particularly mentioned as the center of Japanese military pederasty, and public opinion in Japan held the affection to reinforce the manliness and fighting spirit of its natives. The Tokugawa era has also left to posterity other literary works that describe the adventures of pairs of lovers, their heroism, and self-sacrifice. As late as the Russo-Japanese War (1904–05) such homoerotic relationships persisted in the army, between officers and soldiers, and underlay the defiance of death and sacrifice of life on the battlefields of Manchuria.

Europe. If in the Christian **Middle Ages** in Europe the clergy imposed a formal ban on homosexual activity, it did not diminish the psychological reality of the warrior's need for male comradeship or the social isolation of the soldier from conventional married life. So renowned commanders with homosexual natures continued to write chapters in the history of warfare: **Eugene** of Savoy and **Frederick the Great** of Prussia are only the most brilliant. The male who identifies solely with other men, who disdains and rejects the company of women, and prefers the all-male setting of the camp and the bivouac to the drawing room and the marriage chamber—such a man is a born soldier. That other homosexual types depart extensively if not completely from this ideal does not negate its existence; the contrast proves only how protean in reality are the phenomena grouped under the rubric of homosexuality. It is also relevant in this connection that in some European countries homosexual gratification is regarded by the common people as a pleasure or prerogative of the upper classes, including the warrior nobility with its leisure-class ethos and its sporadic bouts of orgiastic release from the tensions of battle.

The German theoretician Hans Blüher (1888–1955) went so far as to formulate the principle that "When a number of persons of the male sex must live together under compulsion, then the social strivings that exceed the mere organizational purpose develop according to the pattern of the male society," which is to say that male bonding with an unconscious homoerotic content is the psychological cement of the association. Blüher counterposed the "male society" with its primary homoeroticism, which he deemed the basis of the state and the military formations that protect its security, to the family as a social unit grounded in heterosexual attraction and the ensuing reproductive activity. The first assures the political and cultural continuity of the state, the second the biological survival of the nation. He maintained that Judaism had suppressed the homosexual aspect of its culture, with concomitant hypertrophy of the family, so that ultimately the Jewish state lost its independence, and the Jews were doomed to centuries of wandering in exile as a people of merchants and traders without a military caste. The success of the Zionist movement he foresaw, as early as 1919, as dependent upon the ability of diaspora Jewry to generate a true leadership initiated in the mysteries of male bonding and therefore achieve a national identity with a military ethos. And in point of fact the army has grown ever more influential in the politics and national life of Israel since 1948—making a comparatively small country the only first-class military power in the region, even if the Orthodox parties in the Knesset clung to the Pentateuch's prohibition of male homosexuality. Blüher further saw male bonding as crucial to the formation of male elites with a firm sense of group solidarity and loyalty that enables them to play a leading role in the state, of whose strength war is the severest test. The discipline, the comradeship, the willingness of the individual to sacrifice himself for the victory of the nation—all these are determined by the homoerotic infrastructure of the male society.

Prejudices and Stereotypes. In total contrast to this analysis is the attitude of the military establishment toward homosexuality in recent times, since the emergence of mass citizen armies—"the nation in arms"—and the psychiatric concept of sexual **inversion**. Once vast numbers of draftees had to be classified and trained, and the notion of homosexuality as "degeneracy" or "disease" had reached the half-educated public, it was certain to be abused by authoritarian regimes such as the military; and in fact was.

For the American armed forces during World War II, the homosexual posed a particular dilemma: the services badly needed fighting men at the outset of the war for which America was sadly unprepared, and the psychiatric examination given to draftees was perfunctory in the extreme. So, many homosexual men were inducted, served in the fighting lines—and then, when the pressure to draft more recruits waned, were ignominiously released from the armed forces with undesirable or dishonorable discharges. A study of the unfit soldier even classified homosexuals with eneuretics, as presumably both were guilty of incontinence. During the latter part of World War II a systematic effort was made to detect and exclude homosexual men and lesbians from the American armed forces. As a result many lives were blighted and even ruined.

The intolerance of the American military mounted in the wake of Senator Joseph R. **McCarthy**'s charges that the Truman Administration was "harboring sex perverts in government," followed by the report of a seven-member subcommittee that found homosexuals to be security risks at a time when the media were actively propagating fears of Soviet **espionage**, and even commended the army for "ferreting out sex perverts." Even the armed forces of America's allies in NATO, many of which had no penal laws against homosexual behavior, were pressured to do likewise. The procedures used to obtain confessions from suspected homosexuals often violated the rights guaranteed a defendant in a criminal case in civilian life, but the courts have been loath to deny the armed services the option of discharging individuals whose homosexuality has come to light, even if no criminal behavior while on duty could be imputed to them. A series of cases have been appealed and lost on the ground that the concept of privacy has no application in military life, while close observers of the upper echelons of the officer corps have noted an official reaction to homosexuality that borders on the paranoid. It is significant that a postwar study of German military justice in the 1939–45 period concluded that despite the official attitude of the **Nazi** regime, the German tribunals dealt less harshly with homosexual offenders than did the American—in part because the emphasis that Magnus **Hirschfeld** had placed on the constitutional etiology of sexual inversion had convinced the German physicians and biologists that criminal proceedings against such individuals were largely useless, while their American counterparts were for the most part naive and uninformed, or had been persuaded that the homosexual needed only psychotherapy to be converted to a normal mode of life. So the medieval attitudes toward homosexual behavior are perpetuated by the American military (*see* **Law, United States**) with a host of rationalizations such as the authoritarian-bureaucratic mind loves to devise.

BIBLIOGRAPHY. Hans Blüher, *Die Rolle der Erotik in der männlichen Gesellschaft: Eine Theorie der menschlichen Staatsbildung nach Wesen und Wert*, Jena: Eugen Diederichs, 1917–19, 2 vols; Félix Buffière, *Eros adolescent: la pédérastie dans la Grèce antique*, Paris: Les Belles Lettres, 1980; Edward Carpenter, *Intermediate Types among Primitive Folk*, London: George Allen & Unwin, 1919; Colin J. Williams and Martin S. Weinberg, *Homosexuals and the Military: A Study of Less than Honorable Discharge*, New York: Harper and Row, 1971.

Warren Johansson

MILK, HARVEY
(1930–1978)

American gay political leader. Born into a Jewish family on Long Island, NY, at the beginning of the Depression, Milk enjoyed the family's greater prosperity in the 1940s, when he began to journey to Manhattan to attend opera and theatre performances. Yet the adolescent Harvey, becoming aware of his homosexuality, nonetheless absorbed the dominant idea of the period, that conformity was the sine qua non of success. He attended a college in upstate New York, served a hitch in the Navy, and then settled down to an inconspicuous life in a New York apartment with a male spouse. He joined a Wall Street firm and campaigned for Barry Goldwater in 1964. It was the theatre—the musical *Hair* in which he had invested—that began to erode Milk's social and political conservatism.

Moving to San Francisco also helped to shift his perspectives. He had the good fortune to open his camera shop on Castro Street when the neighborhood had not yet achieved its renown. His notoriety grew with that of the street itself, for Milk not only absorbed the *genius loci* but was largely instrumental in creating it. With a kind of outsider's holy simplicity, Milk blithely proceeded to upset the applecart of San Francisco's carefully nurtured gay establishment. Behind the flamboyant façade he proved a shrewd wheeler-dealer, cultivating an improbable but effective alliance with the city's blue-collar unions. He would hire people off the street for his political campaigns, sometimes because of physical attraction, sometimes on a hunch. The hunches often paid off, and a number of members of San Francisco's 1980s gay establishment owed their start to Milk's intuitions. But his last lover, Jack Lira (who committed suicide in their apartment), was a disaster. Milk neglected and mismanaged his camera business so that at times he scarcely had money for food. Yet somehow he pulled the whole thing off. On his third try, in 1977, he was triumphantly elected to the coveted post of San Francisco supervisor. He quickly became a nationally known figure, whom many believed destined to rise to higher office.

Later mythology has portrayed Harvey Milk as a radical leftist, but more careful scrutiny shows that he retained elements of his conservative background to the very end. At bottom he held an almost Jeffersonian concept of the autonomy of small neighborhoods, prospering through small businesses and local attention to community problems. His belief in citizen participation led him to stress voting, something radicals often reject as irrelevant. Above all, by not painting himself into a corner through a set of inflexible doctrinaire principles, Milk was able to develop the broad base he needed for acquiring and keeping power.

Milk's public career was tragically short. On the Board of Supervisors he was frequently opposed by his colleague Dan White, a militant defender of "family values." After White first resigned and then sought vainly to reclaim his post, he decided to shoot Mayor Moscone, who had thwarted him. On November 27, 1978, he shot not only Moscone but his enemy Harvey Milk. In the subsequent trial White's lawyers mounted the notorious "twinky defense," claiming that his judgment was impaired through consuming too much junk food. The judge sentenced him to only seven years, eight months for voluntary manslaughter. This verdict triggered a major riot on the part of San Fransciso's gay community. After White's release from prison he took his own life, ending the sordid chapter in American politics that he had begun.

Despite his differences with the San Francisco gay establishment and his occasionally unethical behavior, Milk succeeded in riding the crest of a wave that had been gathering strength for some years. During the **beatnik**/hippie period the city had become a mecca for all sorts of disaffected people, while retaining its old ethnic mosaic. Milk anticipated the later strategy of the "rainbow coalition," but because of his personal gifts, and the time and place in which he lived, he was able to make it work more effectively for gay and lesbian politics than any other single individual has done before or since.

BIBLIOGRAPHY. Warren Hinckle, *Gayslayer*, Virginia City, NV: Silver Dollar, 1985; Randy Shilts, *The Mayor of Castro Street: The Life and Times of Harvey Milk*, New York: St. Martin's Press, 1982.

Wayne R. Dynes

MILLAY, EDNA ST. VINCENT (1892–1950)

American poet. Born in Rockland, Maine, she attended Vassar College (1913–17), and then settled in New York's Greenwich Village, where she was at first associated with the rebellious bohemianism then at its height. However, her 1923 volume *The Harp-Weaver and Other Poems* confirmed an independent maturity, which she had already projected in her precocious "Renaissance" of 1912. Her work drew not only on the austere landscape of her childhood in Maine, but on the Elizabethan and Cavalier poets which, thanks in part to T.S. **Eliot**, were then undergoing a revival. She was one of the last poets of the twentieth century to master the sonnet.

Millay's poetic drama, *The Lamp and the Bell*, written during a stay in Paris after her graduation, concerns the undying devotion between two women. Octavia, the authority figure in a school that seems to be Vassar, holds that the friendship between her own daughter and the princess is unhealthy and will not last. But she is mistaken, and the women prove their passionate devotion until one of them dies. While Millay had always written heterosexual verse, several of her sonnets of this period are deliberately ambiguous as to gender. She became more specific after her marriage in 1923, excising the ambiguity from her new work—a tacit confession that the earlier poems concern women. Many critics believe that the quality of her poetry gradually declined as Millay grew older (she wrote nothing in the last decade of her life). This decline may be linked with her felt need to suppress one half of her sensibility.

BIBLIOGRAPHY. Jeannette Foster, *Sex Variant Women in Literature*, New York: Vantage Press, 1956.

Evelyn Gettone

MINIONS AND FAVORITES

Since the late sixteenth century these terms have been given to the intimates of kings and queens who accorded sexual favors to their royal protectors in return for honors, gifts, and positions of influence. In particular, the *mignons* were the openly effeminate courtiers of **Henri III** of France, who behaved in a manner well calculated to scandalize the puritanically minded. But this was no new phenomenon in European history: as far back as classical antiquity, when homosexual conduct was not so stigmatized, rulers had bestowed titles, honors, and estates on handsome youths who shared their beds— and often exercised a decisive role in the political life of the court. The relationship of the Roman emperor **Hadrian** to his favorite **Antinous** was the outstanding instance of such a liaison. **Edward** II and Piers Gaveston, **James** I and the Duke of Buckingham, **William of Orange** and William Bentinck are later examples from British history.

In an age when power was concentrated in the hands of a sovereign whose every whim was law, those who could gratify his sexual tastes often became his advisers as well, though the two functions could also be kept rigorously distinct. The power could also be exercised in the opposite direction, so that the term acquired a pejorative nuance as designating an individual with no political will of his own, totally dependent upon his protector or benefactor. The role of female favorites has been more frequently acknowledged by historians who so titled the chief mistress of the monarch, who was often the de facto ruler of the court, with the power to disgrace and exile a rival and her clique of followers. The favorites might have their own entourage of lesser courtiers anxious for the favors to be had through the intermediary of the royal bed partner, so that elements of jealousy and ambition complicated the political struggles behind the scenes. Naturally heterosexual animosity, particularly in eras when homosexuality was strongly tabooed, could lead to conspiracies that would endanger the position or even the life of the favorite.

The status was therefore a coveted but precarious one. A favorite whose beauty was fading or had made a false move in the deadly game of court politics could be supplanted by a younger and more adroit rival, as others were always ready and waiting to occupy the monarch's couch. But the rewards of such a position were great enough to ensure a constant stream of aspirants, often the ambitious sons of members of the lesser nobility who capitalized on their looks and virility— and were not infrequently requited with arranged marriages into influential families that betokened wealth and power. There was no sharp dividing line between the heterosexual and homosexual spheres in antiquity and even in much of the later period of European history. For some rulers marriage was largely pro forma, as in the case of **Frederick the Great** of Prussia, who made no secret of his preference for the male sex.

With the coming of the constitutional state and of parliamentary rule in the nineteenth century the significance of the minions faded. Their modern counterpart would be the intimates of figures in the musical and entertainment world (such as Rock **Hudson** and **Liberace**)—intimates who bask in the fame and multimillion dollar incomes of these celebrities in return for the sexual pleasures they bestow.

And in other spheres of life physical beauty and sexual versatility can still be rewarded with access to the private domains of the wealthy and powerful. The history of the minions and favorites reveals the erotic undercurrents beneath the surface of political life that could direct the tide which led some on to fortune, others only to disappointment and death.

Warren Johansson

MINORITY,
HOMOSEXUALS AS A

In the 1970s some U.S. gay leaders began to speak confidently of gay men and lesbians "emerging as a people"—a stable minority within an America made up of a mosaic of such groups. Apart from the problem of whether there is to be one people or two—homosexuals per se vs. gay men *and* lesbians—such claims raise serious conceptual, historical, and sociological issues.

Historical Precedents and Parallels. Minorities in the sense of an array of peoples ruled by a dominant group have existed at least since the formation of the Assyrian empire in the ninth century B.C. Yet as long as the rule of the Herrenvolk remained unchallenged, the status of the incorporated groups remained unproblematic. The question of ethnic minorities first attracted modern analysis in the Austro-Hungarian monarchy at the end of the nineteenth century, when the introduction of a parliamentary system had made the issue acute. In 1898 Georg Jellinek contrasted the older concept of a parliamentary minority, that is a fluid and changeable interest group, with the more fixed situation of the minority as an ethnic or religious collectivity, whose membership is determined not by the changing tides of political opinion but by loyalty to the community in which one was born.

To be sure this late nineteenth-century situation had parallels. The Ottoman Empire retained its *millet* system, granting official recognition to what might be called national minorities, though these were organized on a religious basis. In the United Kingdom from 1707 onwards there were three subordinate entities: Wales, Ireland, and Scotland—the last possessing de jure, but not de facto, equality with England. Two characteristics seem essential in minorities of this general type: (1) they are communities of lineage or genealogy in the sense that a Romanian child is born of Romanian parents, a Welsh child of Welsh ones; and (2) each ethnic group has a territory which it occupies or occupied and which its members regard as their homeland, even if they reside, say, in Vienna or London.

The minority issue took on general European urgency when the representatives of the powers met in Paris in 1919 to redraw the map of Europe in the wake of World War I. The attempt to square logic with the principle of allocating the spoils to the victors led to many anomalies. In this atmosphere of the clash of conflicting rights, Kurt **Hiller**, the German left thinker and homosexual activist, conceived the idea of the sexual minority. In an address of September 19, 1921, he insisted that "human beings are marked not only by differences of race and character type, but also of . . . sexual orientation."

The coming of the world Depression in 1929 caused the issue to fall dormant, as economic problems dwarfed all else. In the 1940s in the United States, however, the second-class status of Negroes evoked increasing discussion and concern, which were to eventuate in the mass Civil Rights movement of the 1960s. As early as 1951, however, Donald Webster Cory (pseud. of Edward Sagarin) organized his widely read book *The Homosexual in America* around the idea of gay men and women as a minority who should be accorded their just rights. Cory and other leaders of the new homophile rights movement saw the opportunity of making a persuasive appeal to the traditional Anglo-Saxon virtue of fairness, while at the same time allying themselves with a powerful emerging social movement.

Changes in American Society. During this period it was becoming all too evident that America could no longer sustain the "melting pot" myth of a society moving rapidly toward homogeneity. The process of assimilation predicted by such classic sociologists as Weber and Durkheim, as well as by the Marxists, was not proceeding smoothly—and this continuing exceptionalism is not owing solely to lingering irrational discrimination. It was becoming apparent that minority resistance was sustained not merely by way of response to pressures from a nonaccepting society but by an internal sense of pride. In-group cohesiveness was becoming a function of a "quest for community," a felt need for intermediate structures between the atomized individual, on the one hand, and the universal institutions of the State, on the other. Alongside assimilation (which some groups were still experiencing) arose the "deassimilation" of groups that consciously rejected the supposed imperatives of the melting pot.

Once the cause of blacks had been taken up by the Civil Rights movement of the 1960s, other groups, first Hispanics then white ethnics, came forward to demand their place in the sun. With a few exceptions the new "unmeltable ethnics" differed from earlier groups in other countries, in that they were usually not territorial (though a few idealistic individuals were heard to voice a demand for a black homeland). Some of the newly recognized ethnic groups have little salience, that is to say they are on the way to being assimilated (Armenian-Americans) or largely have been (German-Americans). For many, ethnic consciousness lingers only in street fairs and such events as the annual marches on Fifth Avenue in New York City (which include a gay/lesbian one on the last Sunday in June).

Nonetheless, these social movements generated an academic counterpart in the form of ethnic studies in the universities. Some came to cherish a vision of a rainbow nation, in which most citizens would be bicultural. This exaltation of pluralism implicitly discounts the still-ongoing counterprocesses of amalgamation and homogenization—as shown by the fact that many recent immigrants and their children do wish simply to "be American." It is highly significant that homosexuality has not been admitted within the discourse of ethnicity, though (illogically) women's studies sometimes are. One can search through vast bibliographies of American minorities without finding a single reference to gay men and lesbians.

Problems of Treating Homosexuals as a Minority. While this exclusion may to some extent reflect prejudice and academic rigidity, it is also supported by real differences. In the personal process of psychoindividuation, homosexuals generally achieve self-awareness in defiance of the norms and counsels of the family. By contrast, among ethnic groups the family is the incubator for group consciousness and a refuge from the intolerance of the majority. Another difference is that homosexuals can "pass" more easily than most, which they tend to do in the belief (true or not) that in this way they are perceived like anyone else. Another key point is that homosexuals never constituted an ethnic group with contiguous territory, state formations, a distinctive language, and the like. Paradoxically, homosexuals do not rank as a minority in the usual sense because they were *always* a minority, usually unrecognized as such (there having been, until recently, no concept of sexual orientation as distinct from overt behavior). Lastly, the (ethnic) minority is typically a group that has immigrated into a country far more recently than the majority which claims to be autochthonous and resents the "self-invited guests" who have "disrupted its unity." This situation has no parallel with the distinctiveness of the homosexual group, which is disenfranchised for quite different reasons.

Still if one examines such indicators as residential enclaves ("gay **ghettoes**"), self-help groups, religious organizations, travel **guides**, and distinctive taste preferences, homosexuals do indeed qualify—perhaps more than most groups. How many American ethnic entities can count as many bookstores, for example, as gays and lesbians? Another feature is the sense of identity and shared fate with homosexuals in other countries, cultures, and political and social systems—together with the emergence of gay **subcultures** modeled on the American one throughout the non-Communist world. With minimal social skills a foreign homosexual can pick up partners in a bar, bath, or cruising area. This facility suggests another paradoxical concept: that of a transnational minority.

The idea of homosexuals as a minority has obvious appeal to would-be political leaders as an organizing tool. But it also meets resistance from the rank and file who reject the role of "professional gays." Moreover, the concept of homosexual identity is of recent origin, and it may not last. As yet unmeasured is the impact of the **social construction** theory of historical development, which denies the stability of the homosexual orientation. To put it most sharply, if there are no homosexuals, they cannot be organized—as a minority or anything else. Then again, to the middle class, "minority" usually connotes underprivileged, oppressed, persecuted people, not members of a group who may on average be wealthier, more educated, and more intelligent than the majority in the given country. The affluent homosexual can retreat into a world of private clubs, social groups, and exclusive institutions invisible to the larger society. Thus the concept of homosexuals as a minority may appeal rather to the two extremes—street people and gay leaders—while having little to offer to the mass of homosexuals in between. While in principle the matter of political practicality should be separated from the epistemological question of whether homosexuals are a minority, in real life the two are closely related.

In recent years the magnitude of the overall minority question has been recognized not only in the United States, but in such European countries as Britain, France, and Germany, where populations are changing. World demographic shifts and new migration patterns are likely to make the minority concept even more complex, while the place of homosexuals within it will remain scarcely less problematic.

BIBLIOGRAPHY. Stephen O. Murray, *Social Theory, Homosexual Realities*, New York: Gay Academic Union, 1984.

Wayne R. Dynes

MISHIMA YUKIO (1925–1970)

Japanese writer of fiction, drama, and essays. Born in Tokyo as Hiraoka Kimitake, the son of a government official and grandson of a former governor of Karafuto (now southern Sakhalin), he preferred to emphasize his descent from the family of his paternal grandmother, which belonged to the upper **samurai** class. He attended the Peers' School, where non-aristocrats were often treated as outsiders, and where Spartan discipline prepared young men to be soldiers rather than poets. A story entitled "The Boy Who Wrote Poetry" has strong autobiographical elements stemming from this period of his life, and describes the boy's fascination with words.

Mishima's mentors at the Peers' School not only encouraged him to study the Japanese classics but brought him into contact with the Nipponese Romanticists, a group of intellectuals who stressed the uniqueness of the Japanese people and their history. His later devotion to Japanese tradition, however, was tempered by fascination with the West. As a student he was much taken with the essays of Oscar **Wilde**, and even after war broke out with Great Britain and the United States, Mishima continued to read—generally in Japanese translation—authors who had been denounced as "decadent." But unlike most postwar writers, who distanced themselves from the literature of the Tokugawa period and earlier, he read the classics for pleasure and inspiration.

A story entitled "The Forest in Full Flower" so impressed Mishima's adviser that he proposed publishing it in *Bungei bunka* (Literary Culture), a slim magazine of limited circulation, but of high quality and with a nationwide readership. To protect the identity of the author, still a middle-school boy, the editors gave him a name of their own invention, Mishima Yukio. The work was published in book form even during the war, when the paper shortage was acute. Mishima himself took care not to be conscripted, and was more concerned about his own writing than about his country's defeat in 1945.

His first full-length novel, *The Thieves* (1948), was an implausible and unsuccessful portrayal of two young members of the aristocracy who are irresistibly drawn toward suicide. In the same year he was invited to join the group that published the magazine *Kindai bungaku* (Modern Literature). He was an outsider here too, because he was essentially apolitical in a left-leaning milieu, though his criticism of postwar Japan's business and political elite was that in their craze for profit they had forgotten Japan's traditions.

In July 1949 Mishima published the most self-revealing of all his works, the novel *Kamen no kokuhaku* (Confessions of a Mask), which made his reputation and continued to be ranked among his finest work, even when his corpus had grown to some 50 books. Yet the homosexual tendencies of the hero, which keep him from desiring the girl he loves, so baffled the critics that some imagined the intent to be parody. Neither then nor later was the novel read as a confession of guilt. Japanese readers interpreted the work as

an exceptionally sensitive account of a boy's gradual self-awakening, with the homosexual elements attributed to sexual immaturity or explained as symbolic of the sterility of the postwar world. In *Confessions of a Mask* Mishima boldly countered every convention of the novels that had served him as models: the hero fails to win the hand of the girl he loves because he can no longer endure the mask of the "normal" young man that society and literature forced him to wear. The intensity and truth of his revelatory insights justify the novel's reputation, and the combination of truth and beauty made the work a landmark in his development as an artist.

With his literary reputation in hand, Mishima then began to compose works of popular fiction with largely financial motives in mind. He continued until the year of his death to devote about a third of his time each month to writing popular fiction and essays in order to be free the remainder of the time for work on serious fiction and plays. In a novel entitled *Kinjiki* (Forbidden Colors; 1953), Mishima sought to show the discrepancies and conflicts within himself, "as represented by two 'I's." The first "I" is Shunsuke, a writer of sixty-five, whose collected works are being published for the third time. Despite the acclaim accorded to his literary work by the world, he experiences only a horror of his aging self. The second, contrasting "I" is Yuichi, a youth of exquisite beauty, first seen by the older man as he emerged from the sea after a swim. Yuichi is a spiritually uncomplicated sensualist who enjoys the act of love, but for that reason far more a narcissist than a homosexual—true to Mishima's own character in this respect. The novel is strongly misogynist: Shunsuke uses Yuichi to wreak his revenge on several women whom he detests. The novel was also chauvinistic: the foreigners among the characters are deliberately absurd.

Mishima's private life at this time resembled Yuichi's. He patronized Brunswick, a gay bar in the Ginza, where he met the seventeen-year old Akihiro Maruyama, who had just begun a golden career from which he was to graduate to the theatre, where he became the most celebrated female impersonator of his day. Mishima had reservations about the gay bars, as (in keeping with the pederastic tradition) he intensely disliked effeminate men and sought both male and female company—in the Japanese phrase "a bearer of two swords"—while preferring the male.

After passing the peak of his literary career, he became more of a public figure than ever. In 1967 he secretly spent a month training with the Self Defense Forces, and in 1968 he formed a private army of 100 men sworn to defend the Emperor, the Tate no Kai (Shield Society). From the same period is an essay deploring the emphasis given by intellectuals to the mind and glorifying the body instead. On November 25, 1970, he committed suicide in samurai style to publicize his appeal for revision of the postwar Japanese constitution that would allow his country to rearm. However one may judge his political views, Mishima was the most gifted Japanese author of his generation, and he retains a secure place in the literature of his country and the world.

BIBLIOGRAPHY. John Nathan, *Mishima: A Biography*, Boston: Little, Brown, 1974; Henry Scott-Stokes, *The Life and Death of Yukio Mishima*, New York: Farrar, Straus and Giroux, 1974; Marguerite Yourcenar, *Mishima, ou la vision du vide*, Paris: Gallimard, 1980.

Warren Johansson

MODERNISM

The literary and artistic currents that came forcefully to public attention at the end of the nineteenth century and favored stylistic and thematic experiment are known collectively as modernism. High modernism, the age of the pioneers, is generally accepted as lasting until about 1940. After that date modernism expanded beyond its early base, becoming more diffuse. In the 1970s many critics and historians concluded that modernism had, for all intents and purposes, come to an end, having been overtaken by post-modernism. Even though there was no consensus as to the meaning of the new term, its introduction signals the possibility of assessing the meaning of modernism itself as a period which had attained closure.

Although some would trace its roots to the later eighteenth century, most scholars concur that modernism was a response to the complexities of urbanization and technology as they reached a new peak in the later decades of the nineteenth century. The hallmarks of modernism vary from one medium to another, but they may be summed up as a new self-consciousness, irony, abstraction, and radical disjunction of formal elements. Among the trends highlighting the first stage of modernism are **aestheticism**, with such figures as Oscar **Wilde** and Walter **Pater**, and **decadence**, with Paul **Verlaine** and Arthur **Rimbaud** as central figures. Modernism entered a new phase in the second decade of the twentieth century, with such movements as Cubism and non-objectivism in painting, imagism in poetry, and twelve-tone music. This phase is sometimes known as high modernism, with late modernism ensuing about 1940.

The bearers of high modernism, such as Ezra Pound and Wyndham Lewis, Guillaume Apollinaire and F. T. Marinetti, Pablo Picasso and Marcel Duchamp, were reacting against some features of incipient modernism as they perceived them: the so-called "fin-de-siècle," associated with over-refinement, decadence, and homosexuality. Consequently, we find in these writers and artists a strong element of masculism, leading them loudly to disdain "pansies," and to treat women as mere adjuncts in their creative endeavors.

The case of Pound shows a gradual hardening of attitudes. In the winter of 1908 he was dismissed from Wabash College, ostensibly for a minor heterosexual escapade. Yet to a friend he remarked afterwards, "They say I am bi-sexual and given to unnatural lust." Later in 1908, in a letter from London, he remarked that "in Greece and pagan countries men loved men"; although he did not share this taste, he did not feel it necessary to condemn it. After World War I, however, he inserted a coarse homophobic joke in Canto XII, and connected sodomy with **usury** as two evils of the age. Although he continued to cherish his friendships with Jean **Cocteau** and Natalie **Barney**, Pound could be heard inveighing in the 1950s against the "pansification" of America. Illustrating the fact that bigotries tend to come in sets, Pound's thinking showed a simultaneous increase in **anti-Semitism**. It is probably too simple to attribute this growth of homophobic attitudes to the poet's involvement with Mussolini's **fascism**. Even before World War I, Pound had had a portrait sculpture made depicting himself as a phallus. And he associated artistic creativity with the aggressive performance of heterosexual coitus.

It is interesting to observe the interplay of trends in a more conflicted figure, such as D. H. **Lawrence**, who railed against **Bloomsbury**'s effeteness, but at the same time recognized his own homoerotic component. Nonetheless, he felt that maturity required commitment to a heterosexual relationship, which he maintained through thick and thin with his wife Frieda. The artist Marcel Duchamp twice had himself photographed in feminine clothing as "Rrose Sélavy," but seemed to compartmentalize his flirtation with this identity, and otherwise showed no gender-bending or homosexual tendencies.

An exception to the link between modernism and machismo is the activity of lesbian innovators. Margaret **Anderson** and Jane Heap, the lesbian editors of the avant-garde magazine *The Little Review*, never had any difficulty with the most advanced literary modernism. At considerable risk from the forces of Comstockery they issued the first, serial publication of James Joyce's *Ulysses*. Later the complete volume was to be issued by Sylvia **Beach** from her bookshop, Shakespeare and Co. in **Paris**. Gertrude **Stein** created a prose style that was consciously aligned with Cubism and other avant-garde movements in the visual **arts**. For many years she was close to Picasso, an arch-sexist. In conversation Stein tended to put down male homosexuals, going so far as to impugn even the masculinity of Ernest **Hemingway**, though she did collect paintings by the minor homosexual artist Sir Francis Rose. Her younger modernist contemporary Djuna **Barnes** seemed to have more sympathy for gay men. Other lesbian writers working in Paris, such as Natalie Barney and Renée **Vivien**, were relatively traditional in style. The case of Virginia **Woolf** is complex, because she belonged to Bloomsbury, where she was on intimate terms with other lesbian, bisexual, and homosexual figures. At the same time she strove to innovate in her own prose style.

On the Mediterranean fringe of European industrial civilization, two of the most significant modernist poets, Constantine **Cavafy** (Greek, residing in Alexandria) and Fernando **Pessoa** (Portuguese) were homosexual. In America the gay poet Hart **Crane** was a chief modernist innovator, while Marsden **Hartley** and Charles **Demuth** were advanced painters who were homosexual. Perhaps the most visible figure of late modernism in the visual arts was Andy **Warhol**, whose public persona combined elements of **camp** and **dandyism**. In the experimental **film** genre sometimes known as the "Baudelairean cinema" a number of leading figures were gay, including Kenneth Anger and Jack Smith. These last examples suggest that, among men at least, modernist machismo was most characteristic of the European core where it all began; at the periphery there was more room for variation.

In a bizarre twist in the 1980s, a few architectural critics hostile to the new trend of post-modernism, have attacked it as homosexual, claiming that the contrasting treatment of façades and interiors is a form of "transvestism."

There can be no simple, one-to-one correlation of literary and artistic styles, on the one hand, and **gender** concepts, on the other. Yet an interplay does exist, and working out its details in the case of modernism—in its several varieties—is a challenge for future scholarship.

Wayne R. Dynes

MOLL, ALBERT (1862–1939)

Berlin neurologist who helped shape the medical model of homosexuality that was created in late nineteenth-century Germany. His first treatise on the subject, *Die konträre Sexualempfindung* (1891), differentiated between innate and acquired homosexuality and proceeded to focus on the former, describing the homosexual as "a stepchild of nature." He proposed that the sex drive was an innate psychological function which could be injured or malformed through no fault or choice of the individual himself.

Moll refined his theory in his more general treatise on sexuality, *Untersuchungen über die Libido sexualis* (1897), and placed more stress on the nature of homosexuality as an illness, often an "inherited taint." With his *Handbuch der Sexualwissenschaften* (1911), he turned his attention to the cases of acquired homosexuality, for which he offered association therapy (replacing same-sex associations with those of the opposite sex) as a cure.

As the years passed, he became increasingly hostile to Magnus **Hirschfeld** and his **Scientific-Humanitarian Committee**. Alienated in part by Hirschfeld's polemical mode of dealing with the subject, in part by certain ethically dubious sides of Hirschfeld's activity, he became the major "establishment" opponent of the Committee. At the same time, he lessened his emphasis on the innate character of homosexuality in favor of one that could be used to justify penal sanctions by the state.

In his autobiography, *Ein Leben als Arzt der Seele* (1936), he stated his belief that most homosexuality is acquired by improper sexual experiences, and only a small percentage can be said to be innate. He even went so far as to attack those (especially Hirschfeld) who believed homosexuality an inborn condition and sought social and legal acceptance for homosexuals.

Although his name is largely forgotten today, his works were widely read in their time. His *Sexualleben des Kindes* and *Handbuch der Sexualwissenschaften* were the first works to appear on their respective topics. His theory on the sex life of the child had a profound (but largely unacknowledged) effect on **Freudian concepts**.

BIBLIOGRAPHY. Edward M. Brecher, *The Sex Researchers*, Boston: Little, Brown, 1969; Max Hodann, *History of Modern Morals*, trans. by Stella Browne, London: William Heinemann Medical Books, 1937, p. 48ff; Frank Sulloway, *Freud, Biologist of the Mind: Beyond the Psychoanalytic Legend*, New York: Basic Books, 1979, 309–15.

James W. Jones

MOLLIS

The primary meaning of this Latin adjective is "soft," but it was also used in a secondary, sexual sense. From the first century B.C. onwards the Romans used the word as an equivalent *malakos/malthakos*, "soft, passive-effeminate homosexual." Other Latin words in this semantic field are *semivir*, "half-man," and *effeminatus*. The compound *homo mollis* ("softy") is also found. The abstract noun *mollities* meant "softness, effeminacy" but also "masturbation," with the underlying notion that "only a sissy has to masturbate." In St. Jerome's translation of I Corinthians 6:9 the *molles* (pl.) are (along with the *masculorum concubitores*, "abusers of themselves with mankind,") excluded from the Kingdom of God; the former term denotes the passive, the latter the active male homosexual. This usage was continued in medieval Latin and even found its way into the early literature of sexology composed in the learned tongue. As late as 1914 Magnus **Hirschfeld** commented on the appropriateness of the term by claiming that 99 percent of the homosexual subjects he had interviewed described their own character as "soft" or "tender."

The Latin *mollis* may well be the origin of the eighteenth-century English **molly** (or *molly-cull*) = effeminate homosexual, a term given publicity by police raids on their clandestine haunts in London (1697–1727) following the relative tolerance of the Restoration era that had seen a homosexual subculture emerge in the British metropolis. The term *molly* also suggests the personal name *Molly*, a diminutive of *Mary*, so that the folk etymology introduces a separate nuance of the effeminate.

See also **Effeminacy; Women's Names for Male Homosexuals.**

MOLLY HOUSES

The molly houses were gathering places for male homosexuals in **London** during the eighteenth century. The public was first made aware of them by the prosecuting zeal of the Societies for the Reformation of Manners. These public houses were at times relatively informal, or there could simply be a special room for "mollies" at the back of an ordinary public house. Other establishments were quite elaborate. Mother Clap, as she was called, kept a house in Holborn which on Sunday nights in particular—the homosexuals' "night out"—could have from twenty to forty patrons. The house had a back room fitted out with beds. In 1726 a wave of repression led the authorities to discover at least twenty such houses; a number of their proprietors were convicted and made to stand in the pillory, while three indi-

viduals were actually hanged for the crime of buggery.

The term *molly* for an effeminate man may be simply the feminine name *Molly*, often applied to a prostitute, but it may derive in part from Classical Latin **mollis**, "soft", which designated the passive-effeminate partner in male homosexual relations. It is also the first component in *mollycoddle*, which alludes to the manner of childrearing that makes a pampered, effeminate adult.

Outside the clearly defined setting of the molly house, it was exceedingly dangerous to approach another man for sexual favors. The descriptions of the subculture of the molly house always emphasized the effeminacy of the denizens. All the patrons were likely to be addressed as "Madam" or "Miss" or "Your Ladyship," and in conversation they spoke as though they were female whores: "Where have you been, you saucy quean?" Sometimes the diversions entailed mimicry of heterosexual respectability, such as enactments of childbirth and christening. Intercourse was referred to as "marrying," and the dormitory in the molly house was termed the "chapel." A prostitute remarked that his procurer had "helped him to three or four husbands." On occasion there were collective masquerades in which all the participants dressed as women.

The male homosexuals who frequented these establishments were from eighteen to fifty years old. Those who sought adolescent partners had the far more risky undertaking of meeting and courting them outside the bounds of this subculture. The popular notion of sodomy at the time made it a vice of the idle and wealthy, and there is some evidence that members of the upper classes frequented the molly houses, mainly in search of male prostitutes, but in so doing they also exposed themselves to scandal and **blackmail**. The records of prosecutions and executions contain no aristocratic names; the justice of eighteenth-century Europe was class justice. There were about a third as many trials for attempted blackmail as for sodomy committed or attempted. Blackmail was the form of extortion practiced by the criminal or semi-criminal classes at the expense of the individual with means and social position who was nevertheless in the grip of forbidden sexual desires. When a blackmailer was convicted, the penalty was usually the same—pillory, fine, and imprisonment amounting to ten months in jail—as for attempted sodomy.

The subculture of the molly houses tried to protect itself from discovery and from betrayal by its own members. The worst foe of all was a vindictive participant in the molly houses' activity, or an individual who had kept records and documents which later fell into the hands of the authorities, indirectly revealing the whole clandestine network of sexual interaction.

For the ordinary Englishman with no powerful protectors, access to the shielded environment of the molly house was the sole way of making homosexual contacts with ease. The absence of a highly organized police force and of a vice squad with regular infiltrators and paid informers actually gave such houses more security than comparable establishments in the first half of the twentieth century enjoyed. It was religious fanaticism in the form of societies "for the protection of morals" that persecuted the subculture from above, while the criminal underworld preyed on it from below—a situation that remained into the twentieth century until the campaign to enlighten the public on the nature of homosexuality and reform the the archaic criminal laws made possible a new social environment for the homosexual community.

BIBLIOGRAPHY. Randolph Trumbach, "London's Sodomites: Homosexual Behavior and Western Culture in the 18th Century," *Journal of Social History*, 11 (1977), 1–33.

Warren Johansson

MONASTICISM

Originating in late antique Egypt, the monastic movement had as its goal to achieve an ideal of Christian life in community with others or in contemplative solitude. Monastic asceticism required the rejection of worldly existence with its cares and temptations. The institution, one of the formative elements of medieval society, transformed the ancient world. The **asceticism** it demanded stands at the opposite pole from what most modern (and classical) thinkers would deem a healthy attitude toward sex, diet, sleep, sanitation, and mental balance.

Institutional History. St. Anthony of Egypt (died 356), a son of Coptic peasants, came to be regarded as the father of the monks, though he was not the founder of monasticism. The Egyptian anchorite movement began, perhaps under the influence of **Buddhism**, just before the end of the persecutions, about 300. The *Life of Anthony* by Athanasius of Alexandria (circa 357) emphasizes Anthony's orthodoxy, the gospel sources of his renunciation of the world, his fight against the demons, and his austere way of life. Later depictions often stressed the sexual aspect of the temptations to which Anthony was subjected. Anthony found a number of imitators who lived in solitude, separated by greater or lesser distances, but coming to him at intervals for counsel; eventually he agreed to see them every Sunday.

Farther to the south, a younger contemporary of Anthony's, Pachomius, who had become a monk about 313, began organizing cenobitic communities. He founded monasteries that were divided into houses where men lived in common, performed remunerative labor, and practiced self-imposed poverty joined with organized prayer. A novelty in the ancient world, monastic communities were rigidly homosocial, consisting of members of only one gender but, needless to say, genital sexuality was proscribed. Monasticism began in the eastern provinces of the empire and was strongly colored by the ascetic trends found in that part of the world. It included not just members of religious communities, but also hermits who preferred to wander far from civilization, in wild and desert places, choosing a primitive and eccentric mode of life. Systematic practice of deprivation of food and sleep produced a hypnotic effect designed to obviate direct need for sexual release, in part by stimulating a kind of ecstasy that was its surrogate.

Monasticism reached the West through the exile of Athanasius to the Italian peninsula, while John Cassian from Egypt set up houses near Marseilles. There it characteristically penetrated the clergy in the service of the local church. From the end of the fourth century monasticism based on communal life spread in the West, and the Oriental monastic texts were early translated into Latin by Jerome, Rufinus, Evagrius, and others. The Latin genius multiplied and codified the Oriental rules, until St. Benedict of Nursia (ca. 480–ca. 543) synthesized them, mainly shortening the *Rule of the Master*. The monks had their own culture, independent of the world of classical antiquity and strongly permeated with the ideal of asceticism, new forms of worship such as the recitation of the Psalter, and a cultivation of the inner life.

Western monasticism was at first not organized into an order, nor did it have a common rule. Oriental, Celtic (most of these usually hermits, not cloistered), and Benedictine elements were combined to form various rules, but in the course of the seventh century these rules incorporated ever larger parts of the Rule of St. Columban and St. Benedict. It was the latter that spread and finally became obligatory for all monks and nuns under Carolingian authority. Missionaries when abroad, at home the good monks labored in the school and scriptorium, composing and copying theological, hagiographical, and historical works, and managing the lands of the abbey. They also copied (and sometimes composed) secular Latin and Greek texts, in-

cluding some sexually explicit ones. Bad monks, some even under lay abbots, enjoyed the good life and observed the Rule, though also transgressing it.

Following the foundation of the Abbey of Cluny in 910, Western monasticism entered a new phase. The monastic institutions of that congregation, which came to have hundreds of daughter houses, were centralized in a single order. Monks were no longer primarily missionaries and teachers, manual labor was curtailed or rather shifted to serfs, and the Divine Office was made longer and more solemn. Many great churchmen of the tenth to twelfth centuries such as the fanatical enemy of Judaism St. Bernard were monks. As bishops and popes others led the struggle of the church for freedom from secular authority and like Hildebrand, Pope Gregory VII, for political domination in Christendom. Until the rise of the cathedral schools in the mid-twelfth century (followed by the universities), the monks enjoyed a near monopoly on intellectual life.

In the thirteenth and fourteenth centuries monasticism lost much of its initial fervor and sincerity. The abbeys had become immersed in secular affairs, some had become resorts for members of the nobility, and others restricted their membership so that the professed monks could enjoy a larger income. The Friars, who at first begged for their living—Dominican, Franciscan, and Augustinian—wandered among the people and gained much of the prestige formerly enjoyed by monks. The Hundred Years War and the Black Death intruded on the self-isolated existence of the monasteries, while the office of abbot and other monastic dignities were treated as benefices and commitment to personal poverty all but vanished.

Erotic Aspects. As communities composed of members of but one sex, the monasteries were a Christian innovation—and one that could hardly have been free of homosexual desire. St. Basil (ca. 330–ca. 379) had to warn against the dangers which a handsome monk in the pride of his youth could pose to those in his entourage, yet in so doing he indirectly admitted the homoerotic character of the attraction which the novice inspired. As early as the reign of Charlemagne (died 814), accusations of sodomy among the monks begin to appear in documents, and not without evidence. The immediate forerunner of the Rule of St. Benedict provided that all monks were to sleep in the same room, with the abbot's bed in the center. Benedict refined this principle by decreeing that a light had to be kept burning in the dormitory all night, the monks had to sleep clothed, and the young men were to mingle with the older ones, not being allowed to sleep side by side (chapter 22). This precaution had its precedents in the Eastern Church, where the purpose was explicitly to forestall homosexual relations. The St. Gall plan of an ideal monastery (ca. 820) clearly shows these preoccupations about sleeping arrangements. All this, naturally, was in the context of an institution whose members had taken a vow of celibacy.

The tradition of friendship that had survived from antiquity gave the homoerotic feelings of the literarily gifted monks an outlet in the form of passionate verses addressed to a "friend" or "brother." These outpourings belong to a specific legacy of erotic attachment between males with a wealth of strands and nuances both pagan/secular and biblical/religious. The guilt that was later to envelop such intense feelings had not yet ensconced itself in the Christian mind.

It is not easy for the modern reader to penetrate the mind of the author of texts written in a dead, even if still cultivated tongue, where so much is cast in the form of clichés and commonplaces. St. Anselm (1033–1109), the prior of Bec and later archbishop of Canterbury, who advised mitigating punishments, especially against sodomitical clerks, and St. Aelred of Rievaulx (ca. 1109–1166), the abbot of a Cistercian monastery and adviser of Henry II of England, whom some suspect of homosexuality, gave Christian friendship a quality that united human and spiritual love and rendered it an avenue to divine love. A great intellect may have been capable of the self-discipline that denied such feelings any physical expression, but lesser souls probably were not. A German manuscript of the twelfth or thirteenth century contains two eloquent Latin poems of nuns who were lovers. Not surprisingly many of the penalties for homosexual misconduct in the early penitentials applied specifically to monks and novices, not to the laity. The thin line between pure emotion and sensuality could be crossed imperceptibly and—from the standpoint of Christian morality—fatally.

The question legitimately arises as to what extent the monastic life attracted individuals whom the modern world would label homosexual. The Russian Vasiliĭ Vasil'evich **Rozanov** (1856–1919), in *Liudi lunnogo sveta* (Moonlight Men), claimed that the monastic orders were an ideal refuge for such individuals from the cares and obligations—more often the latter, in an age of arranged marriages—of heterosexual life: an instance of the psychological "I cannot" masquerading as the moral "I will not!" The outward celibacy of the monks and nuns was a cover for homoerotic involvements shielded from the arm of the secular power—which was to take an interest in the matter only much later—by the high walls of the abbey. Rozanov likened monasticism to a hard crystal indissoluble within Christian civilization, the embodiment of the Christian ideal of life—rejecting this world, and preparing the soul for its transition to the next. Some medieval writers compared monasteries to prisons, and they are the prototype of the "total institution" in Western society. It would be of no small interest to compare the sexual mores of the inmates of such institutions—boarding schools, reform schools, prisons, military units—in different settings. For women the nunnery meant an escape from the world of male domination and the drudgery imposed upon the wife and mother in an ever-growing household.

Aftermath. By the early sixteenth century the great days of the monasteries were long over. **Protestant** reformers and monarchs greedy to confiscate their wealth, found them easy targets for their charges of idleness, self-indulgence, and vice—fornication, masturbation, and sodomy. For the most part abbeys and nunneries survived only in Catholic and Orthodox countries, where they eventually came under attack by secularists and in not a few instances saw their property sequestered by the state power. The link between religious mysticism and sexual ecstasy was inadvertently brought out in the vivid imagery of the Spanish mystics St. John of the Cross (1542–1591) and St. Teresa of Ávila (1515–1582). In an unusual, sensational case (1619–23), the lesbian sister Benedetta Carlini of Pescia, near Florence, created a complex visionary world of magic in which she enveloped her lovers. *La Religieuse*, a posthumously published novel by Denis Diderot (1713–1784), portrays graphically, even melodramatically, the distress of a nun at the hands of a lesbian prioress. After the end of the Old Regime this work was followed by a large class of exposé literature, perpetuated by the anti-clerical movement at the close of the nineteenth century, and designed to flay the Catholic church as a redoubt of the vicious and depraved and to undermine its self-proclaimed sanctity.

At the present time it is hard to know (and harder even to appraise the situation in historical epochs) what proportion of Catholic and Orthodox members of religious orders are homosexual and, of these, how many are practicing. Probably both figures are much higher than the ecclesiastical authorities would care to admit. As in former times, abbots seek to inhibit the formation of erotically charged pair-bonds by separating "particular friends." But declining vocations and applications of religious for return to lay

status make such interventions seem counterproductive: if monasteries are to survive as an institution a less harsh regime may be required. In 1985 considerable stir was caused by the publication of *Lesbian Nuns: Breaking the Silence* (edited by Rosemary Curb and Nancy Manahan), which contains autobiographical accounts by some fifty women.

Though it has its obvious sociological aspect (the magnetism of a homosocial environment), the question of gay and lesbian religious is part of a broader interface between homoeroticism and religious feeling that extends from the **shamanism** of the paleo-Arctic cultures to the occult underground of today. Albeit explored by such pioneers as Rozanov and **Edward Carpenter**, it is yet to be fully recognized or understood by researchers into the phenomena of religion.

See also **Christianity; Clergy, Gay; Medieval Latin Poetry; Middle Ages; Patristic Writers.**

BIBLIOGRAPHY. John Boswell, *Christianity, Social Tolerance, and Homosexuality*, Chicago: Chicago University Press, 1980; James A. Brundage, *Law, Sex, and Christian Society in Medieval Europe*, Chicago: Chicago University Press, 1987.
Warren Johansson

MONTAIGNE, MICHEL EYQUEM DE (1533–1592)

French courtier, essayist, and thinker. In 1571, during the French religious wars, he retired from the *Parlement* of Bordeaux and, after inheriting his father's estate, lived in seclusion at his chateau. Here, isolated in a tower to avoid visitors, he wrote his *Essais*, published in 1580. After a stint as mayor of Bordeaux he again returned in 1588. Inspired by the Latin classics and by **Plutarch**'s *Parallel Lives of Famous Greeks and Romans*, he skeptically considered the careers and beliefs of the prominent figures of his own time. His *Essais* influenced both French and English literature, being considered models of precise style and of accurate analysis. Although France has no universal writer like **Shakespeare**, **Cervantes**, **Dante**, and **Goethe**, Montaigne, who like all of them had a homosexual or at least homoerotic side, is one of the outstanding French writers before the classical age of the seventeenth century. With his elder contemporary François Rabelais (ca. 1494–1553), he helped modernize French prose, soon after his death standardized by the Académie Française, founded in 1635 by Cardinal Richelieu and the homosexual Abbé de **Boisrobert**.

About 1558 Montaigne, while serving on the parlement of Bordeaux, developed an intense affection for a young judge, Etienne de La Boétie, author of an essay, "Against One Man," honoring liberty against tyrants. This passion inspired his composition "On Friendship" in the *Essais*. There he asserts that **friendship** is more passionate than the "impetuous and fickle" love for women and superior to marriage, which one can enter at will but not leave. He concedes that physical intimacy between males "is justly abhorred by our moral notions," while the "disparity of age and difference of station" which the Greeks demanded "would not correspond sufficiently to the perfect union that we are seeking here." Montaigne condemns pederasty because of the age asymmetry between the partners, "simply founded on external beauty, the false image of corporeal generation," but approves fully of intense friendship between men of the same age, "friendship that possesses the soul and rules it with absolute sovereignty." In this respect he is a forerunner of modern, age-symmetrical, androphile homosexuality. Physical beauty means less than the "marriage of two minds" such as he contracted with his friend, who died some five years later, in 1563, of dysentery, leaving Montaigne with a memory that haunted him all the rest of his days. Never again would such an enthralling experience befall him, but the great love of his life underlay his classic essay on friendship.

Also relevant to homosexuality are the "Apology for Raymond Sebond" and "On Some Verses of Vergil." So if Montaigne could not openly defend physical intimacy between men, he at least evoked the ancient ideal of friendship, anticipating the modern notion of **homosociality**.

BIBLIOGRAPHY. John Beck, "Montaigne face à l'homosexualité," *Bulletin de la Société des amis de Montaigne*, 9/10 (1982),41–50; Maurice Riveline, *Montaigne et l'amitié*, Paris: Félix Alcan, 1939.

William A. Percy

MONTESQUIOU, COUNT ROBERT DE (1855–1921)

French aristocrat, poet, and aesthete. Descended from the d'Artagnan of *The Three Musketeers*, he spent most of his wealth on collecting art objects and throwing parties, as well as vanity-press editions of his own books. He was the model for Jean des Esseintes in the novel *A Rebours* by Joris-Karl Huysmans (1884), Phocas in Jean Lorrain's novel *Mons. de Phocas* (1902), the Peacock in Rostand's play "Chantecler" (1910), and Baron de Charlus in **Proust**'s *Sodome et Gomorrhe* (1921), all of which portray his flamboyance and homosexuality. However, he was so afraid of scandal that he avoided associating with notorious homosexuals and was so discreet in his sexual life that there is no proof that he ever had sex with any of the handsome young men in his entourage. The great love of his life was a South American, Gabriel Yturri, whom he met in 1885 and who died in 1905. Montesquiou wrote some poems on homosexual themes. Although he was a glittering center of Parisian society, he is remembered today only as the original of Charlus and des Esseintes, and Giovanni Boldini's portrait of him is on the cover of the Penguin paperback edition of Huysmans' novel.

BIBLIOGRAPHY. Philippe Jullian, *Prince of Aesthetes*, New York: Viking, 1968.
Stephen Wayne Foster

MONTHERLANT, HENRY DE (1895–1972)

French novelist, dramatist and essayist. A Parisian by birth, Montherlant was educated in an elite Catholic boarding school, whose atmosphere of particular friendships and ambivalent student–teacher relations left an abiding impression. At the age of sixteen he fell passionately in love with a younger boy—an interest evoked in *La Ville dont le prince est un enfant* (1952) and *Les Garçons* (written in 1929 but published posthumously).

In World War I he used family connections to make sure that he had a taste of combat without really being endangered by it. His first novel, *Le songe* (1922), is an account of the war initiating a lifelong personal cult of virility and courage that many have subsequently found spurious. In ensuing novels, as well as in his plays (1942–65), Montherlant presents resolute heroes and heroines who are steadfast in their confrontation of God and nothingness, embodying audacity, patriotism, purity, and self-sacrifice as opposed to cowardice, hypocrisy, compromise, and self-indulgence. Throughout his life, Montherlant labored to polish an image of a manly stoic, and it was in this key that he took his own life in 1972, as blindness set in.

The postumous publication of his correspondence with the openly gay novelist Roger Peyrefitte threw a new light on Montherlant, one that could only prove disconcerting to many of his erstwhile admirers. In April 1938 the thirty-one-year-old Peyrefitte met Montherlant, then forty-three, at an amusement arcade in Place Clichy in Paris. Both had discovered independently that, in a Paris that had still not entirely recovered from the Depression, these commercial undertakings provided good opportunities for picking up impoverished teenaged boys, taking them to the movies, and then home to bed. Montherlant soon fell in with one particular youth, who was fourteen, with the knowledge of the boy's mother. Although not a novice in these matters, the older novelist came to rely on Peyrefitte's advice as to how to conduct the affair. After Montherlant settled in the south of France, their friendship continued on a weekly, sometimes daily postal basis, though with verbal dodges to fool the censor. Through the tragic events of the declaration of war, the defeat of France, and the beginning of the Occupation, the two remained obsessively preoccupied with their affairs with boys. Both men got into scrapes with the authorities, but while Montherlant was able to use influence to smooth things over, Peyrefitte lost his job with the Quai d'Orsay.

Although a first version of the novel *Les Garçons* was written in 1929, the full text, which shows the pupils of Sainte-Croix in an almost frantic ballet of love affairs with each other (though not with the teachers), did not appear until after the writer's death. The book captures the sultry mixture of passion, religion, and (a very definite third) study in an elite French school as well, if not better than any other in this well populated genre. Before his death Montherlant seems to have foreseen that the truth about himself would come out, and even to have given this process some anticipatory encouragement.

In their lives Montherlant and Peyrefitte offer a vivid contrast: the one striving to retain and even polish the mask of heterosexuality, the other frank about his homosexuality from his first novel, *Les amitiés particulières* (1945). Yet after Montherlant's death a truer picture has emerged, and the divergent perspectives of work and life have become visible without growing together. In fact his work abounds in divided characters: a colonial officer who does not believe in imperialism, an artist who does not care for painting, a priest for whom God is an illusion, and an anarchist who has never believed in anarchism.

BIBLIOGRAPHY. Henry de Montherlant and Roger Peyrefitte, *Correspondence*, Paris: Robert Laffont, 1983; Pierre Sipriot, *Montherlant sans masque*, I: *L'Enfant prodigue, 1895–1932*, Paris: Robert Laffont, 1982.

Wayne R. Dynes

MOTION PICTURES
See Film.

MOVEMENT, HOMOSEXUAL

Modern life has seen many movements for social change, including those intended to secure the rights of disenfranchised groups. The *homosexual movement* is a general designation for organized political striving to end the legal and social intolerance of homosexuality in countries where it had been stigmatized as both a vice and a crime, and where the revelation of an individual's homosexuality almost inevitably led to social ostracism and economic ruin. Only at the end of the nineteenth century did such organized movement endeavors become possible in continental Europe, in no small measure because of the impact of scientific thinking on the political discourse of that epoch. Characteristic of such movements is their capacity to give the homosexual individual not just a sexual but a political identity—as a member of a **minority** with a grievance against the larger society. These movements varied in the size of their membership and the scope of their activity, as well as in the specific goals which they pursued and the arguments by which they sought to persuade the decision-making elites and the general public of the justice of their cause.

Origins. The **Enlightenment** of the eighteenth century, which took up arms against every form of arbitrary oppression, may be regarded as the spiritual parent of all later homosexual liberation movements. Yet such leading Enlightenment thinkers as **Voltaire** and Diderot had ambivalent attitudes toward sexual nonconformity. While opposing barbaric oppression, they clung to the notion that the church remained the arbiter of "morality," which in practice meant sexual morality, and that same-sex relations, being "unnatural," were destined to disappear in a truly enlightened polity. During the French Revolution two pamphlets appeared, *Les enfans de Sodome* and *Les petits bougres au manège*, purporting to give information on adherents to a proto-liberation movement for homosexuals, but this anticipation remains shadowy.

A lonely precursor was Heinrich **Hoessli** (1784–1864), a Swiss milliner from the canton of Glarus, who in 1836–38 published in two volumes *Eros: Die Männerliebe der Griechen: ihre Beziehungen zur Geschichte, Erziehung, Literatur und Gesetzgebung aller Zeiten* (Eros: The Male Love of the Greeks: Its Relationship to the History, Education, Literature and Legislation of All Ages). Amateur that he was, Hoessli collected the literary and other materials—mainly from ancient **Greece** and medieval **Islam**—that illustrated male homosexuality. His writings, issued in very small editions, had no immediate effect on public opinion or the law.

Second in the prehistory of the movement, the German jurist and polymath Karl Heinrich **Ulrichs** (1825–1895) began in January 1864 to publish a series of pamphlets under the title *Forschungen zur mannmännlichen Liebe*. The first of these was entitled *Vindex*, a name meant to vindicate the homosexual in the eyes of public opinion. The second had the name *Inclusa*, taken from Ulrichs' formula *anima muliebris corpore virili inclusa*, "a female soul trapped in a male body." The pamphlets rambled over the entire field of ancient and modern history and sociology, with comments on contemporary scandals. Although he even conceived the idea of an organization that would fight for the human rights of Urnings, as he called them,

Ulrichs' efforts to ameliorate the legal plight of the homosexual in **Germany** failed, since the North German Confederation and then the German Empire adopted the Prussian law penalizing "unnatural lewdness" between males. He ended his days in poverty and exile, befriended by an Italian nobleman who wrote a short tribute to him after his death.

Emergence. Two years after Ulrichs' death, the world's first homosexual organization came into being: the Wissenschaftlich-humanitäre Komitee (**Scientific-Humanitarian Committee**), founded in Berlin on May 14, 1897 under the leadership of Magnus **Hirschfeld** (1868–1935), a physician who became the world's leading, if controversial, authority on homosexuality in the years that followed. The Committee's first action was to draft a petition to the legislative bodies of the German Empire calling for the repeal of **Paragraph 175** of the Penal Code of the Reich. For this petition the Committee solicited the signatures of prominent figures in all walks of German life, and ultimately it obtained some 6,000 names, an impressive cross-section of the intellectual elite of the Second Reich and the Weimar Republic. It also began to publish the world's first homosexual periodical, the *Jahrbuch für sexuelle Zwischenstufen* (Yearbook for Sexual Intergrades), whose title embraced not only homosexuality but also transvestism, pseudohermaphroditism, and other departures from the norm of masculinity or femininity.

The Committee professed the view—which did not go unchallenged even within homosexual circles—that homosexuals belonged to a "**third sex**" which represented an innate "intermediate stage" between male and female. All traits of mind and body it assigned to the masculine or the feminine, while insisting that there was a continuum between the two in every human being. It also issued pamphlets and brochures for the lay public, trying to break down the layers of prejudice and ignorance that had encrusted the subject over the centuries. Gathering some 1500 members from all parts of Germany, the Committee never became a mass or "activist" organization; unlike some later groups, it never even sought this status.

Outside Germany the Scientific-Humanitarian Committee only gradually attracted imitators, as in countries that had adopted the Code **Napoleon** where no criminal statute remained in need of repeal. In the **Netherlands** a branch was founded in 1911 in the wake of the passage of a law which ominously raised the age of consent from 14 to 21—discriminating against homosexual acts for the first time in the twentieth century. This Dutch branch had been preceded by the participation of several writers—Arnold **Aletrino**, L. S. A. M. von **Römer**, Jongherr Jacob van Schorer—in the international aspect of the German movement. Aletrino had courageously spoken in defense of homosexuals at the Congress of Criminal Anthropology in Amsterdam in 1901 and been roundly abused by the other delegates. Another offshoot of the Committee was founded in Vienna in 1906 to seek reform of the Austrian law of 1852 which penalized both male and female homosexual expression.

By the second decade of the twentieth century the various organizations or groups of friends such as those around John Addington **Symonds**, Edward **Carpenter**, and Havelock **Ellis** that were concerned with changing the law and public opinion in regard to the legitimacy and morality of sexual behavior began to coalesce into a larger "sexual reform movement." All rejected the traditional ascetic morality of the Christian Church and its more modern variants to a greater or lesser degree, though some affected a neutral pose on this issue. The birth control movement was joined by the eugenics movement and by an organization that sought to abate the stigma attaching to unwed motherhood—the *Deutsche Bund für Mutterschutz* (German League for the Protection of Motherhood). Also, voices were raised against the laws prohibiting voluntary abortion as a method of birth control and the religiously based laws which made divorce difficult—if not impossible, as was the case in most of Catholic Europe. Despite entrenched opposition, the women's suffrage organizations were becoming ever more influential in countries such as Germany and Great Britain.

Throughout the industrial world, the old order in the realm of sexuality—a kind of Old Regime of social control—was under attack on many fronts. By and large, the protagonists of these various reform movements saw one another as natural allies and clerical and traditionalist parties in the national legislatures as natural enemies. So the homosexual movement was part of a much larger wave of social agitation against nineteenth century sexual morality. This positive development was paradoxical in that its roots lie in part in the "social purity" campaigns of the late Victorian era. In their conviction that social hygiene required repressive as well as fostering aspects, the social purity advocates were hardly unambiguous supporters of sexual freedom. Social purity sought reform in the context of normative management and social engineering, not liberation. But in the actual situation, which was one of revolt against the corseted restraints of High Victorianism, reformers of various stripes were swept along in a wave of libertarian or quasi-libertarian openness. Yet the contradictions exposed in this era were to reemerge in the 1970s in the feminist campaigns against pornography and child abuse.

The 1920s. World War I brought the efforts of the sexual reform movement to a temporary halt, but then ushered in the far more radical rejection of Victorian norms of sexuality of the 1920s. The preoccupation of the police with **espionage**, sabotage, and other crimes directly affecting the war effort, the mood that youth had "so little time" to enjoy the pleasures of life when death was always imminent, the breakdown of authority in the wave of revolution that swept Central and Eastern Europe in 1917–18—all created a new setting for efforts at homosexual emancipation.

Germany, now the Weimar Republic, remained the center of the movement, which barely existed in most other countries, even where a semi-clandestine subculture flourished, as it had in **London**, **Paris**, and the major Italian cities since the late **Middle Ages**. The Deutsche Freundschaftsverband [German Friendship Association] was founded in 1920 as an expression of the displeasure felt by many homosexuals at the academic and political orientation of the Scientific-Humanitarian Committee and the narrow elitism of the Community of the Exceptional. The Association was more oriented toward the needs of the average homosexual; it opened an activities center in Berlin, held weekly meetings, sponsored dances, and published a weekly entitled *Die Freundschaft* [Friendship]. Some 42 delegates from chapters throughout Germany attended the second annual conference of the Association. A period of rivalry with the Committee ensued that lasted until 1923 when the Association renounced its involvement in the struggle for legal reform and changed its name to the *Liga für Menschenrechte* (League for Human Rights), while *Die Freundschaft* changed from a weekly to a monthly and took on a more literary and cultural focus. A third journal *Uranos* also competed with Adolf **Brand**'s *Der Eigene* in the artistic sphere. The *Jahrbuch* itself was forced to discontinue publication after the inflationary spiral of 1923 had destroyed its resources. Its 23 volumes remain the classic repository of information on all aspects of homosexuality from the first quarter of the twentieth century.

Most of the organizations and periodicals that flourished in the 1920s had a more social than political purpose, though Hirschfeld and the Committee continued their struggle against the "paragraph." In 1922 Gustav Radbruch, the Social Democratic Minister of Justice, drafted a far more progressive criminal code, but it never came before the Reichstag. The indifference of conservative jurists to legal reform led to the formation in 1925 of the Kartell für Reform des Sexualstrafrechts [Coalition for Reform of the Law on Sexual Offenses], which under the direction of the lawyer and litterateur Kurt Hiller (1885–1972) set about drafting a comprehensive alternative. Only one of the seven member-organizations of the Coalition, whose own draft was published as a compact volume of legal texts and commentaries in 1927, was a homosexual group (the Committee).

The country that had the most sweeping revolution of all was Russia, where the codes of the fallen autocracy were abolished in one stroke, and when the Soviet regime drafted its penal code in 1922, homosexual offenses were not included. Only crimes involving force or the corruption of minors were punishable, and the definition of minor was a sliding one, to be determined by physical examination of the subject, not by chronological age. The actual degree of freedom that homosexuals enjoyed during what later came to be seen as the "golden age" of the Soviet regime remains moot. No publications on homosexuality for the general reader are known from this decade, and no organization comparable to the Scientific-Humanitarian Committee or the League for Human Rights was formed. A group of medical experts did seek to enlighten the masses on sexual matters in general, and a rather tolerant attitude of the regime toward heterosexual promiscuity, divorce, birth control, and abortion facilitated some public discussion of homosexuality. But no direct benefits for homosexuals ensued, and a number of individuals suffered repression or persecution.

The English-speaking world lagged sadly behind Europe, as the traditional "Anglo-Saxon attitudes" toward sexuality changed but slightly in spite of protests after the condemnation of Oscar Wilde. At the end of the 1920s Bertrand Russell wrote that it would be virtually impossible to discuss the findings of modern psychologists on sexuality in print because of the English laws on "criminal obscenity," which the courts had defined as the power to corrupt any individual "into whose hands the publication might fall." A British Society for the Study of Sex Psychology had been established in 1914, but its real interest focused in the subcommittee on sexual inversion which was surreptitiously a "committee of the whole." Between 1915 and 1933 the Society published 17 pamphlets, one of them a translation of a German tract issued by the Scientific-Humanitarian Committee.

In the United States, Henry Gerber, who had served in the American Army of Occupation in the Rhineland, attempted to transplant the ideas and organizational forms of the German movement. In December 1924 the (Chicago) Society for Human Rights received a charter from the state of Illinois; it was officially dedicated to "promote and protect" the interests of those who, because of "mental and physical abnormalities" were hindered in the "pursuit of happiness." It lasted only long enough to publish a few issues of the newspaper *Friendship and Freedom*, modeled on the German periodical *Freundschaft und Freiheit*. One member of the ill-fated group was a bisexual whose wife complained to a social worker, with the result that all four members of the group were arrested without a warrant. Gerber lost all his savings and had only the bitter memory that no one came to the aid of the organization.

In France *Inversions* published a few issues in 1925 but was halted by a prosecution inspired by Catholic members of the National Assembly. The prosecution appealed to anti-German sentiments (the movement drew its inspiration "from across the Rhine") quite as much as to the traditional intolerance promoted by the church; the defendants lost. Still, in the absence of any penal law comparable to Paragraph 175, French homosexuals had little reason to organize. The frightful loss of life in the trenches during World War I coupled with the declining French birth rate even led in 1920 to anti-birth control legislation.

On the international front, a World League for Sexual Reform on a Scientific Basis was founded in Berlin in 1921 at the recently created *Institut für Sexualwissenschaft* (Institute for Sexual Science) headed by Magnus Hirschfeld. The founders included world leaders in law, sex education, contraception, endocrinology, eugenics, and sexual research in general. At its peak, the League united groups with a total membership of 130,000, and had members in countries from the Soviet Union to Australia. All were devoted to the task of replacing the ascetic morality of the church with a new standard of rights and obligations shaped by the findings of biology and medicine as well as by a modern conception of society's interests and of the individual's claim to happiness. Further congresses of the League were convened in Copenhagen (1928), London (1929), and Vienna (1930). The London conference, attended by many prominent figures in British intellectual and public life, may have had the greatest influence. In the following year, 1930, the Lambeth Conference of the Church of England approved the use of birth control by married couples. Breaching the long tradition of intolerance on this subject, Anglicans began to abandon the old ascetic norms of morality, thereby opening the way to ultimate acceptance of sexual pleasure as legitimate in its own right.

Setbacks. The 1930s—the Depression era—saw the sexual reform movement, as a whole, retreat. While it fostered radical movements throughout the world, the economic crisis made sexual problems seem secondary if not irrelevant. Worst of all, the rise of National Socialism and its seizure of power spelled the end of the homosexual movement in Germany. As early as 1929 **Nazi** harassment had forced Hirschfeld to leave the country. In 1933 the Scientific-Humanitarian Committee had to dissolve, and on May 6 the Institute for Sexual Science was invaded by Nazis who seized the library and files and burned them publicly four days later. Many of the homosexual and lesbian cafés and bars in Berlin were closed; all publishing activity of the organizations ceased for twelve years of National Socialist rule. The World League for Sexual Reform lasted until 1935, when the death of Magnus Hirschfeld in Nice led to its collapse, because the leadership was split over the issue of whether to remain a centrist movement or to form an open alliance with the Communist Party—which, as it happened, would have been a dead end.

The Soviet Union amended its penal codes to make homosexual acts between males—though not females—criminal. The "Law of March 7, 1934" patently alluded to the day of National Socialist assumption of power in Germany the previous year. Repudiating most of the other reforms of the 1920s, the Stalin regime prohibited abortion, suppressed the sale of birth control devices, and returned to a puritanical "petty bourgeois" code of sexual morality. Communist parties under Soviet domination lost all interest in sexual reform and became—and mostly remain—foes of homosexual emancipation.

Towards the Present. In Switzerland, just as the movement in Germany was coming to an end, a new homosexual organization began. In 1933 a monthly journal called *Schweizerisches Freundschaftsblatt* (Swiss Friendship Bulletin) came under the editorship of Karl Meier ("Ralf"), a former contributor to *Der Eigene* and *Die Freundschaft*, publishing articles, short stories and photographs of interest to the general gay reader. Subsequently the name was changed to *Der Kreis/Le Cercle*, and French (1943) and English (1952) sections were added, so that the publication took on an international character. The headquarters of the publication in Zurich became a social center for the subscribers; foreigners were admitted upon presentation of a passport. From their observation post in neutral Switzerland the contributors recorded the death of the older movement as the Nazis occupied one European country after another, but after the war they watched the rebirth of the movement, in due course, with an ideological and social base in the Anglo-American world.

The movement revived only slowly after the liberation of Europe from Nazi rule. The first country to have a postwar movement was the Netherlands, where the "Amsterdam Shakespeare Club" held its first meetings on December 8–9, 1946. This group and its journal *Levensrecht* (Right to Life) formed the nucleus of the Cultuur- en Ontspanningscentrum [Culture and Recreation Center] with the publication *Vriendschap* (Friendship), both of which began early in 1949. Despite the Catholic Center Party's efforts at repression in the Parliament, the organization grew in size from 1000 members in 1949 to 3000 in 1960. In preference to the term "homosexual," the Dutch group preferred the coinages *homofiel*, "homophile," and *homofilie*, "homophilia," which gained a certain currency in other languages and served to designate the first phase of the movement in the United States.

For a time the Netherlands became the refuge of the reviving homosexual movement. Supported by such world-renowned figures as Alfred C. **Kinsey**, whose pathbreaking studies (1948–53) had begun to reorient public opinion, the International Committee for Sexual Equality (ICSE) held its first conference in Amsterdam in 1951 and for a number of years issued an *ICSE-Newsletter*. In France André Baudry founded the monthly *Arcadie* in 1953 as a forum for the discussion of homosexual issues; like *Der Kreis*, it had a membership of Arcadiens who gathered at intervals for political and social purposes. Although France and Switzerland had no laws against homosexuality between consenting adults, the pressure of public opinion and the refusal of the establishment

media to open its channels to the homosexual cause left the leaders and supporters of these publications with a painful sense of their outsider status.

The Early American Movement. The United States had no tradition of homosexual movement activity, though many Americans had lived in Central Europe and Hitler's persecution brought **exile and émigré** homosexuals to such centers of the American gay underworld as **New York** and **Los Angeles**. "Vice squads" of the metropolitan police forces regularly entrapped homosexual men, raided bars, and generally intimidated public manifestations of same-sex proclivities. As early as 1948 in Southern California "Bachelors for Wallace" had appeared as a cover for the gathering of homosexuals, but Wisconsin Senator Joseph McCarthy's campaign against "sex perverts in government" put the gay community on the defensive: its response was the founding of the **Mattachine Society** in Los Angeles by Henry (Harry) Hay in December 1950. With leadership modeled on the organizational forms and practices of the American Communist Party and of freemasonry, it designed a five-tiered structure that would preserve the anonymity of members while allowing the highest tier to control the entire group. The founders conceived homosexuals in a separatist manner as a minority deprived of identity and rights, and needing a new consciousness of its history and place in society. Initial successes of the group led to growth in Southern California and spread to the **San Francisco** Bay Area, with chapters elsewhere in the country (these became independent in 1961). Mattachine also had a nationally circulated monthly, *ONE*, which for the first time provided American homosexuals with a forum for discussion of their problems and aspirations. In the course of time **ONE** emerged as a separate organization, while the original group's San Francisco branch issued *Mattachine Review*.

The anti-Communist campaigns

of the cold war could not leave the Mattachine Society untouched, and in 1953 an open struggle developed between the founders and a new set of leaders who challenged their "separatist" ideology, instead stressing the normality of homosexuals as differing from other Americans only in sexual identity. With this assimilationist program went a rejection of activism, so that the group could only by proxy appeal for toleration and understanding—through psychiatrists, jurists, sociologists, and the like who would come forward as seemingly disinterested authorities.

In San Francisco in 1955 Del Martin and Phyllis Lyon founded the lesbian counterpart to Mattachine, the Daughters of **Bilitis**. Its monthly publication, the *Ladder*, provided an English-language forum for homosexual women analogous to the *Mattachine Review* and *ONE*. The three organizations worked together in the face of the indifference and hostility of the Eisenhower years, in which "deviation" and nonconformity were relentlessly decried.

Law Reform. In 1953 a series of sensational trials in England brought the subject of homosexuality to the attention of Parliament. Urged by the Church of England and a number of prominent intellectuals, the Conservative government appointed a Committee on Homosexual Offenses and Prostitution headed by John **Wolfenden**. After hearing the testimony of witnesses from the British establishment, the Committee voted 12–1 in favor of repeal of the existing laws punishing male homosexual acts between consenting adults in private. Its Report, published in September 1957, proved a major landmark in the evolution of public opinion in the English-speaking world. It held that sexual acts belonged to the realm of private life which was not the law's business, rejecting the theological arguments that these were "crimes against nature," "contrary to the will of God," and the like, just as it dismissed the notion of homosexuality as a disease, finding it—to the

chagrin of the psychiatric establishment—compatible with full mental and physical health.

In a country where the whole subject had been taboo since time immemorial, and where German homophile literature had remained largely unknown, the public discussion of the Wolfenden Report put the issue on the agenda and set the precedent, though ten years were to pass before a Labour government enacted the recommendations. The Homosexual Law Reform Society (later known as the Albany Trust) was founded to press for repeal of the criminal laws; it issued brochures and a magazine, the first specialized periodical in Great Britain.

The United States followed in 1961 with the American Bar Association's drafting of a model penal code that omitted homosexual offenses from the roster of punishable acts. Illinois, in 1961, became the first state to enact this recommendation. Furthermore, professors of criminal law at the major schools began to teach the coming generation of lawyers that "victimless crimes" had no place on the statute books because they violated the freedom and privacy of the individual, and in time half of the states of the Union struck the archaic laws from the books either by legislative act or by an appellate court decision holding them unconstitutional.

Warren Johansson

America in the 1960s. The period from 1961 to 1969 saw the evolution of the American homophile movement from a defensive, self-doubting handful of small, struggling groups in California and the Boston–Washington corridor to an assertive, self-confident, nationally organized (if ideologically divided) collection of some three score organizations with substantial allies and a string of major gains for which it could take credit.

A characteristic figure in the ideological change was Franklin E. Kameny, a Harvard-trained astronomer, who became president of the Mattachine Society of

Washington after unsuccessfully fighting his dismissal from a government job. Where the previous leaders of the movement emphasized "helping the individual homosexual adjust to society," Kameny and such associates as Barbara Gittings, Randy Wicker, and Dick Leitsch urged a program of militant action designed to transform society on behalf of a homosexual community which was perfectly capable of speaking for itself. Not the psychiatrists, not the theologians, not the heterosexual "authorities," but homosexuals themselves were the experts on homosexuality, they insisted. Progress would come not by accommodation to the powers-that-be but by publicly applied pressure, legal action, demonstrations, and aggressive publicity.

Operating from his base in Washington, Kameny targeted the federal government's discriminatory practices in employment, military service, security clearances (a key to employment in large sectors of private industry), and other areas. Finding that government officials were relying on the doctrines current in psychoanalytic and other psychiatric circles to the effect that homosexuality was a debilitating mental illness, Kameny launched a systematic and rigorously formulated attack on the medical model in July 1964. While this effort would make considerable progress during the 1960s, gaining support from a National Institutes of Mental Health task force under Dr. Evelyn Hooker (1969), it was not to reach its triumphant conclusion until a 1973 vote by the American Psychiatric Association. More importantly, the campaign transformed the self-image of the American homosexual from one which internalized many of the most negative characteristics attributed to homosexuals by homophobic "authorities" to one which embraced his slogan "Gay is good."

Other activists, such as Laud Humphreys and Arthur Warner, preferred to work more quietly, though their efforts too reflected the new mood of urgency.

The National Committee for Sexual Civil Liberties, headed by Warner, orchestrated a subtle and resourceful campaign of sodomy **decriminalization**, which proceeded methodically on a state-by-state basis through the 1960s and 1970s.

Throughout the decade, mass media coverage of homosexuality snowballed, starting with Randy Wicker's publicity barrage of 1962 in New York and extending through articles on homosexual lifestyles in national magazines, until the once-forbidden topic had become a common subject for television and newspapers. In the process, previously isolated homosexuals became aware of the gay subculture and the homophile movement in large numbers and the ground was laid for substantial shifts in public, as well as professional, opinion on issues of concern to the movement. Notable also was the favorable publicity and financial support extended to the hard-pressed movement from the *Playboy* empire.

The movement's involvement with the social life of homosexuals was another major development of the sixties, originating in San Francisco. First came the organizing of gay bars there in the Tavern Guild (1962), then the founding of the Society for Individual Rights (S. I. R.) in September 1964, combining a militant stance with social activities. This led to the first gay community center in April 1966, and made S. I. R., with nearly a thousand members, the largest homophile organization in the country.

Other milestones in San Francisco saw the involvement of liberal clergymen and then whole religious groups (Council on Religion and the Homosexual, founded by the Rev. Ted McIlvenna in December 1964, and spreading to a number of other cities later in the decade); and the beginnings of productive political involvement with candidates for office and city officials (August 1966). These innovations heralded San Francisco's later reputation as the "gay capital" of the United States.

Southern California contributed the first nationally distributed large-circulation homophile news magazine, *The Advocate* (1967 onward). Dick Michaels, the magazine's editor, represented a new type that became influential: the journalist–activist. In October 1968, Los Angeles witnessed the founding by the Rev. Troy Perry of the first gay **church**, the Metropolitan Community Church; from the start the MCC and its leaders were heavily involved in the homophile movement and provided major financial and personnel support.

Another organizational breakthrough of lasting importance was the establishment of the homophile movement in academia, beginning with the founding of the Student Homophile League at New York's Columbia University by Stephen Donaldson (Robert Martin) in October 1966. Granted a charter by the university in April 1967, and making front-page headlines around the world, the student movement spread quickly and contributed a major impetus first to the spread of militancy and later to the radicalization of the homophile movement.

An important victory on the issue of employment discrimination came with the Bruce Scott case, in which the U.S. Court of Appeals reversed Scott's disqualification for federal employment in a June 1965 decision. This set the ground for the Civil Service Commission's acceptance of homosexuals in the 1970s. Piecemeal progress was made on the issue of security clearances, while efforts to gain admission to the armed forces remained stymied.

Another result of the new militancy was the recognition by the American Civil Liberties Union of the movement as a legitimate civil rights activity. The national ACLU reversed its policy in 1967 under pressure from the Washington, D.C., area affiliate, which began backing homophile causes in 1964, supported by the two California affiliates; this decision did much to legitimize the movement and gave it much-needed support on a wide range of legal and legislative issues.

On a local rather than a national scale, homophile organizations were often involved in contesting police practices, and were successful in halting raids on gay bars and entrapment of homosexuals in New York, San Francisco, and other cities. This effort probably had the greatest impact on the life of the average homosexual in the cities concerned.

A major transformation in the movement of the 1960s led from the closeted, fearful members of the early 1960s, operating under pseudonyms and avoiding involvement with the public, to the highly visible and equally vocal activist of the latter part of the decade. Landmarks in this evolution were the first public demonstrations organized by the movement in the spring of 1965 at the United Nations in New York in April and at the White House on May 29. The latter picket, with seven men and three women participating, gained nationwide television coverage, thus exposing the new gay militancy to a nationwide audience for the first time.

These changes in philosophy, strategy, and tactics did not come easily, but were accompanied by bitter struggles within the movement between the new militants and the old-guard "accommodationists"; the New York Mattachine Society, which was captured by militants in a crucial election in May 1965, and the Daughters of Bilitis in particular were wracked by internal struggles and eventually foundered. New groups took their place; a tendency by the movement to devour its leaders generated continual organizational instability. Despite these problems, the period witnessed a growth in the total membership of its groups from under a thousand in 1961 to an estimated eight to ten thousand by the spring of 1969.

While there is a popular tendency to believe that nothing of importance happened in the homophile movement until it expanded to the dimensions of a mass movement in the summer of 1969, such a view proves on examination to be highly superficial. The explosion of the 1970s was made possible only by the laborious efforts of the pioneers of the 1960s, and in particular by the victory of the militants. As John D'Emilio points out, "their decisive break with the accommodationist spirit of the 1950s opened important options for the homophile cause. The militants' rejection of the medical model, their assertion of equality, their uncompromising insistence that gays deserved recognition as a persecuted minority, and their defense of homosexuality as a viable way of living loosened the grip of prevailing norms on the self-conception of lesbians and homosexuals and suggested the contours of a new, positive gay identity."

North American Conference of Homophile Organizations (NACHO). One of the characteristic developments of the homophile movement in the 1960s was its attempt to forge a semblance of first regional, then national, and finally continental unity under the umbrella of a common organization. Frank Kameny initiated this effort, stimulating the formation in January 1963, in Philadelphia, of the East Coast Homophile Organizations (ECHO). It was this loose confederation of four groups which sponsored the series of public demonstrations launched in May of 1965 at the White House, and it played a major role in gaining control of the movement on the East Coast by the militants.

The next step was the formation of a national grouping, established at a Kansas City conference of fifteen groups in February, 1966, as the National Planning Conference of Homophile Organizations. Meeting in San Francisco in August of 1966, this loose assembly reconvened in Washington a year later, where it changed its name to the North American Conference of Homophile Organizations (NACHO), developed an organizational structure with officers, by-laws, and established three regional subsidiaries (ECHO became ERCHO).

Though wracked by infighting among the groups, NACHO provided a largely informal but no less important boost to a sense of common purpose and identity among the leaders who attended its annual meetings and more frequent regional conferences, and to a certain extent among the rank-and-file members who read of its activities. It facilitated the spread of a militant approach on a nationwide basis, and presented the national media and other nationally-organized groups with a more formidable-looking movement.

Much credit for holding NACHO together was due to its secretary and coordinator, Foster Gunnison. Among its more tangible accomplishments, it established a national legal fund, coordinated public demonstrations on a nationwide basis, undertook a number of regional projects, and officially adopted and publicized the "Gay Is Good" slogan (adopted in Chicago in 1968). Furthermore, NACHO and its regional affiliates were instrumental in spreading the movement from its bicoastal base by colonizing the major cities of the North American heartland. And from 1968 until its demise in 1970 it provided a major forum for the growing radical wing of the movement.

The Stonewall Uprising and After. The slow pace of the American movement in the 1950s was accelerated in the early and mid-1960s in part under the influence of the black civil rights movement ("Gay Is Good" derives from "Black Is Beautiful"), then injected with the tremendous energies that accompanied the opposition to the war in Vietnam. With American involvement in Vietnam at its peak, student uprisings shook the campuses of Columbia and Harvard Universities in 1968 and 1969, and by the late spring of 1969 the country was in a mood of unprecedented mass agitation. It was against this background that the **Stonewall Rebellion** of June 27–30, 1969, marked the start of a new, radical, and even more militant phase of the homosexual movement in the United States.

Beginning as violent resistance to a police raid on the Stonewall Inn, a bar in New York's Greenwich Village, the popular movement found a new expression in the Gay Liberation Front (GLF). The GLF was conceived as uniting homosexuals (without guidance or even participation from sympathetic heterosexuals) around their own identity and grievances against an oppressive American society and as organizing them to force their own **liberation** from the persecution and powerlessness that was their lot even in the "land of the free." The radicals saw themselves as part of a broad alliance of oppressed groups developing autonomously but in an atmosphere of mutual support.

Superficial as was the New Left rhetoric of the Gay Liberation Front, since its analysis of the whole problem began virtually "from scratch," it had the merit of giving its followers a sense of identity as a group inevitably oppressed by the established social structure. The black and feminist movements as well as their homophile predecessors supplied the ideological resources that the growing organization needed to legitimate itself in its own eyes, if not those of the larger society.

The new Gay Liberation activists quickly collided with the pre-Stonewall movement leaders, whom they saw as part of an established structure too rigid for the kind of gay guerrilla warfare unleashed by Stonewall. Only two months after the riot, at the August 1969 NACHO convention in Kansas City, the Youth Committee under Donaldson issued a 12-point "radical manifesto" which stated, "We regard established heterosexual standards of morality as immoral and refuse to condone them by demanding an equality which is merely the common yoke of sexual repression." The youth leaders further demanded the removal of strictures against prostitution, public sex, and sex by the young; urged the development of independent "homosexual ethics and esthetics," denounced the Vietnam War and declared "the persecution of homosexuality" to be "part of a general attempt to oppress all minorities and keep them powerless."

The committee report was voted down, but the battle had just begun. The next confrontation came at the November 1969 meeting of ERCHO in Philadelphia, when GLF and SHL delegates pushed through a resolution declaring "freedom from society's attempts to define and limit human sexuality," a step beyond the movement's previous insistence on equality into the realm of social autonomy. Chaos ensued and the meeting broke up in disorder.

The handwriting was on the wall: when NACHO reconvened in San Francisco in August, 1970, gay liberation was over a year old and had no use for complex continental organizations with their by-laws, officers, and parliamentary procedures. Deeply divided between reformers and revolutionaries, itself the object of disruption by feminists on its first day and by radicals on its last, NACHO broke up in disorder as the more conservative delegates fled before an invasion by non-delegate radicals. Thus the five-year effort to bring all of North America's movement groups under a single roof collapsed in a tidal wave of gay activists.

In New York, those who called for a return to the "single issue" approach seceded to found the Gay Activists Alliance, which retained radical tactics of confrontation but focused on the specific problems of homosexuals in American society. "Zaps," sit-ins, blockades, seizures of lecterns and microphones, and disruptive tactics of all kinds were featured in highly publicized scenes which astonished the American public, long used to an image of homosexuals as passive and weak. And now it was not just repeal of the sodomy laws that the movement demanded, but the enactment of positive legislation protecting the rights of homosexual men and women in all spheres of life. None of this would have been possible without the ability of the new groups to call out hundreds and then thousands of supporters, drawing on the post-Stonewall mass base which the homophile movement had never been able to mobilize.

This new wave of mass "coming out" led to the formation of hundreds of gay associations with particular identities: political clubs, student groups, religious organizations, professional caucuses, social clubs, and discussion groups in towns and neighborhoods from one end of the country to the other. Far from the margin to which it had been confined until the end of the 1960s, the movement became an institutionalized part of American life. In the two decades that followed the Stonewall uprising, the movement grew to a network of interest groups as diverse in its origins, as multi-faceted in its identities and aspirations as America itself. National marches held in Washington in 1979 and again in 1987 brought tens of thousands of participants from all sections of the country, rallying behind the banners of hundreds of different groups all demanding their place in the sun.

The proliferation of gay groups in the 1970s led to a fragmentation of concerns and a lessening of a sense of focus for the homophile movement as a whole. Victories were attained on the psychiatric front (the American Psychiatric Association's vote in 1973 and subsequent defeat of a campaign to reverse that vote) and in a number of nationwide professional associations, but the struggle for decriminalization continued to be fought on a state-by-state basis, and with the demise of NACHO there was no longer a clearly legitimized national leadership. The Rev. Troy Perry was the most visible homophile spokesman as his Universal Fellowship of Metropolitain Community Churches expanded to nearly two hundred congregations and Perry engaged in highly publicized hunger strikes, led marches, and addressed protest meetings, even as arson destroyed a number of his church buildings. In 1974, Dr. Bruce Voeller, formerly president of GAA in New York,

founded the National Gay Task Force (NGTF), a membership organization rather than a federation. The NGTF lobbied on nationwide issues and in the next decade moved to Washington, but it never developed a mass following.

Much of the movement was turning its attention in the seventies to the adoption of gay civil rights laws, ordinances, and executive orders, and to the blocking of numerous attempts to repeal their scattered successes. In the absence of major progress towards a federal civil rights law, this was a local effort, though the campaigns pro and con often drew considerable nationwide publicity. Portland, Oregon, and St. Paul, Minnesota adopted rights ordinances in 1974, San Francisco in 1978, Los Angeles and Detroit in 1979, and New York City in 1986; Wisconsin adopted the only statewide gay rights law in 1981. Two Christian fundamentalists, the singer Anita Bryant and the Rev. Jerry Falwell led extensive homophobic campaigns which produced repeal of rights measures in Miami (1977), St. Paul, and Wichita, Kansas. Their efforts, however, suffered a major setback with the defeat in a California statewide vote of the Briggs Initiative, which would have banned gay teachers, in 1978.

Gay men and lesbians became visible in party politics and sent openly homosexual delegates to Democratic national conventions, forcing battles over "gay rights" planks (a weak one was adopted in 1980), and making homosexuality a presidential campaign issue; under the Carter administration a gay delegation was received by aide Midge Costanza in the White House and military discharge policies were changed to provide for fully Honorable Discharges, though the exclusion of known homosexuals from the armed forces remained intact. Notable here was the effort to avoid discharge by Air Force Sgt. Leonard Matlovich, whose fight brought him a *Time* cover in 1975. In San Francisco, the movement rallied behind supervisor (councilman) Harvey **Milk**, who was first elected and then assassinated in 1978; elsewhere the movement welcomed the emergence (usually but not always involuntary) of gay legislators and congressmen from their closets.

Reinforcing this movement activity was a thriving gay **subculture**, with its bars, baths, bookstores, guest houses, and services of all kinds, and above all a press that discussed the issues that confronted the gay community as a segment of American society.

World Perspectives. Given the extent of America's influence on popular culture throughout the world, this subculture became a model for gay life everywhere, from Norway to Taiwan—though the Islamic world still resisted this aspect of Westernization. The American example inspired countless imitators of the **"life style"** of the affluent and hedonistic America of the 1970s. In Europe **bars** adopted incongruous American names, such as The Bronx and Badlands, while gay rights organizations, retreating from their earlier radical stance, adopted American terminology and tactics.

Canada, being most intimately related to the United States, developed a homophile movement early on with the establishment in Vancouver of the Association for Social Knowledge (ASK) in 1964. Decriminalization passed in Canada in May of 1969, followed by emergence of the main Canadian group, the Community Homophile Association of Toronto (CHAT) in February, 1971. The influential gay newsmagazine, *The Body Politic,* also began publishing in 1971, surviving government harassment until 1986. The Canadian province of **Quebec** adopted an antidiscrimination law in 1977, followed a decade later by the provinces of Ontario and the Yukon, while the city of Vancouver passed a rights law in 1982.

In **Latin America** the first organization seems to have been Argentina's Nuevo Mundo (1969), but this promising development was cut short by the imposition of a cruel military dictatorship. Other organizations, often short-lived, appeared in **Mexico** (FHAR, 1978, followed by street demonstrations in 1979), Colombia, and Peru (Movimento Homosexual de Lima, 1982). In **Brazil** a major journal, *O Lampião,* began in 1976, and stable organizations appeared in Bahia, Rio de Janeiro, and São Paulo.

In **Japan** economic prosperity contributed to the expansion of the gay subculture, but traditional reticence impeded the formation of gay associations. Elsewhere in Asia, gay conferences were held in both **India** and **Indonesia** in 1982. In 1988 Israel discarded the sodomy law that it had inherited from the British mandate.

The Movement in Europe and Australasia. The watershed year of 1969 saw law reform in West Germany, while the next year witnessed the establishment of a gay Italian journal, *Fuori,* in Turin. By 1971 there was a proliferation of gay liberation groups in Britain and West Germany, while the Front Homosexuel d'Action Révolutionnaire was getting established in France. London's sole wide-circulation gay newspaper, *Gay News,* was established in 1972 and soon ran into major problems with the government, including an obscenity conviction which was upheld by the House of Lords. In Milan, 1973 saw the establishment of the Italian Association for the Recognition of Homosexual Rights.

By the mid-70s, the gay church in the form of the UFMCC was putting down roots in Britain, France, Denmark, Belgium; it even found a predominantly heterosexual congregation in Nigeria. Northern **Ireland** got a Gay Rights Association in 1975. In **Spain**, the Front d'Alliberament Gai de Catalunya (FAGC) was launched with marches in Barcelona in 1977. Catalonia remained the most important focus of activity, though other groups appeared in Madrid, the Basque country, and Andalusia.

Coventry, England, was the site of the formation in 1978 of the International Gay Association, like the defunct NACHO, a coalition of independent groups. The same year saw gay marches in Sydney, Australia. In the following year **Austrians** organized the Homosexuelle Initiative (HOSI) in Vienna.

The 1980s saw major advances in the European and Australian movements, with British decriminalization extended to Scotland in 1980. In 1981 the Assembly of the Council of Europe voted in favor of gay rights, the European Court of Justice in Strasbourg struck down a homophobic statute in Northern Ireland, and Norway adopted antidiscrimination legislation. In the same year Greece organized the group AKOE and Finland began the Sexuaalinen Tasavertaisuus (SETA). The **Australian** state of New South Wales adopted gay rights legislation in 1982, while New Zealand not merely repealed its criminal laws, but enacted a gay rights measure in 1986.

The European Parliament went on record in favor of gay rights in 1984, with France becoming the largest jurisdiction to adopt such protections in 1985. Progress, however, has not been uniform. In Great Britain in 1988 Parliament adopted Clause 28, which prohibited the use of public money for any activity deemed to "promote" homosexual behavior. Conversely, in the Netherlands gay studies programs became established in all major Dutch universities. The officially supported international conferences in Amsterdam in 1983 and 1986 set new standards for gay and lesbian scholarship.

The Challenge of the 1980s. The 1980s, with their conservative trend in most major industrial countries, confronted the movement with new obstacles and challenges. The spread of Acquired Immune Deficiency Syndrome (**AIDS**) in the United States and Western Europe meant that ever larger resources of time and money had to go into lobbying around the issues of research on the causes and cure of AIDS and the financing of health care for victims of the syndrome.

The stigma that linked homosexuality with a contagious and fatal condition was exploited by sensation-mongering media eager to profit from public curiosity and fear. The columns of the gay press began to print, week after week, the obituaries of those who had died of the consequences of AIDS, and new organizations such as New York's Gay Men's Health Crisis and ACT UP (AIDS Coalition To Unleash Power) were formed to deal specifically with this new challenge. In October 1988 AIDS activists from across the country staged a blockade of the Food and Drug Administration in Rockville, Maryland, charging that it was dilatory in making newly developed drugs available to the public. The AIDS Memorial Quilt was displayed first in Washington in 1987 and then in other major cities, providing a public symbol of grief. The new activism showed some similarities with that of the sixties, but it was accompanied by a battle-scarred realism regarding means and ends.

Homosexuals may take no small comfort from the ability of the movement to adapt to this crisis in creative and publicly effective ways, sustaining a sense of community and gaining a strong voice in government efforts to deal with the disease. Efforts to protect the rights of AIDS victims, recently being pressed as a medical necessity, may end in opening the door to long-denied measures on behalf of homosexuals in general.

The movement everywhere still faces the task of articulating the concerns of a minority in a society that continues to harbor hostility toward homosexuals. Fearing this hostility, the majority of male homosexuals and lesbians tend to remain in the **closet**, and the claims of the gay movement to represent them rest at best on silent consent. Movement leaders seek to become players in a political process still largely geared toward responding to economic interest groups mobilized to influence officeholders and alter public opinion, and toward accommodating ethnic minorities that have achieved voting cohesion. In the closing years of the century, the movement still aspires to achieve for its followers the same degree of political rights and social acceptance that the democratic countries have gradually accorded to other minorities in their midst.

Stephen Donaldson

BIBLIOGRAPHY. Barry D. Adam, *The Rise of a Gay and Lesbian Movement*, Boston: Twayne Publishers, 1987; John D'Emilio, *Sexual Politics, Sexual Communities: The Making of a Homosexual Minority in the United States, 1940–1970*, Chicago: Chicago University Press, 1983; Hans Hafkamp and Maurice van Lieshout, eds., *Pijlen van naamloze liefde: pioniers van de homo-emancipatie*, Amsterdam: Uitgeverij SUA, 1988; Laud Humphreys, *Out of the Closets: The Sociology of Homosexual Liberation*, Englewood Cliffs, NJ: Prentice-Hall, 1972; John Lauritsen and David Thorstad, *The Early Homosexual Rights Movement (1864–1935)*, New York: Times Change Press, 1974; Jim Levin, *Reflections on the American Homosexual Rights Movement*, New York: Gay Academic Union, 1983; Toby Marotta, *The Politics of Homosexuality*, Boston: Houghton Mifflin, 1981; James Steakley, *The Homosexual Emancipation Movement in Germany*, New York: Arno Press, 1975; Donn Teal, *The Gay Militants*, New York: Stein and Day, 1971; Rob Tielman, *Homoseksualiteit in Nederland*, Amsterdam: Boom Meppel, 1982.

MUJUN

This Arabic word denotes frivolous and humorous descriptions of indecent and obscene matters in stories and poems, what is sometimes called **pornography**. It is an important theme in Arabic literature, appearing often in combination with *sukhf*, scurrilousness and shamelessness. The most famous example of mujun is the stories of the *Thousand and One Nights*, in which the story-teller saves herself through the power of her imagination. Mujun can be considered as a verbal liberation from the shackles of decency, a kind of literary protest against social, and therefore also **Islamic**, norms and values.

With its obscenity, slander, and blasphemy, it meant to shock society. It stood for enjoyment of pleasure, drinking of wine, and spending the night with wide-but-tocked beardless youths or licentious women—not secretively as Islamic morals required, but openly, ignoring blame which would arise from behaving in such a sinful and shameful way. In principle it ought not to go beyond words, but of course it did. Nonetheless, mujun texts undoubtedly went far beyond practice and therefore have to be used very carefully when drawing conclusions about reality. But **fantasies**, especially when they are popular, give us insight into a social reality which exists next to official Islamic morals.

For the most part, sexual and scatological humor of this kind would be covered only in the language of the people, and not in literature. Only in periods of cultural bloom and a high level of social tolerance did it acquire a place in literature.

In the ninth and tenth centuries mujun was highly popular with the ruling elite of the Abbasid caliphate in Baghdad. Learned and religious people became fascinated by it, as for example the vizier Ibn 'Abbad (ca. 936–95). The most popular mujun writer of that time was Ibn al-Hajjaj (ca. 941–1001), whose work consisted of obscenity and scatology in its purest form. He compared his poetry with a sewer and with an involuntary emission from the anus: "When I speak the stench of the privy rises up towards you." Ironically, he himself served for some time in Baghdad as the official in charge of public morals!

Mujun was also used in an educational sense, rationalized by the idea that humor would stimulate and refresh the mind. Highly learned and respectable theologians and lawyers suddenly diverted their readers by digressions of mujun. Shaykh Salah ad-din as-Safadi for example wrote an essay about the size of the body-openings of women and boys in the middle of a very serious juridical work. Probably the best mujun, written with style and wit, can be found in the work of **Abu Nuwas**. One also finds mujun in Arab erotic works like Al-Tifashi's *Les délices des coeurs* (thirteenth-century Egypt) and Al-Nafzawi's *The Perfumed Garden* (fifteenth-century Tunisia). Most mujun, however, is not yet translated, which is most regrettable, because it would provide a major source of information, especially in regard to homosexual behavior.

Maarten Schild

MUKHANNATH

This Arabic and Persian word (plural *mukhannathūn*) denotes boys or men who dress and behave effeminately. In particular, the term refers to those who work as homosexual **prostitutes**, and who combine this trade with singing, dancing, or domestic chores. Mukhannathun imitate women in their movements and voice, and also in their use of perfume, make-up, and ornamentation. While their hair-style and clothing are effeminate, differing from the male's, they are also distinct from female styles: this differentiates the mukhannathūn from both sexes and symbolizes their social position. Socially, they are neither men nor women. Mukhannathūn are not regarded as men, because their appearance is not manly. Moreover, their unmanly occupations (particularly homosexual prostitution, in which they take the passive, female role) make them even less suitable for a man's position in society. Because they are "inferior" to men and have renounced their manhood through their behavior, they are allowed to associate openly with women (Koran 24:31), and women treat them practically as equals. However, the mukhannathun have more freedom than the traditional Islamic woman, not being hindered by the female role. They are not accepted as women because of their provocative behavior, and their occupations are just as unsuitable for virtuous women as for men. As a result, they find themselves in a position which might be called intermedi-ate, outside of the male/female dichotomy. Neither the prescribed role behavior of men or women is applicable to them, and sanctions against them are not necessary because they are not judged as men or women. Since they have no social role at all, they are regarded as "outsiders."

The mukhannath can be viewed as a socially acknowledged form of **effeminate** behavior, and, in particular, passive homosexual behavior. Although the occupation of prostitute is considered shameful, the mukhannathun fulfil a social need by indirectly protecting the honor of women; because they do not have a defined social role, their behavior can be generally accepted. The reasons for becoming a mukhannath are not clear, but probably result from a refusal of the masculine role or an inability to perform it, which may stem from a preference for passive homosexual behavior and/or a sort of psychological effeminacy which can result in transvestism or, in the extreme case, transsexualism. Economic motives can also play an important role in this process.

In former times, the mukhannathun had a bad reputation, probably as a result of their provocative behavior as singers and dancers, and, of course, their sexual behavior, which was no secret. From time to time, harsh action was taken against them, ranging from banishment to castration. Often they were the victims of mockery. In **Sufism**, the mystic current of Shi'ite Islam, mukhannathun were sometimes considered as symbols of unreliability, since they alternately presented themselves as men and women. The noted Sufi poet **Rumi** described them as ridiculous creatures, who thought like women and who were attached to worldly pleasures; he regarded them as caught up in "forms" and not in "meanings," the latter being the province of the truly masculine.

Western observers have traditionally been mystified by the phenomenon of the mukhannath, which they tried to define as hermaphroditism or transsexuality; both terms are oversimplifications of a social role they clearly did not understand.

Contemporary examples can be found in Turkey (köcek) and in Oman (khanith), and probably throughout the entire Middle East. Other societies of the past and present have presented similar phenomena: the constellation of homosexual prostitution, cross-dressing, singing and dancing is reported from Greece and China, and the hijra in **India** also appear similar. These transcultural similarities should be carefully studied, for the presence of general similarities may conceal more important differences.

BIBLIOGRAPHY. Ahmad al-Tifachi, *Les délices des coeurs*, trans. by René R. Khawam, Paris: Phébus, 1971; Unni Wikan, "Man Becomes Woman: Transsexualism in Oman as a Key to Gender Roles," *Man*, 12 (1977), 304–319, plus criticism and reply in *Man*, 13 (1978), 133–134, 322–333, 473–475, 663–671; and *Man*, 15 (1980), 541–542.

Maarten Schild

MUNRO, HECTOR HUGH (PSEUDONYM SAKI; 1870–1916)

British fiction writer, playwright, and journalist. Saki is best known for his witty and exquisitely crafted short stories, which often satirize the mores of Edwardian society, or describe a world of supernatural horror underlying the tranquil English countryside.

Munro was born in Burma, the son of a career officer in the British military police. Following the death of his mother when he was two, he and his older siblings, Ethel Mary and Charles Arthur, were sent to live with his grandmother and two aunts in western England. Though an old Scottish family with aristocratic pretensions, the Munros had only a modest income. Nevertheless, the boys were raised to be gentlemen, and throughout his life Munro thought and wrote as a Tory. The despotism and intolerance of the aunts informed a recurrent theme of his fiction:

the tyranny of dullards over their natural superiors, and the eventual revenge and triumph of the latter.

Munro was educated at Exmouth and at Bedford grammar school. In 1887 his father retired from the military, returned to England, and took his three children on a series of travels throughout Europe. In Davos, Switzerland, Hector Hugh, then eighteen years old and uncommonly attractive, was a frequent visitor at the home of John Addington **Symonds**, a prominent British writer who was the foremost authority on "masculine love" among the ancient Greeks. Munro appears to have accepted Symonds as his mentor in matters of literary style as well as sexual philosophy.

In 1893 Munro joined the military police in Burma. Here he observed the exotic customs of the inhabitants, and acquired a collection of animals, including a tiger cub. He discovered the advantages of having a houseboy, and throughout the rest of his life was seldom without one. Contracting malaria, he was invalided out of the service. He then turned to journalism, writing satirical pieces for the *Westminster Gazette*. He adopted the pen name, Saki, a word with esoteric homoerotic connotations. (Poems by **Hafiz** and other Sufi writers, as well as by **Goethe** in his collection, *West-östlicher Diwan*, are addressed to the "saki" or cupbearer, a beautiful boy, the object of male desire.)

After a number of years as a foreign correspondent for *The Morning Post*, Munro settled in London. Here he wrote a series of short stories: *Reginald* (1904), *Reginald in Russia* (1910), *The Chronicles of Clovis* (1912), and *Beasts and Super-Beasts* (1914). The stories are in turn playful, cynical, uncanny, and hilariously funny—a singular blend of urbanity and paganism. At their best, they represent the highest of high camp.

Though Munro's penchant for young men was well known, he was neither secretive nor blatant. The short stories contain numerous sly allusions to the "unmentionable vice" and occasional flashes of homoeroticism. The two most prominent characters, Reginald (no last name) and Clovis Sangrail, are dandies. Reginald is a vain and good looking young man, with nice eyelashes, who compares himself with **Ganymede**, wears "a carnation of the newest shade", and takes special delight in shocking people. A few of his epigrams have become famous ("To have reached thirty is to have failed in life."). At the same time that Reginald is courted by both men and women, he himself has an interest in lift boys, gardener boys, choir boys, and page boys. Clovis Sangrail, a bit older and more sophisticated, frequents the Jermyn Street baths (as did Munro himself) and is an admirer of male beauty, in others as well as himself.

Among the gayer stories are *Gabriel-Ernest* (a masterpiece which can be read on at least three different levels: a werewolf horror story, a comedy, and a parable of pederastic temptation), *Adrian, The Music on the Hill, Reginald's Choir Treat, The Innocence of Reginald*, and *Quail Seed*. A central figure in *Quail Seed* is a boy, "about sixteen years old, with dark olive skin, large dusky eyes, and thick, low-growing, blue-black hair" who works as an "artist's model"; the story concludes with the artist's statement: "We enjoyed the fun of it, and as for the model, it was a welcome variation on posing for hours for 'The Lost Hylas.'"

When World War I broke out, Munro, then 43 years old, enlisted in the army. Rejecting several offers of a commission, he remained in the ranks. His two years at the front, in the company of young working class men, were apparently the happiest time of his life. He was killed by a sniper's bullet in 1916, his last words being: "Put that damn cigarette out!"

His sister Ethel, in her *Biography of Saki*, wrote his epitaph: "He had a tremendous sympathy for young men struggling to get on, and in practical ways helped many a lame dog."

BIBLIOGRAPHY. A. J. Langguth, *Saki: A Life of Hector Hugh Munro*, New York: Simon & Schuster, 1981.

John Lauritsen

MURDERERS

More homosexuals have been the victims of murder than its instigators, but the popular imagination has seized on certain sensational exceptions to promulgate the legend of the lust-driven, antisocial sadist preying on young men. Cheap fiction likes to show the homosexual murderer as effete and flamboyant, but this is seldom true in reality. Occasionally, as in the case of Kenneth Halliwell, lover and slayer of the playwright Joe **Orton**, the violent act is a domestic crime of passion, the culmination of long self-loathing and humiliation. More often, the motive is profit, as when a hustler kills a john in his apartment: the files of the European police are packed with such cases going back to the eighteenth century. Homosexual *Lustmord* or sexual murder is less common than believed, and its practitioners rarely carry on lengthy torture sessions. Serial killers are generally closeted, with an emotional life arrested in childhood; their murders may be violent, but are often prompted by an inability to make emotional contact with another human being. They are unilateral in their taking of sexual pleasure and unimaginative in the recurrent patterns of their crimes.

The earliest criminals on record to mix homicide and homosex are monarchs or nobility, whose power enabled the crimes and whose prominence lent them notoriety. Zu Shenatir, fifth-century tyrant of El-Yemen, enticed young men and boys to his palace, sodomized them, and tossed them out of windows. He is alleged to have died, stabbed through the anus by the youth Zerash. Tipu Sahib (1751–1799), the Sultan of Mysore in **India**, convinced that he was the chosen servant of Mohammed with a mission to destroy infidels, would customarily sodomize every European he captured, including General Sir David Baird; their children would be burned over slow fires, or sodomized while drugged, or defenestrated, or castrated and trained as catamites.

Gilles de Rais. Gilles de Rais (1404–1440), companion-in-arms of Joan of Arc and one of France's richest noblemen, a youth of "rare elegance and startling beauty," was renowned for piety and courage. After Joan's death, he separated from his wife, retired to his castle at Tiffauges, and gave himself over to extravagance and dissipation. To repair his fortunes, he had recourse to alchemy and under the influence of Prelati, a comely Italian sorcerer, commenced torturing and murdering young boys, to use their blood for pacts and spells. Hundreds of children in his territories disappeared (up to 800 according to some authorities). At his trial in 1440, he and his confederates confessed that he used the children sexually as he tortured them and enjoyed orgasms as they died, arranging beauty contests of their decapitated heads. Although sentenced to be strangled and burned, his body was retrieved by his family and given a Christian burial. Gilles de Rais has achieved mythic status and is the subject of a study by Georges Bataille, a play by Roger Planchon, and a novel by Michel Tournier. But one may question whether the trial testimony, extorted from underlings, was authentic or fabricated by the civil and ecclesiastical authorities in order to seize the holdings of a lord who had grown too independent and powerful. As an emblem of divine good turned diabolically evil, the image of Gilles de Rais still exercises a powerful hold on the imagination.

Báthory. Erzsébet Báthory (1560–1614), the "Blood-Thirsty Countess" of a family which long showed a strain of madness and cruelty, is credited by legend with the death of more than 600 girls and young women. An adept in witchcraft and alchemy, with the aid of her handmaiden-lovers Barsovny and Ötvös, she kidnapped local girls and imprisoned them in her castle in Csej, northwest Hungary. Here she fattened and regularly bled them to provide beauty baths for her white skin. She would then have herself licked dry by virgins and anyone showing disgust would be tortured in various ingenious ways. Although her cousin was prime minister, he could not protect her castle from being raided and she was arrested and tried. Her accomplices were burned and decapitated, but in view of her high birth Báthory herself was immured in her apartments, where she died after four years of this living tomb.

The Rise of the Common Murderer. A signal difference between these slayers of the past and those of the present is that of rank. Royal or aristocratic murderers were in a position of privilege; their sexual tastes were considered as out of the ordinary as their crimes. The rise of the common man seems also to herald the rise of the common murderer, whose depredations and lusts must be rationalized within his society. With the emergence of forensic psychiatry and "criminal anthropology," the connection between sexual inversion and homicide has been studied in considerable, often obtuse, detail. It does seem certain that the anonymity of sexual promiscuity in the modern metropolis is both a temptation and a facilitation of mass murder.

The first "Romantic everyman" murderer was Pierre François Lacenaire (1800–1835), who wrote his memoirs while awaiting the guillotine. Although Lacenaire admitted to homosexual liaisons during earlier prison terms, he denied that he continued them in "civilian" life; nevertheless, police authorities were convinced that he and his accomplice Avril were more than good friends. Their last victim was a notorious *tante* ("auntie"). But, except for his self-aggrandizement and pretensions to literature, there was little to distinguish Lacenaire's criminal career from that of any heterosexual felon. The same might be said of Joseph Vacher (1869–1897), the "Ripper of Southeast France," who raped and ripped both sexes without discrimination; or of Ronald Kray (b. 1933), who with his twin brother Reggie terrorized the London underworld in the 1960s: Ronald was gay, his brother straight, but their records for brutality and viciousness were almost identical.

Although the number of heterosexual mass murderers is high, the homosexual serial killer exercises a special fascination for alienists and journalists alike. However, social taboos have prevented the homosexual murderer from being idealized by the media, with the exception of Wayne Williams, whose guilt was questioned in a TV special; so far, even homophobes have boggled at exploiting the crimes of Dean Corll and Dennis Nilsen. The most celebrated cases of murder by homosexuals in modern times are the following.

Haarmann. The German Fritz Haarmann (1876–1924) was an escapee from an asylum to which he had been sent because of child molestation. Once an exemplary soldier in a Jäger regiment, he turned petty criminal and police informer. In Hannover during World War I he became a successful smuggler, aided by his police connections. During the postwar inflationary period, Haarmann, posing as a detective, would pick up unemployed lads at the railway station, take them back to his room, and murder them, often by biting their throats during the sexual act. He would dismember the body and dispose of it in the river that ran outside his lodgings; charges that he sold the flesh for butcher's meat were never proven, but it is a strong likelihood. Infatuated with a petty thief and hustler, Hans Grans, who encouraged his activities, Haarmann stepped them up and may have been responsible for over 50 deaths of good-looking youths from 13 to 20. Despite complaints from parents, po-

lice were very slow to take action until bones and clothes too numerous to ignore began to turn up. Haarman and Grans were indicted for 27 murders in 1924; the former behaved with remarkable insouciance during the fortnight's trial and wrote a confession that revealed his delight in his sexual tastes and homicidal practices. He was decapitated; Grans was sentenced to twelve years' imprisonment. Haarmann's career formed the inspiration for the film, *Zärtlichkeit der Wölfe* (1973), made by Fassbinder's disciple Ulli Lommel.

Seefeld. Adolf Seefeld (1871–1936), a German tramp and religious fanatic, killed boys with natural poisons. When arrested and tried in 1936, he confessed to 12 murders, committed at ever-decreasing intervals between April 16, 1933, and February 23, 1935. (There may have been more, since he had been charged with a murder as early as 1908.) The Nazi court moralized over his deeds and sentenced him to be executed.

Leopold and Loeb. Nathan Leopold, Jr. (1905–1971) and Richard Loeb (1906–1936), brilliant scions of wealthy Jewish families in Chicago, were lovers who, under the influence of Nietzsche's "superman" philosophy, decided to commit a "Raskolnikovian" crime. In 1924, they kidnapped a younger acquaintance, Bobbie Franks, battered in his skull with a chisel, drowned him in a culvert, disfigured his face with hydrochloric acid, and hid the body in a drainpipe, before phoning ransom demands to the parents. They were traced by eyeglasses Leopold dropped at the culvert and, under police interrogation, Loeb confessed; both men accused the other of wielding the chisel. At their trial, they were defended by Clarence Darrow, who argued they were paranoid schizophrenics, thus irresponsible for the crime. They were both imprisoned for life plus 99 years; in the Joliet prison showerroom, "Dickie" Loeb was stabbed to death in a brawl; "Babe" Leopold, believed to be the mastermind of the Franks crime, was paroled in 1958 and served as a health worker in San Juan, Puerto Rico, until his death.

Corona. Juan V. Corona, Mexican labor contractor, was convicted in 1971 of killing 25 vagrants and migrant workers, whom he buried in the fruit orchards near Yuba City, California. The motive was apparently sexual, since most of the victims had their pants off or down, and one had gay pornography in his pocket; they had been stabbed and hacked about the head with a machete. Corona's defense tried to argue that he was a married man with children and therefore not a homosexual, whereas his half-brother Natividad, convicted of an earlier attack on a young Mexican, was a homosexual who returned to Mexico. Corona was sentenced to 25 consecutive life terms, although doubt remains as to whether he had an accomplice or was in fact the guilty party.

Corll. Dean Allen Corll (1939–1973) was the child of a broken home, a "mamma's boy" who allegedly "came out" during his service in the U. S. Army. In 1969, while living in Houston, he began to exhibit signs of moroseness and hypersensitivity, organized glue-sniffing parties, and indulged in sadistic activities. He would pick up boys for sex, torture and murder them; eventually he enlisted two youths, Elmer Wayne Henley and David Owen Brooks, as procurers and assistant torturers. The victims were often tormented for days at a time, occasionally castrated, before being despatched and buried in beaches and boathouses. Henley later claimed there were 31 victims, but only 27 bodies were recovered. The end came in 1973 when Henley made the mistake of bringing a girl to a party; the enraged Corll threatened to kill him, and Henley shot him. Henley and Brooks were sentenced to life imprisonment.

Toole. Otis Toole of Jacksonville, Florida, ex-hustler and arsonist, claims to have committed his first murder at the age of 14. Between 1975 and 1981, he and his close friend Henry Lee Lucas killed ap-

proximately 50 persons, including a six-year-old boy they beheaded; the victims were often tortured before death and sexually molested afterwards. Toole concentrated on the boys, Lucas on the girls. Although they confessed to some 700 crimes, they have since repudiated their confessions; Toole is serving a life sentence in Florida State Penitentiary, Lucas is on Death Row in Texas.

Cooper. Ronald Frank Cooper (1950–1978) was an unemployed laborer in Johannesburg who recorded in his diary in 1976 the intention to "become a homosexual murderer . . . [I] shall get hold of young boys and bring them here where I am staying and I shall *rape* them and then kill them. I shall not kill all the boys in the same ways." He then went on to list the ways, planning 30 murders, following which he would begin a campaign against women. After three unsuccessful attacks, he managed to throttle a 12-year-old, failed at raping him and, with a change of conscience, sought to loosen the rope. Identified by another boy he had molested, he was soon arrested, convicted with the aid of the diaries, and hanged.

MacDonald. William MacDonald was responsible for the murder and mutilation of four men in Sydney, Australia, in 1961; one of them was found castrated in a bathhouse, another castrated in a public toilet. MacDonald passed himself off as his last victim, Allan Brennan, but was picked up from Identikit descriptions. Sentenced to life imprisonment, he was later transferred to a home for the criminally insane.

Bartsch. Jürgen Bartsch (b. 1946) was a West German butcher's apprentice who between 1962 and 1967 lured four boys from a carnival in Langenberg, slaughtered them in an abandoned air-raid shelter, attempted anal intercourse, cut them up like beef carcasses, and masturbated over their bodies. On trial, he declared attempts to abduct 70 more. The fact that Bartsch had confessed his first crime to a priest shortly after committing the murder and that the priest had observed the confidentiality of the confessional occasioned debate about the sacrality of such confidence. Bartsch was condemned to life imprisonment.

Gacy. John Wayne Gacy, Jr. (b. 1942), Chicago salesman and contractor, may have suffered a personality disorder when struck on the head at the age of eleven. A man desperate to be liked, often serving as a clown at children's parties, he was a sorry mythomaniac, pretending to be a precinct captain and a friend of President Carter. Twice married and twice divorced, Gacy, who had a history of forcing sex on young men, lured at least 33 of them to his house in Des Plaines, sodomized them, often with violence, before murdering them. The bodies were buried there until he ran out of space and dumped the last five in the Chicago River. He was sentenced to life imprisonment in 1980.

Bonin. William G. Bonin (b. 1947) was a truck driver. Occasionally accompanied by friends, he cruised the streets and freeways of Los Angeles in his self-styled "death van," picking up young men. Inside the van, the victims were robbed, raped, tortured, and killed, their bodies strewn along the highway. Bonin varied his techniques, strangling with T-shirts, puncturing with an icepick, castrating, and stabbing endlessly. Altogether 44 bodies were recovered in the "Freeway Killings," which began in the mid-1970s. Bonin stood trial for ten of them in 1980, four more subsequently. He was sentenced to death and is awaiting execution.

Williams. Atlanta's Wayne Bertram Williams (b. 1958) is a problematic case: many are persuaded of his innocence and James **Baldwin**, in *The Evidence of Things Not Seen* (1985), writes: "It is unlikely, as well as irrelevant, that he is homosexual." For 22 months, between 1979 and 1981, 28 corpses of poor black children, two of them girls, were found murdered, shot, stabbed, bludgeoned or strangled. The spoiled and arrogant Williams, himself black, was charged with the murders of two grown men, Jimmy Raye Payne and Nathaniel Cater; the prosecution relied heavily on circumstantial evidence and innuendo, implying that the children's murders could be put down to Williams as well. He was sentenced to life imprisonment and the police declared the earlier cases closed.

Nilsen. Dennis Nilsen (b. 1945), a Scottish civil servant, holds the record for multiple murder in Britain. After a career in the army and the police, Nilsen became known as an excellent worker in the London Manpower Services Commission, a frequenter of gay bars, he often took young men, both homosexual and heterosexual, home for the night. Overwhelmed with a sense of loneliness and convinced that only death could keep his companions from leaving him, Nilsen began to strangle many of them, finishing them off by drowning in the bathtub. He would sleep beside the corpses, occasionally masturbating, or retain them on his premises, until corruption or overcrowding compelled him to dissect them and dispose of the remains under the floor-boards, in bonfires, or, in his last residence, down the toilet. It was the clogged drains which led to his discovery. On his arrest in 1983, he made a full confession, later amplified by circumstantial diaries; in prison, awaiting trial, he fell in love with David Martin, the bisexual murderer of a policeman. Nilsen was sentenced to life imprisonment. Of all homosexual serial killers, although he conforms in some respect to the standard profile, Nilsen seems the most intellectual, the most questioning of his own motives: these appear to be a profound need for affection, combined with a sense of the permanence and stillness to be found in death. It is significant, though not exculpatory, that he always committed his murders when thoroughly drunk, the alcohol releasing his inhibitions and permitting the suppressed violence in his nature. He seems to have finally located his identity as a reviled mass murderer.

Paulin. Thierry Paulin (b. 1963), a black cabaret performer from Martinique, appeared in drag as Diana Ross in Parisian night clubs. In tandem with a Guyanian boyfriend Jean-Thierry Mathurin (b. 1965), he brutally murdered 29 elderly widows betwen 1985 and 1987, until he was identified by a survivor. His motive was apparently mere robbery.

See also **Violence**.

BIBLIOGRAPHY. J. P. de River, *The Sexual Criminal: A Psychoanalytic Study*, Springfield, IL: Charles C. Thomas, 1949; Laurence Senelick, *The Prestige of Evil: The Murderer as Romantic Hero from Sade to Lacenaire*, New York: Garland, 1987; Colin Wilson and Patricia Pitman, *Encyclopedia of Murder*, New York: Putnam, 1962; Colin Wilson and Donald Seaman, *The Encyclopedia of Modern Murder 1962–1982*, New York: Putnam, 1983.

Laurence Senelick

MURET, MARC-ANTOINE (1526–1585)

French Renaissance humanist. Born at Muret in the Limousin, he was an autodidact who became a professor at the age of eighteen. Recommended by Julius Scaliger to the magistrates of Bordeaux, he taught literature at the college of Guienne. Among his pupils was the young Michel Montaigne, who later boasted that he had played the lead in the Latin tragedies composed by his teacher. Settling in Paris, Muret taught at the college of Cardinal Lemoine, delivering lectures so brilliant that Henri II and Catherine de' Medici attended them. By 1552 he was giving courses on philosophy, theology and civil law all at the same time, while publishing his poetic *Juvenilia*. But accused of unnatural vice, he was imprisoned at the fortress of Châtelet, and would have died of self-starvation had his friends not intervened to secure his release. Disgraced in Paris and reduced to poverty, he fled to Toulouse, where he eked out a living by giving lessons in law. He was accused a second time of having committed sodomy, in this instance with a young man named L. Memmius Frémiot, and on the advice of a councilor in the parlement he absconded once more. He was sentenced to death in absentia and burned in effigy with Frémiot in the Place Saint-Georges as a Huguenot and sodomite. He crossed the Alps in disguise and was warmly received for a time in Venice, while in France his memory was ceaselessly vilified. Théodore de Bèze remarked that "For an unnatural penchant Muret was expelled from France and Venice, and for the same penchant he was made a Roman citizen."

Muret found his fortune only under the patronage of the princes of Ferrara, in whose palace everything was at his disposal: several libraries, the precious manuscripts of the Vatican, and his protector's villa. In Rome he lectured on Aristotle, taught civil law, and was one of the first to apply it to the study of history and philosophy. His Latin was judged so perfect that his auditors believed that they were hearing the voice of another Cicero. In 1576 he entered religious orders and there conducted himself in a manner that won the approval and generosity of Pope Gregory XIII. As a defender of the Catholic party he even composed a eulogy of the massacre of Saint Bartholomew's eve. In addition to works on law he wrote numerous Latin commentaries on the Greek and Roman classics.

Muret was a type of Renaissance scholar and intellectual who had his brushes with the law because of his homosexual activity, but thanks to his enormous talent and the protection of influential friends managed to escape the penalty which the law then decreed and even to have a distinguished academic career. His mastery of Latin and his commentaries on the ancient authors belonged to an age that saw as its main task the recovery and assimilation of classical antiquity rather than original scholarship.

BIBLIOGRAPHY. Charles Dejob, *Marc-Antoine Muret: un professeur français en Italie dans la seconde moitié du xvi° siècle*, Paris: E. Thorin, 1881.

Warren Johansson

MUSIC, POPULAR

Popular music is not only of interest in its own right as an important area of popular culture, but in times for which major documentation of homosexuality and attitudes towards it on the part of the lower and middle classes is lacking, it is one source of value to historical inquiry

In the broadest sense, popular music includes everything that is not funded by elites for an elite, usually upper class or ecclesiastical, audience. This is usually art music (that is to say, sonatas, symphonies, lieder, operas, etc., and their equivalents in non-Western music). It is, moreover, useful to distinguish "popular" music from folk music—the older forms of anonymous, noncommercial expression. Popular music made use of mechanical means of reproduction of musical scores and text, beginning with song books and sheet music in the Renaissance. The commercialization of popular music appears first in cabaret and concert performances to which tickets are sold to a general audience, later in the sale of recordings.

Although some scholars believe that they can detect erotic motifs in instrumental music, this is certain only in the few cases where the composer has so indicated, as in the "Love Death" music from Wagner's *Tristan und Isolde*; it has been suggested that **Tchaikovsky's** *Symphonie Pathétique* has a homosexual theme. But the field of inquiry is in practice limited to songs with words, and the texts are the principal criterion of interpretation. In practice intonation (broadly defined to include lilt, timbre, and accentuation) is also important as a second level of meaning, which may supplement or even contradict the denotative one; sound recordings largely retain these intonational registers.

Early Indications. A fourteenth-century ordinance from Florence bans the singing of "sodomitical songs." Although the words and music of these are lost, the need to prohibit them attests that homosexuality was part of the bawdy repertoire of urban life as early as the late Middle Ages. The arrival of printing made possible the diffusion—no doubt with establishment encouragement—of a counterflow of antihomosexual songs. A characteristic example is an English single-sheet folio of a ballad, "Of the Horrible and Woefull Destruction of Sodom and Gomorra, to the Tune of the Nine Muses" (London, ca. 1570). In France during the time of Louis XIV satirical songs pilloried the homosexual peccadillos of Jean-Baptiste **Lully**, master of the king's music, and the indiscretions of other notables.

In the nineteenth century the music hall saw a vogue for both male and female impersonators, leading to drag performances of songs appropriate to the opposite sex. In 1881 Gilbert and Sullivan's *Patience*, incorporating a character based on Oscar **Wilde**, created the archetype of a gay man in popular music—though the character (Bunthorne) was officially simply an "aesthete." In the inner cities of Europe and North America a few clandestine gay establishments offered sung entertainments, a tradition that survived into the second third of the twentieth century with the performances of Rae Bourbon.

Modern Commercial Popular Music. At the turn of the present century, the English-speaking world saw the emergence of a new category of music with mass appeal, the commercial popular song. What made this music distinctive was its broad availability through phonograph recordings, radio, and eventually sound motion pictures and television. Suggestive elements had been present in the nineteenth-century music hall, in vaudeville and minstrelsy, but these live entertainments lacked the standardization of style, tempo, and intonation found in songs diffused by a New York-centered grouping of highly professional songwriters, collectively styled Tin Pan Alley, that were fixed in form and sold by the millions in recordings. Of course each recorded version would have its own standardization, but many songs retained in the popular mind the qualities given by the first major recording. Erotic suggestiveness appears in these songs not only in the lyrics, where the innuendo may be subtle, but in intonation, which served to bring out any underlying ambiguities. Consequently, it is necessary to listen to the audio recordings themselves to obtain the full effect.

A surprising number of examples escaped the tacit censorship that prevailed until the 1960s. One category is that of songs intended for one sex to be sung by a singer of the other—without benefit of the drag disguise as seen in the music hall. As early as 1898 John Terrell recorded "He Certainly Was Good to Me," and in 1907 Billy Murray longed for his absent sailor "Honey Boy," while in the 1930s Bing Crosby was to essay "There Ain't No Sweet Man (Worth the Salt of My Tears)." Ruth Etting sang a 1927 song about the charms of a woman friend, "It All Belongs to Me" (1928), and Marlene Dietrich became celebrated for such renditions as "I've Grown Accustomed to Her Face." There has been a tendency to interpret the female-to-male songs as more threatening than the male-to-female ones (as shown by censorship in later versions), corresponding to the fact that the **sissy** is more disapproved than the tomboy.

Some songs, such as Bing Crosby's 1929 "Gay Love," simply refrained from revealing the sex of the love object, leaving it to the listener's imagination. A few others were more explicit, such as Ewen Hall's thirties tune "Delicate Cowboy," who not only sang "gay" but preferred to ride side-saddle.

America's wars helped to stimulate a certain interest in buddy songs. Thus in 1922 the singer of "My Buddy" laments the departure of his comrade, reminiscing about "gay" times. As World War II approached this song was revived by Bing Crosby, Frank Sinatra, and others.

Other songs show mockery of gender conventions. The 1938 story "Ferdinand the Bull," about an animal that preferred sniffing flowers to fighting, became a Disney film and song. In *The Wizard of Oz* Bert Lahr played and sang the part of the cowardly lion, a dandified incompetent.

The interwar years saw the rise of a special category known at the time as "race records." These songs, whose verve made them increasingly attractive to white audiences, drew upon an existing genre of very frank black folk music, which they to some extent bowdlerized. Nonetheless, blues singers Ma Rainey and Bessie Smith recorded a number of clearly lesbian songs. In 1928 Rainey sang: "Went out last night,/ with a crowd of my friends,/ they must be womens/ Cause I don't like mens" ("Prove It on Me Blues"). As confinement was a common part of the black male experience, blues songs frequently dealt with jailhouse life, and occasionally referred to the necessarily homoerotic sexuality therein. Thus in one old song the prisoner asks the jailer to "put another gal in my stall," "gal-boy" being one of many Southern black slang terms for a sexually passive prisoner.

Stephen Foster (1826–1864), who began the tradition of distinctively American popular songs, was almost certainly gay—he ran away with another composer, George Cooper—but his lyrics sedulously avoid any hint of his orientation.

Such concealment is hardly characteristic of the work of Noel **Coward** (1899–1973) and the uncloseted Cole **Porter** (1893–1964). The witty lyricist of Broadway musicals Lorenz Hart (1895–1943) seems to have been gay, but it has not been possible to confirm rumors about George Gershwin (1898–1937). Although bisexual composer–conductor Leonard Bernstein (1918–) aspires to renown in the classical field it may be that his most lasting work is the music for *West Side Story* (1957).

The 1959 Broadway musical *The Nervous Set* featured an indirect but widely understood "Ballad of the Sad Young Men," which despite its gloomy perspective became popular in gay bars. Although musicals were much patronized by gay men, in order to retain their heterosexual audience they tended to be circumspect about sexual references. (Later, after the **Stonewall Rebellion**, the Reverend Al Carmines was to create a series of openly gay musicals in Greenwich Village, beginning with *The Faggot* in 1973.)

No survey of gay-related music would be complete without a mention of the phenomenon of "conscription," whereby a song without ostensible gay reference would become adopted by gay people as special to them and be widely played in gay bars as well as at home. Often such songs would deal with furtive love, such as The Lettermen's "Secretly," but the most famous one of the sixties was interpreted by homosexuals to deal with cruising and eye-contact: Frank Sinatra's "Strangers in the Night" (1966).

Rock and Roll. A new, youth-oriented popular music, rock and roll, developed in the United States in the mid-1950s out of a fusion of black rhythm and blues, gospel, doowop harmonic singing, white rockabilly, and other elements.

One of the black pioneers of rock and roll was the singer Richard Penniman ("Little Richard"), who appeared onstage wearing mascara eyelashes and a high, effeminate pompadour, having been kicked out of his home at age 13 for homosexuality. His cleaned-up 1956 recording of "Tutti Frutti" sold over three million copies, leaving an indelible mark on the new genre. A year later, however, Little Richard left rock and roll to become a Seventh Day Adventist and later denounced his own homosexuality, claiming to have "reformed" to heterosexuality.

When white singers such as Elvis Presley started recording black rock and roll tunes, radio took up the new music and it quickly came to dominate the commercial mass market, displacing to a large extent the old Tin Pan Alley hegemony.

In its origins, however, rock and roll was a type of "underground" music. As such, it was not aimed at widespread radio airplay and was therefore less subject to censorship. This, however, does not explain the widespread airplay of Presley's big hit, "Jailhouse Rock" (1957), which contained a hardly disguised allusion to homosexuality in the context of a song containing black code-words for sex, most notably "rock" itself: "Number 47 said to Number 3/ 'You're the cutest jailbird I ever did see./ I sure would be delighted with your company/ come on and do the jailhouse rock with me!'" With the commercial breakthrough of rock and roll, such uncensored references quickly disappeared and were not to reappear until broadcast censorship standards had been seriously weakened in the upheavals of the late sixties and early seventies.

In the 1960s, rock and roll broadened out into "rock," incorporating such diverse elements as electrified quasi-folk music (among whose stars were the publicly bisexual or lesbian/gay singers Janis Joplin, Donovan, and Joan Baez), political protest songs, and complex "psychedelic" constructions. The decade was dominated by the British, who invaded American rock starting in 1964, led by the Beatles and the Rolling Stones. The Beatles released the sexually ambiguous "Obladie Oblada" on the "White Album" in 1968, while the Stones included some esoteric but clear self-ascribed references to homosexual prostitution in "When the Whip Comes Down" and some references (slightly disguised through the use of British slang) to oral sex by transvestites in "Honky Tonk Women" (1969). The very popular Doors opened up the previously taboo subject of anal intercourse in 1968 when Jim Morrison lyrically proclaimed "I'm a Backdoor Man."

The Explicit Seventies. In 1970 the Rolling Stones, trying to get out of a contract with their record company, Decca, recorded "Cocksucker Blues"; Decca did refuse to release it, but the song became well known to the legions of Stones fans through bootleg recordings and discussions in the music press. Lyrics asked "Oh, where can I get my cock sucked? Where can I get my ass fucked?"

Following in the wake of "Cocksucker Blues" came a wave of explicit songs in the rock genre, some of which managed to get mass airplay and thus become major hits. The relaxation of broadcast censorship standards was no doubt related to the explosion of homosexual visibility which began with the 1969 **Stonewall Rebellion** and which brought discussion of homosexuality into all the mass media.

Among the first of these was "Lola" from the very popular British group The Kinks (1971). In this hit, which reached the number nine position on the bestseller charts, Ray Davies sang of a virgin boy who takes a fancy to Lola, only to discover that "I know I'm a man/ and so is Lola"; the discovery doesn't seem to lessen the boy's ardor at all. This eye-opener was followed by the American Lou Reed's 1972 Top Ten hit, "[Take a] Walk on the Wild Side," which recommended not only male prostitution but also transvestism. The campy Reed (who was presumed homosexual but who got married in 1980) and his producer on this record, the androgynous, married, and (according to a 1972 statement he later qualified) homosexual David Bowie, were major figures in a rock movement of the early seventies called "glitter rock," which was frequently associated with homosexuality in the music press. Another notable feature of the glitter movement was the New York Dolls, who appeared in drag and female makeup.

More in the mainstream of commercial rock was Rod Stewart's popular 1976 song, "The Killing of Georgie," an outright attack on "queerbashing." Elton John, who "came out" as bisexual in 1976, achieved considerable commercial success

with a 1972 homoerotic love song, "Daniel." In France Charles Aznavour's "Ce qu'ils disent" (1972) was a somewhat mournful ballad about a transvestite entertainer who lives with his mother. And at the end of the decade Peter Townshend, lead singer for the supergroup The Who, was ready to release a solo album with a song called "Rough Boys" describing his erotic attraction to young toughs.

A footnote to the seventies was the 1978 "coming out" of Mitch Ryder, who had become a Top Ten singer in 1966 and 1967, and now discussed his experiences with anal intercourse in his album "How I Spent My Vacation."

Disco, Punk, and New Wave. Even as rock music was turning its attention to homosexuality, however, the gay audience was turning away from rock. As early as 1972, disc jockeys in gay bars and clubs were putting bits and pieces of black dance music together into a new genre, disco, which at first had little appeal to heterosexual whites. Disco music featured mechanical studio productions using canned rhythm tracks overlaid with a live singer, and thus did away with the necessity of hiring bands either for clubs or for recording purposes. Even as disco swept rock off the airwaves in 1977, it retained many of its previous associations with the gay subculture.

Most notable of the gay-associated disco performers was a group (in itself rare for the genre) of New Yorkers called The Village People, which dressed like a collection of gay stereotypes. With songs like 1978's "Macho Man," "YMCA" (a number two hit in 1979), and "In the Navy," The Village People appealed with little indirection to the gay disco audience, but found themselves becoming a mass commercial success as well. The United States Navy at one point agreed to use "In the Navy" as part of a recruiting campaign, but quickly dropped the idea when it was pointed out to them that the song was full of only thinly disguised homoeroticism. The openly gay black disco singer Sylvester, based in San Francisco, managed a fairly successful career for some years (he succumbed to AIDS in 1988). Generally, however, the mass commercial success of disco, which lasted into the early eighties, discouraged producers from including frankly homosexual themes in their lyrics.

In reaction to the dominant position of disco in the mid-seventies, there arose in 1975 a new underground movement with inspirations going back to the rock and roll of the fifties: **punk rock**. As an underground, with little hope for substantial airplay, the punks were able and encouraged to break all the taboos they could find, protesting against the "safe" homogeneity of disco lyrics.

Both founders of punk, singer Patti Smith (a bisexual) and the group The Ramones, sang about homosexuality in their debut albums. When the movement reached Britain in 1976, it sparked a similar reaction with groups like the Sex Pistols and the Buzzcocks singing about explicitly homosexual themes; punk ideology opposed homophobia. Rather than frequent the disco-oriented gay bars, homosexual rockers went to punk clubs and made their presence notable in an atmosphere of general acceptance.

Punk began to make an impression on the wider gay audience when gay punk singers began to move out of the genre and into the wider "new wave" musical movement; in this fashion London gay activist Tom Robinson and ex-Buzzcock Pete Shelley became widely known. Robinson's 1978 "Glad to Be Gay" drew wide attention even as a punk song, perhaps the only widely successful song to treat homosexuality as a political issue; the telephone numbers of the New York and Los Angeles gay switchboards were listed on the inner sleeve of his "Power in the Darkness" album. Shelley's "Homosapien" love song became a commercially successful (especially in England) dance song in 1981 despite explicit lyrics. Meanwhile, punk has continued as a thriving, if "underground," music through the eighties, and it is still notable for producing explicitly homoerotic songs and singers.

The trend towards musical diversification led to women's music sung by lesbians. As early as 1969 Maxine Feldman was proudly singing "Angry Atthis," which became the first example to be issued as a 45 rpm single. Later, Holly Near, Meg Christian, and Cris Williamson were to become long-term favorites, frequently performing in cabarets and women's festivals. The firm of Olivia Records was created to record and market this music. No one of comparable stature appeared from a purely gay-male context, but in the 1970s gay (and lesbian) choruses sprang up in major cities of North America, spreading to Europe as well.

Early in the 1980s, radio programmers and mass audiences began to tire of disco, opening the way for the popular acceptance of the once-underground "New Wave," which evolved into "electropop" by incorporating synthesizers and other electronic music. In Britain a number of new wave figures such as the androgynous Boy George and the Culture Club and the outright gay groups Bronski Beat, Soft Cell, and Frankie Goes to Hollywood achieved widespread commercial success; Bronski Beat in particular produced a string of popular gay-oriented songs. Towards the end of the decade this tradition was carried on by singers in the bands Erasure and the Pet Shop Boys. The Broadway version of *La Cage aux Folles* showed that even a musical about transvestites could be successful, but it did not start a trend. By and large, explicit gay music retreated from the American mainstream in the 1980s as AIDS put a damper on gay romanticism.

Conclusion. As we have seen, the forces of censorship often operated to keep gay elements in mainstream popular songs on the level of ambiguity and innuendo. Yet this need for covertness bonded with the homosexual talent for camp humor to produce examples that are not only creative but throw light on the consciousness of gay men and lesbians in earlier as well as recent times. For a brief time in the 1970s it looked as if explicitly gay-related music was successfully breaking into the commercially successful mainstream of popular music. Nevertheless, for examples of explicit treatment of gay/lesbian themes the contemporary listener must often turn to relatively uncommercial sources such as the feminist groups or the punks.

Stephen Donaldson

MUSICIANS

The mythical archetype of the homosexual musician is the figure of the Greek **Orpheus**, noted for his magical art in music and poetry. After the loss of his wife Eurydice, Orpheus gathered together an entourage of young men, whom he wooed with song. In some **inventor legends** he is regarded as the discoverer of pederasty itself. A more humble ancestor is Corydon, the love-sick shepherd of **Vergil**'s Second Eclogue, who poured out his unrequited affection for the youth Alexis in song, accompanying himself on the pipes.

Baroque Music. **Opera**, arising at the start of the seventeenth century in southern Europe where the Counter-Reformation had its baleful sway, nonetheless provided an umbrella for a certain amount of nonconformity. For musical reasons, many of the most important roles were sung by eunuch males, the **castrati**, who sometimes became the objects of male devotion among the rich and cultivated admirers of the art.

For Jean-Baptiste **Lully** (1632–1687), a native of Florence who dominated music-making at the French court of Louis XIV, scholars have been able to piece together a complex picture of the trials and triumphs of a major gay musician. After composing numerous ballets, in 1672 Lully obtained a patent for the production of opera and established the Académie Royale de Musique, which he used to ensure a virtual monopoly of the operatic stage.

Skillfully adapting the conventions of Italian grand opera to French taste, he set the pattern for French opera down to the late eighteenth century. His homosexual conduct generated endless gossip, which he forestalled temporarily by marrying in 1661. In the end he owed his survival to the support of the king, who could not do without the sumptuous entertainments Lully provided.

Pietro **Metastasio** (1698–1782) was by far the most important librettist of baroque opera. The son of a Roman grocer, Pietro was adopted at the age of eleven by a noble who was undoubtedly in love with him and who provided the classical education needed for his career. His tempestuous later career was marked by dramatic involvements with women as well as with men, including the famous castrato Carlo Broschi (better known as Farinelli; 1705–1782).

George Frideric Handel (1685–1759), born in Germany, but active mainly in Italy and in England, wrote many operas and oratorios. In striking contrast to his great contemporary Johann Sebastian Bach, Handel never married or had children. His associations point to homosexual inclinations, but if he exercised this taste, he covered his tracks so successfully that modern research has not been able to find the evidence.

Romanticism and After. The key figure for musical romanticism was the great Viennese composer Franz **Schubert** (1797–1828), whose unique melodic gift enabled him to reach the heart of every musical task he attempted. In Vienna Schubert moved in bohemian circles, which teemed with homosexual and bisexual lovers of the arts. Schubert never married, rejecting suggestions that he do so with outbursts of temper. His romantic attachments to men appear in veiled form in a short story he wrote in 1822, "My Dream." The composer died of syphilis just after reaching the age of thirty.

The sexual tastes of Schubert's lesser French counterpart, Camille Saint-

Saens (1835–1931) transpire from a quip attributed to him: "I am not a homosexual but a pederast!" However, it is uncertain whether this pleasantry reflected real activity, though in his later years the composer took up residence in North Africa where opportunities were legion.

Peter Ilyich **Tchaikovsky** (1840–1893) was the greatest Russian composer of the nineteenth century. His attempt at marriage was a complete failure, and his closest emotional relations were with men. His sixth symphony, the *Pathétique* (1893), was dedicated to his beloved cousin Bob Davydov, and was the fullest outpouring of the emotions he had felt during a lifetime. In the Soviet Union, where the composer's musical achievement is deeply revered as a national treasure, an impenetrable veil of silence has been drawn across his homosexuality, but in the West it is generally acknowledged. There seems to be no truth, however, in the claim that he was forced to commit suicide because of his homosexuality.

The Polish composer Karol **Szymanowski** (1882–1937), who became director of the Warsaw Conservatory, had a passion for handsome young men. He also wrote a homosexual novel, though it was never published.

Dame Ethel **Smyth** (1858–1944) achieved more success in Germany than in her native England. In addition to full-scale choral and orchestal works, she wrote and produced six operas. A strong-willed, sometimes flamboyant personality, Smyth threw her energies into to the British movement for women's suffrage, for which she wrote a "March of the Women." She fought for equal treatment of women as artists, chivying conductors and performers, and staging grand scenes of temperament. After a number of affairs with women, at the age of seventy-one Smyth fell in love with Virginia **Woolf**.

In the United States, Stephen Foster (1826–1864), who wrote such popular songs as "My Old Kentucky Home" and "Come Where My Love Lies Dream-ing," and Edward MacDowell (1861–1908), composer of many symphonic poems, were probably homosexual. The picturesque wanderer Francis **Grierson** (1848–1927), who resided for a time in France, achieved success as both a pianist and a singer. The gay life of Charles Tomlinson **Griffes** (1884–1920), perhaps America's first cosmopolitan composer of distinction, is well attested. Katherine Lee Bates (1859–1929), the Boston professor who wrote the text of "America the Beautiful," was lesbian.

Modern Music. Twentieth-century musical life has witnessed a number of famous gay couples, including the French Francis **Poulenc** (composer) and Pierre Bernac (tenor), the English Benjamin **Britten** (composer) and Peter Pears (tenor), and the Americans Samuel Barber and Gian-Carlo Menotti (both composers). The major avant-garde composer John Cage has long shared a residence with the influential choreographer Merce Cunningham. Henry Cowell (1897–1965), a pioneering American modernist composer, was convicted on a morals charge in California and imprisoned at San Quentin. Charles Ives, who had been a close ally, reacted with virulent homophobia, suggesting that Cowell should kill himself. In his several volumes of *Diaries*, Ned Rorem has been frank about his homosexuality, both during his early career in France and his later one in New York. Other American composers of distinction are Aaron Copland, David Diamond, Lou Harrison, and Charles Wuorinen.

Among performers the high correlation of homosexuality and the instrument of choice is particularly striking among organists. Many contemporary pianists are also gay. What is the reason for this link? Surely, it cannot be simply that touching the ivories has some special affinity with homosexuality. The explanation of why most organists are gay, and many pianists are, appears to reflect the fact that both instruments are normally played solo. Only on special occasions is an organ or piano used in conjunction with a symphony orchestra. Contrast the violin. Although this instrument can be played solo, the vast majority of violinists earn their living playing in string ensembles in orchestras. This contrast between solo and group activity has its counterpart in the world of sport, where swimmers and runners are more likely to be homosexual than baseball and hockey players. Like all such generalizations, this one has exceptions. Nonetheless, gay musicians and and athletes seem more drawn to individual performance than to team participation.

Many contemporary gay pianists and organists, for understandable professional reasons, have chosen to keep their sexual orientation private. This is not the case with the great Russian virtuoso Vladimir Horowitz (1904–1989), who did not object to Glenn Plaskin's frank biography of 1983. A child prodigy, Horowitz' homosexuality became evident in his early maturity in Russia and Germany. In the 1930s the pianist came under the influence of the charismatic Arturo Toscanini, who encouraged him to marry his daughter Wanda. Despite the husband's resort to psychoanalysis, the marriage proved troubled, and Wanda objected to Horowitz' close relationships with a series of young men. The pianist's temperament became legendary: he would cancel concerts at the shortest notice, sometimes apparently in order to complete a sexual rendezvous. In the 1970s, responding to New York's upscale version of the counterculture, Horowitz became more gregarious, and his sexual tastes became widely known. Accompanied by his lover, the aging pianist essayed frequent trips to gay bars and clubs.

Less clear is the instance of the distinguished harpsichordist Wanda Landowska (1877–1959), who revolutionized the aesthetics of baroque music. Her companion seems to have been lesbian, but Landowska's own orientation is uncertain.

There is one exception to the solo–group contrast. Homosexuality has long been particularly decried in the field of conducting, where the role seems to call for macho assertiveness. Nonetheless, the Greek conductor Dimitri Mitropoulos (1896–1960) quietly defied the ban, at the same time taking risks in championing avant-garde music. His protégé, Leonard Bernstein (1918–) has broken the mold altogether, insisting on his right to live openly as a gay man. Active also as a composer and educator, Bernstein has probably also attained the status of the most successful conductor of all time—certainly the wealthiest. His achievement is a beacon of light to countless young musicians.

See also **Music, Popular; Opera; Punk Rock.**

Wayne R. Dynes

MYSTERY AND DETECTIVE FICTION

The impression that homosexual and lesbian characters and situations are rare in mystery and detective fiction is true for earlier decades, but not for more recent ones. Lesbian characters can be found in some British mysteries of the late 1920s, including Dorothy L. Sayers' *Unnatural Death* and *Strong Poison*, and gay male characters began to appear in the next decade. In most of the early fiction, however, the homosexual characters are incidental, often introduced to complicate the plot.

The "Hard-Boiled" Novel and After. Gay male characters begin to appear in the work of those American writers classified as "hard-boiled" because sexuality of all sorts along with drugs, alcohol, and violence were displayed without moralizing in these naturalistic novels. The first example is in Rex Stout's 1933 novel *Forest Fire*. The protagonist is a macho forest ranger who is sexually attracted to a summer helper. Stout then proceeded to the Nero Wolfe novels where homosexuality seems sublimated in misogyny, gourmet meals, and cultivating orchids. More typical of the hard-boiled school treatment of gay men is the work of three of its leading practitioners, James Cain, Ross Macdonald, and Raymond Chandler. Gays are effeminate (often cross-dressers) and unhappy. Cain's *Serenade* features a bisexual hero and a homosexual villain who is killed in the end. Chandler's *The Big Sleep* and Macdonald's *Dark Tunnel* include weak and psychologically impaired gay men, but the extreme examples of effeminate gay men and masculine women occur in the works of Mickey Spillane, especially *I, the Jury.*

About the only exception to these negative views in the earlier detective fiction are three excellent whodunits by Gore Vidal, written under the pseudonym of Edgar Box. *Death in the Fifth Position* (1952) includes the first attractive gay men in mystery fiction and also includes some realistic pictures of the gay subculture. However, other works of the 1950s such as Margaret Millar's *Beast in View*, Meyer Levin's *Compulsion*, and Anne Hocking's *A Simple Way of Poison* show the influence of psychoanalytic ideas of homosexuality as an illness that can lead the unbalanced individual into murder.

The number of homosexual characters in mystery fiction grew enormously in the 1960s, and the picture was slightly less negative. Lou Rand's *Rough Trade* is an early example of a novel with a gay detective and a gay setting published for a gay readership. George Baxt's three Pharaoh Love novels reached a general audience. Love was a black gay detective and the novels included other gay characters and pictures of the gay subculture presented in a comparatively positive manner. Several novels by Patricia Highsmith in the fifties and the sixties including *Strangers on Train* and *The Talented Mr. Ripley* include gay men as their main characters, but the homosexuality is so cunningly described that it was often avoided by those who did not care to see it. However, in most mysteries homosexual men and lesbians were still pictured as emotionally deformed killers and villains. Such works as Ellery Queen's *The Last Woman in His Life* and Roderick Thorp's *The Detective* are examples.

After Gay Liberation. After the advent of the modern American gay liberation **movement**, there was a radical change. Joseph Hansen had written his first gay mystery novel, *Known Homosexual*, in 1968, but in 1970 he published *Fadeout* featuring David Brandstetter, a gay detective in Los Angeles drawn in the hard-boiled tradition of Philip Marlowe and Lew Archer. The enormous success of the work led to a series numbering about ten novels as of 1987. Within a few years there were also excellent whodunits published by openly gay writers Richard Hall (*Butterscotch Prince*) and John Paul Hudson (*Superstar Murder*). These works depicted the gay subcultures of New York and Los Angeles as well as any fiction of the time, in addition to being excellent representatives of the mystery genre. A popular novelist who was less gay identified, James Kirkwood, Jr., published the successful *P.S. Your Cat is Dead* in 1972. The novel had a gay man as a protagonist. At the end of the decade Felice Picano utilized the secret agent concept in *The Lure,* and Paul Monette recreated the secret panels and hidden caves of older adventure novels in the brilliant satire of Hollywood, *The Gold Diggers,* all within a highly professional whodunit.

The success of these works led to an explosion of mystery fiction featuring gay characters and settings in the 1980s. At least three writers followed Hansen's plan of a whodunit series featuring the same gay detective. Richard Stevenson's Don Strachey novels are set in Albany, New York; Nathan Aldyne's Daniel Valentine books take place in Boston and Provincetown, and Tony Fennely's Matt Sinclair novels utilize a New Orleans background. All these whodunits present an accurate picture of the gay subculture in the area and a range of gay characters. Probably intended for a mainly gay audience, they are all such good examples of the genre that they reach a much broader cross-section of readers. Many other mysteries intended for gay audiences (usually of a far less professional character) have appeared. Gay and lesbian characters are also much more prominent in the general mystery fiction of the two decades after 1970 in both the United States and Britain, their numbers far too numerous to mention. Such well known authors as Ian Fleming, Ngaio Marsh, Ruth Rendell, Josephine Tey, John MacDonald, and Amanda Cross have included both lesbian and gay characters in their novels. In most cases the gay characters are far more well-rounded and emotionally balanced individuals than those created in earlier decades.

The success of mystery novels with gay male detectives has also led to an increase in novels with lesbian characters and at least one series with a lesbian detective. Three novels by Heron Carvic published between 1968 and 1971 featuring Miss Seeton as the detective have lesbian characters, as do three mysteries by Peter Dickinson published between 1972 and 1976, and three well-received works of P. D. James published between 1971 and 1980, including *Death of an Expert Witness*. The well known mystery novelist Robert Parker wrote about lesbian characters and the lesbian subculture in his 1980 work *Looking for Rachel Wallace*. In the early 1980s, Vicki P. McConnell started a series of whodunit novels featuring the lesbian detective Nyla Wade.

See also **Novels and Short Fiction.**

James B. Levin

Mythology, Classical

The concept of mythology in Greek civilization refers not merely to the gods, but to the demigods as well—the heroes renowned in song and story. Nineteenth-century German scholars, reversing the formula that "God created man in his image," held that man had created the gods in his own image, endowing them

with his attributes and passions. Since *paiderasteia* was institutionalized in Greek civilization, boy-loving gods and heroes figure prominently in Greek mythology, in contrast with the suppression of the homoerotic theme in the Judeo-Christian scriptures.

The Loves of the Gods. Zeus, the father of the gods, is renowned principally for his love of the Phrygian boy **Ganymede**, the fairest of mortals, whom the god carried off to make him his cup-bearer. By the time of **Pindar** Ganymede is enshrined as the *eromenos*, the beloved boy of his heavenly patron. In earlier myth Ganymede is abducted by a whirlwind, but from the fourth century B.C. onward he is seized by Zeus in the form of an eagle. This later became a common theme of literature and art, despite the unlikelihood that an eagle could carry an adolescent boy in its talons. The name Ganymede was also extended in time to any handsome boy with a male lover and protector. Moreover, Ganymede never ages; he is the mythical embodiment of the *puer aeternus*, the pederast's dream of the beloved lingering forever in the prime of his adolescent beauty. Another theme that appears in the following centuries is the rivalry of Ganymede and Hera, which suggests that in the Greek household the *eromenos* and the wife could find themselves competing for the husband's favors. Ultimately the opposition served for debates over the merits of homosexuality (boy-love) and heterosexuality (woman-love). By contrast, Zeus has no heavenly mistress; his amorous adventures with mortal women are conducted solely on earth.

The pederastic affairs of the other gods, while mentioned sporadically in classical literature, never attained the celebrity of Zeus' passion for Ganymede. However, Poseidon, according to Pindar, preceded Zeus in loving Pelops, the son of Tantalus, the ancestor of the Atrides. Tradition had it that his father cut the boy into pieces and served him to the gods, but only Demeter, famished and distraught, consumed a shoulder. The gods recognized him and repaired his body with a shoulder of ivory, of which the city of Elis boasted that it had the relic. Pindar himself rejected the myth that ascribes cannibalism to the gods and instead had the boy carried off by Poseidon in a golden chariot. Later the boy invoked the aid of the god of the sea as recompense for his amorous favors.

Apollo, himself of exquisite beauty, had one unhappy affair after another—twenty in all—even if, as *paiderastes*, he was worshipped as the ideal and patron of man-boy love, and his image accompanied those of Hermes and Heracles in every Greek gymnasium. The most prominent of his *eromenoi* were Cyparissus and Hyacinth. The former was the son of Telephos who dwelt on the isle of Ceos. The boy was especially fond of the tame stag with golden horns who was his companion at play. On a hot summer day the boy accidentally killed his pet with his javelin, and wishing to die, he had himself transformed into a cypress in order to sympathize eternally with the grief of others.

Hyacinth had a tragic death when struck by a discus thrown by the god while the two were playing on the shores of the river Eurotas. In Ovid's version of the story Apollo is driven to despair when he sees that he is powerless to heal the wound, yet he exclaims: "My only crime is that of having loved!"

Dionysus, the god of the vine, is given a lover named Ampelos, who is the vine itself. First treated by Ovid, this episode was further elaborated by Nonnus of Panopolis in the *Dionysiaca*, where in the course of a march to India Ampelos is carried off by a homicidal bull, but is reborn metamorphosed into the fruit of the vine.

Another story reflecting the homosexual aspect of ancient fertility rites has Dionysus, to descend into the nether world, ask the way of a peasant named Polymnus, who as a reward wished to be penetrated anally by the god. Dionysus promised to grant the favor on his return, but in the meantime Polymnus died. Dionysus then carved a branch of a fig tree in the form of a phallus and thrust it into the tomb, thus symbolically performing the sexual act that would have gratified the deceased.

Heros. The story of Laius and Oedipus has a pederastic background that is often overlooked or suppressed in modern treatments of the myth, including the psychoanalytic derivatives. The first author who treated this affair was Pisander of Cameiros, who lived late in the seventh century B.C. Laius, bannished from Thebes by Zethus and Amphion, took refuge at the court of Pelops, where he fell in love with Chrysippus, the son of his host and the nymph Axioche, and abducted him. Defiled by Laius, Chrysippus took his own life with his sword. Because the Thebans did not punish the perpetrator of this outrage, Hera avenged the crime by sending them the Sphinx. Pelops for his part uttered the fateful curse on Laius: that he would have a son who would "kill his father, marry his mother, and bring ruin on his native city." In the tragedy of Euripides entitled *Chrysippus*, Laius is made to express his pederastic desires openly, while in a later version of the story, Laius' motive for becoming a boy-lover is exactly to avoid having the son who would fulfill such a dire curse. In **Plato's** *Laws*, 836, Laius is held to be the inventor of pederasty, while before him the law "in accord with nature" had forbidden such relations. The deeper meaning of the legend suggests that the Greeks were ambivalent on the subject of sexual aggression between males: Laius' violence against Chrysippus is avenged, in accordance with the principle of the *lex talionis*, by the murderous act of his own son that Sigmund **Freud** chose as the symbol of the rivalry of the son with the father, the conflict between the younger generation and the older one. Oedipus compounds his crime by marrying his own mother Jocasta in violation of the incest taboo.

Hercules, the very model of the Greek hero, is the lover of Hylas, whom he teaches everything that he needs to fulfill the ideal of the noble warrior, including the military arts that the young squire had to master in order to play his role in combat. His most faithful companion, however, is Iolaos, the son of Hercules' twin brother Iphicles. In the version of Hercules' combat with Cycnos, in the *Aspis* of pseudo-Hesiod, Hercules is clad in the conventional costume of the warrior of the period, while Iolaos is to him the "dearest of mortals," just as Patroclus was to **Achilles**. *Ioläus* was to be chosen by Edward **Carpenter** as the title of his 1902 anthology of homoerotic passages from world literature.

Orpheus figures in the list by virtue of his having invented male love after losing Euridice; his *eromenos* was Calais, the son of Boreas, who had also taken part in the expedition of the Argonauts. This novelty so angered the Thracian women that they murdered him and severed his head from his body; but attached to his lyre it was carried by the waves to the isle of Lesbos. Those who found the head buried it together with the musical instrument.

Orestes and Pylades were another pair of faithful lovers who accomplished great feats because of the erotic bond between them. After they kill Clytemnestra as if they had both been the sons of Agamemnon, Orestes is pursued by the Erynies, but Pylades supports him in his great trial against the avenging furies.

Androgynous Themes. Highly developed in Greek mythology was the myth of the *androgynos*, the man-woman. Ovid tells the story of Hermaphroditus, a dazzlingly handsome boy, who at the age of fifteen kindled the love of Salmacis, the nymph of a spring of the same name in Caria; against his will she enticed him down into the water and forced him to copulate with her; the gods granted her plea never to be separated from her lover by uniting them into a single being of two sexes. But Hermes and Aphrodite granted the wish of Hermaphroditus by giving it the magical property of turning every man who bathed in it into a *semivir*, an effeminate half-man. In Hermaphroditus the Greek mentality expressed its consciousness of the androgynous unconscious of human beings who worship in an artistically refined and perfected guise as the good spirit of the household and private life. The importance of Hermaphroditus for plastic and pictorial art was enormous: after the fourth century B.C. rooms in private houses, gymnasia, and baths were adorned with statues or painting representing him, and especially beautiful are the numerous sleeping hermaphrodites that have survived from antiquity. Openly sensual and even obscene are the depictions of Hermaphroditus having sexual connection with Pan or with Satyrs, shown in a half or wholly completed embrace.

The figure of Tiresias has an androgynous motif. Hesiod asserts that Tiresias once watched two snakes copulating in Arcadia and wounded one of them, after which he became a woman and had intercourse with men. But Apollo told him that when he again watched the serpents and wounded one, he would be turned into a man again. This happened; and so when Zeus and Hera were disputing whether man or woman experiences greater pleasure in orgasm, they asked Tiresias, who answered that the male experiences one-tenth of the pleasure, the female nine-tenths. Offended by the reply, Hera made him blind, but Zeus compensated him with the gift of prophecy and long life.

All the homoerotic myths of ancient Greece pertain to male homosexuality; lesbianism was invisible to the mythopoetic consciousness of the Hellenes. The figures of antiquity associated with lesbianism were all historical, the poetess **Sappho** being merely the most celebrated among them.

Plato in the *Symposium* has Aristophanes relate a myth that is meant to explain the origin of the differences in sexual orientation among human beings. The first such creatures were double beings, male-female, male-male, and female-female; to weaken their potency Zeus cut them in half, then refashioned them so that each half could find and unite with the other. The members of the androgynous pair would accomplish the act of reproduction. Deriving from a Babylonian myth reported by Berossus, this fanciful account of the cause of homosexuality shows that the ancients, aware of the phenomenon, invented an etiological legend that covered all the facts of sexual attraction, unlike the Judaic version in the book of Genesis that leaves only the proto-heterosexual pair.

Afterlife. The suppression of the homosexual element in the anthropology of Biblical Judaism later contributed to the defamation of homosexuality as "contrary to the will of the creator," but since the classical texts preserved into the Middle Ages and the Renaissance kept alive the homosexual mythology of Greco-Roman paganism, this offered an inexhaustible source of inspiration for writers and artists, and also a code by means of which tabooed and unnamable subjects could be raised with subtlety and double entendre. Although the conventional treatments of Greek and Roman mythology, especially in school texts, bowdlerized homoerotic themes, they persisted in the literature which those versed in the ancient languages were always free to consult. Allusions to heroes of homosexual love affairs were enough to suggest to the initiated the author's intent, as in the case of **Whitman's** *Calamus* poems; the language of Aesop conveyed the message despite Christian and then Victorian censorship. So the afterlife of the Greek myths undercut the heterosexual bias of Judeo-Christian theology, and for the sophisticated modern reader these legends revive the profoundly homoerotic ambiance of the "glory that was Greece and the grandeur that was Rome."

BIBLIOGRAPHY. Félix Buffière, *Eros adolescent: la pédérastie dans la Grèce antique*, Paris: Les Belles Lettres, 1980; Hans Licht, *Sexual Life in Ancient Greece*, London: Routledge and Kegan Paul, 1932; Bernard Sergent, *Homosexuality in Greek Myth*, Boston: Beacon Press, 1986.

Warren Johansson

MYTHS AND FABRICATIONS

Prejudice against any human group manifests itself in stereotypes. Male homosexuals are said to be effeminate, superficial, and clannish, while lesbians are accused of being mannish, homely, and aggressive. Apart from these characterological ascriptions, however, historical study brings to light antihomosexual myths—purported true stories which are invented and propagated to validate bigotry.

Myths of Judeo-Christian Origin. The most ancient and influential of these myths is the Biblical story of **Sodom** and Gomorrah. Genesis 14, 18 and 19 tell of these arrogant cities and of their destruction by a rain of brimstone and fire. Over and over again, Christian statesmen and preachers have used the tale to demonstrate that if people do not renounce their wicked acts, they will go the way of Sodom and Gomorrah—whose historicity modern critical scholarship has utterly rejected and consigned to the realm of geographical legend.

According to a medieval legend, on Christmas eve, at the very moment of the Nativity of Jesus, all mankind guilty of homosexual sin died a sudden death. Unless human nature were purged of unnatural vice, the Savior could not be persuaded to assume human flesh. Although the story is often ascribed to St. Jerome in the fourth century (and in part to his contemporary, St. **Augustine**), in fact it cannot be traced back in manuscript sources before the Biblical Commentary of Hugh of St. Cher (about 1230–35), who claimed to have learned it from Peter the Chanter of Paris.

It may have been inspired by a Jewish midrash on the death of the Egyptians in the last of the ten plagues (Exodus 12:29). The tale reached a wide public through an uncritical compilation of saints' lives known as the *Legenda Aurea* of Jacobus of Voragine (1290). For a long time no one cared to challenge this homophobic absurdity, and it was repeated by such worthies as St. Bonaventure (1221–1274), Roberto Caracciolo (1425–1495), and the Viennese preacher Abraham a Sancta Clara (1644–1709), who was apparently the last to take it seriously.

Another cluster of legends presents sodomites not as the victims of disasters but as their cause. Primitive cultures associated rainwater with the fertilizing effusions of the gods. Hence an equation of semen with rain water: if the males of a community waste their semen, the consequence will be a shortfall of rain and ensuing drought and famine. Homosexuals are the Jonahs who endanger the commonwealth; in the interest of public safety they must be eliminated, otherwise droughts and other injury to crops will follow. Then in **Byzantium** in the sixth century the Emperor Justinian proclaimed that unchecked homosexual activity provoked the wrath of God to visit earthquakes on districts where it was rampant—the superstitious echo of the Sodom legend. A millennium later folk accretions had increased the number of sodomy-caused disasters to a roster of six: earthquakes, floods, famines, plagues, Saracen incursions, and large field mice. Such superstitions might be thought safely dead, yet in 1976 the entertainer and crusading homophobe Anita Bryant produced a version of her own, alleging that droughts in Northern California had been caused by the gay mecca of **San Francisco**. And in the 1980s moralists have insisted that **AIDS** is the revenge of Mother Nature—or of the godhead itself— on unnatural practices.

Notions of Decadence. There are also myths about the course of universal history and the fate of nations within it.

Those do not learn from history, it is said, will be condemned to repeat it. One of the things learned from history, purportedly, is that the decline and fall of **Greece** and Rome were caused by their tolerance of homosexuality. More careful study of the development of these civilizations fails to substantiate this charge. The institution of **pederasty** is documented in the Greek city states almost from their inception. The training that a boy received was held to be character building in that it prepared him for service to the state. The military successes of the Greeks, especially in defending themselves against the Persians, would be unthinkable without the loyalty of male comradeship and the skills that it fostered. Only after the inception of the Hellenistic age in 323 did pederasty decline as an institution; and only after the neglect of this ancient institution did Greek civilization succumb to Roman conquest. Among the Romans themselves homosexual behavior is most clearly evident in the first and second centuries, which are generally regarded as the most flourishing period of the Empire. Only after the Christian emperors tried to repress homosexual behavior in the fourth and fifth centuries did the Western empire disintegrate and collapse in the wake of barbarian invasions. Furthermore, ancient authors themselves disagree as to whether "luxury and **effeminacy**" invaded Rome from the conquered provinces of Asia, or the Romans corrupted the subject peoples by introducing their lavish and ostentatious way of life to the Eastern regions of the empire. Historiography has witnessed a long debate over the causes of Rome's **decadence**, and a definitive answer has yet to be found.

A claim that recurs in the writings of heterosexual observers of society is that homosexual behavior is increasing, dangerously so. This notion has been documented from so many authors over the last several centuries that it is a virtual commonplace, yet it probably reflects at most the ability of the particular author to discern the presence of homosexual activity that is not immediately evident to the outsider. The implication is that a growing number of individuals are renouncing marriage and family obligations, and that if this trend persists the end result will be race suicide, because homosexual activity is intrinsically sterile, is a form of biological "death in life." This belief ignores the well-attested fact that superfetation cannot occur in homo sapiens, which is to say that nature has already set a limit on the number of children a women can bear: once impregnated, she cannot conceive again until she has borne the child. Where "natural" fertility prevails, and nothing is done to check the results of sexual intercourse, a very small amount of heterosexual copulation would be enough to keep the entire female population of childbearing age continuously pregnant. Of course, no modern society could tolerate such a level of fertility; in a nation where 95 percent of all children born live to maturity, this would mean that in a mere two generations the population would increase 80 times! In point of fact, the fall of the birth rate in the last hundred years can be mainly ascribed to economic factors: the economic burden and liability that a child represents in urban middle-class society, where the cost of educating a child for a future career can consume a large portion of a family's financial resources. Only a few percent of the population is exclusively homosexual—not enough to have an appreciable effect on **demography**. Subsidies and other incentives for middle-class families have not succeeded in altering the negative ratio of births to deaths, and even the pronatalist policies of the National Socialist regime yielded a marked increase in births only in rural areas. Moreover, less developed areas of the globe are today afflicted with overpopulation that in the coming decades may lead to political crises as the demand for foodstuffs and public services makes it impossible for these countries to export enough of their natural resources or products of cheap labor to service their debts to the lending nations, while advanced countries close their doors to immigration because the market for unskilled labor is dwindling.

Homosexuals as Antisocial. There is also the notion that homosexuals form a secret society, a **freemasonry** whose rites of initiation exclude "normal," morally righteous members of society. Gay people are alleged to prefer one another for employment and advancement and to demand sexual favors from subordinates, especially young ones, in return for furthering their careers. Further, homosexuals are purportedly "uncomfortable" in the presence of normal people and prefer to be among their own as much as possible. But homosexual circles make the contradictory observation that "closet cases" deliberately shun and reject others of their ilk as a means of protecting their own covert identity.

Myths Originated by Homosexuals. These several myth types are the creation of societies seeking to rationalize discrimination and persecution of homosexuals. Gay people themselves have propagated others. The venerable archetype is the explanation of the source of sexual orientation presented in **Plato**'s *Symposium* positing that human beings are in reality the sundered halves of original dual persons. Those who trace their origin to a male-female combination are heterosexual, yearning for union with a member of the opposite sex, while those who derive from male-male or female-female conjunctions are male homosexuals or lesbians, respectively. While Plato is not likely to have taken it seriously, this tale has a background in a Babylonian myth of primordial human androgyny. Imagined or not, for some today **androgyny** has a renewed appeal as a solution to the problems of **gender** identity.

A more sinister myth, invented and spread only in recent decades by homosexuals, is that the word **faggot** recalls the supposed medieval practice of using male homosexuals as kindling at the public burning of witches and heretics. There is no historical record of such a practice, and the slang use of the pejorative term faggot (originally applied to a fat, slovenly woman) cannot be traced before American English of the twentieth century. Yet the myth, which may reflect an unconscious longing for martyrdom, has now taken on a life of its own, and will be hard to eradicate, particularly as dictionaries that list the several meanings of the word are not likely to include an explicit refutation of the false etymology.

A few homosexuals cherish the belief that a majority of the members of society would prefer same-sex acts if it were not for the pressures for conformity that are deployed to prevent this result. This view seems clearly a case of projection, for there is no indication that in an erotic "free-market" situation such choices would prevail, though it may be that bisexuality of some sort would be followed by the majority. But here one is dealing with hypothetical—and unlikely—scenarios, since no society yet known has renounced its capacity for social melding by seeking to channel sexual behavior. The social sciences do not know, and are un-

likely soon to learn, how people would behave in a hypothetical free market, unaffected by external conditioning. A related phenomenon is the gossip, once particularly common among gay men, claiming this or that noted figure in public life as a secret homosexual. The underlying assumption is that such instances could be multiplied ad infinitum.

Conclusion. The eighteenth-century Enlightenment bequeathed to educated society a hope of eliminating social myths that stood in the way of human happiness. Regrettably, the expectation that such a goal could be totally achieved is probably **utopian**: new myths spring up as others fade. Myths that flourished under Christian auspices survive under the aegis of officially atheist Communist states. Yet by exposing the myths, and the processes that lead to their formation, to the light of reasoned examination, the critical scholar may seek to limit their spread and noxious effect.

BIBLIOGRAPHY. Wayne Dynes, *Homolexis: A Historical and Cultural Lexicon of Homosexuality*, New York: Gay Academic Union, 1985.

Wayne R. Dynes

NAMELESS SIN (OR CRIME)

The designation of homosexuality as "the nameless sin" derived from the belief that it was unfit even to be mentioned in Christian society. In 1769, for example, the influential English jurist Sir William Blackstone described the "crime against nature" as "a subject the very mention of which is a disgrace to human nature. It will be more eligible to imitate in this respect the delicacy of our English law, which treats it in its very indictments, as a crime not fit to be named, peccatum illud horribile, inter Christianos non nominandum." Blackstone alludes not to the statute of 1533 (*see* **Sixteenth-Century Legislation**), but probably to a single celebrated case, the arraignment of Lord Castlehaven in 1631, where the indictment speaks (in Latin) of "that detestable and abominable sin . . . 'buggery' [in English in the text] not to be named among Christians." (Similar language occurs in a text of Sir Edward Coke, published in 1644.)

Comparable expressions enjoyed the favor of canonists and authors of confessionals on the European continent; in 1700, for example, Ludovico Sinistrari d'Ameno records the terms *peccatum mutum* ("silent sin"), *vitium nefandum* ("unspeakable vice"), and *vitium innominabile* ("unnameable vice"), all designating the crime against nature or sodomy. A century before, the **Andean** historian of Peru, Garcilaso de la Vega, claimed that sodomy was so hated by the Incas and their people that the very name was odious to them and they never uttered it; while the Incas were apparently hostile to male homosexuality, Garcilaso's claim that they refused to name it is probably a projection of Christian attitudes. Significantly, Gar-

cilaso also mentions a city that, like **Sodom**, was destroyed by fire for its addiction to homosexuality. In late antiquity, through a false etymology based upon the Greek form of the place name, Sodom was interpreted as meaning *pecus tacens*, "silent herd," a gloss that may have influenced the later formula *peccatum mutum*. William of Auvergne (ca. 1180–1249) said that it was the "unmentionable vice," noting Gregory the Great's claim that the air itself was corrupted by its mention.

Thus it was against an extensive and varied background of usage that Oscar **Wilde** was to seek to turn the tables in his eloquent plea during his 1895 trial for the "love that dare not speak its name," taking up a phrase from the poem "Two Loves" by Lord Alfred **Douglas** (1894). As used by Douglas, the phrase applied allegorically to a pitiful uninvited companion to the true Love, and is called "Shame" by the latter; the poem itself gives little clue as to the nature of this bogus Love. In Wilde's statement under cross-examination, however, the phrase was transformed into "a great affection of an elder for a younger man. . . . It is intellectual . . . when the elder man has intellect, and the younger man has all the joy, hope and glamour of life before him." In subsequent usage, the phrase became synonymous with homoeroticism in general.

In the **New Testament** Paul remarked mysteriously "For it is a shame even to speak of the things that they do in secret." (Ephesians 5:12). Although this passage has been taken to refer to homosexuality, there is no conclusive evidence to pinpoint the sin (or sins) in question. Nonetheless, the words show that the notion of a transgression too horrible to be named directly was familiar to the early Christians. The Book of Wisdom (14:17) had spoken of "worshipping of idols not to be named." Latin pagan usage supplies *infandus*, "unspeakable, abominable" and *nefandus*, "impious, heinous," both sometimes used of sexual conduct (cf. the later *vitium nefandum*; in some Spanish texts sodomites are curtly termed *nefandarios*). Primitive societies, of course, observe taboos on certain words either because the objects they designate are too dangerous or too numinously sacred to be mentioned outright. In early Christian thought, Dionysius the Areopagite (ca. 500) evolved his "negative (or apophatic) theology," which held that God's attributes are too incomprehensible to limited human reason even to be mentioned. Thus by a curious irony, the Christian Trinity and the sodomites are linked in their ineffability/ unspeakability.

In ordinary parlance today, this taboo on naming homosexuality sometimes takes the form of deleting any specific word for it, e.g., "Is he. . . ?" "Is she that way?" or "Could he be one?" (often accompanied by a raising of the eyebrows or the simulation of a limp wrist). One can find numerous instances of it in twentieth-century fiction, **film**, and lyrics, where oblique references are left as clues but the clear words are missing. With the widespread publicity accompanying the gay liberation movement in the 1970s, however, the taboo seems to have been finally vanquished, its obituary phrased in the apocryphal enhancement: "The love that dared not speak its name . . . now scarcely ever shuts up."

Wayne R. Dynes

NAPOLEON BONAPARTE (1769–1821)

General and Emperor of France. Homosexuality was ascribed to Napoleon by such writers as Sir Richard Burton and Auguste Cabanès, and more recently, though no more convincingly, by Major

General Frank M. Richardson in *Mars without Venus* (Edinburgh, 1981). In particular the Emperor was accused of an erotic liaison with General Duroc, the Grand Marshal of his palace. Duroc, born in 1772, became the adjutant of General Bonaparte in 1796 and was one of his close collaborators until fatally wounded by a grenade splinter at the battle of Wurtzen in 1813. During the height of Napoleon's power Duroc had been the one who attended to all his personal needs, both in **France** and on his travels, and the one who was privy to all the Emperor's love affairs. The death of such a faithful attendant naturally grieved Napoleon enormously, but there are no grounds for seeing their relationship as a homosexual one. Also, Napoleon never lacked women to gratify his sexual needs and desires, and all the evidence points to the heterosexual character of his passions. The only well-attested trait that would have given rise to the allegation of homosexuality is a somewhat feminine body build that became more pronounced as the Emperor grew older.

However, the personal attitude of Napoleon toward homosexuality needs to be mentioned, as it contrasts markedly with the homophobia of his contemporaries in England, where a virtual paranoia prevailed into the second decade of the nineteenth century. Napoleon selected the homosexual **Cambacérès** as his Arch-Chancellor, and because of his legal talents entrusted him with the redaction of the Code Napoléon (1810)—not a new document, but a collection of 28 separate codes that embodied all the legal reforms enacted since 1789, including the quiet disappearance of the provisions against sodomy that had been part of the penal law everywhere in Europe under the Old Regime. Hence Napoleon allowed to stand the decision of the Constituent Assembly in 1791 to omit sodomy from the list of sexual offenses—following the line of thought of **Enlightenment** criticism of the criminal legislation and practice of previous centuries. The prestige which Napoleon imparted to the new code by placing his name and seal on it was responsible for its widespread adoption, not only by the Catholic nations of Europe but by nearly the whole of Latin America as well. In this area of the law the First Empire completed and consolidated the work of the French Revolution, while in England the law reform of 1828 under Robert Peel not only left the law against **buggery** on the books but actually made it more punitive by narrowing the evidence required for conviction. So while there was no more psychological understanding of homosexuality in nineteenth-century France than in the eighteenth, the legal oppression of the homosexual as a capital offender whose crime was scarcely less heinous than murder ended forever, and the homophile movement in France was spared the need to fight decade-long battles for the irreducible minimum of toleration. The reign of Napoleon I is thus a landmark in the emancipation of the homosexual from medieval intolerance and outlawry.

BIBLIOGRAPHY. Numa Praetorius, "Homosexualität und Napoleon I," *Zeitschrift für Sexualwissenschaft*, 8 (1921), 95–105.

Warren Johansson

NARCISSUS
Greek mythological figure. A beautiful youth, he rejected the advances of the nymph Echo and was punished by Aphrodite with boundless self-love. One day, while drinking at a spring, he was smitten with his own image. With the object of his love unreachable, he fell more and more into lassitude and despair until he was changed into the **flower** that bears his name. His fate recalls that of other Greek youths who were changed into plants, such as **Calamus** and Ampelos, the companion of **Dionysus**.

His fame was revived in the Renaissance when Narcissus was often shown in paintings, where the depiction of the image seen in reflection offers a pretext for bravura effects of illusionism. Havelock **Ellis** cited the name in his discussion of self-contemplation as a psychodynamic fixation in 1898, and the term Narzissismus was coined in German by Paul Näcke in his book *Die sexuellen Perversitäten* of the following year. The term was picked up by **Freud** in 1910. In his view it applied to homosexuals, "who take themselves as a sexual object; they begin with narcissism and seek out young men who resemble them whom they can love as their mother loved them." In the following year, in his discussion of the Schreber case, Freud suggested that narcissism was a stage in human psychic development: "the subject begins by taking himself, his own body as love object." In his revised perspective it was the original universal condition, out of which object love later developed, without necessarily effacing the narcissism altogether. Inevitably **psychoanalysts** linked narcissism to homosexual behavior and masturbation as immature forms of gratification. Later Jacques Lacan was to make the "mirror stage" a cornerstone of his own creative reinterpretation of Freud's thought.

In popular-culture criticism of the 1970s narcissism became an epithet that served to excoriate the self-absorption of the "me generation." Such journalistic usages illustrate the trickle-down of psychoanalysis into the general culture. In this polemical sense it is just a high-sounding term for selfishness.

Wayne R. Dynes

NATIONALISM
Born of the French Revolution, mass nationalism spread across Europe during the nineteenth century, and, in reaction to colonialism, beginning with **Japan** in 1867, to the rest of the world. It triumphed after World War II even in areas in Africa that had never been distinct or unified before they became colonies a century earlier.

The link between nationalism and sexuality is subtle but real. On the one hand, nationalist movements have tended to foster male bonding that is **homosocial**. On the other, they have favored inherently heterosexist pronatalist policies in the belief that population is power. One should be careful to avoid a simplistic equation to the effect that nationalism corresponds flatly to right-wing ideology and this in turn to antihomosexuality. There have been many nationalists whose emphasis on male bonding has carried them on to sympathy, at some level, with homosexuality itself.

Forerunners. Modern nationalism profoundly differs from the aristocratic and haut-bourgeois nationalism, related to dynastic loyalty, that began in the late **Middle Ages** with Henry V of England and Joan of Arc, leaders in the Hundred Years War, and with Jan Hus' revolt that stirred Czechs against Germans as well as against popes. Lutheranism kindled nationalist pride among Germans. Like his Hussite inspirers, Luther, and soon Calvin too, whose followers used the vernacular, appealed to the bourgeoisie as well as to princes and nobles, criticizing the moral laxity of Catholics, of the **penitentials**, and of the **canon law**. Although at first universalist like Catholicism, **Protestantism** reinforced nationalism throughout Teutonic lands by translating the Bible into the vernaculars and thus helping to standardize languages and literatures. All these earlier forms of nationalism, even those formed or reinforced by Catholic reaction in lands such as **France**, **Poland**, and **Ireland**, were tempered by aristocratic reservations and regional variations.

Mass Nationalism. Not until the French Revolution swept away royalty and nobility and attacked the altar did the bourgeoisie triumph. Like Italian, Flemish, and Dutch burghers of earlier centuries, their French counterparts felt themselves to be more industrious, moral, and deserving than the decadent, spendthrift **aristocracy** and superstitious, indolent clergy. Revolutionary lawmakers in 1791 and **Napoleon's** code of 1810, which was adopted in Holland, Belgium, Germany (except for Prussia and Austria), Italy, and Spain, decriminalized sodomy between consenting adults in private along with other survivals of medieval superstition and fanaticism.

After the Restoration in 1815 homosexuality, though not recriminalized in France and certain German states, suffered greater disapproval as it was associated with Spain, Naples, and the papal states. Homosexuals were ostracized after the model of triumphant England, Prussia, Austria, and Russia, none of which decriminalized the offense before the twentieth century. In fact the repressive English sentenced sodomites more than ever before to prison, the pillory, and even hanging during the Napoleonic Wars and afterwards, in part to display their moral superiority over the French. In the post-Napoleonic reaction romantic outcasts like Lord **Byron** and Count **Platen** suffered, while Catholic and Protestant moralists, not to mention Orthodox in less advanced lands, joined and encouraged the petty bourgeoisie in condemning sexual freedom. To unify their people, nationalists suppressed dissidents. After the suppression of the revolutions of 1848, when many nationalists became anti-liberal, homosexuals and Jews were increasingly suspect and persecuted by an enlarged and strengthened bureaucracy and police, even in those countries where the Code Napoléon had emancipated them.

The Age of Imperialism. Prussia's annexation of western areas of Germany in 1866 and the formation of the German Empire in 1871 brought about the imposition of Prussian laws against male homosexuality (lesbianism was not criminalized) in the Rhineland, Bavaria, and Alsace-Lorraine, and inspired the homosexual emancipation **movement** pioneered by K. H. **Ulrichs**. Repressive measures in England after the adoption of the **Criminal**

Law Amendment Act, with the Labouchere amendment, in 1885, as well as police raids and other harassment in France paralleled by growing anti-Semitism, led to the trials of Alfred Dreyfus in 1894 and of Oscar **Wilde** in 1895. In Imperial Germany, the Harden-**Eulenburg** affair (1907–09) resulted from the jingoist editor Maximilian Harden's discovery that the First Secretary of the French Legation in Berlin, Raymond Lecomte, had infiltrated the circle of homosexuals around Wilhelm II and was using the confidential information that he collected there to France's advantage, as Andrew Dickson **White**, founding President of Cornell University, had done for his country in 1898, when as Ambassador to Berlin he skillfully kept Germany neutral during the Spanish–American war. Homosexuals have often been outstanding spies and intelligence officers, as were in the present century W. Somerset **Maugham**, Alfred **Redl**, and Anthony Blunt. (*See also* **Espionage**.)

Disregarding official promulgations, a number of imperialist nationalists and missionaries deviated from sexual norms. Marshal Lyautey (1854–1934), who conquered Morocco for France, reputedly said that he could not work with men with whom he had not previously had sex. The British hero General Charles George "Chinese" **Gordon**, who perished at Khartoum in 1885, was homosexual. Cecil Rhodes (1853–1902), creator of an economic empire in southern Africa, had his closest emotional relationships with handsome young men. The British government, which circulated his homosexual diaries, caught and executed the Irish nationalist Roger **Casement** in 1916. Most famous of all, T. E. **Lawrence** inspired the Arabs with whom he rode and to whom he made love to revolt in the desert against the Turks and promised their sheiks kingdoms after the fall of the Ottomans. These men shared a predilection for male companionship under challenging conditions and an intuition that in what Alfred Sauvy later named the Third World they could pursue their interests away from direct surveillance by the moral guardians of their home countries.

In Europe the iconography of extreme nationalism, which often featured muscular men in heroic poses derived from the classic art of **Greece**, promoted eroticization of the male body. In the 1930s such German artists as Fidus (Hugo Höppener) and Arno Breker manipulated the overtones of this macho (but ambivalent) imagery—with full official approval. Also, especially in Teutonic nations the cult of fitness produced the boy scouts and the Wandervogel movement, both nationalistic, the latter often practicing nudity. The **Olympic games**, revived in 1896, emphasized nationalistic competition. The stadium Mussolini prepared for their celebration in Venice in 1940 was adorned with muscular male nudes so beloved by **fascists**.

World Wars and Totalitarianism. The repression of homosexuality under Hitler and Stalin went hand in hand with nationalism and **anti-Semitism**, both conspicuous among **Nazis** from their very outset, and reviving—the latter covertly but also effectively—in the Soviet Union from the late 1930s onward and especially during the "Great Patriotic War" (1941–45). Also, both dictators, like the fascist Mussolini, favored pronatalist policies subsidizing and honoring mothers of large families without regard for their genetic quality; they wanted not intellectuals but cannon fodder for the wars they were planning. By nature as well as by definition totalitarian governments demand more conformity and enforce greater repression than any other type.

Social Democracy at first resisted bourgeois nationalism but, caught up in the enthusiasm for the war of 1914–18, it was (unlike **anarchism**) not immune to homophobia and other petty bourgeois sexual prejudices.

It is difficult to apportion the blame for anti-Semitism and homophobia between **Christianity** and nationalism. The teachings of the medieval church in regard to Jews as deicides, not repudiated until the Second Vatican Council in 1963, and to sodomites as guilty of a mortal sin that might provoke the wrath of God against the whole society that tolerates it, still influenced many in the first half of the twentieth century. Extreme nationalist definitions of "racial identity" that labeled the Jew as a foreign body which had to be removed from the political and economic life of the country, undoubtedly fed the irrational hatreds that culminated in the **Holocaust** and other persecutions of the 1930s and 1940s, while the ideas that homosexuals undermined the country by failing to reproduce and even betraying the nation because they were degenerates and targets of blackmail are still voiced by many homophobes. Many Communists and Third World nationalists, especially in Africa, even today claim that homosexuality is a foreign import or a bourgeois vice.

Right-Wing Nationalism in the Democracies. In the early 1950s, United States Senator Joseph **McCarthy** directed his smears not only at Communists and fellow travelers but also at "sex perverts in government." The conviction that homosexuals were security risks led to a wave of dismissals from government service in the United States and to pressure on America's allies to undertake similar purges in their own ranks. In England, a number of spies who had been involved in homosexual activity as undergraduates at **Cambridge and Oxford** were exposed as Soviet agents.

Even today the British and American right combines nationalistic appeals with homophobic prejudice to win the electorate over to policies that are against its own economic interests. The campaign of Margaret Thatcher against the "looney left," which had openly sympathized with the cause of gay liberation, and Ronald Reagan's pro-family and traditional morality patriotism, supported by television evangelists and moralizing Catholics, both gained resounding victories at the polls in

the 1980s. In 1988 Senator Orrin Hatch, a Republican, denounced the other major American party, the Democratic, as the "party of the homosexuals."

The left has not dealt effectively with the irrational forces in the mass psyche the right is uncannily adroit at sensing and exploiting. National Socialism in Germany, like fascism elsewhere, made no secret of the value that it attached to the irrational in all its forms as contrasted with the "sterile intellectualism" of the liberals and the left, and especially of Social Democracy. Conservative and clerical parties unfailingly stress the virtues of morality, the family, religion, and all the other institutions that are symbolically opposed to the "uninhibited, immoral" gay lifestyle. With the coming of the **AIDS** crisis in the 1980s, many became apprehensive that homophobia might be destined to play much the same role in the political maneuvering of the right as did anti-Semitism between 1880 and 1945. Because conservatives of all sorts still reject and condemn homosexuality, they can unite around this issue, even where economic and other factors would keep them apart. If anti-Semitism is no longer respectable because of the mass murder to which it led, homophobia has kept the blessing of fundamentalist and most mainstream churches—a formidable right-wing bloc. Whether from Christian backgrounds or not, many Third World nationalists, of democratic as well as of authoritarian bent, the late Ayatollah Khomeini being the most notorious, have imported Western homophobia.

Homosexual "Nationalism." Scholars of nationalism have pointed out that many modern nations have come into being as "imagined communities," where charismatic leaders have arisen with a vision of drawing divided human groups together, endowing them with national symbols, promoting a common (sometimes ersatz) language, and then demanding independence—as occurred in eastern Europe in the early decades of the present century (Poland, Czechoslovakia, Yugoslavia) and more recently in the Third World (Indonesia, Kenya, Nigeria). Inspired by such examples, some gay **liberation** leaders have suggested that homosexuals may be undergoing such a process of crystallization into a new nationality. Yet the mere mention of such a project shows how chimerical it is. Homosexuals do not possess a territory of their own on which to erect a state; were they to seek to create such a haven, as in the abortive Alpine County project in California in the 1970s, it would immediately become a target for homophobes of all stripes. Moreover, the vast majority of homosexuals, as patriotic citizens of their own countries, have no wish to transfer their political loyalties. Spread thinly across the territory of the democracies, they have difficulty electing an avowed gay representative to a state legislature, Elaine Noble in Massachusetts being the first of a handful of exceptions, or to a city council except in a few districts where they form a significant plurality. Still, the quicksilver appeal of the political fantasies of gay nationalism attests the continuing refulgence of the nationalist model.

BIBLIOGRAPHY. George Mosse, *Nationalism and Sexuality: Respectability and Abnormal Sexuality in Modern Europe*, New York: Howard Fertig, 1985.
William A. Percy

NATIVE AMERICANS
See **Indians, North American.**

NATURE AND THE UNNATURAL

As Raymond Williams has observed in *Keywords* (New York, 1976), the term "nature" is one of the most complex in the language; it is also one of the most dangerous. An adequate study of the problem must also focus on the emotionally charged antonym: the "unnatural," which

needs to be distinguished from the supernatural and the praeternatural, from second (and for the Greeks, third, fourth, and fifth) nature, and from the peculiarly Thomistic concept of the "connatural" (which, as the personal and habitual, stands in a kind of intermediate zone between the natural and the unnatural).

Historical Semantics of the Concept. The ancient Greek word for nature, *physis*, was unique to that language and to Hellenic thought; no equivalent can be found in the Semitic and Oriental languages, or in other intellectual traditions. The term physis derives from a verb meaning "to grow," and hence retains strong connotations of organic completeness and development toward a goal. The primary notion of physis is a magical, autonomous life force manifesting itself not only in the creation and preservation of the universe, but even in the properties and character traits of species and individuals. Thus in medical usage it even leads into the sphere of the pharmacopoeia and of constitutional biology.

Its use among the Greeks can be further understood in the light of three contrasting pairs of terms: physis/nomos (law or custom); physis/techne (art); kata physin/para physin (against nature). The last of these antinomies, which is of particular significance for our enquiry, received a decisively influential formulation from the aged **Plato** (ca. 427–347 B.C.) in his *Laws*. In this book the philosopher condemns same-sex relations because, unlike those in which animals naturally engage, they cannot lead to procreation. In the so-called intertestamental period this Hellenic idea found its way into the *Testaments of the Twelve Patriarchs* and into the apologetic writings of **Philo Judaeus**, who equated the Mosaic Law with the "law of nature," and thence into the **New Testament** with the fateful formulation of Romans 1:26–27, which speaks of changing "the natural use to that which is unnatural." This language—which in the Pauline text cited sets the stage for a condemnation of male homosexuality—made its way into other contexts, including that of jurisprudence.

The path for this development was smoothed by the earlier Roman acceptance of the concept of "natural law," defined by Cicero as "right reason in agreement with nature." Cicero ascribed this law to God, hence giving legal standing to Biblical injunctions in the eyes of Christian interpreters, and went on to insist that "it is a sin to try to alter this law." On the other hand, the Christians tended to overlook Cicero's statement that in practice God is also the enforcing judge of natural law; that role they took on themselves. The twelfth-century groundswell of interpretation of Roman law and canon law had a major emphasis on natural law perspectives, both classical and Christian. Natural law underpinned arguments justifying antihomosexual legislation throughout the Middle Ages and into early modern times, when its legacy passed from church to secular penology, retaining much of its influence. This secularization notwithstanding, natural-law arguments play a major role today in the continuing Roman Catholic condemnation of homosexual behavior.

It is curious that the notion of "crime against nature," so familiar to us from the penal codes of the American states, did not figure in Henry VIII's English statute of 1533 or its successors. Sir Edward Coke, however, did affirm it in his seventeenth-century *Institutes* and *Reports*, whence it became part of the not-fully-investigated Anglo-American legal tradition down to the present time.

In medieval Europe the semantically iridescent concept of *natura* was perpetuated and even given some new twists and images by moralists (Peter **Damian**), literary figures (Bernard Silvestre, **Alan of Lille**, and Jean de Meun), and philosophers (Albertus Magnus, Thomas **Aquinas**). Later French usage coined the adjective *antiphysique* (taken into English

in the rare "antiphysical") for unnatural sexual behavior.

Eighteenth-century aesthetics saw a broad shift from a view of nature as rule obeying and rule enforcing to one in which the awesome complexity and sovereign fecundity of nature was emphasized—the source of the admiration which naturalists of today profess for the unspoiled wilderness, untrodden by man and unaltered by human hands. This shift is part of the change from neo-Classicism to Romanticism. By providing a more flexible definition of nature the new approach gave it new life as a normative (though more diffuse) principle.

The contemporary scene offers a curious paradox in that conservative thinkers continue to denounce homosexuality as "unnatural" (Ezra Pound), while some homophile apologists have revived the ancient **Hippocratic** definition to claim that homosexuality is inborn and thus "natural" (K. H. **Ulrichs**, Magnus **Hirschfeld**). For its part, the counterculture has glorified natural foods and the environmental protection of nature (which are in themselves valuable) without addressing the contradiction that the sexual freedom and tolerance that it cherishes have been historically denounced as "unnatural."

Inadequacy of the Traditional Arguments. The arguments thus far discussed may be briefly refuted as follows. If nature is truly all-embracing, it is impossible to depart from it. Only things that do not exist at all, such as centaurs and phlogiston, would be unnatural. In this perspective, the supposed criterion of naturalness provides no means for separating existing acts that are judged licit from those regarded as illicit; some yardstick other than "naturalness"—since all acts possess that attribute—must be supplied. If, however, one chooses the other path, regarding some things within the world as natural and others not, the dichotomy becomes culture-bound and subjective. Thus clothing, cosmetics, and airplanes have been sometimes stigmatized as unnatural. Perhaps they are. But then it is hard to see how, say, life-saving heart surgery can be regarded as anything other than an unnatural intervention in otherwise inevitable processes. How many proponents of "naturalness" would be willing to revert to a Stone Age economy and Stone Age medicine? In short, opponents of "unnatural" sex need to demonstrate that they have at their disposal a comprehensive and even-handed theory of the natural and its opposite. What usually happens in practice is that some other assumption, or assumptions, are imported to provide a basis of decision. Thus the natural–unnatural contrast becomes essentially a rhetorical device to provide a pseudo-confirmation of moral presuppositions reached on quite other grounds.

Another critique is that the image of Natura is a survival of the mother goddess figures of pagan antiquity, in which God is the male principle of creation and "Nature" the female counterpart. Discarding such relics of polytheism, modern scientific thought does not concern itself with the supposed "purposes" or "aims" of nature, and in general rejects teleological concepts as empirically undemonstrable. The standard claim is that nature has intended sexuality solely for the purpose of procreation and that any sexual pleasure obtained from non-procreative activity is therefore "unnatural" and wrongful. To this assertion it can be rejoined that only a tiny fraction of all human sexual activity has reproductive consequences, and that to restrict it to such a narrow goal would doom most of the population to virtually lifelong abstinence—though the ascetic ideal would regard such a state of affairs as a desirable end.

From a scientific perspective, the debate over the "naturalness" of homosexuality has been joined by the eminent sex researcher Alfred C. **Kinsey** who, holding that norms of naturalness are in the last analysis historically contingent and arbitrary, concluded that anything sexual which can be done is natural. The older arguments deployed by theologians and moralists were, in his view, accompanied by a considerable charge of emotionality. "This has been effected, in part, by synonymizing the terms clean, natural, normal, moral, and right, and the terms unclean, unnatural, abnormal, immoral, and wrong."

Anthropologists have reported homosexuality in many tribal societies (presumed "close to nature"); a wide range of ethologists have described homosexuality among other species (presumed more "natural"); and theorists in sociobiology have sought to provide an evolutionary rationale for human homosexuality. Perhaps as a reflection of these efforts as well as of other scientific embarrassments involving earlier cultural assumptions about "naturalness," it is no longer scientifically respectable to maintain the argument against homosexuality as "unnatural." This development has not yet had a major impact on Judeo-Christian homophobes or popular demagogic rhetoric, nor on public opinion among the less educated, but over time it can be expected to undermine the credibility of the position that "homosexuality is unnatural."

BIBLIOGRAPHY. A. P. d'Entrèves, *Natural Law*, London: Longmans, 1951; Alfred C. Kinsey, et al., "Concepts of Normality and Abnormality in Sexual Behavior," in P. H. Hoch and J. Zubin, eds., *Psychological Development in Health and Disease*, New York: Grune and Stratton, 1949, pp. 11–32; Donald Levy, "Perversion and the Unnatural as Moral Categories," *Ethics*, 90 (1980), 191–202; C. S. Lewis, *Studies in Words*, Cambridge: Cambridge University Press, 1960, pp. 24–74; Arthur O. Lovejoy, "'Nature' as Aesthetic Norm," *Essays in the History of Ideas*, Baltimore: Johns Hopkins University Press, 1948, pp. 69–77; Clément Rosset, *L'Anti-nature*, Paris: Presses Universitaires de France, 1973.

Wayne R. Dynes

NAVY
See **Seafaring**.

NAZISM

The ideology and practice of National Socialism, which under the leadership of Adolf Hitler ruled Germany from 1933 to 1945, united several virulent strands of hostility to homosexuality. Inheriting the repressive attitudes of the nineteenth-century sexual purity movements, Nazi ideologues reacted also to the licence they perceived as eroding the social fabric of **Germany** under the Weimar Republic (1918–33). Popular sentiment among the Nazis favored a strong polarization of male and female roles, which the perception of homosexuals as "the third sex" contradicted. Equating population growth with power, the Nazis also pursued a vigorous pronatalist policy. Their attitude toward male homosexual behavior, regarded as a threat to the survival of the German people, was unequivocally negative. Heinrich Himmler, the Nazi leader most concerned with the question, advocated drowning homosexuals in bogs as a return to the tribal custom of the ancient Germans recorded by **Tacitus**.

It is a historical paradox that the presence of a few known homosexuals in the ranks of the early Nazi Party, notably Ernst **Röhm**, the head of the paramilitary Brownshirts (SA), gave unscrupulous opponents and propagandists of the **left** the leverage required for the superficial plausibility of their myth of the "**fascist perversion**"—a supposed affinity between sexual deviation and Nazism. In fact, Rohm and his associates were liquidated on Hitler's orders in the Night of the Long Knives, June 30, 1934.

The jurists of the Third Reich reinforced the existing antihomosexual clause of the Reich Penal Code by adding a new section (175a), but at the same time inserted an article in the Code of Criminal Procedure (154b) that allowed the public prosecutor to take no action in a case in which the offender had been the object of blackmail—thus acknowledging the validity of Magnus **Hirschfeld**'s claim that the existing law encouraged the extortion of homosexuals. The prohibition was not extended to lesbians, so that female homosexuality remained legal.

When detected, male homosexuals were arrested and consigned to the concentration camps, where they were placed in the lowest category of prisoners. In the camps homosexual inmates were required to wear the **pink triangle** as an identifying mark; subsequently, this emblem was adopted as a positive symbol by the gay liberation movements of the 1970s. Estimates of the number of pink triangle men killed vary from 10,000 to 250,000; probably the true number will never be known. Sadly, homosexual victims of the Nazis were the only such group denied monetary compensation from the West German government after World War II because of their continuing illegal status. Even today commemorations of the **Holocaust** often fail to mention them. A bizarre footnote is the appearance of two tiny groups of "gay Nazis" in California in the mid 1970s; this episode is a reflection, probably of ephemeral significance, of the lingering myth of the "fascist perversion."

BIBLIOGRAPHY. Heinz Heger, *The Men with the Pink Triangle*, London: Gay Men's Press, 1980; Manfred Herzer, "Nazis, Psychiatrists, and Gays," *Cabirion*, 12 (1985), 1–5; Rüdiger Lautmann, "The Pink Triangle," *Journal of Homosexuality*, 6 (1980–81), 141–60; Richard Plant, *The Pink Triangle: The Nazi War Against Homosexuals*, New York: Holt, 1986.

Wayne R. Dynes

NEOPLATONISM

A revival and recasting of Platonism—mingling with it Pythagorean, Aristotelean, Stoic, and mystic ideas—Neoplatonism supplanted **Stoicism** as the dominant philosophy of the classical world from the mid-third century to the closing of the pagan schools at Athens and elsewhere by Justinian in 529. Philosophers from Antiochus (d. ca. 68 B.C.) to Plotinus (205–269/70), who opposed all sex, including homosexuality of every type, evolved this new synthesis. In Rome when he was forty, Plotinus founded a circle of leading politicians and scholars, including his most important disciple, Porphyry (232/3–ca. 305), who arranged for the publication of Plotinus' *Enneads* almost on the eve of the official recognition of **Christianity** in 313. In the fourth century, from its chief centers in Syria and then Pergamon, its star proponent being Iamblichus, Neoplatonism became the creed of the pagan antagonists of Christianity, which had been made the state religion by Theodosius ca. 390.

Neoplatonism even influenced Christianity through St. Gregory of Nyssa and other theologians of the **Byzantine Empire**, and through St. **Augustine**. Neoplatonism survived at Athens and Alexandria into the sixth century. It appeared in the writings of the pseudo-Areopagite (about 500) and John Scotus Eriugena in the ninth century, as well as in the work of the middle Byzantine polymath Michael Psellus. One of the principal features of Neoplatonism was its spectrum of gradations between "the One" and "matter': the world-mind, the world-soul, and nature—each stage being characterized by diminishing unity. Mystical as well as rational, Neoplatonism encouraged Christian belief in intermediate powers such as angels and demons. One of Porphyry's works in five books, *Against the Christians*, of which fragments survive, though the source was condemned to the flames by the Christians in 448, used historical criticism to prove the lateness of composition of the Book of Daniel, as elsewhere he proved the "Book of Zoroaster" a forgery. His work on logic became the standard Byzantine text and his critique of Homer a philological landmark.

Marsilio **Ficino** (1433–1499), the Florentine philosopher and humanist who was also homophile, was the chief exponent of **Renaissance** Neoplatonism. Exposed to Greek thought by the arrival in **Italy** of learned Byzantines fleeing Constantinople after its fall to the Turks in 1453, the young Ficino discovered **Plato** and his later followers, learning Greek in order to study the original texts. (Plato had been known in medieval Europe only through often faulty Latin versions, some of them secondary translations from the Arabic.) An eclectic, Ficino sought to reconcile Platonism and Neoplatonism with Christianity, using another body of Greek texts, the Hermetic Corpus compiled in late antiquity.

Of special significance is his resurrection of the Platonic ideal of love, as it is known from the *Phaedrus* and the *Symposium*. In the sixteenth century Ficino's version was repackaged in countless treatises on love, becoming the prototype of a new concept of "courtly love" that was very different from the medieval variety. Ficino advocated a profound but highly spiritual love between two men, ideally united by their common quest for knowledge. This love is caused, following Plato's conception, by the vision of beauty conveyed by the soul of the other individual—a beauty that reflects the celestial perfection of God. Through the physical beauty of a young man—women were in Ficino's view unsuitable as catalysts of this sublimity—the conscience of the enlightened man ascends to the Beauty which is the archetypal Idea (in Plato's sense) on which the beauty that he responds to depends—to God himself. With Cosimo and Lorenzo de' Medici's patronage, he founded—in imitation of Plato's Academy in Athens—the Platonic Academy in **Florence**, which was to be a major center of Italian Renaissance thought.

In the course of the sixteenth century those who followed Ficino became increasingly uncomfortable with the homoerotic aspects of his **philosophy** of love. Deploying an intellectual sleight of hand, they heterosexualized the ideal—so that today "Platonic love" usually means the love of man and woman that includes no physical expression.

William A. Percy

NERO (37–68)

Roman emperor. Exiled as a result of the disfavor of the Emperor Caligula, the boy Nero and his ambitious mother Agrippina were rehabilitated and allowed to return to **Rome** after the emperor's death in 41. Several years later Agrippina married the emperor Claudius and, on his demise in 54, was able to secure the throne for her son. Guided by the philosopher Seneca, the empire then entered an auspicious period of sound government. Growing bored of the tedium of rule, however, Nero became addicted to luxury and to his artistic pursuits—he imagined himself a distinguished poet and performer. He constructed for himself a great palace known as the Domus Transitoria. This proved insufficient, and Nero apparently ordered a large part of Rome set on fire in 64, to serve as a site for the construction of his Golden House. As foreign relations became more difficult, his connections with the Senate soured, and the plots against him required increasingly repressive measures. A revolt by the army and Senate caused him to commit suicide, uttering the words, "What an artist is perishing in me." His death ended the Julio–Claudian dynasty.

Nero's appetite for luxury and self-indulgence emerged in his sexual escapades. After enjoying sexual relations with his mother (or so **Suetonius** claims) he grew tired of her when she disapproved of his liaisons with the freedwoman Acte and the glamorous sophisticate Sabina Poppaea. He then devised a special collapsing boat on which he sent her with great ceremony for a short cruise. But Agrippina escaped and swam to shore, where she was dispatched. Nero had a youth, Sporus, whom he castrated and treated as his wife. Sporus was escorted through the streets, receiving the homage due an empress.

Reversing roles, Nero made his husky freedman Doryphorus marry him (though dispensing with the castration).

Nero's many misdeeds have earned him an infamy outstanding even for the profligate age in which he lived. Recent historians, however, have sought to redress the balance. His early years were marked by a serious effort at governmental reform. Unlike his cruelty, his sexual irregularities no longer seem monstrous. And Nero presided over what has been called the Roman architectural revolution, the beginning of the great phase that made the empire's accomplishments in this field unsurpassed. The image perpetuated by Henryk Sienkiewicz' novel *Quo Vadis* (1896) and by Hollywood films is not confirmed by sober historical analysis.

BIBLIOGRAPHY. K. R. Bradley, *Suetonius' Life of Nero: An Historical Commentary*, Brussels: Latomus, 1978; Miriam Tamara Griffin, *Nero, the End of a Dynasty*, New Haven: Yale University Press, 1984; Villy Sørenson, *Seneca, the Humanist at the Court of Nero*, Chicago: University of Chicago Press, 1984.

Warren Johansson

NETHERLANDS, THE (HOLLAND)

A European kingdom of fifteen million Dutch-speaking inhabitants, the Netherlands has in recent times acquired a reputation as the most tolerant country in the industrialized Western world on the subject of homosexuality.

History. The (northern) Netherlands emerged as a national entity (the Republic of the United Provinces) during the Eighty Years War (1568–1648), a revolt against the Spanish Habsburg empire, which separated them from the southern Netherlands (**Belgium**). A great commercial and maritime power, until 1795 they were a loose federation of seven virtually independent provinces. The House of Orange, by no means a monarchy, held only limited rights. Until 1748 the princes of Orange, the so-called *stadtholders* (viceroys), held no hereditary office but each time had to be appointed by each of the provinces separately.

A process of unification of the seven provinces started in 1795 when, after a decade of democratic uprisings, a French invasion put an end to the old system and turned the United Provinces into the Batavian Republic. In 1806 **Napoleon** made the Republic one of his satellite kingdoms with his brother Louis Napoleon as its monarch. After an annexation by France in 1810, the end of the Napoleonic era in 1813 saw the restoration of the House of Orange, now turned into a monarchy, and a short-lived (1815–1830) reunification with the southern provinces.

During the nineteenth century the Netherlands gradually changed into a parliamentary democracy with universal suffrage (including women) finally established in 1917. From an almost absolute monarchy in the early nineteenth century, the House of Orange changed into a constitutional monarchy. From the second half of the nineteenth century onwards the country grew from an agricultural into a modern industrialized nation. It remained neutral in World War I, but was invaded by Nazi Germany in 1940 and occupied until the end of World War II in 1945.

Legislation. Lack of centralization and the indistinctness of "the crime" make it hard to obtain a general view of legislation concerning same-sex behavior in the period prior to the unification of the nation and the law. In the absence of a central legislature each of the provinces (or parts of them) was responsible for its own legislation. Only some of them had articles of law against sodomy or unnatural acts. In the absence of—or next to—such explicit articles, Roman and Mosaic law, legal comments, and tradition could be applied. All of them provided capital punishment for **sodomy**. The *Constitutio Criminalis Carolina* (1532) of the Habsburg emperor Charles V, to a certain extent authoritative in the Netherlands, provided that bestiality and sodomy should be punished by burning at the stake (article 16). Legal texts or comments in many cases included under a single heading such different things as masturbation, rape, bestiality, parricide, arson, as well as sexual acts with Jews or Saracens. Where the articles were explicit, they usually referred to sexual acts with animals, between men or between women, and to non-procreative, "unnatural," sexual acts involving members of both sexes.

Soldiers and sailors were subject to martial and admiralty law respectively. The 1590 *Artikul-Brief*, meant for the military forces, threatened those who had committed sodomitical acts, whatever these were considered to be, with the death penalty, as did admiralty law at least from the early eighteenth century onwards.

It was not until 1730 that a wave of persecutions of sodomites swept through the country and prosecutions indeed had already started, where the province of Holland (because of the diversity of punitive measures) felt the need for anti-sodomy legislation. On July 21, 1730, an edict was issued which stipulated that those who had committed sodomy should be executed publicly, leaving the method of execution to the discretion of the judges. A week before, on July 14, 1730, the province of Groningen granted anonymity to whomever denounced anyone suspected of the *crimen nefandum*. (Since only two men were executed in the city of Groningen in that year, the announcement can hardly be considered to have been successful.) In 1764 a slightly modified version of the edict of 1730 was issued in Holland, whereupon Amsterdam especially was hit by a new wave of persecutions.

In 1777 A. Perrenot, legal adviser to Stadtholder William V, published anonymously the treatise *Bedenkingen over het straffen van zeekere schandelijke misdaad* (Thoughts About the Punishment of a Certain Shameful Crime). In this he pleaded for the abolition of the death penalty for sodomy in the enlightened tradition of **Beccaria** and **Voltaire**. Sodomy, though a sin, in his opinion could not be considered a crime. Far from being a **Bentham**, he still wanted sodomites guilty of seduction to be imprisoned. Perrenot's treatise was soon followed by another anonymous pamphlet, *Nadere bedenkingen over het straffen van zeekere schandelyke misdaad* (Further Thoughts About the Punishment of a Certain Shameful Crime), whose author argued sodomy to be a crime because it weakened male power and thus the power of the state. For practical reasons he argued against the death penalty: if sodomites were imprisoned and occasionally shown to the public in shameful clothes, employed in cleaning toilets and doing other filthy jobs, it would inspire more horror of the crime to the public than the short-lived impression of a public execution.

In 1798 separation of church and state was declared. It inspired a member of the Amsterdam Court, J. Gales, to publish a treatise in which he rejected the possibility that this separation automatically meant the abolition of the 1730/1764 edicts. Indeed, no such abolition followed.

Between 1795 and 1809 a new national criminal code was drafted, coming into force in the latter year. It threatened those who were guilty of unnatural acts with man or beast with a long term of imprisonment and banishment from the kingdom, and maintained the death penalty for those guilty of seducing others. The new criminal code had little or no effect since a necessary restructuring of the legal system still had to be prepared. Besides, with the annexation of the Netherlands by **France** in 1810 and the introduction of the French penal code in 1811, the 1809 code became redundant. The French code, which contained no article against sodomy, was left in force until 1866 despite new drafts of a Dutch criminal code that still provided penal sanctions against same-sex behavior.

The criminal code of 1886, because of liberal dominance in parliament, did not provide a penalty for same sex behavior, but set the age of consent for all sexual behavior at fourteen. Yet all through the nineteenth and part of the twentieth centuries local legislation against public indecency and sexual acts in public made it possible to prosecute those who had given public offense.

It was only in 1911, when Christian influences permeated Dutch politics, that a new Morals Statute included a discriminatory provision: Article 248bis added to the Criminal Code set the age of consent for same-sex behavior at 21, fixing that for heterosexual behavior at 16, and providing an imprisonment for offenders. This provision was abolished in 1971 after the so-called Speyer Report had ascertained that no youth became a homosexual because of early homosexual experience.

With the exception of the period of Nazi occupation of the Netherlands (1940–45), no law prohibiting homosexuality as such was ever reintroduced. Regulation 81 of the German occupiers provided for punishment of all same-sex behavior with imprisonment. This regulation, like other exactments of the occupation, was abolished immediately after the Liberation.

Prosecutions. Until the eighteenth century prosecutions because of same-sex behavior in the Netherlands were a rare phenomenon. Some verdicts are known from fourteenth- and fifteenth-century courts in Utrecht. In the same period some cases with political overtones are known to have been tried in The Hague, one of them involving the president of the States of Holland. Most cases prior to the eighteenth century dealt either with men who had sexual relations with children or with misuse of marriage, for instance women dressed as men who "married" other women. Until 1795 all cases in which women were involved dealt with cross-dressing.

Best known are the prosecutions of 1730. The discovery of a nationwide network of sodomites caused an avalanche of verdicts. Courts all over the country dealt with some 300 people, about half of them by default. Seventy death penalties were carried out. The most notorious were the 1731 prosecutions led by the country squire Rudolph de Mepsche in the Groningen provincial counties. On September 24, 1731, 22 men and boys from Faan and other nearby villages were put to death after dubiously obtained confessions. Several others were kept in prison without a verdict until 1747. The case caused wide disbelief and political upheaval. De Mepsche was accused of an attempt to get rid of political opponents.

Less known is the fact that in Rotterdam as early as 1702 two men were put to death and in 1717 a small local network was discovered which led to the banishment of several people. Equally less known are waves of prosecutions later in the eighteenth century. Such waves occurred in 1764–65 in Amsterdam and in 1776 in the province of Holland, in both cases following the discovery of networks of sodomites. Especially between 1795 and 1798 prosecutions in Amsterdam reached a new peak in a number of isolated trials (without the death penalty), which for the first time involved women, who without any reference to cross-dressing were accused of sexual acts with one another. Prosecutions stopped in 1811 with the introduction of the French penal code. Altogether throughout the eighteenth century some 600 people were prosecuted because of same-sex behavior.

In the eighteenth century capital punishment was only applied when anal intercourse with an ejaculation in the body of a partner was considered proven by a confession and eyewitness accounts or confessions of accomplices. Other genital acts, or the absence of either a confession or some other part of the necessary evidence in charges of anal intercourse, resulted in long-term solitary confinement.

To obtain a confession the courts had torture (shin screws or whipping) at their disposal, though this was subject to rules. It could only be applied in cases that might result in a death penalty (anal inter-course) when eyewitness accounts or confessions of accomplices were available. Moreover, bailiffs had to ask their court's permission to submit a suspect to torture. A confession obtained under torture had to be repeated "free from pain and restraint."

Until 1795 in sodomy cases the rules for torture were observed even more than usual, with the exception of the trials in the village of Faan in the province of Groningen, where suspects seem to have been beaten up regularly and at least one man died as a result of torture. Judicial torture was abolished in 1798.

Before the eighteenth century, death penalties for sodomy were usually carried out by burning at the stake. In the eighteenth century garroting, the usual punishment for women guilty of a capital crime, was mostly applied to sodomites as well. In this period no sodomite was burned alive. The last death penalty for sodomy in the Netherlands was carried out in Schiedam in 1803. Prosecutions in the Netherlands in the eighteenth century, though no doubt the severest in the early modern period in Europe, were never systematic, but the result of accidental discoveries.

During the nineteenth century same-sex behavior was liable to prosecution only in case of public indecency, sexual acts in public places, which could be punished by imprisonment or sometimes led to confinement in a lunatic asylum. In the second half of this century such prosecutions increased tenfold as a result of improvements in policing, the introduction of rules concerning the use of public lavatories, and changes in the design of the latter which made activities in the lavatories visible from the outside.

The history of Article 248bis is one of a trail of **blackmail**, ruined reputations, and derailed careers. The number of trials under this article gradually grew from about fifty per year before the war to several hundred per year in the first decade after the war. In 1936 the case of General Treasurer Ries became notorious. He was accused by a minor, fired from his office, and abandoned by the government, even though the accusations against him were withdrawn. Equally notorious was a series of 1939 prosecutions in the Dutch East Indies (**Indonesia**), which were covered by Dutch newspapers in a sensational manner.

Contrary to popular belief, prosecution of homosexuals by the Nazis during the Occupation was rare. Only a small number of trials in regard to Regulation 81 are known to have happened, usually resulting in a few months of imprisonment. The number of trials under Article 248bis decreased compared with the number of such trials before the war. Homosexual behavior was left to the Dutch police, who were no more repressive than before the war. Though a couple of raids on pubs where homosexuals gathered did occur, historians so far have failed to uncover any case in which a homosexual was sent to a concentration camp, just for being a homosexual. Which does not mean to say that no Dutch homosexual was sent to a concentration camp, but that such a person was there either for being Jewish, as a member of the Resistance, or for political reasons.

Social Organization. The earliest references to a sodomite **subculture** have been traced to the last quarter of the seventeenth century. Public buildings like the City Hall in Amsterdam, a park in The Hague, and public lavatories in different cities were widely used by sodomites as meeting places from the last decades of the seventeenth century onwards.

It was especially through the trials of 1730 and those in later years that the extent of the subculture came to the attention of the authorities (and modern historians). To a large extent sodomite contacts were organized through a network in which men of all classes and ranging in age from 20 to 60 participated. Most of the participants (or at least those that are known because they were prosecuted) occupied professions that easily could bring them in touch with numerous other people: they were merchants, shopkeepers, peddlers, footmen. Many were married. The women involved in persecutions in the 1790s did not form a network or a subculture and were of a poorer, sometimes prostitution, background. Only some of them were married.

Brothels and pubs existed in The Hague, Utrecht, Amsterdam, and Leiden. Special go-betweens provided footmen for gentlemen. Public buildings like the Amsterdam City Hall, the Bourse in Amsterdam, churches, theatres, as well as numerous lavatories which sometimes were specially nicknamed, city walls, specific streets, the underbrush in and outside city walls: all were known to sodomites as places where they either could have sex or find a casual partner.

At some of these places they used special codes to make contact with one another, like tapping with one hand on the back of the other, or putting the hands on the hips and hitting with the elbow against that of somebody who did the same thing.

In some places rituals existed, e.g., a group of sodomites in Haarlem used to elect one of them when they met under a tree and gave him the first choice of a partner. Though drag was not as popular among sodomites in the Netherlands as in England, some were described by accomplices or witnesses as effeminate.

The eighteenth-century subculture was essentially a street culture and by its very nature an urban one. Sodomite contacts in rural areas seem to have had an even more casual and much less organized character. In the village of Faan, men and boys more or less accidentally engaged in games which included sexual acts, without being aware that these acts were considered criminal and sinful.

The nineteenth century showed a gradual growth of this street culture and it has survived well into the second half of the twentieth century. The number of pubs and brothels showed an equal growth, while at the same time coteries of male as well as female friends, usually of higher class, either with or without a sexual purpose, came into existence. During World War II, "tearoom trade" prospered as never before, mostly owing to the blackout. Even some pubs kept their largely homosexual clientele during the war. Though still existing, the street culture now seems to be giving way to a large commercial subculture, and also to more intimate forms of homosexuality.

A lesbian subculture has been much slower in coming into existence and today is much smaller than its male counterpart, though it provides not only pubs but also archives, bookshops, and health organizations.

Organizations. The first homosexual movement in the Netherlands was founded in 1911 as the Dutch branch of Magnus **Hirschfeld's Scientific-Humanitarian Committee** (Nederlandsch Wetenschappelijk Humanitair Komitee—NWHK) by the nobleman and jurist Jacob Schorer in response to the introduction of article 248bis. He intended to fight this law and to give support to homosexuals whenever and wherever they got into trouble.

The NWHK published yearbooks and brochures, which were sent to students, politicians, medical doctors, and key figures in society. Schorer collected a huge library of publications on homosexuality, which was seized by the Nazis in the early days of the Occupation. Not a genuine movement per se, the NWHK was what it said it was, a committee, mostly personified by Schorer himself, financially dependent on the gifts of homosexuals who wanted to support it. Throughout its existence the NWHK met with fierce opposition from Protestant and Catholic groups. It came to an end in 1940 when Schorer wisely destroyed his membership records at the outbreak of war with Germany.

The editors of the newly founded homosexual magazine *Levensrecht* (Right to Live) also destroyed their records in May 1940, as well as the recently-printed fourth issue of their magazine. In 1946, after World War II had ended, the editors decided to revive *Levensrecht*. The authorities were obliged to give them a permit since, having ended the publication in 1940, the editors had obviously not collaborated with the Germans. Like the editors of the Swiss magazine *Der Kreis/Le Cercle*, which the Dutch editors took as their model, they started to organize special evenings in Amsterdam and other places with lectures and cultural events for a homosexual audience. Shortly thereafter, they founded the Shakespeare Club, forerunner of the COC.

Neither the publication of *Levensrecht* nor the existence of the Shakespeare Club was welcomed by the Dutch authorities, who sought reasons to prohibit both. Through the careful policy of one of its founders, Niek Engelschman, who managed to keep on speaking terms with the vice squad of the police, and through tough negotiations, such a prohibition was prevented. The police, however, made Engelschman stop publication of *Levensrecht* before a legal prohibition was issued. Yet shortly afterwards, the board of the Shakespeare Club decided to start a new magazine, *Vriendschap* (Friendship), which was left undisturbed by the authorities. (In 1986, at the COC's fortieth anniversary, Engelschman was awarded a royal decoration by the Dutch government for his role as one of the founding fathers of the organization and for his activities in later years.)

In 1948 the Shakespeare Club changed its name to COC (Cultuur en Ontspannings Centrum, "Center for Culture and Recreation"). Unlike its predecessor, the NWHK, the COC wanted to organize homosexuals and offer them the opportunity to meet and relax in "decent" surroundings. Its principal goal was to strengthen the self-consciousness of homosexuals by acquainting them with the "great" cultural, literary, and political homosexuals of past and present and with scientific research on homosexuality. Like the NWHK, the COC in its external policy focused on key figures in society.

Social changes, including more openness about (homo)sexuality, caused the COC in 1964 to change its rather introverted policy into a more extroverted one, reflected by its new "open" name, Nederlandse Vereniging van Homofielen COC (Dutch Organization of Homophiles COC). With a new journal *Dialoog* it literally hoped to enter into a dialogue with society.

Hardly aware of things happening elsewhere in the world and without any knowledge of the **Stonewall Rebellion**, at the end of the sixties the Dutch homosexual movement went through a series of changes that were not unlike those in America. Vietnam, radical student protests, sexual revolution, the feminist movement and, not least, radical gay groups affected the COC and turned it into a more radical movement that increasingly focused on society. Homosexuality was no longer considered to be the problem of homosexuals but society's problem. Once again these changes forced the COC to change its name: from 1971 onwards it called itself Nederlandse Vereniging tot Integratie van Homoseksualiteit COC (Dutch Society for the Integration of Homosexuality COC). In 1973, having been refused in 1963 and 1968, it was granted legal status.

From the very beginning women had been involved with the COC, though only as a small minority. Since the second half of the seventies, when the COC started to provide special facilities for women, this minority has been growing. Yet numerous lesbians prefer women-centered organizations and meeting places.

Perceptions. Until the persecutions of 1730, neither secular nor ecclesiastical authorities in the Netherlands paid much attention to sodomy. It was considered a crime and a sin that eventually would be punished. But until 1730, the church councils in their constant diatribes against "crying sins" (card-playing, swearing, whoring, etc.) never mentioned sodomy. Secular authorities seemed to consider sodomy as an incidental crime or, as Michel **Foucault** claimed, as a temporary aberration from the norm. All this changed in 1730. In several books published by ministers after the persecutions had already started, they presented interpretations of the Biblical chapters on Sodom and Gomorrah that provided an etiology of same sex behavior on both a collective and an individual level. At a collective level such behavior was mostly seen as the result of an abundance of food and the absence of enemies of the state. At an individual level such abundance made people yield to the successive stages of the "crying sins" which in the end would make the individual vulnerable to seduction into same sex behavior by an individual who had reached that (new) nadir of sinfulness already. This was supposed to have happened on a large scale in 1712–1713 during the negotiations in Utrecht to end the War of the Spanish Succession, when numerous Catholic diplomats visited the city.

Once an individual had been lured into such a behavior he would cling to these practices and seduce others. Indeed, in 1730, faced with men who had not committed their sins just accidentally but deliberately and in an organized manner, these were the questions and sometimes unprovoked answers to and from suspects on trial: how long had they persisted in their behavior and who had been their seducers? From an accidental sin, sodomy became a permanent state of sinfulness. Same-sex behavior was understood in a religious manner and the secular and ecclesiastical authorities, the general public, and the men involved in the trials referred to acts "for which cities had been destroyed."

So far as the existence of a vague sodomite identity is reflected in such statements, this may have derived from the subculture and been acknowledged by the trials. Women seem not to have had such an identity.

As elsewhere in Europe, the Netherlands in the nineteenth century gradually put more emphasis on the prevention than on the punishment of same-sex behavior; this brought the discussion of such behavior into the sphere of medicine. Same-sex behavior became pivotal in the discussion, mostly conducted within the medical profession, of cellular imprisonment, the spread of venereal diseases, and prostitution. Yet no original contributions in the process of the medicalization of homosexuality were published in the Netherlands in this period. The writings of K. H. **Ulrichs** and other authors on the Third Sex in the second half of the nineteenth century became known there among physicians and those directly involved. Terms like "Urning" replaced "sodomite" and in 1892 for the first time the word "homosexuality" was used in the Netherlands, conveying the biological or medical meanings attached to same sex acts.

It was two members of the medical profession, Arnold **Aletrino** (also a literary author) and Lucien von **Römer**, who, as forerunners of the NWHK, were the first to defend "Urning rights," though the former wanted them to abstain from sexual acts, thus separating desire and behavior. Both of them believed that "uranism" originated in biological deviations, though Aletrino preferred to compare it to variations in plant life rather than see it as a perversion or sickness. Both of them published on the subject, not seldom putting their reputations at risk.

The extensive Dutch press coverage of the Oscar **Wilde** trial in England and later scandals in Europe provided further opportunity for homosexuals to identify with the accused. The Radclyffe **Hall** case and her *Well of Loneliness* (1928) provided such an opportunity for women.

The NWHK mostly followed Hirschfeld in his "intermediate type" theory, although Schorer was not espe-cially interested in any theory about homosexuality. On the eve of World War II, such biological theories were firmly established among homosexuals. This is best reflected in the book *De Homo sexueelen*, which the lawyer Benno Stokvis published in 1939. In a series of short autobiographies men and women claimed to have felt that they were different from an early age onwards. Most of the men considered themselves effeminate and in their relationships they thought of themselves in husband/wife roles, each complementing the other.

In the early years after the war, the COC continued to think of homosexuality in biological terms. It tried to pay attention to new theories as well, including obscure eugenic ones. Gradually such thinking gave way to a psychological (Freudian) concept. In the late sixties any concept that included an etiology became suspect and was made a taboo, though the existence of homosexuals and lesbians as a separate category still goes largely unquestioned.

Conclusion. As far as homosexuality is concerned today's Netherlands enjoys a reputation as one of the most tolerant countries in the world. The popularity of the Amsterdam "scene" with its more than 50 bars, representing many different lifestyles, rivals that of much larger cities. The Dutch government officially carries out a gay and lesbian emancipation policy and so do many municipalities, one of the cabinet ministers being responsible for coordinating such policy. In Amsterdam, the first official gay and lesbian monument (widely mistaken as a tribute to homosexual victims of Nazi persecutions) has been built with government support. At an institutional level—government, parliament, press—there seems to exist a taboo on anti-homosexuality, to which even fundamentalists have at least to pay lip service. Yet attempts in the 1980s to introduce anti-discrimination legislation concerning same-sex behavior have been frustrated by fundamentalist and Christian Democratic opposition and seem to have entered a deadlock. As neither Christian Democrats, Liberals, nor Socialists have a majority in parliament, no party is able to enforce its views. Christian Democrats, though in agreement with such legislation, want exceptions to be made for schools and other institutions of a Christian character, exceptions which are unacceptable to the other parties. Equally frustrated have been attempts to lower the age of consent to twelve or to grant gay couples the right to adopt children.

Long considered to be the only representative of homosexuals and lesbians in the Netherlands, the COC nowadays is no longer the only gay and lesbian organization. Homosexuals and lesbians have organized in gay and lesbian caucuses in professional groups such as in health care, teachers' and civil servants' unions, in the police forces and the army, in religious groups, groups of elderly people and youths. Special groups or organizations have been set up for gay and lesbian (mental) health especially in regard to AIDS, and against anti-gay and -lesbian violence. At three universities (Amsterdam, Utrecht, Nijmegen) it is possible to take courses in gay and lesbian studies or research. Dutch universities organized two of the world's major gay and lesbian academic events: the "Among Men/Among Women Conference" in 1983 (University of Amsterdam) and the "Homosexuality, Which Homosexuality? Conference" in 1987 (Free University, Amsterdam).

In the eighties the Netherlands entered the **AIDS** era. This crisis seemed to reenforce the taboo on anti-homosexual expression, as a result of a widely-proclaimed compassion toward AIDS victims. In AIDS prevention, the gay and lesbian movement has become a negotiating partner of the government, carrying out a policy of restraint.

Despite all this progress, anti-gay **violence** seemed to increase; the Netherlands joined other countries in their hysteria about child abuse and incest, creating an exceedingly dangerous atmosphere for pedophiles and homosexuals alike. Moreover, question marks should be put beside some of the government's efforts to support gay and lesbian emancipation, since they are also used to control homosexuality in a heterosexual manner. Despite these shortcomings, the Netherlands continues to point the way to true homosexual emancipation.

BIBLIOGRAPHY. Gert Hekma, *Homoseksualiteit, een medische reputatie*, Amsterdam: Sua, 1987; Pieter Koenders, *Homoseksualiteit in bezet Nederland*, Amsterdam: Sua, 1984; Theo van der Meer, *De Wesentlijke sonde van sodomie en andere vuyligheeden*, Amsterdam: Tabula, 1984; A. X. van Naerssen, ed., *Interdisciplinary Research on Homosexuality in the Netherlands*, New York: Haworth Press, 1987; Rob Tielman, *Homoseksualiteit in Nederland*, Meppel: Boom, 1982.
Theo van der Meer

NEW ORLEANS

This major port (population ca. 600,000) at the mouth of the Mississippi River was founded in 1718 as capital of the French colony of Louisiana. Sold to the United States in 1803 as part of the Louisiana Purchase, New Orleans has long ranked as a major gay center and mecca for homosexuals from all over the American South.

Two main factors fostered the early development of New Orleans' exceptionally large gay community and continue to shape that community's unusual contours: the city's cosmopolitan character and its French heritage. To the diverse, largely male, French, Spanish, German, Indian, and African populations (including Jean Lafitte's **pirates**) assembled during the port's colonial decades, the nineteenth and twentieth centuries added successive, and still largely male, waves of Americans, Irish, Italians, Jews, Yugoslavs, Greeks, Filipinos, Latin Americans, still more French, and most recently a number of Vietnamese. And from its French colonial period, New Orleans also inherited a high degree of racial, ethnic, and social toleration; a certain almost feminine *gentilesse*; a sure urbanity; and a distinctive public culture that still sets it apart from other American cities.

The Nineteenth Century. In the nineteenth century the lower strata of New Orleans' day-to-day illicit sex world centered, as in many other ports, on the waterfront, as well as in the grog shops and upstairs rooms of the French Quarter's Gallatin Street that ran along the wharves behind the French Market. The waterfront bars catered, from the beginning, to an unusually high number of Greek **seafarers** brought to the port by the **Mediterranean** trade patterns inherited from the city's French and brief Spanish (1763–1800) period. Such Greek bars even today remain heavily mixed, straight and gay.

A cut above the nightly grime of Gallatin Street, a number of public dance halls, called "ballrooms," catered to a sexually, racially, and socially mixed assortment of masked revellers. Each winter season these masked balls also became centers of the city's most famous, and traditionally its most sex-oriented, public festival, **Mardi Gras.**

The top stratum of nineteenth-century New Orleans gay society, while it might periodically drag through Gallatin Street and the ballrooms, more often frequented cafés, theatres, and restaurants. Unlike the rest of the United States, where bars, theatres, and restaurants remained largely rough male preserves, New Orleans, from the beginning, afforded respectable women the pleasure of attending. Consequently these institutions took on, in New Orleans, a gentle character, in the French mode, combining restaurant, bar, and coffee house, often along with music, into a neighborhood café. Moreover, New Orleans perpetuated the close connection the French had long made between food and sex. From their inception in the 1830s and '40s, great restaurants always had a series of private dining rooms upstairs,

each equipped not only with the usual dining furniture but, *de rigueur*, also with an ample and armless couch. The *intime* dinner and the *déjeuner galant* became, and remain today, fixtures of New Orleans social-sexual life for the affluent of all orientations.

At the same time, the institution of *plaçage* (the keeping, by many white men, of free women of color as mistresses) found a parallel, albeit small by comparison, in some white men's keeping of free **black** youths as lovers. The latter practice continued after the abolition of slavery, more often than not with a black lover disguised as a manservant in a bachelor white man's house.

From the Turn of the Century to World War II. At the opening of the twentieth century, Gallatin Street died as a waterfront, crowded out by an expansion of the French Market's food stalls. New Orleans' new "monkey wrench corner," as sailors traditionally called the center of any port's tenderloin district, became lower Canal Street and the first blocks of Decatur, Chartres, Exchange Alley, and Royal streets, which run from Canal into the French Quarter. On these seedy blocks seamen's bars, pool rooms, penny arcades, and cheap hotels proliferated, and hustlers and prostitutes abounded, even as they do today.

Prohibition had little effect on heavy-drinking New Orleanians. Cafés kept their liquor under the bar instead of on top of it, and served it in coffee cups instead of glasses. Otherwise the city's social-sex life continued virtually as before. In addition to the national trends of the 1920s, the major changes the Prohibition decade saw were: (1) a largely homosexual nightspot, mixed male and female, operated as a sort of gay speakeasy in an apartment of the Lower Pontalba building, facing Jackson Square; (2) the fad of private "ether parties" involving that substance along with marijuana and cocaine; and (3) the rise of literary and theatrical circles that had heavy homosexual components.

Theatre devotees gathered at a small restaurant in the Upper Pontalba building that continued into the 1960s as Dottie Reiger's Alpine Café. The chief literary circle formed around Lyle Saxon and his black lover, whom Saxon fictionalized in his last work, *The Friends of Joe Gilmore*. Victor's Café, situated at the Chartres/Toulouse corner which had earlier been the site of the House of the Rising Sun (the city's most famous prostitution parlor, which gained international reknown when an old blues song about it became a worldwide hit after being recorded in 1964 by Eric Burdon and the Animals), became the literary circle's watering place.

With the end of Prohibition in 1933, bar-restaurants immediately blossomed in New Orleans. The heavily mixed (gay and straight) James' Beer Parlor on Royal Street at Toulouse became such a favorite with gay men and women that its corner remained the chief gathering place for gay people to watch nighttime Mardi Gras parades until these processions ceased entering the Quarter in 1972. A number of other bars also developed sizable gay components in the 1930s, most notably Mom's Society Page on Exchange Alley, Pat O'Brien's on St. Peter Street, and the Old Absinthe House on Bourbon Street.

The nineteenth-century masked ball tradition continued in the decayed form of shows featuring **transvestite** female impersonators, especially in black bars, of which the Dew Drop Inn off Louisiana Avenue uptown and the Caledonia Inn on St. Philip Street just outside the Quarter were the most celebrated. Both drew considerable white patronage, straight as well as gay. And by the late thirties, drag shows at the Wonder Bar and the My-Oh-My Club on the Lake Charles marina had become two of the city's most frequented tourist attractions. In the long view, the era's most important contribution, the architectural restoration of the French Quarter and its official recognition as an historic district, was spearheaded,

and has since been maintained, largely by the city's gay community.

During World War II, gay activities increased in New Orleans as in other American cities. The pool halls, poker rooms, and bookie joints that lined lower Canal Street functioned as easy pick-up spots, and any number of small hotels in the vicinity, such as the Teche, by then decayed from their former elegance, served as convenient trick parlors. Jackson Square in the middle of the Quarter, a jungle of overgrown vines, trees and shrubs at the time, became an all-night cruising ground, and the public men's room across the street in the French Market achieved national notoriety as "the blue grotto." The leader of one of the thirties' most famous all-girl orchestras opened Dixie's Bar of Music on St. Charles Avenue, a straight bar but favored by female and male gays as well. Exchange Alley added Wanda's Seven Seas and Mack's Oyster Bar to its collection of hustler dives.

The postwar forties saw the opening of the Starlet Lounge at Chartres and St. Philip streets and of Tony Bacino's on Toulouse near Bourbon; both remained infamous for a decade. In the front room of Bacino's a bartender called the "White Roach" and black pianist and singer Ginny and Gracie entertained a mixture of tourists and locals under the eye of black doorman "Tune," while in the slave-quarter bar to the rear, across the patio which connected via typical narrow passageways to neighboring bars, an outrageous French-speaking Cajun drag queen called "Candy Lee" regaled a largely gay crowd with coarse humor. And a few blocks away on the corner of Bourbon and St. Philip, the Café Jean Lafitte opened in an old blacksmith shop to become one of the most elegant gay bars in the country, though it continued, as did all New Orleans bars of the period, to have many straight patrons as well.

The Postwar Period. When authorities closed the poker halls and bookie joints of lower Canal Street in the 1950s, their back-room sexual activities moved into several old cinema theatres, by then reduced to showing bawdy films: the Avenue Theater on St. Charles, the Globe, the Tudor, and the Center on Canal, and the Gaiety in the Quarter. At the same time, Exchange Alley's House of the Fencing Masters, a rough bar commonly called Ivan's after its owner, inherited some of the spillover. Air travel in the fifties also greatly increased the city's daily number of tourists and the annual Mardis Gras crowds. Dixie moved her bar into the Quarter, at Bourbon and St. Peter, and it, along with the Café Lafitte in Exile, which moved from the blacksmith shop to the corner of Bourbon and Dumaine, became the twin hubs of gay life, with exclusively gay patronage. New black bars such as the Golden Feather on St. Bernard Avenue and the Dream Castle on Frenchmen Street also sprang up. At the same time the Missisippi Gulf Coast, the city's nearby beach resort, developed gay bars such as the Cafe Ko-Ko and Charley's Hideaway, but they remained, like the black bars in New Orleans, a straight–gay mix.

The increased crowds of the 1950s not only forced a certain anonymity upon individuals, but also caused bars to dispense first with food service and later with live entertainment, both long their hallmarks. These changes had two profound effects on the city's gay life. Without food and entertainment to bind them together, male and female homosexuals began to drift apart, and a few lesbian bars opened, the earliest ones on the Tchoupitoulas Street waterfront uptown, well outside the Quarter. Sheer numbers also produced the phenomenon of bar sex. The 1957 Mardi Gras crowds in Dixie's developed small groping circles that suddenly became daisy-chains, the idea of which, despite Dixie's and other bar owners' efforts to stop it, rapidly spread. Before 1960 such "public" sex was a commonplace in New Orleans gay bars, precursors by over

a decade of the orgy rooms that became a national fad in the 1970s.

The baby-boom generation reached its twenties in the late sixties and seventies and their presence multiplied the number of gay bars and baths in New Orleans, as elsewhere. Establishments followed the sixties' bifurcated sense of style: urbane elegance on the one hand and hippy hedonism on the other. But in New Orleans the two mixed more than elsewhere, for the **Counterculture**'s emphasis on freedom of choice and street life found easy accommodation in New Orleans' traditionally tolerant attitude and festival culture.

Dancing, for example, which had never before been part of the New Orleans gay bar scene, became common, if only briefly, for dancing was traditionally so much a part of the city's daily life that gay natives saw no advantage to having it in their ever more crowded bars.

The unusual mix of the 1960s produced one particularly notable bar, Las Casa de los Marineros at the corner of Decatur and Toulouse. Beginning in the fifties as a Latin American seaman's bar, it nightly assembled in the sixties an extraordinary collection of artists, intellectuals, street people, gays, workers, college students, and young society couples, to become a remarkable microcosm.

The 1970s saw another enormous jump in the number of gay bars and the New Orleans version of coming out of the closet. By 1980 the city had nearly thirty gay bars, almost all within the one square mile constituting the Quarter, an average of a bar every third block. Even the Greyhound Bus station sported a gay bar, black and wild. And the local bars reflected something of the segmentation of the gay community that was occurring nationally, but with a difference. The specialization that characterized bars in other American cities during that decade remained in New Orleans a cosmetic difference. Leather bars, for example, never became exclusively, much less rigidly, leather. Most gay men, from all social strata, now went periodically to all bars. Hence, below surface differences, the bars of the seventies actually were more alike than they had ever been before. That fact represented the major change the decade brought, a loss of focus for the gay community. When Dixie's closed and Lafittes in Exile installed disco music, there ceased to be centers of the city's gay life; it lost its stratification to become diffuse and disorganized.

By contrast the gay pride movement in New Orleans proved notably effective, especially its political arm. In 1977 the Gertrude Stein Democratic Club grew out of a somewhat older gay literary salon called the Gertrude Stein Society and began political lobbying. In 1982 the GSDC gave way to NORCO, the New Orleans Regional Chapter of the Louisiana Gay Political Action Committee. NORCO has succeeded in electing a number of city council members and state legislators sympathetic to gay rights and in influencing gay rights ordinances and legislation.

Other aspects of the gay pride movement, for reasons directly traceable to the city's general lifestyle and its public culture, had both somewhat less as well as considerably more success than their founders hoped. *Impact*, the gay newspaper established in 1977, has, save for the brief period it was edited by Jon Newlin, never made a dent on the city's largely non-reading public. A new publication aimed at gay Christians is called *The Second Stone*. But gay parades and public drag contests, designed to pique, instead delighted the local population who simply coopted them and turned them into new civic festivals. "Southern Decadence," for example, a drag parade originated in 1974 as a protest march, is today the center event of the New Orleans Labor Day celebration.

The main effects of the **AIDS** epidemic of the eighties on the New Orleans scene have been the diminution of drugs and the associated lifestyle, the disappearance of most public and bar sex, and the closing of most, but not all, bathhouses. There has been no official suppression, and gay life continued quite public, especially in the Quarter. Young people were markedly few on the public gay scene, and bars became more social and more entertainment-centered than at any time since the 1950s. Live music and even food again made their appearance in gay bars, whose patrons reflected the highest female-male ratio seen in over thirty years.

Lucy J. Fair

NEW TESTAMENT

Consisting of twenty-seven short writings, the New Testament forms the second part of the Christian Bible. The first part of the Christian Bible, the Hebrew Bible or **Old Testament**, is considered authoritative by Jews, but the New Testament is not. Apart from this, the New Testament does have some value as a source book for the history of both the synagogue and the church, although a great part of it is of dubious merit as historical source material because it amounts to a series of testimonials of faith.

The Gospels. The four gospels, Matthew, Mark, Luke, and John, with which the New Testament begins, are not biographies of **Jesus** but statements of belief. Mark, the earliest, was written as homiletic material to the new church in Rome, Matthew as a tract to convert Jews, Luke as a tract to convert Greeks, and John as a pseudo-gnostic treatise to win the pagans of the Orient, positing Jesus as the True Light of the world. Though the historical school would assign these gospels to the reigns of Vespasian, Titus, and Domitian, all four may have been composed as late as the time of Hadrian (117–138), as they begin to be mentioned and quoted only in the third quarter of the second century, and are recognized by all Christendom only in the last quarter. To take any one of them as an accurate life of

Jesus is to misunderstand them from the outset, though some of the information about Jesus may be accurate. He is depicted as an itinerant preacher, faith healer, and miracle worker who wandered through Judea, Galilee, Syria, and Trans-Jordan in the reign of Tiberius, when the prefect of the province of Judea was Pontius Pilate. He was accompanied by a small group of devoted followers of diverse social backgrounds, some with extensive property, others marginal types in the eyes of Pharisaic Jewry, the inner circle of his disciples being entirely male, but with some devoted women in their entourage.

The four gospels record Jesus as making no statement that focused explicitly on homosexual behavior or rendered a judgment in favor of either the Jewish or the Hellenic attitude toward it. The omission of this narrow area of sexual morality in no way means that he had no moral judgment on such matters. His statements on adultery and divorce (Matthew 5:27–32) and on that which "defileth the man: . . . adulteries, fornications . . . lasciviousness" (Mark 7:20–23) imply no weakening or abrogation of the code of sexual morality recognized by both Palestinian and Hellenistic Jewry, but instead a higher standard of morality that goes far beyond the conventional Judaic one; it is not just overt acts, but even thoughts and intentions that are condemned and banished from consciousness. Even if one takes the Sermon on the Mount to be a new ethical standard meant only for the elite of the proto-Christian community in contrast with the ritual and ceremonial observances minutely prescribed by the Old Testament for the priests and Levites—the elite of the old covenant—it still urges a broadening rather than a narrowing of the sexual taboos in the Holiness Code of Leviticus. The word **racha** in Matthew 5:22 may be a vulgar loanword (from Hebrew *rakh)* in Hellenistic Greek signifying the passive-effeminate homosexual whom both Jew and Gentile held in contempt; the meaning of the passage would then be that not

simply physical aggression and violence, but even verbal insults directed at the masculinity of the addressee are forbidden by the higher morality of the new faith.

Other Aspects. The Christian tradition as we now have it, however, must have been purged by James the pious brother of Jesus, who took charge of the infant church soon after Jesus' death and held onto it until he himself was executed (ca. 44). He would hardly have let anything salacious about the relationships of the earliest apostles survive. The same is true of Paul of Tarsus, a Jew who came upon the Christian scene about six or seven years after the death of Jesus and reshaped the new sect largely according to his own thinking, in the process writing about one third of what later became the canonical New Testament. Letters attributed to him number thirteen, although several of these (I–II Timothy, Titus, Philemon, Hebrews, and Ephesians), should be called pseudo-Pauline, for to attribute them entirely or at all to him raises numerous critical objections that are not easily answered by the traditional arguments.

There are explicit references to the morality of homosexual acts in Romans 1:26–27, I Corinthians 6:9–10, and I Timothy 1:9–10. The first is often mistakenly understood as the sole reference to lesbianism in the Bible, but is in fact a reinterpretation of the sin of the "daughters of men" who had intercourse with the "sons of God" (= fallen angels) in Genesis 6:1–2, 4, echoed in Testament of Naphtali 3:5, an **intertestamental** writing. The opening statement that "the wrath of God is revealed from heaven" (Romans 1:18) shows that the whole passage is a commentary on the Deluge and the destruction of **Sodom**, in both of which Paul sees retribution for violations of the natural order. There is no reference in the passage to the sexual behavior of Paul's Roman contemporaries, though implicitly the conduct of the gentile world is excoriated as transgressing the Judaic norms.

The passage in I Corinthians

6:9–10 is modeled on the Decalogue: those who violate its precepts will find themselves excluded from the Kingdom of God. The words *malakoi,* "effeminate," and *arsenokoitai,* "abusers of themselves with mankind," signify the passive and active partners in male homosexual relations respectively, rephrasing the explicit condemnation of both in Leviticus 20:13, which **Philo Judaeus** and Flavius **Josephus** alike show to have been universally upheld in the **Judaism** of the first century. The reference in Timothy parallels the one in Corinthians, with the same catalogue of evil-doers who are deserving of ostracism and punishment. For fundamentalists the sanctions expressed in these passages are absolute and beyond question, while the liberal Christian would seek to "reinterpret the Bible in the light of contemporary knowledge," and the gay Christian advocate must use every exegetical stratagem at his disposal to excise the offending texts from the canon of authority.

Apart from this standard group of three passages, the references to "dogs" in Paul and in Revelations 21:8 and 22:15 are probably not allusions to the *kelebh,* the Canaanite and Phoenician hierodule who prostituted himself in honor of Astarte. The story of the Centurion's servant in Matthew 8:5–13 and Luke 7:1–10 may suggest a pederastic relationship, since the servant "who was dear (*entimos*) unto him" may have been both orderly and bed partner. But the emotional or physical overtones of the tale are less important than Jesus' remark that "I have not found so great faith, no, not in Israel," which foreshadows the conversion of the Roman Empire alongside the rejection of the new faith by Jewry. The "**beloved disciple**" in the Gospel of John alone is sometimes, usually not in a pious vein, asserted to have been a youth for whom Jesus' love was tantamount to a Greek pederastic attachment of the mentor to his protégé.

An eighteenth-century manuscript recently discovered and published by Morton Smith includes a passage that refers to the "young man having a linen cloth cast about his naked body," amplifying Mark 14:51–52, with the innuendo that Jesus had an homoerotic relationship with this otherwise mysterious disciple as well.

So the New Testament references to homosexuality fully echo the Judaic origins of primitive **Christianity**, even if the customs of the Hellenic world occasionally emerge from the backdrop of the narrative. These passages indicate that the primitive Church implicitly ratified Leviticus 18 and made its strictures part of its own constitution (Acts 15:20, 29). In due time the sexual morality of Hellenistic Judaism, interpreted in a rigoristic and even ascetic manner, became normative for Christian civilization.

BIBLIOGRAPHY. Tom Horner, *Homosexuality and the Judeo-Christian Tradition: An Annotated Bibliography,* Metuchen, NJ: Scarecrow Press, 1981; idem, *Jonathan Loved David: Homosexuality in Biblical Times,* Philadelphia: Westminster, 1978; Robin Scroggs, *The New Testament and Homosexuality: Contextual Background for Contemporary Debate,* Philadelphia: Fortress Press, 1983; Morton Smith, *Clement of Alexandria and a Secret Gospel of Mark,* Cambridge: Harvard University Press, 1973.

Tom Horner and Ward Houser

NEW YORK CITY

Settled by the Dutch in 1624 and acquired by the English in 1667, the New York colony (unlike most other American colonies) lacked the character of a religious haven; its emphasis was overtly commercial from the start. After American Independence (1783), the city became the major port of entry for millions of immigrants, chiefly European, some of each ethnic group staying behind to establish the city's cosmopolitan society. Given this demography, it would be expected that its gay **subculture** would be largely European in type, as it was—though with significant modifications for local conditions. In modern times, New York and **San Francisco** vied for leadership of the American gay subculture.

Colonial Times. Dutch Roman law punished sodomy with death, and cases are recorded from 1646, 1658, and 1660. After the English conquest a new capital statute was enacted in 1665, but it seems rarely to have been enforced. Lord Edward Cornbury, governor of New York and New Jersey in 1702–08, had a penchant for women's clothing, but appears to have been entirely heterosexual.

The Nineteenth Century. The newly independent American states were spared the recrudescence of antisodomy bigotry that disfigured Britain during the Napoleonic wars, and for the first seven decades of the nineteenth century, New York City's homosexuals seem to have been largely left alone. There were two competing and somewhat ineffectual police forces, which were not proactive, which is to say they undertook no entrapment, raids, or other activity to bring sodomites to justice, unless the matter was brought to their attention in an unavoidable way. Thus in 1846 a man was prosecuted for making lewd advances to a police officer. As we know from Horatio **Alger**'s novels, the streets were full of footloose teenage boys, a constant temptation for some. Churches, which were generally kept open and relatively dark, seem to have been a regular place of assignation. Walt **Whitman**'s laconic diary entries give evidence of one man's pursuit of ephebic sex objects.

After the Civil War this easy-going atmosphere changed. The social purity and censorship movements put pressure on public authorities to "clean up" America's cities. The importation of recent European ideas about "inverts" and "degenerates" increased the glare of publicity, provoking the indignation of the respectable. At the same time, New York City developed a vibrant **bohemian** and entertainment subculture. As a result of vice investigations of the 1890s, we know of such establishments as the Golden Rule Pleasure Club, Manilla Hall, Paresis Hall, The Palm, the Black Rabbit, Little Bucks, and the Artistic Club. Some of these places were essentially male brothels, while others offered drinks and entertainment. In the Bowery and lower Broadway areas, the streets were cruised by aggressive male hustlers, identifiable by their painted faces and red ties.

The Twentieth Century. The first two decades of the twentieth century were the original heyday of Greenwich Village as a cultural center and also as a place of some toleration for lesbians and gay men. Others preferred to visit the nightspots in Harlem, which was also the scene of a major black intellectual movement with several significant gay and bisexual participants: the **Harlem Renaissance**. Among the notables who enlivened New York during these years were Djuna **Barnes**, Willa **Cather**, Hart **Crane**, Marsden **Hartley**, and Edna St. Vincent **Millay**. At this time the modern gay **bar** and **bathhouse** began to take shape. For the bars, however, Prohibition (1919–1933) meant devastation, though some gay bars continued as speakeasies. An unintended consequence of the legal change was to make gay and straight bars more similar, since both were now invested with the same atmosphere of clandestinity. Until the rise of the American gay liberation movement, the gay bar represented the premier institution—virtually the only institution—for male homosexuals. In the late 1930s, however, a kind of satellite appeared in the summer **resorts** on Fire Island, notably the all-gay village of Cherry Grove.

As the country veered away from Prohibition attitudes in the 1930s, bars became legal but subject to supervision, in New York by the State Liquor Authority. This agency could revoke the licence of any tavern for permitting "degenerate disorderly conduct," and campaigns of particular virulence were waged in 1939 and in the early 1960s, in order to sanitize the city for the two world's fairs. With a sword of Damocles hanging over them, so to speak, bar owners themselves tried to keep "obvious" types and behavior at a minimum. Dancing and kissing, though they sometimes occurred, were particularly liable to bring down the wrath of the public guardians. In addition, many bars were owned or partially controlled by organized crime, while payoffs to the police were de rigueur. This tyrannical situation in the bars was finally ended by the New York Mattachine Society and the election of John Lindsay as Mayor in 1965.

From the late 1940s to the early 1960s an average of at least a thousand men were arrested annually on solicitation charges, which were usually occasioned by police entrapment. Public dislike and fear of homosexuals continued to be fanned by campaigns in the tabloid press; the first major series occurred in 1892, and such yellow journalism was often repeated on the eve of municipal elections.

The Gay Movement and New Visibility. After World War II New York was the scene of a proto-gay rights organization, the Veterans Benevolent Association (chartered in 1948). But the real gay **movement** came to New York from California in the form of the **Mattachine Society** (1955). Other groups followed, including a chapter of **ONE**, the West Side Discussion Group, a chapter of Daughters of **Bilitis**, and the **Student** Homophile League, which established chapters at Columbia (1966) and New York (1967) universities. These groups began meeting together in 1964, sponsoring demonstrations and conferences, and eventually coalescing into the East Coast Homophile Organizations (ECHO). In the 1960s the increasing efforts by Mayor Robert Wagner, Jr., and others to repress homosexuals and homosexual behavior collided with a mood of intransigence and rebellion heightened by outrage against the Vietnam War. The result was the 1969 **Stonewall Rebellion**, in which a huge crowd of angry gay people imprisoned the police for a time in a bar in Greenwich Village. This landmark event,

commemorated each year in marches or parades on the last Sunday in June in New York City and throughout the world, led to a heady but turbulent period. A New **Left** organization, the Gay Liberation Front, elbowed the Mattachine Society out of the limelight, only to be itself replaced by the single-issue Gay Activists Alliance, which promoted the **lambda** symbol. Disputes among gay leaders and entrenched opposition by old-line politicians were to delay the passage of a gay rights bill in the city council until 1986. In 1973 the Gay Academic Union was founded, holding a series of annual conferences that promoted a comprehensive sense of gay studies. Contributions from the many homosexual and lesbian artists resident in New York led to its flourishing as a gay cultural center, notable for a strong presence in **theatre**, **film**, popular **music**, visual **arts**, and literature. In different ways Frank **O'Hara** and Andy **Warhol** had influential roles in **poetry** and painting, while gay **novelists** banded together to form the Violet Quill Club.

As a result of gay political activity and legal pressure, an atmosphere of unprecedented openness, almost a continuous carnival, developed in the 1970s. Bathhouses, backroom bars, clubs such as the Mine Shaft, and even open-air places of sexual encounter attracted a national and international clientele of tourists seeking a gay Mecca—a title that New York disputed with San Francisco.

In the 1980s, however, increasing awareness of the city's many social problems, together with the **AIDS** crisis, dimmed this festive atmosphere, and New York's gay and lesbian leaders settled into the slower and more arduous task of community building. A persistent problem is that because of the high degree of stratification and social distance which the gay community shares with the larger New York City society, no organization bringing together the leadership of all the diverse groups has been able to survive.

New York City as Pioneer. Significant firsts in gay history that New York claims are the publication of Donald Webster Cory's *The Homosexual in America* (New York: Greenberg, 1951); the beginning of the homophile phase of the man–boy love movement in the United States with the publication of J. Z. Eglinton's *Greek Love* (New York: Oliver Layton Press, 1964); the founding of the Student Homophile League at Columbia University by Stephen Donaldson (1966); the opening in November 1967 of the Oscar Wilde Memorial Bookshop, the first to be devoted solely to gay/lesbian books, by Craig Rodwell, who had earlier organized a gay youth group; the Stonewall Rebellion (June 1969); the founding of the Gay Liberation Front (July 1969); the founding of Gay Activists Alliance (December 1969); the first Gay Pride March [simultaneously with Los Angeles] (June 1970); the launching of the Gay Academic Union at John Jay College (1973); the founding of the National Gay Task Force (1974); the establishment of Gay Men's Health Crisis (1981); the founding of Gay and Lesbian Alliance Against Defamation (1985); the founding of ACT UP [AIDS Coalition To Unleash Power] (1987); the Stonewall commemorative postal cancellation initiated by Warren Johansson (1989).

Wayne R. Dynes

NICOLSON, HAROLD (1886–1968)

British diplomat, gardener, publisher, and prolific writer of biographies, diaries, and letters. Born into the British diplomatic service (in Teheran, where he would later serve), Nicolson helped write the Balfour Declaration during World War I, and was a junior adviser (along with John Maynard **Keynes**) at the Paris Peace Conference which launched the League of Nations. In his spare time Nicolson wrote popular biographies of **Byron**, Swinburne, and **Verlaine**. In 1929 he retired to write for the *Evening Standard*, published by Lord Beaverbrook, and to create formal gardens.

Nicolson met Vita **Sackville-West** in 1910, and married her in 1913. Both had a series of homosexual affairs with persons of their own station, in marked contrast with the British upper-class pattern of seeking proletarian homosexual partners. Nicolson's liaisons with younger aristocrats were emotionally cooler than his wife's passions for Virginia **Woolf** and Violet Trefusis. He was quite devoted to her, while she was less promiscuous than he and more devoted to the women she loved than to her husband. Their third-born son published Vita's account of their open marriage and her unhappy affair with Violet Trefusis in 1973.

BIBLIOGRAPHY. Nigel Nicolson, *Portrait of a Marriage*, London: Weidenfeld & Nicolson, 1973.

Stephen O. Murray

NORTH AFRICA
See **Africa, North**.

NOVELS AND SHORT FICTION

Fiction in the form of novels and short stories ranks as a particularly characteristic feature of modern imaginative life, continuing to flourish even in an era dominated by electronic entertainment. Gay and lesbian characters and situations sometimes appear in mainstream novels whose major context is heterosexual. Less well known to the general public is the "gay novel," a modest though surprisingly hardy variant. Few works of this type have garnered acclaim as masterworks, and gay/lesbian novels are perhaps best regarded as forming a genre, such as **mystery** or **science-fiction**.

Classical Antiquity. As a literary category the novel was a late-comer in ancient **Greece**, becoming popular only in the second century B.C. Achilles Tatius' romance *The Adventures of Leucippe and Clitophon* mingles heterosexual and homosexual episodes with nonchalant impartiality, though Longus' *Daphnis and Chloe* is less favorable to male same-sex love. A proto-science-fiction story, the *True History* of **Lucian** of Samosata, tells of a man who voyaged to the moon, where he found an all-male society in which offspring emerged from plants. Finding favor with the king, the hero was invited to marry his son.

A major landmark is the Latin *Satyricon* of **Petronius** Arbiter (first century of our era), which recounts the picaresque adventures of Encolpius (the narrator) and his boyfriend Giton in southern Italy. The present fragments, running to some 160 pages in modern editions, are believed to amount to only a tenth of the original, which would have been a work of almost Proustian scope.

From the Middle Ages to the French Revolution. The medieval legend of *Amis and Amile* is a tale of intense male bonding of two devoted friends, the **David and Jonathan** of their age. To save his friend from leprosy, the other agreed to slay his own two children. However, after he made the sacrifice they were miraculously restored to life.

The **Renaissance** revival of ancient models paved the way for the bawdy novel of early modern times, diffused by the printing press, though often clandestinely. With its great pioneering figure of **Aretino** at the head, **Venice** early took the lead. Here the homosexual classic is the mid-seventeenth-century *L'Alcibiade fanciullo a scola* (Alcibiades the Schoolboy), attributed to Antonio Rocco. This little book is a plea for pederasty that takes the form of a conversation between the young Alcibiades and his lustful teacher. A work that belongs in a class of its own is *La Cazzaria* of the Sienese Antonio Vignali ("Arsiccio Intronato," 1501–59), which presents a series of playful fantasias on a variety of sexual subjects. In France Nicolas Chorier took the lead in his *De arcanis amoris et Veneris* (ca. 1658), which, though primarily heterosexual, has both lesbian and male homosexual passages. In order to avoid repercussions, Chorier disguised his book as the product of a Spanish woman author as adapted by a Dutch Latinist. A disapproving, voyeuristic homosexual episode appears in John Cleland's *Memoirs of a Woman of Pleasure* ("Fanny Hill," 1748–49), and in *Roderick Random* (1748) Tobias Smollett includes two unmistakably homosexual characters, Lord Strutwell and Captain Whiffle, both presented negatively.

The French eighteenth century, combining the **Enlightenment** with libertine trends, saw a plentiful production of erotic literature, most of it heterosexual. Only in the last decade of the century were the pansexual works of the Marquis de **Sade** published, as well as Denis Diderot's *La Religieuse*, which concerns lesbianism inside a convent.

The Nineteenth Century. Through the nineteenth century a copious flow of clandestine erotic novels appeared for the well-heeled purchaser. Near the century's beginning is a lurid novel *Gamiani* (1833), attributed to Alfred de Musset, that features lesbianism. At its end is the still mysterious English *Teleny* (1893), about a gay Hungarian pianist. A mainstream author, Honoré de **Balzac**, left an example of a noteworthy homosexual character, Vautrin, embedded in his vast tapestry, *La Comédie humaine*. The secret of the character is that he does not love women, but his homosexuality is woven skillfully into the fabric of the narrative, as Balzac had mastered the technique of suggesting in an unobtrusive manner the erotic motives and actions of the subject. Balzac was also aware of the political dimension of homosexuality, of the "freemasonry of love" that it represented.

The end of the century saw a greater flow of relevant works, though the authors still had to tread a careful path to avoid prosecution for pornography. Catulle Mendès' *Mephistophéla* offers a broad panorama of lesbian life, though inscribed in a judgmental framework. The mystic Joséphin **Péladan**, leader of the Rose+Croix group, gave novelistic form to his obsession with androgyny in *L'androgyne* and *La gynandre* (both 1891). From a literary point of view, probably the finest work of the decade is *Escale-Vigor* (1899) by the Belgian writer Georges Eekhoud, which concerns the love of a Flemish nobleman for a middle-class youth.

The Modern French Achievement. In the early years of the twentieth century Marcel **Proust** took up the challenge of the great French novelists of the past: his vast *A la recherche du temps perdu* includes extensive male homosexual and lesbian materials refracted in a special concept of love. For his younger contemporary, André **Gide**, the pivotal novel is *The Counterfeiters* (1926), though his autobiographical works surpass his fiction in frankness. Although she wrote also about heterosexuality, the lesbian counterpart to these giants is **Colette**, who drew upon her experiences at school and on the Parisian stage. Her friend Jean **Cocteau** was multitalented, but could not concentrate his gifts in a single masterwork. Marcel **Jouhandeau** and Julien Green (the latter a gallicized American) have been much preoccupied with religion and homosexuality. A place apart belongs to the searing novels of Jean **Genet**, which reflect his experiences among the underclass—on the road and in **prison**. Marguerite **Yourcenar**, who spent many years in the United States, has preferred male-homosexual themes to lesbian ones.

After a hiatus in the wake of World War II, a new crop of French writers has confronted gay themes. By all odds the leader is Michel Tournier, the author of intricately wrought philosophical fables. Other significant French gay novelists of the late twentieth century are Renaud Camus, Tony Duvert, Dominique Fernandez, and Yves Navarre. Among lesbian novelists Monique Wittig stands out for her formal innovations reflecting French and American feminism.

Germany and Austria. The distinguished Austrian writer Robert Musil produced a novel based on his military school experiences, *Young Törless* (1906), that shows the exploitation of a vulnerable, effeminate boy by two bullies. Using the pseudonym of Sagitta, the German anarchist theorist John Henry **Mackay** wrote what was probably the first completely sympathetic novel of boy-love, *Fenny Skaller* (1913). In 1926 "Sagitta" published *Der Puppenjunge* (The Hustler) which details the milieu of boy prostitutes in Berlin in the 1920s.

Thomas **Mann**, a Nobel prize winner, was much troubled by his homosexual side, to which he succeeded in giving powerful artistic form in his novella *Death in Venice* (1912), which depicts the downfall of an aging writer who falls in love with a beautiful Polish boy. His son Klaus **Mann** was entirely homosexual, and all his novels deal with the matter either directly or indirectly. Like the Manns, Hans Siemsen found it necessary to emigrate because of his anti-Nazi opinions. The journals *Der Eigene* and *Der Kreis* offered opportunities for lesser German-speaking gay writers to publish short fiction. Not well known outside of Germany, Bruno **Vogel** combined explicit, positive homosexuality with socialist–anarchist politics as seen in his antiwar novel *Alf* (1929). The lesbian novelist Anna Elisabet **Weihrauch** produced a panorama of German lesbian life in her *Skorpion* (1919–21). Christa Winslow's *The Child Manuela* (1931) has been repeatedly filmed as *Mädchen in Uniform*. Hermann Broch, considered by some as one of Europe's great modern novelists, completed his *The Death of Vergil* (1946) while in exile in America.

Bridging the war years was the pacifist Hans Henny **Jahnn**, who was based in Hamburg. Now recognized as a major figure is another Hamburg writer, Hubert **Fichte**, who explored themes relating to the counterculture and the Third World. Alexander Ziegler's message novel of gay emancipation, *Die Konsequenz* (1975) was made into a film. Other contemporary German writers of note include Guido Bachmann, Friedrich Kröhnke, and Martin Sperr.

Britain. As Henry Spencer Ashbee has remarked about erotic literature, "The English nation possesses an ultra-squeamishness and hyper-prudery peculiar to itself, sufficient alone to deter any author of position and talent from taking in hand so tabooed a subject." In the wake of the Oscar **Wilde** trials this caveat applied particularly to homosexual literature. E. M. **Forster** wrote his homosexual novel *Maurice* in 1913, but showed it only to a few friends; the book was not published until 1971. In 1928 Radclyffe **Hall**, an established writer since before World War I, created an enormous furor with her lesbian novel *The Well of Loneliness.* Although Virginia **Woolf**'s novel of androgyny *Orlando* (also 1928) was about her lover Vita **Sackville-West**, the tale was so fantastic that no one seemed to mind. Similarly, Ronald **Firbank**'s *Concerning the Eccentricities of Cardinal Pirelli* (1926) was done in such a coy and gossamer style of high camp that it could hardly give offense. Compton Mackenzie's *Vestal Fire* (1927) paints a delightful picture, based in part on the doings of Count **Adelswärd Fersen**, of the international set on the island of Capri. In the 1930s Christopher **Isherwood** included homosexual motifs in his Berlin stories, but carefully "balanced" with heterosexual material.

Only after World War II did this situation begin to change—though censorship kept out many foreign writings on homosexuality even into the 1980s. Mary **Renault**, who specialized in writing about male homosexual experience, began her career with a wartime novel, *The Charioteer*, in 1953; she soon switched to historical novels about ancient Greece which enjoyed a popular following among gay readers throughout the English-speaking world. Perhaps the best-known of these are *The Last of the Wine* (1956), set in the Athens of the Peloponnesian War, and the second of her books on Alexander the Great, *The Persian Boy* (1972).

Leading British middle-brow authors, such as Angus Wilson (*Hemlock and After*, 1952) and Iris Murdoch (*The Bell*, 1958; and *A Fairly Honourable Defeat*, 1970), presented sympathetic homosexual characters in a context of social comedy. The coming of gay liberation created a larger market, but the new gay writers were characteristically traditionalist: among the best are David Galloway, Adam Mars-Jones, David Rees, and David Watmough. Alan Hollinghurst's *The Swimming Pool Library* (1988) earned widespread admiration for its poignant contrast between the sexual-revolution era and pre-1969 oppression.

Other Countries. The fall of Mussolini opened Italian literature to foreign influences, especially American ones. The realistic novelists Alberto Moravia and his wife Elsa Morante have both treated homosexuality, though it is not their main theme. A small masterpiece is Giorgio Bassani's *The Gold-Rimmed Spectacles* (1958), which shows the dovetailing of **homophobia** and **anti-Semitism** at the end of the 1930s. The homosexual Pier Paolo **Pasolini**, later better known as a filmmaker, wrote frank treatments of Roman proletarian life, as well as pederastic sketches, which were published only after his death. The reception of French influences led to a new experimentalism in the Italian gay novel, as seen in the work of Mario Appignano, Francesco Merlini, Pier Vittorio Tondelli, and Dario Trento. Aldo Busi, author of *The Standard Life of a Temporary Pantyhose Salesman* (1985), ranks as a writer of European stature.

In the Russia of the Silver Age Mikhail **Kuzmin** produced *Wings* (1906), a delicately etched portrait of a young man's gradual self-understanding. The great Dutch novelist Louis **Couperus**, wrote two relevant historical novels, *De Berg van*

Licht (1905), on the Emperor **Heliogabalus,** and *De komedianten* (1917). His contemporary Jacob Israel de **Haan** wrote the realistic *Pijpelijntjes* (1904), commenting on the homosexual scene of the day. After World War II, Gerard Reve repeatedly scandalized the Dutch public with his frank novels, featuring sardonic wit and a mixture of gay liberation and Catholicism. The Dane Herman **Bang's** *Mikaël* (1904) is a sensitive portrait of artistic circles that a decade later was made into the first gay film. Pre-Meiji Japan had an extensive tradition of gay **samurai** stories, as exemplified by the prolific **Saikaku** Ihara. After World War II, the spectacular **Mishima** Yukio produced two sardonic portraits of Japanese gay life: *Confessions of a Mask* and *Forbidden Colors.*

An early standard bearer in Latin America was Brazilian Adolfo Caminha's *Bom Crioulo* (1895), concerning the tragic love of a black sailor for a white cabin boy. Since World War II the emergence of a vibrant gay scene in **Brazil** has nourished a number of fiction writers, including Gasparino Damata, Caio Fernando Abreu, Aguinaldo Silva, Edilberto Coutinho, and Darcy Penteado. Several little known Spanish-speaking writers treated same-sex themes, including Enrique Gómez-Carrillo and Rafael Arévalo Martínez (both Guatemala), Augusto D'Halmar (Chile), and Porfirio Barba-Jacob (Colombia). Since its publication in Havana in 1966, José **Lezama Lima's** *Paradiso* has been recognized as a Proustian masterpiece and translated into many languages. The Argentinian Manuel Puig's *Kiss of the Spider Woman*, about two men in a jail cell, has been turned into a notable film. In Spain the openly gay Juan Goytisolo has established himself as a major writer.

French-speaking Canada has produced a number of distinguished gay and lesbian writers (*see* **Quebec**). In 1986 Scott Symons, born in Toronto, published *Helmet of Flesh*, offering a vision of culture shock in Morocco that mingles reality and fantasy. Australia's Patrick White, author of *The Twyburn Affair* (1980), received the Nobel Prize in literature in 1973.

Wayne R. Dynes

The Gay American Novel. Homosexuality as an explicit subject appears relatively late in American fiction, though much has been made of homoerotic themes which critics have found in works by Herman **Melville** (*Billy Budd* and *Moby-Dick*), James Fenimore Cooper, Mark Twain (*Huckleberry Finn*), and Henry **James.** Not until the 1899 publication of Alfred J. Cohen's *A Marriage Below Zero* was explicit homosexuality the central theme of an American novel. Cohen, concerned that a lack of information about homosexuality was leading young women into marriages with homosexuals, also established the tradition of ending the major homosexual character's life with suicide.

In 1908 Edward I. Prime-**Stevenson** ("Xavier Mayne") published the first positive picture of homosexuality, *Imre: a Memorandum.* Also a distinguished scholar of the field, Prime-Stevenson believed homosexuality congenital but found justification in achievements by many homosexuals in history. After much hiding and self-doubt, his lovers find true and lasting bliss, but probably only a few people read this privately printed book. Before 1920, Henry Blake **Fuller's** *Bertram Cope's Year* (published in 1919) is the only other example of an American novel with explicit homosexuality as a theme.

The 1920s showed little further development, but in 1931 Blair Niles wrote *Strange Brother*; attempting to be comprehensive and sympathetic, she achieved a result that is mainly of use in understanding contemporary ideas and for a glimpse of the homosexual subculture in New York. Two other novels of the thirties, *Butterfly Man* and *Twilight Men*, offer a less clinical picture of gay lifestyles, but in both suicide is still the fate of the protagonists. The anonymous "underground" novel *Scarlet Pansy* satirized many of the prevalent negative views of homosexuality, but also ends with the death of the hero.

Two exceptions to the generally bleak picture of homosexuality in this decade are the sentimental *Better Angel* by "Richard Meeker" (Forman Brown) and the campy bohemian novel *The Young and Evil* by Charles Henri Ford and Parker Tyler. While around a dozen novels treated homosexuality as a major theme between the wars, none of them was written by a major novelist.

In the years immediately following World War II (1946–50), the dam of silence was clearly collapsing, with numerous works, some by renowned writers, making an impact on the American market. First-hand information about the sexual habits of males in an all-male environment seems to have influenced many of the authors, and about half the novels deal with war or military experiences. James Jones, often acclaimed as the leading American war novelist, described homosexuality in the peacetime army in *From Here to Eternity* (1951); eleven years later Jones gave a sympathetic account of "situational homosexuality" in the combat zone in *The Thin Red Line*.

The most famous novel of this period (and probably the first novel with homosexuality as a major theme to reach general circulation) was Gore Vidal's 1948 *The City and the Pillar*. The author's later outspoken positive ideas on homosexuality are barely visible in this early work; none of the gay characters is able to find lasting love or emotional fulfillment, but at least suicide is avoided. Other major writers employing homosexual characters or themes include Norman Mailer, Truman **Capote**, John Horn **Burns**, and Vance Bourjailly. The first novels to discuss homosexual problems as a result of intolerance appear at this time and include Richard Brooks' *The Brick Foxhole* and Ward Thomas' remarkable *Stranger in the Land* (1949), in which homophobia is com-

pared to racism and anti-Semitism. Pseudo-Freudian views can be seen in Isabel Bolton's *The Christmas Tree* and Michael DeForrest's *The Gay Year*. James Barr's 1950 *Quatrefoil* has remained popular in the gay subculture as an idealized picture of a gay relationship, though its depiction of homosexuality is less positive than appears at first glance. None of these works seems very enlightened by the standards of two or three decades later, but they represented a great advance in tolerance at the time.

In the fifties, with its political conservatism (Senator Joseph McCarthy was linking homosexuality with Communism) and high regard for **Freudian concepts**, fiction about homosexuality is less salient and less positive. The subject is exploited as titillation in Meyer Levin's *Compulsion* and Allen Drury's *Advise and Consent*. Only James **Baldwin** in *Giovanni's Room* and Christopher **Isherwood** (a British expatriate) made homosexuality a main theme.

The dominant psychiatric view of homosexuality as an illness led to a prevalence of novels ending in suicide or death such as Fritz Peter's *Finistère*, Oakley Hall's *The Corpus of Joe Bailey*, and the Baldwin work. The best example of this tendency can be found in Jean Evans' *Three Men*, which was used in psychology classes in some universities. So dominant were these views that only Isherwood, Vidal, and **counterculture** writers such as Paul **Goodman** and William Burroughs were able to avoid them. Burroughs, a member of the **beat** writers group, wrote a series of phantasmagoric novels which included nearly pornographic descriptions of male homosexuality. His best-known work, *Naked Lunch* (1959), was the subject of obscenity trials in the early 1960s.

The social changes which swept through the American landscape in the sixties brought about a major liberalization and extension of treatments of homosexuality in fiction. Early in the decade, Isherwood wrote *Down There on a Visit* and *A Single Man*, both treating homosexuality as an ordinary alternative lifestyle. Baldwin's *Another Country* (1962) was more positive than his work from the fifties. John Rechy's *City of Night* (1963) carried much of the old negative baggage, but it presented an honest and insightful look into the seamier side of gay life, with its theme of male prostitution. By 1968, Vidal's *Myra Breckinridge* showed a radical view of acceptance, while many minor novels served to convey the varied sociology of gay life.

When the fiction of the seventies caught up with the gay liberation movement, major works for a general reading public such as Patricia Nell Warren's 1974 book, *The Front Runner*, and Laura Z. Hobson's *Consenting Adult* began to reflect a view that equated homosexual with heterosexual behavior and depicted problems as owing to social intolerance. By the end of the decade, homosexual themes appeared in such genres as **mystery**, humor, and **science fiction**, while styles varied from the elegant symbolism of Edmund White to explicit realism and literary quality ranged from the highly literate to gross pornography. By 1978, two novels which expressed negative views, Larry Kramer's *Faggots* and Andrew Holleran's *Dancer from the Dance*, were coming under fire from many gay leaders for ideological deficiencies.

With the 1980s, bookstores catering to a gay market proliferated and with them novels with major homosexual themes. Following the lead of Joseph Hansen with his David Brandsetter mystery series, several authors began series of novels with gay detectives. Felice Picano, Paul Monette and others produced novels set in the gay community or with major gay characters. Charles Nelson made homosexuality a major theme in his Vietnam novel *The Boy Who Picked the Bullets Up*. Christopher Bram, Robert Ferro, and David Leavitt were among the authors who attracted attention for the literary quality of their work.

Most of the newer authors depict a homosexual orientation as unproblematic in itself. In general, however, the "gay" fiction of the eighties has become as diverse as the subculture and behavior it describes, making it impossible to generalize in the manner in which works of earlier decades were treated. In many ways it is melting into the general body of American fiction.

James B. Levin

The American Lesbian Novel. In the first few decades of the twentieth century the archetypal figure was the expatriate Gertrude **Stein**, who lived in Paris with her lover Alice B. Toklas. Stein's prose was too experimental and formalistic for most to make out much lesbian content, but she remained a formidable symbolic figure. Her contemporary Parisian-by-adoption, Natalie **Barney**, wrote in French. More directly related to the "lost generation" was Djuna **Barnes** who, however, returned to live in New York City; her major works were *Ladies' Almanac* (1928) and the darkly claustrophobic *Nightwood* (1936). The latter work knits together the story of five troubled characters, told from the perspective of a transvestite doctor.

The Great Depression caused a reaction against twenties preoccupations, which were seen as frivolous and decadent. Nonetheless, Gale Wilhelm published two novels in this period that address the dilemma of lesbian women: *Torchlight to Valhalla* (1935) and *We Too Are Drifting* (1938). In the first the heroine resigns herself to separation from her beloved, but in the second two women are united—an unusual ending for a novel of the period.

After World War II the spread of mass-market paperbacks led to a considerable production of lesbian pulps—some of them "lesbian trash," that is potboilers aimed at the prurient interests of straight male readers. This period nonetheless saw the start of the building of a lesbian audience which sought out the somewhat melodramatic novels of Ann Bannon and Paula Christian. A little later new standards of quality were set by May Sarton (*Mrs. Stevens Hears the Mermaids Singing*, 1965; *A Reckoning*, 1978) and Jane Rule (*Desert of the Heart*, 1964; *Contract with the World*, 1980). Sarton linked lesbianism with creativity and artistic inspiration, though her Mrs. Stevens seems to have found more fulfillment with men. With rare veracity, Rule's work portrays lesbian and gay male characters interacting with heterosexual friends. A widely read historical novel, set in early nineteenth-century America, is Isabel Miller's *Patience and Sarah* (1972; originally published in 1969 as *A Place for Us*).

Resolute lesbian feminism made a splash in Rita Mae Brown's *Rubyfruit Jungle* (1973). This book's preachy earnestness is relieved by its occasional humor, tenderness, and heartfelt anger, and it has rightly become a landmark in the field. Brown subsequently became a "cross-over" writer, gaining mainstream attention and commissions for Hollywood film scripts, but at the cost of some loss of verve. Ann Shockley pioneered in writing about the black lesbian experience, and others wrote from chicana, American Indian, and Asian points of view. Alice Walker's mainstream *The Color Purple* (1982) contrasts love between two poor southern black women with the brutality of relations with men, while Maureen Brady's less well known *Folly* of the same year deals with both black and white working-class women in a Carolina mill town. In several fast-paced novels that break new ground, Sarah Schulman has explored aspects of violence and emotion in lesbian life in the inner city.

Evelyn Gettone

The Gay/Lesbian Novel as History. Attempts to trace out a history of homosexual behavior are seriously handi-capped both by a lack of empirically valid research from earlier periods and by the taboos on the subject which have led to enormous gaps in documentation. Given such uneven, often threadbare materials to work with, historians can only rejoice in the glimpses which fiction gives us of the texture and ideational context of homosexuality in days long gone by. The efforts of novelists have bequeathed us pictures of homosexualities which no amount of culling of archival records, law cases, and polemical works can equal. They open a window to local variations and to the various mores of homosexuality in such diverse and otherwise undocumented worlds as ancient **Rome** and medieval **Japan**, Renaissance **Venice** and Fascist **Italy**, 1930s **Berlin** and turn-of-the-century Amsterdam. They portray the homosexuality of soldiers and junkies, street hustlers and pederasts, black women and prisoners, wooden-ship sailors and military-academy schoolboys. They shed light on the subjective as well as objective realities faced by homosexuals of many times and cultures in ways that no social scientist can hope to match.

Conclusion. The great variety of novels and short fiction that treat male homosexuality and lesbianism gives the impression of almost limitless horizons. Yet reflection suggests that the achievement of this body of work depends upon a complex network of publishers, editors, critics, and bookstores. In the past this network often operated to shift narratives into a negative key as authors scrambled to "play the game" by satisfying the changing demands of the gatekeepers of the book world. Today such publishers as Alyson, Gay Sunshine Press, and Naiad Press in the United States, Gay Men's Press (GMP) in England, Persona in France, and Rosa Winkel Verlag in Germany assure an alternative to mainstream publishing houses. The many gay and lesbian periodicals provide reviews, and specialized bookstores make the fiction available. Although such specialization has often been decried, this infrastructure assures that gay and lesbian creativity will not be constricted by hostile or indifferent outsiders.

Stephen Donaldson

BIBLIOGRAPHY. Roger Austen, *Playing the Game: The Homosexual Novel in America*, Indianapolis: Bobbs-Merrill, 1977; Jeannette H. Foster, *Sex Variant Women in Literature*, 3d ed., Tallahassee: Naiad Press, 1985; Francesco Gnerre, *L'eroe negato*, Milan: Gammalibri, 1981; Barbara Grier, *The Lesbian in Literature*, Tallahassee: Naiad Press, 1981; James Levin, *The Gay Novel*, New York: Irvington Press, 1983; Jane Rule, *Lesbian Images*, Garden City, NY: Doubleday, 1975; Ian Young, *The Male Homosexual in Literature*, 2nd ed., Metuchen, NJ: Scarecrow, 1982.

NUDE IN ART, THE

As an art form the monumental nude was perfected by the Greeks in the fifth century B.C. It was, and remains, one of the major vehicles for the realization of the concept of beauty in art. Commonly the nude is automatically equated with the female nude, despite the relatively recent origin of this predominance.

Classical Antiquity and the Middle Ages. The beginning of the sixth century B.C. saw the realization of the Dorian concept of the nude youth in the *kouros* type. Only later, toward the middle of the century, did the female counterpart, the *kore*, appear. Developing in the Ionic sphere, the *kore* is finer, lighter, and—clothed. The male statues, conveniently termed Apollos, are the primordial expression of the young male body, forming an essential component of the art of ancient **Greece** from the Archaic period until the end. Stemming from a society in which young men regularly exercised naked, in the **gymnasium** and at athletic competitions, they incarnate the most cherished ideals of the Greeks. The flowering of the male nude in Greek art (sixth–fifth century B.C.) was situated during the period in which the **pederastic** institution was at its height. Moreover, the depiction of homosexual relations in Greek **vases** occurred mainly between 570 and 470 B.C., constituting, together with statuary, the fullest repertoire of nudes surviving from classical antiquity.

A radical break took place in the **Hellenistic** period, in which large monarchies replaced the earlier city-states. Formed in association with the city-state tradition of citizen participation, the classic ethos of earlier times became increasingly less satisfying and less relevant for the average Greek. Women demanded more personal freedom, while at the same time seeking to bind men to their family duties. New phenomena, including the growing **Stoic** flight from the world, a contrasting **Epicurean** quest for creature comforts, sophisticated cosmopolitanism, and the rising mystery cults, made their appearance. In this atmosphere, it is not surprising that pederasty lost its sociocultural centrality, becoming more and more a matter of personal preference. In the fourth century B.C. themes of female beauty and heterosexual love made their way into poetry. The appearance and increasing popularity of the nude Aphrodite symbolized the considerable social and psychological changes. Sculptors sought to endow their figures with human passions: joy, sorrow, anger, despair. The development of the male nude shows a tendency to polarization, so that the figures are either too virile or too effeminate.

In the Middle Ages the male nude underwent a kind of etherealization. The Crucified Christ is a symbol of suffering, passion, abnegation, and death. The contrast with classical antiquity could scarcely be greater.

The Renaissance Tradition. The **Renaissance** rediscovery of the ideas and values of antiquity created an inexhaustible source for artistic creation. The male nude body claimed a central place and, especially in fifteenth-century **Florence**, reclaimed its status as an aesthetic object; in this climate outstanding figures were created, studied, and judged. Several factors contributed to this development. First is the relation between the male body and architecture, which goes back to the Greeks. They were the first to develop post-and-lintel architecture based on the archetype of the male body. The vision of the male body as an architectural form depended on a system of proportion. The male body, with its clear relationships among the various component parts, can itself be viewed as a kind of post-and-lintel architecture. The nude **David**, as seen in works by **Donatello** and **Michelangelo**, was popular for another reason. Thanks in large measure to the advocacy of **Ficino**, ideas of Platonic love came to be cherished in Florentine artistic and intellectual circles during the late fifteenth century. Even Greek love enjoyed a certain popularity among the elite. The mitigation of legal prosecutions for sodomy was for a time an enabling factor.

During the following century the female nude gradually came to predominate. The first artists to give the female nude pride of place in their work were the early sixteenth-century Venetian painters. These artists preferred a recumbent Venus—simultaneously vulnerable and inaccessible—to a standing David. The nude female body was easily assimilated to the soft contours and valleys of a verdant landscape, where each part readily flows into another. At this same time, **Venice** pioneered in launching the tradition of the independent landscape, one that is not simply a foil for the figures. Moreover, courtesans, who were important in the social and economic life of the Adriatic city, probably played an ancillary role: the Venuses may be regarded as idealized versions of them. Three underlying factors contributed to the success of the female nude in Venetian painting. First, nudes symbolized the city's independence from the church. In comparison with neighboring lands, the Venetian republic was openly refractory with regard to the power of the church. Significantly, this type of erotic painting flourished also in conjunction with a similar spirit of independence of kings and princes with regard to the church. North of the Alps, Lucas Cranach in Germany and the School of Fontainebleau in France depicted female nudes in this political context. Secondly, for the elite these female nudes symbolized privileges not shared with the common people. Finally, the female nude was popular because their male counterparts had come to be regarded as suspect. The artistic presentation of suspect sexual preferences was something that even the most powerful rulers could not countenance, certainly not after the onset of the rigorism of the Reformation and Counterreformation. For reasons of state Venice had its own intolerance of deviant sexuality; the earliest mass campaign against sodomy is documented in the archives of the Adriatic city. These factors help to explain an epochal development: the identification of the female nude with the erotic itself. This predominance even allowed occasional presentation of scenes of female–female eroticism, as in the scenes of Diana at the bath—but only at the behest of male patrons.

Baroque, Rococo, and Neo-Classicism. In seventeenth-century art the male nude retained a major role in the form of models for the training of artists in the academies. Male models were more readily obtainable than female ones. In compositions intended for sale, however, the female nude gradually became universal as a symbol of freedom and pleasure (eroticism and sensuality). The art market, which had attained maturity in this period, seized every opportunity to promote genres: still life, landscape, portraiture, the nude. In this context the female nude became ever more common throughout western Europe.

The rococo was a style that was particularly susceptible to erotic fascination with the female body. The very creation of the rococo has been hailed as a female achievement: women painted, purchased, and collected more than ever before, as earlier in the Hellenistic period women had gained more importance in society. Toward the end of the eighteenth century there occurred a break in costume history, which J. C. Flügel characterized as the "Great Masculine Renunciation"; this change entailed a drastic reduction of decorative exuberance in male attire. The male abandoned all claims to beauty in exchange for a clothing code of "sobriety." The wish to be seen was transformed into a wish to see. Exhibitionism became a female privilege.

Nonetheless, there were some attempts to rehabilitate the male nude. Johann Joachim **Winckelmann**, the homosexual archeologist who was also an influential herald of Neo-classicism, cultivated his personal preference for the male body, making it the hallmark of a whole artistic movement—though the male nude had lost its earlier symbolic value. An effort was made to give it a new significance, resulting in nude statues of such figures as Voltaire and Napoleon, but with little success. After 1800 the nude portrait statue became an academic cliché. Nineteenth-century artists drew the male nude during their studies, but mostly chose the female nude as the major subject of their mature work. Painters such as Hans von **Marées** who emphasized the male nude were exceptional.

Toward the Present. In the twentieth century both the rise of abstract art and of photography tended to discourage a revival of the male nude. Through their tacit voyeurism, photographic nudes of the nineteenth and twentieth centuries usurped the erotic function that had previously been reserved to the fine arts. One exception was the erotic work of the American painter Charles **Demuth**, which included all-male nude bathhouse and beach scenes.

Outside the realm of art, other trends, such as dress reform, nudist colonies, body building, and sun bathing, contributed to a renewed appreciation of the beauty of the human body. The **Nazi** idealization of beautiful, healthy, and "pure" bodies fit with the claim that classic Greek beauty reached its full perfection in the Nordic race. Earlier, some of the first **photographs** of the male nude, such as those of Wilhelm von **Gloeden**, had appeared in the budding homosexual **press** of Germany. A highly ambiguous relationship existed between the Nazi male ideal and homosexuality.

Pop art of the 1950s and the **counterculture** of the sixties renewed interest in the nude male body. But the male body returned as a focus of artistic interest only in the 1970s, stimulated in part by the international homosexual **movement**. Also, feminism and the ever more numerous women artists became a major factor. Especially in photography the male nude served as a fount of inspiration. Yet even in the twentieth century the male nude caused uneasiness. The guardians of public morality regard the penis, however artfully it is presented, as more threatening than the vagina. And frontal male nudes are less acceptable than female ones.

The interest of lesbian artists in the female body is as yet insufficiently demonstrated. If they wish to give expression to their own sexuality, lesbians must first secure the necessary financial and social means. After the end of World War II women became somewhat more comfortable with investigating their own sexuality and giving it artistic value. Leonor Fini's surrealism underlines the way female desire tends not to be as passionate and outspoken as male lust. Lesbian artists who do not simply use their sexual nature as a source of inspiration, but employ it as a central focus of their work, remained the exception in the early eighties. Images of nude women could be interpreted by men—and by feminists as well—as soft-core pornography specially produced to give pleasure to the consumers.

In general the domination of the female nude began in the sixteenth century as part of a "sexualization" of the nude as an object of enjoyment. The female nude in the art of the last four centuries was viable precisely because it was an icon of male desire. With male nudes the matter is different: those that are erotic (though not openly so) seem to have flourished in periods that may be regarded as **homosocial**—classical Greece, early Renaissance Florence—or under the umbrella of trends that had a definite homoerotic aspect—Winckelmann's circle, early twentieth-century homosexual emancipation, and elements of the German right that overlapped with National Socialism.

BIBLIOGRAPHY. Kenneth Clark, *The Nude: A Study of Ideal Art*, New York: Pantheon, 1956; Emmanuel Cooper, *The Sexual Perspective: Homosexuality and Art in the Last 100 Years in the West*, London: Routledge & Kegan Paul, 1986; Edward Lucie-Smith, *The Male Nude: A Modern View*, Oxford: Phaidon, 1985; David Martocci, *The Male Nude*, Williamstown, MA: McClelland, 1980; Margaret Walters, *The Nude Male: A New Perspective*, London: Penguin, 1978.

Daniël Christiaens

OBESITY

From ancient Egyptian times onwards the appearance of being well nourished, extending to what we would call overweight, has been a sign of power and wealth. Through gargantuan feats at the table such kings as Louis VI of France and Henry VIII of England turned themselves into mountains of flesh. By contrast thinness tended to connote poverty or neurasthenia. In the nineteenth century, as food supplies became more regular and plentiful, poor people could become fat, and in consequence the rich began to prize thinness. Standards of ideal weight are therefore culturally conditioned.

In our society women are bombarded with advertising and exhortations to maintain their attractiveness by keeping thin, and fashions are designed to suit those who succeed. Predictably, some overdo it and become anorexic. While men too are enjoined to keep trim, many fail to achieve the ideal. Gay men are more successful in this struggle than straight men, and the styles they favor tend to show off slender bodies. Yet even within the overall "thinist" aesthetic there are variations. In the 1960s and early '70s an almost emaciated look prevailed, promoted by the **counterculture** and no doubt conditioned by appetite-suppressing drugs. With the increasing popularity of **gymnasia**, however, gay men began to admire a more hefty look, though one characterized by muscle rather than fat.

At the turn of the century some researchers believed that homosexual men, being in their view a third sex, tended to have broad hips. This assumption has not been statistically confirmed. More generally the German psychiatrist Ernst Kret-schmer (1888–1964) believed that a person's temperamental reaction patterns reflected physiological type, with heavy-set persons behaving in one way and slender ones another. These theories too have not found general acceptance.

On average gay men tend to be more prejudiced against obesity in their sexual partners than women, whether straight or lesbian. The sexual **advertisements** of gay papers teem with the admonition: "no fats." Still, there are a few individuals, known as chubby chasers, who admire what most reject, typically preferring partners who are over 300 pounds. People of these two complementary persuasions, the chubbies and their chasers, join Girth and Mirth clubs. In Japan travelers find that "well padded" older men are in considerably greater demand among homosexuals than in Western countries, a difference that tends to confirm the culturally determined character of the preference.

Wayne R. Dynes

OBJECTIFICATION, SEXUAL

This expression, which became popular only in the 1970s, denotes an attitude of treating others as mere vehicles for sensual or ego gratification—or simply as sexual partners—rather than as full human beings deserving of equality of respect. An individual who is so treated is a *sex object*. These terms were spread by adherents of the women's movement, who sometimes refer the phenomenon to a mental pattern which they term *objectivism*, the unwarranted assumption that male (or patriarchal) values are simply objective reality, rather than cultural constructs imposed upon it.

However this may be, the concept has been adopted by some sectors of the gay movement as a tool for internal criticism. In **bars** and other places where encounters are intended to lead to sexual contact, the treatment of other individuals as sex objects may be said to be reasonable and expected. But where this procedure passes over into business or political activity, to the point that articulate and persuasive individuals who do not happen to be goodlooking are ignored or passed over in favor of men who are "cute," this seems a waste of human resources as well a source of unhappiness to those who are the victims of it. Some critics of the pattern have proposed the alternative term *looksism* as a more convenient descriptor. A similar phenomenon, known as **ageism**, works to the disadvantage of older gay people. This overemphasis on sexual attractiveness is to some extent explainable by the fact that gays as a group are united only by their sexual preference, and by the fact that they have been stigmatized by the host society because of it. Still, to the degree that it is prevalent in gay male circles—less so in lesbian ones—it may serve to bolster **stereotypes** that gay people are superficial and frivolous.

The concept of sexual objectification has been traced to the German philosopher Immanuel Kant (1726–1804), who in his *Lectures on Ethics* presented the sexual act as the mere manipulation of an object by a subject, in effect masturbation *à deux*—unless the relationship is redeemed by the altruism of marriage. In the twentieth century, the notion of objectification has been widely diffused by Freudian psychoanalysis, where *object* may be defined in three ways: (1) the goal toward which the organism's instincts or drives are directed, be it a person, a thing, or a fantasy; (2) the focus of love or hate; and (3) that which the subject perceives and knows, in keeping with the traditional philosophy of knowledge. This analysis has the advantage of showing that confusion has been caused by conflating the neutral sense (3)—from which it follows that the very process of cognition continually and inescapably enmeshes one in subject–object relations, without thereby imposing any distorting or reductive effect—with (1) and (2), which entail a charge of emotion suffusing the object so as to enhance or demean it. Moreover, the everyday sense of the word object suggests a tendency to turn persons into things, though this is in no way required by sense (3).

While the existing terminology is not ideal, it must be conceded that the psychosocial phenomenon of sexual objectification exists, and that when it is allowed to intrude into all sorts of spheres of human activity where it is in fact dysfunctional, it may stifle the personal development of those who are subjected to it. At the same time, it is necessary to recognize that sexual selection is indeed selection, and human beings are unlikely to free themselves from this component of their phylogenetic legacy, or the ongoing physiological processes that underlie such selection. Thus the ideal of treating human beings in terms of equality of respect, discarding inappropriate sexual objectification, should be inculcated and promoted, but one should harbor no illusions about the imminence of its universal realization. This tension is one of the many complications of civilization itself.

Wayne R. Dynes

O'HARA, FRANK (1926–1966)

American poet and art critic. Raised in Worcester, Massachusetts, O'Hara served in the Navy from 1944 to 1946, and then attended Harvard and Michigan Universities. The most important experiences during his college years were probably his visits to New York, where he met a number of poets, as well as painters of the rising Abstract Expressionist school. He settled in New York in 1951, working for the Museum of Modern Art, where he organized exhibitions of contemporary art. O'Hara wrote books of art criticism (*Jackson Pollock*, 1959; *Robert Motherwell*, 1965), and also sought the collaboration of artists in his own creative endeavors. He believed that the support of painters in particular was useful to him in escaping the suffocation of the reigning academic tradition in poetry.

His plays, which were often produced in avant-garde theatres, included *Love's Labour*, *Awake in Spain!*, and *The Houses at Fallen Hanging*. He published only six small collections of poems; others were found only in letters to friends or written on a hoarded scrap of paper. During his lifetime, however, O'Hara enjoyed an extensive word-of-mouth reputation, and his inclusion in anthologies began to bring him to a wider audience. On the morning of July 24, 1966, he was accidentally struck by a beach buggy on Fire Island, the gay resort where he spent his summers, and died shortly thereafter.

Like his older contemporary Wallace Stevens, O'Hara was influenced by the French avant-garde poets; indeed his relation to his favorite painters recalls that of Guillaume Apollinaire and the Cubists. Yet O'Hara tempered his mandarin sources of inspiration with eclectic infusions of popular culture and the kaleidoscope of the New York scene. His use of everyday-speech rhythms recalls the **beat** cult of spontaneity. Less observed by many critics is the fact that many of his poems are sophisticated transcriptions of the bantering "queens' talk" common among gay men at the time. After his death O'Hara's work did much to free American poetry from the domination of a fading academic tradition. At the same time however, his fondness for ephemeral, campy, and trivial motifs restricted the scope of all but a few poems.

BIBLIOGRAPHY. Bruce Boone, "Gay Language as Political Praxis: The Poetry of Frank O'Hara," *Social Text*, 1 (1979), 59–92; Marjorie Perloff, *Frank O'Hara: Poet Among Painters*, New York: George Braziller, 1977.

Ward Houser

OLD TESTAMENT

This conventional term is the Christian name for the Hebrew Bible, which the Church incorporated into its own scriptural canon. The **New Testament** constitutes the additional scriptures of Christianity, and some churches supplement the Hebrew Bible with the Deuterocanonical (or Apocryphal) books. Jewish tradition divides the Old Testament into three parts: the Law (the first five books ascribed to Moses), the Prophets (most of the historical books and all of the prophetical writings except Daniel), and the Writings (all the other books including Daniel). For Jews it is the first five books, the Torah, that are authoritative; and in the third of these the death penalty is explicitly prescribed for male homosexuality (Leviticus 18:22 and 20:13). Although there is scant evidence for the actual enforcement of this law by Jewish courts, it is known that in later Christendom it cost the lives of thousands of homosexual men from the later **Middle Ages** to modern times.

Negative Texts. The Old Testament itself is an intricate body of literature, varied and complex; each of the literary units is a product of its own time and place, and a great deal of it is not easily understood without extensive delving into the languages and cultures of the principal nations of the ancient Near East that influenced the nascent monotheism of Israel and the later Jewish community in the Persian Empire. Genesis, the opening book, contains in chapters 18 and 19 the infamous story of **Sodom**. This narrative never actually says that the Cities of the Plain were destroyed because of homosexuality, but indicates that their sins "cried to heaven for vengeance." In the story the male inhabitants of Sodom are shown attempting to commit gang **rape** on two visitors who have taken shelter in the house of Lot, and the Biblical tradition made Sodom proverbial for its inhospitality and injustice toward strangers. For most cultures of the ancient world, according to the surviving sources, consensual homosexual activity entailed no stigma or penalty; the subject rarely finds mention unless prominent persons or extraordinary circumstances are involved. And even in such circumstances the homosexual element is not deemed worthy of emphatic mention. For example, a midrashic source tells us that Joseph in Egypt was bought by Potiphar for pederastic purposes (cf. Genesis 37:36 and 39:1). The *New English Bible* translation finds this theme explicit in the text itself, but other versions ignore it.

The outrage at Gibeah (Judges 19–21) begins, it is true, with an attempt at homosexual gang rape but is diverted into a heterosexual one in which the Levite's concubine is violated and killed. The outcome is a tribal war against the Benjaminites, who are overwhelmed and massacred. Two curious episodes in Genesis merit discussion. First, there is the epilogue to the Deluge narrative in which Ham "saw the nakedness of his father" (Genesis 9:22), an action interpreted in the Talmud as an assault on Noah's masculinity. The second is the scene in which Sarah encounters Ishmael "playing with Isaac her son" (Septuagint of Genesis 21:9), with overtones of a homosexual initiation rite. Both have puzzled or eluded modern commentators who cannot admit the overt aspects of male–male sexuality in cultures of antiquity.

Positive Figures. That Naomi and Ruth had a lesbian love affair has been, improbably, derived from the text by some (e.g., Jeannette Foster in *Sex Variant Women in Literature*, new ed., Baltimore, 1975), and the surmise that **David and Jonathan** had not merely a strong friendship but a homosexual liaison has long been popular. While it is true that Naomi and Ruth make one of the strongest declarations of fidelity ever written (Ruth 1:16–17), not much else attests the claim, since the purpose of the narrative is to authorize the acceptance of converts into the "house of Israel." In the case of the men there is more evidence. The book of Samuel relates that "Jonathan and David made a covenant because he (Jonathan) loved him as his own soul. And Jonathan stripped himself of the robe that was upon him and gave it to David, and his garments even to his sword, and to his bow, and to his belt" (I Samuel 18:3–4). From other Eastern Mediterranean heroic love affairs armor is known as a pledge of affection from the more important member of the duo to the lesser. Jonathan often speaks of his concern for David, and there is a scene of intense emotion and probably sexual release between them. After Jonathan's death David sings in his lament that Jonathan's love for him "was wonderful, passing the love of women" (II Samuel 1:26).

Modern Westerners tend to view homosexuality in other times and places in the light of the way in which it has been understood (or misunderstood) in their own culture. The Israeli anthropologist Raphael Patai cautions against such an approach, arguing that "male homosexuality was rampant in Biblical times and has so remained in the Middle East down to the present day. It may not have been as general as it was in Greece, but the folk mores certainly did not regard it with any degree of disapproval."

References to men in the ancient world who engaged in homosexual activity may generally be assigned to three categories. First of all, there was the military or virile type; such men usually bonded with another, similar male: examples are **Gilgamesh** and Enkidu, **Achilles** and Patroclus, and David and Jonathan. A second group of references mention the passive-effeminate male who took the "female" role in sexual intercourse. Such men might wear women's clothes; they might engage in sacral prostitution (the **kādēsh**) or its commercial counterpart. Other texts mention a type of male, a third type, who patronized the second category described above.

Cultic Prostitution. Difficult for the modern religious consciousness to understand is that male cult prostitutes, specifically homosexual prostitutes, with both erotic and mantic functions, were part of the religious life of Syria and Palestine, including pre-exilic Israel (i.e., from about 1200 to 587 B.C.). References to their activity are found in I Kings 14:24, 15:12, 22:46, II Kings 21:2, 21:11, 23:7, the Septuagint of II Chronicles 35. 19a, Isaiah 2.6 and Job 36:14, as well as in place names such as "En-mishpat [Spring of Judgment], which is Kadesh" (Genesis 14:7). The references in Kings cover a period of some 400 years, so that the custom survived down to the reforms of King Josiah. Ten years after his death the Temple was destroyed and the Jews were carried off into captivity in Babylon. (*See also* **Kadesh Barnea.**)

Later Prohibitions. Under Persian rule (beginning in 538 B.C.) the Jewish community reestablished itself in Palestine. The Persians proved more tolerant than previous conquerors, allowing the Jews and other subject peoples to run their own affairs, but they did not tolerate homosexuality. In the Persian period the male cult prostitutes no longer functioned in the rebuilt Temple in Jerusalem or in the province of Judea. There is good reason to assume that at this time—under the influence of **Zoroastrianism**—the verses Leviticus 18:22 and 20:13 were added to the Holiness Code of Leviticus 12–20, forbidding male homosexuality under pain of death.

All forms of male homosexual behavior were odious to later Jewish religious thinkers and apologists, both those who wrote in Hebrew or Aramaic and those, such as **Philo** and **Josephus**, who were Hellenized and composed their works in Greek. Persian rule ended with the capture of Jerusalem by **Alexander the Great** in 333; but the Greek rulers who followed him (except for Antiochus

Epiphanes in the brief period from 168–65) and the Romans in later times allowed the Jews to enforce the norms of their own cult. Hence the Levitical laws stood and became an integral part of the Judaic moral code.

There may be an allusion to the homosexual aspect of the slave trade in Joel 3:2, to homosexual rape in Lamentations 5:13 (cf. St. Jerome's version), and in other passages that have been claimed as relevant. It is safe to conclude that by the end of the Persian period **Judaism** officially reproved all expressions of male–male sexuality. Although it might be argued that some distinctly modern forms of homosexuality, including **andro-philia**, were not an issue in Old Testament times, one has no grounds to assume that they would be regarded as permissible.

BIBLIOGRAPHY. Tom Horner, *Homosexuality and the Judeo-Christian Tradition: An Annotated Bibliography*, Metuchen, NJ: Scarecrow Press, 1981; idem, *Jonathan Loved David: Homosexuality in Biblical Times*, Philadelphia: Westminster, 1978; Raphael Patai, *Sex and the Family in the Bible and the Middle East*, Garden City, NY: Doubleday, 1959.

Tom Horner and Ward Houser

OLYMPIC GAMES

For over 1000 years, the Olympic games helped mold a common Hellenic outlook linking sports and religion with the art of the great temples and statues that adorned the precincts of Olympia in the northwestern Peloponnesus.

The Olympic Games in honor of Zeus, traditionally founded in 776 B.C., were held every four years thereafter. Eusebius of Caesarea preserved Julius Africanus' list of winners from the founding to A.D. 217. It was probably the tyrant Phaidon of Argos in the seventh century who, seizing the site from the Elians (who Plato in the *Symposium* claimed practiced pederasty in a more uninhibited physical manner than did other Greeks), reorganized the games from one-day contests in track or wrestling to include chariot and horse races ("racing" in the modern sense). However, the competition between runners on foot always remained central to the games. Between 720 and 576, 46 of the 81 known Olympic winners were Spartans, but Athenian, Sicilian, and Italian Greeks as well as ones from elsewhere figure on the lists. After 472 the games lasted for five days, the boys' games (the "junior competitions") falling on the third day. Cities nobly rewarded the victors with expensive prizes, at **Athens** equaling several years' pay for a common worker, and pensions. They became heroes, they won political power and fame, and the games in some ways resembled **beauty contests**. Some victors even received divine statues after death.

All these games honored gods portrayed as pederastic from 600 B.C. The legendary *aition* (cause) of the games was a wrestling match between Heracles and Iolaus, which may be a parallel of the story of Jacob wrestling with the angel in Genesis 32:24–32—possible evidence for the origin of the contests in a northwest Semitic athletic tradition. Games were held by the Phrygians and by the Homeric heroes where they pulled each other down by the belt in wrestling—proving that they competed while clothed. Elsewhere men and boys competed in the nude and women were unequivocally barred from attendance, even as spectators. It was, however, a myth that Orisippus of Megara, a runner in the twentieth Olympiad in 720 B.C., accidentally lost his tunic and thus introduced nudity; it was imported from **Crete** ca. 600 B.C. Once an *erastes* (senior lover) rushed up to embrace his bloodied teenaged *eromenos* (beloved), who had emerged victor in the *pankrateia*, a sort of free-style boxing match and roughest of the five main competitions.

The Olympics were more prestigious than their competitors. The Isthmian Games, where wreaths of cedar leaves were the prize, held every four years at Corinth in honor of Poseidon, owed their origin to a mythical founding by Sisyphus, king of Corinth, or alternatively by Theseus. The Pythian games honored Apollo at Delphi every eight years until the Amphyctionic Council reorganized them in 582 B.C., to be celebrated in the third year of each Olympiad, with crowns of bay leaves—later apples—as the award (with musical competitions still enjoying greater prestige than the equestrian and athletic contests modeled on the Olympic games, which were added). The Nemean games became pan-Hellenic in 573 B.C. and were eventually managed by Argos on the same lines as at Olympia, the prize being a crown of wild celery. Other contests included kissing matches held by the boys at Megara and endurance of flogging at the altar of Artemis Orthia in Sparta (in which some boys actually died), which became a tourist attraction in Roman times. **Pindar's** odes celebrated victors in the Olympic, Pythian, and Isthmian games.

Archaic tyrants competed avidly for prizes, usually in the expensive chariot races, which could be compared to modern trotting races, Dionysius and Agathon of Syracuse being among the victors.

Women's athletic contests were likely more widespread than indicated in the exclusively male sources that have survived. In cultic contests they raced on foot. At Olympia a women's festival honored Hera, paralleling the games for her husband Zeus, with victors receiving an olive crown. The male victors were awarded parts of the animal sacrificed. These may have sprung from races connected with marriage as in the myth of the swift Atalanta who would consent to marry only the man who could outrun her, or of King Oenomaus who forced suitors to race for the hand of his daughter, won by Pelops, beloved of Heracles and buried at Olympia. But in all sports, male or female, the Greeks competed most aggressively to win, not to overturn records, which with their poor means of timekeeping they could not measure as do modern referees. Nor did they compete to win for their team, as teamwork was foreign to sports at the time and applied only to dance and to the military.

After triumphing under Theodosius, Christians insisted that the religious rites integral to the Olympic games be suspended in 393–94, though the games may have continued until the middle of the fifth century.

The Olympic games, now worldwide, were revived in 1896 at Athens. They bear the impress of modern athletic traditions: the mass physical training of the Turnverein in Germany and the Sokol in the Czech lands, and the aristocratic ideal of the sportsman and gentleman cultivated on the playing fields of the British **public schools** during the previous hundred years.

The **Gay Games** of the 1980s were denied use of the term Olympic by United States courts responding to a suit of the American Olympic Committee. Classical scholars remain reticent about the homoerotic aspects of the ancient games. Sansone's theory that **athletics** and **theatre**, which involved masks like those primitive hunters wore, and males taking female parts, arose exclusively from primitive sacrifice and self-enhancing rituals, can no more be sustained than the hypothesis of **Indo-European** initiatory pederasty.

BIBLIOGRAPHY. Wendy J. Raschke, ed., *The Archaeology of the Olympics: The Olympics and Other Festivals in Antiquity*, Madison: University of Wisconsin Press, 1988; David Sansone, *Greek Athletics and the Genesis of Sport*, Berkeley: University of California Press, 1988; Waldo E. Sweet, "Protection of the Genitals in Greek Athletics," *Ancient World*, 11 (1985), 45–50.
William A. Percy

ONE, INC.

The oldest surviving homosexual organization in North America began in **Los Angeles** as a monthly magazine in January 1953. Although formally independent of the **Mattachine Society**, most of the early staffers were members of that recently formed organization. In 1958 the magazine won a landmark legal victory when the United States Supreme Court overturned a decision by the postmaster of Los Angeles that made the periodical unmailable. This success opened the way for the present profusion of the gay and lesbian press.

In the course of time, ONE developed other activities. Responding to a need for public education, the group held small classes beginning in 1956, supplemented by the midwinter institutes which took place in January. A research facility began to take shape in the Baker Memorial Library. Early in the history of ONE it was realized that there was need for a new comprehensive bibliography of the whole interdisciplinary field of homosexual behavior. After many delays, this goal was finally achieved in the *Annotated Bibliography of Homosexuality* (2 vols., New York, 1976), which remains the largest work of its kind.

In 1965 the organization was split by a schism, leading to the secession of a number of members, who formed the Tangents group, later known as the Homosexual Information Center (Hollywood). Under the vigorous leadership of W. Dorr Legg, the original group successfully rebuilt itself, though *ONE Magazine* itself was a casualty of the dispute, publishing its last regular issues in 1968. The magazine was replaced for a time by *ONE Institute Quarterly of Homophile Studies* (1968–73), the first scholarly journal of its kind in North America.

In 1981 the state of California granted ONE, Inc. the right to operate as an accredited graduate school. A regular program of classes and student supervision was begun with the collaboration of a number of leading scholars. In due course several students earned the degree of Ph.D. in homophile studies. In spacious new quarters ONE Institute continues to host a variety of scholarly and community activities in Los Angeles.

Ward Houser

OPERA

A composite art fusing words, music, and stagecraft, opera has flourished for five centuries. Although the lavish support the medium requires has, until recently, placed limits on overt representation of variant sexuality, careful scrutiny reveals significant homoerotic aspects.

Origins. Opera began in late **Renaissance** Italy with Jacopo Peri's *Dafne* (1597) and *Euridice* (1600), and homosexual themes and characters initially appeared during the form's first half-century or so of existence. In director Gerald Freedman's 1973 New York City Opera production of Claudio Monteverdi's *L'Incoronazione di Poppea* (1642), concerning the marriage of the bisexual first-century Roman emperor **Nero** to his mistress, Poppaea Sabina, the erotic nature of Nero's relationship with the poet Marcus Annaeus Lucanus—called Lucano in the libretto—was made explicit. In Pier Francesco Cavalli's *La Calisto* (1651), Jove, the supreme Roman deity, must disguise himself as Diana, goddess of the moon and the hunt, in order to seduce the nymph Calisto. Among the musicians of the seventeenth century, Jean-Baptiste **Lully** (1632–1687), court music master to King Louis XIV of France and composer of 20 operas, was homosexual. The poet Pietro **Metastasio** (1698–1782), the greatest librettist of the Baroque period, was erotically linked to several men of his day.

In her study *Sex Variant Women in Literature* (1956), Jeannette Foster characterized the heroic Bradamante in Ludovico Ariosto's epic *Orlando Furioso* (1531) as a "young Amazon in full armor" who finds, between martial exploits, that she attracts female admirers. In George Frideric Handel's *Alcina* (1735), Bradamante's loving champion is the eponymous enchantress' sister Morgana, who remains unaware until the last act of her beloved's actual sex.

In 1974, Dominique Fernandez wrote a novel entitled *Porporino, ou les mystères de Naples*, about Italian **castrati**, many neutered as boys in order to preserve the treble timbres of their singing voices, and drawing on historical fact, depicting them as having hetero- and homosexual relationships. In 1979, the French Aix Festival presented a staged *Porporino* using dialogue from the novel and a pastiche of arias by Alessandro Scarlatti, Giovanni Battista Pergolesi, and other eighteenth-century composers, assembled by musicologist Roger Blanchard. Countertenor James Bowman and high *coloratura* tenor Bruce Brewer portrayed castrati Porporino and Feliciano.

Two of Wolfgang Amadeus Mozart's major operas concern homosexual monarchs from antiquity. **Alexander the Great**, the fourth-century B.C. conqueror of the Persian Empire (whose orientation is discussed in a biography by Roger Peyrefitte and in novels by Mary **Renault**), is a central figure in *Il Re Pastore* (1775). In *The Twelve Caesars*, the Roman historian **Suetonius** wrote that first-century emperor Titus, the protagonist of *La Clemenza di Tito* (1791), "owned troops of inverts and eunuchs" and had "relations with . . . favorite boys [who] danced . . . on the stage." The finales of both operas find the heterosexual lovers paired up while the rulers remain alone: eighteenth-century sensibilities would never have tolerated on-stage male mates for Alessandro and Tito. This situation parallels Hollywood's development of the "harmless sissy" image for **films** of the 1930s and 1940s, rendering gay male characters asexual to avoid provoking public outrage. In a Salzburg intermezzo *Apollo et Hyacinthus*, composed when he was eleven, Mozart had approached the forbidden theme more directly, though in the Latin libretto the love of the god for the boy is in part obscured by a female interest.

Nineteenth Century. Passionate letters Ludwig van Beethoven (1770–1827) wrote to his nephew, Carl Obermayer, have led to speculation that the German composer may have been homosexual. In his only opera, *Fidelio* (1805), the fearless Leonore, who dons male clothing to penetrate prison walls in order to rescue her husband, Florestan, a political prisoner, attracts a female admirer, Marzelline, jailer Rocco's daughter. When Leonore reveals her true identity to all in the finale, Marzelline bewails her choice of love object. In Otto Schenk's 1970 Metropolitan Opera production, choristers made much homophobic merriment over Marzelline's discomfort.

The fifteenth-century transvestite and French patron saint, Joan of Arc, was given male lovers in Giuseppe Verdi's *Giovanna d'Arco* (1845) and in Russian homosexual Peter Ilyich **Tchaikovsky's** *The Maid of Orléans* (1881), just as the Lesbian poet was in Charles Gounod's *Sapho* (1851). St. Joan's life was later dramatized in *Joan* (1971) by openly gay, New York-based composer and minister Al Carmines (born 1936), whose eclectic works, drawing on classical, popular, and liturgical music, are variously termed operas, oratorios, and musicals. In *Joan*, the martyred heroine's story is updated to the present and relocated to New York's East Village and Joan and the Virgin Mary are depicted as lovers.

Daniel Auber's *Gustave III ou Le Bal Masqué* (1833) and Verdi's *Un Ballo in Maschera* (1859) have as protagonist homosexual Swedish King Gustavus III (1746–1792), whose reign began in 1771, but stress his heterosexual amorous pursuits. Magnus **Hirschfeld** cited possible liaisons between the king and Adolf Fredrik Muell, Johann Aminoff, and Gustav Mauritz Armfelt, men to whom he gave the title of Count. In a production of *Ballo* at the Royal Opera in Stockholm (1959), director Göran Gentele suggested an erotic tie between the king and the page Oscar, who is played by a soprano. In his 1972 Met production of Georges Bizet's *Carmen* (1875), realized posthumously by Bodo Igesz, Gentele had the smuggler Remendado played as gay on the basis of his rhapsodizing over the "distinguished" Englishmen he has seen in Gibraltar, and other passages of dialogue.

While *Eugene Onegin* (1879) and *The Queen of Spades* (1890) by Tchaikovsky show heterosexual love frustrated or in a cynical light, they offer no gay alternative. In an *Opera News* article (1986), American gay composer and diarist Ned Rorem contrasted Tchaikovsky, whose "homosexuality . . . was 'realized' though tragic," with his compatriot Modest Mussorgsky (1839–1881) who, Rorem opined, "was homosexual . . . [but] probably unfilfilled." Mussorgsky set his masterwork *Boris Godunov* (completed 1870, revised 1871–72) in the homosocial halls of government and the exclusively male environment of the monastery. The sole heterosexual liaison, between Marina and Dimitri, spurred by power, not love, was only added later to fulfill the Imperial Theatre's directors' demand that the opera have a *prima donna*. In *Khovanshchina*, on which Mussorgsky worked between 1872 and 1880 but left unfinished, the composer included gay-baiting among Prince Andrei Khovansky's other unsavory attributes. When his abandoned fiancée Marfa prevents his pursuit of the frightened Emma, Andrei snidely wonders if Marfa is herself "inappropriately attracted" to Emma. Dignified Marfa calmly ignores his charge.

French composer Camille Saint-Saëns (1835–1921) is best known to operaphiles as the composer of *Samson et Dalila* (1877). In a *Gay Sunshine* interview, Edouard Roditi recalled that Saint-Saëns, "a notorious homosexual," was trailed by plainclothes police bodyguards protecting him from "scandal" and harassment as he searched for sex partners. Though the Biblical spectacle and lush orchestration of *Samson* seem to hint at a gay sensibility, these also characterize works of the presumably heterosexual Jules Massenet and likely merely show Saint-Saëns to be typical of creative artists of his time.

A profound influence on late-Romantic and later composers was the German Richard Wagner (1813–1883). His principal patron was the homosexual King **Ludwig** of Bavaria (1845–1886), who had the court opera in Munich give the premieres of *Tristan und Isolde* (1865), *Die Meistersänger von Nürnberg* (1868), *Das Rheingold* (1869), and *Die Walküre* (1870), though it is questionable whether the king's ardor was requited.

Some directors of *Das Rheingold* have depicted as gay the gentle god Froh, who pines for his sister Freia when the giants abduct her and conjures up the rainbow bridge leading to Valhalla. Father M. Owen Lee, in *Opera News* (1987), and other writers have explored homoerotic themes in *Parsifal* (1882), concerning the youth who joins the homosocial society of the Knights of the Grail. In his 1983 film, director Hans Jürgen Syberberg found in Parsifal an androgynous duality and split his scenes between an actor and an actress.

The Earlier Twentieth Century. Wagner influenced the compositions of Dame Ethel **Smyth** (1858–1944), whose lesbianism is well attested. Smyth wrote six operas, one of which is the only opera by a woman ever presented by the Metropolitan Opera, *Der Wald* (*The Forest*, 1902), given two performances there in 1903. A participant in the women's suffrage movement in England, Smyth wrote its anthem, "Shoulder to Shoulder" (1911), which has been sung by the New York City Gay Men's Chorus. *The Concise Oxford Dictionary of Opera* says that Smyth's "entertaining series of memoirs conveys considerable relish for the long struggle against suspicion of a woman who composed, and did so with a robust professionalism that took men's breaths away."

Ned Rorem, writing in *Opera News* (1978), wondered if the reticent Pelléas, protagonist of Claude Debussy's *Pelléas et Mélisande* (1902), should be seen as gay and asked if the dying Marcellus, who lures him from his ailing father's side, is more than a friend.

Wagner's heir as preeminent German composer of his day was Richard Strauss. The earliest Strauss opera in the regular repertory is *Salome* (1905), a setting of the 1893 play by Irish/English homosexual writer Oscar **Wilde** (1854–1900). Lines of Herodias' page, which imply his intimacy with Narraboth, Syrian captain of the Tetrarch's guard—"He was my brother and nearer to me than a brother," and so on—were omitted from librettist Hedwig Lachmann's adaptation, but Herod's observation that Narraboth "was fair to look upon" remained. Other operas based on works of Wilde include Alexander von Zemlinsky's *Der Zwerg* and *Eine Florentinische Tragödie*, Mario Castelnuovo-Tedesco's *The Importance of Being Ernest*, William Orchard's *The Picture of Dorian Gray*, Hans Schaeuble's *Dorian Gray*, Renzo Bossi's *L'usignuolo e la rosa*, and Jaroslav Kricka's *The Gentleman in White*. Wilde and the **aesthetic** movement were satirized in Sir William Gilbert and Sir Arthur Sullivan's operetta *Patience* (1881), but without mention of his homosexuality.

In Strauss' *Elektra* (1909), the outcast, rebellious heroine, who inspires the admiration and affection of one of the solo serving women, all but makes love to her timid, conformist sister Chrysothemis in her attempt to convince her to join in avenging their father, Agamemnon's death, and some performers have made their embraces quite graphic. Created in the spirit of Mozart's Cherubino, the pubescent pageboy in *Le Nozze di Figaro*, Octavian, in *Der Rosenkavalier* (1911), is a young nobleman played by a woman. Gender lines blur still more when, like Cherubino, this male character dons female clothes for a ruse. Early productions faced censorship problems not only because the first scene finds Octavian in bed with or in close proximity to the Marschallin, but also because both performers in this erotic scene are women.

In a 1987 German production of Austrian composer Franz Schreker's *Die Gezeichneten* (*The Branded Ones*, 1918), hedonistic Duke Adorno and his close friend Count Tamare were played as bisexual.

The homosexuality of Polish composer Karol **Szymanowski** (1882–1937) is well documented. His *King Roger* (1926) concerns a historical twelfth-century Sicilian ruler who is torn between the Apollonian, represented by the intellectuals he summons to his court, and the Dionysian, personified by an Indian shepherd who leads a wild bacchanal. Staging *King Roger* for the Long Beach (California) Opera in 1988, director David Alden highlighted homoerotic themes he detected there. Szymanowski's earlier opera *Hagith* (written 1912–13, first performed 1922) was modeled on *Salome*.

Austrian composer Alban Berg's *Lulu*, based on Frank Wedekind's plays *Earth Spirit* (1895) and *Pandora's Box* (1901), had a posthumous premiere (1937). Its third act, long suppressed by Helene Berg, the composer's widow, was edited and orchestrated by Friedrich Cerha and first performed in 1979. The lesbian Countess Martha Geschwitz, who belongs to an exclusive society of women artists, has seen Lulu's portrait *en travesti* as Pierrot, and invites her to attend a ball dressed in male costume. In her masochistic devotion, the countess contracts cholera in order to substitute for her adored "angel" Lulu in a prison hospital. Called mad, mannish, and unnatural by her love, the countess never loses her dignity despite the sordid circumstances into which her love leads her. She declares her determination to attend law school and fight for women's rights but soon dies, with Lulu, at the hands of Jack the Ripper. It is never made clear whether or not the countess' relationship with Lulu develops into a physical one.

The Mid- and Late Twentieth Century. French homosexual composer Francis **Poulenc** (1899–1963) wrote three operas. In the whimsical *Les Mamelles de Tirésias* (1944, first performed 1947), with a text by Guillaume Apollinaire, husband and wife exchange sexes. She grows a beard and moustache, while he gives birth to thousands of babies. In *Dialogues des Carmélites* (1957), after Georges Bernanos' play, set during the French Revolution in the single-sex environment of the convent, the relationship between the protagonist Blanche de la Force and young Soeur Constance is depicted as a particularly loving one. The monodrama *La Voix Humaine* (1959), a setting of a play from the 1930s by gay writer Jean **Cocteau**, consists of a woman's anguished telephone conversation with the male lover who has left her. *La Voix* has an air of autobiography, understandably transmogrified with an alteration of pronouns at a time when it would have been nearly impossible to gain acceptance for a dramatization of a breakup of a homosexual relationship.

Homoerotic themes, both overt and covert, figure prominently in the *oeuvre* of gay English composer Lord Benjamin **Britten** (1913–1976). Leading roles in most of his works were created by his long-time lover, Sir Peter Pears (1910–1986), one of the few opera singers to come out publicly during his lifetime. A number of writers, including Philip Brett—author of the Cambridge opera handbook *Benjamin Britten: Peter Grimes* (1983) and subject of an extensive *Christopher Street* magazine interview by Lawrence Mass (1987)—have probed the parallel between the composer's emphatic portrayals of oppressed and ostracized individuals and his own experience as a gay man living and writing in a hostile, repressive society.

In Britten's *Peter Grimes* (1945), based on George Crabbe's poem "The Borough" (1810), the protagonist, sensitive, poetic and deeply troubled beneath his gruff fisherman's exterior, is shown in a brief tender moment with his boy apprentice. Grimes' attachments to John and to his late predecessor William Spode are definitely obsessive, if questionably erotic. Grimes' neighbors in the small fishing village suspect him of abusing his apprentices and galvanize into a lynch mob which drives Grimes to suicide. *Billy Budd* (1951), with libretto by Eric Crozier and gay novelist E. M. **Forster,** after Herman **Melville's** *Billy Budd, Foretopman* (1924), traces the disastrous effects of the repressed attraction of two British naval officers—one irredeemably evil, whose feeling turns to jealous hatred, the other good, but dutybound—for the handsome sailor Billy, who is falsely accused of inciting mutiny.

In *The Turn of the Screw* (1954), based on Henry James' 1898 novella, the ghostly servant Peter Quint, who "made free" with young Miles while living, continues to exert influence over the boy from beyond the grave, as the late governess, Miss Jessel, does over her former charge, Miles' sister Flora.

Britten's church parable *Curlew River* (1964), which incorporates elements of the Japanese Noh style, includes the first serious female role in Western music drama composed for male voice in modern times, that of the madwoman. (Stephen Sondheim wrote additional such parts in his 1976 opus about Japan, *Pacific Overtures.*)

Death in Venice (1973), which Britten based on Thomas **Mann's** 1913 novella, concerns the struggle of the intellectual novelist Gustav von Aschenbach with his erotic awakening, inspired by the ethereal youth Tadzio. The climax of the first act, preceded by a driving crescendo, is Aschenbach's realization and declaration, "I love you."

Slightly outside the realm of opera, but sometimes staged by opera companies, Carl Orff's scenic cantata *Catulli Carmina* (1943) is based on sexually explicit verses by bisexual Roman poet Gaius Valerius **Catullus** (87–54 B.C.) and concerns his love for the bisexual

Lesbia as well as their other same-sex amorous adventures.

In a *Gay Sunshine* interview, openly gay American composer Lou Harrison (born 1917) said of his colleague Virgil Thomson (born 1896) that, though he "hasn't openly declared himself, . . . his gayness is an open secret." Thomson collaborated with lesbian writer Gertrude **Stein** on two operas, *Four Saints in Three Acts* (1928, first performed 1934), dealing with the lives of Spanish saints, and *The Mother of Us All* (1947), which had its premiere after Stein's death and has as its subject Susan B. Anthony's long crusade for American women's suffrage. Openly gay English conductor Raymond Leppard (born 1927), who led an American bicentennial production of *The Mother* in Santa Fe, noted in a public television documentary (1977) that the relationship of Anthony and her companion Anne Howard Shaw, depicted in the opera as devoted and mutually supportive, parallels that of Stein and Alice B. Toklas (1877–1967), which he called one of the great love affairs of the century. Thomson's third opera was *Lord Byron* (1961–68, first performed 1972). Other composers who have used Stein's texts as librettos include Ned Rorem, for the short opera *Three Sisters Who Are Not Sisters* (1968), and Al Carmines, who set her words in *What Happened* (1963), *In Circles* (1967), *The Making of Americans* (1972), *Listen to Me* (1975), and *A Manoir* (1977). As "Gertrude S." and "Virgil T." appear as characters in *The Mother of Us All*, so are Stein and Toklas, and Oscar Wilde and Lord Alfred Douglas as well, in the cast list of Carmines' coming-out work *The Faggot* (1973).

As Britten, working in an era before gay liberation, made pacifism his primary cause, so did gay American composer Marc Blitzstein (1905–1964) channel his social consciousness into music theatre works dealing with laborers struggling against scoundrelly bosses, and with related issues, in *The Cradle Will Rock*

(1937), *Regina* (1949), and a 1952 adaptation of Bertolt Brecht and Kurt Weill's *Threepenny Opera* (1928). At the time of his death at the hands of sailors in Martinique, Blitzstein was at work on an opus, commissioned for the Metropolitan Opera, about anarchists Bart Vanzetti and Nicola Sacco. Blitzstein's biographer Eric A. Gordon has pointed out a homoerotic touch in the original Broadway staging of the opera *Regina*. Two black male servants observe (through a window) a party given by their rapacious white employer and imitate actions of the guests. Among the targets of the men's mockery is an extravagant romantic scene, which they reenact.

In Samuel Barber's *Antony and Cleopatra* (1966), Antony and his young shield-bearer, Eros, have a tender farewell scene. On the verge of defeat by Octavius Caesar, Antony bids Eros to run him through with his sword. After words of affection and praise, the youth kills himself to avoid having to slay his master. The libretto, after William **Shakespeare**'s play, is by Franco Zeffirelli (born 1923), filmmaker, and director and designer of many operas, who came out publicly in an *Advocate* interview. Zeffirelli was a protégé of gay film director Luchino **Visconti** (1906–1976), who also staged and designed opera. Other gay opera directors or designers have been the Metropolitan Opera's Bruce Donnell, actor Charles Ludlam, choreographer Mark Morris, photographer Cecil Beaton, and artist David Hockney. Gay librettists include lovers Wystan Hugh **Auden** and Chester Kallman, for Igor Stravinsky's *The Rake's Progress* and Hans Werner Henze's *Elegy for Young Lovers* and *The Bassarids*; Langston Hughes for Weill's *Street Scene*; and William M. Hoffman, author of *As Is*, a play about AIDS, for John Corigliano's *A Figaro for Antonia*, commissioned by the Met for production in 1991.

Operas of Ned Rorem, who came out in his *Paris Diary* (1966) and *New York Diary* (1967), include *Miss Julie* (1965),

after August Strindberg, and *Bertha* (1973), about a Queen of Norway.

In Argentine composer Alberto Ginastera's *Bomarzo* (1967), Pier Francesco Orsini, the hunchbacked Duke of Bomarzo, is impotent with his wife, Giulia Farnese, and with the courtesan Pentasilea, but "dearly loves" his powerful male slave Abul. Orsini dreams that wife, courtesan, and slave compete for possession of him. At Orsini's command, the faithful Abul kills Maerbale, the Duke's brother, who dressed Orsini in female clothing as a child and later became Giulia's lover.

The Seventies and Eighties. The year 1970 brought the premieres of Ben Johnston's *Carmilla*, based on Sheridan La Fanu's novel, which influenced Bram Stoker's *Dracula*, and concerning Laura's seduction by the vampire Carmilla, and Sir Michael Tippett's *The Knot Garden*, in which interracial male lovers Dov, a musician, and Mel, a writer, undergo trials, including humiliation, and separation by heterosexual partners, before their reunion. Operas based on plays by gay writers Federico García **Lorca** (1899–1936)— *Yerma* by Heitor Villa-Lobos, a posthumous premiere—and Tennessee **Williams'** (1911–1983) *Summer and Smoke* by Lee Hoiby, with libretto by Lanford Wilson— were introduced in 1971. (A Williams short story, "Lord Byron's Love Letter," received operatic treatment by composer Rafaello de Banfield in 1955.) Conrad Susa's *Transformations* (1973) uses as a text Anne Sexton's poetic versions of fairy tales and includes a lesbian interpretation of the story of Rapunzel. The historical homosexual figure Henry, Lord Darnley (1545–1567), husband of the titular monarch, is a character in Thea Musgrave's *Mary, Queen of Scots* (1977). His enemies in the opera call him vain, ambitious, weak, and foppish. Slightly tangential, but pertinent to the topic of opera, is the oratorio *The Return of the Great Mother* (1977), by composer Roberta Kosse (born 1947) and librettist Jenny Malmquist. The work celebrates matriarchy and women's relationships with women. *A Lesbian Play for Lucy* (1978), with music by Tamara Bliss and libretto by Eleanor Hakim, examines the relationships among Demeter, Hecate, Persephone, and Athena.

While during the 1970s, gay opera fans were spoken of with hostility and contempt in print by soprano Régine Crespin (*High Fidelity*, 1977) and actor and *aficionado* Tony Randall (*Opera News* and *After Dark*, 1972), the decade also found writers in the gay press, including the *Bay Area Reporter*'s George Heymont and *Gay Community News'* Nicholas Deutsch, a director, and Michael Bronski, beginning to write about opera from a gay angle.

In *A Quiet Place* (1983) by Leonard Bernstein (born 1918), bisexual François is Dede's husband as well as her brother, Junior's former lover. While—to the consternation of gay activitists—relatively few people who work in opera have openly declared their homosexuality (apparently fearing loss of prestige or employment in a profession heavily dependent on voluntary public subsidy), in the scurrilous, homophobic *Bernstein: A Biography* (1987), Joan Peyser discussed the homosexual orientations of numerous musicians who had not come out publicly, including the subject of her book, composers Aaron Copland, Virgil Thomson, Samuel Barber, and Gian Carlo Menotti; and conductor Dimitri Mitropoulos (Menotti later came out in an *Advocate* interview).

Homophobia mars Dominick Argento's *Casanova's Homecoming* (1985), also called *Casanova*, in which the Marquis de Lisle, described as asexual but depicted as a mincing stereotypical homosexual, is made the butt of the opera's climactic joke for his failure to indulge in heterosexual intercourse. Sam Michael Belich's *Laius and Chrysippus* (1986), with a text by *Opera Monthly* contributor Sam H. Shirakawa, depicts the love affair of Laius, father of Oedipus, and Chrysippus, son of Pelops, in music the *New York* *Native* called "Straussian." A major character in Jay Reise's *Rasputin* (1988) is homosexual Russian prince Feliks Feliksovich Yusupov, one of the murderers of the mad monk Rasputin in 1916.

During the 1980s, opera lost many talented individuals to AIDS, including New York City Opera baritones and stage directors David Hicks and Ronald Bentley, Met tenor James Atherton, and *Opera News* editor Robert M. Jacobson. Singers and conductors have participated in AIDS benefit concerts, such as "A Gala Night for Singing" in East Hampton, New York (1985), organized by Jacobson and openly gay manager Matthew A. Epstein and featuring Aprile Millo, Jerry Hadley and others, and "Music for Life", at Carnegie Hall (1987), which benefited Gay Men's Health Crisis and starred Leontyne Price, Marilyn Horne, Luciano Pavarotti, Samuel Ramey, Leonard Bernstein, and James Levine.

During the 1980s, gay choruses were formed and began interacting with the opera world. Opera singers Faith Esham and Jane Shaulis have appeared with the New York City Gay Men's Chorus, while the San Francisco Gay Men's Chorus participated in San Francisco Opera performances of Wagner's *Der Fliegende Holländer* and *Parsifal*. In 1988, the Portland, Oregon, Gay Men's Chorus presented Lou Harrison's opera *Young Caesar*. While Handel's *Giulio Cesare* focuses on Julius **Caesar**'s (102–44 B.C.) involvement with Cleopatra, Harrison's work explores the Roman general and statesman's affair with the Oriental king of Bithynia, Nicomedes IV. During this decade, Ira Siff, who sang tenor in Al Carmines' works, formed La Gran Scena Opera (1981), which presents opera parodies, blurs gender with transvestite diva portrayals (notably Siff's Madame Vera Galupe-Borszkh), and includes gay *double-entendres* in performances. Similar work has been done by David Clenny, who sang male soprano with the Handel Society in the 1970s and took the *travesti* title part in his own *La Contessa dei Vampiri* (1987), and by Englishman Michael Aspinall, who is billed as "the Surprising Soprano."

BIBLIOGRAPHY. David Hamilton, ed., *The Metropolitan Opera Encyclopedia*, New York: Simon and Schuster, 1987; Harold Rosenthal and John Warrack, eds., *The Concise Oxford Dictionary of Opera*, Oxford: Oxford University Press, 1979.

Bruce-Michael Gelbert

OPPRESSION, GAY

The concept of gay oppression was disseminated by the Gay Liberation Front founded in New York City in the summer of 1969 and by similar groups elsewhere that took GLF as their model and ideological paradigm.

Early Statements and Background. In a typical statement, the British Gay Liberation Front declared (December 1970) that its first priority was "to defend the immediate interests of gay people against discrimination and social oppression." It added that "the roots of the oppression that gay people suffer run deep in our society, in particular to the structure of the family, patterns of socialization, and the Judeo-Christian culture. Legal reform and education against prejudice, though possible and necessary, cannot be a permanent solution. While existing social structures remain, social prejudice and overt repression can always re-emerge. . . . GLF therefore sees itself as part of the wider movement aiming to abolish all forms of social oppression." Among the social groups suffering from one of the multifarious forms of oppression, its manifesto listed women, black people and other national minorities, the working class, young people, and peoples oppressed by imperialism.

This bill of grievances grew out of the experience and the thinking of the New Left in the late 1960s, which saw repressive practices at work in many areas of Western society where the inferior status of particular segments of the population had been taken for granted or justified as necessary on utilitarian grounds. The analogies with the disadvantaged condition of the aforenamed social categories shaped the notion of "gay oppression" as a pervasive set of wrongs inflicted by an establishment that imposed a heterosexual norm on the whole of society. Obligatory heterosexuality, the need to conceal one's sexual identity, the social ostracism and economic boycott to which known homosexuals were subjected, **police** harassment and sporadic **violence** at the hands of hooligans, the entire structure of privilege which the Judeo-Christian tradition conferred on the patriarchal family—all these burdens that the homosexual had to endure in an intolerant society were ascribed to a system of oppression that the Gay Liberation Front aspired to overthrow, along with the rest of the injustices for which the capitalist order was held responsible.

An Italian writer appealing to the classical **Marxist** tradition, Mario Mieli, went even further, asserting that "the monosexual Norm . . . is based on the mutilation of Eros, and in particular on the condemnation of homosexuality. It is clear from this that only when we understand why the homoerotic impulse is repressed in the majority, by the whole mechanism of society, will we be able to grasp how the exclusive or at least highly predominant assertion of heterosexual desire in the majority comes about." He added that the process of repression began in childhood, when homosexual tendencies are branded as "feminine" and shameful, and the whole subject is treated as unspeakable.

Realities of Oppression. Such concepts were undoubtedly shaped in large measure by the personal experiences which many gay activists had to undergo at various times in their lives, when they confronted head-on the hostility of society and its relentless pressure to conform to the norm of heterosexuality. Still later, they were able to see how across centuries of European history homosexuals had been the object of persecution as ferocious as that inflicted on religious minorities and ethnic groups, how the very existence of the homosexual minority had been denied by a church which claimed to uphold ideals of justice and humanity. In some respects the oppression of homosexuals was greater than that of demographic categories which may have been denied political and economic rights and been marginalized by the practice of segregation and ostracism, but at least had a recognized place, however unenviable, in the social order. The most crying aspect of the injustice was its invisibility to the rest of society, which either tacitly accepted it or was simply unaware that it existed.

Appeals to the courts for the recognition of homosexual rights had met with flat rejection on the grounds that homosexual behavior was per se immoral and illegal, while the validity of the ascetic morality was unchallenged. The further pressure of ostracism served to keep the victims of oppression from fighting back, because their efforts would only intensify the rejection and marginality. Worst of all was that many homosexuals internalized the guilt and self-reproach instilled by the attitudes of society.

All these phenomena found parallels in the oppression of other social and economic groups in the contemporary world, and the sense of kinship and solidarity with them buoyed the spirits of the founders of the radical organizations that "took to the streets" as part of the radical upsurge of the late 1960s. The goal of "ending gay oppression" became part of the universal struggle for justice and equality which seemed to be inching forward with every independence movement in the former colonies and every campaign of a minority for the rights which it had been unjustly denied.

Problems. Some difficulties arise with this overall analysis of the situation of homosexuals in terms of oppression. First, the situation of homosexuals presents notable differences from that of eth-

nic minorities. These incompatibilities emerge when gay leaders meet exasperating rebuffs, as they often do, in their efforts to build coalitions with leaders of ethnic blocs. Significantly, the late Harvey **Milk**, one of the most successful practitioners of coalition politics, achieved his goals mainly with San Francisco's old-line labor movement rather than with the city's ethnic leaders.

Another difficulty has to do with the broader contextualization of the idea of oppression. As practiced up to now, the analysis of oppression tends to be embedded in two broader ideologies, neither of which now enjoys hegemony in any western society. A major strand of the Judeo-Christian worldview sees the rich and powerful as obstacles to the work of redemption, for their heartless subjugation of the poor and downtrodden stands in the way of the achievement of a just society. While this critique is currently most salient in Liberation Theology, it has a substantial biblical foundation, for the concept was a creation of the Hebrew prophets of the **Old Testament**, who lent it the full force of their moral authority and powerful eloquence. A not dissimilar value-contrast appears in Marxism, with its perception of the class struggle between the exploiters and the proletariat—though it seeks to ground its interpretation of the phenomenon of oppression in an economic analysis rather than an appeal to religious eschatology. Quite apart from the growing disenchantment of the larger society with both these ideologies, gay people have many reproaches to address to both, owing to their histories of homophobia.

There is also a **counterculture** concept that was loosely invoked in the late 1960s as the right to reject as "oppressive" every cultural norm or every demand made on the individual by society. Such an approach ill coincides with the mounting need of advanced industrial societies for a highly self-disciplined citizenry, and is wholly incompatible with the renunciation of individual self-interest that collectivist ideologies such as Marxism formally entail.

As has been noted, all subsequent analyses of oppression stem from the original insights of the Hebrew Prophets. While it is theoretically possible to devise a critique of oppression independent of both the Judeo-Christian tradition and its Marxist offshoot, the task has not been seriously attempted, and it is hard to see what framework might serve the purpose. Detached from the larger intellectual context that would give it meaning, the discourse of oppression now seems rhetorical. While it undoubtedly encapsulates social and psychological realities, it does so in a partial way that many find unsatisfying.

BIBLIOGRAPHY. Dennis Altman, *Homosexual Oppression and Liberation*, New York: Outerbridge and Dienstfrey, 1971; Norman Gottwald, *The Bible and Liberation: Political and Social Hermeneutics*, Berkeley: Radical Religion, 1976; Mario Mieli, *Homosexuality and Liberation: Elements of a Gay Critique*, London: Gay Men's Press, 1980; Jacques Pons, *L'oppression dans l'Ancien Testament*, Paris: Letouzey et Ané, 1981; Aubrey Walter, ed. *Come Together—the Years of Gay Liberation*, London: Gay Men's Press, 1980.

Ward Houser

ORAL SEX

Human oral sex may be said to be the one family of sexual practices that is truly universal, inasmuch as it is common to heterosexuals, male homosexuals, and lesbians. Although oral sex is widely diffused among the world's societies, past and present, no detailed studies have been made as to the reasons for its relative popularity—in comparison with anal sex, for example—and the relevant correlations with other cultural traits. One reason why many prefer it to anal sex is the absence of the pain and discomfort often initially experienced by the passive partner in the latter activity, particularly if the sphincter has not been sufficiently loosened.

Mouth-to-Penis Activity. The ancient Mediterranean peoples were familiar with this behavior in both its homosexual and heterosexual forms. The Romans distinguished between fellatio— in which the penetrating partner remains relatively motionless, allowing his receptive partner to do most of the work—and irrumation, in which the penetrator engages in vigorous buccal or laryngal thrusts. Depending on the individual, both are felt to enhance the penetrator's masculinity: in fellatio the beneficiary of the action luxuriates in making the other service him completely, while in irrumation he has the converse satisfaction of being able to give full vent to the impulse to aggressive penile thrusts. In modern writings, however, it is usual to refer to both forms simply as fellatio; the street terms "cocksucking," "blow job," and "(giving/getting) head" are also current.

There are three common positions in this form of sexual activity. In the first, the penetrator stands, while his partner kneels, sits, or crouches to take the erect member in his mouth. In the second main position, the penetrator lies on his back, and the insertee crouches over him or lies between his legs. In the third position, especially suitable for irrumation, the insertee lies on his back with head propped up, and the penetrator straddles his chest, leaning forward over his head while thrusting forward. Of course there are many variants and intermediate positions.

The novice fellator tends to be inexpert in various ways that may prove frustrating to his partner. Since he has usually not yet overcome the gag reflex, he may take only the head of his partner's member in his mouth rather than deepthroating it, which is optimal. Furthermore, anxiety about ejaculation may cause him to slow his movements or even freeze up at the stage in which the tempo of the action should be increased. With relaxation and experience these difficulties are usually overcome, and many practitioners learn to swallow the semen, even developing an appreciation of variations in its taste.

There is a tendency to associate the two very different roles in fellatio—penetration and reception—with a hierarchy of beauty, age, and sexual orientation, wherein the favored position is that of penetrator. With respect to the latter, many men who regard themselves as heterosexual will accept a blow job ("**trade**"), claiming that there is little difference between a female and a male mouth; yet they show revulsion at the slightest suggestion that they should return the favor. This attitude is characteristic of a certain type of adolescent male **prostitute**. In **toilet** sex contacts it has been observed that younger men expect to be fellated, but as they get older will switch to the receptor role. Some older men are only active as cocksuckers, having long since given up the expectation of having their own member orally stimulated. By convention, regardless of the source of effort, the penetrator is considered "active" and the insertee "passive."

Some hold that sixty-nine, in which the two partners fellate one another simultaneously, is ideal because of its mutuality. Certainly this reciprocity offers a psychological advantage. Yet sixty-nine has real drawbacks. First, the position decreases each partner's maneuverability. Secondly, the distraction at one end tends to cause a slowdown or even cessation of activity at the other. Finally, the tongue is of necessity on the upper side of the penis, where it is less stimulating than it would be if it were placed on the lower side. For these reasons, many prefer serial fellatio to the simultaneous mutual form known as sixty-nine.

In the 1980s oral–penile activity has become more popular as it has been shown that the risk of contracting the **AIDS** virus is either insignificant, especially for the penetrator, or at least enormously lower than with penile–anal activity. However, oral activities do not usually lend themselves to shielding the penis in a rubber condom, while anal ones do.

Lesbian Oral Activity. Physically, lesbian cunnilinctus does not differ in any essential way from heterosexual cunnilinctus, the configurations of the mouths of women and men being essentially the same. However, the fact that a woman is better able to gauge the physiological responses of another woman than is a man (a factor which also favors male fellators) allows for lengthy and subtle sessions that take advantage of the capacity of women for multiple orgasms. As with men, the oral activity may be sequential, one woman sucking another first and then having the favor returned, or the sixty-nine position may be assumed. However, lesbian relations are less likely to be hierarchical, so that neither partner is "left in the lurch" by receiving an inadequate amount of stimulation. Contrary to popular belief, modern lesbians rarely resort to dildoes, though electrical vibrators—usually not phallus-shaped—may be employed as a supplement to oral activity.

There is virtually no risk of venereal disease, including AIDS, in lesbian activity. However, yeast and other infections of the vaginal region may on occasion be transferred to the mouth.

Variations. Some people enjoy giving their partner a tongue bath, though the extent of this procedure is usually limited by the exhaustion of the tonguer's saliva. Many restrict themselves to French kissing, laving the inside of the outer ear, nipple sucking, or (less commonly) toe sucking.

Anilinctus or "rimming" is the tonguing of the anus. Although this is mildly enjoyable to the recipient of the action, the main benefit appears to be the psychological effect that the rimmer has of accepting his partner totally. In other cases, however, the rimmer may be enacting his own self-abasement, and in a few extreme scenes his partner may even expel faeces which he then ingests. One need scarcely stress that anilinctus in all of its versions is dangerous to health; it has been implicated in hepatitis and probably transmits other diseases as well. Erotic **urination** may take place in or into the mouth, sometimes as an adjunct to oral sex; unlike faeces, however, fresh urine is normally sterile and thus poses no comparable health problem.

Legal aspects. In the **canon law** of the medieval church the definition of sodomy included all forms of oral sexuality, whether the partners were of opposite sexes or of the same sex, because the possibility of fecundation was excluded in both. The prosecution of participants in oral sexuality, however, has certainly been less frequent than legal action against those engaging in anal penetration, and in regard to lesbians, virtually non-existent.

While English **common law** took over many of the canon law definitions, in 1817 a court decision excluded oral sexuality from the definition of **buggery**, so that the crime was later prosecuted under other statutes such those prohibiting gross indecency, lewd and lascivious conduct, and the like. In entrapment cases, however, the unsuspecting victim of the plainclothesman's advance may have agreed to nothing more than one of the forms of oral sex in order to find himself under arrest.

In the recent Georgia case of *Bowers v. Hardwick*, which went to the United States Supreme Court (1986), the party under indictment had been accidentally observed in the act of fellating another male; the court ruled that the American legal precedents extending the right of privacy to heterosexual intercourse did not apply to sodomy.

BIBLIOGRAPHY. Gershon Legman, *Oragenitalism*, New York: Julian Press, 1969; Joann Loulan, *Lesbian Sex*, San Francisco: Spinsters Ink, 1985; Charles Silverstein and Edmund White, *The Joy of Gay Sex*, New York: Crown, 1977.

Ward Houser

ORGANIZATIONS
See **Movement, Homosexual**.

ORIENTATION, SEXUAL

The expression sexual orientation, which came into general use only in the 1970s, denotes the stable pattern established by an individual of erotic and affectional response to others with respect to gender. Commonly two orientations, **heterosexual** and **homosexual**, are recognized; many would add **bisexual**. Attractions to sectors within the male and female populations with respect to age, race, and the like are not normally regarded as orientations, nor are such paraphilias as eroticization of **urine** and **sadomasochism** (S/M).

In comparison with older judgmental terms, such as sexual **deviation** and **perversion**, sexual orientation has the advantage of value neutrality. In comparison with the expression sexual preference, it emphasizes that erotic attraction stems from the deep structure of the personality, and is not a mere choice or taste which can be easily altered. Moreover, the metaphor of orientation, which originally referred to alignment according to the points of the compass, suggests the possibility of variety among individuals, rather than the rigid either/or contrast that a strict polarity of heterosexual/homosexual implies. Finally, the concept of sexual orientation conveys something of the complex interactions between the individual personality (itself made up of conscious and unconscious components), on the one hand, and the changing scripts and cues being transmitted by the social environment, on the other. One responds to a subtle "landscape of eros" as posited by society, but one does so in keeping with one's individual character and experience.

In the view of some, the expression should be altered to *affectional* orientation, to indicate a broader concern with the whole person, rather that overtly expressed erotic or genital acts. Restriction to the specifically erotic has also been felt to be a defect of the term homosexual itself, hence the temporary popularity of the word **homophile**.

In its remote origins, the term orientation stems from architecture, where it signifies the alignment of temples and churches on an east–west axis (from *oriens*, "east"). In psychology it has come to mean awareness of one's position or direction with reference to time, place, or identity of persons; also it denotes a tendency to move toward a source of stimulation or a particular direction, as in tropisms. From this nexus it is but a short step to the concept of *sexual* orientation. The widespread adoption of the expression is related to the 1970s popularity of such compounds as action-oriented, identity-oriented, and success-oriented. It is possible that the semantic modulation into the erotic sphere was anticipated by the late-nineteenth-century German use, with respect to sex, of the term *Richtung*, "direction."

Wayne R. Dynes

ORIGIN MYTHS
See **Inventor Legends**.

ORPHEUS
Greek mythological figure, the son of the muse Calliope, noted for his magical art in music and poetry. Whether Orpheus was a historical personality is disputed, but if so he lived in the generation before the Trojan War, therefore in the thirteenth century B.C.

Orpheus in Antiquity. A number of important aspects of the career of Orpheus are recounted by ancient Greek writers. Of Thracian origin, Orpheus possessed musical skill that could enchant animals and plants and cause them to do his will. Trees would transplant themselves for him, while birds and even fish gathered to hear his song. As a member of the expedition of the Argonauts, he beat time for the rowers and stilled harsh winds.

When his wife Eurydice died of the bite of a poisonous snake and was taken to Hades, Orpheus obtained her release by giving a concert for the ruler of the Underworld. Warned not to look at Euridice on the trip home, Orpheus yielded to temptation and lost her forever. Orpheus then gathered around him a group of Thracian young men, to whom he introduced the new practice of **pederasty**. Greek vase paintings show this ephebic entourage enchanted by the splendors of his song. Yet Orpheus' influence provoked resentment among the forsaken female companions of his new lovers. The women—sometimes identified with the maenads of the Dionysiac cult—ganged up on him, attacking the musician with spears, axes, and stones. Orpheus was dismembered, his head separated from the rest. Eventually the head floated away, still singing, together with his lyre. Orpheus' head washed ashore on the island of Lesbos, where it received the honor of a shrine. The shrine could still be visited in ancient times, and reputedly the head might be heard faintly singing. Some scribes claimed to have taken down the words, which then presumably provided the texts for the Orphic hymns. Around these hymns developed a religious cult, Orphism, whose role and significance are still the object of debate by historians.

Most images of Orpheus in Greek and Roman art are either representative depictions of him as singer or dramatic scenes of his later career—his leadership of the male band in Thrace, his death, and the survival of the head. These last events were important to the Greeks not only because they laid the foundation for his influence after death, but because he was regarded as the **inventor** of pederasty. Although he was not the only candidate for this honor, his nomination reflects the Greek penchant for attributing significant cultural achievements to particular individuals. The Eurydice episode, which in modern consciousness has become virtually synonymous with Orpheus, was less important to the Greeks, and may even be a later grafting onto the earlier torso of legend.

The Fortunes of Orpheus. The Middle Ages had a curiously divided concept of Orpheus. To some early Christian writers, such as Clement of Alexandria, the element of cosmic harmony seemed uppermost, and he was even compared to Christ. During the later Middle Ages, however, the singer was subject to moralization: as a sodomite, he was seen as deserving his fate.

It was left to the neo-Platonic circles of fifteenth-century Florence, with their fondness for merging pagan wisdom with a rarified Christianity, to rehabilitate Orpheus as seer, musician, and lover of men. The Greek Orphic hymns, now read once more, were hailed as evidence of Orpheus' skill as a mystical theologian. In 1480, apparently, Angelo **Poliziano** (Politian) created for the court of Mantua his brilliant short play, *La Favola di Orfeo*. At Mantua Poliziano could have inspected the frescoes of the life and death of Orpheus done by Andrea Mantegna six years before. In his play Poliziano boldly states that after losing Eurydice Orpheus turned with great zest to his own sex. The Italian humanist's description of Orpheus' later career echoes the Latin poet Ovid, with some touches of his own. A lover of youths, Orpheus "plucks the new flowers, the springtime of the better sex when men are all lithe and slender."

The finest artistic representation of the revived ancient Orpheus is by a northern painter, Albrecht Dürer. In a masterly drawing of 1494 he reworked an earlier Mantegna design to show a heroic Orpheus—virtually a pagan martyr—dying at the hands of frenzied maenads. The banderole contains a German inscription reading "Orfeus der erst puseran" (Orpheus the first bugger), a blunt expression by which Dürer acknowledged the musician's distinction as the inventor of homosexuality.

In the second half of the sixteenth century the chill winds of the Counterreformation gradually suppressed knowledge of the homoerotic themes of classical antiquity. Thus Ottavio Rinuccini's Florentine **opera** *Euridice* of 1600 deals only with the married Orpheus—he even brought Eurydice back to her husband in a happy ending. This tradition of suppressing his later career has been generally followed in all the arts. Toward the end of the nineteenth century there was a revival of the tragic Orpheus, as seen in paintings by Odilon Redon and Álvarez de Sotomayor, but usually as an emblem of the alienated artist, and not as a sexual innovator. To the modern gay movement was left the task of reviving the homoerotic Orpheus.

BIBLIOGRAPHY. Wayne Dynes, "Orpheus without Eurydice," *Gai Saber*, I (1978), 278–86; Dorothy M. Kosinski, *Orpheus in Nineteenth-Century Symbolism*, Ann Arbor, MI: UMI Press, 1989; Charles Segal, *Orpheus: The Myth of the Poet*, Baltimore: Johns Hopkins University Press, 1988; John Warden, ed., *Orpheus: The Metamorphosis of a Myth*, Toronto: University of Toronto Press, 1982.

Wayne R. Dynes

ORTON, JOE (JOHN KINGSLEY) (1933–1967)

English playwright and novelist. In the 1960s, Orton's works shocked British audiences and had a significant impact on the direction of contemporary drama, despite the slender canon he had produced before he was bludgeoned to death in 1967 by his long-time lover, Kenneth Halliwell, in a murder–suicide, sparked by artistic as well as sexual jealousies.

Orton, self-educated under Halliwell's guidance after the two met while students at the Royal Academy of Dramatic Arts, offered a cynical view of human nature, grounded in violence, sexuality, exploitation, greed, narcissism, and ruthlessness, in plays that are nonetheless witty, urbane, and stylized. An artistic descendent of Oscar **Wilde**, Orton wrote drama that can be thought of as either social farce, moral satire, or ethical parody—or all three simultaneously. His dramatic world is comedic, but blackly so, and homosexuality pervades the sex-infused world of his theatre, in every work he produced.

Before his and Halliwell's conviction and jail sentence in 1962 for defacing library books (a situation worthy of an Orton plot), he had written little, collaborating with his lover on the manuscripts of four unpublished novels. After his release, however, Orton began to write furiously, affected both by incarceration and his first separation from Halliwell. In 1964, he wrote *The Ruffian on the Stair* and his brilliant *Entertaining Mr. Sloane*, the latter a touchstone to his vision of inherent human depravity as a brother and sister try to outmaneuver each other to seduce the charmingly dangerous young man who has begun to dominate and exploit them and their home. Also in 1964, he completed *Loot*, whose 1966 production made him a celebrity, and his television play, *The Good and Faithful Servant*, an unusually bitter examination of the condition of the working classes—if still quite witty in form. In 1966, he wrote *The Erpingham Camp* and an unproduced screenplay for the Beatles, *Up Against It*; in 1967, Orton produced another television play, *Funeral Games*, and the play many consider to be his finest achievement, *What the Butler Saw*, staged posthumously in 1969. His only other independent work was a novel completed in 1961, *The Vision of Gombold Proval*, published in 1971 as *Head to Toe*.

Orton's drama was designed to shock and disorient, motives clearly revealed in the diaries he kept, and his work accomplished just that: it challenged the comfortable assumptions of London's traditional and safe West End and offered theatre audiences an amoral view of themselves with an impact and shock of recognition unmitigated by its witty and intelligent presentation. As a boost to the "school of anger" of the previous decade, Orton's drama coupled with the works of Harold Pinter (one of the few fellow dramatists Orton admired) to jar the British theatre from the complacency that had characterized it for the many years previous, allowing both America and France to forge ahead into much more adventurous dramatic territory.

Orton, however, never believed his plays were as outrageous and improbable as did his audiences and critics, for his diaries demonstrate that much of his vision came directly from his own life rather than from fanciful literary imagination. For example, his addiction to sexual encounters in public toilets explains much about the pervasion of anonymous and indifferent sexuality in his written work. Had he lived, his would have no doubt been one of the most pervasive presences in the drama of the last two decades, but his few works have still had a profound influence in shaping the dual vision of current drama and its multiplicity of effect.

BIBLIOGRAPHY. John Lahr, *Prick Up Your Ears: The Biography of Joe Orton*, New York: Knopf, 1978; Simon Shepherd, *Because We're Queers: The Life and Crimes of Kenneth Halliwell and Joe Orton*, London: Gay Men's Press, 1989.

Rodney Simard

OWEN, WILFRED (1893–1918)

English poet. Born in Oswestry, Shropshire, Owen was educated at the Birkenhead Institute, Liverpool, and at University College, Reading. His relationship with his affectionate, devout but not intellectual mother was the closest of his life, but a source of many difficulties. Despite her hopes and prayers Owen did not become a clergyman but even lost his faith. A tutor at Bordeaux at the moment World War I broke out, he returned to England and enlisted in the Artists' Rifles in 1915. In January 1917 he was sent to the Somme with the 2nd Battalion Manchester Regiment. He was soon recording the horrors of life at the front in letters he wrote home, and as a victim of "shell shock" he was sent to convalesce at Craiglockhart War Hospital, near Edinburgh, where he met Siegfried Sassoon, another patient. For Owen it was the friendship of a lifetime, far more important to him than any previous literary encounter. Their conversations and subsequent correspondence gave Owen's poetic vocation focus and meaning, and Sassoon's supportive criticisms helped to curb his friend's tendency to lush overwriting. Recovered from his ordeal, Owen returned to France in August 1918. He was awarded the Maltese Cross, but was killed a week before the Armistice while leading his men across a canal.

His brother, Harold Owen, deliberately tried to keep the poet's reputation under the control of the family, turning away researchers prying into Wilfred's personal life. He dreaded particularly that someone might raise the "frightful implication" of homosexuality. He even claimed that when pressed on the subject Wilfred had denied any personal involvement but admitted to an "abstract" interest because homosexuality seemed to attract so many intelligent people. At the poet's own request his mother burned "a sack full" of his papers, and remarkably few letters to him have survived. Only four poems by Owen were published in his lifetime; the great ones, the chief poems, written during the last twelve months of his life, were issued from the press in 1920 with an introduction by Siegfried Sassoon, next to whom he is the greatest of English war poets.

Having grown up in a world in which homosexuality was unthinkable, Owen may have repressed and denied his inclinations until Sassoon introduced him to one of the very few literary circles where "Uranianism" was accepted and casually discussed. Sassoon's own ideas came from the circle around Edward **Carpenter**, who preached a gospel of idealized Uranian love. From him Owen derived the awareness of these matters that illuminates his last poems and his thoughts on religion and war. His interest in young male beauty became one of the sources of his poetry. Owen discovered that the artistic temperament which he sought in himself was a function of his homosexuality, or to reverse the equation, that his sexual tendencies were a boon for art and for humanity. He also made the acquaintance of Robert Ross, the intimate of Oscar **Wilde**, whose life was ended by a scandal that occurred in 1918. Thus Owen was heir to two major strands of homosexual thought in the early twentieth century—the ethical and the aesthetic—and only his premature death precluded their further unfolding in his verse.

BIBLIOGRAPHY. Dominic Hibberd, *Owen the Poet*, Athens, GA: University of Georgia Press, 1986.

Warren Johansson

OXFORD
See **Cambridge and Oxford**.

Pacific Cultures

The immense territory of the Pacific islands is customarily divided into three major regions: Melanesia, Micronesia, and Polynesia. Culturally related to the Melanesians are the aborigines of **Australia**. In the present state of our knowledge, which requires sensitivity to far-flung relationships, some parts of the **Philippines** and **Indonesia**, as well as aspects of **Korea**, **Japan**, and Siberia, are also significant.

Age-Defined Patterns. Voluminous descriptions of homosexuality in Pacific cultures exist in several languages. To start arbitrarily from the south, Gilbert Herdt (1984) noted explicit reference to ritualized homosexual practices of Australian aborigines, especially those of Kimberly and Central Desert. Intriguing, though suspect, are early Western Australian reports that, until pledged young wives attained the marriage age, their brothers would be used as their surrogates. Later, more detailed reports of Nambutji and Aranda exogamous homosexuality are somewhat more reliable.

Although Géza Roheim (pp. 70, 324–37) argued that the Australian data mirrored the Melanesian, Melanesian homosexual intercourse is prescribed, not just condoned. Moreover, the male cult and its practices are supposed to be unknown to women. Although male informants probably overestimate this ignorance, it is difficult to picture the women freely discussing ritualized homosexuality in highland New Guinea cultures, let alone reporting who was linked to whom. Moreover, the partners in New Guinea seem to show less tendency to pair off.

Nevertheless, in both areas, homosexuality is clearly age-defined—it is not just that the insertees are younger, but that the insertors are young men in transit to marriage, marriage being a hallmark of adult status.

Melanesian ritualized homosexualities in their cultural context have been analyzed in sometimes florid detail by Herdt. These cults co-occur with intense gender antagonism and fears of semen depletion (apparently applying only or mostly to coitus with women). A number of Melanesian tribes "share the belief that boys do not become physically mature men as a result of natural processes. Growth and attainment of physiological maturation is contingent on the cultural process of initiation, and this entails insemination because it is semen which ensures growth and development" (Kelly, p. 16). In the native views, "Semen does not occur naturally in boys and must be 'planted' in them. If one does not plant sweet potato [a diet staple throughout the area] then no sweet potatoes will come up in the garden, and likewise semen must be planted in youths if they are to possess it as men" (ibid.). Since boys lack semen and men who have all gone through the initiation process can produce it, the native theory is verified anew with regularity. The means of insemination vary: oral for the Etero studied by Kelly and the Sambia studied by Herdt (1981), anal for the Kaluli and by masturbation and the smearing of semen over the bodies of the initiates among the Onabasulu. Despite the shared belief in the necessity of inseminating boys if they are to grow into men, and the whole complex of beliefs about pollution by females and the life-threatening loss of semen to them, the differences in means of insemination used are ethnic markers, used to justify warfare with tribes that employ differing means.

Melanesian work is of obvious import for questioning the contention that there are lifelong homosexual preferences in all societies, as well as the notion widespread in American culture that homosexuality is "incurable": once a youth is involved ("corrupted"), he can never marry. (Of course one need not look so far away as Melanesia to learn that.)

The Melanesian evidence also challenges the still popular theorizing about the diseased **effeminate** "essence" of homosexuality. As Herdt (1984, p. 39) explains, Melanesian homosexuality is masculinizing for both participants: "The boy believes that this act will make him grow and strengthen. He is demonstrating his desire to be masculine, to act in accord with ritual ways, to be unfeminine. On the other hand, his counterpart, the postpubescent inseminator, demonstrates his superordinate maleness [and recently achieved sexual maturity] by the homosexual act of masculinizing the boy. Moreover, both (along with their elders) are participating in a cult of masculinity, affirming its superiority to feminity, and helping both inseminators and inseminated to achieving warrior masculinity."

Gender-Defined Patterns. In Australian and Melanesian cultures homosexuality was and is age-defined, and often mandatory. In Polynesia it is gender-defined, and, while not punished, it is also not prestigious. From the time of European contact until the present, most Tahitian villages have a *mahu*. There is never more than one, one informant explained, "because when one dies, then another substitutes. God arranged it like that. . . . Only one mahu and when that one dies, he is replaced" (Levy, p. 132).

Cross-dressing is not an invariable concomitant of the mahu role, and there is some native disagreement about

whether homosexuality is essential either, though younger men in the village where Levy lived claimed the village mahu serviced most of the young males. "Males describing their relationships with mahu tend to stress their passive participation in the relationship and the lack of symmetry . . . [e.g.] 'He ate my penis. He asked me to suck his. I did not suck it.'" (Levy, p.135). Social tolerance was summarized as follows: "It is stated that there is nothing abnormal about this as far as the male *tauréaréa* bachelors are concerned. Some adults in the village found the idea of homosexual relations with the mahu 'disgusting,' but they did not seriously stigmatize those males who engaged in them. Sexual contact with the mahu tends to be treated in conversation as a standard kind of sexual activity." (Levy, p. 134).

The reported sexual activity of the mahu is invariably reported to be "'ote moa' (literally, 'penis sucking'). Anal sodomy is categorically denied as a mahu activity. . . . Intercourse between the thighs is said not to be done" (ibid.). As in other gender-defined systems, such as those in **Latin America** and the **Mediterranean**, mahu concur "that a male who engages as a partner with a mahu is not at all a mahu himself, nor in any way an abnormal man" (ibid., 138). That some men are "like that" is accepted as natural, both by the mahu who reports no shame about his sexual behavior or by non-mahu.

In the Tahitian capital city of Papeete, in addition to the mahu role, a non-gender-defined role appears to be emerging: the *raerae*. A man who lives a female role in the village and who does not engage in sexual activity would be a mahu but not a raerae, whereas somebody who does not perform a female's village role and who dresses and acts like a man, but who indulges in exclusive or preferred sexual behavior with other men would be raerae but not mahu.

When Levy made his study in Tahiti (1962–64), the mahu role was one of a limited number of cultural forms which still persisted in Tahitian communities. In those years, the tradition of there never being more than one mahu to a community still held. These days, that rule no longer applies, for in some communities such as Vaitape on the island of Bora Bora, several mahu now live in close proximity to one another. When elderly mahu die, no more will emerge to take their place. Instead, they will be replaced by raerae.

Although it is somewhat peripheral to the main Pacific area, the Sulu archipelago of the Philippines offers some relevant comparisons. Nimmo reported that few, if any, of the major communities of Sulu lack male homosexuals. Some of these are transvestites who assume the dress and sexual role of women, and some are men who retain male attire but prefer other men for sex. Some islands are known locally for their large numbers of homosexuals, whereas others are known for having few. A group of male transvestites, renouned throughout southern Sulu as the *dahling-dahling* dancers, are professional entertainers who travel among the islands, singing and dancing at major festivals and ceremonies (p. 92).

Nimmo's paper discusses exogamy for homosexual relations between ethnic groups. Although the case may have more to do with "Islamic accommodations" than with Polynesian cultural traits, Nimmo (p. 94) reported, "None of the five acknowledged Bajau male homosexuals I interviewed admitted to having sexual relationships with Bajau males. . . . Numerous non-Bajau males are available in Sitangkai [the port which was the site of his research]."

Also from the Sulu archipelago, Kiefer reported a professional niche for "sensitive men" (*bantut*) among the Tausug. Professional musician (*mangangalang*) is a role providing "opportunities for temporary sex-role reversal in an expressive situation, female-like voice and mannerism, expressive bodily movements," especially in *pagsindil*, a popular performance of stylized courtship repartee

in which the bantut takes the female role (p. 108).

Returning to Polynesia, the isolated, deviant, feminine mahu role stands in marked contrast to the Melanesian prescription of homosexual insertee behavior as a necessary part of any warrior's masculinization. Explaining how this great contrast arose is an interesting task that will not be attempted here, beyond suggesting that Polynesian societies were slave societies with all-powerful chiefs, whereas Melanesian warriors were not subordinated to a divine chief. Rather than look for ecological-geographical differences, differences in social structure (which are quite considerable) should be the starting point for such explanation.

An Intermediate Pattern: Profession. Continuing the overview of the organization of homosexuality in Pacific cultures, a somewhat intermediate type between the Melanesian and Polynesian organizations of homosexuality (but not located between the two areas) is offered by several sets of warriors. Javanese warriors' kept boys (*gemblakan*) were young and effeminate, whereas the Korean *hwarang* were age-stratified, but apparently not effeminized.

In Japan there has been (and remains) the gender-defined role of kabuki actors. Especially during the Tokugawa period "love between comrades" flourished among **samurai** warriors. Mahayana Buddhist monks had their own forms of relationship with novices.

The classic exemplar of profession-defined homosexuality is the Chukchi **shaman** of Siberia, but as Bogoras' classic study reveals, the shamans are not just homosexual, but occupy a cross-gender role—one quite like the **berdache** in tribes down the Pacific coast of North America. These tribes presumably crossed from Northeast Asia to Northwest America more recently than Indian peoples further south and east, so there are close genetic connections of cultures across the North Pacific.

There are also reports of cross-dressing shamans scattered elsewhere (Borneo, Vietnam).

Lesbians. The only relatively clearly documented instance of institutionalized lesbianism in Melanesia comes from Malekula Island in the New Hebrides. A. B. Deacon was able to learn that among the Big Nambas of the northern part of the island lesbianism was "common": "Between women, homosexuality is common, many women being generally known as lesbians, or in the native term *nimomogh iap nimomogh* ('woman has intercourse with woman'). It is regarded as a form of play, but, at the same time, it is clearly recognized as a definite type of sexual desire, and that women do it because it gives them pleasure" (p. 170).

Blackwood suggested something close to ritualized lesbian behavior: homosexual play during the coming-of-age (menstruation) celebration in the Solomon Islands. Such reports are uncommon. One should be wary of the general lack of data on lesbian behavior, however, since most Melanesianists have been males studying males. Whether lesbian activity existed elsewhere in Melanesia will probably never be known because of the increasing tempo of westernization.

From the Philippines, Hart described females who cross-dressed and engaged in male occupations. These females were sometimes referred to with the term for male cross-dressers (*bayot*), sometimes with their own: *lakin-on*, and sometimes pass as men away from their natal village (pp. 223–26).

In Tahiti, "Transient homosexual contacts between women are said to be frequent. These are said to involve mutual mouth–genital contact or mutual masturbation. These contacts are not considered particularly abnormal or signs of altered sexuality. They involve women who also engage in ordinary heterosexual behavior" (Levy, p. 141). There is lesbian behavior, but "no evidence for a full homosexual role corresponding to the mahu.... Mahu

[as a term] is considered by many to be misused for describing female homosexuals" (Ibid.). The term *raerae* [see above] is sometimes used, also *vahine pa'i'a* which means "woman rubbing together genitals without penetration" (Levy, p. 140). Scattered, inconclusive reports from the Indonesian archipelago exist but contain nothing that would parallel the profession-defined male homosexuality.

BIBLIOGRAPHY. Beatrice Blackwood, *Both Sides of the Buka Passage*, Oxford: Clarendon Press, 1935; Waldemar Bogoras, "The Chukchi of Northeastern Asia," *American Anthropologist*, 3 (1901), 80–108; A. Bernard Deacon, *Malekula*, London: Routledge & Kegan Paul, 1934; Donn V. Hart, "Homosexuality and Transvestism in the Philippines," *Behavioral Science Notes*, 3 (1968), 211–48; Gilbert H. Herdt, *Guardians of the Flutes*, New York: McGraw-Hill, 1981; idem, *Ritualized Homosexuality in Melanesia*, Berkeley: University of California Press, 1984; Raymond Kelly, *Etero Social Structure*, Ann Arbor: University of Michigan Press, 1977; Thomas M. Kiefer, "A Note on Cross-sex Identification among Musicians," *Ethnomusicology*, 12 (1967), 107–09; Robert I. Levy, *The Tahitians*, Chicago: University of Chicago Press, 1973; H. Arlo Nimmo, "The Relativity of Sexual Deviance: A Sulu Example." *Papers in Anthropology*, 19 (1978), 91–97; Géza Roheim, *Social Anthropology*, New York: Boni & Liveright, 1926.

Stephen O. Murray

PAINTING
See **Art, Visual; Nude in Art.**

PALEO-SIBERIAN PEOPLES
Several anthropological accounts of the indigenous peoples of eastern Siberia and Alaska describe a widespread practice of same-sex marriage between gender-mixed and gender-consistent males, and to a lesser extent, females. Sexual relations between men and between women fall into the **berdache** pattern common among circum-**Pacific** cultures from **Indonesia** and Polynesia to North and South

America, but the Paleo-Siberian peoples also associate gender-mixed individuals with **shamanism**. Though not unique to this cultural area, in that gender-mixed shamans have been noted among the Araucanians of Chile, the Sea Dyaks of Kalimantan, and the Sami of Lapland, these Siberian and Alaskan people present a consistent cultural pattern.

The transition to gender-mixed or cross-gender status may take the form of a profound spiritual-psychological experience at any point during the life course from childhood to old age or may be an identity experienced virtually from birth. The form of the transition varies as well from assuming a token trait of the other gender to a complete shift in comportment, dress, and location in the division of labor. Waldemar Bogoras noted the example of a Chukchee widow of middle age with three children who cut her hair, assumed masculine attire and speech, and learned to use a spear and a rifle. She subsequently married a girl who bore two sons. A male may make a similar gender transition, then "seeks the good graces of men, and succeeds easily with the aid of 'spirits.' Thus he has all the young men he could wish for striving to attain his favor. From there he chooses his lover, and after a time takes a husband." (1909, p. 450).

The association of special powers with interstitial or ambiguous persons is a widespread human idea and among foraging societies where the division of labor is often only by gender, it is gender-mixed individuals who present occupational innovations often as proto-artist or intellectual. Mircea Eliade notes that "the poetic vocabulary of a Yakut shaman contains 12,000 words, whereas the ordinary language—the only language known to the rest of this community—has only 4,000. [The shaman is] singer, poet, musician, diviner, priest, and doctor, appears to be the guardian of religious and popular traditions, preserver of legends several centuries old." (p. 30). Just as gender-mixed individuals bridge gender boundaries, they

are called to bridge between the sacred and the profane. Chukchee shamans show virtuosity in ventriloquism, spells, and divination in calling forth spirit voices. The Koryak and Kamchadal berdache is regarded as a magician and interpreter of dreams, who is "inspired by a particular kind of guardian spirits called *eien* [?], by the help of which he treats patients, struggles with other shamans, and also causes injury to his enemies." (Jochelson, p. 420).

Homosexuality is a frequent but not indispensable socially recognized component of the shaman identity among the circumpolar Samoyed, Ostyak, Tungus, Buryat, Aleut, Kodiak and Tlingit. It is noteworthy that in keeping with the gender cosmology, the gender-consistent marital partners of berdaches and shamans are not thought peculiar or worthy of differentiation from their counterparts who marry heterosexually.

Homosexuality among Paleo-Siberian peoples, then, is culturally recognized as an element in a social constellation of characteristics including "mixed" or anomalous placement in the division of labor and gender expectations, which sets certain persons apart as "special," "destined," or "gifted."

BIBLIOGRAPHY. Waldemar Bogoras, "The Chukchee," *Memoirs of the American Museum of Natural History*, 11 (1909); idem, "The Chukchi of Northeastern Asia," *American Anthropologist*, 3 (1901), 80–108; Marie Antoinette Czaplicka, *Aboriginal Siberia*, Oxford: Clarendon Press, 1914; Mircea Eliade, *Shamanism*, New York: Pantheon, 1964; Vladimir Jochelson, "The Mythology of the Koryak," *American Anthropologist*, 6 (1904), 413–25.

Barry D. Adam

PANIC, HOMOSEXUAL

The condition known as homosexual panic was first posited by Edward J. Kempf in the book *Psychopathology* (1920) and hence is sometimes styled *Kempf's disease.* In the moralizing language of the period, he there defined it as "panic due to the pressure of uncontrollable perverse sexual cravings," ascribing its importance to the frequency with which it occurred whenever men or women had to be grouped apart from the opposite sex "for prolonged periods, as in army camps, aboard ships, on exploring expeditions, in prisons, monasteries, schools and asylums."

According to Kempf, the homosexual cravings threaten to overcome the individual's ego, his sense of self-control, which has been weakened by fatigue, debilitating fevers, loss of love object, misfortunes, homesickness, the seductive pressure of some superior, or erotic companions. The affective homosexual desires cause delusions about situations, objects, and persons that tend to gratify the craving, or even hallucinations of them. When the erotic hallucination is felt to be an external reality and the subject can find no defense, panic ensues. The erotic affect may be symbolized as visions, voices, electric injections, "drugged" feelings, "poison" and "filth" in the food, seductive and hypnotic influences, irresistible trance states, crucifixion, and the like. It may be more or less severe, lasting from a few hours to several months, and the metabolic disturbances attending such dissociations of the personality, because the autonomic reactions produced by fear may be quite serious. When the subject's compensatory striving to retaliate or escape increases his liability to punishment, a tendency to lowering of blood pressure, irregularity of pulse, difficulty in breathing, and a tendency to assume a catatonic attitude seem to follow, as in young monkeys, puppies, terrified soldiers, and catatonic patients. Further, the individual incarcerated in a mental hospital may be caught in a vicious circle, because the deteriorating, monotonous existence forced upon him reduces his powers of adaptation and social competition. The panic state may be the first acute episode in schizophrenic disorders, and is more frequent in males than in females. The prognosis in such cases depends largely upon the extent of the defensive systematization of the delusions, and whether or not the patient is reacting with hatred. The presence of hatred is always to be considered as dangerous and certain to prevent the development of insight. Instead of overt sexual delusions, the individual suffers anxiety on account of fears of undue malignant influence, physical violence, or impending death. Such an episode is termed *acute aggression panic.* Prognosis is usually favorable, but a relapse is liable to occur if the individual does not make a successful heterosexual adjustment. The recurrence of panic results from inability to control or repress the homosexual tendencies, which may eventually become dominant and incurable. Such was the psychiatric discourse generated to deal with a problem that, in the socially repressive atmosphere of the period, undoubtedly possessed a certain reality.

It is significant that the concept of homosexual panic emerged in the United States just after World War I, when for the first time since 1865 large numbers of men were brought together in training camps and military bases with no members of the opposite sex present. While homophobic literature makes much of the alleged tendency of one-sex institutions to cause homosexual behavior, just the opposite reaction can and does occur. The fear of being socially defined as "homosexual" was in the past so intense that the perception of homosexual desires within oneself could precipitate the symptoms described above, particularly since the popular mind failed to grasp the psychiatric distinction between exclusive homosexuality and homosexual attraction of a sporadic or episodinal kind, and the religious sanctions could attach even to erotic desires, independent of any overt activity. The anxiety created by this confusion and by the affective character of the imagined homosexual identity was demoralizing for the patient and perplexing for the therapist. The phenomenon of homosexual panic stems in no small part from the internalization of society's futile attempt to stigmatize and prohibit homosexual behavior.

BIBLIOGRAPHY. Edward J. Kempf, *Psychopathology*, St. Louis: C. V. Mosby Company, 1920.

Warren Johansson

PAPACY

Given the custom of monastic sex-segregation and the extension of celibacy to the priesthood in the Western church beginning in the eleventh century, it is not surprising that a number of Roman pontiffs should have been involved in homoerotic sentiments and behavior. Details of the personal biographies of the early Christian popes are scanty, but beginning with the so-called dark age of the papacy (ninth–eleventh centuries) we begin to find information on wayward and self-indulgent behavior on the part of the bishops of Rome.

John XII (938–964) was the son of Alberic II, the civil ruler of the eternal city, and connected to other patrician families. On being elected pope at the age of eighteen, he modeled himself on the scandalous Roman emperor **Heliogabalus**, holding homosexual orgies in the papal palace. To counter opposition to his rule, he invited the German ruler Otto the Great to Rome, where he was crowned emperor in 962. John was thus instrumental in establishing the Holy Roman Empire, an institution that lasted in a formal sense until 1806. Benedict IX (1021–ca. 1052) was the son of the count of Tusculum. He imitated John XII in staging licentious orgies. These and other excesses caused such indignation that Benedict was deposed in 1045, but then reinstated, only to be deposed again. He disappeared into such deep obscurity that his actual date of death is unknown. John's activities may have helped to incite the reaction of the puritanical theologian Peter **Damian** (1007–1072), whose *Liber Gomorrhianus* is an attack against all kinds of sexual irregularities among the clergy. Under his associate Pope Gregory VII (ca. 1021–1085) reform ideas triumphed, and clerical celibacy was made obligatory for the Catholic priesthood, an injunction that remains in force to this day. The licentious "Pope Joan," who is supposed to have lived during this period, is entirely mythical.

As might be expected, it is the **Renaissance** period, with its revival of classical antiquity and love of art, that sees the greatest number of sexually active popes. The Venetian Paul II (1417–1471) was so vain that he had originally intended to take the name Formosus ("beautiful"). He was a collector of statuary, jewelry, and (it was said) of handsome youths. Given to the most sumptuous ecclesiastical drag, he was lampooned by his enemies as "Our Lady of Pity." His successor, Sixtus IV (1414–1482), is remembered for his art patronage, which included the erection and first decorations of the Sistine chapel. Among the artists most prominent in his reign was the Florentine homosexual **Botticelli**. This pope favored his scheming nephews, one of whom himself became pope under the name of Julius II. However, Sixtus was most devoted to another nephew, Raffaele Riario, whom he made papal chamberlain and bishop of Ostia. He elevated to the cardinalate a number of other handsome young men.

The Borgia pope, Alexander VI (1431–1503) was believed to have reduced Rome to unparalleled depths of depravity, and the city teemed with assassins and prostitutes of both sexes. Alexander was himself much given to womanizing, having sired eight or more children, but he was apparently not averse to the charms of young men as well. His successor Julius II (1443–1513) positioned himself for high office during the reign of his uncle Sixtus IV. A lover of art, he patronized both **Michelangelo** and Raphael, and in 1506 he laid the foundation stone for the magnificent church of New St. Peters. However, Julius' military conquests caused friction with the king of France and the German emperor. At their behest a council met in Pisa in 1511 to consider his deposition. Arraigned as "this sodomite, covered with shameful ulcers, who has infected the church with his corruption," Julius nonetheless managed to prevail by calling his own council, which was still in session when he died in May 1513. His successor, the Medici Leo X (1475–1521), was also a great patron of the arts, so much so that his extravagance is said to have helped bring on the Reformation. Like several of his predecessors he was involved in intrigues to advance favorite nephews, an expensive hobby that strained the treasury to the utmost.

Before becoming pope, Julius III (1487–1555) had presided over the Council of Trent, which was to result in the Counterreformation and a new sobriety at the papal court. However, Julius III was granted one last Indian summer period of licentiousness. He was often seen at official occasions with a catamite, Innocente (Prevostino), whom he created a cardinal, together with a number of other teenage boys.

The dour Pius V (reigned 1566–1572) issued two constitutions, the first (V, *Cum primum*) of which turned sodomites over to the secular courts and ordered degradation of members of the clergy who were guilty of the vice; a second (LXXII, *Horrendum*) provided that religious found guilty be deprived of the benefit of clergy, but only if the sodomitic acts were frequent and repeated, as it were from habit; this presumably exempted individuals who had only occasionally strayed.

Little is known of sexual irregularity of modern popes, at least during their pontificates. According to Roger Peyrefitte, John XXIII (1881–1963) and, more plausibly, Paul VI (1897–1978) conducted homosexual affairs. The Polish pope, John Paul II (1920–), had enounced conservative views on sex and marriage long before his election in 1978. After becoming pope he encouraged Joseph Cardinal Ratzinger to issue a statement reaffirming disapproval of homosexuality, terming it an "intrinsic moral evil" (letter of the Vatican Congregation for the Doctrine of the Faith, October 30, 1986). Also under this pope the American gay Catholic organization Dignity was forbidden to use church premises for its activities, and gay Catholics would appear to have entered a phase of banishment *extra ecclesiam*, as least as far as the practice of their sexual preference is concerned.

BIBLIOGRAPHY. J. N. D. Kelly, *The Oxford Dictionary of Popes*, New York: Oxford University Press, 1988.

Wayne R. Dynes

PARAGRAPH 175

This was the notorious article of the Imperial Criminal Code (*Reichsstrafgesetzbuch*) that was adopted in 1870 for the newly-formed North German Confederation and then took effect on January 1, 1872 on the entire territory of the empire, replacing the criminal codes of the 36 sovereign entities that had existed in **Germany** since 1815. Paragraph 175 penalized *widernatürliche Unzucht*, "lewd and indecent acts contrary to nature" between males (but not between females), and provided for a maximum penalty of five years' imprisonment. Although the original scope of the law had been solely anal intercourse, it was subsequently expanded by the appellate courts until it covered all "acts similar to coitus" (*beischlafsähnliche Handlungen*), but not mutual masturbation. The major aim of the **Scientific-Humanitarian Committee**, founded by Magnus **Hirschfeld** and his collaborators on May 14, 1897, was to secure repeal of the offending paragraph, and to that end a petition was circulated among prominent and cultured figures of Wilhelmine and then Weimar Germany. The petition was in the course of more than three decades signed by some 6,000 Germans from all walks of life, a number of them world-famous to this day.

The arguments against Paragraph 175 included: the injustice of stigmatizing as criminal the sexual activity of those whose homosexual orientation was inborn and unalterable; the danger of **blackmail** to which it subjected those who engaged in homosexual activity; the futility of attempting to penalize activity that in any case occurred in private and was thus inaccessible to police surveillance; and the number of illustrious figures of past and present whose homosexual inclinations would have made them liable to prosecution and social ruin.

Despite the support given to the campaign for repeal by the **Social Democratic** (and later by the Communist) Party, beginning with a speech in the Reichstag by August Bebel in 1898, the conservative opponents of repeal retained a majority on the commissions appointed to revise the penal code, and a 15–13 victory in 1929 proved hollow, as the National Socialist assumption of power led to an even more punitive version of the Paragraph in the novella of June 28, 1935, whose constitutionality was later upheld by the Federal Constitutional Court in Karlsruhe on May 10, 1957 on the pretext that "homosexual acts indisputably offend the moral feelings of the German people." In line with this reasoning the government of the Federal Republic has denied all compensation to those who during the Nazi period were for violations of Paragraph 175 interned in concentration camps, where they were forced to wear the **pink triangle** that later became a symbol of gay liberation.

Hirschfeld's vigorous campaign against Paragraph 175 made it a household word in Germany, and a slang expression for homosexual is *geboren am 17.5*, literally "born on the 17th of May." Only in 1969 did a Social Democratic government in Bonn repeal that portion of the law which penalized consenting homosexual activity between adult males. Even in the Nazi period Paragraph 175 was not extended or applied by analogy to lesbians. But it had taken 72 years of struggle, interrupted by the renewed persecution under National Socialism, to secure the abolition of a criminal law that in **France** the Revolution had stricken from the books in 1791.

BIBLIOGRAPHY. Günther Gollner, *Homosexualität: Ideologiekritik und Entmythologisierung einer Gesetzgebung*, Berlin: Duncker & Humblot, 1974; James D. Steakley, *The Homosexual Emancipation Movement in Germany*, New York: Arno Press, 1975.
Warren Johansson

PARANOIA

In current usage the word paranoia has two senses. The older meaning, stemming from nineteenth-century **psychiatry**, is that paranoia is a psychosis characterized by systematized delusions of persecution or grandeur. Hallucinations may be present, though they are not necessary for a diagnosis. Recent popularization of the term—a consequence of the general diffusion and vulgarization of psychiatric concepts characteristic of our society—has tended to reduce its meaning to a tendency on the part of an individual or group toward excessive and irrational suspiciousness and distrustfulness.

As part of his overall concern with mental conditions that impaired functioning, Sigmund **Freud** had sought to grapple with paranoia in the original psychiatric sense. From his mentor in the 1890s, Wilhelm Fliess, Freud took the notion that paranoia was dependent on repressed homosexuality. Only later, in 1915, did he formulate this interpretation as a general rule. He believed that the paranoic withdrawal of love from its former object is always accompanied by a regression from previously sublimated homosexuality to narcissism, omitting the half-way stage of overt homosexuality. This claim of a special link between paranoia and (male) homosexuality has been one of the most thoroughly examined of all **Freudian concepts**. Although some **psychoanalysts** cling to it, the results of a variety of investigations make the conclusion inescapable that it is untenable.

It may well be that, for reasons independent of the Freudian system, a somewhat larger proportion of homosexuals and lesbians incline to paranoia in the clinical sense. This finding would not be surprising in view of the **homophobia** to which they have been subjected. However, no serious or sustained consideration has been given to the matter.

In recent decades members of some gay organizations have also shown paranoia in the more ordinary sense of collective fearfulness that some sectors of society, primarily the government, are out to get them. To some extent these fears came in the baggage of the **leftist** sects who were influential in the years of gay liberation following the **Stonewall Rebellion** of 1969. They were not entirely groundless, inasmuch as the Federal Bureau of Investigation did engage in surveillance of gay groups. Nonetheless such fears can take exaggerated form, as in the belief that the **AIDS** virus was deliberately spread by some governmental agency. Prudence requires that one be on guard against inimical activities by state agencies, but—in the absence of any real evidence—this is a belief that clearly illustrates the possibilities of exaggeration and panic that lie in wait for those who are overly eager to detect conspiracies.

BIBLIOGRAPHY. Gary Anton Chalus, "An Evaluation of the Validity of the Freudian Theory of Paranoia," *Journal of Homosexuality*, 3 (1977), 171–88; Kenneth Lewes, *The Psychoanalytic Theory of Male Homosexuality*, New York: Simon & Schuster, 1988.

Wayne R. Dynes

PARENTS, LESBIAN AND GAY

Society has traditionally treated parenting as the exclusive prerogative of heterosexual couples whose union is sanctioned by marriage. Of course when children were born outside of wedlock, both parents and children have been made to feel the stigma of illegitimacy. In advanced industrial countries, however, recent social changes have eroded the dominant position of the nuclear family, and made single-parent units virtually of equal significance. In this context families headed by lesbians and gay men have become more numerous and more visible.

Origins of Lesbian and Gay Parental Units. Some persons, who eventually come to acknowledge their homosexuality, marry while still under the impression that they are bisexual or that their homosexual feelings are merely a phase that they will leave behind once they enter a stable union with a member of the opposite sex. Although they may become uneasy as the feelings emerge or persist, nonetheless children may be conceived and born in the initial years of the **marriage**. A few persons, mainly gay men, discuss their homosexuality with their fiancées before the wedding and, with candor and mutual understanding, the marriage may hold. However, increasing numbers of parents who become aware of their different orientation seek and obtain a divorce. In keeping with the tradition of allowing the children to remain with the mother, lesbian parents then raise the children. It is much less common for a gay father to retain custody of the children. In other instances childless lesbians and gay men may adopt children, though this has led to some controversy.

Some lesbians have conceived and given birth as a result of artificial insemination by donors. Since many doctors frown on this practice, associations have been formed to help prospective parents to accomplish the insemination themselves. As in the case of childless heterosexual couples seeking artificial insemination, the potential donor must be screened for genetic and health reasons. In many instances a gay man is the semen donor, and in a few cases both parents agree to bring up the child together ("coparenting"). In the latter situation it is essential for the parties to sign an agreement drafted by a lawyer, so that custody battles do not occur later. Some potential lesbian mothers prefer to obtain the semen from a sperm bank—where the donor renounces all rights—so as to avoid the possibility of a custody dispute.

After establishing a new household, the lesbian or gay male parent will date others of the same sex, which often leads to a permanent arrangement. There are then two persons of the same gender to raise the child. Sometimes the lover is called "aunt" or "uncle," but many children accept calling both "mother" or "daddy."

The Children. It is generally considered advisable for the lesbian or gay parent to "come out" to the children at an early age, indicating that she or he is "different." If the child learns of his or her parent's homosexuality through hostile remarks of playmates and relatives, they may have a negative reaction. In general girls accept the news of the orientation with some ease; boys initially resist, but then also usually come to accept.

Studies have shown that children of lesbian and gay parents are no more likely to become homosexual than those of heterosexual parents. Many lesbian and gay parents raise their children in traditional sex roles, others in less determinate modes. Sometimes boys are subject to "reverse sexism" on the part of lesbian separatist parents, or this result may occur indirectly, as when a lesbian mother is told to leave an all-women commune when her son reaches the age of twelve. On the whole, however, lesbian mothers and gay fathers—despite the economic difficulties that they often face—prove loving and supportive parents for their children.

Custody Problems. For the last hundred years, the usual position has been that when divorce occurs the mother is the best person to raise the children. With the current general questioning of sex-based privileges, this principle too is less firmly situated than formerly. Hence the heterosexual father in a divorce case is more likely to contest the granting of custody to a lesbian mother. In many instances the court battles that ensue are the result of bitterness that has accumulated over the course of an unhappy marriage. Such procedures are expensive for the litigants and often disturbing to the children. Inasmuch as custody decisions are never final, a lesbian mother may later have her right to keep her children challenged. In some cases the lesbian or gay parent is simply seeking visitation rights, but these too may be contested. Gradually a body of law is being developed which makes custody and visitation decisions more predictable, if not always more just.

To deal with these and other problems support groups of lesbian mothers and gay fathers have been formed. Many members find, however, that they derive benefit from these groups even when they are not experiencing any problems. Being a homosexual parent is a life situation all its own, and sharing experiences in a positive atmosphere is rewarding.

BIBLIOGRAPHY. Joe Gantz, *Whose Child Cries: Children of Gay Parents Talk about Their Lives*, Rolling Hills Estates, CA: Jalmar Press, 1983; Donna J. Hitchens and Ann G. Thomas, eds., *Lesbian Mothers and Their Children: Annotated Bibliography of Legal and Psychological Materials*, 2nd ed., San Francisco: Lesbian Rights Project, 1983; Joy Schulenburg, *Gay Parenting: A Comprehensive Guide for Gay Men and Lesbians with Children*, Garden City, NY: Anchor Press, 1985.

Evelyn Gettone

PARIS

From the high **Middle Ages** onward Paris was the political and cultural capital of **France**. After the religious and political turbulence of the sixteenth and seventeenth centuries the city emerged in the eighteenth century with its modern role as the *ville-lumière*, a major international center of intellectual endeavor and tastemaking.

The Eighteenth Century. Although the philosophes, the era's influential intellectuals, did not always reside there, Paris was the natural fulcrum of the **Enlightenment**'s effort toward social reform. Significantly, the last public executions for sodomy, those of Bruno Lenoir and Jean Diot, were carried out in the Place de Grève in 1750. Despite the advance of the new ideas, the Old Regime remained an uncertain environment for sexual experimentation, as the Marquis de **Sade**'s twenty-six years of imprisonment, much of it in the Bastille, attests. As early as the eighteenth century, it is clear that the Paris **police** kept records of the "infâmes," as they were called, even if no individual or mass arrests ensued. Certain areas of the city, notably dark and dead-end streets, were cruising grounds and even the scene of orgies after nightfall. The safest path to pleasure was membership in an erotic club. In 1777 *L'Espion anglois* of Pidansat de Mairobert carried an account of the Société des Anandrines, a group of lesbians who assembled for mutual gratification. A few years later the novel *Le Diable au corps* by Andréa de Nerciat, published only in 1803, described the doings of an aristocratic orgy club.

Denounced by the philosophes as relics of medieval barbarism, the old laws against sodomy were swept away in the wake of the French Revolution, and a brief epoch of freedom of the press ensued, as illustrated by two surviving pamphlets, *Les enfans de Sodome* and *Les petits bougres au manège*, which implicate several prominent members of the National Assembly.

The Nineteenth Century. The **Napoleonic** period and the Restoration saw the emergence of a new bourgeois capitalist culture, by definition amoral and pleasure-seeking—an ethos well captured in the many volumes of Honoré de **Balzac**'s *Comédie humaine* which has as its backdrop the France of the July Monarchy. In the 1840s the **bohemian** subculture of the Latin quarter emerges fully into view. A **subculture** characterized by freedom from family ties and restrictions, and therefore by erotic licence, it was immortalized in Henry Murger's *Scènes de la vie de Bohème* (1847–49). Also, at this time the first studies of the criminal underworld of Paris were published, with information on the **blackmail** that could still be practiced against wealthy and prominent homosexuals because of an intolerant public opinion.

It was the Second Empire (1852–1870), in the massive urban reconstruction projects of Baron Haussmann, that created the modern visage of the Paris of the great boulevards. Behind their showy façades lurked a fascinating underworld—a second city as it were. The contrast between the wealth of the aristocracy and haute bourgeoisie and the poverty of the masses favored prostitution in different forms, especially on the part of the handsome and well-built but poorly paid professional soldiers. It was this type of sexual commerce that underlay such groups as the Société des Emiles, a circle of prominent figures of the Second Empire who were discovered by the Paris police in 1864 to have members of elite regiments of the French army at their disposal. Other records kept by the police showed how young men who had prostituted themselves could then drift into crime as a profession. While homosexual activity as such was not a crime, the authorities could still intervene when they saw fit under statutes that loosely penalized sexual "immorality" (*délits contre les moeurs*).

From 1871 to 1945. Under the Third Republic, Paris did not lose its reputation as a center of vice; it even became a haven for wealthy homosexuals and lesbians who chose or were forced into exile from the English-speaking world with its prudery and intolerance. Englishmen such as Oscar **Wilde** could find Paris an inviting haven for their pleasures, while the bohemian quarter could shelter Paul **Verlaine**, whose poems include a series that frankly celebrate homosexual love. Lesbians from the English-speaking world, such as the wealthy Natalie **Barney** and her lovers Renée **Vivien** (Pauline Tarn) and Romaine **Brooks**, as well as the **modernist** Gertrude **Stein** and her companion Alice B. Toklas, found Paris a congenial home. The world of the upper-class French homosexual was recorded on the immortal pages of Marcel **Proust**'s *Sodome et Gomorrhe*, in which the character of the Baron de Charlus is supposed to have been modeled on Robert de **Montesquiou**-Fézensac.

Under the Third Republic erotic publishers such as Isidore Liseux and Robert Carrington could produce their wares in both French and English, reprinting the classics and bringing out new volumes, including translations of the early studies on "sexual science" that had begun to appear in Germany and Austria but could not be sold openly in England. French erotic literature flourished at the turn of the century, with lesbian love as a frequent theme, though usually from the standpoint of the male voyeur. One of a series of novels celebrating the adventures of a fictional Club Gérando even ascribed a different sexual practice to each of the Cities of the Plain, with sodomy as the starting point.

Interwar Paris remained a mecca for the foreign homosexual, some with literary pretensions ("the lost generation"). For foreigners and locals alike, a clandestine gay subculture existed unknown to the average citizen. Each **Mardi Gras** there was a Magic City gay costume ball on the left bank which thousands of people attended following an old tradition. However, the attempt to create a homosexual monthly entitled *Inversions* (1924–25) foundered when a prosecution inspired by the interpellation of Catholic deputies triumphed in court. The Paris of the 1920s lagged behind **Berlin** in the extent and openness of its homosexual activity.

The Depression years were far more sombre, but one significant event occurred whose homosexual background has not been fully appreciated: the 1938 assassination of Ernst vom Rath, a secretary at the German Embassy, by a young Polish Jew, Herschel Grynszpan, who had met him at the café Tout va bien in the capacity of a pimp arranging encounters with French hustlers. This event served as the pretext for "Crystal Night," November 9, in which Jewish synagogues and businesses in Germany fell victim to pogroms organized by the Nazis that spelled the virtual end of Jewish community life in that country. Paradoxically, the murderer fell into the hands of the Germans when France fell in 1940 but could never be tried because Hitler feared the humiliating exposure of the "martyr" vom Rath as a homosexual.

After World War II. Postwar Paris saw the appearance of the first French homophile organizations and their publications. An early journal named *Futurs* (1952–55) had contacts with the movement organized around the C.O.C. group in the **Netherlands**, but expired after 17 issues. Longer lived was *Arcadie*, a monthly that began in 1954 and lasted into the early 1980s. Its pages carried the most serious and intellectual discussions of that period, when the German **movement** was barely reviving and the American one was young and inexperienced.

The coming of the Fifth Republic was a setback, as the De Gaulle regime had its clerical-authoritarian overtones of puritanism, but the radical demonstrations of May 1968 and after saw the dam break, and Paris sprouted a diversified gay subculture inspired by that of the **United States**, with its network of organizations, bars, bathhouses, and erotic bookstores, some with incongruous American names such as Fire Island and The Broad. Gay political groups spanned the spectrum from far left to far right. Beginning in 1979 the journal *Gai Pied*, explicit in its illustrations and advertising, became the leading French gay publication, covering life in both Paris and the provinces. Homosexuality became a respectable theme in the world of the literary salons and publishing houses whose debates set the tone for the intellectual life of France and many other countries. After the decline of the influence of Jean-Paul **Sartre** and his existentialism, new sets of intellectuals, structuralist and post-structuralist, took the stage in Paris, attracting followers at home and abroad; prominent among them were Roland **Barthes** and Michel **Foucault**.

The steadily increasing prosperity of France as a whole has brought the consumer society within the reach of many gay Parisians, who have not spurned the pleasures of fine clothing, entertainment, and foreign travel. A gay radio station, Future Génération, broadcasts twenty-four hours a day, and the Minitel system makes computer dating possible. Paris hosts the only successful gay **church** that originated in Europe, the Centre du Christ Libérateur. Less favored by the new prosperity is the large section of the working class of North **African** origin, known colloquially as "les Beurs." Retaining a strong sense of family solidarity and aspects of **Mediterranean homosexuality**, these mainly Muslim French citizens are subject to stereotyping by the majority, a situation complicated by the fact that many hustlers are Beurs. An attempt to establish a gay mosque in Paris failed. Although the French capital is less renowned as a gay center than Amsterdam and **Berlin**, the overall attractions of Paris still suffice to draw enormous numbers of foreign gay and lesbian visitors.

BIBLIOGRAPHY. Gilles Barbedette and Michel Carassou, *Paris Gay 1925*, Paris: Presses de la Renaissance, 1981; Catherine van Casselaer, *Lot's Wife: Lesbian Paris, 1890–1914*, Liverpool: Janus Press, 1986; *Guide Homo*, Paris: Gai Pied Hebdo, 1989; Michel Rey, "Parisian Homosexuals Create a Lifestyle, 1700–1750: The Police Archives," *Eighteenth-Century Life*, 9 (1985) 179–91.

Warren Johansson

PARTICULAR FRIENDSHIPS

This term has been applied mainly to the emotional attachments of adolescents, particularly in closed institutions such as boarding schools, monasteries, and convents, who are passing through the "homosexual phase" of their development, but it is sometimes extended to the affectionate pairings of adults. Used in French as early as 1690 in a text entitled *Examen des amitiés particulières*, it was adopted by Joseph-François Lafitau to describe male–male relationships among the members of Amerindian tribes. In 1945, the novelist Roger Peyrefitte adopted the term for the title of his novel (*Les amitiés particulières*; in English, *Special Friendships*) about the tragic love affair of two schoolboys at an exclusive Catholic boarding school in France on the eve of World War I. Internationally famous, the work has become a classic of adolescent male love and so consecrated the term in that specific meaning.

The text of 1690 describes those involved in a "particular **friendship**" as constantly seeking each other's company, sharing their most intimate cares and griefs, and covertly violating the rules of the institution, while keeping others at a distance and excluding them from their conversation. The authors who recount such friendships agree that physical intimacy may, but need not be part of the mutual affection. Such writers include the novelists Honoré de **Balzac** (*Louis Lambert*), Paul Bonnetain (*Charlot s'amuse*), Camille Ferri-Pisani (*Les pervertis—Roman d'un potache*), Jehan Rictus (*Fil de fer*), Alain-Fournier (*Le grand Meaulnes*), and Amédée Guiard (*Antone Ramon*).

The British **public school** has an analogous phenomenon, but far more strongly tinged with sadomasochistic elements because of the system of "fagging" (not related to the modern American meaning of *faggot/fag*), in which a younger boy had to serve an upperclassman as his menial. The diaries of John Addington **Symonds** and other sources portray the Harrow of the 1840s as a virtual jungle where adolescent lust and brutality reigned unchecked. Every good-looking boy was given and addressed by a female name, and was regarded either as public property, in which case he could be forced into (often public) acts of incredible obscenity, or else made the "bitch" of an older boy. On the other hand, there could also be romantic friendships at public schools, in which one boy was younger, handsome, in another house, and in need of protection; such relationships were usually left asexual, to preserve the romantic glow. The participants would probably have liked to give them physical expression but were restrained by the pressures of the milieu. A modern classic novel on this theme is Michael Campbell's *Lord Dismiss Us* (1967); an American counterpart, John Knowles' *A Separate Peace* (1960), has a tragic ending.

The analogous relationships in girls' schools were named *crushes* or *smashes*. Because the sexual element in these feminine attractions is often deeply sublimated, the pattern appears unmistakably in books written for adolescents themselves, even in the era of Victorian prudery. Just because intense emotion between girls was less interdicted and more overt physical expression allowed, the lesbian equivalent of particular friendship could be delineated more clearly. **Colette** depicts such an attachment in her early work *Claudine à l'école* (1900), Dmitry Merezhkovsky another in his *The Birth of the Gods* (1925). In the film *Mädchen in Uniform* (1932), based on the novel *The Child Manuela* by Christa Winsloe, a lesbian "special friendship" ends in terror and tragedy.

For many participants in special friendships, the whole experience was a moment of adolescent romance and ideal-ism which they would leave behind as they matured into the heterosexual affairs of adulthood. For a few, it was an initiation into the realm of homosexual experience that would remain forever tinged with the afterglow of youthful tenderness and mutual devotion.

BIBLIOGRAPHY. Marion Zimmer Bradley, "Feminine Equivalents of Greek Love in Modern Fiction," *International Journal of Greek Love*, 1/1 (1965), 48–58; Jonathan Gathorne-Hardy, *The Old School Tie: The Phenomenon of the British Public School*, New York: Viking, 1978; Martha Vicinus, "Distance and Desire: English Boarding-School Friendships," *Signs*, 9 (1984), 600–22.
Warren Johansson

PASOLINI, PIER PAOLO (1922–1975)

Italian novelist, poet, filmmaker, playwright, and polemical essayist.

Life. Born in Bologna, during World War II he took refuge in rural Friuli, where he remained until 1949, becoming a member of the Communist Party. In 1949 anticommunist political enemies made his homosexuality public, creating a scandal that led to his expulsion from the Party, ruining his career as a teacher, and causing him to move to Rome.

In Rome Pasolini came into contact with the world of the slums on the outskirts of the city, which he portrayed in his novels *Ragazzi di Vita* (1955) and *Una vita violenta* (1959). His novels were accompanied by poetry of high quality, as seen in the volumes *Le ceneri di Gramsci* (1957), *La religione del mio tempo* (1961), and *Poesia in forma di Rosa* (1964). These publications brought him fame, but also a series of prosecutions (often for "obscenity") that were to dog him periodically throughout his life.

By the early 1960s Pasolini's name had become one of the best known in postwar Italian culture. He had also published essays and anthologies which served to keep him in the public eye. International renown came, however, not from his literary works, but from his activity as a filmmaker, which began in the sixties. Alongside this work Pasolini wrote plays, which were published in 1973 and 1979. The seventies represented the height of his fame. His political and journalistic work found easy entry into the Italian press, stimulating major debates.

On November 1, 1975, Pasolini was murdered at Ostia by a male prostitute with whom he had just had sexual relations. The slayer was a street tough ("ragazzo di vita") of the type he had so often portrayed in his works.

Critical Evaluation. Probably no contemporary author has so fully incarnated the cultural and social contradictions of Italian homosexual life as has Pasolini. Catholic by upbringing and Communist by conviction, throughout life he was tormented by the conflict between a lay and progressive concept of life and a conservative one laced with Catholic sexual guilt.

The 1949 scandal had a major impact on this conflict inasmuch as it forced him to "come out" before he was psychologically prepared to do so, when he was in fact traumatized. From these circumstances stemmed a certain diffidence, sometimes tinged with paranoia, in his relations with society in general and the homosexual world in particular. In fact the homosexuals who appear in such works as *Ragazzi di vita* and *Una vita violenta* are stereotypically effeminate, distasteful caricatures. Their role is to be victims.

The conception of sexuality that emerges from Pasolini's works is a nostalgic one, linked to traditional **Mediterranean homosexuality**, and hence inimical to the sexual revolution that was taking place in Italy as in the rest of the industrialized world. A good example is the famous "trilogy of life" that is made up of the **films** *Decameron* (1971), *The Canterbury Tales* (1972), and *The Arabian Nights* (1974), in which Pasolini sought to capture an innocent, "pure" sexuality, untouched by the Catholic conditioning and sense of guilt. He sought it sentimentally in the peasant society of the past, or in Third World countries that remain outside the orbit of Western civilization and Christian morality.

Toward the end of his life Pasolini repudiated this trilogy of films, publicly confessing that the sexuality he had been in search of had no existence— not in the past and not in the Third World. From this crisis came his last, posthumous film *Salò*, which is shot through with desperation. As in the work of **Sade** which inspired it, sex here is an instrument of power and oppression.

Despite his conflicts, Pasolini several times started debates on sexuality which were discussed throughout Italy, including the famous one on abortion. In these acts of setting forth his position one sees his love of being scandalous and of going against the tide, even at the cost of contradicting himself. His willingness to shock did not prevent him from withholding much of his homoerotic writing from publication, an abstention that reflects his prudery on the subject, together with his diffidence.

With Pasolini's consent, however, theatre works in which homosexuality was important were released, including *Orgia* (performed in 1968) and *Calderón* (1973), to which was added *Affabulazione* after his death (1977). Entirely posthumous were the long autobiographical stories *Amado mio* and *Atti impuri* (both 1982), sensitive evocations of his adolescent turmoil and of Pasolini's first loves for young peasants of the Friuli region. These last are probably the works in which homosexuality is evoked with the greatest serenity, and with a gentle lyricism absent elsewhere.

Although individual love poems appeared in Pasolini's works, his specifically homoerotic production remains unpublished, including for example the cycle known as *L'hobby del sonetto*, written for Ninetto Davoli, the smiling, curly-haired actor who starred in several of his films.

After Pasolini's death a veil of obscurity descended in Italy to cover the "embarrassment" of his sexual "deviation." Hence the effort some of his friends made to have his murder treated as a political rather than as a sexual crime; though the evidence was flimsy, this hypothesis was considered more respectable. Only recently, however, through the initiative of the Italian gay movement, has an analysis been undertaken of the enormous influence that Pasolini's homosexuality exercised on his achievements.

BIBLIOGRAPHY. Stefano Casi, ed., *Cupo d'amore: l'omosessualità nell'opera di Pasolini*, Bologna: Il Cassero, 1987; Enzo Siciliano, *Pasolini: A Biography*, New York: Random House, 1982.

Giovanni Dall'Orto

PASSIVE
See **Active–Passive Contrast.**

PATER, WALTER (1839–1894)

British writer and critic. Born the third child of a surgeon in the London slum of Stepney, Pater lost his father at an early age. He overworked himself to the point of illness to win a scholarship to Oxford. Pater early attempted writing in verse; yet lacking any poetic instinct or command of rhythm, he abandoned poetry to become a master of English prose style, a highly refined, allusive and personal style that gave him a potentially stirring instrument of self-expression. At Oxford he heard lectures by Matthew Arnold, appreciating their wide, topic range of literary references and the author's serious belief in the importance of culture. He learned French and German, studied the literature of both countries, and acquired a combination of French **aestheticism** and German learning, yet he never became a profound thinker or a conventional scholar.

In 1864 he won a classical fellowship at Brasenose College, Oxford—the beginning of his career. A discreet essay on the homosexual archeologist J. J. **Winckelmann** (written for *Westminster Review* in 1867) betrayed to discerning readers a sympathy for Greek *paiderasteia*. Pater's marked preference for the company of young and good-looking men, joined with the intellectual currents in his work and the personality of several of his friends, was enough to win some admirers and make some enemies. Added to this heterodoxy was Pater's rejection of Christianity and affinity for paganism; and over him these aspects of his character cast a shadow that later efforts at hiding his private self never dispelled.

A friendship with Charles Lancelot Shadwell, a former pupil of his who became a fellow of Oriel College in 1864, inspired an essay entitled *Diaphanéité* (1864), and to him was dedicated the fruit of Pater's first visit to Italy, *Studies in the History of the Renaissance* (1873). This was not a true history, but a study of a set of chosen personalities whom he recognized as kindred spirits in subtlety, sophistication, and love of beauty. Collected and read together, the essays in the volume sounded a sensuous verbal music, adumbrating a novel view of life that made the tone of the work more fascinating than its contents. But even more provocative to Pater's contemporaries was the Conclusion, ending with the words "To burn always with this hard gem-like flame, to maintain this ecstasy, is success in life." Nothing could better have summed up the repugnance provoked by the volume than the pungent characterization of the author—attributed to Benjamin Jowett—as a "demoralizing moralizer."

In the second edition of *The Renaissance* (1877), he deleted the Conclusion, but revised the first chapter by adding passages on *The Friendship of Amis and Amile*, a thirteenth-century French romance centered on male **friendship**. As part of the plot Amis lays down his life for Amile by taking his place in single combat, while Amile in turn lays down his life in proxy by slaying his children so that Amis may be healed. In the discussion of the tale Pater made both more explicit and more nuanced his appreciation of the libidinal aspects of human culture and specifically of the Christian culture of the **Middle Ages**.

Two others who appealed to Pater were Algernon Charles Swinburne, protodecadent poet, and Simeon Solomon, a Pre-Raphaelite painter, frankly homosexual, whose career was destroyed when a morals charge revealed his proclivities to Victorian society. From 1869 to his death, Pater lived in Oxford with his two spinster sisters in a curious sort of household that took the place of a conventional marriage.

In 1885 Pater published a novel entitled *Marius the Epicurean*. It was a sustained portrait of an invented, non-historical figure, a fictitious biography in two volumes set in the reign of Marcus Aurelius, when the alternatives of paganism and Christianity coexisted. In writing the book the author shifts from sensations to ideas, as the hero Marius replaces his love for the poetic and pagan Flavian with friendship for the Christian soldier Cornelius. Marius—with whom Pater strongly identifies—dies at the end of the novel, but since he intervenes to set Cornelius free when both are taken captive, the Christians with whom he has associated deem his death a sort of martyrdom.

Other works of his were in the field of literary criticism, such as *Appreciations: with an Essay on Style* (1889). Though containing nothing that could not have been read before, it elicited highly favorable reviews, with the recognition that the author was "beyond rivalry the subtlest artist in contemporary English prose." Pater was famous at the end of his life, when he published *Plato and Platonism* (1893), in which, however, there are only a few neutral and scholarly references to homosexuality, while the book closes with an admonition to love the intellectual, disciplined, patiently achieved "dry beauty" which **Plato** recommends and is

shown to have achieved against his own instinctual urgings. In the spring of 1894 he became ill and died suddenly just before his fifty-fifth birthday.

Heterosexual love and marriage receive scant attention in his work, and the attitude toward Christianity in his early writings contained more animosity than wit. In a review of William Morris' poetry in 1868, he commented that medieval religion "was but a beautiful disease or disorder of the senses." With intimates he could engage in a provocative mockery and sarcasm that he rigorously suppressed from his published writings and even more from his private letters, which reveal none of the arcana of his existence.

The refined and academic hedonism of Walter Pater mark him as a type of homosexual with profound aesthetic sensibilities who functions both as a critic of art and as a creator, in this instance, of a prose style whose formal perfection and musicality make it one of the highwater marks of nineteenth-century English literature. Only subtly does his fascination with male beauty betray the real focus of his interests, while he kept his private self deliberately elusive and hidden in his lifetime. His career as a lecturer at Oxford followed a path distant from the one trodden by "decadent" contemporaries such as Oscar **Wilde** whose unconventional sexuality he secretly shared.

BIBLIOGRAPHY. Richard Dellamora, "An Essay in Sexual Liberation, Victorian Style: Walter Pater's 'Two Early French Stories,'" *Journal of Homosexuality*, 8/3–4 (1983), 139–50; Michael Levey, *The Case of Walter Pater*, London: Thames and Hudson, 1978.

Warren Johansson

PATRISTIC WRITERS: THE FATHERS OF THE CHURCH

The Patristic writings are usually defined as the surviving texts of the Christian teachers from the end of the first century—when the **New Testament** was being completed—until the seventh century. Some would extend the term to the thirteenth century, when the tradition of Scholasticism took hold. Although the New Testament itself properly precedes the Patristic texts, the latter presume it as a canonical source, so that some attention must be given to it at the outset.

The New Testament. The Secret Gospel of Mark (as reconstructed by Morton Smith) may have treated **Jesus'** implied homoerotic relationship with a male catechumen before the theme was expunged from the surviving text of canonical Mark. As we know them, the gospels are so reticent that disputes still rage over whether Jesus recommended the chastity he apparently practiced over the marriage he praised, although subsequently disciples abandoned wives as well as parents to follow him.

Jesus criticized those who followed the letter of the law instead of the spirit of love. More than any other evangelist, St. Luke portrays Jesus as contradicting rabbinical conventions on sex, for example by teaching that to follow him a man must reject his wife's love or that celibacy might be necessary for salvation. In the early church, before tradition took shape or the texts of the gospels were fixed, though praising and practicing every variety of sexuality from virginity to promiscuity, most Christians, conscious of standing apart from and above pagans in sexual mores, accepted the Judaic view that homosexuality, like infanticide, was a sin.

Deemed the second founder, St. **Paul**, whose epistles are the earliest of preserved Christian writings and came to comprise one-third of the New Testament when its canon was established about A.D. 200, was explicit about sex. He prescribed marriage only for those too weak to remain chaste, but forbade divorce, available at the whim of Jewish, Greek, and Roman husbands, as well as polygamy, then common among Jews, and levirate marriage, which had been mandatory, of a brother's widow. In other ways, however,

greatly influenced by the Old Testament, by pharisaic **Judaism**, and by the melange of ascetic Platonism and theosophical Judaism best exemplified by **Philo** Judaeus, he forbade sex outside of marriage. This included concubinage, and he singled out homosexuality, even between females, for special condemnation, as well as transvestism of either sex, long hair on males and other signs of effeminacy or softness, and masturbation. Romans 1:18–32, Titus 1:10, Timothy 1:10, and I Corinthians 6:9 all emphatically condemn male homosexuality.

Greek (and Coptic) Fathers. The earliest post-Biblical (non-canonical) Christian homophobic writing that has been preserved, the Epistle of Barnabas, explained that the Mosaic law declared the hare unclean because it stood for sodomites. The *Acts of Paul and Thecla* claimed that Paul demanded total renunciation of sex. The *Acts of Andrew the Apostle* told a lady that her renunciation of sex with her husband would repair the Fall. In the *Acts of John* Christ thrice dissuaded the apostle from marrying. By the mid-third century, the *Acts of Thomas* were enthusiastic about the sexless life. The **Gnostic** *Gospel According to the Egyptians* argued that Adam and Eve by introducing sex brought about death.

On returning to the Near East from Rome in 172, Tatian, a student of Justin Martyr (who had even approved another young man's wish to be castrated), enjoined chastity on all Christians. Many Syrian churches allowed only **celibate** males to be baptized. By the second and third centuries, certain heretics argued that marriage was Satanic. Marcionites described the body as a nest of guilt. The *Gospel According to the Egyptians* had Jesus speak of paradise in which the sexes had not been differentiated. Libertine sects were exceptional in this period. Thus the second-century Alexandrian heretic Carpocrates' teen-aged son Epiphanes, who succeeded him as head of the sect, allowed women and goods to be held in common.

St. **Clement** (ca. 150–ca. 215), who studied at **Alexandria** under Pantaenus, whom he succeeded as head of its catechetical school until he fled the persecution of 202, combined the Gnostic belief that illumination brought perfection with the Platonic doctrine that ignorance rather than sin caused evil. Borrowing phrases from neo-Platonism and **Stoicism**, Clement condemned homosexuality as contrary to nature and idealized a sexless marriage as between brother and sister. After him most Christians wrote far less positively of the married life. Pseudo-Clement opined that one had to look far away to the *Sinae* (to China) for a people who lived justly and moderately in sex and thus were not afflicted with famine or disease (*Recognitions*, 8, 48).

The learned Origen, prevented from seeking martyrdom by his mother in 202, succeeded Clement as head of the catechetical school in Alexandria. Fasts, vigils, and poverty he reinforced with self-castration, which he understood Matthew 19:12 as recommending. Deposed as head of the school, he left Alexandria in 231 for Caesarea, where he founded a rival school. He succumbed a few days after being released from torture during the persecution of 250. Some of his many works, including commentaries on almost every book of the Bible emphasizing the allegorical interpretation open only to the enlightened, were destroyed after their condemnation in 400.

From 235 to 284 the "Thirty Tyrants" rapidly succeeded one another as emperors of Rome, only one dying peacefully, to the accompaniment of invasions, plagues, and famines. These catastrophes undermined trade and cities' wealth, particularly in the west, causing **gymnasia**, **bathhouses**, and **symposia** to diminish or fail. Thus these disasters undermined **pederasty** while driving the majority to seek salvation in Oriental mystery religions. In desperation several tyrants unleashed great persecutions against the scapegoat Christians.

In 257 St. Cyprian, bishop of Carthage, opined that the plague had the merit of letting Christian virgins die intact, but no Christian invoked medical arguments about the benefits of virginity or (as frequently among late pagan physicians) of moderation. The third-century forgeries made by a Syriac author but ascribed to St. Clement, bishop of Rome, worried about the abuses and perils from unmarried females besetting the celibate male virgin traveling from one community to another.

The Coptic St. Anthony (ca. 251–356), father of Christian monasticism, gave away his inheritance at the age of 20 and devoted himself to asceticism, retiring first into a tomb and then in 285 into the desert, in both of which he fought with hordes of demons. When the Devil failed to seduce him alone in the guise of a woman, he reappeared as a black boy. Around 305 Anthony organized the community of hermits he had attracted under a loose rule. He lent Athanasius, Patriarch of Alexandria, who wrote St. Anthony's life, crucial support against a priest of Alexandria, Arius, founder of the greatest Trinitarian **heresy**. The end of the persecutions gave ascetics the glory formerly gained by martyrs for the faith and spawned Christian **monasticism**. Like St. Anthony, other anchorites found sexual desire the most difficult bodily urge to control and ordained severe fasts to weaken it. The success of monasticism increased the sexual negativism of the rest of the church.

Converted after his discharge from the army in 313, the Copt St. Pachomius (ca. 290–346) founded a monastery near the Nile in the Thebaid about 320. By his death he ruled over 9 such institutions for men and 2 for women as abbot general. His rule, the first for cenobites, influenced those of St. Basil, John Cassian, Caesarius of Arles, and Benedict, as well as that, anonymous, of "the Master." Pachomius said that "no monk may sleep on the mattress of another" (Ch. 40) or come closer to one another "whether sitting or standing" than one cubit (about 18 inches) when they had meals together. It was only about 500 in Gaul that a common dormitory was instituted in place of the solitary cells (Benedict, Ch. 22) after the old building burned.

The Cappadocian Fathers defined orthodoxy and defended it against the Arian heresy in the mid-fourth century: Sts. Basil, Gregory of Nazianzus, and Gregory of Nyssa. St. Basil the Great, brother of Gregory of Nyssa, forsook the world, having received a classical education in Constantinople and Athens, where he had been a fellow student with Julian the Apostate under the pagan rhetorician Libanius. After a stint with ascetics in Syria and Egypt, he settled as a hermit in Pontus, renewing his friendship with Gregory of Nazianzus, third of the Cappadocian fathers. In 370 Basil became bishop of Caesarea, a post earlier held by Eusebius, the friend and biographer of emperor Constantine the Great and historian of the church (ca. 260–ca. 340). After 313, as a moderate Arian rather than a puritan, Eusebius advised Constantine's Arian sons, who first decreed capital punishment for passive homosexuality in 342, two years after their mentor's death. Basil was much influenced by Origen, most brilliant of the theologians of **Alexandria**, which remained an intellectual center even after Christians murdered Hypatia and began to burn books. Basil continued to fight the Arians and also composed the liturgy still used by the Eastern church. His monastic rule, though strict, eschewed the more extreme austerities of the hermits of the desert. As revised by St. Theodore of Studios (died 862), Basil's rule still regulates Orthodox monasteries.

First of the pillar ascetics, St. Simeon Stylites (ca. 390–459) lived on a column for about 40 years working miracles near Antioch. These "athletes for Christ" mortified the body more than any Olympic athlete improved his, but the lack of discipline of Simeon and other hermits, and scandals about them, encouraged the growth of monasteries. In these, repression of homosexuality became an obsession.

With Eusebius, Athanasius, the Patriarch of Alexandria (who authored the Nicene Creed against the followers of Arius), and the Cappadocian fathers, John Chrysostom, the most influential of the Desert Fathers, closes the list of the most important Greek Fathers. He also set in motion the intensifying of Christian homophobia from Jesus' "Let him who is without sin cast the first stone" to "How many hells shall be enough for such [sodomites]?" in Homily IV on Romans 1:26–27, and to the assertion of Luca da Penne (ca. 1320–ca. 1390) that "sodomy is worse than murder" because the murderer seeks to destroy only a single human being, but the sodomite means to destroy the entire human race by frustrating its reproduction.

Latin Fathers. Spreading westwards, the Church won its earliest converts among urban Jewish and Greek communities. All the early bishops of Rome were Greek. The long struggle with the synagogues, which St. Paul had begun in the heartland of Christendom, Asia Minor, continued in Rome and North Africa, leaving a stain of anti-Judaism in Christianity. Like the eastern churches, the western ones flourished in cities rather than in the countryside and drew non-Jewish or non-Greek converts more often from oppressed urban minorities: the poor, women, and slaves. The first surviving Christian writing in Latin was Tertullian's *Apologeticum* of 197. The Latin church was thus later than and modeled on the Greek, and the earliest translation of the Gospels or Epistles from Greek to Latin was done in North Africa at the end of the second century (the so-called *Afra*).

Just as Latin Christians borrowed anti-Judaism from Greeks, who had long clashed with them in Alexandria, as well as from Copts and Armenians, oppressed ethnic minorities in the east whose urban representatives turned early and eagerly to Christianity, they also borrowed homophobia from the Jews which they reinforced with the hostility of Rome to effeminacy. The disapprobation of the ancient Romans, which persisted under the **Roman emperors**, helped the Catholic Church to become even more homophobic than the Orthodox, which grew upon the more tolerant soil of ancient **Greece**.

Made head of the church in Lyons in 177 after the martyrdom of its bishop Pothinus, St. Irenaeus attacked **Gnosticism**, especially as advanced and practiced by Valentinus. Perhaps the most influential Gnostic, Valentinus was said to recommend free love for the "pneumatics," spiritual men freed from the Law by *gnosis*. Unlike his eastern contemporary Clement of Alexandria, who condemned sodomy as "against nature," a Greek concept, and brandished other Platonic arguments, Irenaeus fought Gnosticism by emphasizing tradition, the canon of Scriptures, and the episcopate.

Reared a pagan in Carthage and educated in liberal arts and law, Tertullian, father of Latin theology, converted in 197 but eventually joined the Montanist sect. His apologies and controversial and ascetic tracts were written in Latin and occasionally in Greek. He rebutted accusations of immorality, including homosexuality and cannibalism. Ironically, Christians were soon to hurl these charges against heretics. Tertullian demanded separation from pagan society to escape its immorality and idolatry. He may have edited the *Passion* of Saints Perpetua and Felicitas, whose virginity he made central. Following Irenaeus in stressing tradition and attacking the Valentinians, he pessimistically dwelt on the Fall and original sin. Eschatological expectations led him to asceticism and perfectionism. In the 220s in *De pudicitia*, as a Montanist he condemned Pope Callistus' and a bishop of Carthage's laxity toward sexual sinners, urging a legalistic system of rewards and punishments. He probably used a Latin version of the Bible and, though influenced by Stoicism, stressed the literal and historical interpretation of revelation. Another Latin author, probably Novatian, wrote about 250: "Virginity makes itself equal to the angels."

Son of the Pretorian Prefect of Gaul, St. Ambrose, after practicing law and being governor, became bishop of Milan in 374. First of the four Latin "Doctors of the Church" with Jerome, Augustine, and Gregory the Great, this famous preacher and upholder of orthodoxy against pagans and Arians converted St. Augustine in 386. A familiar of emperors, as Bishop of Milan, which had replaced Rome as the Western capital, Ambrose upheld the independence of the church and made Theodosius the Great, who in 390 issued the second imperial law ordering death for homosexuality, do penance for a massacre at Thessalonica. Knowing the works of Cicero and other Latin thinkers, as well as Greek Christians, many of whose ideas he introduced to westerners, Ambrose wrote a treatise on clerical ethics, *De Officiis*, which encouraged asceticism and Italian monasticism.

After studying at Rome, St. Jerome devoted himself to asceticism with friends in his native Aquilea. In 374 he departed for Palestine but tarried at Antioch for further study before retreating as a hermit to the Syrian desert for 4 or 5 years, during which he learned Hebrew. Back in Rome, he was secretary to Pope Damasus, who ordered him to revise the Latin text of the Bible on the basis of the Hebrew and Greek originals. Finally settling in a monastery in Bethlehem, Jerome dedicated his life to study. The best patristic scholar, he produced many commentaries on the books of the Bible, of which his Latin version became authoritative in the Western church (in a late medieval edition known as the Vulgate). Attacking heretics, he advised extreme asceticism in *Against Helvidius* and *Against Jovinian*.

He asserted that "Christ and Mary were both virgins, and this consecrated the pattern of virginity for both sexes."

St. **Augustine**, who towered over all the Greek and Latin fathers, developed doctrines that held sway throughout the Dark Ages, were challenged and modified by Thomas **Aquinas** in the thirteenth century, but revived again by **Protestantism** in the sixteenth century. Leaning heavily on the Old Testament and rejecting **Manichaeanism** to which Augustine had once adhered, he taught that all non-procreative modes of sexual gratification were wrong because pleasure was their sole object.

St. Benedict of Nursia withdrew from the licentiousness at Rome, where he was educated, for a cave at Subiaco. He organized the monks attracted to his hermitage into twelve monasteries but in 525 moved to Monte Cassino where the "Patriarch of Western Monasticism" composed his rule by altering and shortening "The Rule of the Master" and also drawing freely upon those of Sts. Basil, John Cassian, and Augustine. Chapter 22 of his Rule prescribed that monks should sleep in separate beds, clothed and with lights burning in the dormitory; the young men were not to sleep next to one another but separated by the cots of elders.

From a noble family that fled Cartagena when it was destroyed by the Arian Goths, St. Isidore (d. 636), who had entered a monastery ca. 589, succeeded his brother as Archbishop of Seville in 600. Presiding over several councils in Visigothic Spain, the only Germanic realm whose laws punished homosexual acts, he founded schools and convents and tried to convert Jews. His often fanciful *Etymologies* (such as *miles quia nil molle faciat,* "*miles* [soldier] because he does nothing *molle* [effeminate]") became the encyclopedia of the Dark Ages. In his theological writings, Isidore borrowed from Augustine and Gregory the Great, condemning non-procreative sexuality and approving marriage hesitantly and solely for the begetting of children.

Adopted *in toto* from such Hellenistic Jewish authors as Philo Judaeus and Flavius Josephus, the homophobia of the early fathers was never contradicted or opposed by any Christian thinker accepted as an authority by later generations. The Third Lateran Council in 1179 prescribed for sodomitical clerics only degradation or penitential confinement in a monastery. This was carried out according to **canon law**, but secular legislation under clerical influence usually prescribed burning alive. Gratian in the *Decretals* devoted little space to homosexual and other "unnatural" sex acts but clearly considered such sins more heinous than fornication or adultery. The final triumph of homophobic thought and practice within the Western church occurred only in the thirteenth century, when at the Fourth Lateran Council under Pope Innocent III (1215) the Church attained its all-time height of power and influence over European society. From the close of the century onward, all expression of homosexual feeling and activity was forbidden and penalized not just by criminal sanctions, but by ostracism and social **infamy**.

BIBLIOGRAPHY. Peter Brown, *The Body and Society: Men, Women, and Sexual Renunciation in Early Christianity*, New York: Columbia University Press, 1988; James A. Brundage, *Law, Sex, and Christian Society in Medieval Europe*, Chicago: University of Chicago Press, 1987; Robin Lane Fox, *Pagans and Christians*, New York: Knopf, 1987; Elaine Pagels, *Adam, Eve, and the Serpent*, New York: Random House, 1988.

William A. Percy

PEDERASTY

Pederasty is the erotic relationship between an adult male and a boy, generally one between the ages of twelve and seventeen, in which the older partner is attracted to the younger one who returns his affection, whether or not the liaison leads to overt sexual contact. It is probably the most characteristic, if not normative, form of male homosexual relationship in the majority of human societies throughout history, though not in Western Europe and North America in modern times.

In contemporary writings on the subject of age-asymmetrical relationships there is an increasing tendency to merge pederasty into a larger context of **pedophilia**, comprising all adult–child relationships. Although it is common today, this trend has the disadvantage of suggesting that the adolescent partner in a pederastic relationship is a child, with all the connotations of vulnerability and innocence that such a term conveys. However this may be, it is best to examine the phenomenon, at least initially, in a nonjudgmental manner.

There is also reason to consider the attraction to young men of ages roughly eighteen to twenty-one as a separate phenomenon, termed **ephebophilia**.

Phenomenology. In tribal and premodern societies pederasty occurred chiefly as a form of initiation into the world of male adulthood through sexual intimacy between the older partner who serves as patron, protector, and mentor, and the younger, who is the pupil or protégé. Like marriage, the pederastic relationship may assimilate the junior partner to the status of the senior one, may incorporate him into the structure of a society dominated by aristocratic families and their clients and servitors. In terms of psychological functioning, the liaison can allow the younger male to experience sexuality in a nonprocreative mode (the "homosexual phase"), as it were a "dry run," before he masters the heterosexual aggressiveness of adult manhood, and at the same time to eroticize the tasks of the mature male in such a way that they are experienced not as a chore and a burden, but in a context of sexual pleasure and fulfillment. It also allows the older individual to trans-

mit his cultural identity to the younger one in a manner paralleling the bequest of genetic identity through marriage and fatherhood.

Traditionally, the pederast begins to lose sexual interest in his adolescent partner with the first signs of the growth of the beard. Some modern pederasts also report aversion to the inception of adult male pheromones, the "man scent" that the boy still lacks. Finally, some are erotically concerned with the hip-shoulder ratio, which is more nearly equal in the willowy adolescent youth than in the well-developed adult male with his V-chest configuration. Choosing adults as his sexual objects, the **androphile** typically likes prominent pectorals; the pederast does not.

In its most archaic forms, pederasty was an outgrowth of the comradeship in arms of warrior societies in which the older male instructed the younger in the arts of combat and self-defense. Even now in many primitive cultures the rite of passage into manhood entails pederastic activity that is obligatory for every member of the tribe. This aspect of pederasty is in itself a proof of the capacity for homosexual arousal and activity that is part of the macroevolutionary heritage of homo sapiens. Pederasty has also flourished in a number of high cultures, including ancient **Greece**, medieval **Islam**, **Japan**, and **Korea**.

Ancient Greece. The most celebrated model of man–boy relationship is the *paiderasteia* of the ancient Greeks, whose culture was thoroughly permeated by the institution. The pederastic element in Hellenic culture was part of the whole system of *paideia*, the education that is intended to make a boy a good soldier, a good father, a good citizen, a good statesman—to endow him with the combination of qualities which Greek civilization cherished and admired in the adult. While the Greeks practiced several varieties of pederasty, a particularly admired form was that of Sparta with its military culture; Plutarch's life of Lycurgus mentions edicts of that archetypal lawgiver to the effect that a man was obligated to form such a union, and that a boy was disgraced if he could not find an honorable lover who was in turn held responsible for his conduct on the battlefield. The actual origins of the pederastic institution in **Greece** are lost in the mists of prehistory. At the point that our sources allow us to monitor the phenomenon (the sixth century B.C.), pederasty flourished in the Greek city-states with varying degrees of emphasis on the content of the ethical/educational basis, from mere athletic prowess to training for leadership in the boy's later public career.

The myth of the abduction of **Ganymede** by Zeus served as the prototype of such a relationship, which was commemorated in **Crete** by a symbolic ravishment of the youth who then spent two months with his lover in the wild, finally being sent home with legally prescribed gifts symbolic of the liaison. Such an attachment supplemented the rather limited content of the education imparted in school, which was confined to rote learning reinforced by severe discipline. The principal concern of the Greeks was that the youth should choose a worthy lover and ever after be faithful and devoted to him, instead of engaging in the selfish conduct typical of the kept boy or "hustler" of today. It is worthy of note that a slave could not be a pederast, just as he could not contract a legal marriage: the older party had to be a free citizen who could inspire the boy to perform his duties to the city-state in an outstanding manner.

The aesthetic emphasis in pederasty, then and now, was on the ephemeral, **androgynous** quality of the youth that is lost the moment he crosses the developmental threshold of manhood—the negative event to which the Greek poets devote no little attention. The transient "bloom" (*anthos*) of the adolescent is a union of male and female beauties, a work of Eros and an object of adoration. The pederast, it should be stressed, has no interest in proselytizing for androphile (adult–adult) homosexuality; he is normally repelled by adult males and has no wish to be the object of their sexual attention. It is solely the charm of the youth in his mid-teens that attracts and captivates him.

While allusions to pederasty are found in many of the surviving works of Greek literature (distinct from the clearly negative attitude toward effeminacy in the plays of **Aristophanes**), the largest single collection of such writings is the twelfth book of the **Greek Anthology**, the so-called *Musa paidike* (Boy-Love Muse) of Strato of Sardio, who lived in the middle of the second century of the present era. The 250 poems of this work—and others scattered throughout the Anthology—reveal the customs of pederasty down to the smallest detail. It is remarkable that in the face of this unambiguous evidence—supplemented by the countless works of **art** consecrated to the beauty of the adolescent male—some recent authors have tried to claim that the "boy" (*pais*) of Greek literature was the adult male courted by the homosexual of today.

As known to us in literary sources, the Greek institution presents pederasty in a particularly elaborate form, with not only aesthetic and personalistic dimensions, but also those of state-building and military preparedness. Because of the lasting prestige of Greek civilization this type of pederasty has continued to occupy scholarly attention, though modern sensibilities sometimes present it in an altered version that is not true to the historic reality. Still the Greek phenomenon, however misunderstood, has been a tracer element revealing the permutations of the Western tradition of male same-sex love.

Cross-Cultural Manifestations. Comparative study discloses many societies in which the principal homosexual love object for males is the adolescent boy. The Far East provides the closest parallels to the elaborated form of Greece. In Korea in the first millennium the *hwarang* were pages chosen for their beauty and military prowess alike. In Japan the **samurai** class, arising in the late twelfth century, fostered an idealized love between the older warrior and his young protégé. There are many accounts of one partner dying to preserve the other's honor. Japanese **Buddhism** also permitted the admission of young novices who became the lovers of older priests. In China a more aesthetic variety of pederasty flourished, and there are a number of accounts of royal favorites, as well as everyday boy **prostitution**. The seclusion of women in Islamic countries led to an almost universal diffusion of boy love. Yet only in some regions of that civilization—as in **Mamluk** Egypt and modern **Afghanistan**—did the practice take on a military and state-building character.

Evidence from tribal cultures, though often obscured by inadequate reports, suggests that several modes approximating pederasty were prevalent. In New Guinea, as among other **Pacific** cultures where the matter has been carefully studied, a number of tribes believe that younger boys can become men only if their bodies are "primed" through the ingestion or insertion of the semen of older partners. In most cases the active partners seem themselves to be boys in their late teens, who were then expected to marry and lead a totally heterosexual life. A participant may be a receiver one year and the giver the next. Thus this initiatory homosexuality fits the pederastic pattern somewhat imperfectly, since the sexual connection is not truly intergenerational.

Modern Perspectives. The dominance of **androphilia**, the erotic relation between two post-adolescent males, is of comparatively recent origin, emerging among the Germanic-Celtic populations of northwestern Europe. Its characteristic subculture—the bars, bathhouses, and similar trysting places that flourish in the anonymity of the large city—lacks the educational/initiatory function of pederasty. The merits attaching to the latter are, however, the theme of much traditional apologetic literature on behalf of homosexuality. In harking back to ancient Greece, the androphile advocate of the late nineteenth and twentieth centuries appealed to the glories of a tradition which his own culture did not share or continue. As a recurring trait of Western civilization, Neo-classicism involves much editing and refashioning of the Hellenic sources. Such adaptive changes are usually ignored by the modern **Hellenist**, who insists that he is following the ancient models with complete fidelity. The evocation of Greek pederasty has not been immune to this process of adaptation and idealization—a process that makes it difficult to understand the character of ancient and modern pederasty alike. Ironically, Western civilization ultimately derived its negative official attitude toward homosexuality from the "evil empire" with which the Greeks had to wage their heroic wars—the Persia that had **Zoroastrianism** as its state religion. As a client-ethnos living under Persian rule, the Jews adopted an antihomosexual moral code which they exported in the guise of Christianity to the Greco-Roman world that had tolerated if not glorified pederasty.

The modern pederast suffers from the double obloquy that is visited not just upon the homosexual, but also upon the age-asymmetrical relationship in which he is implicated. From the very outset of the modern homophile **movement**, its leaders sought to distance themselves from the pederast (not without criticism, for example, from the Youth Committee of the North American Conference of Homophile Organizations at its 1969 convention), even urging an age of **consent** so high as to exclude the boy-lover from any benefit accruing from the law reform which was their goal. Hence the pederastically oriented part of the movement has had to found its own organizations, beginning with the *Gemeinschaft der Eigenen* (Community of the Exceptional) in Wilhelmine **Germany**, and create its own literature. The first writer of note in this field was the anarchist John Henry **Mackay**, who from 1905 onward under the pseudonym of Sagitta composed a whole series of works (*Die Bücher der namenlosen Liebe*) in defense of man–boy love. Others who defended the pederastic tradition were Adolf **Brand** and Benedict **Friedlaender**, and to a lesser extent Hans **Blüher**, who laid stress upon the role of homoerotic ties in what he called the "male society," as opposed to the family with its basis in procreative heterosexuality. He singled out the *Wandervogelbewegung* (the German equivalent of the Boy Scout movement) as a modern expression and institutionalization of the initiatory relationship.

In the English-speaking world the pederastic ideal inspired a whole coterie of minor poets in Late Victorian England (the **Calamites**), where the **public school** had a curiously pederastic ambience that undercut the official taboo. But the first major treatment of the subject was J. Z. Eglinton's *Greek Love* (1964) which, in contrast to the defense of homosexuality "between consenting adults" that followed the publication of the **Wolfenden Report** in 1957, reasserted the right of the pederast to the love-object of his choice and affirmed the value of the man–boy relationship in modern society. In Italy, the Netherlands, West Germany, and other countries, pederasts have formed their own groups, separate from the androphile organizations that dominate the gay movement at the present day. Yet even if the pederast cherishes the aristocratic ideal of being the lover and mentor of a promising youth, he remains obliged to live in a furtive, clandestine, semi-criminal subculture, hiding his attachments with chance partners from the prying eyes of the neighbors and the police. Although the police may no longer prosecute androphile homosexuals, they can still engage in frequently questionable tactics to deliver the pederast to courts that can impose draconian sentences for what is consensual behavior, if the adolescent has not yet reached the artificially high "age of consent."

It is also a curious fact that individuals attracted to prepubescent children—pedophiles in the narrow sense—have tried to ally themselves with pederasts, as if to claim shelter under the ideological umbrella of pederasty that historically excluded them, since the man–boy relationship was strictly defined by the membership of the latter in the appropriate age cohort. This conflation has even led to the demand for abolition of all age-of-consent laws, a step which would presumably sanction heterosexual pedophilia as well—the activity that provokes the maximum of public condemnation and censure. By and large, organizations with such an impractical program have been rejected by the mainstream homosexual-rights movement and excluded from its coalitions.

Modern society has yet to make the effort to understand the historical and phenomenological significance of pederasty as a mode of human behavior. Having accorded a grudging tolerance to androphile homosexuality, public opinion would still deny it to the boy-lover, ostensibly in the interest of the younger partner. Although genuine ethical questions do arise, much confusion has stemmed from equating intergenerational sexual relations with child abuse per se, and the latter with physical mistreatment and neglect. The resolution, if at all possible, of the entire complex of issues—empirical and political—will be a task for future decades.

BIBLIOGRAPHY. Frits Bernard, *Paedophilia: A Factual Report*, Rotterdam: Enclave Press, 1985; Edward Brongersma, *Loving Boys*, New York: Global Academic Publishers, 1986; Felix Buffière, *Eros adolescent; la pédérastie dans la Grèce antique*, Paris: Société d'édition "Les Belles Lettres," 1980; J. Z. Eglinton, *Greek Love*, New York: Oliver Layton Press, 1964; Hans Licht, *Sexual Life in Ancient Greece*, London: Routledge & Kegan Paul, 1932; Parker Rossman, *Sexual Experience between Men and Boys; Exploring the Pederast Underground*, New York: Association Press, 1976; Theo Sandfort, *Boys on*

Their Contacts with Men: A Study of Sexually Expressed Relationships, New York: Global Academic Publishers, 1987.
                    Warren Johansson

PEDOPHILIA

This article refers to mutually consensual affective relationships betwen adults, on the one hand, and pre-pubertal children, those undergoing puberty, and adolescents, on the other, occurring outside the family, and which include a sexual component. The adult participant in such a relationship is termed a *pedophile* by the authors. While various forms of such relationships (distinct from those within the family, which are properly incest), with various social meanings, have existed throughout history and worldwide, the term "p[a]edophilia" was first used in English only as recently as 1906, by Havelock **Ellis**. It had previously appeared as a specific form of sexual pathology in a German article of 1896 by Richard von **Krafft-Ebing.**

Because the term "pedophilia" originated in a medical context and today connotes disease, efforts have been made to replace it. **Pederasty** is sometimes used as a synonym, or as a term restricted to post-pubescent adolescents, but in the present writers' view, it should properly be restricted to the Greek custom it originally designated, which, though a form of pedophilia as we understand it, is not congruent with it. Apologists for homosexual relations with adolescents who seek to separate "pederasty" from "pedophilia" in hopes that the former might share the social tolerance gained by **androphile** (adult-male-to-adult-male eroticism) homosexuality, and who appeal to the Greek model for support, err in their understanding of it, for these relationships often began before the boy entered puberty. The earlier average age for puberty within the last century also means that classical texts (and even more recent ones) which speak of relations with mid-teenage boys were not necessarily referring to sexually mature individuals. (The term **ephebophile** has been used to describe erotic attraction to boys in their late teens, who are considered adults in many if not all cultures.) Similar problems are encountered with the expression "Greek love." "Man/boy love," which posits a symmetry in the relationship and stresses its affective nature, refers to only one variant of pedophilia (the homosexual one), and for that reason is rejected by those who seek terminology inclusive of man/girl, woman/boy, and woman/girl (or "korophile") relationships. "Child molestation" or "abuse," terms current in the media, and in psychological and legal discourse, are neither descriptive of the phenomenon, nor value-free, as academic discourse requires.

That variant of pedophilia occuring between men and boys—male homosexual pedophilia—will be the chief focus of this article. This choice is dictated by several considerations, including the context of the article, the dearth of research on korophile relationships, and the fact that until very recently man/boy relationships were accepted as a part, and indeed were a major part, of male homosexuality.

Comparative Perspectives. Before beginning a cross-cultural survey of male homosexual pedophilia, Gisela Bleibtreu-Ehrenberg's thesis ("The Paedophile Impulse," *Paidika* 1/3, Winter 1988) about the etiology of pedophilia should be mentioned. Based on her survey of animal behavior studies and anthropological literature, she proposes that pedophilia might be considered a remnant, more evident in some persons than others, of the instinct to nurture and protect the young of the species, which in human development has come to serve an educational (including sex-educational) or initiatory purpose in some societies. The attempt to root pedophilia in man's biological inheritance is controversial, but a cross-cultural survey of man/boy pedophilia at least suggests that it is a universal phenomenon, which, when accepted by a society, generally carries a socially constructed meaning related to the acculturation process for boys.

Several studies of the Melanesian societies of the **Pacific** describe the role played by institutionalized sexual relations between pubertal boys and the man or men responsible for the boys' preparation for initiation into full participation in these societies. Several of these societies believe that without receiving the man's semen through fellatio the boy cannot physically mature.

In pre-modern **Japan**, among the **Samurai** warriors, knights took boys as pages and trained them in their ideology and military arts. The popular literature of the day idealized such relationships, which included a sexual component.

A military pattern similar to that of the Samurai was found in Central Africa among the Azande, where warriors took boy-wives who accompanied them during military campaigns, and were in return trained and provided with military equipment by the man upon their "graduation" to adult status in the late teens.

In the above instances, where pedophilia exists in relation to education, initiation or acculturation for boys, it is generally not an exclusive sexual orientation for the adult, but co-exists with the fulfillment of marriage and family responsibilities. In other societies, including our own, man/boy relationships—not sanctioned by the society and viewed with various degrees of intolerance—reflect affective choices of the individuals involved. These relationships may have a generalized educational function, but can be constructed around companionship, substitute parenting, recreation, or simply sexual pleasure. While for some of these pedophiles these relationships do not exclude marriage and family responsibilities, where pedophilia is a personal rather than a socially sanctioned phenomenon, for a higher percentage it will be their only form of sexual contact.

Man/boy pedophile relationships have taken many forms in **Islam**, including religious significance among the **Sufis**. Arabic, Persian, and Urdu literature contain a rich tradition of man/boy love in both sacred and secular forms.

The West. Western cultural traditions were heavily influenced by ancient **Greece**, a society in which man/boy love was the normative form of male homosexuality. Classical scholars, examining the oldest strata of Greek **mythology**, have established that Greek pederasty originated in a situation where a man was responsible for preparing the boy to fulfill his adult civic and **military** responsibilities, through a relationship which involved both educational functions and sexual activity. After the initial military necessity for the practice receded, it remained a central cultural institution; the role it played, the social system surrounding it, and its influence on Greek art and thought have been amply documented. Although relations between males of the same generation existed— what Bernard Sergent calls "Homeric love" and defines as "homosexuality in all but name"—man/boy relationships were clearly the dominant form of same-sex relations, and rhetorical criticism of or comic attacks on individuals who persisted in such relations beyond the culturally sanctioned age limits make it clear that androphile (adult–adult) relations were dimly regarded.

Pederastic traditions remained influential through **Hellenistic** and **Roman** times, though freer from educational goals and more oriented to pleasure. It is symptomatic of this shift that while by law in Greece only free-born boys, who could attain citizenship, could be the younger partner in a relationship, in late Roman times it was illegal for a free-born boy to be the object of the relationship. Yet, as shown by the case of **Hadrian** and **Antinous** (a relationship which began when the boy was eleven or twelve), man/boy relationships retained much of their vigor and meaning as late as the first two centuries of the Christian era. As the function of same-sex relationships increasingly became hedonistic, the age limits broke down: we find increasing references to homosexuality between men (particularly in the satiric poets, who make it clear that this was still scorned) and, to a lesser extent, to the sexual use of very young children.

By the beginning of the Middle Ages a pattern of pedophilia was in place which remained until rather recent times. Despite strong attempts of the church, and later, at the behest of the church, of civil law, to suppress all homosexuality, man/boy relationships continued to exist both in forms reflecting the Greek pederastic model (attested in **medieval Latin poetry** written to their pupils by Alcuin, Hilary, Baudri, and other monastic figures), and in relationships outside of lofty educational contexts, often between masters and apprentices. That the latter remained a frequent form of male homosexuality among common people, coexisting with androphile relations, is demonstrated by the persistence of legal charges involving such activity on into the nineteenth century, in Venice, the Netherlands, and England and its maritime empire.

During the **Renaissance**, the culture temporarily became more open to pedophile relationships. The symbol of **Ganymede** in literature and art reflects this development. Re-entering European culture with the rediscovery of the classics, both love between men and boys and the Ganymede image burst forth in the fifteenth and sixteenth centuries, appearing in the work of such varied figures as **Michelangelo**, Correggio, Parmigianino, and **Cellini** in Italy, and Richard **Barnfield** and Christopher **Marlowe** in Tudor England. By the time the symbol lost its power by the end of the seventeenth century, there had been a flowering of boy imagery in the work of artists including Pontormo, **Caravaggio**, and the Flemish sculptor Jérôme Duquesnoy. That Ganymede was more than an artistic convention is shown by the number of artists who were charged with sodomy with boys, especially their studio assistants. Histories of the Renaissance record similar charges involving popes, poets, and nobles.

The Romantic Movement. A "Grecian" ideal of **friendship**, as interpreted by the German idealists, also influenced the Romantic movement in the late eighteenth, nineteenth, and early twentieth centuries. In addition to the cult of friendship between males, the movement's orientalism also exhibited strong pedophilic influences.

Although also found in androphile figures, these currents were expressed by, among others, Lord **Byron**, with his relations with young teenagers. William **Beckford** was ostracized from society for the scandal of his relationship with William Courtenay, commencing when the boy was eleven. André **Gide**, although today regarded as androphile, is revealed in his diaries as a pedophile. Stefan **George**, a Symbolist poet, was leader of an aesthetic cult centered around the fourteen-year-old Maximin. The pioneer photographers Wilhelm Baron von **Gloeden**, whose imagery was not restricted to adult male nudes, and F. Holland **Day** both produced highly romanticized images of boys.

Besides individuals there were the circles of writers and artists, such as the Uranian poets in England, the circle that produced *Men and Boys* (America's first anthology of homosexual poetry), and the circle around Adolf **Brand**'s magazine *Der Eigene,* all of which included androphiles and pedophiles alike.

Between 1880 and 1920 there was a flowering of boy imagery in painting and sculpture, including work by H. S. Tuke, Lord Leighton, Georges Minne, Charles Filiger, Ferdinand Hodler, Joaquín Sorolla, and Elisàr von **Kupffer**. In education, pedophilia contributed to the formulation of pedagogical eros, with its discussion of the role of a man's erotic love in nurturing and educating boys. Perhaps symbolic of the destruction of all of the Romantic notions of "friendship" by the growing intellectual and political power of forensic medicine and its theories of sexual pathology was the 1920 trial of the German educator Gustav **Wyneken**. He and his supporters defended his actions as expressions of Pedagogical Eros, based on cultural models, but the trial ended in his conviction for sexual indecency, based on the medical model.

Activism. Arising within the Romantic movement, but in sharp contrast to it, was "Sagitta," John Henry **Mackay**, the German anarchist, poet, and propagandist for man/boy love in his *Bücher der Namenlose Liebe* (1913). Refusing to drape his love in a toga, Mackay's was the first voice to speak for liberation for "the love of the older male for the younger" (and, by extension, of all sexual orientations) in political terms, and for its own sake, rather than offering any cultural justifications. Although his publications were suppressed, and it would be half a century before pedophiles began to organize as pedophiles, his work prefigured present pedophile activism.

The homosexual **movement** has had an ambiguous relation to pedophile activism. On the one hand, since Mackay's time it has served as an inspiration for pedophiles and, in both the Netherlands and pre-**Stonewall** America, provided a supportive context; in 1969, the **Youth** Committee of the North American Conference of Homophile Organizations (NACHO), chaired by Stephen Donaldson, issued a manifesto calling for the elimination of all age-of-consent limitations, though the adults at the NACHO plenary session rejected it. On the other hand, there has been a tendency on the part of some "respectable" homosexual leaders to sacrifice and denounce pedophiles for political goals. It has been particularly obvious in contemporary American gay politics, but present from the earliest days in Magnus **Hirschfeld**'s efforts, denounced by Mackay, to trade an age of consent for legalization of adult homosexuality. This rejection has served to spur independent pedophile organizing.

Among the earliest separate pedophile organizing attempts were those in the Netherlands, beginning in the late 1950s, a decade later developing into still ongoing national and local workgroups for pedophiles and the sexual emancipation of youth within the Netherlands Association for Sexual Reform, and the Vereniging Martijn, with its information and support publication *O.K.* (Ouderen-kinderen-relaties). Similar groups have been formed in Scandinavia, West Germany, Belgium, and Switzerland. The North American Man/Boy Love Association (NAMBLA), formed in response to prosecutions and hysteria in Boston in 1978, has been successful in fighting off attempts by American authorities to suppress it, and continues to publish its *Bulletin* and to organize. Other groups were less fortunate. The Pedophile Information Exchange (P.I.E.), organized in England in 1974, was crushed by vicious press attacks and the conviction and imprisonment of its leaders for conspiring to corrupt public morals, and disbanded in 1985.

Incarcerated pedophiles continue to be subject to coercive procedures to alter their sexual interest or reduce its level. Although surgical castration is no longer employed, chemical dosages and **aversion therapy** may be used without the subject's consent.

Research Perspectives. Much of the "research" that exists on pedophilia today reflects a predetermination that adult–child sexual contacts are evil or pathological, and merely documents the point of view with which the authors began. There has been no lack of evidence by which such negative pre-suppositions could be supported, because in the same way that studies of homosexuality until quite recently were limited by the source of their research subjects, resulting in a portrayal of homosexuals as criminal, troubled, and unhappy, most studies of pedophilia examine only cases which have come before either courts or psychiatrists, precisely those where the subjects are most under stress or disturbed. In many countries, research into pedophile relationships under other circumstances is legally impossible: if a researcher should find a healthy, quietly functioning relationship he or she would be required to report it for prosecution under "child protection" laws. These factors, plus the sensationalism surrounding the topic, assure that much of what is written on the subject is, and will continue to be, worthless.

The first multi-disciplinary study in English of pedophilia was J. Z. Eglinton's *Greek Love* (New York: Oliver Layton Press, 1964). As indicated by the title, the author views man/boy relationships in light of the Greek model, and the book is limited by a "pederast" politics that defends relationships with teenagers while declining to consider them for younger boys. Nonetheless, it remains the starting point for study of the cultural history of pedophilia, and a vital source of information. The fullest edition of Frits Bernard's study *Pedophilia* is available in German (*Kinderschänder? Pädophilie— von der Liebe mit Kindern*, Berlin: Foerster, 1982); the Dutch original was not updated, and the English version (Rotterdam: Enclave, 1985) is only a summary. His study concentrates on the psychological dimensions of the phenomenon, with attention to both partners. Parker Rossman's sociological study *Sexual Experience Between Men and Boys* (New York: Association Press, 1976) is less academically rigorous and more popular in its presentations; it is however reliable and far superior to other popular books by Banis or Dodson. In Dutch, Monique Moeller's *Pedofiele relaties* (Deventer: van Loghum Slaterus, 1983) is a fair and thorough sociological treatment. The first volume of Edward Brongersma's *Loving Boys* (Amsterdam: Global Academic, 1986), like Eglinton's book, is as much a defense as a study, and has the largest bibliography

to date, which provides starting points for further study. Though his conclusions about "sickness" seem gratuitous, Morris Fraser's *Death of Narcissus* (London: Secker and Warburg, 1976) is a perceptive Jungian analysis of images and themes in pedophile literature. Kenneth Plummer's article "Pedophilia: Constructing a Sociological Baseline" (in *Adult Sexual Interest in Children*, M. Cook and K. Howells, eds., London: Academic Press, 1981) reviews the sources available at the time and argues for an assessment of pedophilia free from prejudice and stereotyping. *Paidika: The Journal of Paedophilia*, which began publication in Amsterdam in 1987, is a scholarly, cultural magazine examining the phenomenon from the perspective of various disciplines.

Three studies of pedophiles which are both academically rigorous and value-free can be recommended. In Dutch, there is Monica Pieterse's *Pedofielen over Pedofilie* (Zeist: NISSO, 1982), a survey-study of the background and attitudes of a sample of Dutch pedophiles, including women. *The Child Lovers*, by G. D. Wilson and D. N. Cox (London: Owen, 1983), was the result of personality tests administered to 77 English pedophiles contacted through P.I.E. They found that the men were not notably more neurotic or psychotic than any other sample of the general population; nevertheless, their conclusion, based on "moral considerations," is that pedophilia should be suppressed. Australian sociologist Paul Wilson is author of *The Man They Called a Monster* (North Ryde, New South Wales: Cassell, 1981), a study of the case history of Clarence Osborne, a 61-year-old court clerk who committed suicide upon public exposure of his more than two thousand sexual contacts with boys, which he had thoroughly documented. After studying Osborne's history and relationships, and interviewing some of the boys—now adults—Wilson concludes that the condemnation that drove Osborne to suicide was entirely unwarranted.

In addition to Dr. Bernard's work, there are two major sources dealing with the experience of the younger partner in pedophile relationships. The work of the Dutch social psychologist Theo Sandfort, presented in *The Sexual Aspect of Pedophile Relations* (Amsterdan: Pan/Spartacus, 1981) and *Boys on their Contacts with Men* (Amsterdam: Global Academic, 1987), collects and analyzes the attitudes of 25 boys during their participation in pedophile relationships. R. H. Tindall's "The Male Adolescent Involved With a Pederast Becomes an Adult" (*Journal of Homosexuality* 3:4 [1978]) presents data from longitudinal studies. Though the evidence assembled by these sources is slim, they establish that these relationships can be, both at the time and in retrospect, considered consensual, and often beneficial, by the younger partner, and disprove the assumption that such relationships are invariably harmful in either the short or long term. The latter conclusion is supported by "The Effects of Early Sexual Experiences," by L. L. Constantine (in *Children and Sex*, Constantine and F. M. Martinson, eds., Boston: Little, Brown, 1981), a survey of literature concerning childhood sexual experiences (including incest), in which he notes that many studies have reported neutral or even positive reactions to intergenerational sexual experiences, and suggests that the positive evaluations correlate with the degree of mutuality and voluntariness of the child's participation.

Issues. A number of themes recur in debates about pedophilia. Several obviously involve issues the significance of which is not limited to pedophilia.

It is generally recognized that the possibility for adults to have sexual relationships with children is dependent on the right of children to make choices about expressing their sexuality. Pedophile organizations have linked their arguments to support of the rights of children. While emphasizing that these rights most certainly include the power to say no to any unwanted sexual contact as well as the opportunity to say yes to contacts children desire, some groups go further than others in espousing a broad range of children's liberation issues.

Related to the question of legal rights for children is the issue of the child's consent in pedophile relationships. Those speaking for the protection of children frequently assert that children are incapable of consenting to such sexual relationships, sometimes justifying this assertion by the child's lack of experience or knowledge of long-range consequences of an act. It has been answered that children can and do consent, or at least are quite capable of rejecting experiences they find distasteful, and that the proper response is to empower children to be able to say no effectively. This impasse raises the issue of what consent means—freedom to refuse, simple assent, or an "informed" consent that is probably not realized in most human relationships. Closely related to this is the issue of power, and the assertion that the power imbalance between the adult and the younger partner in a pedophile relationship is so great that it inevitably leads to coercion and exploitation. Various responses have been made: either that the power imbalance is not so clearcut as the critics state, particularly citing the power of the child to terminate the relationship; or that while power imbalances are inherent in all human relationships, they do not necessarily lead to exploitation, but can be used for benevolent ends, and the real issue is not the power imbalance but the use of power.

"Child **pornography**" is the sharpest point of attack on pedophilia and pedophiles. Included in this attack are the imputation that children are always abused in the production of such images, and the fear that such images will stimulate the abuse of children. It has been shown that this issue has been exploited for political purposes, and the statistics on the amount of such material exaggerated beyond proportion. Despite rhetoric, it has not been demonstrated that any more connection exists between pedophilia and child pornography than between any other sexuality and its pornography: either to show that pedophiles are more likely to create or use pornography than other persons, or that child pornography encourages sexual contacts with children. Indeed, the Kutschinsky study of the Danish experience with pornography, which has never been refuted, demonstrated that sexual assaults on children declined with the availability of pornography. Pedophiles who have responded to this issue have noted that there is no reason that depictions of children nude or even engaged in sexual actions should be any more or less objectionable than such depictions of adults, and argue that the true issue, as with all pornography, is whether coercion actually is employed in making it.

The issues of child **prostitution** and the sexual exploitation of children in Third World countries have also been used to attack pedophiles and, by implication, pedophilia. Once it is acknowledged that pedophiles are by no means the only persons who engage in "sex tourism" or patronize prostitutes, the debate again seems to resolve itself into issues of power and consent. A defense has been offered that the right of self-determination in sexual behavior for the individual choosing prostitution should apply here. Poverty, however, may diminish the individual freedom of choice in these situations.

BIBLIOGRAPHY (in addition to references in the text). Tom O'Carroll, *Paedophilia: The Radical Case*, London: Peter Owen, 1980; Daniel Tsang, ed., *The Age Taboo: Gay Male Sexuality, Power and Consent*, Boston: Alyson, 1981.

Joseph Geraci and Donald H. Mader

PÉLADAN, JOSÉPHIN (1859–1918)

French novelist and mystic. Péladan was the son of a schoolmaster who edited a fanatically Catholic and royalist paper called *Le châtiment* and was constantly trying to find new meanings in the Apocalypse. His elder brother Adrien, a homeopathic physician and student of the Kabbala, introduced him to the literature of mysticism. As early as 1880 Péladan's Catholic convictions brought him into conflict with the law, when he was arrested for demonstrating against the prohibition on unauthorized religious congregations, but fined a mere fifteen francs because his action was ascribed to eccentricity.

In 1883 he arrived in **Paris** where he quickly penetrated literary circles. His criticism of the Salon of 1883 created a sensation with its text "I believe in the Ideal, Tradition, and Hierarchy." His **aesthetic** ideas, though akin to those of the pre-Raphaelites in England, were attuned to their own time and place. He declared that "all artistic masterpieces are religious, even among unbelievers" and "for nineteen centuries artistic masterpieces have always been Catholic, even among Protestants." Both in the aesthetic and in the occult worlds he stood squarely at the extreme of Catholic reaction. His first book, *Le Vice suprême* (1884), prefaced by Barbey d'Aurevilly, prophesied the fall of the Idea into materialism. The hero, Merodack—a name culled from Assyrian mythology—is a magician whose vocation compels him to conquer all natural vices.

Péladan further developed his mystical and anti-materialist philosophy in a vast "éthopée" of nineteen volumes called *La Décadence latine* (1885–1907), of which the eighth and ninth volumes (1891) were entitled *L'Androgyne* and *La Gynandre*. In the occult circles where Péladan reigned as *sâr* (king), the figure of the **Androgyne** possessed a recondite significance. Part of the seventh treatise in Péladan's *Amphithéâtre des sciences mortes* expounds the theory of the Androgyne under the heading *Erotologie de Platon*; the Androgyne is the artistic sex par excellence, realized in the creations of **Leonardo da Vinci**, "it confounds the two principles, the masculine and the feminine, and balances one against the other. Every exclusively masculine figure is lacking in grace, every exclusively feminine one is lacking in strength." The women in Péladan's novels are generally of thc androgynous type; he asserted that "the number of women who feel themselves to be men grows by the day, and the masculine instinct leads them to violent actions." Péladan never wearied of androgynous and lesbian themes in his monumental "éthopée," and in *Typhonia* (1892), the *Journal d'une vierge protestante* is a tale of lesbian love. His own marriage, in 1895, was a failure, and he gained the homophobic nickname of "La Sâr pédalant," but there is no evidence that he ever had an active sexual life.

In 1885 Péladan had declared himself Grand-Master of the Rose+Croix on the death of his brother Adrien, who had been initiated into a branch of **freemasonry**, by that time moribund, that claimed succession from the legendary Rosicrucians. In 1888 he and Stanislas de Guaita revived the *Ordre Kabbalistique de la Rose+Croix*, in whose occult carryings-on there was a great deal of foolishness and self-importance. Péladan himself fused a real sense of mission with an exhibitionism and a flair for the dramatic—with transvestite overtones—worthy of an Oscar **Wilde**. His dress ranged from the medieval to oriental robes with a nuance of the androgynous and from ecclesiastical vestments to the traditional raffish garb of **bohemia**. His hair and beard were luxuriant and remarkable. Péladan's work is a veritable encyclopedia of **Decadent** taste permeated by his obsession with the Androgyne. The novel of this name he resumed as "a restitution of Grecian ephebic impressions by way of Catholic mysticism," and wrote: "Intangible Eros, uranian Eros, for the coarse men of moral epochs you are but an infamous sin; you are named Sodom, the celestial despiser of all beauty. This is the need of hypocritical ages to accuse Beauty, that living light, of the darkness contained in vile hearts."

The work of Péladan, blending the occult and the homoerotic, is a curious reaction to the prevailing naturalism of the late nineteenth century. Péladan himself is a striking example of the flamboyant, eccentric leader of a cult strongly tinged with evocations of a legendary past and claiming to possess a unique mystical tradition, in contrast with the mundane religion of the conventional believer. He is the prototype of later homosexual figures in the religious life of the twentieth century, and even of certain leaders on the mystical fringe of the gay **churches** of today.

BIBLIOGRAPHY. Robert Pincus-Witten, *Occult Symbolism in France: Joséphin Péladan and the Salons de la Rose+Croix*, New York: Garland, 1976; Mario Praz, *The Romantic Agony*, London: Oxford University Press, 1951; James Webb, *The Occult Underground*, La Salle, IL: Open Court Publishing Company, 1974.

Warren Johansson

PENITENTIALS

The penitentials are Western Christian confessional manuals whose origins can be traced as far back as the sixth century, and which were used until the twelfth century. The purpose of the penitentials was to aid the priest or spiritual guide of the lay Christian by providing descriptions of various sins and prescribing appropriate penances. Many of the manuals go far beyond mere lists of sins and penances, containing introductions and conclusions for the instruction of the confessor that remind him of his role as spiritual healer and urge him to appreciate the subjective mentality of the patient. Modern scholars do not know exactly how these manuals were used in practice, but in all likelihood they served as works of reference, informing the priest of the different kinds of sin, of aggravating and mitigating circumstances, and of the appropriate penance to impose. Most of the penitentials are brief enough to be committed to memory, so that the material amounted to a questionnaire for interrogating the penitent—an important aspect of early medieval penance. Such interrogation was designed to ensure that penitents knew what grave sins were and would confess all of them. In fact, a ninth-century theologian had to warn priests not to corrupt the minds of penitents by suggesting sins which their simplicity had never imagined.

Sexual Aspects. The penitentials have long been recognized as valuable sources for the study of the social, legal, and moral institutions of the early **Middle Ages.** They mediated between the formulations of Christian theology and concrete practice in the everyday life of the lay Christian. One of the most striking features of these documents is the breadth and detail of their treatment of human sexual behavior. Recent works make some use of these manuals for the study of homosexuality in the medieval period.

The general principles of the Christian sexual ethic had been established long before the sixth century, indeed they were adopted in their totality from the Hellenistic **Judaism** of the first century. The testimony of such different personalities as **Philo Judaeus** and Flavius **Josephus** confirms that the prohibition of male homosexual activity was absolute and uncompromising. Sexual intercourse was morally permissible only between a man and a woman who were married and for the purpose of procreation. At the beginning of the fifth century St. **Augustine** reiterated this principle and made it normative for Latin Christendom. All forms of sexual expression falling outside these limits were to be deemed immoral and grievously sinful. The debates over sexuality within the early Church, moreover, led to a standard of sexual morality that set virginity above marriage and idealized an asexual way of life as embodied in monastic orders and in priestly celibacy. For five hundred years the penitential literature was the principal agent in the formation and diffusion of the Christian code of sexual morality. Hence these texts are crucial to the history of the social attitude toward homosexual behavior in that period. They supplement the law codes of Theodosius and Justinian as well as the tribal legislation of Western Europe that dealt with sexual offenses, since these did not cover many areas of individual conduct and were far removed from the interpersonal sphere of confession and penance and the private realm of everyday life.

It cannot be denied that the treatment of sexual behavior in general in the penitentials tends to be authoritarian, apodictic, legalistic, and sex-negative. This ascetic approach to sexuality left its imprint upon Western attitudes in the course of time—and that is what the penitentials were meant to do, to shape the collective consciousness of sexual morality along the lines formulated by the church. They failed to provide a parallel reflective and critical discussion of human sexuality: this they were not meant to do. The penitentials and those who consulted them were engaged in a strenuous—and ultimately futile—combat with urges and drives in the human personality that were regarded as evil and demonic in origin. The peoples of Western Europe, many of them brought into the fold by the missionary campaign initiated by Pope Gregory the Great at the end of the sixth century, remained attached to a more diverse, overt, and freely expressed pagan norm of sexuality than Christian ethics could ever countenance. This archaic morality underlay and undercut the superstratum of ascetic teaching which the clergy sought to inculcate. By comparison with earlier rigoristic practice, the introduction of penitentials constituted an injection of pastoral realism— what almost might be called plea bargaining in modern terms. By bringing forgiveness for even grave sins within reach of the believer, the system was relieved of its most dire aspect, that of automatic eternal damnation, but only in order to make the underlying morality more effective.

Homosexuality. Modern apologists for Christianity have dealt with the attitude of the penitential literature toward homosexuality and with the specific contributions of Regino of Prüm, the *Penitential of Silos*, and Burchard of Worms, claiming that the penitentials are not "an index of medieval morality" and that their treatment of the homoerotic implies "a relatively indulgent attitude adopted by prominent churchmen of the early Middle Ages toward homosexual behavior." The penitentials are an index of what the medieval church—if not the entire laity—thought morally reprehensible on the basis of the Christian revelation.

All the penitentials have at least one canon condemning what later came to be designated *sodomy*, and many offer a relatively extensive treatment of the subject. Two factors influence their analysis: the specific character of the offense and the participants. The types of homosexual behavior distinguished in these manuals may be grouped as follows: (1) general references to males copulating with other males, (2) specific mention of *sodomites* or of a sin or practice labeled *sodomitic*, (3) references to relations *in terga*, mainly with reference to adolescent behavior, (4) references to specific practices other than anal penetration, (5) references to simulations of sexual intercourse by very young boys, (6) references to cases in which an older boy violates a younger one, (7) sexual relations between natural brothers.

The range of persons addressed or implicated shifts the focus of the canons: (1) those addressed to unspecified persons censure all of the specific forms of homosexual intercourse, (2) those addressed to church dignitaries and religious speak only of "acting as did the Sodomites" and grade the penance according to the ecclesiastical rank of the offender, the higher position meriting the higher penance, (3) canons addressed to adolescents censure all forms

of homosexual activity but vary the allusions to the Sodomites.

There is a striking consistency in the weighting of the different offenses. In canons whose subjects are unspecified male persons, the general, not further specified practice of sexual relations between males usually carries a penance of ten to fifteen years; censures using a variant of *sodomite* usually carry a penance of ten years but may range from seven to twenty; relations *in terga* (involving the posterior) invariably carry a penance of three years; intercrural relations are censured with one to three years' penance; mutual masturbation, mentioned only three times, carries a penance from 30 days to two years; oral–genital relations carry a penance ranging from three to seven years, most often the former.

Lesbian relations are almost as neglected in the penitentials as they are in the Judeo-Christian tradition generally. However, they are mentioned, and provide an interesting confirmation of a text from Hincmar of Reims who says: "They are reputed to use certain instruments of diabolical function to excite desire," presumably single or double dildoes. Several penitential reproaches directed at lesbian relations mention such devices.

It should be borne in mind that the penitentials are cumulative works, each compiler incorporating into his own work previous texts, often excerpted without change. The rather explicit descriptions of homosexual acts in Burchard of Worms seem to reflect a personal view of such behavior. Another significant point is that "sodomitical" acts had in Christian thinking come to include bestiality, for obvious reasons a common enough practice among rural populations constantly exposed to the sight of animals copulating or preparing to do so. If homosexuality was to a certain degree tolerated in the early Middle Ages, it was not because of the church but in spite of it. Fundamental moral attitudes are not altered overnight, and a substratum of pagan belief and practice undercut the new religion imported from the Mediterranean world. A situation prevailed that in Russian historiography is termed *dvoeverie*, "dual belief"—the Christian doctrines and practices coexisted with the older heathen ones for several centuries, until the teachings reiterated generation after generation became the folk ethos of Western Christendom.

The penitentials, and the canonical collections into which they were incorporated, enjoyed wide circulation for some four centuries or more, and in the course of time shifted moral judgment in the direction of Christian asceticism. The evangelization of Western Europe involved the inculcation of the moral teachings of Christianity as well as the preaching of its myths and dogmas, and sexual morality from the outset was a significant part of its theology, if not the very cornerstone of its ethical system. The creative elaboration of the material found in decisions of the church councils and in papal letters was accomplished by the middle of the eighth century; after that time the penitentials simply copy previous manuals. This tradition in its Irish, Frankish, and Anglo-Saxon variants is comparatively unanimous both in range of content and manner of treatment. Even original contributions such as those of Burchard of Worms are simply added to an existing penitential tradition, the end result of which was the moral outlawry of homosexual behavior and the marginalization of those engaging in it as criminals and outcasts with no rights that a Christian society needed to respect.

BIBLIOGRAPHY. John Boswell, *Christianity, Social Tolerance, and Homosexuality*, Chicago: University of Chicago Press, 1980; Pierre J. Payer, *Sex and the Penitentials: The Development of a Moral Code*, Toronto: University of Toronto Press, 1984.

Warren Johansson

PENNA, SANDRO (1906–1977)

Italian lyric poet and prose writer. Born in Perugia, where he took a degree in accounting, Penna moved at the age of twenty-three to Rome, where he lived until his death. Shy and diffident, he led a highly private existence for most of his life, refusing invitations to elegant gatherings to be with his *fanciulli* ("lads"), and making a living in various ways, including the gray market during the war and art dealing afterwards. Yet he did show some affinity for the company of such homosexual writers as Pier Paolo **Pasolini**, Elio Pecora, and Dario Bellezza.

Penna was "discovered" by another great twentieth-century Italian poet, Umberto Saba (1883–1957). Thanks to Saba's help he was able to publish even during the fascist period (the first book is from 1939), despite the homoerotic and pedophile content of his work.

Alongside his exiguous poetic production—the compositions up to 1970 are collected in *Tutte le poesie* (Milan: Garzanti, 1970)—he also wrote fiction, some of which appears in *Un po' di febbre* (Milan: Garzanti, 1973). Love for boys is omnipresent in the delicate lyrics of Penna. To critics who, while acknowledging his high artistic quality, found his insistence on homosexual themes "inappropriate," Penna replied with scorn: "The sexual problem/ engages my whole life./ Is it good, is it bad?/ That's what I keep asking myself." Provocatively, he styled himself a "love poet." He was so proud of his *eros paidikos* that in one interview he made his own the saying attributed to Camille Saint-Saëns, "I am not a homosexual, but a pederast."

In his poems—which are usually brief, four lines or a few more—Penna used only a few strokes to sketch a situation, a thought, or a portrait. The source of inspiration was his "lads," adolescents or young boys; his desires (which had a physical dimension) were stated with extraordinary delicacy and a circumspection amounting almost to prudery. Even the poems that he did not want to release because he thought them "pornographic," have been found, after their publication, to be quite chaste.

Sandro Penna ranks among the most significant Italian poets of homosexual love, and is particularly significant in the twentieth-century context. In recent years his work and personality have undergone an unceasing process of critical reevaluation, though this had begun before his death. Penna's influence on young Italian homosexual poets is clearly evident today, so that it is not excessive to speak of his formative influence on contemporary Italian gay poetry.

BIBLIOGRAPHY. Gualtiero De Santi, *Penna*, Florence: La Nuova Italia, 1982; Elio Pecora, *Sandro Penna: una cheta follia*, Milan: Frassinelli, 1984.

Giovanni Dall'Orto

Pérez, Antonio (1540–1611)

Spanish author and political figure. Antonio was publicly the son of King Felipe II's secretary, the priest Gonzalo Pérez, although he may really have been the son of a court noble; he was probably of Semitic ancestry, as were many thinkers and administrators in sixteenth-century Spain. Antonio was well-educated, especially at the universities of Venice and Padua, and was further tutored by Gonzalo for a career in government. He succeeded Gonzalo in the powerful position of royal secretary, and was especially charged with Italian affairs. His hobby was perfumery, and he is also remembered for advances in dental hygiene.

The victim of conservative courtiers, Pérez was arrested on charges of murder and heresy; charges of sodomy were later added. He escaped from prison and fled to Aragon, terrifying the king because of Pérez's possession of documents containing official secrets, probably assassi-

nations. After popular demonstrations prevented the king from immediately recapturing Pérez, he fled to France. His wife and children, whom he was never to see again, were kept as hostages in Madrid to ensure that he did not reveal secrets. In exile in France and England, surviving assassination attempts, Pérez wrote and published on Spain, beginning the long tradition of study of Spain's problems. His works have had considerable influence on Spanish reformist and anti-clerical thinking.

The testimony of the witnesses against Pérez, which has been published only in heavily censored form, speaks of a homosexual underworld among the Spanish nobility. Pérez's cousin Juan de Tovar, also implicated in the scandal and one of the witnesses, is presumably the same Juan de Tovar who composed the first known work in Spanish in which homosexual love is presented positively. This is a lengthy *Eclogue* first published, minus a page torn from the manuscript, in 1985. In it, a boy dies rather than reveal the identity of the man he loves.

BIBLIOGRAPHY: José J. Labrador, C. Angel Zorita, and Ralph A. DiFranco, "La *Egloga* de Juan de Tovar: extenso poema del Siglo de Oro sobre el amor 'que no quiere decir su nombre,'" *El Crotalón—Anuario de Filología Española*, 2 (1985), 365–400; idem, "'A su albedrío y sin orden alguna' (*Quijote*, II, 69), Autor y coincidencias con la *Egloga* de Juan de Tovar," in *Cervantes and the Pastoral*, Cleveland, 1986, pp. 213–33; corrections to their text in *Boletín de la Biblioteca de Menéndez Pelayo*, 63 (1987), 105–06; Gregorio Marañón, *Antonio Pérez*, in his *Obras completas*, VI, Madrid: Espasa-Calpe, 1970, Chapter 13. For the censored testimony, *Colección de documentos inéditos para la historia de España*, XII, Madrid, 1848, pp. 190–95, 224–42, 255–59.

Daniel Eisenberg

Peru
See **Andean Societies.**

PERVERSION

Historically, *perversion* may be the most affect-laden, ambiguous, and misleading term in the whole lexicon of the study of sexual behavior. "Some form of sex gratification . . . preferred to heterosexual coitus and habitually sought after as the primary or only form of sex gratification desired" is the definition offered by *Webster's Third New International Dictionary* (1961). Although the original negativity of the word has weakened in recent decades, it still retains the connotation of a departure from the norm. Fortunately, most serious researchers recognize the problematic character of the word and use it—if at all—with caution.

History of the Term. Perversion entered the semantic field of sexuality only in the last third of the nineteenth century. Until then it had meant simply "any qualitative alteration of a function in disease." Against this background, "perversion of the sexual instinct" meant a change in the direction of the sexual desires, as opposed to a quantitative change (satyriasis and nymphomania on the one hand, impotence and frigidity on the other). The medical criteria for perversion were its involuntary exclusiveness and fixation. It was never asserted, as many laymen were to assume, that all "perverse" behavior stemmed from pathology, but only that certain individuals were in the grip of an **abnormal** sexual orientation beyond their control.

It was Richard von **Krafft-Ebing's** ill-fated notion that the etiology of perverse (= non-procreative) sexual acts (*perverse Handlungen*) could be ascribed either to *Perversion* (pathology) or to *Perversität* (vice). This novel distinction was important for the forensic psychiatrist because it separated persons accused of sexual offenses who were unwilling victims of inner compulsions from others who willfully embraced illicit behavior and were therefore responsible for their actions. Though popularized in Krafft-Ebing's best-selling *Psychopathia sexualis*

(1886; 12 editions in his lifetime), the distinction eluded the public mind, all the more as there had been in classical Latin the phrase *perversio morum* that left its imprint on the modern languages in the form of "moral perversion." Worse still, in English the word *pervert* had from the middle of the seventeenth century possessed the meaning "(religious) apostate," so that in the mind of the English speaker the word easily took on the sense of "one who willfully and obstinately departed from the moral norm of sexual behavior."

To complicate matters still further, the Italian physician Paolo Mantegazza had in his best-seller *Gli amori degli uomini* (1885) used the word *pervertimento* in the meaning that Krafft-Ebing assigned to *Perversität*, and in Emilien Chesneau's French translation of Mantegazza's book, *L'Amour dans l'humanité* (1886) the word was rendered by *perversion*. Richard Francis **Burton** in the "Terminal Essay" appended to his translation of the *Thousand Nights and a Night* (1886) then wrote of "the wide diffusion of such erotic perversion, and its being affected by so many celebrities." Havelock **Ellis**, having both Krafft-Ebing and Burton before him when he wrote his pioneering *Sexual Inversion* (1897), used the word alternately in one and the other sense. On one page he could state: "We have no reason to suppose that this physician practiced every perversion he heard of from patients" while on another he wrote that Krafft-Ebing's treatise "contained over two hundred histories, not only of sexual inversion but of all other forms of sexual perversion." Thus the all too subtle distinction conveyed by the two suffixes was confused at the source, and a physician who used the word in one sense could unwittingly be understood by a layman in the other. The final stage was reached by Canon Derrick Sherwin **Bailey** in his book *Homosexuality and the Western Christian Tradition* (1955), where he employs the word *perversion* in exactly the sense that Krafft-Ebing had allotted to *Perver-*

sität. He thus ratified the error that had been made by the very Havelock Ellis whom he berates for his supposed anticlericalism.

However, Bailey's confusion only repeated the misuse of the word that was especially characteristic of two groups of writers: the authors of pornographic novels and the clergy. In Louis Perceau's *Bibliographie du roman érotique au XIXe siècle* (1930), the entries in booksellers' catalogues from 1907 onward show the word *perversion* used consistently in the sense of *plaisir raffiné*, a "refinement of erotic pleasure." And understandably the Christian clergy seized upon the new term as a pseudo-scientific weapon with which to castigate the practice of "unnatural vice."

Results of the Development. The upshot of this imbroglio is that homosexuality has had to bear the further stigma of being a "sexual perversion" (however ambivalently understood) whose spread "threatened to corrupt the youth of the nation," "undermined the moral fabric of society," "raised the spectre of race suicide" and the like, while abusive letters addressed to gay organizations abound in affronts such as "You filthy perverts." Through its inherent ambiguity and acquired sinister penumbra, the word perpetuated the semantic confusion that enveloped the subject, hindering the emergence of a rational attitude toward homosexual behavior—and indeed of all conduct that departed from the **ascetic** norm of Christian theology. Since the underlying assumption of moralizing **psychiatry** was that nonreproductive sexual activity was somehow "perverse," it served to reinforce the normative edict of Scholastic theologians that sexual acts are legitimate only when performed within marriage and for purposes of procreation. If a scientific term is to be employed for such a deviation of the sexual instinct, then the elegant neologism *parhedonia* would be the logical choice.

An Attempted Reformulation. In recent years several professional philosophers have proposed a redefinition of the concept of perversion. Thomas Nagel, for example, argues that perversion is more psychological than physiological, and that perversions are "truncated or incomplete versions of the complete figuration." Thus bestiality, where there is lack of reciprocity, would be perversion, while homosexuality is not. Unfortunately, these philosophers' discussions are conducted in the afterglow of the earlier history of the set of terms—the adjectives *perverse* and *perverted*, the nouns *perversity* and *perversion*, and the verb *to pervert*—rendering problematic their intended reconstruction of it.

Warren Johansson

PESSOA, FERNANDO (1888–1935)

Leading modern Portuguese poet. Born in Lisbon, he was educated in Durban, South Africa, where he became fluent in English and acquired a good knowledge of English literature. He returned to Portugal in 1905 and led an outwardly uneventful life, earning a modest but comfortable living as a translator of commercial correspondence until his death in 1935.

Though active in Lisbon's literary circles, Pessoa published only a small amount of poetry and some literary criticism during his lifetime. Since his death, however, he has been recognized as the greatest Portuguese poet after Camões and a major European writer. Pessoa is most famous for his invention of the heteronyms Alberto Caeiro, Ricardo Reis, and Álvaro de Campos, poetic creations with distinct personalities, philosophies, and styles, which were intended to add a dramatic element to his writing. Pessoa wrote poetry in both Portuguese and English, revolutionizing the use of the Portuguese language through his classical English education and his familiarity with English literature. The influence of Walt **Whitman** can be seen in some of his major poems.

Pessoa's verse is intellectual and metaphysical rather than emotional or confessional. His poems are a constant reflection on the meaning of life and on different attitudes to the mystery of living. They convey states of mind and the manifold dimensions of experience, suggesting possibilities rather than certainties. Even in his lyrical moments Pessoa remains detached, an observer of life rather than an active participant.

Although there is no conclusive proof that Pessoa was homosexual, the fact that he never married, the extreme reserve he maintained about his private life, and his friendship with the openly gay poet António Botto point in this direction. Three episodes in his literary career have a homosexual theme. The Portuguese poems "Ode triunfal" ("Triumphal Ode") and "Ode marítima" ("Maritime Ode"), both published in 1915 under the heteronym Álvaro de Campos, have overtones of sado-masochistic fantasy. *Antinous* (1918), a long poem written in rather stilted English and published under his own name, commemorates the relationship between the Roman emperor **Hadrian** and his beloved **Antinous**; the passages in which Hadrian recalls their physical love-making are unusually sensuous and explicit. In 1921, a revised version appeared under the title *English poems, I–II*, in which Pessoa systematically removed all words expressing shame or wrong-doing in the relationship. Finally, the publication under Pessoa's Olisipo imprint of *Canções* ("Songs") (1922), a book of openly gay poetry by António Botto, led to a controversy in which Pessoa took a prominent part in Botto's defense. Underlying all Pessoa's work, however, are themes of particular relevance to gay readers, such as the multi-faceted aspects of personality and the many levels of perceived experience.

Among the writers in Pessoa's circle, two are also worthy of note. Mário de Sá-Carneiro (1890–1916) was more subjective in his poetry than Pessoa, writing on the crisis of personality and the sense of frustration, regret, and inadequacy which eventually led to his suicide. He also wrote a short novel, *A confissão de Lúcio* ("The Confession of Lucio") (1914), with a thinly-veiled homosexual theme open to various interpretations. António Botto (1902–1959) published poems on the themes of love, passion, sexual desire, disillusionment, longing, regret, humiliation, and shame. The poems are generally addressed to males and deal with the pleasures and disappointments of physical love and casual encounters, reflecting on the impossibility of complete fulfillment in any relationship. Botto's narcissism is pervasive and his poetic talent is frequently not equal to his themes, but his work is refreshing for its openness in dealing with gay male love.

BIBLIOGRAPHY. Jose Blanco, *Fernando Pessoa: esboço de uma bibliografia*, Lisbon: Imprensa Nacional-Casa da Moeda/Centro de Estudos Pessoanos, 1983; João Gaspar Simões, *Vida e Obra de Fernando Pessoa*, third ed., Lisbon: Bertrand, 1973.

Robert Howes

PETRONIUS ARBITER (D. A.D. 66)

Roman satirist. Petronius is usually identified as a high official and Nero's favorite, "arbiter of taste" at the court, whose career and then suicide when he lost the Emperor's good will are recorded by **Tacitus**: "His days were passed in sleep, his nights in social engagements and the pleasures of life. The fame which other men attain by diligence he won by his use of leisure." The lengthy extant fragments of the fifteenth and sixteenth books of Petronius' *Satires* (usually called the *Satyricon*) amount to about one-tenth of the original.

Claiming that it had Hellenistic antecedents or models (in addition to the obvious borrowings such as the "Milesian Tales," the widow of Ephesus, and the boy of Pergamon), some scholars deny the originality of the *Satyricon*. Some modern authorities believe that there were two prominent men named Petronius who lived at the time of Nero, and that they have been wrongly conflated. Others have maintained that this novel may not have been composed before the third century. Yet the overwhelming majority believe it the highly original creation of Petronius Arbiter.

In a famous set piece, the rich parvenu freedman Trimalchio stages an ostentatious feast of many courses to be vomited up in turn, accompanied by garish entertainment, all in the worst possible taste—a classic literary example of "life as it ought not to be." Set mostly in Southern Italy, Magna Graecia, and involving slaves or freedmen of Greek descent, the work is a veritable gold mine for students of Roman manners and of colloquial language and idiom. The disreputable youth Giton, a freedman of Greek extraction, deflowers a seven-year-old girl in full view of an amused audience. One of his lovers, the hero or anti-hero Encolpius, considers castrating himself when temporarily impotent (in a public bath) "and while the boys just ridiculed me as a lunatic . . . a huge crowd surrounded him with applause and the most awe-struck admiration. You see, he had such an enormous sexual organ that you'd think the man was just an appendage to his penis." Made-up eunuchs, transvestites, prostitutes of both sexes abound.

Typical of the casual attitudes is the inserted story of the boy of Pergamon. A visitor to the boy's father's home offered progressively more expensive gifts to the boy, who feigned sleep, in exchange for sexual favors. However, the boy was disappointed when the visitor failed to deliver the final present, a Macedonian stallion.

Petronius thought that most ladies were fascinated by and preferred low-life lovers. In spite of titillating scenes, the language is less coarse than **Catullus'** or even Horace's. The speech varies with the rank and education of the character: slave, freedman, aristocrat, foreigner, or Roman. Each episode is almost an independent mime, stage-managed by the author.

No ancient work survives as perverse, bizarre, and titillatingly amusing as this one, which with allusions to **Epicureanism** ridicules the pompous "gravitas" of the leading contemporary courtier Seneca, the philosopher of **Stoicism**, litterateur, and tragedian. Doubtless Petronius continued the tradition of Varro's lost *Menippean Satires*, interspersing prose and verse, perhaps in parody of the *Pharsalia* of Lucan, Seneca's nephew. The *Satyricon* is often considered a forerunner of the picaresque novel in which adventurous episodes follow one another without rhyme or reason.

Historians of eroticism have found the *Satyricon* rich in meaning not only for its portrayal of total sexual abandon with equal interest in homosexual and heterosexual escapades, but also as the best ancient documentation of voyeurism, exhibitionism, scopophilia, scopomixia, as well as of castration fantasies, and sadomasochism, all erotic penchants found much more in Latin than in Greek literature. Petronius thus bequeathed to later ages an imperishable record of the sexual life of the early Roman Empire with its unabashed and overt homosexuality.

The "sexual revolution" of the 1960s saw a revived interest in the author. Federico Fellini's extravagant 1969 **film** *Satyricon*, though only loosely based on the original, documents this intersection.

BIBLIOGRAPHY. Joachim Adamietz, "Zum literarischen Charakter von Petrons *Satyrica*," *Rheinisches Museum für Philologie*, 130 (1987), 329–46; Charles Gill, "The Sexual Episodes in the Satyricon," *Classical Philology*, 68 (1973), 172–85; J. P. Sullivan, *The Satyricon of Petronius: A Literary Study*, London: Faber and Faber, 1968.

William A. Percy

PHILIPPINES

The Republic of the Philippines comprises over seven thousand tropical islands off the mainland of southeast Asia, settled by approximately fifty million predominantly Roman Catholic people; a Muslim minority is found in the South.

History. Colonized by Spain in the mid-sixteenth century, the islands passed into American control as a result of the Spanish–American War (1898). A three-year armed revolt against the new American colonial power was crushed in 1901. During World War II, Japan occupied the islands between 1942 and 1944–45. Following the war, the United States granted the Philippines independence in 1946. The post-independence history of the Republic has featured a series of guerrilla wars and considerable civil strife.

Homosexuality and Transvestism. The Philippines enjoys a reputation as one of the contemporary societies most tolerant of homosexuality. Philippine criminal law is silent on the subject of consenting same-sex relations and there is little or no prosecution under other statutes. Filipinos tend to hold benign attitudes toward homosexuals and in certain areas of the country transvestic (cross-dressed) homosexuals even are accorded special status. In Bacolod, for example, a sugar-cane capital of some 300,000 inhabitants, cross-dressed homosexuals traditionally participate as dancers in the main social event of the town, the Christmas Eve pageant, held in the city's principal hotel. The queen of the Christmas pageant is usually a cross-dressed male homosexual.

Transvestic homosexuals are well-known for their fashion shows or beauty pageants which are presented in all parts of the Philippines for the general public and frequently sponsored by civic clubs such as Rotary or Kiwanis. Such drag presentations are regarded as family entertainment and are popular with children as well as adults. Philippine children are socialized to regard homosexuals as interesting and amusing people. Many Tagalog movies contain homosexual comic characters often portrayed as friends of the leading men. The appearance of homosexual characters in Philippine movies inevitably elicits claps and shouts of approval from the many children in the audience.

Terminology. While it is the cross-dressed male homosexuals in the Philippines who are most conspicuous, masculine male homosexuals and masculine and feminine lesbians are also found. Because of the rather complex language usage patterns in the Philippines it is somewhat difficult to generalize about terminology referring to homosexuals. While Tagalog is the official language, English is widely used in the universities and among educated Filipinos as a second language. Several other major regional languages are commonly used. The most widely known terms for male homosexuals probably are *bakla* (Tagalog) and *bayot* (Cebuano). These terms may be used as general terms for male homosexuals and may apply to masculine, non-transvestic homosexuals or may refer to effeminate or cross-dressed homosexuals.

While the Cebuano term *lakin-on* is sometimes used to refer to lesbians, the more universally understood term in most parts of the Philippines is the English-derived term *tomboy*. As the term implies, some lesbians are viewed as mannish and some cross-dress and hold traditionally male occupations. Like male homosexuals, they are well-treated. Lesbians, for example, may flirt with neighborhood girls, sending them small presents and love notes without provoking the hostility of parents and neighbors, who are likely to joke and tease about such "crushes." Lesbians tend to lead more private lives than male homosexuals and have no developed social organizations such as bars, networks, coffee shops, or clubs. They tend to pair off relatively early sometimes with a partner, usually a heterosexual female, called a "live-in." Because of widespread crowding, unmarried homosexuals—both male and female—usually are not able to set up households independent of extended families unless they are affluent.

"Callboys." Courtship patterns of male homosexuals are characterized by the "callboy" system, wherein heterosexual males usually between 15 and 25 engage in sexual relations or in more permanent relationships with homosexuals in exchange for money and sustenance paid by the homosexual. Callboys may be found in all parts of the Philippines and it is estimated that as many as 80 percent of the young males from the working and lower middle classes at some point in their youths work as "callboys." In some areas the callboy system has become institutionalized. In Pagsanjan, for example, a resort town of 3,000, practically all of the heterosexual males between 15 and 25 work as "callboys." Male homosexuals have few sexual relationships with other homosexuals. Most sexual relations of homosexual men are with bisexual or heterosexual youths.

The Roots of Tolerance. Despite its many social and economic problems the Philippines has been able to develop a society which is relatively democratic in terms of sex and gender. Filipinos often say "We don't need women's liberation; we have had it for years." There is considerable truth in this statement. The Philippines has a long tradition of egalitarianism with regard to the sexes. Many women hold positions regarded as traditionally male occupations. For example, 60 percent of accountants, 67 percent of chemical engineers, 70 percent of dentists, and 52 percent of physicians in the Philippines are estimated to be women. Tolerance for homosexuals may well be related to these more general patterns of gender equality. Philippine attitudes are part of the benign system of attitudes prevailing in southeast Asia and the South Pacific and may well be a long-standing aspect of Philippine society as suggested by the pervasive presence of such attitudes in rural areas and small towns as well as in the cities. That homo-

sexuals were indigenous to the Philippines before the the arrival of the Europeans is suggested by the observations of Father Juan de Plascencia, who wrote in 1589 that the native Filipinos had among their priests, "bayoguin . . . a man whose nature inclined toward that of a woman." In a list of "ministers of the devil" of the pre-Spanish religion practiced by the natives, the Spanish friar Juan Francisco de San Antonio, writing in 1738, includes the *bayoguin,* who was "an effeminate man . . . inclined to being a woman and to all the matters of this feminine sex." These scant passages suggest that effeminate homosexuals held places of honor in pre-literate, pre-Hispanic Philippines, a fact which may be related to widespread attitudes of tolerance accorded contemporary Philippine homosexuals.

Crackdowns on Prostitution. By the spring of 1988, two crackdowns occurred to compromise the picture of idyllic tolerance, although both applied only to prostitution: widespread raids on bars in the tourist district of Manila (the capital), and the arrest and deportation of homosexual pedophiles in Pagsanjan.

The spring and summer of 1988 saw the emergence of a moral crusade against prostitution, pornography, and live sex shows (both heterosexual and homosexual) in Manila's famous Ermita tourist belt. The most highly publicized aspect of this crusade was a series of raids led by Manila police chief Brigadier General Alfredo Lim against nearly 300 bars which allegedly were operating as fronts for prostitution. Some two thousand prostitutes, including some male prostitutes catering to homosexuals, were involved in the raids. While most establishments remained open during this period, one of Manila's most famous homosexual establishments "the Retiro 690 Club," a disco with male prostitutes and sex shows, was closed. By May, 1988, a power struggle developed between police chief Lim and Manila Mayor Mel Lopez, who opposed the raids. President Corazon Aquino, who approved the raids, stepped in and called Lim and Lopez to Malacañang Palace to mediate the dispute. While homosexual establishments were not singled out, they were conspicuously included in the generalized attack on "vice" in Manila.

For years the town of Pagsanjan in the province of Laguna has been a favorite of both tourists who visit Pagsanjan Falls and foreign pedophiles who form liaisons with the many boys in that town who readily (and usually with the knowledge and approval of their parents and townspeople) make themselves available for money. In late February, 1988, a surprise raid on Pagsanjan was conducted by constabulary agents, police, and immigration officials, and 22 foreign pedophiles were arrested. The raiding team left Manila early in the morning, arrived in Pagsanjan at 7 A.M., entered the Pagsanjan Lodge and eight private houses without warning or warrants, finding those arrested sleeping with or in other compromising positions with pre-pubertal Filipino boys. Those arrested (from the United States, Germany, Belgium, Australia, the United Kingdom, Japan, the Netherlands, Spain, and Canada) were fined 1,000 pesos ($50) each and deported. Four of them remained to contest their deportation on the grounds that they had done nothing illegal in view of the absence of an "age of consent" for males in Philippine criminal law.

These events are probably related directly or indirectly to the threat of AIDS, coupled with a new government characterized by a growing sense of xenophobia fed by unfavorable international publicity describing the Philippines as a sexual marketplace.

BIBLIOGRAPHY. Donn V. Hart, "Homosexuality and Transvestism in the Philippines," *Behavior Science Notes*, 3 (1968), 211–48; Frederick L. Whitam and Robin M. Mathy, *Male Homosexuality in Four Societies: Brazil, Guatemala, the Philippines, and the United States*; New York: Praeger, 1986.

Frederick L. Whitam

PHILO JUDAEUS (CA. 20 B.C.–CA. A.D. 45)

Jewish thinker and exegete. Philo belonged to a wealthy Hellenized family of **Alexandria** in Egypt. In 39 he took part in an embassy to Rome, described in his *Legation to Caius*; otherwise little is known of the outward circumstances of his life. Philo's fusion of Greek allegory and moralizing with biblical **Judaism** made his work appealing to Christians; significantly, his extensive writings—all in Attic Greek rather than in Hebrew—owe their survival to Christian copyists.

Philo discusses homosexuality in three passages of some length (*On Abraham*, 133–41; *The Special Laws*, III, 37–42; and *The Contemplative Life*, 59–63). These texts disclose a tripartite classification of male same-sex behavior, affording us a glimpse of social reality in a great Hellenistic-Roman city at the time of Christ. The three modes, which to some extent overlap, are those of (1) the latterday Greek adherents of *paiderasteia*, which changed political circumstances had shorn of its positive state-building character, making it an easy target for caricature by hostile observers such as Philo as mere love-sickness; (2) the ostentatious effeminates, whom Philo dubs "men-women"; and (3) the *galli*, or religious-ecstatic castrates. Although it is edged throughout with hostility, Philo's account showed that cosmopolitan Alexandria had a more varied panorama of homosexual **lifestyles** than did earlier communities, anticipating the variety of "scenes" of gay life in more recent times.

The larger significance of Philo, however, stems from his historical position at a pivotal junction of religious and ethical thought. Born into a wealthy and cultivated Jewish family in learned Alexandria, he benefited from a thorough education in the Greek classics. Having absorbed both the allegorical techniques of the literary critics of Homer and the ethical ideals of Middle Platonism, Philo resolved to write a series of apologias for Judaism as he knew it. He had scarcely any Hebrew or Aramaic and much of the tone and fabric of his work is strongly Greek, so that when later normative Judaism came to assume its classical form his writings were rejected by the Synagogue. Conversely, their very synthesis of the Judaic and Hellenic worlds made his texts appealing to Early Christian theologians and apologists. Through this adoption his ideas passed into the mainstream of medieval and early modern European thought.

Central to Philo's project is the notion that the Law of Moses is coterminous with the Law of Nature. On the Hellenic side, the elevation of **nature** as a universal norm of human conduct had for some centuries been a major preoccupation of the Platonic tradition. By reinterpreting the prohibitions of male homosexual conduct in Leviticus 18 and 20 as not simply the ordinances of a particular people—the followers of the god who had revealed his law to Moses on Mount Sinai—and functioning in fact to set them apart from other nations, but as a categorical imperative for all of mankind, Philo made the repression of homosexual behavior virtually a state duty. Thus an ideal of continence, which had been largely a matter of individual choice and the mark of an educated elite in Stoic philosophy, became a moral obligation for all. Following the Mosaic texts, Philo affirms that homosexual conduct among males deserves death, and interprets the legend of the destruction of Sodom as God's judgment upon the wicked. In this way he foreshadows the penal sanctions enacted by the Christian emperors of the fourth century, which were renewed by Justinian and many later authorities and embellished with allusions to the Cities of the Plain, whose destruction Philo attributed to homosexual vice.

Some other antihomosexual motifs found in Philo also echoed through the centuries. In his view, homosexual activity is so disgusting that it scarcely bears mention, foreshadowing the later Christian view of "that horrible sin not to be named amongst Christians." Philo claimed that if homosexual conduct were to spread it would depopulate whole cities, even imperilling the very survival of the human race. Sodomy, in a view reiterated by bigoted jurists as late as the beginning of the twentieth century, is implicated in a plot to murder the human race. Last of all, Philo put into circulation two hostile metaphors that were to have a long life: the idea that homosexual conduct is equivalent to a farmer's sowing on stony ground; and the image of the sodomite as one who debases the sterling coin of nature. The latter notion is a cousin to the medieval identification of **usury**, lending at interest, with sodomy. Philo's blending of Judaic and Hellenic arguments thus supplied nascent Christianity with a sophisticated rationale for interdicting homosexual activity among its followers.

Although they were virtually contemporaries, Philo and the **New Testament** authors wrote independently of one another. Nonetheless, they reflect a similar stage in the development of antihomosexual beliefs derived from biblical Judaism and integrated into the syncretistic mind-set of the early Roman empire. These negative ideas were to play a major role in Early Christian and medieval homophobia.

BIBLIOGRAPHY. Richard A. Baer, Jr., *Philo's Use of the Categories of Male and Female*, Leiden: E. J. Brill, 1970; Samuel Sandmel, *Philo's Place in Judaism: A Study of Abraham in Jewish Literature*, Cincinnati: Hebrew Union College Press, 1966.

Wayne R. Dynes

PHILOSOPHY

From the Greek word meaning "love of wisdom or knowledge," the definition of philosophy has varied over the ages. It includes logic, metaphysics, epistemology, aesthetics, and **ethics**—and formerly comprised physics, cosmology, and **psychology** as well. Concepts from **India**, **Egypt**, and **Mesopotamia**, if not yet from **China**, influenced the Greeks. Greek philosophy itself—like its close ally Greek **science** under the Ionian physicists—began in Ionia, on the coastal fringes of Anatolia, just when **pederasty** was introduced there and to the Ionian islands from **Crete** and **Sparta**, and intellectualized to provide each beloved boy a loving inspirer.

The Pre-Socratics. From the time of Thales of Miletus (flourished ca. 585 B.C.) Western philosophy has its own distinct history; however, many foreign influences may be traced, from the neo-Platonists down to **Schopenhauer** and even the New **Left**. Although Western philosophy embraces, as do the others, materialism and idealism, atheism and pantheism, monism and dualism, pragmatism and mysticism, it adheres more strictly to logic as developed by pederasts in late archaic and classical Greece.

The Ionians conceived nature as operating in a non-mythological, impersonal manner. Reflecting the maritime setting of Greece, Thales thought water the basic element, which Anaximander expanded to air, earth, fire, and water. The Persian conquests ended such speculations and apparently also finished institutionalized pederasty, as when the conquerors crucified Polycrates of Samos in 521, with the consequent flight of the pederastic poets **Ibycus** and **Anacreon** who had been drawn to his court.

Having already fled Polycrates' tyranny, Pythagoras returned to Southern Italy ca. 530 and founded his brotherhood at Croton, something between a college and a cloister, being pederastic, stressing form rather than matter. Study of music taught him the value of proportions and the necessity of numbers, often conceived geometrically. The correct proportions of hot and cold, wet and dry became fundamental to **medicine**.

Another refugee from Ionia, Xenophanes of Colophon, who attacked Homer and Hesiod for their anthropomorphic conceptions of the immortals, founded the Eleatic school at Elea in southern Italy, the first metaphysical school: "But if oxen or horses had hands, oxen would make gods like oxen and horses would make gods like horses." His *eromenos* (beloved) Parmenides of Elea (d. ca. 480) regarded the cosmos as eternal, uncreated, and imperishable. Zeno of Elis (d. ca. 420) contradicted the Pythagorean notion of multiplicity, arguing instead by paradoxes for monism.

Heraclitus (ca. 540–475 B.C.) saw fire as the primary element: "This one order of all things was created by none of the gods" but is always changing and always moving. Anaxagoras (d. 428) believed that "intelligence" and "reason" had brought order out of chaos in the universe, a theory adopted by Aristotle. Empedocles of Agrigentum proposed two principles, love and hate or attraction and repulsion, which organized the four elements. The atomists opposing the Eleatic concept of reality as an immutable static one, culminated in Democritus (d. 370), whose mechanistic explanations of a materialistic universe underlay the Epicurean school.

The significance of these advances in philosophy is that they broke decisively with the notion of a universe created by the gods, presumed by late Babylonian cosmology, that furnished the starting point for Greek philosophical and scientific speculations. But incorporated into Genesis and the other books of the Old Testament, this Semitic mythology, albeit in a monotheistic guise, became the patrimony of all three **Abrahamic religions**. The incompatibility between the divinely created universe of these revealed faiths and the mechanistic model of the cosmos, which evolved into the world picture of modern physics and astronomy, predetermined the conflict between religion and science that reached its peak in the late nineteenth century and still echoes in the antagonism between the Judeo-Christian tradition and the secular ideals of the gay liberation **movement** a hundred years later.

The Golden Age. After defeating the Persians in 480, the confident Greeks accelerated the building of their unique culture, with greater material wealth and more democracy, and with Athens as the center of commerce and innovation. Knowledge was sought as a good in itself as well as a way to win trials and public office. Sophists, "wise men," lectured for fees. Often in the **gymnasia**, Protagoras, Georgias, Hippias, and Prodicus taught debating skills, how to make the best of even a bad case and how to defend lost causes or strange and even absurd theories. As the conservative **Aristophanes** lamented, they could "make the better seem the worse case," demoralizing some Athenian youths and bringing into question established norms and ethics. Protagoras proclaimed: "Man is the measure of all things," denying universally valid knowledge.

Regarded by some of his contemporaries as a sophist, **Socrates** like them educated the young by dialectic, proving that the "experts" knew as little as he about ethics, but he did believe in the possibility of discovering truth through the inductive method of elimination of falsehood by constant questioning. No man knowing good would do evil. Sticking to his guns he was condemned to death by an Athenian jury in 399, the first martyr to philosophy, accused of "corrupting the youth and questioning the existence of the gods." His protégé **Alcibiades** had betrayed Athens to Sparta, and another disciple Critias had tyrannized Athens as one of the "Thirty Tyrants" installed by the Spartans from 404 to 403, when they were expelled and the democracy Socrates so criticized restored.

The most important of Socrates' disciples was **Plato**, who met him at the age of 20. After the master's death he traveled to Italy, where he encountered the Pythagoreans. He opened his school, whose elitism reflected the Pythagorean brotherhood and like it encouraged "love"—at least male bonding—among members. The Academy, in Athens in 387, had inscribed on the doorway "Let no one who knows no geometry come under my roof," echoing the Pythagorean emphasis on harmony. He adapted Heraclitus' belief that all matter is in constant flux, unknowable, hence one may only formulate opinions about it. Plato changed his views during his long life, repudiating in the *Laws*, his last work, many of his earlier, more open principles, including pederasty. His earlier dialogues, masterpieces of style almost like the dramas so popular at Athens since Aeschylus, reflect opinions then discussed at **symposia** and **gymnasia**.

Aristotle was Plato's most important pupil. Even in the imperfect form in which we have them, often as notes taken by students, his treatises articulate every branch of philosophy, gathering up more systematically and comprehensively than Plato all the best arguments of the predecessors. Having studied twenty years in Plato's Academy, he founded after travels abroad his own school, the Lyceum. He was more realistic and empirical than his master. A biologist, Aristotle emphasized becoming from potential to actual, from seed to final form, more teleologically than Plato, the geometrician concerned rather with eternally static truth. In his "scale of nature" things were ranked, the highest being God, the unmoved mover who induced preexisting matter to develop its potentialities by taking on higher forms. Not hailing from the pederastic high society of Athens, as Plato did, but from the provincial bourgeoisie, Aristotle was less inspired by the pederastic lyrics of **Ibycus**, **Anacreon**, **Theognis**, and **Pindar**, and being more biologically oriented, felt that pederasty, natural to some, was a vice acquired by others and limited the teleological potential of reproduction. But pedagogy in Greece, since the late Archaic Age, rested on pederasty, which flourished among philosophers, many of whom broke the taboo that made marriage almost mandatory for the upper class: Plato, Diogenes the Cynic, and all the early Stoics.

The latter kept eromenoi to the age of 28, at least a decade after the eromenoi were customarily abandoned.

Later Greek Philosophy and Rome. The troubles and tyranny that ensued after Philip of Macedon conquered Epaminondas of **Thebes** at Chaeronea in 338 rendered people more anxious for individual ethical guidance, upon which **Epicureans**, **Stoics**, and Skeptics, three principal schools concentrated.

The Epicureans valued knowledge only for its usefulness. Knowledge of nature emancipates man from superstition and baseless fear and study of human nature aids in self-control. They preferred Democritus' mechanistic materialism to the idealism and teleology of both Plato and Aristotle. Even the soul was composed of atoms "hence those who call the soul incorporeal talk foolishly." In late republican Rome Lucretius (d. 55 B.C.) composed *On the Nature of Things*, the classic account, to preserve their teaching. It was neglected and even banned by Christians who disapproved of the hedonism the Epicureans had adopted from the Cyrenaics, although they ranked mental pleasures, especially those deriving from the practice of virtue, higher than any others.

Likewise denying the intrinsic value of knowledge, **Zeno** of Citium and the Stoics valued it only as it aided virtue. They substituted "body and soul" for the Aristotelian "matter and form." Reason providentially directs the organic universe by natural law, leaving no room for chance, or *Tyche*, so dear to their Epicurean rivals. Life should conform to a pantheistic **nature**. Rational self-control, the only good, rendered one free of external forces and hence content. Appealing to old-fashioned Romans like the Catos, **Cicero**, and Marcus Aurelius, these trends tended to uphold the *mos maiorum*, the ancestral peasant customs which stood against the degeneracy of the Hellenizing gilded youth exemplified in Lucullus, Sulla, and **Caesar** in the Republic, all of whom employed Epicureanism to justify hedonism. In the Empire Caligula used Epicureanism to rationalize his extreme excesses such that he helped to discredit it. Stoicism was used by Christian Fathers, especially after **Clement** of Alexandria who set the fashion, but **Patristic** literature everywhere reveals merely superficial borrowing to shore up an anti-rational, anti-sexual mystery religion influenced by **Gnosticism**.

Unlike Stoics and Epicureans, Pyrrho and other Skeptics stressed epistemology, asserting that things cannot be calculated or accounted for sufficiently to warrant any conviction whatever. By renouncing attempts to acquire knowledge one might attain peace of mind.

Not one of these pagan philosophers failed to practice pederasty, except perhaps Musonius Rufus (ca. A.D. 30–101), the only one to condemn it in his writings—if one excepts the *Laws*, the last of Plato's dialogues, which so contradicts the *Phaedrus* and the *Symposium*, where he had Eros alone excite knowledge and virtue.

The Confluence of Judaic and Platonic Trends. The Macedonian conquests had thrown the Greeks together with other ethnic groups in the **Hellenistic monarchies**, making them more cosmopolitan, especially in **Alexandria**, which replaced Athens as the intellectual center, and its rivals Antioch, Seleucia, Pergamon, and Beirut (Berytus), all of which created libraries, schools, gymnasia, and symposia, all of which fostered pederasty. But the Jews, especially numerous in Alexandria, felt scandalized. Chief of a learned group of Jews seeking in the early decades of the first century to harmonize the Bible, allegorically interpreted, with reason, **Philo Judaeus** combined this religion with Platonism, the most religious of the Greek philosophies. This line of thought formed a school known as neo-Platonic under Plotinus (d. 270), who proclaimed God the ultimate source, who created the Spirit who created the world-soul and so forth on down to the lower kind of material things.

Thus creation emanates from God. **Asceticism** and mysticism can help the soul escape from its body after a series of successive goals. Adapted to support paganism, neo-Platonism encouraged polytheism and credulity in spirits and spectres, giving paganism a new lease on life and criticizing Christianity's exaggeration of man's place in the universe and the efficacy of prayer without work. Julian the Apostate (r. 361–363) revived neo-Platonism in his losing struggle against Christianity.

Patristic Thinkers. Moralists now determined right conduct from Scripture as jurisconsults interpreted a law code, with ultimate sanctions in the next world and immediate ones in this by penance or excommunication so that canon law evolved along Jewish models. Christians substituted faith and love for knowledge and wisdom as sources of virtue, giving ethics a theological instead of a philosophical base, an arbitrary, inscrutable law, and an aversion to impurity regarded as a defilement. Deriving more from Plato, neo-Platonists, and Stoics than from the Ionians, Aristotle, Skeptics, and Epicureans (the last being their *bête noire*), the fathers of the Church were more theologians than philosophers. Patristic writers from the second to the seventh century warned against the philosophical schools which Justinian closed in 529, ending both the Academy and the Lyceum which had flourished in Athens for almost a millennium.

Although **Clement** of Alexandria began borrowing phrases from pagan philosophers, St. Jerome, far more educated and brilliant, relaxed the incompatibility between Athens and Jerusalem. Extreme intolerance, however, began with Theodosius the Great (r. 379–395), who banned rival religions and reiterated the death penalty against sodomites prescribed by the sons of Constantine the Great in 342. Whereas Anaxagoras, Socrates, and Aristotle had been persecuted for their hostility to popular religion, philosophy now became the handmaiden of religion. The authority of the Book and of tradition subordinated Western philosophy throughout the Middle Ages to religion in **Christianity** as in **Judaism** and **Islam**. When these Abrahamic religionists of the Book did not denounce or ignore philosophy, they fitted bits and pieces of it borrowed from Greek and Roman writers into a mosaic to buttress the "true faith." Around 400 St. John **Chrysostom** and St. **Augustine** absorbed into Christianity the asceticism of the desert fathers and the goals of **monasticism**, making blind faith in inscrutable providence the guide for the chaste hermit.

The Middle Ages. In the early Middle Ages that descended on the Latin West after Pope Gregory the Great (r. 590–604), nothing worthy of the name philosophy was composed in Latin. **Penitentials** and the beginnings of **canon law** reflect the absence of analysis even during the "Renaissance" under the Carolingians (751–887), when Alcuin, head of Charlemagne's cathedral school, and John Scotus Eriugena actually attempted philosophy. But the triple invasions of the ninth and tenth centuries, by Saracens, Magyars, and Northmen, swept away almost all of the cathedral schools the great Charlemagne had ordered every bishop to establish.

After 1000 invasions ceased, **Scandinavians**, Magyars, and Slavs converted to Christianity, and Europe revived. Teaching the seven liberal arts divided into trivium (grammar, rhetoric, and logic) and quadrivium (arithmetic, geometry, astronomy, and music), the *doctores scholastici* also broached philosophy in the revived cathedral schools more than did their rivals in the monastic schools, the mainstay of the early Middle Ages. Out of these and municipal schools—stronger in Italy, where trade had never as completely declined and sooner revived than in the north—there grew during the twelfth century the universities of Paris and Bologna, which dispute primacy. Paris soon sent offshoots to Oxford and Cambridge, which also claim twelfth-century origins, while Bologna branched out to Padua, Naples, and Salamanca. The university as an institution of higher learning was created in Europe by the Roman Catholic Church; the Byzantine and Islamic cultural spheres produced nothing comparable in the way of a hierarchical course of instruction with examinations leading to ever higher academic degrees. The University of Nalanda in India taught Buddhist philosophy throughout the first millennium, but was unknown in Europe.

During the Renaissance of the twelfth century ideas flowed into Catholic Europe from **Spain** and other Muslim lands, often through Jewish translators. While Christians languished in ignorance and proscribed homosexuality, Muslims kept philosophy (and pederasty) alive: al-Kindi (d. 870), Alfarabi (d. 950), Avicenna of Baghdad (d. 1037), and Averroes of Cordoba (d. 1198)—knowing nearly all of Aristotle's and several of Plato's extant works. Avicenna struggled to relate universals to particulars and Averroes, most Aristotelian of the Moslems, asserted the eternity of matter against the creation myth of the Koran, claiming that the soul died with the body but that man's immortal reason rejoined after his death the universal "active reason." In Spain the kingdom of **Granada** long served as a bridge to western Christendom.

The two principal texts of Jewish mystical teaching, the Kabbala, were completed in Muslim lands: the *Book of Creation* ca. 900 and the *Zohar* (The Shining Light) in 1290. Alongside such speculations, sensual philosophy influenced by Plato and Aristotle as well as by Alexandrians such as Philo appeared, especially in Cordoba and Toledo, but also in Baghdad and Cairo between the tenth and the fourteenth centuries, when tolerated Jews flourished in a Muslim world then at its intellectual zenith: Maimonides (d. 1204), Gersonides (d. 1344), and Crescas (d. 1410). Like the Muslims they influenced the scholastics directly and through their trans-

lations of the Greek philosophers from Arabic into Latin. Doctrines absorbed by the scholastics, such as the Latin Averroists combatted at Paris by Thomas **Aquinas**, made the universities rivals in disputes between Franciscans and Dominicans and between them and the secular hotbeds of heresy, as well as foci of the dogmatic orthodoxy imposed by the **Inquisition**. Other "students" often wandering from university to university preferred the wine, women, and song celebrated in the Goliardic poems.

Gerbert of Aurillac, pope from 999 to 1002, who had imbibed deeply of Moslem learning in Spain and had made the cathedral school at Reims preeminent when archbishop there, may have begun scholastic thought by emphasizing that reason can aid faith. St. Anselm, promoted from Abbot of Bec in Normandy to Archbishop of Canterbury in 1110, recommended light penalties, especially for young sodomitical clerks in opposition to the growing homophobia fanned by Peter **Damian**. As a philosopher Anselm logically explained why God became man (*Cur deus homo*).

From the start scholasticism at the medieval schools and universities was tainted with undercurrents of **heresy**, heterodoxy, sexual license, sorcery, and homosexuality. Clerics all, most in minor orders, students and faculty were forbidden to marry, a tradition abolished only by the French Revolution but continued at **Cambridge and Oxford** until 1877, at least for the dons. Some students entered the universities as early as the tender age of 13, since their curriculum overlapped with that of the modern preparatory school. The **public schools** like Eton and Harrow where rich boys came to be prepared for the universities in the later Middle Ages on the models of the Italian theorists Vittorino da Feltre and Guarino da Verona eventually also became hotbeds of pederasty.

Renaissance and Reformation. Unlike the ancient Greeks, medieval

Western man subordinated thought to authority. Scholars fleeing the sack of Constantinople by the Turks in 1453 brought manuscripts with them to Italy where, since affirming its independence from Milan in 1402, Florence had exuberantly developed its arts, ideas, and democracy, initiating the Italian **Renaissance**. Already devoted to the later classics, Florentines eagerly studied the Greek originals that lay behind their cherished Latin imitations. At the suggestion of the Greek exile Pletho, Cosimo de' Medici founded the Platonic Academy in Florence. There Marsilio **Ficino** with the help of Pico della Mirandola helped to revive Platonic and neo-Platonic philosophy, undermining the Aristotelianism of the scholastics, while Lorenzo Valla criticized their poor literary form. Paracelsus and Jan Baptista van Helmont denounced "authority" as a source for knowledge of nature and Bernardino Telesio's academy at Naples studied nature scientifically. Although Giordano Bruno, who was burned by the Inquisition in 1600, has been hailed as a forerunner of modern skepticism, recent research has shown that he was deeply involved in the hermetic (magical) tradition—illustrating the complex interplay of science and speculation in that period. **Montaigne** and Tomás Sánchez pleaded for toleration, skeptically attacking dogmatism. The Renaissance was more given to poetry than to philosophy, which was in any case soon threatened by the Protestant and Catholic Reformations.

The **Protestants** were as hostile to secular philosophy as to sodomy. Luther dubbed reason the devil's mistress. John Calvin condemned Michael Servetus to the flames in 1553. Ulrich Zwingli was only a bit more reasonable. But the terrible quarrels, mutual denunciations, persecutions, tortures, and religious wars helped to undermine Christian authority. Sir Francis **Bacon** is credited with heralding modern science, though like Bruno he was sensitive to the hermetic tradition.

Early Modern Philosophy. Hostile to scholastic dependence upon authority, René Descartes (1596–1650) posed instead the mathematical method by which one reasoned by axioms as in geometry deductively to unchallengeable conclusions. Like Augustine, he found that the only thing that could not be questioned was existence of his own doubt. "It is easy to suppose that there is no God, no heaven, no bodies. . . . I think, therefore I am." Like his contemporary Galileo, who was silenced by the Inquisition, Descartes explained natural phenomena mechanically. At the end of his life he became an adviser to Queen **Christina** of Sweden, whom he may have subtly counseled to understand her erotic proclivities.

In the Netherlands, Benedict Spinoza (1632–1677) also vindicated reason against every type of authority, including the scriptures. He set in motion the Higher Criticism of the Old Testament that was ultimately to discredit the Mosaic Law as a supposed "revelation" made by God on Mount Sinai and therefore eternally binding upon mankind. His pantheism appealed to "Deus sive Natura," bringing the Renaissance love of nature to a culmination as opposed to the characteristic medieval Christian equation of "the world, the flesh, and the devil."

Gottfried Wilhelm von Leibniz (1646–1716) denied the reality of matter, which can be infinitely divided into an infinity of monads which God had created. Thus each had an end as in medieval teleology: "The best of all possible worlds." He also conceived of "infinitely minute sensations" inaccessible to consciousness in the way that microscopic phenomena were invisible to the naked eye, and so adumbrated the concept of the unconscious (discussed in Buddhist philosophies in India two millennia previously) that beginning with Sigmund **Freud** would play an enormous role in the discussion of sexual psychology and of the determinants of homosexuality.

The Enlightenment. In 1690 John Locke (1632–1704) revolutionized Western epistemology with his *Essay Concerning Human Understanding*, rejecting innate ideas and tracing all mental activity to experience. Each man was convinced of his own and God's existence.

Pushing Locke's theories to the extreme, Hume advocated skepticism in philosophy and positivism in science. He rejected mental substances and mental causes. He reduced even mathematical knowledge from certainty to mere probability.

British skepticism helped inspire the French *philosophes* who had begun with Pierre Bayle and Bernard Fontenelle to disprove miracles and denigrate the church, and to criticize monarchy as well as all other established institutions and received morality. Montesquieu (1689–1755) offered a subtle new interpretation of the European legal tradition. In his *Persian Letters* (1721) he laid the groundwork for a criticism of Western civilization from an exotic point of view, an idea subsequently pursued by Diderot. In a tireless stream of polemical and imaginative works, **Voltaire** attacked abuses of church and state, including the persecution of sodomites. Jean-Jacques Rousseau (1712–1778), a more ambiguous figure, has sometimes been regarded as a forerunner of modern totalitarianism. The most radical offshoot of the French **Enlightenment** was the bisexual Marquis de **Sade**, who anticipated Nietzsche and other modern nihilists.

German Idealism and After. Immanuel Kant (1724–1804), the founder of transcendental idealism, denigrated all his predecessors as dogmatic philosophers. He sought to prove the a priori existence of pure reason. While in ethics Kant is best known for his "categorical imperative," the belief that each person should act as if his own conduct were a universal rule, he also set forth the bases of the modern critique of sexual **objectification**, for he held that sexual relations should be a matter of two loving persons and not just bodies.

Founding a logical idealism, G. W. F. Hegel (1770–1831)—who like Plato elaborated a philosophy of the state—insisted that the whole universe "can be penetrated by thought." He also held that "the real is the rational and the rational is the real." The philosopher's followers divided into Right and Left Hegelians; among the latter were Marx and Engels, so that indirectly Hegel came to have a great influence on political radicalism. **Marxism** was also affected by the revival of Enlightenment materialism that took place in the middle of the nineteenth century.

Associated with "voluntarism" and "pessimism," Arthur **Schopenhauer** identified reality with an irrational will. He advocated a kind of neo-Buddhist principle of renunciation. Unmarried like many major philosophers, Schopenhauer offered perceptive remarks on pederasty (which he does not seem, however, to have practiced). His sexual ethic began a separation of erotic expression from procreation that was to be carried further by Friedrich Nietzsche (1844–1900). The radical skepticism expressed with biting irony by Nietzsche was to prove a corrosive solvent of many seeming certainties that had bolstered established institutions. Often banished to the outer margins of professional philosophy, his writings have shown remarkable staying power, influencing Michel **Foucault** in the 1970s.

Pragmatism and Positivism. Following Locke and his empiricist predecessors, English and French philosophy diverged in the nineteenth century from German thought which, as has been seen, flowed from Kant. Jeremy **Bentham** went from the public school of Westminster to Oxford, where he was hazed for lack of robust manliness. He derived his principle of utilitarianism, especially the so-called "felicific calculus" (the greatest good of the greatest number) from the Italian reformer Count **Beccaria**. Bentham did not dare to publish his papers recommending the decriminalization of **sodomy** during his own lifetime (they began to appear only in 1931).

The creator of positivism, Auguste Comte (1798–1857) thought, like the British empiricists, that knowledge was acquirable only by observation and experience, but agreed with Kant that the ultimate principles were unknowable. Generally regarded as the founder of **sociology**, Comte emphasized human improvement through the application of ostensibly objective social laws. One of a number of thinkers sometimes known as the "prophets of Paris," his ideas about society have been ambiguous in their relation to sexual variation since they tend to emphasize uniformity and universality, rather than pluralism. However, Comte's eccentric contemporary Charles **Fourier** did not hesitate to include both lesbianism and male homosexuality in his Phalansteries, **utopian** cells of a new society.

Son of Bentham's friend James Mill, John Stuart Mill (1806–1873), who may be called a positivist, empirically stressed logic, utilitarian ethics, liberal politics, and laissez-faire approach to economics (which he derived from Adam Smith). His *On Liberty* (1859) sets forth the most eloquent defense of freedom of speech that has ever been devised, and has proved of enormous value in combatting **censorship** of both political and erotic materials.

Twentieth-Century Philosophy. Idealism, in the form of Hegelianism, lingered in Britain and North America in the early years of the century. Related to this trend are the individualist works of George **Santayana**, which are today read more for their literary qualities than for their technical acuteness.

A break with the idealist tradition was signaled by the **Cambridge** thinker, G. E. Moore (1873–1958), who though not himself homosexual was widely influential on several prominent gay men in the Apostles group, who then went to shine in **Bloomsbury**. Also a student at Cambridge was Ludwig **Wittgenstein**, who is arguably the most influential thinker of the twentieth century. His followers, fearing damage to his reputation, continue to deny Wittgenstein's homosexuality, but it is well established.

Although it has earlier roots in such thinkers as Kierkegaard and Husserl, existentialism is generally associated with the Frenchman Jean-Paul **Sartre**, who was also active as a novelist and political polemicist. An atheist, Sartre held that existence precedes essence, and that we are therefore radically challenged to embrace the freedom that is inherent in our situation. Although he seems never to have had a homosexual experience, Sartre was familiar with gay men and women through his left-bank circle in Paris, and included them in his overall concern with marginalized groups.

In Britain and America at mid-century the most visible philosophers adopted the austere credo of "analysis," which excluded most traditional themes from its purview. By about 1970, however, philosophers began to descend from the mountaintop to address themes of life and death, human destiny, and moral dilemmas. Such topics as capital punishment, abortion, incest, and homosexuality became accepted—at least in some academic philosophy departments. Feminism also made a strong impact, and women philosophers began to address what they held were the distortions of androcentric thought. It was even debated whether men and women might have fundamentally different styles of thinking that admit of no common denominator. Other thinkers, especially such neo-Marxists as Herbert Marcuse and Louis Althusser, addressed questions of **political theory**. All these currents came to have a considerable, though indirect, influence on the ideas of gay **liberation**.

BIBLIOGRAPHY. Robert Baker and Frederick Elliston, ed., *Philosophy and Sex*, second ed., Buffalo: Prometheus,

1984; Vern L. Bullough, *Sexual Variance in Society and History*, New York: Wiley-Interscience, 1976; Laurence J. Rosán, "Philosophies of Homophobia and Homophilia," in *The Gay Academic*, L. Crew, ed., Palm Springs: ETC, 1978, pp. 255–81; Alan Soble, ed., *Philosophy of Sex: Contemporary Readings*, Totowa, NJ: Littlefield and Adams, 1980.

William A. Percy

PHONE AND COMPUTER SEX

Phone sex is **masturbation** while communicating by telephone with another person. It is an emerging pastime and industry, with franchises and telephone equipment designed for it. An offshoot of the **pornography** industry, phone sex has built its legal base on the freedom accorded to pornographic utterances and shows signs of attracting a significant fraction of its revenues. A number of small, non-profit clubs facilitate obscene phone calls among their members.

History. Dirty talk over the telephone is nearly as old as dial telephones, on which no one could eavesdrop, and has a precedent in obscene letters exchanged by lovers. Also helpful was the telephone industry's early stand in favor of confidentiality of communications, which soon became law. As a commercial phenomenon, though, it originated in the 1970s with recorded tapes of dirty talk sold by Old Reliable and a number of smaller publishers. Beginning in the early 1980s advertisements appeared in sex publications for phone sex services, in which for a fee of $10 to $40, usually paid via credit card, a voice at the other end creates fantasies or discusses any topic that will stimulate orgasm in the customer.

"976" phone services were introduced in the United States in the mid-1980s; the number refers to a telephone company prefix. They provided recorded messages of short duration for a fee of $2 or less, billed through the telephone company. An important legal ruling stated that providers of sexual messages should have equal access to this facility, and the primary use of the "976" capacity was for masturbatory sexual messages, gay and straight. The unrestricted availability of these recorded messages to minors led to such a parental outcry that they were effectively ended by the late 1980s. They were also a problem for businesses, which were faced with charges for surreptitious calls by employees. So many calls were made from Mexico to 976 numbers that international access was discontinued at the request of the Mexican telephone company.

Various adaptations of this highly profitable service were tried: the use of access codes furnished upon validation of age; changes in telephone company prefixes and equipment so that parents could remove access to such services from their phones; a requirement of payment by credit card, which few minors could effect. The adaptation which seemed to meet with the most immediate success was the abandonment of recorded messages altogether in favor of simply connecting callers to one another, in pairs or groups, or providing contact advertisements via telephone. Thus the service provider could disclaim responsibility for, and indeed remain ignorant of, the message content.

Computer Sex. An offshoot of phone sex is computer sex or compusex, in which the connection is made by modem, parties being linked over telephone lines with a host computer. This began with mainframe-based services such as CompuServe and American PeopleLink, which have been friendly to their numerous gay customers. Computer sex then spread to smaller, exclusively gay services operated by individuals; while they started as hobbies, several have outgrown that status. Providers of computer communication services encourage callers, in private messages or when connected in private with one or more other callers, to be as explicit as they wish; part of the appeal is that one can converse anonymously using a pseudonym or "handle." They also provide contact advertisements and gay news and commercial advertisements. Main-frame-based services offer popular "party line" type discussions; services usually have a gay conversation line, accounting for a third to a half of the party line conversations, and on which a cruisy atmosphere sometimes develops. Computer communications are quickly being given the same legal rights to privacy as telephone messages. In France, since the national telephone system distributed simple computer terminals to all customers, sexual message services, called *messageries roses,* have been highly successful; indeed, the sexual message services have ensured the success of home computer terminals in France, just as X-rated videos made a hit of the video tape recorder in the United States.

BIBLIOGRAPHY. Dave Kinnick, "From Floppy to Hard: Computer Dating at Home," *The Advocate*, 516 (January 17, 1989), 42–45.

Daniel Eisenberg

PHOTOGRAPHY

"Gay" or "homosexual" photography is an ambiguous concept. While a person can be described as homosexual because of sexual activities, or as gay because of sexual preference or expressing a certain consciousness, an inanimate, unconscious object cannot. Nonetheless, to the extent that a photographic image reflects a particular consciousness on the part of the photographer, it might be termed gay, though that consciousness is notoriously hard to define. Thus images by gay or homosexual photographers are sometimes described as "gay photography," although not every image by a gay person is necessarily marked by gay sensibility. On occasion the term is used to describe the documentation of gay events or meeting places, or of homosexual behavior. At still other times the term is used almost as a synonym for male **nudes**, though feminist-inspired male nudes (while a gay man may appreciate the images) could not be called

gay images. Yet in each case there is some justification for the usage, if "gay" or "homosexual photography" is defined as those images which consciously or unconsciously portray or evoke homoerotic associations shared by the creator and viewer. Homosexual photographers would be most likely to express such associations, the places or behaviors to be charged with such meanings, and certainly the male nude is the central focus of such homoerotic references.

Until recently, such expression of homoerotic interests had to be masked by a "top dressing" of one sort or another—artist's reference studies, ethnological studies, mythological or classical subjects, nudism, and physical culture. While these cover categories provided an area of safety in which homoerotic photography could exist in the face of social hostility, they also imposed artificial limits on what the photographer could create and how he could present his work, and contributed to a sense of the marginality of the work.

Pioneers. From the very earliest processes—daguerreotypes, ambrotypes, and the like—very few images of male nudes exist, even as compared with the number of female nudes, and those are rare. It was not until the development of albumen paper and, later, of dry plate negatives, that any significant number of homoerotic images were created.

Photography, in its earliest phases, was not considered as an art form in itself, but as a technique for recording reality in the service of science or art. It was this rationale that provided the cover for the first major development of photographic images expressing homoerotic intentions, in the form of "études," nude studies of men and boys ostensibly for the use of artists who were unable to obtain the services of live models. Such studies flourished in the years 1875–1900, from studios such as Calavas in France, but were also produced in other countries. As in images of women and girls created for similar purposes, the subjects are displayed in "statuesque" poses against studio backdrops. Contemporary reports of their availability, and the number that still exist, indicate that the clientele for these was far wider than the artists.

Among the first to treat photography as an independent art form was a German living in Sicily, Wilhelm Baron von **Gloeden** (1856–1931), whose aesthetic reflected the academic school of painting in which he had been trained. The classical allusions that were standard in this academic art—though certainly used quite sincerely by von Gloeden, at least most of the time—provided a cover for his homoeroticism. While conservative in his aesthetic, he was a technical innovator in moving his models outdoors. His work—including but not limited to his well-known "classical" male nudes—made him one of the best known and best selling photographers in the world at the turn of the century. Similar nudes were produced by von Gloeden's cousin Wilhelm Plüschow, and by the Italians Vincenzio Galdi and Gaetano d'Agata.

Photography as an art, however, did not follow von Gloeden's academic aesthetic. Another important homosexual photographer, the American F. Holland **Day** (1864–1933), figured in the development of pictorial photography, which modeled itself on impressionism. His New School of American Photography, a predecessor to the Photo-Secession movement, promoted an aesthetic "soft-focus," manipulated prints, and narrative themes. Day's "Grecian" subjects of nude boys and men remain key pictorialist images.

Surrealist photography, though strongly dominated by heterosexual eroticism, also included homoerotic images in the work of the German photographer Herbert List (1903–1975). Another important figure who explored the erotic meanings of the male body was the American photographer George Platt **Lynes** (1907–1955). Although he did exhibit male nudes, influenced by surrealism, in which mythological references cover the homoerotic subtext, his precisely observed studies of the male form, in which the body itself becomes an object for contemplation, were created primarily for a close circle of acquaintances or published pseudonymously in a European homophile magazine. Another American photographer who shared this interest in the erotic implications of the closely regarded male body was Minor White (1908–1976), while the German Herbert Tobias (1924–1982) produced homoerotic work which shares Lynes' more dramatic vision.

Popular Aspects. Two popular expressions of homoerotic photography, which had no pretensions to art, also developed between 1900 and 1950. Physique photos originated with publicity photographs of Eugene Sandow, Bernarr McFadden, and other turn-of-the-century health and physical culture practitioners. With the 1930s images of Tony Sansone and movie stills of Johnny Weissmuller as Tarzan, these developed into an equivalent of the contemporary pictures of glamorous actresses. The naturist (nudist) movement, flourishing particularly in Germany between 1920–1933, contributed outdoor studies of relentlessly healthy, active male groups. The display of the male body inherent in both these genres became explicit by the late 1950s as they intermingled in the work of photographers like Alfred Heinecke (1915–1975), who had been involved in German nudist photography before coming to America, and later, in more overtly homoerotic images of Anthony Guyther's New York-based Capital studio, Bob Mizer's California-based Athletic Model Guild, and Bruce Bellas ("Bruce of Los Angeles," d. 1974), who still used physique studies or naturism as a cover while acknowledging the increasing distance between what the image purported to be and what it really was by adding such "camp" references as cowboy hats, motorcycle jackets, and construction equipment.

The habit of covering real intentions for the sake of safety, of "things-being-what-they-aren't," is perhaps one of the elements that fed into **camp** sensibility, with its elevation of the artificial, of appearances, style, and the theatrical. A number of homosexual photographers, including Baron de Meyer (1868–1946) and Lynes, have been involved with fashion and theatre, but perhaps the "campiest" photographer was Sir Cecil Beaton (1906–1980), known for his exquisitely superficial (in the sense of being absolutely concerned with surface appearances) portraits of society and theatre figures.

Contemporary Trends. With the climate of sexual liberalization in the 1960s, gay photographers found themselves increasingly free to explore overt homoerotic themes without the excuses previously necessary, and stripped of the formulas that provided cover in the past, they also have been more able to explore their personal visions. Healthier social attitudes and more positive self-perceptions among homosexuals that followed the rise of gay liberation have also encouraged personal expression.

In the years since 1970, homoerotic photography has become both more personal and more intimate. Examples of the former are explorations of private imagery by such stylistically diverse photographers as Duane Michaels, Arthur Tress, Bernard Faucon, and David Lebe. The uncovering of personal intimacy is a common thread which connects the work of such photographers as George Dureaux, Peter Hujar, Erwin Olaf, and Hans van Manen, whose friends or acquaintances are often their subjects. In addition to exploring the erotic meanings of the male body, their nudes frequently also explore the implications of the photographer's relationship with the subject of the photograph. Robert Mapplethorpe (1947–1989), whose reexamination of the studio techniques of the 1930s and 1940s, often with homoerotic or sadomasochistic subjects, led to a rethinking of the possibilities of the studio nude and portrait, is the central figure in this development.

Lesbian Elements. Although there are isolated figures such as Viscountess Clementis Hawarden (1822–1865) and Alice Austen (1866–1952), owing largely to the historical underrepresentation of women in the photographic profession lesbian photography has no broad heritage. What lesbian images exist may be characterized as more concerned with affective relationships, and less concerned with erotic meanings, than their male counterparts. An important figure in this tradition is the American "JEB" (Joan E. Biren), noted for her portraits of lesbian women. The last few years have seen the emergence of photographers like Diana Blok and Marlo Broekmans (The Netherlands), whose imagery more openly explores women's eroticism.

BIBLIOGRAPHY. Judith Schwartz and Joan Biren, *Eye to Eye: Portraits of Lesbians*, Washington, D.C.: Glad Hag Press, 1979; Tom Waugh, "Photography, Passion and Power," *Body Politic*, 101 (March 1984), pp. 29–33; Peter Weiermair, *The Hidden Image: Photographs of the Male Nude in the Nineteenth and Twentieth Centuries*, Cambridge, MA: MIT Press, 1988.

Donald Mader

PINDAR (518–438 B.C.)

Ancient Greek poet of **Thebes**. Pindar's works exemplify the classical Greek tradition of male devotion to the *kouros*, or beautiful young man, witnessed also in surviving statuary and vase painting, and in the poetry of Pindar's near-contemporary **Theognis** of Megara. Pindar's epinician odes, or songs of victory, were commissioned to celebrate the exploits of athletes at the great games, the most famed of which were the **Olympian** (in Elis) and the Pythian (in Delphi), held every four years; and the Nemean (in the northeast Peloponnese) and the Isthmian (on the isthmus of Corinth), held every other year.

The express purpose of these odes, classified by the festivals they celebrate, was praise both of the victor and of the noble who paid for the composition and performance of these lavish choral works.

Pindar's patrons included the wealthy families and military aristocrats throughout **Greece** and **Sicily**, notably Hieron of Syracuse and Theron of Akragas. Although the poet lived in a time of political upheaval and social democratization, particularly at Athens, following the Persian Wars, his outlook, in accordance with that of his patrons, remained conservative and unabashedly aristocratic.

The odes offer in fact a veritable paradigm of the noble Greek youth who best embodied that composite abstraction, so dear to the hearts of later Athenian eugenicists, *kalokagathia*, that is a mixture of *to kalon* (physical beauty) and *to agathon* (valor). Indeed, the first quality already implied the second. The adolescent hero possessed quasi-divine strength and manly virtue; he was an ideal man-boy, and thus could be compared to the mighty Heracles (*Nemean* 1), swift Achilles (*Isthmian* 8, *Nemean* 3), or **Ganymede**, the archetypal ephebe (male in his late teens) snatched up to heaven by Zeus (*Olympian* 1).

Pindar normally incorporated into his epinician odes an illustrative myth meant to enhance further and to "immortalize" the athlete's victory. These myths were naturally heroic, but often (homo)erotic, since praise of a youth implied, in the Greek mind, at least a measure of love for and devotion to him. The fabled Ganymede (*Olympian* 1) provides one example; but the most provocatively homosexual use of myth occurs, again, in *Olympian* 1, which celebrated Hieron of Syracuse, winner of the horse race in 476 B.C. There Pindar introduced a new myth of Tantalus and Pelops to show how dear he (Pelops and, by extension, Hieron) was to the gods. The poet, rejecting the grisly story of Pelops' dismemberment by his father Tantalus, explained Pelops' "disap-pearance" by his having been spirited away, like **Ganymede**, by the god Poseidon, who, once he saw the boy, fell in love with him. But the myths extolling youthful male beauty also had their darker side: Tantalus abused his divine privilege by stealing the gods' ambrosial food, and so suffered eternal punishment in Hades. His son Pelops, "cast out" by the immortals, had to resume his place among men, but, before his death, he gained glory for himself.

In a non-mythic context, youth could be looked on merely as an ephemeral glory, the prelude to old age and death. As Pindar succinctly moralizes in *Pythian* 8:95, "Man lives but a day." Therefore, since everyone must die, what use is it to "sit in darkness" and to "cherish an old age without a name, letting go all lovely things" (*Olympian* 1:82–84). This *carpe diem* motif which, in the context of the Pindaric ode, urged young men to win a glorious name for themselves while they still could, was a staple of both Greek and Latin pederastic poetry meant to cajole an often petulant ephebe: normally a boy's best period encompassed those years immediately preceding the first growth of beard (cf. *Nemean* 5:5–6).

Pindar also composed poems in many other forms, notably *partheneia*, or maiden songs, which survive only in fragments. These partheneia, sung by choruses of women, praised the beauty and grace of young girls, sometimes in sexually loaded descriptions strikingly similar to the lesbian verses of **Sappho**. The maiden song, like the male-oriented victory ode (and, like it, composed by men), appears to have been a popular genre; a large fragment of a partheneion by the poet Alcman (seventh century B.C.) survives.

BIBLIOGRAPHY. C. M. Bowra, *Pindar*, Oxford: Clarendon Press, 1964.

Eugene M. O'Connor

PINK TRIANGLE

In the **Holocaust** camps effected by the German National Socialist regime (1933–45), the prisoners in the concentration camps were obliged to wear markings that indicated the category into which they fell. The triangle was a piece of colored fabric, about 5 centimeters across, sewn on their clothing. The **color** scheme was: yellow for Jews, red for political offenders (Communists), green for professional criminals, black for asocial individuals (criminal psychopaths), violet for Jehovah's Witnesses, blue for illegal émigrés, brown for Gypsies, and pink (in German *rosa*) for male homosexuals. This scheme was not applied uniformly, and other symbols could perform the same function: a yellow band on the upper arm with the letter A for "Arschficker" [Arsefucker], or a large numeral 175 (the number of the paragraph of the Reich Penal Code which the wearer had violated). However, the pink triangle was the most frequent badge imposed on prisoners who had been convicted of homosexual offenses.

The colored triangles could also be used to isolate prisoners and prevent them from playing a role as organizers of resistance within the camps, for example as when a Communist was labeled with the black triangle and relegated to the company of asocials in whose midst he could accomplish no political task. Also, many of those convicted under **Paragraph 175** were not homosexual: some were opponents of the regime such as Catholic priests or leaders of youth groups who were prosecuted on the basis of perjured testimony, while others were street hustlers from Berlin or Hamburg who had been caught up in a police dragnet. The yellow star of David with the word "Jude" (or its equivalent in the language of the occupied country) was inspired by the medieval Jew badge that had been imposed on Jewish communities in Christian Europe by the Fourth Lateran Council (1215). Under the **Nazis** it had to be worn by Jews in civil life and exposed them to all the discriminatory statutes and regulations, while the triangles were strictly confined to the concentration camps.

In the early 1970s the pink triangle was discovered by gay activists in the United States and adopted as a symbol of resistance and solidarity. Since then it has become, together with the Greek letter **lambda**, one of the worldwide emblems of the gay liberation movement, as well as a reminder of the homosexuals who perished in the Nazi extermination camps during the Second World War.

BIBLIOGRAPHY. Richard Plant, *The Pink Triangle: The Nazi War Against Homosexuals*, New York: Henry Holt, 1986; Hans-Georg Stümke and Rudi Finkler, *Rosa Winkel, Rosa Listen: Homosexuelle und "gesundes Volksempfinden" von Auschwitz bis heute*, Hamburg: Rowohlt, 1981.

Warren Johansson

PIRATES

Because pirates or buccaneers belonged to all-male organizations which tended to be isolated from women for long periods of time, **situational** homosexuality (as in prisons) has probably flourished in their midst over the centuries. For various reasons, however, there is little documentation, let alone detailed accounts, of this conduct. It is known that homosexuality was widespread among the Barbary corsairs of the North African coast, but this may be better categorized as **Mediterranean** or **Islamic** homosexuality than as pirate homosexuality.

The Buccaneers of the West Indies. Professor B. R. Burg has attempted to deal with homosexuality among the pirates of the Caribbean during the seventeenth century. He was handicapped by the lack of documents, and sought to reason backwards in many cases from what is known today about the sexual behavior of men in all-male groups to the patterns of sexuality among the pirates.

In his research, Burg discovered only one book, of dubious authenticity, offering material on pirate homosexuality. This was the autobiography of a French pirate named Louis Le Golif, who said that he had engaged in passive sodomy when he was young. Beyond this, Burg found some legal records, and close friendships between adult pirates, as well as considerable affection between captains and their cabin-boys. Because of these methodological problems, Burg's reconstruction of a widespread, thoroughly homosexual society among the West Indies pirates has elicited scepticism.

Nevertheless, Burg's work does shed light on the subject. He establishes that the pirates did not show much interest in acquiring women, and often went to lengths to keep their distance from them even when the pirates could easily have procured them for sexual purposes. Burg infers that the pirates preferred the all-male society and its homosexuality. This conclusion departs from a strictly situational model, such as is applied to **prisons**, boarding schools, and **seafaring**, where the participants express a preference for heterosexuality which is, however, unobtainable. On the other hand, Burg paints a picture of impoverished youths growing up in all-male environments in which they were socialized to homosexuality from puberty onward and found it "normal" to continue such patterns in their careers as pirates.

Burg also found no evidence for effeminacy or for quasi-female roles among the pirates, in marked contrast to prison patterns in which the insertees are assigned such roles; all the pirates, from the most aggressive sodomizers to the cabin boys, were considered thoroughly male.

According to Burg's analysis, the common members of the pirate crews practiced **androphilia**, that is the adults engaged in sex with each other; he also found a marked preference for anal sex and little or no reference to oral sex. **Pedophilia**, however, could be found as a practice of captains and certain other crewmembers with specialized skills who were socially not integrated with the rest of the pirate crew.

The institution of *matelot* was also found to be widespread among the Caribbean pirates, with one pirate taking on a boy or man as a personal servant, either from a captured ship or from a port, and forming very close emotional bonds to him. The matelots even had inheritance rights in the event of the death (not uncommon among the pirates) of their masters.

In England of the Stuart period, according to Burg, attitudes toward homosexuality were relatively relaxed, and the practice flourished among those from whom pirates drew their crews: groups of vagabond youths, merchant mariners, and Royal Navy crewmen. In the absence of heterosexuality, one is left with the options of sexual abstinence (which for many is scarcely credible), masturbation (which is not too plausible either), or widespread homosexuality. While it is easy to criticize the dearth of documentary material offered by Burg, his conclusions cannot be readily dismissed.

Pirates of the China Coast. Thanks to reports by Chinese governors to their emperors, there is a good deal more documentation for homosexual practices on the part of Chinese pirates operating in the South **China** Sea around the turn of the nineteenth century, when a confederation of six pirate fleets defeated the Chinese Navy and raided coastal villages between 1790 and 1810.

The chief of this confederation was first Cheng-I, who kidnapped the 15-year-old fisherman's son Chang Pao (1783–1822) and made him his lover and later his adopted son. It was common for Chinese pirates to rape anally their captives of both sexes, and captured boys often became the lovers and/or adopted sons of the pirates. At the death of Cheng-I, Chang Pao inherited the chiefdom and married his adoptive mother to consolidate his power.

Chang Pao terrorized all of southeast China, threatening to attack Macao and Canton, and even dreamed of becoming emperor. However, his plans were forestalled by the governor of Canton in 1810 when the latter offered pardons and rewards to all pirates who would surrender, and this pulled out the rug from under Chang Pao, who eventually settled for a colonelcy in the Chinese army.

Dian Murray's study of the Chinese pirates describes them as moving "easily and freely" between men, women, and boys as sexual partners. Unlike their West Indies counterparts, the top pirates usually carried women on board, with one captain noted for having five or six wives living on the ship with him. Murray suggests that forcible sodomy may have been used as a rite of initiation into the pirate crew. Certainly, to judge from Chang Pao's story, it was not considered a dishonor or a bar to future leadership, in marked contrast to the contempt accorded by ancient Romans or modern prisoners to any male who has been sexually penetrated.

If the data on Chinese and Carribean pirates are both scanty and tantalizing, there is even less information on other periods of great pirate activity, such as occurred in the late Roman republic or the sixteenth-century heyday of the Spanish Main. If any conclusion can be drawn from what is recorded, it is that the study of pirate lifestyles confirms earlier knowledge that patterns of homosexuality differ extraordinarily from one culture to another and resist easy generalization.

BIBLIOGRAPHY. B. R. Burg, *Sodomy and the Perception of Evil*, New York: New York University Press, 1983; Dian H. Murray, *Pirates of the South China Coast*, Stanford: Stanford University Press, 1987.

Stephen Wayne Foster and
Stephen Donaldson

PLATEN-HALLERMÜND, AUGUST VON (1796–1835)

German Romantic poet. Born in Ansbach of one of the oldest aristocratic families of the city, he was by rank a count.

His outward life was uneventful, consisting mainly of brief military service, an extensive stay at the university, and some dozen years of residence or travel in Italy. The poet's inner life, however, was a profound psychological drama. He was attracted to the late adolescent or male in his twenties; and although he had lifelong friendships that lay outside the sphere of his homosexual tendencies, when his attraction to another man began with a note of sexual passion, it remained so to the bitter end—and often meant intense torment for him. In religion a Protestant, in character a sensitive, refined individual of idealizing temperament, Platen was virile in mind and body, yet only the male appealed to his sense of beauty.

At the close of the Napoleonic wars Platen served in a Bavarian regiment in Munich and even accompanied it onto French soil, but returned home without a baptism of fire. He then studied foreign languages, literature, political history, and philosophy at the universities of Würzburg and Erlangen, furnishing his mind with an encyclopedic knowledge of these subjects. Before his student days were over, Platen had attracted notice, even in high literary circles, by his poems and his brilliant satirical dramas, and he understood that his calling was to be a writer. The oriental poems known as the Ghazels, the profound human feeling in the Sonnets, and the passion, rhythmic sense and melody of the Odes still command admiration. His comedies are precursors of the sort of social satire that Gilbert and Sullivan later immortalized for the British stage. After 1826 the poet was increasingly alienated from his German homeland, and his contempt for most aspects of its literary life grew biting. In part because of his homosexual interests, it was Italy that beckoned him, and he spent the last decade of his life there, a life prematurely ended by an outbreak of cholera in Syracuse in 1835.

The clearest record of his homosexuality is in the diary, kept from childhood, which he wrote not just in German, but in considerable portions in French, Italian, and Portuguese. Meant for the writer's eyes alone, the diary records not only his intellectual growth and literary studies, but also his homosexual passions. During his lifetime he allowed no one else to read it, except perhaps in a single unfortunate instance that enabled one of his best friends to detect Platen's true sexual nature—with an ensuing painful scene in a public circle of their acquaintances. After his death his literary executors were shy of publishing this revealing document, which was kept with restricted access in the Royal Library in Munich until in 1896–1900 the entire text was published in two large volumes of over 2000 pages. The entries chronicle the intense erotic friendships of his student days and later passions that tormented and thrilled him, as some of his *innamorati* were wholly unresponsive to his overtures.

Toward the close of his life Platen became embroiled in mortal enmity with Heinrich Heine, who shared many of his political views and yet was his antipode as a poet. Heine maliciously seized upon the poet's homoerotic side to attack him in *The Baths of Lucca*. Platen did in 1834 publish a poem with the code word "Vernünft'ge" [= gay] that to the initiated was a declaration of homosexual self-consciousness and solidarity ("Sollen namenlos uns länger," written January 31, 1823). He is a classic example of the homosexual in whom talent is joined with an intensity of feeling that can betray him in his private and his public life, but also with a strength of character that enables him to surmount these vicissitudes.

BIBLIOGRAPHY. Xavier Mayne (pseudonym of Edward Irenaeus Prime-Stevenson), *The Intersexes: A History of Similisexualism as a Problem in Social Life*, Rome: Privately printed, 1908, pp. 563–620.

Warren Johansson

PLATO
(CA. 420–347 B.C.)

Greek philosopher and prose writer. He was the son of Ariston and Perictione, both Athenians of distinguished lineage. His writings show the enormous influence that the philosopher **Socrates** had upon him by his life, his teaching, and his death. The spectacle of contemporary politics, both during the ascendancy of his own supporters and under the democracy, gradually turned him away from the career of a statesman and forced him to the paradox that there was no hope for cities until **philosophers** became rulers or rulers philosophers. After the trial and execution of Socrates in 399 he chose with other Socratics to leave Athens and reside for a time in Megara. In the next twelve years he traveled to many places, including Egypt. In 387 he visited Italy and **Sicily**, where he initiated lifelong friendships with Dion of Syracuse and the Pythagorean Archytas of Tarentum. On his return he began teaching formally and continuously at a place near the grove of Academus about a mile outside the wall of Athens. This was his chief occupation during the last forty years of his life; he departed only to make two further visits to Syracuse, where he involved himself fruitlessly in its internal politics under Dionysius II.

Plato's writings consist of some twenty-five dialogues and the *Apology* of Socrates. As a prose stylist in Attic Greek he is one of the great figures of classical literature. His style possesses infinite variety, his language is tinged with poetry and rich in metaphors, especially from music, to which he can return even when their implications seem exhausted. His sentences can range from the briefest to long, straggling periods, sometimes even more powerful than those of the orator Demosthenes, but quite different from them. His later style betrays traces of mannerism, including subtle interlacings of word order and affectations of assonance. No other author attains such sustained power and beauty in Greek prose.

The subject of homosexuality in Plato is primarily a question of *paiderasteia*, the erotic attachment of an adult male for an adolescent boy that was the normative form of homosexual expression in the society in which he lived. Wherever he depicts or alludes to the power of sexual desire, the context is homosexual. The principal works in which he treats the matter are the *Symposium* and the *Republic*, which belong to his middle period, and the *Laws*, which was probably written at the end of his life. Only secondarily does Plato, in the *Gorgias* of his early period, deal with the *kinaidos*, the passive-effeminate male who accepts the role, seeks to be sexually possessed by other men, and so behaves like a woman. Though the participants in the dialogue admit that the *kinaidos* derives pleasure from his shameful practices, his disgrace reaches the level of taboo and so contaminates those who even allude to his existence. The example of the *kinaidos* proves conclusively that pleasure does not equal goodness. The stigma which even Hellenic society attached to passive homosexuality was for Plato a source of ambivalence that colored the negative evaluation even of *paiderasteia* in his last writings.

In the *Symposium*, moreover, Plato is forced to deal with a non-Greek conception of the origin of homosexuality in the speech of Aristophanes, who relates a mythical account of the origin of the erotic attraction between members of the same sex. All human beings today are the halves of primordial ancestors who had two heads, four arms, four legs, and two sets of genitalia. At that time there were three genders: male-male, male-female, and female-female. To punish these creatures for their insolence, Zeus divided them in half, so that the sexual drive is the attempt of the original dual beings to reunite. The male-male halves are homosexual men, the male-female halves are heterosexuals, and the female-female halves are lesbians, to use the modern terminology—which was not Plato's, it should be emphasized.

This myth echoes a Babylonian account of the origin of the sexes reported by Berossus, and to some extent underlying the story of the separation of Eve from Adam in Genesis, in which of the three only the heterosexual pair remains.

In the *Symposium* Pausanias holds that pederasty is justified, but that admiration for the physical beauty of the boy should be paralleled by concern for his moral qualities and their development. The dialogue further develops the notion that there are two forms of love: the vulgar one, Aphrodite Pandemos, can be that of a male subject for either women or boys, while the heavenly one, Aphrodite Uranios, is directed solely toward males and rises above the desire for physical gratification. The lover cherishes the vigor, the intelligence, and the potential for maturation of the *eromenos*, the beloved youth to whom he remains devoted throughout life. Thus *paiderasteia* is accepted as a fact of social life, but the philosopher seeks to orient the man–boy relationship toward non-sexual goals.

In the *Republic* Plato's attitude toward pederasty is more negative; he finds males who have sexual relations with other males, even in age-asymmetrical pairs, guilty of "vulgarity and lack of taste." The ideal of chastity in the life of male society is coupled with the notion that love of the soul should replace that of the body. Then in the *Laws*, probably written at the end of his life and in a mood of bitterness, Plato condemned pederasty as *para physin*, "contrary to **nature**," and called for complete suppression of the homoerotic drive by defaming it so continuously that it would, like incestuous desire, vanish from consciousness. The feeble argument that supports this doctrine is that "one cannot know in advance how boys will turn out," so that the efforts of the pederast to educate his beloved boy are futile. In the Hellenic society of Plato's own time, and even later, this teaching found no resonance, but when fused with the condemnation of male homosexual relations in the book of Leviticus—of which the Greeks of the Golden Age knew nothing—it became the nucleus of the intolerance of homosexuality that has characterized Western civilization since the Roman state adopted **Christianity** as its official religion.

Plato's influence has been manifold, and cannot be reduced to a simple formula. The enemies of homosexual expression have used Plato's arguments selectively and have even tried to depict the more negative ones as typical of the whole of ancient Greek society—which they never were. On the other hand, homosexual apologists have over the centuries looked to the *Symposium* as justifying and ennobling sexual liaisons between males and even exalting them above heterosexual ones in their utility to society, and at times have conveniently disregarded the crucial point that these are age-asymmetrical relationships with an educational purpose—of which modern **androphile** homosexuality has none. Just because of his importance in the history of philosophy and his mastery of Greek prose, Plato has for more than twenty-three centuries been read, studied, and translated. His ambivalent legacy has shaped and even today informs the attitudes of Western man toward love of beauty and its sexual expression.

BIBLIOGRAPHY. Félix Buffière, *Eros adolescent: la pédérastie dans la Grèce antique*, Paris: "Les Belles Lettres," 1980; David M. Halperin, "Plato and Erotic Reciprocity," *Classical Antiquity*, 5 (1986), 60–80; Gregory Vlastos, *Platonic Studies*, Princeton: Princeton University Press, 1981.

Warren Johansson

PLAUTUS, TITUS MACCIUS (D. CA. 184 B.C.)

The greatest Latin comic playwright and earliest Latin of whom substantial writings survive. Of the 130 plays attributed to him, the 21 that have come down from a second-century collection are certainly his. Modeled on plays by Menander, greatest of the Greek New Comedians, who wrote at the very end of the Golden Age of Athens, Plautus' comedies are not merely translated from the Greek, but also incorporate new material not only from other Middle and Late comedies but from Roman life as well. Nowhere is this combination clearer than in his treatment of homosexuality, which the Middle and Late Greek comedies, in marked contrast to **Aristophanes'** and others' Old Comedies, tended to avoid in favor of marriage and slapstick heterosexual street scenes.

Plautus featured pederasts and pathics and portrayed relationships, primarily between masters and slaves, a dominance–submission pattern that was the normal practice in Rome, far removed from the mentor–disciple paradigm of Greek **pederasty**, which was theoretically (and often in practice) between upper-class males for pedagogic aims. Likewise in *Pseudolus* (The Confidence Man), Plautus transformed the refined hetaira of a Greek original into the coarse inmate of a low Roman brothel. Slaves in general figured far more in his plays than in the Greek models, presumably because after the wars of expansion, they represented a much greater part of the Roman than of the classical Athenian population. Plautus portrayed the stereotypical characters from Greek comedies with a distinctively Roman twist.

His successor Terence (ca. 190–159 B.C.) stuck closer to the Greek originals, especially to Apollodorus of Carystus, a disciple of Menander, and to Menander himself, and consequently made few allusions to homosexuality (only three have been detected). Perhaps this dearth explains why Terence, more than Plautus, was assigned to Roman schoolboys and enjoyed greater vogue in the **Middle Ages**.

In Greek comedy it is always the effeminate male who is satirized, whereas Plautus portrays macho characters such as braggarts and soldiers in *Miles Gloriosus* who lust in their bisexual aggressiveness. His adult males are bisexual as a matter of course. Thus Plautus reveals the prevalence and character of homosexuality in the Roman Republic at the close of the Punic Wars, when, although the civilizing role of Hellenism was just beginning, homoerotic relationships already flourished in uncouth, indigenous forms.

BIBLIOGRAPHY. Jane M. Cody, "The senex amator in Plautus' Casina," Hermes, 101 (1976), 453–76; Saara Lilja, "Homosexuality in Plautus' Plays," Arotos, new series, 16 (1982), 57–64; Amy Richlin, The Garden of Priapus: Sexuality and Aggression in Roman Humor, New Haven: Yale University Press, 1983.

William A. Percy

PLETHYSMOGRAPHY

According to Masters and Johnson, sexual arousal consists (among other things) of the engorgement of the blood vessels in the pelvic region. Scientists can directly measure this physiological engorgement using a technique called plethysmography. A *vaginal photoplethysmograph* records an electronic signal that measures the reflectivity of the vaginal wall, which is correlated with the amount of engorgement of the blood vessels in the region. A *penile strain gauge plethysmograph* records a signal that reflects the circumference of the penis it encircles. A *volumetric penile plethysmograph* reports the total volume of air around a penis it encloses. A *groin temperature thermocouple* reports the temperature at the surface of the skin on the inside upper thighs, a temperature that reflects the rise in warm blood pooling in the groin during sexual arousal in either sex.

The scientific validity of penile plethysmography is no longer much in dispute—it is, after all, practically valid prima facie—though it is not settled which of the two kinds of device is more accurate. Vaginal photoplethysmography has almost attained the same status. Groin temperature reading is a new technique which has not yet been completely tested.

Origins and Basic Procedures. Plethysmography was first applied to the study of sexual orientation issues by Kurt Freund, a Czech researcher, who was conducting studies of aversion therapy to change the sexual **orientation** of gay men who came to him for such help. Freund found that these patients' self-reports of "cures" due to the aversion therapy did not last long, and that plethysmography failed to confirm these cures. Accordingly, he stopped performing such aversion therapy and, in Canada, he has popularized the technique in basic research on sexual topics. Other researchers (notably Nathaniel McConaghy of Australia) have also discovered, through plethysmography, that it is very difficult to change sexual orientation in men.

In research on sexual orientation, plethysmography is useful because it assesses which stimuli cause sexual arousal independent of a person's conscious knowledge or reporting thereof. Age preferences can also be roughed out in cooperative subjects.

In a typical experiment, subjects wear a plethysmograph while they watch a screen and/or listen to an audiotape involving a variety of stimuli: some sexually neutral stimuli (as controls), and some depictions or descriptions of situations or objects thought to be sexually arousing. A mixed bag of plethysmographic results will give the flavor of the kinds of experiments conducted. (1) Male cross-dressers who have been erotically aroused by women are also somewhat aroused by stories of themselves wearing women's clothes, while cross-dressers never aroused by women (i.e., homosexual "drag queens") are not. (2) Ordinary heterosexual men who are *most* aroused by pictures of naked adult women sometimes show small but measurable arousal to pictures of naked prepubescent girls, but ordinary homosexual men who are *most* aroused by pictures of naked adult men apparently do not show measurable arousal to pictures of naked prepubescent boys. (3) Very few if any men show significant amounts of sexual arousal *both* when viewing naked adult women and when viewing naked adult men. (4) Substantial numbers of heterosexual women can be aroused by descriptions of group sex. (5) The best stimuli for separating homosexual from heterosexual men are those in which several members of the preferred sex are shown participating in sexual behavior. Thus, pictures of two women are typically more arousing to groups of heterosexual men than pictures of heterosexual copulation are.

Implications. The use of such studies and techniques in political or social contexts of course cannot be ignored. It is hotly debated among sexologists whether plethysmography is scientifically valid if used on nonconsenting subjects (i.e., **pedophiles** or others whose sexual fantasies involve acts that remain illegal). Masturbating several times just before the procedure would, of course, make it useless in men and nearly useless in most women. Repressive regimes would also have difficulty using it surreptitiously. Nevertheless, the potential for abuse is clear, and it is fortunate that so many of those who used it in dangerous ways have now disavowed those uses.

Erotic Taxonomy. Scientifically, plethysmography's best successes have been in erotic taxonomy. It has helped show that male-to-female transsexuals can be dichotomized into two groups: those sexually attracted to men and those sexually attracted to women, and that those sexually attracted to women always or almost always have been aroused by cross-dressing. (Asexual and bisexual male-to-female transsexuals are now considered subtypes of the group attracted to women.) It has helped sharpen definitions by showing that certain types of bisexuality are very uncommon in men but not rare in women. In theory, it could be used over

time to establish precisely how (and whether) one's erotic inclinations change as one gets older, and to throw light on situations where one's genitals are doing one thing and one's mind is doing another. And perhaps most important, it has established the validity of talking about one's sexual orientation, since it can establish that it exists independently of what one consciously reports. In so doing, it has challenged the notion that one's sexual proclivities are mere preferences on the level of what route one prefers to drive to work, even as it has made explicit the dangers and consequences of assuming that one's sexual orientation is far more important than one's handedness or one's leggedness.

BIBLIOGRAPHY. Ray Blanchard, I. G. Racansky, and Betty Steiner, "Phallometric Detection of Fetishistic Arousal in Heterosexual Male Cross-dressers," *Journal of Sex Research*, 22 (1986), 453–62; Kurt Freund, F. Sedlacek, and K. Knob, "A Simple Transducer for Mechanical Plethysmography of the Male Genital," *Journal of the Experimental Analysis of Behavior*, 8 (1965), 169–70; Kurt Freund, "Male Homosexuality: An Analysis of the Pattern," in J. A. Loraine, ed., *Understanding Homosexuality*, New York: Elsevier, 1974, pp. 27–81; idem, "Should Homosexuality Arouse Therapeutic Concern?" *Journal of Homosexuality*, 2 (1977), 235–40; Peter W. Hoon, "The Assessment of Sexual Arousal in Women," *Progress in Behavior Modification*, 7 (1979), 1–61; Nathaniel McConaghy, "Is a Homosexual Orientation Irreversible?" *British Journal of Psychiatry*, 129 (1976), 556–63.

James D. Weinrich

PLUTARCH
(CA. 50–CA. 120)

Greek eclectic philosopher and biographer. Widely traveled in the Mediterranean, this noble, who became a priest at Delphi but resided at his native Chaeronea in Boeotia, knew many leading Greeks and Romans and may have received appointments from Trajan and **Hadrian**. He advocated partnership between Greeks and Romans. An ancient catalogue of his works listed 227 items, of which 87 survive, most lumped together under the title *Moralia*, in addition to 50 biographies in *Parallel Lives of Famous Greeks and Romans*. His "On Moral Virtues" is Aristotelian and anti-Stoic: piety being a mean between superstition and atheism. In his dialogues, Plutarch, essentially a Platonist, discussed the fate of the soul after death. His antiquarian works are a mine of information about paganism, music, and education.

Plutarch's "Dialogue on Love" presents an imaginary debate (an example of **contest literature**), between a pederast and an advocate of the love of women. Declaring that "the one true love is the love of youths," the pederast, reciting a list of famous heterosexual lovers, attacks heterosexual love as self-indulgent, vulgar, and servile. The advocate of the love of women, equally cutting, condemns pederasty as unnatural and innovative in the bad sense. With passionate arguments on both sides, this example reveals that the days when the superiority of **pederasty** could be taken for granted had long passed.

In a vivacious sketch, Plutarch sets forth a conversation between Odysseus and one of his men who, through enchantment, has been turned into a pig (Gryllos). To the hero's surprise the pig who was once a man does not want to return to his human state: he prefers to remain a beast because, in his view, animals live a life in conformity with **nature**, while human beings do not. According to Gryllos, one evidence of the superiority of animals is the supposed fact that they do not practice male or female homosexuality. While this claim has been disproved, over the centuries Plutarch's little dialogue exercised a good deal of influence as a touchstone of the "happy beast" conceit (*see* **Animal Homosexuality**), which argued that human conduct could be reformed for the better by adopting the "natural, healthy" standards of animals.

In his vivid and gripping *Lives*, Plutarch stressed the vices and virtues in the personalities of the great as well as their family, education, personality, and changes of fortune. Their accuracy varies according to the sources available to him. Many portray pederasty flatteringly, particularly in the case of heroes of **Sparta** and **Thebes**, sometimes unflatteringly as in Otho and other **Roman emperors**, and amusingly as in the case of Demetrios Poliorcetes. They were extremely influential and much read from the Italian **Renaissance** through the Napoleonic era, when they were central to the Exemplar Theory of **history**—the concept that history teaches through the lives of great men who excelled either in virtue or vice. With the emergence of the idea of history as a supraindividual process, the accomplishment above all of the nineteenth-century German school, the centrality of Plutarch's biographies faded.

Plutarch shows that if pederasty was an ambivalent and disputed subject in late pagan antiquity, still no general taboo on the discussion or even more, the practice of it existed before the Christian church began to exert its influence on law and public opinion.

BIBLIOGRAPHY. R. H. Barrow, *Plutarch and His Times*, Bloomington: Indiana University Press, 1967; Curt Hubert, *De Plutarchi amatoria*, Kirchhain: Max Schmersow, 1903.

William A. Percy

POETRY

Through most of history, poetry has been a vital form of literature, and one which has often lent itself to the expression of erotic or romantic sentiment. At the same time, poetry displays an inherent capacity for ambiguity which has provided a cover for homoerotic elements which might otherwise never have reached the printed page. In light of these considerations, and the long period during which the poetry of ancient **Greece** and **Rome** (often **pederastic**) has been held up as a model and inspiration, it is not surprising to find an abundant homoerotic tradition expressed in poetic form.

Traditionally, poetry has been classified as epic, dramatic, and lyric. While some homosexual elements appear in early epics, most relevant poetry belongs to the lyric genre, which permits expression of individual feelings.

Antiquity and the Earlier Middle Ages. The history of homosexual poetry begins with the epic theme of the loving friendship between two warriors. In **Mesopotamia**, this theme was exemplified by the love between **Gilgamesh** and Enkidu, and in Greece between **Achilles** and Patroclus, depicted respectively in the anonymous *Epic of Gilgamesh*, and **Homer's** *Iliad*. **David's** "Lament for Jonathan" in the Old Testament (II Samuel 1:17–27) contains the famous phrase "surpassing the love of women," although it has never been explained whether this means that Jonathan's love for David surpassed a man's love for women, or woman's love for men.

The first lesbian poems were the ones that ultimately gave lesbianism its name, the intense lyrics of **Sappho** of Lesbos, a Greek island. **Theognis** of Megara introduced pederastic ideals into Greek poetry, establishing a long-lived tradition, and many of the leading poets of ancient Greece dealt with the love of boys. In the Hellenistic and Roman periods, Greek poets turned to this subject in large numbers. **Theocritus** excelled as an exponent of the pastoral conventions for such poetry. The twelfth book of the **Greek Anthology** is the *Mousa Paidike* ("boyish muse") edited by Strato of Sardis, a collection of over 250 brief pederastic poems expressing a remarkable range of sentiment.

Among the Romans, most of the leading poets dealt with homosexuality at some point. **Vergil** wrote a pastoral poem about Corydon, which gave André **Gide** the title for his modern defense of ped-erasty. The sardonic **Martial** composed many poems on this subject. **Catullus** wrote several which were so explicit that only recently have they been honestly translated into English.

After the fall of the Roman Empire, there were a few poets who treated this theme and whose works have survived, including Luxorius in Vandal North Africa and the Greek Nonnus in Egypt; the latter's *Dionysiaka* counts as the only surviving "Byzantine" poem to deal extensively with homosexuality. The later Byzantines reputedly burned the poetry of Sappho, but preserved the *Mousa Paidike*.

The central **Middle Ages** (eleventh and twelfth centuries) saw the appearance of a number of **medieval Latin poets**, mainly clergy in France, who wrote homosexual works, including Abelard, Baudri of Bourgueil, Hilary (an Englishman), Marbod of Rennes, and Walter of Châtillon. The "Debate Between Helen and Ganymede," an imitation of the ancient **contest literature**, concerns the relative merits of women and boys. The early Portuguese-Galician *cantigos de amigo* were poems written by men in which a female persona describes her love for a man; some of these poems must have been written by homosexuals.

Non-Western Poetry. It was not long after **Islam** spread across much of the world that pederastic poems began to appear, especially in **Iran** (Persia) and Andalusia. The Persian poets were generally **Sufis**, mystics whose love for youths was disguised as an allegorical love for God; these included such famous poets as **Hafiz, Rumi,** and **Sa'di.** One of their favorite themes was the love of Sultan Mahmud of Ghazna for the boy Ayaz. Omar Khayyam mentions this topic in his *Rubaiyat* ("where name of Slave and Sultan is forgot, and peace to Mahmud on his golden throne"). The Andalusian poets of **Granada** who extolled pederasty were too numerous to mention, but it must be noted that the Jewish poets of Spain also wrote such poetry, including the most famous of them, Jehuda Halevi (*see* **Judaism, Sephardic**). The **Turks** also cultivated pederastic poetry, drawing upon the earlier rich Islamic tradition. In **India**, Hindu poets avoided it, but Islamic poets, including Babur, founder of the Mughal dynasty, addressed it.

Outside Arab North Africa, only two "African" poets are known to have been homosexual, Roy Campbell of modern South Africa, and Rabearivalo of the island of Mauritius in the Indian Ocean, the latter writing in French. There is little record of homosexual poetry in Southeast Asia, Australia, New Zealand, and the Pacific Islands.

Although pederasty was widespread in **Japan**, and often expressed in short stories and other works of fiction, the only Japanese poet noted for dealing with it is the modern Matsuo Takahashi.

China is a different matter. Arthur Waley once observed that there were an enormous number of Chinese poems dealing with male friendships instead of heterosexual love. Unfortunately, very few of them have been translated into English. One pederastic poet has been the subject of a biography by Waley, Yüan Mei (eighteenth century). Some homosexual items appear in *New Songs From a Jade Terrace*, a anthology of Chinese love poems compiled in ancient times. This has been translated into English, and is the best introduction to Chinese homosexual poetry available. As a large portion of all homosexual verse is probably Chinese, it is to be regretted that so little of this heritage is accessible to Westerners.

Europe in the Later Middle Ages and the Renaissance. The later Middle Ages were a dry period for homosexual poetry. There are sections of **Dante's** *Divine Comedy* and brief passages in Chaucer's *Canterbury Tales* which bear on homosexuality; there were brief mentions of homosexuals in some of the eddas and sagas of Scandinavia. Some of the friendships between warriors in medieval narrative poems seem to have homosexual

overtones. These, however, are merely bits and scraps to be found over a long period of time.

With the coming of the **Renaissance** and its rediscovery of the classic poetic tradition, homosexual poetry began to flourish anew. Antonio Beccadelli wrote elegant scurrilities in Latin about sodomites. **Poliziano** described the homosexuality of **Orpheus** in *La Favola di Orfeo*. The sculptor **Michelangelo** expressed his passion for handsome young men in sonnets and other forms. The homosexual poetry of Italy during this period is vast in quantity, and much of it, including work in the **Bernesque** and **Burchiellesque** genres, has never been translated into English.

In England, Richard **Barnfield** composed openly pederastic poems, but stopped when he was condemned for this ("If it be sin to love a lovely lad, oh then sin I"). **Shakespeare** wrote his famous sonnets to a youth mysteriously known as "Mr. W. H." Christopher **Marlowe** and Michael Drayton both dealt with **Edward II**. In France during this period, there were some poets who wrote about homosexuality, especially Denis de **Saint-Pavin**, the "king of Sodom."

Most of the seventeenth century showed a dearth of homosexual poetry. There were poems about beautiful boys written by Giambattista Marino in Italy and by Don Juan de Arguijo in Spain, but it is a long haul until the Restoration in England, when John Wilmot (Lord **Rochester**) wrote about pederasty, only to be followed by an even longer silence.

Modern Times. From the Romantic period, the number of poets increases until the present day, so that it becomes more and more difficult to evaluate the extant material. Numerous poets must remain unmentioned in order to concentrate on some of the more important or interesting figures.

Russia discloses only one poem by Pushkin, but it does boast Vyacheslav Ivanov, Mikhail **Kuzmin**, and the modern poetry of Gennady Trifonov. The Netherlands and the Scandinavian countries produced a few minor poets, especially Vilhelm Ekelund of Sweden. Spain and Latin America gave us Federico García **Lorca**, Porfirio Barba-Jacob, and Luis **Cernuda**. Portugal rejoices in the lyrical António Botto and Fernando **Pessoa**, who ranks as one of the greatest modernist poets in any language. Italy claims Pier Paolo **Pasolini**, Mario Stefani, and Sandro **Penna**, all pederastic. Alexandria, Egypt, hosted Constantine **Cavafy**, a Greek and arguably the finest openly homosexual poet of the twentieth century. Canada produced E. A. Lacey, Ian Young, and some other poets. There are also homosexual poems written in little-known languages such as Basque, Lithuanian, and Friulian.

Britain. Though most of the British homosexual poetry has come from England, it was a Scot, Lord Alfred **Douglas**, who created one of the most famous poems on this theme, the one which calls it "the Love that dare not speak its name." George Gordon, Lord **Byron** wrote a number of covert love poems to his boyfriends, and to him was (falsely) attributed the authorship of *Don Leon* (ca. 1836), a verse defense of pederasty which is a masterpiece of its kind. The true author may have been Thomas Love Peacock, but this cannot be proven. Shelley was also interested in homosexuality, as is seen in his translations of Plato. Alfred Lord **Tennyson** created the great *In Memoriam* after the death of his beloved Hallam, and Queen Victoria loved it in spite of the condemnation that came from homophobic critics ("It is better to have loved and lost, than never to have loved at all."). Thomas Lovell Beddoes wrote one of the most beautiful of homosexual love-poems, also on the theme of the lost lover, "Dream-pedlary."

The latter half of the nineteenth century and the early twentieth century saw a tremendous amount of homosexual (mostly pederastic) poetry produced in England. The full details of this golden age appear in Brian Reade's *Sexual Heretics* (London, 1970) and in Timothy d'Arch Smith's *Love in Earnest* (London, 1970), but some overview of this material must be given here. The British **public school** system, along with the sexual segregation at the universities of **Cambridge and Oxford**, stimulated a vast outpouring of love poems aimed at (mostly) boys. A few of these compositions, such as those by John Addington **Symonds** and Edward **Carpenter**, concerned working-class men in their twenties. The pederastic poets included John Gambril Nicholson, Edward Cracroft Lefroy, Frederick **Rolfe** ("Baron Corvo"), Aleister **Crowley**, Edwin Bradford, Edmund John, and many others. A place apart among these writers is reserved for Ralph N. **Chubb**, who created extraordinary privately-printed books illustrated by himself.

This flourishing was somewhat interrupted by the uproar over the "**decadents**," especially Oscar **Wilde**, at the end of the nineteenth century. This uproar started with Theodore Wratislaw's poem "To a Sicilian Boy" and Douglas' poem (noted above) and culminated with Wilde's going to prison. However, this poetic movement continued after things had calmed down, producing such lyric masterpieces as Edmund John's "The Seven Gifts" and Richard Middleton's "The Bathing Boy." James Elroy Flecker translated a Turkish poem, "The Hammam Name" (*name*, Turkish for "piece of writing"), into English.

This traditional poetry gradually gave way to **modernist** poetry, among the practitioners of which may be counted such homosexuals as Wystan Hugh **Auden**, Thom Gunn, and others. Auden moved to America and fell in love with young Chester Kallman. James Kirkup wrote a poem about a Roman soldier who was sexually attracted to the naked, dying Christ, and when this was published in London's *Gay News* in 1976, the British government prosecuted the publisher for violating the law against blasphemy. However, the pornography laws were meanwhile liberalized to the point where explicit poems could be published, such as Auden's pornographic "Platonic Blow."

The United States. There were some American romantic poems written before the Civil War on homoerotic themes, such as Henry David Thoreau's "The Gentle Boy," which were protected from public outrage by the pre-Freudian belief that it was possible for two men or two women to love each other in a non-sexual manner.

Outrage did greet the publication of Walt **Whitman**'s *Leaves of Grass* in 1860 with a homosexual section, "Calamus." Whitman defended himself by claiming he was heterosexual, but the poems speak for themselves; a group of English minor poets called themselves "Calamites" in his honor. Whitman had a tremendous influence on American poetry in general and on homosexual literature in particular, and he is often mistakenly considered the only American homosexual poet of the nineteenth century, but there were a host of minor, now largely forgotten, versifiers (see Stephen W. Foster, "Beauty's Purple Flame"). Many of these poets, such as the unlucky James Bensel, tended to deal with the Tennysonian theme of the lover who has died.

The most important of these writers was the pederastic George Edward Woodberry. Another interesting poet was the highly precocious Cuthbert Wright, whose volume of homosexual verse, *One Way of Love* (1915), completed when he was only sixteen years old, was published both in America and England. George Sylvester Viereck also wrote "decadent" poems.

After World War I, the chief modernist poet in America was the homosexual Hart **Crane**, who preferred sailors and young Mexican boys. The painter Marsden **Hartley** also produced poetry.

Lesbian Poetry in English. After classical antiquity, little lesbian poetry worth noting was written until the end of the nineteenth century in Europe and America, and no lesbian poetry at all is known from Africa, Asia, or Latin America. There was a brief flourishing of lesbian verse among educated women in England during the seventeenth century ("The Matchless Orinda" and some others), but it is not until Emily **Dickinson** that the theme reappeared. In England, there had been "lesbian" poems written by Swinburne (from the male point of view) and Christina Rossetti ("Goblin Market"), but the apogee of lesbian poetry was reached by the international (part Hawaiian, among other strains) poet Pauline Tarn, who wrote in French under the pen-name of Renée **Vivien**, and who had a love affair with Natalie Clifford **Barney** in Paris.

An attentive reading of the lyrics of Edna St. Vincent **Millay**, who was bisexual, shows them to treat tender feelings for young women. Some other American lesbian poets who should be mentioned are Amy **Lowell**, the imagist and literary impresario, and Katherine Lee Bates, a professor at Wellesley College. Bates produced *Yellow Clover*, a sort of lesbian version of *In Memoriam*, and she also wrote "America the Beautiful," which almost became the American national anthem.

Germany. Count August von **Platen** was a homosexual poet who was the victim of a homophobic attack by Heinrich Heine. Xavier Mayne wrote a long study of Platen and Platen's sonnets have been translated into English. There appears to have been a tremendous upsurge of homosexual poetry in Germany at the same time as in England, but very few of these poets have been rendered into English, and in any case most of them were minor. In the midst of a vast amount of inferior homosexual poetry, there appeared a giant, Stefan **George**, whose *Seventh Ring* was written in honor of his boyfriend, Maximilian Kronberger, a teenager known poetically as Maximin—a quasi-divine figure who died young. There has not been another German homosexual poet of similar stature since George, but there has been no dearth of poets, except during the Nazi period.

France. Charles Baudelaire (along with Swinburne) introduced intimations of lesbianism into poetry written by men, and founded the "decadent" school of literature, which caused French and English poets to explore sexual themes hitherto taboo, including homosexuality. Some of these writers seem to have been heterosexuals experimenting with "horrifying" themes, and it must be noted that some of the poets who wrote about homosexuality also wrote about necrophilia, for example. Their aim was to create shudders, not to express their personal feelings. Isidore Ducasse, called **Lautréamont**, created the phantasmagoric *Les chants de Maldoror* before dying young; this has some pederastic scenes.

Arthur **Rimbaud** stoppped writing at the age of twenty, after having had a tempestuous love affair with Paul **Verlaine**; both were major poets. Some of their poems deal with homosexuality, especially in the volume *Hombres/femmes.* Pierre Louÿs devised *Les chansons de Bilitis*, a volume of lesbian poems supposedly translated from the Greek. This book provided American lesbians with the name of their first organization, the Daughters of **Bilitis**. A host of other French poets at this time ("fin de siècle," end of the nineteenth century) wrote decadent or pseudo-decadent poems and even song lyrics (Aristide Bruant's songs about boy prostitutes, sung in the Chat Noir). Much of the French homosexual poetry of the twentieth century has been produced by writers more famous for other things, such as novels (**Crevel**, **Cocteau**, and **Genet**). Contemporary French poetry in general lacks great names, and this is also true of homosexual poetry.

Postwar American Poetry. After World War II, some new homosexual poetic voices were heard in America, such as Paul **Goodman**, Jack **Spicer**, and Allen Ginsberg, with the latter attaining world-wide fame in the context of the **beat generation**. Honesty increased as more and more poets "came out" at the same time that **pornography** laws were being struck down by the courts. There are now numerous homosexual poets in North America, such as Edward Field, Richard Howard, Dennis Kelly, James Merrill, and James Schuyler. Of the lesbian poets associated with the second wave of feminism possibly the most important is Adrienne Rich, author of the volumes *Of Woman Born* (1976) and *The Dream of a Common Language* (1978). Rich has also been influential as a critic. Catherine R. Stimpson has characterized Rich's major themes as "the analysis of male power over women; the rejection of that power; the deconstruction of dominant images of women; the need for women to construct their own experience, history, and identity; and the tension between two possible futures"—androgynous and separatist. Other lesbian poets have written from the black, Chicana, and American Indian experiences. The cultures from which these poets stem retain a loyalty to poetry that has been eroded elsewhere.

The Present Situation. This flourishing of gay literature has taken place at a time when poetry as such has moved out of the cultural mainstream. Most of the public no longer reads poetry at all, its function being usurped in part by popular **music** lyrics, and as a result the writing of poetry is not financially viable. In a sense, poetry has "gone underground," claimed by cultural minorities for whom commercial success is not an expected result. In a crude form, it continues to demonstrate vitality, if not much originality, among the uneducated, as seen in the emergence of "rap" rhyming, metrical verse from the inner city. But there is little incentive for highly talented writers to write poetry.

The rise of the gay liberation **movement** stimulated the appearance of numerous small-circulation publications aimed at an exclusively homosexual or lesbian audience, and these provide gay poets with an outlet for their work, since what remains of "mainstream" poetry periodicals show little interest in publishing homosexual material. The problem is that most of this material is published because of its theme rather than its literary merit. Furthermore, it has fostered a ghettoization of gay literature: homosexual writings aimed at an exclusively homosexual audience.

Heterosexual Americans do not buy or read homosexual poetry, with the exception of classics from the past like Whitman. One would think that if homosexuals can appreciate heterosexual love stories, heterosexuals could relate to homosexual love stories (or poetry), especially since thousands of heterosexuals never noticed that A. E. **Housman** was writing about boy and boy, not boy and girl. But modern homosexual poetry is no longer about love as a human universal, expressed in homosexual terms; it is specifically about homosexuality as such.

Conclusion. For better or worse, this is a prosaic, not a poetic age. Much of the current spate of gay male poetry may be attributed to the retrospective, nostalgic side of homosexual **taste**, as seen in the predilection for antique furniture and grand **opera**. Formally, however, much of the current gay male poetry reflects a shallow modernism of omission—it lacks rhyme, meter, significant imagery. In his exaltation of everyday experience, the pioneer of this kind of work was the New York writer Frank O'Hara. Yet despite its seeming casualness, O'Hara's poetry shows the impress of his study of models from the French tradition. By contrast, much of current gay male production seems to display little acquaintance with the history of literature. Instead, it is a "home brew" purveying, all too frequently, a bald, explicit recitation of some recent sexual experience—lurid exhibitionism of a not very interesting sort.

Lesbian poets, such as Olga Broumas, Judy Grahn, Joan Larkin, and Audre Lorde, are more concerned both with the demands of craft and the addressing of subject matter of weight and substance. Inasmuch as their work forms part of the literary currents associated with feminism, it transcends the lesbian/gay paradigm, and deserves to be addressed in a different, larger context.

As has been noted, heterosexuals do not read homosexual poetry. Generally speaking, male homosexual poems are not read by lesbians, and lesbian poems are not read by male homosexuals. This tribalism and subtribalism rob homosexual poetry of universality. It is perhaps a hopeful sign that similar restrictions that once narrowed the audience for black literature have been largely overcome—though gaining the attention of white readers was accomplished only after a considerable effort on the part of critics of both races. It may be that the **AIDS** crisis and the waning of the sexual revolution have slowed, but not blocked, a similar critical enterprise on behalf of gay and lesbian literature. In the 1980s mainstream acceptance has been gained for the work of a few gay and lesbian novelists (e.g., David Leavitt and Rita Mae Brown). The prospects for poetry of same-sex concerns are probably dependent on a revival of interest in poetry as such, which would require the deployment of factors not now on the horizon.

As poetry has been losing its general audience, it is being chosen as an art form by homosexuals in a sort of cultural "hand-me-down" syndrome; yet even among homosexuals it reaches only a very small segment of its target audience. Under such circumstances, it is questionable how much longer traditional printed-page verse can survive as a meaningful literary vehicle for the expression of homoerotic sentiment. Perhaps the future lies in mixed-media combinations, spoken poetry with sound and/or visual images (as in Laurie Anderson's work) or other sensual dimensions yet to be explored (smell, taste, feel).

BIBLIOGRAPHY. Paula Bennett, *My Life a Loaded Gun: Female Creativity and Feminist Politics*, Boston: Beacon Press,

1986; Anne Birrell, ed., *New Songs from a Jade Terrace*, London: Penguin, 1986; Stephen Coote, ed., *The Penguin Book of Homosexual Verse*, London: Penguin, 1983; Jeannette H. Foster, *Sex Variant Women in Literature*, 3d ed., Tallahassee: Naiad Press, 1985; Stephen Wayne Foster, "Beauty's Purple Flame: Some Minor American Gay Poets, 1786–1936," *Gay Books Bulletin*, 7 (1982), 15–17; Barbara Grier, *The Lesbian in Literature*, 3d ed., Tallahassee: Naiad Press, 1981; Robert K. Martin, *The Homosexual Tradition in American Poetry*, Austin: University of Texas Press, 1980; Carl Morse and Joan Larkin, eds., *Gay & Lesbian Poetry in Our Time: An Anthology*, New York: St. Martin's Press, 1988; Brian Reade, ed., *Sexual Heretics*, New York: Coward-McCann, 1971; Timothy d'Arch Smith, *Love in Earnest*, London: Routledge & Kegan Paul, 1970; Gregory Woods, *Articulate Flesh: Male Homo-eroticism and Modern Poetry*, New Haven: Yale University Press, 1987; Ian Young, *The Male Homosexual in Literature*, 2nd ed., Metuchen, NJ: Scarecrow Press, 1982.

Stephen Wayne Foster

POLAND

This major nation of east-central Europe has undergone many vicissitudes. The western Slavs who occupied the area of present-day Poland were first united under the Piast dynasty and Christianized beginning in 966. The crown passed to the Jagiello dynasty, under which Poland, having lost its western territories, then expanded eastward, so that by 1568 the Polish–Lithuanian commonwealth embraced not just those two nations but most of Belorussia and the Ukraine as well. The confluence of the Renaissance and the Reformation brought Poland to the zenith of its political and cultural greatness, while a policy of toleration in religion not only spared the country the Protestant–Catholic wars that ravaged Western Europe but also allowed Polish Jewry to enjoy its golden age, while dissenting groups such as Socinians and Unitarians found refuge within its borders. Declining from the mid-seventeenth century onward, Poland after 1718 was virtually a protectorate of the great powers. Between 1772 and 1795 the country was thrice partitioned by Russia, Austria, and Prussia. Under the oppressive rule of the tsars the Poles twice rebelled, while Catholicism kept a grip on the masses as a symbol of opposition to the Lutheran Prussians and the Orthodox Russians. **Nationalism** ultimately triumphed in 1918 with the reconstitution of an independent republic as one of Woodrow Wilson's Fourteen Points. It was the discussion of nationality problems in central Europe that introduced the concept of an ethnic or religious **minority** to the English-speaking world. Interwar Poland was racked by economic problems and the inability to find a modus vivendi with the non-Polish components of its population. Once again partitioned by Nazi Germany and Soviet Russia in 1939, Poland was restored in 1945 with a new set of boundaries, the eastern territories having been annexed by the Soviet Union, with large areas of Prussia and Silesia being ceded to the country as compensation for its losses. The Communist regime that long ruled Poland has had to cope with constant unrest from a nation unwilling to be a Russian satellite.

Religious and Legal Background. Although the reception of Latin **Christianity** and of the medieval version of Roman law entailed the adoption of laws against **sodomy**, there is evidence that the anti-Trinitarian sects which found refuge in Poland were influenced by the Nicodemites and similar trends of thought in Italy to abandon the notion that homosexual sins were the "crime of crimes" which the Scholastic theologians had proclaimed them to be. Even if they did not proclaim this departure from orthodox Christianity openly, they influenced the Quakers in western Europe. Their heritage was still active in the thought of William Penn who reduced the penalty for buggery to a nominal one in his law code for the colony of Pennsylvania (1682).

The partition of Poland meant that four separate codes—the German, the

Austrian, the Hungarian, and the Russian—all of which penalized male homosexual acts and the second and third of which also penalized lesbian acts before 1918, were in force on its territory when it was reunited. The discussion of a uniform code for the entire country led to proposals such as one by the physician Andrzej Mikulski in 1920: "Poland is waiting for a reform of these laws or rather their abrogation.... Even those who advocate the need to penalize homosexual acts are forced to admit that Paragraph 516 of the Russian and Paragraph 175 of the German Penal Code prove a total want of logic."

When the new Penal Code (*Kodeks karny*) came into force in 1932 under the authoritarian regime of Marshal Piłsudski, the model of the Code **Napoléon** prevailed: homosexuality ceased to be criminal on the entire territory of the Polish Republic, and the age of consent was uniformly fixed at 15 for both heterosexual and homosexual acts. The revised Penal Code introduced by the Communist regime on April 19, 1969 did not depart from this basic principle; its Article 176 condemns only a person (regardless of sex) who engages in acts of a sexual character with a person under the age of 15 regardless of the latter's degree of physical or psychological development.

Poland's homosexuals have to contend, not with legal repression, but with the long-standing prejudice and intolerance instilled by the prevailing Roman Catholicism of the country's population, a legacy that reached its peak in the Counterreformation. As in **Cuba**, this repressive tendency has been augmented by Stalinist homophobia stemming from the Soviet Union.

Cultural Aspects. The nationalistic emphasis of Polish literature hindered writings that emphasized physical love. It was only in 1917 that a literary outsider, the homosexual composer Karol **Szymanowski** (1882–1937), composed a two-volume autobiographical novel, *Ephebos*, written in 1917 but published only in fragments; the manuscript was burned during the bombing of Warsaw in 1939. Jarosław Iwaszkiewicz (1894–1980) was hailed by the Communist regime as one of Poland's greatest contemporary writers. Though homosexual, he carefully maintained a façade of conventional married life, and homoerotic themes are rare in his uneven work. They emerge most clearly in a story entitled "The Teacher," in which an aging, disappointed woman accuses a tutor of "unworthy acts" with a young gardener, whereupon he is dismissed and the oldest son of the family, platonically in love with the teacher, commits suicide.

Jan Lechoń (1899–1956) was also unable to reveal the homoerotic side of his personality in his work, but in his *Diary*, written in exile in New York in 1949–56, he justified his reserve, but at the same time composed interesting critical sketches on the homoerotic literature of France (**Gide**, **Genet**, Peyrefitte).

In the novel by Tadeusz Breza *Adam Grywałd* (1936) homosexuality was treated as a modern psychological problem. The hero, at first enamored of a young woman who fails to reciprocate, then finds consolation in her brother. The Adlerian theory of homosexuality as an acquired, neurotic condition forms the theoretical background of the narrative.

The avant-garde writer Witold Gombrowicz (1904–1969) was far more overt in his treatment of the homoerotic, first in his *Diary* of 1933 and then in *The Happenings on the Brig Banbury*, which deals with the sexual cravings of sailors that find expression in sexual contact between them. Inclined to mock the conventional patriotism and religiosity of his countrymen, he continued to write while in exile in Argentina during the war. His novel *Trans-Atlantic*, published in Paris in 1953, develops an amusing conflict situation with a gay character.

Jerzy Andrzejewski (1909–1983) was at first a supporter of the Communist regime, and then a leading dissident. His *Gates of Paradise* (1960), a historical novel about the medieval children's crusade, includes a love affair between two young men. In a short story he retells the Biblical story of Cain and Abel, with the boys as lovers. *No One*, a particularly explicit homosexual retelling of the Odysseus story, was published posthumously in 1983. Despite the repressiveness of the military regime, other fictional works dealing with homosexuality have also been published.

The media have also shown a surprising openness. In 1974 Tadeusz Gorgol published a remarkably positive article in *Zycie literackie*. At the end of the 1983 the Warsaw monthly *Relaks* began printing gay "contact" personal ads, though this policy was discontinued in July 1984. On November 23, 1985, Krzysztof Darski published in *Polityka* an article, "We Are Different," that called for a homophile organization. By 1988 informal gay groups had formed in Wroclaw, Lodz, Gdansk, and Warsaw. Information bulletins, however, were limited to a printing of one hundred copies to avoid censorship.

BIBLIOGRAPHY. Homosexuelle Initiative (HOSI) Wien, *Rosa Liebe unterm roten Stern: Zur Lage der Lesben und Schwulen in Osteuropa*, Hamburg: Frühlings Erwachen, 1984.

Warren Johansson

POLICE

The regulation of sexual behavior would be incomplete without an administrative branch of government to enforce the laws on the statute books, and in Western society this task has traditionally fallen to the police. However, the police as an institution came into being only gradually, between the second half of the seventeenth century and the first half of the nineteenth.

The word stems from *politeia*, in turn derived from Greek *polis*, "city." Originally it referred to civic organization and administration as instruments for shaping citizenship and *politesse*. In French usage the meaning gradually narrowed from this broad sense to the more specific denotation of the corps of agents who carried out the instructions of the lieutenant of police. Among the special functions of this authority was the suppression or at least the monitoring of vice, the so-called *police des moeurs*, out of which the English-speaking world developed the "morals squad" or "vice squad."

Functions and Practices. One of the primary tasks of this branch of the police force has always been the regulation of **prostitution**, at least to the extent that prostitutes had to be registered with the authorities and to confine their activities to certain areas of the city and particular times of day. Male prostitution far less often was controlled in this manner because the acts in which the prostitute and his client engaged were ipso facto criminal, quite apart from any payment which the hustler or call boy received, so that the whole relationship had to be exceedingly clandestine. And despite social disapproval and periodic campaigns aimed at driving **sodomy** out of existence, the principal cities of Europe from the late **Middle Ages** to the present have always had a homosexual **subculture** of parks, streets, taverns, and other places where men seeking partners of their own sex habitually congregated. These areas came under police surveillance, and at least from the early eighteenth century onward, the Paris police kept lists of such persons, even if it did not proceed to arrest them. These "homo-files," to use a modern play on words, often included the names of thousands of individuals from all classes of society. In 1725 Lieutenant General Lenoir estimated that there were 20,000 sodomites in Paris, and in 1783 Mouffle d'Angerville gave an account of a ledger in which the names of 40,000 pederasts were inscribed, "almost as many as there were whores."

Another practice of the police was entrapment, whereby a plainclothesman would encourage the victim to make an advance and then—often with accomplices hidden nearby—proceed to arrest him. Entrapment was to continue in many large cities down to the sixties of the twentieth century. And with fear of arrest and exposure came the danger of **blackmail**, which hung like a Damocles' sword over the head of every homosexual who led a double life. Since denizens of the homosexual subculture often had to pay off the police in order to function unmolested, the police themselves could be enmeshed in a network of bribery, extortion, and blackmail. The fact that Western society tacitly assigns sexual activity to the realm of the private and unseen has meant, moreover, that the police could maintain their surveillance only over sexual activity that occurred in public places or was implied by the attempt of a suspect to establish rapport with a prospective sexual partner. This last fell into the category of **"loitering"** or "disorderly conduct," an ill-defined concept that gave the authorities a free hand in dealing with anyone of whose actions they disapproved. Also, when national prohibition was repealed in the United States (1933), premises serving alcohol came under the supervision of regulatory bodies with power to close them if "degenerates" were engaging in "disorderly conduct." The ambiguous status of the bars led to a continuing pattern of raids in which employees and patrons would be arrested; these culminated in the famous **Stonewall** tavern raid of June 27–28, 1969 in **New York's** Greenwich Village, when for the first time homosexuals fought back. Occasionally private parties were also raided and the guests hauled off to the police station.

Surveillance and the Morals Squad. It was only in the last third of the nineteenth century that a morals squad came to be a regular part of the metropolitan police force. Gustave Macé of the Paris Sûreté reported that in 1872—thus at the beginning of the Third Republic—a brigade composed of eight agents was formed to maintain surveillance over the pederasts of the French capital, but that he had to disband it because the head of the squad began to keep dossiers on political figures as well as professional hustlers. Léo Taxil held that despite the reform of the penal code by the Constituent Assembly in 1791, every French government from that of Napoleon I to the 1880s had used the knowledge of the homosexuality of individuals in public life for purposes of political blackmail. Thus the surveillance exercised by the morals squad served to increase the hold of the state power over those "to whom no crime could be imputed," as Gibbon said it had done since the time of Justinian.

The object was not to prosecute the culprits or to destroy their social existence, but to monitor their activities and, it goes without saying, survey the functioning of the clandestine networks of homosexual contact and influence. In fact, the police authorities in the large cities of the Western world were aware that they should not proceed too vigorously in tracking down "vice rings" because sooner or later influential and wealthy individuals were bound to be implicated. This truth was lost on the police in small towns and cities, where a campaign against "unnatural vice," more often than not provoked by a member of the local clergy, could lead to a chain of arrests in which the most prominent families would be compromised. The most recent well-publicized example of such a chain is the "cleanup" undertaken in Boise, Idaho in 1955. Also, since the metropolitan police could not touch those who were privileged by their own social standing or by powerful protectors, they targeted for arrest or extortion the "small fry" who fell into their nets—the street hustler, the drag queen, the lower middle class denizen of the homosexual underworld. Lesbians were less often victims of police harassment except in connection with statutes against cross-dressing which they could be accused of violating.

Tensions between Homosexuals and the Police. Naturally the police were hated by the homosexuals on whom they preyed, and whom they in turn resented because their own superiors used discretion in proceeding against those guilty of the "crime against nature." At the same time homosexuals who were victimized by common criminals feared to turn to the police for help because they would encounter no sympathy and even expose themselves to investigation or worse. So the absence of great numbers of prosecutions for sodomy attests to an ambiguous situation: comparatively few individuals were ever caught "in the act" and prosecuted for the maximal offense, but many were entrapped or subjected to semi-legal forms of harassment such as raids on gay bars in which the patrons would be arrested and their identity—and the motive for the arrest—made known to family members, employers and the like, so that, even though they were charged with a misdemeanor at most, their careers and lives could be ruined by the simple act of disclosure. The police themselves could engage in "shakedowns" or outright blackmail.

The police thus functioned in three ways to embitter the existence of participants in the homosexual **subculture**: (1) by harassing patrons of establishments known to be frequented by homosexuals, or individuals simply observed in cruising areas, (2) by allowing criminals, or private persons hostile to homosexuals, to victimize and assault them with impunity, and (3) by conducting campaigns of repression at the behest of politicians who wanted to impress the electorate with their zeal in "upholding morality." When an establishment failed to pay the sums demanded by the police for protection, or a crusading mayor or district attorney wanted the newspapers to report that he had "cracked down on vice," the arm of the law would descend in full fury. So long as the gay **community** was unorganized, powerless, and itself a "fugitive from justice," nothing could be done to minimize or halt these practices. While the United States saw national waves of repression,

especially in the 1940s and 50s, local variations were considerable. A city with an energetically homophobic police chief (as was repeatedly the case in **Los Angeles**) could make life difficult for homosexuals, in contrast with one in which the authorities were more lax—and more susceptible to bribery.

Improved Relations. In the latter part of the twentieth century, with the rise of the homosexual liberation **movement**, gay and lesbian organizations have made efforts at establishing liaisons with urban police forces and at cultivating better relations with the local police. Enlightened district attorneys and their counterparts in major European cities have been persuaded to halt the practice of entrapment and to restrict their repressive activity to sexual behavior that caused public scandal or entailed corruption or abuse of a minor, and also to educate the members of the police force in a spirit of toleration for the gay subculture. In such cities as **San Francisco** and **New York** the police have actually begun to recruit gay and lesbian candidates for the force, while homosexuals who already belong have formed benevolent organizations of their own.

BIBLIOGRAPHY. John J. Gallo, et al., "The Consenting Adult Homosexual and the Law: An Empirical Study of Enforcement and Administration in Los Angeles County," *UCLA Law Review*, 13 (1966), 643–832; Gustave Macé, *Mes lundis en prison*, Paris: Charpentier, 1889; Michel Rey, "Police et sodomie à Paris au XVIIIe siècle: du péché au désordre," *Revue d'histoire moderne et contemporaine*, 29 (1983), 113–24; Steven A. Rosen, "Police Harassment of Homosexual Women and Men in New York City 1960–1980," *Columbia Human Rights Law Review*, 12 (1980–81), 159–90.

Warren Johansson

POLITICAL THEORY, HISTORY OF
Political theory seeks to analyze and envision things political, originally of the *polis* or city-state of ancient **Greece**. Thus the subject begins with the Greeks of

Athens at the end of the fifth century B.C. in close association with **philosophy**.

As institutions and modes of thought have changed, so has political theory. While it may aspire to universality, it is, among theories, particularly dependent on context. What counts as political is subject to continuing controversy. Thus **pederasty** was politically important in classical Athens, where it was a basic aspect of educating male citizens, while contemporary **libertarians** view it as politically neutral. What is political is not restricted to affairs of state; it extends to embrace all matters of legitimate public concern. Thus issues of morals, education, custom, language, and culture are politically germane.

Homosexuality as a Topic for Political Theory. That **homosexuality** is a term of the second half of the nineteenth century is well known. To what extent it can be applied to earlier periods is an issue rightly debated. As with all phenomena over time and space, which are complex both conceptually and evidentially, so with erotic same-sex bonding: there are similarities and differences. Practices, norms, conceptualizations, and consciousness vary significantly. What is now taken to be homosexuality was not so viewed in earlier periods. No effort is here made to resolve the essentialist–**social constructionist** dispute, which has addressed the issue of similarity vs. difference. It is assumed only that from the current vantage point a sufficient family resemblance can be descried in discussions by major political theorists of pederasty, **sodomy**, the crime against **nature**, and so forth to yield some coherence.

The main course of political theoretical discussion of homosexuality can be periodized: (1) the subtle discussion of pederasty in fourth-century-B.C. Athens; (2) the long period of Christian condemnation; and (3) the **Enlightenment** critique of received ideas. The extant writings are all by male authors, and they devote virtually all their attention to male homosexuality.

Greek Thinkers. **Plato** (d. 347 B.C.), a student of **Socrates**, is the first great writer of political philosophy, notably in the *Republic*, *Statesman*, and the *Laws*. The *Symposium* and *Phaedrus* are his major dialogues on eros. The Greek practice of pederasty—courtship and love of an adolescent (never child) by a somewhat older man—was the form of homosexuality on which he reflected. He viewed this not as a distinct category or problem in itself but rather in the context of discussions of appetite, desire, temperance, education, and law. Given Plato's use of dramatic dialogues, the difficulty in determining which of the views that he attributes to Socrates are his own, and the differences between early and late dialogues, it is difficult to state Plato's views concisely. He clearly assumes that male homoerotic desire is ubiquitous.

The *Symposium* is less a dialogue than an account of a banquet at which successive speakers praise and explain the nature of love, that is, eros. In the discussion Pausanias distinguishes between two loves, the heavenly, Uranian Aphrodite and the younger, earthly Pandemian Aphrodite. The latter is the common love which seeks bodily pleasure only and pertains to both sexes. Uranian love is entirely male and involves cultivation of the mind and spirit. Indeed, Uranian love is associated with political freedom and resistance to tyranny. Pausanias also notes a tension between Athenian support for the lover's (*erastes*) ardent pursuit as well as for resistance on the part of the beloved (*eremenos*). This he explains as supporting his distinction between noble and base love, which means that a youth should not yield too readily or for a reason other than gaining virtue. The nineteenth-century usage of "**Uranian**" (stemming from K. H. **Ulrichs**) to denote a male homosexual derives from this speech.

In the *Symposium* Plato makes **Aristophanes**, the celebrated writer of Old Comedy, give a remarkable speech in which he develops the compelling myth that once there had been three "sexes," who were spherical beings, solar double men, lunar double women, and earthly fused men-women. Zeus, angered at these creatures' arrogance, severed them in two; later, he rearranged their genitals. Ever after, each creature seeks wholeness in coupling with the lost half of its own kind. The women drawn to women are clearly lesbians, and this is one of the rare references to lesbianism in the political-theory canon. The males attracted to males, the most virile, are as youths drawn to men and as men love youths; they marry and beget children only in response to social custom.

Socrates, however, in the concluding speech in which he recounts what the priestess Diotima had told him of love, rejects Aristophanes' view. Love is that which one lacks; love is not a god but a *daimon*, a being halfway between a god and a man and also between wisdom and ignorance. It is an intermediary. Love begins with attraction to one particular body, but the truest love ascends a ladder, as it were, and culminates in a vision of beauty itself. Since beauty and goodness are the same, love is a longing for possession of goodness eternally. Indeed, love's association with propagation reveals that love is really a longing for immortality. At the conclusion of this famous speech of Socrates, the drunken **Alcibiades** bursts into the party and tells the revealing story of how Socrates, his sometime lover, had resisted any physical gratification despite Alcibiades' best efforts.

The effect of the *Symposium* on the western mind, a great one, has been deeply equivocal. While what is recognizably homosexual desire is unforgettably celebrated, only a chaste, idealized expression of it is finally permitted.

In the late dialogue, the *Laws*, Plato proposed outlawing physical homosexual relations, readily acknowledging that such a proposal was contrary to practice and opinion. Indulgence in such practice, it is held, leads to intemperance and effeminacy. It is suggested that a custom

whereby the sanctions against incest would be extended to all "unnatural" sex would do untold good. Plato here uses unsound arguments from animal behavior and fatefully introduces the idea that sex between men is "against nature" (*para physin*).

While there are several scattered references to homosexuality in the prodigiously learned **Aristotle** (384–322 B.C.), they convey no strong view. The existence of pederastic attraction is taken for granted; there are several nonjudging references to such love affairs. Aristotle shares a common Greek concern about the tension between friendship, which requires equality, and the pederastic relationship, characteristically an unequal one. Reciprocity and constancy, though, can be attained through the mutual love of character.

A text from the Aristotelian school (*Problemata*, IV, 26) engages the question, most puzzling to the Greeks, of how the sexually passive male could enjoy the sexual act. The somewhat confused discussion concludes that though such a pathic (*kinaidos*) acts contrary to nature, habit can become nature. Clearly the ancient Greek view of nature was ambiguous, and the arguments from nature were problematic, as they continue to be.

Christian Thinking. In the next period of political theory, that dominated by Christian thinkers, the figures of St. **Augustine** and St. Thomas **Aquinas** stand out. While each was deeply influenced by the classical heritage, what distinguishes them is the presence of Christian revelation as the decisive criterion for truth and rightness.

St. Augustine (354–430), after his conversion to **Christianity**, took a dark view of sexual activity generally. Lust, concupiscence was the shameful result of original sin. He viewed involuntary sexual arousal as a consequence of Adam and Eve's disobedience. Only intercourse for procreation was justified and that solely within marriage. In a famous passage in his *Confessions* (III, 8, 15), he refers to detestable crimes against nature, such as those of the Sodomites, which "even if all nations should commit them" are contrary to divine law. In Augustine we find a mixture, characteristic in Christian discussions, of reference to the Bible, to nature, and to divine law.

St. Thomas Aquinas (1225–1274), most influential and authoritative of Roman Catholic theorists, developed a complex, architectonic philosophic and theological system which included significant treatment of politics and morals. These are regulated by a structure in which four kinds of law intermingle: eternal, natural, divine, and human (or positive). The universe is an ordered whole carrying out a special plan; each entity within it is to carry out its appropriate ends within that plan. Each naturally seeks its own good: preservation for all substance, procreation for animals, an orderly social life and knowledge of God for human beings. "All things have a natural tendency toward activity befitting their natures." To seek good and avoid evil is the first principle of natural law. To sin is either to offend God or to injure men.

Sexual matters are discussed under the general category of temperance and that applied to matters of touch. *Sodomiticum vitium*, the vice of sodomy, of which one form is intercourse between persons of the same sex, is carefully distinguished from related sexual sins *(Summa Theologiae,* IIa–IIae.154.11–12). Sodomy is peculiarly a sin against nature in that it is contrary not only to man's uniquely human nature but also to that which he shares with animals. Further, this sin against nature, the plan of which comes from God, is a sin against God: it is an affront to God, the ordainer of nature. On a scale of gravity, masturbation and non-missionary-position intercourse are lesser sins than sodomy, only bestiality is worse. Unnatural vice is worse than incest.

While the 1986 Vatican pronouncement on homosexuality (*Letter to the World's Bishops on the Pastoral Care of Homosexual Persons,* by the Congrega-

tion for the Doctrine of the Faith) relies more on biblical citation, the view developed by Thomas Aquinas remains that of the Roman Catholic Church.

Early Enlightenment Thought. The sixteenth and seventeenth centuries saw the next great period of political thought with figures such as Machiavelli, Hobbes, and Locke addressing issues central to the emergent modern state: action, sovereignty, legitimacy, and consent. While they appear in law and literature, references to homosexuality in political theory in this period are scant.

In a characteristic remark, modern, derisive, and reductive, the caustic Thomas Hobbes (1588–1679), commenting on Socrates, suspects that platonic love was sensual, "but with an honorable pretence of the old to haunt the company of the young and beautiful" (*Human Nature,* 17). Since multitude, increase of population, is a temporal good, the law of nature obliges the sovereign to forbid "unnatural copulation."

It is with the Enlightenment of the eighteenth century, a broad movement of opinion rather than a doctrine, that the possibility of new views emerged. Enlightenment thinkers subjected received ideas and established authority, political, cultural, and especially religious, to scrutiny. They raised doubt about existing categories, principles, and judgments, suggested new ones, and promoted practical reform of laws, institutions, and taste.

The sage Baron de Montesquieu (1689–1755) exemplifies the cautious humanity of the early phase of the Enlightenment. Montesquieu's attempt both to respect general principles of justice (natural law) and to understand the needs of particular peoples in particular circumstances led to confusion but also to creative insight.

In his major work, *The Spirit of the Laws* (XII, 6), he professes abhorrence of the crime against nature which "religion, morality, and civil government equally condemn." He suggests that it gives to one sex "the weakness of the other," and he avers that where social custom does not promote it, the crime against nature will make "no great progress."

Yet he also expresses concern over "the tyranny that may abuse the very horror" that ought to be felt for the vice. He is distressed that in prosecuting the crime, the deposition of a single witness, a child, a slave, opens the door to calumny. Most tellingly, he notes the oddity that in contemporary France three crimes are "punished with fire": witchcraft, which does not exist; heresy, which is susceptible to infinite interpretation; and the crime against nature, which is "often obscure and uncertain." Despite the continuing muddle of the concept of crime against nature, a cool scepticism begins to subvert it.

Bentham. Jeremy **Bentham** (1748–1832) represents at once the later, more radical phase of the Enlightenment and also the founding of nineteenth-century British philosophical radicalism. With Bentham the cautious questioning of received views, still couched in natural-law language, is replaced by the slashing critique of utilitarianism. This influential doctrine posits judgment of morals and legislation by the consequentialist criterion of the greatest happiness of the greatest number, happiness considered as pleasure and calculable in terms of probability, duration, and so forth. Whatever its defects as philosophy, which are considerable, this doctrine directed to the question of the crime against nature had the great merit of instantly demystifying it. Why is this crime (punished in England by hanging until 1861) treated so severely? Wherein lies the offense? Is this even a crime?

Given the few, brief, and oblique references to this topic in centuries of previous political theory, it is stunning to find that Bentham wrote over 600 manuscript pages on the subject, at several times during his long career. Yet none of these were published in his lifetime and most

still have not been. (See J. Bentham, "Essay on Paederasty," Louis Crompton, ed., *Journal of Homosexuality*, 3:4, Summer 1978, and 4:1, Fall 1978, written ca. 1785. The best discussion of all Bentham's writings on the subject is in Crompton, *Byron and Greek Love*, Berkeley, 1985.)

While Bentham expresses his own disapproval of homosexual practices ("preposterous," "unnatural," "odious"), he can find no basis in reason for the severity with which they are treated. "Let us be unjust to no man: not even to a paederast." With his accustomed thoroughness, Bentham marches forth arguments against private consenting homosexual acts and finds them wanting.

They produce no primary mischief, only pleasure. It is not a crime against peace, nor an offense against security. If it is debilitating, as Montesquieu said, then it is an offense against oneself, but there is no physiological evidence that this is so, and historical evidence reveals the vigor of ancient Greek and Roman soldiers who practiced it. It cannot be argued that it is prejudicial to population (at this time Bentham assumed as did most that population growth was desirable), since "prolific venery" is quite adequate to that end. If this were a reason, why is not monkish celibacy outlawed? Nor can it be argued that it robs women; marriage remains popular.

Bentham goes on to explore "the ground of antipathy." He finds it to lie in the propensity "to confound physical impurity with moral," in "philosophical pride" against pleasure, and in religion. In his later unpublished nineteenth-century writings on this subject, Bentham goes even further. He abandons the conventional language of disapproval that he had used earlier; he saw actual merit in nonprocreative sex.

With Bentham's effort to demystify this subject by rational instrumental and normative analysis, his considered arguments for decriminalization, and his pioneering attempt to explore the sources of hostility to homosexuality, one reaches, at last, a turning point in political reflection. Yet this writing remained unpublished until recently, and the nineteenth century saw no further sustained, serious discussion of the subject by a major political theorist.

Conclusions. It has been remarked that the European philosophical tradition simply fails in its discussion of women, not just in the falseness of its conclusions but in the collapse of its usual standards of thought. The same is true for political theory's treatment of homosexuality. It is scarcely accidental that with Plato and, if not with Bentham, then with his intellectual grandson, John Stuart Mill, the treatment of women is considerably more intelligent. Between Plato and Bentham there is scarcely a discussion of homosexuality instructive for other than historical purposes. Even here, the account focuses on the classical Greek male practice of pederasty, only a small part of what is now thought of as homosexuality. From the late Plato of the *Laws* through Montesquieu, much of the intellectual confusion is rooted in the tortuous ambiguities of the concepts of nature, natural law, and the crime against nature. With Bentham's eventually effective assault on this mode of theorizing, largely a negative achievement, the way was cleared for more searching views to be developed. In the twentieth century, the quest for an adequate account of that aspect of homosexuality which is of legitimate public concern remains far from complete.

See also **Conservatism; Left, Gay; Liberalism; Liberation, Gay; Libertarianism; Marxism; Movement, Gay.**

BIBLIOGRAPHY. Richard D. Mohr, *Gays/Justice: A Study of Ethics, Society and Law*, New York: Columbia University Press, 1988; Laurence J. Rosán, "Philosophies of Homophobia and Homophilia," in L. Crew, ed., *The Gay Academic*, Palm Springs, CA: ETC Publications, 1978, pp. 255–81; George H. Sabine and Thomas L. Thorson, *A History of Political Theory*, Hinsdale, IL: Dryden Press, 1973.

David J. Thomas

POLIZIANO (POLITIAN), ANGELO AMBROGINI KNOWN AS (1454–1494)

Italian Humanist and poet. Born at Montepulciano, he was taken to **Florence** at a tender age, where he received instruction from outstanding teachers, including Marsilio Ficino. While still quite young he undertook a partial translation of Homer's *Iliad* into Latin (1469–73), which attracted the attention of Lorenzo de' Medici, who gave him free run of the private library of the Medici family. In 1475 Lorenzo made Poliziano tutor of his children. Two years later he became prior of San Paolo, giving him the leisure and prestige he deserved.

Then friction with the Medici family, brought on partly by questions having to do with the education of the children, led him to abandon Florence in 1479, though he returned the following year. Henceforth he dedicated himself to teaching and to the philological study of the ancient classics.

In addition to his works in Italian, Poliziano wrote with ease in Latin and in classical Greek. Among his chief texts are the *Sylvae*, the *Stanze per la giostra di Giuliano* (1475–78), the *Detti piacevoli* (1477–79), the secular drama *La Favolo di Orfeo* (1480), as well as historical works, translations from the Greek, and works of philology.

The theme of homosexual love emerged on at least three occasions in Poliziano's oeuvre. The best known is the above-mentioned *Orfeo*, a theatre composition which marks the transition in Italy from sacred to secular drama. In this play **Orpheus**, having lost Eurydice forever, swears that he will love no other woman and that he will turn to boys instead. He meets his death at the hands of a vengeful group of maenads. The story was culled from ancient **mythology**, which Poliziano simply clothed in elegant Italian words.

More extended is the treatment in the love poetry that Poliziano wrote in Latin and Greek (significantly, this sensitive theme does not occur in his Italian verse). In these poems he talks of a certain Chrysocomus ("golden locks") and a Corydon, extolling his love in the manner of prestigious Greek and Latin models.

Finally, a lighter note appears in the *Detti piacevoli*, the attribution of which has been disputed for some time, though recently the scholar Gianfranco Folena has restored them to Poliziano. This collection consists of jokes involving various Florentine figures, including homosexual motifs involving the artists **Botticelli** and **Donatello**.

Today it is difficult to say to what extent Poliziano's interest in homoeroticism went beyond that of the imitation of the antique, which was a common feature of the period. According to a story spread by some contemporaries (including Paolo Giovio, 1483–1552), Poliziano died of strain after having played the lute one night underneath the window of a Greek youth named Argo. Isidoro Del Lungo has collected several versions of the tale.

In any event, even during his lifetime Poliziano was accused of harboring homosexual tastes, as shown by the poems of Andrea Dazzi (which belong, however, to a vein of invective cultivated by the Humanists, and cannot be simply taken at face value). Some attestations, like those reported by Gustavo Uzielli, make Poliziano's position suspect, but do not take us out of the realm of speculation. Further uncertainty is cast on the subject by positions such as that maintained by Giovanni Semerano, who condemns all the homosexual poetry as being somehow unworthy of "Poliziano's true nature."

BIBLIOGRAPHY. Isidoro Del Lungo, *Florentia*, Florence: Barbera, 1897; Gianfranco Folena, "Sulla tradizione dei 'detti piacevoli' attribuiti al Poliziano," *Studi di filologia italiana*, 11 (1953), 431–48; Giovanni Semerano, "La lirica greca e latina del Poliziano: 'Epigrammata,'" *Convivium* (1951), 234–48; Gustavo Uzielli, *La vita e i tempi di Paolo Dal Pozzo Toscanelli*, Rome: Forzani, 1894, pp. 232–33.

Giovanni Dall'Orto

POLYMORPHOUS PERVERSE

This expression for a disposition toward multifarious sexual experience stems from **psychoanalysis**. In *Three Essays on the Theory of Sexuality* (1905) Sigmund **Freud** states: "[U]nder the influence of seduction children can become polymorphously perverse, and can be led into all possible kinds of sexual irregularities. This shows that an aptitude for them is innately present in their disposition." Children have not yet built up the mental dams that would guard them against such sexual excess. They also do not yet know to focus their sexuality on their genitals, but allow it to roam, as it were, over the entire body. Some adults, such as prostitutes, may deliberately revert to this infantilism for their own purposes. Thus, in Freud's view, the inclination to the polymorphous **perverse** is built into the plan of human development, and a more mature sexuality must be created out of it as a result of organic growth and the introjection of psychic inhibitions. In a like manner, psychoanalysis tends to assume that the adult homosexual orientation is a relic of an early bisexual disposition, and therefore amounts to an arrest of development. This notion implicitly reinforced the ascetic belief that sexuality had only a reproductive function and that mere pleasure-seeking fell short of the goal which "mature" individuals should attain.

In the 1960s, owing in part to Freudian revisionists such as Norman O. Brown and Herbert Marcuse, a more positive version of the idea came into circulation. The internalization of repressive mechanisms was no longer regarded as essential for the maintenance of civilization. Hence there was room for sexual experimentation, even for excursions into the polymorphous perverse. Yet orthodox psychoanalysis continued to assert that polymorphous perverse adults were either psychotic or unable to form stable human relationships, and therefore driven from one sexual episode to the next. With the gradual decline of the influence of psychoanalysis the term no longer occurs in general writing with any frequency, being replaced by more neutral designations, such as "sexual pluralism."

Wayne R. Dynes

POLYNESIA
See Pacific Cultures.

POPPERS
See Drugs.

PORNOGRAPHY
Originally referring mainly to writings, today pornography includes a whole range of sexually explicit cultural artifacts intended to produce immediate sexual arousal. The term first appeared in eighteenth-century France, a coinage from Greek *pornegraphos*, "a painter of prostitutes." It is documented in English from the mid-nineteenth century.

Definition. Considerable thought has been devoted to the definition of pornography. Proposed definitions are of three types. The first is by content: the portrayal or discussion of genitalia or specific sexual acts is pornographic; this definition fails because sexual acts and genitalia may be portrayed for medical purposes, or in educational material, without the intent to arouse. A second approach is by the observer's use of the materials: those materials which produce sexual arousal are pornographic. This approach fails because images not intended for arousal, and not found arousing by most, can be used to produce sexual arousal; conversely, some are not stimulated by scenes which the majority finds intensely erotic. Finally, there is the intent of the producer: those materials which are intended to arouse the viewer, reader, or listener are pornographic. As a legal criterion this approach also fails, because intent can be disguised or denied,

and can never be established directly or with absolute certainty. However, it is sufficient for critical purposes and is the definition used in this article.

Value of Pornography. Pornography has often been considered a symptom of societal illness, and its demise predicted. That the gradual removal of restrictions on sexual activities has not produced a parallel decline in pornography, but rather the reverse, suggests that it satisfies a deep need. While animal sexual excitement is produced by odors, a consequence of the estrus cycle, human beings use their minds. The separation of sexuality from reproduction, the increased lifespan civilization has brought, and the anti-erotic trends in modern society mean that glandular impulses toward sexual activity are insufficient. Hence the production and consumption of pornography as a stimulant of sexual activity.

The production of pornography, then, is a naturally human activity, stemming from the same sorts of inner drive that lead to the production of music, art, and literature. It has been found among many tribal peoples. That sexual excitement, like laughter, is contagious lies at the root of pornography's power.

Pornography is, for many people, pleasurable, directly and indirectly producing orgasm, and that alone is a powerful argument for it. It relieves guilt over sexuality, encourages **masturbation** and **fantasy**, and is a substitute for risky sexual encounters; as such, it can be relationship-enhancing. Through pornography the creator and consumer can explore and accept aspects of their sexuality which cannot be acted upon. Although some pornography transmits misinformation, on the whole it provides education about sex and contributes to public acceptance of sexuality. Through pornography society does its thinking about sex and to some extent about relationships. Pornographers and the legal struggles they have fought have made it possible for non-pornographic sex education materials to circulate freely. Pornography also provides the historian and anthropologist with evidence of sexual activities and attitudes.

Homosexual Pornography. It has been argued that almost all pornography is homosexual. Save for those small portions consumed by women, or created by women for consumption by men, pornography has been created by men in order to stimulate other men. Even if heterosexual activities are described or portrayed, even if the producer and consumer are heterosexually identified, the intent and, in some way, the true nature of such pornography is homosexual. That homosexuality and pornography tend to be accepted or condemned together gives further support to a probable deep relationship, perhaps that they both encourage and require societal tolerance of non-procreative sexuality. There has also been significant involvement of homosexuals in the production and sale of materials directed to the heterosexual public.

However, pornography is usually considered homosexual if it has homosexual content or subject matter. While erotic portrayals of men, and descriptions or expressions of homosexual love, are widely found, homosexual pornography is much more restricted. Where it exists it shows an acceptance by society, however begrudging and limited, of homosexuality and homosexual sexual relations. The occasional exposure of non-homosexuals to it has in turn contributed to further societal acceptance of homosexuality.

History. Pornography is exceptionally subject to destruction, homosexual pornography doubly so, and the following discussion is presumably incomplete. The earliest homosexual pornography occurs in Greek **vase paintings**, which show much sexually explicit homosexual activity (oral, anal, and intercrural intercourse). Primarily pederastic, these depictions constitute a body of work unsurpassed in artistic value and positive attitude toward sex.

Little is known in the West about the homosexual pornographic writings (**mujun**) of the classical Islamic cultures or the pederastic paintings of Persia. In China the Ming period (1368–1644) saw the appearance of sexually explicit literature and prints, including same-sex material. Despite the disapproval of the rulers, these interests continued in the succeeding Manchu dynasty, when **China**'s greatest novel, *The Dream of the Red Chamber*, which has a bisexual hero and many homosexual episodes, appeared. One of **Japan**'s major writers, **Saikaku** Ihara, specialized in frank writing about both amorous women and the male–male loves of the **Samurai**.

Until the nineteenth century, homosexual pornography in the West was often combined with defenses of sodomy. Such works include **Alcibiade fanciullo a scola**, an erotic defense of pederastic love from seventeenth-century Italy; the bisexual, philosophical fiction of the Marquis de **Sade**; and *The Sins of the Cities of the Plain, or the Recollections of a Mary-Anne* (1881), the earliest such work that survives in English and the first that is unabashed masturbatory fiction, with brief appended essays on "Sodomy" and "Tribadism." Pornographic scenes are found in the famous *Teleny* (1893), a novel falsely attributed to Oscar Wilde. The number of published works, however, was small. Well into the twentieth century pornographic stories, such as *Seven in a Barn*, circulated in typewritten form.

The Pulp Novel. The vast majority of written gay male pornography in the United States is issued in the form of paperback novels printed on pulp. Most of this material is of no literary value whatsoever, being typically composed at a rate of over 50 pages a day by writers who often have little or no understanding of the settings (interstate trucking, rodeos, the Navy, etc.) involved. Typical pay for a full book is $250. Writers may churn out scores of books using the same basic ingredients: several pages of sexual description followed by several pages of "plot/character" in a pattern repeated throughout the book. Occasionally, however, one finds well-written pornography, often by professional writers "moonlighting" under pseudonyms, in which a talent for almost poetically concise description of characters and setting is clearly visible, and sometimes an exotic setting is portrayed with such telling detail that one must presume the author is drawing on personal experience or thorough research.

A wary consumer is well advised to browse such novels before purchase, as the title and cover illustration may have no relation to the contents. Until the 1970s, novels invariably were introduced by pseudo-scientific statements, supposedly from psychiatrists or clergymen, often denouncing the behavior depicted therein, and intended to provide the "redeeming social value" then required by the American courts, but actually providing no little humor in a genre seldom noted for a comic touch.

The sexual scenes in these books are surprisingly varied, given their mass-production origins, and reflect the great diversity of exotic styles and tastes among their readers and writers. While male organs are invariably huge, ejaculations copious, and recuperation of potency instantaneous, and there is a definite bias in favor of youthful characters and settings (teenagers being most popular, perhaps reflecting **ephebophilia**), working-class occupations, and **macho** rather than refined or effeminate characters, nevertheless a considerable age range, a rainbow of racial types, and a wide palette of sexual styles is to be found in these novels.

Among writers who have sought to find a place in the territory between purely ephemeral pornography and literature are Richard Amory (*Song of the Loon* trilogy), Casimir Dukahz, Gordon Merrick, John Preston, John Rechy, Samuel M. Steward ("Phil Andros"), Larry Townsend, Dirk Vanden, and Marco Vassi.

Modern Visual Pornography. The invention of **photography** in the nineteenth century provided a new medium for the pornographer. The best-known creator of sexually stimulating male portraits was the Baron von **Gloeden**, although there were others in both England and Germany. Sexual activity was often the subject of photographs, though legal restrictions kept them underground.

Twentieth-century homosexual visual pornography in the United States and Germany, other than that which was underground, began as an offshoot of the naturist and physical-culture movements. Erotic "physique" magazines, picture sets, and films were published under the pretense of non-sexual interest in body development. More explicit were the drawings of "Blade" (Carlyle Kneeland Bate; 1917-1989).The devastation of German culture by the Nazis and World War II left the United States as the principal center of gay erotica. Eight and 16mm homosexual films, progressively more straightforward in subject matter and more open in their circulation, were made and screened. A major figure is Bob Mizer, who founded the Athletic Model Guild in Los Angeles in 1945.

The last two generations have seen a continual attack through the courts on **censorship** of pornography. Supported by an ever more tolerant public, these efforts have gradually brought upholdable convictions for publication or distribution of pornography to an end in most of the United States (except for child pornography). However, legal harassment and prosecutions have continued, and increased toward the end of the Reagan years. The freeing of the mails to pornography in the 1970s was an influential step; another was the Danish decision, in the late 60s, to end all legal restrictions on pornography.

Pornographic Filmmaking. Gay porno films typically have much lower budgets than their heterosexual counterparts, being limited to a smaller market, and pay their actors less: a few hundred dollars for a couple of days' work is typical. In the heterosexual business, actresses are paid much more than actors, but for gay films their absence helps keep expenses down. The primary requirement for a male pornography actor is the ability to maintain an erection while being aware of such technical matters as camera angle, director's instructions, soundtrack, and so forth. This is no mean feat, and a production can be held up for many hours for lack of an erection; sometimes skillful editing can disguise this failing.

Filmed pornography has always been **"safe sex"** in that, by convention, ejaculation is always external (in order to be visual). Producers may, however, resort to such tricks as using beaten egg-white to simulate semen.

Early films tended to have rock-bottom budgets and were intended only for cinematic use; as home videos became more popular, budgets expanded to the point where lush background scenery is common and even special effects are used.

Leading recent gay pornographers of films and videos include Jean-Daniel Cadinot, Jack Deveau (Hand in Hand Films), Joe Gage, Sal Grasso ("Steve Scott"), Fred Halsted (d. 1989), William Higgins, Christopher Rage, and Peter de Rome.

The Porno Film Theatre. In the United States, the gay pornographic cinema arose in the late 1960s, originally featuring "soft-core" films but switching over to "hard-core" features in the more tolerant 70s. These movie houses soon came to be features of the gay subculture in all major cities, serving not only as places of visual entertainment, but often as sites for sexual activity as well. Spaces behind the screen or off to a side were sometimes in effect reserved as orgy rooms, while other activities took place in the seats of the theatre. Some cinemas added dance floors, bars, and other facilities so that they came to rival the **bathhouses** as leisure centers. With the development of the **AIDS** crisis, overt activity came to be

frowned upon, but **cruising** remained a major activity.

Long before the opening of specifically gay cinema houses, theatres showing heterosexual pornographic films had become sites for homosexual cruising, being particularly favored by those homosexuals attracted to "straight **trade**," heterosexual males who, upon arousal by the images of females on the screen, became less choosy about their means of relief. Even if the gay cinema should disappear in favor of home videos, this tradition is likely to endure.

Recent Developments. Increased gay self-awareness and self-acceptance, greater public acceptance of homosexuality, and the dropping of most legal barriers to the publication and circulation of pornography have all helped homosexual pornography to grow explosively. It has today a major role in the gay male world, in which it is not controversial; few legal cases have involved homosexual pornography. While figures are unavailable, anecdotal evidence suggests that per capita consumption is higher in the gay than in the straight community. It has shown a classic sign of economic health, the division into specialties, and the conservatism which has come to characterize part of the pornographic industry is also a sign that it is well-established. Inexpensive **video** equipment has made it easier for new pornographers to enter the field, although to date there has been more straight amateur pornography than gay. A number of glossy monthly magazines, following the model of *Playboy* and its successors, have strong pornographic components in pictures and text (*Blueboy, Honcho, In Touch,* etc.); *Stroke* proclaims openly that it is and wants to be pornographic and masturbatory.

In the 1980s there has been a renewed interest in written and drawn pornography, in which fantasies are not limited by what models can actually do and in which laws, as on intergenerational sex, can be broken without consequence.

The new **phone sex** industry offers personalized, oral pornography. The division between pornography and high art loses its rigidity as painters, photographers, and authors of fiction and poetry produce works which stimulate sexually, and pornographers exceed the limits of popular art.

The New York editor and publisher Boyd McDonald pioneered the collection, for pornographic ends, of confessional, reader-written material, an undeterminable but large proportion of which is not fantasy but reports of authentic sexual adventures; his magazine *Straight to Hell* has been succeeded by *First Hand* and *Friction*. Most of McDonald's magazine material has been reprinted in book form by Gay Sunshine Press (now Leyland Publications of San Francisco), and there are original books of the same type from that publisher, from Gay Presses of New York, and from Bright Tyger Press. Jack Fritscher, before turning to "documentary" erotic videos (Palm Drive Video), wrote and edited stories and confessions (*Man 2 Man* magazine). Among the other pornographic titles published by Leyland Publications is Mike Shearer's *Great American Gay Porno Novel* (1984). David Hurles ("Old Reliable") has recorded, first on audio and then on video tape, hustlers and ex-convicts, often filled with anger. Two leading pornographic visual artists are Tom of Finland and Rex. Pornographic **comics** have been collected and reprinted by Leyland Publications. In the 1980s a gay pornographic industry emerged outside the United States, first in France, then in Japan and on a smaller scale, for export only, in Thailand, Brazil, and Mexico. Just as American pornography has had considerable influence in the spreading and homogenization of gay male culture, foreign pornography has the potential for broadening American gay eroticism.

Women's Pornography. Most allegedly lesbian pornography has consisted of fantasies for heterosexual male consumption. As a genre of sexual fantasy women have had romances, abundant pulp fiction with a strong sexual component. A development of the 1980s is the birth of a true women's pornographic movement, in which women create and market erotic materials for female consumption, both homosexual and heterosexual. A precedent is the feminist erotica of Anaïs Nin.

There are now published anthologies of women's erotica (*Herotica*, edited by Susie Bright, *The Leading Edge*, edited by Lady Winston, and several other collections), magazines both lesbian (*Bad Attitude, On Our Backs, Outrageous Women, Yoni*) and heterosexual (*Eidos, Libido, Yellow Silk*), a major novelist, Anne Rice ("A. N. Roquelaure," "Anne Rampling"), and filmmakers (Fatale Video; the heterosexual Candida Royalle). Lace Publications has published several volumes of Lesbian erotica, including the adventure fantasies of Artemis Oak Grove and Cappy Kotz' *The First Stroke*. Pat Califia's *Macho Sluts* appeared in 1988 (Alyson Publications). In comparison with men's, women's pornography is less visual, and includes more emotional context for the sexual acts. While pornography has been controversial in the feminist movement, and fantasies of violence or domination especially so, the emergence of women's erotica has helped to defuse the issue. Its continued strong growth seems very likely.

Bisexual Pornography. As many men find lesbian lovemaking stimulating to watch, and the division between homosexual and heterosexual women has not been as rigid as the modern dichotomy between gay and straight men, much pornography has presented women bisexually. The mid-1980s saw the emergence of pornography portraying men bisexually, usually using sexual trios consisting of two men and one woman. Not of "grassroots" origin, as other forms of pornography have been, it has been a successful creation of the pornographic film industry, with only trivial written precedents, though books have followed in the wake. Although a product of the homosexual rather than the heterosexual branch of the industry, among non-bisexuals it seems to appeal more to heterosexual men than to the gay-identified.

BIBLIOGRAPHY. *Al's Male Video Guide, 1986,* New York: Midway Publications, 1986; Varda Burstyn, ed., *Women Against Censorship,* Vancouver and Toronto: Douglas & MacIntyre, 1985; Emmanuel Cooper, *The Sexual Perspective: Homosexuality in Art in the Last 100 Years in the West,* London: Routledge & Kegan Paul, 1986; Gordon Hawkins and Franklin E. Zimring, *Pornography in a Free Society,* New York: Cambridge University Press, 1989; Walter Kendrick, *The Secret Museum: Pornography in Modern Culture,* New York: Viking, 1987; John W. Rowberry, *Gay Video: A Guide to Erotica,* San Francisco: Gay Sunshine, 1986; Betty-Carol Sellen and Patricia A. Young, *Feminists, Pornography, and the Law: An Annotated Bibliography of Conflict, 1970–1986,* Hamden, CT: Library Professional Publications, 1987; Alan Soble, *Pornography, Marxism, Feminism, and the Future of Sexuality,* New Haven: Yale University Press, 1986; Tom Waugh, "A Heritage of Pornography," *The Body Politic* (January 1983), pp. 29–33; idem, "Photography, Passion & Power," *The Body Politic* (March 1984), pp. 29–33; Jack Wrangler and Carl Johnes, *The Jack Wrangler Story,* New York: St. Martin's, 1984.

Daniel Eisenberg

PORTER, COLE
(1891–1964)

American composer and lyricist. Porter was born to wealthy parents in Peru, Indiana; Cole was his mother's maiden name. After studying music and law at Harvard and Yale Universities, he served in the military in France in World War I. There he met Linda Lee Thomas, and they were married in December 1919. The couple spent most of the following decade conducting a lavish version of the "lost generation" lifestyle in Europe, though Porter occasionally returned to the United States for triumphal productions of his songs in Broadway musicals. On his various travels he was sometimes accom-panied by his comrade-in-arms Monty Woolley, and the two made no secret of their attraction to handsome young men.

In 1936 Porter wrote the score for the Hollywood musical *Born to Dance,* the first of a number of such films. The following year he suffered a riding accident in which both legs were crushed; in the course of his life he required more than thirty operations to avoid amputation. For long he bore the pain stoically, but in his later years he became reclusive, his days enlivened only—so it has been claimed— by a sadomasochistic relationship with actor Jack Cassidy. In 1946 Cary Grant impersonated Porter in a slick Hollywood film, *Night and Day,* which, true to form, entirely omitted the homosexual aspects of his life.

Porter, who wrote both the lyrics and the music to his songs, chose to operate in the field of commercial music. Through his often sly wit he almost single-handedly raised the medium to an art form. Evidently he relished seeing just how far he could go in a era that exercised strict watchfulness on sexual innuendo. He was not always successful, and such songs as "Love for Sale" and "My Heart Belongs to Daddy" were long kept off the radio, while others underwent bowdlerization. In his 1929 song "I'm a Gigolo," the evidently bisexual character admits that he has "just a dash" of lavender. "But in the Morning, No" disturbed the prurient on several occasions, and alterations were made. Needless to say, these and other songs have enjoyed continuing popularity as cult favorites among homosexual audiences.

BIBLIOGRAPHY. Robert Kimball, ed., *The Complete Lyrics of Cole Porter,* New York: Random House, 1983; Charles Schwartz, *Cole Porter: A Biography,* New York: Da Capo, 1977.

Ward Houser

PORTUGAL

This nation of almost ten million people in the southwestern corner of Europe has had a disproportionate effect on world history through its colonies in the New World (**Brazil**), and in Africa and Asia. Sexual attitudes, though related to those of Spain, are nonetheless distinct.

Legal Sources. The earliest information on Portuguese homosexuality stems from the legal prohibitions, which antedate the beginning of national identity in 1128. The Visigothic Code (506) of Alaric II specified the death penalty. Other punishments included public ostracism, shaving of the head, and whipping. Castration was also inflicted as a penalty.

In troubadour poetry of the thirteenth century accusations of "vice" (i.e., **sodomy**) were directed in poetry against men and women of the court, including troubadours themselves.

The *Leys e Posturas Antigas* of Afonso IV (1324–57) condemned homosexuality. Influenced by the strong Castilian repression in **Spain**, they specified that homosexuals did not have (as did other offenders) the right of refuge in a church. Two centuries later, Afonso V specified burning as the punishment, and used the hitherto-unknown terms "sodomites" for homosexuals and "sodomy" for the practice. In 1499, Manuel included punishments for women engaging in homosexual practices.

The most complete government documents are from 1571: the "ordenações Filipinas" of Felipe II of Castile (ruling also over Portugal as Felipe I). Restating the punishment of death by burning, they denied sodomites the right of burial so that their bodies would "not be remembered"; all the descendents of the victim were tainted by **infamy** and could not inherit. These laws employ the terms *o pecado nefando* (infamous sin), *contra natura* (against **nature**), and *molície* (weakness; from the Latin **mollis**). The latter term included anal and oral intercourse, solo or mutual masturbation, and frottage.

Gay Subcultures. However, the recent research of the Brazilian scholar Luiz Mott in the archives of the Portu-guese Inquisition has shown that conditions in the seventeenth century were considerably more lenient than the draconian laws would suggest. In sixteenth- and especially in seventeenth-century Portugal, there grew up a rich and energetic gay subculture. There were recognized slang terms, modes of dress, and wide use of female nicknames. There were also recognized cruising areas and sympathetic private houses in Lisbon and elsewhere where homosexuals could meet and consort with each other. A transvestite dance troup, the Dança dos Fanchonos, existed at the beginning of the seventeenth century. Homosexual practices within the clergy were also widespread, and some, including ones in positions of authority, defended sodomy, calling it "the most delicious sin," or not a sin at all. Several monarchs, including Pedro I and Afonso VI, had homosexual inclinations. The Inquisition tribunals were anything but vigorous in pursuing cases brought to their attention. While some victims were burned and others condemned to life imprisonment, the proportion suffering severe penalties, compared with countries such as Switzerland and the Netherlands, was not high.

Toward the Present. With the promulgation of the **Napoleonic** Code, legal prohibitions of homosexuality were removed. Homosexuality was covered only under the more general prohibitions of public scandal and mistreatment of minors. As a result, in nineteenth- and twentieth-century Portugal homosexuality has not been the subject of great legal persecution. During the dictatorship of 1933 to 1974, for example, while the police did arrest homosexuals found in public places, they were then taken to a police station, their identities recorded, and a symbolic fine assessed. There was no imprisonment and the cases were not pursued. Discreet activity was widespread.

The fall of the dictatorship and institution of a liberal regime in 1974 permitted the establishment of Portugal's first openly gay organization. Gay periodical publications began in 1977. Lisbon has a number of gay bars, discos, saunas, and hotels, and beach cruising is frequent. The monthly *Homo 2000* and the irregular *Órbita Gay Macho* permit contacts through advertisements. AIDS has not had a major impact in Portugal, and thanks to intelligent information campaigns, it is not seen as a gay disease.

Writings. The first novel dealing openly and tolerantly with homosexuality was *O Barão de Lavos* (1902) by Abel Botelho. A destructive poem ridiculously accusing a bishop followed. In 1918 the great Fernando **Pessoa** published *Antinous*, a treatment, in English, of the love of the Greek youth **Antinous** and the emperor **Hadrian**. In 1920 the lyric *Songs* of António Botto appeared. A minor controversy ensued, whose peak was the pamphlet *Sodoma Divinisada* of Raúl Leal (1923). This exalted pederasty as "the highest form of masculinity," which "leads to a theometaphysical unification of life."

In 1922 Portugal produced one of the landmark monographs on the whole history of homosexuality, Dr. Arlindo Camillo Monteiro's massive *Amor Sáfico e Socrático*, a volume now rare. In 1926 Dr. Asdrúbal de Aguiar published another major study, *Evolução da Pederastia e do Lesbismo na Europa*, followed by his *Medicina Legal: A Homosexualidade masculina através dos tempos* (1934). It was not until 1979, however, that the concept of homosexuality as illness disappeared from Portuguese scientific writings, with the appearance of the first volume of Júlio Gomes' work.

BIBLIOGRAPHY. Júlio Gomes, *A Homossexualidade no Mundo*, 2 vols., Lisbon: The Author, 1979–81; R. W. Howes, "Fernando Pessoa, Poet, Publisher, and Translator," *British Library Journal*, 9 (1983), 161–70; Luiz Mott, "Pagode português: a subcultura *gay* em Portugal nos tempos inquisitóriais," *Ciência e Cultura*, 40:2 (February 1988), 120–39; Mandy Vale, "Portugal," *Blueboy* (January–February 1979), 64–68.

Júlio Gomes

POULENC, FRANCIS (1899–1963)

French composer. Born into a well-to-do Parisian family of pharmaceutical manufacturers, Poulenc received his musical formation from his pianist mother. Her brother, "Oncle Papoum," introduced his nephew to the racier aspects of the entertainment world of the French capital. At the age of sixteen he began taking lessons from the homosexual pianist Ricardo Vines.

After World War I Poulenc was linked to the younger innovative French composers known as Les Six, though he was not a formal member of the group. He followed their trend of reacting against romantic sentimentality and vagueness in favor of crisp frankness of statement. Following Erik Satie, the young Poulenc sometimes imitated the comic songs of the popular music hall. In 1924 the impressario Sergei **Diaghilev** commissioned a ballet score from him, "Les Biches" (The Does), which spread his reputation throughout Europe. The saucy impertinence of his early music masked technical deficiencies—and probably personal emotions as well. After a period of aesthetic uncertainty, he reached a new maturity in 1935, signaled by his liaison with the baritone Pierre Bernac (also born in 1899). Over the years he wrote many songs for Bernac, and the two frequently appeared together in concert—foreshadowing a similar relationship between the English composer Benjamin **Britten** and the tenor Peter Pears.

After World War II Poulenc emerged as a champion of the moderate avant-garde as against the iconoclastic rigorism of Olivier Messiaen and the twelve-tone composers. Assessing his own position, he said: "I know perfectly well I'm not one of those composers who have made harmonic innovations . . ., but I think that there is room for *new* music that doesn't mind using other people's chords." His first opera, *Les Mamelles de Tirésias* (1947), was set to a proto-surrealist text by Guillaume Apollinaire. The 1957 *Dialogues des Carmélites*, about a group of nuns condemned to death in the French Revolution, is one of the few operas of the second half of the twentieth century to have secured a place in the repertory. Poulenc also wrote concertos for various combinations of instruments, incidental music for plays and films, the Mass in G (1937), and the famous "Gloria" (1959).

Although the composer is said to have had some flings with Arab boys in North Africa, during the latter part of his life he lived in an essentially spousal relationship with Bernac. Apparently he had no difficulty reconciling this liaison with his return to the Catholic faith. Often marked by witty sallies, his music was highly regarded as the outstanding exemplar in his time of the distinctive French tradition of *mélodie*. Poulenc influenced composers of many nations, including the American gay composer and diarist Ned Rorem.

BIBLIOGRAPHY. Henri Hell, *Francis Poulenc*, London: Calder, 1959.

Wayne R. Dynes

PREJUDICE

The term prejudice and its equivalents in many European languages refer primarily to a negative prejudgment reached before the pertinent information has been collected or examined and therefore based on insufficient or even imaginary evidence. As a rule, prejudice entails a negative attitude and an element of emotional charge; in addition there is usually, though not invariably, a readiness to express in deeds the rejection of others. The resulting actions are also described as embodying various degrees of **discrimination**. In practice the term prejudice has been applied primarily, if not exclusively, to populations distinguished by race, ethnic identity, language, or any combination of these. It denotes a negative evaluation of human groups perceived as different in genetic origin or in significant behavioral traits from one's own.

In his classic study of the nature of prejudice, Gordon W. Allport stated that "Prejudgments become prejudices only if they are not reversible when exposed to new knowledge." This principle implies that some irrational, unconscious determinant is shaping the feelings and opinions of the subject. The hostility which prejudice (as an umbrella term for antipathies of all kinds) engendered and the discrimination to which it may inspire the dominant segment of the population have caused so much harm and suffering (the Hitler era is the supreme example) that many investigators in the social sciences have directed their energies toward understanding and controlling what they interpreted as a form of social pathology. A crucial aspect of the maintenance of prejudice is the transmission of **stereotypes** about members of the group—beliefs that may be true in regard to a small number, but are projected onto one and all. These notions may be supported by more elaborate **myths and fabrications**, such as the fable of the destruction of **Sodom** because of the sexual indulgence of its inhabitants.

Prejudice is not a monopoly of any group, as oppressed **minorities** can develop their own ethos that includes a rejection of anything associated with the race and culture of the oppressor. Yet it would be wrong to assume that prejudice is a normal and ineradicable phenomenon of social life; its absence in young children who have not undergone acculturation argues that learning rather than nature is the crucial factor in its development.

Sexual Aspects. Sexuality plays a leading role in the maintenance of prejudice. The restriction of legitimate sexual expression to indissoluble monogamous marriage had its counterpart in the fantasies of unbridled sexual aggression, of demonic instincts lurking in tabooed, outsider groups which could at the same time be sexually exploited by the dominant one, as when its younger members were forced to become concubines, kept boys, or prostitutes serving the erotic needs of the male members of the dominant group. Pervasive fear of aggression on the part of male homosexuals (but not lesbians) underlies the accusation that homosexuals will seduce or molest anyone whom they encounter. Public opinion polls in the United States have found that 59 percent of those questioned believed that "homosexuals have unusually strong sex drives," and 35 percent agreed that "frustrated homosexuals seek out children for sexual purposes." Employers deny homosexuals jobs on the ground that they will approach fellow employees with lewd propositions.

At the same time a secret glamor attaches to the forbidden conduct; the pleasure derived from tabooed sexuality is believed more intense, more addicting than ordinary heterosexual coitus. The lure of uninhibited, promiscuous sexual gratification hovers over the gay **subculture** with its far more relaxed norms of sexual contact. The outgroup represents a threat to the moral values of Christian society, a force undermining civilization and leading to its downfall, and a violation of the order of nature. Also, the homosexual is linked with a vast conspiracy, an international **freemasonry** from which the "normal" citizen is excluded—to his professional and economic detriment—and which (so it is believed) secretly decides the fate of crucial institutions or even of the whole society.

Although an extensive literature on prejudice was produced between the 1930s and the 1960s, in no small part in reaction to the policies of Nazi Germany, the subject of antipathy to homosexuals was scarcely mentioned. Even toward the end of that time the gay movement was tiny and semi-clandestine, and those who advocated a minimum of toleration often had to mouth the traditional defamatory clichés. The fact that the Communist movement had disowned sexual reform endeavors in the mid-1930s also diminished concern with the attitudes toward sexual "**deviates**." Toward the end of the 1960s terms such as *racism* and **sexism** tended to replace the notion of prejudice. The counterpart to this in the gay movement was the expression *heterosexism*, which has achieved only a limited acceptance, and the more widely used **homophobia**. The word prejudice by contrast seemed too weak and indefinite an expression, and the role of ethnic minorities, particularly of Third World origin, in shaping the new political ambience contributed to the terminological shift.

Another relevant point is that analysts of prejudice in Western Europe and the United States tended toward interpretations derived from depth psychology, which was officially banned in the Soviet Union and little known in the revolutionary Third World. **Marxism** itself favors a simplistic, strongly economistic explanation of social phenomena, which cannot easily be transposed onto the situation of the homosexual in a culture whose tradition of intolerance stems from the later Middle Ages. The feminist notions of "patriarchy" and "male domination" have been evoked to explain the hostility visited upon the homosexual in Western culture; but conversely the notion of "homosexuality" was itself created in Western Europe in the late nineteenth century as a political response to the definitions of certain forms of sexual activity in theology and law. The particular intensity with which the taboo on homosexual activity was enforced—the imposition of compulsory heterosexuality—went so far beyond ethnic or racial prejudice, which could never deny the existence of the object of the hatred, as to be in another class of psychological phenomena altogether. Hence the term prejudice finds little application in the current discussion of the attitude of Western society toward homosexual behavior and those identified by themselves or others as homosexual.

BIBLIOGRAPHY. Barry D. Adam, *The Survival of Domination: Inferiorization* and Everyday Life, New York: Elsevier, 1978; Gordon W. Allport, The Nature of Prejudice, Reading, MA: Addison-Wesley, 1954.

Warren Johansson

PRESS, GAY

A minority group such as homosexuals needs a press of its own for particular reasons. Only at the end of the nineteenth century did periodicals meant primarily or exclusively for a homosexual or lesbian readership come into being. Such publications supplemented the mass media addressed to a general readership by providing news, commentary, advertisements, and later personal columns for individuals with special needs or interests. Thus the gay press cannot be compared to a Chinese-language or Russian-language periodical in the United States, or to an English-language newspaper in Buenos Aires or Jerusalem, which provides general news and information to a public that cannot read the idiom of the country. In other respects, however, it has had problems similar to those of the Lithuanian and Ukrainian speech communities in Tsarist Russia, which before 1905 were not allowed to have publications in their own language; these were printed in East Prussia and Austrian Galicia and smuggled across the border. Publishing houses in Paris and elsewhere on the Continent performed an analogous function by issuing books in English with homosexual themes, though it was only in the early 1950s that the Swiss monthly Der Kreis/Le Cercle began to include English articles on its pages.

Pioneers. The earliest serial publication of this kind was the *Jahrbuch für sexuelle Zwischenstufen*, edited by Magnus **Hirschfeld** in Berlin from 1899 to 1923. Modeled on an academic journal, the *Jahrbuch* featured long and sometimes ponderous articles abounding in footnotes and learned references; it also carried a remarkable annual bibliography of new books and articles compiled by Eugen Wilhelm under the pseudonym of Numa Praetorius. A second major journal was *Der Eigene*, which had originally been devoted to the arts but became the organ of the **pederastic** wing of the German homosexual **movement**, the Gemeinschaft der Eigenen; it was a de luxe publication on fine paper with illustrations in black and white, in sepia, and in color that imitated such foreign models as the *Yellow Book*. On its pages the adolescent male nude played a prominent role. With a number of significant interruptions, *Der Eigene* appeared from 1898 to 1930.

France had only two publications in the period before World War II: *Akademos*, which was issued monthly during 1909 in Paris by Count **Adelswärd Fersen**, and *Inversions*, which appeared briefly in 1925 before it was suppressed by the police at the instigation of clerical members of the Chamber of Deputies. Because of the intolerance that prevailed in the English-speaking world, no counterpart could be published. In the mid-1920s a few issues of *Friendship and Freedom* were produced by Henry **Gerber**, who was promptly arraigned for having created a homophile organization. Later, in 1934, he and Jacob Houser issued a mimeographed newsletter entitled *Chantecleer*. At this time only semi-clandestine newsletters and similar ephemeral publications could exist in the United States, while the German movement of the 1920s had a whole set of journals, from *Freundschaft und Freiheit* to *Freundin* (for lesbians).

In Switzerland a bilingual monthly called *Der Kreis/Le Cercle* began to appear in the mid-1930s, when the National Socialist seizure of power had obliterated the gay press in Germany proper. None of these early publications could appeal to a mass readership; most existed in the shadows of the world of journalism, dreading the intervention of the authorities under one pretext or another, as the sacred freedom of the press even in democratic countries never applied to journals that defended homosexuality.

After World War II. The revival of the homophile movement after World War II saw new journals emerge: in the United States *ONE* (1953–72) and *Mattachine Review* (1955–66), and for lesbians an early clandestine effort, *Vice Versa* (1947), and then the stable *The Ladder* (1956–72); in France *Arcadie* (1954–82); in the Netherlands *Vriendschap* (1948 et seq.); and in West Germany *Der Weg* (1952 et seq.). These were monthlies discreetly mailed in unobtrusive wrappers, often at first-class rates to deter postal inspection. The contents were limited to news, editorials, commentary, and illustrations more suggestive than explicit; personal advertisements could not yet appear because these would have been construed as "inciting to immorality." Only a limited readership had access to these journals, although the American ones were at times sold on newsstands.

The radical wave of the late 1960s furthered the growth of a so-called "underground press," which claimed and largely enjoyed a freedom from the taboos that had long excluded explicit treatment of sexual topics from the mainstream media. Besides using obscene language galore, they carried personal ads whose authors could uninhibitedly express their most intimate wishes. Among the best known of the underground papers were the *Berkeley Barb* and the *Berkeley Tribe*, published on the outskirts of what was to become the gay mecca of the United States. Following their example, the gay liberation movement that began with the **Stonewall** Uprising of June 1969 soon found its voice, and publications such as *Come Out!* and the *Advocate* were joined by the *Body Politic* (Toronto), *Gay* (New York City), *Gay Community News* (Boston), *Gay Sunshine* (Berkeley), and many others.

Also characteristic of the 1970s was the emergence of magazines and newsletters for gay and lesbian readers with a more specialized identity—religious, political, or professional. These were often issued by organizations or caucuses of gay members of a larger professional society or religious denomination, or local groups communicating with a membership drawn from a specific locale and carrying news of events in their own area. Some of these periodicals did not survive one or two issues; others—there are now hundreds—have become monthlies of 4 or 8 pages regularly mailed to the list of members.

For the mass reader, glossy illustrated magazines modeled on their heterosexual counterparts, with unabashedly erotic illustrations and short stories and personal and classified **advertisements** rich in explicit detail, now became part of the press. The *Advocate* and *Blueboy* in the United States, *Gai pied* and *Samouraï* in France are the best-known examples of this genre. Their articles and editorials reach a nationwide audience and create a norm of taste and opinion within the gay community. In the United States even smaller cities, such as Anchorage, AL; Raleigh, NC; and Sacramento, CA, have tabloid size newspapers; these depend heavily on advertising and are usually distributed free in bars, bookshops, and other commercial establishments. Many of these newspapers have joined together to form the Gay and Lesbian Press Association. The United States has also created scholarly periodicals: *Gai Saber* (1977–78) and *Gay Books Bulletin/Cabirion* (1979–85), both published by the Scholarship Committee of the Gay Academic Union, New York; and *Journal of Homosexuality* (1974 et seq.; edited by John De Cecco at San Francisco State University). In the Netherlands *Homologie* (1978 et seq.) provides an excellent current bibliography, while the Turin annual *Sodoma* (1984 et seq.) has achieved a particularly distinguished level of quality.

Conclusion. The existence of a periodical addressed specifically to a gay readership is a crucial part of the building of a movement in any country. Only when a common vocabulary, a shared framework of ideas and aspirations can be communicated by a specialized press can a true "gay identity" develop. Otherwise the members of the gay subculture are isolated and atomized, thrown back on their own, often limited intellectual and moral resources. It is characteristic of the Communist bloc that even where the sodomy laws tenaciously retained by previous bourgeois regimes have been repealed by fiat, no gay periodicals are allowed, even under strict Party supervision. This prohibition confirms that such regimes are unwilling to grant their homosexual citizens the right to a corporate personality, the status of a legitimate interest group with its own voice in public affairs. The gay press is the collective voice of the homosexual minority in society, and its right to exist should be defended as part of the irreducible minimum of toleration which such a community requires. It has the function of disseminating news of importance to its readers, defending their interests in public debate, and combatting efforts at defamation and persecution on the part of their political and religious foes.

BIBLIOGRAPHY. David Armstrong, *Trumpet to Arms: Alternative Media in America*, Boston: South End Press, 1981; Joachim S. Hohmann, ed., *Der Eigene: Ein Blatt für männliche Kultur*, Frankfurt am Main: Foerster, 1981; idem, *Der Kreis*, Frankfurt am Main: Foerster, 1980; H. Robert Malinowsky, *International Directory of Gay and Lesbian Periodicals*, Phoenix: Oryx Press, 1987.

Warren Johansson

PRINCE-AND-PAUPER SYNDROME

See Working Class, Eroticization of.

PRISONS, JAILS, AND REFORMATORIES

Incarceration facilities have for some time provided data for those seeking a comprehensive understanding of the full range and potential of homosexual behavior. These facilities host social worlds in which sexual acts and long-term sexual pairing between people of the same gender, who consider themselves and are generally considered by others both to be **heterosexual** ("man"/"punk" pairs), are not only common but validated by the norms of the prisoner's subculture.

General Features of Incarceration Facilities. Incarceration centers constitute a subset of the "total institution," a category which includes the several branches of the armed forces and boarding schools. Along with monasteries and nunneries, incarceration facilities are characterized by gender segregation, a limited interface with the outside world, and an official norm of sexual abstinence. Like other total institutions, confinement facilities witness a good deal of resistance on the part of their inmates to the regimentation demanded by the institution; such resistance can take the form of involvement in officially censured sexual activity.

There is a great deal of diversity among institutions holding prisoners sent to them by government as a result of criminal charges. Probably the most salient differences exist between confinement centers for males and for females, at least with regard to the prevalent sexual conditions; unless otherwise noted, the account below pertains to facilities for males, who are still nearly 19 out of every 20 prisoners in the United States, with similar ratios elsewhere. Confinement institutions for the mentally disturbed and for privately-committed juveniles have been omitted from this article for lack of data. For similar reasons, there is a focus on contemporary American institutions, which held nearly three-quarters of a million prisoners in the late 1980s at any one time and saw nearly eight million admissions over the course of a year (mostly short jail lockups for minor offenses such as public drunkenness).

Confinement institutions for adults (most commonly 18 or over, though there is considerable variation in age limits) may be divided into *prisons* and *jails*. Prisons are places of incarceration for persons serving a sentence, usually of a year or longer; they are divided by security level into maximum (long-term), medium, and minimum (short-term) security. A jail, properly speaking, is a place of detention for defendants awaiting trial or sentencing and for convicts serving misdemeanor or very short sentences. This division, which is characteristic of modern penal systems, is replicated at the juvenile level with reformatories (going by a wide variety of names) and juvenile detention centers. Both "prison" and "jail," though especially the latter, are also used as comprehensive terms for all confinement institutions.

The proportion of the general population which is incarcerated varies enormously from jurisdiction to jurisdiction; the countries with the highest rates are said to be South Africa, the Soviet Union, Cuba, and the United States. Demographically, the incarcerated population is overwhelmingly young, with the late teens and twenties predominating, and lower or working class.

Historically, widespread confinement is a relatively recent development, replacing previous criminal sanctions of execution, banishment, and short times in the stocks and pillories. Imprisonment as a punishment for crime is unknown to the Mosaic law, whether for sexual or for non-sexual offenses. The first penitentiaries were built in the United States in the nineteenth century and were soon copied by other countries, although debtor's jails existed for some time previous.

Not all penal systems have sought to banish sex from the prisoners' lives; conjugal visits were common in English jails of the seventeenth century, while in South American countries today conjugal visits are common and in many places the prisoners are allowed visits from female prostitutes. Originally, solitary confinement was the rule in the penitentiaries, but so many of the prisoners became in-sane as a result that this regime was dropped. Evidence for widespread homosexual activity in confinement is generally lacking until the twentieth century, handicapping attempts to trace its historical development; there are, however, indications that sexual patterns similar to those found today prevailed in the nineteenth century as well.

Sexual Roles in Confinement. The inmate **subculture** has its own norms and definitions of homosexual experience, which are to some extent archaic: they derive from the period before the modern industrialized-world concept of homosexuality had become even imperfectly known to the educated public, much less to the criminal underworld. In general, they seem to reflect a model of homosexuality found in ancient **Rome**, medieval **Scandinavia** and the Viking realms, and in **Mediterranean** countries into modern times: any man can be active in the sexually penetrating role without stigma, and does not thereby compromise either his masculinity or his heterosexuality. A male, on the other hand, who submits to penetration has forfeited his claim on "manhood" and is viewed with contempt *unless* he is too young to make the claim, is a powerless slave, or has become sufficiently feminine so as to never raise the claim. A salient difference from the Greek model is that the sexually passive youths are not being trained to become men, but are expected instead to become increasingly **effeminate**.

That this model is not limited to jails, prisons, and reformatories, but is also widespread (if not so sharply drawn or so clearly legitimized and institutionalized) in the lower class of the general population from which prisoners are drawn, is clear to students of sexual patterns.

Discussion of conditions in confinement, including sexual mores, is common among outlaws, so that even a juvenile delinquent who has never been locked up has some idea of the sexual system prevalent among prisoners. The model is introduced in the reform schools and reinforced in the local jails, so that by the time a convict reaches a prison, he has already been saturated with it and considers it "normal" for such institutions.

The Role of the "Man." The prison subculture is characterized by a rigid **class** system based on sexual roles. The majority of prisoners are "men" (used in quotation marks as a term of jail slang, not as a reflection on the masculinity of such individuals), also known as "jockers," "studs," "wolves," "pitchers," and the like. These prisoners are considered to be heterosexual, and most of them exhibit heterosexual patterns before and after incarceration, though a small number of macho homosexuals blend with this group by "passing." The "men" rule the roost and establish the values and behavioral norms for the entire prisoner population; convict leaders, gang members, and the organizers of such activities as the smuggling of contraband, protection rackets, and prostitution rings must be "men."

Sexually, the "men" are penetrators only; a single incident of being penetrated is sufficient for lifelong expulsion from this class. The sexual penetration of another prisoner by a "man" is sanctioned by the subculture and considered to validate the "man's" masculinity. "Manhood," however, is a tenuous condition as it is always subject to being "lost" to another, more powerful or aggressive "man"; hence a "man" is expected to "fight for his manhood."

Middle-aged and older "men" are most likely to abstain from sexual activity while incarcerated. A minority of the younger "men" also abstain, but most of the young "men" who have been incarcerated for a significant amount of time will take advantage of any opportunity for sexual relief, despite its necessarily homosexual nature. The latter, however, is not recognized by the prisoner subculture, which insists that aggressive-penetrative activity is *not* homosexual, while receptive-submissive activity is.

Some of the reasons for such involvement go beyond the necessity of relieving the sex/intimacy drive. One is that aggressive sexual activity, especially rape and possession of a known sexual receptive, are considered to validate masculine status and hence tend to protect the "man" from attempts to deprive him of that status. There is considerable peer pressure in many institutions to engage in "masculine" sexual activity because it validates such activity on the part of other "men" already engaged.

Other motivations are not as directly sexual: deprived of almost all areas of power over his own life by the regime of incarceration, a "man" often seeks to stake out a small arena of power by exerting control over another prisoner. The existence of such an island of power helps the "man" retain a sense of his own masculinity—the one social asset which he feels the administration cannot take from him—because of his identification of power and control with the masculine role or nature. For an adolescent prisoner, this motivation is often even stronger, as he has few other means of acquiring "manhood" stature. Furthermore, involvement in prohibited homosexual activity is an act of rebellion against the total institution, hence a demonstration that the institution's control over that person is less than complete.

Prisoners serving long terms are often looking for a companion to "do time" with; such "men" tend to rely less on aggression and more on persuasion in their search for someone to "settle down" with, but they are not above arranging for a confederate to supply the coercion needed to "turn out" someone for this purpose.

As the demand for sexual partners always far exceeds the supply, however, only a minority of the "men" succeed in obtaining possession of a partner; these tend to be the highest-ranking "men" in the prisoner power structure. The remainder, including some "men" who would be able to claim and retain a sexual partner but who choose not to do so for various reasons, make use of prostitution, join in gang-rapes, borrow sexual submissives from friends who control them, or do without. "Men" who are without sexual outlet altogether may be considered marginal in their claim to "man" status, and targeted for violent demotion.

The Role of the "Queen." A second class consists of the **"queens,"** also known as "bitches," "ladies," and so forth. These are effeminate homosexuals whose sexual behavior behind bars is not markedly different from their patterns "on the street." They are strictly receptive (penetrated) and are generally as feminine in appearance and dress as the local administration will allow. By prison convention, these prisoners are considered to be females in every possible way, e.g., their anus is termed "pussy," they take female names, and are referred to using female pronouns. The queens are submissive to the "men" and may not hold positions of overt power in the inmate social structure.

Known or discovered homosexuals who enter confinement without a feminine **identity** are relentlessly pressured to assume one; the idea of a homosexual who is not a substitute female is too threatening to be tolerated. The more extreme the contrast between the effeminized homosexual and the super-macho "men," the more psychologically safe distance is placed between the "men's" behavior and the notion of homosexuality.

In some prisons and many jails and reformatories, queens are segregated from the general population and placed in special units, referred to by the prisoners as "queens' tanks." There they are often denied privileges given to the general population such as attendance at the recreation hall, yard exercise, library call, hot food, and the like. The rationale given for such units is to protect the homosexuals (who generally would prefer to pair off with the "men" instead) and reduce homosexuality, though in practice it simply increases the frequency of rape among the remaining population.

The actual life of prison homosexuals, it should be clear, has little or nothing to do with the ideals propagated by the gay movement, which have barely affected prison life. There is little room for the independent, self-affirming homosexual, who upon entering confinement faces the choice of "passing" as a heterosexual "man," submitting to the subservient role of the "queen," or risking his life in combat time after time. Only the toughest of homosexuals can even seriously consider the third option.

The Role of the "Punk." The lowest class (though the difference between the two non-"men" classes is often minimal) consists of those males who are forced into the sexually receptive role; they are called **"punks,"** "fuck-boys," "sweet kids," and other terms. The overwhelming majority of these punks are heterosexual in orientation; they are "turned out" (a phrase suggesting an **inversion** of their gender) by rape, usually gang rape, convincing threat of rape, or intimidation. Punks retain some vestiges of their male identity and tend to resist the feminizing process promoted both by the "men" and by the queens; upon release they usually revert to heterosexual patterns, though often with disruptions associated with severe male rape trauma syndrome.

Punks often try to escape their role by transferring to another cell block or institution, but almost always their reputation follows them: "once a punk, always a punk."

Punks tend to be younger than the average inmate, smaller, and less experienced in personal combat or confinement situations; they are more likely to have been arrested for non-violent or victimless offenses, to be middle class, and to belong to ethnic groups which are in the minority in the institution.

Relations between queens and punks are often tense, as the former tend to look down on the latter while trying to recruit them into their ranks, a process which the latter resent, though some may succumb to it over the years.

In subsequent usage, when both queens and punks are meant, the American prison slang word "catcher," which includes both (as the opposite of "pitcher," both terms derived from the sport of baseball) will be used here.

The percentage of queens in an incarcerated population is usually very small, from none to a few percent. The number of punks is usually much larger, given the unrelenting demand on the part of the "men" for sexual catchers; nevertheless, the supply of punks never approaches the demand, so that the majority of the population is always "men." The number of punks tends to rise with the security level of the institution, as the longer the prison term, the more risks will be taken by an aggressive "man" to "turn out" a punk for his own use. Big-city jails and reform schools are also considered to have relatively high populations of punks.

Relationships. In ongoing sexual relationships, a "man" is paired ("hooked up") with a catcher; no other possibilities, such as a pair of homosexuals, are tolerated, but this one is not only tolerated but sanctioned by the prisoner subculture. These relationships are taken very seriously, as they involve an obligation on the part of the "man" to defend his partner, violently if necessary, and on the part of the catcher to obey his "man." Catchers are required to engage in "wifely" chores such as doing laundry, making the bunk, keeping the cell clean, and making coffee. Owing to the shortage of catchers, only a minority of "men" succeed in entering into such a relationship, and the competition for available catchers is intense, sometimes violent.

The impetus manifested by the "men" to form pairs is remarkable in light of the many disadvantages in doing so, for the "man" not only risks having to engage in lethal combat on behalf of someone else and hence suffer for his catcher's blunders, seductiveness, or good looks, but he also greatly increases his vulnerability to administrative discipline by increasing his profile and the predictability of his prohibited sexual activities. The fact that so many "men" seek to form pairs rather than find sexual release through rape, prostitution, etc. is strong testimony for the thesis that such relationships meet basic human needs which are related to, but not identical with, the sexual one, such as a need for affection or bonding.

Sometimes the "man" part of the relationship is actually a collective, so that a catcher may belong to a group of "men" or to a whole gang. Ownership of a catcher tends to give high status to the "man" and is often a source of revenue since the "man," who is often without substantial income, can then establish himself in the prostitution business. These relationships are usually but not always exploitive and they often result from aggression on the part of the "man"; the catcher may or may not have consented before the "man" "puts a claim" on him.

The relationship of involuntary to voluntary sexual activity inside prison is a complex one. Many continuing and isolated liaisons originate in gang rape, or in the ever present threat of gang rape. Prison officials can label such behavior as "consensual," but fear on the part of the passive partner is certainly a prime stimulus.

"Free-lance" or unpaired catchers are not very common, since they are usually unable to protect themselves and are considered to be fair game for any aggressive "man." Usually, a gang-rape or two is sufficient to persuade an unattached catcher to pair off as soon as possible. A catcher who breaks free from an unwanted pairing is called a "renegade."

Pair relationships are based on an adaptation of the heterosexual model which the prisoners bring with them from the street; the use of this model also validates the jail relationship while confirming the sense of masculinity of the "man." The "men" tend to treat their catchers much as they habitually did their female companions, so a wide range of relationships ranging from ruthless exploitation to love are encountered.

Emotional involvement by the "men" is less common than "on the street," but not rare; long-term prisoners may even "get married" in an imitation ceremony to which the whole cell block may be invited. A little-noted emotional significance of the relationship for almost all the "men," however, is that it becomes an island of relaxation away from the constantly competitive jungle, with its continual dangers and fear of exposing anything which might be considered a "weakness," that mark social relations between the "man" and other "men." Confident in his male role, the "man" can allow himself to drop the hard mask which he wears outside the relationship and express with his catcher the otherwise-suppressed aspects of his humanity, such as caring, tenderness, anxiety, and loneliness.

Sexual reciprocation is rare, and when it does occur, is almost always kept highly secret.

Another noteworthy alteration from the heterosexual model is that the "men" tend to be considerably more casual about allowing other men sexual access to their catchers than they would with regard to their females. The catchers are frequently loaned to other "men" out of friendship or to repay favors or establish leadership in a clique, and are commonly prostituted. Unlike their females, the jail catchers will not get pregnant by another man. It is very important, however, for a "man" to retain control over such access to his catcher.

The punks, who retain a desire for an insertive role which they cannot find in sex with their "men," sometimes reciprocate with one another, giving each a tem-porary chance to play the "male" role which is otherwise denied them.

As queens are highly valued, being both scarce and feminine-appearing, they tend to have a little more autonomy than the punks, who are for all practical purposes slaves and can be sold, traded, and rented at the whim of their "man." The most extreme forms of such slavery, which can also apply to queens, are found in the maximum-security institutions and some jails.

Rape. Perhaps the most dreaded of all jailhouse experiences is forcible **rape**. This phenomenon, while it has much in common with rape of males in the community, is distinguished by its institutionalization as an accepted part of the prisoner subculture. Most common in urban jails and in reformatories, gang rape (and the common threat of it) is the principal device used to convert "men" into punks.

In the subculture of the prison those with greater strength and knowledge of inmate lore prey on the weaker and less knowledgeable. Virtually every young male entering a confinement institution will be tested to see whether he is capable of maintaining his "manhood"; if a deficiency is spotted, he will be targeted. Sometimes an aggressive "man" will seek to "turn" the youngster using non-violent techniques such as psychological dependence, seduction, contraband goods, drugs, or offers of protection. There is a great variety of "turning out" games in use, and with little else to do, much time can be spent on them.

If these techniques fail, or if the patience or desire to use them is absent, or if a rival's game is to be pre-empted, violent rape may be plotted. Usually this is a carefully planned operation involving more than one rapist ("booty bandit," "asshole bandit"). The other participants in a gang rape may sometimes have little sexual interest in the proceedings, but need to reaffirm that they are one of the "men," to retain membership in the group led by militant aggressors. In the absence of such positive identification, they would expose themselves to becoming victims.

The aggressor selects the arena for the contest, initiates the conflict, and deliberately makes the victim look as helpless, weak, and inferior as possible. The usual response is a violent defense which, if successful, will discourage further attempts. Frequently the target is seized by a number of rapists under circumstances which do not even allow a defense. Sometimes the attack will be discontinued even when the attacker (or attackers) has the advantage, so long as the victim puts up a vigorous fight and thereby demonstrates his "manhood." In other cases, especially with particularly young and attractive newcomers, the assault will be pressed with whatever force and numbers it takes to subdue the victim. If the victim forcibly resists, he is liable to be wounded or mutilated, in no small part because he has no experience or skill in the use of knives and the like.

Defenses used to preempt a rape by knowledgeable but vulnerable newcomers include paying for protection, joining a gang, and being sponsored by relatives or friends already locked up.

Rape in prisons is less frequent than in jails and reform schools because most prisoners who are vulnerable to rape will have already learned to accommodate themselves to the punk role in jail or reform school and will "hook up" with a protector shortly after arrival. Nevertheless, rape remains a feature of prison life since the testing process is never really concluded and the demand for punks is always high. In a minimum-security prison, rape is uncommon because few "men" want to assume the risks involved and the separation from females tends to be short or release imminent; in a maximum-security prison rape is far more prevalent because the prisoners are more violent to begin with, are more willing to take the risks involved, and feel a more intense need for sexual partners.

The psychological roots of jail rape are complex, but it is clear that the primary motivation for the rapist lies more in the area of power deprivation than sexual deprivation, though the role of the latter should not be underestimated. In the eyes of the perpetrator the victim is less a sexual object than a means of exhibiting male dominance and superiority of the rapist. That physical qualities are significant, however, is shown by the fact that obese or older inmates are rarely selected as victims.

From a sociological perspective, rape functions as a violent *rite de passage* to convert "men" into punks in order to meet part of the demand for sexual partners. Most jail rape victims quickly "hook up" with a "man" (not necessarily the lead rapist) in order to avoid repetitive gang-rapes; some enter "protective custody" (often called "punk city") but usually find it impossible to remain there indefinitely, or find the promised protection to be illusory; some take violent revenge on their assailant(s) at a later date, risking both death and a new prison term; others commit suicide.

The rape of an "attached" catcher is also a direct challenge to his "man," who must retaliate violently, according to the prison code, or give up his claim on the catcher and be targeted for rape himself.

It should also be mentioned that when the combination of easy victims and administrative pressure against pair-bonding arises, as it often does, it becomes less risky to commit rapes than to commit oneself to an ongoing consensual relationship.

The rape problem has **class** aspects as well: the middle-class white who finds himself in an institution where he is a total stranger to its subculture, its language, even the tricks and stratagems played on unwary newcomers, simply lacks the survival skills requisite for the prison milieu, while the repeated offender of lower-class or delinquent background has mastered all of them, even if he is not adroit enough in his calling to escape the clutches of the law.

A further dimension of prison rape is the racial issue. In the United States, rape often takes on a racial dynamic as a means by which the dominant ethnic group (usually but not always black) in the institution intimidates the others. Whether or not blacks constitute a majority or plurality of the prison population, the aggressor in rape tends to be black, the victim to be white or Puerto Rican. A study by Alan J. Davis of 129 separate incidents in the Philadelphia prison system showed that:

13 percent involved white aggressors and white victims

29 percent involved black aggressors and black victims

56 percent involved black aggressors and white victims

Hence 85 percent of the aggressors were black, 69 percent of the victims were white. The motivation for the crime is not primarily sexual; it is conceived as an act of revenge against a member of white society collectively regarded as exploiting and oppressing the black race. Among older boys in a reform school, the white victim was often forced to submit to a black in full view of others so that they could witness the humiliation of the white and the domination by the black. Gang rapes are typically perpetrated by black inmates from urban areas serving sentences for major crimes such as armed robbery and assault with a deadly weapon. The white inmates are often disadvantaged in the prison setting if they have not been part of a delinquent subculture in the outside world, and they lack the sense of racial solidarity that furnishes the blacks with a group ethos and the collective will to oppose the official norms of the prison and to risk the penalties attached to fighting, even in self-defense.

Further, in some institutions blacks commit acts of sexual aggression to let the white inmates collectively know that the black inmates are the dominant element, even if they are involuntarily behind bars. It is essential to their concept of manhood to make white prisoners the victims of their assaults, and they resent the black homosexuals in the prison, whom they identify as weak and effeminate. This whole pattern of symbolic acts is first inculcated in reform schools and then carried over into the penitentiaries where the offenders are sent for the offenses of their mature years. As the black population of the United States has ceased to be concentrated almost entirely in the states of the historic Confederacy, as it was before World War I, and is now spread more evenly over the territory of the Union, the share of blacks in the prison population of other states has risen, so that a more homogeneous institutional subculture now exists in which whites are the dominated and exploited class.

Thus far the white prisoners have generally not developed their own sense of solidarity in order to cope with the threats inherent in the situation.

Prevalence. As noted above, reliable statistics on the extent of homosexuality in confinement are notably lacking. However, some figures are worth citing from a study by Wayne Wooden and Jay Parker. It must be kept in mind that these figures derive from a low-medium-security prison, that they apply only to incidents affecting the prisoners while in that particular prison (thus omitting previous "turn-outs" by rape), that the percentages apply to prisoners of all age groups and races taken together, and that the authors themselves emphasized that "our study is likely *underreporting* certain types of sexual behavior (i.e., sexual coercion and assault)."

This study found that 55 percent of all (self-designated) heterosexuals reported being involved in sexual activity while in that prison, this figure breaking down into 38 percent of whites, 55 percent of Hispanics, and 81 percent of blacks; that 14 percent of all the prisoners (9 percent of heterosexuals and 41 percent of homosexuals) had been sexually assaulted there; that 19 percent of all the prisoners (100 percent of homosexuals and 10 percent of heterosexuals) were currently "hooked up."

Looking at the (self-designated) homosexuals alone, 64 percent reported receiving some type of pressure to engage in sex (82 percent of whites, 71 percent of Hispanics, 19 percent of blacks) and 11 percent had been forced into it. Disciplinary action for sex had been taken against 71 percent, while 35 percent were engaged in prostitution. An eye-opener for some gay consumers of pornography featuring jailhouse sex may be the report by 77 percent of the homosexuals that they had better sex "on the street" and by 78 percent that they were "looked down upon and treated with disrespect by other inmates."

The Davis study of the Philadelphia jail system, based upon interviews with 3,304 prisoners, estimated that the number of sexual assaults in the 26 months of the study was about 2000; during this period some 60,000 men passed through the system. Of these assaults, only 96 were reported to prison authorities, only 64 were mentioned in prison records, only 40 resulted in disciplinary action, and only 26 were reported to the police for prosecution.

Jailhouse Sexual Mores. Sexual activity in confinement may take place nearly anywhere; the expectation of privacy which prevails in other circumstances often gives way to necessity. Furthermore, it is often to a "man's" advantage to be seen engaging in "masculine" sexual activity by other prisoners, enhancing his reputation as a "man." For these reasons, sex is often a group activity with some participants taking turns standing "lookout" for guards or shooing away uninvolved prisoners from the area being used.

While disciplinary codes in confinement institutions are nearly unanimous in outlawing all sexual activity, these codes usually have little more effect than to ensure that sex takes place outside the view of the guards. They do, however, inhibit catchers from enlisting the aid of administrators in avoiding rape situations, given the fact that such avoidance usually requires pairing off with a protector. The furtive nature of consensual activities and pairings necessitated by the disciplinary codes also works to dehumanize them and favor the quick mechanical relief as distinguished from an affectionate relationship.

The severe sanctions provided by the prisoner code against informers protect even rapists from being reported to the administration by their victims. These fear retaliation from the perpetrators, who can be well placed in terms of the inmate power structure—and famed for their criminal ruthlessness and daring. The aggressor is usually guilty of the far more serious crime, while the victim may have committed only a trivial one. Officials usually have a general idea of what is going on, based on reports from informers, but these reports cannot be made openly enough to provide a basis for disciplinary action.

The openness of jailhouse sexuality, in spite of disciplinary codes, is one of its most remarkable features. The institution of "hooking up" that is the heart of the system, and that specifies that any catcher who is "hooked up" may be "disrespected" only at the risk of violent retaliation from his "man," is dependent on general knowledge of the specifics of such pairings among the entire incarcerated population. Virtually the first result of a claim being laid on a catcher is its announcement to the prisoner population at large; sex is the number one topic of conversation, and the news that a new punk has been "turned out" spreads like wildfire throughout an institution.

Under such circumstances, guards and administrators with their eyes open can hardly fail to be aware of pairings.

Often, in fact, housing moves are made to facilitate keeping the pair together; practical experience has shown that this tends to minimize fights and therefore keeps the general peace, which is the first priority of all officials. Thus when a "man" in a double cell acquires a catcher, he "persuades" his current cellmate to request a move out, the new catcher requests a move in, the catcher's current cellmate is prompted to request that he be moved out, and the administration approves it to keep the peace among all concerned. A particularly dangerous situation is one in which a catcher is bunked with a "man" other than the one he is hooked up with. For this reason punks are often celled together, as are queens.

Female Institutions. It is not known whether the incidence of homosexuality in prison is higher in male or female populations. One survey that used the same criterion for male and female inmates reported the same incidence in both.

The role of the female inmate in lesbian activity is precisely defined by the prison subculture. The "penitentiary turnout" is the woman who resorts to lesbian relations because the opposite sex is unavailable; in contrast, the "lesbian" prefers homosexual gratification even in the outside world, and thus is equated with the queen in the men's prison. The lesbian is labeled as sick by some of the other inmates because the preference in a situation of choice is deemed a perversion. The participant in lesbian relations who does so for lack of choice is not so stigmatized.

The "femme" or "mommy" is the inmate who takes the female role in a lesbian relationship, a role highly prized because most of the inmates still wish to play the feminine role in a significant way in prison. In the context of a pseudo-marital bond, the femme continues to act out many of the functions allotted to the wife in civil society. The complement is the "stud broad" or "daddy" who assumes the male role, which in its turn is accorded much prestige for three reasons: (1) the stud invests the prison with the male image; (2) the role is considered more difficult to sustain over a period of time because it goes against the female grain; (3) the stud is expected not just to assume certain symbols of maleness, but also to personify the social norms of male behavior.

In sharp contrast with the men's prison, homosexual relations are established voluntarily and with the consent of the partners; no physical coercion is applied to the weaker or feminine partner. Interpersonal relations linked with homosexuality play a major role in the lives of the female prisoners. Cast as a quasi-marital union, the homosexual pair is viewed by the inmates as a meaningful personal and social relationship. Even though for previously heterosexual women this mode of adjustment is difficult, the uniqueness of the prison situation obliges the inmate to attach new meaning to her behavior.

When a stud and a femme have established their union, they are said to be "making it" or to "be tight," which is to say that other inmates recognize them socially as a "married" pair. Since the prisoners attach a positive value to sincerity, the "trick"—one who is simply exploited sexually or economically—is held in low esteem by the inmate subculture. Tricks are also regarded as "suckers" and "fools" because their lovers dangle unkept promises in front of them. The "commissary hustler" is the woman who establishes more than one relationship; besides an alliance with an inmate in the same housing unit, she also maintains relations with one or more inmates in other housing units for economic advantage. The other women, labeled tricks in the prison argot, supply her with coveted material items which she shares only with the "wife" in her own unit. The femme may even encourage and guide the stud in finding and exploiting the tricks. The legitimacy of the primary pseudo-marriage is not contested, though the tricks may anticipate replacing the femme when a suitable opportunity arises.

Writers on female institutions agree that, apart from sexual relationships, such institutions are marked by quasi-family social units which provide emotional support to their members, in sharp contrast to the ever-competitive male environments.

Administrative Attitudes. There is, as may be expected, a wide range of administrative attitudes toward both violent and consensual homosexuality in their confinement institutions. Consensual activities are accepted as inevitable by some, hunted out and seriously punished when discovered by others, while most tend to look the other way so long as the behavior does not become disruptive or too open.

Convicts have charged that administrators too often exploit rape as a tool to divide and control the inmate population, particularly in connection with racial tensions. A state commission investigating the unusually violent New Mexico prison riot (1980) found that officials used the threat of placement of new inmates in cells with known rapists to recruit informers. Other administrations have been charged with setting vulnerable prisoners up for gang rape in order to discharge tensions within a housing unit or reward it for keeping quiet. Administrators are aware that a difficult or disliked prisoner can be maneuvered into a position where he will be sexually victimized by his fellow inmates. In other cases the staff is simply resigned to what is happening inside the institution and turns a blind eye to the sexual violence. Administrators themselves deny such actions and universally proclaim their opposition to rape, while often saying that it is no problem in their own institution.

The uniformed guards often have a different set of attitudes. Some of them consider all participants in homosexual activity to be homosexuals; some display considerable homophobia and engage in private witch-hunts. Others, especially those with long experience as guards, may encourage a "man" whom they consider to be dangerous to get "hooked up" with a catcher on the theory that paired-off "men" are less likely to cause major trouble. Guards are also involved in setting up some rapes and sexual encounters, in exchange for payoffs or for such diverse reasons as to destroy the leadership potential of an articulate prisoner. The guards are capable even of ignoring the screams of a prisoner who is being raped. The guards may even tell the prisoner that to file charges against the aggressor would be tantamount to publicizing his own humiliation, just as a public rape trial in the outside world exposes the female victim to shame and embarrassment.

Writings on Sex in Confinement. A good deal has been written in scholarly style, in North America at least, concerning homosexual behavior in prisons, jails, and reformatories. Much of this literature is fraught with controversy, and the views of penologists, often concerned more with institutional control and abstract theorizing on "the problem of homosexuality" than with actual behavioral patterns, tend to differ both normatively and descriptively from the accounts of inmates. Penologists reflect the concerns of their employers, who usually seek to minimize aspects of life in their institutions which would arouse public indignation, and who are usually hostile to all forms of sexual contact among prisoners. The conclusions of a recent paper cited in *Criminal Justice Abstracts*, that "greater efforts to deter . . . consensual homosexual activity" are needed, are not untypical for penological writings.

Complicating the matter is the extreme difficulty, which is often glossed over, of a non-imprisoned investigator, usually someone associated with the administration (at least in the eyes of the prisoners), seeking to obtain reliable data on behavior which violates disciplinary codes and which is as secretive as the most sensitive aspect of underworld life can be to the prying eyes of outsiders. As a result, armchair theorizing, remote from the actual behavior which is supposed to be its subject, is endemic to the formal literature.

A few non-penological psychologists and at least one sociologist (Wayne Wooden) have published useful studies in the 1980s, but it is noteworthy that only one comprehensive survey of sexual behavior in a prison (a low-medium-security California institution) has found its way into print (the Wooden-Parker book *Men Behind Bars*, for which Jay Parker gathered information while a prisoner). The only systematic investigation of sexual behavior (in this case rape) in jails (the Philadelphia system) was reported in 1968 by Alan J. Davis. Reliable statistics for juvenile institutions are apparently non-existent, though reform schools have been described as the incarceration facilities where sexual activity is most common, and as the locus in which habitual criminals first acquire the mores governing sexual expression in the prisoner subculture.

Accounts written by prisoners or ex-prisoners have usually taken the form of autobiography or fiction, and these also tend to draw veils over areas which might reflect unfavorably on the writer in presenting himself to the general public, such as rape and homosexuality. Former prisoners also tend to remain silent concerning their sexual experiences in confinement when conversing with people who have not shared that environment, former "punks" being most loath to disclose anything about their humiliating sexual role.

Novels by Jean **Genet** have depicted homosexuality in French reform schools and prisons, and these are the only widely read books dealing with the subject, though one must hesitate to conclude too much from Genet's hallucinogenic-fantastic writings. Billy Hayes' autobiographical *Midnight Express* (1977)

gave an explicit account of the author's homosexual experiences in Turkish prisons. Karlheinz Barwasser wrote from a gay inmate's point of view on German prisons in *Schwulenhetz im Knast* (1982), while Robert N. Boyd did the same on the California prison system in *Sex Behind Bars* (1984). The only systematic account from a "punk's" perspective can be found in Donald Tucker's revealing "A Punk's Song" in Anthony Scacco's 1982 anthology, *Male Rape*. A third-person novel which has dealt candidly with prison sex, based on the author's experience in the California system, is *On the Yard* (1967) by Malcolm Braly; a play by Canadian ex-inmate John Herbert, *Fortune and Men's Eyes* (1967), made into a movie in 1971, revolves around sexuality in a reformatory. There are numerous gay pornographic books featuring an incarceration setting, but very few of them have been written by former inmates and they are generally extremely inaccurate.

Theories of Prison Homosexuality. Two major theories have been advanced by penologists to account for prison homosexuality: the Importation Model and the Deprivation Model. The Importation Model suggests that the "problem" of homosexuality exists in a prison because it has been brought in from outside, the Deprivation Model assigns it to the conditions of incarceration where it is found.

The Importation Model rests on studies showing that the variable of previous homosexual experience is significant for predicting homosexual activity in prison. It alone accounted for 29 percent of the variance of the individuals' scores on an index of homosexuality. Its major flaw is that much of the prior homosexuality— including aggression against other prisoners—is likely to be imported from other incarceration programs rather than from the larger society outside prison. The variable of prison homosexuality is not a pure measure of importation free of the effects of imprisonment, since convicts have often served previous sentences, some as adolescents in reform schools. The aftereffects of such periods of incarceration are difficult to unravel from the impact of the outside world. In one study, two-thirds of those reporting prison homosexuality indicated that their first experience had occurred in a reform school. However, the validity of this finding is weakened by the absence of comparable data from non-correctional institutions: how many young adults involved in homosexuality had their first experience while enrolled in high school?

An Importation Theory might more legitimately be focused on the concepts applied to sexual activity in confinement by the prisoners. There is little doubt that the dominant group seeks to apply the heterosexual models with which it is familiar from the outside world to the female-deprived prison society; if there are no females around, they will be created. The particular application of this model draws from **working-class** ideas of masculinity and homosexuality already mentioned. Only with respect to the punks—admittedly an indispensable element—does the prisoner culture depart from these ideas in upholding the notion of the "fall from manhood" and rationalizing its violent inducement through the act of rape.

The Deprivation Model focuses on the negative aspects of the prison experience as a cause of homosexuality. The deprivation model predicts that persons and institutions that associate high pains and intense suffering with imprisonment are more likely to have homosexual experience. Advocates of this view also assume that the harsh, depriving conditions of custody-oriented, maximum-security prisons would favor the development of homosexual patterns. Yet this prediction is belied by a study finding more prison homosexuality in a treatment-oriented prison (37 percent) than in a custody-oriented one (21 percent). The only positive correlations found are with the degree of isolation from the prisoner's family and friends, and the distance from home. The

element of loneliness caused by the deprivation of the prison experience may contribute to the need for sexual affection and gratification.

Perhaps it would be too much to suggest that penologists consider a Deprivation Theory which posits that homosexuality results from the sexual, affectional, and emotional deprivation of prisoners who would, if given the opportunity, otherwise continue their heterosexuality. Such a theory, however, would also have to take into account the question of power deprivation, which might motivate sexual assaults on other prisoners even if females were readily available. Another question which has yet to be addressed is why pecking-order contests are resolved in a sexual rather than some other manner.

Incarceration as Punishment for Homosexual Conduct. Imprisonment for homosexual offenses is a comparatively modern innovation. For no infraction of its commandments does the Mosaic Law prescribe imprisonment as a penalty, and as the punishment for sodomy, late medieval law decreed castration, banishment, or death. In practice, if not in law, eighteenth-century England commuted the death penalty for buggery to exposure in the pillory—a fate almost worse than death—together with a term of imprisonment, and when the punishment of hanging established by 5 Eliz. I c. 17 was finally abolished in 1861, the sentence was reduced only to penal servitude for life. In 1885 the **Criminal Law Amendment Act** prescribed a sentence of two years for "gross indecency" between males. One can question the logic of sentencing a man found guilty of homosexual acts with other males to confinement for years or even for life in an exclusively male community, but the legislatures of the nineteenth and early twentieth centuries evidently had no qualms.

Though until recently homosexual acts were illegal in most American states, relatively few men and fewer women were imprisoned for violating such laws.

More frequent was the incarceration of convicted pedophiles, which still continues. Far more homosexuals arrive in local jails for prostitution (particularly "street transvestites"), and other—usually nonviolent—offenses.

Conclusion. The patterns of sexual behavior and sexual exploitation documented in recent studies have a long history. In the nineteenth century such behavior could simply be dismissed as another sordid aspect of "prison vice," but with the coming of a more scientific approach prison administrators have had to confront this issue at least in terms of the effect on the inmates whom they held in custody. Isolation and maximum-security wards for obvious homosexual prisoners were attempted, but they did not keep the young and physically slight prisoner with no previous homosexual experience from being victimized. The lurking danger for the individual prisoner has become so overt that an appellate court has even upheld the right of a prisoner to escape if he surrenders to the authorities within a reasonable time, and courts of the first instance have hesitated to send convicted persons to prison because of the likelihood that they would be exposed to sexual violence.

Proposals for reform include new systems of inmate classification based on scoring devices designed to indicate the level of security required for each prisoner. However, the state often does not have available space within suitably differentiated facilities to provide the correct berth for each prisoner. A more fundamental flaw with such proposals is that they do not address the reasons for sexual aggression, so that present patterns are likely to replicate themselves within each classification level.

One strategy which, so far, has yet to be tried would be to legalize consensual sexuality in prison and encourage the formation of stable, mutually supportive pair-bonds in that context, while reserving the full weight of administrative attention and discipline for rape. With administra-tors continuing to regard both rape and consensual homosexuality as problems to be equally eliminated, such suggestions have produced only "we can't sanction homosexuality" replies.

So long as the sex-segregated prison remains society's answer to crime, the issues of rape and of consensual homosexual behavior behind prison bars are likely to persist. So, also, will the strong suggestion that most sexually active heterosexuals, deprived of access to the opposite sex and not discouraged by their peers from doing so, will eventually turn to another person of the same sex, and may even become emotionally attached to that person. The full implications of that statement, supported as it is by a considerable body of experience, for our concepts of sexual **orientation** and potential, have yet to be explored.

See also **Situational Homosexuality.**

BIBLIOGRAPHY. Robert N. Boyd, *Sex Behind Bars: A Novella, Short Stories, and True Accounts,* San Francisco: Gay Sunshine Press, 1984; Alan J. Davis, "Sexual Assaults in the Philadelphia Prison System and Sheriff's Vans," *Transaction,* 6:2 (1968), 8–16; Rose Giallolombardo, *Society of Women: A Study of a Women's Prison,* New York: John Wiley, 1966; Alice M. Propper, *Prison Homosexuality: Myth and Reality,* Lexington, MA: Lexington Books, 1981; Anthony M. Scacco, Jr., *Rape in Prison,* Springfield, IL: Charles C. Thomas, 1975; Anthony M. Scacco, Jr., ed., *Male Rape: A Casebook of Sexual Aggressions,* New York: AMS Press, 1982; Hans Toch, *Living in Prison: The Ecology of Survival,* New York: The Free Press, 1977; Wayne S. Wooden and Jay Parker, *Men behind Bars: Sexual Exploitation in Prison,* New York: Plenum Press, 1982.

Stephen Donaldson

PRIVACY

The right to privacy—freedom from unauthorized or unjustified intrusion—has become relevant to the issue of homosexuality because of the role that has befallen it as an argument for homosexual rights. Legal and philosophical literature of the 1980s abounded in pieces arguing that the right of privacy should or should not be extended to the homosexual behavior of consenting adults in private.

Antecedents. Recent in its practical application, the right is nonetheless grounded in a long-established dichotomy. The notion of the private as distinct from the public realm goes back to classical antiquity, to the contrasting Greek adjectives *idiotikos* and *demosios*, for which Latin used the equivalents *privatus* and *publicus*. In a much-discussed passage, **Cicero** has the phrase *res publica, quae . . . populi res est*, which means simply that the adjective *publicus* is equivalent to the genitive of *populus*: the commonwealth is the property of the people (*De re publica*, I, c. 26). Hence the public is that which belongs to or concerns the *demos*, the *populus*; the private is a matter for the individual citizen. Privacy, be it noted, was not a term of Roman law or in the Romance languages; it made its appearance in English only at the close of the Elizabethan era, while French legal texts must still resort to the paraphrase *vie privée* to express the notion contained in English *privacy*.

Common Law. The right of privacy entered the **common law** tradition in the middle of the eighteenth century as the heir to a long series of judicial precedents dating back almost to the Norman Conquest (1066) that protected the sanctity of individual property rights. The initial logic was that the law should protect a man's letters from unauthorized use by others, not on the ground that his privacy had been invaded, but rather that his property had been stolen. In three English cases of 1741, 1820, and 1849 respectively, the right of privacy was asserted as a kind of property right. Further than this the English courts did not go, and it was left for the American interpreters of the common law to develop the modern concept of privacy.

American Law. It was a technological innovation, not a theoretical one, that proved the catalyst. Photography at its outset was a time-consuming procedure that required the full consent and self-discipline of the subject. However, the moment that instantaneous photography was introduced commercially, pictures could be taken "in a flash" without the knowledge or permission of the subject. The unauthorized use of such photographs by the "yellow" press of the 1880s for purposes of scandal inspired two young Boston lawyers to act. On December 15, 1890 the *Harvard Law Review* published an article "The Right to Privacy" by Samuel D. Warren and Louis D. Brandeis—an article so splendidly conceived and executed that Dean Roscoe Pound later deemed it to have done nothing less than add a chapter to the law. Warren, a scion of a socially prominent and wealthy Massachusetts family, had been offended by the press coverage of his own social life in his home in Boston's exclusive Back Bay, and the outcome was the article written literally *pro domo*.

The article began with a succinct account of how the common law principle that "the individual shall have full protection in person and in property" had developed so that in the case of property its principles extended to the products and processes of the mind. It went on to assert that "Instantaneous photographs and newspaper enterprise have invaded the sacred precincts of private and domestic life; and numerous mechanical devices threaten to make good the prediction that 'what is whispered in the closet shall be proclaimed from the house tops.'" The two authors concluded that "the protection afforded to thoughts, sentiments, and emotions expressed through the medium of writing or of the arts, so far as it consists in preventing publication, is merely an instance of the enforcement of the more general right of the individual to be let alone." They appealed to the common law notion, not always honored in practice, that "a man's house" is "his castle, impregnable, often, even to its own officers engaged in the execution of its commands." Even at the time the article appeared, reasonable men differed widely as to how much this so-called right of privacy owed to history and how much to imagination. The article partook of both the past and the future, and in the course of the twentieth century, the positions taken on the issue have determined in large part whether the courts or the legislatures would emerge as guardians of privacy.

This argument applied only to the sphere of civil law. Criminal acts as such were crimes whether committed in public or in private. However, the common law also knew offenses that were criminal because they were committed in public or in such a manner as to become a public nuisance. The **Criminal Law Amendment Act** of 1885, moreover, had made acts of indecency between males punishable whether "committed in public or in private," and the supporters of the recommendations of the Wolfenden Committee focused attention exactly on those "committed in private" as the ones which they sought to remove from the concern of the law. While Parliament was debating this step, the United States Supreme Court in *Griswold v. Connecticut* (1965) found unconstitutional a Connecticut statute prohibiting all persons from using contraceptives, on the ground that the statute and its enforcement violated a married couple's right of privacy. Writing for the majority, Justice Douglas conceded that such a right could not be found on the face of the Constitution, but maintained that the right was created from "penumbras" of the Bill of Rights "by emanations from those guarantees that help give them life and substance."

In the wake of *Griswold*, the Supreme Court had little difficulty in expanding this right of privacy to protect an interracial couple's decision to marry, a person's right to view obscene material in the privacy of his home, and a woman's decision to abort a pregnancy. In these decisions the Court employed a "substantive due process analysis" rather than the *Griswold* penumbra rationale. This procedure has not gone unchallenged, indeed it has been attacked as judge-made law and an expression of judicial ideology, but the Supreme Court has remained steadfast in asserting that a right of privacy exists as a product of the Constitution.

Application to Sodomy Statutes. Once recognized, the constitutional right of privacy developed in *Griswold* and its offshoots was advanced as a ground for attacking the constitutionality of state sodomy statutes, but the courts were uncertain as to whether this right should extend to consensual sexual activity. Since sodomy in medieval usage extended far beyond homosexuality, certain heterosexual acts fell within its scope, and these the courts have had no difficulty in treating as protected by the right of privacy, so that they could in good conscience strike down the laws prohibiting them. However, because of the particular intensity with which the taboo on homosexual acts has been maintained in American culture, these same courts have been reluctant to extend equal protection to homosexual activity.

The issue came to a head in two cases, *Doe v. Commonwealth* (1976) and *Bowers v. Hardwick* (1986). The first summarily affirmed the decision of the District Court for the Eastern District of Virginia upholding a Virginia sodomy statute on the ground that the right of sexual privacy extended only to decisions relating to the home, marriage, and the family. In the second, a majority of 5–4 denied that the Court's prior decisions have construed the Constitution to confer a right of privacy on homosexual activity; "No connection between family, marriage and procreation on the one hand and homosexual activity on the other has been demonstrated." The assertion that a right to engage in homosexual sodomy is "deeply rooted in this Nation's history and tradition" was dismissed as absurd. Last of all, the plaintiff's argument that his conduct should be protected because it had occurred in the privacy of his own home was rejected. The majority argued that a decision rendered in 1969 was "firmly grounded in the First Amendment" and therefore inapplicable as the present case did not deal with printed material. The minority opinion held that homosexuals, like everyone else, have a "right to be let alone" and that "A way of life that is odd . . . but interferes with no rights or interests of others is not to be condemned because it is different."

Broader Implications. The battle line remained drawn between those who defend the right of the state to uphold a moral code derived from the **canon law** of the medieval church, and those who cherish the **Enlightenment** principle that offenses against religion and morality, so long as they do not violate the rights of others or the interests of the state, do not fall within the scope of the criminal law. In that respect the concept of privacy is a legal weapon, an ideological innovation which the defenders of homosexual rights seek to interpose between the received law, the *jus receptum*, and the individual having overt sexual relations with a person of the same sex in the interest of a *jus recipiendum*, a more just law which if adopted would protect homosexuals in the exercise of sexual freedom.

The paradox of this situation is that the "deep structure" of society prescribes that sexual acts be private, that is to say, performed out of range of the sight and hearing of others who would rightly take offense if the acts were inflicted upon their consciousness. A legal commentator in Nazi Germany recognized that private sexual acts harm no one and are seldom detected, but argued that if they were committed in public they would cause outrage and scandal; the law should therefore proceed *as if* the private acts had been performed in public. In other words, although the state power is invading the

privacy of the participants and exposing them to humiliation and punishment, they should be punished on the fiction that they had deliberately violated the moral feelings of others by behaving indecently in public. One could hardly imagine a better example of paranoid logic, yet it is this type of thinking that underlies the refusal of the courts to extend the protection of privacy to homosexual behavior. By contrast, in the Dudgeon case (1981) the European Commission of Human Rights in Strasbourg held that laws penalizing private homosexual acts violated the right of privacy embodied in Article 8 of the European Convention on Human Rights of 1950. The struggle for the recognition of the right of privacy in this sphere of sexual conduct will likely continue unabated into the twenty-first century.

See also **Law: United States**.

BIBLIOGRAPHY. "Dudgeon v. United Kingdom," *European Human Rights Reports*, 3 (1981), 40–75; Morris L. Ernst and Alan U. Schwartz, *Privacy: The Right to Be Let Alone*, New York: Macmillan, 1962; Richard D. Mohr, *Gays/Justice: A Study of Ethics, Society, and Law*, New York: Columbia University Press, 1988; David A. J. Richards, "Sexual Autonomy and the Constitutional Right to Privacy: A Case Study in Human Rights and the Unwritten Constitution," *Hastings Law Journal*, 30 (1979), 957–1018; Ferdinand David Schoenman, ed., *The Philosophical Dimensions of Privacy: An Anthology*, Cambridge: Cambridge University Press, 1984; Roger D. Strode, Jr., "The Constitutionality of Sodomy Statutes as Applied to Homosexual Behavior," *Marquette Law Review*, 70 (1987), 599–611.

Warren Johansson

PRIVATE PRESSES

Presses that produce books in limited quantities not intended for the regular channels of the book trade are termed "private." Some of them have had to operate clandestinely, as the contents of the books would have attracted the attention of the authorities by their political or sexual nonconformity.

Historical Development. The invention of the printing press in fifteenth-century Europe, whose cultural life was still largely under the domination of the church, did not at first promote the spread of literature on homosexuality. The pagan classics, rich as they were in homoerotic passages and allusions, were in time printed and made accessible to a far larger public than would ever have seen them in manuscript. But the potential of the new medium for reproducing books and pamphlets on homosexual themes was realized only through clandestine private presses that eluded the repression and **censorship** exercised by the state and the church. The issuance of such works was a side activity of aristocratic orgy clubs that could flourish on the privacy of estates to which the authorities had no easy access. One of the first presses of this kind was created by the Duc d'Aiguillon on his estate at Verets in Touraine, which in 1735 issued the *Recueil de pièces choisies, rassemblées par les soins du Cosmopolite*. In England Horace Walpole, Earl of Oxford, had his own private press somewhat later in the century.

Subsequently the actual work of producing such books in a limited edition was transferred to master-printers in the publishing capitals of Europe, who issued them as custom pieces for wealthy patrons and connoisseurs. With the coming of the French Revolution, the breakdown of authority made it possible for printers to produce a variety of erotica, some of which had an explicitly homosexual content, and at this time the works of the Marquis de **Sade** transformed pornography itself by admitting themes of aberrant and forbidden sexuality. While Holland had been the principal source of clandestine literature under the Old Regime, in the nineteenth century France and Belgium took the lead in this area. The phenomenon that has gained the Russian name of *tamizdat* ("publication elsewhere") is characteristic of erotic literature: books were published in France in English for sale to Englishmen, in Brussels in French for sale to Frenchmen, because it was too dangerous to produce them in the country for which they were destined. Thus the earliest defenses of homosexuality in English were printed on the continent in the 1830s; of these only the so-called *Don Leon* poems have survived.

Typical of erotica issued by private presses is the use of false imprints on the title page. The place of publication may be given as "Sodom and Cythera" or "Eleutheropolis" = "Ville Franche" = "Freetown" or even "Partout et nulle part" (Everywhere and Nowhere); the publisher may have a facetious name such as "Uriel Bandant" or a classic pseudonym like "Pierre Marteau" = "Peter Hammer" or a parody of some institutional name such as "Society for Propagation in Foreign Parts." Even the year of publication, if not given wrongly to mislead the authorities into believing that this is *not* a new edition, may take the form of "An de la liberté."

Later in the nineteenth century such publishers as Auguste Poulet-Malassis, Isidore Liseux, and Charles Carrington issued editions of the erotic classics, translations of foreign works, and even contemporary writing for clandestine sale to lovers of erotica. The British collector Henry Spencer Ashbee assembled some 1517 volumes of erotica and kryptadia, among them many books enlarged with additional illustrations, which upon his death he bequeathed to the British Museum Library. For the purpose of illustrating such volumes the talents of artists and engravers of the first rank could be employed, as the price of a *de luxe* volume on fine paper ran into several pounds or scores of francs. Works written primarily or exclusively for a homosexual readership began to appear only toward the end of the nineteenth century, when the emerging movement awakened a consciousness that homoerotic literature had a past of its own, together with a public that would buy and collect such writings. In Leipzig the Max Spohr firm began openly issuing scholarly publications in the field during the last decade of the century.

Ephemeral and Popular Material. Naturally private presses could also turn out an ephemeral literature, some of it today known solely from references in booksellers' catalogues or bibliographers' lists, in the form of pamphlets, brochures, and similar trivia meant only for brief diversion. In the United States and England the restrictions on publishing even medical and anthropological literature that dealt with homosexuality remained in such vigor that as late as the 1930s private presses were issuing reprints and translations "in 1500 numbered copies for subscribers only." The Nonesuch Press and the Fortune Press in England—which had ties to Carrington's firm in Paris—were two such ventures. Also, little coteries of boy-lovers published their verses and apologetic writings in tiny editions for circulation solely among the initiate. Such works could never be advertised or sold through conventional channels, but the international publishing underground saw them to their destination. Even in the 1950s it was common for American travelers to purchase sexually explicit works in Paris—usually under the imprint of Maurice Girodias' Olympia Press—and then to hide them in their baggage to escape the attention of customs officers.

Another class of literature was the paperback novel or piece of reportage with a homosexual theme, typically sold in a particular sort of bookshop tolerated by the police in return for regular payoffs. For the United States market crude homosexual **pornography** was published in the 1940s and 1950s in Mexico (mainly in Tijuana) and smuggled across the border. As restrictions were relaxed in the 1960s, some of the firms moved across the border to San Diego and Los Angeles. At the same time the incipient gay **movement** tried to set up presses for book publishing, but with little success. It was the upsurge of underground newspapers that probably laid the groundwork for such gay and lesbian publishers of today as Alyson, Gay Sunshine Press, and Naiad. The advent of desktop publishing in the 1980s doubled and then tripled the number of small presses, and made it possible for authors to publish and distribute their own works if they wish.

During the closing years of censorship, photographs of the male body in a state as close to nudity as current mores would allow were circulated in the form of pictorial magazines, or in a more elegant guise, as art books on glossy paper. Much of this clandestine literature is fast disappearing, as the volumes could not find their way into public or scholarly libraries, and in a private collection they were as likely as not to be dispersed or simply destroyed on the death of the owner.

Conclusion. The significance of the private press was that it undercut the monopoly of the commercial publishers and also the control exercised by the state in the form of prior censorship or the prosecution for obscenity of works that violated the "moral standards of the community." In a time when homosexuality was virtually unmentionable in public, and every oblique reference to it in the media had to be accompanied with execration, such publishers issued a trickle of independent writing, and also preserved and disseminated classics of homoerotic literature that had survived from earlier centuries. With the advent of a general tolerance for public discussion of sexual matters, and the rise of publishing houses openly issuing erotica—and more serious works—for a gay readership, as well as the emergence of electronic non-print media, the older form of the private press is receding into the past.

BIBLIOGRAPHY. Patrick J. Kearney, *The Private Case*, London: Jay Landesman, 1981; Gershon Legman, *The Horn Book: Studies in Erotic Folklore and Bibliography*, New Hyde Park, NY: University Books, 1964; Pascal Pia, *Les Livres de l'Enfer*, 2 vols., Paris: C. Coulet et A. Faure, 1978; Timothy d'Arch Smith, *Love in Earnest: Some Notes on the Lives and Writings of English 'Uranian' Poets from 1889 to 1930*, London: Routledge & Kegan Paul, 1970.

Warren Johansson

PROSTATE

The prostate is a male gland surrounding the urethra, between the bladder and the penis. It secretes seminal fluid, which is almost the entire component of semen; the sperm cells are only a minute part. Adjacent to it are seminal reservoirs, which when full contribute to sexual desire, and when empty diminish it. Muscles around the prostate play a key role in the sensations of orgasm.

It seems to have been as a result of treatment of prostate disorders that its function in the male sexual cycle was discovered. It is the prostate, not the testicles, that is necessary for ejaculation. It was discovered that the screening procedure of palpation (feeling) of the prostate by a finger inserted in the rectum could be surprisingly pleasurable. Part of the pleasure of **anal** intercourse, for the male recipient, lies in the stimulation the penis provides to the prostate. The prostate may also play a role in the pleasure produced by other anal practices such as **handballing** and enemas. Direct anal stimulation of the prostate with a finger or a toy which cannot cut, scratch, or get "lost" can produce orgasm in men.

The Grafenberg or G-spot in women, located on the upper wall of the vagina, is anatomically related to the prostate, and women report that stimulation of it can be especially pleasurable.

Daniel Eisenberg

PROSTITUTION

Male homosexual prostitution is and has long been a widespread phenomenon attested in all high civilizations. At the same time it has in the course of the centuries been strongly conditioned by the attitudes of the host society toward homosexual behavior. By prostitution is meant a sexual relationship in which one partner is paid by the other to perform a specific act or set of acts on a particular occasion. The prostitute may himself be the employee of a service that arranges the encounter and collects a portion of the fee, or may simply be an entrepreneur whose clandestine income is more often than not unreported to the tax collector.

Because of the legal and social stigma attaching to homosexuality itself, only rarely in modern times has the state power attempted to regulate and control male prostitution ("hustling"). By contrast, heterosexual prostitution has in some countries been the object of rigorous **police** measures intended not just to prevent the phenomenon from becoming a public nuisance, but also to inhibit the spread of disease and to hinder the movement of prostitutes across national or state boundaries (the so-called "white slave trade").

History. Over the centuries, prostitution has taken three forms: guest prostitution, sacred prostitution, and commercial prostitution. The ancient world was familiar with the second category as both male and female hierodules plied their trade at the shrines of the deities of paganism. The k̇ādēsh of the Bible sold his sexual favors in the service of Ishtar, to the scandal and outrage of the priests of the cult of Yahweh who branded the practice an "abomination." A large measure of the condemnation of sexuality in the **Old Testament** stems from the association of orgiastic sexual activity with the rites of Semitic polytheism.

In ancient **Greece** cities such as Corinth were famed for the extent of their commercialized erotic life, just as today resort towns are a prime source of business for the hustler encountering clients in search of sexual pleasures as part of a vacation. Prostitutes were usually either **slaves** or freedmen; the free citizen who sold his body to other males incurred loss of civic rights (*atimia*). In Athens and other Greek cities male **brothels** flourished, as they did in ancient **Rome**, where male prostitutes even had a holiday of their own (April 25). In recent centuries, servicemen (such as **London's** guardsmen) have made their services available for a fee.

Phenomenology. In the simplest terms, prostitution exists because there is a demand for it, that is to say, the physical beauty and virility of the male in his teens or twenties are a commodity for whose enjoyment homosexually oriented males are willing to pay in accordance with an informal scale that is usually fixed by social convention in a given geographical area at a particular time. The fee varies depending on the length of time the prostitute is expected to stay with the client (least for an encounter of a few minutes, most for a whole night) and with the character of the service demanded (the more aberrated, demanding, or painful forms of sexual submission being the most costly). There are rendezvous where the client and the prostitute (hustler or call-boy) can meet or indirectly make contact; in recent times there have been gay publications that accept **advertisements** (ordinarily billed as "Models and Masseurs") for prostitutes who describe their formulaic attributes and range of services in concise but appetizing detail.

The complexity of the world of male prostitution forbids any generalizations in regard to either the prostitute or the client. The youth may come from the stereotypical impoverished, broken family or may be attending an exclusive secondary school or college; he may hustle only occasionally or may have prostitution as his sole source of income; he may be little more than moderately attractive or may be an aspiring actor or model temporarily out of work. Many hustlers refuse the label "homosexual" entirely, insisting that they perform sexually "only for money," or that they are at least "bisexual." Call-boy services generally screen out applicants who assert that they are heterosexual.

Social Structure. The world of the male prostitute has a hierarchy that runs from the street hustler and the bar hustler to the call-boy and the kept boy. The first of these types encounters his client in a zone where any boy idling casually on the street announces thereby that he is "for sale"; the bar hustler meets his "trick" in the atmosphere of a gay bar known for its hospitality to the prostitute; the call-boy either prints his number in an advertisement or secures his customers through a commercial service; the kept boy lives wholly at the expense of a single client for a longer or shorter period of time. A significant difference between male and female prostitution is that the client of the female prostitute never thinks of her as a potential marriage partner, while even the street hustler occasionally receives offers of a long-term relationship from his clients; in other words, there is no sharp or absolute dividing line between the hustler and the kept boy.

In motivation and degree of involvement, there are three subcategories of male prostitute: the professional, the amateur, and the runaway. The professional is typically in his late teens or older, has had a good deal of experience with commercial sex, and is able to make a steady living or to supplement his earnings from other sources—acting or modeling—by the sale of his services. The amateur performs only sporadically, when he needs the money or for the thrill or adventure involved in the activity. The runaway may be quite young, may have been disowned by his family and find himself struggling to survive "on his own" by selling his body. Since there is always an element of competition in this field, and the aging hustler finds little demand for his services (although a few manage to pursue their commercial activity into their mid-thirties, or may become managers of call-boy services), the career of male prostitutes is relatively brief.

Sexual Services. The range of physical acts which the male prostitute is willing and able to perform runs the whole gamut of erotic possibilities, though the individual offering his sexual services usually specifies in advance what he is willing to do with a specific client. Fear of disease was not a particularly inhibiting factor until **AIDS** made its appearance in the chief centers of homosexual life; today some prostitutes refuse to engage in more than erotic massage and mutual masturbation, while others insist on wearing a condom for acts that involve penetration of the body. The subculture of male prostitution has its norms (including ethics), its folklore, its camaraderie, even a certain agreement to keep a floor on the minimum price asked of a prospective client.

Clientele. The client (or "john") is ordinarily somewhere between his thirties and his sixties; he may be of undistinguished middle-class background or may come from the very top of society. His choice of a commercial partner may be determined by a variety of factors: the wish for a brief, impersonal contact with no later commitments or compromising self-revelation, the desire to have a partner with the highest degree of beauty and virility, or even the need to make an erotic quasi-conquest by displaying his wealth. Famous clients rely upon the reputation of a call-boy service and its boys for maintaining the confidentiality of their clientele, a marked point of prostitution ethics. If he finds a particular hustler exceptionally to his liking, he may try to establish a permanent relationship, or at least to retain the youth for a time as a "traveling companion" or under some other guise.

Many clients prefer to seek their boys in other cities than the one in which they live in order to avoid the possibility of being recognized. Not a few even prefer to travel abroad to Third World countries where there is an abundant supply of young hustlers, many straight identified, and prices are cheap. The Arab countries of North **Africa** enjoy a time-honored reputation for such sexual tourism. In recent years **Latin America** has increased in popularity, while those in search of really young partners are said to prefer **Thailand**, the **Philippines**, and **Korea**.

The Boys. Initially, at least, prostitution can be a highly attractive means of earning money for many youths. Not only is the "work" often if not always enjoyable, but it is tax-free, the hours are set by the worker at his convenience, and there is no paperwork involving social security numbers, working papers, and the like. The rate of pay, even when time spent "on the street" awaiting a client is considered, is usually much higher than what a youth can find in other lines of work. In addition, there are often considerable fringe benefits such as free liquor or drugs, meals, entertainment, even vacations and foreign travel.

There are, however, other motivations for remaining involved in prostitution: the continuing ego-boosts provided by the tangible evidence of one's desirability, the opportunity to witness and (to a small degree) experience the private lifestyles of the wealthy, and the often interesting clients to be met.

Since for many hustlers their earning ability is dependent on the number of times they are able to ejaculate in the course of an evening, teenagers often find their income declining as they grow older. This may cause them to drop out, to take sexually passive roles they had previously declined, or to leave the streets in favor of listing with a call-boy service.

Enlistment with a call-boy service is generally considered to be the career goal of the serious street hustler. The better services greatly increase a boy's earnings, despite their commissions, because their customers tend to be wealthier and pay more to begin with, and because the boy need not waste time hanging out in bars and on street corners. The services furthermore provide security (not only for the client), advice, and professional tips, health care, and quasi-family functions such as Thanksgiving dinners and picnic outings. Both a brothel and a call-boy service can provide a pleasant environment in which the boys can "hang out" with their peers when not actively working. Male madams of call-boy services can steer their boys to lucrative work in the pornography industry, and can teach their boys the social graces needed to operate in upper-class environments.

Legal Aspects. The focus which heterosexual society long kept on female prostitution, and the illegality of homosexual acts per se, often led to a situation in which the law and the police authorities took far more cognizance of the woman as prostitute than of the man. On the other hand, some legislation has tried to suppress commercial homosexual activity, or to prevent the "corruption of minors," while leaving private consensual acts outside the scope of the law. With the creation of vice squads within the police forces of the large cities of Western Europe and the United States, the authorities of necessity became aware of the extent of male prostitution, even if they only intermittently and haphazardly acted to repress it. They were obliged to maintain a certain surveillance if solely to obtain information on other illegal activities that overlapped with male prostitution: assault, robbery, **blackmail**, murder, more recently the clandestine traffic in **drugs**. With increasing availability in the 1970s and 80s, many hustlers found the attractions of drugs irresistible, even though persistent use of stimulants may reduce their capacity for sexual performance.

Because of the illegality and clandestinity that until quite recent times attached to homosexual prostitution, the whole phenomenon existed in the shadow of violence, extortion, and blackmail, all the more because the victim, no matter how well placed in society, could not complain to the police if he was assaulted and robbed; even when the hustler murdered his client, he could plead that "his masculinity had been insulted" by the other male. Some adolescents even made a regular practice of attacking and robbing

men whom they allowed to approach them with requests for their sexual services, or in some cases of going through the act and then assaulting the partner. Houses of male prostitution could exist, though they usually had to pay off the police or other authorities charged with the suppression of vice. Such male brothels exist even today in some large European cities. The police most of the time chose the path of least resistance and preferred to arrest the street hustler, the transvestite, and other marginal elements of the world of prostitution.

Unlike his female counterpart, the male prostitute usually has no need of a pimp and retains the whole of his earnings, unless he works for a call-boy service with which he splits his fee in a prescribed ratio.

Contemporary Scene. With the rise of a flourishing commercial gay subculture in the wake of the homosexual liberation movement of the late 1960s and early 1970s, male prostitution thrived, and individual hustlers or call-boy services were able to advertise their wares on the pages of the magazines, some of them elaborate productions on glossy paper, that addressed themselves to a homosexual readership. The organized gay movement has paid little attention to the phenomenon of prostitution, probably thinking it one of the less defensible aspects of the homosexual subculture; Vanguards, an organization of San Francisco hustlers, however, was admitted to the North American Conference of Homophile Organizations (NACHO) in the late 1960s. A positive side of recent developments has been action by the police to protect the client who is victimized by the male prostitute. The accessibility of bathhouses and hotels that cater to prostitute–client liaisons has also removed some of the problems attendant on the commercial relationship. The interest of society does not lie in trying to suppress prostitution, but in acting to minimize the abuses that have historically been linked with it: to prevent the spread of disease, to counter violence or robbery committed on the margin of the activity, and to offer an escape for the runaway who against his own wishes finds himself trapped in a life of prostitution.

Not to be omitted from any serious consideration of the role of prostitution in society are those who are most in need of its services: unmarried men well past their prime, those lacking in their society's standards of beauty, the physically and mentally handicapped, and those with unusual **fetishes**. For these men, whose access to non-commercial sexuality is severely restricted, the denial of the use of prostitution effectively denies them a sexual life.

With continuing changes in the structure of the labor market throughout the advanced countries, it is likely that prostitution (perhaps redefined as "intimate personal services") will serve as an alternative occupation for those displaced from more traditional careers. Apart from the financial rewards, the successful male prostitute can utilize his contacts with the upper strata of male society as a springboard for later economic advancement, provided that he has proved his reliability and discretion. But whatever the economic situation, the prevalence of unfulfilled homoerotic desires—and of income earmarked for "leisure activity"—will ensure that prostitution continues into the indefinite future.

BIBLIOGRAPHY. Iwan Bloch, *Die Prostitution*, Berlin: L. Marcus, 1911–25, Bd. 1 and Bd. 2, Hälfte 1; Debra Boyer, "Male Prostitution and Homosexual Identity," *Journal of Homosexuality*, 17 (1989), 151–84; Eli Coleman, "The Development of Male Prostitution Activity Among Gay and Bisexual Adolescents," *Journal of Homosexuality*, 17 (1989), 131–49; Neil R. Coombs, "Male Prostitution: A Psychosocial View of Behavior," *American Journal of Orthopsychiatry*, 44 (1974), 782–89; Mervyn Harris, *The Dillyboys: The Game of Male Prostitution in Piccadilly*, Rockville: New Perspectives, 1973; David F. Luckenbill, "Entering Male Prostitution," *Urban Life*, 14 (1985), 131–53; Paul W. Mathews, "On 'Being a Prostitute,'" *Journal of Homosexuality*, 15:3/4 (1988), 119–35; John Rechy, *City of Night*, New York: Grove, 1963; A. J. Reiss, Jr., "The Social Integration of Queers and Peers," *Social Problems*, 9 (1961), 102–20.

Warren Johansson

PROTESTANTISM

Of the approximately one billion adherents of **Christianity**, 630 million are Catholic, 100 million Orthodox, 375 million Protestant, and a few million are Copts, Nestorians, and others. Of the 142 million Christians in the **United States** (60 percent of the population), 52 million are Roman Catholic and 79 million Protestant.

General Features. Late medieval Albigensian, Waldensian, Lollard, and Hussite **heretics** had criticized the hierarchy for worldliness, greed, luxury, and sins of the flesh, including **sodomy**. Intensifying these proto-Protestant critiques, Lutherans, **Anglicans**, Calvinists, and Anabaptists agreed that no Scriptural basis existed for clerical **celibacy**, which encouraged sexual depravity. Luther himself denounced homosexuality in **Old Testament** and Pauline terms, condemning **penitentials**, scholasticism, and **canon law** for laxly allowing a mortal sin to be confessed and atoned through penance. All Protestant churches and governments continued the Catholic policy of prescribing death for sodomites whom they too considered enemies of God and allies of the Devil.

Protestants elevated marriage above celibacy but condemned simple fornication more than had the medieval church. Harking back to the precedents of Biblical Judaism, they opposed clerical celibacy, excoriating the clergy, including nuns, for indulging in sodomy among themselves and with the laity. In their view, a principal advantage of abolishing **monasticism** and allowing marriage of priests and bishops was to discourage clerical sodomy. Reformers also tried to abolish prostitution which Catholics before the Counterreformation had condoned as less evil than adultery or homosexuality. But in making that choice less available, they increased the risk of homosexual activity which some of them denounced more vehemently than did Catholics. Lutherans and Calvinists, as well as Dominicans and Jesuits, persecuted Jews, Moriscos, and heretics as well as sodomites to effect conversion or repentance through force and intimidation. Witches were sometimes confounded with sodomites; the *Theologia moralis* (1625) maintained that sodomy led to **witchcraft**.

Monter's study of sixteenth- and seventeenth-century Switzerland shows that Geneva Protestants and Fribourg Catholics condemned sodomites with much the same zeal. After 1628, when the Spanish **Inquisition** quit burning sodomites, Protestants increased their executions. A great persecution in the **Netherlands** in 1730–31 resulted in the hanging, burning, and drowning of fifty-seven men and boys. In England an average of two hangings a year took place between 1806 and 1836. Most Catholic countries had by then abolished the death penalty, following the lead of **France** in 1791.

The Lutheran Tradition. The Augustinian monk Martin Luther (1483–1546) condemned clerical celibacy as part of his attack on the efficacy of good works. Only a few, he maintained, could remain continent. Marriage he praised as the foundation of society, begun in Paradise, and endorsed by the Fifth and Seventh Commandments. It eliminated lust. He himself set the example by marrying Katherine von Bora, an ex-nun, and producing five children. Sex he limited strictly to marriage and for procreation. Perhaps influenced by the spread of syphilis that had begun in Western Europe in 1493, he broke with the indulgent medieval church and denounced prostitution.

Regarding sodomy as more heinous than fornication, Luther fulminated against all non-procreative sex: "The hei-

nous conduct of the people of Sodom is extraordinary, in as much as they departed from the natural passion and longing of the male for the female, which was implanted by God, and desired what is altogether contrary to nature. Whence comes this perversity? Undoubtedly from Satan, who, after people have once turned away from the fear of God, so powerfully suppresses nature that he beats out the natural desire and stirs up a desire that is contrary to nature."

Converting **Denmark** (1520), Finland (1523), **Sweden** (1521), and Norway (1534), Lutheranism became the official religion of most north German states as well, with 35 million adherents in Germany and 25 in Scandinavia today. Scandinavian and German immigrants made it one of the most important denominations in the United States with 8 million members in various branches. Over the opposition of Lutheran pastors, Denmark in 1866 abolished **capital** punishment for all offenses, including homosexual acts, while Sweden mitigated its penalties for sodomy in 1864. Between 1930 and 1948 the Scandinavian countries under **Social Democracy** abolished sodomy laws in spite of Lutheran opposition. Mostly Lutheran Prussia, however, extended its punishments to all citizens of the German Empire in the infamous antihomosexual **Paragraph 175** in the Penal Code of 1871, which was stiffened by the Nazis in 1935. Traditionally subservient to the state, Lutherans became notorious for failing to oppose Hitler, with rare exceptions such as pastors Dietrich Bonhoeffer and Martin Niemöller.

Secularism, which helped undermine clerical power, has not led twentieth-century American Lutherans to accept homosexuality. The moderate Lutheran Church in America at their convention in 1970 stated that "homosexuality is viewed biblically as a departure from the heterosexual structure of God's creation. Persons who engage in homosexual behavior are sinners only as are all other persons—alienated from God and neighbor. However, they are often the special and undeserving victims of prejudice and discrimination in law, law enforcement, cultural mores, and congregational life. In relation to this area of concern, the sexual behavior of freely consenting adults in private is not an appropriate subject for legislation or police action. It is essential to see such persons as entitled to understanding justice in church and community." Three years later the conservative Missouri Synod convention resolved: "Whereas, God's Word clearly identifies homophile behavior as immoral, and condemned it (Lev. 18:22; 20:13 and Rom. 1:24–27); and Whereas, The Law and the Gospel of Jesus Christ are to be proclaimed and applied to all conditions of mankind; therefore be it Resolved, That the Synod recognize homophile behavior as intrinsically sinful. . . ." In 1977 the American Lutheran Church's Standing Committee for the Office of Research and Analysis declared: "We believe that taken as a whole the message of Scripture clearly is that: a. Homosexual behavior is sin, a form of idolatry, a breaking of the natural order that unites members of the human community; b. Homosexual behavior is contrary to the new life in Christ, a denial of the responsible freedom and service into which we are called through baptism; c. God offers the homosexual person, as every other person, a vision of the wholeness He intends, the assurance of His grace, and His healing and restoration for the hurting and broken. Nevertheless, we recognize the cries of our homosexual brothers and sisters for justice in the arena of civil affairs. We cannot endorse their call for legalizing homosexual marriage. Nor can we endorse their conviction that homosexual behavior is simply another form of acceptable expression of natural erotic or libidinous drives. We can, however, endorse their position that their sexual orientation in and of itself should not be a cause for denying them their civil liberties."

Anabaptists and Others. Anabaptists, various continental groups in the sixteenth century who refused infant baptism, including Thomas Münzer and the Zwickau prophets, and who sympathized with the Peasants' Revolt of 1525, taught the doctrine of the inner light, later adopted by Quakers. The Swiss Brethren, who in Zurich in 1525 reintroduced from **Patristic** sources believers' baptism (i.e., of conscious adults), taught non-resistance and rejected participation in the magistracy. Their views spread into the Rhineland and southwest Germany. The Brethren took refuge in Moravia under Jacob Hutter (d. 1536) with community of property. The Melchiorites from northwest Germany and the Low Countries learned from Melchior Hoffmann chiliastic expectations. Vigorously denounced by Luther, Zwingli, Calvin, and Catholics, the Mennonites, reorganized in the Netherlands and Friesland by Menno Simons, strongly emphasized pacifism. Hostility to Mennonites, today numbering 700,000, continues today. Denounced and persecuted by mainstream Protestants, tens of thousands of Anabaptists were probably put to death by the Inquisition, mainly in the Low Countries and in Bohemia—less developed regions where they had sought refuge before being attacked by the Counter-Reformation. Subject to severe persecution, Anabaptists, like the Socinians, early favored toleration.

A place apart belongs to the Socinian sect. Fausto Sozzini (1539–1604), a Sienese jurist settled in **Venice**, the most sophisticated city of the Italian **Renaissance**, before visiting France, England, the Netherlands, and stopping in Calvin's Geneva, from where he visited Melanchthon, Luther's assistant, and Poland, spreading radical ideas. His even more radical nephew, who denied the essential divinity of Christ and the immortality of man, eventually settled in remote Transylvania and then in Krakow, Poland, out of which the Jesuits eventually hounded him. Socinian ideas were among the formative influences in the emergence of Quakerism.

Quakers. First mentioned in Oliver Cromwell's proclamation of 1654 persecuting them for refusal to serve in the military and to take oaths, the Quakers, officially designated the Religious Society of Friends, grew from a wave of religious ferment in seventeenth-century England. Disdaining ordained ministers and consecrated buildings, George Fox proclaimed after 1647 the immediacy of Christ's teachings. After their "yearly meeting" in London in 1675, which established a "meeting for sufferings," Friends have been in the forefront of race relations, penal reforms, social relief, and conciliatory work. Before the Toleration Act of 1689, 15,000 had been sentenced and more than 450 died in prison in Great Britain. In 1682 William Penn founded the British colony of Pennsylvania on Quaker principles. Pennsylvania's law code of 1682 all but decriminalized sodomy for the first time in Christian lands since 342, when the **Roman emperors** introduced the death penalty.

Quakers have been in the forefront of homosexual toleration. As early as 1963 English Friends published *Towards a Christian View of Sex*: "One should no more deplore homosexuality than left-handedness.... Homosexual affection can be as selfless as heterosexual affection, and therefore we cannot see that it is in some way morally worse." Ten years later the influential Philadelphia Yearly Meeting of Friends declared: "We should be aware that there is a great diversity in the relationships that people develop with one another. Although we neither approve nor disapprove of homosexuality, the same standards under the law which we apply to heterosexual activities should also be applied to homosexual activities. As persons who engage in homosexual activities suffer serious discrimination in employment, housing and the right to worship, we believe that civil rights laws should protect them. In particular we advocate the revision of all legislation imposing disabilities and penalties upon homosexual activities."

Baptists. Largest of Protestant sects, the Baptists have a total formal membership of 30,000,000 that extends to every continent. They look to John Smyth, an English Separatist under Mennonite influence, who in 1609 in Amsterdam exile reinstituted the baptism of those believers able to understand and commit themselves to the faith. Like the earlier Anabaptists, he rebaptized those whom the established churches had christened as infants. Members of his congregation established the first English Baptist Church in 1612. As the church grew, attracting some converts from Calvinism, complete immersion became their normal form of baptism. Baptists pioneered religious liberty and freedom of conscience and in the seventeenth century with Independents and Presbyterians formed the three denominations of Protestant Dissenters.

Roger Williams' church in Rhode Island began America's Baptist history in 1639. The Great Awakening in New England (1740) quickened Baptist missionary activity, particularly on the western frontier. By 1980 the 26 million North American Baptists were organized into four major conventions (as well as twelve splinter groups): the Southern, largest and most conservative, the American, and two black ones. Over 66 percent of black churchgoers in the United States, including the late Martin Luther King, are Baptists. Perhaps out of recognition of their own persecuted past, black Baptists have been helpful in the passage of ordinances in New York in 1986 and Chicago in 1988 protecting gay rights. The American Baptists recently proclaimed: "We, as Christians, recognize that radical changes are taking place in sex concepts and practices.... [W]e call upon our churches to engage in worship, study, fellowship and action to provide for meaningful ministries to all persons as members of the 'Family of God' including those who are homosexuals."

Southern Baptists, however, inspired by and recently presided over by Bible-thumping Adrian Rogers of the Bellevue Baptist Church of Memphis, who defeated the moderates to become president of that largest Protestant group in the United States (membership 14.7 million), are adamantly homophobic. At their convention in 1976 they passed the following resolution: "Whereas, homosexuality has become an open lifestyle for increasing numbers of persons, and Whereas, attention has focused on the religious and moral dimensions of homosexuality, and Whereas, it is the task of the Christian community to bring all moral questions and issues into the light of biblical truth; Now therefore, be it resolved that the members of the Southern Baptist Convention . . . affirm our commitment to the biblical truth regarding the practice of homosexuality and sin. Be it further resolved, that this Convention, while acknowledging the autonomy of the local church to ordain ministers, urges churches and agencies not to afford the practice of homosexuality any degree of approval through ordination, employment, or other designations of normal lifestyle."

"Fundamentalists" are now purging "moderates" from their colleges and six seminaries, even though these "moderates" themselves anathematize homosexuality. In March 1988 a theological conservative, Lewis A. Drummond, an associate of Billy Graham, was elected president of the Southeastern Baptist Theological Seminary. Declaring that he would hire only faculty who accepted the Bible as literally true even in science and history, he pledged to carry out the agenda of the conservatives. Of the 25 American states which have decriminalized sodomy, not one is in the Bible Belt in the South—of which Memphis is described as the buckle—where Baptists predominate. Virginia-based Jerry Falwell, who pioneered in the use of contemporary media in his Moral Majority (disbanded in 1989), has emphasized opposition to homosexuality.

Anglicans. Declaring Henry VIII (1509–1547) supreme head of the Church of England in 1535, Parliament instituted a political church close in liturgy and doctrine to the Roman Catholic but abolishing monasteries, whose estates and revenues the king desired, and translating the liturgy into English. In the spirit of Henry's daughter Elizabeth I (1558–1603), who maintained that she did not want "to open windows into men's souls," Archbishop Matthew Parker issued the Book of Common Prayer, beautifully written but ambiguous so that all but extreme Catholics and ultra-Protestants could interpret it to their liking, giving the church a latitudinarianism which it has preserved. It has never executed a single heretic and to the disgruntlement of Puritans rather laxly enforced morality. Trials and executions of sodomites remained rare under Henry VIII's statute of 1533 and Elizabeth I's of 1561, the first being the Earl of Castlehaven in 1631. William Blackstone argued in his *Commentaries on the Laws of England* (1765–69) that "the express law of God. . . by the destruction of two cities by fire from heaven . . . [commands] such miscreants to be burned to death." A wave of anti-Jacobin nationalism resulted in the hanging of about 60 sodomites between 1806 and 1836; in 1861 English law was reformed to abolish execution for sodomy. The **Wolfenden** Report of 1957, inspired by Canon D. S. **Bailey**'s *Homosexuality and the Western Christian Tradition* (1955), recommended eliminating the penalties for consenting homosexual behavior, which was achieved for England and Wales in 1967 with considerable church support.

The Church of England (Episcopalian in the United States) claims, by dividing the orthodox into their various national churches, to be second only to the Roman Catholic in size with 70 million members. Not without controversy, it has given support to women's and minority rights, installing the first female bishop in all history in the apostolic succession, Barbara Harris, who is also black, in the

Massachusetts diocese in 1988. Bishop Desmond Tutu combats apartheid in South Africa. In America and the Commonwealth, in all of which the church has had a largely upper-class membership with many only rarely attending services, Episcopalians have been in the forefront of homophile movements, spurred by their active gay organization, Integrity, largest next to the Catholic, Dignity. In 1973 the *Report of the Commission on Homosexuality of the Episcopal Diocese of Michigan* declared that "homosexuals seriously seeking to build such (loving) relationships with one another are surely as deserving as heterosexuals of encouragement and help from the Church and its ministry. . . . Historical studies disclose that persecution and discrimination have been the homosexual's lot in Western society and that the Church bears a heavy share of responsibility for this state of affairs." In 1976 the American Episcopal Church resolved: "that it is the sense of this General Convention that homosexual persons are children of God, who have a full and equal claim with all other persons upon the love, acceptance, and pastoral concern and care of the Church [and] that homosexual persons are entitled to equal protection of the law with all other citizens, and calls upon our society to see such protection is provided in actuality."

Since then, in Britain at least, there has been a backlash, caused by concern over AIDS, but urged on by Prime Minister Margaret Thatcher, who for the first time in history, on January 1, 1988, elevated a rabbi to the peerage in England, Immanuel Jakobovits, Chief Rabbi of the British Commonwealth, because, some claim, he declared homosexual acts "morally wrong. My creator tells me it is grievously wrong under the heading of immoral acts. I want to cultivate a moral sense in which society will differentiate between what is acceptable and what is morally unacceptable." His views run counter to the official position of the state of Israel, which in March 1988 decriminal-

ized homosexuality. Although on November 11, 1987, by a vote of 388 to 19, leaders of the Church of England rejected a move to expel its homosexual priests, calling instead for them to repent and to be treated with compassion, an Anglican Synod in England has since passed a motion calling for practicing homosexuals to change their lifestyle and turn their back on homosexual activity as contrary to the will of God. In an editorial of January 3, 1988 in the *Sunday Times* Peter Nott, Bishop of Norwich, perhaps angling for Thatcher's support to be designated Archbishop of Canterbury, denied the right of practicing homosexuals to be ordained and called for the reassertion of the normality of the single and the celibate. Church authorities in London have taken legal action to force the closure of the headquarters of the Lesbian and Gay Christian Movement at St. Botolph's Church, Aldgate.

The backlash has also had some effect among Episcopalians on the other side of the Atlantic. On November 7, 1987, Episcopalian laity in Boston voted down by 82–140 a resolution approved by a 114–79 margin among the clergy to develop a liturgy blessing gay couples. Shepherded through by the liberal Bishop John S. Spong, in January 1988 the Diocese of Newark voted to encourage its priests to bless gay **couples**. Spong quoted a proposed rite to bless a same-sex union: "The joining of two persons in heart, body, and mind is intended by God for their mutual joy, for the help and comfort . . . in prosperity and adversity . . . in accordance with God's intention for us." None of the other dioceses or any mainstream Protestant denominations followed suit. Bishop Arthur E. Walmsley of the Diocese of Connecticut denied that Spong spoke for the Church and retorted that "the sanctity of holy matrimony is not a debatable issue in the Episcopal Church." Indeed, despite the 1976 pronouncements of the national church calling homosexuals "children of God" entitled to participate in all church services, three years later it denied practicing homosexuals entrance into the priest-hood.

Calvinists. Generally more fa-natic than the other Protestants and more prone during the religious wars to torture monks and priests, Calvinists vehemently denounced clerical homosexuality when shutting down monasteries, often looting and always expropriating wherever they could. John Calvin (1509–1564), who pub-lished his *Institutes of the Christian Reli-gion* in 1536, created a theocracy in Ge-neva which drew like-minded preachers from all over Europe, sending them out when indoctrinated to establish congrega-tions everywhere. It has been said that paradoxically "Calvin abolished the mon-astery but made every man a monk." With his legal training, Calvin in his *Institutes* gave his Church a consistency greater than any other denomination's. Not going as far as Luther in equating the Sodom story with homosexuality, Calvin followed Thomas **Aquinas** in condemning all non-procreative intercourse as unnatural. In Geneva thirty sodomites were put to death between 1555 and 1680. Catholic writers published scurrilous writings charging Calvin with pederasty. While these charges are lacking in foundation, those laid at the door of the Reformer's lieutenant, Théodore de **Bèze**, are more plausible.

In Scotland, John Knox drove out the lascivious Mary Stuart in 1568 and established the Kirk, henceforth known as Presbyterian because elders governed each congregation. Presbyterians gained a repu-tation for severity with executions. Scot-land with its own criminal law continued to uphold the statute against sodomy longer than England, from 1967 to 1980. In 1976 the 188th General Assembly of the United Presbyterian Church in the United States, with over 3 million members in addition to those of various splinter groups, de-clared: "The 188th General Assembly calls to the attention of our Church that, ac-cording to our most recent statement, we 'reaffirm our adherence to the moral law of God . . . that . . . the practice of homosexu-

ality is sin. . . . Also we affirm that any self-righteous attitude of others who would condemn persons who have so sinned is also sin.'. . . [O]n broad Scriptural and confessional grounds, it appears that it would at the present time be injudicious, if not improper, for a Presbytery to ordain to the professional ministry of the Gospel a person who is an avowed practicing homosexual."

In the **Netherlands**, where the Dutch Reformed helped inspire the Revolt against Spain in 1566, the dour Calvinists of the rural churches were tempered by the suave urbanity of the merchants and sea-men of Amsterdam, both joining to domi-nate the Catholic minority. Anti-sodomite hysteria reached a zenith in 1730–31 with fifty-seven executions and nearly two hundred expulsions from the country, but afterwards it waned. When **Napoleon** annexed Holland in 1811 the French codes were introduced at one stroke, effectively decriminalizing sodomy. The fight for toleration began as a branch of the German emancipation movement founded in 1897 when in 1911 a clerical ministry passed a bill raising the age of consent from 14 to 21—the first such innovation in modern times. The Netherlands branch of the **Scientific-Humanitarian Committee** con-tinued until the German occupation of the country in May 1940.

Being a minority in a Catholic land, the French Huguenots nevertheless continued to persecute sodomites in the towns they controlled but with less vehe-mence than elsewhere. After publishing *Juvenilia* in 1548, describing affection for his mignon Audébert, Théodore de Bèze converted, becoming a leader of the Hu-guenots and succeeding Calvin as leader in Geneva. Catholic polemicists claimed that he remained a sodomite at heart although he married. Following release from his first imprisonment, Bèze's contemporary Marc-Antoine **Muret**, although in his youth his writings harshly disapproved of sod-omy, was charged a second time with sodomy and of being a Huguenot as well.

Found guilty in absentia, he was burned in effigy. In 1558, this time in Padua rather in France, he was again charged but fled and died a Catholic. In *The Princes* the Huguenot poet Agrippa d'Aubigné accused the royal family, including **Henri III**, of acting contrary to nature, blaming Henri's problems on his mother, Catherine de' Medici, for encouraging the depravity of her children so that she could rule.

Calvinists, Puritans disapproving all frivolity and strictly enforcing Old Testament morality, failed to rule England under Parliament, Oliver Cromwell, and his son from 1649 to 1660, but in New England they predominated, outlawing sodomy in the colonies that they ruled. In 1629, on the vessel *Talbot* sailing for Massachusetts, "5 beastly Sodomiticall boyes" were examined and after landing in New England sent back by the governor to "ould England" for punishment, where they were probably hanged. In 1642, three of the most distinguished clergymen of the Plymouth colony, founded by Pilgrims rather than Puritans, concluded that the Bible ordained the death penalty for sodomites and executed several. In 1646 William Plaine, accused of sodomy, masturbation, and atheism, was executed in New Haven, where ten years later the Puritans prescribed death for lesbians following the current interpretation of the law against buggery originally promulgated by Henry VIII in 1533. Wealthy merchants from Boston and Salem and increasing Anglican influence lessened homophobia in New England during the eighteenth century. New England Puritans evolved into more tolerant Congregationalists, while those who did not defect to Anglicanism later turned into highly tolerant Unitarians.

Methodists. Formally founded in 1784 by John Wesley (1703–1791), whose *Notes on the New Testament* (1754) and four volumes of sermons form their standard doctrine, Methodists have debated whether ordination was conferred by the imposition of hands, with or without bishops being merely supervisors. Disputes over discipline and polity have caused offshoots and reunifications, as in 1857 with the establishment of the United Methodist Free Churches in England. The Northern and Southern Methodist Churches, the two main branches in the United States, split before the Civil War but reunited in 1939. The United Methodist Church now has 9.3 million members, with another 4 million, mostly blacks, in splintered churches. Actively concerned with evangelism and social welfare, one of the Church's glories is William Wilberforce's efforts to end the slave trade. Methodists have a worldwide membership of over 20 million and a total community of nearly 50 million.

As an organization, Methodists have generally stood between Episcopalians and Baptists in their attitude to sexuality and homosexuality. Spurred by United Methodists for Lesbian/Gay Concerns, the United Methodist Church published the following manifesto at its Quadrennial Conference in 1976: "Homosexuals no less than heterosexuals are persons of sacred worth, who need the ministry and guidance of the church in their struggles for human fulfillment, as well as the spiritual and emotional care of a fellowship which enables reconciling relationships with God, with others and with self. Further we insist that all persons are entitled to have their human and civil rights ensured, though we do not condone the practice of homosexuality and consider this practice incompatible with Christian teaching." In a retreat from toleration, on May 2, 1988, the General Conference of the United Methodist Church meeting at St. Louis, Missouri voted to maintain its stance that homosexual behavior is "incompatible with Christian teaching" and a bar to the ordained ministry.

Unitarianism. A pupil of Reuchlin, Martin Solarius (1499–1564), in his *De operis Dei* in 1527 became the first exponent of Unitarianism. Juan Valdés, Michael Servetus, and Bernardino Ochino were sympathetic. The first organized communities appeared in seventeenth-century Poland, Hungary, and England. Rejecting Trinitarian doctrines and the divinity of Christ, Unitarians possess no formal creed, but in the nineteenth century James Martineau in England and Theodore Parker in the United States developed a rational Biblical Unitarianism with reason and conscience rather than tradition as the criteria of belief and practice.

In 1658 the Jesuits suppressed Unitarianism in **Poland**. England enforced penal acts against Unitarians until 1813. The first Unitarian congregation in America, King's Chapel in Boston, in 1785 adopted a liturgy modified to suit Unitarian doctrines. Descended from Puritan groups, many other Congregational churches adopted Unitarianism in the early nineteenth century. William Ellery Channing and Ralph Waldo Emerson emphasized ethical and philosophical aspects. By 1900 American Unitarians had become very liberal, with great influence at the Harvard Divinity School as reconstituted in 1880 by President Charles W. Eliot. In 1961 the Unitarian Association joined the Universalist Church to form the Unitarian Universalist Association. Unitarians acquired a gay offshoot, Unitarian Universalists for Lesbian and Gay Concerns, and like Episcopalians have assisted gay brethren threatened with AIDS. Unitarians were the first group to establish a lesbian/gay office, eventually merged with their office of elderly affairs. The General Assembly of the Unitarian Universalist Association of Churches in North America in 1970 stated: "1. A significant minority in this country are either homosexual or bisexual in their feelings and/or behavior; 2. Homosexuality has been the target of severe discrimination by society and in particular by the police and other arms of government; 3. A growing number of authorities on the subject now see homosexuality as an inevitable sociological phenomenon and not as a mental illness; 4. There are Unitarian Universalists, clergy and laity, who are homosexuals and bisexuals; therefore be it resolved: That the 1970 General Assembly of the Unitarian Universalist Association: 1) Urges all people immediately to bring an end to all discrimination against homosexuals, homosexuality, bisexuals, and bisexuality, with specific immediate attention to the following issues: Private consensual behavior between persons over the age of consent shall be the business only of those persons and not subject to legal regulations."

Disciples of Christ. Claiming 1,132,000 members, the Church of Christ (Disciples of Christ) broke off in Kentucky in 1804 and in Pennsylvania in 1809 as Evangelical Presbyterians protesting the decline of fervor and Protestant factionalism. Organized in 1832 in congregational fashion with adult baptism, trying to avoid any ritual or doctrine not explicitly present in the first century of the Church, they claim: "Where the Scriptures speak, we speak; where the Scriptures are silent, we are silent." Highly tolerant, the General Assembly declared in 1977: "It has never acknowledged barriers to fellowship on the basis of dogma or life style. . . . Homosexuals may be included in the fellowship and membership of the community of faith where they are to love and be loved and where their gifts of ministry are to be welcomed."

Mormons. Founded in 1827 in New York by Joseph Smith (1805–1844), who received a divine revelation on golden tablets, the theocratic Mormons (Church of Latter Day Saints; 3.6 million members in the United States) practice adult baptism as well as baptism for the dead. Although the faith emerged from the American tradition of religious pluralism, Mormonism is not a Protestant denomination, but an independent religion. It had conflicts with the authorities for practicing polygamy, officially renounced in 1890. After the lynching of Smith, the Mormons emigrated in the 1840s to Utah, then still Mexican territory, where they founded their own commonwealth. In 1860 they reorganized their church, abandoning the greater part of their peculiar beliefs and practices except their scripture, the *Book of Mormon*. The ideal Mormon is temperate, hard-working, communal-minded, and implacably hostile to sexual freedom. Affinity, a group of lesbian and gay Mormons, is officially shunned by the church.

Adventists. The Adventists, Christian groups expecting the imminent Second Coming, numbering over 600,000 in the United States, date as a denomination from 1831 when William Miller proclaimed in Dresden, New York, the Second Coming in 1843–44. With combined world membership over three million, both chief branches, Second Advent Christians and Seventh-Day Adventists, emphasize that the human body, a temple of the Holy Spirit, requires strict temperance and mandate abstinence from alcohol and tobacco. They baptize adults with total immersion. In January 1988, the Seventh-Day Adventists asked a US District Court in California to bar a support group for homosexuals, the Seventh-Day Adventist Kinship International Inc., from using the church's name, declaring that homosexual and lesbian practices are "obvious perversions of God's original plan" for the proper association of the sexes.

Jehovah's Witnesses. In the 1870s a Congregationalist draper from Pittsburgh, Pennsylvania, Charles Taze Russell, founded Jehovah's Witnesses, originally called the International Bible Students Association, now counting 1.3 million members, 700,000 of them in the United States. "Pastor" Russell published *The Object and Manner of Our Lord's Return*, predicting the secret second coming of Christ in 1874 and the end of the world forty years later. Through a spate of books, pamphlets, and magazines, including *The Watchtower*, the movement's chief literary organ, which is still published, he attracted a considerable following. Proclaiming a workers' revolution as the prelude to the resurrection of the dead, the Last Judg-

ment, and the reign of the Messiah, when only the "elect of Jehovah" would be members, and denouncing institutional churches, governments, and business enterprises as instruments of Satan, Jehovah's Witnesses suffered persecution not only in liberal Australia and New Zealand but in totalitarian Soviet Russia and Nazi Germany. During Hitler's **Holocaust** thousands of the "Ernsten Bibelforscher" perished in concentration camps. On the other hand, the United States Supreme Court has time and again upheld their rights under the First Amendment, thus strengthening the principle of freedom of conscience and separation of church and state.

Christian Scientists. Of New Hampshire Calvinist background, Mary Baker Eddy (1821–1910), believing in healing by prayer alone, claimed to have rediscovered Christ's healing spiritual influence through revelation. Publishing *Science and Health* (1875), she opened her first church in Boston four years later. Christian Science teaches the unreality of matter, sin, and suffering. The Church, wealthy from the bequests of the elderly it exhorts to avoid doctors, publishes *The Christian Science Monitor*, a purportedly liberal newspaper that is as homophobic as the mother church and even in the 1980s purged homosexuals from its staff. Christian Scientists have, however, organized gay groups. Membership has declined from 270,000 in the 1930s to 170,000 in the 1980s and licensed practitioners from 8,300 in 1960 to 3,500 in 1989.

Pentecostals. Splintering from Methodism and other sects in 1901 in Topeka, Kansas, and in 1906 in Los Angeles as a response to the decline of Protestant fervor, the Pentecostal Church evolved from a "holy roller" movement to organized bodies with an informal service marked by hymns and spirit baptism. Standing apart from middle-class mainstream churches, Pentecostalism stresses perfection and lifestyle austerity.

United Church of Christ. Founded in 1957 by the union of Calvinist Congregationalist with Lutheran Evangelical and Reformed Churches, the United Church of Christ features infant baptism and the Lord's Supper with a simple liturgy centered on the sermon. Tolerant, it pays attention to social problems, declaring in 1975: "Therefore, without considering in this document the rightness or wrongness of same-gender relationships, but recognizing that a person's affectional or sexual preference is not legitimate grounds on which to deny her or his civil liberties, the Tenth General Synod of the United Church of Christ proclaims the Christian conviction that all persons are entitled to full civil liberties and equal protection under the law. Further, the Tenth General Synod declares its support for the enactment of legislation that would guarantee the liberties of all persons without discrimination related to affectional or sexual preference."

Orthodox Christians. Often united with Protestants to oppose Catholicism, Orthodoxy with its autocephalous national offshoots has roots in Greece and the **Byzantine empire**. Based on the first seven ecumenical councils (325–787), during which the Monophysite, Jacobite, Armenian, Coptic, and Ethiopian Churches split off, it has celibate monks, bishops, and patriarchs and married priests but does not recognize the authority of the Pope, and assigns a great role to secular monarchs and the state. The majority live in **Russia**—where ecclesiastical homophobia often eclipsed that of Roman Catholics until the end of Tsarism in 1917. The Churches of Serbia, Macedonia, Romania, Bulgaria, Georgia, Russia, the Ukraine, Cyprus, Greece, Lebanon (the Malekites), and Albania, all weakened by centuries of Tatar (1227–1783) and/or Ottoman (1354–1913) oppression, today profess Orthodoxy. All except Greece, Cyprus, and Lebanon suffered under Communist hostility after 1945. Axios is its American gay group, imitating Dignity and the Protestant analogues.

In 1976, before AIDS, in its Biennial Clergy–Laity Congress, the Greek Orthodox Church, with 3.5 million members in the United States, declared: "The Orthodox Church condemns unreservedly all expressions of personal sexual experience which prove contrary to the definite and unalterable function ascribed to sex by God's ordinance and expressed in man's experience as a law of nature. Thus the function of the sexual organs of a man and a woman and their biochemical generating forces in glands and glandular secretions are ordained by nature to serve one particular purpose, the procreation of the human kind. Therefore, any and all uses of the human sex organs for purposes other than those ordained by creation, runs contrary to the nature of things as decreed by God. . . . The Orthodox Church believes that homosexuality should be treated by society as an immoral and dangerous perversion and by religion as a sinful failure."

Conclusion: A Variegated Picture. In spite of the growing homophobic backlash, some hopeful signs have recently appeared. On December 10, 1987, 150 clergy and religious professionals from the United Methodist, Presbyterian, United Church of Christ, Episcopal, Unitarian Universalist, and American Baptist denominational leaders as well as officials of the American Jewish Congress, the American Jewish Committee and individual congregations appealed in vain to the Massachusetts Senate to approve a gay rights bill, opposed by Cardinal Bernard Law. In 1988 after a bitter debate, the United Church of Canada, consisting of Presbyterians, Methodists, and Congregationalists, voted by a narrow margin to ordain open homosexuals. Moreover, at the end of the 1980s the sex scandals of the charismatics Jim Bakker of the PTL Ministries (who has been accused of homosexual conduct) and Jimmy Swaggart undermined the self-styled "moral majority." In 1988 Jerry Falwell endorsed George Bush rather than Pat Robertson for President, and the failed candidacy of Robertson indicates that the strength and influence of the homophobic New Christian Right may be waning. But even today, with the exception of Episcopalians, Unitarians, and Quakers, and of course the Metropolitan Community Church founded in 1968 by Troy Perry as part of the gay **movement**, many American Protestants tend to be as homophobic as Orthodox and Roman Catholics, the last now in full retreat from Vatican II liberalism and reaffirming as perennially valid the thirteenth-century doctrines of St. Thomas Aquinas.

As has been noted, most American denominations have acquired gay/lesbian affinity groups, which provide a sense of fellowship and press for change within the denomination. Perhaps paradoxically, the most successful of these groups in the 1970s and early 1980s was Catholic; Dignity, whose membership once reached 7,000, by 1989—after the devastation of two antihomosexual Vatican pronouncements and expulsion from church premises—counted only half as many. Integrity, the Episcopalian counterpart, has had difficulties, though these are less serious. As a rule, these affiliates are found only in English-speaking countries. In 1976, however, Pastor Joseph Doucé, a gay Belgian Baptist, founded the Centre du Christ Libérateur in Paris; its mission subsequently spread to a number of other European countries.

See also **Churches, Gay; Clergy, Gay.**

BIBLIOGRAPHY. Edward Batchelor, Jr., ed., *Homosexuality and Ethics*, New York: Pilgrim Press, 1980; Vern L. Bullough, *Sexual Variance in Society and History*, New York: Wiley, 1976; F. L. Cross and E. A. Livingstone, eds., *The Oxford Dictionary of the Christian Church*, 2nd ed., London: Oxford University Press, 1974; Tom Horner, *Homosexuality and the Judeo-Christian Tradition: An Annotated Bibliography*, Metuchen, NJ: Scarecrow Press, 1981; Malcolm Macourt, ed., *Towards a Theology of Gay Liberation*, London: SCM Press, 1977; E. William Monter, "Sodomy and Heresy in Early Modern Switzerland," *Journal of Homosexuality*, 6 (1980–81), 42–55; John Shelby Spong, *Living in Sin!*, San Francisco: Harper & Row, 1988.

William A. Percy

PROUST, MARCEL (1871–1922)

French novelist. Born to wealthy bourgeois parents at the beginning of the Third Republic, he suffered from delicate health as a child and was lovingly tended by his mother. Despite his partly Jewish origins he aspired to mingle in the high society of a Paris that had entered the *belle époque*, and in 1896 he published his first work, *Les Plaisirs et les jours* (Pleasures and Days), in which an astute reviewer discerned "a depraved Bernardin de Saint-Pierre and an ingenu **Petronius**."

Plagued by asthma, after the deaths of his parents he increasingly withdrew from social life, and after 1907 lived mainly in a cork-lined room where at night he labored on a monumental novel, unfinished at his death, and ultimately published in 16 volumes between 1913 and 1927, *A la recherche du temps perdu* (Remembrance of Things Past). If the first part went unnoticed, the second, *A l'ombre des jeunes filles en fleurs* (Within a Budding Grove) won the Goncourt Prize for 1919. The semi-autobiographical novel is superficially an account of the hero's account through childhood and through youthful love affairs to the point of commitment to literary endeavor. It is less a narrative than an inner monologue; alive with brilliant metaphor and sense imagery, the novel is rich in sociological, philosophical, and psychological understanding. A vital theme is the link between outer and inner reality found in time and memory, which mock man's intelligence and endeavor; if memory synthesizes past experience, it also distorts it. Most experience produces only inner pain, and the objects of desire are the causes of suffering. In Proust's thinking man is isolated, society is false and ridden with snobbery, and artistic endeavor is elevated to a religion and judged superior to nature. His ability to interpret man's innermost experience in terms of such forces as time and death gives the novel transcendent literary power, assuring its place as one of the great works of the twentieth century.

Proust was the first major novelist to deal extensively with the theme of homosexuality, and more than any other writer, he bears the responsibility for introducing the topic into the mainstream of modern literature, ending the centuries of spoken and unspoken taboo on mentioning it in other than a subtle and oblique manner. Yet so strong was the negative attitude in the 1920s and later that the adjective *Proustian* served in literary circles as a euphemism for *homosexual*, and critics who grasped the full importance of homosexuality in Proust's life and art avoided the subject out of shame, embarrassment, prejudice, and the tendency in academic circles to suppress the realistic and erotic sides of French literature when addressing undergraduate audiences or the general public. Only in the late 1940s did critics begin to evaluate in print the homosexual element in Proust's novel, and then with biases and superficial generalizations. Even later work was marred by an exclusively **psychoanalytic** approach to Proust's psyche or a vulgar **Freudian** attitude toward sexuality as a whole. The novelist's sexual orientation could be written off as a fixation, a dead-end of psychological development, rather than as the logical and inevitable maturation of a psychic nucleus inseparable from the constitution of the subject and from his artistic experience of self and the world.

Homosexuality is an integral part of Proust's literary creation. Many of the major and minor characters of the novel—Saint-Loup, Morel, the Prince de Guermantes, Jupien, Legrandin, Nissim Bernard, and of course the immortal Baron de Charlus—prove to have homosexual inclinations. And lesbianism is no less one of Proust's preoccupations: the narrator spends much of the novel pondering the implications of female homosexuality and trying to discover whether Albertine has ever loved other women. The role of homosexuality in Proust's work was not accidental; it was to him a theme of capital importance on which he lavished a great deal of reflection and painstaking craftsmanship. When the novelist began to write, the theme was so shocking and unacceptable that he had to approach his publisher, Gaston Gallimard, rather diplomatically to assure him that the subject would not be treated in a sensational manner, but integrated into the narrative.

The crucial date in Proust's career was April 30, 1921, on which the Nouvelle Revue Française issued a book containing the second part of *Le Côté de Guermantes* (Guermantes' Way) and the first part of *Sodome et Gomorrhe* (Cities of the Plain). In the latter, the narrator discovers the homosexuality of the Baron de Charlus (modeled on the real-life Robert de **Montesquiou**-Fézensac) and presents his famous essay on the nature of homosexual love, seen by many critics as an indirect confession of Proust's own orientation and an oblique plea for understanding and tolerance of the homosexual and his way of life. The novelist's own sexual life, as far as can be judged, was marred by pain, rejection, and unrequited love—which is often the bitter experience of the homosexual attracted to a heterosexual man who cannot return his affection. Proust's relationship with his dashing secretary–chauffeur Albert Agostinelli partook of this character; it was cruelly disappointing, because it not only went unrequited but was cut short by the tragedy of unexpected death. (Agostinelli perished while piloting an airplane Proust had given him.)

The mature Proust also witnessed two scandals: the Dreyfus case that divided France—and the salon society of which the writer was a part—into irreconcilable camps, and the Harden-**Eulenburg** affair in which the favorite of Kaiser Wilhelm II was pilloried for his homosexual proclivities. These current events sank into his mind, and the former plays no slight role in the novelist's depiction of the evolution of French society from the early years of the Third Republic down to 1919. At the same time Proust was conscious of the complex, Protean quality of homosexuality itself, of the nuances and contradictions that invalidate any formula which movement apologists were promoting as the politically correct understanding of the matter in their effort to reform public opinion. Sometimes Proust created homosexual stereotypes in order to shatter them, utilizing the artist's freedom to project an image and then reshape it. Internalized self-hatred was not alien to his personality, and from time to time it irrupts into the novel. But the total picture of homosexuality combines great structural and expressive beauty with unprecedented insights into human nature, and the overall artistry of the novel resisted the tendency of a still intolerant Western society to relegate the work to the "memory hole" of literary oblivion. Proust was thus a trailblazer who made the literary treatment and analysis of homosexuality possible, and reached an audience that would never have read a medical study or a movement brochure. In the emancipation of homosexuality from post-medieval taboos, Marcel Proust played a central and incomparable role.

BIBLIOGRAPHY. Henri Bonnet, *Les amours et la sexualité de Marcel Proust*, Paris: A.-G. Nizet, 1985; George D. Painter, *Marcel Proust: A Biography*, 2 vols., London: Chatto & Windus, 1959–65; J. E. Rivers, *Proust & the Art of Love: The Aesthetics of Sexuality in the Life, Times, & Art of Marcel Proust*, New York: Columbia University Press, 1980.

Warren Johansson

PRZHEVALSKY, NIKOLAÏ MIKHAÏLOVICH (1839–1888)

Russian army officer, geographer, and explorer. Descended from a small Cossack landowner, Przhevalsky finished school at Smolensk in 1855 and entered military service, becoming an officer in the following year. In the summer of 1866 he met Robert Koecher, a young Pole of German ancestry who was to be the first of his traveling companions. Each of Przhevalsky's expeditions into Central Asia was planned with the presence of a young male traveling companion between sixteen and twenty-two. On these protégés he lavished expensive gifts, he sponsored their educations, and arranged for them to be commissioned as army officers; in return they had to shun women, share his tent, and give him unquestioning obedience. In the village of Sloboda (today Przheval'skoe) in the northern part of the government of Smolensk he acquired a remote country estate where he was surrounded by a retinue of male visitors. Throughout his life he basked in an all-male ambience from which the presence of women was rigorously excluded. His biographers ascribe his loathing of the coarseness and debauchery of the towns in which he resided to the cultured side of his personality; more likely he had little use for the interests and preoccupations of the heterosexual men who would otherwise have been his boon companions.

Przhevalsky led four major expeditions: in 1870–73 to Mongolia, China, and Tibet, in 1876–77 to Central Asia (Lobnor and Dzhungar), in 1879–80 to Tibet, and in 1883–85 a second to Tibet. At the start of a fifth expedition in the fall of 1888 he died not far from Lake Issyk-Kul', where today his grave and museum are found in the city of Przheval'sk.

During his lifetime Przhevalsky's travels and the books in which he recorded them captured the imagination of a worldwide audience. His books were translated into English at a time when the classics of nineteenth-century Russian literature were barely glimpsed in Great Britain and the United States. He discovered species of wild plants and animals that still bear his name: poplar, rose, and rhododendron;

gerbil, carp, and lizard; but above all *Equus przewalskii*, the only species of horse that survived undomesticated into modern times and caused a major revision of the evolutionary history of the animal.

With Fyodor Eklon, whom he met in the summer of 1875, he had a liaison that lasted until the summer of 1883, when the youth summoned up the courage to tell him that he was to be married and that he could not accompany him on the next expedition to Tibet. This confession led to a bitter scene and rupture, as Przhevalsky never forgave the women who deprived him of the male companionship that he needed. But in the winter of 1881–82 he met a distillery clerk, Pyotr Kozlov, who proved to be "the young man who had been eluding him all his life: alert, submissive, loyal and handsome." Kozlov not only accompanied his protector on his last and most important journeys, but after his death went on to a distinguished career of his own as explorer, archeologist, and author of travel books. He also fulfilled the dream that his mentor's premature death prevented him from attaining: to visit the forbidden city of Lhasa and meet the Dalai Lama.

Przhevalsky was a hunter and explorer who revived an almost archaic homosexual personality type: that of the leader who willingly faces hardship and danger with only other males as companions, and a younger male as his beloved protégé.

BIBLIOGRAPHY. Donald Rayfield, *The Dream of Lhasa: The Life of Nikolay Przhevalsky, Explorer of Central Asia*, Columbus, OH: Ohio State University Press, 1977.

Warren Johansson

PSYCHIATRY

The discipline of psychiatry addresses the problem of mental illness and its treatment, in contrast with **psychology**, which is the academic study of mental processes and functions in human subjects. There is an assumption on the part of the public—and often of psychiatrists themselves—that anything with which psychiatry deals falls into the category of the pathological. The profession of psychiatry has not always been interested in the phenomenon of homosexuality, and when it has considered the subject its approach has not been detached and impartial, but reflected prevailing social attitudes, derived as these were from the cultural and religious beliefs of the community.

Origins of Psychiatry's Concern with Homosexuality. It was only in the last third of the nineteenth century that psychiatry began to study what it called "sexual **inversion**," and it did so not spontaneously, but at the prompting of the earliest spokesmen for the emerging homosexual liberation movement, Karl Heinrich **Ulrichs** and Károly Mária **Kertbeny**. Thus it was not the psychiatrist's own insight, or the data collected from patients under observation, that enabled such authors as Karl Friedrich Otto Westphal and Richard Freiherr von **Krafft-Ebing** to reach the formulations which they published in their pioneering papers, it was the claim of homophile writers that there were human beings without attraction to members of the opposite sex, but with a paradoxical inborn attraction to members of the same sex which they experienced as perfectly natural and consonant with their inner selves.

However, the character of the patient universe from which the earliest cases were drawn—mainly individuals observed in prisons, psychiatric wards, and insane asylums—led the psychiatrists to hold that sexual inversion was, if not an illness itself, at least a symptom of a psychopathic personality. At first homosexuality was thought to be an extremely rare condition: in fact the book published in 1885 by Julien Chevalier, *De l'inversion de l'instinct sexuel*, listed the total number of known cases in the entire world—35! At that time the paper which Vladimir

Fiodorovich **Chizh** had read in St. Petersburg in 1882 was still unknown in Western Europe; in it the author remarked that so far from being rare, the phenomenon in question could account for many of the cases of pederasty that daily came before the courts.

From the outset of the discussion in modern times, psychiatry has found itself in an ambivalent position: on the one hand, it sought to present itself to an increasingly secular society as an objective discipline that could replace the traditional moral authority of the **Christian church**— and for many the psychiatrist took the place of the confessor in the religious culture of the past; on the other hand, it found itself invoked as a source of scientific authority by the church itself to bolster its "revealed" teachings on the subject of sexual morality. Caught between two fires, most psychiatrists have opted for one party or the other; and by and large those who accepted the principle that homosexuality was inborn and unmodifiable have supported the homosexual emancipation **movement**, while those who believed that it was an acquired condition, a pathological fixation, a mental illness have sided with the theologians and formulated their judgments in terms that amounted to condemnation, when they did not openly reaffirm the traditional attitudes.

Homosexuality as a Congenital vs. Acquired Condition. At the moment when Krafft-Ebing summarized the early papers that had appeared in psychiatric journals between 1869 and 1877, psychiatry was so strongly influenced by the belief in the congenital origins of mental illness that homosexuality quite effortlessly fell into this category. His views were echoed by many others down to the early decades of the twentieth century: Arrigo Tamassia, Julien Chevalier, Albert **Moll**, Paul Näcke, Havelock **Ellis**. Only at the end of the nineteenth century did the pioneering work of Albert Freiherr von Schrenck-Notzing in the use of hypnosis open the way to a developmental theory of sexual orientation in which **Freudian** psychoanalysis was to occupy a prominent place. **Psychoanalysis** began as a particular method for the treatment of mental and emotional disturbances that were psychogenic in origin, but expanded into a psychology of all "unconscious" mental processes, including those of normal individuals. The psychoanalytic school claimed rather that homosexuality was the outcome of faulty psychological development in childhood, that it represented an inhibition of the heterosexual potential present in all human subjects. Thus homosexuality tended rather to be classified as a neurosis or as the expression of a neurotic personality disorder than as an erotic monomania.

Forensic Aspects. The forensic evaluation of homosexuality has had its own history since the 1870s. On the one hand, psychiatric testimony was at times introduced in trials for sodomy with the aim of proving that the defendant was suffering from a mental illness that diminished or abolished his legal responsibility; on the other, the notion that the homosexual was a "psychopathic personality" led to the introduction of many disabilities in civil and administrative law that were added to the criminal statutes already in force. In the English-speaking world the latter trend actually made the legal position of the homosexual even worse than it had been when the defendant was simply "guilty of unnatural vice." Down to the 1960s the psychiatric profession remained largely indifferent to the legal problems of the homosexual, even if individual psychiatrists would at times testify on behalf of a particular defendant. The fact that psychiatrists obtain the largest segment of their referrals from the clergy made them unwilling to argue for a change in the traditional punitive attitudes, or for liberalization of the statutes which maintained penalties for private sexual acts far more severe than those for such crimes as armed robbery or beating or neglecting a small child. As late as 1956 a report by a group of

American psychiatrists could criticize the law only on the ground that "some innocent persons" might be punished.

Psychiatric "Cures" vs. Gay Rights. Also included in the psychiatric confrontation with homosexuality was the matter of enforced therapy—individuals required by court order to undergo psychiatric treatment, or in other cases compelled by their parents to submit to therapy for their unwanted "tendencies." This treatment could take exceptionally cruel and humiliating forms, including shock therapy and other painful procedures designed to create an **aversion** to homosexual stimuli.

Even when the **Wolfenden Report** (1957) heralded the movement for criminal law reform, the psychiatric profession remained indifferent, insisting only that homosexuality was "a serious disease" and that measures had to be taken to combat its spread. It was the gay liberation **movement** itself that had to rouse the psychiatrists out of their inertia, and specifically put pressure on the American Psychiatric Association to drop homosexuality from its roster of mental illnesses— which it did in 1973. In 1986 even the substitute "**ego-dystonic homosexuality**" disappeared from the list (DSM-IIIR). The importance of this change, as mentioned above, was that in the meantime the notion of homosexuality as disease had been used to deny homosexuals a whole range of civil rights, including immigration, employment, adoption, service in the armed forces and other benefits accorded to the rest of the population. But the decision of the American Psychiatric Association was more the outcome of political pressure and manipulation than an expression of the sincere belief of the members. The psychiatrists who have been the most outspoken in proclaiming homosexuality to be a "disease"—Edmund **Bergler**, Abram Kardiner, Irving Bieber, Charles Socarides—usually express reservations if not outright opposition to any demand for gay rights in the sphere of civil or administrative law—a clear proof that their belief rationalizes the traditional condemnation of homosexual expression by Judaism and Christianity.

A number of psychiatrists have claimed success in "curing" homosexuality, but their results have been questioned on a number of grounds, including the lack of follow-up studies. In some instances the individual merely became far more inhibited in expressing his homosexual desires, which is to say more guilt ridden and unhappy than before. Nearly all practitioners conceded that only carefully selected subjects could benefit from their proposed therapy; Edmund Bergler, for example, maintained that the patient had to experience conscious guilt over his homosexual practices. Many practitioners would admit that some foundation of heterosexuality is necessary for even a temporary "cure" to be effected; that is to say, they choose to treat bisexuals in whom it is possible to suppress one side of the equation. There are few, if any, well attested cases of permanent reversal from complete homosexuality to complete heterosexuality. In any event, the inability of the psychiatrists to distance themselves from traditional morality has often been striking, even if they were oblivious of the normative dimension of their practice.

Exclusion of Homosexuality from the Realm of Mental Illness. The contemporary gay liberation movement has been characterized by an effort to remove the stigma of "mental illness" from homosexuality and therefore to renounce any benefits that might have accrued from the appeal to psychiatry as a shield from the law. The virtual cessation of prosecutions for consenting homosexual activity between adults has made this degrading démarche a thing of the past. A number of psychiatrists now practice a line of therapy that enables the patient and his family to accept the homosexuality as an integral part of his personality, and then to optimize his personal adjustment to a society with many vestiges of intolerance. Self-acceptance and openness are recognized as preferable to a forced adherence to the ascetic morality once regarded as the absolute norm.

BIBLIOGRAPHY. Ronald Bayer, *Homosexuality and American Psychiatry: The Politics of Diagnosis*, 2nd ed., Princeton: Princeton University Press, 1987; Peter Conrad and Joseph W. Schneider, *Deviants and Medicalization: From Badness to Sickness*, St. Louis: C. V. Mosby, 1980; Martin S. Weinberg and Alan P. Bell, *Homosexuality: An Annotated Bibliography*, New York: Harper & Row, 1972.

Warren Johansson

PSYCHOANALYSIS

Psychoanalysis is the movement that takes its start from the ideas set forth by Sigmund **Freud** at the turn of the present century. The movement, which has had a vast influence on many realms of modern thought, remains hard to classify. The lay public tends to confuse it with **psychology**, yet academic psychologists remain among the most determined doubters of the value of psychoanalytic techniques and concepts. Although psychoanalysis claims to be a form of mental therapy—indeed the only truly serious one—the efficacy of its procedures in promoting mental health has never been conclusively demonstrated, and indeed an increasing number of observers question whether they possess any intrinsic therapeutic value. The popular mind associates the views of Freud and his followers with sex, believing that psychoanalysis is centrally concerned with the erotic, or that it was the first discipline to discuss the matter in an ordered way. These assertions are false. Freud actually arrived as a late-comer at the crest of a period of sex research, the main center of which lay in Berlin, not in Vienna. Moreover, the views of Freud and his followers are addressed primarily to nonsexual issues. In addition to its concern with the mind, psychoanalysis also has a metapsychological side, in which it offers views and speculations on human destiny and the nature of civilization. Finally, psychoanalysis has had an enormous influence over modern literature and art, where it may be said to play a role similar to that of **mythology** in the creative work of classical Greece and Rome. Increasingly questioned by scientists, the lasting significance of psychoanalysis is now seen more and more to reside in this cultural realm.

History. Freud founded the Vienna Psychoanalytic Society in 1902 and the International Psychoanalytic Society in 1910. His organizations attracted a number of talented followers, but their history was marred by defections, notably those of Alfred **Adler** in 1911 and Carl Gustav **Jung** in 1914. Although, as has been noted, Freud's theories are not exclusively or even centrally sexual, he rightly criticized both men for their excision of the sexual element from psychoanalysis.

At first psychoanalysis was largely restricted to German-speaking countries, but it was diffused to some extent in France thanks to the work of Marie Bonaparte and in England through Freud's faithful follower Ernest Jones. Although Freud visited the United States in 1911 (in the company of Jung), he came to dislike the country, in part because of personal financial losses in World War I.

On at least two occasions, in 1905 and 1935, Freud gave statements that were remarkably sympathetic to homosexuals as individuals. The lesbian tendencies of his favorite daughter Anna (which were quietly, though discreetly acknowledged in his immediate circle) may have helped to soften his views. Yet, when all is said and done, his theory relegates homosexuals to a category of the mentally second class. Human psychosexual development Freud sees as an arduous journey through the oral and anal to the mature genital stage, which he equates with heterosexuality. Instead of obeying the summons to complete this journey, homosexuals have lingered along the way. Important psychic developments have been "inhibited," and they remain immature.

In the 1920s professional psychoanalytic circles debated the question of whether a homosexual might be qualified to become an analyst. Freud answered that under certain conditions such a person could be accepted. Ernest Jones, however, disagreed, and this ban came to be the dominant view, so that overt homosexuals in the course of a training analysis presumably had to lie blatantly to their analyst, while the exclusion practiced by the psychoanalytic profession provided a model for discrimination in other fields calling for confidentiality and intimacy.

Ironically, in view of Freud's dislike, America seemed the nation in which psychoanalysis achieved its greatest triumphs, thanks the the large number of émigré analysts who settled there in the 1930s because of Hitler's persecutions. In fusing with the American ethos, psychoanalysis blurred some of its essential features. The notion of primordial **bisexuality** was thrown overboard (especially in a key paper by Sandor Rado), and new handicaps were discovered in homosexuality (e.g., the supposed tendency to **"injustice collecting"** promoted by Edmund **Bergler** and the "close-binding mother" of Irving Bieber). Seeing only homosexuals who came to them for help as patients, the practicing psychoanalyst is tempted to project the neuroses of this selected group on the entire homosexual population.

All too frequently American psychoanalysis seemed to wish nothing more than to acquiesce in, and even to abet, the then prevailing demands for adjustment and conformity. In this way it lost whatever emancipatory vigor it had originally possessed. In the period after World War II countless numbers of homosexuals and lesbians were analyzed at enormous expense, the result usually being misery in that they could not "adjust" to society's norms by overcoming the "neurosis" of homosexuality.

Critiques. In the 1960s discordant voices came to be heard, including those of Wilhelm **Reich** (1897–1957) and Herbert Marcuse (1898–1979), both well-informed central Europeans. Different as they were, Reich and Marcuse seemed to offer a more "revolutionary" brand of psychoanalysis which would meld personal change with radical societal reconstruction. Yet these new trends reckoned without the social pessimism of the founder, who had counseled, in effect, "repression will ye always have with you."

More damaging were challenges that went to the heart of the therapeutic claims of psychoanalysis. In the 1950s H. J. Eysenck produced a statistical study showing that psychoanalytic patients recovered no more quickly (in fact somewhat more slowly) than those who received no therapy at all. While the psychoanalytic establishment has sought to pour cold water on this and similar studies, it has yet to produce conclusive evidence that psychoanalysis has any distinctive therapeutic efficacy. Considering the length and expense of the treatment, and the increasing availability of more concise therapies, this critique has struck home. When asked to supply empirical evidence of the success of their therapeutic sessions, psychoanalysts commonly reply that the analyst–client relationship is privileged, and must not be monitored by a third party. Thus the efficacy of psychoanalytic procedures is presented as self-validating. Such defensive measures cannot be employed by any true science, which by definition must always take the risk that it will be falsified by independent tests.

Nor are self-reports even of patients who have enjoyed "successful" analyses uniformly encouraging. Some even return for a "retread" program. Forced to renounce even the claim that psychoanalysis makes one happy, its defenders have retreated into the position that prolonged analysis offers the benefit of showing the tragic ambiguity of life. This claim would suggest that it is a poetics or lay philosophy rather than a therapy. Such assertions would seem to be buttressed rather than countered by the opaque writings of Jacques Lacan, a French "deconstructionist" psychoanalyst much in vogue in the 1980s in some circles in England and America.

In the 1980s criticism mounted. Jeffrey Moussaieff Masson and Martin Swales presented evidence that showed the personal ethics of Freud to be questionable. It has also been charged that he remained a cocaine addict through the 1890s, when he began to present his distinctive theories. Other researchers have emphasized the eclecticism of his ideas, their lack of originality: the idea of the unconscious came as part of the legacy of German romanticism; universal bisexuality derived from Freud's mentor Wilhelm Fliess; and infantile sexuality was purloined (without acknowledgement) from Albert **Moll**. Individually these critiques may not suffice to overturn psychoanalytic theory, but they have seriously eroded the popular perception, so carefully nourished by the psychoanalytic establishment over the years, that Freud was a secular saint. More generally, it has been justly remarked that psychoanalysis is culture-bound, a product of middle-class Viennese society at the end of the nineteenth century. Thus the "penis envy" that is supposed to be a universal stage of women's self-understanding is nothing more than the confluence of Victorian prudery and the subjection of women. Yet the most damaging critiques are those which challenge the very core of psychoanalysis: its logical status. Adolf Grünbaum and Morris Eagle argue that psychoanalysis works essentially as a placebo. Forming an emotional bond with the analyst ("transference"), the patient gradually internalizes the concepts of psychoanalysis. For example, patients of Freudian analysts tend to have "Freudian" dreams with "Freudian" symbols, those of Jungian analysts have "Jungian" dreams with matching symbols. This process of assimilation is then labeled therapeutic progress.

The ultimate value of psychoanalysis remains hard to assess. There can be no doubt that in the early decades its ideas, novel to the lay public, helped to undermine conventional moral certainties and to stimulate new thought. Yet once psychoanalysis was itself assimilated into the conventional wisdom this benefit was lost. The problems experienced by analysands (therapeutic clients) were compounded for gay men and lesbians. Many believed that they benefited from analysis, but a great many more have emerged with negative feelings about the process and recurrent difficulty in accepting their sexual nature.

Despite its problematic character, psychoanalysis has proved a hardy perennial through the twentieth century. Although the twenty-first is unlikely to see its final triumph, this trend in modern thought may yet have new contributions to make.

BIBLIOGRAPHY. Frederick Crews, *Skeptical Engagements*, New York: Oxford University Press, 1986; Richard C. Friedman, *Male Homosexuality: A Contemporary Psychoanalytic Perspective*, New Haven: Yale University Press, 1988; Robert Friedman, "The Psychoanalytic Model of Male Homosexuality: A Historical and Theoretical Critique," *Psychoanalytic Review*, 73 (1986), 483–519; Adolf Grünbaum, *The Foundations of Psychoanalysis: A Philosophical Critique*, Berkeley: University of California Press, 1984; Richard A. Isay, *Being Homosexual: Gay Men and Their Development*, New York: Farrar, Straus & Giroux, 1989; Kenneth Lewes, *The Psychoanalytic Theory of Male Homosexuality*, New York: Simon and Schuster, 1988; Timothy F. Murphy, "Freud Reconsidered: Bisexuality, Homosexuality, and Moral Judgment," *Journal of Homosexuality*, 9:2/3 (1983–84), 65–77; Paul Roazen, *Encountering Freud: The Politics and Histories of Psychoanalysis*, New Brunswick, NJ: Transaction, 1989; idem, *Freud and His Followers*, New York: Basic Books, 1976.

Wayne R. Dynes

PSYCHOLOGY

Psychology is the discipline that studies the phenomena of mental life and the conditions that produce them. Psychology differs from **psychotherapy** in being a strictly empirical field: it observes human mental processes and behavior but does not try to change them. Social psychology, which is concerned with the group aspect of human behavior, with the collective counterpart to the individual personality, stands on the borderline of **sociology**. Psychology must be distinguished from **psychiatry**, the branch of medicine which studies and seeks to cure mental illness.

History and Character of the Field. Psychology originated in the eighteenth century as that branch of philosophy which studied the phenomena of mental life, that is to say, what is introspectively observed as happening in the mind, together with perception, memory, thought, and reasoning. Only in the closing decades of the nineteenth century did psychology as an academic discipline escape from the tutelage of philosophy and become an independent department of the university, with its own methods, books and periodicals, courses, and professional societies. The two leading figures were Wilhelm Wundt and William James. In 1875 Wundt founded the first laboratory dedicated to the experimental study of sensation, memory, and learning. In 1890 James published the classic *Principles of Psychology*, which defined the branches of the discipline; the chapters of today's textbooks are still devoted to perceiving, remembering, thinking and language, concepts and reasoning, as well as emotions, needs, and motives, learning, coping behavior, and conflicts, intelligence and skills, and attitudes and beliefs in regard to social and cultural phenomena.

The growth of the discipline was accompanied by mounting specialization, and also by the formation of schools such as behaviorism, physiological psychology, Gestalt psychology, psychoanalysis, purposivism, factor analysis, and ethology. Behaviorism had the effect of narrowing the definition of the subject to exclude all that could not be directly observed and rather to focus on those aspects of behavior that could be mechanically recorded and measured, while **psychoanalysis** addressed those phenomena which could not be observed—because inaccessible to the conscious mind—but only inferred from the observable ones. The rigorous definition of scientific psychology came to mean that the study must be systematic, with observations made under controlled conditions that allow reliable conclusions to be drawn, and with inclusion of the subject's responses to external events or stimuli, whether occurring naturally or under the manipulation of the experimenter. Psychology remains on an uncertain borderline between the natural sciences and the social sciences, and it has further opted to concentrate on particular sets of mental phenomena that are only to a limited extent the subject of political or ideological controversy.

These circumstances, and the legacy of nineteenth-century positivism, have given psychology a peculiar emphasis on the quantifiable, so that the development of tests and scales of all kinds for measuring intelligence, aptitude, and the degree of mastery of academic subjects in relation to native ability has become a prime task of the psychological establishment, which justifies its existence by providing society with the means for determining who is qualified for higher education, employment, and advancement. This very fact led academic psychology to ignore the issue of homosexuality, and of attitudes toward homosexuality—a rather different matter—because these topics rarely intersected with the goals of the discipline as it had come to be defined. Even the specialty of abnormal and clinical psychology, which overlapped with psychiatry, since the Ph.D. in that field could practice psychotherapy, could deal with homosexuality only as a form of pathology, as a deviation that needed to be cured.

Psychology and Prejudice. The study of **prejudice** against minority groups within society began in the 1940s, and received a tremendous stimulus from the publication of the work of T. W. Adorno and his associates in *The **Authoritarian Personality*** (1950), which found common denominators in personality types that accepted or rejected individuals who differed markedly from themselves. When the subject of homosexuality became more acceptable, numerous questionnaire studies addressed the problem of attitudes toward homosexuals and the factors that tended to alter them, either positively or negatively. The evaluation of such findings suffers from numerous biases, in particular the tendency of academic psychologists to rely almost entirely on college student populations as the ones most easily accessible and also the most easily instructed in the manner of taking the test, as contrasted, one might say, with barely literate juvenile-delinquent populations. Likewise the pressure exerted by the makers of mass opinion to indoctrinate the general public with a "correct" set of attitudes on sundry issues leads to a certain conformity, as the subject senses that there is a right answer to particular questions—which may differ profoundly from his spontaneous reactions and inner beliefs.

Identity. In general, **identity** means a person's self-definition in relation to others, but more specifically it connotes the definition derived from membership in various social groups. Identity has both social and personal aspects, the former having to do with the experience of belonging to a defined group, the latter having to do with individual psychodynamics. The concept of social identity has occupied a central place in both social psychology and sociology. Kurt Lewin, for example, whose field theory inspired a whole generation of postwar social psychologists, did extensive research on the psychological significance of group affiliation, especially for minority and marginal groups. Social identity is also a factor in intergroup discrimination, even in the absence of real conflicts of economic interest, and sheds light on such problems as the dilemma of minority groups, industrial conflicts over pay differentials, and linguistic differences between classes and ethnic groups.

A homosexual identity is a problem for the individual in that it entails first, the discovery of being psychologically different from the norm of the population, and second, the acceptance or rejection of affinity with the collectivity of persons labeled "homosexual" (or "gay") by themselves and by the larger society. It further imposes upon the individual the task of managing a self-concept that in many circumstances of life is perceived as a distinct liability, even an impossible handicap. Because of the attitudes toward homosexuality that have prevailed in Western society the individual with an "inner" homosexual identity has often had to cultivate an "outer" heterosexual one— to function in two social worlds simultaneously.

The range of **subcultures** and **lifestyles** within the gay community requires that the individual identify with one in order to be accepted as a full-fledged member and to interact sexually with others in the subculture. This identity must be validated not just by appropriate sexual behavior, but also by the adoption of the style of dress, the mannerisms, the argot, and the ideology of the particular segment of the homosexual world into which the subject desires acceptance. Psychological studies have focused on the process by which the homosexual identity is acquired (or rejected) and the skills needed to cope with the accompanying stigma are developed and internalized.

Functioning. Psychological **functioning** is another major concern of the academic psychologist. A whole series of papers and monographs has produced evidence to support the claim that homosexuals function in the circumstances of public and private life as well as heterosexuals, in opposition to the charge that they are neurotically disturbed and conflict-ridden to the point of being dysfunctional. Some authors have even found that their homosexual subjects functioned better than the matching heterosexual control group. Mark Freedman, for example, did a Ph.D. dissertation at Case Western University which concluded that his lesbian subjects differed from heterosexual women in having more independence and inner direction, more acceptance of aggression, and more satisfaction in work. It is remarkable that advocates of gay rights have had to substantiate the claim that their constituency functioned as well as the heterosexual majority despite the psychological pressures imposed by society's intolerance, while for others no such attestation is required to seek escape from inferior status. The inferior performance of some (but not all) members of ethnic minorities is generally ascribed to centuries of **discrimination** and prejudice, but this insight is withheld in respect to members of sexual **minorities**.

Attitudes Toward Homosexuality. Only recently has the study of attitudes toward homosexuality been differentiated from psychological inquiry into the phenomenon itself. Here again, the demand for moral conformity in sexual matters made it impossible until then even to suggest that there could be another attitude than one of uncompromising rejection. Comparative studies have shown that dislike of homosexuals parallels negative attitudes toward other "outsider" groups, but with the difference that decades of propaganda against racial and religious prejudice have compelled most of the general public to profess a formal tolerance of such minorities in reply to questionnaire or interview studies, while open hatred and contempt for homosexuals can still be voiced with no social disapproval.

Hence homosexuals come at the very bottom in nearly all polls of attitudes toward minority and deviant groups. In general, the greatest intolerance is found among the elderly, the poorly educated, and those most involved with traditional religion—categories that overlap to a considerable extent—while the most tolerant are those who have been exposed to the modern psychological and sociological literature on homosexuality.

Conclusion: Structure and Limitations of the Discipline. To a great extent the discipline of psychology, emerging as it did on the threshold of the second Industrial Revolution, has come to reflect the needs of an increasingly complex society to ensure that its members fitted into the model of a self-regulating component of a production team, whether in the office or on the assembly line. Aptitude and performance tests measured whether the educational system was effectively sorting and processing the human raw material fed into it to be readied for active participation in the labor force. Thus academic psychology was oriented toward predominantly utilitarian ends, not toward idle speculation on the "mind–body dichotomy" and other classical issues in philosophy. In a pluralistic society like the United States, moreover, psychology felt summoned to address issues of intergroup relations and the tensions and conflicts which these engendered, including the relationship of the mass culture shared by all Americans to the particular value systems of ethnic and socio-economic subgroups.

The findings of academic psychology are often limited in value by the lack of cross-cultural comparison, although as the discipline grows in other parts of the world it is becoming possible to administer standard tests and questionnaires to individuals raised in very different cultures. The notion of homosexuality, which originated in Northern Europe and has only partially spread into non-Western countries, poses real problems for the psychologist studying the issues of identity formation, functioning, and public opinion on the subject. Also, the campus-bound inertia of many psychologists makes the base of their investigations too narrow and too divorced from everyday life. College sophomores figure in small print as the subjects in paper after paper, hence the findings apply to this upwardly mobile, middle-class population. Public opinion sampling has addressed the issue of constructing representative groups of respondents who accurately reflect the range of attitudes within a heterogeneous society, but also of ascertaining regional and class dimensions of political and social belief. These inquiries, however, often lack the precision and depth of the psychologist's elaborately constructed and administered questionnaire or interview.

The number of papers and dissertations in which homosexuality figures in one connection or another continues to grow, and the stigma that once attached even to the academic investigator of the subject is waning. So psychology will in the future confront the problem of homosexuality with all the issues that arise from the subject's interaction with the special areas of investigation that comprise the discipline.

BIBLIOGRAPHY. John Gonsiorek, *Psychological Adjustment and Homosexuality*, Washington, DC: American Psychological Association, 1977; Stephen F. Morin, "Heterosexual Bias in Psychological Research on Lesbianism and Male Homosexuality," *American Psychologist*, 32 (1977), 629–37; Lon C. Nungesser, *Homosexual Acts, Actors and Identities*, New York: Praeger, 1983; Alan T. Watters, "Heterosexual Bias in Psychological Research on Lesbianism and Male Homosexuality (1979–1983), Utilizing the Bibliography and Taxonomic System of Morin," *Journal of Homosexuality*, 13 (1986), 35–58.

Warren Johansson

PSYCHOTHERAPY

The effort to treat mental or emotional disorders by **psychiatric** means, sometimes accompanied by drugs and surgery, is a characteristic modern phenomenon, stemming originally from a "social engineering" belief system—the idea that societal ills may be attacked and banished in the same way as public health problems such as epidemics and poor sanitation. Recent experience indicates that more modest expectations are in order.

History and Rationale. Medieval and early modern society regarded the insane as simply irretrievable, and relegated them permanently to the margins of society. Toward the end of the eighteenth century, however, a new group of alienists, influenced by the **Enlightenment**, sought to cure the insane by humane treatments. Their success in this recuperative effort, qualified as it was, nonetheless contributed to the growth of the idea that there was no sharp break between the insane and the mentally healthy, but rather a continuum, with various states of neurosis occupying the zones between the two poles. Human hypochondria being what it is, the spread of this nuanced view had the unfortunate side effect of causing many **functioning** human beings to regard themselves as neurotic and to seek psychotherapy. Also, many individuals whose problems were essentially ones of morale—an indefinable malaise, lack of purpose in life, boredom at work, the drying up of the creative impulse—sought relief from the psychotherapist as if their difficulties were medical, although they were suffering from no known clinical entity.

Recent social critiques distinguish sharply between coercive and voluntary psychotherapy. It is recognized that coercive therapy, which ranged from family-compelled visits to the therapist to such brutal treatments as psychiatrist-ordered electric shock, has been overused. Even with voluntary treatments, however, clients were kept attending sessions for years, being bled white of their money and developing a crippling emotional dependence on the therapist. To all intents and purposes, the psychotherapist had taken the place of the priest or astrologer of former times, but with such a heavy baggage of medical and pseudomedical assumptions that consultation of the priest or astrologer might have been more effective. Many now recognize the limitations of psychotherapy, and shorter, result-oriented programs are more common. For the individual seeking voluntary treatment today, however, a bewildering variety of therapies—as many as 250 according to one account—are available.

Homosexuals and Psychotherapy. During the height of the modern coercive therapy trend in the first half of the twentieth century, many homosexuals were treated against their will. Such barbarous treatments as lobotomy and electroshock were widely practiced. In many instances the victims of these procedures were young people who had been committed by their parents or guardians. In keeping with the law in some American states homosexuals were even castrated. Even when these steps were not actually taken, dread that they would be applied, often accompanied by open threats, served to reduce many to the status of miserable accomplices in their own degradation. Adverse publicity and the abandonment of the idea that homosexuality is an illness eventually greatly reduced the prevalence of these appalling punitive practices. Yet incarcerated pedophiles are still subjected to a variety of involuntary treatments— some amounting to chemical castration.

The subjection of homosexuals to barbaric therapies, an accepted procedure within living memory, is one of the factors that have caused a healthy skepticism of the ethics of psychotherapy. In most countries of the First World greater sensitivity is found among professionals. In countries of the Soviet bloc and many Third World nations arbitrary use of coercive psychotherapy persists as a way of coping with political dissent.

Over the years there have undoubtedly been many closeted homosexual therapists, professionals who concealed their orientation in order to retain their positions. The most famous example is Harry Stack **Sullivan** (1892–1949), who headed the William Allenson White Foundation in New York City. Because of this factor of professional concealment, homosexuals could be undertaking treatment from another homosexual without realizing it. Apart from this problem, many earlier treatment programs were simply exercises in futility with the patient agreeing pro forma to the goal of change of orientation, but in fact continuing to cherish his deeply rooted wishes and desires.

Realism requires one to concede that even overt identity of the client's sexual orientation with that of the therapist offers no guarantee of a satisfactory outcome—or even inception. Today, however, there are many affirmative gay and lesbian therapists who are concerned not with changing the client's orientation but with making possible a richer and more rewarding life within that orientation. Many hold that a lesbian should seek a lesbian therapist, a gay man a gay male therapist. The main point is that the procedures should be affirmative and constructive in the best sense. To this end, client and therapist should achieve a firm understanding of goals and commitments, including costs, before undertaking work together. It should be recognized that other complications, such as **alcoholism** and family relations, may need to be taken into account. Even so, therapy is at best an art, not a science, and no exaggerated hopes should be entertained of any major personality transformation. The most that therapy is likely to achieve is to permit the client more effectively "to play the hand he or she is dealt."

Under the editorship of Professor David Scasta (Temple University Medical School), a *Journal of Gay and Lesbian Psychotherapy* was founded in 1989 (Haworth Press).

BIBLIOGRAPHY. Sidney Bloch and Paul Chodoff, eds., *Psychiatric Ethics*, New York: Oxford University Press, 1981; Eli

Coleman, ed., *Psychotherapy with Homosexual Men and Women: Integrated Identity Approaches for Clinical Practice*, New York: Haworth Press, 1987; John C. Gonsiorek, *A Guide to Psychotherapy with Gay and Lesbian Clients*, New York: Harrington Park Press, 1985; Marny Hall, *The Lavender Couch: A Consumer's Guide to Psychotherapy for Lesbian and Gay Men*, Boston: Alyson, 1985; Michael Ross, ed., *Psychopathology and Psychotherapy in Homosexuality*, New York: Haworth Press, 1988.

Wayne R. Dynes

PUBLIC SCHOOLS

This is the British name for the private secondary schools that educate, for sizable fees, upper-class and upwardly mobile middle-class children between the ages of twelve and eighteen—the future elite of the nation. Their educational methods and the environment in which adolescents spend the formative years of their adolescence have done much to shape British character. Although some of them were founded in the mid-fourteenth century beginning with Winchester in 1378, whose statutes, enacted in 1400, governed it until 1857, they took on their present character only with the reforms of Thomas Arnold (father of Matthew) toward the middle of the nineteenth century, but during the eighteenth and early part of the nineteenth the study of Latin and Greek formed practically the entire curriculum.

Basic Features. Traditionally boarding schools with harsh living conditions (including physical discomfort and corporal punishment for misdemeanors), public schools permitted a good deal of autonomy, allowing the adolescent subculture—with all its cruelty and demand for conformity—to dominate the lives of the boys. The curriculum introduced by Arnold was strongly classical, Latin and Greek being the principal subjects; but public schools also emphasized athletics and teamwork that made for success on the playing field. At the same time Victorian evangelism invested the schools with

the pietistic ideal of creating "Christian gentlemen." Graduates of the "public schools," the best secondary institutions in the country, have an enormous advantage in competing for admission to the leading universities—**Cambridge and Oxford** as well as London, or to Sandhurst or the Royal Naval College. And to boot, access to the nine great public schools, led by Eton and Harrow, was limited to the sons of alumni, who had to be registered with the school at the time of their birth.

Homosocial and Homosexual Aspects. The public schools have a homoerotic ambiance that may not find overt expression; but confined as they are with members of their own sex, at what is for many the "homosexual phase," and approaching the peak of their physical beauty, the boys are perforce involved in intense friendships that amount to love affairs. The degree of acceptance of these attachments has varied over the decades, but there is abundant evidence for homosexual affairs between public school boys and between them and their teachers, who are in some instances homosexuals of the pederastic type—attracted solely to boys of that age, not to adults.

At the same time the public schools inculcate an ethos of duty, of loyalty, of service to king and country that amounts to an initiation into what Hans Blüher called the "male society," the form of social organization based on male bonding that is the foundation of the state and of its administrative and military apparatus. And the public schools, whatever defects their curriculum may have had, did train and instill in the men who governed the Empire the virtues requisite for ruling.

Evidence for homosexual activity within the public schools is slight from the early modern period, although Nicholas Udall, the headmaster of Eton, was in 1543 exposed as a result of an unsuccessful attempt of two of his pupils implicated in the theft of silver objects to **blackmail** him into silence. The death penalty for buggery to which he would have been subject was commuted to imprisonment by the Privy Council, and in 1547 he was released and appointed headmaster of Westminster.

In the nineteenth century C. J. Vaughan, the headmaster of Harrow, was compromised when a good-looking boy named Alfred Pretor revealed to John Addington **Symonds** that Vaughan had been having an affair with him. Symonds kept the secret for eight years, then revealed it to a professor at Oxford who told him to disclose the information to his father. The elder Symonds promptly forced Vaughan to resign as headmaster and to promise that he would never hold any high position in the Church of England. This scandalous (but suppressed) episode explains why Vaughan mysteriously "curbed his ambition" for the rest of his life.

If only a fourth of the public school boys are involved in overt homosexual activity, far fewer become lifelong homosexuals, yet they all share a lingering attachment to the camaraderie and the group identity crucial to the "male society." That sense of solidarity and cohesiveness stood Britain in good stead during the two world wars; but weaknesses in the public schools' curriculums share in the blame for the decline of Britain in an age when science and technology are increasingly important factors in a nation's competitiveness.

The American boarding schools, especially ones in New England, are modeled on the British public schools, though they are less rigorous and less insistent upon the Greek and Latin classics. But like their counterparts in the (British) Commonwealth, they foster homoeroticism. The same is true of the military schools that predominate in the American South, more removed as they are from the British public school model. Thus much of the elite of the whole Anglo-Saxon world passes through this male bonding process before college and the military.

In the eighteenth century Count **Beccaria** recommended abolishing one-sex schools precisely because they served as breeding grounds for "Greek customs." The spread of the coeducational model in Western industrial societies reflects in part such cautionary views, as well as feminist aspirations for equality.

Female Parallels. Girls' schools in many respects mirror the male ones, but they earlier introduced more modern subjects—science, history, and living languages. Not a few of the teachers are lesbians who cherish a dislike of men and a resentment of male privilege which they subtly convey to their pupils. The universal feature of the sexual life at girls' schools is the "crush"—the love of a younger girl, one between eleven and fourteen, for an older one who often played the role of surrogate mother. Older girls tend to be attracted to teachers and are rivals for their favor as in the school of **Sappho**. The embargo placed on heterosexual relationships—with the perils of loss of virginity and pregnancy—encourages strong physical attraction to members of one's own sex. Measures to discourage contact between members of different age-cohorts and the ensuing "sentimental friendships" have not been able to suppress the emotional needs of those experiencing the first flush of adolescence.

Literary Aspects. Its rigors notwithstanding, the sentimental attachment to the public school has fostered a genre of popular **novels** in which homoerotic sentiments pervade—but usually only as a subtext that the casual reader may miss. The archetype of the genre is Thomas Hughes' *Tom Brown's School Days* (1857). H. A. Vachell's *The Hill: A Romance of Friendship* (1905) is a chaste version of the **David and Jonathan** theme. Michael Campbell's *Lord Dismiss Us* (1968) captures some of the emotional intensity of (unconsummated) love between two sixteen year olds.

The French diplomat and novelist Roger Peyrefitte wrote candidly of his school in *Les Amitiés particulières* (1945), his friend Henry de **Montherlant** less so.

Catholic boys in French boarding schools were educated by Jesuits and other celibate members of the clergy, who (though usually chaste) were often inclined to homoerotic sentiments. **Colette** recalled her schoolgirl lesbianism in a matter-of-fact way, while the German writer Christa Winsloe (in *The Child Manuela*, and its several film versions entitled *Mädchen in Uniform*) emphasized the conflicts stemming from an idealistic love affair between a teacher and her girl pupil.

Conclusion. The overall pattern of public school homosexuality is one of intense emotional bonds between adolescents, sometimes encouraged or facilitated by pederastic homosexuals or corophile lesbians on the staffs. For most these erotic attachments are transitory; for a few, they mark the onset of a homosexual career. In Britain especially, the collective experience does much to strengthen the kind of same-sex bonding that gives elite society its distinctive ethos and value system.

BIBLIOGRAPHY. John Chandos, *Boys Together: English Public Schools 1800–1864*, New Haven: Yale University Press, 1984; Jonathan Gathorne-Hardy, *The Old School Tie: The Phenomenon of the English Public School*, New York: The Viking Press, 1977; Claude Pujada-Renaud, *L'Ecole dans la littérature*, Paris: Editions ESF/Science de l'Education, 1988; Jeffrey Richards, *Happiest Days: The Public Schools in English Fiction*, Manchester: Manchester University Press, 1988; Martha Vicinus, "Distance and Desire: English Boarding-School Friendships," *Signs*, 9 (1984), 600–22.
Warren Johansson and William A. Percy

PUBLIC SEX
See Impersonal Sex.

PUNK
In American **prison** and **hobo** usage this word has had (at least since the beginning of the twentieth century) the meaning of a young, usually smaller and heterosexual, male who is exploited as a female surrogate by older, tougher, more powerful (and for the most part essentially heterosexual) males, or "jockers." Since less is known about hobo punks, the following discussion focuses on the jailhouse punk.

Jail Punks. A punk in this sense is involuntarily recruited to the role, usually through gang **rape**, though he is likely to adapt to it over time if he does not commit suicide; in the prison class structure, he stands apart from the "man" and the "**queen**," or effeminate homosexual. Often there is considerable tension between the two sexually passive classes, as the "queens" reinforce the feminizing process initiated by the "men," and the punks resist it. The "queens" also tend to look down on the punks as weak, while seeing themselves as doing what they want.

The process of converting someone into a punk is called "turning out" and its climactic point is the moment of sexual penetration, after which the punk is said to have "lost his manhood," considered by prisoners to be irreversible; hence "once a punk, always a punk."

Studies of prison sexual patterns indicate that considerable numbers of heterosexual young males are "turned out" in this manner. A careful sociological survey by Wayne Wooden and Jay Parker defined punk as "an inmate who has been forced into a sexually submissive role" and reported that at least nine percent of the heterosexual inmates (of all ages and ethnic groups) in a medium-security prison had been sexually assaulted in that prison. The frequency of "turning out" for youngsters in a big-city jail or high-security prison or many juvenile prisons is likely to be much higher, though never sufficient to meet the demand. Factors which raise the likelihood of a prisoner's becoming a punk, in addition to youth and small size, are lack of combat skills or experience, middle-class background, lack of familiarity with jail and criminal mores (first-timers), lack of gang membership, non-violent offenses as reason for incarceration, and adherence to an ethnic group which is in an unfavorable power situation in that particular institution.

After being "turned out," a punk is usually paired off with a dominant male who "owns" him, providing protection from gang rape in return for sexual and other services (such as doing laundry, cellkeeping, and other tasks). Punks are comparable to slaves in that they are commonly sold, traded, and have no rights of their own; their social status in the jailhouse society derives from their owners, who tend to be high-ranking, since there is always a considerable amount of competition for the punks. They are frequently directed into prostitution for the profit of their owners. "Commissary punks," in contrast, voluntarily engage in prostitution in order to obtain goods from the prison store.

It is not, however, uncommon for emotional bonds to form over time between jockers and their punks, resulting in the distinctive situation of a sexual-emotional pair bonding between two heterosexual males. While very little research has been done on the psychology of punks (or of their jockers), investigation may throw considerable light on the nature of homosexual relationships as intensely experienced by the heterosexually oriented.

Punks do retain some fraction of their original masculine **identity** and usually revert to heterosexual or bisexual patterns after release, though their sexuality may be seriously warped by their experience and sense of compromised manhood. Punks characteristically exhibit the symptoms of male rape trauma syndrome, usually heightened if they are caught in the punk role for any length of time and are forced to adapt to it. Some punks seek to "reclaim their manhood" through rape or other acts of violence after release, in sharp contrast to the non-violent offenses which they committed before undergoing rape trauma.

In many ways, the punk role replicates or perpetuates into contemporary times the tradition of the *pathic* as seen in ancient Roman and Viking cultures. A similar pattern prevails today in many **Mediterranean** cultures and in **Latin America**. Other terms used in prison slang for punks include "sweet boys," "kids," "fuck-boys," and "catchers."

Other Senses of the Term. The prison/hobo meaning, until recently unknown in the general society, may descend directly from the Elizabethan *punk* or *punck(e)*, a harlot or kept woman, though its usage in this sense is not documented in America. (The variant form, *punquetto*, suggests an origin from the Italian *panchetta*, a pallet on which the woman would lie.) An alternative derivation may come from the usage, which dates to at least the 1920s, of "punk" as "a juvenile delinquent, a young outlaw, a young hoodlum," since it was such persons who ended up in jails and as the youngest were particular targets for "turning out." Another possibly related usage is punk as "a person of no importance, someone worthless or inferior."

In the circus "punk" designated untrained animals, while in other usage the term could simply mean an inexperienced young man or novice, without sexual implications. To the ordinary middle-class person a faded adjectival meaning was all that was usually recognized: "poor, inferior"; thus someone who is under the weather might remark, "I feel punk today."

This situation changed in the middle 1970s with the appearance of the punk (rock) **subculture**, with its characteristic music, types of dress, and attitudes, bringing the term into wide currency with connotations of "rebellious youth."

BIBLIOGRAPHY. Anthony M. Scacco, ed., *Male Rape*, New York: AMS Press, 1981; Wayne S. Wooden and Jay Parker, *Men Behind Bars: Sexual Exploitation in Prison*, New York: Plenum Press, 1982.

Stephen Donaldson

PUNK ROCK

"Punk rock" is a genre of rock and roll **music** which originated in an "underground" musical protest movement in New York in 1975 and quickly spread, first to Britain in 1976 and later throughout the industrialized world, as the unifying focus of a "punk" youth **subculture** which considers itself a defiant alternative to commercial popular music and to the general social order. With an "underground" form of music that had little hope for airplay on commercial or state radio, the punks were able and encouraged to break all the taboos they could find. Punk lyrics have from the beginning frequently touched on homosexual topics and the punk subculture has been notable for its ongoing discussion of **homophobia**, which is generally condemned as incompatible with punk ideology.

The "Classic" Period (1975–79). The American founders of punk rock, the singer Patti Smith and the band The Ramones, both included songs on homosexuality in their debut albums. In 1975 Smith released "Horses" with a long song of the same name which describes the **rape** of a boy and his consequent suicide, and the bisexual singer followed it on the same album with a lesbian love dirge, "Redondo Beach." The Ramones' 1976 self-titled album contains a song, "Fifty-Third and Third," describing a male prostitute working that New York street intersection. In a later song, "We're a Happy Family," the chorus line comments: "Daddy likes men." Bassist DeeDee Ramone is reported to have had a long affair with singer Neon Leon.

Not to be outdone, the English band The Sex Pistols also referenced homosexuality in their debut album "Never Mind the Bollocks, Here's the Sex Pistols" (1977) in the song "New York," when singer Johnny Rotten (Lydon) urged a "faggot" to "kiss me!" Lydon and Sex Pistols bassist Sid Vicious (John Ritchie) were occasionally involved with each other sexually during the early days of the band, before Vicious met up with Nancy Spungen, according to several reports, and Vicious was photographed wearing a Tom of Finland type gay T-shirt.

Many of the early leaders of the punk rock movement had been heavily influenced by early-seventies American bands such as the New York Dolls (who appeared in drag and with female makeup) and singers like Lou Reed, who was sometimes assumed to be homosexual after releasing his 1972 hit, "Walk on the Wild Side."

During the later 1970s, British punk rock saw the rise of Tom Robinson, who had been a volunteer for the London Gay Switchboard and whose bitterly ironic anthem "Glad to Be Gay" became a surprise underground hit in 1978. The song, which angrily catalogues a long list of English homophobic practices and is probably the only commercially successful song in the history of rock and roll to treat homosexuality as a political issue, drew thousands of predominantly heterosexual young punk rockers to sing along with Robinson at concerts throughout the United Kingdom and helped to establish the condemnation of homophobia as a part of the punk ideology. As the leading band The Jam put it (in "Alone in a Strange Town [1980]"): "We have our own manifesto/ we are kind to queers." Robinson's American double album "Power in the Darkness" listed the telephone numbers of the New York and Los Angeles gay switchboards on the inner sleeve.

Singer Pete Shelley of the very popular Buzzcocks (whose first single, "Orgasm Addict," describes a bisexual) eventually went solo with a gay love song, "Homo Sapien," which crossed over to mainstream dance charts. Also notable in Britain were Elton Motello's "Jet Boy Jet Girl" (with the chorus "He gave me head") and Alternative TV's "Sniffin Glue."

Back in the United States, the singer Wayne County eventually became transsexual Jane County, while Lance Loud, who sang for The Mumps, "came out" to his family while being filmed for the television series *An American Family*, and for a while was one of the most famous homosexuals in America. Many of the clubs which served as centers for the growing punk subculture, such as New York's Mudd Club and Max' Kansas City, were openly "mixed," drawing a considerable anti-disco gay crowd (musically alienated from gay bars) as well as the punk rockers.

Throughout this period, the general emphasis was on becoming free of society's concepts and moral prescriptions, on being experimental and breaking "rules" of all kinds, on freedom from the boundaries restricting sexual expression, rather than endorsing a ghettoizing "gay" **identity**. To a certain extent, there was also an undercurrent of hostility, derived from the association of homosexuals with disco music (which the punks detested) and the early-70s "glitter rock," but this was not a serious concern.

American "Hardcore" in the Eighties. Around the turn of the decade, punk underwent a transformation with the introduction of "hardcore" punk, originating in California. A new emphasis on machismo and the emergence of homophobic right-wing "skinheads" (modeled on the British variety) as a violent part of the otherwise anarchistic–leftist punk subculture brought with them an open **homophobia**, represented musically by the Rastafarian-influenced Bad Brains and the satiric Angry Samoans ("Homosexual"). At the same time, G. G. Allin was promoting a polymorphously perverse "slut rock" and a quartet of Texan bands (many of whom relocated to more hospitable San Francisco) was taking up the gay theme in a positive way. The Butthole Surfers, Millions of Dead Cops (MDC), the Dicks and the Big Boys all featured gay singers or songs. MDC, whose anthemic "Dead Cops" complains about police homophobia and whose singer, Dave, occasionally performed in drag, engaged in a celebrated feud with the Bad Brains over the latter band's homophobic statements, fueling a vigorous discussion of homophobia in the flourishing punk press. This debate continued throughout the decade in such publications as the international monthly *Maximum Rock & Roll*, with homophobia becoming disreputable among punk rockers as a result, though it is still found occasionally among "rank and file" punks and among skinheads, some of whom have been involved in "queerbashing." There are also gay punk publications originating in Toronto (*J.D.s*) and San Francisco (*Homocore*).

Stephen Donaldson

QUEBEC

A province of **Canada**, Quebec cherishes its historic continuity with New France, settled in the early seventeenth century. It includes two of the most attractive cities in North America, Montreal and Quebec. Montreal is a modern metropolis that has escaped the fate of many big cities in the United States. Public transportation (subway and bus) is modern, efficient, and clean, there is no litter in the streets, which one can walk at any time of the day or night (weather permitting) without danger of being mugged, and pollution remains at tolerable levels. Quebec is the political and administrative capital of the province. The old city, surrounded by walls, occupies a picturesque site atop a hill high above the Saint Lawrence River.

Montreal is more cosmopolitan, with diverse ethnic neighborhoods formed by the Canadian policy of encouraging immigrant groups to settle and preserve their native cultures, while Quebec has remained purely French in character and language. Both cities have excellent universities, Montreal four, two English-speaking and two French-speaking, while Quebec has two, both French-speaking.

The Front de Libération Homosexuelle was founded in Montreal in 1971. In 1977, in a police raid on the Truxx bar in Montreal, 146 men were arrested and charged just for being on the premises. The subsequent outcry by homophile activists led the Quebec government to include sexual orientation in its Charter of Human Rights the same year. However, as Gary Kinsman points out in *The Regulation of Desire*: "Sexual orientation protection ... still permits our arrest under the criminal code if we engage in prohibited sexual acts, or if we engage in these acts in the 'wrong' place." The *Guide Gai du Québec* emphatically warns its readers about the danger of cruising public places and parks in Montreal. Parks are officially closed from midnight to 6 a.m., whatever the season. Just being there at the wrong hours is punishable by a fine. The most famous and largest cruising area, situated in Parc Mont-Royal, in the center of the city, is regularly raided by the police.

However, harassment of gay and lesbian bars has ceased. Montreal boasts many gay bars, including several where nude dancers perform. The *Guide Gai* lists 29 gay bars and 3 lesbian ones. Quebec, a much smaller city, has only 12 gay bars and 1 lesbian one. Both cities have several gay sauna baths, still open in spite of the **AIDS** crisis.

The province of Quebec has its share of **AIDS** patients, and in contrast with other areas in North America, 90 percent of these are gay men. In Montreal two organizations (one for each of the two main communities) have been formed to help people with **AIDS**.

The Literary Scene. Contemporary Quebec is rich in talented writers. Homosexuality ranks as a major theme in the works of two of its most famous contemporary writers: novelist Marie-Claire Blais and playwright Michel Tremblay.

Born in the city of Quebec in 1939, Blais published her first novel, *Tête Blanche*, in 1959. In 1966 she obtained one of the most prestigious French literary prizes, the Prix Médicis, for *Une saison dans la vie d'Emmanuel*. Other works include *David Sterne* (1967), *Manuscrits de Pauline Archange* (1968), *Le Loup* (1972), and *Un Joualonais sa joualonie* (1973).

Most of her books have been translated into English. Homosexuality, chiefly male, plays an important part in her works, most particularly in *David Sterne* and *Le Loup*. In both novels, the main characters are gay men. In 1983, a long-time friend of Marie-Claire Blais, Mary Meigs, published an autobiographical work, *The Medusa Head*, in which she describes with great talent a devastating attempt at a *ménage à trois* by a French woman writer, Marie-Claire Blais, and herself.

Michel Tremblay is generally considered the most important living playwright in Quebec. His plays, which have been translated into many languages, have enjoyed tremendous success among his fellow Québecois, in spite of the initial scandal caused by his writing in "joual," the local dialect of lower-class Montreal, which contains a good many English words. In a way, Tremblay has become a sort of national icon, despite the presence in many of his plays of transvestites and homosexuals. It has been suggested that the people in Quebec, after centuries of oppression by the English overlords, understood and sympathized with Tremblay's unhappy and alienated characters. His most important plays are *Les Belles-soeurs* (1968), *La Duchesse de Langeais* (1969), *A Toi pour toujours, ta Marie-Lou* (1971), *Damnée Manon, sacrée Sandra* (1972), *Hosannah* (1973), and *Les Anciennes odeurs*. About *La Duchesse de Langeais*, a monologue by an aging transvestite, playwright and critic Jean-Claude Germain has written: "Half man, half woman, oversophisticated and vulgar, impotent, unable to look at himself as a person and talking about himself as if he were a thing, the character in *La Duchesse de Langeais* epitomizes the alienation of the Québecois man."

Two younger playwrights have recently entered the Montreal stage with two gay plays: René-Daniel Dubois (*Being at Home with Claude*, 1985) and Michel Marc Bouchard (*Les Péluettes*, 1987). *Being at Home with Claude*, in spite of its original English title, is written in French. Its subject is a police interrogation of a young male hustler who murdered his gay lover out of love. *Les Péluettes*, a brilliant melodrama in which all the female parts were played by men, is a beautiful mixture of poetry and satire. To sum up, gay subjects and gay writers have played and continue to play a major part in the literary life of French-speaking Quebec.

BIBLIOGRAPHY. Michel Belair, *Michel Tremblay*, Quebec: Les Presses de l'Université de Québec, 1972; Alain Bouchard, *Le guide gai du Québec*, Montreal: Editions Homeureux, 1988; Thérèse Fabi, *Marie-Claire Blais, sa vie, son oeuvre, la critique*, Montreal: Editions Agence d'A.B.C., 1973; Ed Jackson and Stan Persky, eds., *Flaunting It*, Vancouver: New Star Books; Toronto: Pink Triangle Press, 1982; Gary Kinsman, *The Regulation of Desire: Sexuality in Canada*, Montreal: Black Rose Books, 1987; Alain Poutant, *Dictionnaire critique du théâtre québecois*, Ottawa: Leméac, 1972.

Michel Philip

QUEEN

This vernacular term denotes an effeminate homosexual, often one who is perceived as inclined to put on airs and is easily offended. The word is more loosely applied indiscriminately to anyone thought to be homosexual. Queen is one of those terms, like ethnic epithets, that can (sometimes) be used nonjudgmentally, even affectionately, among gay people, but which are always perceived as bearing a hostile charge when uttered by outsiders.

Historically, the term results from the rejoining of the divergent paths followed by two related Old English words, *cwen* and *cwene*, rooted in the common **Indo-European** base *gwen*, "woman." One form ensconced itself at the top of the social scale, producing "queen" as "consort of a king, woman having sovereign rule." The sibling word *quean* experienced downward mobility so that it came to mean "impudent woman, jade, hussy." It is this latter usage which led to its derisive application to homosexuals. An early attestation of this semantic development may lie in the Latin hexameter alluding to James I of England: *Rex fuit Elisabeth, nunc est regina Jacobus* (Elizabeth was a king, now James is a queen/quean).

In recent years, the compound formula noun + queen has become popular, producing such compounds as "drag queen" (a homosexual who wears feminine attire), "tearoom queen" (one who cruises toilets), "seafood queen" (one who pursues sailors), "rice queen" (one who prefers Asian partners), and so forth. The word queen has parallels in Spanish (*reina*) and Italian (*regina*), but these are minor items in the homosexual argot of those languages, probably largely sustained in popularity by contamination from English-language usage.

A curious folkway of American gay men, the "imperial courts," is limited to the western United States, where it apparently arose not long after World War II. The courts are fraternal (some would say sororal) societies which each year elect an "empress" or supreme drag queen—and sometimes a muscle-bound "emperor" as well. The custom probably arose as a refinement of annual drag balls, which go back at least to the end of the nineteenth century. There is also an implicit comparison to the prom queen on American college campuses. Apparently the empress is conceived as the superlative of queen. Although they have their risible aspects—which are fully acknowledged—the courts perform charitable and public service activities during the rest of the year.

Wayne R. Dynes

QUEER

In twentieth-century America this epithet has been probably the most popular vernacular term of abuse for homosexuals. It was also common in England, producing Cockney rhyming phrases such as "ginger beer" and "King Lear." Even today some older English homosexuals prefer the term, even sometimes affecting to believe that it is value-free.

The current **slang** meaning is probably rooted in the use of "queer" for counterfeit (coin or banknote) in the mid-eighteenth century, with an antonym "straight"; hence an expression popular in the recent past, "queer as a three-dollar bill." As a verb, "to queer" means "to spoil, to foul up." At one time the adjective could be used unselfconsciously to mean "queasy" ("This muggy weather makes me feel ever so queer."). The word can also be used in a less pejorative sense with the meaning "fond of, keen on", e.g., "He's queer for exotic cuisine."

As used for homosexuals, the term queer has connoted strangeness and "otherness," rooted in the sense that gay people were marginal to society's mainstream. It has also conveyed the sense of fear and aversion that many heterosexuals felt for emotions that they could not share and acts that they could not understand. The term served to express (and reinforce) a kind of heterosexual ethnocentrism that branded difference as per se alien and unacceptable. The ignorance in which the establishment media kept the general public reinforced all these anxieties. The word's declining popularity may therefore reflect today's greater visibility and acceptance of gay men and lesbians and the growing knowledge that most of them are in fact quite harmless, ordinary people.

See also **Deviance and Deviation**.

Wayne R. Dynes

R

RACHA

This word is found only in some manuscripts of the **New Testament** Gospel of Matthew at 5:22, where the King James Version reads:

> But I say unto you, that . . .whosoever shall say to his brother, Racha, shall be in danger of the counsel. . . .

The text of the gospel includes no explanatory gloss, as is usual with foreign words that would otherwise have been unintelligible to the Greek reader, and the majority of modern commentators understand the word as Semitic: *raka* = Hebrew *réqā* "empty, emptyheaded, brainless." Yet there is an alternative meaning proposed in 1922 by Friedrich Schulthess, an expert in Syriac and Palestinian Christian Aramaic: he equated the word with Hebrew *rakh,* "soft," which would thus be equivalent to Greek *malakos/malthakos,* which denotes the passive-effeminate homosexual. Further, in 1934 a papyrus was published from Hellenistic Egypt of the year 257 before the Christian era that contained the word *rachas* in an unspecified derogatory sense, but a parallel text suggests that it had the meaning *kinaidos* ("faggot"). It would thus have been a loanword from Hebrew in the vulgar speech of the Greek settlers in Egypt. A modern counterpart is the word *rach,* "tender, soft, effeminate, timid, cowardly" in the Gaunersprache, the argot of German beggars and criminals, which has absorbed many terms from Hebrew and Jewish Aramaic because of social conditions that created a linguistic interface between the Jewish "fence" and the gentile thief.

The import of the Gospel passage is that whereas the old Law forbade only murder, the new morality of the church forbids aggression even in purely symbolic, verbal forms; and the ascending scale of offenses and penalties is tantamount to a prohibition of what is called in Classical Arabic *mufaḥarah,* the ritualized verbal duel that is often the prelude to combat and actual bloodshed. So **Jesus** is represented as forbidding his followers to utter insults directed at the other party's masculinity—a practice that has scarcely gone out of fashion in the ensuing nineteen centuries, as the contemporary vogue of **faggot** well attests.

So it cannot be maintained that Jesus "never mentioned homosexuality," as some gay Christian apologists claim. In the sphere of sexual morality Jesus demanded an even higher standard than did contemporary Palestinian and Hellenistic Judaism, which uncompromisingly rejected and condemned the homosexual expression that was commonplace and tolerated in the Gentile world. Thus **Christianity** inherited not merely the Jewish taboo on homoerotic behavior, but an ascetic emphasis foreign to Judaism itself, which has always had a procreation-oriented moral code. What the text in Matthew demonstrates is that he forbade acts of violence, physical and verbal, against those to whom homosexuality was imputed, in line with the general emphasis on self-restraint and meekness in his teaching. The entire passage is not just a legalistic pastiche of Jewish casuistry, but also a polished gem of double entendre and irony.

BIBLIOGRAPHY. Warren Johansson, "Whosoever Shall Say to His Brother, *Racha* (Matthew 5:22)," *Cabirion*, 10 (1984), 2–4.

Warren Johansson

RADICALISM
See Left, Gay.

RAPE OF MALES

Rape is a sexual act imposed upon a nonconsenting partner. The method of imposition is often violent, though it may be by threats or intimidation or abuse of positions of authority. Rape is one of the most misunderstood of all crimes, and when the victim is male, the misconceptions are severely compounded. Many legal jurisdictions do not even recognize a crime of rape against a male victim, but instead use terms such as "forcible sodomy" or "child abuse." Nonetheless, rape of males in the non-legal sense is a much more common event than is usually supposed, covered as it is with a blanket of silence. If prisoners are included, on any given day in the United States there may be more males raped than females.

It appears that the rape of females by females, while not unknown, is very rare, and little is known about it.

The rape of males by males is a practice protected by the silence observed by its victims, responding to a set of popular beliefs centering around the notion that a "real man" cannot be raped. The phrase "homosexual rape," for instance, which is often used by uninformed persons to designate male–male rape, camouflages the fact that the majority of the rapists as well as of the victims are generally heterosexual.

History. In antiquity, the rape of males was more widely recognized. In Greek mythology, Zeus, king of the gods, abducted **Ganymede** for sexual purposes. In the Oedipus myth, Laius, king of **Thebes** and Oedipus' father, abducted Chrysippus, son of his host, King Pelops; the boy killed himself out of shame, occasioning

Pelops' curse on Laius that he should be slain by his own son.

In some societies the rape of a defeated male enemy was considered the prerogative of the victor in battle, and served to indicate the totality of the former's defeat. Even in ancient times, we find the widespread belief that an adult male who is sexually penetrated, even by force, thereby "loses his manhood," and hence can no longer be a warrior or ruler. In the twentieth century, the best-known instance of this kind of humiliation occurred when the Englishman T. E. **Lawrence** ("Lawrence of Arabia") was captured by the Turks, who were well known for this custom, during World War I. The subsequent disruption of Lawrence's life, while a surprise to his contemporaries, can now be recognized as a typical consequence of male Rape Trauma Syndrome.

Gang-rape of a male was also considered an ultimate form of punishment, and as such was known to the Romans (for adultery) and Iranians (for violation of the sanctity of the harem).

In modern Western societies, until recently, rape of one male by another was considered rare outside of the special context of incarceration. Virtually all the non-penological literature on rape assumes that the victim is female; police did not (and usually still do not) even collect statistics on "male rape."

When the feminist movement led to the establishment of rape crisis centers in the United States in the 1970s, however, it became obvious that there was a large number of hidden cases of male rape. Most of these came to the attention of rape counselors owing to injuries inflicted on the victims (usually anal) which could not be hidden from medical personnel. Rape crisis centers willing to deal with male victims found that anywhere from three to forty percent of their counselees were male, with the higher figures resulting from specific efforts to publicize the availability of the centers for male victims.

This development led to research aimed at discovering the extent of male rape, and in 1982 to an anthology on the subject, Anthony M. Scacco, Jr.'s *Male Rape*. The results of this research have surprised virtually everyone by indicating the vast extent of rape of males in North America.

Extent of Male Rape "in the Community." Students of sexual abuse, drawing upon a wide number of studies conducted in the 1980s which sought to overcome the reluctance of the abused to discuss their experiences, have now concluded that boys and girls up to the early teen years have an *equal chance* of being sexually victimized; a summary of these studies was published by Eugene Porter in 1986.

For the later teens and adult males, figures are harder to come by, but a consensus appears to be forming that "in the community" (a phrase excluding incarceration facilities) between one-seventh and one-fourth of all rapes involve male victims. A household survey conducted for the United States Bureau of Justice Statistics stated that the rapes of males reported to their interviewers were 25.9 percent of the number of completed rapes reported by females in the same survey; when applied to the national population that would be about 12,300 rapes of males per year. These figures are believed to be underestimates owing to a reluctance of male victims to identify themselves to the interviewers.

Phenomenology of Male Rape. Research in America indicates that the most common sites for male rape involving post-puberty victims "in the community" are outdoors in remote areas and in automobiles (the latter usually involving hitchhikers). Boys in their early and mid teens are more likely to be victimized than older males (studies indicate a median victim age of 17). The form of assault usually involves penetration of the victim anally and/or orally, rather than stimulation of the victim's penis.

Comparing rapes of females with rapes of males, it has been found that in cases involving male victims, gang-rape is more common, multiple types of sexual acts are more likely to be demanded, weapons are more likely to be displayed and used, and physical injury is more likely to occur, with the injuries which do occur being more serious than with injured females.

Whereas cases of sexual assault of young girls usually involves a relative or family friend, young boys are more likely to be sexually abused by strangers or authority figures in organizations such as church, school, athletics, or scouting. It is also noteworthy that men who rape boys, according to one study, have on the average well over three times as many victims each as men who rape girls. One perpetrator kept records showing he had sexually assaulted over three hundred boys in one summer, mostly hitchhikers; he was arrested only when one of the boys complained to the police, the rest having remained silent.

While gay males are also raped, there is no evidence that they are victimized in appreciably greater numbers than their proportion of the general population; most male rape victims are heterosexual.

What is even more surprising to the average man is that, according to several studies, most rapes of males are committed by men who are heterosexual in their consensual sexual preference and self-identity; only 7 percent of the rapists of men in the Groth-Burgess study were homosexual. (Indeed, it has been reported that homosexual men are far less likely to engage in rape than heterosexual men.) Half or more of these rapists choose victims from both genders.

Theorists have sought to explain this as rooted in the nature of rape as primarily a crime of power and domination through **violence** rather than a sexually motivated act, though it is clear that sexuality has something to do with it. The exact relationship between the quest for power and dominance on the one hand and sexual drive on the other is little understood, and probably varies a great deal from one rapist to another. It is clear that rapists are often not erotically attracted to their victims, and examples of sexual dysfunction (impotence, inability to ejaculate) are common in "community" rape. On the other hand, one can cite instances of "marital rape" among gay couples where an erotic element is clearly present.

One of the most interesting findings of recent research on rape has profound implications for public policy regarding male rape: anywhere from 80 to 100 percent (depending on the study) of adult male rapists (of women) have a history of childhood sexual victimization themselves. The implication is that rape is a vicious cycle in which boys, unable to even discuss their own rape traumas, much less find effective treatment for them, grow up to take revenge on others in the same fashion.

Public Attitudes Toward Male Rape. Generally speaking, rape of males is a taboo subject for public discussion, so that for most women and many men, it does not exist. On the popular level, however, there are numerous mistaken beliefs which are common among the male population. These include the notions that male rape is very rare; that to be raped indicates a weakness which is not to be found in a "real" male, hence "real men" cannot be raped; that rapists of males are necessarily homosexual; that being raped turns the victim into a homosexual; and most importantly, that for a man to be raped is to "lose his manhood" permanently.

It is because of these attitudes, which surround male rape with an aura of total humiliation for the victim, that it is rare for a male rape victim (especially past the early teens) to acknowledge his victimization even to his family or friends, much less to the police. If ever there was a crime hidden by a curtain of silence, it is male rape. For the same reason, most vic-

tims outside of jail consider themselves to be almost unique, and loathe to call attention to themselves.

Given such pervasive silence, there is no demand for treatment programs for male victims as there is for female victims; there is no pressure for law enforcement activity; and the perpetrator is usually protected from even being accused, much less convicted. So powerful is the suppression of knowledge of male rape that criminals such as burglars and robbers sometimes rape their victims as a sideline solely to prevent them from going to the police.

Rape Trauma Syndrome. Rape is an extremely traumatic experience centering on the total loss of control of one's own body and usually the inside of that body, the most intimate sanctum of self. On top of this trauma, which is common to all rape victims, the heterosexual male survivor must deal with the experience of sexual role **inversion** and the pervasive popular mythology revolving around "loss of manhood" and homosexuality. The psychological devastation of rape is difficult to imagine for a male who has not been through such an experience.

Survivors of rape, and often of rape attempts, usually manifest some elements of what has come to be called Rape Trauma Syndrome (RTS), a form of Post-traumatic Stress Disorder (PTSD). The effects of RTS often last for years or decades, and can be lifelong. Apart from a small number of therapists and counselors specializing in sexual assault cases, few **psychotherapists** are familiar with the literature on RTS. For this reason, a rape survivor is usually well advised to consult with a rape crisis center or someone knowledgeable in this area rather than relying on general **counseling** resources. The same applies to those close to a rape victim, such as a lover or parent; these people are termed "secondary victims" by rape crisis counselors.

Typically, the first stage of RTS involves a phase of denial and disbelief.

Child victims commonly experience amnesia, partial or total, regarding the assault; memory, however, may return years later and initiate a psychological crisis.

A sense of guilt, shame, and humiliation is commonly found, exacerbated by the common tendency of those who should be supportive to instead "blame the victim." The sense of stigma, whether internalized or reinforced by others (in the case of public knowledge of the rape), is pervasive. Heterosexual male survivors typically show enormous anxiety and confusion regarding issues of masculine **identity** and homosexuality. The survivor's sexuality may show severe distortions and malfunctions. Serious depression is likely and **suicide** may result. The victim's rage may explode under unpredictable circumstances.

Other manifestations of RTS include a sense of heightened vulnerability, anxiety, powerlessness, helplessness, nightmares, **paranoia**, sleep disturbances, fixation on the incident, inability to concentrate, dependency, fear of intimacy, chaotic relationships, multiple personality development, drug and alcohol abuse, and revictimization.

Survivors of childhood sexual assault and of rape in institutional surroundings often have to contend not with a single incident, but with a continuing series of involuntary sexual activities which may stretch over years. In such cases, the adaptation process by which the victim learns to live with the continuing pattern of assault further complicates and strengthens the RTS pattern.

As mentioned above, a certain number of male rape survivors become rapists themselves. It is not known how large this number is, though it appears to be more common among those victimized as boys than as adults.

It has also been suggested that "queer-bashers," violently homophobic males, are likely to be survivors of childhood sexual abuse, laboring under the usually mistaken idea that the male who assaulted them must have been homosexual.

Jail Rape. While rape of males is a serious problem in the community, it is in the institutions of confinement (**prisons and jails**, reformatories, mental institutions) and, to a markedly lesser extent, in other all-male residential settings (boarding schools, hobo camps, the military) that male rape is most common, even an accepted part of institutional life.

Rape of males in confinement differs from male rape in the community in that it is generally open, is accepted if not condoned by the prisoner subculture, usually involves repeated patterns of sexual assault following the initial rape, is far more likely to be interracial, and serves a social function in converting heterosexual young prisoners into sexual slaves to be acquired by more powerful men. Thus, once raped, the victim is forced into a pattern of perpetual sexual abuse which may in time appear consensual to a casual observer, but which is rooted in the need for protection of the rape survivor from further mass assaults.

Confinement institutions furthermore have the effect of legitimizing to their graduates the use of rape as a means of validating their masculinity, and of converting non-violent offenders, by raping them, into ex-convicts full of rage and potential for violence (often rape) once released. In these ways the institutions help perpetuate the practice of rape of women and of men.

Conclusion. Rape of males, while a widespread and extremely serious problem, has escaped the attention of society because of deep taboos springing from popular conceptions that to be raped is to forfeit one's masculinity. The actual dynamics of rape are only beginning to be explored, and very little of what is known to students of the phenomenon has penetrated the public consciousness.

Rape crisis centers in the United States have developed much of what is known about rape and its effects, including Rape Trauma Syndrome, yet many if not most such centers, run by feminist women, still see rape as a "women's issue" only and have made little or no effort to reach out to boys and men who have experienced rape. The public media have continued to treat rape of males as a taboo subject.

Until this taboo is broken, there can be little hope that survivors of male rape will be enabled to deal constructively with rape trauma or that the vicious cycle of rape will be effectively undermined.

BIBLIOGRAPHY. Stephen Donaldson, *The Rape of Males: A Preliminary Statistical Look at the Scope of the Problem*, 2nd ed., Ft. Bragg, CA: People Organized to Stop Rape of Incarcerated Persons, 1985; A. Nicholas Groth and Ann W. Burgess, *Men Who Rape*, New York: Plenum Press, 1979; idem, "Male Rape: Offenders and Victims," *American Journal of Psychiatry*, 137 (1980), 806–10; Arthur Kaufman, et al., "Male Rape Victims: Noninstitutionalized Assault," *American Journal of Psychiatry* 137 (1980), 221–23; Eugene Porter, *Treating the Young Male Victim of Sexual Assault*, Syracuse, NY: Safer Society Press, 1986; Anthony M. Scacco, Jr., ed., *Male Rape: A Casebook of Sexual Aggressions*, New York: AMS Press, 1982; Wayne S. Wooden and Jay Parker, *Men Behind Bars: Sexual Exploitation in Prison*, New York: Plenum Press, 1982.

Stephen Donaldson

RAUCOURT, STAGE NAME OF FRANÇOISE MARIE ANTOINETTE JOSEPH SAUCEROTTE (1756–1815)

French tragédienne and foremost lesbian of her time. Daughter of a third-rate actor, she served an apprenticeship in the provinces before making her debut at the Comédie française in 1772 as Dido. It was a prodigious success, owing to her beauty, expressive mime, melodious voice and "prodigious intelligence," as well as to a short-lived reputation for virtue. Within two years she was embroiled in scandals that made her notorious. She and the Opera soprano Sophie Arnould (1740–1802) vied for lovers of both sexes; virtually bankrupt, she and her inseparable companion, the German Jeanne-Françoise-Marie Souck or Sourques, were summoned for bad conduct, insolence, and threats to creditors. Her early popularity faded and she was hissed in 1776. Expelled from the Comédie for absenteeism, she went to Russia but was recalled to the Comédie to take on the *emploi* of tragedy queens and mothers. Her new masculine manner and coarsened voice enabled her to do so with magnificence, but without tenderness. When she made a hit as a captain of hussars in *Le Jaloux*, her rival Mlle. de Saint-Val remarked, "What a pity she persists in wishing to play women's roles."

According to the scandal-sheets, Raucourt was president of the sapphic Sect of Anandrynes, founded in 1770 by Thérèse de Fleury; it met in the Rue des Boucheries-Saint-Honoré, where novices were stripped and examined for the seven marks of beauty that would ensure them membership. Surviving documents suggest that the Anandrynes subscribed to **Enlightenment** principles. A quarrel arose between Arnould and Raucourt over the admissions policy: the former insisted on women exclusively, the latter wanted to admit as voyeurs men who practiced women's ways (she had in mind the homosexual Marquis de Villette). Arnould's rallying-cry "Either whores or tribades" signaled the dissolution of the Sect in 1784. By then Raucourt had become synonymous with lesbianism and was exploited as a character in erotic fictions such as Pidansat de Mairobert's *Confessions of a Young Girl*.

A rabid royalist, Raucourt was imprisoned by the Jacobins in 1793, but released thanks to former actor Charles Labussière, a clerk of the Committee of Public Safety. She inaugurated the Second Théâtre Français in 1796, and when the Comédie was reconstituted, returned to it.

Napoleon, an admirer, sent her with two troupes to Italy to spread French culture, but she had scant success. Retiring to her estate on the banks of the Loire, she devoted herself to horticulture and died of an inflammation. Her funeral caused another scandal, for the curé of St. Roch, who had benefitted financially as her almoner in her lifetime, refused to admit her body to the church. A mob of over 15,000 persons broke in bearing her coffin, and an order of Louis XVIII assured her the last rites. She is buried in Père Lachaise cemetery in Paris.

BIBLIOGRAPHY. Jean de Reuilly, *La Raucourt & ses amies*, Paris: Bibliothèque de Vieux Paris, 1909.

Laurence Senelick

RECRUITMENT CONCEPT

Recruitment is a military term referring to the outreach whereby soldier candidates are solicited for enlistment. As applied to homosexuality, it represents, on the one hand, a heterosexual fantasy or **myth**, on the other, a recognition that rites of passage are part of the process of joining any group. There are no "recruiting stations" for homosexual behavior, but individuals may seek to join their fellows and, in this sense only, become recruits.

The Myth. The recruitment myth is the notion that since homosexuals for the most part, and exclusive homosexuals by definition, do not reproduce, they must constantly recruit new acolytes to their forbidden practices from the ranks of the society in which they live. This assertion then becomes the basis for the claim that young people need to be "protected" from homosexuals and even kept in ignorance of the facts of homosexual behavior as long as possible. Also, the pederast is in the light of this assumption seen as an "aggressive homosexual" vigorously recruiting adolescents for the gay **subculture** that flourishes in the large cities of every Western country.

The truth of the matter is otherwise. Most of those who are predominantly or exclusively homosexual as adults become aware of their feelings long before they make their first contact with the world of gay **bars** and **bathhouses**, homophile groups and organizations, the vast majority of which are composed solely of adults. It is principally on the college campuses that **student** organizations are active, and these serve as a focus of social life for those who are already fully aware, at seventeen or later, of the direction of their sexual interests.

Initiation. Because of the semiclandestine nature of the gay subculture, even in recent times, there is a phase of initiation in which the newcomer learns the rules of behavior, the argot of the group, and the fund of information that permits him to interact with other members of the subculture in the manner of his choice. But this is true of any social group that differs in some degree from the dominant, mainstream culture of the nation in whose midst it is located. The most important single fact is that the individual who cannot experience sexual relations with members of his own sex pleasurably will be repelled by such contacts, and even if he experiments with them, will decide never to return.

Religious Analogues. The analogy that is undoubtedly present, at some level of consciousness, in the minds of those who cherish the recruitment myth is with religious conversion and apostasy. It is perhaps not fortuitous that **pervert** in English was originally the antonym of *convert*, hence "religious apostate," and that the modern meaning appears only in the 1880s under the influence of German *pervers* as used by forensic psychiatrists. But all the evidence shows that the homosexual **orientation** emerges in individuals who have been exposed from the beginning of their lives to every form of direct and indirect promotion for heterosexuality. If any "recruitment" occurs, it is to heterosexuality. The apologetic discourse of the homophile movement serves in most cases to give the subject a political identity and a sense of pride and self-worth that he could never extract from writings in which his sexual feelings are branded an **abomination**. That many homosexuals still cling to the religious faith of their upbringing, despite official refusal to accept them into the organized churches and synagogues, proves the element of apostasy to be absent.

The Pederastic Subculture. Another crucial point is that the pederastic subculture is totally distinct from the main gay subculture of the late twentieth century; in many respects the two are in watertight compartments. The **pederast** has no sexual interest in adult males and does not wish to be the object of their attention; even the handsomest college athlete has no appeal whatever for him. He does not frequent the bars, baths, clubs, and other rendezvous of the **androphile** (adult-oriented) homosexual, because he can find there no one for whom he would feel the slightest attraction. Moreover, the androphile political groupings generally, though not always, bar the North American Man–Boy Love Association and similar organizations of boy-lovers from membership and participation in their activities. And finally, the pederast usually has an upper age limit after which he has no further erotic feelings for the boy and does not care if as an adult the latter gravitates toward exclusive heterosexuality.

Biological Aspects. The homosexual is a good and true member of the racial and ethnic group to which he belongs; in **demographic** terms, the protoplasm of his ancestors is continued in him, even if not by him. In each generation a certain percent of the offspring of heterosexual unions are homosexually oriented, but this fraction does not diminish the vitality or the evolutionary capacity for survival of the race. The variations in the birth rate in modern times, just as in antiquity, are explained by economic and cultural factors, not by the occurrence of homosexuality. In early modern China the number of reported male births was almost twice that of female, but this is explained simply by the practice of infanticide on unwanted female babies. Likewise the low birth rates of some strata of the intelligentsia in contemporary society result from the deliberate choice of married couples to employ birth control devices and techniques rather than to have one child after another, as was the norm among all classes well into the nineteenth century.

A minority of the members of any society will always by virtue of inner predisposition be predominantly or exclusively homosexual, and no "recruitment" is needed to swell the number. The homosexual does not reproduce, but nature reproduces him. The evolutionary dialectic that produced exclusive heterosexuality in homo sapiens has exclusive homosexuality as its necessary antithesis and complement.

Warren Johansson

REDL, ALFRED (1864–1913)

Chief of espionage and counterespionage for the Austro-Hungarian Monarchy who divulged military secrets for financial gain to the intelligence service of Tsarist Russia. The seventh of thirteen children born of middle-class parents, Redl possessed an intellect and creativity (along with the pension and special allowances granted upon his father's death in 1875) that quickly led him into a military-school education. From the very outset of his military career, he was rewarded with promotions, and by 1900 Redl had joined the General Staff. During a year spent in Russia (1898–99), learning the language and training as an **espionage** operative, he came to the attention of Russian officials who, since Redl had no private income like many other members of the officer corps, took advantage of his financial dependence. By 1902 he was functioning as a double agent. His information proved invaluable, for Redl was promoted to Chief of Counter-Intelligence and chief of the Operations Section of the Austro-Hungarian intelligence apparatus.

Alfred Redl maintained his double secret—that of his work for the Russians and that of his homosexuality—until his death. He fell in love with Lt. Stefan Horinka (referred to as Hromodka in some works) and financed his military career. Horinka knew nothing of Redl's involvement with the Russians and kept a certain distance from him on the emotional plane by having a liaison with a woman at the same time he was seeing his protector.

On May 24, 1913, Austrian authorities discovered Redl's treason when he picked up two letters full of cash which the Russians had sent to him under a code name and which had aroused the suspicions of the Austrian postal authorities. The military representatives confronted Redl in his hotel room and left a pistol on the table. He committed suicide in the early morning of May 25. Upon searching Redl's apartment, the authorities discovered the rest of his secret life when they found perfumed letters from men, photographs of nude males, and copies of documents with state secrets.

Redl's treason has been appraised as a major factor in Austria's defeat in World War I, as her enemies knew most of her plans before the outbreak of hostilities. The additional fact that Redl was homosexual was exploited by the opponents of the homosexual emancipation movement which was then growing in the German-speaking countries, and even found mention in a United States Senate subcommittee report of 1950—during the epidemic of **McCarthyism**—as proof that homosexuals were "security risks."

Redl's life has been the subject of several fictionalized treatments, including John Osborne's play *A Patriot for Me*

(1965) and four German-language films (1925, 1930, 1955, 1984).

BIBLIOGRAPHY. Robert B. Asprey, *The Panther's Feast*, New York: Putnam, 1959; Egon Erwin Kisch, *Der Fall des Generalstabschefs Redl* (Aussenseiter der Gesellschaft: Die Verbrechen der Gegenwart, 2), Berlin: Verlag die Schmiede, 1924; Georg Markus, *Der Fall Redl*, Vienna: Amalthea, 1984; Valentin Pikul', "Chest' imeiu. Ispoved' ofitsera rossiiskogo genshtaba" [I Have the Honor. Confessions of an Officer of the Russian General Staff], *Nash sovremennik*, No. 9 (1988), pp. 74–76.

James W. Jones

REFORMATION
See **Protestantism**.

REICH, WILHELM (1897–1957)

Psychoanalyst and sexual reformer. Born to an assimilated Jewish family in Galicia in 1897, he suffered a severe trauma when his mother committed suicide, as he feared that he had been unwittingly responsible in revealing her love affair with one of his tutors. His attitude toward his father may be judged from his belief that he was not really his father's son.

After serving in the Austrian army in World War I, Reich studied medicine in Vienna. He spent his internship in the clinic of the Nobel Prize winner Julius Wagner-Jauregg, and married a fellow medical student, Annie Pink, who also became a psychoanalyst. In the Jewish intellectual circles of interwar Vienna, both **Marxism** and **psychoanalysis** were fashionable, and Reich set about the task of synthesizing them. How could the discoveries of Marx and **Freud** be placed at the service of the masses? He first joined the Austrian Socialist Party and became a clinical assistant at Freud's Psychoanalytic Polyclinic, which gave him close contact with the working class. Reich aspired to put knowledge of sexual hygiene within the reach of the industrial worker and remove the reproach that psychoanalysis was a middle-class luxury. Five years later, in 1929, he opened the first sex hygiene clinic in Vienna that offered free advice on birth control, child rearing, and sex education.

Reich's political interests soon led him to question the neutrality required of orthodox Freudian analysts. In 1927 his book on *The Function of the Orgasm* was issued by the International Psychoanalytic Publishing House, and in 1928 he published a paper on "Character Analysis" that he subsequently elaborated into a book which is still regarded by many as his most important contribution to the discipline. Idealizing the Soviet Union for the reforms it had undertaken after the Revolution of 1917, he went to Moscow in 1929 expecting to find a new society, but discovered instead that the need to industrialize backward **Russia** had taken precedence over sexual hedonism, and that under Stalin reaction was slowly but inevitably setting in.

The rapprochement between Marxism and Freudianism for which Reich was striving was doomed to fail, so that in the end he was expelled from both the International Psychoanalytic Association and the Communist Party. Moving to Berlin in 1930, he promoted the German Association for Proletarian Sexual Politics, which advocated abolition of the laws against homosexuality, and also reform of the marriage and divorce laws, free birth control counseling and contraceptive devices, abolition of laws prohibiting sex education, and an end to the restrictions on abortion—all measures that have since won general acceptance by reformers.

After publishing *The Mass Psychology of Fascism* Reich returned to Vienna, but the rise of **Nazism** in Germany and the complete repudiation of the sexual reform movement in Stalinist **Russia** marked the onset of a period of trials and reverses that undoubtedly embittered him. Rejected in one country after another, he

found refuge in Norway, where he was able in 1936 to found the International Institute for Sex-Economy to study the way the human body utilizes sexual energy. The unifying principle of his theories was the concept of energy, by which he meant no mystical *élan vital*, but an actual, physical component of man and the universe that could be measured and harnessed. The pursuit of this idea degenerated into an obsession in the last phase of his life.

Advised by a psychiatrist at Columbia University, Theodore P. Wolfe, to emigrate to the United States, he joined the throng of Jewish refugees from Nazi-ruled Europe in New York a few days before the outbreak of war in 1939. In Forest Hills, New York, he established the Orgone Institute, a laboratory and later a hospital. Despite his vicissitudes, he was now convinced that he had found a new kind of energy that could be stored in accumulators and used to strengthen the body against disease. He even ventured to treat cancer patients by placing them in boxes resembling telephone booths which supposedly collected orgone energy. This practice spawned the rumor that orgone accumulators could restore waning potency.

Such activities were not only denounced by the American Medical Association, but also investigated by the Food and Drug Administration, which in 1954 enjoined him from distributing orgone accumulators and operating the Orgone Institute Press. When a court order was issued for the destruction of all accumulators, Reich defied it and soon found himself the defendant in a trial that ended with a verdict of guilty and a two-year prison sentence. In March 1957 he entered Danbury Penitentiary where he was diagnosed as paranoid, but he disdained treatment and died of heart disease in Lewisburg Penitentiary on November 3.

Although Reich has become almost synonymous with "sexual freedom" in some quarters, and his admirers include some gay activists and theoreticians, there is not a single favorable reference to homosexuality in his writings. He loathed homosexuals, never knowingly accepted a homosexual for treatment, and avoided overt homosexuals in his social and professional life. When a Norwegian physician recommended an individual for training with Reich, no sooner had the latter learned of the candidate's homosexuality than he rejected him with the words; "*Ich will mit solchen Schweinereien nichts zu tun haben*" (I want nothing to do with such filthiness). In a letter to A. S. Neill in 1948, Reich stated that while his discipline of sex economy dealt with the problems of natural genitality, the sexology promoted by the World League for Sexual Reform (**Hirschfeld**'s bailiwick) concentrated on lingams, condoms, and homosexual perversions. He had earlier maintained that homosexuality was a disease of **fascism** that would "wither away" under socialism. Despite all this, the radical wave of the 1960s and later saw **counterculture** homosexuals turn to Reich as an authority for repudiating conventional morality and equating socialism with the untrammeled gratification of their own sexual impulses.

BIBLIOGRAPHY. David Boadella, *Wilhelm Reich: The Evolution of his Work*, London: Vision Press, 1973; Eustace Chesser, *Reich and Sexual Freedom*, London: Vision Press, 1972; Ilse Ollendorff Reich, *Wilhelm Reich: A Personal Biography*, New York: St. Martin's Press, 1969.

Warren Johansson

RENAISSANCE, ITALIAN

In **Italy** the term Renaissance designates a period somewhat different from that in the rest of Europe: the Italian Renaissance embraces the epoch that stretches from the late fourteenth century through the later decades of the sixteenth century, when the Catholic Counterreformation took hold. On the other side of the Alps, the Renaissance did not commence until the beginning of the sixteenth century, when it was introduced from Italy; yet it lasted somewhat longer there, at least in **Protestant** countries.

The word Renaissance (literally: rebirth) alludes to the impression, widespread in the period itself, that the ongoing cultural and artistic flowering was a kind of revival—on a Christian base, to be sure—of the glory of the ancient Romans, a revival attained on the very soil from which Rome itself had arisen.

A notable feature of the Italian Renaissance was an intense drive to recover the authentic character of classical antiquity. This impulse led to the rediscovery of original texts, chiefly Latin ones—though the study of Greek and Hebrew was also promoted. As a result of this trend, ancient manuscripts thought to have been lost were copied and disseminated, and a new branch of learning, philology, was founded.

The roots of the Renaissance lie in the great upsurge of commerce and industry that occurred in Italy after the year 1000. These advances required cultural changes: merchants needed to know how to read and write and to keep accounts. A surplus of wealth accumulated that sufficed to maintain a number of scholars and investigators in "full-time employment." Since the traditional training that religious schools provided was inadequate, lay schools appeared, from which a number of prestigious Italian universities developed. Becoming famous throughout Europe, the universities were one of the channels that diffused the Italian Renaissance, permanently injecting its values into Western civilization.

Social Background. With respect to homosexuality the Renaissance attitude was not uniform. The beginning of the Renaissance—the late fourteenth century—coincided with increased persecution of homosexuals. Toward the middle of the fifteenth century, however, a more tolerant atmosphere began to prevail, and capital punishment became uncommon.

The upper classes—in part under the umbrella of **libertine** currents of thought—witnessed the spread of a mood of "live and let live," which did not approve of homosexual behavior, but felt no obligation to condemn it either.

Evidence of the mindset that lies behind this trend is found for instance in the letters Nicolò Machiavelli (1469–1527) and his friend Francesco Vettori (1474–1539) exchanged between 1513 and 1515 commenting about the homosexual behavior of this or that friend as the most natural and obvious thing in the world. Similarly, Baldassare Castiglione (1474–1529) treated homosexuality quite nonchalantly in his famous classic of manners, *Il Cortegiano* (1529).

In short it is not an accident that beginning in the fifteenth century information proliferates on the rise of a sodomite subculture in the major Italian cities. Even in the previous century documents lament the existence of sodomite coteries. That these complaints were not baseless is shown by the documents of mass trials preserved in municipal archives, and in the literary allusions to the existence of specific zones in the cities where the sodomites went to look for sexual partners. The sermons St. Bernardino of Siena (1380–1444) preached against sodomites in 1424–25 seem an almost inexhaustible source of relevant anecdotes.

Italian Renaissance Literature and Homosexuality. If society tolerated the subculture, the world of letters did not lag behind. Because of the boundless affection that humanist men of letters cherished for the Ancients, few had the courage to condemn, or even to refuse to condone, the tastes which the great Latin and Greek poets accepted without question. In emulation of the antique there appeared a rich literature of homosexual themes both in Latin and in Italian—so rich that it has no equal in quantity and quality until the twentieth century.

Naturally, one should not conclude that every declaration of homosexual love stemming from the Renaissance corresponds to experiential reality, rooted in the emotional preference of the author. Often writers of the fifteenth century contented themselves with imitating **Vergil, Martial, Catullus**, and other major figures of the past. A similar trend appeared in Elizabethan **England**.

Nonetheless, it is a mistake to interpret, as is often done, every homosexual utterance as simply the product of literary convention. In the Italian Renaissance no risk attended the expression of homosexual sentiments and wishes. Hence many, profiting from literary and amatory conventions, took advantage of this freedom to set down their own homosexual feelings, though in the guise of "imitations" of the revered models of antiquity.

For these individuals the coming of the Counterreformation was a real tragedy that effectively ended the Renaissance. Shortly after the middle of the sixteenth century this rigorist trend brought a chill climate of moralism and censure that proved intensely hostile to the expression of homoerotic themes.

Classical Imitation. Italian Renaissance homosexual discourse was much given to donning the garments of classical antiquity. Latin Renaissance poetry often shows it proximity to its sources by its choice of terms and themes. On the one hand, one finds recyclings of specific authors, of **Martial**, as in the case of the *Hermaphroditus* (1425) of Antonio Beccadelli (1394–1471), and of less jocular authors, as in the *Hecathalegium* (1489) of Pacifico Massimo of Ascoli (ca. 1400–1500)—not to mention the invectives that Italian Humanists launched against one another. One finds classical trappings in the accusations of sodomy that Francesco Filelfo (1398–1481) launched against Cosimo de' Medici in 1448; or in those of Giovanni Pontano (1426–1503) against a certain "Antonino," or yet again by Andrea Dazzi (1473–1538) against **Poliziano**. As regards invectives against behavior **Juvenal** remained the obvious point of reference, as had occurred earlier in the **Middle Ages**. Imitation also involved other authors (e.g., Vergil), as seen in Niccolò Lelio Cosmico (before 1420–1500), who was accused by contemporaries of being a sodomite; Angelo Ambrogini, known as Poliziano (1454–1494), who wrote also in classical Greek; Pomponio Leto (1421–1498), who was also arrested on suspicion of sodomy; and Pietro Bembo (1470–1547).

Jocose Poetry. Jocose or burlesque poetry enjoyed particular favor. In Florence it became so popular that as early as 1325 a law explicitly forbade the composition and singing of sodomitical songs, which were usually in verse.

Satirical poetry in Italian continued the traditions of medieval jocose and burlesque poetry; thus one finds the invectives (in which accusations of sodomy abound) of Matteo Franco (1447–1494) against Luigi Pulci, and of Nicolò Franco (1515–1570) against Pietro **Aretino** (1541).

To this general class belong the pasquinades, or public satires, in which the accusations of sodomy are unceasing. Valerio Marucci has provided an excellent sampling of this material, but much of it remains unpublished.

In burlesque poetry, as early as 1406–7 one finds two significant documents, the so-called "Tenzone fra Dante e Forese" (long attributed to **Dante** himself) and the work entitled *L'Aquettino.* From 1407–9 comes a long poem entitled *La Buca di Monteferrato* of Stefano Finiguerri (d. after 1422), in which a large number of Florentines were accused of sodomy and chastised for it in allusive language that abounds in double entendres.

This kind of cryptic language was carried to perfection in the so-called **Burchiellesque poetry**, and utilized also in **Bernesque poetry**, which enjoyed immense fame in the fifteenth and sixteenth centuries. A later development of of burlesque poetry was to give rise to **Fidentian** verse, which was also homoerotic in theme.

Prose. Relying upon the precedent of Giovanni Boccaccio (1313–1375), one of the "fathers" of the Italian language, who included stories with homosexual motifs in his *Decameron,* Italian writers did not flinch from offering an abundance of new tales and anecdotes featuring homosexual characters. Citing only the most important, one may note short stories and jokes on homosexual themes by the following: Gentile Sermini (fifteenth century), Poggio Bracciolini (1380–1459), Sabbadino degli Arienti (1450–1510), Niccolo dell'Angeli dal Bucine (ca. 1448–1532), Matteo Bandello (1485–1561), Agnolo Firenzuola (1493–1543), Girolamo Morlini (sixteenth century; wrote in Latin), Francesco Molza (1489–1544), and Sebastiano Erizzo (1528–1585).

A particular type of writing, a mock essay on an erotic theme, appeared in the *Commento alla "ficheide" di Padre Siceo* of Anibal Caro (1507–1566) and with the audacious *La Cazzaria* (1531) of Antonio Vignali de' Buonagiunti (d. 1559).

In prose writing a special place belongs to the numerous treatises on love, starting with that of the neo-Platonist Marsilio **Ficino**, in which the discussion of the permissibility of love between men is almost an obligatory commonplace. Among authors of treatises discussing this question are Tullia d'Aragona (1508–1556), Girolamo Benivieni (1453?–1542), Giuseppe Betussi (1512?–1573?), Giovanni Pico della Mirandola (1463–1494), Flaminio Nobili (1530–1590), and Francesco Sansovino (1521–1583).

Theatre. Homosexual characters and situations appear in the *Janus Sacerdos,* a Latin comedy of 1427, as well as dramas by Ludovico Ariosto (1474–1533), Pietro Aretino, and Poliziano.

Love Lyrics. Lyrical love poetry addressed to persons of the same sex was cultivated during the Renaissance by poets who often assembled a genuine *canzoniere* or personal anthology for the beloved.

From the imposing collection of Tuscan lyrics of the fifteenth century edited by Antonio Lanza, one must note at least Giovanni Gherardi (ca.1367–1446), Andrea Bellacci (fifteenth century), Filippo Scarlatti (1442–after 1487), and Antonio di Guido (d. 1486). Also noteworthy is the love poetry of **Michelangelo**, Francesco Beccuti (1509–1553), Benedetto **Varchi**, and Torquato Tasso (1544–1595).

Sermons. The social historian will find much material in sermons, providing anecdotes and detailed descriptions of elements of the homosexual life. Among the most important are, besides those already cited by Bernardino of Siena, the sermons of Antonino of Florence (Antonio Pierozzi; 1389–1459), Roberto of Lecce (Roberto Caracciolo; 1425–1495), and the famous Girolamo Savonarola (1452–1498).

Visual Arts. In the late Middle Ages, artists were organized in workshops whose personnel were made up, for the most part, of members of a single extended family. In fifteenth-century Florence, however, rising prosperity and new technical advances made it possible for gifted artists to set up studios of their own. In these independent establishments they hired unrelated young men (*garzoni*) who served as apprentices, models, and servants. Women did not function as models and, in an era in which ideal beauty was a supreme value, comely youths posed for renderings of both the male and female form. At the same time, artists became familiar with the ancient heritage of pederasty that the humanists had been uncovering. The homosexual character of classical themes, such as **Ganymede** and **Orpheus**, became known and cherished. In this climate it is not surprising that some artists succumbed to the charms of their *garzoni* and to those of other attractive youths. Such major figures as **Donatello**, **Leonardo**, and **Botticelli** are known to have had homosexual affairs. At the end of the fifteenth century a period of religious and political disturbances began, which made the situation of the artists, then reaching the zenith of prestige in what subsequently came to be known as the High Renaissance, more uncertain, though their same-sex amours by no means ceased. Here the names of Michelangelo, Giovanni Antonio Bazzi (called "Il **Sodoma**"), Benvenuto **Cellini** (twice accused), Jacopo Pontormo, and **Caravaggio** must be recorded. Eventually, however, the Counterreformation put an end to this period of efflorescence of homoeroticism in the arts.

See also **Art, Visual; Florence; Papacy; Venice.**

BIBLIOGRAPHY. Giovanni Dall'Orto, "La Fenice di Sodoma: essere omosessuale nell'Italia del Rinascimento," *Sodoma*, 4 (1988), 31–53; Antonio Lanza, ed., *Lirici toscani del quattrocento*, 2 vols., Rome: Bulzoni, 1973; Valerio Marucci, ed., *Pasquinate romane del Cinquecento*, 2 vols., Rome: Salerno, 1984; James Saslow, *Ganymede in the Renaissance*, New Haven: Yale University Press, 1986.

Giovanni Dall'Orto

RENAULT, MARY (PSEUDONYM OF MARY CHALLANS; 1905–1983)

Born in England in 1905, Mary Challans was educated at St. Hugh's College, Oxford, in preparation for a teaching career. When she decided to become a writer instead, she concluded that she needed to see more of life and trained as a nurse from 1933 through 1937. After World War II broke out, she worked as a nurse and wrote in her off hours.

After the war, Challans settled in South Africa, where she spent the rest of her life, traveling periodically to mainland Greece, Crete, and other points. She was an intensely private woman, as shown by her use of a pseudonym, and never sought the "writer-celebrity" limelight, despite the fact that she was world-famous and highly esteemed. Since she never married, and since homosexuality and the nature of male and female are constant leitmotifs of her fiction, it would be only sensible to presume that she wrote about things which concerned her; from this one would conclude that Challans was a lesbian—or at least bisexual—but there is, as yet, no direct biographical evidence.

She began her career with an apprenticeship in the world of popular fiction, or romance novels. She later asserted that if everything she had written before *The Charioteer* were to perish, she would only feel relief. Her first novel, *Promise of Love* (1939), dealt with lesbianism as a subtheme, and her other romance novels continued to probe the nature of male and female in a very nonstandard way for the genre. Also nonstandard was the continued development of her writing style and a constant background of ancient **Greek** themes.

With *The Charioteer* in 1953, Challans began to break new ground for the popular novel. (The book's publication was delayed until 1959 in America, a fact which Challans attributed to **McCarthyism**.) The ancient Greek subthemes assume a much more prominent role, and the foreground tale is an overt account of male homosexual love. The novel describes physical love largely through ellipses (Challans was never to vary this habit of restraint), but otherwise pulls very few punches.

With her next book, *The Last of the Wine* (1956), Challans left popular romances behind her and took up a career in historical fiction. This is a problematic genre, since it has been so often abused. Yet, very early on, she was receiving the highest possible accolades for her faithful recreations of ancient Hellas. She typically included a bibliography and an "Author's Note" in each novel, explaining what was historical fact and what was not.

The Last of the Wine is one of the few classic novels of male homosexual love, and has been cherished by many gay men since it first appeared (it has never gone out of print). Other novels followed in steady progression: *The King Must Die, The Bull from the Sea, The Mask of Apollo,*

Fire from Heaven, The Persian Boy, and *The Praise Singer.* She also published a non-fiction work describing her research into **Alexander the Great**: *The Search for Alexander.* Almost all her historical novels seem assured of a healthy life for many years to come. The theme which is dating the novels most quickly is the **Freudian** mythology which Challans unfortunately decided to weave into her tales.

Challans' significance is similar to that of Marguerite **Yourcenar**, another lesbian who wrote magnificent books about male homosexuality. It is a somewhat puzzling phenomenon, in that one would expect them to write novels about women in love, and the beauty of women. But somehow these two women (and they are not alone) had extremely strong perceptions of male beauty and of love between men. In Challans' case, that has left *The Charioteer, The Last of the Wine,* and *The Persian Boy* as a literary heritage.

BIBLIOGRAPHY. Bernard F. Dick, *The Hellenism of Mary Renault*, Carbondale and Edwardsville: Southern Illinois University Press, 1972.

Geoff Puterbaugh

RESORTS

Resorts frequented by homosexual men—and to a lesser extent by lesbians—tend to be at the shore. A few inland exceptions, such as Palm Springs and Russian River in California occur, but winter resorts, such as skiing sites, have rarely developed a visible homosexual presence. The reason for this specialization lies probably in the association of sun and sensuality, and gay resorts function more clearly as places of sexual assignation than those favored, say, by family groups. An interesting contrast is that between nude beaches, which attract a gay clientele, and nudist camps, which rarely do.

Some well-heeled gay visitors travel to resorts in the company of their regular lovers, while others hope to find romance there—either with other visitors or with hustlers. The availability of the latter depends in large measure on the economic situation of the region in which the resort is situated; those which are remote from a demographic reservoir of impoverished individuals tend not to have many hustlers. Apparently, gay resorts do not favor the migratory legions of prostitutes that work the heterosexual circuits, so that local talent is necessary. In a wealthy town, such as Palm Springs, this pool of sex workers is simply lacking. Hence the attraction of Third World countries for some "sexual tourists."

This article observes a distinction between resorts proper, which are located away from major population centers (their attraction lying in part in this very distance), and metropolitan **beaches**. Distance lends enchantment—or at least a sense of security inasmuch as those employed in such conservative occupations as banking and law often do not feel that they can truly relax except far from their business associates and family. During the tourist season the typical resort town functions around the clock: **bars**, restaurants, and other places of relaxation and social contact are open into the wee hours of the morning, in contrast with an industrial town where all night life ends by eleven in the evening. In resorts frequented by homosexuals, many of the guest houses are owned by gay proprietors and solicit patrons through advertisements in the gay **press**. Occasional exceptions to the separation between resort towns and metropolitan centers occur, as Rio de Janeiro, which has beaches for its residents, but which functions as a resort for foreign gay men, especially during the **mardi gras** or carnival season.

History. The sources for the popularity of modern gay resorts are various, including the old **arcadian** dream of a place apart from hostile heterosexual pressures, a long-standing tradition of homosexual **travel**, and the sexual **exiles** and remittance men who tended to flock together during their involuntary foreign sojourns. The first stirrings of the impulse to the gay resort stem from the beginnings of mass travel to the Mediterranean in the nineteenth century. During the previous century the homosexual archeologist J. J. **Winckelmann** had been responsible for popularizing, in elite circles at least, a notion of **Italy** as the homeland of aesthetic paganism. This idea was subsequently reinforced by such writers as Walter **Pater** and John Addington **Symonds**. As a practical matter the opening of trunk railway lines linking northern Europe to the Mediterranean made the fabled spots available to a considerably enlarged clientele. By the end of the nineteenth century **Florence**, Capri, and **Sicily** had well developed colonies of homosexual and lesbian expatriates. The Tuscan capital tended to attract the more intellectual and artistic visitors for longer stays, the southern islands a more hedonistic and nomadic crowd. The special qualities of Capri have been captured by such novelists as Norman **Douglas**, Compton Mackenzie, and Roger Peyrefitte. Later in the twentieth century, as Capri's attractions faded, other Mediterranean islands, including Mykonos, Lesbos, and **Crete** in Greece, became centers of gay tourism. At the end of the 1980s the top three gay summer resorts were all in Spain: Sitges, Ibiza, and Torremolinos.

The French acquisition of North **Africa** (beginning in 1830) had opened up historic Islamic countries with a long tradition of available youth. Thus André **Gide** was to find Oscar **Wilde** and Lord Alfred **Douglas** visiting Algeria for sexual purposes in 1894; he was surprised not so much by the purpose of their visit as the frankness with which it was avowed. Because of its international status, the city of Tangier in Morocco remained a gay center at least through the 1960s. More adventurous travelers could, of course, visit Turkey, Syria, and Egypt, but these countries seem not to have developed any specific sites of fascination for the sexual tourist.

Contemporary Patterns. In the United States, the east coast boasts two resorts of particular renown: Provincetown, Massachusetts, and Key West, Florida. Just when these locales emerged as gay meccas is hard to say because they began their careers as places favored by artists, writers, and theatre people, with a considerable though not originally dominant gay admixture—"tipping" probably only in the 1960s. Fire Island, easily accessible on day trips from New York City, belongs to a special category intermediate between the metropolitan beach and the true resort. In a number of states of the United States enterprising individuals have set up gay ranches for private customers. To some extent this practice parallels nudist camps, which are themselves part of a large, but little known subculture.

BIBLIOGRAPHY. James Money, *Capri, Island of Pleasure,* London: Deutsch, 1987; *Odysseus ... An Accommodations Guide for Gay Men,* New York: Odysseus Enterprises, 1989; *Spartacus International Gay Guide,* Berlin: Bruno Gmünder, 1989.

Wayne R. Dynes

RICHARD I THE LION-HEARTED (1157–1199)

King of England. Richard was famed for his reckless courage and extreme cruelty—he massacred 3,000 brave Moslems who had surrendered Acre to the Crusaders under his safe conduct—as well as for gallantry to many, including Saladin. Favorite of his mother, Eleanor of Aquitaine, who set him against his royal father Henry II of England—himself falsely accused of having loved Thomas Becket, with whom he did share a bed on occasion while carousing and wenching together before Becket became Archbishop of Canterbury—Richard has been seen by some as a mama's boy.

The Norman and Angevin (Plantagenet) kings of England were, along with their courtiers, regularly accused by monk-ish chroniclers of sodomy. It was not true of Henry II, who made his son's fiancée Alice of France his mistress to the outrage of Eleanor and Richard. The accusation rings true, however, for William II Rufus (ca. 1056–1100), as for his nephew Prince William (son of his brother Henry I), who was coasting down the Channel with his frivolous, effeminate companions, when the White Ship capsized—"God's vengeance on the sodomites," as the chroniclers declared.

Richard was the great-grandson of Henry I and scion on the other side of the brutal, vicious, exuberant counts of Anjou, thought by some to be genetically sadistic. It is perhaps not true that Richard fell in love with the young king of France, Philip II Augustus. Their intimate friendship was occasioned by their plotting against Richard's father. But Richard never showed any serious interest in women. He waited very late to marry Berengaria of Navarre; he spent practically no time with her, and failed to sire any heir, an important obligation of kingship. During a stay in Messina in 1190 he seems to have decided to abjure his preference for male sexual partners. He appeared barefoot in a chapel and, surrounded by high ecclesiastics, Richard confessed his past misdeeds. Although he was absolved on promise of good behavior, he apparently relapsed later.

When Richard, who spent only ten months of his eleven-year reign in England, was imprisoned or captured on his way back from Jerusalem by the Duke of Austria, an ally of Philip II of France, now his enemy, a visitor sang outside the prison a troubadour's song, composed long before by the king, as a signal of his arrival. Perhaps this was a lover, but the sources do not name a single one of them.

To Richard's reign belongs the account of the **London** underworld and its homosexual denizens composed by Richard of Devizes. Like **Edward II** (1284–1327), Richard II (1367–1400) probably practiced sodomy. None of the medieval sodomitical monarchs and princes of **England** died a natural death, unlike almost all their exclusively heterosexual royal rivals in France, the Capetians.

BIBLIOGRAPHY. James A. Brundage, *Richard Lion Heart*, New York: Scribner's, 1974.

William A. Percy

RIMBAUD, ARTHUR (1854–1891)

French symbolist poet. The son of an army officer who deserted his wife and family in 1860, he had an unhappy childhood under his mother's harsh discipline that may explain the spirit of adolescent rebellion that characterizes his first poems, written in 1870–71. Some of these astonishingly mature pieces attack those in authority, while others dream of a different world of total freedom. The most celebrated is "Le Bateau ivre," in which the poet imagines himself as a boat completely out of control, drifting wildly down rivers, into seas, and across oceans. Immediately after writing this poem, he set off for Paris in September 1871, where he was welcomed by Paul **Verlaine**, ten years his senior, whose unorthodox versification appealed to him. He then put into practice the code that he had formulated in his famous "Lettre du voyant" of May 1871, that the poet should sharpen his perception by submitting to every sort of experience and then transmitting what he has perceived directly, without conscious control.

Nearly all of his poetry belongs to the period of his homosexual love affair with Verlaine, which ended in July 1873 when the two quarreled violently and the older man shot him in the wrist. He had broken away from verse forms and adopted the prose poem in a group of some forty passages called the *Illuminations*, which however obscure in meaning, have a unique and compelling poetic quality that springs from the vividness of the imagery, the rhythm of the phrases, and the directness of the language. In the summer of 1873 he wrote *Une Saison en enfer*, again in an obscure but often compelling prose, in which he admitted to having lived in a fool's paradise and to have spent a "season in hell" with his lover.

After this he abandoned literature, and in a sense abandoned life, becoming a solitary wanderer, first in Europe and then the East Indies, and finally in Ethiopia, where he may have had some homosexual liaisons with the natives. He died in a hospital in Marseille in 1891 at the age of 37, indifferent to the extraordinary reputation as a youthful genius of the poetic that he had acquired after Verlaine wrote an essay on him in his *Poètes maudits* in 1884.

The homosexual elements in Rimbaud's work are slight, even if the creative period of his life was one of his liaison with Verlaine, and some modern critics have seen in his adolescent eroticism the key to his life's work, a rebellion that transcends the mere personal and culminates in the shattering of society's moral conventions and the negation of its traditional values. By seeking inspiration through narcotics that placed him on the margin of respectable society and its realm of experience, Rimbaud reinforced the image of the poet as outsider, as one who has the right to create his own mode of expression rather than adhering to the received canons of literature. He remains the unmatched archetype of the adolescent poet whose homoerotic feelings lifted him far above the imitation of which most youthful writers alone would be capable—into the sphere of creative genius.

BIBLIOGRAPHY. Robert Montal, *L'adolescent Rimbaud*, Lyon: Les Ecrivains réunis, 1954; Enid Starkie, *Arthur Rimbaud*, New York: New Directions, 1961.

Warren Johansson

ROCHESTER, JOHN WILMOT, EARL OF (1647–1680)

English poet and intellectual. After receiving the privileged education of a Restoration nobleman—Wadham College, Oxford, followed by the grand tour of the continent—Rochester became a member of a clique at the court of Charles II, where he was famous for his wit, skepticism, and ostensibly dissolute life. His surviving works are few: about 75 poems, an adaptation of a tragedy, and a scene from an unfinished play. Although his free use of sexual language earned him censure and bowdlerization over the centuries, his satirical bite has always guaranteed him admirers. Restoration culture underwent strong French influence, and it is from the libertine poets of that country, as well as the Latin satirists that were a common source, that Rochester seems to have derived his main impetus. As understood in the seventeenth century, **libertinism** meant not praise of licentious excess, but a skeptical attitude toward received values that went hand in hand with an effort to set forth a new and more rational approach to living. Thus the light-heartedness and flippancy of some of Rochester's poetry must be viewed within a larger context of serious purpose.

Contemporary testimony leaves little doubt that Rochester was personally bisexual. His account of a rake's reminiscence is probably not too far from his own attitudes: "Nor shall our love fits, Chloris, be forgot,/ When each the well-looked linkboy strove t'enjoy,/ And the best kiss was deciding lot/ Whether the boy fucked you or I the boy." ("The Maimed Debauchee," ll. 37–40). The same approach, recalling Horace's statement that a woman or a boy would suit his needs equally well, recurs in "The Platonic Lady," "Love a Woman? You're an Ass!," and "Upon His Drinking Bowl."

There has been some dispute about the canon of poems to be attributed to Rochester. It seems generally agreed, however, that the obscene play in rhyming couplets *Sodom*, first published in 1684 and frequently reprinted under his name, is not by him.

BIBLIOGRAPHY. *Works: The Complete Poems of John Wilmot, Earl of Rochester*, David M. Vieth, ed., New Haven: Yale University Press, 1968. *Criticism*: R. M. Baine, "Rochester or Fishbourne: A Question of Authorship," *Review of English Studies*, 22 (1946), 201–6; Dustin H. Griffin, *Satires Against Man: The Poems of Rochester*, Berkeley: University of California Press, 1973.
Wayne R. Dynes

ROCK AND ROLL
See **Music, Popular; Punk Rock.**

RÖHM [ROEHM], ERNST (1887–1934)

German soldier and politician; leader of the Schutz-Abteilung (SA) of the **Nazi** Party during its rise to power in the Weimar Republic. Röhm was an organizer of right-wing paramilitary groups who, in 1919, first made Hitler aware of his own political potential, and for the following fifteen years the two were close friends. Magnus **Hirschfeld** remarked that the only photograph in which Hitler appeared smiling was one in which he was in Röhm's company.

From the fall of 1930 onward Röhm transformed the SA Brownshirt militia from a handful of unemployed thugs and embittered veterans of World War I into an effective fighting force some half a million strong—an instrument of Nazi terror. He had in 1928–30 lived abroad as an instructor of the—largely Amerindian—Bolivian Army and boasted in letters to his friends in Germany that he had introduced the recruits not only to Prussian discipline but also to homosexual love—which until then had supposedly been unknown there. Röhm, who made no secret of his homosexual proclivities and of his aversion to women, was well known in the gay subculture of **Berlin**, and had down to the end of 1932 been the object of five different court proceedings for his "immoral" conduct. Hitler had resolved to rid himself of his chief of staff, all the more as the Social Democratic newspaper *Münchner Post* had published letters that established Röhm's homosexuality beyond doubt. Also, opponents of Röhm within the Nazi ranks and the psychiatrist Oswald Bumke had written to Hitler denouncing the SA leader and the homosexuals in his entourage as a corrupting example for the youth of Germany. One opponent went so far as to say that even intellectuals could not understand how it was that so many homosexuals occupied leadership positions in the Nazi Party. Röhm for his part proudly asserted that the homoerotic, male-bonding element within the Nazi paramilitary units had given them the crucial edge in the struggle with the Reichsbanner and the Communists.

After the accession of the National Socialists to power in March 1933, Röhm remained in Hitler's good graces, but as part of a compromise with the Reichswehr leadership, whose support he needed to become Führer. Hitler allowed Göring and Himmler to murder Röhm together with dozens of loyal SA officers on the night of June 30–July 1, 1934—the "Night of the Long Knives." It was later said, somewhat dubiously, that with Röhm the last socialist in the Nazi Party died, but so perished the quixotic hopes of homosexuals such as Hans **Blüher** within the right-wing, pro-Nazi groups that Hitler's rule would mean greater toleration. The regime hypocritically used Röhm's sexual life as a pretext for claiming that it was "protecting German youth from corruption" by liquidating Röhm and his clique, but a newspaper in Kassel created a scandal by publishing stories to the effect that the truth had long been known to Hitler and his chief associates.

See also Fascist Perversion, Myth of.

BIBLIOGRAPHY. Max Gallo, *The Night of the Long Knives*, New York: Harper and Row, 1972; James D. Steakley, *The Homosexual Emancipation Movement in Germany*, New York: Arno Press, 1975.

Warren Johansson

ROLE

In social science usage, the concept of role contrasts with that of self (or **identity**). In dramaturgical **sociology**, as on theatre stages, an actor plays many roles over the course of a career, or even on a single night. Some actors always play the same kind of character. Some are swallowed up in one role, while others have extensive repertoires of different types and do not live onstage roles when they are offstage. Similarly, "homosexual roles" are enacted in appropriate settings by persons who play other roles at other times or places. As important as affirming homosexuality may be to some individuals, or as recognizing homosexuals may be in some cultures, no one is onstage as "a homosexual" and nothing but "a homosexual" all the time.

Theoretical Considerations. In the basic social science introduction to the concept, Ralph Linton (1936) defined status as "a collection of rights and duties," and role as dynamic status: how rights and duties are realized in interaction. Each person in a society has more than one status, and therefore plays multiple roles. Moreover, a particular status involves, not a single role, but an array of associated roles, e.g., the "teacher role" in relation to students is not the same as the "teacher role" to administrators (or to the Parent–Teachers Association, etc.). There are overlapping simultaneous statuses so that different roles may be played even within a single setting. For instance, in a women-only bar it may not matter that one is a lesbian lawyer. Entry depends upon being a woman and of legal age. If there is a raid on the bar, the attorney role may be activated. Responding to a sexual proposition makes sexual status salient. Within this interaction, being a mother, daughter, wife—all roles that she plays in other times and places—may not matter, although these outside statuses may affect where or whether the sexual proposition is accepted, if one of the perceived requirements of the mother, daughter, or wife role is not to bring sexual partners home. Obligations to another person not present may impinge on interaction, and may do so whether or not the woman explicitly defines herself as, say, "wife" (to herself, to others present, or to those with whom she resides).

Analysis of shifting, overlapping, and multiple simultaneous status enactment in roles easily becomes very complex. Sometimes, it seems that an abstract "situation" determines (rather than merely limits) statuses; at other times it seems that role theorists believe that any sort of role can be presented (that is, that there are no constraints of plausibility on acting in public). Phenomenological analysis can make the "local accomplishment" of even the simplest communication seem miraculous. Perhaps even more confusingly, as Goodenough noted, use of the term "role" often drifts from this definition of enacted rights and obligations to any and all kinds of statements about social categories, selves, and "personality structures." In the case of "homosexual role," discussion blithely posits psychological entities detached from any interaction, although to be meaningful "role" must be a relational term, involving relation to actors of other roles and/or to an audience. Enacting a role plausibly does not require full commitment to a role or total self-identification with it. Indeed, an individual's "role distance" may facilitate plausible performance, whereas totally embracing a role may land a person in the realm of psychopathology (Goffman). And role strain is "normal: in general the individual's total role obligations are over-demanding" as well as incompatible (Goode).

Homosexual Aspects. In an often cited paper which consolidates Anglo-American stereotypes into a "theoretical construct," McIntosh (1968) posited a dichotomous homosexual/heterosexual categorization apart from any interaction and, indeed, based on no empirical data. McIntosh's "homosexual role" lacks any of the subtle multiplicities of situated meanings of role as used by classical role theorists (none of whose writings she cited). It is a functionalist, not an interactionist construct, in effect a bogeyman to scare boys away from homosexuality. What those enacting a (the?) heterosexual role expect from those playing "the homosexual role," according to McIntosh, is exhibition of (1) effeminacy, (2) more or less exclusive homosexual feelings and behavior, (3) attraction to and (4) attempted seduction of all young men, or, perhaps all men ("sexuality will play a part of some kind in all his relations with other men"). Where, when, or whether the person playing McIntosh's version of "the homosexual role" has a right to act effeminately and seduce men and/or boys is matter she does not discuss. Implicitly, this un-male "role" was enacted to/for a heterosexual male other. In some other cultures (especially Polynesian ones) in which there is a societal conception of gender-crossing homosexuality, blatant specimens of failed masculine socialization could be tolerated, because such persons provided vivid warnings of what boys must avoid becoming.

Although, as Whitam noted, McIntosh's treatment "violates the prevailing definition and conventional usage of this concept in sociology," and cannot "explain homosexuality," there are homosexual roles to analyze apart from the monster of the heterosexual imagination conjured up by McIntosh. Within homosexual interactions and relationships, complementary roles exist, e.g., mentor/initiate or sodomite/catamite occur where homosexuality is organized by age; hustler/trick or patron/protégé in class societies, especially where there are "homosexual occupations" such as dancing boys; trade/queer, hombre/maricón (in **Latin America**), or brave/berdache (among the

North American **Indians**) where homosexuality is organized by gender distinctiveness. Each of these pairs has been listed in insertor/insertee order, although sexual behavior is only one aspect of these roles. A person may play one or more of these roles without possessing a homosexual identity, any strong commitment to or preference for homosexuality. Indeed, some of the roles may not require even feigned homosexual desire.

How to perform the sexual and other rights and obligations of these roles is learned. One does not learn how to be a homosexual any more than one learns how to be a husband or a wife directly in primary socialization with one's natal family. One may learn *about* such roles, that is, learn the cultural script for each. Boys may learn about "the male role" without male role models, just as they may learn about **queers** without seeing any. Similarly, girls may hear about **dykes**. Learning about a "homosexual role" of the sort McIntosh portrayed may motivate suppressing homosexual desires, and may also motivate acting out exaggerated cross-gender behavior before realizing that such behavior is not a necessary attribute of homosexuality within a homosexual **subculture**. Some observers have discerned a transient effeminate stage in the uninitiated boy's or man's process of distinguishing societal expectations of effeminacy from actual subcultural expectations. Similarly, a **butch** phase may have made a woman's sexual interest in other women visible. Such a traditional phase of cross-gender role exaggeration may be attenuated or altogether lacking for those who, growing up with homosexual desires, are able to perceive a lesbian or gay role for themselves unmarked by cross-gender behavior and demeanor. More recently, a phase of hypermasculinity ("**macho**") has been central to socialization into some gay male worlds.

Prior to contact with other gay or lesbian people or groupings, gender exaggeration (toward either extreme of the gender continuum) may be the only conceivable way to signal desired sexual variance. Generally, anticipatory socialization is incomplete and either ambiguous or stereotyped. Moreover, anticipatory socialization "helps only to the extent it is accurate. . . . If it is not accurate, it may actually impede adjustment, for performing the acquired role will necessitate unlearning as well as further learning" (Thornton and Nardi). The gender-crossing idiom for recognizing homosexuals, is learned in early socialization in many societies (including the United States) in which age-grading is not central to organizing homosexual relations.

"Learning about" may heavily condition initial attempts to do what is expected of a sexual partner (husband, wife, or homosexual), but there is also secondary socialization onstage in the role, as well as intra-psychic rehearsal for playing it. **Gender** roles (how to act male or female) are part of primary socialization in Anglo-Saxon North America, but the roles enacted in heterosexual marriage, as well as those enacted in gay subcultures are part of later learning/socialization. Breaking the externally imposed notion that homosexuality requires having to live out society's stereotypes of what "a homosexual" is a key part of secondary socialization within gay and lesbian subcultures. Nonetheless, neophytes tend to play their preconceptions of a role rigidly, or even ritualistically (Goffman). Within gay or lesbian communities or networks, most people discard the "queer" or "dyke" role (at least as conceived in the dominant society) and learn what others involved in homosexual scenarios expect. Such expectations may be only slightly conditioned by societal stereotypes, although residues of such images may be eroticized, or otherwise unconsciously maintained.

In all cultures, whatever the dominant conception or valuation of homosexuality, a merger of self and role is not inevitably achieved. Not only is there homosexuality outside subcultures, and behavior contrary to societal expectations, but there are individual conceptions of all roles in all societies. The process of role acquisition is not mere training in automaton-like replication of fixed roles. Human beings create meaning even when they are trying to follow a social script exactly. Conceptions of what homosexual roles require vary within as well as among societies.

BIBLIOGRAPHY. Erving Goffman, *Encounters*, Indianapolis: Bobbs-Merrill, 1961; William J. Goode, "A Theory of Role Strain," *American Sociological Review*, 25 (1960), 483–96; Ward Goodenough, "Rethinking Status and Role," in S. Tyler, ed., *Cognitive Anthropology*, New York: Holt, 1965, pp. 311–30; Ralph Linton, *The Study of Man*, New York: Appleton, 1936; Mary McIntosh, "The Homosexual Role," *Social Problems*, 16 (1968), 182–92; Russell Thornton and Peter M. Nardi, "Dynamics of Role Acquisition," *American Journal of Sociology*, 80 (1975), 870–84; Frederick J. Whitam, "The Homosexual Role Revisited," *Journal of Sex Research*, 13 (1977), 1–11.
Stephen O. Murray

ROLFE, FREDERICK WILLIAM ("BARON CORVO"; 1860–1913)

English adventurer, novelist, and historian. Born in London as the son of a dissenting piano manufacturer, he left school at 15, then studied briefly at Oxford. He served as a tutor and made ends meet as a poorly paid hack writer. He found a number of patrons during his career, but his lifelong attempt to convince the Catholic Church—to which he had become a convert—that he had a vocation for the priesthood developed (or rather accented) a pathological state of mind that bordered on paranoia, and inevitably led to his break with it.

In 1890 he received from Caroline, the Duchess of Sforza-Cesarini, the title of Baron Corvo, and she regarded him as her adopted grandson. While working for the firm of G. W. Wilson & Co. in London in 1893, he invented underwater photography, but with no financial gain. To the *Yellow Book* he contributed six "Stories Toto Told Me" (1898); these legends of the saints, with 26 additional ones, were printed as *In His Own Image* (1901). A work written on commission for the money, the *Chronicles of the House of Borgia* (1901), displays his curious fund of knowledge, vivid but undisciplined imagination, and considerable prose talent. His self-deluded, self-justifying, spiritual dreams of a rejected convert who became the noblest of popes furnished the material for his best work of fiction, *Hadrian the Seventh* (1904), to which he added malicious sketches of his supposed enemies. The central character, Hadrian, though endowed with Rolfe's identity, still blurs the boundaries between autobiography, while the secondary characters, all puppets manipulated as part of the drama of Hadrian, stem directly from Rolfe's experience. Although the work is remarkable for its passages of wit and erudition, it spoils its effect by yielding to anti-socialist melodrama. The last years of his life were spent as a parasite in **Venice**. An idealized chronicle of the period from December 1908 to July 1909, with parting shots at his enemies, is contained in *The Desire and Pursuit of the Whole*, edited by A. J. A. Symons in 1934. To this subject matter Rolfe added a tender account of homosexual love, disguised as the hero Nicholas Crabbe's love for Zilda, a girl who lived and dressed as the boy Zildo.

Homosexuality, and more particularly **pederasty**, as subjects for literature, were much in Rolfe's mind while he was writing this work. Sometime in 1909 he had sent to the British pederast John Gambril Nicholson a "specimen" of some ten thousand words, an experiment in formulating homosexual experiences as though they were his own. In September of the same year he began writing to an English visitor to Italy, Charles Masson Fox, a series of letters that may well be the most painful and the most erotic homosexual correspondence in English. Readers have found in them evidence that Rolfe was a corruptor of innocent youth, an insatiable and unrepentant sodomite, or contrariwise mere begging letters concocted out of the literature of homosexuality and the author's own imagination. They in effect promise his patron the sexual services of fourteen- or fifteen-year-old boys, many of them inexperienced.

Rarely has any man left so clear an account of his own sexual nature and his passionate hunger for its fulfillment, along with the tragic evidence of its constant frustration. Rolfe's own preference was for boys sixteen to eighteen years old—the upper limit of the pederast's range of interest. But with his slender and uncertain means he simply could not pay hustlers' fees or rent suitable premises for the rendezvous. He felt real sympathy for the Venetian boys—gondoliers and the like—with whom he associated, and bitterly regretted that he could do no more for them. His failure to achieve the erotic conquests for which he longed paralleled all of the other disappointments of his life. He succeeded in nothing that he attempted, and was denied everything that he sought from the church except faith itself.

Rolfe has been the object of a cult, inspired perhaps by the fascination which the career of a pretender with equal touches of the holy and the demonic exerts on those fated to live their adventures vicariously through literature. He is a classic type of the homosexual "begging intellectual," constantly trying to live by his wits and to bask in the favor of the wealthy and powerful, yet doomed by the inner flaws of his personality to the margin of society and even of sanity. Born without the means and social position to realize his grandiose ambitions, he nevertheless left a heritage that is part of English literature.

BIBLIOGRAPHY. Miriam J. Benkovitz, *Frederick Rolfe: Baron Corvo*, New York: G. P. Putnam's Sons, 1977; A. J. A. Symons, *The Quest for Corvo*, New York: Macmillan, 1934.

Warren Johansson

ROMAN EMPERORS

Although many Roman sovereigns took their official duties seriously, others—especially in the first century of the empire—used their almost limitless powers to secure personal pleasure. Roman biographers and historians supply abundant records of their careers, including their characteristic weaknesses. The first emperors, known as Julio-Claudian, came from the family of Julius **Caesar**. Although no Roman emperor ever failed to marry, Edward Gibbon remarked that "of the first fifteen emperors Claudius was the only one whose taste in love was entirely correct" (heterosexual).

Julio-Claudian Dynasty. Julius Caesar (ca. 102–44 B.C.), notorious as "the husband of every woman and the wife of every man," prostituted himself as a teenager to the **Hellenistic monarch** Nicomedes of Bithynia. His grand-nephew and successor Octavian—known as Augustus when emperor from 31 B.C. to A.D. 14—was a handsome lad beloved, perhaps physically, by **Cicero**, although in later life his wife Livia, the sole empress, provided him with as many women as he wished. The slide of Tiberius (ruled 14–37) into debauchery in his old age, analyzed by the genius of **Tacitus** in his *Annals*, on the isle of Capri, from whose fatal cliffs he pushed 76 suspect senators, is embellished by **Suetonius**, who in his *Lives of the Twelve Caesars* described the swimming pool he kept filled with his "minnows," young boys and girls he taught to swim through his ancient legs and nibble his private parts. His vicious minister Sejanus had once been a senator's catamite.

Tiberius' nephew and assassin, the mad Caligula (37–41), who made his horse consul, ripped open the womb of his sister Drusilla out of fear that the progeny might succeed him and also indulged in pederasty with the patricians Marcus Lepidus and Valerius Catullus, Mnester the Comedian, and even foreign hostages. The drooling hunchback and stutterer Claudius (41–54), who survived Caligula's tyranny by pretending to be an imbecile, was dragged from his hiding place in a closet in the palace by the Praetorian guards who after assassinating Caligula made him Emperor, although his own sympathies were republican. He later had his first wife Messalina beheaded after she "married" a courtier in a revel without divorcing the Emperor. Claudius' son-in-law was, however, found dead in bed with a boy, and he himself was poisoned with a bowl of deadly mushrooms by his beautiful niece Agrippina, whom he had forced to marry him in spite of his repulsiveness, but she did so to arrange the succession of her son by a previous marriage, Nero.

Nero (54–69), who succeeded in murdering his mother on the third attempt and forced his tutor Seneca, the greatest Latin writer and philosopher of **stoicism**, of the Silver Age, to commit suicide, was quite effeminate, but took as his bride in an elaborate wedding the eunuch Sporus because his face resembled that of his former wife Poppaea. Nero's patrician contemporary Sempronius Gracchus, who degraded himself to fight as a gladiator, married a young male cornet player.

Year of the Four Emperors and Flavian Dynasty. The suspicious, parsimonious Galba, who replaced Nero, was succeeded by the effeminate Otho, and he then by Vitellius, the last of the four emperors to die in the year 69. The victor in the civil war, doughty Italian Vespasian (69–79), of equestrian rather than senatorial background, tried to restore to the principate the rectitude that the elderly Augustus pretended to have, but the elder of his sons Titus (79–81) owned a troop of pathics and eunuchs. The embittered, tyrannical Domitian (81–96) went mad, indulging in heterosexual and homosexual orgies, although pretending to enforce chastity. Before conspirators, including his wife, succeeded in assassinating him, he executed three Vestal Virgins unfaithful to their vows and enforced the Lex Julia against pederasts.

Adoptive and Antonine Emperors. Although Suetonius and Tacitus, the main sources for the sexual lives of the first twelve Roman emperors, as pro-republican senators denigrated their character with scandal, their mostly creditable tales only slightly exceed the accounts of the immorality common in the late Republic in avant-garde aristocratic circles. About the five "good emperors" who succeeded one another "by adoption of the best" more than by the close family ties of the Julio-Claudian and Flavian dynasties and came from the provinces, the historian is far less well informed. They seem to have been more moderate sexually as well as less tyrannical. Nerva (96–98), septuagenarian when proclaimed Emperor, is, however, rumored to have buggered his younger predecessor Domitian.

Trajan (98-117), the hero whom the army forced the old senator to adopt as successor, descended from Roman colonists in Spain. A heavy drinker, Trajan practiced pederasty uninhibitedly and "without harming anyone." His cousin and successor, the philhellenic **Hadrian** (117–138), who composed pederastic verses in Greek imitating Anacreon—though respecting his wife Faustina—had a passionate affair with the beautiful **Antinous**. After the favorite drowned himself in the Nile, Hadrian declared him a god and erected so many statues for his cult that no other figure of antiquity has so many surviving representations.

Of Antoninus Pius (138–161) the least is known, but his successor Marcus Aurelius (161–180) noted that he had overcome any passion for boys. Unlike the other "good emperors," Marcus unfortunately produced a son and heir, the mad Commodus (180–192), sexually wild and impossibly tyrannical. Fancying himself a gladiator, he butchered cripples and other handicapped and otherwise shackled victims before seventy or eighty thousand spectators in the Colosseum. He is said to have prostituted himself to men and to have kept a harem of 300 girls and 300 boys.

Severans. Although Commodus' successor the elderly Pertinax (193) reigned only 87 days and auctioned off Commodus' harem (except those who had been introduced into the palace by force, whom he freed), the old man bought some of them back for his own pleasure. The Praetorians sold the Empire to the wealthy, hen-pecked Didius Julianus, whose wife wished to be the first lady of Roman society, but murdered him after two months. Upon his assassination the "pax Romana" permanently ended in a bloody civil war in which Septimius Severus (193–211), of Punic descent, triumphed. The African Septimius married Julia Domna, the heiress of the priestly family of the sun god Baal from Emesa in Syria. She and her sister and daughter became the powers behind the throne during the reign of their mad progeny. Beside the unreliable continuators of the biographer Suetonius, known as the "Augustan historians," who wrote lives of the emperors from Hadrian to the last of the Thirty Tyrants in 284, the modern scholar has better sources, Herodian and Dio Cassius, to tell him of the political and sexual exploits of the Severi.

Using the term *Dominus* (Lord) to replace *Princeps Senatus* (Chief of the Senate), the Severi transformed the Empire into an overt military dictatorship that began to use the trappings of Oriental despotism and forbade Christians to proselytize, forcing **Clement** to flee Alexandria. Septimius was the first emperor to learn Latin as a foreign tongue, as in the eastern half of the Empire Greek remained the language of administration and Latin was used only in the army.

Septimius' elder son and successor Caracalla (211–217) treacherously murdered his brother and coemperor in his mother's arms. By enfranchising all free inhabitants of the Empire citizens in 212, Caracalla accidentally made it harder to find a legal homosexual partner because only freedmen, slaves, and foreigners were fair game, Roman citizens being shielded from *stuprum* by Domitian's extension of the Lex Julia to homosexuality among citizens, if not by earlier decrees. In other words, provincials and members of other ethnic groups, henceforth Roman citizens, could no longer assume the passive role.

Julia Domna's and Septimius' great-nephew, the effete transvestite **Heliogabalus** (218–222) attempted to popularize the worship of the Black Stone, a symbol of Baal. Accompanied by eunuch priests in saffron robes with cymbals, he officiated in public, the soldiers cheering his dancing. Twice married, once to a Vestal Virgin, Heliogabalus had agents scour the Empire for men with "large organs and bring them to court so that he could enjoy them." He also offered a great reward to the physician who could perform a transsexualizing operation on him, but this feat lay far beyond the Greco-Roman art of medicine.

After his assassination, his cousin Alexander Severus (222–235), who ascended the throne at fourteen and at seventeen married the daughter of a senator, saw his jealous domineering mother banish his wife and afterwards remained single until his assassination.

Imperial Crisis. Of the Thirty Tyrants who reigned in the fifty years that separated the death of Alexander to the accession of Diocletian (235–284), only two died peacefully, if we exclude the one stricken by plague. Famine, pestilence, and war civil and foreign devastated the Empire during that half-century. Debasement of the coinage and ruinous overtaxation exacerbated the crisis. The barracks emperors who fought their way to the throne, if not illiterate, were generally peasants, often from Illyricum and unfamiliar with upper-class Greek (and Roman) pederastic traditions. **Neoplatonists** who attempted to refute Christians came to resemble their adversaries in trying to escape from a hopeless world and resorting to mysticism, and the majority of them were sex-negative and disapproving of homosexuality.

The crude giant from Thrace, Maximus (235–238), who assassinated the whimpering Alexander Severus in his tent along with his mother and faithful friends, was the first Emperor never to visit Rome. Descended from the Gracchi, Gordian I managed only 36 days, but his grandson Gordian II (238–244) lasted under the control of his mother's eunuchs and then his father-in-law until assassinated by followers of Philip the Arab (244–249), reputed to be black and even Christian. Celebrating the thousandth anniversary of the founding of Rome in 247, he also attempted unsuccessfully to suppress male prostitution and to enforce the Lex Scatinia. Decius (245–251) began the great persecution of the Christians, but Gallienus (253–268) refused his father Valerian's (253–257) policy of persecution and replaced it with toleration, hoping to win over the Christians with his neo-Platonic arguments.

The grave disorders may have destroyed one-third of the population, devastated the cities, which had been the focus of classical pederasty, and destroyed the old upper classes. Provincial and even villa autarky (self-sufficiency) replaced the capitalistic trading network that had sustained the old cities. They also had to be walled to protect against marauders and invaders. Pederastic writing, like all other non-religious literature, declined sharply under the Thirty Tyrants. Physicians and philosophers increasingly recommended sexual restraint.

Christian Emperors. Even with the accession of Christian Emperors, who soon imposed the death penalty for sodomy, classical pederasty did not die out at once. Constantine's sons Constantius and Constans (the latter's bodyguards chosen for their beauty rather than their competence), following the lead of Church councils and ascetic theologians, first decreed death for even consenting, adult sodomites

in 342. In 390 Theodosius the Great (379–395) with his sons Arcadius and Honorius and coemperor Valentinian II prescribed burning at the stake for those found guilty of anal intercourse with another male. In two novellae appended to his summation of previous Roman laws condemning pederasty in the *Corpus Juris Civilis*, Justinian the Great (527–565), who married the former showgirl Theodora, decreed death at the stake for unrepentant sodomites because the Biblical account of the conflagration of **Sodom** proved that they had brought ruin upon society, causing famines, earthquakes, and pestilences. Justinian, who closed the pagan schools of philosophy, also ended the classical pederasty institutionalized by the Greeks in **Crete** and **Sparta** toward the end of the seventh century B.C., 1300 years earlier. He set the tone for the persecution codified by **Patristic writers**, **penitentials**, **canon law**, and scholastic **philosophy**, as well as **laws (feudal and royal)** and **laws (municipal)** that still endures in Christian society, only relieved of the death penalty beginning with reforms of the French Revolution and of Joseph II of **Austria** inspired by the **Enlightenment** ideas of **Beccaria**.

BIBLIOGRAPHY. Eva Cantarella, *Secondo Natura*, Rome: Riuniti, 1987; Michael Grant, *The Roman Emperors: A Biographical Guide to the Rulers of Imperial Rome, 31 BC–AD 476*, New York: Charles Scribner's, 1985; Otto Kiefer, *Sexual Life in Ancient Rome*, London: Routledge & Kegan Paul, 1934.

William A. Percy

ROME, ANCIENT

The erotic life of ancient Rome—the Republic and the Empire—has long fascinated philologists and historians, novelists and moralists. Whether on account of its long dominance of Western civilization, its role as the primary antagonist of early **Christianity**, or its apparently contradictory images of robust, virile military power and orgiastic, "polymorphously perverse" **decadence**, Roman sexuality has provided fodder for unceasing polemics, ranging from the moralism of the church fathers to the lauding of antiquity by homophile antiquarians. Some assert with seeming assurance that law and custom forbade male homosexuality as incompatible with civic virtue, while others are confident that the Romans casually accepted homosexuality or at least bisexuality as a natural, common part of their society.

These discordant images stem from the contradictory attitudes of Romans whose works have survived into modern times, from the scanty documentation for actual practices, especially among the bulk of the Roman population, and, most important, from the anachronistic application of a modern concept of homosexuality to a period which, not recognizing it as a unitary phenomenon, separated it into discrete practices based on **class** and **role**.

Historical Background. According to tradition, the city was founded in 753 B.C., but archeologists have unearthed remains of settlements from as early as the middle of the second millennium, when the several hamlets on the site were beginning to coalesce. **Etruscans** dominated the nascent city-state for at least a century setting examples of sexual promiscuity, but in time Romans supplanted their tutors, exiling Tarquin, the proud last Etruscan king. They then overcame the Carthaginians, from whom they learned to crucify rebel slaves and pirates and to cultivate latifundia worked by slaves, and between 202, the defeat of Hannibal, and 30 B.C., the death of Cleopatra, imposed their rule on the entire Mediterranean. Preeminent among the older cultures on whom the Romans imposed their rule were the Greeks. To paraphrase the poet **Horace**, politically prostrate Greece triumphed culturally over the barbarous victor, and Rome became the first exemplar of a post-Hellenic civilization in the wake of ancient **Greece**. Roman borrowings were accompanied by a hounding sense of inferiority to Greek culture. In reaction, some Romans withdrew into a kind of anti-intellectualism that abandoned such fripperies as literature and the arts to the decadent Greeklings. In the sixth book of the *Aeneid*, **Vergil** portrays Anchises recommending that the Romans specialize in governing, and freely acknowledging that the peoples of the eastern Mediterranean with their far older civilizations would always surpass his own in the arts and sciences. Another defensive response to perceived inferiority stressed Rome's primordial simplicity and purity before alien luxury corrupted its people. According to the patriotic fables of historians like Livy, the early Romans were paragons of guileless virtue. Toiling in the fields kept them too busy to plot intrigues against their neighbors, and yielded too few worldly goods to incite envy. This idealized picture of the early Republic served as a foil for castigating ubiquitous luxury, corruption, and coveting of goods and sex objects in the later times. Wide acceptance of such myths of a vanished golden age of virtue legitimized attacking contemporaries for "un-Roman" behavior, especially sexual indulgence. The invidious contrast between present corruption and past simplicity increased in popularity during the last century of the Republic (146–27 B.C.), a period marked by brilliant military success abroad and political disaster at home. Rome's modest institutions were not designed to cope with the sudden influx of booty—luxury goods, art objects, and, especially, slaves—from foreign conquests. The rise of many, some not even citizens, from straitened circumstances to great wealth stimulated a vulgar opportunistic tone which grated on those loyal to the old ways, whose relative status was declining. Despite the earnest striving of Augustus to reform imperial Roman society, the ostentatious nouveau riche style persisted for several generations, into the second century of the present era.

The Role of Slavery. A massive influx of slaves accompanied Roman rise to domination in the Mediterranean. Although, like almost all ancient peoples, Romans had probably always countenanced slavery, the early peasant community had few. However, success in the Samnite, Punic, and eastern Mediterranean wars yielded enormous infusions, as many as 25,000 captives in a single day. By the end of the Republic, slaves comprised 30 to 35 percent of the population of Italy, a proportion comparable to that of the antebellum American South. Their cheapness and abundance clearly invited arbitrariness and maltreatment. Slaves were routinely beaten for "sport" and to relieve masters' frustrations. Until the time of Hadrian, Roman law permitted owners to execute slaves summarily. Slaves were objects for lust as well as sadism. As Seneca remarked, "Unchastity (*impudicitia*) is a crime in the freeborn, a service (*officium*) for the freedman, and an obligation for the slave" (*Controversies* IV, 10). This common situation made the role of slavery in same-sex relationships far more salient than in Greece, where of course it was not absent, but was on a much reduced scale and counterbalanced by the concept of **pederasty** as an instrument of education and state-building. The comedies of **Plautus** (who died ca. 184 B.C.) already make the master's lust for his slave boys the chief same-sex theme. Attractive slaves in the great houses of the rich were expected not only to cater to their master's lust, but also to be sexually available for guests (see Horace's *Satires*, 1.2.116–119). For all its importance, tantalizingly little is known about the sexual aspects of the Roman trade in slaves. The paucity of information reflects not only the prudery of modern scholars, but also the very banality of the activity in ancient times. Slaves were part of the taken-for-granted background of life, omnipresent but little noticed. It is certain that many slaves were sold by free but indigent parents. Others were foundlings.

Captives taken in military campaigns supplied the bulk of young flesh for the slave markets and thence the numerous brothels. Slaves would be set upon a slowly rotating platform, while the auctioneer lifted the garments so as to display not only the musculature and general physical condition of the specimen, but also the sexual endowments. Often deprived of access to women, sometimes even shackled slaves enjoyed one another sexually.

Roman Roles. Although Roman women had somewhat more power and influence than those of ancient Athens and were not secluded, Roman society was overwhelmingly male-dominated, with a consequent dearth of surviving references to lesbianism except for epigrams scattered throughout **Martial's** collected poems. Roman custom accepted a paradigm of sexuality which observed a stark dichotomy between the penetrator, who was seen as engaging in normal aggressive and dominating masculine behavior regardless of the gender of his object, and the penetrated (pathic), who was considered to be weak, submissive, and powerless. Under this system, any Roman male citizen could be a penetrator without fear of aspersions or disgrace, though some criticized any homosexual activity. On the other hand, the penetrated role was considered appropriate only for those who were submissive because of their exclusion from the power structure: women, slaves, and provincial or foreign boys, but not free boys destined to become citizens. A male adult Roman citizen who became a sexual receiver was seen as yielding his birthright of power and hence compromising the power position of all other male adult citizens. As so much of the homosexuality took place between penetrating masters and receptive slaves, the conception of master–slave relationships became entangled in the agent–pathic one. The salience of the former, implying that the man who "takes it" enslaves himself to his penetrator, is characteristically Roman. Moreover, as Eva

Cantarella has pointed out, this asymmetry was reinforced by the Roman imperative to rule over subject peoples, so that the position of the sexually penetrated was analogous to that of a conquered province. This concatenation of degradations lent itself to particularly vicious exploitation in Roman political campaigning, as in **Cicero**'s attacks on Mark Antony, whom he accused of being not only a woman but a slave for being pathic. This notion of self-abasement through accepting the role of pathic, even though Antony was a boy when with Curio, seems to have struck a particularly sensitive nerve. Perhaps it was being so outnumbered in their empire that confirmed Roman citizens in their sense that an instance of one member of their collective yielding himself to sexual "degradation" was a lessening of the strength of the community. In the army, sex with a male citizen was punishable by death, but in times of war, according to Cicero, soldiers were permitted to **rape** (enemy) freeborn youths and virgins. Male **prostitution** was extremely widespread—the boys even having their own annual festival day (Robigalia, April 25)—and was not only looked upon with general favor but was taxed by the state. While most of the prostitutes were slaves, a few of them were freedmen, and most were boys. Pederasty did not, as in Greece, play a compensating role in the training and toughening of young men for duty to the State. Relatedly, the Romans before the introduction of **gymnasia** on the Greek model permitted nudity only in the **bathhouses**, a milieu of selfish and hedonistic indulgence, in contrast to the Greek consolidation of the link between pederasty and male character formation through public nude athletics. Very little is known about the sexual life of the Roman proletariat, the lower class of citizenry—after 200 B.C. often of Oriental or Greek origin—that owned no slaves. According to some graffiti at Pompeii, there were, however, prostitutes for the poor available for the equivalent of an unskilled laborer's hourly wage or even

less. A large number of the graffiti discovered in the ruins of Pompeii are bisexual or homosexual in content. Moreover, they do not seem to include any real "homophobia," and even romantic sentiments appear occasionally. Frequently signed, these homoerotic graffiti indicate no fear of social repercussions. The graffitists appear to be penetrative males, usually directing their attentions to boys.

Roman Law. The earliest and most problematic landmark is the shadowy Lex Scantinia (or Scatinia), purportedly dating from the third century B.C. The text has not survived, and the question of its meaning still defies adequate interpretation. To interpret this moot testimony as indicating the Romans were antihomosexual because "they had a law against it" goes beyond the evidence. As is so often the case, part of the problem stems from applying the modern comprehensive notion of homosexuality to an earlier era which had no such overall concept. The Latin *stuprum* covered a whole range of prohibited sexual behavior. The same act might or might not be stuprum according to the circumstances. To copulate with a freeborn teenage girl was stuprum; but not with a teenage girl who was a slave or freedwoman, but officially registered as a prostitute. It was the status of the actors rather than the act itself that determined whether or not it was licit. It seems likely that the boundaries of stuprum varied over time, but the late imperial codifications, extending from Ulpian to Tribonian, failed to preserve earlier legislation. If there were restrictions on same-sex behavior in the Lex Scantinia, they do not seem to have been enlarged, or even reaffirmed at any later stage of lawmaking. In fact, there were complaints from some moralists that the statute had fallen into disuse like modern blasphemy statutes. The few cases under the republic typically refer to a superior pressuring an inferior in the army to submit to him sexually. Interestingly, pronatalist legislative initiatives of the early Imperial period, most famously the

Lex Julia de adulteriis of Augustus, were entirely devoted to curbing men's activities with prohibited women, completely disregarding any dalliances with boys.

Literary Evidence. Valuable evidence from Roman writers begins with Cicero, who Latinized many Greek technical concepts, accusing opponents—as Attic orators routinely did—of pathic behavior. How much irritation at his tiresome moralizing provoked the triumvirs' secret decision to proscribe him can only be a speculation, but such scurrilous accusations became a common feature of Roman political life. If Cicero was hostile, the **Epicurean** Lucretius was merely indifferent, nowhere condemning same-sex relations. Nonetheless, by elevating generation through the pivotal principle *nihil ex nihilo fit* ("nothing can come from nothing"), he unwittingly laid a foundation for later prescriptivists' obsession with procreation. Allegedly at least the later Stoics opposed same-sex pleasure, and indeed all sex outside marriage, and bequeathed this view to Christian rigorism. On the whole, evidence fails to support so austere a view, although **Stoics**, like most **Epicureans**, their main philosophical rivals, did stress the advantages of moderation and indifference to passion. One could, however, be a moderate pederast, instead of a frenzied one. Only Musonius Rufus, seemingly following the track of **Plato** in *The Laws* in rejecting same-sex copulation as "against nature," specifically sought to discourage homosexuality (a citation of Seneca offered by St. Jerome being of dubious import shorn of its original, now lost context). In the sphere of sexual morality, the early church fathers' debt to the Stoics was slight. **Patristic** thinkers used Stoic and Platonic phrases mainly as window-dressing for a sex-negative, other-worldly, at times dualistic, oriental, anti-intellectual dogma. In sum, a few Romans denounced or discouraged some aspects of homosexuality, but most did not comment on the matter—and in the general setting of Mediterranean social life, it can reasonably be concluded that their silence implied consent.

Evidence from poetry and belles lettres is more abundant. **Catullus** wrote some of his most piercingly eloquent lyrics on the joys and sorrows of being in love with a boy. Recent research has shown how extensively Catullus relied on Hellenistic prototypes, exemplifying the Roman duality between immediate experience and hallowed Greek models. Catullus' pederastic love poetry is echoed in more muted fashion by his contemporary **Tibullus**. Vergil's Second Eclogue, with his immortal homosexual swain Corydon, an object case of the Greek–Roman duality, imitates a heterosexual idyll of **Theocritus**—who wrote his own share of homosexual verse. Crossovers of this kind, anomalous only in light of a rigid heterosexual–homosexual dichotomy, occurred as a matter of course in antiquity. Even Ovid, exiled under the Lex Julia for being one of many lovers of Augustus' daughter Julia, and apparently the most heterosexual of the Latin poets, wrote nonchalantly of pederasty and magical changes of sex.

Satire is the only distinctly Roman literary form. Although claiming to act from the high motive of purging the body politic of hypocrisy and corruption, often the satirist was actuated by personal spite and love of gossip. **Juvenal's** criticism of Roman same-sex customs in the first century of the present era revolves around the familiar contrast between the artless simplicity of the revered past and the luxury of the depraved present. For him a symptom of this degeneration was the violation of class barriers in the obsessions of Roman aristocrats for low-born favorites, usually of foreign descent. His *Second Satire* had scions of patrician families offering themselves in marriage, replete with Oriental rites, to their darlings. As in analogous cases from Martial (e.g., XII.42) and Suetonius (*Life of Nero*), they sought to dignify their male–male unions by assimilating them to religious rites wherein the initiate "weds" the god. Stripping away Juvenal's veneer of moral indignation, one can see that these weddings in fact reflected an innovatory striving to regularize a type of relationship that, however well-worn in practice, was nonetheless marginal to the official structure of Roman ideology and institutions. Some may have been merely travesties. Very different is **Petronius'** ambitious picaresque novel, the *Satyricon*, of which only about a tenth has survived. These fragments recount the bawdy adventures of two friends, rivals for the favors of Giton, a fickle pretty boy. Holding very definite opinions about literature and art, Petronius was as nonjudgmental about sexual behavior as anyone could be. **Martial**, too, has been considered unedifying, often even accused of sensationalism and of purveying scurrilous gossip for mere titillation. Yet he operated within certain cultural restraints, e.g., believing it better to fuck than to be fucked, better to have the means to invite others to dine with one than to cadge invitations, and, best of all, to be open about one's tastes rather than hypocritical. His writings are a cornucopia of information on Roman customs relating to sex, such as the cutting of the hair of slave boys to signal the end of their availability as sexual utensils. Martial throws some light also on the vexed question of the *cinaedus*, a kind of gigolo, often trained as a dancer or entertainer, who would perform as the agent for adult pathics. Martial alleged that cinaedi often serviced wives as well. His favorable comments on *pueri delicati*, handsome boys who seem to have appealed to his own taste, leave the impression that in his time there was a definite bifurcation between the ephebe (in his teens) and the cinaedus (in his twenties) as sexual objects, the former being pathic, the latter not.

The mass of Roman literature—all of which could be printed in about 500 modern volumes—is not large, and much of it does not provide any information on sexual customs and attitudes. Even so, from the historians, notably **Suetonius** and **Tacitus**, the reader quickly learns that the emperors were—to say the least—polymorphous perverse, and that their omnisexuality served more to titillate than nauseate the Roman populace.

Debates over the Fall of Rome. Modern historians have assembled a bewildering variety of contradictory explanations for the fall of the Roman Empire: external pressures vs. internal decay, failure of leadership at the top vs. festering anger welling up from below; a shortage of manpower vs. maldistribution of resources; physical causes such as plagues vs. collective psychic exhaustion signified by the fading of Rome's ancient religion and civic spirit before cults from the East, such as **Manichaeanism** and **Christianity**. Drawing in part on the harsh judgments of their satirists and historians, the modern stereotype was mainly shaped by nineteenth-century French writers and painters, who were uncomfortably aware of parallels between the decline of their own cultural hegemony and that of their Latin forebears. Popular culture (including the film *Caligula* and the television series "I, Claudius") has picked up their lurid images. This moralistic sleaze is completely irrelevant to the fall of Rome, for most of it is firmly set in the first century of our era, before the Empire reached its zenith with the Five Good Emperors and even before the starting point of the narrative of Edward Gibbon's *Decline and Fall*.

In order to relate this varied material causally to Rome's fall one would have to assume a "latency period" of six to eight generations. Indeed, as early as 180 B.C. Cato the censor condemned Scipio, conqueror of Hannibal and of Antiochus III, for importing luxury and Greek profligacy to corrupt the *mos maiorum*, the strict ancestral morality of the early Romans such as Cincinnatus. This plaint continued with Sallust, who had Jugurtha, king of Numidia say upon leaving Rome that there was nothing in the city that was not for sale. Cicero too argued that moral and social decadence epitomized by Catiline and Antony caused Rome's disgrace. But these laments ceased in the second century, and it was only long after those halcyon days of sexual abandon that the fall ensued. To conflate Caligula (much less Catiline or Antony) and the fall of Rome is like finding in Sir Walter Raleigh's behavior the cause of the decline of the British Empire. Caligula had no more to do with the fall than Raleigh with the Boer War.

What were the views of the Romans themselves? Many castigated the falling away from the sturdy virtues of the Republic, and saw such conduct as individually and collectively shameful without threatening the foundations of the Empire. For Rome had been given *imperium sine fine*, dominion without limit. Even during the dark days of the third century, orators celebrating the thousandth anniversary of the founding of the city regularly summoned up the image of *Roma aeterna*. Only after the fact was the idea expressed that indulgence, sexual or otherwise, caused Rome's collapse. The first instance of what was later to become a commonplace reproach is in *De gubernatione Dei*, a moralistic diatribe composed by Salvian, a Christian presbyter of Marseilles, about A.D. 450. In discussing Carthage (by then a Roman city, not the old Semitic realm) Salvian contrasted the former degenerate effeminacy of the city, its ostentatious queens on parade, with the severe, highly moral regime instituted by the Germans after their successful siege. Thus, in Salvian's overoptimistic view of the horrible Vandals, the most destructive of all the Germanic tribes that overran the western provinces, the material and intellectual losses caused by the barbarian incursions were compensated for by a moral advance. The contrast between the older pluralistic civilization and obsessive early Christian moralizing could scarcely be clearer, and in longer historical perspective, Salvian's arbitrary linking of sexual freedom, particularly same-sex activity, with political weakness and instability was to become a pernicious legacy, one of the cornerstones of the later **decadence** myth. Besides this, the eastern provinces of the Empire, just as corrupt and sexually permissive as the west, in fact more given to pederasty, survived for another thousand years until conquered by the Ottoman Turks in 1453, though Justinian in the early sixth century voiced the **Judeo-Christian** belief that sodomites caused earthquakes, plagues, and famines.

Conclusion. Rome shared with Greece (and other Mediterranean cultures) the fundamental agent/pathic distinction in sexual transactions. Apart from a common **Indo-European** heritage, its origins lost in the proverbial mists of prehistory, Rome was subject to a massive and continuing influx of Greek culture with Greek models adapted to and merging with Latin and Etruscan tendencies, Oriental ones appearing later with the conquest of Syria and Palestine by Pompey in 66 B.C. and of Egypt by Julius Caesar. Nevertheless, significant differences make the conventional compound term Greco-Roman civilization questionable. (1) Rome generally lacked the Hellenic concept of pederasty as contributing to the collective (civic) good quite beyond the pleasure afforded the agent. (2) There was an absence of public nudity— except in the baths, where men and women were often nude together—in the socially sanctioned pedagogical setting of the gymnasium. (3) With hordes of slaves, imperial Rome differed from the Greek city-states, and the master–slave relationship was the paradigmatic locale of sexual pleasure in Rome, but not earlier in Greece. (4) In the nouveau-riche atmosphere of the late Republic and early Empire, the role of cinaedus with respect to his patron paralleled the more respectable asymmetrical relationship of parasite and client, less extreme but still akin to the slave–master disparity. (5) Greek idealism about sexual passion as a motive for improving the mind of the sexually receptive contrasts sharply with the thoroughly materialistic Roman use of property for sexual gratification. (6) Rome's exploitation of a vast empire created an inequity between rulers and ruled that influenced paradigms of sexual conduct.

BIBLIOGRAPHY. J. N. Adams, *The Latin Sexual Vocabulary*, London: Duckworth, 1982; Eva Cantarella, *Secondo Natura*, Rome: Riuniti, 1987; Danilo Dalla, *"Ubi Venus mutatur": omosessualità e diritto nel mondo romano*, Milan: Giuffrè, 1987; Françoise Gonfroy, "Homosexualité et idéologie esclavagiste chez Cicéron," *Dialogues d'histoire ancienne*, 4 (1978), 219–65; Pierre Grimal, *L'Amour à Rome*, Paris: Belles Lettres, 1980; Otto Kiefer, *Sexual Life in Ancient Rome*, London: Routledge & Kegan Paul, 1934; Saara Lilja, *Homosexuality in Republican and Augustan Rome* (Commentationes Humanarum Litterarum, 74), Helsinki, 1982; Beert Verstraete, "Slaves and the Social Dynamic of Male Homosexual Relations in Ancient Rome," *Journal of Homosexuality*, 5 (1980), 227–36.

Wayne R. Dynes

RÖMER, L. S. A. M. VON (1873–1965)

Dutch physician, historian, and student of homosexuality. Lucien Sophie Albert Marie von Römer was born in Kampen as the scion of a noble family that had lived in the Netherlands since the eighteenth century. He studied medicine at Leiden and Amsterdam, passing the licensing examination in 1903. Thereafter he studied and worked in Berlin with Albert **Moll** and Magnus **Hirschfeld**, and met two well-known transvestites, Willibald von Sadler-Grün and Freiherr Hermann von Teschenberg, who made no secret of their predilection and let themselves be photographed for Hirschfeld's *Jahrbuch*. Von Römer had an idealistic philosophy of life and a great reserve of personal dynamism; he was an admirer of Erasmus, Spinoza, and Nietzsche, whose *Thus Spake Zarathustra* he translated into Dutch. A trip to Greece in 1912 interrupted his term of service as health official in the Royal Navy. After 1913 he settled in the Dutch East Indies, where he occupied various functions in the health service until 1932. In the course of his career his campaign against injustice earned him the hostility of many of his colleagues, and his energetic measures against unhygienic conditions won him the title of "the medical Napoleon." After his retirement he practiced neurology and psychiatry in Malang, where he lived until his death at the age of 92.

Von Römer's articles on various aspects of homosexuality were for their time major, path-breaking studies that assembled a vast amount of material that was little-known or had been deliberately ignored by official scholarship. His first article was a biography of "**Henri** the Third, King of France and Poland," which appeared in the fourth volume of the *Jahrbuch* in 1902; in the same volume he commented on the abusive reception of Arnold **Aletrino**'s paper at the Congress of Criminal Anthropology in Amsterdam the previous year. In the fifth volume (1903) he issued a study of more than two hundred pages on "The Androgynous Idea of Life," a survey of myths and beliefs concerning **androgyny** and **hermaphroditism** from remote antiquity to the present. In 1904 he published in Dutch a book entitled *Unknown People: The Physiological Development of the Sexes in Connection with Homosexuality*, and in the following year *The Uranian Family: A Scientific Investigation and Conclusions on Homosexuality*. This latter work examined disparities from the normal sex-ratio in the siblings of homosexuals in the aim of demonstrating that they were biologically disguised members of the opposite sex. A German version was published in 1906, together with an article in the *Jahrbuch* on "Uranism in the **Netherlands** before the Nineteenth Century, with Especial Reference to the Great Uranian Persecution in the Year 1730," the classic study of a wave of intolerance in which 250 men and boys were prosecuted and 57 put to death. His last work on the subject appeared in 1908, an anthology of passages from Nietzsche on homosexuality in the *Zeitschrift für Sexualwissenschaft*. In the same year he unsuccessfully attempted to have a medical dissertation on homosexuality accepted by the University of Amsterdam, but it was rejected on the ground that a number of passages were judged "in conflict with morality and offensive to others." The hostile climate engendered by the Harden-**Eulenberg** affair in Germany may have influenced him to turn away from the subject. Following Hirschfeld, von Römer always laid stress in his writings on the social obloquy and **blackmail** that embittered the lives of his homosexual subjects, and by defending the existence of innate homosexuality he sought to deliver them from the reproaches of sin, sickness, and degeneracy. He also combatted the Dutch version of the "social purity" movement of his time and idealization of sexual abstinence. A last work of his, the fruit of thirty years' labor, he showed in manuscript to Magnus Hirschfeld when his former teacher visited the East Indies in 1931; it has remained unpublished.

BIBLIOGRAPHY. Maurice van Lieshout, "Stiefkind der natuur. Het homobeeld bij Aletrino en von Römer," *Homojaarboek I*, Amsterdam: Van Gennep, 1981, pp. 75–105.

Warren Johansson

ROOSEVELT, ELEANOR (1884–1962)

American public figure and journalist. Born into an old New York family of Dutch patroon ancestry, she was the niece of President Theodore Roosevelt and a distant cousin of Franklin Delano Roosevelt, whom she married in 1905. Even before her marriage she had been an active and able promoter of social causes, and she continued this career after becoming the wife of a rising star in the Democratic Party who was its vice presidential nominee in 1920. When Franklin was stricken with poliomyelitis in 1921, she overcame her shyness in order to be his liaison with the political scene. When her husband, returning to the political arena, was elected first governor of New York (1928) and then president of the United States (1932), she played a leading role in women's organizations, in promoting consumer welfare, in struggling against unemployment and poor housing, and in furthering the rights of minorities. In 1933 she held the first press conference ever staged by a president's wife, and in 1935 she began a daily column "My Day," which, syndicated in newspapers throughout the country, gave her the opportunity to focus attention on social problems of the time.

Eleanor Roosevelt recast the role of president's wife in a far more activist, political tone, breaking with older conventions and earning the intense hatred of the foes of the New Deal. In an era when the feminist movement, having achieved the goal of women's suffrage in 1920, was in abeyance, she symbolized the career-oriented, politically active, socially concerned woman of modern times.

From 1945 to 1953, and again in 1961, she was United States delegate to the fledgling United Nations Organization, and in 1946 she was named chairwoman of the Commission on Human Rights, a subsidiary of the Economic and Social Council. In the 1950s she remained in politics as a leader of the liberal wing of the Democratic Party and a supporter of Adlai Stevenson. As one of the most prominent women of the first half of the twentieth century, she won an enduring place in American political and social history.

The question of a lesbian component in Eleanor Roosevelt's life and personality is somewhat complicated by the problematic of lesbian self-definition as it emerged in the middle decades of the twentieth century. It is clear that the wife of an American president in the 1930s could have had no part in an overt lesbian subculture, but on the other hand Eleanor exchanged passionate letters with the journalist Lorena Hickock. These Doris Faber first tried to suppress out of fear that others might "misunderstand" them, but failing this, she wrote a book, *The Life of Lorena Hickock, E. R.'s Friend* (1980), as a lengthy polemic to the effect that neither "of these women can be placed in the contemporary gay category." Arthur Schlesinger, Jr., a noted apologist for the Roosevelt administration, tried to defend the two women by placing them in "a well established tradition" as "children of the Victorian age." It is impossible on the basis of surviving evidence to assert that they had an overt lesbian relationship, but they undeniably had an emotional friendship with homoerotic overtones.

Those attuned to the theme of "great lesbians in history" will no doubt wish to include such a notable as Eleanor Roosevelt on their list, while her enemies will seize upon the label as a confirmation of their dislike. The affairs of the heart are not so easily categorized as the alliances and affinities of political life. Eleanor Roosevelt overcame the feminine shyness and passivity into which she had been socialized to play a role in American politics of the 1930s that was not in her husband's shadow, and possibly she overcame sexual conventions as well. Her need for intense female companionship may have been the equivalent of male bonding—with its nuances and ambiguities. Her role as promoter of women's rights and as a symbol of the emancipated woman of the New Deal era is her chief legacy to the lesbian/feminist movement of today.

BIBLIOGRAPHY. Doris Faber, *The Life of Lorena Hickock, E. R.'s Friend*, New York: Morrow, 1980; Jess Flemion and Colleen M. O'Connor, *Eleanor Roosevelt: An American Journey*, San Diego: San Diego State University Press, 1987.

Evelyn Gettone

RORSCHACH TEST

The Rorschach test is the invention of the Swiss psychiatrist Hermann Rorschach (1884–1922), a disciple of Eugen Bleuler. In 1921 he published *Psychodiagnostik*, which was the outcome of a decade of work with a very large number of bilaterally symmetrical inkblot cards administered to a variety of psychiatric groups. After supplementary testing with so-called normal subjects, retarded persons, and other special categories he issued the first German edition with its 10 standard cards that have been used ever since. The crucial feature of the test is that there is no meaning in the inkblots, it is simply "projected" from the mind of the subject onto the shapes and colors which he sees on the cards. The projective principle had been familiar to artists since the time of **Leonardo** da Vinci; new was its application to depth psychology. The test was scored primarily for the ratio of color to movement responses, and Rorschach's somewhat typological scoring system was based upon a combination of the observable with clinical insight or intuition. In the 1920s some 30 titles relating to Rorschach technique were published, in the next decade some 200 more, and in the following decades the literature swelled into thousands of items.

The popularity of the Rorschach stemmed from a time when **psychoanalytic** views predominated, and inner processes and the unconscious were the object of clinical assessment. Enthusiastic users claimed that the Rorschach test was a foolproof x-ray of the personality not subject to any situational set, but others rejected the test and predicted its abandonment. The current mean of opinion is that "The Rorschach is a field of study in research which permits workers to investigate such diverse concepts as body image, primary process thinking, hypnotizability, orality, and ego strength." It is further understood that the Rorschach is a complex instrument that cannot yield a simple score, rather the entire configuration must be compared with the clinical picture obtained from other procedures such as psychiatric examination.

From 1945 onward, a number of investigators sought to establish the usefulness of the Rorschach test in the diagnosis of male homosexuality. In a paper of 1949, W. M. Wheeler developed 20 content signs which he attempted to make as unambiguous and objective as possible, and found a low, but consistently positive relationship between them and clinical diagnoses of homosexuality. Five years later, R. Shafer published a book in which he outlined a number of themes in Rorschach content relating to homosexuality.

In 1954 Evelyn Hooker set out to compare the incidence of the Wheeler homosexual content signs in the Rorschach protocols of overt male homosexuals as compared with the protocols of heterosexuals, and also to compare the two groups with respect to the frequency of occurrence of Shafer's content themes relating to homosexuality.

Hooker's findings, published four years later, were that the Wheeler signs did, as a whole, differentiate a homosexual from a heterosexual group, but only when matched pairs were considered. When highly qualified Rorschach experts attempted to distinguish the homosexual records, the process was marked by uncertainty and precarious vacillation. Agreement was primarily in the correct identification of records characterized by open anality, perverse or parhedoniac sexuality, and "feminine emphasis." In other words, the Rorschach test served to diagnose homosexuality correctly only in a limited number of cases in which specific elements of personality distortion were present. The relationship of the Rorschach picture to overt behavior depended upon many complex variables in the subject's life situation which tended to be overlooked in the clinical picture of homosexuality that prevailed in the 1950s. Continued use of the Rorschach technique alone for diagnosis of homosexuality, without other substantiating evidence, Hooker concluded, would lead to erroneous findings, both positive and negative, and perpetuate false concepts that disregarded the cultural aspect of the problem by focusing on the supposed clinical one.

BIBLIOGRAPHY. Evelyn Hooker, "Male Homosexuality in the Rorschach," *Journal of Projective Techniques*, 22 (1958), 33–54; R. Shafer, *Psychoanalytic Interpretation in Rorschach Testing*, New York: Grune and Stratton, 1954; W. M. Wheeler, "An Analysis of Rorschach Indices of Male Homosexuality," *Journal of Projective Techniques*, 13 (1949), 97–126.

Warren Johansson

ROUGH TRADE
See **Trade**.

ROUSSEL, RAYMOND (1877–1933)

French poet, novelist, and playwright. Roussel was born into an upper-class Parisian family, friends and neighbors of Marcel **Proust**. Jean **Cocteau** (who spent time with him in a drug treatment program at St. Cloud) called Roussel "the Proust of dreams."

The young Raymond studied piano, composed songs but at seventeen turned to poetry because "the words came easier." Publication of his first book *La Doublure* (1897) led to a deep depression and treatment by the noted psychiatrist Pierre Janet, who published an account of his patient. Another book of poems, *La Vue* (1904), followed and two novels, *Impressions d'Afrique* (1910) and *Locus Solus* (1914).

In 1909, Roussel won a gold medal for his marksmanship; he was an avid chess player and adored the writings of Jules Verne. He was an early fancier of **camp** since he enjoyed melodramas and in 1914 had his own *roulette* (housetrailer) built.

In 1912 *Impressions d'Afrique* ran as a play with a distinguished cast and important praises by Apollinaire, Duchamp, and Picabia, but its unorthodoxy aroused vehement public ridicule. *Locus Solus* was likewise adapted for the stage in 1922, and Roussel wrote two additional plays, *L'Etoile au Front* (1925) and *La Poussière de Soleils* (1927). The surrealists defended *L'Etoile* and confronted the jeering audiences; the fighting aroused public scandal.

Roussel's sexuality is described by Houppermans as not unlike his writing: "Pluperversity, that fundamental elasticity, that continuous back and forth of libidinal drives, was to be the hallmark of a new universe." Roussel found a new realm of libidinal pleasures (including both drugs and men) in travel: in 1920–21 he visited India, Australia, New Zealand, Tahiti, China, Japan, the United States, and other developing areas. His greatest fascination was with Africa, where he often visited and found inspiration.

In 1933 he took up lodgings in Palermo, Sicily, with his platonic companion Madame Du Frêne, who never established whether his death was by accident or suicide. His ending, like his writing, remains (as he said of the surrealists) "a bit obscure." Roussel's obscurity was not entirely clarified by his posthumous (1935) explanations of *How I Wrote Certain of My Books* (perhaps an echo of Nietzsche's "Why I Write Such Good Books"). "Taking the word *palmier* I decided to consider it in two senses: as a *pastry* and as a *tree*. Considering it as a pastry, I searched for another word, itself having two meanings which could be linked to it by the preposition *à*; thus I obtained (and it was, I repeat, a long and arduous task) *palmier* (a kind of pastry) *à restauration* (restaurant which serves pastries); the other part gave me *palmier* (a palmtree) *à restauration* (restoration of a dynasty). Which yielded the palmtree in Trophies Square commemorating the restoration of the Talou dynasty."

Michel **Foucault** analyzed the relation between Roussel's cryptology and homosexuality: "When Cocteau wrote his works, people said, 'It's not surprising that he flaunts his sexuality and his sexual preferences with such ostentation since he is a homosexual.' . . . and about Proust they said, 'It's not surprising that he hides and reveals his sexuality, that he lets it appear clearly while also hiding it in his work, since he is a homosexual.' And it could also be said about Roussel, 'It's not surprising that he hides it completely since he is a homosexual.'"

BIBLIOGRAPHY. François Caradec, *Vie de Raymond Roussel*, Paris: Pauvert, 1972; Michel Foucault, *Death and the Labyrinth, The World of Raymond Roussel* [1963], trans. C. Ruas, Garden City, NY: Doubleday, 1986; Hanns Grossel, *Raymond Roussel, eine Dokumentation*, Munich: Edition Text und Kritik, 1977; Sjef Houppermans, *Raymond Roussel, écriture et désir*, Paris: Corti, 1985. Trevor Winkfield, trans., *How I Wrote Certain of My Books*, New York: Sun, 1977 (includes two essays by John Ashbery and a bibliography).

Charley Shively

ROZANOV, VASILIĬ VASIL'EVICH (1856–1919)

Russian writer and social critic. Rozanov came of a poor middle-class family from the government of Vetluga. Educated in a classical high school, he then studied history at the University of Moscow. He taught history and geography for many years in various provincial secondary schools, but had no vocation as a pedagogue. About 1880 he married Apollinaria Suslova, a woman near forty, who in her youth had been intimate with Dostoevsky. Apollinaria was a cold, proud, "infernal" woman, with unknown depths of cruelty and sensuality, who left Rozanov after three years but refused him a divorce. Several years later Rozanov met Varvara Rudneva, who became his unofficial wife and with whom his liaison was completely happy.

In 1886 Rozanov published a book, *On Understanding*, an attack on the positivism and official agnosticism that prevailed at the University of Moscow. Though it had no success, it attracted the attention of the historian N. N. Strakhov, who began a correspondence with him, introduced him to the conservative literary press, and finally arranged an official appointment in St. Petersburg for him, which did not help him much, as he remained in straitened circumstances until 1899, when he was invited by Suvorin to write for *Novoe vremia* (New Times), the only conservative newspaper that paid its contributors well. The editor gave him not only a comfortable income, but also a free hand to write whatever he liked and as often as he liked, so long as each article did not take up too much space. Among his early writings was *The Legend of the Grand Inquisitor* (1890), a commentary on the episode in Dostoyevsky's *The Brothers Karamazov*. Having obtained through his wife access to certain hidden aspects of Dostoyevsky's mind, he discerned with wonderful acuteness the novelist's striving toward absolute freedom, including the freedom of not desiring happiness.

As the years passed Rozanov's Russian style matured, and so did his intellectual personality. He had a profoundly mystical and religious temperament, was a born Slavophile, and detested the cosmopolitanism of the Russian intelligentsia just as much as their agnosticism. Recognized and lauded only by the right, he somewhat inconsistently wrote conservative articles for *Novoe vremia* under his real name, and radical ones for the progressive *Russkoe slovo* (Russian Word) under the pseudonym V. Varvarin. At the time of the trial of Mendel Beilis in Kiev (1911–13), he wrote pieces accusing the Jewish people of ritual murder, so that he gained the reputation of a conscienceless hack journalist. In his last work, *Apoka-lipsis nashego vremeni* (The Apocalypse of Our Time; 1918), he decried the October Revolution as the coming of the Antichrist. Reduced to extreme want and misery, he died in 1919.

On the subject of homosexuality he composed a work entitled *Liudi lunnogo sveta: Metafizika khristianstva* (Moonlight Men: The Metaphysics of Christianity; second edition, 1913), which was inspired by the writings of the pre-Freudian investigators of abnormal sexuality, notably **Krafft-Ebing** and Forel, but far transcended their narrow psychiatric approach by virtue of his insight into the role of the homosexual character type in the history of Christianity. He rejected the late nineteenth-century conception of the **invert** as "perverted" or "sick," arguing instead that such an individual had a divinely appointed mission in society, that he was not intended for heterosexuality and marriage. He claimed that the homosexual is "a third person around Adam and Eve, as a matter of fact, the 'Adam' from whom 'Eve' has not yet emerged—the first, complete Adam." In the cosmological scheme of things, androgyny and bisexuality preceded sexual dimorphism and reproduction. As an archaic, primordial type, the homosexual has more of the intuitive, more of the metaphysical perception of the world that underlies the religious vocation.

Such anomalous individuals, Rozanov believed, were the backbone of **asceticism**, pagan and Christian, ancient and modern. It was **Christianity** that elevated the ascetic ideal to the center of its moral teaching. From the lives of Russian saints with their insurmountable refusal to marry or submit to the conventions of heterosexual life, Rozanov concluded that the moral "I will not!" was only the mask of a much deeper, psychological "I cannot." "A fact of Nature unknown to the compilers of the saints' *vitae* was taken for an especially profound, especially pure profession of a religion of chastity." Unknown in the West, and reduced to the status of a non-person in Soviet Russia, Rozanov nevertheless should be remembered for having probed one of the mysteries of Christian history: the affinity of many homosexual men and women for a religion that formally condemned and excluded them.

BIBLIOGRAPHY. Vasilii Vasil'evich Rozanov, *Four Faces of Rozanov: Christianity, Sex, Jews and the Russian Revolution*, New York: Philosophical Library, 1978; Prince D. S. Mirsky, *Contemporary Russian Literature, 1881–1925*, New York: Knopf, 1926.

Warren Johansson

RUMI (1207–1273)

Persian poet and mystic; founder of the Malawiyya order of dervishes. His name was derived from Rum (Central Anatolia), where he mainly lived, but he was also known by the sobriquet Mawlana. Rumi was born in Balkh and died in Konya.

After schooling in theology and mysticism, Jalal al-Din Rumi followed in the footsteps of his father Baha' al-Din Walad (d. 1231) and became a preacher. In 1244 he fell in love with a wandering dervish, Shams al-Din (ca. 1185–1248), who became the sun in his life: "A burning candle came and fired me with its naked flame." It was a mutual attraction, and each found in the other something for which he had been looking all of his life. Rumi saw Shams as "the Beloved," while Shams found in Rumi a true master and friend.

For six months they were inseparable, which made Rumi neglect his religious and social duties. This caused complaints from his wife and children and especially from his pupils, who jealously resented the intruder and even threatened him. Shams fled because of this, leaving Rumi behind full of grief: "Sweet moon without thy ray like a cloud I weep." But fortunately, Shams was found in Damascus and brought back by Rumi's son Walad. When they met again they embraced and kissed each other warmly, and according to Walad nobody knew who was the lover and who the beloved.

But the jealousy and hate of the pupils knew no bounds and in 1248 they killed Shams with the help of Rumi's own son 'Ala' al-Din. All of this was concealed from Rumi, who thought that Shams had just left again. He felt desolate, his eyes and soul had gone, without him life was unbearable. He searched through Syria and wrote many poems with lamentations and cries of despair, but after a time he gave up hope and found comfort by identifying with Shams, so they were one after all.

The relationship between Rumi and Shams was unique because it was not the usual adoration for Divine Beauty in the form of a beautiful youth, as in **Sufism**, but a love between two older mystics of great personal strength and character. According to some sources, Shams was killed by having a wall thrown upon his head, which could symbolically refer to the **Islamic** story of Lot. Although this may suggest homosexual behavior, the writer thinks it designates the resentment of the pupils against a person whom they considered evil in general, because he had seduced their master away from the true religion. Rumi and Shams had a quite intimate and, probably, a purely spiritual friendship, in which sex had no part because it would interfere with the equality of friendship and the purity of love.

During the last twenty-five years of his life, Rumi found inspiration in music and dance and in relationships with the goldsmith Salah al-Din Zarkub (d. 1258), who became a mirror to his sun, and after his death, with Celebi Husam al-Din (d. 1283), who inspired him to write down his wisdom. This time he was more careful with his pupils, and threatened to desert them if they would not stop their malicious slander of his friends. In 1273 Rumi died at sunset; it is told that his cat refused food and died one week after him.

Rumi's attitude toward homosexual behavior was probably not different from that of his contemporaries. Dislike of passive homosexual behavior of adult men is reflected in his excoriation of the **mukhannath** as models of unreliability, who are bound to worldly pleasures, caught up in "forms" as women are, and not in "meanings" like real men. Loving boys was understandable because of their divine beauty, but Rumi warned against indulgence. Real love had to be spiritual, because love of forms was only relative to the love of God. "Human beauty is a gilt-gingerbread phenomenon, or else why does your beloved become an old ass? He was formerly an angel, but now seems to be a demon. The beauty he had was merely ephemeral."

BIBLIOGRAPHY. William C. Chittick, *The Sufi Path of Love: the Spiritual Teachings of Rumi*, Albany: SUNY Press, 1983; Annemarie Schimmel, *The Triumphal Sun: A Study of the Works of Jalaluddin Rumi*, London, 1978.

Maarten Schild

RUSSIA AND USSR

As an entity with links first to Byzantine and then to Western European culture, the Russian state may be said to have begun with the conversion to Christianity in 988. This development, which provided the foundation of a vast territorial expansion over the course of the centuries, brought much with it of cultural significance, including the characteristic Judeo-Christian ambivalence toward male homosexuality.

The Middle Ages. Male homosexual love appears in one of the earliest extant works of Russian literature, the *Legend of Boris and Gleb*, written by an anonymous but, one suspects, homophile monk at the beginning of the eleventh century. Combining history, hagiography, and poetry, this work enjoyed a remarkably wide circulation in subsequent centuries. It tells of the assassination in 1015, for dynastic reasons, of two young Kievan princes by minions of their half-brother Sviatopolk the Accursed. Describing the murder of prince Boris, the author of *The Legend* brings up the favorite squire of Boris, "Hungarian by birth, George by name" (Hungarians and Kievan Russians had a common border at the time). Boris had a magnificent golden necklace made for George the Hungarian, for "he was loved by Boris beyond reckoning." When the four assassins pierced Boris with their swords, George flung himself on the body of his prince, exclaiming "I will not be left behind, my precious lord! Ere the beauty of thy body begins to wilt, let it be granted that my life may end." The assassins tore Boris out of George's embrace, stabbed George, and flung him out of the tent, bleeding and dying. While the *Legend of Boris and Gleb* is couched in the standard life-of-saint format that was imported from Byzantium, the author's sympathy for the mutual love of Boris and George comes clearly through as does his realization that the gratuitous murder of George resulted from his open admission of the nature of this love.

George's brother Moses, later canonized by the Orthodox church as St. Moses the Hungarian, was the only member of Boris' retinue to have escaped the massacre. His fate is told in *The Life of St. Moses the Hungarian*. Moses was captured by the troops of Sviatopolk the Accursed and sold as a slave to a Polish noblewoman who became enamored of his powerful physique. He spent the next year resisting this woman's efforts to get him to marry her, preferring the company of his Russian fellow prisoners. At the end of the year, exasperated by his refusals and taunts, the noblewoman ordered that Moses be given one hundred lashes and that his sex organs be amputated. Eventually, Moses found his way to the Kievan Crypt Monastery, where he lived as a monk for ten more years, constantly admonishing other monks against the temptations of women and sin. *The Life of St. Moses* was obviously influenced by the biblical story of Joseph and Potiphar's wife. Its text is permeated with the hatred of women and all sexuality that is typical of the medieval monastic tradition. Yet, as the modern scholar Vasilii **Rozanov** maintained, the legend of St. Moses is clearly the story of a male homosexual punished because he is unable to enter a conventional heterosexual marriage.

Muscovite Russia. The culturally rich Kievan period (eleventh to thirteenth centuries) was followed by 250 years of Mongol invasions and occupation by nomadic warrior tribes. The Russia that regained its independence, with a new capital in Moscow, had taken over many of the ways and customs of the Mongol occupiers. Women were now segregated, kept in special quarters, and received virtually no education. Marriages in Muscovite Russia were arranged by the families and the two spouses were usually strangers who met for the first time only during their wedding ceremony. Romantic attachments between men and women, if there were any in sixteenth-century Russia, remain unrecorded. What one finds instead, all foreign and domestic observers agree, is that male homosexuality was astoundingly widespread.

Grand Prince Vasily II of Moscow, who ruled from 1505 to 1533, seems to have been totally homosexual. For reasons of state he married Princess Helen Glinsky, but he was able to carry out his conjugal duties with her only if one of the officers of the guard joined them in bed in the nude. His wife strongly resented this behavior, not (as one might have supposed) on moralistic ground, but because she was afraid that this practice would expose her children to the charge of being illegitimate. The domestic life of Vasily and Helen was hell on earth, with no quarter given on either side. One of their sons was born mentally retarded; their other son ruled Russia as Ivan IV, better known as Ivan the Terrible.

As bloody and sociopathic a ruler as his reputation credits him with being, Ivan married almost as many times as Henry VIII of England, but he was also attracted to young men in drag. One of the most ruthless chieftains of Ivan's political police, Feodor Basmanov ("with the smile of a maiden and the soul of a snake," as a later poet described him) rose to his high position through performing seductive dances in female attire at Ivan's court.

But Muscovite homosexuality was by no means limited to royalty. Sigmund of Herberstein, who visited Russia during the reign of Vasily III as the ambassador of the Holy Roman Empire, states in his *Rerum moscovitarum commentarii* that male homosexuality was prevalent among all social classes. The minor English poet George Turberville came to Moscow with a diplomatic mission in 1568 during one of the bloodiest phases of Ivan IV's regime. Turberville, however, was shocked not by the carnage but by the open homosexuality of the Russian peasants.

Apparently neither laws nor customs restrained homosexual practices among the men of Muscovite Russia (there is no record of what went on among the women). The only recorded objections came from the church. Archpriest Avvakum, the leader of the Old Believers during the religious schism of the seventeenth century, considered every man who shaved his beard a homosexual. "Sermon No. 12" by Metropolitan Daniel, a popular Moscow preacher of the 1530s, is almost entirely dedicated to denouncing the gay blades of the day. These young men, Daniel thundered, behaved like whores: they shaved off their beards, used lotions and ointments to make their skins softer, rouged their cheeks and perfumed their bodies, plucked out their body hair with tweezers, changed their clothes several times a day, and wore scarlet boots several sizes too small for them. Daniel likened these young men's elaborate preparations before going out of their houses to a cook preparing a spectacularly decorated dish and ironically asked to whom the finished dish was to be served.

The Eighteenth and Nineteenth Centuries. Peter the Great, who pulled Russia into the modern world at the beginning of the eighteenth century, was one of those heterosexuals who dabble in bisexuality when the occasion is suitable. Peter's relationship with his protégé Alexander Menshikov, the baker boy whom the tsar made his orderly, then a generalissimo, and finally a prince, apparently had its sexual aspects. In battle conditions, Peter used soldiers as bed companions, preferring those with big, flabby bellies on which he liked to rest his head.

Another ruler of the Romanov dynasty with a bisexual streak was Peter's niece, Anna Ioannovna, who was empress of Russia from 1730 to 1740 and who, according to some memoirists, had intimate relations with some of her ladies-in-waiting. The German-born Catherine II (the Great) may have had a brief lesbian fling with Princess Dashkova, the noblewoman who helped Catherine overthrow her husband Peter III and to seize the throne. But Catherine's overpowering yen for well-endowed males prevented her from forming any emotional ties with other women.

Among the western ideas that were imported into Russia after Peter's reforms was homophobia. In the eighteenth and nineteenth centuries, the visible male homosexuality of the Muscovite period went largely underground. Among the poorer classes and in remote northern regions, tolerance and acceptance of homosexual behavior survived the peasant eschatological dissenters that separated from the Old Believers. Two of these sects, the Khlysty (distorted plural of "Christ") and the Skoptsy (Castrates) had recognizable homosexual, bisexual, and sadomasochistic strains in their culture, folklore, and religious rituals. The Skoptsy who engaged in commerce had an institutionalized practice of an older merchant adopting a younger assistant–lover as his son and heir. After the older man's death this heir would repeat the process with a still younger man, thus giving rise to a mercantile dynasty.

At the opposite end of the social spectrum, we find a succession of ultra-conservative gay statesmen–writers, who moved in the highest echelons of tsarist Russia in the eighteenth and nineteenth centuries. Ivan Dmitriev (1760–1837), the leading Russian sentimentalist poet and an author of witty satires, saccharine love songs, and didactic fables, was Minister of Justice under Alexander I. In his government career Dmitriev was noted for his nepotism, surrounding himself with handsome male assistants, some of whom owed their advancement to the fact that they were his lovers. In his poetry, however, he wore a heterosexual mask.

Equally nepotistic was count Sergei Uvarov (1786–1855), Minister of Education under Nicholas I. To improve his financial situation, Uvarov married a wealthy heiress and had several children by her. His great love, however, was the handsome but not-too-bright prince Mikhail Dondukov-Korsakov. Other prominent and politically conservative nineteenth-century Russian gays were Filip Vigel (1786–1836), Konstantin Leont'ev (1831–1914), and prince Vladimir Meshchersky (1839–1914).

Not all the gay people of pre-Revolutionary Russia were reactionary or conservative. There was, for example, the marvelously anarchic figure of Nadezhda Durova (1783–1866), a woman who today would probably be classified as a transsexual. Forced by her parents to marry a government official, Durova left her husband and child three years later, and donning a cossack uniform, joined the army to take part in the Napoleonic wars.

Nikolai Gogol (1809–1852) is one of the most harrowing cases of sexual self-repression to be found in the annals of literature. Exclusively gay, Gogol spent his whole life denying this fact to himself and others, primarily for religious reasons. His stories and plays are permeated with fear of marriage and other forms of sexual contact with women, but Gogol enveloped this theme in such a cloud of symbols and surrealistic fantasies that his contemporary readers failed to discern its presence. Gogol's personal involvements consisted mostly of falling in love with straight men unable to respond.

Contemporaries of Gogol were already enriching Russian literature with explicitly gay poetry. One collection of these poems in a classical Russian, which had originated in the exclusive educational institutions of St. Petersburg in the late 1830s and 1840s, was published in Geneva in 1879 (*Eros russe*); the longest piece is entitled "Pokhozhdeniia pazha" (The Adventures of a Page).

The theme of homosexuality in the life of Leo Tolstoy (1828–1910) deserves a special study which will undoubtedly be written one day. In his childhood, Tolstoy kept falling in love with boys and girls. In Tolstoy's later writings homosexuality is portrayed in a negative light and in only a few instances. *Resurrection* (1899), is the aged Tolstoy's great indictment of the inequities and corruption of tsarist Russia; tolerant treatment of homosexuals and of those who advocate equal rights for them figure in this novel as one of the many symptoms of the country's moral decay.

One of the greatest Russian celebrities of the 1870s and 80s, both nationally and internationally, was the explorer and naturalist Nikolai **Przhevalsky** (1839–1888). Each of Przhevalsky's expeditions was planned to include a male lover–companion between the ages of 16 and 22. His renown was so great that he could require the Russian government to pay for the education of each new lover and to commission the youth as a lieutenant in the army.

Reform and Cultural Flowering. The abolition of serfdom, the replacement of a corrupt judiciary system with trials by jury, the reduction of military service from 25 years to 5, and other liberal reforms initiated by Alexander II in 1861 did not make Russia a democracy, but they did set the stage for change. In this new atmosphere homosexuality became far more visible in both Russian life and literature.

Prominent on the Russian literary scene during the last two decades of the nineteenth century were two lesbian couples. Anna Yevreinova (1844–1919) was highly active in the feminist movement. She was the founder of the literary journal *The Northern Herald*, which she edited jointly with her lover–companion Maria Feodorova. Polyxena Soloviova (1867–1924), a Symbolist poet, shared her life with Natalia Maneseina. Among the notable and overt gay male figures of the period were the popular poet Alexei Apukhin (a classmate and one-time friend of Peter Tchaikovsky); the previously mentioned prince Vladimir Meshchersky; and of course the famous Sergei **Diaghilev**, who headed the World of Art (Mir iskusstva) Group, before achieving international fame in the West as a ballet impresario. During this period there were at least seven gay grand dukes—uncles, nephews, and cousins of the last two tsars. The antihomosexual articles 995 and 996 of the penal code of the 1830s (and their successor, article 516 of the 1903 project) were hardly ever enforced. For this reason—and others— the legend that the great composer Peter **Tchaikovsky** (1840–1893) was forced to commit suicide is untenable.

The uprising of 1905 forced Nicholas II to issue his October Manifesto, authorizing a parliamentary system and virtually abolishing preliminary censorship of printed material. In 1906 the sexual reform movement reached Russia, and in its wake there appeared gay and lesbian poets, fiction writers, and artists who saw in the new freedom of expression a chance to depict their lifestyle affirmatively. Mikhail **Kuzmin** (1872–1936), the most outspoken of Russia's gay writers, made his literary debut in 1906, when he published his autobiographical novel *Wings*, the story of a young man who slowly realizes that he is homosexual. Frequently reprinted, this book became the catechism of Russian gay men. Lydia Zinovieva–Annibal's (1866–1907) novel *Thirty-Three Freaks* (1907) and her collection of short stories *The Tragic Zoo* (1907) did for Russian lesbians what *Wings* had done for gay men: they showed the reading public that lesbian love could be serious, deep, and moving.

About 1910 there appeared in Russia a group of poets called peasant—not only because of their origin, but because the fate and survival of the peasant way of life was their central theme. The undisputed leader of this group was the homosexual Nikolai Kliuev (1887–1937), who was born into a peasant family belonging to the Khlysty sect. The great love of his life was Sergei Esenin (1895–1925), who was a remarkable poet in his own right. Although successively married to three women (including the dancer Isadora Duncan), Esenin could write meaningful love poetry only when it was addressed to other men.

The Post-Revolutionary Situation. The provisional government, formed after the abdication of Nicholas II in February 1917, lasted for only eight months. Constantly harassed by the monarchists on the right and the Bolsheviks on the left, the regime managed to promote human rights and freedoms on a scale not experienced in Russia before or since. That was when women and minorities were given full civil and political rights including the vote. The seizure of power by Lenin and Trotsky in October 1917 was hailed by many then (and is still often regarded) as an enhancement of the rights gained by the revolutions of 1905 and February 1917. But as far as rights (including gay rights) and personal freedoms are concerned, the October Revolution was actually a reversal and a negation of the two earlier revolutions rather than their continuation. To

be sure, articles 995 and 996 disappeared, but this was simply part of the abolition of the entire Criminal Code of the Russian Empire.

When the civil war ended, a new Soviet criminal code was promulgated in 1922 and amended in 1926. In the sexual sphere, this code prohibited sex with minors under the age of 16, male and female prostitution, and pandering. It did not mention sexual contacts between consenting adults, which meant that adult male homosexuality was legal. The provisions of this code extended only to the Russian and the Ukrainian republics of the USSR. But the previously widespread homosexual practices in the Caucasus and the Muslim areas of Central Asia were persecuted and punished during the 1920s as "survivals of the old way of life."

In Central Russia, including Moscow and Leningrad, two forms of the Soviet government's negative attitude to homosexuality became evident after the end of the civil war: morbidizing it by treating it as a mental disorder; and dismissing or ignoring its manifestations in literary works that appeared in the 1920s. If the nineteenth century considered homosexuality as a crime to be punished, the Soviet regime in the 1920s saw it as an illness to be cured. It is significant that although the Soviets reject psychoanalysis on ideological grounds, they are willing to use arguments purloined from depth psychology to justify their condemnation of homosexuality.

The growing hostility of the Soviet government and press to homosexuality, observable in the 1920s, culminated in the new Stalinist law, article 121 of the Soviet Penal Code. This law, announced on December 17, 1933 and made compulsory for all the republics of the Soviet Union on March 7, 1934—the first anniversary of the National Socialist seizure of power in Germany—outlawed sexual relations between men and prescribed 5 years of hard labor for voluntary sexual acts and

8 years for using force or threats and for sex with a consenting minor. However, just as in Nazi Germany, lesbian relations went unpunished throughout the Stalin era. The opinion that homosexuality equaled opposition to the Soviet system became entrenched in the minds of the bureaucracy. In 1936 the Commissar of Justice Nikolai Krylenko proclaimed that there was no reason for anyone to be homosexual after two decades of socialism; no one from the working class could possibly be homosexual so that the people who hang out "in their vile secret dens are often engaged in another kind of work, the work of counter-revolution."

Nonetheless, during the Stalinist era, Soviet persecution of gay men was neither continuous nor total. In the case of well-known personalities, such as the great director Sergei Eisenstein, the operatic tenor Sergei Lemeshev, the pianist Sviatoslav Richter, and numerous ballet dancers, the authorities were willing to look the other way—provided the man was married and kept his homosexuality out of public view.

The Post-Stalin Decades. During the decades that followed Stalin's death in 1953, foreign scholars and tourists were again able to come to the USSR for extended stays. Homosexuality was—and still is—a state crime. But foreign visitors were able to find clandestine gay communities in all major cities. As they had done under Stalin, the Soviet political police still used homosexuals as informers and for recruiting foreign gay men for espionage. In a police state, the existence of a sexual outlaw was necessarily precarious; his "weakness" constantly put him at the mercy of the authorities.

Still, the post-Stalin years were a time of slow social change. The decade of the 1970s witnessed the emergence of gay and lesbian writers, the first under the Soviet regime (writers who treated gay and lesbian themes in the 1920s had all come out before the October Revolution). Unable to publish their work, they had to resort to *samizdat* ("self-publishing") or *tamizdat* ("publishing over there," i.e., abroad). Well documented is the case of Gennady Trifonov, who served a hard-labor sentence in 1976–80 for privately circulating his gay poems and who since 1986 has been allowed to publish essays and reviews in Soviet periodicals, provided he makes no reference to gay topics. More light has been shed on the situation of lesbians in the Soviet Union in recent years in memoirs published abroad by women who had served time in Gulag camps and were able to observe lesbian behavior there, and in works of fiction by Soviet writers expelled from the USSR.

Under Gorbachev the situation remained uncertain. The glasnost campaign made homosexuality a mentionable topic in the Soviet press, but initiatives dating back to the early 1970s that evinced a tentative approach to change with regard to gay rights do not seem to have been followed up. As the historical record shows, Russia's past gives indications both of hope and despair.

BIBLIOGRAPHY. Simon Karlinsky, "L'omosessualità nella letteratura e nella storia russa dal' XI al XX secolo," *Sodoma*, 3 (1986), 47–70; idem, "Russia's Gay Literature and Culture: Liberation and Repression," in Martin Duberman, Martha Vicinus, and George Chauncey, Jr., eds., *Hidden from History: Reclaiming the Gay and Lesbian Past*, New York: New American Library, 1989.

Simon Karlinsky

RUSTIN, BAYARD (1912–1987)

American black civil rights leader. Born in West Chester, Pennsylvania, the illegitimate son of an immigrant from the West Indies, Rustin was reared by a grandfather who worked as a caterer. In the 1930s he joined the Young Communist League, which he regarded as the youth group of the only party then truly dedicated to civil rights. In 1941 he became race relations director of the Fellowship of Reconciliation, a nondenominational group seeking solutions to world problems through nonviolence. He spent 28 months in prison for refusing military service in World War II. From 1953 to 1955 Rustin was director of the War Resisters League, a pacifist organization, and from 1955 to 1960 he worked with Martin Luther King, Jr. Having organized several earlier mass protests, he achieved his greatest success in the 1963 March on Washington for Jobs and Freedom. A believer in progress through the labor movement, he served for many years as president of the A. Philip Randolph Institute.

Because of his "gradualist" labor emphasis, as well as his advocacy of black–Jewish harmony and support for Israel, Rustin was labeled conservative by some black radicals. In 1953 he was arrested and briefly imprisoned on a morals charge in Pasadena, California. His homosexuality, which was known to his associates but not to the general public, is believed to have been used by enemies to deny him the position of leadership to which he was rightfully entitled.

SACKVILLE-WEST, VITA (1892–1962)

British novelist, poet, biographer, and travel writer. The granddaughter of a Spanish dancer, and daughter of the imperious Lady Victoria Sackville, Vita Sackville-West was brought up on the family's palatial estate at Knole. In 1913 she married the homosexual diplomat Harold **Nicolson**. The partners agreed that the institution of marriage was "unnatural," but with care, frankness, and deep mutual affection theirs lasted forty-nine years.

In 1918 Sackville-West "rediscovered" Violet Keppel whom she had known as a child. Both were immediately smitten and embarked on a tempestuous affair, which Vita presented in fictionalized form in her novel *Challenge*, published in 1924 in the United States but not in England. She wrote a franker account for the drawer (which was not published until it was included in her son's memoir of 1973). In 1919 Violet contracted a marriage—which was not intended to be consummated—with Denys Trefusis, but she and Vita continued to escape for love trysts at various locales in Britain. Harold, for his part, was preoccupied with the peace negotiations at Versailles.

At the end of 1922 Vita met Virginia **Woolf**, ten years her senior, who enchanted her. Prompted by caution on both sides, their affair was slow to ripen, but it proceeded intermittently through much of the 1920s. Woolf wrote *Orlando* (1928), her novel of androgyny, as an act of homage to Vita; Sackville-West's *Letters to Virginia Woolf* was published in 1984.

Although Vita Sackville-West's books achieved considerable popularity in her day (as did those of Violet Trefusis), it cannot be said that she ranks as a major writer. Her life showed, however, the varieties of experience open to a privileged woman in an era in which social controls were gradually lifting.

BIBLIOGRAPHY. Victoria Glendenning, *Vita: The Life of V. Sackville-West*, New York: Knopf, 1983; Nigel Nicolson, *Portrait of a Marriage*, New York: Atheneum, 1973.

Evelyn Gettone

SADE, DONATIEN ALPHONSE FRANÇOIS, COMTE DE, KNOWN AS MARQUIS DE (1740–1814)

French writer and thinker. A playboy in his youth, Sade was imprisoned in Vincennes and in the Bastille for twelve years while a cabal of relatives prevented his release. Here he did most of his writing. Liberated by the outbreak of the French Revolution in 1789, he served for a time in Paris as a minor official. Having fallen afoul of the Napoleonic regime, he spent the last years of his life in the insane asylum at Charenton.

In the popular mind Sade is simply a scribbler of **pornography** who lent his name to the paraphilia known as sadism. Closer study of his writings reveals not only their elegant style and inventive plotting, but an astute, bitingly corrosive analysis of society and human motivation, which was forged by his solitary meditation and reading during his long years of confinement. The **philosophy** he evolved stems in large measure from the ancient **Epicurean** stress on the maximization of personal pleasure and the minimizing of pain. He adds the corollary that to the extent that one's own pleasure can be increased by the pain of others so much the better for the beneficiary. Cruel as they may seem, such views accord with a recurring trend in human thought to find the ultimate motor of human action in self-interest. Applied to sexual conduct they link up with the ancient contrast between the **active** (enjoying) vs. the passive (suffering) partner. Denying the existence of **God**, he sees no barrier to the pursuit of self-interest as the goal of human life. A century before Friedrich Nietzsche, Sade anticipated most of his key insights about power and motivation. He also provided a striking example of the "transvaluation of values." As Lester Crocker has shown, Sade is the most radical and disturbing of all the **Enlightenment** thinkers. Yet because his books were hard to obtain until the 1960s, awareness of their importance has come late.

It is not generally realized that Sade was personally bisexual. In actual life—the murderous scenes in his books are not to be taken as records of real experience—one of his favorite sexual positions was to be penetrated by his valet as he penetrated a woman. He commended **anal** intercourse both for contraception and for (male) pleasure. Not surprisingly, in view of his prison years, he was also a connoisseur of **masturbation**.

Sade is sometimes taken to be misogynistic. Yet several of his books feature strong-willed women who are just as adept as the most ruthless man, if not more so, in obtaining their way. The didactic dialogue *Philosophy in the Bedroom*, which is perhaps the best introduction to his work, has a character (Dolmance) who defends male homosexuality. His masterpieces are the novels *Juliette* and *Justine*, the one showing the manifold satisfactions of those who follow his precepts of self-interest, the other the endless sufferings that are the lot of one who obstinately clings to virtue.

BIBLIOGRAPHY. Angela Carter, *The Sadeian Woman and the Ideology of Pornography*, New York: Random House, 1978; Lester G. Crocker, *Nature and Culture*, Baltimore: Johns Hopkins University Press, 1963; Gilbert Lely, *The Marquis de Sade: A Biography*, New York: Grove, 1970; Jean-Jacques Pauvert, *Sade vivant: une innocence sauvage, 1740–1777*, Paris: Robert Laffont, 1986.

Wayne R. Dynes

SA'DI (CA. 1213–1292)

One of the most famous Persian poets and writers. Sa'di ("felicity") was his poetical name. He was born in Shiraz and attended the University in Bagdad. Thereafter he studied the mysticism of the **Sufis** and educated himself by traveling for years through almost the whole **Islamic** empire. In or about 1255 he settled in Shiraz where he earned himself a great reputation as a writer. His most famous works are the *Gulistan* (Rose Garden) and the *Bustan* (Orchard), both consisting of stories and poems which are moralistic, didactic, mystical, and amusing.

An important theme in the works of Sa'di is the love for beautiful young boys, which he describes in all its facets, ranging from purely platonic and spiritual in the mystical love poems to obscene and lustful in what can be called his "pornographic" works. In his mystical love poems Sa'di invokes chaste love for boys as a way to transcend the self and ultimately achieve union with God. Beautiful boys can serve as mediators because they are considered as witnesses (*shahid*) of God's beauty on earth. In his more worldly poems and stories he is more cynical and down to earth about the problems and joys of loving boys. Love ended, of course, when the boy's facial hair besmirched him: "Sa'di admires the fresh down of youth and not hairs rigid like a packing needle."

In general, Sa'di shared the attitude of his contemporaries toward homosexuality and consequently showed a strong aversion to passive homosexual behavior of older boys and men. Typically, he had a low opinion of women and marriage. His own wife and children are neglected in his writings. As friends and companions men were important, and for love there were boys. In a poem he says of himself: "Sa'di's fame has spread everywhere for his love of boys (*shahid bazi*). In this there is no blame among us, but rather praise."

BIBLIOGRAPHY. Minoo S. Southgate, "Men, Women and Boys: Love and Sex in the Works of Sa'di," *Iranian Studies*, 17 (1984), 413-52.

Maarten Schild

SADOMASOCHISM (S/M)

This term is conventionally defined as the giving or receiving of pain for erotic gratification. However, nonphysical elements, such as verbal abuse and humiliation, often play a large role. Bondage (restraint) is also common. A more comprehensive definition situates physical and nonphysical aspects in a larger framework of dominance and submission that engages the **fantasy** life of the participants. S/M differs from mere cruelty in that it is—expressly or implicitly—consensual: the partners define limits that must not be transgressed. The activities found in S/M are not radically different from the "horseplay" that sometimes occurs in ordinary lovemaking: teasing, biting, pinching, and wrestling. But in the S/M scene there is, superimposed on these ordinary behaviors, a range of specific S/M activities in a continuum ranging from harmless play to the most elaborate ritual "torture."

Clinical Theories. The first element of the compound *sadomasochism* derives from the Marquis D. A. F. de **Sade** (1740–1814), whose works depict the inflicting of pain for the erotic enjoyment of the active partner. The term masochism stems from writings of the German Leopold Ritter von Sacher-Masoch (1836–1895), which concentrate on the element of humiliation experienced by the passive partner, notably the novel *Venus im Pelz* (Venus in Furs), in which Wanda and Gregor are the active and passive participants in flagellation. From clinical evidence nineteenth-century psychiatrists—above all Richard von **Krafft-Ebing**, author of *Psychopathia Sexualis* (1886)—created an analysis of sadism and masochism as pathology. Modern S/M practitioners hold that what they do has very little in common with the compulsive patterns analyzed by psychiatrists. Instead, they employ their techniques as symbolic interpersonal play that deals in intensities that approach the actual pain threshold and may surpass it, but generally avoid crossing the level of tolerance.

In modern street parlance the two complementary aspects are described as "top" and "bottom" or "S" and "M." In keeping with the dichotomy cherished by abnormal psychology, sadism and masochism are often regarded as diametrically opposed capacities, yet this dichotomy is belied in practice by the fact that individuals can exchange roles. Many S's actually began their involvement as M's, for this is often the best way for a novice to learn.

Homosexual Aspects of S/M. Culturally, the practice of S/M is a commentary on the dominance—submission pattern inculcated by the **gender** roles of advanced industrial society. Hence it is not surprising that women willing to take the role of dominatrix should be in demand, for reversal of the "normal" roles of dominance and submission offers not only a temporary relief from expectations imposed by patriarchal social traditions, but constitutes a kind of symbolic restitution. In like fashion, gay and lesbian S/M practices incorporate culturally defined ideas of active and passive. Here, however, there is a paradox, for S/M adepts will often insist that the M, who in theory is completely subservient, actually controls the pace, direction, and intensity of the experience by communicating his or her needs and limits. In such a dynamic, the S is often "on trial" to demonstrate true competence and sensitivity. From this crisscross effect many participants derive stimulation and, they believe, insights into human relationships in general.

In most gay and lesbian S/M circles today, the wearing of leather garments, together with chains and other accoutrements, is common. Such apparel is often the focus of **fetishistic** attachments. It also emphasizes the element of theatre and performance, so that the S&M scene—and more broadly one's presentation of self as a "leather person" in social contexts—becomes a matter of enactment.

Entering the S/M subculture is not a matter of a simple one-time conversion. Some individuals flirt with the idea for years before taking the plunge. Once the novice has decided to enter the subculture, he may progress through several stages of increasing depth of involvement as experience grows and inhibitions about particular acts wane. This stagelike progression has led sociologists to speak of S/M "careers"—the individual trajectories of those who sustain their commitment. Some observers have noted increasing "tolerance levels" on the part of adepts who find that previous levels of involvement no longer deliver the intensity they once did, requiring progression to deeper levels.

In addition to flagellation, bondage, verbal abuse, role playing, genitorture, use of hot wax, and abrasion, S/M scenes may include "watersports," urinating on the M or causing him to swallow **urine**. Depending on the relationship, this may be regarded either as a gift, a humiliation, or a degradation. Much less common is the similar use of faeces ("scat"). **Handballing** or fisting, in which the hand or even the lower arm is inserted in the anal passage, formerly enjoyed some popularity, but with the spread of safer sex techniques it has become less common. Handballing is not necessarily an S/M activity any more than fellatio or masturbation; it depends entirely on the attitudes and intentions of those engaging in it. Although S/M practices have the reputation of being "far out," many of them are less risky in terms of disease transmission than the penetrative practices that are the central feature of the mainstream male gay world. In S/M scenes, sexual toys of various kinds—whips, straps, handcuffs, tit clamps, etc.—are freely used. Those who are seriously involved may have their nipples or genitals pierced and adorned with small rings; although quite popular, this practice is not universal. In ordinary S&M practice, however, there is almost invariably an avoidance of any activity that would lead to permanent marking or bodily harm.

As with any other subculture, S/M people tend to socialize with others who share their tastes. Most big cities in North America and northern Europe have at least one "leather **bar**," usually for gay men only. Prominent among the icons displayed in such establishments are trophies and photographs relating to motorcycle clubs, to which many serious S/M enthusiasts belong. There are also artists who have created imagery that is clearly S/M in its appeal; among the best known of these are Cavello, Etienne, Rex, Sean, and Tom of Finland (though some of the latter's work is not relevant).

Sociological studies have shown that in North America most S/M participants are of northern European ancestry, rather than from Mediterranean or African stock. Contrary to the stereotype that associates them with conservative or even quasi-Nazi views, surveys in the United States have shown that a majority are politically liberal. On the whole, they are well educated and hold upscale professional jobs. Few S/M people share the obsessive preoccupation with youth that is found in other sectors of the gay world; with a very few exceptions, boy lovers are not found among them. In fact, older individuals are notably visible at S/M gatherings, which are relatively free of **ageism**. The premium placed on technical expertise seems to cancel out ageism with its attendant privileging of youth.

While some S/M practitioners seek new partners constantly, others may wish to form a more-or-less permanent relationship. In this case the M becomes the "slave" of his S, who will symbolize the ownership in various ways, such as the shaving of body hair, or the slave's wearing of a prominent dog collar, or being required to perform various services for the master and the master's friends. The appeal of the slave relationship is ostensibly the freedom from the crushing burden of responsibilities and decisions that modern urban life imposes. In some instances, however, the slave role is much less demanding and may even be carried out in an almost humorous fashion. There is a large range of activity between these two extremes of total slave–master bonding and playfulness, whereby the two participants limit the enactment to specific occasions, in the bedroom or elsewhere, when they perform their tasks with the utmost seriousness.

Seemingly objective presentations of the nature of S/M almost invariably slight the less tangible elements that are of supreme importance to those who are seriously committed. In the view of some who are experienced in the scene the real appeal of S/M is that it promotes a state of consciousness that transcends ego. Such "egoless" states are inherently blissful. Moreover, participants have the sense that they are involved in a form of magic or alchemy. In a state of perfect trust, their "vibrations" become perfectly attuned to one another, and blows that would normally be unwelcome are transmuted into a choreography of pleasure.

Literary Manifestations. The pioneering novels of the Marquis de Sade and Leopold von Sacher-Masoch have been noted above. William Carney's *The Real Thing* (New York: Putnam, 1968) presents a historically accurate picture of the now-vanished scene in the United States in the late 1950s and 1960s. It is cast in the form of a series of letters from an experienced S to his nephew, a novice whom he is instructing in the traditions of the subculture he wishes to enter. Although Carney's view of S/M is ultimately negative, it offers theorizing that is still of interest. Terry Andrews' *The Story of Harold* (New York: Holt Rinehart and Winston, 1974), of unusual literary quality, is revealing because S/M is integrated with other themes. The novels of "A. N. Roquelaire" (a pseudonym of Anne Rice) are ostensibly heterosexual, but include considerable relevant psychological speculation. Story collections by Phil Andros (*Stud*, Boston: Alyson, 1982; repr. of 1966 issue; and *Below the Belt*, San Francisco: Perineum) and Jack Fritscher (*Corporal in Charge of Taking Care of Captain O'Malley*, San Francisco: Gay Sunshine, 1984; and *Stand by Your Man*, San Francisco: Leyland Publications, 1984) offer material of varied interest.

Parallels. Analogies for the physical side of the S/M relationship have been found in some tribal societies, where warriors must undergo trials of pain before being admitted to the military elite. (Fraternity hazings are a faded modern version of these customs.) In ancient Thessaly the all-women rites of Aphrodite Anosia included erotic flagellation. The Romans delighted in gladiatorial shows and in watching condemned criminals devoured by lions in the arena. Yet these were not voluntary submissions to pain, and they seem—despite assertions to the contrary—to have no direct connection with eros.

The beautiful frescoes of the Villa of the Mysteries at Pompeii, which have never been completely interpreted, show women's flagellation in the context of a religious and erotic initiation. Paintings of the martyrdom of the Christian saints —Catherine tormented by her wheel, Agatha suffering the assault on her breasts—are more explicit in their depiction of pain. In one instance, that of the handsome St. Sebastian pierced by arrows, a Christian image has acquired (since at least the end of the nineteenth century) a secondary status as the focus of contemplation by gay men. Of course it was not the aim of Christian hagiography and art to stimulate S/M thoughts. It may be, however, that these legends of fortitude under suffering were one of the elements that helped, however unintentionally, to prepare for the modern S/M sensibility.

The adage "spare the rod and spoil the child" attests to the use of flogging by parents and schoolmasters. In the English **public school** this practice became a veritable cult, with masters and pupils alike developing erotic feelings in conducting it. Through this imprinting some members of the upper classes developed a lifelong flagellomania; hence the expression "English vice" for erotically stimulating caning.

There may even be phylogenetic sources for the connection between corporal pain and sexual performance, as with cats where the male cat bites the neck of the female during intercourse. Some students of the question hold that the human experience of erotic release of pain is governed by a distinctive physiological process, characterized by the release of certain endorphins; this physiological dynamic is, however, still imperfectly understood.

BIBLIOGRAPHY. Ian A. Gibson, *The English Vice: Beating, Sex and Shame in Victorian England and After*, London: Duckworth, 1978; Michael Grumley and Ed Gallucci, *Hard Corps: Studies in Leather & Sadomasochism*, New York: Dutton, 1977; John A. Lee, "The Social Organization of Sexual Risk," *Alternative Lifestyles*, 2 (1979), 69–100; Geoff Mains, *Urban Originals: A Celebration of Leather Sexuality*, San Francisco: Gay Sunshine Press, 1984; Michael Rosen, *Sexual Magic: The S/M Photographs*, San Francisco: Shaynew Press, 1986; Samois Collective, *Coming to Power: Writings and Graphics on Lesbian S/M*, 3d ed., Boston: Alyson, 1987; Andreas Spengler, *Sadomasochisten und ihre Subculturen*, Frankfurt am Main: Campus Verlag, 1979; Larry Townsend, *The Leatherman's Handbook II*, New York: Modernismo Publications, 1983; Thomas Weinberg and G. W. Levi Kamel, eds., *S and M: Studies in Sadomasochism*, Buffalo: Prometheus Books, 1983.
Wayne R. Dynes

SAFE SEX

Safe sex refers to activities with no risk, or very small risk, of undesirable consequences. Safe sex need not be conservative or monogamous sex, and it certainly does not mean less sex. Sex can indeed be "safe," not just "safer."

Disease. Partners who are free of **sexually transmitted diseases** can engage in any sexual activities they wish. Since there are diseases which can be transmitted sexually although the carrier is symptom-free and is even unaware he or she has been exposed—hepatitis and **AIDS** are by far the most serious—such a disease-free state can be known only through medical examination. In the case of AIDS, since it takes months before tests can detect antibodies to the HIV virus, testing indicates the subject's infectious state as of several months previously. For a result valid at the time of the test, the test must follow a period of no potential exposure. As a practical matter, activities which can transmit disease can only be safe within a relationship monogamous so far as those activities are concerned.

There are, however, many ways of having enjoyable sex, even kinky and adventurous sex, with little if any risk of disease and without need for examinations and tests. **Masturbation** in pairs and groups is totally without risk. Among consenting partners, dirty talk, exhibitionism, and photography are safe. No one has gotten a disease from an odor, from **fantasy**, role-playing, erotic **clothing**, or bondage. One can safely be promiscuous with such activities, if desired, and those who are HIV-positive can fully participate.

Kissing and licking of unbroken skin cannot transmit AIDS. Intercourse with a barrier, such as a strong condom (extra-strength condoms are available and recommended for **anal** sex), is safe as long as the barrier remains unbroken. Ample use of a water-based lubricant reduces the risk of breakage.

The activities which can transmit disease are those in which one receives orally, anally, vaginally, or through broken skin a substance from inside someone else's body: semen, seminal fluid (pre-cum), vaginal secretions, blood, urine, feces. Sexual toys can harbor microorganisms, and if they cannot be cleaned thoroughly or covered with a condom they should not be shared. A finger or penis can transfer disease organisms from one orifice to another, or one partner to another; washing before changing to a different orifice or partner is sensible. If fingers are inserted into the anus, a rubber glove is recommended; it also prevents dangerous internal scratches from fingernails. While the HIV virus is absorbed through the colon or breaks in the skin, and there are few known cases of its transmission via oral–genital sex, the hepatitis viruses, gonococcus, and other microorganisms are hardier and are readily transmitted orally. A condom or (for women) a dental dam makes **oral** sex safe.

Injury. Sexual play, like other recreations, has various additional hazards; pornography tends to ignore these. The colon is easily injured, and such injuries require immediate medical attention. Sharp or breakable objects should never be inserted into the anus, and any anal play should be slow and careful, with lots of lubricant. While restraint (bondage) can be very erotic, for safety it should be limited to partners one knows and trusts. Ropes can injure the skin or nerves, and specialty stores sell safer hardware, such as padded cuffs. Abnormal weight distribution, as in suspension, can cause injury. Restriction of breathing is potentially fatal, and gagging or any other type of restraint requires constant monitoring and provision for immediate release in an emergency.

Planning, negotiation, and communication are essential components of safe erotic play. An agreed-upon "safe word" can be used to signal the need to lessen or stop activity which is undesirable. The use of alcohol or other **drugs** increases risk.

Eroticism and Danger. For many people a touch of danger enhances a sexual encounter, and there are those for whom sex without danger is uninteresting. One may rationally decide that the enjoyment an activity offers makes its possible negative consequences acceptable. Some behaviors have such a high risk, however, that they must be considered self-destructive, and may indicate the need for **psychotherapy**; these include unsafe sex with partners not checked for disease, public or semi-public sex without concern for possible legal consequences, and exposing oneself to assault from unstable partners (e.g., rough **trade**). It is possible, though, to incorporate limited and controlled danger in sexual activities. The presence of a caring and vigilant third party reduces risks. Some semi-public sex involves only minimal risk, and for willing partners to enact fantasies of danger— a pretended assault and rape, for example— can be very enjoyable.

BIBLIOGRAPHY. Pat Califia, ed., *The Lesbian S/M Safety Manual*, Denver: Lace, 1988; Richard Locke, *In the Heat of Passion: How to Have Hotter, Safer Sex*, San Francisco: Leyland, 1987.

Daniel Eisenberg

SAIKAKU, IHARA (1642–1693)

Japanese novelist. The novels and short stories of Ihara Saikaku rank among the masterpieces of the literature of **Japan**. His work is a product of the urban townsman class that developed in the cities of Kyoto, Osaka, and Edo (modern Tokyo) in the early decades of the Tokugawa period (1603–1868). Saikaku was known for most of his life as a poet of comic linked verse, but in the last decade of his life he turned to writing prose fiction. One of his favorite topics was male homosexual love, which in his day always took the form of a relationship between an adult man and a teenage boy. In *The Great Mirror of Male Love* (1687), his longest collection of short stories, Saikaku divided his discussion of boy love into two parts: the non-professional love exemplified in relations between **samurai** men and boys; and the love of professional actor/prostitutes in the kabuki theatre. He establishes a romantic ideal for boy love in his own townsman class based on the loyalty and self-sacrifice of samurai man–boy relations. Saikaku takes a deliberately misogynistic stance in the book in order to dramatize the single-minded dedication demanded of male lovers, but the stance is full of irony and may have had humorous appeal for his readers.

In addition to *The Great Mirror of Male Love*, Saikaku treated the topic of male love in the story of "Gengobei, The Mountain of Love," the last of five stories in *Five Women Who Loved Love* (1685). The heroine of the story, Oman, manages to seduce Gengobei, a confirmed lover of boys, by dressing as a handsome youth. By the time Gengobei realizes the error, it is too late, for he has fallen madly in love. The humor of the discovery scene must have appealed greatly to Saikaku's readers. In *The Man Who Loved Love* (1682), the hero, Yonosuke, is a man of insatiable sexual appetites, meant obviously to be understood as a plebeian version of the courtly lover Prince Genji in the *Tale of Genji*. At the end of Yonosuke's life of love, he numbers over 3,000 women and almost 900 men and boys among his lovers. One story tells how Yonosuke as a young boy surprised and confused a samurai by aggressively attempting to seduce him, a reversal of the normal pattern. The story implies that Yonosuke was ultimately successful.

Saikaku dealt with female homosexuality only once in his writing, and only briefly, in a scene in *Life of an Amorous Woman*. The book is a parody of Buddhist confessional literature from the fourteenth century, and records the tale of the heroine's progress through respectable married life, high-class courtesanship, low-class harlotry, further degradation, and ultimately spiritual enlightenment. At one point in her checkered career, she took work as a housemaid. The mistress of the house was impressed with her beauty and summoned her to her bed. The heroine is shocked to discover that the woman wants to make love to her, but cannot protest. After a night of love-making, the scene concludes with the woman's comment, "When I am reborn in the next world, I will be a man. Then I shall be free to do what really gives me pleasure!"

BIBLIOGRAPHY. Robert Lyons Danly, *In the Shade of Spring Leaves*, New Haven: Yale University Press, 1981; Howard Hibbett, *The Floating World in Japanese Fiction*, London: Oxford University Press, 1959.

Paul Gordon Schalow

SAILORS
See **Seafaring**.

SAINT-PAVIN, DENIS SANGUIN DE (1595–1670)

French poet and libertine writer. The son of a counselor in the Parlement, he studied with the Jesuits and thought of becoming a priest, but soon renounced this career and lived without a profession as writer, poet, and freethinker. In his lifetime he enjoyed the title of "The King of Sodom" and made no bones about his sexual interests in his poetry. Unlike such contemporaries as Théophile de **Viau**, he was more a sensualist than a philosopher—and therefore less of a threat to the Church and its orthodoxy. Too indecent for the press, his poems circulated only in manuscript, and it was not until 1911 that a French scholar named Frédéric Lachèvre ventured to publish some of the least offensive; others still await their editor. Lachèvre had the naïveté to deny Saint-Pavin's homosexuality, claiming that it was a literary pose, a mere imitation of

Martial, an expression of displeasure at the frivolity of the opposite sex which he inwardly loved, or simply a wish to scandalize the conventionally minded. The poet seems in fact to have preferred the active role in anal intercourse, and—when he had sexual relations with women at all—to have practiced this only, so that he indignantly rejected the imputation that he had fathered the child of a woman of whom he had carnal knowledge. His interest in women was limited to those whose **androgyny** awakened the genuine attraction which he felt for the male sex.

His poems express a fondness for pages and their costumes, and in particular for a youth who is named "Tireis"—who later entered a monastery, inspiring the poet to allude to the pederastic practices of the monks by claiming that "in the same place he can find both his salvation and his pleasures!" Saint-Pavin evidently had contact with contemporary lesbian circles, as he wrote verses likening women's fondness for their own sex to his male–male attachments. In his imitations of Martial he defended homosexual love against the accusation of being "unnatural." Intimate with the homosexual cliques of his day, he revealed his inner thoughts in verses addressed to their members with a frankness that anticipated no censure or incomprehension. With the great Condé he was on such familiar ground that he could send him a poem declaring that "**Caesar** was as a great a *bougre* as you, but not so great a general." He was in modern terms a self-proclaimed homosexual who made no secret of his identity, even in an age when death at the stake was not a wholly remote possibility for one of that persuasion. The publication of his complete corpus will shed much light on the homosexual subculture of France in the mid-seventeenth century and on the antecedents of the Enlightenment.

BIBLIOGRAPHY. Maurice Lever, *Les bûchers de Sodome*, Paris: Fayard, 1985; Numa Praetorius (pseudonym of Eugen Wilhelm), "Ein homosexueller Dichter des 17. Jahrhunderts: Saint-Pavin, der 'König von Sodom,'" *Zeitschrift für Sexualwissenschaft*, 5 (1918) 261–71.
Warren Johansson

SAMURAI

The samurai class developed in **Japan** from what were originally soldiers who served courtiers and great aristocratic families in defending and managing their country estates, which in some cases were far from the capital in Kyoto, during the Heian period (794–1185). By the end of the Heian period, the soldiers had in many cases usurped their employer's landholdings and carved out large territories where they ruled by the sword. During military campaigns, soldiers were accompanied by boy attendants who saw that their physical needs were met. From this probably followed the tradition of man–boy bonding that seems to have been a feature of samurai life almost from its inception.

The Ashikaga shoguns, who ruled Japan's heartland from the fourteenth to sixteenth centuries, seem to have brought the homosexual ethos of the samurai to the seat of power in Kyoto from which they ruled, for there was a marked "homosexualization" of court culture during this period, particularly in the aesthetics of the Noh theatre. When Francis Xavier and the Jesuits came to Japan in the sixteenth century to proselytize, they were horrified by the openness with which homosexuality was practiced among the ruling samurai class and condemned it furiously, apparently with little effect.

Homosexual love was a major component of samurai sexuality right up until the samurai class was abolished in the early years of the Meiji period (1868–1912), after which it was deliberately suppressed by the Meiji government as part of its effort to modernize Japan. The novelist **Mishima** (1925–1970) sought to revive samurai traditions in order to revitalize Japan spiritually, and respect for the homosexual bond was apparently part of the revitalization he envisioned.

BIBLIOGRAPHY. Caryl Ann Callahan, trans., *Tales of Samurai Honor*, Tokyo: Monumenta Nipponica, 1981; Edward Carpenter, "The Samurai of Japan and their Ideal," in *Intermediate Types Among Primitive Folk*, reprint, New York: Arno Press, 1975, pp. 137–60; E. Powys Mathers, trans., *Comrade Loves of the Samurai*, Rutland, VT: Tuttle, 1972.

Paul Gordon Schalow

SAN FRANCISCO

It may seem surprising that for the first hundred years after its incorporation in 1850 as a city of the new State of California, San Francisco (population ca. 700,000) was not particularly noted as a homosexual center. Certainly, as in the case of other cosmopolitan port cities such as **Boston** and **New Orleans**, gayness was not absent. With the rise of the modern homosexual rights **movement** in the 1960s, however, San Francisco assumed a paramount status, highlighting the triumphs as well as the setbacks of homosexual affirmation in the United States

Early History. San Francisco began as a Spanish settlement in 1776 as Yerba Buena, passed into Mexican hands in 1821, and was conquered by the United States and renamed in 1846. The Gold Rush days of 1848–49 brought prosperity to the city—and a typically Western disproportion of numbers of men and women. The red-light district was the Barbary Coast, but thus far little information has come to light on specifically homosexual activities there (the catastrophic 1906 earthquake and fire destroyed many records from earlier days). The more genteel atmosphere of the century's later decades, with the presence of gay people in the arts, is subtly evoked in Charles Warren Stoddard's novel *For the Pleasure of His Company: An Affair of the Misty City* (1903).

After the turn of the century, travelers reported the availability of servicemen for sexual purposes (the Presidio was a major army center). Henry Hay, who later was to start the American homosexual movement, enrolled in Stanford University in 1930. He recalls being helped to come out by his visits to friendly speakeasies in the city. Joe Finocchio's establishment featured drag entertainment; after the repeal of prohibition it moved to new quarters at 506 Broadway, becoming the city's premiere nightspot and gathering place for homosexuals. Such female impersonators as Rae Bourbon, Walter Hart, and Lucian Phelps played an important role as focal points of the gay identity at that time. Finocchio's location in the North Beach area, a Bohemian redoubt, was also important, and the neighborhood later became noted for its **beat** population.

World War II and After. During the war San Francisco was the chief port of embarkation for the Pacific Theatre of War. While awaiting their orders or returning from battle many American servicemen and -women from less sophisticated regions had their first taste of some sexual freedom. After being mustered out, a certain number of gay men and lesbians decided to settle in the Bay City, where they often became involved in a coupled situation, rather than return to their home towns.

Understandably, then, shortly after the American homosexual rights movement began in Los Angeles it spread to San Francisco. In January 1955, the *Mattachine Review* began to appear, patiently watched over by Hal Call, the guiding spirit of the San Francisco chapter of the **Mattachine** Society. At the end of the year, eight Bay Area women formed the Daughters of **Bilitis**, which became the national organization with its own monthly, *The Ladder*. Two of the founders, Phyllis Lyon and Del Martin, remained significant figures in San Francisco into the eighties.

Gay-baiting charges lodged by an unscrupulous candidate in the 1959 mayoral election introduced a phase of unprecedented public discussion of homosexuality. Public talk about a hitherto taboo subject, including revelation of police payoffs, in turn engendered a backlash in which the police arrested large numbers of gay men and lesbians in sweeps in the bars. Gay organizations, including the Society for Individual Rights (SIR) and the Tavern Guild, found an unexpected source of support in sympathetic members of the clergy, who formed the Council on Religion and the Homosexual in 1964. The gay leaders and church people combined to monitor and eventually stem the homophobic backlash.

Maturity. Although San Francisco's gay community was well advanced in many respects by the late sixties, New York's **Stonewall Rebellion** of 1969, coming in the wake of the Civil Rights movement and the anti-Vietnam War movement, represented a national watershed which can also be used to divide historical periods in San Francisco. Attention in the mainstream media was reinforced by the brash input of new "underground" **Counterculture** publications such as the *Berkeley Barb*, as well by a series of newspapers written by and for homosexuals. In the late 1970s San Francisco alone boasted four gay newspapers. Under the direction of Winston Leyland the journal *Gay Sunshine* turned into a major gay press, issuing books of all kinds. In the scholarly realm Professor John De Cecco established a center for the study of sexuality at San Francisco State University, where he edited a research tool of great prestige, the *Journal of Homosexuality*.

Three neighborhoods emerged as gay zones. Polk Street gulch was the oldest and most traditional of these. Eventually it was surpassed by the Castro, with its stereotypical **clone** type. Finally, Folsom Street became the center for those committed to, or dabbling in, the leather and S/M subculture. Backrooms and glory hole establishments for **impersonal sex** proliferated, and the income generated by tourists soared. Yet old-line politicians continued to deplore San Francisco's reputation as "Sodom by the Bay."

For their part gay men and lesbians had not neglected politics, but this realm was galvanized and transformed by the energies of an outsider from New York, Harvey **Milk** (1930–1978), who owned a shop on Castro Street. To the dismay of the city's established gay leaders, Milk forged an improbable but solid alliance with the city's blue-collar unions. His methods were often amateurish, sometimes even unethical, but they worked, and he was elected Supervisor on his third try in 1977.

Triumph turned to tragedy when Milk was murdered a year later, together with Mayor George Moscone, by a resentful former colleague and police officer, Dan White. When a jury acquitted White of the most serious charges after an inept prosecution, widespread riots erupted in the vicinity of City Hall, and some gay activists were seen setting fire to police cars. Milk was replaced by Harry Britt, another gay officeholder, and the lesson dawned on the city's straight establishment that gay power had come to stay.

After 1981 the **AIDS** crisis hit San Francisco particularly hard, but new organizations and coalitions arose to cope with the medical emergency. A prolonged controversy led to the closing of San Francisco's gay bathhouses. Even without these events, some dimming of the exuberance and sheer craziness of the 1970s was probably inevitable. Despite bickering, however, San Francisco's gay infrastructure held firm and seemed destined to remain a major part of the city's life.

BIBLIOGRAPHY. John D'Emilio, "Gay Politics, Gay Community: San Francisco's Experience," *Socialist Review*, 55 (1981), 77–104.

Ward Houser

SANTAYANA, GEORGE (1863–1952)

American poet and philosopher. Born in Madrid, he came to the United States at the age of nine. He graduated from Harvard College *summa cum laude* in the class of 1886. From 1889 he taught philosophy at Harvard, and in 1907 was appointed professor there. In 1912 he retired and spent the remainder of his life abroad, mainly in France and Italy.

Having had to learn English at the age of nine, Santayana had a firm command of the literary language, but not the spontaneity in diction that marks the true poet in his mother tongue. His verse diction was a pastiche of **Shakespeare**, Shelley, Keats, and **Tennyson**, together with Victorian translations of the classics. The poetic outcome was sentimental, insincere, and abstract. As a philosopher Santayana was unoriginal in logic, taking his ideas from **Plato** and Leibniz. He rebelled against the tradition of American **philosophy** with its Calvinist background, which made the philosopher the moral guide of the community, a clergyman without a church. Santayana created no school of philosophy, though he was appreciated by his pupils at Harvard; he was an excellent lecturer, his voice even and melodious, his diction perfect, his whole manner aristocratic.

The content of his philosophy was that reality has different levels that cannot be forced into a comprehensive, universally valid scheme. For the purpose of giving his thought a realistic basis, he located that particular form of reality at the material level, but claimed that vital, spiritual, and ideal entities have qualitative traits of their own and cannot be reduced to material elements. The material realm of facts is wholly independent of the ideal realm of essences, as well as of their specific modes of apprehension. Beauty is a pure essence, whose contemplation cancels out the struggle for existence and forms the noblest and happiest human experience. Human reason is unable to penetrate intuitively into the regions of existence beyond the senses, but from this skeptical position Santayana developed a pragmatic attitude which he judged one of "common sense," one that accepts the possibilities and limits that its material origin imposes upon the human mind. Human institutions are tokens of the progress of the human spirit that is realized thanks to the growth of consciousness, from the primitive forms of human experience to its highest stages, a growth that is based in human nature itself.

In a genteel society where all sexuality was suspect, Santayana frankly preferred homosexuality to heterosexuality. He referred scornfully to the outcome of heterosexuality as "breeding," while studiously maintaining a façade of coldness and detachment that hid his true feelings from a scornful world. His first love was a Harvard undergraduate named Ward Thoron, seventeen, and three years younger than himself. All his love poems, beginning with a sonnet to Thoron, betray an origin in genuine homosexual emotion usually veiled in Christian imagery and allusion, or by the convenient fiction that the love object belonged to the opposite sex. He later admitted that he must have been homosexual in his Harvard days, like A. E. **Housman**, although he was "unconscious of it at the time." This may simply mean that the new concept of homosexuality, which reached the general public only after 1886, did not become part of his self-definition until later. Certainly no one of his urbanity and familiarity with the Greek and Roman classics could have been ignorant of the pederastic moods of the ancient world. Writing of this at the age of twenty-four, he asserted that paiderasteia "has been often preferred by impartial judges, like the ancients and orientals, yet our prejudices against are so strong that it hardly comes under the possibilities for us." Later he could speak of the profound irrationality of love in terms that reflect his homosexual experience. Outsiders like Charles W. Eliot, the President of Harvard, suspected the abnormality of Santayana's character, though they veiled their criticisms in disapproval of his "unworldliness." His gradual withdrawal and then departure from a still puritanic America was an immersion in a warm humanity and Old World wisdom that American culture and simple prudence both forbade. His novel *The Last Puritan* (1935) has a character who is washed out of midshipmen's training school in the Royal Navy for being implicated in a homosexual scandal aboard ship. Today Santayana's reputation has considerably faded, yet he retains interest as a homosexual academic philosopher who after inner struggle against the intolerance of the American society in which he lived, then sought a more congenial atmosphere in the urbanity of the Old World.

BIBLIOGRAPHY. John McCormick, *George Santayana: A Biography*, New York: Paragon House, 1988.

Warren Johansson

SAPPHO
(CA. 612–CA. 560 B.C.)

Classical Greek poet. Celebrated in antiquity as the "tenth Muse," Psappha, as she styled herself in the Aeolic dialect, was born at Eresus on the island of Lesbos, or according to others, in Mytilene. The daughter of Scamandronymus, she had three brothers, one of whom, Larichus, was appointed cupbearer in the prytaneum of Mytilene because of his remarkable beauty. Political struggles on Lesbos forced Sappho into exile in **Sicily**, but in time she returned to her homeland and there became mistress of a school for daughters of the aristocracy that achieved such fame as to attract pupils from distant parts of the Hellenic world of the early sixth century B.C.

To understand Sappho's life and creative personality is especially difficult for the modern reader because of the enormous cultural distance that separates the milieu in which she loved and immortalized her love in poetry from that of the lesbian of today. In antiquity, and perhaps in all of historic time, she ranks as the outstanding singer of woman's love for her own sex, but this was expressed as an age-asymmetrical relationship that exactly paralleled the *paidon eros*, the love of a man for an adolescent boy. It was not an unconventional, bohemian passion, but was inspired by the *eros paidagogikos*, the attachment of the teacher for the protégé. And so far from being reproved by religion, the affection was consecrated to Aphrodite, the goddess of love.

Sappho's poetry, edited by the Alexandrian scholars in nine books, has survived only in fragments, some preserved in quotations in later authors, some recovered on papyri buried for two thousand years in the Egyptian sands. It is an intensely personal lyric poetry, saturated with the unutterable happiness of love and also the unbearable pain of rejection. Of all her girls the dearest was Atthis, and even from the imperfect remains of her poetry the love of the woman for the girl emerges with crystal splendor. Out of the anguish of her heart the poet invokes Aphrodite to float down from heaven and relieve her sorrow. Sappho was drawn to her pupils when they were barely emerging from girlhood, when the hour of their betrothal and marriage was still far distant. When they had outgrown this stage in their lives and were on the threshold of womanhood, Sappho composed epithalamia. Assembled in the ninth and last book of her poems, they symbolize her acquiescence in their passage to a new life as mistresses of aristocratic households. A whole set of poems is devoted to the theme of her resignation to the loss of her beloved pupil, her *eromene*.

Lesbian love played the same role in Sappho's circle as did Dorian *paiderasteia* in Sparta. It was the younger partner's first experience with love, and a step in her initiation to womanhood through intimacy with an older member of her own sex, but also a stage that she would leave behind when she passed on to her adult role as wife and mother. The circle of girls with their headmistress and lover formed a *thiasos*, a cultic union that recited the myths which had already received concrete form in the Homeric poems and performed rites in honor of their divine patroness. The mythical is the collective, the shared element of Sappho's poetry and the counterpoise to her individual outpourings of emotion.

Even if Sappho's poetry comes at a comparatively early stage of Greek literary history, it stems ultimately from a long tradition in the Aegean and Near Eastern worlds. The artistic perfection of her writing was made possible by thousands of years of poetic composition in Akkadian, Egyptian, and other languages in which men had sung the beauty of women. In the annals of civilization Sappho stands almost midway between the absolute beginning and the modern era, and the legacy of the past brought her craft to its peak of greatness.

Posterity has dealt ambiguously with Sappho's life and work. Leaving aside the dishonesty and hypocrisy of later critics under the influence of the **Judeo-Christian tradition**, comic authors of antiquity, who in a manner incomprehensible to moderns equated the woman attracted to her own sex with one who takes the aggressive role in relations with men, had Sappho marry Cercylas (from *cercos*, "penis") of Andros ("the city of men"), and invented the story that she committed suicide when rejected by Phaon, the man whose love she craved, by leaping into the sea, a literal interpretation of the metaphor "to spring from the Leucadian rock into the sea," meaning to purify the soul of passions. Generations of classical scholars abused these bits of ancient wit to construct the preposterous image of a heterosexual Sappho whose unconventional love was a legend fabricated by slander or even by misogyny, and their falsehoods continue to be parroted in standard reference works.

For the more discerning, Sappho's poetry has been a perennial inspiration to literary creation. The Latin poets, who could read the entire corpus of her work, often imitated it. The frankly homoerotic component of her poems ultimately, in the nineteenth century, made "lesbian" the designation for a woman enamored of her own sex, and Magnus **Hirschfeld** appropriately entitled his first pamphlet (1896) on the homosexual question *Sappho and Socrates*.

The significance of Sappho's legacy for the modern lesbian movement is another issue. To identify the Lesbian writer's korophilic affection for her schoolgirls with the love of two adult women for each other is as misleading as to equate Greek pederasty with modern androphile homosexuality. The one and the other throve in a cultural context that belonged to their time and place—not that of the resurgent homophile **movement** of the twentieth century. But to disavow the heritage of ancient **Greece** is impossible, because it is one of the wellsprings of Western civilization, and every one of its values is a latent value capable of being revived and reinstituted, even if in a different form. A creative figure of Hellenic and Mediterranean civilization, Sappho gave lesbian love its classic literary expression, and her work is an enduring part of the poetic treasure of humanity.

BIBLIOGRAPHY. Bruno Gentili, "La veneranda Saffo," *Quaderni Urbinati*, 2 (1966), 37–62; Giannes Kordatos, *He Sappho kai hoi koinonikoi agones ste Lesbo* [Sappho and the Social Struggles on Lesbos], second ed., Athens: Epikaroteta, 1974; Hans Licht, *Sexual Life in Ancient Greece*, London: Routledge & Kegan Paul, 1932; Reinhold Merkelbach, "Sappho und ihr Kreis," *Philologus*, 101 (1957), 1–29.

Evelyn Gettone

SARTRE, JEAN-PAUL (1905–1980)

French philosopher, novelist, playwright, essayist, and political activist. Sartre, who enjoyed a life-long partnership with Simone de Beauvoir (herself a major contributor to modern feminism), never had a homosexual experience, as far as is known. Yet as the dominant figure in

French intellectual life in the third quarter of the century, his thoughtful attitude toward the phenomenon, in combination with his sympathy for other marginalized groups, helped to prepare the way for the flourishing of France's gay community after 1968.

Sartre's understanding of homosexuality, like his perception of the situation of women, evolved slowly. His early story "Childhoood of a Leader" (1938) portrays a spoiled upper-class boy who is seduced in preparatory school by an older student, and then joins a parafascist organization by way of compensation. Although not directly homophobic, this presentation did tend to lend some support to the theory (reflected also in Alberto Moravia's *The Conformist*) that there is a link between early homosexual experience and right-wing commitment: the **fascist perversion**. Included in the play *No Exit* (1944) is an articulate lesbian, Inès Serrano. In Sartre's novel sequence *Les chemins de la liberté* (1945–49), the homosexual character Daniel shows a fascination with militarism and fascism: he welcomes the German occupation.

His one major nonfiction study of a minority, *Anti-Semite and Jew* (1946), offers a number of interesting perspectives; in fact, inasmuch as it views the Jews as fundamentally defined by the environing hostility of society, his analysis may be (mutatis mutandis) better applicable to homosexuals than to its ostensible subject. However, Sartre's major involvement with homosexual questions arose from his association with Jean **Genet**, to whom he had been introduced by Jean **Cocteau**. Sartre's project of writing a preface to one of his friend's works grew into a sprawling 600-page book (*Saint-Genet: comédien et martyr*, 1952), in which the philosopher discusses issues of freedom and self-understanding from an existentialist standpoint. Genet's atypical experience, as foundling, thief, and worshipper at the shrine of the dominant male, may have skewed Sartre's view of an identity in which he had no immediate personal stake.

In 1971 Sartre assumed, at some risk to himself, responsibility for publishing the manifesto of the Front Homosexuel d'Action Révolutionnaire, a radical gay-**liberation** group. Nine years later he gave an interview to two French gay journalists. In the colloquy he acknowledged that some key characters in his work, such as Mathieu in *Chemins de la liberté* and Roquentin in *Nausée*, were uncertain of their masculinity, an uncertainty that corresponded to the writer's own sense of self. He likened becoming homosexual to becoming a writer as two creative responses to otherwise intolerable pressure. As regards the status of homosexuals in France in 1980 ("this prudish society"), he held that they should renounce the hope of blending in and remain aloof, seeking "a kind of free space, where they can come together among themselves, as in the United States, for example."

BIBLIOGRAPHY. Annie Cohen-Solal, *Sartre: A Life*, New York: Pantheon, 1987; Jean Le Bitoux and Gilles Barbedette, "Jean-Paul Sartre: The Final Interview," *The Christopher Street Reader*, New York: Coward-McCann, 1983, pp. 238–44.

Ward Houser

SATIATION THEORY

The traditional critique of luxury holds that indulgence in one vice, even a relatively mild one, sets the tyro on a path toward ever more serious involvement. In the modern language of addiction, one develops a tolerance to the intake of the entry-level stage, causing one to increase the dose, to which one then develops a new tolerance, and so on. For writers of nineteenth-century popular medical tracts, **masturbation** was the first step toward ruin; the practiced pervert, in this view, always began by laying "violent hands" on himself.

In the **Old Testament**, Ezekiel 16:49 links the sodomites with other forms of luxurious indulgence. This notion has a current folk version which maintains that older men and women turn to same-sex relations when they can no longer experience the pleasures of "normal" love or have supposedly become impotent with the opposite sex. Such a view was sustained in the otherwise remarkably tolerant remarks of the philosopher Arthur **Schopenhauer**. The common belief, which has little foundation, that prostitutes are often lesbian in their own preferences is ascribed to the fact that they have had too many men. Oddly enough, this notion of homosexual **orientation** as the outcome of surfeit and repletion is the mirror opposite of the **psychoanalytic** claim that homosexuality is a type of arrested development. For critics, the appetite governing same-sex love is always too little or too much, but never "just right."

There seems to be little empirical support for this folk view. Some people do change their sexual orientation, but usually for other reasons than satiation with their previous mode of erotic fulfillment. They may be responding more fully to feelings that they have always had, but have been suppressing; or they may wish to explore a side of their nature that has been neglected through lack of opportunity. But such a shift is rarely undertaken out of a mere sense of "jadedness." It is possible that for some individuals **sado-masochistic** practices have the function of restoring interest in sexual pleasures that have become too anodyne.

Wayne R. Dynes

SAUNAS
See Bathhouses.

SCANDINAVIA, MEDIEVAL
In this article Scandinavia has the extended sense that includes not only the three European countries of Norway, **Sweden**, **Denmark**, but also Iceland. The extant sources for the history of homosexuality in the Scandinavia of the Middle Ages, which is to say the period just before the introduction of Latin **Christianity** (about the year 1000) and the three centuries following, record no positive attitudes toward the phenomenon. There are no accounts of comradely love, of fidelity and heroism on the battlefield, of institutionalized pederasty such as have been transmitted by the literature of other peoples at a similar stage of cultural development. The textual material that has come down to us—undoubtedly reflecting a process of selection and editing—stigmatizes the passive-effeminate homosexual as slothful, cowardly, and unmanly—as the object of other males' sexual aggression and humiliation.

Folk Attitudes and Customs. There is no word in Old Norse or in other Germanic languages for what came to be called **sodomy** in Medieval Latin, so that the criminal offense owes its inception to Christian teaching. Yet there was a term *argr* which was broader in its meaning: the Roman writer **Tacitus** in the twelfth chapter of the *Germania* had to paraphrase it in Latin as *ignavos et imbelles et corpore infames*, "slothful and unwarlike and sexually infamous," specifying that such individuals were punished by drowning in a swamp. And in later vernacular sources the word *argr* (with the variant *ragr*) is mentioned alongside *strod̄inn/sord̄inn* and *sannsord̄inn* as one of three *fullrettisord*, "words whose utterance amounts to a capital offense." The man who is the object of such insults has the right to bring whoever uttered them to court or even to assault and kill him so as to avenge his honor. The three latter terms are past participles applied to one who has been used sexually by another male. In the same category of heinousness were insults likening a man to a female animal (*berendi*). The *argr* carried the further stigma of practicing sorcery (*seid̄r*), which was in principle a female art, as the *Ynglinga saga* says, "such *ergi* [*argr* conduct] accompanies this sorcery that it was deemed shameful for men to busy themselves with it;

therefore this art was taught to the priestesses." The disgraceful component of both the sexual and the ritual aspect of *ergi* was the taking of a female **role** by a male; it constituted the behavioral expression of a character type that was held in contempt by a warrior society. Such was the moral judgment of the people of the age of the sagas and even of later times. Conversely, when applied to a woman the feminine of *argr* meant *manngjǫrn*, that is to say, "man-crazy," aggressive in pursuing men, a quality as much despised in a woman as passivity and unmanliness in a man. It should also be mentioned that these customs applied only to free men, just as the laws against rape protected only free women: **slaves** were the property and responsibility of the master, and while sexual intercourse between two free men in which one had to take the passive role was considered shameful, no such feeling seems to have prevailed toward a slave's playing that part. In this respect the attitude of the pagan Scandinavians did not differ significantly from that of the ancient **Greeks** and **Romans**.

A further concept that bears upon this complex of beliefs is *nið*, a form of ridicule or insult that exposes the object to the contempt of the whole community. The laws distinguished between *tungunið* (tongue *nið*) and *trenið* (carving *nið*). The former was the spoken insult; the latter a carving or statue that represented the injured party in a humiliating position, that of the passive party in anal intercourse. The erection of such a statue was a reproach that called for vengeance—hence the proverb "Only a slave retaliates at once, an *argr* never" (*Grettis saga*, chapter 15). By implication the free man defends his honor, but not impetuously, rather in accordance with an Arab proverb that says "He who waits but forty years for revenge is a man of little patience." The feminine behavior of a free man, whether in a sexual or in a magical function, is an act of baseness; and if he is not guilty, he must behave in a manner that will restore his honor. In another saga the carved *nid* takes the form of a pole with a man's head carved at one end and a runic inscription on the shaft which is then thrust into the body of a dead mare—the symbol of the feminine, implying that the abused party has taken the female role in an obscene act. In all these instances the sexual need not be the exclusive object of the reproach, as in Finnish and Estonian the loan word from *argr* is a complete inventory of the traits ascribed to the passive-effeminate homosexual, while in Modern German the word *arg* means simply "bad." A semantic parallel is Medieval Latin *felo/fello*, "evildoer, criminal," stemming from Classical Latin *fellare*, "to perform fellation."

Legal Aspects. The only written law against homosexual behavior from medieval Scandinavia is Chapter 32 of the Norwegian *Gulathinglog*, a part of the new legislation introduced by King Magnus Erlingsson and Archbishop Eysteinn in 1164: "And if two men enjoy the pleasures of the flesh and are accused and convicted thereof, they shall both suffer perpetual outlawry. But if they deny the charge while common report affirms it, let them deny it with the hot iron. And if they are convicted of the charge, the king shall have one-half of their goods and the bishop one-half." This law was the outcome of collusion between the archbishop and Erlingr skakki, the father and guardian of the King. The provision against male homosexual acts was a convenient tool to rid the Church and the state of their enemies and dispossess them of their property, and was probably modeled on a similar provision in the Code of Justinian which prescribed banishment with confiscation of half of their property for those guilty of an "abominable crime with persons of the male sex."

In conclusion, the material of the sagas and law codes from medieval Scandinavia shows that pre-Christian custom and belief severely stigmatized the free man who took the passive role in a homosexual relationship—a role that was equated with cowardliness and want of manhood.

BIBLIOGRAPHY. Kari Ellen Gade, "Homosexuality and Rape of Males in Old Norse Law and Literature," *Scandinavian Studies*, 58 (1986), 124–41; Joaquín Martínez Pizarro, "On *Nið* against Bishops," *Mediaeval Scandinavia*, 11 (1978–79), 149–53; Preben Meulengracht Sørensen, *The Unmanly Man: Concepts of Sexual Defamation in Early Northern Society*, Odense: Odense University Press, 1983; Folke Ström, *Nið, Ergi and Old Norse Moral Attitudes*, London: Published for University College by the Viking Society for Northern Research, 1973.

Warren Johansson

SCHOPENHAUER, ARTHUR (1788–1860)

German philosopher. Through a large inheritance from his father the celebrated misanthrope enjoyed financial independence so that he could devote his life completely to philosophy. Even today Schopenhauer's ethic of compassion possesses great philosophical significance. In the third edition of his magnum opus *The World as Will and Idea*, Schopenhauer analyzed the the phenomenon of "pederasty" in an addendum to Paragraph 44 on the metaphysics of sexual love. At that time (1859), the technical term **homosexuality** had not yet entered scientific discourse. Nonetheless one must proceed from the assumption that in this addendum Schopenhauer was seeking to find the cause of homosexuality from the philosophical standpoint. In a historical survey he showed that homosexuality has occurred at all times and among all the peoples of the globe. From this finding Schopenhauer concluded that homosexuality could not be unnatural, as his great model Immanuel Kant had held. Schopenhauer's teleologically oriented conception of nature therefore had to assume in male homosexual behavior—the only form he discussed—a "stratagem of nature" (in the words of Oskar Eichler).

Referring to **Aristotle** he hypothesized that young men (supposedly boys just past puberty) and likewise men who are too old (the magic boundary is here the age of 54) are not capable of begetting healthy and strong offspring, because their semen is too inferior. As nature is interested in perfecting every species, in men older than 54 "a pederastic tendency gradually and imperceptibly makes its appearance." When he formulated this argument Schopenhauer himself was 71 years old, so that he could have harbored a homosexual tendency for some years. His ethical evaluation of homosexuality is consistent: What is in the interest of nature cannot be bad. Schopenhauer considered only the seduction of minors as problematic, "since the unlawfulness consists in the seduction of the younger and inexperienced partner, who is thereby physically and morally corrupted." Therefore homosexuality as such is not reprehensible, solely the alleged seduction of minors.

Schopenhauer was himself the father of at least two illegitimate children and had many unhappy affairs with women. He passionately admired Lord **Byron** and like him came to the conclusion that women could be considered beautiful only by "the male intellect clouded by the sexual instinct." In intellectual and aesthetic respects Schopenhauer had homosexual preferences. In a letter to his admirer Julius Frauenstadt he stressed that "even their [women's] faces are nothing alongside those of handsome boys." Bryan Magee hypothesizes that the philosopher systematically suppressed his gay tendencies, a view shared by Oskar Eichler and others. Thirty years after the publication of the third edition of *The World as Will and Idea* Oswald Oskar Hartmann adopted Schopenhauer's teleological explanation of homosexuality, suggesting that the first champions of homosexual rights voluntarily followed Schopenhauer's arguments.

BIBLIOGRAPHY. Oskar Eichler, *Die Wurzeln des Frauenhasses bei Arthur Schopenhauer: eine psychanalytische*

Studie, Bonn: Marcus & Weber, 1926; Oswald Oskar Hartmann, *Das Problem der Homosexualität in Lichte der Schopenhauer'schen Philosophie*, Leipzig: Max Spohr, 1897; Bryan Magee, *The Philosophy of Schopenhauer*, Oxford: Oxford University Press, 1983; Udo Schüklenk, "Arthur Schopenhauer und die Schwulen," *Widerspruch: Münchener Zeitschrift für Philosophie*, 16–17 (1989), 100–16.

Udo Schüklenk

SCHUBERT, FRANZ (1797–1828)

Austrian composer. Franz Schubert was the only great Viennese composer native to the city. While he did not enrich every department of music with a masterpiece, he did create supreme works in orchestral, piano, and chamber music, but above all in song, where he is preeminent because his rich vein of melody and expressive harmony reached the heart of the text as no one before him had done.

Schubert was the son of a Catholic schoolmaster descended from Moravian peasant stock. From an early age he displayed oustanding musical gifts, effortlessly outstripping his father, his elder brother, and his teacher, the organist at the parish church of Liechtental. Toward the end of 1808 he was accepted as a choirboy in the imperial court chapel, and simultaneously as a scholar in the Imperial and Royal City College. Here he impressed everyone with his musical gifts, and he was accorded the privilege of leaving the building for his lessons with Antonio Salieri, the friend of Haydn and rival of Mozart.

From 1810 onward Schubert began to compose music, and in 1811 he attended his first opera. His first settings of Schiller date from this period. Too short for the army, and with poor vision, he was rejected by the military authorities, and by the autumn of 1814 he was teaching at his father's school, but he felt the irksome duties of the classroom as an insuperable barrier between him and the freedom to compose. But 1815 was one of his most productive years in sheer volume: in one year he composed 145 songs with a tremendous range. He also became acquainted with Franz von Schober, a wealthy and cultured young law student who urged him to abandon teaching and devote himself to composition. This he did only at the end of the following year, after his first commissioned work had been performed. In time, after another depressing stint as schoolmaster, Schubert was appointed music master to the children of Count Johann Esterhazy at Zseliz in Hungary, but there he was bored and unappreciated, and longed only for the stimulus of life in the capital, to which he returned in November 1818.

Here he encountered new friends and new patrons, and there is circumstantial evidence that he gravitated to the Viennese *bohème* of the Metternich era, where he became the central figure in a coterie of homosexual and bisexual lovers of the arts. Despite continued and enthusiastically received performances of his songs and vocal quartets, he still found publishers reluctant to issue his work. In the autumn of 1822 he composed his eighth, "Unfinished" symphony in B minor, which dwarfed virtually all his compositions until that time. The reason why he did not finish the work is that he had contracted syphilis, and by the spring of 1823 he was dangerously ill. Despite this handicap and a pressing need for money that forced him into a bad deal with his publishers, he continued to compose. He was never able to fulfill his ambition to write a successful opera, but in other musical genres his fame and reputation were growing. He had a circle of friends at whose social gatherings his pieces were performed, and the press outside of Vienna gave him ever more notice. But by 1828 his health had been fatally undermined by the syphilitic infection and by the feverish pace with which he composed in the last eleven months of his life. His death—in the Romantic tradition—at an early age was followed by decades of neglect and oblivion, and only much later was he recognized as one of the great **Austrian** composers.

What is known of Schubert's lifestyle, his bachelorhood, his intense and loving relationships with other men, and manifold accounts of his disorderly sexual conduct—all this points to a homosexual orientation. His biographers have interpreted unflattering references to the sensual side of his nature in contemporary sources as meaning that he frequented prostitutes, but hedonism of this kind was perfectly acceptable in the "Old Vienna" of his day, and the veiled allusions are probably to a far more unconventional form of sexuality. Schubert never achieved a fulfilled love relationship with a woman; his rejection of marriage was deeply rooted, and Schober recalled his friend's desperate and pathological reaction to the suggestion that he take a wife. Contemporaries ascribed this attitude to misogyny, which was the most that the heterosexual society of the nineteenth century could make of some individuals' failure to be magnetized by the opposite sex.

A modern psychoanalytic biographer of Schubert has concluded, from the study of a brief tale written by Schubert in 1822 entitled "My Dream," that the composer's creativity was fully unleashed by his mother's death on May 28, 1812, when he was in mid-adolescence. Within a month his enormous musical productivity began and continued almost without respite until his final illness and death. Self-conscious both as man and as artist, Schubert knew and treasured his distinctive sexual orientation, even if it had to be hidden from the obscurantist Catholic society of official Vienna. A poem of August von **Platen** dated January 31, 1823 proves that a well-defined homosexual subculture existed in the German-speaking world by that time, and in such a milieu Schubert could find comradeship and acceptance, while submitting to the outward conformity of the "quiet years" of Austrian history.

A psychoanalytic interpretation of Schubert's personality has found the clue to his life in the dialectical irony of homosexuality itself. In this view rebellion and submission are two sides of the same coin, as the subject oscillates between a passive, masochistic stance vis-à-vis the father and other male rivals, and competitive aggression against them. Schubert's creativity expresses the rebellious side of the complex, for although the homosexual refusal to be dominated is undermined by the need to propitiate the father and similar authority figures, the rebellion itself is perpetual. The homosexual aestheticism of the Romantic period defended brotherhood—with political overtones—against authority, creativity against submission to routine, beauty against the ravages of time and reality. In such an emotional and cultural setting Schubert lived out a brief but intensely creative life as one of the great composers of the early nineteenth century.

BIBLIOGRAPHY. Maynard Solomon, "Franz Schubert's 'My Dream,'" *American Imago*, 38 (1981), 137–54.
Warren Johansson

SCIENCE

Assessing the contribution of male homosexuals and lesbians to science is complicated by the fact that it is no longer clear what science is. Until the middle of the twentieth century, it was generally accepted that scientific progress occurred through slow incremental accumulation of factual data, a process requiring periodic revision of theories to accord with the data. Through the work of such thinkers as Thomas Kuhn and Karl Popper, however, it has become clear that, examined as a whole, scientific change is discontinuous, even erratic and willful, and often guided by external and contingent factors. These factors include the overall world view (not excluding religious components), social and economic determinants, and the whims and idiosyncrasies of individual scientists. In its more extreme versions, the new skepticism discards the ideas of progress and rationality altogether, discerning an almost random succession of paradigms. Thus Paul Feyerabend, the gadfly of the field, has commended a Dada concept of science, in which "anything goes." It is not necessary to subscribe to this extreme view to acknowledge that as a result of ongoing reexamination the boundaries between science, on the one hand, and ideology on the other, are blurred. In a recent American educational controversy, for example, most scholars hold that the so-called "creation science"—which seeks to reaffirm the traditional picture of the origin of the cosmos given in the book of Genesis—is mistaken, but they seem unable to offer a conclusive argument as to why this is so.

At the end of the nineteenth century when the homosexual rights **movement** began in the optimistic climate of Wilhelmine **Germany**, it was confidently held that the emancipation of homosexuals would be achieved by the spread of "science." Increase of knowledge, erected on objective, incontrovertible foundations, would inevitably sweep away lingering "medieval" sources of bigotry and discrimination. The cataclysmic political developments of the twentieth century eroded these high expectations in every sphere. This more sober mood is fortunate, because the impact of the natural and social sciences in the first half of the twentieth century on homosexuality was decidedly mixed. Some fair-minded scientists helped to refute older stereotypes, it is true, but other researchers addressed themselves to schemes for the eradication of homosexuality through social engineering.

Antiquity. It is generally acknowledged that the emergence of critical rationalism in ancient **Greece** in the sixth century B.C. was the prerequisite for all subsequent scientific progress. This historic breakthrough depended on earlier advances in ancient **Mesopotamia** and **Egypt**, which pioneered in many areas of technology and scientific measurement. The birth of the critical rationalism of the pre-Socratics did not occur in a social vacuum: the absence of a powerful priesthood and of a central despotic government created zones of freedom in which independent thinkers could flourish. The sixth century also saw the emergence to full historical view of the institution of **pederasty**, the love of an older man for a youth. The Greeks regarded pederasty as itself a contribution to civilization. Hence the belief that, like scientific discoveries themselves, it had an **"inventor,"** **Orpheus** and Laius being the two leading candidates.

Unfortunately, the life records of the pre-Socratics are too scanty to permit much conjecture about the dynamics of sexuality in their personalities. However, the writings of **Plato** and Xenophon indicate that **Socrates**, who has become synonymous with the very spirit of Greek inquiry, was a joyous pederast, who reached some of his most important conclusions in colloquy with a bevy of handsome disciples. In later Greek **philosophy** there is some indication that doctrines were transmitted from one generation to the next by being imparted by an older master to a beloved pupil. **Aristotle**, and after him, the Greek medical writers, attempted to determine biological mechanisms that might determine same-sex preference.

Greek science continued during the Hellenistic age, but declined under the Romans. It is probably not accidental that it revived again among the Arabs, under whose rule pederasty flourished almost as strongly as it had among the Greeks.

The Renaissance Tradition. It was largely from the Arabs that Western Europe of the **Renaissance** received its knowlege of Greek science. In **Florence** (dubbed both the New Athens and the New Sodom) the humanist Marsilio **Ficino** (1433–1499) championed **Neoplatonism**, together with hermeticism and **astrology**. From the modern point of view these last two elements might be thought of as anti-scientific. Yet recent research has established that the boundaries between science and the occult were often fluid, and hermetic ideas played a major role in the scientific revolution in the seventeenth century.

By common consent the most comprehensive Renaissance genius was **Leonardo** da Vinci (1452–1519), scientist, engineer, military expert, writer, painter, sculptor, and architect. The accusation of sodomy that was lodged against him in 1476 seems to have reinforced impressions derived from early life to make Leonardo both reclusive and self-reflective. Apart from the quality of his inventions—he designed a bicycle and a parachute, as well as perfecting the use of chiaroscuro in painting—the enigma of Leonardo's personality has continued to fascinate.

The English Renaissance found its own universal genius in the person of Sir Francis **Bacon** (1561–1626), the creator of the *Novum Organum* and inspiration of the Royal Society. Holding that those who have wives and children give hostages to fortune, he was known for his partiality to handsome youths. Other English scientists who may have been homophile are Sir Isaac Newton (1642–1727), Edmund Halley (1656–1742), and Robert Boyle (1627–1691). In France, René Descartes (1565–1650) was author of the *Discourse on Method*, and thereby the pioneer of modern rationalism. In his last years he was tutor to the bisexual Queen **Christina** of Sweden. Descartes composed some letters to her which have been interpreted as discreet advocacy of freedom of sexual orientation. In America the bachelor Benjamin **Banneker** (1731–1806) was probably the first notable black scientist.

Modern Times. The great explorer, geologist, and ethnographer Alexander von **Humboldt** (1769–1859) received his formation in the Berlin of Frederick the Great. Often accompanied by handsome young men on his travels, Humboldt left his fortune to a servant who was also his favorite. Other notable explorers who were homosexual were the Canadian David Thompson (1770–1857) and the Russian Nikolai Mikhailovich **Przhevalsky** (1839–1888). The sexuality of Sir Richard **Burton** remains obscure, but he certainly used his observations to making notable contributions to the study of same-sex behavior in the tropics (his "**Sotadic Zone**").

In the twentieth century the inventors Nikola **Tesla** and Wilbur and Orville Wright may have been homophile. Study of the psychobiography of scientists is just beginning, and we may expect further breakthroughs. Two cases are of particular interest. The Austro-English philosopher Ludwig **Wittgenstein** (1889–1951), who had been trained as an engineer, was given to furtive homosexual encounters with men he met in parks. Enigmatic and ascetic in his personal life, he was largely successful in concealing his secret, which his executors tried also to keep, fearing that its revelation would damage his standing as a philosopher. The obstacles placed in the effort to open the door to this aspect of the creativity of one of the twentieth century's most influential figures constitute a revealing and all-too-typical instance of the difficulties of this kind of biographical inquiry. Much better documented is the case of one of the founders of computer science, the Englishman Alan **Turing** (1912–1954). Apprehended by the police, Turing was forced to be injected with hormones which resulted in chemical castration. He died of cyanide poisoning.

It is often asked, with wonder or disdain according to taste, why so many artists, poets, and painters, so many actors, dancers, and musicians, have been homophile. In the face of the massive evidence, however, it tends to be assumed that there is some nexus between creativity in the arts and same-sex orientation. Inasmuch as the "scientific personality" counts as the opposite of the artistic one, stereotypical thinking assumes that science is a pursuit somehow inherently "normal." The relative paucity of famous homosexual scientists probably stems from the fact that one does not have much information on the affective lives of investigators of natural phenomena, because such aspects are thought irrelevant to the "objectivity" of science. Yet, as indicated at the outset, the older picture of science as a seamless web of dispassionate inquiry is yielding to a more nuanced picture, in which science draws closer to the arts. As this newer approach takes hold, one may expect to learn more about the emotional commitments of individual scientists and the way in which these commitments in turn interacted with their creativity and the larger world in which they live.

Richard Dey

SCIENCE FICTION

Although the definition of "science fiction" has eluded any real consensus either inside or outside the field, for present purposes science fiction will be treated as a literary (and lately, cinematic, television, and musical) genre which either speculates on life in the future (or "alternative universes" of the present or past) or in which the extrapolated or speculated effects of advances (or declines) in science and technology are important elements to the story. With this definition the article excludes the major genres of fantasy and horror.

General Considerations. Sometimes called "speculative fiction," "sf" (as it is commonly referred to) is a genre of the modern age of science, though some would trace its roots back to such "fantasy travel" writers as the second-century (A.D.) Greek **Lucian**, whose *True History* takes him to a homosexual kingdom on the moon. A wider circle of opinion credits Mary W. Shelley's *Frankenstein* (1818) with being the first sf work, showing a genuine concern for the effects of science on humanity. Jules Verne (1828–1905) and H. G. Wells (1866–1946) are other oft-cited founders of the genre.

As a self-conscious body of literature, sf arose in the Anglo-American world in the 1920s and 1930s, when it found a vehicle for short stories in pulp magazines and an audience among male adolescents. As such sf "predictions" as the atomic bomb became reality in the 1940s, the genre became increasingly respectable, developed an adult readership, and became able to economically sustain book-length works by talented writers. This expansion continued at a slow but steady pace into the 1960s, when an explosion of interest in space travel (accompanying the moon landing program) and science in general raised interest in sf to the point where it became a major part of popular culture, generating films of mainstream circulation (such as *2001: A Space Odyssey*), television series (such as "Star Trek"), and scholarly scrutiny. Today it is one of the most popular genres of fiction in the English-speaking world, has spread to many other languages (notably Russian), and is the subject of hundreds of academic courses. Sf also boasts a highly organized and very vocal fandom constituting what almost amounts to a subculture in itself.

By its nature, sf tends to posit alternatives to contemporary societies, their assumptions, and their mores, while remaining rooted in the cultures of its writers and readers. It should not be surprising, then, that sf has on the one hand dealt imaginatively with issues of sexuality, sexism, and sexual **orientation**, portraying contemporary assumptions about these topics as time-and-culture-limited rather than universal, and on the other hand has had its share both of invisibility for non-heterosexual characters and of homophobic stereotypes. Since the 1970s, the former tendency has become dominant, aided by a good number of acknowledged gay, lesbian, or bisexual writers; it is not too much to say that in the 1980s, homophobia is no longer considered "good form" in sf.

Historical Development. During the "pulp period," sexuality in general was largely neglected, the subject not being considered suitable for adolescent literature, and the magazine editors serving as effective censors. As the demographics of the readership broadened, it became possible to include characters who were more or less undisguised homosexuals, but these, in accordance with the attitudes of the times, tended to be villains: evil, demented, or effeminate stereotypes. The most popular role for the homosexual was as a **decadent** slaveholding lordling whose corrupt tyranny was doomed to be overthrown by the young male heterosexual hero. Lesbians for good or bad remained nearly invisible.

It fell to Theodore Sturgeon, one of the most noted sf writers of the 1950s, to provide the first positive portrayal of homosexuals in a 1953 story "The World Well Lost," published in the June issue of *Universe*. Coming at the height of the homophobic hysteria of the **McCarthyite** period, this story featured a pair of homosexual-androgynous aliens who, exiled from their homeworld, arrive on earth. At first their gender remains unknown and Earth's population fawns on them, dubbing them "lovebirds," but when the truth is discovered they are sent back where they would face execution. In the end, however, the pair is rescued by a spaceman who is a closet homosexual. This landmark story is typical sf in criticizing contemporary mores (here, homophobia) while undermining the threat to the reader (and the current censors) by recasting the protagonists as aliens.

A step backwards to homophobic attitudes was Charles Beaumont's 1955 story "The Crooked Man," a *Playboy* piece which inaugurated a long line of stories in which homosexuality is portrayed as the social norm for one reason or another. Sturgeon came back in 1957 with "Affair with a Green Monkey," examining social stereotyping of homosexuals (again with an alien as the subject).

By 1960 Pyramid was ready to publish the book-length *Venus Plus X*, in which Sturgeon posits a one-gender society; the homophobic attitudes of a heterosexual male brought into this society are unfavorably depicted.

There matters rested until 1967, when Samuel R. Delany, a black gay writer and winner of four Nebula Awards and one Hugo Award, started playing with alternative sexuality in his Ace novel *The Einstein Intersection* (using semi-alien, semi-human hermaphrodites) and the Nebula-winning short story "Aye, and Gomorrah," which posits the development of neutered human "spacers" and then depicts the "frelks"—people who become sexually oriented toward the spacers. In this work the concept of sexual orientation is examined with the desired distance attained by imagining a new one.

Delany followed this in November, 1968, with the dazzling Hugo- and Nebula-winning short story, "Time Considered as a Helix of Semi-precious Stones." This picaresque tour de force featured two human males, H. C. E. and the teenage sexually masochistic singer Hawk, who are still friends after having once been intimates.

Enter Ursula K. Le Guin, a mildly feminist writer, who in 1969 startled the sf world with her Ace-published novel *The Left Hand of Darkness*. This book, which won both major awards and quickly gained the stature of an all-time classic of the genre, broke all previous molds in depicting a planet whose people are sexually neuter most of the time, but who randomly turn male or female for a few days each month.

After Le Guin's searching examination of sex roles and orientations, the field was wide open for further exploration; the coming of the "gay liberation" period starting with the 1969 **Stonewall Rebellion** led to a relative flood of works looking at unconventional sexualities.

It remained only for Delany to break the last barrier, depicting homosexual lovemaking on the part of his bisexual male hero, the Kid, in his 1975 Bantam novel, *Dhalgren*.

In the cinema, where science fiction has been flourishing commercially since at least 1969, the absence of homosexuality has been nearly complete. *Logan's Run* (1976), depicting a future city in which homosexuality is casually accepted, stands out as an exception.

Authors. A number of the most prominent writers working in the field of sf have been publicly identified as gay, lesbian, or bisexual. Two of these, William S. Burroughs and Gore Vidal, made their reputations in mainstream literature but have contributed important novels to the genre, such as Burroughs' *The Wild Boys* (1971) and Vidal's *Kalki* (1978). Writers working primarily in sf who have reached the very top of their field include Marion Zimmer Bradley (b. 1930, prolific author of the Darkover series of novels and also a frequent contributor to gay and lesbian periodicals), Samuel R. Delany (b. 1942 in Harlem, author of the Neverÿon series and a frequent writer on gay themes), and Joanna Russ (b. 1937, a radical lesbian feminist and occasional contributor to lesbian and gay journals). Edgar Pangborn (1909–1976) wrote a number of widely read works and consistently dealt with same-sex love. Less well known are Nikos A. Diaman, the Englishman Henry Fitzgerald Heard, Elizabeth A. Lynn, Tom Reamy, Sally M. Gearhart, and (in this field) the Frenchwoman Monique Wittig.

There is also a body of gay male **pornography** with sf settings; authors in this area include Felix Falkon, Dave Garrett, Peter Harnes, Peter Hughes, Rex Montgomery, Charles Platt, and the more widely known Larry Townsend.

Novels of Interest. A large number of sf novels are of substantial gay or lesbian interest. The largest category of these are works in which the hero(ine) or a major protagonist is either homosexual or bisexual, usually males; books of particular interest to women are so noted. These works include Marion Zimmer Bradley's Darkover books *The Heritage of Hastur* (1975) and *The Forbidden Tower* (1977), which link homosexuality to telepathy; William S. Burroughs' characteristic, widely read *The Wild Boys* (1971); the classic sf writer Arthur C. Clarke's *Imperial Earth* (1975), in which the hero brings back from Earth a clone of his lost lover; Joan Cox's *Mindsong* (1979); Delany's hallucinogenic *Dhalgren* (see above); Thomas M. Disch's *On Wings of Song* (1979); Zoe Fairbairns' *Benefits* (1979), a feminist work set in Britain; M. J. Engh's *Arslan* (1976), in which the title character, a modern Alexander the Great, is bisexual and develops a long-lasting affair with a schoolboy; Sally M. Gearhart's *The Wanderground* (1978), a set of feminist stories with a common background; David Gerrold's *The Man Who Folded Himself* (1973), in which the hero uses time travel to make copies of himself which turn out to be ideal lovers; Leo P. Kelley's *Mythmaster* (1973), whose bisexual protagonist opts for heterosexuality; Elizabeth A. Lynn's *A Different Light* (1978), in which another bisexual protagonist opts this time for homosexuality, and *The Dancers of Arun* (1979), which features fraternal incest complicated by telepathy; a set of novels by Michael Moorcock: *The Final Programme* (1968), featuring a bisexual hermaphrodite, *The English Assassin* (1972), whose female characters are lesbian or bisexual, *Breakfast in the Ruins* (1972) about a gay male, and *The Adventures of Una Persson and Catherine Cornelius in the Twentieth Century* (1976), two bisexual lesbians; George Nader's *Chrome* (1978), the first sf novel published by a major house (Putnam) specifically geared for the gay male market; Frederik Pohl's *Gateway* (1977), a Nebula and Hugo winner about a repressed homosexual; Thomas N. Scortia's *Earthwreck!* (1974); popular writer Robert Silverberg's *The Book of Skulls* (1972), in which two of the four heroes are gay; the great sf philosopher Olaf Stapledon's *Odd John* (1936), whose hero goes through a homosexual phase shortly after puberty; best-selling sf writer John Varley's *The Ophiuchi Hotline* (1977), whose heroine is bisexual, and his Gaia series starting with *Titan* (1979) and continuing with *Wizard* (1980) and *Demon* (1984), featuring a pair of women, one bisexual and one lesbian, who become closer and closer lovers as the trilogy progresses; Paul Welles' *Project Lambda* (1979), depicting concentration camps for male homosexuals in a police-state United States; and John Wynne's *The Sighting* (1978), a coming-out story.

Homosexual villains can be found in numerous books; an interested reader might consult Barry Malzberg's *The Sodom and Gomorrah Business* and *Tactics of Conquest* (both 1974), Fred M. Stewart's *Star Child* (1975), or Kate Wilhelm's Hugo-winning *Where Late the Sweet Birds Sang* (1976).

Novels set in worlds which accept homosexuality as a normal and integrated part of the environment, but without a focus on a major character, include John Brunner's multiple award-winning (Hugo, British Science Fiction Award, Prix Apollo) classic *Stand on Zanzibar* (1968); Delany's *Babel-17* (1966) and *Triton* (1976); Marta Randall's *Journey* (1978) and *Dangerous Games* (1980); and John Varley's "Eight Worlds" series of books. The paucity of novels projecting homosexuality as a not-very-remarkable, accepted part of the landscape, is noteworthy; authors seem either to make homosexuality a major element of their story or to omit it altogether.

A significant number of novels posit a world or society in which homosexuality is the only option, there being but one gender present. The feminist vision of a world without males has no doubt inspired several of these; in short-story form they are represented by James Tiptree's (pseudonym of Alice Sheldon) Hugo-winner "Houston, Houston, Do You Read?" (1976), in which a plague has wiped out men and three male astronauts hurled into the future have to deal with the situation. Novels in this category include Suzy M. Charnas' *Motherlines* (1978), in which women have set up societies completely outside of the men's world, the novel containing no male characters; Charles E. Maine's *Alph* (1972), showing a future Earth in which men have been extinct for half a millennium and civil war erupts over a plan to bring back males; Joanna Russ' *The Female Man* (1975), where the all-woman world is called Whileaway; Joan Slonczewski's *Door Into Ocean* (1986), where an all-female race on a water planet must deal with male invaders; the French-woman Monique Wittig's *Les Guerillères* (1969) and *The Lesbian Body* (1973), which posit all-female lesbian societies; her collaboration with Sande Zeig, *Lesbian Peoples* (1976), which does the same in the far future; and Donna J. Young's *Retreat: As It Was!* (1979), which has an entire lesbian galaxy subjected to warfare by an unknown species: men.

All-male environments have been a staple since the pulp days of sf, but these have usually been limited situations such as spaceships rather than entire cultures. Novels which depict entire all-male societies include: A. Bertram Chandler's *False Fatherland* (1968), in which the arrival of a mixed-crew spaceship precipitates a miraculous conversion to heterosexuality; Auctor Ignotus' *AE: The Open Persuader* (1969), in which gay men have set up their own society; and the Italian Virgilio Martini's homophobic *The World Without Women* (1969), where gay men invent a disease which kills off all the females.

Theodore Sturgeon's oft-cited *Venus Plus X* (see above) sets out a single-sex world which is defined as neither male nor female, while Philip Wylie's *The Disappearance* (1951) separates males and females into two parallel worlds, each of a single gender, where homosexuality is adopted out of necessity.

Another large category of stories involves societies in which both sexes are present but homosexuality is either compulsory or socially favored. These works could be written out of an author's desire to hold a satirical mirror up to the homophobia of his culture, but in practice seem to reflect the writer's own **paranoia** about homosexuality. The classic tale of this type was the short story by Charles Beaumont, "The Crooked Man" (see above). In this story, however, the "genuine" homosexuals are cruel and depraved. Novels dealing with this theme include Anthony Burgess' *The Wanting Seed* (1962), in which homosexuality is required for official employment in Britain and violent warfare breaks out between the sexes, while Nature goes on strike: crops fail and animals will not reproduce; Suzy M. Charnas' *Walk to the End of the World* (1974), which sets out an Earth of sexual apartheid and the subjugation of females; the Frenchman Robert Merle's *The Virility Factor* (1974), in which men are hit by a disease which leaves a despotic lesbian tyranny in charge and the remaining men become second-class citizens; Naomi Mitchinson's *Solution Three* (1975), basically an expansion of the Beaumont setting; and Eric Norden's *The Ultimate Solution* (1973), in which homosexuality is the social norm in a Nazi America.

Settings in which sexuality involves more than two genders have been presented in the venerable Isaac Asimov's *The Gods Themselves* (1972), which depicts a three-sexed race, two of whom are more or less male; Samuel R. Delany's seminal *The Einstein Intersection* (1967), also trisexual; and John Varley's Gaia series, in which the native intelligent species undergoes extremely complex patterns in order to reproduce.

A final major category of novels does away with gender distinctions altogether, presenting worlds of androgyny. Ursula Le Guin's *The Left Hand of Darkness* (see above) is the classic of this type. Other novels in this area include the legendary Robert Heinlein's *I Will Fear No Evil* (1970), which puts a man's brain into a woman's body through a transplant operation; Robert Silverberg's *Son of Man* (1971), where the inhabitants of a future Earth can change sex at will; Frederick Turner's *A Double Shadow* (1978), whose hero is a hermaphrodite; and John Varley's "Eight Worlds" series, in which human beings can and do change gender as easily as haircuts.

BIBLIOGRAPHY. Camilia Decarnin, Eric Garber and Lyn Paleo, eds., *Worlds Apart*, Boston: Alyson Publications, 1986; Samuel R. Delany, *The Motion of Light in Water*, New York: Arbor House/ Morrow, 1988; Eric Garber and Lyn Paleo, *Uranian Worlds: A Reader's Guide to Alternative Sexuality in Science Fiction and Fantasy*, Boston: G. K. Hall & Co., 1983.

Stephen Donaldson

SCIENTIFIC-HUMANITARIAN COMMITTEE

The Wissenschaftlich-humanitäre Komitee, the world's first homosexual rights organization, was founded in Berlin on May 14, 1897, the twenty-ninth birthday of Magnus **Hirschfeld** (1868–1935), a physician of Jewish origin who became the leading authority on homosexuality in the first third of the twentieth century. Under the pseudonym of "Dr. Ramien," Hirschfeld had in 1896 published a book entitled *Sappho und Sokrates, oder wie erklärt sich die Liebe der Männer und Frauen zu Personen des eigenen Geschlechts?* (Sappho and Socrates, or How Is the Love of Men and Women for Persons of Their Own Sex to Be Explained?). Moved by the suicide of a young homosexual officer on the eve of a marriage into which his family had pressured him, Hirschfeld went on to create an organization that would campaign for legal toleration and social acceptance for what he called the **third sex**.

Writing in an era when biology and **medicine** uncritically accepted the notion of "inborn traits" of all kinds, Hirschfeld maintained that homosexuals were members of a third sex, an evolutionary **intermediate** (or intergrade) between the male and the female, and he bolstered his thesis with data of all kinds showing that the mean for the homosexual subjects whom he studied by interview and questionnaire fell almost exactly between those for male and female respectively. Accordingly the journal which the Scientific-humanitarian Committee published from 1899 onward was entitled the *Jahrbuch für sexuelle Zwischenstufen mit besonderer Berücksichtigung der Homosexualität* (Annual for Sexual Intergrades with Special Reference to Homosexuality).

Aims and Methods. The first and foremost goal of the committee was legal reform, as following the establishment of the North German Confederation and then of the German Empire, a new penal code was adopted that went into force on the entire territory of the Reich on January 1, 1872. Its **Paragraph 175** made criminal *widernatürliche Unzucht zwischen Mannern* (lewd and unnatural acts between males), with a maximum penalty of five years. The repeal of this paragraph was the main object of the Committee's endeavors during its 36 years of existence. For this purpose it drafted a petition "to the Legislative Bodies of the German Empire" that was ultimately signed by some 6000 Germans prominent in all walks of life. But it also sought to enlighten a public that as yet knew nothing of the literature that had been appearing sporadically in the psychiatric journals since 1869, or of the earlier apologetic writings of Heinrich **Hoessli** and Karl Heinrich **Ulrichs**. By means of pamphlets, public lectures, and later even films, the Committee sought to convince the world that homosexuals were an unjustly persecuted sport of nature, who could not be blamed for their innate and unmodifiable sexual **orientation**. Because they lived in a society that was wholly intolerant of homosexual expression, they had to hide their orientation and their sexual activity, and so were peculiarly exposed to **blackmail** if their true nature came to the knowledge of members of the criminal underworld. As early as January 1898 August Bebel, the leader of the German Social Democratic Party, spoke on the floor of the Reichstag in favor of the petition, while the other parties denounced it in horror. Among the educated elite Hirschfeld's views soon won a large measure of support, but they were totally rejected by the churches and by the conservative jurists of the Wilhelmstrasse engaged in drafting a new criminal code.

The Committee was in practice the world's first center for the study of all aspects of homosexuality. Though ignored by academic scholars, Hirschfeld collected material from various sources on the frequency of homosexual behavior in the population and the psychological profile of the homosexual personality. In 1904 Hirschfeld concluded that 2.2 percent of the population was exclusively homosexual, and that the figure was surprising only because so many of his subjects successfully hid their inclinations from a hostile world. The private lives of his subjects he examined from numerous aspects, in every one of which he found evidence that supported his theory of an innate third sex.

Difficulties and Rivals. As the years passed, the Committee was beset with problems from within and without. Hirschfeld's theories placed undue emphasis on the effeminate male and the viraginous female as the homosexual types *par excellence*, a standpoint that alienated the pederasts who fell into neither category and were often bisexual as well. Benedict **Friedlaender**, an independent scholar, denounced Hirschfeld's views and contrasted them with the Hellenic ideal of man–boy love which was a virile, state-building phenomenon in his *Renaissance des Eros Uranios* (Renaissance of Eros Uranios; 1904). A rival organization, the Gemeinschaft der Eigenen (Community of the Exceptional), was founded in 1902, and adopted as its journal *Der Eigene*, edited by Adolf **Brand**, which had been publishing literary and art work on the subject of **pederasty** since 1898. The incompatibility of the two approaches shows that the umbrella concept of "homosexuality" united biological and psychological phenomena which had only this in common, that they both ran afoul of the Judeo-Christian taboo on same-sex relations; socially and politically they were—and still are—incompatible. The Committee had even anticipated the split by proposing in its petition an age of **consent** of 16 for homosexual relations—which would in effect have excluded the boy-lover from the benefit of law reform.

The other critical juncture in the history of the Committee was the Harden-Eulenburg affair, which began in November 1906 with accusations by Maximilian Harden, a sort of Walter Lippmann of the Second Reich, in his journal *Die Zukunft*, to the effect that two of the Kaiser's intimates, Prince Philipp zu **Eulenberg** and Count Kuno von Moltke, were members of a homosexual clique whose inner sanctum had been penetrated by another of their ilk, the First Secretary of the French Legation in Berlin, Raymond Lecomte, who had then revealed to the Quai d'Orsay that Germany was bluffing during the Morocco crisis of January–April 1906 that ended in a diplomatic victory for his country at Germany's expense. A series of scandalous trials ensued in which Hirschfeld testified as an "expert witness," Harden was victorious, and Eulenburg was disgraced and ruined, spending the last years of life in isolation on his estate. But the whole series of events associated homosexuality with espionage and treason in the eyes of the press and the public, and the Committee's fortunes took a turn for the worse. Interestingly enough, it was the newspapers' use of the term *homosexual* during the Harden-Eulenburg affair that made it a household word and displaced the medical coinages current until then in the specialized literature of the subject.

The reaction to the Committee's endeavors went so far as a proposal for extending the sanctions of Paragraph 175 to women in Paragraph 250 of a draft penal code published late in 1909. This elicited a statement in support of the Committee from the Deutsche Bund für Mutterschutz (German League for the Protection of Motherhood), an organization devoted to the welfare of the unwed mother, whom public opinion in Germany stigmatized almost as cruelly as it did the male homosexual. In this way the various groups advocating reform in the sphere of sexual morality were brought closer together by the moves of the opposition.

Scholarly Achievements. Aided by the experts in various disciplines who had been attracted to the Scientific-Humanitarian Committee, Hirschfeld set about writing a major work that was published in January 1914 under the title *Die Homosexualität des Mannes und des Weibes* (Male and Female Homosexuality). This vast tome summarized everything that had been learned from the literature of the past, and especially of the preceding decade and a half, as well as the 10,000 case histories that Hirschfeld had taken in that time. All its arguments were directed toward proving that homosexuality was inborn and unmodifiable and that the reasoning (including early psychoanalytic writings) in favor of acquired homosexuality was untenable. As a scientifically documented, carefully argued plea for toleration, it remains along with the 23 volumes of the *Jahrbuch* the committee's principal legacy to the later movement.

Later History. World War I interrupted the committee's work, and for a time some of its publications were suppressed by wartime **censorship**. Hirschfeld took a patriotic stance on the pages of the committee's journal, which also carried letters from homosexual servicemen in the field. The end of the Empire and the proclamation of the Republic in November 1918 gave new hope to the committee's aspirations, but the postwar drafts of a new penal code were no more acceptable than the previous ones.

To propagate the Committee's views, a **film** entitled *Anders als die An-*

dern (Different from the Others) was made in 1919 and shown in almost the whole of Germany before it was banned by a revived censorship. It was the first use of the cinema to promote the cause of homosexual liberation, and a second film called *Gesetze der Liebe* was produced in 1927. Under the Weimar Republic the committee carried on extensive propaganda, but by now organizations of a primarily or purely social character far exceeded the committee in membership. The postwar era saw an extensive gay **subculture** thrive in Berlin and other large German cities.

The growing anti-Semitic movement in Germany made Hirschfeld one of its targets. He was assaulted in Munich in 1920 and again in 1921, the second time receiving a fractured skull and being prematurely reported dead. On the other hand, the **Social Democrats** and Communists supported the Committee's demands in the Reichstag, and in 1929, a 15–13 vote of a committee approved the striking of the "homosexual paragraph" from the draft penal code. However, this victory was premature: no action was taken by the Reichstag, and the mounting economic crisis not only made other issues more urgent, but led to the phenomenal rise of the National Socialist German Workers Party (**Nazis**), which despite the presence of some homosexuals in its own ranks denounced the homosexual liberation **movement**, in part because it was identified with such Jewish figures as Hirschfeld and Kurt **Hiller**, who had participated in a coalition of groups seeking reform of various sex laws in Germany and edited its critique of the official draft of the new code.

After the Vienna Congress of the World League for Sexual Reform on a Scientific Basis (1930), Hirschfeld did not return to Germany, fearing for his life at the hands of the Nazis. His collaborators continued the work of the committee, but the growth of the extreme right doomed its efforts. With the appointment of Hitler as Reichschancellor on January 30, 1933 the Committee sought a modus vivendi with the new regime, as did many others who hoped that by adopting a nationalist line they could placate the National Socialists. However, the accession to full power by Hitler and his supporters meant the end of the Committee and the destruction of the Institute for Sexual Science which Hirschfeld had founded in 1918.

Conclusion. Little known except in homosexual circles, the Scientific-Humanitarian Committee was all but forgotten by the end of World War II, but its publications survived in a few learned libraries and private collections. The homophile movement that began in the 1950s perhaps unjustly neglected this brave and pioneering effort to change the prejudice and intolerance of Western society in regard to homosexuality, and future students of the subject are well advised to consider how it conceived its mission and set about fulfilling it. Small as it was, it was the forerunner of the vast international gay rights movement of today.

BIBLIOGRAPHY. John Lauritsen and David Thorstad, *The Early Homosexual Rights Movement (1864–1935)*, New York: Times Change Press, 1974; James D. Steakley, *The Homosexual Emancipation Movement in Germany*, New York: Arno Press, 1975.

Warren Johansson

SCULPTURE
See **Art, Visual; Nude in Art**.

SCYTHIANS
Scythia is the general name given by ancient authors to the whole area extending from the Danube to the frontiers of China. It was occupied by a warlike, nomadic people who came from what is now southern Russia in the first millennium B.C. Before the ninth century B.C. they formed a kingdom in the eastern Crimea, and in the seventh century they invaded Syria, Mesopotamia, and the Balkan peninsula. Though attacked by Darius

I of Persia (512 B.C.) and then by **Alexander the Great** (ca. 325 B.C.), they survived but were driven back to southern Russia, where in the following centuries they were displaced by the related Sarmatians. Russian and Ukrainian scholars of today regard the Scythian culture, known from extensive archeological finds that supplement the scattered references in classical literature, as part of the prehistory of their country.

What links the Scythians with homosexuality is the long debate over the meaning of a Greek passage in Herodotus' *Histories* which, brief as it is, seems to provide evidence for a sexual culture that was widespread in antiquity, though unknown among the Greeks themselves. Herodotus (I, 105) reports the dire consequences of the fact that some stragglers from the Scythian army violated the temple of Aphrodite Urania at Ascalon, on the coast of Palestine. "On such of the Scythians as plundered the temple at Ascalon, and on their posterity for succeeding generations, the goddess inflicted the *theleia nusos* ("feminine disease"). And the Scythians say themselves it is for this cause they suffer the sickness, and moreover that any who visit the Scythian country may see among them what is the condition of those whom the Scythians call *enarees*." Elsewhere (IV, 67) Herodotus credits the *enarees*—he translates the term as *androgynoi*, "men-women"—with a special method of divination which they have from Aphrodite. The **Hippocratic** work *On Airs, Waters and Places*, 22, ascribes the "disease" of the *anarieis*, understood as a form of impotence, to divine retribution, which struck the wealthy in particular. Finally, **Aristotle** in the *Nicomachean Ethics* (VII, 7) speaks of a *malakia*, "effeminacy"—also defined as *to thely*, "the feminine"—that was a hereditary trait of the Scythian kings. Such is the scanty but significant evidence that survives from antiquity.

Julius Rosenbaum, in an omnium gatherum of texts and comments on the sexual life of the ancients entitled *Ges-chichte der Lustseuche im Altertume* (History of the Plague of Lust in Antiquity; 1839), argued that the "feminine disease" meant a proclivity to pederasty. In 1882 the Russian historian Vsevolod Miller opened a new chapter in the discussion by pointing to survivals of Scythian myth and custom among the Ossetians. Subsequently, Georges Dumézil analyzed an Ossetian legend in which the hero Hamyc offends the god of the sea Don Bettyr and is punished by having to endure pregnancy and childbirth. He concluded that Herodotus had confounded two phenomena, a genuine Scythian tradition from the northern coast of the Black Sea and a piece of folk belief associated with the shrine at Ascalon. This city on the eastern shore of the Mediterranean remained pagan (Canaanite) even after the interior of Palestine had been conquered by the invading Israelites, who because they had no navy could not blockade the port and compel its surrender.

The two elements in this tangle of legends deserve closer analysis. The Scythian element is the variety of **shamanism** with symbolic change of sex, including the wearing of women's clothing, a custom associated with the practice of divination among the peoples of the far north of the Eurasian continent and one that reputedly serves to enhance the magical powers of the shaman. In modern times the practice of gender change was studied among the Chukchees of eastern Siberia by the anthropologist Waldemar Bogoras, who emphasized that no physical hermaphroditism was involved, but rather the adoption in full of the clothing, speech, manners and even marital status of a woman. These customs are believed to be remnants of a once-vast Eurasian cultural realm, which may well have embraced the Scythians.

Turning to the Canaanite element identified with Ascalon, this would lie in the indigenous religion of the country, more specifically in the practices forbidden in Deuteronomy 22:5 and 23:18. The latter form part of the profession of the **kadesh** and the *kelebh*, who donned women's clothing and prostituted themselves to male worshippers at the temples of Ishtar/Astarte, of which the oldest, as Herodotus specifically mentions, was the one at Ascalon. The rendering of the word *kadesh* in the Septuagint by *porneuon* and *teliskomenos*, which are glossed in the lexica by terms indicating that these servitors of Ishtar performed both erotic and priestly functions for the devotees of the goddess, suggests that the hierodules of the Canaanite-Phoenician religion were the counterpart of the shamans in the archaic cultures of sub-Arctic Eurasia. This conclusion reinforces what is known from other sources: the *kedeshim* engaged in homosexual activity as part of their religious calling, which provoked the rivalry and hatred of the priests and Levites in ancient Israel. Hence the Greek observers of Palestinian and Eurasian sacrosexual customs were struck by the similarity between them.

Soviet commentators on the passages in Herodotus and the Hippocratic corpus have preferred to stress the purported survival of matriarchal customs: the male who practiced divination had to adopt the gender of a woman in order to exercise a function that had previously belonged only to women. However, it is more consistent with the whole body of ethnographic data on divination and magic to see in the Scythian institution (and its Canaanite analogue) another instance of the peculiar gift for extrasensory perception that is often linked with inversion of gender role and sexual orientation. The religious culture of the Scythians institutionalized this phenomenon in the guise of a shamanism which survived among the remote Ossetians until comparatively recent times, when the mounting influence of Islam and Christianity led to its disappearance.

BIBLIOGRAPHY. M. I. Artamonov, "Antropomorfnye bozhestva v religii skifov" (Anthropomorphic divinities in the religion of the Scythians), *Arkheologicheskii sbornik Gosudarstvennogo Ermitazha*, 2 (1961), 85–87; S. S. Bessonova, *Religioznye predstavleniia skifov* (The Religious Conceptions of the Scythians), Kiev: Naukova dumka, 1983, pp. 56–59; Georges Dumézil, *Romans de Scythie et d'alentour*, Paris: Payot, 1978; W. R. Halliday, "A Note on the *thelea nousos* of the Skythians," *Annual of the British School at Athens*, 17 (1910–11), 95–102; Karl Meuli, "Scythica. 2. Enarees. Schamanentum verwandter Völker," *Hermes*, 70 (1935), 127–37.

Warren Johansson

SEAFARING

As a closed environment usually involving only one gender, maritime life offers objective conditions favoring **situational** homoerotic behavior. Nonetheless, at the present stage of research, documentation remains incomplete. Historical evidence, which comes mainly from western civilization, is generally of two types: on the one hand, the official policies of the maritime authorities, and their enforcement; on the other, **folklore** and oral tradition, most commonly sailor songs or sea shanties.

In addition to shipboard sexuality, there is a long and reasonably well attested history of sexual interaction between seafaring men in port and homosexuals attracted by a certain "sexual mystique" attributed to sailors at large. As a result, seamen and their images have assumed a role in the gay **subculture** out of all proportion to their minuscule presence as permanent members of that subculture.

Naval Policy and Discipline. Although Greco-Roman culture was suffused with same-sex relations, little has been recorded of this activity in a maritime context, probably because it was taken for granted. In a fourth-century text from Athens, **Aeschines** notes that one Timarchus, who had ostensibly gone to the port of Piraeus to learn the barbering trade, had actually prostituted himself to sailors there.

The introduction of Judeo-Christian norms created the presuppositions for a new and problematic attitude, for the taboo on homosexual relations was supposed to apply everywhere. Nonetheless, evidence of enforcement is patchy, probably because shipboard activities were out of sight of land-based guardians of official ideology and **pirates** paid them no heed anyway. In early modern Europe, three nations—the Venetian Republic, the United Provinces (Holland), and England—felt themselves at risk, because their very prosperity depended on seaborne commerce. Sermons and pamphlets warned against the vengeance an angry god would inflict on a nation that tolerated sodomy. Nonetheless, the only evidence of sustained persecution comes from English naval history. During the eighteenth-century wars, heavy punishment with the lash as well as hanging were inflicted for buggery, reaching a peak during the conflict with Napoleon. From 1806 to 1816, 28.6 percent of all executions in the Royal Navy were for buggery. The punishments abated, but the practice evidently did not. Sir Winston Churchill, for a time First Lord of Admiralty, was to remark that the three traditions of the Royal Navy were "rum, sodomy, and the lash." Although homosexual conduct has been decriminalized in the United Kingdom for consenting adults (1967 and after), this liberalization does not apply to the navy or merchant marine, where it remains subject to discipline.

In the United States, a kind of witchhunt was conducted among naval personnel in Newport, Rhode Island, in 1919–21, but this local action had no immediate sequel. Court records of testimony, however, demonstrate the sailors' casual attitudes. Some Navy men and women were discharged in the late stages of World War II as part of a campaign to rid the armed services of "sex perverts." Introduction of women aboard ship has caused some shifts in emphasis. In the USS *Norton Sound* case in Long Beach, California

(1980), women in the ranks were subjected to investigation for both heterosexual and lesbian activity. Naval discharges for "homosexual involvement" are still occasionally handed out today, though courts-martial for sodomy are extremely rare. Since the mid-1970s administrative discharges have usually been characterized as "Honorable," especially if the "involvement" in question was off-ship and off-base. Admitted homosexuals are not eligible for enlistment or commissioning in the United States Navy. Naval policy toward homosexuality has been under attack from the gay and civil liberties **movements** since the 1960s, when less-than-honorable discharges were common.

Attitudes of the Sailor. The custom of speeding work through singing—the sea shanty—probably goes back to the days of oars when keeping an exact beat was critical. Surviving sailor songs, however, go back to the nineteenth and sometimes eighteenth centuries, handed down from generation to generation in uncensored form and eventually written down by folklorists and collectors. These songs provide a quite different viewpoint on shipboard sexuality from that of the official establishment.

The attitude reflected in these songs is one of casual acceptance of sex among the sailors at sea, though homosexual adventures in port are not described. Thus, the Royal Navy sang "Backside rules the Navy,/ backside rules the sea./ If you wanna get some bum [arse],/ better get it from your chum/ 'cause you'll get no bum from me." An American Navy enlisted man's song, "Turalai," celebrated the navy "for buggering whatever it can" and went on to state flatly that from this activity "comparative safety on shipboard/ is enjoyed by the hedgehog alone." Merchant mariners commonly characterized the cabin boys as sexual recipients.

It is interesting to note that the sailor songs frequently accompanied tales of heterosexual adventures in port with woeful endings involving venereal disease and vengeful husbands, but the songs describing sex at sea among themselves are good-humored and without such warnings.

Sailor slang characterized the passive sexual partner on ship as "sea pussy," implying he was a legitimate substitute in the female-deprived circumstances of an ocean voyage. Thus does the proverbial seaman's expression "any port in a storm" find direct physiological outlet.

Sailors in general have long been noted for a relatively casual attitude toward the standards of sexual "morality" held by landlubbers; this relative tolerance also applies to same-gender sexual activity. Most seamen are of the working class and widely share the attitude common among working-class men that only the passive partner's activity is "homosexual" or "unnatural," while the active, insertive partner's role is not stigmatized.

In the American navy (until pay was substantially raised with the end of the draft in the early 1970s), and in less-well-paid navies to this day, male prostitution in port was quite common among enlisted sailors, sometimes for nominal sums as an excuse for a desired sexual contact. The active, "male" role had to be preserved, however. Not infrequently, the poverty-stricken sailor would first earn some money offering himself for fellatio with a homosexual male, then take the money so earned and spend it on a female prostitute.

While it is clear that sailors in general are more tolerant of homosexuality than a cross-section of the land-dwelling population from which they come, the maritime subculture is not immune from the homophobia of that population. Significant numbers of sailors can also be found to endorse the strictly homophobic norms established by naval (if not merchant marine) authorities. While some captains ignore the official policy, and others enforce it only when inescapably brought to their attention, still others have been known to conduct vigorous witchhunting. As with many other matters of shipboard life, the atmosphere with regard to homosexuality can vary enormously from one ship to another.

It should not surprise that significant numbers of young men who prefer the companionship of other males and feel little or no need for females have for centuries gone to sea. Those inclined toward passive roles have often found themselves welcomed by sexually frustrated crewmates, while those inclined toward active roles have found it relatively easy to camouflage themselves as "straight" while practicing the sex they like best.

The Mystique of the Sailor. For the landlubbing civilian, sailors have often had a romantic aura, and for homosexual males this has been supplemented by an uncommonly strong erotic mystique. This mystique is promoted by many sailors, who traditionally pride themselves on their erotic prowess, their experience of sexual variations from all over the world, their revealing skin-tight uniforms, and their abundant sexual energy stored up over weeks or months at sea. Some seamen speculate that the constant vibrations of the powerful engines on ship make them especially horny. Perceived by homosexuals as hypersexual, relatively casual about homosexual contact, and easily plied with inhibition-loosening alcohol, it is no wonder that even apparently heterosexual sailors were sought out and highly prized as sexual partners. The sailors, of course, were usually aware of this and often played up to it, resulting in a curious symbiosis of maritime and homosexual subcultures. In gay slang, sailors are called "seafood," probably reflecting their well-known (if scientifically undocumented) fondness for oral sex, and the men who are particularly drawn to them are called "seafood queens." In major ports, where the interaction of the two subcultures is strong, there are well-known places, times, and means of making contact. In Norfolk, Virginia (headquarters of the U.S.

Atlantic Fleet), for example, there are so many available sailors that many of the "seafood queens" become specialists, adopting one particular ship and its crew or one occupational speciality (such as radarman or boatswain's mate) to the exclusion of others.

Not well known is the fact that a great deal of the motivation for those generally heterosexual sailors who become repeatedly involved with gay men as **trade** is not sexual or financial at all. The young common sailor, generally at the bottom of the shipboard hierarchy and often dismissed with contempt by civilians at large, finds himself treated like royalty, his male ego enhanced, his gripes given sympathetic attention. Instead of taking orders all the time, he finds himself in a position to give them. Instead of the usual sterile environment of cramped shipboard quarters, he gets to relax in a home environment where he can kick back, watch television, and have his every need attended to.

Literary and Artistic Images. The sexual fascination with sailors was often expressed, though sometimes cryptically, in literary works. Major monuments are the sea novels of Herman **Melville**; in *White-Jacket* (1850) the title character declares, "sailors, as a class, entertain the most liberal notions concerning morality . . . or rather, they take their own views of such matters." In 1895 Adolfo Caminha published a novel, *Bom-Crioulo*, offering a frank view of an interracial affair between two Brazilian sailors. Among twentieth-century novels, Jean **Genet's** *Querelle of Brest* (1947) is outstanding for its transposition of the sailor image into the author's own powerful moral universe. In its turn the book was made into a film by the German gay director Rainer Werner **Fassbinder**. The multitalented Jean **Cocteau** offered a dual homage to sailors in poetry and drawings. Christopher Bram's novel *Hold Tight* (1988) portrays the spy-catching career of a sailor in a male **brothel** in New York City during World War II. The American painters Paul Cadmus and

Charles **Demuth** showed sailors on shore leave as the object of the attention of gay men. Depictions of sailors, often emphasizing the characteristic contours of the bell-bottom trousers and the jaunty set of the cap, have been a staple of pornographic drawings, photographs, and films.

Much research remains to be done, especially as regards homosexual behavior among Muslim, Chinese, Japanese, and other non-Western sailors. There can be no doubt, however, that seafaring, with its characteristic appeal to escape from the constraints of land-based civilization, has been a major focus of male homosexual imagination.

BIBLIOGRAPHY. E. Lawrence Gibson, *Get Off My Ship: Ensign Berg v. the U.S. Navy*, New York: Avon, 1978; Arthur N. Gilbert, "Buggery and the British Navy, 1700–1861," *Journal of Social History*, 10 (1977), 72–98; Lawrence R. Murphy, *Perverts by Official Order: The Campaign Against Homosexuals by the United States Navy*, New York: Harrington Park Press, 1988; Jan Oosterhoff, "Sodomy at Sea and at the Cape of Good Hope During the Eighteenth Century," *Journal of Homosexuality*, 16:1/2 (1988), 229–35; Thomas W. Sokolowski, *The Sailor 1930–45: The Image of an American Demigod*, Norfolk, VA: The Chrysler Museum, 1983.

Stephen Donaldson

SELF-ESTEEM

Self-esteem refers to the evaluative dimension of the self-concept: the attitude that an individual adopts and customarily maintains with regard to the self as good or bad. It reflects the extent to which an individual believes the self to be capable, significant, and worthy. Self-esteem thus implies an overall attitude of self-acceptance, self-respect, and self-worth independent of context. Rosenberg notes that "A person with high self-esteem is fundamentally satisfied with the type of person he is" while a person with low self-esteem "lacks respect for himself, considers himself unworthy, inadequate, or otherwise seriously deficient as a person." In many ways, self-esteem is the quintessential individual characteristic for Western society.

Theories Viewing Homosexual Persons as Deficient in Self-Esteem. Traditional psychological and sociological theories frequently view the homosexual person as living a lonely, depressed life, conceiving and despising the self as inferior. This state exists, it is believed, because of longstanding developmental handicaps that the homosexual condition imposes or because of the negative effects that a **homophobic** social world has on one's sense of **identity**. In either case, it appears inevitable and, to some, even justifiable that the homosexual individual will devaluate the self, resulting in self-contempt and a negative self-image.

A plethora of theoretical and empirical work has appeared to explain the purported deficient self-esteem level of the gay and lesbian population. Most theories of gay and lesbian self-esteem focus on the etiological connection between self-evaluation and sexual **orientation**. For example, some **psychoanalytic** theorists attribute to homosexuality, by definition, a wide range of neurotic problems that relate to how an individual evaluates himself or herself. Because of their developmental history, which is purported to be responsible for both the sexual orientation and the negative self-image, homosexual persons have (in this view) serious personality disturbances, engendering feelings of self-inadequacy, sadistic and masochistic behavior, and suicidal gestures.

Varying the theoretical perspective but not the fundamental conclusions, sociological theorists are far less concerned with inner psychological dynamics. Rather, this perspective emphasizes the state of the external world and its subsequent impact on self-evaluation among homosexual persons. Low self-esteem is the result of internalizing negative values and attitudes—the reflected appraisals—of significant others in her or his world during the childhood years, especially those of parents, siblings, and teachers. There is a clear message given to the growing child: sexual minority **youth** often feel bad about themselves, have a poor self-image and low self-esteem and, especially during their teenager years, feel totally alone.

One need not necessarily experience the negative social reactions directly—say, by being harassed by peers or fired from a job; the imagined sense or expectation of negative sanctions can be more powerful than a direct assault on one's self-image. The mass media frequently incorporate anti-homosexual cultural meanings and behaviors; apprehensions of **discrimination** that can emanate from this exposure may have serious repercussions for one's self-image as a gay or lesbian person.

More Balanced Approaches. Empirical studies testing these theoretical assumptions concerning the negative self-esteem felt by gay men and lesbians were first stimulated by Evelyn Hooker's (1957) research with non-pathological homosexual individuals. She concluded that homosexual persons are not necessarily maladjusted individuals filled with self-loathing and low self-esteem who experience difficulty in **functioning**. In a review of subsequent empirical studies that compared the self-esteem level of gay and lesbian subjects with that of heterosexual men and women, Savin-Williams (1990) found that eight of the 16 studies comparing lesbians with heterosexual women found no difference in mean self-esteem level; six, higher scores for lesbians; and two, higher scores for straight women. Eighteen of the 30 studies comparing males reported no difference in self-esteem level; five, higher scores for gay men; and seven, higher scores for straight men.

Empirical research on the self-esteem of gay men and lesbians not only fails to substantiate the theoretical speculations of a number of writers, in the case of **lesbians** the findings tend to contradict the psychological and sociological theorists. Apparently, despite the "developmental handicaps" of growing up alienated and alone within a heterosexual home and an alien society, most gay men and lesbians manage to evolve a healthy and positive self-image in the process of **coming out**.

Research Perspectives. It is not particularly profitable to focus on group differences in self-esteem level between gay and straight subjects. More important are investigations that explore the developmental experiences of those gay and lesbian individuals who maintain a negative self-image in contrast with those who view the self as a positive entity, thus apparently insulating themselves against societal messages to the contrary. If this focus becomes primary, then there is hope that the social sciences will be in a better position to address the fundamental issues of self-esteem among gay men and lesbians. As a result, policies and programs that attempt to assist those gay and lesbian individuals who experience negative self-feelings and self-images will be better informed and thus more effective.

Equally critical is the need to expand the self-esteem literature beyond the evaluative aspect to embrace perceptual and cognitive dimensions of the self. Especially needed are in-depth longitudinal studies that trace the evolving sense of self as a gay or lesbian person from the first moments of cognition in infancy and childhood to full recognition—and acceptance—during maturity.

BIBLIOGRAPHY. Evelyn A. Hooker, "The Adjustment of the Male Overt Homosexual," *Journal of Projective Techniques*, 21 (1957), 17–31; M. Rosenberg, *Conceiving the Self*, New York: Basic Books, 1979; R. C. Savin-Williams, *Gay and Lesbian Youth: Expressions of Identity*, Washington, DC: Hemisphere, 1990; Martin S. Weinberg and Colin J. Williams, *Male Homosexuals: Their Problems and Adaptations*, New York: Oxford University Press, 1974.

Ritch Savin-Williams

SEMIOTICS, GAY

In general usage semiotics denotes a scholarly discipline concerned with the interpretation of signs. Although the roots of the field go back at least to the time of John Locke (1632–1704), semiotics first drew notice from a larger public with the spread of the structuralist vogue in the 1960s and 1970s.

The expression *gay semiotics* has been proposed with the more limited sense of the repertoire of symbols and artifacts displayed on the person to signal one's membership in the homosexual community or some sector of it—in short, tokens of sexual preference or allegiance. Typically, these attributes of nonverbal communication have been chosen so that the meaning is evident to initiates but obscure to outsiders. In this respect gay semiotics recalls the symbolism of **freemasonry**, with the important difference that it is not decreed or regulated from above by some central authority, but disseminated by piecemeal invention from below. Absolute secrecy is not a necessity: in the case of the **lambda** pendant and the **pink triangle** button, the wearer may seek to elicit questions from the curious, which then give the gay person a cue to present his or her explanatory "rap."

Among **sadomasochists**, or those flirting with the idea, keys are worn externally on the right or left to indicate the S or M respectively (though in some circles the laterality may be reversed). A similar function is served by the red handkerchief protruding from the right or left back pocket. Urban **folklore**—assisted by commercially produced cards—maintains that there is a whole range of different hanky colors identifying different preferences, but the suggested guidelines do not seem to be followed very closely. As the key and handkerchief codes have spread to outsiders—a common feature of the diffusion of mass culture—the meaning has become blurred.

In the early 1980s some gay men took to carrying a small teddy bear in their back pocket to indicate their fondness for gentle personalized sex as distinct from what they perceived as the mechanical, unloving, sometimes brutal encounters of the time.

In the late 1980s the immense quilt sponsored by the Names Project and carried out by scores of local projects, all commemorating thousands who died of AIDS, produced a fascinating array of visual iconography. The images of the individual panels were chosen and sewn by surviving friends and relatives. Some panels show emblems of favorite places where the person memorialized had lived; another shows an image—of Moscow—that the deceased had wished to visit; still others carry the insignia of the schools from which the deceased had received degrees. Passionate avocations, such as music and dance, are represented by appropriate symbols, such as a clef, a piano keyboard, or the outline of a tapdancer. The use of sequins and bright, glittering colors reflects characteristic aspects of the gay image. Some have quotations alluding to the interests or the character of the individual commemorated. In terms of the world history of funerary iconography, the symbols are usually "retrospective"—referring to joys and accomplishments during life—rather than "prospective"—directed toward a future life.

BIBLIOGRAPHY. Hal Fischer, *Gay Semiotics: A Photographic Study of Visual Coding Among Gay Men*, San Francisco: NFS Press, 1977; Cindy Ruskin, *The Quilt: Stories from The Names Project*, New York: Pocket Books, 1988.

Wayne R. Dynes

SENSIBILITY

In eighteenth-century English, under the stimulus of the proto-Romantic trend, the word "sensibility" acquired the meaning of "sensitive or ready capacity for emotional response, as distinct from intellect or will; acuteness of feeling," overlaying the earlier sense of "physical response to stimuli." More recently, the word has served to designate dimensions of feeling that are conceived as flourishing in certain groups, such as "feminine sensibility," "artistic sensibility." Although the possibility has often been canvassed, it seems unlikely that there is any single homosexual or lesbian sensibility, or mode of expressing the group's way of looking at the world (which is scarcely unitary among the members of these groups). What may exist, however, are more restricted sensibilities cultivated by certain groups or schools of homosexual writers and artists, as in Bloomsbury or lesbian Paris in the 1920s.

This problem is related to the question of whether homosexual individuals are endowed with a greater creative potential than other people. It might be thought that over the centuries the very stigmatizing of homosexuals and lesbians has fostered the development of inventive ways of dealing with the world. Thus far, however, such a phenomenon seems to have been shown only for certain types of wit, and then for limited periods of time (as in camp). It has not been possible to glean any empirical data supporting the folk belief in special homosexual creativity.

BIBLIOGRAPHY. Jean H. Hagstrum, *Sex and Sensibility*, Chicago: University of Chicago Press, 1980.

SEPARATISM, LESBIAN

In its strongest form, lesbian separatism means social, cultural, and physical separation from all who are not lesbians. As society is now constituted this option is possible only for a very few. Many lesbians who regard themselves as separatists seek to live and work in circumstances that are as far as possible "women's space," without insisting on the absolute exclusion of men. The term "lesbian separatist" is also sometimes used within the gay/lesbian movement for those who do not wish to work with gay men.

The **Amazons**, figures of Greek mythology rather than historical reality, are supposed to have lived in an all-female society, rejecting men and making war upon them. Aristophanes' play *Lysistrata* (411 B.C.) shows Athenian women seceding from their city in a "sex strike," but only temporarily—until the men agree to make peace. Charlotte Perkins Gilman (1860–1935), a pioneering American socialist and feminist, wrote a novel, *Herland* (1915; reprinted 1979), depicting a utopia in Africa populated only by women. In her own life Gilman's closest bonds were with other women, and she transmitted her distillation of the women-centered aspects of the first wave of feminism to the second.

In 1971 the New York group Radicalesbians published an essay, "The Woman Identified Woman," coining an expression that was to have considerable resonance. Discarding the exclusively sexual identification of the word lesbian, the essay proposed to identify the concept with a woman who chooses to place her energies with other women.

Outsiders tend to label lesbian separatists as "women who hate men." In their defense, separatists often say that what they are opposed to are the domineering, aggressive aspects of male behavior, rather than men themselves. They wish to make a clear statement that will set them apart from the ambivalent stance of heterosexual women, even those who profess feminism. Separatists believe that such straight women enter too readily into complicity with the power structure of patriarchy; by continuing to meet the sexual and emotional needs of men, these women give aid and comfort to the enemy.

Some women choose to form communes on "women's land," setting themselves apart from all males, including male children and animals. In so doing they hold that they are creating liberated zones in which their natures can grow unhampered by the dictates of patriarchy. They also affirm their protest against the practices of the society from which they have seceded. This solution, which never attracted large numbers of women, seemed to ebb in the late 1980s in the United States, though it has found advocates in other countries, notably West Germany.

Other women who identify as separatists have remained in physical proximity to men, while making their position known. They feel that, like members of ethnic minorities, they must be free to go anywhere, while remaining themselves. Some gay men, who assert that they are seeking to strengthen the feminine elements of their own personality, are drawn to seek association with lesbian separatists, but they are usually told that they can make their best contribution through educating other men.

Some women have entered lesbian separatism for a number of years as part of a process of personal growth, only to emerge later with a more complex position. This seems to have been the experience of a principal theorist of the movement, Charlotte Bunch, who remains a radical lesbian feminist.

BIBLIOGRAPHY. Charlotte Bunch, *Passionate Politics: Feminist Theory in Action*, New York: St. Martin's Press, 1987; Sarah Lucia Hoagland and Julia Penelope, eds., *For Lesbians Only: A Separatist Anthology*, London: Onlywomen Press, 1988.

Evelyn Gettone

SETTEMBRINI, LUIGI (1813–1876)

Italian patriot and writer. Born in Naples, Settembrini took an active role in the movement for Italian unity. In 1851 the Bourbon regime condemned him as a conspirator, first to death, and then to prison. In 1859 he was helped to escape by his son, who diverted to Ireland the ship that was deporting him and others to America. He became an exile in England and then in Florence, where he continued to write and work for the cause. After the 1860 proclamation of the kingdom of

Italy, he taught in the University of Naples. In 1876 he became a senator of the kingdom of Italy.

Settembrini was the author of the autobiographical *Ricordanze della mia vita* and many other works, including *Lezioni di letteratura italiana* and a translation of the works of **Lucian** of Samosata from the Greek, which is still used.

His homosexual side was first revealed in 1977, with the unexpected publication of a novella, *I neoplatonici*, a homoerotic fantasy set in ancient **Greece**. Written in 1858–59 while he was in prison, just after he completed the Lucian translation, he sent the manuscript to his wife in the guise of a translation of an ancient Greek text. Remaining in his unpublished papers at the time of his death, the text was examined by Benedetto Croce, who counseled against publication.

I neoplatonici is a short work, but one that conveys the author's intimate fantasies. Devoid of any real plot, it follows the experiences of two boys who fall in love with one another and become lovers, concluding with a double (heterosexual) wedding. The story includes descriptions of sexual acts (anal) which have no parallel in Italian literature of Settembrini's time. Although the modest ambitions of the work place it outside the canon of the author's major works, it is nonetheless a dignified and serious text, written in a fresh, lively style, and endowed with a certain elegance.

Also noteworthy is the wholly positive and serene picture presented of homosexual relations. The author deliberately returned to a pre-Christian concept of (homo)sexuality, presenting same-sex love as an element of human life that is capable of giving joy and satisfaction. Moreover, the novella treats the link as both emotional and erotic—a rare accomplishment for the period.

When the book was published a hundred years after the author's death, some hailed it as a "revelation" that Settembrini had homosexual relations while in prison. This suggestion remains a hypothesis, which as yet has no documentary support.

BIBLIOGRAPHY. Luigi Settembrini, *I neoplatonici* (with introductory note by Giorgio Manganelli and preface by Raffaele Cantarella), Milan: Rizzoli, 1977.

Giovanni Dall'Orto

SEXISM

Sexism is the assumption that the members of one sex collectively are superior to those of the other, together with the resultant differentiation practiced against members of the supposed inferior sex, especially by men against women. The term is also used to designate conformity with the traditional **stereotyping** of social roles on the basis of sex (social sex roles).

Conceptual Foundations. Modeled on racism and racist, the terms sexism and sexist do not seem to have been used before the mid 1960s. Unlike racists, some sexist males profess to cherish and admire members of the other sex, with whom they have intimate and family relations. However, such admiration—the "pedestal theory"—is not incompatible with **discrimination**, as when it is held that women must be barred from certain occupations "for their own protection." The purported admiration of women by sexist men is also linked to sexual **objectification**—the reductive vision of women as simply bodies which are the object of lust rather than as full human beings. Although the matter remains controversial, some hold that overarching biological differences require difference of treatment in a few areas between men and women. Pregnancy leave is one example. More problematic is the question of differences in temperament, and even in styles of thought, between women and men. In any event, an increasing body of opinion in Western industrial society holds that women deserve equality of respect, together with full access to positions of economic and political strength.

In the view of many feminists, sexism is rooted in an age-old system of patriarchy, the institution and ideology of male domination. Usually couched in the form of a blanket condemnation, this discourse fails to allow sufficiently for gradations, which may be all-important to the situation of the individual. Because most positions of power are held by men in Sweden as well as Iran, we may conclude that both are subject to patriarchy, yet few would deny that the situation of women today in the first country is far better than in the second.

The spread of the term sexism has fostered the coinage of *ageism*, *classism*, and even *looksism*, alongside the well-established *elitism*. Despite their seeming usefulness, all these terms have the quality of epithets. In the usage of some they reveal a certain smugness, a confidence that "we" are superior to "them." Another term that has had some circulation is *heterosexism*, defined as the assumption that heterosexuality and its institutional forms are the only valid and socially beneficial arrangement, and that heterosexual values must prevail, without modification. Unfortunately, in the political practice of gay advocacy organizations the term tends to be divisive, alienating potential allies in the civil rights struggle who happen to be heterosexual. It ill behooves a group seeking pluralistic tolerance of its values and lifeways to appear to defame those of the majority.

Effects on Lesbians and Gay Men. Be this as it may, a good case can be made for the point that **prejudice** against male homosexuals and lesbians is rooted in the sense that they are not behaving in accordance with the norm appointed for their sex, and that they are in fact inverting this norm. Victorian society and its twentieth-century prolongation had a strong interest in promoting gender-role conformity and in censuring "**sissies**" and "tomboys."

Still, the effects of the practice of sexism are different for lesbians from what they are for gay men. Traditionally, lesbians (who are often not perceived as such) have suffered discrimination as women. This existence of this pattern leads lesbians to make common cause with heterosexual women in the feminist movement. On the other hand, insofar as there are benefits to women from sexist discrimination these benefits may be endangered by the recasting of existing assumptions. Until recently, it has been assumed that, unless she is clearly unfit, the mother should receive custody of the children in divorce cases. Yet the questioning of this piece of traditional wisdom has been one of the legal strategies used, in many cases surely hypocritically, to deny lesbian mothers their children. On the whole, however, lesbians are willing to risk any complications that might ensue from dismantling discrimination against women, which affects them more severely. This is the case with lesbian couples, where both typically have low-paying jobs, as contrasted with heterosexual couples, where the man at least receives the salary which in his profession is deemed adequate for the male head of a household.

Gay men hold that they too are victims of sexism inasmuch as they are regarded as womanish and not deserving of the same privileges as "true men." Yet discrimination in hiring and housing usually takes the form of outright barring of homosexuals; that is to say, a gay man might be refused a job or an apartment that a woman would receive. Conversely, in an all male social club, gay men would be admitted. In both situations gay men and women are not equated. In promotions, however, gay men may be passed over because they are held to be wimpish, unstable, and unfitted for executive jobs. Here their situation approximates to that of women, whose "flightiness" and "susceptibility to emotional moodswings" ostensibly bar them from positions in the upper echelons of business and government. According to some feminists, such complaints on the part of gay men are trivial, inasmuch as gay men benefit qua men from the privileges accorded to a whole **gender** class. However, these benefits are differently apportioned, as the category of race shows, for black men do not benefit (if at all) to the same degree as white men. These are only a few of the complexities involved, and they suggest that, as an analytical tool, "sexism" is rather blunt.

Modern industrial society is undergoing rapid technological and social change, and in the course of this transition it is impossible to foresee what the ultimate arrangements will be. While the discussion of sexism has often been heated and rhetorical, thoughtful observers of social policy must remain indebted to it for raising essential questions of human dignity and power.

BIBLIOGRAPHY. David L. Kirp, Mark G. Yudloff, and Marlene Strong Franks, *Gender Justice*, Chicago: University of Chicago Press, 1986.

Wayne R. Dynes

SEX NEGATIVE, SEX POSITIVE

This polarity owes its inception to Wilhelm **Reich** (1897–1957), who sought to synthesize **Freud** and **Marx** in a style acceptable to the leftist intelligentsia in Central Europe of the 1920s. The basic hypothesis is that some societies accept the inherent value of sexual expression and indeed insist on it as a prerequisite of mental health, while other human groups despise sexuality and are ceaselessly inventive in devising austerities and prohibitions as a means of social control.

Despite its seeming radicalism, the exaltation of "sex positivism" perpetuated the sentimental idealism of some eighteenth-century explorers and ethnographers who contrasted the supposed sexual paradise of the South Seas (for ex-

ample, the Tamoé of the Marquis de **Sade**'s *Aline et Valcour* [1791]) with the ascetic regimes of pre-Enlightenment Europe, in which Catholic and Protestant vied in cultivating stringent codes of sexual morality. In our own day, some homophile writers such as Wainwright Churchill characteristically see ancient **Greece** as a "sex positive" culture because it tolerated and even fostered pederastic relationships among males of the upper classes. The situation of Greek women these writers pass by in silence. Popular authors of books on "the sexual history of mankind" have reveled in depicting the joys of life in temporally and spatially remote but uninhibited societies where the burdens of chastity are unknown and sexual bliss is the lot of one and all. Such golden-age fantasies are part of the the discourse of **utopianism**.

In truth, all cultures regulate sexual behavior in one way or another. No human society allows its members, whatever their age, sex, or social status, to interact sexually with one another without restriction. Indeed, there are not a few in which heterosexual intercourse, even with the full consent of the adult participants, can be punished by ostracism, mutilation, or even death if it involves, say, a liaison between a male of a lower caste and a female of a higher one. Also, the concern with the legitimacy of one's offspring causes the sexual freedom of the nubile or married female to be severely restricted in nearly all cultures, as no society wants a horde of children with no assignable father deposited "on its doorstep."

If the myth of complete sexual freedom, however appealing it may be to critics of Western sexual mores, is unfounded, what factors promoted its acceptance? One is the greater licence accorded by many cultures to the foreigner—the tourist or anthropologist—for a variety of psychological and economic reasons, including the undeniable appeal of the exotic partner and the practical demand in tourist resorts for prostitutes and hustlers to serve the guests, even though similar behavior would not be tolerated in a native village fifteen miles away. Also, the availability of teenaged partners to the foreigner may reflect only the circumstance that children are virtually forced into prostitution by families for whom this form of exploitation is a lucrative source of income. Such a situation has nothing in common with the "sexual freedom" on which the leaders of the sexual reform movement liked to expatiate, it is rather a survival of slavery and feudalism in the Third World. Also, even if certain practices are tolerated, the circle of persons who may engage in them without being repudiated by their families or punished by the civil authority is much narrower than Westerners—furnished with a foreign passport and a source of income from outside the country—can ever be aware. Everywhere wealth and power do impart a degree of freedom to gratify one's sexual desires, including even those tabooed by the larger society, but this is not an egalitarian right, it is a privilege of the elite in a hierarchical, class regime of the kind that the **left** would abolish if it could—at least in theory. The concrete practice of the states in the socialist bloc is another matter. Finally, many cultures have puberty rites that entail exceedingly painful practices such as circumcision, subincision, clitoridectomy ("female circumcision"), tattooing, mutilation, and the like —scarcely the Western ideal of an uninhibited adolescence.

What probably forms a line of demarcation is whether **asceticism** ranks as an ideal of behavior for everyone, or only as a norm for those with a religious vocation that does not affect the rest of the community. Medieval **Christianity** did profess an ascetic ideal that would forever place homosexual activity outside the pale of morality, since it can never serve the end of procreation within lawful marriage, and all other forms of attachment were denied the right of sexual expression.

Other cultures have seen pleasure as a good in itself, quite apart from the procreative aspect, but the pursuit of pleasure, as in the case of the prostitute, could also entail becoming a social outcast with no prospects of conventional marriage. So the freedom of one was purchased at the price of another's degradation or servitude.

All these considerations reveal only how far modern Western civilization is from a solution to the "sexual problem," a solution that must take into account the risk of contracting **sexually transmitted diseases,** the possibility of unwanted pregnancy, and similar misfortunes. Even if a future society adopts a wholly positive attitude toward sexual pleasure, the need to shield both the individual and the collective from the negative consequences of unregulated sexual practice poses a problem that cannot be wished away.

Warren Johansson

SEXUAL LIBERTY AND THE LAW

Sexual liberty has been of particular interest in Anglo-Saxon thought. The reception of the **Enlightenment** from the Continent, from **Beccaria**, Filangieri, the French *philosophes*, and the Code **Napoléon** mandated a reexamination of **common law** traditions that long resisted the wave of criminal law reform.

The ideas of John Stuart Mill (1806–1873) have been enormously influential in this sphere. Perhaps unaware of his father James' friend Jeremy **Bentham's** incisive unpublished treatises arguing for the decriminalization of sodomy, Mill defended individual liberties and in the tradition of the *philosophes* urged minimal state interference with speech and conduct of individuals. Mill's ideas have not gone unchallenged. Champions of traditional **Judeo-Christian** morality, including Sir James Fitzjames Stephen in 1874 and Baron Patrick Devlin in the 1960s, argued that a society that failed to control the morality of individuals would disintegrate.

1183

Hart's Defense of Liberty. In *Law, Liberty and Morality* (1963) Professor Herbert Lionel Adolphus Hart sets forth the best analytical argument against the suppression of victimless sexual offenses: the criminal law itself inflicts suffering by requiring that some persons repress their "anti-social" urges. This is of particular importance in the case of the laws enforcing a sexual morality that may create misery of a special degree. For both the difficulties involved in the repression of sexual impulses and the consequences of repression are quite different from those involved in the abstention from "ordinary crime." The imposition of sexual morality by state power interferes with the personality of the individual far more than do laws simply meant to curb the criminal underworld.

As to the outrage of tradition-minded and religious individuals Hart replied: "For offense to feelings, it may be said, is given not only when immoral activities or their commercial preliminaries are thrust upon unwilling eyewitnesses, but also when those who strongly condemn certain sexual practices as immoral learn that others indulge in them in private." The law can offer no relief to those who experience moral outrage at the thought that others may be engaging in conduct which they deem immoral. "To punish people for causing this form of distress would be tantamount to punishing them simply because others object to what they do; and the only liberty that could coexist with this extension of the utilitarian principle is liberty to do things to which no one seriously objects. Such liberty is plainly quite nugatory." Individual liberty entails the right to engage in conduct which others find objectionable or distasteful; this is inseparable from the very notion—"unless, of course, there are other good grounds for forbidding it. No social order which accords to individual liberty any value" could also confirm the adherents of the Judeo-Christian tradition in the right to live in a society free of behavior which that tradition condemns. They may rightly insist on being protected from public display of such behavior, but not from private.

Rebuttal of Devlin. In reply to Devlin's assertion that a society requires a shared morality, Hart claims that "[t]here seems, however, to be central to Lord Devlin's thought something more interesting, though no more convincing, than the conception of social morality as a seamless web. For he appears to move from the acceptable proposition that *some* shared morality is essential to the existence of any society to the unacceptable proposition" that any change in the moral code of a society is coterminous with its destruction.

Devlin's views evidently reflect the wish to restate the sexual morality of medieval or Reformation **Christianity** in the guise of an abstract concept of morality as tantamount to the loyalty which the citizen owes to the modern state: "It is clear that only this tacit identification of a society with its shared morality supports Lord Devlin's denial that there could be such a thing as private immorality and his comparison of sexual immorality, even when it takes place 'in private,' with treason. No doubt it is true that if deviations from conventional sexual morality are tolerated by the law and come to be known, the conventional morality might change in a permissive direction, though this does not seem to be the case with homosexuality in those European countries where it is not punishable by law." For the Christian moralist, though not the liberal thinker, any departure from a moral code held revealed and immutable is divine lèse-majesté, which a secular state must convert into the notion of "treason" to find an equivalent.

Devlin upholds the view now totally disavowed by reputable historians that "history shows that the loosening of moral bonds is often the first stage of [social] disintegration." This kind of generalization about the dangers of **deca-**

dence filled the moralizing history text-books of past generations, and was even the standard explanation of the fall of **Rome**. Today this **myth** lies buried under the weight of the accumulated mass of anthropological, sociological, historical, and other scholarly evidence and is invoked only by the half-educated when they need a generalization to support their resistance to change—which is an inescapable characteristic of human institutions. Devlin's wish to confer immutability upon the Judeo-Christian condemnation of homosexuality through claiming that morals do not change, only the degree of society's toleration of their violation, amounts to a play on words. The increased toleration is a proof that people's ideas about the validity of the principle have in fact changed, even if religious conservatives who believe in the divine origin of moral norms would like to maintain that having once been "revealed" they cannot change throughout eternity.

Legislation and Public Opinion. Hart next takes up the argument—a serious one when one considers the motives of legislators who must submit their voting records to the approval of their constituents—that the irrational aversion and **disgust** caused by homosexuality justify the retention of penal sanctions: "The conviction that such practices [homosexuality] are morally wrong is surely inseparable in the mind of the majority from instinctive repulsion and the deep feeling that they are 'unnatural.'" Devlin maintained that English law had a standard of its own—the reasonable man, the right-minded man, "the man in the Clapham omnibus"— who should not be obliged to argue why conduct that he instinctively feels to be abominable is abominable. Such thinkers as Kurt **Hiller** in his legal dissertation on *The Right Over One's Self* (1908) and Coenraad van Emde Boas in his thesis on *Shakespeare's Sonnets and the Double Disguise Plays* (1952) had earlier discussed this issue of the subjective response to homosexual behavior ("the vital aversion")

which exists quite independent of anything in the book of Leviticus or in the **canon law** of the Christian church, freely admitting that the barely educated "masses" still shared the medieval beliefs and attitudes, and that only an enlightened minority of intellectuals were actively promoting the new credo of sexual freedom. In this matter Hart seems to retreat into the defense that the minority should be allowed the right to its tolerant views, even if the majority persists in rejecting them.

Intellectual Liberty. The free play of ideas in the marketplace, Hart pointed out, has undermined traditional platitudes: "The real solvent of social morality, as one critic of Lord Devlin has pointed out, [Richard Wollheim, *Crime, Sin, and Mr. Justice Devlin,* p. 40] is not the failure of the law to endorse its restrictions with legal punishment, but free critical discussion. It is this—or the self-criticism which it engenders—that forces apart mere instinctive disgust from moral condemnation. If in our own day the 'overwhelming moral majority' has become divided or hesitant over many issues of sexual morality, the main catalysts have been matters to which the free discussion of sexual morals, in the light of the discoveries of anthropology and psychology, has drawn attention." This amounts to little more than saying that because the sexual reform movement has called the traditional beliefs into question by undermining the complacency with which they were accepted—since this rested in the last analysis on their supposed divine origin—they should no longer be enforced even if the majority still upholds them. Moreover, Hart replicates Mill's and the eighteenth-century liberals' fear of the tyranny of the majority: "It seems fatally easy to believe that loyalty to democratic principles entails acceptance of what may be termed moral populism: the view that the majority have a moral right to dictate how all should live. This is a misunderstanding of democracy which still menaces individual liberty." In other words, if the authoritarian state of the **Middle Ages** had the right to legislate personal morality, it has not bequeathed it to the majority in a modern democratic one, though conservatives may in this case appeal to the tradition-minded majority against the reformers.

Hart summarized: "Whatever other arguments there may be for the enforcement of morality, no one should think even when popular morality is supported by an 'overwhelming majority' or marked by widespread 'intolerance, indignation, and disgust' that loyalty to democratic principles requires him to admit that its imposition on a minority is justified."

Conclusion. Although National Socialist and Communist totalitarians have repressed both religion and sexual freedom, the history of the struggle for homosexual rights within democratic societies has been in some sense a duel between the sexual reform movement on the one hand and the church and its heirs and allies on the other. The latter have been able to win not a few victories at the polls and in the legislatures by appealing to the residue of medieval "intolerance, indignation, and disgust" in the electorate. Gay liberation is confronted with the task of fighting an uphill battle against the defenders of traditional sexual morality, in no small measure because in the English-speaking world classical **liberalism** long shirked its task of reforming criminal laws of sexual offenses.

On the positive side, President Reagan's nominee, Robert Bork, failed to gain confirmation by the Senate to the Supreme Court (1987) in large part because he was regarded as the leading exponent of attempts to legislate morality in the Judeo-Christian tradition of Stephen and Devlin, against the pragmatic tradition of minimizing societal control over the individual embodied in the American Bill of Rights and later amendments, and so eloquently supported by Bentham and Mill in the nineteenth century and Hart in the twentieth. Modifying his views, Devlin himself was later to write in *The Judge* (1979): "It is generally agreed that there was no consensus, probably not even a bare majority, . . . for the reformation of the laws against homosexuality. Nevertheless [the change was made and] has surely helped to promote a more tolerant attitude to homosexuals." He thus conceded that legislative reform could justifiably be enacted in advance of changes in public opinion, and that the effect of such legislation might feed back onto that public opinion in a salutary way.

BIBLIOGRAPHY. Carl F. Cranor, "The Hart–Devlin Debate," *Criminal Justice Ethics*, 2:1 (1983), 59–65; Patrick Devlin, *The Enforcement of Morals*, London: Oxford University Press, 1965; Coenraad van Emde Boas, *Shakespeare's sonnetten en hun verband met de travesti-double spelen: een medisch-psychologische studie*, Amsterdam: Wereld-Bibliothek, 1952; H. L. A. Hart, *Law, Liberty, and Morality* (The Harry Camp Lectures), London: Oxford University Press, 1963; Kurt Hiller, *Das Recht über sich selbst: eine strafrechtsphilosophische Studie*, Heidelberg: Carl Winter, 1908; Richard D. Mohr, *Gays/Justice: A Study of Ethics, Society and Law*, New York: Columbia University Press, 1988; David A. J. Richards, *The Moral Criticism of Law*, Encino, CA: Dickenson Publishing Company, 1977.
William A. Percy and Arthur C. Warner

SEXUALLY TRANSMITTED DISEASES

Sexually transmitted diseases (STDs), also called venereal diseases, are among the most common infectious disorders in the world at the end of the twentieth century. They affect men and women of all backgrounds and economic levels. However, they are most prevalent among teenagers and young adults; nearly one-third of all cases occur in teenaged subjects. Homosexual men suffer disproportionately from STDs, while lesbians are scarcely affected by them, for reasons having to do with the anatomical and physiological differences in their manner of sexual intimacy and greater male promiscuity.

The incidence of STDs in the general population is rising; after World War II young people began to cross the threshold of sexual maturity earlier, becoming sexually active at an earlier age, and having multiple sexual partners. The tendency of homosexual men to engage in promiscuous sexual activity was reinforced by the freedom that came in the liberal 1970s, when much of the illegality and clandestinity attached to the search for partners of the same sex vanished. But the new condition called Acquired Immunodeficiency Syndrome (**AIDS**), first reported in the United States in 1981, struck down thousands of homosexual men until studies of the etiology and transmission identified the specific practices that were responsible for its spread. Since then, the greater number of new cases has shifted to intravenous drug abusers. However, no effective immunizing agent or therapy for the condition had been discovered as of 1989. Lesbians, on the other hand, were no more subject to AIDS than they had been to the classical STDs.

Gonorrhea. The classic venereal disease is gonorrhea, attested since classical antiquity; it was, down to the appearance of AIDS, the most common STD among homosexual men. It is caused by the gonococcus, a bacterium that grows and multiplies rapidly in moist, warm areas of the body such as the urinary tract or the rectum (it does not survive long in the mouth, but can sometimes lodge in the throat), while in women the cervix is the most common site of infection. Gonorrhea is usually localized; however, the disease can spread to the ovaries and fallopian tubes, resulting in pelvic inflammatory disease, which can cause infertility and other serious conditions. The early symptoms of gonorrhea are mild, and some infected individuals display no symptoms of the disease; this is one reason why it is so readily transmitted. Men

infected in the urinary tract usually have a discharge from the penis and a burning sensation during urination that may be severe. Symptoms of rectal infection include discharge, anal itching, and sometimes painful bowel movements. The disease is treated with antibiotics such as penicillin, though there is increasing concern about the emergence of new strains of penicillin-resistant gonorrhea. Regardless of the drug prescribed, the patient should take the full course of medication and then return to the clinic for a follow-up test to determine whether the infection has been completely eliminated. In the 1970s, because of the ease with which gonorrhea could be treated, not a few homosexual men developed a nonchalance about the frequency with which they contracted gonorrhea and an indifference to prophylactic measures, so that the incidence of the disease was far higher than among heterosexuals of the same race and social class.

Syphilis. The disease of syphilis made its appearance in the first stage of the formation of the global metasystem, which is to say, the network of economic and political relations that includes all of the regional subsystems. This initial stage occurred in the years 1480–1520, when the voyages of discovery reshaped the image of the world and laid the foundation for the global economy that was to be created in the following centuries. Although the matter is still disputed by medical historians, the weight of the evidence inclines to the view that syphilis was confined to the Caribbean until the sailors of Columbus brought it back to Spain on their return voyage in 1493. Carried by sailors and soldiers—even today high-risk groups for STDs—syphilis rapidly spread to the other end of the Old World, so that by 1522, when Magellan's ships arrived at the Philippine Islands, it was already known there as "the Frankish [= European] disease."

Syphilis is today readily treated with antibiotics, but if left untreated, in its tertiary stage it can cause mental disorders, blindness, and death. It is caused by a corkscrew-shaped bacterium called *Treponema pallidum*. The systemic infection is acquired by direct contact with the sores of someone who has an active infection. Though usually transmitted through the mucous membranes of the genital area, the mouth, or the anus, the bacterium can also pass through lesions on the skin of other parts of the body. A pregnant woman with syphilis can give the disease to her unborn child, who may be born with serious damage to the central nervous system. Also, in the sixteenth and seventeenth centuries, when the practice of bleeding was common, syphilis was occasionally transmitted by shared cupping glasses, much as AIDS is now contracted by the shared needles of IV-drug users.

Because the early symptoms of syphilis may be quite mild, many people fail to seek treatment when they first become infected. Such untreated carriers can infect others during the primary and secondary stages of the disease, which may last as much as two years. The first symptom of *primary syphilis* is an open sore called a chancre, which can appear from 10 days to 3 months after exposure (usually 2–6 weeks). Ordinarily painless and sometimes even inside the body, the chancre may go unnoticed. It is usually found on the area of the body exposed to the bacteria, such as the penis, the vulva, or the vagina. A chancre may also develop on the cervix, tongue, lips, or fingertips. Within a few weeks it disappears, but the disease continues its progress, and if not treated in the primary stage, may evolve through three further stages.

Secondary syphilis is marked by a skin rash that appears from 2 to 12 weeks after the chancre disappears. The rash may extend to the whole body or be confined to a few areas such as the palms of the hands or the soles of the feet. In these sores active bacteria are present that may spread the infection through contact with the broken skin of the infected party. The rash may be accompanied by influenza-like symptoms such as mild fever, fatigue, headache, sore throat, and patchy hair loss, swollen lymph glands throughout the body, and other disorders. The rash usually heals within several weeks or months, and the other symptoms subside as well. The signs of secondary syphilis occasionally come and go over a period of one to two years; like those of the previous stage, the symptoms of the secondary one may be mild enough to go unnoticed.

If untreated, syphilis lapses into a latent stage during which the patient is no longer contagious. Many individuals who are not treated will suffer no further consequences of the disease. However, 15 percent to 40 percent of those infected go on to develop the complications of late, or tertiary syphilis, in which the bacteria inflict damage on the heart, eyes, brain, nervous system, bones, joints, or almost any other part of the body, sometimes causing paralysis. This stage can run into years or even decades.

There are three ways of diagnosing syphilis: a physician's recognition of its symptoms, microscopic identification of syphilitic bacteria, and blood tests, of which the last are not always reliable, as they can result in false positive results in people with autoimmune disorders or certain viral infections.

Syphilis is treated with penicillin, administered by injection; for patients allergic to penicillin other antibiotics can be used. Twenty-four hours after beginning therapy a carrier of syphilis usually can no longer transmit it. A small number of patients fail to respond to the standard doses of penicillin, so that it is necessary for patients to have periodic repeated blood tests to ascertain that the infectious agent has been completely destroyed and that there is no further trace of the disease in his organism. Proper treatment will cure the disease at any stage, but in late syphilis the damage done to body organs is irreversible.

AIDS. Acquired Immunodeficiency Syndrome made its appearance in the last phase of the formation of the global metasystem—the period after 1960. Somewhat hypothetically, scientists have reconstructed its origins as follows. When the former African colonies were emancipated from the tutelage of the metropolitan countries and a network of commercial air lines was established that brought hitherto remote areas of Central Africa within 36 hours' flying time of the major cities of the globe, a rare condition that had been found in isolated cases in the neighborhood of Lake Victoria began to spread to the United States, Brazil, and Western Europe. Others dispute this theory of African origin.

Individual cases occurred in the United States in the late 1960s and 1970s, but only in 1981 was the condition recognized and named. The majority opinion was that it was caused by a virus (Human Immunodeficiency Virus; HIV) that destroys the body's ability to fight off infection, so that the victim becomes susceptible to many fatal diseases, called opportunistic infections, and to certain forms of cancer, as well as a characteristic malignant form of Kaposi's sarcoma.

At the outset, most victims of the condition in the United States were homosexual men in their late twenties or thirties, though in Central Africa it is principally an affliction of heterosexuals. After some floundering, researchers ascertained that passive **anal** intercourse was at the highest risk in sexual transmission, though many continued to assert that all exchange of bodily fluids must be avoided. Health officials, the media, and gay organizations vigorously promoted "**safe sex**" techniques as a means of avoiding **AIDS**. The gay community voiced urgent demands for more funds for research, therapy, and care for people with AIDS, but an effective cure eluded the best efforts of medical science. Other victims of AIDS were intravenous (IV) drug users, hemophiliacs, and children born to women who had contracted the condition mainly by sharing needles with other IV-drug users. Lesbians remained essentially untouched by the epidemic because of the different techniques which they employed to achieve sexual gratification.

Other STDs. Other sexually transmitted diseases include chlamydial infections, genital herpes, and genital warts. Chlamydial infections are now the commonest of all STDs, with some three to four million new cases occurring each year. They often have no symptoms and are diagnosed only when complications develop. Occurring in both men and women, they are treated with an antibiotic drug such as tetracycline. Genital herpes is a disease primarily of heterosexuals that has remained incurable; the major symptoms are painful blisters or open sores in the genital area. Even though the sores disappear in two or three weeks' time, the virus remains in the body and the lesions may recur. Genital warts are caused by a virus related to the one that causes common skin warts. They are generally treated with a topical drug applied to the skin, or by freezing. If the warts are very large, surgery may be needed to remove them.

Infectious hepatitis, a disorder of the liver, may be transmitted through poor sanitation and infected food. For this reason its additional status as a sexually transmitted disease, was for a long time ignored. Yet it was commonly acquired by gay men, sometimes through oral–anal contact ("rimming"). In fact, until the introduction of a vaccine in the early 1980s, the gay male rate of hepatitis was ten times the United States national average.

Prevention. The danger posed to the gay male community—and to a sexually more permissive society—by STDs has led to the adoption of "safe sex" guidelines for intimacy with casual partners or complete strangers, and to the revival of the condom, a sheath for the penis which was invented in England about 1705. Originally it was made of animal intestine, but now it is usually fashioned of very thin rubber. As a simple, cheap, and largely effective if not aesthetically pleasing device it was used in heterosexual intercourse earlier in this century mainly to prevent conception, but found little application in homosexual pairing since the chance of impregnation was non-existent. In the 1980s this attitude changed, and the gay media paid much attention to condoms. Special models appeared that are claimed to be superior for anal (as distinct from vaginal) penetration, and fear of disease has inspired the use of the sheath even for oral–genital contact. In any event, the sexual abandon that characterized much homosexual life in the 1970s has become fraught with danger, and the adage "An ounce of prevention is worth a pound of cure" has gained renewed meaning.

BIBLIOGRAPHY. King K. Holmes and Per-Anders Mardh, et al., eds., *Sexually Transmitted Diseases*, New York: McGraw-Hill, 1983; M. Laurence Lieberman, *The Sexual Pharmacy: The Complete Guide to Drugs with Sexual Side Effects*, New York: NAL Books, 1988; Pearl Ma and Donald Armstrong, eds., *The Acquired Immune Deficiency Syndrome and Infections of Homosexual Men*, Brooklyn, NY: Yorke Medical Books, 1984; David G. Ostrow, ed., *Sexually Transmitted Diseases in Homosexual Men*, New York: Plenum, 1983.

Warren Johansson

SHAKESPEARE, WILLIAM (1564–1616)

Playwright and poet, often considered to be the greatest writer in the English language. Of tenant farmer stock and the son of a glover, Shakespeare was born in the provincial town of Stratford-upon-Avon in England; however, the very few facts known about his life are derived from various legal documents. In 1582, he married Anne Hathaway, with whom he had three children within the next three years; the following five years are unaccounted for, but by 1594 he was involved in the theatre world in London as both an actor and a playwright. He enjoyed an increasingly successful theatrical career until his retirement in 1612 and his return to Stratford.

With so few substantiated facts about his biography, one can only turn with some reservation to his works for insight into the man. An undisputed master of both poetry and human nature, Shakespeare is the author of some of the most enduring classics in world literature: *Richard III* (1591), *Romeo and Juliet* (1595), *As You Like It* (1599), *Hamlet* (1600), *Twelfth Night* (1601), *Othello* (1604), *King Lear* (1605), *Macbeth* (1606), and *The Tempest* (1611), among his 37 plays. Given the almost complete range of human experience chronicled in these works, one can state little about the author's own character and personality without conjecture.

Shakespeare's prolonged separation from his wife and the stipulation in his will that she inherit his "second best bed" has, however, sparked much debate about his sexuality.

The Plays. A search of the plays reveals little advocacy for homosexuality, if much tolerance and compassion for all types of benign variations of human behavior. While his plays are peopled with many passive and introspective men (such as Hamlet and Richard II) as well as aggressive and independent women (such as Rosalind in *As You Like It* and Beatrice in *Much Ado About Nothing*), no distinctly gay characters are evident. Some critics have singled out the sensuous and seemingly asexual Enobarbus of *Antony and Cleopatra*, the effete fop who incites the aggressively masculine Hotspur in *1 Henry IV*, or the doting and infatuated Sebastian of *Twelfth Night* as prototypes, but such designations are inconclusive.

Historically, however, theatrical companies of Shakespeare's time did not employ women; instead, their roles were played by boys, apprentices to the companies. In adherence to the laws and sympathies of the times, the plays were, therefore, unable to display any overtly sexual behavior, but one of Shakespeare's most frequent plot devices was to have his heroines disguise themselves as boys, particularly in the comedies. Thus, what in reality was a boy pretending to be a woman pretending to be a boy leads to some psychologically acute and complex scenes with homoerotic suggestions, such as the encounters between Rosalind (as **Ganymede**, a name rich in suggestiveness) and Orlando in *As You Like It* and Viola (as Caesario) and Orsino in *Twelfth Night*.

The Sonnets. For more substantive evidence, one must turn instead to Shakespeare's sequence of 154 poems in the form of sonnets, published surreptitiously in 1609 and immediately protested by their author. Probably intended as a personal exercise for private circulation, the sonnets may be the works that reveal something of the man himself; in them, Shakespeare names the persona "Will," an obviously personal and intimate diminution of William, and, as in most of the Renaissance sonnet sequences, their subject is erotic love.

Dedicated to "Mr. W. H.," who has been variously identified as the Earl of Southampton, a boy actor named Willy Hewes, Shakespeare himself (in a misprint of his initials), someone unknown to history, or someone invented, the first 126 are clearly homoerotic, while most of the others concern a woman conventionally called "the Dark Lady." Historically, those scholars who begrudgingly admit to their subject matter try to discount their message. Most claim that the attraction the persona feels for the fair young man is either platonic or unconsummated; others assert that the poems are only examples of the Renaissance male **friendship** tradition. Still others insist on the fallacy of equating the persona with the poet and confusing literature with autobiography.

However, a close reading reveals a genuine emotional bond quite clearly consummated physically, one that grows and develops over a period of time, one threatened by a rival poet as well as the Dark Lady herself, also the mistress of the persona and also in pursuit of Mr. W. H. If not homosexual, the sensibility behind the poems is decidedly **bisexual**, and if not William Shakespeare, "Will" is a voice that speaks with convincing experience. Those who minimize the homoeroticism of the sonnets fail to consider why a heterosexual poet would choose homosexual love and desire as his subject matter. They also fail to give credit to the persona, in Sonnet 121, when he says "I am that I am."

Conclusion. Shakespeare's sexual identity will probably always be speculative, but this in no way diminishes the achievement of a playwright who could sensitively chart the full range of human involvement in a compassionate portrait of human diversity. But without question, Shakespeare is the author of some of the finest lyric poems to describe gay love and passion.

BIBLIOGRAPHY. Alan Bray, *Homosexuality in Renaissance England*, London: Gay Men's Press, 1982; Marilyn French, *Shakespeare's Division of Experience*, New York: Ballantine, 1981; Joseph Pequigney, *Such Is My Love: A Study of Shakespeare's Sonnets*, Chicago: University of Chicago Press, 1985; Samuel Schoenbaum, *William Shakespeare: A Compact Documentary Life*, Oxford: Oxford University Press, 1977.

Rodney Simard

SHAMANISM

In the strict sense, shamanism is a phenomenon of the magical and religious life of Siberia and Central Asia. At its core lies a specific technique of ecstasy of which the shaman alone is the master, specializing in a trance during which his soul is believed to leave his body and either ascend to the heavens or descend to the underworld. The shaman further controls his spirits in the sense that as a human being, he is able to communicate with the dead, with demons, and with nature spirits without becoming their instrument. He is invested with power over fire and enjoys a unique method of healing. Shamans belong to the elect who have access to a region of the sacred that is closed to other members of the community.

Siberia. The connection of homosexuality with shamanism was noted by the classic investigators of the subject. Waldemar Bogoras mentions that, under the influence of a Siberian shaman, a Chukchi lad at sixteen years of age will suddenly relinquish his sex and imagine himself to be a woman. He adopts female dress, lets his hair grow, and devotes himself entirely to female occupations. Disclaiming his sex, he takes a husband into the hut and performs all the work usually incumbent upon the wife. This change of gender **identity** is strongly encouraged by the shamans, who interpret such cases as an injunction of their individual deity. The **gender** shift coincides with entry into shamanhood, and nearly all the shamans are individuals who have left their sex.

There are three degrees of effemination of the male. The lowest grade consists simply in the feminine style of the hairdo. The second is marked by the adoption of female clothing, which can be for shamanistic or therapeutic purposes; it need not entail a complete change of sex. That is the third stage, in which the subject, aided by the spirits, learns all the female handicrafts, begins to speak in a feminine mode, and even acquires the physical weakness and helplessness of a woman. He becomes a woman with the physical appearance of a man. He contracts a marriage with a man which is then solemnized in the usual fashion, and the couple lives together as man and wife, with the "wife" taking the passive role in sexual relations. The shaman also has a special protector among the spirits who functions as a kind of supernatural husband, regarded as the real head of the family who gives orders through the "wife," which the husband is duty-bound to execute. The effeminate shaman is feared by other shamans who have not undergone the change of sex, because he alone has the spirit protector who can avenge any wrong done to his protégé.

In speaking of the Koriaks, Stefan Krasheninnikov refers to men who occupy the position of concubines, comparing them in turn to the "men transformed into women" of the Kamchadale. Every one of the latter is regarded as a magician and interpreter of dreams, wears women's clothes, does women's work, and has the status of a concubine. The homoeroticism of the Koriaks was interpreted by Bogoras and Waldemar Jochelson as an outgrowth of the shamanic, but in turn as a monopoly of the profession of shaman held by the homosexual. In olden times, according to Jochelson, shamans "transformed" into women were not rare among the Koriaks, and were even regarded as the most powerful of their ilk. They entered into marriages with men, or became second wives when a female wife was already present. Professional shamans have guardian spirits who appear to them in the guise of animals or birds, typically as wolves, bears, seagulls, eagles, or lapwings. The future shamans are often nervous youths who suffer from attacks of hysteria during which the spirits order them to devote themselves to shamanism. Those in the process of becoming shamans pass through a stage of fits of wild paroxysm alternating with states of total exhaustion. The phenomenon was declining among the Koriaks early in the twentieth century following their conversion to Russian Orthodoxy.

The Broader Context. Edward **Carpenter** understood the shaman as the precursor of a higher stage of cultural evolution, a variation of the human type that sprang from a variant of the sexual orientation itself, or rather of the germ plasm that underlies that orientation. Such classes of men and women, diverging as they do from the norm of sexuality, become repositories and foci of new kinds of lore and new techniques of control over the world of spirits and divinities feared and adored by the rest of their tribe. The primitive development of the intellectual, as opposed to the purely physical, aspects of culture was first embodied in the shamanistic type, which rejected the customary activities of the hunter and warrior in favor of a sacral occupation. The superstitious belief that the spirits had conferred supernatural powers upon them reinforced their commitment to the profession of trance medium and healer—one exercised by many homosexual men and women in different cultures, even in the high civilizations of later centuries. In the whole process the homosexual-transvestite orientation is primary, the shamanic calling secondary. Shamanism is a distinctive feature of the archaic paleoarctic cultures that has fascinated students of primitive religion, though not all have acknowledged the homoerotic component of the phenomenon.

BIBLIOGRAPHY. Waldemar Bogoras, "The Chukchi of Northeastern Asia," *American Anthropologist*, 3 (1901), 80–108; Edward Carpenter, *Intermediate Types Among Primitive Folk*, London: George Allen & Unwin, 1919; Ferdinand Karsch-Haack, *Das gleichgeschlechtliche Leben der Naturvölker*, Munich: Reinhardt, 1911; Åke Ohlmarks, *Studien zum Problem des Schamanismus*, Lund: C. W. K. Gleerup, 1939.

Warren Johansson

SHAWN, TED (1891–1972)

American dancer and choreographer. Born in Kansas City, Missouri, to a father who was a successful newspaperman and a mother related to the famous Booth family of actors, Shawn at first planned to be a Methodist minister. But while at the University of Denver he contracted diphtheria and the experimental serum that saved his life left him temporarily paralyzed from the waist down. As he began to recover, he turned to therapy, to exercise, and then to **dance**. When he decided upon a dance career, he appraised the potential of his own body and found it incompatible with the demands of ballet, but he surmised that he could infuse the decorativeness and technical polish of the ballet into a contemporary dance style that was still rather trivial. This gave him a new vision of dance in America whose culture was then scarcely receptive to such an innovation, and he devoted his life to realizing it.

His first partner was a dancer named Norma Gould, but she was soon eclipsed in Shawn's life by Ruth St. Denis, a star of the day. They met in 1914, and not long afterwards he proposed to her, although at 22 he was some fourteen years the younger, and despite her objections they were married on August 13. The union was not consummated until some time in October, and then only after she had convinced herself that contraceptive methods would shield her from pregnancy and childbirth, which, she felt, would destroy the beauty of her body. During much of their marriage, however, she was unfaithful to him; he did not disapprove of her conduct on moral grounds but took it as an affront to his vanity.

As a teacher and employer of male dancers he was paternalistic and generous. Shawn paid his dancers higher wages than the union demanded, even during the lean depression years. He sought never to invade the privacy of his boys, or to impose himself on them. He required only that they maintain an unbroken façade of masculinity and never display any sign of effeminacy. He was fighting an uphill battle in the America of the interwar period to prove the manliness of dance. If in his instructional readings he touched upon the Greek ideal of male love, he never tried to convert anyone to homosexuality. He himself was bisexual, and not a few of his male dancers were bisexual or homosexual, but he did not make advances to them. Unlike his wife he was not promiscuous, but sought an enduring relationship with his partners. Had she not been unfaithful to him, he might not have chosen a life of homosexual liaisons despite his own erotic ambivalence.

Together Ted Shawn and Ruth St. Denis founded the Denishawn school, an academy of dance and the related arts with classes in as many dance techniques as they could offer, music, drama, stage, and costume design. It created and propagated an entirely new concept of American dance that was to circle the globe and end America's provincial backwardness in this branch of art. Conversely, their tours of other areas of the world, particularly the Far East, gave their art a cosmopolitan quality. Shawn had the gift of transmuting something that had stimulated him intellectually and spiritually into theatrical terms whose surface sheen even untutored audiences could appreciate. After the Ted Shawn Dance Theater, the first theatre designed especially for dance, opened in 1942, the debuts and premieres acquired national and even international significance. Shawn was thus an American pioneer in the choreographic art, and a major figure in the dance culture of the twentieth century.

BIBLIOGRAPHY. Walter Terry, *Ted Shawn, Father of American Dance*, New York: Dial Press, 1976.

Warren Johansson

SIBERIA
See **Paleo-Siberian Peoples; Shamanism.**

SICILY
Dividing the Mediterranean into eastern and western basins, Sicily, largest of its islands, became pivotal when the Phoenicians opened the West to maritime trade after 1000 B.C.

Antiquity. In the eighth century **Greeks** began colonizing eastern Sicily and southern Italy, to control the straits between the island and the toe of Italy, and to establish farms to which to export their burgeoning population. To control the western passage around the island, their Phoenician rivals colonized Western Sicily, their greatest foundation being Palermo, opposite Carthage, their main African site. Until the Roman conquest in the third century these two great merchant peoples contended for Sicily. Both early introduced **pederasty**; Phoenicians with temple prostitutes (*kelabhim*), eunuchs, and effeminate boys, Greek warriors with young aristocratic athletes.

Greek settlements, beginning with Cumae (ca. 750 B.C.), occurred before the Hellenes institutionalized pederasty about 650 on **Crete**. Shortly afterwards Zaleucus introduced pederasty for the colony at Locri on the toe of Italy. While colonists sometimes all came from one "metropolis" (mother-city), often founders of a single colony came from various old cities. The need for constitutions was imperative and many were written. Zaleucus, the earliest known colonial lawgiver and author of a constitution, composed the laws for Locri using the even then prestigious Cretan models. He was the student of Onomacritus or Thaletas, the Cretan "musicians" (poets–statesmen) who first institutionalized pederasty and may have antedated "Lycurgus," as the reformers at **Sparta** who introduced the Eunomia ("good order") institutionalizing pederasty on Cretan models styled themselves. Whether Zaleucus antedated the Spartan reform institutionalizing pederasty or not, it soon spread to all the Greek poleis of Sicily and Magna Grecia and to all other western outposts of Hellenism, including Massilia (the modern Marseilles; founded ca. 600), where it did not shock the **Celts** who practiced their own version of it. Too little is known about the sexual practices of Sicels and Siculs, the aboriginal Sicilians, to form a judgment of their attitudes toward pederasty before the arrival of Greeks and Phoenicians.

Frequent interchange of population and travel fostered a common Hellenic civilization with only local variations, but Sicilian Greeks, partly because of the Carthaginian menace, retained tyrants after most were overthrown in the homeland. Most Sicilian tyrants were pederasts. In the sixth century Phalaris of Acragas (Agrigentum) roasted his enemies alive in a bronze bull which seemed to bellow with their agonizing death screams. At Syracuse, Hiero (died 467/6) competed in the **Olympic Games** and patronized **Pindar**, greatest of the pederastic poets, and Dionysius patronized **Plato** along with his mentor **Socrates**, the principal theoretician of pedagogical pederasty. Hiero's older brother Gelon, who defeated the Carthaginian attempt to take over the island in 480, had made Syracuse the greatest western polis. First of the homosexual **exiles and émigrés**, Pythagoras founded at Croton ca. 530 the pederastic school of philosophy that flourished in Magna Grecia. At the end of the sixth century Parmenides of Elea in southern Italy founded the pederastic Eleatics. Both bucolic poets, **Theocritus** (fl. ca. 250), who migrated to **Alexandria**, and Moschus (fl. ca. 150) were born at Syracuse.

After the **Roman** conquest, during which in 212 a soldier sacking Syracuse slew the scientist Archimedes, Greeks from Southern Italy and Sicily introduced **Hellenism** including pederasty to the more cultivated members of the Roman aristocracy, and Latin writers such as **Vergil** and **Petronius** often placed their pederastic scenes there. In addition, latifundia (great estates) filled Sicily with gangs of **slaves** and other impoverished agricultural workers, normally isolated from women. With inordinately high female infanticide, lower-class males must also have often satisfied their drives homosexually or with farm animals. Under the Romans Sicily became an intellectual backwater and declined further in the fifth and sixth centuries of our era with Vandalic piracy and Byzantine reconquest.

Islamic and Medieval Sicily. Seizing Sicily from the **Byzantine Empire** between 827 and 902, Arabs turned the Mediterranean into a Muslim lake, thereby isolating and accelerating the decline of Western Europe. They reinvigorated Sicily with new crops, often irrigated, such as sugar, cotton, and citrus fruits, and industries such as silk and cotton textiles. The Arabs reestablished its position as an entrepôt of international trade, lost when the Roman Empire crumbled. Though the subject has hardly been studied, polygamy, eunuchs, seclusion of women in harems, and female infanticide must have encouraged both male and female homosexuality in Muslim Sicily, and a high proportion of Arabic poetry is pederastic.

The Normans, who conquered Sicily between 1061 and 1090, and their descendants and successors, the Hohenstaufen kings (1194–1266), were rightly regarded by the **papacy** with suspicion as having imbibed too deeply of Islam, which they tolerated. They played off one group of subjects against another: Muslim, Jew, Greek, and Lombard (in southern Italy, which they also ruled). His Guelph (propapal) enemies accused **Frederick II** (r. 1198–1250; so well depicted by Ernst **Kantorowicz**) of keeping a harem and practicing pederasty with his black slaves. Brother of the fanatic St. Louis, the greedy and bloodthirsty Charles of Anjou (r. 1266–1285), who beheaded Frederick II's 16-year-old grandson Conradin and his coeval "friend" when they tried to regain the Sicilian throne, finally stamped out Sicilian heterodoxy. The bloody rising against tyranny and overtaxation known as the Sicilian Vespers (1282), plunged the central Mediterranean into a century of wars between the islanders, who called in the Aragonese dynasty to protect them from the Angevins, Charles' descendants, who kept the mainland provinces of the former kingdom of Sicily. This conflict created the "two Sicilies," albeit they were reunited by Alfonso the Magnanimous of Aragon in 1437. Sexual imbalance on the island persisted, with 136 males for 115 females and 40 percent of adult males unmarried in some areas during the fifteenth century, indicating the persistence of female infanticide, which other evidence likewise indicates for England, France, and Tuscany.

Antonio Beccadelli (1394–1471), a humanist of the early **Renaissance**, was born in Palermo. In 1434 he was called to Naples, where he served king Alfonso as ambassador, secretary, and historian. He is best known, however, for his learnedly scurrilous *Hermaphroditus*, which contains a number of homosexual epigrams modeled on **Martial** and other Latin poets.

Modern Times. By the fifteenth century Sicily had become a colonial economy owned by a few aristocrats supplying—with the backbreaking labor of landless proletarians and slaves who made up the bulk of the population—grain, sugar, cotton, and other commodities to Genoa, Barcelona, and other Mediterranean ports. Aragonese Inquisitors relentlessly suppressed dissent and non-conformity, but tried in vain during the second half of the sixteenth century to obtain a papal bull so that they could "relax" pederasts, a veritable "social plague," as they stated, to secular courts. Sicilian sodomites were therefore tried and punished in the local secular courts rather than by the **Inquisition** as in Aragon. The Greek language and Arabic pederastic traditions persisted among the lower classes, where males greatly outnumbered females.

The Spanish Bourbons ceded the Kingdom of the Two Sicilies (1759–1860) to their cadet Neapolitan branch, which misgoverned the island as badly as had its Habsburg predecessors, so that the Mafia and a general disrespect of all authority, including clerical, flourished. One of the chief opponents of Bourbon misrule was the bisexual patriot Luigi **Settembrini** (1813–1877), who was fascinated by ancient Greek pederasty.

After Garibaldi liberated Sicily and southern Italy in 1860, but turned it over to the House of Savoy, northern industrialists began a new form of exploitation of the mezzogiorno (south of Italy) and Sicily. Millions escaped poverty by emigrating to the Americas as well as to northern Italy. Americans tended to stereotype Italians as oversexed and morally loose. Sicilians and Neapolitans brought **Mediterranean homosexuality** to the United States, but adjusted their sexual mores rapidly to the new transatlantic climate conditioned by **Protestantism**. A significant contribution of the Italian underworld to the American gay **subculture** was its ownership of gay bars and speakeasies during Prohibition at a time when no respectable businessman would touch such an ill-famed enterprise. A Sicilian-American, the fine gay novelist Robert Ferro, died of AIDS together with his lover in 1988.

Like Capri in the bay of Naples, favorite resort of homosexual **exiles and émigrés**, Taormina in Sicily became in the nineteenth century and remains today a **resort** for gay tourists, along with the seedier violence-prone large cities of Palermo and Naples, abounding as they are even now with dashingly attractive *scugnizzi* (street urchins), often available at a price. Baron Wilhelm von **Gloeden** just after 1900 published provocative pictures of nude Sicilian boys from the region of Taormina, and continued to reside there until his death in 1931. Since World War II even ordinary gay tourists have frequented these once exclusive enclaves, driving those seeking greener pastures to Mykonos, Ibiza, and increasingly, as those have also become overrun, to Muslim sites in North **Africa**.

William A. Percy

SISSY

A diminutive of "sister," the term "sissy" originated in mid-nineteenth-century America as an epithet for a weak, cowardly, or **effeminate** boy or man. Popular works, such as the novel, *Little Lord Fauntleroy* (1886) by Frances H. Burnett, and H. T. Webster's cartoon strip, "The Timid Soul," featuring Caspar Milquetoast, helped to solidify the **stereotype**. The sissy, it was held, was not born but made, through pampering or mollycoddling in childhood by well-meaning, but overprotective female guardians. Such mistakes of training could in many cases be corrected (it was believed) by strict discipline and exercise in such manly pursuits as **athletics**, hunting, and military life. The great exemplar of the redeemed sissy was Theodore Roosevelt (1858–1919), the delicate youth who turned into the roughrider and flourisher of the symbolic big stick.

Twentieth-century America continued to be preoccupied by the contrast between the rugged frontiersman, the stalwart embodiment of the country's abiding strength of character, as against the effete, overcultivated, sissified European. In literature, such expatriates as Henry **James** and T. S. **Eliot**, with their recondite allusiveness, were contrasted with such standardbearers of the forthright native tradition as Jack London, William Carlos Williams, and Jack **Kerouac**. Ernest **Hemingway**, both an expatriate and a he-man, was an exception—though perhaps he protested too much.

While the word sissy may be relatively recent, the sissy concept takes up the older tradition of attacks on luxury as a solvent of manly virtue. Like the dandy before him, the sissy was not necessarily homosexual, but this status was often implied—particularly in the first half of the twentieth century when the word was a favorite stand-in or euphemism for the harsher "queer" or "fairy." In their heyday, Hollywood **films** made considerable use of the ambivalent image of the sissy, as personified by such players as Franklin Pangborn and Clifton Webb.

Significantly, the term "tomboy," the female counterpart, never bore a comparable negative charge, inasmuch as imitation of the male in the young female was considered essentially harmless and transitional.

In the 1970s the popularity of ideals of **androgyny** did something to soften the negativity of the sissy stereotype. Through writings and face-to-face discussions promoting ideas of the women's movement, men learned that it was acceptable to show emotions and sensitivity, and even to cry. The he-man role, though conferring status in a patriarchal society, now seemed a barrier to personal expressiveness and creativity. Many accepted, in principle at least, the idea that there was a range of types between the male and female poles, rather than a stark opposition. Although these arguments made some impact on many men, particularly those who entered sensitivity-training groups influenced by feminist ideas, the concept of sissihood has shown a remarkable capacity to survive; it largely retains its negative aura. In the yuppie eighties the appropriate symbol of this survival was the updated version of the milksop, the trendy quiche eater; *Real Men Don't Eat Quiche* (1982) was the title of a goof book by Bruce Feirstein.

Recently the word "wimp" has become popular as a derisive epithet, conveying a sense of insufficient maleness, but it lacks connotations of overt effeminacy or homosexuality despite its origins as a slang term for a female.

See also **Macho**.

Wayne R. Dynes

SITUATIONAL HOMOSEXUALITY

This term refers sociologically to widespread same-sex behavior in total institutions where no partner of the opposite sex is available. In some cases, as in **prisons, jails and reformatories,** the inmates are there involuntarily; in others, as ships at sea, monasteries and nunneries, and mines in southern Africa, participation has been freely chosen. The term is also applied to cultures where adolescents are gender-segregated. The assumption behind the notion of psychological situational homosexuality is that the individual's behavior is dependent on the heterosexually deprived situation, and that those performing homosexual acts *faute de mieux* under these circumstances will revert to heterosexual behavior once they regain access to the opposite sex, while the "true" homosexual prefers his own sex even when the other is freely accessible.

The situation of deprivation does not affect all people equally. Even late nineteenth-century authors realized that some individuals never engage in homosexual activity no matter how long or how intense the deprivation from heterosexual contact they endure. Similarly, many homosexuals fail to take up heterosexual activity even though homosexuality may be so severely repressed as to be practically unavailable. Nevertheless, cross-cultural evidence abundantly documents higher incidences of homosexual activity in situations of heterosexual deprivation, and markedly so for males in their sexual prime.

SIWA OASIS

A town in the Libyan desert of western Egypt, Siwa is the site of an ancient civilization which retained a form of institutionalized homosexuality into the modern era. The oasis was the location of an oracle consulted by **Alexander the Great** and modern observers have stressed how the Berber population conserved its own language, religious rites, and sexual customs despite the later overlay of Islam and Egyptian administration.

Sexual relations among men fell into the ancient pattern of pairing between usually married adult men and adolescent bachelors. In the nineteenth century, families lived within the walls of a town constructed rather like a single large adobe "beehive" while all unmarried men lived together on the edges of town where they made up a warrior class (zaggalah) protecting the oasis from desert marauders. In the twentieth century, as the military function declined and the townspeople have moved out of the walled center, the zaggalah have become agricultural laborers retaining their customs and clubhouses. The anthropologist Walter Cline, writing in 1936, found "All normal Siwan men and boys practice sodomy. . . . Among themselves the natives are not ashamed of this; they talk about it as openly as they talk about love of women, and many if not most of their fights arise from homosexual competition."

Among the zaggalah, man–boy relationships were formally recognized when the man offered the boy's father a gift (or brideprice) as in heterosexual marriage. Abd Allah notes that "Siwan customs allow a man but one boy [vs. four wives] to whom he is bound by a stringent code of obligations." In the zaggalah clubhouse "laborers come together on any occasion for communal rejoicing and assemble on moonlight nights for drinking, singing, and dancing to the merry rhythm of flute and drum" (Cline). This festive and erotic tradition culminates in a three-day bacchanal dedicated to the medieval sheik, Sidi Soliman, following the Islamic fast of Ramadan. The various accounts of Siwa agree on the openness and fluidity of sexuality, in that divorce is casual and serial polygamy common, men having as many as a dozen wives over time. Male and female prostitution was noted and Cline remarked that the role in homosexual relations was variable and voluntary.

BIBLIOGRAPHY. Mahmud Mohammad 'Abd Allah, "Siwan Customs," *Harvard African Studies*, 1 (1917), 1–28; C. Dalrymple Belgrave, *Siwa: The Oasis of Jupiter Ammon*, London: Lane, 1923; Walter Cline, *Notes on the People of Siwah and El Garah in the Libyan Desert*, Menasha, WI: George Banta Publishing, 1936; Robin Maugham, *Journey to Siwa*, London: Chapman and Hall, 1950.

Barry D. Adam

SIXTEENTH-CENTURY LEGISLATION

This era brought to completion the trend toward criminalization of homosexuality throughout Christendom. The Jewish and Christian antihomosexual tradition that goes back to the fifth century

B.C. had crystalized in the **canon law** of the Christian church, whence it passed—from the end of the thirteenth century onward—into the criminal codes of the various European jurisdictions. The imposition of a Christian sexual morality that saw in homosexual acts a violation of the order of nature went hand in hand with the church's expansion of its organizational and spiritual control over a recalcitrant or even heretical population. The only conflict with the secular power was over the jurisdiction of its courts as opposed to the ecclesiastical ones.

The Reformation did not break with this trend or reverse it. By the close of the sixteenth century the whole of Christian Europe—**Protestant**, Catholic, and Orthodox—held sodomy a **capital** offense. The English statute of 25 Henry VIII c. 6 (1533) imposing the penalty of death by hanging for "the detestable and abominable Vice of Buggery committed with mankind or beast" is but a single example of the laws enacted by the Christian states and principalities in that era.

Central Europe. A condemnation of sodomy committed by *"eyn mensch mit eynem vihe, mann mit mann, weib mit weib"* (a human being with a beast, man with man, woman with woman) appears in Article 141 of the Constitutio criminalis Bambergensis (criminal code for the German city of Bamberg) of 1507, in the same article of the Constitutio criminalis Brandenburgensis (criminal code of Brandenburg) of 1516, in Article 122 of two drafts of a penal code for the Holy Roman Empire dating from 1521 and 1529, and finally in Article 116 of the Constitutio Criminalis Carolina that was formally adopted at the session of the Diet (Reichstag) in Regensburg on July 27, 1532. This was the end result of the work of codification that had been begun at the Diet in Freiburg in 1498 and was completed only in the reign of the Catholic emperor Charles V, who was one of the bitterest opponents of the Reformation. The time span involved—starting 19 years before the division of the Western church and ending 15 years after it—proves beyond a doubt that the rise of Protestantism had nothing to do with the enactments in question. The Carolina had an enormous impact on European criminal law, both substantive and procedural, in countries as far apart as France and Russia, from the time of its enactment to the end of the Ancien Regime; even the *widernatürliche Unzucht* (unnatural lewdness) of the notorious **Paragraph 175** of the Penal Code of the German Empire (1871) merely rephrases the *unkeusch, so wider die natur beschicht* (unchastity contrary to nature) of the German codes of the early sixteenth century. The earlier German code had no force or influence, however, in **England**, which had already gone far down the path of developing its own distinctive legal tradition—the so-called **common law**.

The origin of all these statutes is probably to be sought in the writings of the Italian jurists of the fifteenth century who are cited as sources of the imperial law which displaced the local codes of the individual German cities. What happened was simply that offenses which had been crimes in canon law were now made criminal in the secular courts as well. In this whole process of criminalization of sodomy the teaching of the Christian church is primary; the legal enactments and social attitudes are secondary and tertiary developments, so that the English statute of 1533 independently parallels the Continental enactments.

England. Monks—against whom accusations of sodomy had been voiced since the ninth century—were of course targets of the Reformers. Henry VIII's letter of April 4, 1543 to his agent in Scotland, Ralph Sadler, envisages what one would nowadays call a "covert action" in that country that would dispossess the monasteries of their holdings in a more effective manner than a publicly decreed statute might have allowed. With respect to his own realm there is no evidence that the statute of 1533 (included as it was in a group of miscellaneous statutes having nothing remotely to do with this subject) was motivated by the Reformers' intent to prosecute the monks for "crimes against nature" and then to dissolve the monasteries and confiscate their property. Dissolution of monasteries and enactments against sodomy were two different issues.

The unique features of the English tradition in this sphere are first, the use of the term **buggery** as the legal designation for the crime, though in ordinary speech in England the word was long considered obscene and offensive; and second, the frequent commutation of the penalty of death by hanging (not burning at the stake, as some wrongly assume) to exposure in the pillory, which was described by contemporary observers as worse than death because of the ferocity with which mobs, and particularly women eager to punish enemies of their sex, pelted the defenseless sodomites with missiles and filth of every kind. It is uncertain just how and when this penalty began, but there is evidence that the pillory was used to punish sexual immorality well before the reign of Henry VIII, possibly even as early as the time of Richard II (late fourteenth century). The standard histories of English law begin in medias res by relating the abuses to which the pillory led in the mid-eighteenth century and then its abolition for all offenses except perjury in 1816. In Great Britain it was finally abandoned in 1837, and the United States Congress followed suit in 1839.

The sixteenth-century sodomy statutes remained on the books until the thinkers of the **Enlightenment**, beginning with Cesare **Beccaria** in 1764, denounced the death penalty as a relic of medieval superstition and intolerance.

The number of persons executed for "buggery," "crime against **nature**," and the like in jurisdictions subject to the British crown was probably no more than three a year for the whole period from 1561 to 1861, when the death penalty was abolished in favor of life imprisonment. Thus the scores of victims of the law cannot be compared with the hundreds and thousands who were executed or simply killed just for holding "heretical" beliefs during the Reformation conflict in the sixteenth century. In fact, the really significant feature of the English legal development is its lateness in both directions: the criminalization of sodomy only in 1533, the abolition of the death penalty only in 1861, and the retention of the offense in the criminal codes of the English-speaking world long after the influence of the Enlightenment and of classical liberalism had reshaped almost every other area of the law. But few as the executions may have been, they left an enduring stamp on public opinion. And the United States Supreme Court's fateful decision in *Bowers v. Hardwick* (1986) denying the right of privacy to consensual adult homosexual behavior keeps alive the legal tradition that stems from the law of 1533, reinforced by the unrelenting hostility of religious conservatives and fundamentalists.

See also **Canon Law; Law, Feudal and Royal; Law, Municipal.**

Warren Johansson

SLANG TERMS FOR HOMOSEXUALS IN ENGLISH

The several national varieties of English offer hundreds of slang terms for homosexuals, a few of them traceable to the seventeenth century, but most dating from the nineteenth and twentieth centuries. Some may be heard wherever English is spoken (e.g., **gay, queer**); many more are limited in their area of use ("jasper," "poofter," "moffie"). Nearly all these terms were devised by heterosexuals and so tend to express in their meaning or derivation the hostility, the contempt, the hatred, and the fear that straight people have felt toward gay sex and those who practice it.

The corpus of slang also reflects long-standing and still prevalent misunderstandings of homosexuality. Recent exposures of and challenges to these misconceptions have made as yet little impression on the **language**, and although individuals may have modified their usage, offensive, misconceived, and otherwise objectionable terms continue to be used.

Gay people have themselves adopted many of these terms, because until recently their understanding of themselves and their sexuality differed little from the views of the society in which they lived.

Basic Categories. Almost all terms for male homosexuals fall into four simple categories: first, those taking or assumed to take the "active," masculine role, the insertor role, in **anal** intercourse; secondly, the "passive," feminine role, the receptor role, in anal intercourse; thirdly, effeminate men who may be gay (there is some overlap between the latter two categories). Finally, for United States English, a category of fellator (cocksucker engaged in **oral** activity) is needed.

A similar typonymy, without a fourth category corresponding to fellator, applies to terms for lesbians. First, masculine, "active"; secondly, (ultra-) feminine, "passive"; and, thirdly, mannish women who may be lesbian. Again, there is some overlap between the first and third categories. Even though early sexology distinguished cunnilinctrixes from **tribades**, calling the former "sapphists" and "Lesbian lovers" (this original sense became obscured when these terms became generic for female homosexuals), English slang does not seem to have developed similar categories. There are many slang terms for those who perform oral sex on women ("cuntlapper," "-licker"; "muffdiver," "plater"; "gamahucher," "gamahucker," "gamarucker," and so forth) but none is specifically homosexual in application.

These categories mirror the traditional equation of biological sex and **gender** role, whereby male anatomy entails masculinity and female anatomy femininity. From this psychobiological determinism flow crude popular notions of male and female sexuality generally and an erroneous conception of homosexuality that has not yet been completely dispelled. It is the belief that for a man to renounce the "active," definitively male role of penile penetration and submit to the "passive," female role of accepting the intromission of a penis, he must be a female, either psychically or both mentally and behaviorally.

Slang embodying this simple **active vs. passive** categorization according to roles in sexual activity can be found reduplicated again and again, in different English-speaking countries, in different periods, and in specific close knit or exclusive groups. In particular, whenever men are kept in isolation from women, it is likely that a system of slang corresponding to this pattern will arise. Examples of such masculine worlds in which **situational** homosexuality occurs are **prisons**, navies (and other armed forces to a lesser extent), boarding schools, among **seafarers** and **hoboes**. Even today there are relatively few slang terms that do not assign or imply a role in sexual activity, and these—"queer," "homo," "poof(ter)," "les," "lez," "lezzie," "gay"—have usually become general only recently. A few other words are sometimes neutral when used by homosexuals: **fag(got)**, queen, **dyke**.

Male Terms. By far the largest number of male slang terms fall into the categories of male passivity and **effeminacy**, which imply the renunciation of one's maleness. By contrast, the active insertor terms seldom imply femininity or the loss of masculinity. Very often they refer expressly to taking the active role in anal intercourse: "arse-king," "arse/ass-bandit," "arse-burglar," "booty-bandit," "bud sallogh" (Irish, "shitten prick," obsolete), "backdoor('s) man," "gentleman of the backdoor," "backgammoner," "inspector of manholes," "dirt-track rider," "turd-packer," "dung-pusher," "poo-jabber." The Australian prison slang for the active partner "hock" has the same implication, for it is rhyming slang on "cock." One of the equivalent American terms, "jocker," is likewise probably derived from "jock," which means "fuck" as a verb and "cock" as a noun. In the case of the synonym "wolf" the association is the same but metaphoric rather than direct.

The key to understanding a large number of passive/effeminate terms is the supposed reversal of gender and sex roles: the adoption of behavior deemed "natural" or appropriate to the opposite sex. A man who is passive must in some sense be a woman; even one who is **raped** is judged to have "lost his manhood" and becomes *de facto* a woman. Many slang terms for the passive homosexual directly personify him as a vagina or an anus: "gash," "pussy," "gentleman pussy," "sea-pussy," "boy-pussy," "boy-snatch," "boy-cunt," "bumboy," "poonce" (from Yiddish for "cunt"), "brownie-queen," "browning-sister" or "-queen," "mustard-pot," "jere."

Another common procedure is to apply a word that has female reference. The most direct method is to use a female name. The oldest known slang term "Molly" is an example, and "Marjery," "Mary-Ann," and "Charlotte-Ann" are further obsolete instances. Other nineteenth-century examples still survive: "Miss Nancy," "Nance," "Pansy" (and other **flowers**), "Mary," "Betty," "Dinah," "Ethyl," "Nola" have been recorded in the United States and in Australia the (obsolete?) "Gussie" (from Augusta). Or it may be any one of the large number of words normally used of females: "aunt(ie)," "chicken," "fem(me)," "girl," "bitch," "belle," "mother," "queen," "sis(sie)," "sister," "wife," and the like. Or it may be a word that refers to stereotypically feminine behavior: "limp-wrist," "broken-wrist," "flit," "mince," "prissy," "swish." (*See* **Women's Names for Male Homosexuals.**)

Another way of seeing male homosexuals as women is to view them as **hermaphrodites**. This confusion has seen the word "hermaphrodite" corrupted into "morphodite," "morphydite," "morphrodite," and in South Africa "moffie." It has also yielded "freak."

One of the most prolific sources of feminine words has been male **prostitution**. Evidence of this phenomenon in **London** exists from the **Middle Ages**, and late nineteenth-century writers on homosexuality such as Havelock **Ellis** and "Xavier Mayne" (E. I. Prime-**Stevenson**) state that it was widespread throughout Europe and the United States. The prostitution took two main forms. Highly masculine men, especially soldiers, who were poorly paid, made themselves available as "active" partners. The older tradition involved very effeminate men, often cross-dressers, who frequented certain taverns or bars; sometimes their activity was outright arse-peddling, but often it seems to have been sex in return for a good time paid for by the masculine male. In the seventeenth and eighteenth centuries such effeminate men were called **mollies** (from "Moll," the pet-form of Mary, which meant "harlot" or "hussy") and the places where they operated were molly-houses.

The semantic transition from "harlot" and/or "slatternly woman, hussy" to "effeminate passive homosexual" and hence "homosexual" generally is the source of some of the most common terms for homosexuals. Such words include **fairy,** "nancy" or "nance," "**queen**/quean," and, contrary to popular myth, "fag" and "faggot." Above all there is the term "gay" itself, which in its present sense has not been traced earlier than the 1920s but which clearly derives from the earlier slang sense of "sexually dissolute, promiscuous, libertine," a sense often applied to female prostitutes. Other less familiar examples of this shift include "aunt(ie)" (originally meaning "brothel-keeper, old prostitute"), "ginch," "hump," "kife," "twidget," and "skippy."

The long tradition of male prostitution in London has meant that working-class Londoners have had a long exposure to it. London slang, particularly Cockney rhyming slang, is very rich in terms for effeminate homosexuals, many of which live on in Australian slang. One nineteenth-century term was "sod," which survives a mild term of abuse, its original sense largely forgotten. It in turn gave rise to the rhyming slang "Tommy Dodd," shortened to "Tommy." More important is "poof" ("pouf"), attested from 1833, which has yielded the elaborated Australian form "poofter" (now spread to New Zealand and Britain) and the rhyming slang "horse's hoof" or "horses" (Australian variant, "cow's hoof") and "iron hoof" or "iron." The variant form "puff," attested from 1902, may have originally been only a spelling variant rather than representing a different pronunciation; however that may be, it has spawned "collar and cuff" or "cuff" and "nigh enough" or "enuff." "Queer" has yielded "Brighton Pier," "ginger beer," shortened to "ginger," "King Lear," and, some have argued, "jere" and "gear." In Australian English "queen" has given rise to "pork and bean" and (poor example) "submarine."

United States English is rich in terms for homosexual fellators. Other varieties of English have no such slang, although associated terms such as "blowjob" and "head" (neither necessarily homosexual) have recently begun to penetrate other Englishes. The earliest written record of the word "cock-sucker" occurs in John S. Farmer and W. E. Henley's *Slang and its Analogues*, vol. 2 (1891), and interestingly they define it as "fellatrix." In the United States, however, the word applies to a homosexual, is one of the most taboo of words, and is also one of the strongest terms of abuse. The American homosexual's predilection for fellatio is long-established, for already in 1915 Havelock Ellis recorded the slang term "head-worker." Later synonyms include "blowboy," "flute(r)," "cannibal," "gobbler," "larro" (back-slang), "mouser," "muzzler," "dick-sucker," "dick(ie)-licker," "skindiver," "nibbler," "lapper," "lick-box."

Lesbianism. Terms for lesbians are far less common than those for homosexual men, a fact that is consonant with the greater invisibility of the lesbian in the past. No term now current can be traced earlier than the 1920s. In the eighteenth century lesbian practices were referred to as "the game of flats," but there was apparently no term for the practitioners. In the late nineteenth century two spinsters living together were referred to, in parts of the United States, as being in a **Boston marriage**. The phenomenon of "tomboyishness" was widely recognized and far less deprecated than the male equivalent "sissihood," yet it was not commonly or usually associated with lesbianism.

The word lesbian itself has given rise to many shortenings: "les(s)," "lessie," "lez," "lezzie," "lezzo," "lesbie" and the associated pun "lesbie-friends," "lesbo," "lesley"; and the jocular elaboration "lesbyterian." All of these are generic. Most other terms fall into the **butch-fem**/"fluff" categories and most seem to be of United States origin.

The oldest term seems to be "bull-dyke(r)" or "bull-dyking woman." The latter was also shortened to "B.D. woman." These terms first appear in black circles in the 1920s, and "bull-dyking" and "B.D." occur in the blues. The most plausible etymology of the "-dyke" element, which later became an independent word with the same sense, is that it derives from the late nineteenth-century slang "dike" meaning "to dress up formally or elegantly." This derivation would suggest the priority of "bull-dyker" over "bull-dyke," which accords with the evidence. There are also corrupt forms "bull-dagger" and "boon-dagger," and "bull" too has become an independent word. "Dyke" has spread to other English-speaking countries, and is often reinforced with the word "diesel."

Other masculine-lesbian terms include "butch," "amy-john" (from "amazon"), "jasper," "stud," "baby-stud," "tootsie."

The feminine, "passive" lesbian is a "fem(me)," "fluff," "fairy-lover," and "lady-lover." This last is used generically.

Conclusion. Language and particularly slang mirrors salient facts about the society in which it is used, and this is true of all the slang names for homosexuals that have accumulated over the past two centuries. They show in their meaning and derivation the popular understandings of homosexuals and homosexual behavior and sexual activity. That the understanding and perceptions involved are so frequently wrong makes the task of overcoming prejudice and ill-will so much harder, for the detritus remains embedded in the language. It is no accident that English has so few slang terms that mean homosexual, pure and simple, without reference to sexual roles and acts.

Studies of the slang vocabularies of other Western European languages have shown that they are as rich as English. In all modern languages, apparently, money, inebriation, and sex are all especially productive of popular terms. However, homosexual vocabularies are highly insular: even Spanish and Portuguese, so similar in other ways, show hardly any commonality in their slang terms for gay men and lesbians. Nonetheless, the whole group of Western languages displays some common semantic elements: gender reversal (imputation of effeminacy to gay men and masculinity to lesbians); use of **women's names** as generic terms for male homosexuals; inheritance of medieval Christian words of the "bugger" and "sodomite" families; and adaptations of psychiatric and medical terms. Occasionally slang terms migrate from one language to another, as French *tante* to German (also variant: *Tunte*), and (probably) in loan-translation form to English as *aunt(ie)*. In recent years the English word "gay" has entered these languages, and others as well.

BIBLIOGRAPHY. Wayne R. Dynes, *Homolexis: A Historical and Cultural Lexicon of Homosexuality*, New York: Gay Academic Union, 1985; Gershon Legman, "The Language of Homosexuality: An American Glossary," in George W. Henry, *Sex Variants*, New York: P. B. Hoeber, 1941; *Guild Dictionary of Homosexual Terms*, Washington, D.C.: Guild Press, 1965; Bruce Rodgers, *The Queens' Vernacular*, San Francisco: Straight Arrow Books, 1972.

G. S. Simes

SLAVERY

The institution of slavery, under which one human being was the property of another and his labor power could be exploited by the owner with no remuneration beyond bare subsistence, existed from the dawn of history down to modern times. In some countries of the New World the agricultural sector abandoned slavery only in the second half of the nineteenth century. Most studies of slavery have concentrated on the economic aspect, fewer on the social and political. Only a very few have entered into the sexual exploitation that slavery entailed, and these tended to focus on the problems of marriage and childbearing rather than on the homosexual side.

General Considerations. The person of the slave belonged to the master, and could be used for sexual gratification as well as for economic gain. The slave could not in most cases refuse the master's advances, whether they were heterosexual or homosexual. The inferior status of the slave translated into the passive role in homosexual intercourse, which was always assigned to the party of lower rank. In ancient city-states the free citizen was forbidden to prostitute himself without loss of status, so that the profession of **prostitute** could be exercised only by slaves or foreigners and sometimes by freedmen. For this reason handsome young males captured in battle or in slavehunting raids were likely to find their way into **brothels**, a fate preferable to the hard labor imposed on slaves in the mines and latifundia of the magnates and great landowners. It was no disgrace for the slave to be subordinated sexually to the master, but simply part of his function as an "animated tool," an instrument of pleasure. The slave in ancient Greece was forbidden to be a pederast, that is, to take the active role with a boy. In situations of this kind, as in relationships between male slaves and upper-class women, the law and society could be harshly punitive.

So extensive was the sexual abuse of captives and slaves that it was assumed, tacitly and even explicitly in law codes, that any woman who had been in a city taken by force or had been a slave had been sexually violated. The same was to a lesser extent true of males taken prisoner, who were exposed to the aggression of their captors in a world where homosexual activity was considered part of everyday life. The slavemonger engaged in practices typical of the modern call-boy service, grooming and depilating his wares, concealing their physical blemishes as best he could, and falsifying their ages and other personal data. Such behavior earned the slave dealer the contempt of polite society, an inferior status that lingered as long as slavery itself.

At the same time intimacy with the master could afford a slave a relatively comfortable existence, the superiority of the personal or household servant over the one who toiled in the fields or in the mines. In the ancient world particularly, slaves were educated for all occupations, even the highest in the administrative hierarchy, so that the condition of slave did not imply intellectual inferiority or lack of culture. It has even been asserted that the market in slaves provided for a rational distribution of labor power in ancient society, and the ability to provide "intimate personal services" must have contributed to the overall value of a boy offered for sale.

The status of the slave set the parameters of the sexual activity that was obligatory, permitted, or forbidden. The overriding principle in the ancient world was that the active role was reserved to the superior partner and forbidden to the infe-rior one, while the passive role was prescribed for the inferior partner and forbidden to the superior one. In ancient Athens slaves and boys were often classed and treated similarly, but with this crucial difference: for the upper-class Athenian boy the status was temporary and transitional, the homosexual liaison partook of a rite de passage rather than of an obligation contingent upon the servile role.

Historical Development: Ancient Greece. Among the **Greeks** the pederastic relationship—the legally and socially sanctioned form of male homosexuality par excellence—did not occur between equals. In Greek **vase paintings** the passive partner shows no sign of pleasure, has no erection, and usually faces straight ahead during intercourse. For an adult member of the aristocracy, dalliance with a handsome slave boy was a fleeting pleasure, not a serious involvement. On the other hand, the passion of the *erastes* (lover) for the *eromenos* (beloved) could be as intense and enthralling as any of which the individual was capable. In **Plato's** *Symposium* Parmenides likens the obsession of *erastai* to their young boy friends to that of men "wishing to endure slavery as no slave would," while in the *Phaedrus* Socrates speaks of the lover's soul as "ready to be a slave, to sleep wherever allowed, as near as possible to the beloved." Xenophon's Socrates, in the *Memorabilia*, calls a man such as Critobulus, who has dared to kiss Alcibiades' beautiful son, likely to become a slave forthwith instead of a free man, and in the *Symposium* the *eromenos* who uses his physical beauty may rule the *erastes*. So for the youth in possession of the pride of his adolescence the pederastic relationship could entail a reversal of the role that was imposed upon him as a child; his physical beauty gives him power over his adult lover—the first experience of dominating another male. The slave can never have such power, and **Aeschines** cites a law forbidding slaves to frequent the palestra—a favorite trysting place for young Athenians and their admirers. A second law prohibited slaves from using free boys as sexual partners at all. **Plutarch** ascribed the authorship of both laws to Solon, with the significant proviso that he did not ban relations between slaves and free women— as the **Roman emperors** were later to do.

Rome. Roman pederasty never had the educational role which Greek society had assigned to the phenomenon. The same aspect of dominance and submission prevailed: the behavior that is obligatory for the slave is unworthy and demeaning when practiced by a free man. But a Roman of the upper class had abundant opportunity to acquire a male slave as a bed partner if he so chose. The nonchalance with which Roman society judged such matters is demonstrated by **Catullus'** wedding poem in honor of Manlius Torquatus and his new bride Junia, which alludes at length to the groom's liaison with a young male slave of the household in the jocular manner typical of Roman straightforwardness in dealing with sexuality. However, for the Roman, marriage and procreation were duties; homosexual affairs were casual matters or opportunities for relaxation. The male **prostitute** must have been a characteristic figure of the night life of the metropolis, as during the reign of Augustus such hustlers had their own specially designated holiday, duly recorded in the State Calendar. But the mentor–pupil relationship that was the hallmark of Greek *paiderasteia* at its best never found entry into Roman mores, which always fell short of the Hellenic ideal.

From the Introduction of Christianity to Early Modern Times. **Christianity** influenced the sexual life of slaves by making a breach in the distinction between *matrimonium*, the legal marriage of citizens, and *contubernium*, the union of convenience between slaves. In principle Christian morality upheld a single standard for all, slave or free—which implied that the slave could not be compelled to take the passive role in a homosexual relationship. Byzantine historians record that after the legislation of Justinian on sodomy, it became "the crime of those to whom no crime could be imputed," and that convictions were obtained solely on the word of a child or a slave. In this way the incipient Christian norms of sexual behavior played into the hands of those who needed a political weapon to strike at their enemies. In a society where overt homosexuality had been a matter of everyday life, the adherents of the "old lifestyle" now exposed themselves to the death penalty if the authorities got wind of what was happening inside their households. The innovation of Christian moralists and legislators lay, in a sense, in equalizing master and slave: extending the old prohibitions on the active homosexual role from the slave to the free man, and those on the passive role from the free man to the slave. It was the former act that led Friedrich Nietzsche to characterize Christianity as having a "slave morality," since it reduced the whole population to the lowest common denominator, even if in practice the slave had little opportunity to bring charges against his master unless he found political protectors outside the household.

It is sometimes alleged that the anti-sexual animus of primitive Christianity stemmed from its being a religion of slaves and of the "oppressed" who were forced to submit to their owners, but this view is now being abandoned. The sexual morality of Hellenistic Judaism which the Church ratified and reinforced with an ascetic bias had nothing to do with the institution of slavery, in fact the Mosaic Law held that Israelites should not keep other Israelites in permanent bondage, just as Plato taught that Hellenes should not enslave other Hellenes. The coincidence of the two doctrines led ultimately to the abolition of slavery in the center of Christendom, though not on its periphery, where "barbaric" peoples continued to be enslaved and to be utilized as the labor force of a slaveholding economy from the early Middle Ages until the suppression of the slave trade in the nineteenth century.

In the eighth to tenth centuries Jewish slave dealers transported Slavic captives from Itil and Kiev in Khazaria to the slave markets of Moorish **Spain**, but en route at Verdun the males were castrated, with the result that in Arabic the word *saqaliba* meant not just "Slavs" but "eunuchs," who had their own special role in the sexual economy of the time. The eunuchs were employed as harem guards and as part of the military force of the Moorish rulers, but a feminized eunuch could also be the passive partner in a homosexual relationship. The Arab world preserved vestiges of slavery down to the twentieth century, and only international pressure and intervention have terminated the practice in quite recent times.

Relatively little study has been made of homosexual activity among the **black** slaves of the New World. In the seventeenth century Portuguese sources show, however, that homosexuality was common among the peoples of Angola, from which many Brazilian slaves were recruited. **Inquisition** reports beginning at the same time show considerable interracial sodomy, in most cases involving free white men and black slaves. There is also evidence of direct transfer of the social forms, including transvestism, documented in Angolan homosexuality to the slave population of Brazil.

Conclusion. In various cultural contexts, slavery augmented the element of dominance and submission implicit in many traditional homosexual relationships, and also enhanced the economic value of offspring in societies where parents could for mere financial gain sell a child into slavery knowing full well that it was destined for a brothel in some distant city. Even today the "sexual paradises" of Western tourists in Southeast Asia continue practices such as these that have survived from pre-modern societies, so that the champions of "sexual freedom" are profoundly wrong in imagining them as utopias of any sort. Rather they perpetuate a legacy of sexual exploitation and bondage that is incompatible with modern notions of liberty and self-determination.

BIBLIOGRAPHY. Mark Golden, "Slavery and Homosexuality at Athens," *Phoenix*, 38 (1984), 308–24; Beert C. Verstraete, "Slavery and the Social Dynamics of Male Homosexual Relations in Ancient Rome," *Journal of Homosexuality*, 5 (1980), 227–36.

Warren Johansson

SMYTH, ETHEL, DAME (1858–1944)

British composer and memoirist. The daughter of a Frenchwoman and a British general, Smyth obtained her musical training in Germany. She also spent some time in the multisexual foreign colony in **Florence**, where she came under the influence of Henry Brewster, who wrote the librettos for some of her compositions. From him she derived a quasi-mystical **Neoplatonic** philosophy. Her symphonic choral work *The Prison* (1930) bears the epigraph: "I am striving to release that which is divine within us, and to merge it in the universally divine." Her first major work, the Mass in D Major (1893), was hailed for its expansive construction, robust enunciation, and rich orchestration—all qualities that were then unexpected in a woman composer. From 1898 to 1925 she wrote and produced six operas. She also composed choral and orchestral works, chamber music, and songs.

An extroverted and even flamboyant personality, Smyth made a significant contribution to the British movement for women's suffrage. For this cause she wrote a "March of the Women," which was much used in demonstrations. Her opera *The Boatswain's Mate* (1916) revolves around a strong female personality, that of the landlady. She battled for equal treatment of women as artists, tirelessly canvassing conductors and executants, and staging grand scenes of temperament when her exacting performance requirements were not met. Smyth also cultivated royalty and golf. In 1922 she was made a Dame of the British Empire.

She fell in love with a number of women, most notably with Virginia **Woolf**, whom Ethel Smyth met when she was seventy-one. "I don't think I have ever cared for anyone more profoundly," she noted in her diary. "For eighteen months I have thought of little else." By this time she was suffering from deafness, and had to stop composing. She shifted her energy to her autobiographical volumes, which became renowned for their frankness and excellent prose style. Always forthright, she declared in 1935: "I am the most interesting person I know, and I don't care if anyone else thinks so." Her own summation of the three reasons for her remaining undefeated was: "An iron constitution, a fair share of fighting spirit, and, most important of all, a small but independent income."

BIBLIOGRAPHY. Christopher St. John, *Ethyl Smyth: A Biography*, London: Longmans, 1959.

Evelyn Gettone

SOCIAL CONSTRUCTION APPROACH

In the 1980s a seemingly new approach to the study of homosexual behavior arose, which its advocates termed social construction. Denying the existence of any "transhistorical" definition of same-sex behavior, the social constructionist scholars hold that sexual behavior is, in all significant aspects, a product of cultural conditioning, rather than of biological and constitutional factors. Thus same-sex behavior would have an entirely different meaning, say, in ancient **Egypt** or Tang **China** from what it would have in nineteenth-century Europe. In the view of some proponents of this approach, the "modern homosexual" is sui generis, having come into existence in Europe and North America only about 1880; hence it is vain to conduct comparative research on earlier eras or non-Western societies.

The social constructionists contrast their own approach with that of the "essentialists" (a term of their own devising), who ostensibly believe in an eternal and unchanging homosexuality. Yet most critics of social construction are not essentialists, and to label them as such amounts to a caricature that has proved tactically useful for polemical purposes but has advanced understanding very little. One should also bear in mind that the discussion is not current in the gay/lesbian community as a whole, but is confined to scholars.

Strengths and Weaknesses. What is valuable about the social construction approach is the fact that it alerts researchers to the dangers of anachronism. It makes no sense, for example, to refer to such ancient Greek figures as **Socrates** and **Alexander the Great** as gay without noting that their erotic life was conducted in a framework in which **pederasty**, the love of an adult man for an adolescent boy, was the rule, and not the **androphilia**—male adult–adult relationship—that is dominant today.

Granting this point, social construction errs too far on the side of difference in denying any commonality whatever among same-sex love in ancient **Greece**, in the **Middle Ages**, and in contemporary Western society. This denial of commonality and continuity would deprive scholars of the fruits of cross-cultural study of same-sex behavior. Another consequence of social construction orthodoxy is to exclude biological factors from any role in the shaping of sexual desire. Some extreme adherents claim that the body itself is a mere social construct— implying a rejection of material reality itself.

Sources. It has been suggested that the conflict between social construction and its opponents is another version of the old debate about nature versus nurture, between those who believe that human conduct is largely conditioned by biological forces and those who attribute the leading role to culture (the environmentalists). One's first response is to say that human behavior is the result of a confluence of the two forces, but this compromise is usually rejected by those in the environmentalist camp. In similar fashion, the social constructionists hold that culture is supreme, and are little prepared to concede biological constants. The social construction debate has also been compared to the medieval philosophical dispute between the realists and the nominalists, those who believed that the world contained real essences as against those who believed that we know only names for primal qualities. The parallel is inexact, however, since few social constructionists would be willing to adopt the nominalist views they are said to hold. Indeed, thoroughgoing nominalism would make the social constructionist claims meaningless, since there would be no stable social categories to contrast with the purportedly labile ones of sexual orientation.

The actual roots of social construction as a theory are twofold. First is the heritage of German historicism, which (emerging in the late eighteenth century), saw successive historical epochs as each having a distinct character, radically different from those that precede and follow. This trend, which posits a series of historical eras almost hermetically sealed from one another, accounts for the social constructionist belief that there is a "modern homosexual," a type that has existed only since ca. 1880. This eighteenth-century source shows that the social construction approach is not as new as its proponents suggest.

The second source is the tendency of modern **sociology** and **anthropology** to attribute human behavior solely to cultural determinants. In some social constructionists this tendency is tinged with late **Marxism**—which may itself be regarded as a sociological doctrine. These two main sources were given focus by the writings of the French social thinker and historian Michel **Foucault**, who though not self-identified as a social constructionist seminally influenced such proponents of social construction as Kenneth Plummer and Jeffrey Weeks. These and other adherents picked up Foucault's ideas of historical discontinuity, of "ruptures" radically segmenting periods of historical development.

Two Key Questions. A major objection to the social constructionist position is that homosexual behavior existed in Western society during the hundreds of years in which its existence was formally denied by the dominant culture; the authorities imposed obligatory heterosexuality upon the entire population and subjected anyone known for "sodomitical" behavior to economic boycott and social ostracism, if not to criminal prosecution. A curious outcome of these centuries of oppression is that when the first writings on homosexuality reached the general public at the end of the nineteenth century, some individuals revealed to psychiatrists that, although they had responded solely to members of their own sex since adolescence, until then they imagined themselves unique in the whole world. They had "constructed" their own sexual consciousness without any social input—a feat that should be impossible according to social constructionist postulates.

Another fact that contradicts the social constructionists is the abundant evidence for gay **subcultures** in Europe and the United States for at least a hundred years before the modern, political phase of homosexuality began—a subculture whose participants, however, merely thought of themselves as members of an erotic freemasonry from whose forbidden pleasures the vulgar mass was excluded. (While the evidence becomes sparser as one goes back in time, in some sense these subcultures can be traced back to the twelfth century in the **Middle Ages**.)

The "modern homosexual" is a *political* concept; the phenomenon began when individuals oriented toward their own sex, in the wake of trials such as those of Oscar **Wilde** and Prince Philipp zu **Eulenburg**, came to regard themselves as part of an oppressed minority cherishing a grievance against late Victorian society and its norms of sexual morality, and demanding their own "place in the sun." This trend was for a long time characteristic of northern Europe (where generally homosexual conduct was criminalized) and was foreign to the dwellers of **Mediterranean** lands. Since the 1960s, the "gay" **identity** has had an undeniable component of political **activism**; it was the badge of the individual who proclaimed his sexual nature openly and campaigned for the **liberation** of himself and others like him from the unjust prohibitions and discriminations of "straight" society. One can readily grant that in ancient **Greece** and **Rome** no one was "gay" in this sense. Such a political stance arose only in dialectical opposition to the **Judeo-Christian** attitude toward homosexual behavior and those who engaged in it. Even today many of those who participate in homosexual activity far from the mass meetings and rallies of the "gay ghettoes" are heedless of this political aspect of homosexuality, which they perceive as irrelevant to their desires for erotic gratification.

Conclusions. As has been noted, social construction theory has made a contribution in warning against anachronism, the tendency to project back into the past one's own familiar experiences and life ways. Yet the idea that cultural climates shift, changing the expression of sexuality with them, is scarcely a new discovery. What is disappointing about social contruction is that it offers no explanation of the "grounding" of such change. What mechanisms—economic, political, intellectual—cause a society to move from one dominant cultural climate to another? Moreover, social construction has gone too far in seeking to discourage transhistorical and cross-cultural investigations of homosexual desire. Implied roadblocks of this kind must not stymie the investigation, for comparative studies across time and across social systems are a vital prerequisite to the emergence of a satisfactory concept of human homosexual behavior in all its fullness and complexity.

BIBLIOGRAPHY. John Boswell, "Revolutions, Universals and Sexual Categories," *Salmagundi*, 58–59 (1982–83), 89–113; Wayne R. Dynes, "Wrestling with the Social Boa Constructor," *Out in Academia*, 2:1–2 (1988), 18–29; Robert Padgug, "Sexual Matters: On Conceptualizing Sexuality in History," *Radical History Review*, 20 (1979), 3–23; Kenneth Plummer, ed., *The Making of the Modern Homosexual*, Totowa, NJ: Barnes and Noble, 1981; Will Roscoe, "Making History: The Challenge of Gay and Lesbian Studies," *Journal of Homosexuality*, 15:3/4 (1988), 1–40.

Wayne R. Dynes

SOCIAL DEMOCRACY

This term has acquired various meanings in the course of the past century and a half. Late nineteenth-century Europe saw the formation of **Marxian** working-class parties that called themselves Social Democrats. These gained in numbers and influence, but were beset by the unresolved problem of whether to limit themselves to parliamentary maneuvering, or else to resort to such extra-parliamentary means as general strikes and working-class violence to achieve power.

The Bolshevik Revolution of 1917 triggered a major crisis within the **left**, in which the parliamentary and reformist elements sided with Social Democracy, while those committed to violent revolution joined Communist Parties organized on the Leninist model. This splitting of the left provoked internecine struggles that weakened it in the face of the emerging fascist and National Socialist movements in the years of the Great Depression. Social Democracy tended to become the party of the petty bourgeoisie and the intellectuals, while the working class proper rallied to its Communist rivals.

Germany. The first party to welcome the new homosexual emancipation **movement** was German Social Democracy. In January 1898 August Bebel, the leader of the party in the Reichstag, took the floor in defense of the first petition submitted by the newly founded **Scientific-Humanitarian Committee**, while—with the exception of a single National Liberal—the representatives of the other parties expressed outrage and disgust at the subject of the petition. In the wake of this intervention, Magnus **Hirschfeld** was personally received by Secretary Nieberding, the head of the Imperial Office of Justice, who cautioned him that the government could do nothing until the public had been reeducated as to the justice of abolishing the antihomosexual **Paragraph 175**. The Social Democrats—with a few exceptions in their own ranks—continued to be the only party that supported the demands of the Scientific-Humanitarian Committee, while the opposition was spearheaded by the Catholic Centrist Party. At first the whole issue was limited to Germany, as the Social Democratic parties in other nations, for a variety of reasons, had no "homosexual question" to debate.

As happened elsewhere, German progressives took notice—often uncritically—of Soviet **Russia**. The Bolshevik Revolution of 1917 not only swept away the old order in a cataclysm of blood and violence, it gave the appearance of turning the new Soviet Russia into a huge experimental laboratory in which official support was accorded all kinds of pioneering social innovations. The penal codes of the RSFSR in 1922 and 1926 omitted all reference to voluntary homosexual acts committed in private, and among reformers in the West the myth arose that the Soviet Union was the "country of the future" in which the injustices and inequalities of the past were being overcome. This stance naturally affected the leftist parties abroad.

In 1922 a highly progressive penal code was drafted by the German Minister of Justice, Gustav Radbruch, who had been the teacher of Kurt **Hiller** at the University of Heidelberg, but Radbruch did not succeed in bringing his draft before the Reichstag. The Communist Party, with its principle of strict intraparty discipline, made support for law reform part of its platform. The Communist lawyer Felix Halle formulated its approach to the issue by writing: "The class-conscious proletariat, uninfluenced by the ideology of property and freed from the ideology of the churches, approaches the question of sexual life and also the problem of homosexuality with a lack of prejudice afforded by an understanding of the overall structure of society."

On October 16, 1929, decriminalization of homosexual acts between consenting adults was voted by a committee of the Reichstag 15 to 13, with the Communists, Social Democrats, and German People's Party (classical liberal) supporting the change. However, the American stock market crash a week later—heralding a world-wide depression—provoked a crisis in which law reform was shelved as the Reichstag struggled with the deteriorating economic situation and the mounting polarization of political forces within the country.

The Social Democratic Party supported the demands of the homosexual organizations less out of any principled commitment than because of its devotion to the principle of individual liberty which it had taken over from the classical liberal parties of the nineteenth century, but for just this reason it countenanced defection within its own ranks.

Other Countries. In countries other than Germany the Social Democratic parties and their equivalents often had no clearly defined "sexual politics," suffered embarrassment by the issues which sexual reform raised, and were intimidated by the negative response of the uneducated and religious strata of the population. The only country where law reform was realized under Social Democratic leadership in this period was **Denmark**, which repealed its sodomy law in 1930 (followed by **Sweden** in 1944 and Norway in 1948).

In the Soviet Union, Stalin set about repudiating all concessions to liberalism as he consolidated his power in a one-party state. A law dated March 7, 1934—a year after the National Socialist seizure of power—restored criminal sanctions against male but not female homosexuality. Various contradictory pretexts were offered for the change, but in practice it meant that—even as the myth of the "humanist Stalin" was propagated abroad in the interest of the Popular Front formed to halt the rising tide of reaction in Central and Western Europe—the Communist parties lost all interest in sexual reform, and Social Democracy had to carry the ball alone.

The World League for Sexual Reform on a Scientific Basis itself collapsed after Hirschfeld's death on May 14, 1935, as the two wings—one desiring a centrist approach with the cooperation of the bourgeois parties and the other seeking an open alliance with the Communist Party, even at that late date—could not work together. The movement of the preceding twenty-five years had pursued a number of different goals which now proved ideologically incompatible. The sexual reform aspect tended to become the province of the left, while the birth control movement and sex education were anchored in the center and the eugenics movement became identified with the right, particularly after the **Nazi** accession to power in Germany, where Hitler forced upon his cabinet a series of negative eugenic measures, including compulsory sterilization. The Soviet Union relentlessly dismantled progressive social laws, prohibited homosexuality, forbade abortion and the sale of birth control materials, and conformed to the model of the clerical-fascist states with their pronatalist policies. Some leftist scholars have argued that such retrograde policies were a tem-

porary aberration under Stalin. Yet long after his death, the Communist regimes of **China, Cuba**, and Vietnam—not to mention that of the Soviet Union itself—have continued to adhere rigidly to these policies, with antihomosexuality prominent among them.

In Western Europe after 1945 the Social Democratic parties sympathized with the homosexual liberation movement but were often timid in defending it, while the conservative parties were solid in their opposition to law reform and quite willing to use homosexuals as scapegoats in the anti-Communist furor of the 1950s. It was only in 1969 that Paragraph 175 was finally repealed under a Social Democratic government in Bonn.

In Britain a special situation prevailed. Much of the Labour Party's rank and file persisted in regarding homosexuality as a product of the elite **public schools**, as (in effect) an **aristocratic vice.** Initially it was easier to obtain support for the work of the **Wolfenden** Committee from Liberals and even Conservatives than from Labour stalwarts. When George Brinham, who had been chairman of the Labour Party from 1959 to 1960, was murdered by a hustler in 1962, the party offered no sympathy, only silence.

Nonetheless, in Parliament the chief support for the Abse Bill (1967), which decriminalized homosexual conduct among consenting adults in England and Wales, came from Labour Party members. Yet this step was taken in the form of a private member's bill not officially supported by the Labour government of Harold Wilson.

Subsequently, homosexuality emerged as an issue in dispute between the "modern" sector of the party, consisting of intellectuals and elements of the upper middle class, as against the old-line trade unionists. The latter remained deeply suspicious of the championing of gay rights and other progressive social issues by the modern faction. In the 1980s Thatcherite electoral successes caused frustration that heightened cleavages over social questions. In the Bermondsey by-election of February 1983, when openly gay Peter Tatchell sought to be returned to Parliament as the official Labour candidate, his campaign suffered from systematic vilification at the hands of party stalwarts. In 1988 many Labour M.P.s voted for Clause 28, the notorious measure banning "promotion" of homosexuality.

Despite the checkered record in some countries, on the whole the growth of Social Democracy promoted a climate of liberalism in which, other factors permitting, a visible gay movement could flourish. In the early 1980s the French Socialist Party of François Mitterand proved receptive to a number of requests from the homosexual movement, eliminating the last vestiges of the Vichy restrictions on homosexual conduct. The Spanish Socialists under Felipe González enormously increased the whole sphere of sexual freedom. In Greece, however, the Socialist regime of Andreas Papandreou continued to repress homosexuality.

Conclusion. On the whole, the ideology of Social Democratic parties has been eclectic rather than doctrinaire, absorbing traits of nineteenth-century liberalism repudiated by the conservatives. At the same time they have been gingerly about offending lower middle-class deference to sexual "respectability," and they loathe to engage in a vigorous defense of gay rights in crucial electoral contests where the right (and sometimes the left) openly appeals to anti-homosexual prejudice. Despite these reservations, the progress achieved by the gay movement in Western and Central Europe would have been unimaginable without the intervention and support of the Social Democracy, however qualified in particular situations it may have been.

BIBLIOGRAPHY. Bob Cant and Susan Hemmings, eds., *Radical Records: Thirty Years of Lesbian and Gay History*, London: Routledge, 1988; W. U. Eissler, *Arbeiterparteien und Homosexuellenfrage: Zur Sexualpolitik von SPD und KPD in der Weimarer Republik*, Hamburg: Verlag Rosa Winkel, 1980; Harry Oosterhuis, "The Guilty Conscience of the Left," *European Gay Review*, 4 (1989), 72–80; James D. Steakley, *The Homosexual Emancipation Movement in Germany*, New York: Arno Press, 1975; Peter Tatchell, *The Battle for Bermondsey*, second ed., London: GMP/Heretic Books, 1984.

William A. Percy

SOCIAL WORK

This umbrella term comprises a range of professional services, activities, and methods concretely addressing the investigation, treatment, and material assistance of those perceived to be economically disadvantaged and socially maladjusted. Social work began in late Victorian England as a volunteer response to the wide disparity between the "two nations"—the comfortable class and the poor—and spread quickly to America and northern Europe. In the course of the twentieth century the field became professionalized, and today most social workers are state employees. Large claims have sometimes been made for social work: that it can cure society of its ills, and that it represents the conscience of a people, but these assertions are usually rejected as grandiose. Lacking a methodology of its own, social work has sometimes seemed a prisoner of the varying mixtures of economics, **sociology**, and **psychoanalysis** that have been imported to sustain its practice. Social work should probably be viewed not as a science but as a humanistic endeavor, though one in which the imperatives of bureaucracy loom large. At its best, however, social work avoids ascriptions of pathology, seeking to build on the strengths of clients so that they may take an active part in reclaiming their own lives.

Social Work and Homosexuality. The rise of the modern gay and lesbian **movement** after World War II has exposed the inadequacy of the publicly supported social services for members of sexual minorities. It is not so much that professional social workers are **homophobic**—surveys have shown that they are less so than most segments of society—as that they are ignorant of the special needs of gay and lesbian clients, and hence prone to insensitivity, however unintentional. In part this situation reflects the earlier prevalence of the cultural norm of Western society which decreed heterosexual marriage to be the only acceptable, recognized form of sexual relationship; other types of liaison had to be hidden from the prying gaze of the neighbors, social workers, and the police. Moreover, most gay and lesbian clients, not being members of economically deprived families, or having severed conventional family ties, are seen as middle class, and hence outside the area of the social worker's concern. Of course not all students of social work are the same, and some individuals attend schools of social work as a prerequisite to the practice of **psychotherapy** with middle-class clients.

Gay Self-Help. Almost from the beginning of the **Mattachine Society**, America's first successful homosexual rights organization, the need to organize volunteers to supply **counseling** and—as far as possible—jobs and temporary economic assistance was recognized. Today this need is particularly acute with **youth**, with the elderly, and with people with **AIDS**. Many gay and lesbian teenagers feel compelled to leave home ("runaways"), or may even be pushed out by intensely homophobic parents ("throwaways"). If they are to escape the self-destructive subculture of drug abuse and **prostitution**, they need positive assistance. This has sometimes proved a sensitive issue, as caregivers may incur suspicion of impure motives. As regards older gay men and lesbians, research has shown that the stereotype of a lonely, desperate, unhappy old age is false. Nonetheless, older gay people have special needs, and these are the focus of such organizations as New York's Senior Action in a Gay Environment (SAGE).

The AIDS crisis has caused new organizations to be created in major cities in North America and western Europe. The remarkable social response of the gay community to this baffling disease contrasts with the situation of the intravenous-drug-user group of AIDS patients, where dependence on public sources of therapy and counseling is total.

Even gay-organized social services may display inadequate attention to some sectors of their population. Because most gay volunteers are middle class, they may not have a full understanding of those from poor backgrounds; put differently, commonness of sexual orientation may mask difference in social **class**. It is often forgotten that many lesbians and gay men are parents, and their concern for their offspring is a central aspect of their lives. Finally, gay men and lesbians of color may have not only economic problems but psychological ones as well; the latter stem not only from the racism of the larger society but from lack of understanding within their own ethnic communities.

Experience has shown that the gay community need not continue to rely mainly on its own largely volunteer efforts, but that real successes can be gained in sensitizing social workers employed by the state, either during their training period or in the course of their professional activity. After all, homosexuals are entitled to a return on their tax dollars just as much as any other group, and the social disorganization caused by **prejudice** against them ultimately impacts the larger community. In some cases much may be accomplished by sitting down with the (presumably) heterosexual social workers and patiently explaining the problem. However, the bureaucratic constraints of public agencies can make progress slow. Here external pressure, including lobbying efforts and voting drives, is required. The success of gay groups in organizing is known to politicians and can be used to advantage in changing the social-work profession from the top.

BIBLIOGRAPHY. A. Elfin Moses and Robert G. Hawkins, *Counseling Lesbian Women and Gay Men: A Life-Issues Approach*, St. Louis: C. V. Mosby, 1982; Robert Schoenberg, Richard S. Goldberg, and David A. Shore, eds., *With Compassion Toward Some*, New York: Harrington Press, 1985; Natalie Jane Woodman and Harry R. Lenna, *Counseling with Gay Men and Women: A Guide for Facilitating Positive Life-Styles*, San Francisco: Jossey-Bass, 1980.

Wayne R. Dynes

SOCIOBIOLOGY

Sociobiology is the study of behavior (in human beings and animals) from the point of view of its evolution by natural selection. The term was popularized in 1975 (the field is sometimes also called "behavioral ecology"). Narrowly, sociobiology has come to mean the study of the "why" questions of behavior: why does a particular species of fish have males that act as females do just before they lay their eggs? Broadly, it can also take in the "how" questions: how do the fish's central nervous system and hormones collaborate to produce this behavior?

Nature and Nurture. There are, of course, other approaches that have been called "biological." To the lay mind, if a trait "is" biological then it cannot be changed; if the trait "is" environmental then it can be. This is a false dichotomy, and is self-contradictory. For example, an "environmental" event like a car accident can have very fixed and unchangeable consequences (such as permanent injury), while a "biological" trait such as the growing of a beard can be routinely overridden by a cultural mandate (shaving). Establishing the steps leading up to a trait helps one to understand the trait and perhaps to change it, regardless of whether the causation turns out to "be" biological, environmental, or some combination. The sizes, shapes, and spatial distributions of footprints are all socially determined within certain limits set by the biology of walking. But if the footprints are in sand, they are easily changed; if they are in wet concrete, they are unchangeable (short of jackhammering) after just a few hours.

Unfortunately, this naive nature–nurture dichotomy has been widely taken up in the social sciences. The most common view is to say that biology has an influence in the womb and very early in life, but that soon after birth the family and society socialize the infant and make the influence of biology negligible. A variation of this view maintains that biology sets the limits but socialization sets the precise outcome. A few social scientists, including a few in sexology, believe so strongly in the power of socialization that they claim that students of behavior should not bother with biology at all.

This point of view is rapidly crumbling, even within the narrow confines of sexology itself. The massive Kinsey Institute study of male and female homosexuality in blacks and whites (Bell, Weinberg, and Hammersmith, 1981) attempted to correlate hundreds of environmental factors (number and age of siblings, childhood rearing practices, social class, and the like) with adult homosexual outcome and came up with almost nothing. They very nearly found that the only powerful predictor of adult homosexuality is childhood gender nonconformity, a finding that has been replicated often, both retrospectively and prospectively. This predictor is so strong that the authors of the study considered it evidence that such nonconformity is closely linked to homosexuality developmentally—i.e., that the commonest type of adult homosexuality is just the adult expression of the childhood nonconforming trait. That is a reasonable conclusion, though one cannot thereby assume that biology has been shown to be the likely cause of sexual **orientation** differences.

Yet sexual orientation does run in families, according to a study conducted by Richard Pillard and James D. Weinrich. If the results are extendible to the population at large, then about 20 to 25 percent of the brothers of gay men are also gay, and 20 to 25 percent of the sisters of lesbian women are lesbian or bisexual. These findings per se do not show the reasons for the trait running in families. But it is interesting that in recent history, social scientists have not conducted studies like this one, even though they would quite properly point out that they would use socialization theory to explain the results.

When homosexuality and biology have been discussed together before the advent of sociobiology, results have been mixed. Alfred **Kinsey** approached homosexuality and biology just as he approached heterosexuality and biology: by considering the natural evolutionary heritage of our species. Heterosexually, he noted that a sense of smell is extremely important in the courtship rituals of many mammalian species, and so he thought it not surprising that some human beings would be sexually excited by particular smells. Likewise, he found sexual activities between members of the same sex to be common enough in other mammals to conclude that homosexuality, too, was within the evolutionary heritage of the human mammal. However, he resisted finer distinctions (might something be natural for mountain sheep but unnatural for human beings?) and seemed to be uninterested in the Why questions, even though he was a well-enough regarded expert in evolutionary biology to write a textbook about it.

Genetic Basis for Homosexuality? The Kinsey group's surveys did, however, find an incidence of homosexuality among men and women that was very high, evolutionarily speaking. This significance of Kinsey's statistics was picked out by the pathbreaking evolutionary biologist G. Evelyn Hutchinson, who read the Kinsey statistic that roughly 10 percent of American males had only or mainly homosexual experience for 3 or more years of reproductive life, and argued that there might be a genetic predisposition to such behavior. This number is evolutionarily extremely large if one assumes that homo-

sexuality is merely an evolutionary "mistake." Had the actual incidence of homosexuality turned out to have been what biologists consider the normal range for evolutionary mistakes—very rare, say one in 10,000—Hutchinson would not have taken note of it, because (rightly or wrongly) he could have assumed that if there were a genetic mechanism promoting homosexuality it was no commoner than any of several genetically transmitted diseases. But 10 percent is at least 1,000 times as high a level as 1 in 10,000 is, and so Hutchinson had to ask why natural selection would have "allowed" the evolution of a species that had sexual learning patterns in which 10 percent of its male members reproduce at a level significantly lower than they otherwise seemed able to—not because of some incurable defect but because they are not attracted to women. After all, attraction to the opposite sex is one of the first things one might expect evolution to arrange. So if there were any genetic predisposition to even a portion of male homosexuality, then Kinsey's statistics pose a puzzle: how could a genetic mistake come to be so common? Even if one takes an estimate as low as 4 percent, this is still 40 times higher than the highest mutation rates.

Hutchinson's answer was to find the sense in which homosexuality is not an evolutionary mistake, and in following this radical (for 1959) line of thought he showed a preference that was also shared by the earliest sociobiological investigators of homosexuality. When sociobiologists see variation in a trait in nature, they tend to look not for what went wrong, but rather for what went right. In Hutchinson's day, the way to see something "right" in a trait that lowered reproductive success was heterozygote advantage. This was the first in a number of theories developed in an attempt to explain the evolutionary value of homosexuality.

Heterozygote Advantage. This is commonly illustrated in textbooks by the example of sickle-cell anemia, but there is no reason why the principle has to be illustrated with a disease. The essential point is that sometimes an organism can need two different genes to maximize its reproductive success. Owing to genetic recombination, a parent usually passes only one of these two genes on to any particular offspring, and so only some of that organism's children will get one of each kind of gene (i.e., be heterozygous like the parent), even if both parents have both genes (i.e., are are heterozygous themselves). Some children will get two copies of one and others will get two copies of the other (i.e., they will be homozygous). Natural selection will be unable to eliminate either of the two kinds of homozygote, even if one of them (as in sickle-cell anemia) is extremely deleterious to the carrier's reproductive success, because there is natural selection for heterozygosity.

Hutchinson's idea could be loosely applied to homosexuality as follows. If there were a gene which predisposed its carriers to be heterosexual, and another one at the same locus that predisposed them to be homosexual, and if those who got one of each gene on average raised more children than those who got two of either kind, then there could well be a number of nonreproductive, homozygous individuals who got two copies of the homosexuality-predisposing gene—a number much higher than the levels of 1 in 10,000 or so discussed above, and quite possibly in the 4–10 percent range. So Hutchinson viewed homosexuality not as an out-and-out mistake but perhaps as the inevitable result of selection for heterozygosity in sexual preference.

It was evolutionary biologists John Kirsch and James Rodman who put flesh onto this idea in 1982 by proposing that people with one copy each of the hypothetical homosexuality- and heterosexuality-predisposing genes might be bisexuals with a higher average reproductive success than either the average "pure" homosexual or the average "pure" hetero-sexual. There are, for example, many societies in which everyone is expected to marry but in which male members are expected to engage in extensive homosexual relationships before marriage (or throughout life). These relationships can be of profound benefit throughout the men's lives. A "pure" heterosexual might have more difficulty forming such bonds, and a "pure" homosexual might have trouble forming a marital bond, and thus both groups might not fare as well reproductively as the man with bisexual potential. How this might apply to societies in which extramarital homosexuality was disadvantageous was not explained in detail.

An entirely different model of homosexuality in sociobiological thought concerns certain so-called "cross-gendered" individuals such as the berdache among American Indians, the mu-khannath (or khanith) among the Arabs of Oman, and the hijra in India. In certain societies (with endless variation in detail), boys (and sometimes girls) with marked childhood gender nonconformity are channeled into specialized adult roles. In the case of berdaches, these specialized positions often combine the roles of drag queen, healer, psychotherapist, and teacher. The theory proposed to account for such people is called kin selection, and in its previous application to insect societies it constitutes one of sociobiology's theoretical triumphs.

Kin selection theory points out that Darwin was wrong when he proposed that, as a result of natural selection, individual animals will act so as to maximize their reproductive success (or RS: the number of offspring one has which survive to reproductive adulthood). Instead, says kin selection, natural selection acts to maximize individuals' inclusive fitness (IF), which is the number of surviving offspring plus the number of relatives' surviving offspring, with each such offspring being devalued by a fraction that reflects the percentage of genes shared with the individual by direct descent. One's own children are valued at 1, a full sibling's children at 1/2, one's half-sibling's children at 1/4, and so on. Accordingly, some people might maximize their IF even if they have an RS of zero—which means that one can no longer automatically assume that an animal without offspring is acting contrary to how evolution has selected it to act. Accordingly, the homophobes' most smug argument—that homosexual acts are unnatural because they cannot produce children—collapses at its foundation.

In 1976 Weinrich pointed out that this model might be applicable to the cross-gendered berdaches (following suggestions made by Robert Trivers, Herman Spieth, and Edward O. Wilson). For kin selection to take hold and allow the evolution of such reproductively altruistic traits, a certain mathematical relationship must hold between the cost to the individual of not reproducing (the cost measured in terms of lost RS) and the benefit to that individual's kin of having a nonreproducing relative (the benefit likewise measured in RS units). Under some conditions, an individual might reproductively be considered "damaged goods," and thus have a lower than average cost of not reproducing. Under others, an individual might just happen to be particularly gifted in a given society's nonreproductive role, and might thus maximize her or his IF by taking up the role—even if taking up the role would require one to forego personal reproduction.

The damaged goods argument often meets with acceptance, perhaps because it does not challenge the cultural assumption that homosexuality should turn out to be below heterosexuality in some sense. But the special-talent explanation often meets with the following question: if the people supposedly covered by it are so talented, why do they not apply their talents to reproduction?

Berdaches. A good answer to this legitimate (even if unfortunately-phrased)

question had to wait until 1987. Recent anthropological research suggests that people like the berdaches are not so much cross-gendered as they are mixed-gendered, and that they serve(d) important roles in their societies as arbitrators in the battle between the sexes. Here, once again, the unique sociobiological perspective (or obsession) of reproductive success steps in with a surprising theoretical argument. If mixed-gender individuals are valuable because they can arbitrate different points of view on gender issues, why is it to the advantage of each side to take the berdaches' advice? Why would they be considered less biased than others in the tribe? If a society is willing to reward them (and their families) for settling gender disputes, arranging marriages, and the like, because they are not particularly biased for or against (say) men who abandon their wives and 20 children or women who cuckold their husbands, it would behoove them not to be men who had abandoned their wives and 20 children themselves or women who had cuckolded their husbands themselves.

Sociobiological theory suggests that these people would in fact be less likely to be biased only if they renounced their sex's point of view, which sociobiologically is seen to result from the different actions each sex is selected to use in its reproductive strategy. If they pursue a nonreproductive strategy, then sexual dimorphism suddenly loses its point, and (according to kin selection) their side in the battle of the sexes would depend not upon their own sex but upon the sex of their relatives. But on average (and certainly on average over time!) one's relatives are about equally divided between males and females. So by renouncing individual reproduction, such people make it possible for their advice in fact to be less biased. This in turn makes their advice more likely to be taken (even if, as is the fate of arbitrators, it is taken grudgingly).

Marriage and Homosexual Behavior. With both the kin selection and heterozygote-advantage theories in mind, in 1987 Weinrich proposed a new theory that put forth a better evolutionary raison d'être for homosexuality in societies in which everyone is expected to marry. In such societies, sexual attraction is often not high on the list of reasons to marry; pure lust is expected to be gratified in extramarital liaisons or not at all. Ancient **Greece**, modern urban **Mexico**, medieval **Japan**, and the **United States** in several of the past few centuries may well constitute such societies. "Being homosexual" in such a society, as opposed to "being heterosexual," means being inclined to having homosexual relations outside of marriage instead of heterosexual ones outside of marriage. Obviously, this kind of homosexuality can be considered a form of **bisexuality**, and interestingly such a bisexual or homosexual person has two reproductive advantages over a pure heterosexual when viewed in sociobiological terms: he or she would be less likely to have children out of wedlock, and she or he would be less likely to protest a marriage arranged by the parents (i.e., one would be less likely to be already in love with a member of the opposite sex to whom one might have wished to become married). Both of these traits had previously been proposed by sociobiologists as reproductively altruistic acts (in work published before this theory was circulated).

Conclusion. Of course, any sociobiological theory worth its salt must be highly aware of social and environmental influences on the traits being considered, because natural selection is extremely sensitive to the social forces at work in the society which sets the rules. If your society offers no berdache **role**, you can try to improvise one (as modern "drag queens" seem sometimes to do) but it is unlikely that your IF will thereby increase. Sociobiological theories help to explain why imprinting of sexual object choices could have evolved in some species to be fixed (like footprints in concrete) and in others to be easily changeable (like footprints in

sand). Indeed, it is even conceivable that "fixed" types may have begun evolving in some societies and "changeable" types in other societies.

BIBLIOGRAPHY. Alan C. Bell, Martin S. Weinberg, and Sue Kiefer Hammersmith, *Sexual Preference: Its Development in Men and Women*, Bloomington: Indiana University Press, 1981; G. G. Gallup, Jr., and S. D. Suarez, "Homosexuality as a By-product of Selection for Optimal Heterosexual Strategies," *Perspectives in Biology and Medicine*, 26 (1983), 315–22; G. Evelyn Hutchinson, "A Speculative Consideration of Certain Possible Forms of Sexual Selection in Man," *American Naturalist*, 93 (1959), 81–91; John A. W. Kirsch and James Eric Rodman, "Selection and Sexuality: The Darwinian View of Homosexuality," in *Homosexuality: Social, Psychological, and Biological Issues*, W. Paul, J. D. Weinrich, J. C. Gonsiorek, and M. E. Hotvedt, eds., Beverly Hills, CA: SAGE Publications, 1982, pp. 183–95; Richard C. Pillard and James D. Weinrich, "Evidence of Familial Nature of Male Homosexuality," *Archives of General Psychiatry*, 43 (1986), 808–12; Michael Ruse, "Are There Gay Genes? Sociobiology and Homosexuality," *Journal of Homosexuality*, 6:4 (1981) 5–34; James D. Weinrich, *Human Reproductive Strategy: The Importance of Income Unpredictability, and the Evolution of Non-Reproduction*, Ph.D. thesis, Harvard University Department of Biology, 1976; idem, "Is Homosexuality Biologically Natural?" in W. Paul, et al., op cit., pp. 197–211; idem, "A New Sociobiological Theory of Homosexuality Applicable to Societies with Universal Marriage," *Ethology and Sociobiology*, 8 (1987), 37–47; idem, *Sexual Landscapes: Why We Are What We Are, Why We Love Whom We Love*, New York: Charles Scribner's Sons, 1987.

James D. Weinrich

SOCIOLOGY

The term sociology was coined by Auguste Comte in 1836. Since his time sociology has developed into a major discipline, with particular resonance in English-speaking countries.

Yet academic sociology is in some respects a codification of knowledge that has always been available. In all societies individuals have some view of what is shared by other individuals known to them. Folk theories exist everywhere about what is common to members of a human group as well what contrasts with qualities found in other groups. Programs for scientific comparison of the evolution of social arrangements were stimulated by reports of social arrangements at variance with European ones made available during the Age of Discovery (after 1492). The Industrial Revolution and the French Revolution helped to augment this stimulus and channel it.

Among those trying to make sense of those changes and their place as part of a process of social evolution were the three architects of sociology's "grand theory": Karl **Marx** (1818–1883), Emile Durkheim (1858–1917), and Max Weber (1864–1919). None of them was professionally trained in sociology, and their precursors in theorizing about social order and structure included **Plato**, **Aristotle**, Machiavelli, Vico, Hobbes, Locke, Montesquieu, and Rousseau.

The Basic Problem. The central concern of sociology elaborating this patrimony is world-historical changes in systems of domination. Its aim is to explain how one system (e.g., capitalism) functions at a particular time and how one system arises from another (e.g., capitalism succeeding feudalism). To those ensconced at the discipline's center, others chronicling the lifeways of "queers" have seemed to be engaged in a dubious enterprise unlikely to contribute to the building of a unified theory of society. Indeed, description of how people actually live has often struck those concerned with abstract, general theories of society as a diversion from the path to knowledge. And when the people described are homosexual, motives such as voyeuristic titillation or special pleading are imputed. Yet the macrohistorical processes projected by Marx and Durkheim from their consideration of European history have not been enacted elsewhere as predicted, nor have subsequent events in Europe followed their scenarios of primordial loyalties eroding with increasing industrialization.

Even the builders of American sociological traditions, who focused on smaller social units over briefer periods of time, expected contrasts of race, ethnicity, and gender to wane. The classic work (1913–18) of W. I. Thomas and Florian Znaniecki on Polish peasants emigrating to the United States exemplified Durkheim's conception of the (necessary) breakdown of traditional (peasant) society with accompanying individual pathology which reflected social disorganization— both of which were expected to disappear with integration into the modern world of, say, Chicago. Empirical work in the Chicago School tradition treated ethnic **subcultures** under the rubric of "social disorganization," an anomaly destined to be resolved as contact with dominant American society reduced differences. This process—variously termed assimilation, acculturation, accommodation—was supposed to eliminate hostility and, by the same token, conflict. Since conflict was regarded as a product of individual attitudes and values rather than of structured inequalities, it was expected to diminish as contact dissolved **stereotypes** and cultural differences—the sources of intergroup conflict. Ascribed characteristics (such as race, **gender**, and possibly sexual **orientation**) have taken on an importance quite out of keeping with the confident expectations of those in the "grand tradition" that these need not be considered, because their significance would decline eventually and disappear.

Historical reality has proved to be quite different. Groups based on characteristics which classical theory regarded as already anachronistic a century ago have not merely "assumed political functions comparable to those of a subordinate class; they have in important respects become more effective than social classes in mobilizing their forces in pursuit of collective ends" (Parkin, p. 622). Insofar as sociology aims to analyze what is actually occurring rather than to invoke the tarrying of the messiah, it must endeavor to explain the continued strength and/or emergence of social movements based on consciousness of shared ascribed characteristics. The emergence of a group consciousness and subsequent mobilization of a "people" who could not seriously have been designated a "group" three decades ago contrasts markedly with the erosion of **class** consciousness and the increasing impotence of organized labor. Not just Marxist theory, but classical bourgeois social theory, including the two major American perspectives descended from Durkheim and from Thomas, functionalism and symbolic interactionism respectively, have ill prepared the investigator to understand the quite unpredicted emergence and successes of racial and ethnic, women's and gay **movements**. Although understanding homosexual socialization has not been a central theme for sociological theory, prominent attempts to encompass American (male) homosexuality in the mid-to-late twentieth century will be discussed below.

Functionalism. The structuralist–functionalist tradition included some recognition that moral consensus requires some target: norm-drenched individuals need before them the cautionary example of negative role models. To be certain that they are within the bounds of propriety, someone else must be condemned to obloquy outside the boundaries. Blatant specimens of inadequate masculine socialization can be tolerated as a butt for jokes (among other things), because such persons serve as a horrible warning of what boys must avoid becoming. Possibly, public punishment of sodomites served the same "function" in Europe during the **Middle Ages**, in Aztec **Mexico**, and in the pre-Columbian **Andes**. Ridicule was sufficient in North American **Indian** tribes and in the **Pacific** cultures of Polynesia. To define the moral unit "us" of a society there must be others beyond the moral

pale. Durkheim wrote of "normal" rates of deviance and crime necessary to provide occasions for exemplary punishments to affirm the moral order, publicly fixing the line between acceptable and unacceptable behavior. Durkheim's intellectual heirs have been concerned with boundary maintenance both between and within societies. Of course, to serve an exemplary role as a moral counterexample a deviant (of whatever sort) must be generally recognized as such. Prior to the **Kinsey** findings concerning **incidence**, when it was assumed a homosexual was a rara avis (the village queer) and that one could be readily recognized by everyone (because of their obvious **gender** non-conformity), homosexuality seemed consistent enough with a moral consensus model of society, i.e., it was "normal deviance" rather than subversion of the moral order.

The landmark study that showed how widespread homosexuality could reinforce rather than challenge the moral order was that of Reiss on hustlers and their clients (1961). For **trade** individuals, masculinity was defined by insertor behavior. In their view, the **"queers"** were the insertees, so their participation did not erode trade masculine status, so long as they gave nothing more than their cocks (and possibly an occasional beating), i.e., so long as they "never took it." **Prostitution** was not perceived as demasculinizing as such; apparently this stigmatizing definition was evaded along with that of "queer." Such a system could persist only with the collusion of clients willing to enact the **role** of the "queer" by not challenging the valuation and self-image of those whose behavior was that of homosexual prostitution. So long as this system's script for the dominance of the masculine actor and the submission (and optimally feminization) of the "queer" was credited, validation of masculinity and depreciation of homosexuality were actually supported by "deviant" acts. The "queers" kneeling to worship the symbols of trade's masculinity quarantined the stigma, protecting the masculine self-conceptions of their sexual partners. Beyond the financial rewards, sexual release, and the reassurance of masculinity, the trade participants were exposed to the dangers of succumbing to any temptations toward passivity. Most presumably "learned" they weren't "queer"—and did not have to be such to get off with men. Reiss' study did not assess the degree of "role distance" of those enacting the "queer" role versus the degree of self-hatred, but to whatever extent those playing the "queer" role credited its truth (and justice), the moral order in general and the superiority of heterosexual males in particular were reinforced by "deviant" acts.

How far men could venture into homosexuality—beyond adolescence and even beyond exclusively insertor behavior—without considering themselves implicated as "queers" either by themselves or by their partners was demonstrated by the preponderance of married men observed by Laud Humphreys in his study of **toilet** sex, *Tearoom Trade*. Not only was homosexuality compatible with the existing moral order, so were homosexuals, for it was not just "trade" who "compensated" for suspect sexual behavior with hyper-conformity in espousing traditional social values (especially in regard to sex and gender). The stratification of sexual encounters (with the "masculine principle" on top in every sense), along with the "consent" to stigmatization of those seeking "real men" as partners was perfectly consistent with the Durkheimian vision.

Blumstein and Schwartz' rich comparative study of married, non-married cohabiting, gay male, and lesbian **couples** follows the functionalist tradition into a social world in which such stratification is mostly obsolete—although both lesbians and gay men in their sample remain sensitive to being fit into the opposite gender role. Functionalists delineated complementary instrumental (the husband oriented toward the world outside the family) and affective (the wife oriented inward to the family) roles necessary to the functioning of small groups (not just families). Blumstein and Schwartz substitute a new polarity—work-centered/relationship-centered—for the instrumental/affective one. They contend that for a relationship to endure, at least one partner must be oriented inward toward keeping the relationship going well, but do not try to sort out whether relationships work better when both partners are relationship-centered, or if there is some advantage to one partner being oriented outward from the relationship to the work world (i.e., whether the roles are genuinely complementary, not merely different).

Symbolic Interactionism. In the pre-contemporary period of relative neglect, most sociological research dealing with homosexuality was done, however, within another, indigenous tradition which rivaled functionalism for hegemony in postwar American sociology: symbolic interactionism. The Chicago School included a tradition of studying "unconventional" careers (e.g., the typical patterns of taxi-hall dancers, jack-rollers, hoboes) in the same way as the subcultures built by practically every imaginable social category that could be found in Chicago, except homosexuals. Like Durkheim, the founders of the Chicago School believed the all too visible social pathology they saw around them would first fade, then gradually disappear (a process to be accelerated by sociological knowledge itself) as a modern moral order emerged, to be consolidated and expanded. The modern society envisioned from Chicago was more ethnically diverse than was the *Gesellschaft* conceived by European theorists. Still, Chicago sociologists believed that the knocking together of those with different cultural backgrounds would break down, or at least wear off the rough edges of culturally distinctive differences. And, for whatever reason, this tradition was far more concerned with documenting the stages in what they were certain was the evolution of antagonistic groups into a future unity (moral order) than with discussing the overall process: the forest of the evolution to a more integrated social/moral order often disappeared from view in Chicago descriptions of particular trees (roles, groups, etc.). Nevertheless, the Chicago tradition focused on socialization decades before functionalists turned to trying to account for the actual transmission of social order. The Chicago model of socialization held that an **identity** (i.e., a self) is an internalization of the view of significant others. If a behavior (say a boy playing with dolls) is interpreted by others (e.g., parents) as instancing a category (say, **sissy**), they will treat the boy as if he is that kind of person. By recognizing their conception of what he is, the boy will learn who (what) he is, and if this self is credible, the behavior will be transformed into a stable pattern (conduct) and a defining feature of self.

According to symbolic interactionist theory, the self is a product of social definition. What transforms behavior into conduct is **labeling** by others. In the social system of "trade" and "queers" discussed above, the homosexual behavior of the "trade" is not transformed into homosexual conduct (or identity), because the "queers" who know about the behavior do not so label them. Unless the **police** chance upon them in the act, no homosexual label is applied. But what of the "queers"? Who labeled them? Within encounters with the "peers," "trade" of course did, but most encounters began with someone already set in the "queer" role, so explanation must look back before the particular occasion to locate the manufacture of the "queer." Unfortunately for the theory, most people with homosexual, gay, or lesbian self-identities report never having been labeled. In his pioneer study of 182 men who considered themselves homosexual, Dank (p. 123) found "no cases in which the subject had come out in the context of being arrested on a charge involving homosexuality or being fired from a job because of homosexual behavior.... 4.5 percent of the sample came out in the context of public exposure." Although labeling theory posits labeling by agents of the state (policemen, judges) in official records, those trying to rescue the theory might extend "labeling" from official acts to internalization of everyday epithets. Such a tack does not, however, salvage the theory, for even in this broader sense, labeling does not account for the data which have been gathered. Even those explaining adult homosexuality on the basis of childhood **effeminacy** do not find more than half of those with the effect reporting the supposed cause, even if labeling as effeminate is widened to self-labeling.

That homosexual conduct is generally reached without ever being labeled by others should suffice to discredit "labeling theory," and some men report having **come out** (and have in some cases joined gay organizations) before having had any homosexual encounters. That is, identity (secondary deviance) sometimes precedes behavior (primary deviance). For lesbians, Ponse (p. 125) lists a series of elements in the process of identity formation that reverses the primary–secondary deviance order. The first element is that the individual has a subjective sense of being different from heterosexual persons and identifies this difference as feelings of sexual-emotional attraction to her own sex. Second, an understanding of the homosexual or lesbian significance of these feelings is acquired. Third, the individual accepts these feelings and their implications for identity, i.e., the person comes out or accepts the identity of lesbian. Fourth, the individual seeks a community of like persons. Fifth, the individual becomes involved in a sexual-emotional lesbian relationship.

Rather than those with a gay identity being a subset of those engaged in some homosexual behavior, the sets intersect with most of those with gay identity within the intersection and most of those with some homosexual behavior not in the intersection. Whether the tinier subset of those labeled is wholly in the intersection of these sets is unknown.

Stigma Theory and the Rejection of the Deviant Role. Having explored adult males who engaged in homosexual behavior, and whose denial of homosexuality correlated with social and political traditionalism, Laud Humphreys became the first sociologist to give sustained attention to the puzzles homosexual reality posed to sociological theory. In *Out of the Closets* Humphreys set out to analyze the then-young gay liberation **movement**, which was composed increasingly of those who had never been labeled, yet openly proclaimed their gayness, adopted various idioms of the **counterculture**, and sought coalitions with other groups challenging the status quo. Humphreys did not attempt to fit the emergence of the gay liberation movement into the functionalist or labeling frameworks discussed above. Instead, he built on Goffman's rambling, but suggestive book, *Stigma.*

Erving Goffman (1922–1982), whose major concern is specified in the title of his first book, *The Presentation of Self in Everyday Life* (1959), was interested in how individuals manage potentially discrediting information. He started with the assumption that in a large-scale, mobile society, no one is quite what he or she seems to be, that is, everyone has some things to hide; **"deviance"** involves not a few "deviants," but everyone (albeit to varying extents, depending on the social standards for the gravity of what they have to hide). For Goffman, everyone who is not discredited is (to some degree) discreditable. The discreditable must cope with anxiety about being found out, the discredited with anxiety about being rejected on the basis (which they themselves may consider legitimate) that they are "that kind of person" (whatever kind does not deserve to be treated as a whole human being). For Goffman, feeling oneself discredited does not require labeling by anyone else, nor for that matter do such feelings require any objective basis (such as "primary deviance"). Since labels are selectively self-applied, being frozen in the naming glare of some representative of Society (parent, teacher, policeman) is far from the only path to a sense of spoiled identity. Goffman's extension of the concept of managing discrediting information from exotic "deviants" to everyone led him to glimpse another way of being in the world: accepting that one is indeed an instance of a discredited category, but challenging the legitimacy of that category's opprobrium—that is, neither trying to deny a category ("I'm not like them") nor living in disgrace ("We deserve it"; "We brought it on ourselves"; and so forth), but instead affirming "I'm fine anyway" (e.g., gay and proud).

Goffman glimpsed the possibility of organizing to challenge the very stigma that is the only common feature of a group, and Humphreys provided an exemplar in his case study of a movement committed to transvaluing the negative valuation of homosexuality. "Normalization" of deviance can be a group strategy, but it required a group. Organization of a movement, in Humphreys' view, had two prerequisites: recognition that present treatment of one's kind is intolerable, and conviction that change is possible. Both conceptions now seem so obvious that one is tempted to forget they were once widely unrecognized, when the sinfulness or sickness that was homosexuality was perceived to be inevitable and just.

Conceiving the existing reality as intolerable and changeable was clearly necessary for the formation of a social movement. Undoubtedly the Kinsey data and the example of the Negro civil rights movement encouraged the early homophile movement. The formation of a critical mass of people who viewed themselves as defined to some extent by homosexual desires was the central precondition for change, and was itself disproportionately facilitated by even tiny organizations challenging the legitimacy of the dominant society's picture of homosexuals. There were other fostering circumstances. Wartime **homosociality** was one, whether or not World War II sped urban migration for those who became involved in the homosexual subculture, and even if official labeling was not part of their experience. Another material change abetting the postwar expansion of public settings for meeting others interested in homosexuality was the introduction of penicillin, and the concomitant reduction of anxiety about venereal diseases. Cultural factors which were important to what the critical mass did include the North American tradition of printing dissident views and some general valuing of freedom of the press—a value missing everywhere else in the Western hemisphere, and a value that was not sufficient in itself for the extension to the homophile press—the tradition of voluntary associations derived from the religious pluralism of the United States, and the welfare state's takeover of insurance against disaster (the "safety net" function formerly discharged by the family).

Growth and Diversification of Gay Culture. Early social science discussions of the "homosexual **community**" treated it as static, rather than recently-emerged (post-World War II). Since at least the mid-1970s, sociologists writing about North American gay culture and gay communities have given nominal recognition to changes, particularly more assertive demands for social respect and the diversification of institutions catering to an open, self-accepting gay market. How did the institutionally elaborated gay communities of the 1970s come about? Obviously, some of the same factors, notably the coalescence of a critical mass, the conception that change was possible, the "mobilization of symbolic resources" (including an embryonic gay **press**, distorted mass media coverage, and public examples), and other factors adduced in the discussion of the "evolution" of gay

political organizations, apply to the "evolution" of gay culture at the same time in the same places.

In folk conceptions of the past, it is well known that "in the beginning was the **bar**"—or more exactly, temporal and spatial segments of bars. Before the rise of the present range of gay institutions, what most lesbians and gay men seeking fellow lesbians and gay men did between working, sleep, and sex was to drink. The gay bar was the first gay institution, and for most members of the "pre-**Stonewall** generation" was often the only one. Before gay people demanded acceptance and forged their own institutions, profitable gay bars provided a modicum of anonymity and protection from official and unofficial interference with gay sociation. Of course, bars provided a setting for arranging sexual liaisons, but their historical importance for the development of a gay people has more to do with revealing to many individuals that they were not unique: not only were there similarly-homosexually-inclined others, but these others were not (all) monsters, and were numerous enough to have meeting places (of varying degrees of furtiveness and friendliness).

"In the beginning was the bar" will strike some as sociology again discovering the obvious. However, what is noteworthy about bars' being the first gay institutions to develop is that it holds true in other cultures (e.g., Latin America, the Philippines) in which only embryonic challenges to the equation of homosexuality with female gender behavior have been made. In cultures where homosexuality is age-defined, neither gay bars nor gay identity have developed. Not that alcohol is a necessary catalyst for the crystalization of gay identity, but drinking together represents a degree of solidarity which is lacking where one is expected to "graduate" from the receptor role with age. Solidarity with peers is what is important, not alcohol dissolving inhibitions and generating addiction. Another reason to consider the (historical) primacy of gay bars is that, given the generally higher prices of drinks, undesirability of locales, and poor service, gay bars are also the prototype of businesses selling their patrons to each other. Manifestly, the business of a bar is to sell drinks, and the central importance of the bar (followed by the institution of the cocktail party) likely explains the high rates of lesbian and gay **alcoholism**. As Nardi put it, "Drinking is not used to escape from something; rather it is used to join something. Initial socialization into a gay community often occurs by attending gay bars and enacting the drinking roles perceived as essential to gay identity" (p. 28). As a result, "Getting drunk . . . is normal trouble in the gay community, rather than deviance" (Warren, p. 58). Other preconditions create other institutions.

Organs for communicating a positive view of a group are essential to positive self-identification, as well as to political organization and social coordination. In the United States early homophile organizations produced periodicals, and **ONE**, Inc. in particular fought a protracted legal battle (1954–58) for the use of the U.S. mail. In Latin America gay periodicals continue to be seized as subversive even when there is no conceivable prurience to interpret as obscene, as in **Mexico**, where the *Ley de Imprenta* gives a judge discretion to condemn printed, written, or duplicated materials as "apologías de un vicio" (vice advocacy). Outside metropolises with gay **ghettoes**, many people learn that homosexuality is a possible way of life from print media, the existence of which is now taken for granted by those living in gay worlds (including gay scholarship).

State provision of insurance against disaster (Medicaid, worker's compensation, unemployment insurance) and old age (Social Security) is perhaps the most important replacement of the traditional family function, and increases the likelihood of residential concentration of homosexually inclined persons. Parental control was eroded by the inability to guarantee a livelihood for the next generation and by increased geographical mobility—opportunity was beyond the reach and often beyond even the view of parents. Partner choice then became a more personal decision. Welfare state protection of individuals clearly reduced the necessity of reliance on the family and may well be a prerequisite to gay society (contrast Latin America).

Whether geographical mobility was necessary to populate contemporary gay ghettoes has been questioned. Similarly, while newly created public places such as railway stations and parks provided anonymous meeting places in the nineteenth century, there had been recognized trysting places in pre-capitalist mercantile centers, such as **Venice**, **Paris**, and Seville. Welfare protection, geographical mobility, voluntary relationships, all releasing individuals from dependence on and control by the family, were at least foreshadowed by **monasticism** and the **military** in Western history —locales in which widespread homosexuality occurred or has been posited.

The timing of the emergence of persons recognized by others in terms of homosexual preference is a major point of contention in the **social constructionist** position formulated at the University of Essex and elsewhere ca. 1981. Suggested dates for this transformation range from the fourteenth century until as recently as the end of the World War II. The flux of possible human desire has so impressed advocates of this view that they have ignored the very limited number of known social organizations of homosexuality (by age differences, gender differences, or egalitarian comradeship), historically attested labels for **roles** (e.g., **sodomite** and **catamite**), and the necessary economy of schematization in all cognitive categorization. Actual comparisons of social constructions across space or time have not generally been made by ostensible social constructionists, who seem more intent on avoiding being labeled themselves than in exploring differences and commonalities of social processes.

BIBLIOGRAPHY. Philip Blumstein and Pepper Schwartz, *American Couples*, New York: William Morrow, 1983; Barry Dank, "Coming Out in the Gay World," *Psychiatry*, 34 (1971), 180–97; Erving Goffman, *The Presentation of Self in Everyday Life*, Garden City, NY: Doubleday, 1959; idem, *Stigma: Notes on the Management of Spoiled Identity*, Englewood Cliffs, NJ: Prentice-Hall, 1963; David F. Greenberg, *The Construction of Homosexuality*, Chicago: University of Chicago Press, 1988; Laud Humphreys, *Tearoom Trade*, 2nd ed., Chicago: Aldine, 1975; idem, *Out of the Closets*, Englewood Cliffs, NJ: Prentice-Hall, 1972; Stephen O. Murray, *Social Theory, Homosexual Realities*, New York: Gay Academic Union, 1984; Peter M. Nardi, "Alcoholism and Homosexuality," *Journal of Homosexuality*, 7 (1982), 9–25; David Parkin, "Social Stratification," in R. Nisbet and T. Bottomore, eds., *History of Sociological Analysis*, New York: Basic Books, 1978, pp. 599–632; Barbara Ponse, *Identity in the Lesbian World*, Westport, CT: Greenwood, 1978; Albert J. Reiss, "The Social Integration of 'Queers' and 'Peers,'" *Social Problems*, 9 (1961), 102–20; Carol A. B. Warren, *Identity and Community in the Gay World*, Boston: Wiley, 1974.

Stephen O. Murray

SOCRATES (469–399 B.C.)

Athenian philosopher. The son of a well-to-do sculptor or stonemason, he was later reduced to poverty. Late in life he married Xantippe, who became proverbial in subsequent ages for her bad temper and shrewishness, though the stories about her may have been exaggerated. In early life he was interested in the scientific philosophy of his time and is said to have associated with Archelaus the physicist, but in the period best known to posterity he had abandoned these interests and was concerned solely with the right conduct of life, a quest which he conducted by the so-called "Socratic" method of cross-examining the individuals whom he encountered. While serving in the army he gained a great reputation for bravery, and as one of the presidents of the Athenian Assembly at the trial of the generals after the battle of Arginusae, he courageously refused to put an illegal motion to the vote despite the fury of the multitude. In 399 he was brought to trial before a popular jury on the charge of introducing strange gods and of "corrupting the youth." There has been considerable dispute over the precise meaning of the indictment, but the first part seems not to have been serious, while the second amounted to a charge that he had a "subversive" influence on the minds of the young, which was based on his known friendship with some of those who had been most prominent in their attacks on democracy in Athens. He made no attempt to placate the jury and was found guilty and sentenced to die by drinking a cup of hemlock. Though his friends could have enabled him to escape, he acquiesced to the sentence.

Socrates left no writings of his own: knowledge of his life and work comes from Xenophon, **Plato**, and **Aristotle**. He probably never formulated a precise **philosophy**. His legacy to his disciples and to later generations consisted in the method by which he analyzed and criticized the fundamental assumptions of existing systems. He probably rejected the conventional Greek religious beliefs of his time, yet professed or created no heterodox religious doctrines. From time to time he had paranormal experiences, signs, or warnings which he interpreted as guideposts to his own conduct.

His sexual life, apart from the unhappy marriage, reflected the Greek custom of *paiderasteia* to the fullest. He was both the teacher of the young men who frequented his circle and the lover of at least some of them. As a boy of seventeen he had been the favorite of Archelaus, because he was in the bloom of youthful sensuality, which later gave place to serious intellectual concerns. As an adult he loved good and noble boys with a passion that he asked only to be requited, but he was never given to a coarse and purely sensual **pederasty**; if the beauty of the young **Alcibiades** made an intense and lasting impression on him, he never forgot his duty as a teacher to guide his youthful pupils toward perfection. He was capable of self-willed abstinence and held this power up to others as an ideal; to have sought to impose it on all others was foreign to the Greek mentality. As a **bisexual** Hellene Socrates was always responsive to the beauty of the male adolescent and craved the companionship of young men; as a philosopher he practiced and taught the virtues of moderation and self-control. He endures as one of the outstanding examples in antiquity of a teacher for whom eros was an inspiration and a guide.

Because Socrates is a major figure in Western tradition, his sexual nature posed a continual problem. From **Ficino** to Johann Matthias Gesner (1691–1761) scholars sought to address the question discreetly. The Marquis de **Sade** was bolder, using *socratiser* as a verb meaning "to sodomize." Even today, however, many classicists choose to evade the problem.

BIBLIOGRAPHY. Hans Licht, *Sexual Life in Ancient Greece*, London: Routledge & Kegan Paul, 1932; V. de Magalhães-Vilhena, *Le problème de Socrate*, Paris: Presses Universitaires de France, 1952; idem, *Socrate et la légende Platonicienne*, Paris: Presses Universitaires de France, 1952; Herbert Spiegelberg, ed., *The Socratic Enigma*, New York: Liberal Arts, 1964.

Warren Johansson

SODOM AND GOMORRAH

These legendary cities have been traditionally located in the vicinity of the Dead Sea, where they constituted two members of a pentapolis, the Cities of the Plain. According to the Old Testament account in Genesis 14, 18, and 19, God overthrew four of the five cities in a rain of brimstone and fire. The names of Sodom and Gomorrah, especially the former, have become proverbial. Echoes of the episode recur in the Bible and in the Koran, as well as in Jewish, Christian, and Islamic exegetical and homiletic writings. From the first city, Jewish Hellenistic Greek formed the derivative *sodomitēs*, from which medieval Latin obtained the noun of agent *sodomita*; as a result the connection with male homosexuality is for many axiomatic. However the matter is more complex.

A number of main constituents of the Sodom legend emerge from the central passages and fragmentary allusions in the **Old Testament** and the **intertestamental literature**, together with the midrashic writings of later centuries:

(1) the geographical legend that sought to explain the peculiarly barren terrain around the shores of the Dead Sea. The ancient world's rudimentary science of geology correctly related this barrenness to the circumstance that the water level of the Dead Sea had in prehistoric times been far higher; the sinking of the water level had exposed the previously inundated, now strikingly arid and sterile region to the gaze of the traveler.

(2) the theme of sterility by which the ancient mind sought to explain the origins of this condition; to the Bedouin living east and south of the Dead Sea it suggested the etiological inference that at one time the area surrounding this salinized body of water had been a fruitful garden belt. Yet the inhabitants of the cities of the plain had even in the midst of their abundance and prosperity denied hospitality to the poverty-stricken and the wayfarer, while the luxury in which they wallowed led them inevitably into effeminacy and vice (the parallel in the Hellenistic world was the city of Sybaris, whose proverbial self-indulgence gave the English language the word *sybaritic*). For this reason they were punished by the destruction of their cities and the conversion of the whole area into a lifeless desert.

(3) a Bedouin folk tale on the perils of city life, of which Lot is the hero who

must be rescued again and again by the intervention of others. In Genesis 14:12 Lot is taken captive when Sodom is conquered by the four kings who have allied themselves against the Cities of the Plain; Abraham saves him by military intervention in the manner of a tribal sheikh with his retinue of 318 warriors. In 19:4–9 the Sodomites threaten Lot's guests with gang **rape**, but are miraculously blinded and repelled, and in 19:13, 15 the angelic visitors warn Lot of the imminent destruction of the city so that he and his family can leave just in time to escape the rain of brimstone and fire. This underlying motif explains why Lot later "feared to dwell in Zoar" (19:30), even though God has spared the place as a reward for his model hospitality toward the two visitors. Over the centuries Sodom and Gomorrah, along with the Babylon of the Book of Revelation, came to symbolize the corruption and depravity of the big city as contrasted with the virtue and innocence of the countryside, a notion cherished by those who idealized rural life and is still present, though fading in twentieth-century America.

(4) the occurrence in the region east and south of the Dead Sea of volcanic activity that persisted throughout antiquity and subsided only after the thirteenth century. These volcanic eruptions, which have left traces still to be seen at the present day, inspired the "rain of brimstone and fire" (burning sulfur) of Genesis 19:24, which supplemented the notion that the four cities had been "overthrown" (destroyed by an earthquake) that figures in Genesis 19:25.

(5) the presence in the geographical vicinity of the tribe of Benjamin, which belonged to the pre-Israelite population of Canaan and had for centuries lived by marauding and plundering at the expense of its more civilized neighbors. The culmination of this brigandage in the period of the judges was the outrage at Gibeah recorded in Judges 19, with its explicit motifs of sexual aggression and gang rape.

(6) the currency in antiquity of world destruction legends, in which the earth is annihilated either by water (*kataklysmos*) or by fire (*ekpyrosis*). The story of Noah and the deluge is the rendering of the first in the book of Genesis, while the destruction of Sodom and Gomorrah is a localization of the second, in which the catastrophe is limited to four cities in the vicinity of the Dead Sea (Sodom, Gomorrah, Admah, and Zeboiim) even though the epilogue involving Lot and his daughters clearly derives from a universal conflagration myth.

(7) world destruction legends that actualize elements of fantasy wish-fulfillment. If the human race were annihilated with the exception of a single family, the earth could be repeopled only by means of sexual unions ordinarily condemned as incestuous. The handful of virtuous human beings preserved from the catastrophe by the gods are the chosen seed of a new mankind.

(8) world destruction fantasies associated in modern clinical experience with the early stages of schizophrenia. These fantasies reveal a key component of the Sodomy delusion: the subject cherishes the belief that particular actions would expose the world to this awful fate, and that only by refraining from them is he virtuously warding off the catastrophe. Astrological literature supplied the ancients with an entire list of calamities that betokened divine wrath, as in Luke 21:11, all of which were later ascribed to retribution for "**sodomy**." Fear of homosexual aggression plays a role in these paranoid fantasies, of the sort analyzed by **Freud** in the classic Schreber case.

The Sodom legend and its gradual expansion into the delusional form that obsesses the Christian mind were therefore overdetermined; the conscious and unconscious associations of the component themes blended to form the later complex of Christian beliefs that may be designated the "sodomy delusion." Its priority in the Old Testament sequence notwithstanding, the more prosaic story in Judges 19 served as the model for the mythical narrative in Genesis 19, where Lot's angelic visitors are miraculously saved from homosexual assault. The whole account, reinforced by the enduring geographical features of the Dead Sea region (the supposed "statue of Lot's wife"), underlay the theological dogma that the destruction of the Cities of the Plain had been divine retribution for the homosexual depravity of the former inhabitants. And so the "sin of Sodom" became synonymous with homosexual activity and then with "unnatural vice"—a Hellenic, not a Judaic concept—in general, and the scriptural fate of the cities and prophecies of future doom made their barren site linger as an eternal warning to any people that tolerated such depravity in its midst.

The notion of *sodomy* is an innovation of Latin Christianity toward the end of the twelfth century; it is not found in Jewish or **Byzantine** writings. Legal usage in various countries has given the word broader or narrower definitions, particularly in regard to the character of the actions that "constitute the offense." In the late **Middle Ages** the tendency of the allegorizing mind to parallelism led to the notion that Gomorrah, the twin city of Sodom, had been a hotbed of lesbianism, even though there was nothing in either Testament that would suggest such a construction. The hold of the legend on the mind of Christian Europe has been such that even in the twentieth century literary works have been composed on the subject, and the less sophisticated part of the population still believes that the destruction of Sodom exemplified the wrath of God that is revealed from heaven (Romans 1:18) against those who practice homosexuality.

Warren Johansson

SODOMA (GIOVANNI ANTONIO BAZZI, CALLED "IL SODOMA"; 1477–1549)

Italian painter. Born at Vercelli, Sodoma studied under a minor Lombard artist (Martino Spanzotti) in Milan, where he sustained a more crucial influence—that of the innovative work of **Leonardo da Vinci**. Between 1505 and 1508 he executed a series of frescoes in the Benedictine monastery of Monte Oliveto near Siena. He then became Siena's leading artist. He was also summoned to Rome, where he painted part of a ceiling in the Vatican's Stanza della Segnatura, as well as some handsome frescoes in the Villa Farnesina. Today his works are less appreciated than those of his Sienese rival, Domenico Beccafumi.

Despite some nineteenth- and twentieth-century scholars who have sought to deny it, his nickname is deserved. According to his biographer Giorgio Vasari, Sodoma loved unchaste entertainments and merrymaking; he surrounded himself with an entourage of boys and beardless youths. Cherishing them greatly, "he acquired the name of Sodoma, which he did not take with annoyance or disdain, but rather gloried in it, making jingles and verses on the subject, which he pleasantly sang to the accompaniment of the lute." Once, while in Florence, his horse won a race, and on being asked what name should be proclaimed, he insisted "Sodoma, Sodoma!" This effrontery earned him a session of fagbashing by the mob. He was moreover an eccentric, keeping a menagerie of animals so that "his house resembled Noah's Ark" (Vasari). In his early years at Siena he did marry, siring a daughter, but his wife left him in disgust after a year. In a tax return of 1531 Sodoma facetiously claimed to have three mistresses and thirty grown children—an assertion that is no more indicative of basic heterosexuality than was Walt **Whitman**'s comparable declaration three and a half centuries later.

Vasari, who furnishes most of the information on Sodoma's personal life, taxes him not with immorality, but with lack of industry and imprudent management, as a result of which he passed his last years in want.

BIBLIOGRAPHY. Elisàr von Kupffer, "Giovan Antonio—Il Sodoma, der Maler der Schönheit," *Jahrbuch für sexuelle Zwischenstufen*, 9 (1908), 71–167; Mario Masini, "Gli immorali nell'arte: Giovanni Antonio Bazzi detto il Sodoma," *Archivio di Antropologia Criminale*, 36 (1915), 129–51, 257–77.
Wayne R. Dynes

SODOMY

As an overarching term for sexual deviation, the word sodomy today has an archaic, somewhat obsolescent ring, though it still figures in some legal discourse ("the sodomy laws"). Sodomite, having shrunk to one syllable in early modern British slang ("sod"), has faded further, so that it is little more than a jocular term of mild abuse. Historically, however, the concept of sodomy has been of immense importance. Moreover, it had several nuances of meaning, which it is essential to distinguish in order to interpret older written evidence.

The term *sodomia* originated in Medieval Latin about the year 1180 as a designation for the "crime against nature" that could be committed in one of three ways: (1) *ratione modi*, by obtaining venereal pleasure with a member of the opposite sex, but in the wrong manner, e.g., by fellation; (2) *ratione sexus*, with an individual having the genitalia of the same sex; or (3) *ratione generis*, with a brute animal. The abstract noun sodomia (for the sin) derives from the noun of agent sodomita (for the sinner), which had originally been used in the Septuagint and Vulgate to mean an inhabitant of the city of **Sodom** (from Old North Arabic *sudummatu* = the [Dead] Sea). According to Genesis 19, Sodom had been destroyed because of the sexual depravity of its male population, which had attempted a gang rape on the two angels who came to deliver Lot and his family from the impending destruction. In time the expressions *peccatum sodomitae* or *crimen sodomitae* came to be used to designate a variety of "unnatural" sexual acts, but only in Latin **Christianity** did the new derivative *sodomia* take hold and become a theological and legal concept; it remained alien to Byzantine Greek and Medieval Hebrew. From Latin the term passed into the modern languages of Western and Central Europe as the technical expression for the crime which was punishable by death everywhere until the second half of the eighteenth century, when the **Enlightenment** began to attack this sacral offense as a relic of the medieval superstition that divine retribution would overtake any community that tolerated "sodomy" in its midst.

The terms sodomy and sodomite thus spread until they embraced a far larger semantic sphere and a higher pitch of affectivity than the later terms (sexual) **inversion** and **homosexuality**, and in reading a medieval or later legal text one must not immediately assume that homosexual behavior is meant thereby. Most prosecutions, it is true, were for either male homosexuality or bestiality; criminal proceedings against lesbians and heterosexuals guilty of fellation or anal intercourse were rare at all times, though an occasional case figures in the (admittedly fragmentary) reports from the pre-modern era. The legal definition of the term—what constituted an "indictable offense"—has also differed from country to country and from century to century down to our own time. Eighteenth-century Poland even recorded an instance in which sexual intercourse between a male serf and a girl of noble birth was punished as "sodomy"—because it had supposedly resulted in a crop failure on the estate where it occurred. As a practical definition one may say that a "sodomite" was one whose aberrant sexual activity had become known to the Christian community and its authorities; the word should not be confounded with the later psychiatric notion of "homosexual," which stems from a different conceptual scheme strongly influenced by the writings of the homophile apologists **Ulrichs** and **Kertbeny** in the 1860s. However, the lay public on learning the new term then superimposed it upon the semantic field occupied by the familiar expression "sodomite," so that the afterglow of the older set of associations has never been fully dispelled.

The verb *to sodomize*, which was rare in European languages until the last third of the nineteenth century, usually has the meaning of anal penetration, whether homosexual or heterosexual. In England it is a more learned variant of the common verb to **bugger**.

Historically, the legend of the destruction of the Cities of the Plain served to tinge sodomy with the aura of a fathomless abyss of depravity, of the unspeakable, the monstrous, of "unnatural vice" that provokes the wrath of God against its perpetrators. The associations were reinforced by the sight of the barren terrain on the shores of the Dead Sea which generation after generation of pilgrims from Western Europe described in their travel accounts. As has been mentioned, the scope of the term expanded to include "unnatural" heterosexual activity and intercourse with animals—not even implied in the tale in Genesis 19 from which it derived. As a result of these manifold enhancements, the diabolical intimations of the notion came to seem perversely glamorous for a few wayward spirits.

Even now sodomy evokes from the unsophisticated a shudder of horror, though Biblical criticism long ago demolished the credibility of the composite narrative in Genesis, analyzing it as the Judaic amplification of a local myth that explained the barrenness and salinization of the shores of the Dead Sea. From the time of Justinian (reigned 527–565) onward, however, the legend was deployed as a theological and pseudo-historical justification for laws intended to stamp out "ungodly practices" that would expose Christian society to divine retribution. Recent legislation has tended to avoid the term because of its ambiguity, its older definitions, and strongly affective character, not to mention the archaic ties with the Bible that would ill become a secular code of law.

Warren Johansson

SOLICITATION

American **law** contains various provisions for the action of soliciting, or seeking to obtain by earnest request, entreaty, petition, or diligent and importunate asking, of the person of the opposite or same sex for sexual favors. The concept derives from English law.

Basic Features. Statutes have been employed to make arrests for solicitation to commit sexual acts in private between consenting adults which are no longer illegal in those American states that have decriminalized sodomy. This practice on the part of the **police** results in inconsistency vis-à-vis the consenting adult acts, violates the First Amendment, and is often supported solely by the uncorroborated testimony of a plainclothes member of the vice squad. If such solicitation contains no offer of or request for money and thus does not involve prostitution or the corruption of minors, its criminalization nowhere antedates the English act of 1898. This act punished with a maximum of two years' imprisonment any "male person who in any public place persistently solicits or importunes for immoral purposes," and thus does not specifically mean homosexual conduct. It was aimed originally at pimps and procurers, but soon became the recognized English vehicle against all forms of homosexual solicitation. A number of American jurisdictions soon adopted the concept. The provision of the old New York Criminal Code (superseded in 1965 by Section 722) was representative, punishing as a "disorderly person" anyone "who, with intent to provoke a breach of the peace ... frequents or loiters about any public place soliciting men for the purpose of committing a crime against nature or other lewdness." The English statute had required "persistent" importuning, intending to limit its criminal sanctions to those who refused to take "no" for an answer and thereby threatened a breach of the peace, thus extending the **common law** concept that underlay the notion of "open or public lewdness," a danger because it could incite violence.

Modern legislators such as those of New York in 1965 have conveniently forgotten that the maintenance of public peace was the purpose of the older laws. They do not insist that the importuning be persistent or continued, rather they emphasize the affront and disgust experienced by the "innocent" bystanders to homosexual solicitation. They meant to protect the public from offensive behavior. Yet it is inconsistent that the *locus per se* (the place itself) converts a conversation otherwise private into a public one unless overheard by others. Rather, most men **cruising** for partners employ ambiguous glances, gestures, and words, often not even noticed by a disinterested heterosexual, to evoke a receptive response before unequivocally soliciting. If not encouraged, they usually desist and seek another partner. Circumspect and cautious as it usually is, homosexual solicitation subtly using innuendo and subterfuge belies the myth of flagrant homosexuals brazenly accosting defenseless and abashed respondents. Instead it is normally plainclothes decoys who entice and entrap those allegedly so open and brazen as to constitute an affront to public decency. Most convictions are secured exclusively on the arresting officer's allegation, particularly in past decades when pocket recording devices did not exist at all; complaints by private citizens are rare, indeed virtually non-existent for solicitation, in contrast with indecent exposure. Such unsavory practices encourage shakedowns and extortion.

Solicitation and Sexual Criminalization. Where sodomy committed in private between consenting adults has been decriminalized, as it has been in 25 of the 50 states, solicitation to commit it should ipso facto have also been decriminalized. But this has not always been the case. In Illinois, the first state to decriminalize sodomy in 1961, arrests actually increased in the next year or so. Over 95 percent of those convicted for sex-related crimes are not convicted of sodomy or of other felonies difficult to prove such as rape, statutory rape, gross indecency, or incest, but for prostitution or lesser crimes and misdemeanors such as solicitation, public or open lewdness, battery, indecent exposure, **gross indecency** between males, and (until its limitation in recent years) loitering.

Need for Reform. The crime of "solicitation for sexual activity" should be stricken from the codes in its entirety. It flies in the face of modern legal thought, is inconsistent with the remainder of most penal codes, and is of doubtful constitutionality. On many occasions it has been argued that if someone who is solicited, so long as the behavior involves only consenting adults in private, is not interested in the proposal, he need only say "no" to the solicitor. In punishing solicitations to commit crimes, the law may even infringe freedom of speech. It might be a matter for the legislature to decide "whether the punishment of solicitations should be curtailed in order to protect free speech," and allow **sexual liberty**. If "a solicitation to commit a crime" constitutes "a substantial step in a course of conduct planned to culminate in" the "commission of the crime," the solicitation in those 25 states that have not decriminalized sodomy is treated as a criminal attempt and is punished accordingly. But some codes limit the "definition of crimes of attempt to those situations where the offense attempted is a crime." "An attempt to commit a disorderly persons offense is . . . not sufficiently serious to be made the object of the penal law. Many disorderly persons offenses are too innocuous or themselves too far removed from the feared result to support an attempt offense." Codes punish solicitations to commit prostitution, but prostitution, by definition, is an offense, while private sexual activity between consenting adults is in 25 states no offense at all. Under some codes, any young man loitering on a park bench who asks a girl to go to bed with him could be sent to prison.

A number of states, including Illinois, Connecticut, Hawaii, and North Dakota, have eliminated such provisions in the course of adopting new criminal codes. New Mexico has managed to live quite comfortably without ever having had a sexual solicitation law on its statute book. These changes are the result of a growing recognition that such laws are nothing but relics of a puritanical past and serve merely to make criminals of otherwise law-abiding people without carrying out any useful social purpose. "To remove criminal sanctions from the conduct itself, yet to continue to punish solicitations to engage in the now licit conduct is not only a masterpiece of inconsistency, but provides blackmailers, extortionists, and others disposed to violence against homosexuals with a substantive vehicle for their operations."

A solicitation to commit a lewd act may be lewd or not depending on its character, not on the nature of the act solicited. Speech is not automatically rendered obscene by its subject matter. More than 30 years ago, Mr. Justice Brennan said: "Sex and obscenity are not synonymous." Neither is a solicitation automatically "fighting words" and hence a threat to public peace and order. Solicitations are thus neither automatically legal or illegal and should not be indiscriminately punished. The crime of solicitation is a relic of attempts by the state to suppress sexual activity on the part of its citizens, attempts legitimate enough under the Old Regime, but without justification in the modern liberal state whose constitution guarantees freedom of conscience and of action to those who reject the tenets of an ascetic morality.

BIBLIOGRAPHY. Thomas E. Lodge, "There May Be Harm in Asking: Homosexual Solicitations and the Fighting Words Doctrine," *Case Western Reserve Law Review*, 30 (1980), 461–93; Arthur C. Warner, "Non-Commercial Sexual Solicitation: The Case for Judicial Invalidation," *SexuaLaw Reporter*, 4 (1978), 1, 10–20.
William A. Percy and Arthur C. Warner

SOLON

Poet, lawgiver, and chief archon (magistrate) of Athens in 594–93 B.C. Overpopulation had caused the exploitation of Attica's poor, who were enserfed or even sold abroad into slavery for debt. Solon canceled all debts secured by land or liberty and ended serfdom but did not redistribute all land as the radicals demanded. He standardized coinage, weights and measures, extended citizenship to immigrant craftsmen, encouraged export of olive oil, and took other measures to improve the economy. He divided the citizens into four classes according to wealth, apportioning political power so that only the rich could serve as archons and *areopagitici* (councilors and judges), but also strengthened the *ecclesia* (assembly of citizens).

Having visited **Crete** to study its laws, Solon institutionalized pederasty in Athens. Copying the spectacularly successful reforms recently introduced to **Sparta** from Crete by Lycurgus to limit the increase of their hoplites (foot soldiers) so that their estates would not become overly subdivided, Solon ordained that men should marry between ages 28 and 35, in the fifth seventh of their lifespan. Setting the example himself, he copied the Cretan and Spartan system of having each aristocratic young man at about age 22, when released from alert for military service, take a 12-year-old upper-class boy as *eromenos* (beloved) and train him until he was 18 and with a beard. Then ready for military service, he was often stationed in barracks. At this time the *erastes* (lover), nearing 30, was eligible for marriage. Solon also imported **gymnasia** and palestra, where citizens exercised nude; the seclusion of upper-class women, which later in Athens was to become more pronounced than elsewhere in Greece; and **symposia**, all-male dinner clubs that encouraged pederastic affairs and, in Athens, became, like the gymnasia, foci of learning. He invited the Cretan "musician" (i.e., sage, lover of the Muses) Epimenides to Athens to quell the plague and perhaps to promote the reforms. When one of Solon's *eromenoi*, his cousin Peisistratus, overthrew his reforms and established a tyranny, Solon traveled abroad for a decade, visiting Crete again.

Peisistratus and his sons Hippias and Hipparchus ruled from about 545 B.C. until the revolution of 510, which was headed by an old family, the Alcmeonidae. This family produced Cleisthenes, Pericles, and **Alcibiades**. The Peisistratids furthered Solon's economic and social reforms. After the collapse of Samos, when the Persians in 522 crucified the pederastic tyrant Polycrates, who out of fear of plots hatched in them had ordered all gymnasia burned, the Peisistratids enhanced Athens' economic and political rise to dominance in the Aegean. Hipparchus had **Homer** recited annually at the Panathenaion, establishing the text, emending it to emphasize the importance of Athens. Hipparchus also patronized immigrant poets, **exiles and émigrés** from Samos and the Ionian states seized by the Persians, including Anacreon, and others fleeing tyranny in Magna Grecia. Some of these myth-makers may have invented the fable that Theseus, after slaying the Minotaur, abandoned Ariadne in Naxos and took an *eromenos*, thus creating a "founder" of pederasty for Athens. Most Peisistratids were *eromenoi* and *eras-*

tai in turn, but Hipparchus, the chief patron, was exclusively drawn to boys. When Harmodius, beloved and cousin of the poor but honest citizen Aristogiton, spurned Hipparchus' persistent advances, the pair decided to assassinate the tyrant brothers. The desperate lovers, intent on overthrowing the overbearing tyrants, succeeded in slaying only Hipparchus and were in turn killed (514). Four years later, when the tyranny was overthrown with Spartan help, these "tyrannicides" (Harmodius and Aristogiton) remained heroes of the democracy, and were always toasted at symposia. Their descendants were accorded the right to dine for all time at public expense at the Prytaneum, and their statues in bronze with an inscription composed by Simonides were prominently displayed as models of civic virtue. Thus male lovers became associated with tyrannicide and the defense of self-government.

BIBLIOGRAPHY. Antony Andrewes, *The Greek Tyrants*, London: Hutchinson, 1956; Charles W. Fomara, "The Cult of Harmodius and Aristogeiton," *Philologus*, 114 (1970), 155–80.

William A. Percy

SOTADIC ZONE

In an attempt to sketch the geography of the prevalence of homosexual relations, Sir Richard **Burton** introduced the expression "sotadic zone" in the famous Terminal Essay appended to his translation of *The Book of the Thousand Nights and a Night* (commonly known as the "Arabian Nights"; 1885–88). Somewhat arbitrarily, Burton took his term from Sotades, an Alexandrian poet of the third century B.C. who wrote seemingly innocuous verses that became obscene if read backwards.

In Burton's words, "There exists what I shall call a 'Sotadic Zone,' bounded westwards by the northern shore of the Mediterranean (N. lat. 43) and by the southern (N. lat. 30), including meridional France, the Iberian Peninsula, Italy and Greece, with the coast-regions of Africa

1235

from Morocco to Egypt. Running eastward the Sotadic zone narrows, embracing Asia Minor, Mesopotamia and Chaldea, Afghanistan, the Sind, the Punjab and Kashmir. In Indo-China, the belt begins to broaden, enfolding China, Japan and Turkistan. It then embraces the South Sea Islands and the New World. . . . Within the Sotadic Zone, the [pederastic] Vice is popular and endemic, held at worst to be a mere peccadillo, whilst the races to the North and South of the limits here defined, practice it only sporadically amid the opprobrium of their fellows who, as a rule, are physically incapable of performing the operation." Possibly Burton's exclusion of sub-Saharan **Africa** contributed to the erroneous modern belief that black people were originally innocent of the "vice," having been corrupted to it by their slave masters.

Burton's theory was an attempt to give a theoretical framework to his own observations of sexual mores in various parts of the far-flung British Empire to which he was posted as a diplomat. Trained as a classicist, he considered pederasty the only form of homosexuality worth investigating. He did not, however, come up with a plausible theory as to the factors responsible for this Sotadic Zone.

The explanation for much of Burton's zone, at least, probably lies in the persistence of ancient Mediterranean pederasty and its diffusion eastwards by **Islam**; this however does not account for China, Japan, Indo-China, the South Sea Islands and the pre-Columbian New World.

This further extension may indeed lend some credence to Burton's theory if one looks for climatological factors prevalent in his zone. Northern Europeans, seeking to explain the differences between their own sexual mores and those of the southern Europeans, often pointed to the temperature difference between the two areas and ascribed sexual excitement to the warm climate of the South. Terms such as "sultry" and "torrid" have a primary meaning of "hot" but acquired the secondary sense of "passionate"; the German terms "schwul/schwül" associate hot-humid conditions with homosexuality directly. As yet, there has been little or no scientific investigation of such notions, which remain largely in the realm of folklore.

Wayne R. Dynes

SOUTH AMERICA
See **Brazil; Latin America.**

SOVIET UNION
See **Russia and USSR.**

SPAIN

Spain is one of the countries with the richest homosexual history, which is gradually becoming better known. An appreciation of same-sex love, along with a cult of beauty and poetry, has been present during many periods of Spain's history.

Antiquity. The rich and mysterious civilization of the pre-Roman south of Spain is known to have been sexually permissive, although evidence on homosexuality in that period is lacking. Hispania was one of the most Romanized provinces, and shared Rome's sexual morality; perhaps it is no coincidence, though, that **Martial**, one of the most homosexual Latin authors, and **Hadrian**, one of the best and gayest emperors, were from Spain. That a special term (*hawi*; see *Encyclopedia of Islam*, "Liwat," pp. 776 and 778) existed in Western Arabic for male prostitutes suggests that such were particularly prevalent there before Islam. The Christian Visigoths, who ruled Spain after the disappearance of Roman authority, were in contrast strongly opposed to homosexuality. Sodomy was outlawed in the seventh century, with castration and exile the punishments; at the same time one finds the emergence of legal measures against Jews. (*See* **Law, Germanic.**)

Islam. In the eighth century most of Spain became Islamic; the inhabitants were glad to be rid of Gothic rule. Andalusia or al-Andalus, which occupied more of the Iberian peninsula than does the modern Andalusia, was an Islamic country from the eighth through the early thirteenth centuries, and in the kingdoms of Granada and Valencia, Islam survived well into the sixteenth century. Al-Andalus is a missing chapter in the history of Europe. During the caliphate and *taifas* periods (tenth and eleventh centuries), cosmopolitan, literate, prosperous Andalus was the leading civilization anywhere on the coast of the Mediterranean—with the possible exception of Byzantium. It has also been described as the homeland of Arabic philosophy and poetry. The closest modern parallel to its devotion to the intellect (philosophy, literature, arts, science) and beauty is Renaissance Italy. The roots of this cultural supernova are the subject of dispute, as is the related question of the ethnic makeup of the Andalusian population. While the culture was officially Arabic, the number of pure Arabs was small; there was a much larger number of North African Berbers mixed with a native population of Iberian, Phoenician, or other origin. Women captured during raids on the Christian states were also an important demographic element.

Al-Andalus had many links to Hellenistic culture, and except for the Almoravid and Almohade periods (1086–1212), it was hedonistic and tolerant of homosexuality, indeed one of the times in world history in which sensuality of all sorts has been most openly enjoyed. Important rulers such as Abd al-Rahman III, al-Hakem II, Hisham II, and al-Mutamid openly chose boys as sexual partners, and kept catamites. Homosexual prostitution was widespread, and its customers came from higher levels of society than those of heterosexual prostitutes. The poetry of Abu Nuwas was popular and influential; the verses of poets such as Ibn Sahl, Ibn Quzman, and others describe an openly bisexual lifestyle. The superiority of sodomy over heterosexual intercourse was defended in poetry. Some of the abundant pederastic poetry was collected in the contemporary anthologies *Dar at-tiraz* of Ibn Sana al-Mulk and *Rayat al-mubarrizin* of Ibn Said al-Maghribi (*The Banners of the Champions*, trans. James Bellamy and Patricia Steiner, Madison, WI: Hispanic Seminary of Medieval Studies, 1988). Under the Muslim rulers of al-Andalus, Jewish culture reached its highest peak since Biblical times; the poetry of Sephardic Judaism suggests that pederasty was even more common among the Jews than among the Muslims.

Medieval Christian Spain. The small northern kingdom of Castile viewed itself as the inheritor of the Visigothic claim to rule over Spain. With encouragement from France, French-born queens of Castile, women elsewhere in Europe, and the papacy, it gradually won economic and then political control over the entire peninsula. In contrast and to some extent in reaction to the hedonism of al-Andalus, Castile was puritanical, although its puritanism was very reluctantly and half-heartedly accepted in the southern and eastern sections of the country. Even within Castile, there was much resistance to the imposition of clerical celibacy at the end of the eleventh century, which Spain had until that time resisted. This change, not fully implemented for 500 years, was from the beginning seen as unwanted meddling from the other side of the Pyrenees.

The *Fuero real*, an early medieval law code, ordered that the "sin against nature" be punished with public castration, followed by death by hanging from the legs and without burial (the corpse, thus, eaten by animals). The *Siete partidas* of King Alfonso the Wise (later thirteenth century) also specified the death penalty, except for those under 14 or victims of rape. Documented executions of sodomites begin in the fifteenth century; the cases known are from Aragon and Mallorca, although this may simply reflect better records in those kingdoms. In fifteenth-century Castile Juan II, his administrator

Álvaro de Luna, and his son Enrique IV were primarily homosexual, and homosexuality was predictably used by their enemies as a political issue. Writers of Juan II's court created Castilian lyric poetry, which was absent, ascetically, from previous Castilian literature.

The Renaissance. With the incorporation of Naples into the crown of Aragon in 1443, Aragon came into close contact with an Italian city in which homosexuality was treated indulgently, at least in aristocratic circles. The great king and patron Alfonso V, who moved his court to Naples, was at the very least tolerant. He employed as secretary, librarian, and historian the famous **Sicilian** bisexual Antonio Beccadelli, as falconer the founder of Catalan poetry Ausias March, who is linked with homosexuality in a single document, and Pere Torroella, fifteenth-century Iberia's archmisogynist, also spent time in his court. Naples was not just the center for Renaissance Latin poetry but a major Aragonese political center, through which passed "Spain's best nobles, politicians, and soldiers." Yet there is no evidence of any reform of what in Spanish are called *costumbres* until the introduction of the **Inquisition**— seventy years after it had been introduced in Spain—brought widespread revolt against Spanish authority.

Several decisive steps in the formation of modern Spain were taken by Isabella with her husband Ferdinand, "the Catholic Monarchs" (1474–1516). Through their marriage Castile and Aragon became ruled by the same sovereigns, and Catholicism became even more linked with marriage in the nation's consciousness. Christianity was seen in Castile, more strongly than elsewhere, as a system for controlling sexual behavior. Female prostitution, however, was always tolerated; it was located in the Moorish quarter, a predecessor of the "zona de tolerancia" of the modern Hispanic city.

Granada was conquered in 1492; its baths, described as the citizens' enter-

tainment, closed shortly thereafter. (Alfonso VI had destroyed Castile's baths two centuries before, believing that the "vices" practiced there made for poorer soldiers.) Jews were expelled the same year, although a majority chose conversion to Christianity and remained in Spain; anti-Jewish propaganda shortly before the order of expulsion identified Jews with sodomy ("sodomy comes from the Jews"). In 1497 Ferdinand and Isabella, presumably responding to the continued existence of sodomites in Spain, ordered that those found be burned, with confiscation of possessions by the crown.

The Hapsburg Era. Hapsburg Spain of the next two centuries was similarly repressive, and records survive of many public executions of sodomites, intended to instill terror into the populace. Yet there were ups and downs, with more freedom in Catalonia, Aragon, Valencia, and Andalusia than in Castile, and more among the economically privileged than among the peasantry. The most oppressive period was the reign of Felipe II (1555–1598), which saw a renewed emphasis on marriage; the prudish Counterreformation, which he championed, opposed sensual pleasure of any sort. Just before his death Felipe II reaffirmed the death penalty for sodomy, and made conviction easier. Felipes III and IV (1598–1665) were more liberal, though only by comparison. Testimony in legal cases, among them those of Felipe II's secretary Antonio **Pérez** and the Count of Villamediana, is the largest body of information that survives on homosexual life in Spain during the period. In Valencia, Inquisition testimony reveals the existence in the seventeenth century of a clandestine homosexual ghetto. It should be remembered, in studying modern Spanish society, that pressures toward marriage were so strong that except for ecclesiastics, most of those who engaged in homosexual activities did marry. At the same time, opposition to the Catholic church could be so intense as to make anything Catholicism opposed, such as non-procreative sexuality, seem especially appealing. It should also be noted that homosexuality could be ascetic, rejecting all sexual activity, a purity of which, according to misogynist literature, men were thought more capable.

As Castile took on a world role for the first time, the official morality interpreted the world in terms of sexual behavior and religion. Protestants instituted divorce and clerical marriage, and closed monasteries. New World Indians were sodomites (see **Andean Societies**), and needed Christianity. The Turkish empire, of which the Spaniards were terrified, was likewise seen as a land of sexual license, where Christians were slaves. Italy was decadent and effeminate, and Spain undertook its defense. There were substantial colonies of expatriate Spaniards in Italy, the Turkish empire, France, and Holland. Just as those who rejected medieval Castile's sexual morality could and did emigrate to the Islamic south and east, in the Hapsburg period there were many among the expatriates who left in search of greater sexual as well as religious freedom. The expatriates were sometimes influential in reinforcing the sexual freedom and anti-Catholicism of their new countries.

Homosexuality appears in classical Spanish literature in subtle forms. In the world of sixteenth-century pastoral and chivalric romance an atmosphere of freedom was established, and sex-variant characters, especially women in male roles, appear. Anonymous chronicles of famous homosexuals (Juan II, Álvaro de Luna, very possibly also the "Gran Capitán" Gonzalo Fernández de Córdoba) were published in the sixteenth century. **Cervantes** presents, through same-sex friendships, relationships with many homosexual overtones. In drama, a wide variety of interpersonal and psychological problems were examined. Female roles were sometimes played by boys. Female characters often used male disguise, and men in female dress are not unknown; Tirso de Molina is especially noted for the use of cross-dressing and female protagonists.

Homosexuality was also treated through the use of classical mythology. The most important, difficult, and innovative poet of seventeenth-century Spain is Luis de Góngora y Argote. In his masterpiece, the *Solitudes*, the alienated young protagonist is described at the outset as more beautiful than Ida's ephebe ("garzón"); the allusion is to **Ganymede**. The *Solitudes* started a furious controversy; the tormented conservative Quevedo repeatedly called Góngora a sodomite and Jewish, although he is not known to have been either. An important follower of Góngora was Pedro Soto de Rojas, author of a lengthy poem on Adonis; another was Villamediana; another was the brilliant feminist Sor Juana Inés de la Cruz. On homosexuality in religious literature and monastic institutions much work remains to be done. In some of the most famous poems in Spanish, San Juan de la Cruz took the female role in fantasized mystical lovemaking with Christ, and the Mercedarian order, to which Tirso de Molina belonged, had the reputation, at least in some quarters, of enjoying sodomy.

Executions of sodomites continued, through in reduced number, into the eighteenth century. The death penalty for homosexual acts was removed in 1822 with the first Spanish penal code, which referred only to "unchaste abuses" (*abusos deshonestos*). In 1868 the crime of causing public scandal was added, but no homosexual cases have been discussed.

The Nineteenth and Early Twentieth Centuries. New contact with mainstream Europe, especially Germany, exposed Spain in the later nineteenth and early twentieth centuries to ideas from which it had long been sheltered. There ensued a great campaign of intellectual and cultural renewal; this movement was anti-Catholic, libertarian, and often Arabophile; some of the leading figures spent time in Granada. The founder is the revered, celibate educator Francisco Giner de los Ríos, called "the Spanish Socrates," whose Institución Libre de Enseñanza had a great influence until its demise with the Spanish Civil War. The Hellenism of Giner and his disciples remains unstudied.

A focus of homosexual life was the liberal Residencia de Estudiantes, an offshoot of the Institución Libre de Enseñanza and much more than what its name would imply. Its small campus, with buildings in Hispano-Arabic style, opened in 1915, and it was in the 20s and 30s a center of the artistic vanguard in Madrid. Among its residents were Federico García Lorca, the poet Emilio Prados, and the painter Salvador Dalí.

In the early twentieth century there was little open or published discussion of homosexual topics, but there were many coded allusions. Figures interested in homosexuality, at least during part of their lives, include Giner's nephew and disciple Fernando de los Ríos, the Greek professor, essayist, and fiction writer Unamuno, the novelist Baroja, and the poets Manuel Machado and Rubén Darío (the former the foremost Spanish dandy; the latter, a Nicaraguan, the author of the first published discussion in Spanish of Lautréamont). The Biblioteca Renacimiento, whose literary director was the playwright Gregorio Martínez Sierra, published the works of Spanish homosexual authors along with translations of Freud.

Writers more openly homosexual were not able to deal with the topic in their works. These include the conservative dramatist Jacinto Benavente (Nobel Prize, 1922), the chronicler of Madrid life Pedro de Répide, the short story writer Antonio de Hoyos y Vinent, and the music critic and historian Adolfo Salazar. Many Spaniards escaped to Paris, among them Gregorio and María Martínez Sierra and the composer Manuel de Falla. Little magazines, such as Grecia of Adriano del Valle, Mediodía of Joaquín Romero Murube, and Renacimiento of Martínez Sierra, remain incompletely studied. Even into the 1920's

the situation for homosexuals was oppressive, as can be seen from the reticence of the Espasa-Calpe encyclopedia and the comments of Gregorio Marañón. It was foreigners living in Spain, the Uruguayan Alberto Nin Frías (Marcos, amador de la belleza, 1913; Alexis o el significado del temperamento urano, 1932; Homosexualismo creador, 1933), the Chilean Augusto d'Halmar (Pasión y muerte del cura Deusto, 1924), and the Cuban Alfonso Hernández Catá (El ángel de Sodoma, 1928) who published the first books on the topic.

One type of covert treatment of homosexuality was study of Andalusian culture or homosexual figures, among the latter the Count of Villamediana. An important event was the tercentenary of the Góngora in 1927; the commemoration gave the name to the famous "generation of 1927." This was a celebration of poetry, of Andalusia (Góngora was from Córdoba), an exuberant revolt against Spain's cultural establishment, and also an affirmation of Spain's homosexual tradition. Among those participating were the poets Lorca, Prados, Luis Cernuda, Vicente Aleixandre (Nobel Prize, 1977), and the bisexual poet and printer Manuel Altolaguirre; Altolaguirre and Prados published in Málaga the magazine Litoral (1926–29). Especially important was the role of the great bisexual love poet Pedro Salinas, called the "inventor" of that poetical generation. Salinas, who introduced his student Cernuda to Gide's writings, was translator of and much influenced by Proust.

Pressures for liberalization were building. Besides Freud, Oscar Wilde's works were available in Spanish, as was Frank Harris' life of Wilde and Iwan Bloch's Vida sexual contemporánea. Gide's Corydon and an expurgated version of Lautréamont's Cantos de Maldoror appeared in the 1920's, translated by Julio Gómez de la Serna; Ramón Gómez de la Serna wrote a long prologue to the latter. Young Spaniards studied in Germany, returning with knowledge of its sexual freedom. Contact with the writings of Magnus **Hirschfeld** is certain. Emilio García-Gómez's *Poemas arábigo-andaluces*, which included pederastic poetry, caused a stir when published in 1930. Also contributing to a much changed climate were the lectures and publications on **gender identity** by Spain's most famous physician, Gregorio Marañón. Marañón believed that homosexuality was a congenital defect, and claimed that "Latin races" were superior because they allegedly had less of it than did Germany and England. Yet he strongly and publicly advocated tolerance, and "treatment" was to be just as voluntary as for any other medical condition. (Impressed by the newly discovered role of hormones in sexual desire, Marañón expected a hormonal therapy to be developed.) Besides *Los estados intersexuales en la especie humana* (1929) and other writings on sexual medicine, Marañón wrote an introduction for Hernández Catá's *Ángel de Sodoma*, a prologue for the translation of Bloch, an "antisocratic dialogue" accompanying the second Spanish edition of *Corydon* (1931), and a historical diagnosis of the homosexual king Enrique IV.

The pressures came to fruition in 1931 with the proclamation of the liberal Second Republic. The fervently anti-Catholic Manuel **Azaña** was president; minister of education and later ambassador to the United States was Fernando de los Ríos; and the author of Spain's new constitution, Luis Jiménez de Asúa, had published in defense of sexual and reproductive freedoms *Libertad de amar y derecho a morir* (1928; an epilogue to Hernández Catá's *Ángel de Sodoma*). The first few years of the republic were very happy times. The Chilean diplomat Carlos Morla Lynch kept a cultural salon, but published only heavily censored excerpts from his diary. A Hispano-Arabic institute was created and it launched the journal *Al-Andalus*; surprisingly, both survived the Civil War. Even more surprising, they produced as offshoots, in fascist Spain at the peak of Nazi Germany's campaign to free Germany and the world of Jews, a Hispano-Jewish institute and its journal *Sefarad*.

Homosexuality moved toward open appearance in Spanish literature: while the *Ode to Walt Whitman* of Lorca was privately published in Mexico (1933), Cernuda published *Where Oblivion Dwells* in 1934, *The Young Sailor* and *The Forbidden Pleasures* in 1936, and Lorca's *Sonnets of Dark Love* and *The Public* were being read to friends shortly before his assassination. As with the Nazis, a motive of the Catholics who began the Civil War in 1936 was to free Spain of homosexuals, although one of their heroes, the assassinated José Antonio Primo de Rivera, is reputed to have been a homosexual and a friend of Lorca.

Toward the Present. From 1939 to 1975 Spain was ruled by the joyless clerical-**fascist** regime of Franco, during which all nonprocreative sexuality was again furtive, although there was liberalization in the 60s. Any positive treatment of homosexuality in the media would itself have been a criminal offense. A recriminalization of "homosexual acts" in 1970 produced an embryonic gay movement, and the first gay magazine in Spanish, *Aghois* (1972–73). Founded by Armand de Fluvià, *Aghois* was prepared in Barcelona, then sent clandestinely to Paris, where it was reproduced and mailed. The Franco criminalization was itself repealed in 1978.

Poetry, especially difficult poetry, attracted the least attention and was, therefore, the preferred homosexual genre. Literary figures of this period are Aleixandre, Aleixandre's protégé the poet and critic Carlos Bousoño, the poets and literary scholars Luis Rosales and Francisco Brines, and the less secretive, and thus more marginal, poets Jaime Gil de Biedma and Juan Gil-Albert (*Heraclés*, written 1955, publ. 1981). From voluntary exile in Paris came the major voice of Juan Goytisolo, who in his novel *Count Julian* presents an Arabophile interpretation of Spanish history and a trip through the vagina of Queen

Isabella. His *En los reinos de taifas* is the first public discussion by a Spanish author of his arrival at a homosexual identification.

After the death of Franco in 1975, Spain entered its most liberal period since the end of the Middle Ages; Catholicism has again been deposed from its position as state religion. While there is not a self-consciously or publicly gay culture, a gay **movement** is now well-established. It is primarily based in Barcelona, home of the Institut Lambda. Bilbao has had a gay center since 1980, and *Gay Hotsa*, the most important gay magazine in Spain, is published there.

Major cultural figures are more or less openly gay-identified. Authors emerging or flourishing during this period include, besides Goytisolo, the novelist Terenci Moix, the playwright Antonio Gala, the poet and essayist Luis Antonio de Villena, translator of the Greek anthology (*La musa de los muchachos*, Madrid, 1980), the Bohemian, self-publishing poet Manuel Gámez Quintana (*Apuntes sobre el homosexual*, Madrid, 1976), the bisexual philosopher Fernando Savater, and, from Paris, the novelist Agustín Gómez-Arcos (*The Carnivorous Lamb*, Boston, 1984). A film renaissance has produced two major gay filmmakers, Eloy de la Iglesia (*Hidden Pleasures; The Deputy; Pals*) and Pedro Almodóvar (*Law of Desire; Dark Habits*), both of whom have been acclaimed abroad; also gay is the country's leading and most admired pop singer, Miguel Bosé. Spain has become a favorite destination of gay tourists, with gay **resorts** located in Ibiza, Sitges, and the Costa del Sol. Gay tourists also go to Barcelona and Valencia, and to a lesser degree Madrid and Seville. **AIDS** has not had a large impact in Spain, and the majority of reported cases are intravenous drug addicts.

Lesbians. Little is known about Lesbianism in Spain. Female–female sexuality is believed to have been enjoyed, along with many other forms of pleasure, by the eleventh-century courtesan and poet Wallada; presumably it flourished among the concubines and multiple wives of Andalusia, but other documentation is lacking. (Later Turkish practice would suggest that eunuchs served as cooperative partners for lengthy sessions of cunnilingus and intercourse.) In Christian Spain, the protagonist of the very popular *Celestina* of Fernando de Rojas (1499) enjoyed lovemaking with women. There is a single report of a woman sentenced to exile for "attempted sodomy" in 1549, and there is also mention of women in prison who strapped on a phallus. Women were simply less cause for concern, perhaps because, as an inquisitor said, they did not have the "instrument" with which to commit sodomy. Women were able to live for years in male dress without detection, even serving in the army. Two well-known cases, Catalina de Erauso (1592–1650) and Elena/"Eleno" de Céspedes (late sixteenth century)—the second, possibly a true hermaphrodite, married first as a woman and then as a man—were only discovered by chance.

The role of lesbians in the early twentieth century and Civil War remains to be examined. The actress Margarita Xirgu was at the center of a sympathetic body of theatre people. The *Songs of Bilitis* were published in Spanish translation by 1913; that they were the work of Pierre Louÿs was not yet known. In the contemporary period a number of women writers have dealt with lesbian topics, without, however, making public their own sexual orientation. Among the most important of these are the novelists Esther Tusquets, who also directs a libertarian publishing house, and Ana María Moix.

BIBLIOGRAPHY. Gail Bradbury, "Irregular Sexuality in the Spanish *Comedia*," *Modern Language Review*, 76 (1981), 566–80; Rafael Carrasco, *Inquisición y represión sexual en Valencia. Historia de los sodomitas (1565–1785)*, Barcelona: Laertes, 1985; Ana M. Gil, "Rosa i lila a la literatura catalana," *El Temps*, October 24, 1988, pp. 104–06; *El homosexual ante la sociedad enferma*, Barcelona: Tusquets, 1978; Victoriano Domingo Loren, *Los homosexuales frente a la ley: los juristas opinan*, Barcelona: Plaza y Janés, 1978; Antoni Mirabet i Mullol, *Homosexualidad hoy*, Barcelona: Herder, 1985; Mary Elizabeth Perry, "The 'Nefarious Sin' in Early Modern Seville," *Journal of Homosexuality*, 14:1/2 (1988), 67–89; Ramon Rosselló, *L'homosexualitat a Mallorca a l'edat mitjana*, Barcelona: Calamus Scriptorius, 1978; Angel Sahuquillo, *Federico García Lorca y la cultura de la homosexualidad: Lorca, Dalí, Cernuda, Gil-Albert, Prados y la voz silenciada del amor homosexual*, Stockholm, 1986; Phyllis Zatlin, "Homosexuality on the Spanish Stage: Barometer of Social Change," *España Contemporánea*, 1:2 (Spring 1988), 7–20.

Daniel Eisenberg

SPARTA

Ancient Greek Sparta was the chief city-state of the Peloponnesus in the archaic and classical ages. Inspired by the Dorian ancestral hero Heracles, who loved Iolaus and taught him to hunt and fight, Spartans developed the strongest Hellenic society under the Eunomia (good order), laws given by an oracle to the semi-mythical regent Lycurgus, but actually promulgated just after the Second Messenian War. Victorious under its peculiar constitution that early provided for two hereditary kings but evolved during the First (735–715 B.C.) and Second (635–615 B.C.) Messenian Wars, Sparta enslaved its neighbors, assigning a certain number of these helots to work the 9,000 cleroi (plots of land), each assigned to a Spartan. Thus relieved of work, each male citizen devoted his days from six to sixty to gymnastics and military training to become a perfect hoplite, as the new-style warrior for the phalanx was called.

Pederasty. The semilegendary Lycurgus banned money except for iron spits and ordered periodic redistribution of cleroi. Faced with the need to limit the population of "equals" so that each would possess a cleros, the reformers after 615 B.C. imported the Cretan customs of de-

layed marriages for men, training nude in **gymnasia**, common messes for citizens, and **pederasty**. Provided only with one rude cloak annually, boys roved in herds (*agelai*), as in **Crete**, each under an older boy—an "ciren" of 20–22—slept outdoors, stole food from helots and harassed and even murdered them. If caught stealing they were flogged publicly, not infrequently to death in order to teach them to steal more craftily and to endure greater physical hardship. At 12 each boy was taken by a 22-year-old "inspirer," who trained him for the next eight years. Then, as the "listener" began to sprout facial and body hair, he went on active full-time military duty and was assigned to a barracks where he had to sleep until he was 30, continuing to return to dine with his messmates until the age of 60. At 30 the inspirer married a girl of 18, who on her wedding night lay face down in a dark room in boy's attire with close-cropped hair, and henceforth he slept at home. Eighteen- to 20-year-old ephebes and 20- to 22-year-old eirens, being constantly together, made the transition from "listeners" to "inspirers."

That Lycurgus borrowed Cretan institutions is attested not only by Ephorus, Herodotus, **Plato**, and **Plutarch**, who state that he traveled in Crete to study its constitution, but also by the fact that common messes in Sparta were at first called by the Cretan term *andreia* (men's house) before it became the classical *syssitia*. The Spartan gymnasia and palestra, from which, as in Crete, helots were excluded and citizens trained nude, were modeled on Cretan *dromoi*, running tracks. Also Thaletas, the Cretan musician (devotee of the Muses, hence poet and scholar) and disciple of the Cretan Onomacritus, who had institutionalized pederasty on Crete ca. 650, came at Lycurgus' request to help improve the Spartan constitution and introduced there from Crete the Dance of the Naked Youths. After institutionalizing pederasty and the related reforms, neither Sparta nor

Crete sent out any colonists, unlike the other *poleis*.

The Spartan Apogee. After implementing the eunomia, Spartans became the greatest warriors and athletes in Greece. Their earlier poets, like Tyrtaeus (fl. ca. 630), had not described pederasty (nor had any other earlier surviving authors) but afterwards other Greeks, except those in the most backward areas such as Macedonia, quickly adapted Spartan institutions though in a less severe form. **Solon**, for example, with the help of the Cretan musician Epimenides, institutionalized pederasty in Athens.

All famous Spartans personally practiced pederasty, but much debate raged in antiquity as in modern times over whether inspirers physically loved their boys. Defenders of the so-called "pure" Dorian form (because Cretans and Spartans were the most famous branch of the Dorians, they and other modern scholars assumed pederasty to be a prehistoric institution common to the "Dorian race") of pederasty range from Xenophon to Karl Otfried Müller (1797–1840) and the contemporary Harald Patzer. The majority, however, adhere to the skepticism of Cicero: "Only a thin veil [the tunic separating the lovers who reclined side by side on a couch at **symposia**] preserves their virtue" (*De Republica* IV, 4). Many charged the Spartans with homosexual and/or even heterosexual promiscuity because Spartans secluded their women far less than did other Greeks, even letting them exercise nude in public as the males did and not marrying them until they were 18 whereas most other Greeks of 30 took brides of 15. **Aristotle** accused the Spartans, like the Celts and other "warlike" races, of being dominated by their women and given to pederasty. Alcman's *Partheneia* indicates that corerasty (love of maidens) was practiced between women and girls, both classes of the population less restricted than elsewhere and, according to Aristotle, women owned two-fifths of the property in Sparta as a result of inheritance from warriors slain in its constant wars.

As the Spartans heroically led in repelling the Persians in 480–479 B.C., their reputation soared. Even at their maritime rival Athens, a pro-Laconian, anti-democratic party, mainly composed of aristocrats, existed during the bitter Peloponnesian War (431–404 B.C.), pitting Sparta's Peloponnesian League against Athens' Delian League. **Socrates'** most famous pupils allied en masse with him in praise of Sparta: **Alcibiades**, Critias, who had headed the "Thirty Tyrants" installed by the Spartans after their victory to control Athens, Plato, and Xenophon. This factor plus his questioning the wisdom of the war and the existence of the gods led an Athenian jury to condemn Socrates to death.

Decline. After Sparta's victory, its commanders and harmosts (governors) often became corrupt, taking bribes and ravishing boys in the territories they controlled. Great inequality of wealth resulted from such plunder as well as from inheritances and many unable to contribute as required to *syssitia* lost their status as equals. At battles in 371 and 362 B.C. Thebans led by the "Sacred Band" of lovers organized by Epaminondas overthrew Spartan hegemony and liberated Messenia, slaying so many Spartan warriors that the city never fully recovered, hampered, some say, by a low birth rate caused by pederasty. Two pederastic kings, Agis III (244–241 B.C.) and Cleomenes III (235–219 B.C.), revived the old constitution, redistributing wealth and restoring discipline, but they were defeated by the Romans, in alliance with the Achaean League, in 222 B.C.

Conclusion. The Spartan system of education discouraged intellectual development and fostered "Laconic" brevity of speech. But when the mercantile societies of Ionia, the Aegean Islands, and Athens, following Sparta's lead, copied and intellectualized pederasty, it became the driving force of the Greek miracle.

Each boy *eromenos* had as a distinguished private tutor his *erastes* or lover.

Sparta was to the Greeks themselves and remains the eternal model of an aristocratic warrior society whose unwritten law combined male bonding with an especially virile, austere form of homosexuality. Neglecting the cultural endeavor that was the particular glory of Athens, Sparta nonetheless made its own contribution to the Greek miracle. Inspired by man–boy love, the heroism of Spartan warriors shielded nascent Hellenic civilization from the menace of Persian despotism.

See also **Greece, Ancient**.

BIBLIOGRAPHY. Paul Cartledge, "The Politics of Spartan Pederasty," *Proceedings of the Cambridge Philological Society*, 207 (1981), 17–36; idem, *Agesilaos and the Crisis of Sparta*, London: Duckworth, 1987; Elizabeth Rawson, *The Spartan Tradition in European Thought*, Oxford: Clarendon Press, 1969.

William A. Percy

SPICER, JACK (JOHN LESTER; 1925–1965)

American poet. Stemming from a Minnesota family, Spicer spent most of his life in California. As a freshman at the University of Redlands (1944) Spicer became interested in Calvinism; later he took a Ph.D. in linguistics. Glimpses of his personal life are found in his letters, whose whimsical style attests his keen sense of language, and in recollections of friends.

The earliest published verses date from 1946, when poems appeared in *Occident*, the Berkeley student magazine. In later years Spicer repudiated his early verses, calling them "beautiful but dumb." They are tender and lyrical, qualities attributable to Spicer's study of Yeats.

For the poet Robin Blaser, his close friend and literary executor, Spicer's poetic career actually begins in 1957 with the appearance of *After Lorca*. This is the first of the books written after he changed his approach to creativity and accepted the notion of "divine poetic infusion," a method he traced to the Greek writer Longinus. Blaser writes, "It is indicative of a new consciousness of the power and violence of language, and in Jack's work, it becomes an insistent argument for the performance of the real by way of poetry." With the publication of *After Lorca* in 1957, Spicer began a steady production of verse in his new style. During this creative phase Spicer exercised a charismatic sway over his San Francisco circle. Among the poets he influenced are Robin Blaser, Harold Dull, Robert **Duncan**, and Richard Tagett.

The dozen volumes he wrote are gathered in the posthumous *Collected Books* (Los Angeles: Black Sparrow, 1975). Uncollected items appear in *One Night Stand and Other Poems* (San Francisco: Grey Fox, 1980). His 1965 Vancouver lectures remain unpublished.

BIBLIOGRAPHY. Paul Mariah, ed., [Jack Spicer Issue], *Manroot* (Fall/Winter 1974/ 75).

George Klawitter

SPORTS
See **Athletics**.

STEIN, GERTRUDE (1874–1946)

American writer. Born in Allegheny, Pennsylvania, Stein spent much of her youth in Oakland, California, where her father had business interests. As an undergraduate at Harvard's Radcliffe College she was influenced by the psychology classes of William James. She then pursued medical studies in Baltimore, where she had an affair with a woman named May Bookstaver. This experience provided the basis for the novel *Q.E.D.*, the only work in which Stein wrote explicitly of a lesbian relationship; she did not allow the book to be published during her lifetime.

In 1903 Gertrude Stein left for Europe, in due course settling into a Paris apartment with her brother Leo. The two had a keen interest in avant-garde art, and began a pioneering collection of contemporary paintings. Gertrude became friends with Henri Matisse and Pablo Picasso—then regarded as an enfant terrible, but about whom she wrote with insight. In 1905 her Baltimore friend Etta Cone came to Paris for some months; she and Gertrude had an affair, while Cone typed the manuscript for Stein's book *Three Lives*. Etta soon came to share the Steins' passion for contemporary art, and after her return to America she and her sister Claribel built up a collection of modern masterpieces, which later entered the Baltimore Museum of Art. Etta continued to rely implicitly on the aesthetic advice and judgment of Gertrude Stein, and in this way the bonding of the two women was to play a role in the introduction of modern art to the United States.

At the end of 1907 Alice B. Toklas arrived in Paris. Toklas, who came from a similar upper-middle-class Jewish family of the Bay Area of California, had an almost immediate rapport with Stein. They were to be together for 38 years. Their relationship was a version of the **butch-fem** dyad: Alice did the cooking and kept house, while Gertrude concentrated on her writing. When heterosexual couples would visit, Gertrude would talk to the men, while Alice made the women feel at home. In her forties Stein wrote love poetry reflecting her relationship with Toklas; although sexual particulars are noted in a private code, this can be deciphered without too much difficulty. Like *Q.E.D.*, these poems were not published in her lifetime.

After World War I, Stein's Rue de Fleurus apartment—in competition with the nearby establishment of Natalie Clifford **Barney**—became a favorite gathering place of the American and English writers of the so-called "Lost Generation," including Robert McAlmon, F. Scott Fitzgerald, and Ernest **Hemingway**. Although Hemingway acquired some of his own style through studying Stein's more experimental work, he was later to write

harshly about her—as she seemed to have struck a tender nerve in his own sexual self-concept. For a fellow Harvard graduate, the homosexual composer Virgil Thomson, Stein wrote an opera libretto, *Four Saints in Three Acts* in 1927; it was successfully produced in Hartford in 1934 with sets by Florine Stettheimer.

In 1933 Stein published *The Autobiography of Alice B. Toklas*, deliberately composed in an accessible style. The next year she followed this book with a triumphant tour of America—her only trip home. While her literary eminence was assured, her artistic judgment in this period seemed less certain; she became very interested in a minor English gay painter Francis Rose, and acquired a number of his undistinguished works.

During the Occupation years of World War II, Stein and Toklas lived undisturbed at their country home in the south of France. After the liberation Gertrude Stein was able to return to her Paris apartment, where she delighted in receiving the visits of American soldiers. She died of cancer in 1946, leaving her manuscripts to Yale University, where they have been gradually brought to publication.

Continuing to live in the Paris apartment surrounded by the paintings, Alice B. Toklas became renowned for her cookbook. After converting to Roman Catholicism, perhaps in the hope that somehow it would assist her in being reunited with Gertrude, Toklas died in 1967.

Stein's writings have acquired a reputation for being difficult and opaque. She sought to develop a literary parallel to her cherished Cubist paintings, with their fragmented presentation of reality. An early interest in automatic writing, which grew out of her classes with William James, fused with the stream-of-consciousness techniques that she shared with James Joyce, Dorothy Richardson, and Virginia **Woolf** to produce work of striking modernity. Apart from these innovative concerns, the obscurity of much of her writing is probably also linked with her desire to advert to aspects of her lesbianism, but without openly avowing it. While Gertrude Stein will probably never become a popular writer, she was a pivotal figure in the development of literary **modernism**, and as such has exercised considerable indirect influence. Her first-hand responses to the work of modern artists, and the little museum of major works that so many saw in her Paris apartment, earned her a secondary role as a tastemaker in the field of modern painting.

BIBLIOGRAPHY. Richard Bridgman, *Gertrude Stein in Pieces*, New York: Oxford, 1970; James R. Mellow, *Charmed Circle: Gertrude Stein and Company*, New York: Praeger, 1974; Linda Simon, *The Biography of Alice B. Toklas*, New York: Avon, 1977.

Evelyn Gettone

STEREOTYPE

The term stereotype had its origin in the printing trade, where it meant a solid metal plate, a printing surface that could be used for thousands of identical impressions without need of replacement. The American journalist Walter Lippmann introduced the concept to the social sciences in his book *Public Opinion* (1922), in which he argued that in a modern democracy political leaders and ordinary voters are required to make decisions about a variety of complex matters which they do not understand, but judge on the basis of stereotypes acquired from some source other than direct experience. The inflow of new empirical data fails to correct the situation because the individual who has embraced a stereotype sees mainly what he expects to see rather than what is really present.

The esteem in which Lippmann was held by Americans in public life furthered the adoption of the term essentially in the meaning he gave it. When a concept is designated a stereotype, it is implied that (1) it is simple rather than nuanced or differentiated, (2) it is erroneous rather than accurate, (3) it has been acquired through secondhand rather than direct experience, and (4) it resists modification by later experience. Very little systematic investigation of the dimensions of stereotyping has been done, apart from the dimension of resistance to change. In empirical research the term has usually been restricted to a pejorative designation for commonly held beliefs about ethnic groups. This "group concept" usage was established in a classic study by Katz and Braly of 1933. The questionnaire asked the subject to select from a list of 84 traits the ones he considered characteristic of each of ten ethnic groups, then to choose the five "most typical" traits for each group. This procedure has been repeated many times, for many ethnic groups, and in many different countries. While most of the studies have dealt with beliefs about ethnic groups, a considerable number have probed attitudes toward occupational groups, social classes, the differences between the sexes, and like topics.

One conclusion that may be drawn from this research is that most individuals are willing to make at least a guess about the traits of almost any defined social group on the basis of information that a social scientist would consider inadequate. Opinions are derived first of all from the mass media, which today by electronic means reach even the uneducated and barely literate masses in backward countries, as well as educated publics in advanced ones. Other individuals and fortuitous personal contact supply further bases for opinion-forming. The circumstances under which stereotypes are likely to be accurate or inaccurate are the object of many hypotheses. A widely held belief which Lippmann himself propagated is that the stereotypes of the educated are in general more accurate than those of the uneducated, and that concepts formed by social scientists are the most accurate of all. This view, however plausible, has never been demonstrated. A secondary problem is a group's self-image, which may be as stereotypical as any other. If the self-image of a collective and a second group's image of it largely coincide, this fact is usually taken as evidence for a "kernel of truth" in both sets of stereotypes.

Stereotypes of Homosexuality. Research on attitudes toward homosexuality is relatively recent, and the dimensions of the stereotyping of homosexuals are not fully defined. Several general observations may, however, be made on the basis of the extant findings and of more theoretical presuppositions. The first is that there are diachronic layers of stereotypes. In the West, the oldest layer, inherited from antiquity and the early **Middle Ages**, is that homosexuals behave like members of the opposite sex, or conversely that they violate the appropriate norms of behavior for their genital sex. Thus terms like "effeminate" and "swish" are applied to male homosexuals by some if not always many of the subjects questioned. Conversely, lesbians are perceived as mannish, crude, and aggressive. Another archaic layer, attested in the Greek comedies of **Aristophanes**, is that male homosexuals and bisexuals are constantly thinking about sex, and even (in many cases) almost indiscriminate in their choice of sex objects. The third layer derives from the central and late Middle Ages, when the church systematically defamed homosexual activity and those who engaged in it, with the outcome that terms such as "immoral," "repulsive," "dangerous," and "sinful" are stereotypical responses to questionnaire studies. The fourth layer is the one propagated by **psychiatry** and **psychoanalysis** from the late nineteenth century onward, to the effect that the homosexual is "sexually abnormal," "perverted," "mentally ill," "maladjusted," "insecure," and "lacking self-control." The most recent layer, and the one characteristic of individuals who have overcome the traditional social distance from homosexuals, holds them to be "sensitive," "individualistic," "intelligent," "imagina-tive," "sophisticated," and "artistic." Undoubtedly the standard **movement** propaganda about the homosexuality of great men and women, and also the image of the creative writer or artist as homosexual, have contributed mightily to the diffusion of the last layer. Although it would appear to be a rare example of positive stereotyping (and to a considerable extent it is), the notion of creativity has been traditionally associated—at least in American culture—with lack of manliness.

Such stereotypes are harbored and propagated not only by members of the host culture (the "heterosexual majority"), but also—to a degree that may seem surprising in the era of homosexual **liberation**—by many homosexuals themselves. As part of the **coming-out** process, the tyro homosexual or lesbian may display "obvious" mannerisms and dress, even in an exaggerated form, to gain adhesion to the group. Later these flaunting signals are likely to be toned down, as the need for them decreases. In a more subtle way, traits redolent of stereotypes may be selectively unfurled in order to signal one's orientation nonverbally to other gay people. Such communication serves a specific function, but it also lends a specious validity to the more baneful stereotypes. Dilemmas of this kind are probably inseparable from the experience of a stigmatized minority as such.

Class Differences. There is a **class** aspect to stereotyping: the lower social classes, being less educated and more given to concrete than abstract thinking, incline more to stereotypic responses because their thinking is in imagery rather than in logical concepts, and their mental life more affective than intellectual. Moreover, the uneducated may cherish a random set of stereotypes that contradict one another, as when the male homosexual is thought inordinately aggressive and "a danger to every boy on the streets," but also timid and wanting in masculinity. Also, in the lower classes far more importance is attached to sex **roles** that are rigidly and unequivocally defined. A man must be masculine, a woman feminine, and there is a relatively low level of toleration for **deviant** behavior. In this situation, if a man is homosexual and therefore behaves sexually "like a woman," his whole personality is expected to conform to this model. Hence the stereotype—or more precisely the most archaic layer of stereotypes—is reinforced by the majority of lower-class homosexuals who opt for a female **identity** and then project that identity through overtly effeminate behavior. Conversely the upper-class individual exposed to homophile propaganda may form his stereotypical notion from the biography of a famous novelist or painter, or from literature that stresses the "positive achievements" of homosexuals in history. In general, the more educated part of the population in a society that prides itself on its individualism can tolerate—if not accept—a deviation in sexual character so long as it is not patently disharmonious or incongruent with other societal norms.

Correlations of Stereotypes. A further question is the correlation of negative stereotypes of the homosexual with attitudes toward other outsider, minority groups. In the wake of the findings of Theodor Wiesengrund Adorno and his associates in *The Authoritarian Personality* (1950), investigators have sought a common denominator in a personality type that relies on authority, is unable to tolerate ambiguity, and is deeply immersed in the specific value system of the ethnic group and social class in which it has been reared. A heterosexual having such traits is likely to be even more intolerant of the homosexual than of other deviant groups, and to perceive homoerotic behavior as threatening to his own sexual identity and potentially harmful to society. That is why the effeminate homosexual may be disliked because he violates the norm of masculinity, but conversely the masculine homosexual may provoke even more anxiety because of the ambiguity which

his even subtler departure from maleness entails. It is also a fact that homosexual behavior is often believed to have originated with, or to be characteristic of, another ethnic group, as when Frenchmen call homosexuality "le vice allemand" (the German vice). The very terms *sodomite* and *bugger* are in English the legacy of such labeling of a people or dissident sect as guilty of "unnatural vice." This general tendency to ascribe undesirable characteristics to disliked groups is termed **ethnophaulism.**

The centuries-long stigmatization of the sodomite as a criminal and an outcast in Western civilization has left behind a negative residue of stereotypes that only an equally lengthy process of education and positive-image building can efface. A conference of gay movement leaders held in 1988 placed the creation of a positive image of the homosexual at the head of its agenda for future activity.

See also **Authoritarian Personality; Discrimination; Homophobia; Myths and Fabrications.**

BIBLIOGRAPHY. Ronald A. Farrell and Thomas J. Morrione, "Social Interaction and Stereotypic Responses to Homosexuals," *Archives of Sexual Behavior*, 3 (1974), 425–42; Robert Gramling and Craig J. Forsyth, "Exploiting Stigma," *Sociological Forum*, 2 (1987), 401–15; Sharon B. Gurwitz and Melinda Marcus, "Effects of Anticipated Interaction, Sex, and Homosexual Stereotypes on First Impressions," *Journal of Applied Social Psychology*, 8 (1978), 47–56; Gregory R. Staats, "Stereotype Content and Social Distance: Changing Views of Homosexuality," *Journal of Homosexuality*, 4 (1978), 15–27; Alan Taylor, "Conceptions of Masculinity and Femininity as a Basis for Stereotypes of Male and Female Homosexuals," *Journal of Homosexuality*, 9 (1983), 37–53.

Warren Johansson

STEVENSON, EDWARD IRENAEUS PRIME- ("XAVIER MAYNE"; 1868-1942)

American novelist and scholar. Born in Madison, New Jersey, and educated in the United States, he began to write for the press while still in school. He was admitted to the New Jersey bar but never practiced. Stevenson was a member of the staff of the *Independent, Harper's Weekly*, and other magazines, and gained a wide reputation as musical, dramatic, and literary critic. He specialized in foreign, including European and Oriental, literatures and claimed fluency in nine languages. Down to 1900 he divided his time between the United States and many parts of Europe, then settled permanently abroad out of dislike for the homophobia of contemporary American society, ultimately dying in Europe in 1942. He wrote many novels and short stories, several of which broach the homosexual theme but in the innocuous guise of "male friendship." In a boys' book about Bonnie Prince Charlie, *White Cockades* (1887), there is "half-hinted" an erotic liaison between the prince and a rustic youth.

Under the pseudonym "Xavier Mayne" he published in Naples in 1908 what was perhaps the first explicit homosexual **novel** by a native-born American: *Imre: A Memorandum*. The novel's simple plot describes the love affair between the thirty-year-old Oswald who is spending a leisurely summer of language study in Hungary and the twenty-five-year-old Imre, a Hungarian cavalry officer.

More important was his nonfiction book *The Intersexes: A History of Similisexualism as a Problem in Social Life* (Rome, 1908), the first large-scale survey in the English language of the subject of homosexuality from all aspects. It was based not just upon his reading of nearly everything that had been published until then in the homophile **movement** press and in the psychiatric literature, but also upon his first-hand observations of the homosexual scene in the major cities of Europe and the United States, with much folklore and gossip thrown in for good measure. The author describes the mores of the gay **subculture** of that era, from the nobleman in his salon to the hustler on the street, with an objectivity that is free of both polemic and condemnatory bias. He alludes to many all-but-forgotten incidents and scandals that made the metropolitan newspapers, and names scores of illustrious figures of the past and present as **Uranians** or Uraniads (lesbians). Stevenson adheres to the line of Magnus **Hirschfeld** and the **Scientific-humanitarian Committee** that homosexuality is inborn and unmodifiable, that homosexuals should not be forced to don "masks" to hide from would-be persecutors, and that religion and the law are powerless to extirpate a predisposition of human nature. So thorough is the volume that not a few of the topics broached on its more than 600 pages have yet to be investigated by modern scholars. As the work of a participant observer, *The Intersexes* remains a precious collection of fact and commentary that anticipates Donald Webster Cory's *The Homosexual in America* of 1951, its first American successor.

BIBLIOGRAPHY. Roger Austen, *Playing the Game: The Homosexual Novel in America*, Indianapolis: Bobbs-Merrill, 1977; Noel I. Garde, "The Mysterious Father of American Homophile Literature," *ONE Institute Quarterly*, 1:3 (Fall 1958), 94–98.

Warren Johansson

STOICISM

Founded by **Zeno** of Citium (335-263 B.C.), Stoicism became the leading philosophical school under the **Roman emperors**, until the triumph of **Neoplatonism** in the third century. Insisting in the trying times of the **Hellenistic monarchies** that even poverty, pain, and death are as nothing to the eternal soul, Stoics vanquished their materialistic rivals, the

Epicureans, who stressed pleasure rather than virtue as the aim of life.

Almost all earlier Stoics, sometimes labeled the First Stoa, praised homosexual love and shocked most Greeks by claiming that, contrary to the convention that one should cease loving a boy once he sprouted a beard, one should keep one's *eromenos* until he reached his twenty-eighth year. Paenatius and other Greeks introduced Stoic doctrines, which appealed to the Latin sense for *gravitas* and endurance of hardships, to the Scipionic circle in Rome. Perhaps fearing the wrath of old-fashioned *patresfamilias*, who disapproved of Greek love and arranged the marriage of their sons during their teens to girls of 12 or 13, in contrast to the practice of upper-class Greeks to postpone marriage to 30 and then take brides whose ages ranged from 15 to 19, they omitted the emphasis on boy-love. Aristocratic Roman women lived with their husbands and circulated in society, in contrast to Greek women who were secluded, shut away in *gynaikeia* (women's quarters). Aristocratic Roman women thereby attained a far higher status than Greek women had and fostered the emphasis of later Stoics on marriage. Often designated the Second Stoa, most of the later Stoics deemphasized homosexual love and some, notably the Roman Musonius Rufus in the first century, demanded reciprocal fidelity to one's wife. Others, however, like the Emperor Marcus Aurelius (reigned 161–180), remained bisexual. The slave philosopher Epictetus (ca. 50–ca. 135) demonstrated the Stoic doctrine that one's station in life was unimportant; only one's virtue mattered.

Many have seen Stoic emphasis on the soul and on virtue and restraint of appetites as a harbinger of **Christianity**. Indeed, **Patristic writers** from **Clement** of Alexandria (150–215) to St. **Augustine** (354–430) dressed up Christian doctrine in Stoic phrases to convert the upper classes. But while Stoic philosophers, like pagan physicians, recommended moderation in

sexual activity as in diet and exercise to improve the body and mind, most Christian Fathers advocated complete chastity and total sexual abstinence. Christians wished to transcend nature, while Stoics preferred to live in harmony with it. To control sexual urges, Christians mortified the flesh, often in the deliberate attempt to achieve male impotence and female frigidity, states that Greco-Roman physicians treated as diseases to be cured. Christians condemned **sodomy** with the Stoic phrase, "against nature." The evolution from uninhibited pagan sexuality through Stoic restraint to Christian **asceticism** and chastity that some philosophers and historians claim to detect is thus more apparent than real, more superficial than fundamental, one of vocabulary rather than essence.

BIBLIOGRAPHY. Daniel Babut, "Les Stoiciens et l'amour," *Revue des Etudes Grècques*, 6 (1963), 55–63; G. W. Bowersock, *Greek Sophists in the Roman Empire*, Oxford: Clarendon Press, 1969; Michel Foucault, *The Care of the Self*, New York: Random House, 1986; J. M. Rist, *Stoic Philosophy*, Cambridge: Cambridge University Press, 1969; Aline Rousselle, *Porneia: On Desire and the Body in Antiquity*, New York: Basil Blackwell, 1988.

William A. Percy

STONEWALL REBELLION

This event, which took place in **New York City** over the weekend of June 27–30, 1969, is significant less for its intrinsic character than as a symbol of self-assertion for the gay **liberation** movement. So successfully has the symbol been propagated that it has largely, though not completely, obscured the history of the preceding century of heartbreakingly slow and arduous work on behalf of homosexual emancipation. The Stonewall Rebellion was a spontaneous act of resistance to the police harassment that had been inflicted on the homosexual community since the inception of the modern vice squad in metropolitan police forces, but it sparked a much greater, indeed national phenomenon—a new, highly visible, mass phase of political organization for gay rights that far surpassed the timid, semi-clandestine homophile **movement** of the 1950s and 1960s.

What Occurred. The event began with a police raid on the Stonewall Inn, a gay bar at 51–53 Christopher Street just east of Sheridan Square in New York's Greenwich Village on the night of June 27–28. A police inspector and seven other officers from the Public Morals Section of the First Division of the New York City Police Department arrived shortly after midnight, served a warrant charging that liquor was being sold without a license, and announced that employees would be arrested. Over the preceding two decades such raids had become almost routine for the **police**, and they were confident that with a little strong-arm and menace the "queers" would go quietly, as usual. The Stonewall was a dimly lit dance bar in a neighborhood that abounded in homosexuals with flamboyant, unconventional lifestyles, including **transvestites** known as "street queens." Partly because their overt non-conformity gave them little to lose, as the patrons were being ejected from the bar by the police others lingered outside to watch the proceedings, and were joined by passers-by, including many street people. Some were attracted from the nearby MacDougal Street entertainment area. It was the arrival of the paddywagons that changed the mood of the crowd from passivity to defiance. The first vehicle left without mishap, though there came a chorus of catcalls from the crowd. The next individual to emerge from the bar was a woman in male costume who put up a struggle which galvanized the bystanders into action. As if prompted by a signal, the crowd erupted into heaving cobblestones and bottles. Some officers had to take refuge inside the bar, where they risked being burned to death. Others turned a firehose on the crowd, while they called reinforcements which in time managed to clear the streets. During the day the news

spread, and the following two nights witnessed further violent confrontations between the police and gay people.

Underlying Causal Factors. To understand why this riot occurred, and why it came to have such resonance, it is necessary to recall that the nationwide wave of opposition to the American intervention in Vietnam, which had culminated in the **student** uprising at Columbia University on April 23, 1968, and in riots in the streets of Chicago during the Democratic National Convention in the summer of 1968, had replaced the conservatism of the Eisenhower era with a mood of radicalism that through the "youth culture" of the late 1960s fed into the subterranean world of the hippies and **beatniks** of the **bohemias** in the large cities. There was among the young, the outsiders, the aggrieved of the land a sense of mounting opposition to an establishment headed by President Richard M. Nixon that persisted in maintaining an American presence in Indo-China, but also embodied "straight" society and everything that stood in the way of the liberation for which the rebellious generation of the late 1960s yearned.

Why did the event occur in New York City? After all, **Los Angeles** had been the birthplace of the American gay movement, and other significant social disturbances took place in the 1960s in **San Francisco** and Berkeley, California. Reinforced by creative **exiles and émigrés**, New York City during the 1940s had become a major center of avant-garde culture, which had brought with it from Europe a bohemian tradition of mockery of authority, revivifying Greenwich Village's reputation for innovative non-conformity. The paintings of New York's Abstract Expressionists, championed by poet–critic Frank **O'Hara**, horrified the establishment with their seemingly anarchic "drip" style. Pop art appeared with its principal shrine in Andy **Warhol**'s "factory." New York was also the home of the experimental New American Cinema, whose "Baudelairean" **films**, some of them made by gay directors, explored aspects of the underground in a highly disjunctive, poetic style. MacDougal Street, the vibrant, often raucous center of the folk music scene, was only two blocks away from the Stonewall Inn. Finally New York, together with London, was the home of a new spirit of innovation in the **theatre**; scores of Off-off-Broadway theatres, some accommodating only a score of patrons, sprang up as sites of sometimes daring excursions into novelty, including nudity and obscenity. The Stonewall Rebellion, which involved some of the same transvestites who hovered around the avant-garde theatre, reflected the confluence of these cultural trends.

Although it had played virtually no role in the first fifteen years of the American homophile movement, New York City—as perhaps nowhere else in the country—sheltered a long radical tradition. In the late 1960s this tradition merged with a **counterculture**—whose geographical center and symbol was Greenwich Village—that openly rebelled against the values of "respectable" American middle-class society and fostered a state of mind that could successfully challenge even so long-standing and unquestioned a taboo as the intolerance of homosexuality. That youthful nonconformity, reinforced by the growing sexual freedom and the **drug** culture that had taken firm hold of the college generation in the mid-1960s, led to the loss of inhibitions and unreflecting bravado which inspired the spontaneous resistance to police harassment. The experience of having their privacy invaded and their civil rights violated, of being the victims of entrapment and of perjured testimony brought home to many heterosexuals the kind of injustice that homosexuals had long suffered at the hands of the police. This overall pattern of assaults— not simply the arrest of bar patrons—was the grievance against the police shared by the youth culture and the homosexual subculture alike, both sensing the officers of the law as villains because of their persecution of drug users, student radicals—and gay people.

Significance. If the Stonewall Rebellion was not self-consciously political, it was still an intensely felt refusal to endure any longer the humiliation, the constant insults, the rightlessness that had been the traditional lot of the homosexual in Western society as long as anyone living could remember. Craig Rodwell, who stumbled upon the crowd in front of the Stonewall Inn—named after the legendary Confederate General "Stonewall" Jackson—tried to set up a chant of "Gay Power!" but almost no one joined in.

But times were changing rapidly. Partisans of the New **Left** saw an opportunity to enlist homosexuals for their movement, and the homophile activists of such groups as the **Mattachine Society** began to rethink their positions in the light of the left's critique of the oppressive and exploitative character of American society. After two days, members of New York Mattachine were in the West Village handing out leaflets hailing "the Christopher Street Riots" as "the Hairpin Drop Heard around the World," echoing Emerson's lines of 1835 on the patriots at Lexington who "fired the shot heard round the world."

The American media, centralized in New York City, diffused and reshaped the image of the event. And the Stonewall Rebellion, however brief and local, however apolitical it may have been, did echo around the globe. Enveloped in legend like the Easter Sunday Uprising of 1916 in Dublin, it has been commemorated by a parade held each year in New York City on the last Sunday in June, following a tradition that began with the first march on June 29, 1970, and by parallel events throughout the United States. From a score of organizations cowering in the shadowy bohemias of the large cities, the gay movement expanded into the Gay Liberation Front, Gay Activists Alliance, and many other groups with chapters the length and breadth of the land. Stonewall became the symbol of an oppressed and invisible **mi-**

nority at last demanding its place in the sun and the freedoms which Americans had been taught since childhood were the right and heritage of everyone. The gay subculture that outlasted this radical episode in American politics—a radicalism which quickly faded once the Vietnam War ended, at least provisorily, in 1973—has been the archetype of a wave of political and cultural innovation throughout the world, so that the modern phase of the gay movement can truly be said to have begun on those June nights in Greenwich Village outside the Stonewall Inn.

BIBLIOGRAPHY. Toby Marotta, *The Politics of Homosexuality*, Boston: Houghton Mifflin, 1981; Donn Teal, *The Gay Militants*, New York: Stein and Day, 1971.

Warren Johansson

STRACHEY, (GILES) LYTTON (1880–1932)

English biographer and critic. The son of a general in the Indian Army, Strachey attended Abbotshulme School, Leamington College, Liverpool University College, and Trinity College, Cambridge. As a boy at Leamington he experienced homosexual crushes, which left him with an abiding vision of his need for ideal male companionship. At Cambridge Strachey, whose gawky and unattractive figure was no bar to recognition of his brilliance, was elected a member of the exclusive Apostles group, together with John Maynard **Keynes** and Leonard Woolf. He embarked on his first grand passion, with the painter Duncan **Grant**, whom he was shortly to lose to Keynes.

After taking his degree at Cambridge, Strachey settled in London, where he was almost immediately integrated into the **Bloomsbury** group. The first years of his literary career were difficult and, apart from reviews, produced only a textbook, *Landmarks in French Literature* (1912). In 1917 he settled into a country house with the painter Dora Carrington, who had fallen in love with him. After

the war, they were joined by an ex-officer Ralph Partridge in a ménage à trois. This arrangement gave Strachey the serenity and support he required to complete his biographical works, *Eminent Victorians* (1918), *Queen Victoria* (1921), and *Elizabeth and Essex* (1928). Written with great panache, these books effected a revolution in biography through their ironic, often mocking distance from their subjects. Strachey's last years were enlivened by several successful affairs with young men, notably Roger Senhouse. After his death from cancer, his companion Carrington committed suicide.

As a result of the reaction against aestheticism occasioned by the Depression and World War II, Strachey's work went out of fashion, along with Bloomsbury itself. In the freer climate of the 1960s, however, this attitude changed, and Strachey's sexual unorthodoxy, which had been largely hidden, became an asset. The major factor in the restoration of his reputation came in the 1,200-page life story by Michael Holroyd, the homage of one major biographer to another.

BIBLIOGRAPHY. Michael Holroyd, *Lytton Strachey: A Critical Biography*, 2 vols., New York: Holt, Rinehart and Winston, 1968.

Wayne R. Dynes

STUDENTS, GAY

Until the end of the 1960s the plight of the gay college student on an American college campus was a difficult, sometimes even a tragic, one. Confronted with the growing consciousness of his own sexual orientation, he found himself in a society where negative attitudes toward homosexuality were reinforced by peer pressure, where the obligations and opportunities of undergraduate life were all cast in a heterosexual mold, and where confidences made to a psychologist or psychiatrist could be betrayed to the college authorities. Such betrayal would entail disastrous consequences: further disclosure to his parents and family, forced psychiatric treatment, or even expulsion. The few courses in which homosexuality might have been mentioned usually treated the subject with evasion or disdain; the books available in the college library relegated the topic to the realm of the pathological or criminal. If the student was fortunate, he could make the acquaintance of another individual who had accepted his homosexuality, found a modus vivendi in the midst of an intolerant society, and begun the arduous task of fashioning a mask to deceive the unfriendly heterosexuals around him. If he failed to make contact with the gay **subculture** that existed on some campuses or the nearby **bohemian** milieu, he could be doomed to lead a lonely life of silent alienation from the world of the rest of the undergraduates. Opportunities for social-sexual contact with others of his age such as the dances and fraternity–sorority life offered the heterosexual were unavailable to the homosexual student.

The introduction of war veterans on American campuses in the late 1940s (through legislation known as the "GI Bill of Rights") might have changed matters, for many of these older students had experienced freer sexual lifestyles in North **Africa**, Europe, and the **Pacific**. Though generally credited with pioneering a new seriousness that competed with the pre-war model of late adolescent hedonism ("Joe College"), the veterans were generally too preoccupied with economic struggles and grades to accomplish much social innovation on campus.

The First Campus Groups and Their Vicissitudes. Only toward the end of the 1960s did this situation begin to change, reflecting a new mood among American youth. Robert A. Martin (b. 1946), a student at New York's Columbia University (which in 1945 had suspended undergraduate Allen Ginsberg for suspected homosexuality), conceived the idea of a student group that would create a movement presence on the campus. Martin, better known under the name Stephen Donaldson, had been a member of the Mattachine Society of New York since the spring of 1965 and had spent the summer of 1966 living with **Mattachine Society** of Washington president Frank Kameny.

Returning to the campus as a bisexually-identified sophomore in September 1966, Donaldson discussed the idea with interested students and, finding resistance within New York Mattachine to an autonomous group on campus, he chose the name Student Homophile League (SHL). The incipient group, which mixed both gender and orientation, found a protector in the courageous Episcopal Chaplain of the University, John Dyson Cannon. In October 1966 the chaplain arranged a meeting in Earl Hall to introduce the organization to the administration and the religious and psychological counselors. A certain amount of opposition was voiced, and to gain official standing the group was required to submit a list of names of members to the university administration—which could have been ordered to disclose them to the government. This proved an insuperable barrier until a set of prominent student leaders agreed to become the official charter members in April 1967.

With this list in hand, the university capitulated, and when the resultant story printed in the *Columbia Spectator* came (a week later) to the attention of the *New York Times*, on May 1, 1967 the front-page news was broken to an astonished world: "COLUMBIA CHARTERS HOMOSEXUAL GROUP." The reaction was all the more violent in that college administrations had everywhere clung to the concept of *in loco parentis*, that they replaced the parents as moral guardians of the students and their sex lives, and often held that students needed "protection" from such corrupting influences as homosexuality. The Columbia administration was flooded with letters from indignant alumni, many of whom assured the school that they would never give it another penny.

The newly recognized Student Homophile League was primarily interested in educating the campus, in promoting gay rights, and in counseling. Lectures and panels drew hundreds, while some 15 to 30 people attended the business meetings, and informal parties were held, though at first no public dances. Many students still in the process of **"coming out"** needed peer **counseling**, while frequent, informal discussions in the dormitories had the aim of enlightening the rest of the student body. A series of leaflets taking uncompromising positions foreshadowing gay **liberation** ideas was issued.

Two other SHL chapters were formed at New York University (under Rita Mae Brown, later author of the lesbian novel *Rubyfruit Jungle*) and at Cornell University (under Jearld Moldenhauer, subsequently an editor of Toronto's *The Body Politic*, and with the sponsorship of well-known anti-Vietnam War activist Rev. Phillip Berrigan), and in the fall of 1968 an independent organization called FREE was established at the University of Minnesota. The fledgling gay student **movement** participated in the North American Conference of Homophile Organizations (NACHO) and its Eastern Regional Conference as a radicalizing force, with Donaldson holding several offices at various times.

On April 23, 1968 (coincidentally the same day radical students began a week-long occupation of campus buildings), the SHL, denied participation on a psychiatric panel on homosexuality held at the Columbia medical school, picketed the event and distributed over a thousand multipage statements to members of the audience, many of whom turned over their tickets to the protesters, who proceeded to dominate the question period. This was the first demonstration against the **psychiatric** establishment's "medical model" of homosexuality.

The Columbia uprising of April 1968 did not involve the gay movement immediately, as the radical groups on campus—following the Old Left and Maoist rejection of sexual reform—kept their political distance from it. The Columbia SHL did, however, join the student strike after a few days and issued its own set of demands.

By the spring of 1969 the gay student organizations were beginning to integrate school dances and sponsor their own, while their ideological positions, originally heavily influenced by Kameny through Donaldson, who broke away in 1968, became even more assertive in enunciating what were to become known as "gay liberation" doctrines.

Then the radical wave of the late 1960s, within which the Columbia revolt had become a worldwide symbol of the rebellion of alienated youth, sparked the **Stonewall Rebellion** of June 1969, which marked the beginning of a new, far more aggressive and activist phase of the homosexual emancipation movement. Following the lead of the antiwar protestors who occupied campuses, marched through the streets with huge banners, and constantly agitated for their cause, the supporters of the Gay Liberation Front defied centuries-old conventions and taboos and "came out" for gay rights. With this model, the student groups multiplied across the country, and by the end of the 1970s virtually every major campus in the country had one. To be sure, the end of the draft for the Vietnam War in 1973 saw student activism fade, but the gay student movement remained, constantly renewed as new generations of homosexual students entered the colleges and universities. The activities of the groups were mainly social, with a certain amount of peer counseling as a sideline. Gay dances became a feature of campus life, the organizations were able to sponsor lectures and public discussions, and each year on Gay Pride Day in June the groups would march behind their banners in the parades held in major cities from Boston to San Diego.

Stabilization. By 1975 at least 150 gay and lesbian groups had been established on American college campuses. They tended to be concentrated in the Northeast and on the West Coast and to be most vigorous in older private universities and major state institutions. A decade later the number had at least doubled, and the groups were well represented in the midwest and south as well as the older areas. Even many religious colleges had their groups, though the gay students at Georgetown University in Washington DC (Catholic) had to take their case to the federal courts. Although the gay groups were sometimes resented by insecure heterosexually identified students (and feared by administrations as a potential focus of alumni grumbling), the new associations fit well enough into the existing kaleidoscope of campus clubs which catered to blacks and Asians, to vegetarians and chessplayers. A new factor is diversification: twenty years after the founding of the Student Homophile League, Columbia University boasted fifteen separate groups spread out among the affiliated institutions on Morningside Heights instead of just one. Some schools even provided special counseling services for gay and lesbian students, though funding shortages tended to make the future of these uncertain.

Gay student groups sprang up in other English-speaking countries, notably Canada and Australia. On the European continent the American model did not take root, because European universities do not usually have campuses as such. In a few countries gay youth groups fulfilled some of the same functions.

A number of North American campus groups sponsored annual conferences attended by hundreds of students from their respective areas, which were an opportunity to hear talks by prominent activists and leaders of the national gay movement, as well as to discuss the problems of coping with enemies on the campus and around it. In recent years regional conferences with a long list of workshops and speakers have been held at major schools in the Northeast and elsewhere.

In the history of the gay movement, the student groups have been significant as pioneers of intellectual innovation, as seminars for leaders who went on to mainstream organizations, and as a source of "out front" militants willing to take risks their job-holding seniors were reluctant to undertake.

Gay studies as a unified academic discipline have not fared so well; after some promising beginnings in the 1970s they largely disappeared from college curricula, and the Gay Academic Union founded in New York City in 1973 was unable even to produce a textbook for an introductory course, while in the same time women's studies were able to take root and create institutes for research and teaching. In 1987 two separate projects for similar institutions that would promote academic investigation of homosexuality were launched at Yale University and the City University of New York; the future of both is problematic. While the social needs of the gay undergraduate and graduate student are far better served than before the late 1960s, the academic side of the movement faces many tasks and challenges in coming decades.

See also **Education; Public Schools; Youth.**

BIBLIOGRAPHY. J. Lee Lehman, *Gays on Campus*, Washington: United States National Student Association, 1975; Robert A. Martin, "Student Homophile League: Founder's Retrospect," *Gay Books Bulletin*, 9 (1983), 30–33.
Warren Johansson

SUBCULTURE, GAY

The term "subculture" (introduced as recently as 1936 by the sociologist Ralph Linton) applies to ethnic, regional, economic, and social groups showing special worlds of interest and identification which serve to distinguish them within the larger culture or society.

Basic Features of the Subculture Concept. A subculture differs from a category of people or a common behavior by virtue of its heightened sharing of values, artifacts, and identification. It is intensified by the degree of social separation between its members and the rest of the larger society. This formulation implies a two-level analysis, society and subculture, but in fact there are multiple layers, so that subcultures themselves have what might cumbersomely be labeled subsubcultures, subsubsubcultures, and so on, almost ad infinitum; in practice the definition of a particular subculture must be seen as relative to the larger context in which it is set by the definer.

There is, furthermore, a range of emotional attitudes between the larger society and the subculture; for the former they range from acceptance (e.g., of yachtsmen) through disdain (gamblers) to hostility (heroin addicts). This range appears also in the response of the subculture, which may support the larger society (radio hams) or actively oppose it (bikers). In the latter case, the term **"counterculture"** is often used; here the sense is of a more broadly applied and more conscious emphasis on an alternative to the larger society rather than an enclave within it. In general, there seems to be a relationship between the degree of alienation from the larger society and the relative powerlessness of the subculture members. Social separation tends to correlate with alienation, so that the more emotional distance between the subculture and the larger society, the stronger the subculture becomes, developing independent values, beliefs, roles, status systems, communications networks, and even economic structures. Conversely, as a larger society attenuates its hostility to a subculture and becomes more accepting (in modern consumer societies often exploiting the subculture as a ready-made market), the hold of the subculture on its members tends correspondingly to weaken; at some point

an expanding subculture crosses the line over into mass culture.

It has also been noted that subcultures play major roles in the process of social change, being both powerful agents for change and bulwarks against it. Examples of the latter would include religious fundamentalists and ecological conservationists. The concept of the subculture remains, however, a somewhat amorphous one, and for that reason perhaps, has resisted attempts to provide a general theoretical explanation accepted by a wide range of scholars.

Sexual Implications. The homosexual subculture is often regarded as constituting the individuals who have **come out** or emerged from the closet and are openly pursuing a gay **lifestyle**, often in the setting of the urban gay ghetto. In keeping with the preceding discussion, emphasis should, however, be laid rather on the self-identification of the participants (as "gay" or "lesbian") and on their common interests (same-gender sex, opposition to **homophobia**), artifacts (publications, jewelry, buttons), and values (sexual autonomy, social pluralism). In this sense, the homosexual subculture is much smaller than the aggregate of those engaging in homosexual acts, or even those who consciously define themselves as homosexual, inasmuch as many of these do not participate in group activities or acquire artifacts. **Sociological** theory also has difficulty in accounting for people who identify themselves not as homosexual but as **bisexual** (or even, in some cases, such as with many male **prostitutes**, as heterosexual), but who are otherwise seen to participate widely in major aspects of the "homosexual subculture."

Even conceding these limitations, it is apparent that the description of an overall "gay subculture" remains problematic, particularly in respect to common values and interests, and retains validity primarily when placed in the context of social separation from the majority (heterosexual) society. The gay subculture or community is far from homogeneous, its members have widely varying individual power positions and attitudes toward the larger society, and the latter displays a considerable spectrum of attitudes (compare those toward, say, a pair of **macho** cowboys and those toward promiscuous **pedophiles**). An even stronger argument can be made against the grouping of lesbians and gay males in the same subculture. For many purposes it seems more helpful to think of the gay or lesbian social worlds as collections of subcultures or subsubcultures: participants in the leather "scene," street **transvestites** (drag queen), **bar**-goers, call boys, **opera** buffs, and so forth.

Stephen Donaldson

Historical Perspectives. Some light is thrown on the origins of European homosexual subcultures by a debate between the **social constructionist** scholars and their opponents. A major thesis of the social constructionist school is that the "modern homosexual" began only in the last two decades of the nineteenth century in response to the **psychiatric** concept of **homosexuality** as a psychological state differentiating a minority of individuals from the remainder of the population.

This view can be challenged on a number of grounds. The major argument against the social constructionist thesis is that there is sound evidence for homosexual cliques and groupings as far back as the **Middle Ages**. The question is rather, how did they define themselves in relation to the environing society? This question can best be answered in three time segments:

(1) 1280–1780. In this period the homosexual groupings probably defined themselves, or would have been defined by Christian society, as part of a heretical or criminal subculture. In not a few respects they paralleled such historical phenomena as the Marranos, the crypto-Jews in Spain and Portugal after the Reconquista; the Recusants, who were secret Catholics in Elizabethan England; the Nicodemites,

secret Protestants in countries where the Counterreformation triumphed over the opponents of the Church; the crypto-Christians in the Ottoman Empire after the conquest of the former Byzantine possessions and the Balkan peninsula; and the crypto-Catholics in Japan between 1630 and 1865. All these are instances of clandestine rejection of the official religion of the state and obstinate adherence to proscribed beliefs and practices—often, if not always, at the risk of death if their covert activities came to the attention of the secular authorities.

(2) 1780–1880. Following the penal reforms of the **Enlightenment** and the granting of religious tolerance, the death penalty for heresy receded into the past, but the homosexual subculture now took on the character of an erotic **freemasonry**, with its rites, passwords, and traditions known only to a limited circle of initiates. Their counterparts in the political macrocosm were the Freemasonic lodges, the Rosicrucians, the Illuminati, and similar bodies that played a signal role in the modernization of European life at the end of the eighteenth century—as nuclei of the "new society" within the old. This is the situation attested by the *Don Leon* poems in England, and by August von **Platen's** poem of January 31, 1823, with the line "Was Vernünft'ge hoch verehren/ Taugte jedem, der's verstünde" ("What gay people greatly honor/ Well served all who understood it"); in this poem *vernünftig*, "rational" was a code word meaning "gay."

(3) 1880–present. This so-called modern period was inaugurated not by the work of the psychiatrists, but by the vanguard of homophile propagandists beginning with Karl Heinrich **Ulrichs** and Károly Mária **Kertbeny** in the 1860s, and continuing with Magnus **Hirschfeld** and the **Scientific-humanitarian Committee** in the late 1890s. The "new homosexual" saw himself as a member of an aggrieved minority, and therefore as a political **activist**, one who not simply gratified his sexual drive

with members of his own sex, but openly called for the emancipation of all individuals so oriented from the taboos and prejudices of Christian society, and above all from its restrictive laws. From 1918 onward, the view formulated by Kurt **Hiller**, that such individuals were a **minority** entitled to the same protection accorded ethnic groups in Central and Eastern Europe by the "minority treaties" appended to the peace settlement in the spirit of President Wilson's Fourteen Points, gained sway among politically conscious homosexuals first in Germany and then in other countries. (Psychiatrists—apart from those who endorsed the homosexual emancipation **movement**—did little or nothing to encourage or promote this view, as they preferred to argue that homosexuals were mentally ill and should be compelled to undergo treatment, not that they had rights of any kind.) The gay **liberation** organizations that sprang up in the English-speaking countries inherited this political tradition, in many cases in the indirect form adopted by racial and ethnic groups struggling for equality, and on it have based their own demands and aspirations for justice, to which only a few countries have thus far adequately responded.

It can be stated categorically that always, even in times of the worst intolerance, beneath the surface of society there has lurked a gay subculture, for the simple reason that the anathemas of the church could no more abolish homosexual activity than they could have altered the function of an internal organ of the human body. Such matters are the outcome of human macroevolution, which probably ended some 57,000 years ago, and certainly would not undergo major change even in a hundred generations. The historical differences lie in the mode of adaptation to the religious and political beliefs and practices of the environment, hence they belong to social and cultural history rather than to sexual psychology.

Warren Johansson

Conclusion. As currently being conducted, the debate between the social constructionists and their opponents masks problems of definition that have been insufficiently addressed. It is necessary to distinguish whether one is dealing with (a) homosexual networking—patterns of association and meeting places, together with a rudimentary argot and "semiotics" as facilitators; or (b) consciousness of belonging to a distinctive segment of society, of being in short a "homosexual" (or "sodomite" in earlier days); or (c) a complementary sense of *not* belonging to the larger society with its obligatory heterosexuality.

It is evident that (a) can precede (b) and (c), and almost certainly did. Those in quest of the origins of subculture, looking for earlier versions of the contemporary gay scene, tend to confuse these separate aspects. Moreover, what is termed the homosexual subculture in the first sense was, in early modern Europe, immersed in the larger sphere of deviance or marginalization, so that homosexuals formed part of an underground comprising thieves, vagabonds, entertainers, cardsharps, sorcerers, and so forth.

Even in recent years the degree of social separation (c, above) exhibited by gay people has displayed considerable fluctuation. Until the late 1960s, the general tint of social rejection was considerably attenuated by the widespread practice of "passing," and this worked against the development of a strong subculture. In the "gay liberation" period of the seventies, social separation increased as large numbers of homosexuals "came out," joined gay baseball teams, attended gay churches, read gay periodicals, marched in gay parades, voted against homophobic politicians, and swelled the "gay ghettoes." The proliferation of gay special interest groups and the radical stance of movement activists in this period tended to push the subculture toward the counterculture pole. In the latter part of the decade, however, the pull of greater acceptance by the larger society and the attractions of increased power (political and financial) for the members of the subculture acting together were already evident. We may expect that a continuation of that trend, once the **AIDS** crisis has ebbed, will tend to undermine the cohesion of the gay subculture further, while conversely strengthening the internal unity of such emerging subcultural-type groupings as **sadomasochists** and **pederasts**.

BIBLIOGRAPHY. Giovanni Dall'Orto, "La fenice del Sodoma," *Sodoma*, 4 (1988), 31–53; Claude S. Fischer, *To Dwell among Friends: Personal Networks in Town and City*, Chicago: University of Chicago Press, 1982; Joseph Harry and William B. Devall, *The Social Organization of Gay Males*, New York: Praeger, 1978; John Allen Lee, "The Gay Connection," *Urban Life*, 8 (1979), 175–98.

Stephen Donaldson

SUETONIUS (BORN CA. 69)

Roman biographer. Suetonius led a largely uneventful life as a bureaucrat, but his access to the records of the imperial palace lends his writings authenticity. Of the books that he wrote the only one to survive in full is the *Lives of the Twelve Caesars*, presenting biographies of **Roman emperors** from Julius Caesar through Domitian.

Suetonius' *Lives* have been criticized for their lack of chronological organization, making it hard for later historians to date the anecdotes he presents. In comparison with his contemporary **Tacitus**, whose powerful moral vision caused him to edit and shape the material to make points, Suetonius presents facts without any particular tendency.

Of the rulers he profiles, only one, Claudius, seems to have been purely heterosexual. Often criticized by earlier generations for the profusion of racy details, his sexual material is used to illustrate the character of his subjects. In the case of Julius **Caesar**, his affair with Nicomedes of Bithynia shows his charm and resourcefulness. But in the Life of **Nero**, the "marriages" with Sporus and Doryphorus reveal the wilful profligacy of that emperor's later years. In a period in which imperial power was absolute, it is not surprising that the emperors should have been tempted to have their way with the attractive bodies that surrounded them at every turn. The mores presented are those of the highest society rather than of the people, whose lives must have remained more prosaic and conventional. Refraining from making such contrasts, in his attitudes Suetonius is a naturalist rather than a moralist.

Much read through the centuries, Suetonius' portraits have—probably contrary to his intention—contributed to the image of the **decadence** of **Rome**. In fact he treats the rising age of Roman rule, with its very height—the second century—still to come. The material he provides therefore represents sidelights on an era of exuberant prosperity and imperial ostentation, rather than object lessons of the decline that was to come two centuries later.

BIBLIOGRAPHY. K. R. Bradley, *Suetonius' Life of Nero: An Historical Commentary*, Brussels: Latomus, 1978; Andrew Wallace-Hadrill, *Suetonius: The Scholar and His Caesars*, New Haven, Yale University Press, 1983.

Ward Houser

SUFISM

Sufism, Islamic mysticism, is that aspect of Islamic belief and practice in which believers seek to find the truth of divine love and knowledge through direct personal experience of God. A difficult term to define, it consists of a great variety of mystical paths that give rise to different kinds of personal feelings and experiences. All paths are aimed at culmination in the ultimate union of lover and beloved, signifying the abandonment of the personality (or self) of the mystic in the Absolute Reality. The western term "Sufism"

(Arabic *tasawwuf*) derives from the Arabic word for mystic (*sufi*), which in its turn is derived from 'wool' (*suf*), referring to the woolen garments of early Islamic ascetics. Sufis are also known as "the poor," yielding the words "dervish" and "fakir."

Basic Features. The origins of Sufism can be found in Islamic asceticism, which developed in the seventh and eighth century in reaction to the increasing worldliness of the expanding Muslim community and to the purely dogmatic and non-emotional trend of orthodox **Islam**. Love mysticism took the place of asceticism in the ninth century and reached its height in the thirteenth century. Sufism still exists among the Muslim communities around the world, often organized, as in earlier days, in mystical orders centering on a mystical guide (*shaykh* or master).

Strict obedience to the religious law, especially to the inner aspects, is basic to Sufism, although some mystics attracted public contempt by acting outwardly contrary to the law, while hiding their inner devotion to God. The absolute indifference of some Sufis to socially accepted norms and values led to a mostly unjustified reputation for Sufism in general as being licentious and libertinistic, which was further strengthened by the use of intoxicants (wine and hashish) and illicit love as symbols in Sufi writings and talk.

Because mystical and intuitive feelings and experiences were hard to express and therefore difficult to convey to others, Sufis used metaphors derived from worldly experiences, especially those of love and intoxication. Love and wine both led to drunkenness, to loss of reason, to an absolute indifference to the world, and ultimately to a loss of self. The cupbearer (*saki*), often a beautiful youth, symbolized the spiritual guide, who helped the lover on his way by making him drunk with love. The use of worldly images in Sufi-symbolism led to a fascinating ambiguity, intensified by the fact that non-mystical writers, such as the famous Persian poet **Hafiz** (ca. 1320–1390), tended also to use mystical symbols. It is especially this ambiguity, combined with the dominating theme of love, which continues to make Sufi literature so attractive and charming.

Forms of Love. Love was essential for all mystics. Some Sufis even explained themselves solely in terms of love, and that is why they have been called the "School of Love," of which **Rumi** is the most famous example.

Mystical reasoning about love and beauty was somewhat like the following: because God in his Absolute Essence could not be known, he created the world as a reflection of it, shining through forms so that lovers could realize part of his Essence through its manifestation in forms. The most perfect manifestation of the Divine Reality on earth was man, "created after His own image," and especially the beardless boy was considered to be the purest witness (*shahid*) of God. As in a saying of the Prophet: "I have seen my Lord in the form of greatest beauty, as a youth with abundant hair." Looking at beautiful faces was considered a religious activity, as Rumi said: "Behold that face on whose cheeks are the marks of His face, contemplate him on whose brow shines the Sun." Looking at beauty would inevitably lead to love, "wherever beauty dwelt in dark tresses, love came and found a heart entangled in their coils."

Some Sufis practiced *shahid bazi*, the game of love with the witness of God's beauty on earth, in which contemplation of its beauty was a central form of meditation. Shahid bazi consisted primarily of looking at the face and form of the beloved, with possibly some embracing and kissing, while the meditation was sometimes accompanied by music and dance, which could lead to ecstatic experiences. Famous Sufi shaykhs who practiced shahid bazi were Ahmad al-Ghazzali (d. 1126), Awhad ad-Din Kirmani (1164–1238), and Fakr ad-Din Iraqi (1213–1289).

The ideal witness was generally a beardless youth because of his almost perfect beauty and purity. His beauty was often described in Sufi literature in lyrical terms: He was as beautiful as Joseph, with a face for love of whom the moon turned upside down, and for which the sun trembled like an epileptic before the new moon. One look at him and day would break in the midst of the night. The fresh down on his cheeks was like calligraphy, and his curls like ambergris rolling over the face of the moon. The lasso of his locks cast over the earth, while his lips caused confusion into the heavens. His eyes were like two Negro children caught in a snare; each Negro child with a bow to shoot arrows in the hearts of desperate lovers. In short, he was the paragon of God's beauty and creative power. Sufis often were misogynistic, and looked upon women as symbols of the material world, caught up in forms, while boys were seen as innocent and pure, unconscious of their attraction, and of course much more available.

Worldly love, also known as the love of outward forms, was considered an education experience which prepared the lover for his path of passion and yearning, suffering and submission, and could serve as a bridge to Real Love. In Sufi literature, stories of worldly love relationships were used to teach mystics what kind of behavior and feelings were expected of real lovers. Apart from some male–female couples, one of the exemplary loves was the legendary relation between Sultan Mahmud of Ghazna (969–1030) and his faithful slave Ayaz (d.1057).

Shahid bazi and worldly love in general were considered positively when chaste and spiritual, and striving for the higher love of God; aimed at the Reality that was reflected, and not at the beautiful form itself, which was only illusory and relative. Mystics were not supposed to linger on the bridge of worldly love, while they should definitely not become entangled in sensual love. The latter was rejected as a desecration of love, leading to unlawful sex, for example with boys. Feelings of lust and desire, the so-called "sinful self," were sometimes designated as "the menstruation of men," signifying the uncleanliness resulting from such feelings, which would make union with God impossible. Therefore the "sinful self" had to be shackled and controlled, struggling against the seductive snares and devilish temptations of worldly entanglements, which diverted from the road to God. Only those mystics who had conquered their "sinful selves" were capable of enduring the irresistable beauty of beardless boys or the seductiveness of women, while loving them. Shahid bazi was therefore only allowed to masters and advanced mystics. Paradise was promised for those who stayed chaste, but were not able to cope with their passionate feelings, and died because of them as "martyrs of love."

Controversial Aspects. There were also mystics, however, who fell victim to sin, and although some of them repented and mended their ways, for which God had promised forgiveness, it gave Sufism a bad name. Even worse for the reputation of mysticism were people who behaved as if they were mystics, but did not follow the rules at all, and only reaped the fruits of behaving indifferently to the world. All this confirmed the orthodox in their criticism of Sufism, and was cleverly exploited.

Because a mystical current deviates from the established, dogmatic path, and therefore threatens the authority of orthodoxy, a clash will become inevitable, often leading to accusations of immorality and heresy. According to orthodox Muslims, the only way to seek knowledge of God was through his words (the Koran) and through the example of the Prophet (*hadith*, Tradition); their path was one of obedience and not one of love.

Looking at and loving beautiful forms was considered immoral and sinful, and a devilish diversion of real love, because it would inevitably lead to passionate love that, in its turn, would give rise to sexual desire and unlawful sex. They maintained it was common knowledge that no healthy man was capable of resisting the seductiveness of a beautiful boy.

Even when chaste, the orthodox argued, passionate love led to an idolization of the beloved, which was blasphemous because there was only one God, and besides, all worldly love had to be subordinated to real love. The orthodox viewed practices like shahid bazi as typical of the hypocrisy of Sufism, which used religion as a cover for sexual debauchery and lustful and perverse activities. The continuing self-criticism among Sufis about the paths taken, intensified out of fear of persecutions because of seemingly heretical ideas, gradually led the mystics to become more careful in their expressions and practices. The path of love became more hidden and discreet, which it still is.

BIBLIOGRAPHY. Joseph Norment Bell, *Love Theory in Later Hanbalite Islam*, Albany: State University of New York Press, 1979; Ahmad Ghazzali, *Sawanih*, trans. N. Pourjavady, London: KPI, 1986; Fakruddin Iraqi, *Divine Flashes*, trans. W. C. Chittick and P. L. Wilson, London: SPCK, 1982; Awhaduddin Kirmani, *Hearts Witness*, transl. B. M. Weischer and P. L. Wilson, Teheran: Imperial Iranian Academy of Philosophy, 1978; Hellmut Ritter, *Das Meer der Seele*, Leiden: Brill, 1955; Annemarie Schimmel, *Mystical Dimensions of Islam*, Chapel Hill: University of North Carolina Press, 1975; idem, "Eros, Heavenly and Not So Heavenly, in Sufi Literature and Life," in A. L. al Sayyid Marsot, ed., *Society and the Sexes in Medieval Islam*, Malibu: Undena, 1979; Mir Valiuddin, *Love of God*, Farnham: Sufi Publ., 1972; Peter Lamborn Wilson, *Scandal: Essays in Islamic Heresy*, New York: Autonomedia Inc., 1988.

Maarten Schild

SUICIDE

Suicide is the voluntary termination of one's own life, either to escape unbearable pain or humiliation, or because one's toleration of grief or disappointment is exhausted. Both types of suicide are known in homosexuals. The constant need to hide and falsify one's sexual **identity**, the burden of leading a double life, the gnawing fear of discovery and social ruin, if not actual prosecution, were motives enough for the homosexual to think of ending his own existence.

Earlier Data. In 1914 Magnus **Hirschfeld** claimed that of the ten thousand homosexual men and women whose case histories he had collected, no fewer than 75 percent had thought of suicide, 25 percent had attempted it, and 3 percent had actually taken their own lives. Similar figures, albeit more fragmentary, were reported by other investigators from the late nineteenth and early twentieth centuries. Hirschfeld frequently observed wounds left by suicidal attempts, such as knife wounds on the wrists or bullet wounds in the vicinity of the heart or the temples. Many homosexuals, he indicated, carried poison on them at all times so that they could end their lives on the spot if arrested or similarly compromised.

The chief cause of suicide in Hirschfeld's time was threat of legal prosecution, double suicides of lovers were second in frequency, and **blackmail** was third. Other motives were family conflicts, depression over one's homosexual orientation, grief at the loss of a lover, and the situation of being pressured by one's family into a heterosexual marriage that entailed an impossible sexual role. Hirschfeld conceded that in many cases the threat was exaggerated and the situation not so hopeless as the homosexual subject imagined, and he did his best to console his patients and make them feel that their lot was at least bearable. However, in his propaganda for repeal of **Paragraph 175** he laid great stress upon suicide as a consequence of the legal plight of the exclusive homosexual, and the theme became a usual one in subsequent homophile literature. Today it is seldom mentioned, even if suicides by **AIDS** patients have figured in the history of that affliction in the gay male community.

The Present Situation. Eric E. Rofes, in his book of 1983, brings Hirschfeld's findings up to date. He mentions that of the respondents to the questionnaire analyzed in *The Gay Report* (1977), 40 percent of the men and 39 percent of the women stated that they had attempted or seriously considered suicide, and 53 percent of the men and 33 percent of the women who had considered or attempted suicide said that their sexual orientation was a causal factor. For many years there was a virtual convention that any novel with a homosexual character had to show him committing suicide, if not being murdered by one of his partners. Since the homosexual had sinned in the eyes of the world, his death was a fitting retribution.

Young homosexuals confronted with the trauma of the discovery that their sexual interests set them apart from others of their age and unable to find trustworthy or sympathetic counsel are especially prone to suicide. The late adolescent years, when one's sexual orientation forces its way into consciousness, despite the indoctrination for obligatory heterosexuality, are often a time of major crisis. The thought of being alienated from one's family and one's peers, of having to lead a perilous and uncertain existence to gratify one's sexual desires, even of loving someone who is totally unable to respond, creates unbearable tensions compounded by guilt and self-hatred.

Even gay activists are not exempt from feelings of alienation and isolation. Rofes recounts several case histories of activists who turned to the movement to resolve their personal conflicts but found these as intense as ever, while the radicalism which they encountered, if not in gay politics, then in the radical organizations that overlapped for a time with the Gay Liberation Front and similar groups, only intensified their sense of helpless rage at a society that inflicted so much suffering and injustice on its homosexual members. The ultimate resolution of the crisis was—suicide. **Alcoholism** and narcotics abuse can play a role in homosexual suicide, much as in the case of heterosexuals who have become dependent upon addicting substances. To combat such tendencies programs are needed specifically oriented toward the homosexual with problems of this kind, since a program that does not face the special situation of the individual who must cope with a homosexual orientation will often miss the crux of the dependency.

Prevention. Suicide prevention and suicide intervention are strategies for alleviating the distress associated with homosexuality. The first is the long-range planning that will decrease a population's risk for suicide, the second is the immediate **counseling** and other services that will deter a subject from taking his own life. The homosexual in need of psychological counsel must find a trained individual who is knowledgeable about his special problems and difficulties and not bent upon exacerbating them for religious or other reasons. Hotlines and crisis intervention agencies can be a good source of advice for gay people beset with suicidal tendencies; such services have developed in many parts of the country, though specifically homosexual-oriented ones are confined to urban areas and college towns.

More important in the long run is eliminating the ramifications of intolerance and **discrimination** that impose intolerable burdens upon the homosexual trying to lead his life within a society that is implacably hostile to his whole personality. Real as this burden is, the conventions of Christian morality until recently forced the subject to endure it in silence, or even to interpret it as his own moral failure that justified the hatred and contempt to which he was exposed. In demanding that society recognize the existence of gay people and the problems that their homosexuality engenders, the gay **movement** has taken a major step toward ending the silence and the hypocrisy of the past—potent factors in isolating homosexuals and driving them to self-destruction.

Comparative Perspectives. Social attitudes toward suicide have varied greatly over the centuries. Severely condemned by Christianity, suicide has been in other cultures regarded as a heroic way of ending one's earthly existence, almost as a defiance of the fate that would have doomed the subject to prolonged unhappiness or physical pain. In circles such as the Japanese **samurai**, with a strongly homoerotic ethos, suicide could even be part of the warrior's code of honor, in particular when a page did not wish to survive the knight whom he had accompanied on the field of battle, or vice versa. Suicide might therefore also be reckoned for situations in which one of a pair of lovers has sought death in war or some especially dangerous mission with the implicit wish that his sacrificial act should reunite him with the other. Suicide missions undertaken for patriotic or ideological motives are the heroic and self-sacrificing facet of the subject, and one that fills the pages of history with deeds of glory.

The literature on suicide includes some classic sociological writings in which the topic of homosexuality never appears, but the invisibility of the motive to outsiders did not mean that it was inoperative. Of course, homosexuals could commit suicide for reasons wholly unrelated to their sexual orientation, just as could others overwhelmed by the difficulties and sorrows of life, or simply the desire not to be a burden to one's family and friends. Suicide is part of the tragedy and the heroism of human existence, and as a resolution of life's dilemmas it will remain a finale of the human condition chosen by homosexuals and heterosexuals alike.

BIBLIOGRAPHY. Magnus Hirschfeld, *Die Homosexualität des Mannes und des Weibes*, Berlin: Louis Marcus, 1914; Eric E. Rofes, *"I Thought People Like That Killed Themselves": Lesbians, Gay Men and Suicide*, San Francisco: Grey Fox Press, 1983.

Warren Johansson

SULLIVAN, HARRY STACK (1892–1949)

American psychiatrist. Throughout his life Sullivan had to struggle with emotional problems in his relationships with other human beings, and these struggles in turn had a marked effect on the **psychiatric** concepts that he evolved. But for just this reason he was never detached from the problems of the patients he was studying.

Born in Norwich, a small town in upstate New York, to an Irish Catholic family, he had a shy, inept father who dwelt on the margin of his son's life, while his mother poured out on the boy all of her resentment at her unhappiness and low social status. Sullivan was a socially awkward boy who felt rejected and ostracized by other children. Scholastic excellence won him esteem, but it further isolated him from those around him. At the age of eight and a half he formed a close relationship with a boy some five years older who introduced him to sex. Neither Sullivan nor the older boy, who also became a psychiatrist, ever developed into heterosexuals. In 1908 he entered Cornell as an undergraduate, but in June of 1909 was suspended for failure in all academic subjects. He may have had a brief schizophrenic illness, but the result of this obscure episode was that he lost his scholarship and never thereafter attended any college. His lack of a college education handicapped him in later life.

In 1911 he entered the Chicago College of Medicine and Surgery, a diploma mill that was closed down some six years later as part of a campaign to raise the standards of American medicine. As a struggling medical student he lived in poverty, taking odd jobs in order to make ends meet. Only in 1922 did he enter psychiatry through an appointment to St.

Elizabeths, a large federal psychiatric hospital in Washington, D.C. There he learned psychiatry in a haphazard, inaccurate manner, more from contact with the patients themselves than from any book or teacher. He was greatly influenced, however, by Edward J. Kempf, who had written the classic paper on homosexual **panic**, named after him "Kempf's disease." In early 1929 Sullivan organized at the Sheppard and Enoch Pratt Hospital the special ward for treating schizophrenics where his success elevated him to the status of a prominent figure in American and then world psychiatry. His therapeutic method focused on fostering comfortable interpersonal relationships with these patients that would enable them to return from the psychotic world into which they had retreated.

Between 1929 and 1933 he composed a book, never published, that acknowledged his own homosexuality, and his belief that a prolonged period of active homosexuality in adolescence is necessary if a person is to have sound mental health in later life. This phase is moreover essential for the later development of heterosexuality, and may protect the individual from other psychiatric disorders. Presumably he had stumbled upon the positive aspect of Greek *paiderasteia*, though to the American society of his lifetime his views were totally unacceptable.

From 1931 to 1939 Sullivan practiced psychiatry privately in New York, and underwent **psychoanalysis** (300 hours in all) by Clara Thompson, who stopped the sessions because she was overawed by Sullivan's intellect. He had ever less patience with colleagues who clung to **Freudian** concepts in preference to his own. He founded in 1938 the journal *Psychiatry*, and after much bitter quarreling with the other editors made it a personal journal. He also elaborated his "interpersonal" theories to emphasize that society itself needed to change in order to create a healthy environment for its members. In 1947 his lecture series, *Conceptions of Modern Psychiatry*, was published in book form and sold essentially on the basis of word-of-mouth advertising. After 1942 he wrote little, but lectured and taught extensively, and after the war ended, he devoted much time to optimistic efforts at decreasing international tension and avoiding another war. He died in Paris on January 14, 1949.

Sullivan did not have a positive attitude toward adult homosexuality. He felt that the therapeutic task in treating a homosexual was to remove the deep-seated psychic barriers that kept him from genital contact with the opposite sex—a goal he himself seems not to have attained. With this irrational dread removed, the patient would no longer seek partners of his own sex but gravitate toward the opposite one. However, his concepts are useful for evaluating and solving the problems of social groups, since they were developed in the context of social settings and expressed in interpersonal terms. He stressed the removal of interpersonal barriers between hostile groups in order to make close, harmonious contact possible. His work therefore has implications not only for the reduction of ethnic conflicts and the gap between generations, but also for coping with the alienation and isolation of homosexuals in a society that has been taught for centuries to hate and fear them. So, however biased his thinking may have been by the tragic circumstances of his early life, he may yet have bequeathed a psychiatric legacy that can contribute toward the reintegration of the gay community into the environing society.

BIBLIOGRAPHY. A. H. Chapman, *Harry Stack Sullivan: His Life and Work*, New York: G. P. Putnam, 1976.

Warren Johansson

SWEDEN

The **Scandinavian** kingdom of Sweden lies in Northern Europe between Norway and Finland and contains over 8 million citizens, who enjoy one of the highest standards of living in the world. Having adopted **Christianity** as its official religion in the twelfth century, Sweden participated in all the social and intellectual currents of Europe. For the earlier centuries of the country's history our information bears chiefly on the legal situation of same-sex conduct. Only after considerable struggle and educational progress was the country's present enviable state of social enlightenment attained.

Legal Developments. For a long period in its history, Sweden lacked any specific laws against same-sex relations. The all-Swedish law codes from 1350 and 1442 contained no prohibitions concerning **sodomy** between men (or women). Instead, the newly established Catholic Church exercised its moral (and economic) power through penitential and local statutes. The bishop of Skara, for instance, proclaimed in 1281 that "a person who sins against nature, must pay a fine of nine marks to the bishop."

Thus, "sodomy" between males was not officially a crime worthy of death (but a sin serious enough) when St. Bridget in a politically motivated attack accused King Magnus in 1361: "You have the most indecent reputation inside and outside this land that any Christian male can have, namely that you have had intercourse with men. This seems likely to us, because you love men more than God or your own soul or your own wife."

Despite such religious and political attacks on heretical sexual behavior, it was in fact not the Catholic **Inquisition**, but the **Protestant** Reformation that would impose severe punishment for sodomy between men in Sweden.

The Protestant King Erik XIV in 1563 made a list of crimes that had to be punished by death to avoid the "wrath of God" (which implied not earthquakes but "plagues, hunger, poverty and other troubles"). Among such crimes worthy of death were "bestiality with dumb animals and other such vices."

"Other such vices" were probably interpreted as sodomy between men. But the fact that no such cases were brought to trial in Stockholm until the seventeenth century seems to imply that this vague reference served more as a warning than as effective new legislation.

It was not until 1608, when the Swedish law code was published in a new version, that the climate became really severe. The old laws were not changed, but Charles IX added as an "appendix" to the 1608 lawbook a new list of crimes "abstracted from the Holy Scriptures." The appendix stated in section IV (on "fornication," and other like offenses): "Thou shalt not sleep with a boy as with a woman, for this is an abomination. And they both shall die, their blood be upon them." This text, echoing the prohibitions in Leviticus, was assumed to include sodomy between adult males.

It was, however, bestiality and not sodomy between men that mostly occupied the imagination of rural Swedish society. Extremely few court cases of sodomy between men are known. There is no evidence of a sodomitical **subculture** in Stockholm at this time, and official campaigns against "sodomites" are unknown.

On the female side, the courts had, as in other European countries, some difficulties with cross-dressing women, who supported themselves as soldiers and even married other women. The fact that the courts failed to see any "sodomitical" dangers in such same-sex marriages, but instead concentrated on marriage legislation and the religious crime of cross-dressing, shows that "homosexuality" as such was not yet the concern of the authorities. (Sodomy between women, according to Swedish courts, demanded some physical hermaphroditical peculiarity in the sex organs.) At the highest level, Queen **Christina** was involved with same-sex sentiments, if not acts.

From 1734 onwards, the official Swedish policy toward sodomy between males became one of total silence. The new law code of 1734 contained no such references at all, despite the fact that sodomy in the form of bestiality was still a crime worthy of death. The law commission stated that it was "not advisable to mention more sodomitical sins; it is instead better to keep silent as if they were not known, and if such a bad thing happens that they occur, let them be punished anyway."

This peculiarly lawless state of affairs seems to have led to a paradox: the scope of punishable sodomitical sins widened, and a few very unclear (and very secret) court cases with only one person involved may imply that also individual sins like masturbation from that point on were punished, if found out.

Very few death sentences for sodomitical acts between males are known from this "silent" period in Sweden. And in 1778 King Gustav III, the "enlightened" king who opposed **capital** punishment as such, issued a new order that all death sentences had to be confirmed by His Majesty. In practice this means that from 1778 on no executions for sexual crimes were carried out in Sweden.

At the beginning of the nineteenth century, Sweden lacked any laws directly applicable to sexual relations between males (or females), and under the impact of the French Revolution and Code **Napoléon**, an era of limited and conditional legal freedom for "sodomitical sinners" seems to have begun, and lasted until 1864 (the period is poorly researched, however). There are no traces of a "sodomitical" or "pederastic" subculture, despite this formal freedom. And even if the regime of Gustav III at the end of the eighteenth century, with its **Hellenic**-classisist ideals, directly or indirectly may have introduced the Greek term "pederasty" into Swedish language, the term surely had lost its Hellenist and poetic overtones by the beginning of the nineteenth century.

The "radical" anti-Gustavian military coup in 1809, directed against the

son of Gustav III, was followed by anti-pederastic gossip about the old regime. Such propagandistic gossip of course also discredited "pederasty" as such, referring it to the former sodomitical and "unnatural" context.

Sweden soon also followed the example of many of the German states, which about the middle of the nineteenth century reintroduced old or obsolete laws against "unnatural behavior" between males. A Swedish law commission in 1832 stated that even if bestiality was a disgusting crime, it was not as dangerous to society as "other unnatural ways of committing fornication, when committed between persons." In 1864 (at the same time as the Swedish parliament was reformed and democratized) a new law against "unnatural" behavior between persons was issued. The new law book stated in paragraph 18:10: "If anyone, with another person, engages in fornication against nature, or if anyone engages in fornication with an animal, he shall be punished with hard labor in prison up to two years."

Paragraph 18:10 was also applicable to relations between women, which however was not officially recognized until 1943, when a few women in a lesbian network were sentenced.

Emergence of Modernity. During the 1880s, when Stockholm (the capital) reached about 200,000 inhabitants, we have the first signs (police records) of a "sodomitical" subculture in parks and public places. At the same time there are on the cultural level expressions of an emerging homosexual **identity**. In 1879 the popular and highly respected Swedish philosopher, Pontus Wikner (1837–1888), secretly wrote a pamphlet, called "Psychological Confessions," which demands the right for people of the same sex to marry and to have sexual relations on the same terms as men and women.

Wikner unfortunately never published his pamphlet, but a famous lecture he held in Uppsala in 1880 about male and female "borderline people," "The Sacrificial System of Our Culture," was a subtle attack on sexual/religious hypocrisy and prescribed **gender-roles**, which caused some alarm in conservative circles.

The author and national poet Viktor Rydberg (1828–1895), who was a friend of Wikner, at the end of the nineteenth century also published poems and essays, where disguised homoerotic Hellenist ideals were brought to a newly formed mass audience of bourgeois readers (who mostly preferred not to understand his homoerotic hints). Vilhelm Ekelund (1880–1949), who was inspired by Count von **Platen**, wrote brilliant, if enigmatic, poems and essays.

The real "homosexualization" of Sweden does not begin until 1906, when a certain Paul Burger Diether, contact man for the German **Scientific-Humanitarian Committee** in Stockholm, announced a lecture on homosexuality with the title "The Revolution of the Twentieth Century." The lecture was treated as a public nuisance and was silenced. But the revolution was not to stop: a "scandal" in Stockholm in 1907, involving a well-known factory-owner and designer, Nils Santesson, gave broad circulation to the term "homosexuality," providing the homosexual cause with its first public martyr in Sweden.

Artists such as Eugen Jansson ("blue painting" and athletes), Gösta Adrian Nilsson ("GAN": modernistic and cubistic paintings of sailors and sportsmen), and Nils Dardel ("decadent" dandyism) also expressed hidden and open homoerotic sentiments during and after this period.

A sign of backlash was the book of Martin Koch in 1916, *Guds vackra värld* ("God's Beautiful World"), which was a crusade not only against social misery, but also against the "sodomites" who seduced, exploited, and corrupted the young.

In 1916, however, Mauritz Stiller and Axel Esbensen also produced the first **film** with a homoerotic theme, *Vingarne*

("The Wings"), based on the novel *Mikaël* by the Dane Herman **Bang** (but having a **Ganymede** statue instead of a painting at the center of the plot). In 1919 the first Swedish sexology book devoted entirely to homosexuality was published by Dr. Anton Nyström, who was a friend of Magnus **Hirschfeld**.

During the twenties, a vivid discussion about homosexuality took place in the "yellow press" of Stockholm and Göteborg, and letters from homosexuals were published on page after page (with reprimands and corrections from the editors, of course).

Another phase of homosexual emancipation started in the thirties, when lawyers and doctors and radical philanthropic organizations, such as the National Federation for Sexual Enlightenment, demanded revision of the old paragraph 18:10 "in accordance with new scientific findings." The Swedish iron-mill worker Eric Thorsell at the same time returned from a study period at Hirschfeld's Berlin Institute in 1932, and started a one-man movement against paragraph 18:10 with public lectures, newspaper articles, and the like.

The campaigns were successful. From 1944 homosexuality in private was declared legal in Sweden, with some discriminating clauses such as a higher age-limit (18 years instead of 15, in the case of **prostitution**, and 21 for dependent relationships).

Toward Today. In 1950, the first homosexual organization in Sweden was founded by the engineer Allan Hellman. At first it was a Swedish branch of the Danish/Scandinavian Federation of 1948, but soon became an organization in its own right, acquiring its present name RFSL (National Federation for Sexual Equality) in 1952.

The fifties, however, also meant a new wave of anti-homosexuality. In Sweden the gay baiters were not right-wing but "radicals" and "anti-fascists." A labor newspaper and the author Vilhelm Moberg played the role of **McCarthy**, accusing the authorities of being corrupted by "homosexual leagues." The campaign was in practice an attack on all homosexuals (and on homosexuality as such). But the RFSL succeeded in strengthening itself in the struggle, and in presenting its goals and aims in the press during a difficult period.

The sixties were politically a silent era for the homosexual movement. But they also meant a consolidation of RFSL and the new indoor subculture: the cafés and small dance halls that had emerged during the fifties.

When gay **liberation** swept in from the West at the beginning of the seventies, gay life in Sweden was vitalized and radicalized. At the end of the seventies, the first sizable gay demonstrations in Stockholm were held, organized by RFSL. They grew from 400 people in 1977 to several thousand in the eighties. The Stockholm Gay Liberation Week held in August every year during the eighties became one of the biggest social and political gay events in Europe.

One of the achievements in the gay struggle during this period was setting the same age of consent, 15 years, as for heterosexual relations (1978). This followed on a statement from the Swedish Parliament in 1973 that "cohabitation between two parties of the same sex is from the standpoint of society a totally acceptable form of relationship."

In 1987 Parliament passed two historic laws. The first forbids **discrimination** against homosexuals by authorities and private enterprises. The second grants homosexuals many of the same economic and legal privileges (and obligations) that unmarried heterosexual couples living together have in Sweden. Thus for the first time a positive homosexual status, *homosexuellsambo* ("homosexual cohabitant"), has been introduced into the Swedish language and Swedish society, after a struggle of more than a century.

BIBLIOGRAPHY. Bent Hansen, *Nordisk bibliografi: Homoseksualiteit*, Copenhagen: Pan, 1984.

Fredrik Silverstolpe

SYMONDS, JOHN ADDINGTON (1840–1893)

English scholar. John Addington Symonds was born into a prosperous London family; his father was a renowned physician and the young Symonds was educated at Harrow and at Oxford.

Symonds realized that he was homosexual at a very early age. Even as a child, he had vivid dreams of being in a room surrounded by naked sailors: odd dreams, since he had not seen a nude adult male, much less a nude sailor. According to his *Memoirs*, the central theme of Symonds' life was his ongoing attempt to deal with what he felt to be an inborn propensity to love the male sex. His innate timidity and romanticism caused him to be disgusted by the abundant homosexual activity available to students at Harrow. This puzzling rejection (of what he was later to value most highly) culminated in his first adult action on the scene of the wide world: he accused the Harrow headmaster, Dr. Vaughan, of loving one of his pupils, and with the cooperation of his father, procured Vaughan's removal from the headmastership and subsequent exile to obscurity. This malicious act caused several of his closest friends to cut him off for the rest of his life, and he was deeply troubled by the remembrance of it. What, after all, was the difference between him and Dr. Vaughan, except for Symonds' vague feeling of spiritual superiority?

He had already, by this time, read **Plato** and become enthusiastic about the ideals of Greek **pederasty**; he was, indeed, in love with an English choirboy named Willie Dyer, with whom he twice exchanged kisses which he would remember to the end of his days. This passionate friendship was terminated on the advice of his father, who pointed out that Symonds might be accused of the same "crime" as his recent victim, Dr. Vaughan.

In his twenties, again at the advice of his father, Symonds married, and eventually fathered four daughters. He never had any passion for his wife. Fortunately, she loathed sex and pregnancy, and soon they were living in separate parts of the house, while Symonds continued to pursue young men as soul mates.

Serious illness made Symonds incapable of any real career, so he turned to literature as an avocation. He pursued another schoolboy named Norman Moor in an ardent Platonic fashion, which eventually culminated in their spending six nights in bed together, nude and kissing, but without doing anything which would offend the laws of the time.

Several things happened in a short space of time, which decisively altered Symonds' life. His father died, he moved to Switzerland for the sake of his health, he had his first "base" homosexual interaction with a nineteen-year-old soldier, his literary output increased substantially, and his health improved. This would perhaps indicate that the beloved father was in fact an obstacle to Symonds' self-actualization.

In any case, he quickly got the knack of making close and passionate friends among the Swiss peasants and Italian gondoliers, and discovered that it was quite possible for two men to share their sexuality, in moderation, without being immediately damned and thrown into jail.

Symonds became one of the foremost men of letters of his time, famed for his reviews, essays, books of art history, and expositions of poetry. He became a cultural arbiter for the Victorian era, and also published several volumes of bad poetry.

Unknown to most of his contemporaries, however, Symonds was pursuing a second career. As he grew more accustomed to his own homosexuality and discovered Walt **Whitman**, he produced the pioneering essay *A Problem in Greek Eth-*ics (1883), published in an edition of 10 copies. As he grew older and read the works of such pioneers as **Krafft-Ebing**, he realized that he was not alone and wrote the larger essay *A Problem in Modern Ethics* (1891), issued in 50 copies. He also began a collaboration with Havelock **Ellis**, which resulted in the publication of *Sexual Inversion* after Symonds' death. (The family made trouble about the book, and demanded that Symonds' name and life history be removed from the English edition.)

Symonds also committed his memoirs to a distant posterity. The sealed memoirs were handed to his literary executor, H. F. Brown, and were willed to the London Library by Brown on his demise in 1926, with instructions to withhold them from publication for fifty years. They finally appeared in 1984.

As Symonds' respectable Victorian persona retires into obscurity (he is mostly remembered for his enormous *Renaissance in Italy*), his fame as a homosexual theorist and apologist takes up the failing torch and secures for him a new and perhaps more lasting reputation. He has certainly been a major influence in the cause of social and legal reform, and, with the sad exception of Dr. Vaughan, a valuable ally for homosexual men everywhere.

BIBLIOGRAPHY. Phyllis Grosskurth, *The Woeful Victorian: A Biography of John Addington Symonds*, New York: Holt, Rinehart and Winston, 1964.

Geoff Puterbaugh

SYMPOSIA

In ancient Greece, symposia were convivial meetings for drinking, conversation, and intellectual entertainment; they were all-male, upper-class drinking parties that beginning ca. 600 B.C. were held following the evening meal.

After pouring libations to the gods, the guests—usually ten or twelve—began to drink wine diluted with various amounts of water. Often garlanded and perfumed, they reclined usually two to-gether—often *erastes* (lover)and *eromenos* (beloved)—on couches propping them-selves up on one arm while servants brought round the calyx, the common drinking cup filled with watered wine. Though some did not drink, others be-came riotous. Besides drinking and con-versing, they told riddles and fables and sang drinking songs (often ribald and ped-erastic) and recited verses, whether ar-chaic (the most popular being those of **Theognis**) or of recent composition. **Athenaeus** preserved a collection of scolia, as the drinking songs were known, from the fifth and sixth centuries B.C. Each sang in turn when he was passed the myrtle branch. Having wrestled nude with his boy in the **gymnasium**, a gentleman might recline with him in the evening on a couch at a symposium sipping wine together and exchanging glances and singing love songs. Flirtation was the rule, and sometimes kisses and embraces. Going farther in public with one another was considered indecorous, although young girl and boy slaves were often pinched and pummeled, and attending musicians, often slaves themselves, were available and often fondled and groped by intemperate guests, and *hetairai* (female companions) often attended. But ladies, after 600 B.C., were shut away in the gynaikeia (women's quar-ters), and children were formally excluded from these parties. They were held in the men's chamber that each greater house possessed, often furnished with stone couches upon which pads and pillows were placed. One of the more popular games was *kottabos* (winethrowing) in which, reclining on their left elbows on the couches, the guests threw the last drops of wine from the *calyx* into a basin set in the middle of the room without spilling any.

In the seventh century, first at **Crete**, then at **Sparta**, lawgivers founded men's houses (*andreia*), where upper-class males messed together. The institution

was imported to Athens and the rest of Greece after 600 B.C., along with **gym-nasia**, **pederasty**, and the seclusion of women, but in Athens the eating clubs, often bound together by pederastic rela-tionships, met only occasionally for din-ner parties and symposia, many of which became very intellectual. Some ended in *komoi*, drinking processions revelling through the streets to serenade an *eromenos* outside his house. Heroes and others whom the state wished to honor, such as the descendants of Harmodius and Aristogiton, were dined at public expense in the Prytaneum, but most upper-class men outside of Crete and Sparta normally dined *en famille*. The symposia fulfilled the need of educated Greeks for relaxation and stimulation, as restaurants and night clubs did not exist. They could, however, also degenerate into drunken orgies that brought out the mutual hostility of the participants.

Plato, Xenophon, and many oth-ers set dialogues in symposia, which be-came a recognized literary form that al-lowed the author to ramble over his choice of barely related themes. Prominent in this genre is the *Deipnosphistae* of **Athenaeus**, who had a most artificial ar-rangement, with 40 guests and a three-day banquet. **Vase paintings** preserve a vivid picture of the proceedings at such affairs. Crude Roman imitations of the Greek banquets were satirized, more in literary form, by **Petronius** in the *Cena Trimal-chionis*, the banquet episode of the *Satyri-con*. Christian hostility to such centers of pederasty and intellectual analysis, as well as the loss of wealth and leisure be-ginning with the third century, led to their decline. In the late fourth century Libanius complained that at Antioch banquets had degenerated, citing an egre-gious case in which a father regularly prostituted his son.

A survival of the symposium is the Jewish Passover meal, where the guests are formally required to recline in the manner of upper-class Greeks, proving that they are no longer slaves after being delivered from bondage in Egypt. Also, a ceremonial part of the meal is the *aphikoman*, from Hellenistic Greek *epicomon*, the final course of the banquet.

English colleges created their own, more sedate versions of the symposia. The common room and dining hall arrangements with sherry, port, and other wines, where a variety of opinions are expressed, parallel those of antiquity. Tutorials, though one-on-one, traditionally end with the quaffing of a glass of sherry.

William A. Percy

SZYMANOWSKI, KAROL (1882–1937)

Polish composer. The son of Polish landed gentry, Szymanowski was born in Tymoszowka, in eastern **Poland** (now part of the Soviet Union). He began to play the piano and compose at an early age, and while at the Warsaw Conservatory quickly acquired a reputation as a composer of talent, and a follower of modern musical trends.

Szymanowski's wide travels (he visited America in 1921) brought him into contact with many European artistic trends. This is reflected in his evolving and somewhat eclectic style, which moves from a Chopin-Scriabinesque early period, through a more Germanic chromaticism, to an impressionist period. His final compositions reflect Polish folk traditions and are more Bartokian in style.

Evidence of Szymanowski's sexual preference is largely indirect but nonetheless telling. He remained unmarried, and once jokingly remarked that the only woman in his life was his mother. Correspondence with several close male friends is extant, although not published in its entirety (no similiar correspondence with women exists). Contemporaries of the composer make reference to his fondness for men. B. M. Maciejewski, in *Karol Szymanowski: His Life and Music* (London, 1967), states that it was common knowledge throughout European cultural circles that Szymanowski was homosexual. The Polish biographer Stefania Lobaczewska is more circumspect, stating only that Szymanowski was regarded in his youth as *zepsuty* (decadent, immoral) and that his music is marked by a strong erotic drive.

The most direct evidence is the composer's two-volume novel, *Efebos*, written in 1917. It is described by the composer as an *apologia pro vita sua*. The hero of the novel is a divinely beautiful young man in whom are united physical and divine love. Unfortunately, all but the introduction to the novel was destroyed during the bombing of the Polish National Archives at the beginning of World War II. Contemporary accounts describe it as the composer's theory of Greek love.

Szymanowski's musical output spans the gamut from solo piano works (three sonatas, preludes, studies, mazurkas) to songs for voice, orchestral works, symphonies, concerti, ballets, and **opera** (*King Roger*, premiered in the United States only in 1988). Szymanowski was director of the Warsaw Conservatory from 1927 to 1931, and was a strong advocate for contemporary music in prewar Poland. At his death, he was widely heralded as Poland's greatest composer since Chopin.

Peter Gach

TACITUS
(BORN CA. A.D. 55–56)

Roman historian and ethnographer. Tacitus had a public career which ended in service as proconsul in Asia circa 112–113, but even earlier he had begun to compose the works on which his later fame rests.

The *Germania* was published in all likelihood in 98, but contains material from sources of earlier decades; it is the most extensive source that has survived from classical antiquity on the customs and beliefs of the Germanic barbarians who lived east of the Roman province of Gaul. The text that is most often quoted as evidence for the attitude of the pagan Germanic tribes toward homosexuality is in the twelfth chapter: "Penalties are proportional to the gravity of the offense; traitors and deserters they hang on a tree, the slothful and cowardly and sexually infamous (*ignavos et imbelles et corpore infames*) they drown in mud and swamps with a wicker basket placed over their heads." This passage has been interpreted as expressing an intolerance of homosexual behavior that preceded any contact with the Christianity of the Mediterranean world, but in fact the three Latin words express a single Germanic one, corresponding to Old Norse *argr*, which is a designation for the male who is in general passive, cowardly, and effeminate; the penalty named is for cowardice and lack of manliness on the battlefield, not for sexual activity per se. However, right-wing circles in twentieth-century Germany conceived on the basis of this text the notion that their pagan ancestors punished homosexuals by drowning them.

The *Histories* and the *Annals* are Tacitus' great contribution to Roman history. Composed in an exceedingly refined and concise style, they are informed by the ideology of the Senatorial aristocracy and its resentment of the power of the imperial regime that had supplanted the Roman republic. These works include occasional references to homosexual matters, such as that under Tiberius men were forbidden to wear thin silk clothing of the sort in which handsome slave boys were appareled (*Annals*, 2:33). He mentions that **Nero** had sexual connections with his stepbrother Britannicus—whom he poisoned shortly after coming to power—(*Annals*, 13:17), with the actor Paris, and with boys of free birth, thus using freemen for his own gratification as if they were slaves. Tacitus also describes Nero's "marriage" with a male favorite whose name is given as Pythagoras or Sporus, and says that he went in disguise to participate in lewd revels in the city of **Rome**, accompanied by other men who robbed and assaulted those who crossed their path (*Annals*, 13:25). Another story (*Annals*, 14:42) tells how Pedanius Secundus, the prefect of Rome, was murdered by one of his slaves, either because he had been refused the liberty that he had purchased or because he was in love with a youth and could not bear to be supplanted by his master. When all the slaves living under the same roof were to be executed as retribution, a mass meeting called to protest this excessive penalty turned into a riot. This incident, like others, shows that homosexual attachments in no way diminished the esteem which even a slave could enjoy in antiquity. Tacitus also recounts (*Annals*, 16:18) the life and death of Nero's favorite **Petronius**, the probable author of the *Satyricon* which, even preserved as it is in a fragmentary form, still affords a panorama of the sexual life of first-century Rome. Thus while Tacitus does not describe the homosexuality of that period in as much detail as do **Suetonius** and **Martial**, his work is a valuable supplement to other contemporary portrayals of Roman eroticism.

BIBLIOGRAPHY. Otto Kiefer, *Sexual Life in Ancient Rome*, London: Routledge & Kegan Paul, 1934; Ronald H. Martin, *Tacitus*, London: Batsford, 1981.

Warren Johansson

TALMUD

A collection of 67 treatises, the Talmud interprets and elaborates the commandments of the Torah and the narratives of the **Old Testament**; the legal portion is known as *halakhah*, the folklore is called *agadah*. There are two redactions of the Talmud, the Jerusalem Talmud and the Babylonian Talmud. Both have as their core the Mishnah, the decisions of the sages of the preceding three centuries that was edited by Rabbi Judah the Prince in 193. Written in late Hebrew, it served as the basis for subsequent teaching and interpretation that lasted from the first half of the third century to the year 499. These secondary deliberations, not in the Mishnah and assembled in the Gemara, were mainly conducted in Aramaic, the spoken language of the Jews of Palestine and Babylonia (each with its own dialect). The final process of redaction probably began before the end of the fifth century and lasted into the seventh. The *editio princeps* of the Babylonian Talmud is that of Venice: Daniel Bomberg, 1520–23, the numbering of whose folios is the basis for later citation; the standard modern edition is that of Vilnius: Romm, 1922, with the classic commentary in Rabbinic Hebrew of Solomon ben Isaac of Troyes (1040–1105) and numerous minor glosses.

The largest part of the material relative to homosexuality in the Talmud is in the treatise Sanhedrin, which deals with the capital crimes adjudicated by the Beth Din, the high court of the Jewish religious community. In Sanhedrin 53a it is stated that death by stoning is the penalty for two groups of offenses, the first of which constitute violations of the *patria potestas*—the authority of the head of the patriachal extended family—the second the propagation or practice of idolatry or magic:

incest with mother	blasphemy
father's sexual intercourse with daughter in law	idolatry
intercourse with another male or with a beast	giving one's seed to Molech
cursing one's father or mother	necromancy or divination
adultery with a betrothed maiden	incitement to idolatry
a wayward and rebellious son	sorcery

In Sanhedrin 54a–55a the Gemara elaborates this prescription as follows: In Leviticus 20:13 "if a man also lie with mankind" means "a man" not a minor, "mankind" both adult and minor; "their blood shall be upon them" is by analogy with Leviticus 20:27 (the penalty for one who "hath a familar spirit" or "is a wizard" is interpreted to ordain death by stoning). Leviticus 18:22 is taken to apply to the active partner, Deuteronomy 23:18 to the passive, proving that the **kadesh** mentioned in the latter verse was the sacred prostitute who served the male worshipper in the Ishtar–Tammuz cult; but Rabbi Akiba derived both prohibitions from the former by reading the consonantal text as both *tishkabh*, "thou shalt lie" and *tishshakebh*, "thou shalt be lain with." Legal responsibility commenced at the age of nine years and a day, which was also the lower limit for the emancipation of the child from the *patria potestas* in sexual matters in later Islamic law.

In Niddah 13b, the tractate that deals with menstrual impurity in women, there is the curious statement that "those who play with children delay the coming of the Messiah." While the assertion is not interpreted solely to refer to pederasty, the underlying notion is that the Messiah will not come until all the unborn souls contained in Guph (literally "body") have been disposed of. This is the probable source of the thirteenth-century Christian accretion to the account of the Nativity which maintained that because of the "crime against nature" the Son of Man repeatedly postponed his incarnation, and even thought of abandoning the project altogether.

Sanhedrin 70a interprets the passage in Genesis 9:22 "And Ham . . . saw the nakedness of his father" as meaning that Ham sodomized Noah, while the alternative explanation is that he castrated him. The allusion is to the legal language of Leviticus 18:7 "The nakedness of thy father . . . thou shalt not uncover," which prohibited homosexual incest with the male parent, an indirect proof that the generalized taboo of Leviticus 18:22 is a later insertion into the Holiness Code.

On the subject of **Sodom**, Sanhedrin 109a–b relates that the "men of Sodom were wicked and sinners" (Genesis 13:23), "wicked" meaning "with their bodies" and "sinners" with their money, hence both depraved and uncharitable. In their prosperity the Sodomites resolved to abrogate the laws which protected the stranger and the traveler, and further inverted the principles of justice so that if someone wounded his neighbor he was ordered to pay the fee for bleeding; if someone crossed the river by ferry he had to pay four *zuzim*, if on foot he had to pay eight. A particular tale of their inhospitality concerned a maiden who gave a poor man some bread hidden in a pitcher. When the Sodomites discovered this, they smeared her body with honey and exposed her on the city wall so that the bees would come and devour her.

The decisions and pronouncements of the sages were later codified, first by Musa ibn Maimun (Maimonides) in the thirteenth century in the *Mishneh Torah*, then by Joseph Karo in the sixteenth in the *Shulhan Arukh*. The latter remains the fundamental code of morality and religious observance for the Orthodox Jew to the present day, and authorizes the fierce opposition of some Orthodox groups in large American cities to the enactment of gay rights legislation. On this issue they can form alliances with conservative Catholics and fundamentalist Protestants, even though they refuse, unlike the Conservative and Reform wings of **Judaism**, to join the contemporary ecumenical dialogue on public policy and social justice with the Christian denominations.

BIBLIOGRAPHY. Immanuel Jacobovits, "Homosexuality," *Encyclopedia Judaica*, 8 (1971), 961–62; Barry Dov Schwartz, *The Jewish Tradition and Homosexuality*, New York: Jewish Theological Seminary, 1979 (unpublished Ph.D. dissertation).

Warren Johansson

TASTE
Traditionally one of the five senses, taste is used in an extended sense to denote critical judgment, discernment, or appreciation. In this broader sense it has played a major role in the history of aesthetics. In addition, sociologists hold that taste preferences characterize specific social groups or **classes.**

The seventeenth and eighteenth centuries saw a reign of "good taste." While most agreed that this taste was formed through experience and cultivation, it proved difficult to determine what its actual defining characteristics were. For some, good taste was unitary and identifiable with classic norms, including such qualities as balance, restraint, and ideal beauty; for others, there were several tastes, each valid in its own sphere. In the latter approach, one might acquire a taste for the sublime, the romantic, or the Gothic, as distinct from the classic. During the later decades of the eighteenth century, the concept of taste meshed with the novel idea of **sensibility**, viewed as a matter of subtle intuition, of attunement to a kind of unheard melody, rather than a simple assimilation of rules. The notion that tastes are personal and variable is sometimes summed up in the Latin proverb *De gustibus non disputandum est*, "There is no arguing about tastes." If, in principle, a plurality of tastes is generally recognized today, it is still possible to speak of, say, a bawdy joke as being "in poor taste."

The idea that sexual interests are appetites probably lies at the root of the concept of homosexuality as itself a taste, though the expression has also had its appeal as a euphemism. In a passage in *The Adventures of Roderick Random* (1748), Tobias Smollett spoke of **Petronius'** (homosexual) "taste in love." The notion is probably more common in French, where older writers spoke of sodomy as *le goût contre nature*, "the unnatural taste." In his great novel *A la recherche du temps perdu*, Marcel **Proust** rang many changes on the word *goût* with relation to homosexuality. French also records an expression *goût florentin*, "Florentine taste," for homosexuality; technically, this is an **ethnophaulism**, an ascription of a disprized behavior to a foreign group.

A different topic is that of homosexuals as tastemakers. As far as can be determined, this role emerged in the second half of the eighteenth century. The presiding genius of this period was the archeologist Johann Joachim **Winckelmann** (1717–1768), whose interpretations of Greek art (which was filtered through his homoerotic appreciation of male beauty) had a formative influence on the course of neo-Classicism in the visual arts throughout Europe. His efforts were reinforced by a noble gadfly, Count Francesco Algarotti (1712–1764), a close friend of **Frederick the Great** of Prussia. It is a curious fact that the rise of the opposing current of romanticism was also promoted by homosexuals, especially the poet Thomas Gray (1716–1771), whose 1751 *Elegy Written in a Country Churchyard* is a major harbinger of the new sensibility, and Horace Walpole (1717–1797), whose villa at Strawberry Hill near London counts as one of the first monuments of the Gothic revival.

The bisexual poet George Gordon, Lord **Byron** (1788–1824), had an incalculable influence over romanticism throughout Europe. None of the romantic critics, with the possible exception of Samuel Taylor Coleridge (1772–1834), seem to have been homosexual. In a lesser realm, Edward **Lear** (1812–1888), with his limericks and other nonsense writings, helped to define the characteristically English genre of humor. On the continent French artists and writers, such as Eugène Delacroix (1798–1863) and Gustave **Flaubert** (1821–1880), took an interest in **Islam**, its art and culture, noting that sexual norms in Arab countries (*moeurs arabes, moeurs levantines*) differed from those of the Christian occident.

Through his Russian Ballet, Sergei **Diaghilev** (1872–1929) not only changed attitudes about dance but, through his patronage, was able to promote avant-garde music and painting as well. Gertrude **Stein** (1874–1946), a friend of Picasso and Matisse, played a major role in the introduction of modern art into the United States. The New York poet Frank **O'Hara** (1926–1966) was one of the chief advocates and definers of Abstract Expressionist painting. On a less exalted level of cultural achievement many modern couturiers, whose sensibilities determine the changing tides of women's fashions, are homosexual. The prominence of gay people in the fashion industry has led hostile observers (such as the late Edmund **Bergler**, a Freudian psychoanalyst) to denounce their influence as perverse and conspiratorial.

In conclusion it is perhaps appropriate to advance some speculative suggestions as to why homosexuals, in some periods at least, have felt a special calling as tastemakers. Participation in a different (but justifiable) mode of sexuality may sensitize one to different (also justifiable) artistic modes. Then the well known affinity of homosexuals for **travel**, and for partners of other races, allows them to immerse themselves in the aesthetic theory and practice of "exotic" peoples, and then to return with these discoveries to their own lands. Finally, the stereotypical ascription of aesthetic sensitivity to male homosexuals may operate—as **stereotypes** generally do—to lure some members of the affected group into the general field. From the host society they have absorbed the idea that they must be "sensitive," and some are impelled to achieve this quality.

Wayne R. Dynes

TCHAIKOVSKY, PETER IL'YICH (1840–1893)

The greatest Russian composer of the nineteenth century. Imbued with Western techniques and attitudes at the conservatory, his artistic personality remained profoundly Russian both in his use of folksong and in his absorption in Russian ways of life and thought. His genius for what he called "the lyrical idea," the beautiful, self-contained melody, gives his music permanent appeal; a hard-won but secure and professional technique and his ability to use it for emotional expression enabled him to realize his potential more fully than did any of his Russian contemporaries.

The son of a mining engineer, he began taking piano lessons at the age of five and quickly evinced a striking talent. In 1840 he was enrolled at the School of Jurisprudence in St. Petersburg, where the homosexual practices common in the institution may have served to bring out or to confirm his own tendencies. After several years as a clerk in the Ministry of Justice, he resigned in 1863 to become a full-time student at the Conservatory and thereafter devoted himself to a musical career. He had a brief attachment to a woman named Desirée Artot, but their wish to marry was opposed by family and friends, and Tchaikovsky had no further direct emotional involvement with any woman until, in 1877, he received a written declaration of love from Antonina Miliukova, whom he married on July 18. Inspired by self-loathing and a desperate effort to escape from his homosexuality, the marriage was—in the euphemistic language of the Victorian era—a complete failure. The composer fled his bride and even attempted suicide, after which he suffered a complete nervous collapse. A medical specialist advised him never to see his wife again. On the other hand, he maintained a correspondence over some 14 years with the wealthy widow Nadezhda von Meck, never meeting her in person so that each for the other could remain a figure of fantasy.

His work has no specifically homosexual themes; the love affairs in his compositions are all heterosexual, as befitted works intended for performance in the Russia of the nineteenth century, especially the repressive regime of Alexander III under which the last years of his life were played out. His Sixth Symphony, the *Symphonie Pathétique*, written in 1893, was dedicated to Bob Davydov, and was the expression of his love, the fullest outpouring of the emotions he had felt during a lifetime. In the Soviet Union, where the composer's musical achievement is deeply revered as a national heritage, a complete veil has been drawn across his homosexuality in historical, critical, and cinematic accounts. In the West, however, his orientation is generally acknowledged. Thus the German homosexual writer Klaus **Mann** devoted to Tchaikovsky a novel that treats the erotic side of his character, *Symphonie Pathétique* (1935).

The circumstances of his death have been disputed. In 1978 a Soviet scholar, Aleksandra Orlova, revealed a narrative dictated to her in 1966 by the aged Aleksandr Voitov of the Russian Museum in Leningrad. According to this source, a member of the Russian aristocracy had written a letter accusing Tchaikovsky of a homosexual liaison with his nephew, entrusting it to Nikolai Jakobi, a high-ranking civil servant, for transmission to the Tsar. Jakobi, also a former pupil of the School of Jurisprudence, feared the disgrace which the scandal would bring on the institution and hastily summoned a court of honor that included six of Tchaikovsky's contemporaries from the school. On October 31, 1893, after more than five hours of deliberation, the court supposedly resolved that the composer should kill himself. The arguments against this story are considerable. Homosexuality was too extensively tolerated among the upper classes in Russia at that period for the matter to have had such serious import. Moreover, the intervals of freedom from censorship that followed the Revolutions of 1905 and 1917 gave sufficient opportunity for the publication of the facts, had the tale been true. It is more likely that Tchaikovsky died of cholera after accidentally drinking a glass of contaminated water.

BIBLIOGRAPHY. Nina Berberova, *Tchaïkovski: biographie*, Paris: Editions Actes Sud, 1987.

Warren Johansson

TEAROOMS
See Toilets.

TELEOLOGY

Teleology (from Greek, *telos* "end") is the character attributed to nature or natural processes of being directed toward an end or shaped by a purpose. As such, the concept has been deployed as a criterion of the morality of sexual acts.

Classical Thought. Teleology was a favorite concern of the Greeks. The pivotal discussion is **Aristotle**'s treatment of final cause, "that for the sake of which a thing exists" (*De generatione animalium*). According to those belonging to the school of Aristotle (the Lyceum) or philosophical sects based on his teaching, each object had an end or purpose at which naturally it should aim. Nature designed the sexual organs, they maintained, for procreation upon which the future of the race depended. To direct the penis to other orifices than the human vagina, its predestined container, was to act against **nature**.

Another strand derives from **Plato**. Although Aristotle recognized that some individuals were homosexual "by nature," that is congenitally, while others acquired that sexual orientation through experience and practice, on the whole his numerous and often contradictory writings argued that homosexuality was something to be explained, and therefore not clearly a part of the given, of the world of nature in the ordinary sense. In the work of Plato, however, the concept of nature was more clearly evaluative. In the *Laws*, his last dialogue, the old Plato—whose earlier dialogues had praised pederasty as inciting love of truth and beauty—condemned homosexual acts as against nature.

While a minority of Greeks observed homosexual behavior among **animals**, those who denied it there argued that its absence was proof that such conduct was at best artificial, rather than natural. Although some argued that what made man superior to animals was exactly his improvement over nature, the majority of later Greek thinkers felt that it was best to act in accord with nature. This doctrine typified the **Stoics**, who dominated ancient philosophy during the late Republic and the first two centuries of the Roman Empire. Most but not all teachers of the "Second Stoa," centered in Rome and catering to old Roman disapproval of pederasty as a Greek import, decried homosexuality as against nature: Seneca, Musonius Rufus, and Epictetus.

Judeo-Christian Attitudes. **Philo Judaeus** of Alexandria combined the Greek doctrine that homosexuality was unnatural with the peremptory injunction preserved in Leviticus that Judaism had taken from **Zoroastrianism**, the Persian state religion. St. Paul merely echoed this ban in the first chapter of Romans, citing the Flood and the destruction of Sodom as proof of divine disapproval of unnatural sexual conduct. William Benjamin Smith (1850–1934) speculated that this Pauline passage, which makes no mention of Christ or **Christianity**, is a self-contained essay on the revelation of God's wrath taken from an anonymous Jewish source. St. **Clement of Alexandria**, an assiduous student of Greek philosophy, held that "one must follow nature herself when she forbade [pederastic] excesses through the disposition she gave the organs, having given virility to man not to receive seed but to eject it" (*Paedagogus*, X, 87, 3).

Constantius and Constans, the sons of the first Christian **Roman emperor**, Constantine the Great, inscribed the condemnation in Roman law. In a tortuously worded edict of 342, they first decreed death for homosexual offenses and forbade sexual relations between man and wife in any fashion that did not involve penetration of the vagina by the penis. Theodosius the Great resumed this tradition, followed most horribly by Justinian, who proclaimed that sodomites if unpunished brought famines, earthquakes, and pestilences on society.

Medieval and Modern Times. Medieval theologians continued and developed this **Patristic** approach, which the Scholastics Albertus Magnus and Thomas **Aquinas** greatly strengthened in accord with the new reverence for Aristotle's teleological system. Aquinas claimed that even rape was preferable to sodomy, because it was, after all, a penis-to-vagina act. The revival of Roman law, as interpreted by Christian jurisconsults in the twelfth century, stressed the idea of nature. Curiously, it was the early **Middle Ages**, and not classical antiquity, that elevated Nature to the status of a goddess, and her supposed decrees were adduced in the condemnations of homosexuality of **Alan of Lille** and Jean de Meun.

Even apart from the peremptory condemnation in the Mosaic law and the legend of the destruction of **Sodom** deriving from Genesis 19, the **ascetic** motif in Christian morality, which sets Christianity apart from the other **Abrahamic religions**—Judaism and Islam—that have no such ideal of an asexual humanity, would alone have sufficed to render all non-reproductive sexual activity immoral. Dualistic and **gnostic** thought imbued Pauline Christianity with an intense pathological rejection of the body and its erotic functions, conditioned by the proximity of the sexual and the excretory organs that made disgust an inescapable component of the Christian attitude toward sexuality and especially toward homosexual activity. The fantasies of Scholastic writers in Latin Christendom bear witness to this irrational hatred of homoerotic feeling and behavior. A legal author of the fourteenth century, Luca da Penne (ca. 1320–ca. 1390), went so far as to call the sodomite worse than a murderer, because he aimed at destroying not just a single human being but the entire human race, and declared that if such a culprit had been executed and could be brought back to life several times, each time he should be punished more severely than the preceding one. Paradoxically enough, such views were maintained alongside the glorification of virginity, which if it became universal would effect the end of the human race just as surely as any form of non-procreative sexuality. Other legal writers held that God could wreak vengeance on an entire community for the crime of a single individual, so branding the sodomite as an enemy of society to be blamed for every manner of collective misfortune.

Modern Critiques of Teleology. The seventeenth and eighteenth centuries saw the popularity of the "argument from design" as a proof of the existence of God. Even deists like Sir Isaac Newton

(1642–1727), himself possibly homophile, argued that the perfect mechanism of the universe required a clockmaker—a "prime mover" as Aristotle and Thomas Aquinas had supposed. The things of the world manifest such order, so it was claimed, that they could only have reached their present state through the purposeful guidance of a creator who endowed each thing with its own specific character, which man should not seek to alter. Hence the penis is suited only for placement in a vagina, not in an anus or mouth. The argument oddly neglects the point that the penis has a dual function: it serves to urinate (presumably not in the vagina) as well as emit semen. If it can have two distinct types of emissions, why must it have only one proper vessel? Conversely, if **God** had been opposed to putting the penis in the mouth or anus, could he not have shaped these latter organs in such a way as to make penetration difficult? **Voltaire** ridiculed the argument from design because by it one could demonstrate that God had foreseen ships, since he provided harbors for them, and eyeglasses, since he gave noses a bridge.

Of course modern biologists recognize purpose in the world, in the limited sense that birds build nests in which to hatch and raise their young and spiders weave webs to trap insects. What they generally do not hold, however, is that some cosmic mind has predetermined the purposes of all living things.

Even today, however, Aristotle's discarded model of a grand teleology ruling nature inspires Roman Catholic and much other Christian doctrine. In spite of all subsequent criticism and the repudiation by the physical and biological sciences of the concept of "Nature" as a personified feminine principle whose intentions are somehow frustrated by non-procreative sexual activity, these religious thinkers persist in their antiquated views. Though scarcely metaphysicians and unwilling to discuss how many angels could dance on the head of a pin, Hitler and Stalin were as convinced as any Roman pope or Southern Baptist that homosexuality is unnatural. The most recent pronouncements of the Roman Catholic church still teach that homosexual acts are "intrinsically disordered because they lack finality," which is to say that they are immoral because they cannot lead to procreation—as if any good would result if every sexual act did have procreative consequences. The prospects for world population densities would be horrifying. In the twentieth century the increasing longevity of the population and the need to maintain the proper equilibrium with available resources has forced heterosexuals to adopt birth control techniques ranging from periods of abstinence and the use of the condom to abortion to keep the procreative consequences of their own sexual activity within bounds. Yet even most of those branches of **Protestantism** which do not completely reject birth control and other forms of non-procreative sex (as the Catholics and Orthodox do), still tend to condemn homosexuality as against the law of God and nature. It is incumbent on thinkers not beholden to a revealed religion to expose such positions as inconsistent, and above all to affirm that they embody no inherent logic sufficient to compel a secular, pluralistic society to adopt them.

William A. Percy

TELEPHONE
See **Phone and Computer Sex.**

TELEVISION

Although the technology on which it is based came into existence as early as 1923, it was only in the early 1950s that television became a fixture of American domestic life, gradually elbowing the Hollywood **film** out of its primacy in the entertainment field. Establishing itself in Europe at the same time, television eventually spread throughout the globe, even to the poorest Third World countries. While in America most television stations are commercially owned, in many countries the medium (like radio) is a government monopoly. It is uncertain, however, whether the exigencies of censorship in state systems are more restrictive than the "tyranny of the ratings" in the United States. The spread of cable TV and increased use of satellite transmissions in the 1970s reduced the stranglehold of the major networks. In a few cities gay people were even able to secure their own programs, thanks to public access legislation. In the 1980s the widespread use of VCRs (recording equipment operating through television sets) further promoted diversity, and users could, if they wished, rent a wide variety of porno films to be shown through their home sets. The new field of video emerged as a means for minority artists to create individualized works which could be shown on television screens.

Gay Men and Lesbians in Television. From the beginning children formed a large portion of the TV audience. Commercial advertisers were sensitive to campaigns by pressure groups. These factors excluded sex of any kind from the small screen, and reduced controversy to a minimum. Only in the news services, which were to some extent insulated from the rest of programming, was some discussion of issues possible. In the view of many, the early decades of television justified the claim of Federal Communications Commission commissioner Newton Minow that television was a "vast wasteland."

The fledgling industry inherited many practices and trends from Hollywood—among them self-**censorship**. However, Hollywood had created a genre of "sissy" character, a figure with veiled gay traits. This type occasionally appeared, in even more disguised form, in such early situation comedy series as "Mr. Peepers," with Wally Cox. When motion pictures that contained references to homosexuality were shown, even on late-night television, the offending sections were ruth-

lessly edited out, a practice that continues to this day. For this reason many now prefer to buy or rent uncensored versions to play on home VCR equipment.

In the 1960s the civil rights movement, and increasingly the women's movement, were big news. This opened the way for some rare excursions into the realm of homosexuality. Mike Wallace's CBS Report, "The Homosexuals," aired nationwide on March 7, 1967, was something of a landmark, but it had been preceded in England by BBC-TV's "One in Twenty" (1966), based on more thorough research by Brian McGee. Occasional discussions on local stations were generally dominated by the judgmental views of psychiatrists.

After the **Stonewall Rebellion** in 1969 coverage increased somewhat, and gay activists appeared on "The Dick Cavett Show," "Jack Paar Tonight," and "The David Susskind Show." In 1972 ABC's "Movie of the Week" aired a sensitive portrayal of a gay-male couple in the San Francisco Bay Area, "That Certain Summer," featuring Hal Holbrook and Martin Sheen. Situation comedy series produced by Norman Lear ("All in the Family" and "Maude") occasionally showed nonstereotypical homosexuals. In the 1980s, prime-time series such as "Cagney & Lacey," "Designing Women," and "L.A. Law" treated the subject. Such popular series as "Brothers" (a cable series), "Dynasty" (with its "sensitive son," Steven Carrington), "Hooperman," "Love, Sidney," and "Soap" have included gay and lesbian characters. A few long and lavish British series based on literary classics have provided portraits of gay people in the round ("Brideshead Revisited," 1980, and "The Jewel in the Crown," 1984), but these have reached only elite audiences. When all is said and done, however, after forty years of the hegemony of network television, gay people have had good reason to feel that they are woefully underrepresented.

Gay Influence over Television. It was to be expected that from the first, television, recruiting much of its talent from Hollywood and Broadway, had many gay and lesbian participants, especially in such behind-the-scenes work as makeup and costuming. Yet an unwritten law (itself inherited from Hollywood) held that the actors who appeared on the screen must be heavily closeted. The revelation of Rock **Hudson's** homosexuality, after he had appeared in several television dramas, sent shock waves through the industry. Symptomatic of the prejudice that exists is the fact that open membership organizations to defend the rights of gay people in television have never really gotten off the ground, and homosexuals have had to rely on informal groups of friends. Fear of loss of work—even blacklisting—continues to be a powerful deterrent to speaking out.

Following the pattern of Jewish and black organizations fighting **stereotyping** in the media, gay "pressure groups" have had some success in reducing blatant expressions of prejudice on television screens. A 1974 episode of "Police Woman" called "Flowers of Evil," about three lesbians who murder patients in an old-age home, provoked justified outrage. Soon afterward, the National Gay Task Force induced the Television Review Board of the National Association of Broadcasters to issue a directive stating that the Television Code's injunction that "material with sexual connotations shall not be treated exploitatively or irresponsibly" applied to homosexuals. In Los Angeles Newton Deiter, a gay psychologist and activist, successfully ran the Gay Media Task Force (GMTF). He and his associates were able to monitor scripts for the networks, and to obtain frank meetings with producers. GMTF was particularly alert for lisping, limp-wristed mannerisms for gay men and truck-driver characterizations of lesbians. Such offensive words as **faggot** and **queer** were taken out.

In the 1980s these lobbying efforts seemed to falter. However, gay newspapers publicized writing campaigns against offensive programs, and new civil rights groups, such as New York's Gay and Lesbian Alliance Against Defamation (GLAAD) organized their own efforts.

AIDS and Television. When the **AIDS** crisis appeared in 1981 mainstream newspapers were the main vehicle of information for the general public. Eventually, through news programs and specials, television made a contribution, though its insensivity sometimes fueled a climate of panic that could have been avoided or at least reduced. In 1983 the hospital series "St. Elsewhere" introduced an AIDS story line, while the made-for-TV film "An Early Frost," about the effect of knowledge of the disease on a middle-class homosexual's family, garnered an Emmy (American television's highest award) in 1985.

Although Hollywood stars lent their support to campaigns to raise money in the fight against AIDS, many felt that a silent backlash was taking place. In the late 1970s several major performers seemed on the verge of "coming out," but the atmosphere shifted radically. Even heterosexual actors who had portrayed gays found that it was hard to get work. If kissing scenes were involved, actresses demanded to be able to veto leading men who were gay. Those in the industry who did contract the disease felt the need to conceal it in order to retain benefits, and to avoid "incriminating" friends.

All in all, the AIDS crisis revealed the inadequacy of television's feeble efforts to mend its ways. Much work remains to be done by activists, but even so it is unlikely that mass-market television will ever be a true friend of gay men and lesbians. Rather, hope lies in the spread of new technologies which will cut the commercial networks down to size by making communications accessible to a full range of viewpoints, not just those that a few opportunistic and amoral TV executives judge appropriate.

See also **Communications**.

Ward Houser

TEMPLARS

Founded in 1119 to protect pilgrims who flocked to the Holy Land after the First Crusade of 1095, the Knights Templars (or Poor Knights of Christ) of the Temple of Solomon were, with the Hospitalers and Teutonic Knights, one of the three great military orders of medieval **Christianity**. Vowed to poverty, chastity, and obedience, as well as to the Benedictine rule for monasticism, the Knights were "to fight with a pious mind for the supreme and true King." They gained immunity from excommunication by bishops and parish priests. Backed by the anti-Jewish fanatic Bernard of Clairvaux, the most influential clergyman in mid-twelfth-century Europe, they adopted a Rule, copies of which exist, giving vast powers to the Grand Master, who did on occasion have to consult the Chapters. No copy has ever been found of their alleged "Secret Rule." Special chaplains under the Grand Master served the order, which married men could enter if they bequeathed it half their property. Through bequests and profits from interest charged on loans and from letters of credit for pilgrims, the Templars became the richest of the orders.

The Templars in the Levant. Rashness on the part of Templars helped provoke defeats, and also led to the recapture of Jerusalem in 1187 by Saladin, who ordered the execution of all Templars and Hospitalers he had captured. The Templars expended much of their blood and treasure in an attempt to hold a few fortresses against the Saracen onslaught. During the Third Crusade in 1190, they tended to side with the sodomitical Richard the Lionhearted against his rival Philip Augustus of France. "First to attack and last to retreat," the Templars heroically saved the Fifth Crusade (1228–1229) from annihilation in Egypt. They did not cooperate with **Frederick II** of Hohenstaufen during the Sixth Crusade (1227–1230), and except in the most dire crises, regularly opposed their rivals the Hospitalers, helping to fragment further the feudal Kingdom of Jerusalem, already rent by factions and quarrels among Italian merchants from rival cities. In the disaster of 1244 at Gaza only 18 of the 300 Templars and 16 of the 200 Hospitalers, and neither Grand Master, survived the slaughter by the Saracens. The Seventh Crusade led by Louis IX was captured in Egypt in 1250. After his ransom the King went on to the Holy Land but his best efforts failed to restore the situation. The few Templars from Palestine who survived the fall in 1291 of the last Christian outpost there, Acre, during the siege of which the Grand Master was slain, sailed for their new headquarters on Cyprus.

The Dissolution of the Order. The order of the Templars, of whom there were about 4,000 in Europe, half of these in France, did not long survive the loss of the Holy Land. They had become the greatest international bankers in Europe. The Paris Temple became the principal money market where popes and kings deposited their funds, which the Templars loaned out at interest, rivaling the Lombard bankers and circumventing **canon law** prohibitions against usury. Philip IV the Fair (Philippe Le Bel) went deeply into debt to the Templars, who sided with him in his quarrel with Pope Boniface VIII (r. 1290–1303), whom the king had arrested at Anagni in 1302. Having taxed the clergy, robbed and expelled Jews and Lombards, and debased the coinage, Philip began to plot the despoiling of the Templars as early as 1305. Having obtained the election of his French puppet Clement V as pope, he struck through venal informers who denounced the Templars for heresy, blasphemy, and sodomy.

Popular suspicion had for half a century attributed strange events to the Templars' secret midnight meetings. In spite of papal procrastination and professions of disbelief in the charges, Philip had the Grand Inquisitor of France proceed. In August 1307 Philip had the suspected Templars arrested, including Jacques de Molay, then Grand Master, who had come from Cyprus to consult about a crusade. Tortured first by royal officials, then if need arose by the papal inquisition, 36 Templars died under torment in Paris alone. Of the 138 examined in Paris, 123 confessed to spitting on or at the cross at the rites when they joined the order. The Grand Master confessed to spitting on the crucifix and denying Christ. When papal opposition collapsed, Templars were arrested in England, Aragon, Castile, and Sicily, but the Pope assumed control and summoned a general council to decide the case. When the public trial began in 1310, many Templars withdrew their confessions, trusting in the pope—in vain. As relapsed heretics 67 were consigned to the flames. In all about 120 died in Paris.

In 1312 Clement abolished the order, transferring its property to the Hospitalers. At last Jacques de Molay revived his courage and repudiated his confession, whereupon he was burnt along with the Preceptor of the order in Normandy, in front of Notre Dame de Paris. This horrible trial confirmed the precedent for burning heretics, blasphemers, and sodomites—something the scholastic philosophers had been preaching for a century—and sealed it with the approval of the mightiest authorities. It was the forerunner of the **witchcraft** trials with their atrocious cruelty and rivaled that of Joan of Arc as the most dramatic trial in medieval France.

Among the chief accusations leveled at the Templars by Philip IV in 1307 when he issued the order to arrest them was that initiates to the Order kissed its receptors on the buttocks, stomach, navel, spine, and mouth and were enjoined to commit sodomy. In spite of the most exquisite tortures, which included roasting the feet until the bones fell from their sockets, only two or three of the accused Templars confessed to committing sodomy, which they either regarded as more heinous than blasphemy and **heresy** or believed themselves innocent of committing, though many more confessed to the other two offenses. Some seventy said that they had been ordered to commit sodomy but denied having done so. Scholarly opinion is about equally divided as to whether recruits had to perform the *osculum infame* (infamous kiss), i.e., rimming the arsehole of their superiors at the secret midnight initiation rituals. No one can deny that in the minds of these tortured heroes, sodomy was a worse sin to confess than heresy and blasphemy, a view cultivated by the scholastic philosophers Albertus Magnus and Thomas **Aquinas** during the thirteenth century. Franciscans and Dominicans, enemies of the order and leaders of the **Inquisition**, helped in the prosecution and propaganda. More than ever since the fall of the Roman Empire, a Catholic secular power, the Capetian monarchy, already inured by its bloodthirsty campaigns against the Albigensians, was exploiting the supposed ties between demonic powers and heretics, blasphemers, and sodomites—against whom the Christian clergy had for so long warned. This was a momentous precedent for Hitler in the twentieth century, but a more immediate one for the torture and murder of Philip's son-in-law **Edward II** of England in 1327, engineered by Philip's daughter Isabella.

BIBLIOGRAPHY. Malcolm Barber, *The Trial of the Templars*, New York: Cambridge University Press, 1978; Alain Demurger, *Vie et mort de l'ordre du Temple, 1118–1314*, Paris: Seuil, 1985; Peter Partner, *The Murdered Magicians: The Templars and Their Myth*, London: Oxford University Press, 1982.

William A. Percy

TENNYSON, ALFRED, LORD (1809–1892)

English poet laureate. The son of a country rector, Tennyson began writing poetry at the age of eight. In 1830 he published his first significant book, *Poems Chiefly Lyrical*. Three years later occurred what was probably the most important event of his life: the death of his close friend Arthur Hallam in Vienna. They had met at Trinity College, Cambridge in 1828, and had taken two continental trips together, which had deeply impressed the poet. Tennyson's continual and intense brooding over the loss yielded many manuscript drafts, which he finally combined in his major poetic sequence, *In Memoriam*, published anonymously in 1850. Later he gained fame for a number of individual shorter poems, as well as for the Arthurian cycle, *The Idylls of the King* (1859). Profiting from the innovations of the romantic poets, Tennyson enjoyed a superb ear, and was able to combine color and richness of imagery with ethical statement. By no means the apologist for Victorian beliefs that he is sometimes taken to be, Tennyson found the way to capture some of the chief moral dilemmas of his age in verse of matchless eloquence.

From the first, *In Memoriam* puzzled and disconcerted many of Tennyson's admirers. It is difficult to avoid the challenge of a prolonged expostulation to a dead friend that speaks of "A spectral doubt which makes me cold,/ that I shall be thy mate no more." For Tennyson, Hallam had once been "the centre of a world's desire," its "central warmth diffusing bliss." The years had only brought more depth of feeling: "My love involves the love before;/ my love is vaster passion now;/ tho' mixed with God and Nature thou,/ I seem to love thee more and more."

In a contemporary review of *In Memoriam*, Charles Kingsley found the poetic sequence a descendant of "the old tales of David and Jonathan, Damon and Pythias, Socrates and Alcibiades, Shakespeare and his nameless friend, of 'love passing the love of woman.'" Benjamin Jowett, wondering whether it was manly or natural to linger in such a mood, excused the poems by speaking vaguely of their "Hellenism." For a century and a quarter after the publication critics twisted and turned to avoid directly addressing the disturbing implications of this pivotal work. To be sure, Tennyson complicated

matters by conflating the love of his dead comrade with the love of Christ. Probably in his own mind the poet laureate was never sure what the meaning of the whole searing experience was. It is significant that he was able to marry his cousin Emily Sellwood, as he had long planned, only after the final publication of *In Memoriam*.

BIBLIOGRAPHY. Christopher Craft, "'Descend and Touch and Enter': Tennyson's Strange Manner of Address," *Genders*, 1 (1988), 83–101; Alan Sinfield, *Alfred Tennyson*, Oxford: Basil Blackwell, 1986.

Wayne R. Dynes

TESLA, NIKOLA (1856–1943)

Serbian-American scientist and inventor. Born the son of an Orthodox priest in the village of Smiljan in the province of Lik, he received his higher education at the Technische Hochschule in Graz and at the Charles University in Prague. In 1882 he worked for the telephone company in Budapest and invented the amplifier, and in February of that year discovered the phenomenon of the reverse magnetic pole. Between 1882 and 1884 he worked in Paris and Strasbourg, rebuilding the Edison dynamos. Then he came to America and worked with Edison himself for a time. In 1886 he invented the arc lamp for lighting city streets, and in April 1887 he founded the Tesla Electric Company. He also built the first high-efficiency multiphasic current machines and motors. In November and December 1887 he applied for patents for the Tesla induction coil and other inventions. In 1888–89 he worked for Westinghouse in Pittsburgh, applied for a patent for the transmission of alternating current, and built the first high-frequency generators, and in 1890 he discovered high-frequency currents. In 1892 he patented a transformer to increase oscillating currents to high potentials, and began his work on wireless telegraphy.

Between then and 1899 he pioneered in the development of radio communication and in the transmission of electricity without wires, which he realized at a distance of more than 1000 kilometers. This marked the end of his creative period, though he continued to be an active inventor for more than twenty years afterward. He became an American citizen and lived in New York until his death in 1943.

Tesla never married; no woman, with the exception of his mother and his sisters, ever shared the smallest fraction of his life. He believed that he had inherited his abilities as an inventor from his mother. As a young man he was not unattractive, though too tall and slender to be an ideal masculine type; he was handsome of face and wore clothes well. He idealized women, yet planned his own life in a coldly objective manner that excluded women entirely. Only the highest type of woman could win his friendship; the remainder of the sex had no attraction for him whatever. In 1924 he gave an interview published in *Collier's* magazine in which he asserted: "The struggle of the human female toward sex equality will end up in a new sex order, with the females superior. . . . The female mind has demonstrated a capacity for all the mental acquirements and achievements of men, and as generations ensue that capacity will be expanded; the average woman will be as well educated as the average man, and then better educated. . . . Women will ignore precedent and startle civilization with their progress."

Tesla tried to convince the world that he had succeeded in eliminating love and romance from his life, but he merely drew a veil over the secret chapter of his life which an intolerant world had no right to know. The mystery of his devotion to science is one of those episodes in the annals of invention and discovery that are illuminated by insight into the androgynous character of genius.

BIBLIOGRAPHY. Margaret Cheney, *Tesla: Man Out of Time*, New York: Laurel, 1983; John J. O'Neill, *Prodigal Genius: The Life of Nikola Tesla*, New York: Ives Washburn, 1944.

Warren Johansson

THAILAND

Previously known as Siam, in 1939 the country was officially renamed Prathet Thai, or Thailand—literally, "the land of the free." The change of name closely followed a change in the country's form of government, from the previous absolute monarchy to the modern constitutional monarchy with a representative legislature. With some fifty-two million citizens, Thailand occupies a key position in the rapidly developing Asian economic sphere, and aspires to join Taiwan and **Korea** as a world-wide economic force.

An ethnically and linguistically diverse nation, Thailand began to assume its present shape only within the last thousand years, and many key elements of Thai culture reached their present form in the relatively recent past. The formation of the nation began with the arrival in Thailand of members of a linguistic and cultural group designated by the term "Tai." (Some important members of this group are the Siamese, the Lao, and the Shans of northeastern Burma; altogether the "Tai" comprise about 70 million persons in southeast Asia.) The modern Thai may be a descendant of the incoming Tai, but he may also come from the indigenous Mon and Khmer groups whom the Tai joined, or from much later Chinese and Indian immigrants to Thailand. The modern Thai is not so much a member of a race as a person claiming fealty to the state of Thailand; secondarily, a Thai is identified by his language ("a speaker of Thai").

During the eighteenth and nineteenth centuries, Thailand managed to avoid colonization by any European power: the primary foreign influence was

British, and later influence came from the United States, but the Thai always retained their independence. King Rama VI (reigned 1910–25), a poet and translator of Shakespeare, was reputed to be homosexual. During the 1930s the Thai government hired the libertarian French sexologist René **Guyon** as an advisor, and he may have had a hand in the Thai retention of their sexual freedom.

Thailand remains well over ninety percent **Buddhist**. Thai Buddha figures are frequently effeminate, especially the so-called "Walking Buddha."

Thai insistence on personal freedom carries with it a logically necessary corollary: a strong tolerance of eccentricities in other people. One result is that Thailand is one of the few countries on earth where homosexuality is not condemned or treated in any special way. During the 1970s, for example, the Minister of Defense won the national Thai contest for best female dresser. The combination was not perceived as dreadful, but as *sanuk*, a key Thai concept which roughly translates as "fun" or "pleasure." The toleration of homosexuality is not a modern development. Somerset **Maugham** remarked long ago that "the Siamese were the only people on earth with an intelligent attitude about such matters." Two recent Thai prime ministers have been reported to be gay.

One result of viewing sexual pleasure as a domain with little moral content is that **prostitution** is not a highly stigmatized activity. In fact, Bangkok is renowned for its thriving "sex industry," which horrifies many Westerners (who are, of course, simultaneously tempted by all the perceived depravity).

The male prostitute is not highly stigmatized; it is perfectly possible to make a transition from a year as a Buddhist monk to a year of working as an "off-boy" in Bangkok, without abandoning any of the religion one has absorbed and without losing self-esteem. (The "off-boy" is a young man employed at a gay bar who may be taken home by clients; the term is British.) The suburbs of Bangkok also have "off-boy" establishments which cater almost entirely to Thai customers, and which are more polite as a result. The misbehavior of foreign tourists has caused some of these Thai institutions to bar foreigners, beginning in 1988. Thai culture is inherently nonconfrontational, and the Thai would never think of trying to correct a foreigner's rude, loud, or stingy behavior. The only way out is a generic ban on the offending parties. As one owner explained: "The foreigners were scaring the boys." Bangkok also has discos, saunas, and clubs where gay men can meet on a noncommercial or free-lance basis.

While Thai society is generally lacking in homophobia, and also has little antipathy to age-graded relationships, an age of **consent** for males was first established (with little publicity) in 1987, at 15.

Thai society lacks Western concepts of homosexuality as a distinct **identity**, though this situation may be changing. Traditionally, the Thai conceptualization of male homosexuality is similar to the **Mediterranean** model: the penetrator is considered a "complete male," and any normal male may find himself in this role; his opposite is the "katoey," a term which embraces **transvestism**, transsexuality, hermaphroditism, and effeminacy. The katoey is expected to remain sexually passive and submissive, and to have no interest in women. While not discriminated against as homosexuals, the katoey suffer from the limited position of women in the male-dominated Thai culture. Not all males who take passive roles are katoey, however, and reciprocity in sex is not unknown.

To these traditional concepts is now being added a more flexible concept, imported from the West, of a "gay" (the term itself is borrowed into the Thai language, which has no counterpart).

Thai homosexuality is seldom discussed in public, although changes in this area are noticeable in the emergence of five homoerotic or bisexual publications, led by *Mithuna* (bi), *Mithuna, Jr.* (gay), and *Neon* (gay), a regular radio program broadcast from Bangkok, and the beginnings of gay literary output in the form of novels and short stories.

Attitudes on homosexuality show marked differences by **class**, relating to power positions. While there appears to be no "queerbashing" **violence** directed against homosexuality, there seems to be a considerable amount of coercion, abuse of authority positions, and **rape** of males. Peter Jackson comments that "the lessened resistance to having sex with a man means that male rape or sexual attacks on men appear to be significantly more common than in the West." As in other cultures, however, rape of males is a taboo subject and is not reported to authorities.

BIBLIOGRAPHY. Eric Allyn and John P. Collins, *The Men of Thailand*, San Francisco and Bangkok: Bua Luang, 1987; Peter A. Jackson, *Male Homosexuality in Thailand*, New York: Global Academic Publishers, 1989.

Geoff Puterbaugh

THEATRE AND DRAMA

As public performance, accessible to a wide range of spectators, the theatre has been more subject to the constraints of **censorship** than any other long-established art. It is expected to confirm and endorse standard social values and to present the heterodox or the taboo in a manner which will incite either derision or revulsion. Consequently, homosexual sentiments, behavior and concerns have, until recently, rarely appeared on stage; when they have, their presentation has often been skewed to the expectations and sensibilities of convention-bound playgoers.

At the same time, the practicing theatre, in its gregariousness, its opportunities for artistic creativity, and its relative tolerance, has been, at least from the sixteenth century, both in Western and Eastern cultures, an arena where talented homosexuals have flourished. From the ancient **Romans** until very recently, performers were distrusted as outcasts, misfits in the scheme of things: the outlaw actor and the sexual heretic were often the same individual (and some psychiatrists are fond of equating the actor's egoist exhibitionism with an alleged homosexual love of display).

As homosexuality has become more conspicuous in everyday life, the stage, traditionally regarded as the mirror of life, has portrayed it more openly, both as a subject worthy of dramatic treatment and as an attitude that informs the production.

Ancient Greek Theatre. **Greek** classical theatre developed in a culture saturated with homoerotic attitudes and behaviors, but owing, perhaps, to deliberate excision by **Byzantine** and monastic librarians, there is little surviving evidence of these aspects in drama. Lost tragedies include **Aeschylus'** *Laius* (467 B.C.), about the man thought by the Greeks to have invented **pederasty**; *Niobe*, which displayed the love-life of Niobe's sons; and *Myrmidons*, concerning **Achilles'** grief at the death of his lover Patroclus. This last was a favorite of **Aristophanes**, who quoted it frequently. Other lost plays on the Myrmidon theme were written by Philemon (436/5–379 B.C.) and Strattis (409–375 B.C.). Sophocles, too, wrote *Lovers of Achilles*, whose surviving fragment describes the intricate workings of passion. The oft-dramatized tragedy of the house of Labdacus was, in the earlier myths, triggered by Laius' lust-motivated abduction of the son of his host during his foreign exile. Sophocles eschewed this episode, but it was the subject of Euripides' lost *Chrysippus* (ca. 409 B.C.), apparently created as a vehicle for his own male favorite Agathon (447–400/399 B.C.), who was noted for his "aesthetic" way of life. (Another lost *Chrysippus* was composed by Strattis.) Euripides' masterpiece *The Bacchae* (405 B.C.) depicts the androgynous god **Dionysus** unsexing and dementing his antagonist and kinsman Pentheus, before he sends him to his doom.

But whereas the love and lust of man for man was considered worthy of tragic treatment, effeminate manners were the stuff of comedy: Gnesippus was ridiculed for inappropriately using a tragic chorus of effeminates. The successful comic poet Eupolis (445–ca. 415 B.C.) was attracted to this theme; his *Those Who Dye Their Hair* (*Baptai*; 416/15 B.C.) satirized members of the circle of **Alcibiades**, who was rumored to have had him drowned for it. Surviving fragments suggest that they were ritual transvestites who spoke an obscene lingo of their own in ceremonies worshipping the goddess Cotytto. Eupolis' *The Flatterers* (*Kolakes*) (431 B.C.), a satire on parasitism with sidelights on compliant sexuality, won first prize over Aristophanes' *Peace*.

The comedies of Aristophanes teem with references to pederasty and cross-dressing. Although his earthy heroes have no hesitation in declaring what fun it is to watch naked boys at the gymnasium and to fondle their scrotums, the effeminate (*euryproktos* or "broad-ass") is mercilessly mocked. In *The Clouds* (423 B.C.), for instance, Right Reason rhapsodizes on the "moisture and down" that bloom on a youth's genitals "as on quinces" and wins his argument. Yet Cleisthenes is regularly made a laughingstock for his lady-like carrying-on, and the central device of the *Women's Festival* (*Thesmophoriazousai*) (411 B.C.) is to have the protagonist disguise himself as a woman, under Cleisthenes' instruction, thus running the danger of being buggered when captured and bound.

Roman Theatre. Buggery on compulsion remained a standard comic *topos* in the **Mediterranean** basin. In Roman comedy, **Plautus'** characters mistake one another for eunuchs and effeminates; his *Casina* (ca. 190–180 B.C.), in particular, is packed with jokes, puns and equivocations on the theme. Sodomy frequently crops up in the farcical *fabula togata*, es-

pecially those of Lucius Afranius (fl. later second century of our era), credited to have introduced homosexuality into the genre. Among the later Greeks, actors were respected as artists (Mary **Renault's** novel *The Mask of Apollo* offers a persuasive recreation); but in Rome, they were legally classified as "infamous," even if popularly regarded as desirable sexual catches. The Emperors Caligula, **Nero**, and Trajan often took their male bedmates from the ranks of actors, dancers, and mimes; the last became notorious for the indecency of their performances. To increase the eroticism of their shows, the mimes introduced women on stage in what had hitherto been an exclusively male preserve.

The Orient. In the Oriental theatre, women were frequently banned from the stage, either for religious or moralistic reasons; the resultant professional female impersonator, the *tan* of **China's** Peking Opera, introduced in the reign of Ch'ien Lung (1735–1796), and the *onnagata* of **Japan's** Kabuki theatre, replacing boy players after 1652, exercised a pseudo-female allure. In China actors, no matter what they played, were frequently prostitutes, sought after by statesmen and scholars: among the most famous of these actor-favorites were Chin Feng (fl. 1590), Wei Ch'ang-sheng (fl. 1780), and Ch'en Yin-kuan (fl. 1790). The boy acting-troupes of nineteenth-century China were often equated with male brothels, and certainly the boys' looks were regarded as more important than their talent. But these **pedophilic** passions were never reflected in the Chinese dramatic repertory. On the Kabuki stage, on the other hand, a bisexual love affair is the pivot of *Tsuwamono Tongen Sogo* (1697), and a homosexual one comprises a subplot in *Asakusa Reigenki*.

The most popular **Korean** entertainment form before 1920 was the Namsadang, a traveling troupe of variety performers; a homosexual commune of 40 to 50 males, it has been described as the "voice of the common people" (Young Ja Kim). The company was divided into *sut-*

dongmo ("butch") and *yodongmo* ("queen") members, the novices serving the elders and playing the female roles. Despite Confucian disapproval of pederasty, the troupe's sexual identity did not put off village audiences, probably because its status as an outcast group made conventional standards irrelevant to it. The institutionalized homosexuality of the Namsadang raises questions about similar itinerant companies in ancient and medieval Europe, and has an analogue in the enforced male bonding of acrobat troupes. Late nineteenth-century commentators on the circus noted that homosexual relationships were common among gymnasts and aerialists, a combination of physical contact and the need for trust. Bands of mummers and mountebanks may have shared such an ethos.

The Middle Ages and Beginnings of the Modern Theatre in Europe. Christianity was antagonistic to the theatre, partly on grounds of immorality; **Clement of Alexandria** specifically rebuked the obscenity of mimes who brought *cinaedia* or male prostitution on stage. When the theatre in Europe was reborn from the Church, the religious teleology of the drama precluded treatment of illicit love, except in imitation of the classics. Nor was the burning of Sodom ever treated by the mystery plays, although Jesuit school-drama in the Baroque age would dramatize it with accompanying fireworks, as in Cornelius a Marca's *Bustum Sodomae* (Ghent, 1615). The Renaissance revived the comic treatment of homosexuality, first in ribald farces by Bolognese students, mocking burghers and clergy: one of these is Ugolino Pisani's *Philogenia* (after 1435), wherein the boy hustler Epifebo deploys his charms to snare the venal priest Prodigio.

Sexual ambiguity is the basis of "gender-confusion" comedy in which a male or female character disguises him/herself as the opposite sex and attracts the amorous attentions of the "wrong" sex. The archetype is Bernardo Dovizi da Bibbiena's (1470–1520) bawdy *La Calandria* (1513), but it was a common device in *commedia dell'arte* as well as in *commedia erudita*. Involuntary buggery remained a basic joke: in Niccolò Machiavelli's (1469–1527) *La Clizia* (1525), old Nicomaco is sodomized in his sleep by his servant Siro. Pietro **Aretino**'s *Il Marescalco* (1526/7) features a pederastic hero, a chief groom of the stables who is obliged by his master to marry a woman only to find to his great relief that the bride is a boy (this served as a source of Ben Jonson's *Epicoene*, 1609).

Although Spanish Golden Age drama dropped the homosexual references when it adapted Italian comedy, it often featured the *mujer varonil*, a woman in men's clothes who takes on the aggressive role in the love-chase; farcical **transvestism** was not uncommon, as in Lope de Vega's (1562–1635) *El mesón de la corte* (The Inn of the Court, 1583?) and Monroy y Silva's *El caballero-dama* (The Lady Cavalier), in which two men in drag are tricked into bed together. Intense Platonic relationships between single-sex couples are often depicted, as in the anonymous *El crotalón* (ca. 1553), but in a society where sodomites were burned at the stake during the **Inquisition**, orthodox sexuality always prevailed by the play's ending.

The Elizabethan Stage. The Elizabethan gender-confusion drama was complicated by the fact that women were played by boy actors, a development from school drama. Thus, in William **Shakespeare**'s *As You Like It* (1599/1600), there is the intricate enigma of a boy actor playing a girl disguising herself as a youth who acts as a woman to aid his/her wooer. The practice also required adjustments in performance convention: nowhere in *Antony and Cleopatra* (1607) do the passionate lovers kiss. This aspect of the stage fueled condemnation by Puritans and reformers, who damned it as a hotbed of sodomy; there is scant hard evidence of homosexual activity among players and playwrights, but the imputation is not without foundation. Clear cases can be made for Nicholas

Udall (1505–1556), headmaster of Eton and author of *Ralph Roister Doister* (between 1534 and 1541), who admitted to "buggery" with one of his students; and for Christopher **Marlowe**, whose own predilections found their way into his work: the grand amour of the king and his favorite Piers Gaveston in *Edward II* (1593), the court of **Henri III** in *The Massacre at Paris* (1593), and the scene between **Ganymede** and Jupiter in *Dido Queen of Carthage* (1594). Whatever the homosexual component of his sonnets, Shakespeare only occasionally portrayed the love of one man for another in his dramatic works: when he did it was as a consuming, unspoken passion that expressed itself in deeds: Antonio's sacrifice for Bassanio in *The Merchant of Venice* (1594 or 1596); the sea-captain Antonio's protection of Sebastian in *Twelfth Night* (1600); and **Achilles'** avenging of Patroclus in *Troilus and Cressida* (1602/3).

Further Developments in England. Tudor Morality plays packed with Protestant propaganda had displayed allegorical characters named Sodomy to stand for corrupt, courtly, and Catholic manners (as in John Bale's *Three Laws*, 1538). Throughout the Jacobean and Caroline periods, pederasty continued to be associated on stage with (usually Italian) luxury and high life, a character called Sodome appearing in Cosmo Manuche's *The Loyal Lovers* as late as 1652. John Marston's *The Turk* (1610) contains an outspoken scene between the erotic tourist Bordello and his page Pantofle. In William Davenant's *Albovine* (1629), the Lombard hero has a minion, and in his *The Cruel Brother* (1630), the Duke of Siena cherishes a favorite who "in his love . . ./ He holdeth thus in his Armes, in fearfull care/ Not to bruse you with his deere embracements."

After the Restoration of the Stuarts and the introduction of actresses on the English stage, the heterosexual ingredient became more realistic in comedy, more idealistic in tragedy, though without entirely ousting the competition.

Montague Summers typically overstates the case when he refers to "the prevalence of uranianism in the theatre" of the time; it must be noted that fops, although mocked for such Frenchified behavior as the exchange of kisses in George Etherege's *The Man of Mode* (1676), long to bed down women exclusively. (Despite their names, for instance, Sir Gaylove and Sir Butterfly in Newburgh Hamilton's *The Doating Lovers* [1715] are both inveterate womanizers.) Pederasty is associated not with effeminates, but with decadent foreign courts or decayed rakes who need a new stimulus: in Edward Howard's *The Usurper* (1664), the comments of Damocles and Hugo de Petra concerning a page are openly pedophilic, and in Aphra Behn's *The Amorous Prince* (1671), Lorenzo tries to seduce the boy Philibert who, however, turns out to be a girl in disguise. In Thomas Otway's *The Soldier's Fortune* (1681), an elderly fool is delighted to discover—or so he thinks—that a girl he is tumbling is a boy. The rhymed extravaganza *Sodom, or The Quintessence of Debauchery* (1684?), attributed to the Earl of **Rochester**, which partly hymns the superiority of buggery to "normal" practices, was never performed.

The matchmaker Coupler is the only blatant "queen" in Restoration drama; in John Vanbrugh's *The Relapse* (1696) "old Sodom" as he is known requests the hero's sexual favors as a reward for his complicity. He represents a new trend, for in the eighteenth century the flamboyant fop character, like the audience itself, underwent a process of *embourgeoisement*. The fop was shown as an overreaching member of the middle class, usually a simpering "molly," more distinctly a denizen of a subculture than his predecessors. The molly's first stage appearance may be the "nice fellow" Maiden "who values himself upon his Effeminacies," in Thomas Baker's comedy *Tunbridge-Walks; or, The Yeoman of Kent* (1703), believed by his contemporaries to be a portrait of the author's former behavior. Other examples are Varnish and Bardach in *Kensington Gardens* (1720) by the actor John Leigh; the much-imitated Fribble in David Garrick's *A Miss in Her Teens* (1747); "The Daffodils" in Garrick's *The Male-Coquette* (1757); and Jessamy in Isaac Bickerstaffe's *Lionel and Clarissa* (1768). A spate of pamphlets and articles about similar "soft gentlemen" suggest that these types did not exaggerate real life models by much. Within the theatrical community, a number of homosexual figures were conspicuous, among them Leigh (1689–1726) himself. Of the boy-actors who continued to play women into the Restoration period, Edward Kynaston (1643–1712) was accused by Dryden of being the Duke of Buckingham's catamite; and James Nokes (d. 1696), who played the title role in *The Maid of the Mill* (1660) and later kept a toyshop, was castigated in the *Satyr on the Players* as "This B[ugger] Nokes, whose unwieldy T[arse]/ Weeps to be buryed in his Foreman's A[rse]." Later, the popular comedian Samuel Foote (1720–1777), who often played old women, was tried and acquitted for sodomy with his man-servant. In the Regency period, a post-mortem revealed the actress and prostitute Eliza Edwards (1814–1833) to have been a male transvestite.

French Theatre. When Mme. de Maintenon, the morganatic wife of Louis XIV, requested the archbishop of Paris to follow the example of Cromwell's parliament and order the closing of the French theatres, he resisted by pointing out that the stage, with its heterosexual concerns, prevented the spread of "unnatural vice." Under the French Regency (1715–23), a number of private pornographic theatres were maintained by the *noblesse*, but homosexual activities were rarely shown; an exception was the private theatre of the Duchesse de Villeroi, where lesbian comedies performed by Opera dancers ended in orgies. One of the erotic authors, Charles Colle (1709–1783), planned a *vaudeville* based on "those gentlemen," but gave it up allegedly because he could find no rhyme for *bougre*. In *La Comtesse d'Olonne*,

attributed to Bussy-Rabutin, Le Comte de Guice, described as a "gentilhomme de la manchette" is finally converted to heterosexuality; similarly, in *Les Plaisirs du cloître*, sapphic flagellation gives way to ordinary love-making. A later parody of these works, *Les Esprits des moeurs au XVIIIe siècle*, attributed to Charles de Nerciat, presents a graphic scene of lesbian lovemaking. The French acting profession harbored many deviants: the great tragedienne Françoise **Raucourt** presided over a lesbian secret society, the Anandrynes; the harlequin Carlo Bertinazzi (1713–1783), admired by Garrick for his eloquent back, had a liaison with the married actor Favart. The handsome young actor Fleury (Abraham-Joseph Benard, 1750–1822), was said to be kept by the Venetian ambassador at an annual pension of eight thousand pounds; he had a declared admirer in Prince **Henry of Prussia**, Frederick the Great's homosexual brother.

Europe from the End of the Old Regime to World War I. From its inception, the most prominent figures in the German theatre were unabashed pederasts, starting with the classical actors August Wilhelm Iffland (1759–1814) and Wilhelm Kunst (Kunze, 1799–1859), both much valued by **Goethe**. Some of the greatest German dramatists are believed to have had similar propensities which nourished their works: Friedrich von Schiller (1759–1805) left behind an unfinished play, *Die Malteser* (The Knights of Malta, 1794–1803), whose Crequi and St. Priest exhibit homophilic feelings; August von Kotzebue's (1761–1819) tendency to lachrymose sentimentality rather than sensuality in his portrayal of love may be attributed to his nature. The tastes of Heinrich von **Kleist** and the Austrian Franz Grillparzer (1791–1872), on the other hand, are not demonstrated in their dramatic works. In Vogtland, a workers' neighborhood in northern Berlin, the Nationaltheater was known before it burned in 1883 as the playhouse of homosexuals, who included its manager, the "last romantic" star Hermann Hendrichs (1809–1871), the tragediennes Clara Ziegler (1844–1909) and Felicita Vestvali (Anne Marie Stegemann, 1829–1880), both of whom played Romeo, and, among the patrons, Prince Georg of Prussia and J. B. Schweitzer, president of the All-German Workers' Union. Later, the Viktoriatheater rightfully inherited its reputation. Josef Kainz (1858–1910), the great leading man of Wilhelmine classical theatre, was, at the age of 27, the final favorite of **Ludwig** II of Bavaria.

Simon Karlinsky has argued convincingly for the homosexuality of Russian playwrights Nikolai Vasilevich Gogol (1809–1852), whose fear of women perspires through his comedies, and Vladislav Aleksandrovich Ozerov (1770–1816), whose verse tragedy *Dmitrij Donskoj* (Dmitry of the Don) (1807) has as a subplot the fervent devotion of a page for his knight. Homophilic sentiment also motivates **Balzac**'s melodrama *Vautrin* (1840), banned not for its content but for the political satire in its costuming.

Homosexuality, as it came to be defined and recognized in the nineteenth century, was not unveiled on stage until the *fin-de-siècle* cult of decadence made it modish. A leading star of the Parisian theatre of that period was the flamboyant Romanian Edouard de Max (1869–1925) who, according to Gide, nursed a lifelong desire to play Nero, Henri III, and **Heliogabalus**; a play about him was written by André Boussac de Saint-Marc: *Sardanapale* (1926).

Oscar **Wilde**'s aphoristic comedies can be seen as manifestations of a **camp** sensibility, and some critics have speculated that the Bunburying of the heroes of *The Importance of Being Earnest* (1895) stands for *sub rosa* excursions into the gay demi-monde. Lytton **Strachey** interpreted the main character of *A Woman of No Importance* (1893) as "a wicked Lord, staying in a country house, who has made up his mind to bugger one of the other guests—a handsome young man

of twenty." Wilde's *Salome* (1893, prod. 1896) had an influence on the usually reticent André **Gide**; *Saul* (1903, prod. 1922), set in the Biblical time of **David and Jonathan**, was his only theatrical paean to an older man's passion for a younger.

Scandinavia's most illustrious homosexual author, the Danish novelist Herman **Bang** (1857–1912), though deeply involved in the theatre, was not an outstanding dramatist. He founded the first Norwegian artistic cabaret (in Christiania, now Oslo, 1892), worked in Paris at the experimental Théâtre de l'Oeuvre in 1894 as "scenic instructor," and was director at the Folketheater, Copenhagen, 1898–1901. Despite his insignificance as a playwright, his intimacy with drama deeply influenced the prose style of his outsider novels. The Swede August Strindberg (1849–1912) at the outset of his illustrious career was led by his complex misogyny to introduce evil lesbians as psychic vampire figures into his writings. In *Comrades* (1888), a mannish female artist seduces the hero's wife into a bohemian career; the heroine of *Miss Julie* (1889) is doomed because her mother raised her as a boy and thus undermined her feminine intuition for survival; and the two-woman one-act *The Stronger* (1889) reflected the author's own insecurities about his wife's womenfriends. Strindberg's later historical dramas about Queen **Christina** (1901) and Gustav III (1902) touch glancingly on their protagonists' sexual nature, the Queen shown to be repelled by the idea of marriage (a common enough distaste in Strindberg). The modern Swedish play *Night of the Tribades* (1975) by Per Olof Enquist (b. 1934) caused a sensation by exploring Strindberg's tortured awareness that his first wife was having an affair with another woman.

A lyrical treatment of the male eros was proffered by the Russian poet Mikhail Afanasievich **Kuzmin**; several of his plays, including *A Dangerous Precaution* (1907) and *The Venetian Madcaps* (1912), vaunt the love of two men over that of a man and a woman. The first professed contemporary gay protagonist in drama is the title character of Armory-Dauriac's comedy *Le Monsieur aux chrysanthèmes* (1908; the title parodies *La Dame aux camellias*), which satirized the popularity of elegant homosexuals in society. Deviant characters crop up occasionally in modernist Italian and Spanish drama—Lorenzaccio in Sem Benelli's *La Maschera di Bruto* (The Mask of Brutus, 1908) and the King in Antonio Buero-Vallejo's *Isabela, reina de corazones* (Isabel, Queen of Hearts). Sholem Asch's Yiddish melodrama *Gott fun Nekoma* (God of Vengeance, prod. 1907), with its saving love between a lesbian prostitute and a brothel-keeper's innocent daughter, created no great *frisson* when produced in Europe, but raised a howl of execration in New York in 1922.

Germany was perhaps the first European nation to treat homosexuality frankly, though as a psychic catastrophe, on the modern stage. Usually historic subject matter justified its introduction, in plays about **Hadrian** (Frederiksen, Paul Heyse), Saul (Wolfskehl), and **Frederick the Great** (Burchard), or else the play was based on ancient myth (Elisàr von **Kupffer's** *Narkissos*) or on stage convention (Karl von Levetzow's pantomime *Die beiden Pierrots* [The Two Pierrots]). As a "problem" of modern society, homosexuality appears disguised as the decadent clown Edi in Hermann Bahr's *Die Mutter* (The Mother, 1891) and undisguised as the tormented youth Rudolf in Ludwig Dilsner's *Jasminblüthen* (Jasmine Blossoms, 1899), who is one of the first of many to find his way out of the dilemma by shooting himself. As early as 1902, the critic Hanns Fuchs was complaining that the denouements of such plays depended too much on the state of the laws: "the ideal homosexual drama, depicting the conflicts in an individual soul and their influence on its action and conception of life of homosexuals, is still to be written." He suggested a dreamer like Grillparzer or a strong-man like **Michelangelo** as models.

Fuchs' wish went unanswered. Herbert Hirschberg's *Fehler* (Faults, 1906) also belonged to the school of problem drama. In his "tragedy of sex" *Frühlingserwachen* (Spring's Awakening, 1891, prod. 1906), Frank Wedekind (1864–1918) included a vignette of teenage homoeroticism amid his spectrum of pubescent anxieties, but again the play's catastrophe was the result of social attitudes. He came closer to offering an inner conflict with the Countess Geschwitz, a full-length portrait of an obsessed tribade in *Erdgeist* (Earth Spirit, 1898, prod. 1902) and *Die Büchse der Pandoras* (Pandora's Box, 1904, prod. 1906).

After World War I. The liberation from Victorian values felt after World War I was reflected in the theatre as well. Expressionist drama often used adolescent homosexuality as a metaphor for youthful rebellion, morbidity, and confusion, as in Arnolt Bronnen's *Vatermord* (Parricide, 1922), Klaus **Mann's** *Anja und Esther* (1925), and Ferdinand Bruckner's *Krankheit der Jugend* (The Disease of Youth, 1926). Bruckner's *Die Verbrecher* (Criminals, 1928) included an attack on the infamous **Paragraph 175** of the penal code. Bertolt Brecht's early plays, *Baal* (1922), *Im Dickicht der Städte* (In the Jungle of Cities, 1924), *Edward II* (1924), and even *Die Dreigroschen Oper* (The Threepenny Opera, 1928), are filled with erotic male-bonding, partly derived from **Rimbaud**. An amateur group, the Theater des Eros, existed between 1921 and 1924 to perform outspoken homosexual liberation dramas in private homes.

Christa Winsloe's *Gestern und Heute* (Mädchen in Uniform, 1930), filmed and widely revived outside Germany, presented a girls'-school crush in a tragic light, but put the blame squarely on old-fashioned values. Throughout the 1920s, in fact, tragedy was the standard dramatic mode for lesbianism. In France, Edouard Bourdet (1887–1945) treated upper-class gay males comically in *La Fleur de pois* (The Upper Crust, 1932), but imbued lesbian attraction with dire consequences in *La Prisonnière* (The Captive, 1926). (Its plot had a foreruner in Catulle Mendès' *Protectrices*, a pale epigone in Roger Martin du Gard's *Taciturne*, 1931, and a German counterpart in Hermann Sudermann's *Die Freundin*, 1913/14.)

Federico García **Lorca** may have channeled his own predilections into the repressed sexuality of his major tragedies, for he puts his praise of masculine beauty in the mouths of his trammelled heroines. More explicit are his early poetic drama *Diálogo del Amargo* (The Bitter One's Dialogue), in which a young man with a death wish is seduced by the horseman Muerte who offers him his highly symbolic knives; and the suppressed surrealistic play *El público* (The Audience, 1930; not published until 1976).

This convention that passion was tragic, but behavioral characteristics comic, was maintained in the United States. The very first American drama of homophilic despair, Henry Blake **Fuller's** "closet" (in both senses) one-act *At Saint Judas's* (1896), ends with the suicide of the best man reviled by the beloved (straight) bridegroom. Mae West's *The Drag* (1927), which devoted a whole act to a transvestite ball, and *Pleasure Man* (1928), which filled the stage with hilarious dishing queens, both had tragic endings tacked on. These plays were prosecuted and banned, whereas Lillian Hellman's ambivalent melodrama of calumny and suppressed desire, *The Children's Hour* (1934), won critical acclaim. The leading dramatic actresses of the New York stage, Eva Le Gallienne (b. 1889), Katharine Cornell (1893–1974), and Lynn Fontanne (1887–1983), were known privately for the intimacy of their female friendships; the last two married gay men, Guthrie McClintic (1893–1961) and Alfred Lunt (1893–1977), respectively.

Broadway was somewhat hamstrung by police censorship, which was less consistent in its bans than was the Lord Chamberlain's Office in London; still, British drama managed to sneak in the occasional reference. Precious chamber plays like Ronald **Firbank's** *The Princess Zoubaroff* (1920) circulated only among the cognoscenti; but in 1925, Arnold Bennett could find the opening scene of Frederick Lonsdale's *Spring Cleaning*, a gathering of homosexuals at a cocktail party, the only genuine thing in the play. That same year, a sentimental attachment formed in a prison-camp was made central to J. R. **Ackerley's** *The Prisoners of War*, and to ken homosexuals also made an appearance in Ronald Mackenzie's *Musical Chairs* (1931). *The Green Bay Tree* (1933) by Mordaunt Shairp (1887–1939), a melodrama about an epicene older man's hold on a languid youth, made a success, repeated, with some changes, on Broadway. Schoolboy crushes, familiar to much of the audience, surfaced in *The Hidden Years* (1948) by Travers Otway and *Quaint Honour* (1949) by Roger Gellert in more or less covert form. It is typical that England's two favorite authors of comedies and musicals, Noel **Coward** (1899–1973) and Ivor Novello (Daniel Davies, 1893–1951), whose sexual orientation was common knowledge in theatrical circles, remained closeted to the general public; the campiness of their works was put down to "sophistication." The same held true for such important playwrights and actors as Somerset **Maugham**, Terence Rattigan (1911–1977), Michael Redgrave (1908–1985), Charles Laughton (1899–1962), Emlyn Williams (1905–1987), Esme Percy (1887–1957), Ernest Milton (1890–1974), Gwen Ffrangcon-Davies (b. 1896), and John Gielgud (b. 1904) (even after Gielgud had been arrested for public indecency), as well as for the powerful producer Hugh "Binkie" Beaumont (1908–1973) and the influential critic James Agate (1877–1942). At the end of his career, Coward, who had put a chorus of "pretty boys, witty boys" wearing green carnations into *Bitter Sweet* (1929) and hinted at a bisexual triangle in *Design* *for Living* (1933), ventured a bit more frankness in *A Song at Twilight* (1966), ostensibly based on Maugham and Max Beerbohm; Rattigan also made the exploitation of a pederast central to his late play *Man and Boy* (1963). William Douglas Home (b. 1912) is a mainstream playwright who has been willing to deal with the taboo subject throughout his career, from his prison play *Now Barrabbas* (1947), to his comedy about a transsexual, *Aunt Edwina* (1960), to his drama *David and Jonathan* (1984).

When the Nazis came to power in Germany, the leading man Adolf Wohlbruck (1900–1966) had to flee to England, where he became known as Anton Walbrook; so did Conrad Veidt, who eventually wound up in Hollywood. Less lucky colleagues perished in the camps. The immensely popular Gustav Gründgens (1899–1963) was forced to marry and suppress his propensities to retain the favor of his masters; after the war, he persisted as the leading director and classical actor in West Germany, but his survival tactics were attacked by his former friend Klaus Mann in the novel *Mephisto.*

After World War II. During the post-war period, the French theatre was dominated by Jean **Cocteau**'s circle, including the stage designer Christian Bérard (1902–1949) and the actor Jean Marais (b. 1913); the bisexual Gérard Philipe (1922–1959) was everyone's favorite leading man. The foremost members of the Comédie Française, such as Jean Weber and Jacques Charon (1920–1975), were familiar faces at gay salons. Julien Green's monumental *Sud* (South, 1953) clothed his doomed love story in Civil War garb and veiled suggestion; the agony of unrequited affection went even deeper in Henry de **Montherlant**'s *La Ville dont le Prince est un Enfant* (The City Whose Prince Is a Child, 1951), set in a Catholic school where an obsessive priest roots out the special friendships of the students. Typically, the secretive and suicidal Montherlant considered it unsuitable for public performance by boys.

New Openness in the Sixties. The drag-ball scene in John Osborne's play about the Austrian spy Alfred **Redl**, *A Patriot for Me* (1965), proved one of the nails in the coffin of official British censorship, whose demands for cuts showed up its absurdity. Joe **Orton** was another strain on it, for, like Wilde, his sense of paradox and sly verbal innuendo informed all his work, making it not so easy to cut offending passages: *Entertaining Mr. Sloane* (1964), with its bisexual protagonist, the amoral male couple in *Loot* (1966), and the polymorphous perversity of the entire cast of *What the Butler Saw* (1969) could not be neutralized by excision. His camp sensibility led him to include arcane references within standard farce set-ups, couched in impeccably elegant utterance; and his successes emboldened him, in rewriting his radio play *The Ruffian on the Stair* for the stage in 1967, to strengthen the sexual bond between the two male characters.

Three plays of the 1966/67 season continued the tradition of homosexual as lonely outsider: Frank Marcus' (b. 1928) cruel lesbian comedy *The Killing of Sister George*, Charles Dyer's (b. 1928) bleak duet *Staircase*, and Christopher Hampton's (b. 1946) examination of adolescent alienation, *When Did You Last See My Mother?* Hampton's next play, *Total Eclipse* (1968), was a skillful exploration of the **Rimbaud/Verlaine** relationship. At least one homosexual was to be found as local color in performances by Joan Littlewood's group (*A Taste of Honey* by Shelagh Delaney and *The Hostage* by Brendan Behan, both 1958). The plays of Peter Shaffer (b. 1926), beginning with *Five Finger Exercise* (1958), generally concern the uneasy relationship between an older man and a younger; and Simon Gray (b. 1936) played with pathetic same-sex desires in *Wise Child* (1967) and *Spoiled* (1968) before presenting a witty bisexual protagonist (but one who is abandoned at the end) in *Butley* (1971). Alan Bennett's (b. 1934) plays have been both more open and more fun.

In the United States, *Tea and Sympathy* (1953) by Robert Anderson (b. 1917) encapsulates a prevalent American attitude: the sensitive hero could be cured of his reputation as a sissy by the love of a good woman. The stage image of the homosexual as outrageous fairy or doomed psychotic was challenged by Ruth and Augustus Goetz' adaptation of Gide's *The Immoralist* (1954); imperfect in its reasoning, it nevertheless presented a man with homophilic tendencies as intelligent and sympathetic. It was, however, less significant than the prominence of Tennessee **Williams** in the American theatre. In Williams' early drama, explicit homosexuality remained marginal; the flashback into Blanche's marriage in *Streetcar Named Desire* (1947), the Baron de Charlus episode in *Camino Real* (1953), and the lesbian undercurrent in *Something Unspoken* (1958). It became more crucial as the hidden motivation in *Cat on a Hot Tin Roof* (1955) and the central secret in *Suddenly Last Summer* (1958), but in a standard mode: the protagonists are both victims, of desires suppressed and expressed, respectively. In later plays like *Small Craft Warnings* (1972) with its transvestite husband, and *Vieux Carré* (1977), the types are grotesque but the motives are somewhat less disguised.

Such themes remained covert in William Inge (*The Boy in the Basement*, 1962, *Natural Affection*, 1963) and Edward Albee (although *The Zoo Story*, 1959, is cryptic only to those who cannot spot one of its two characters). This did not stop hostile critics from declaring that *Who's Afraid of Virginia Woolf?* (1962) was really about two gay male couples. Albee's savage hostility to the nuclear family struck them as symptomatic of a perverted imagination; they were outraged by the musky and enigmatic eroticism of *Tiny Alice* (which one claimed was gay slang for the rectum). Albee's choice of fiction to dramatize— Carson **McCullers'**

Ballad of the Sad Café (1963) and James Purdy's *Malcolm* (1966)—also seemed intent on glorifying the freakish outsider. As homosexual characters proliferated on the Broadway stage, this critical hostility grew until, in the mid- and late 1960s, such widely read pundits as Stanley Kauffmann, Walter Kerr, and Robert Brustein were positing a homosexual conspiracy in the American theatre, which "often poisons what you see and hear." They argued that homosexual playwrights camouflaged their concerns in the guise of heterosexual relationships; also implicit was the fear that show business was in the hands of perverts, from costumers and choreographers to producers. A decade later this paranoia was echoed in Canada, where the actor John Colicos complained "the faggots have taken over."

Canada was the breeding-ground for John Herbert's (b. 1926) harsh play of **prison** life, *Fortune and Men's Eyes* (1967), which pivots on the sexual politics of the cell-block; and the **Quebec** playwright Michel Tremblay (b. 1942), with his drag-queen soap operas *La duchesse de Langeais* (1969) and *Hosanna* (1973). Tremblay, a master of local patois, was also influenced by the French thief-turned-prose-stylist Jean **Genet**, whose dramas, although they explore the mysteries of personality, are less explicitly homoerotic than his novels. His first play, *Les Bonnes* (The Maids, 1947), did not get the all-male cast Genet desired in its premiere production, but since then the two sister-maids and their mistress have frequently been played by men. Similarly, Herbert's play may owe something to Genet's *Haute Surveillance* (Death Watch, 1949), a more oblique and lyrical treatment of sexual subservience in confinement.

The American critics' demand for homosexual honesty in packaging was answered by Mart Crowley's (b. 1935) *The Boys in the Band* (1968); drenched in self-pity, predictable in its stereotypes, carrying on the tradition of the deviant as victim of his own deviance, it nevertheless presented a half-world independent of heterosexual concerns. Its commercial success, which opened the flood-gates to similar confessional dramas, was due in part to its confirming the general public in the view that such a life was emotionally barren. Although *Boys in the Band* did include a campy sissy in its roster, at least it eschewed the drag queen who remained a constant in drama of this period (Lanford Wilson's *Madness of Lady Bright*, 1964; Frederick Combs' *The Children's Mass*, 1973). A rash of commercial farces erupted, using the homosexual as a trendy type in the hackneyed comic situations; in the West End, *Spitting Image* (1966) by Colin Spencer (b. 1933) presented a gay couple about to have a baby; in New York, *Norman, Is That You?* (1972) by Ron Clark (b. 1933) and Sam Bobrick (b. 1932) and *Steambath* (1971) by Bruce Jay Friedman (b. 1930) exploited coming-out and cruising areas for their crude cartoons. (The British critic Kenneth Tynan noted that Broadway humor derived exclusively from Jews and homosexuals.)

The "Liberated" Seventies. In Paris, the phenomenally successful *La Cage aux Folles* (Cage of Queens, 1972) by Jean Poirier ran for four years, its popularity also due to its reinforcing misconceptions with broad caricatures of glamor drag queens, ghettoized in a showbiz setting. (When the actor Michel Serrault was asked how he dared go on in net stockings and ostrich-boa at his age, he explained that he put a spot of red on his nose, and so was not playing a homosexual but a clown in drag.) Gay dramatists attempted to infuse the boulevard farce with insider knowledge, as in A. J. Kronengold's *Tub Strip* (1973), James Kirkwood's (1930–1989) *P.S. Your Cat Is Dead* (1975), and Terrence McNally's (b. 1939) *The Ritz* (1975). But the drag queen remained the favored protagonist, cropping up again in *Torch Song Trilogy* (1983), three plays by Harvey Fierstein which were evolved in a gay theatre and then transferred successfully to Broadway to win a Tony Award. Significantly,

Fierstein's only popular success since was his libretto for Jerry Herman's (b. 1933) musical comedy version of *La Cage aux Folles* (1983), which coarsened an already simplistic sitcom to suit the tired businessman.

Heterosexual playwrights like David Rabe and David Mamet seemed unable to get beyond the notion that same-sex affection spelled doom, a collapse of personality. Meanwhile, homosexual dramatists were moving beyond such clichés. It is noteworthy that Robert Patrick and Lanford Wilson (both b. 1937) first gained recognition on the New York stage in 1964 with oppressed characters: the obsessed older man in Patrick's *The Haunted Host* and the suicidal drag queen in Wilson's *The Madness of Lady Bright*. After treating other themes for more than a decade, they then took a less hysterical approach to the subject: Patrick in *Kennedy's Children* (1973) offered a homosexual as a type of his times, and by 1983 was writing specifically for gay audiences in such plays as *Blue Is for Boys*. Wilson matured to present homosexual relationships and characters as natural features of the American landscape in *The Fifth of July* (1978) and *Burn This* (1987). Similarly, Albert Innaurato (b. 1948) could balance his obese and pathetic freak in *The Transfiguration of Benno Blimpie* (1977) with a humorous, boy-next-door seduction in *Gemini* (1977).

It was the "worthiness" and remoteness of the subject and the familiarity of its treatment which dictated how the general public would react to plays about gay life. *Bent* (1978) by Martin Sherman, an overwrought picture of persecution in Nazi Germany, couched in the prose of Masterpiece Theatre, was acclaimed; *Forty-Deuce* (1981) by Alan Bowne, a much more authentic and original piece of work concerning the teenaged hustlers and their johns who hang out around Times Square, was reviled. Black American playwrights tended to define homosexuality as a decadent white threat to their virility. The work of Imamu Amiri Baraka (LeRoi Jones, b. 1934) grew more homophobic as his political radicalism increased: *The Toilet* (1964), a self-styled "play about love," seems to sanction the embrace of the white "queer" and the black youth, yet Baraka's public statements have attacked homosexuals violently. James **Baldwin** (1924–1987), excoriated by the radical black community for "collaboration," never ventured on a theatrical equivalent of *Giovanni's Room*. Ed Bullins (b. 1935), who portrayed a stereotypical "bull dyke" in *Clara's Ole Man* (1965), boasted that his directors were not "twisted and trying to find the latest fad that the faggots are trying to make a new *Hair* out of."

The reference was to the "hippie" musical *Hair* (1967), which, with the pseudo-sophisticated revue *Oh! Calcutta!* (1969), presented unorthodox sexual practices as natural variants; but the notion of homosexual as villain persisted even in a counter-culture phenomenon like the rock musical *Jesus Christ Superstar* (by Andrew Lloyd Webber, 1971): the disciple who loves Christ most ardently turned out to be Judas, and Herod is played as a sequined screamer. Exclusively gay musicals could not redress the balance: Al Carmines' (b. 1936) *The Faggot* (1973), meant as a populist and ecumenical plea for love, was scorned by activists for stereotyping, and the novelties *Boy Meets Boy* (by Bill Solly and Donald Ward, 1975) and *Lovers* (1975) enjoyed no particular shelf-life. However, *The Rocky Horror Show* (1973) by Richard O'Brien, especially in its cult film avatar, revealed how familiar *psychopathia sexualis* had become to a youthful mass public.

More vital was the explosion of "low camp" **transvestitic theatre** that emerged from New York's underground, in tandem with Andy **Warhol**'s Factory. Characteristically, the earliest of these playwrights were Warhol hangers-on: the transvestite actor Jackie Curtis (b. 1947) with *Glamour, Glory and Gold: The Life*

of Nola Noonan, Goddess and Star (1967), and the scenarist Ronald Tavel (b. 1941) with the jungle extravaganza *Gorilla Queen* (1966). An important hothouse was John Vaccaro's Theater of the Ridiculous, which forged one major talent in the person of Charles Ludlam (1940–1987). The basic technique of the Ridiculous style was pastiche, trashing Western civilization by mingling high culture and popular totems, and lacing it all with genital humor and gender switches. Ludlam's plays, beginning with *When Queens Collide* (1967), and culminating in his own Ridiculous Theatrical Company (*Bluebeard*, 1970; *The Grand Tarot*, 1971; *Camille*, 1973; *Stage Blood*, 1974, etc.) were virtual palimpsests, shrewdly inlaying classical allusions and quotations into pop art. A consummate comedian, best known for his portrayals of Marguerite Gautier and Galas (a monster diva based on Callas), Ludlam was surrounded by lesser talents whose ineptitude made its own comment on the aspirations of the professional theatre. His influence is strong on such an epigone as Charles Busch (b. 1955), whose *Vampire Lesbians of Sodom* (1985) and *Psycho Beach Party* (1987) are less cultured, less threatening, and therefore more accessible than Ludlam's work.

In the wake of the political events of 1968, feminist and gay liberation politics gave rise to a number of agitprop groups, and by the mid-1970s, theatre collectives and "coming-out" plays burgeoned. In London, Gay Sweatshop, organized by Ed Berman in 1975, staged lunchtime bills of short plays dealing with identity, censorship, and relationships; the actors were professionals, many of whom, such as Simon Callow and Anthony Sher (both b. 1949), were to become highly articulate luminaries of the establishment stage. In 1977, the Sweatshop divided into men's and women's groups, the latter tending to revue-like formats. In Holland, the Rooie Flikkers (or The Softies) became prominent.

New York counterparts likes TOSOS (The Other Side of the Stage, New York, 1972–77) and the Stonewall Theater were both more polemical and less professional in their achievements; they developed their own playwrights, such as Doric Wilson (b. 1939), William M. Hoffman (b. 1939), Philip Blackwell and Arch Brown, who preached to the converted, but provided a sense of cultural solidarity. Jonathan Katz' docudrama *Coming Out!* (1975) supplied a useful history lesson for the newly aware. The Glines Theater (founded 1976) nurtured talents like Fierstein, whose early work, such as *Flatbush Tosca* (1975), made comment through reductive comedy; and the gifted Jane Chambers (1937–1983), whose *Last Summer at Bluefish Cove* (1980) has become a staple in lesbian theatre. The proliferation of similar groups in other cities led to the creation of a Gay Theater Alliance in 1978 to provide a network. Gender-fuck troupes like The Cockettes and the Angels of Light in San Francisco and Centola and the Hot Peaches, another Warhol-sponsored enterprise, in New York, combined shock tactics, high camp, glitter rock, and reverse glamor to achieve their effects. They have been succeeded by less strident, more recondite performance artists like Tim Miller and Holly Hughes.

Lesbian Troupes. A score of lesbian ensembles quickly sprang up in the wake of feminist theatre groups, among them the Lavender Cellar in Minneapolis (founded 1973), the Red Dyke Theater in Atlanta (founded 1974), and the Lesbian-Feminist Theater Collective of Pittsburgh (founded 1977). Although they produced plays by Chambers, Pat Surcicle (*Prisons*, 1973), and the poetic imagist Joan Schenkar, their repertories, as in England, emphasized satiric revue. This was especially the case at the WOW Cafe in New York's East Village, founded by Lois Weaver and Peggy Shaw in 1982; Alice Forrester's subversive parody *Heart of the Scorpion* and Holly Hughes' self-regarding satire *The Well of Horniness* (both 1985) were typical offerings.

Developments in World Theatre. Australia, perhaps because of its willfully macho image, tended to dramatize homosexual life in transvestite terms, equating the gay male with the drag queen. The best-known examples are Peter Kenna's (b. 1930) *Mates* (1975), whose catalytic character is yet another depressed and depressive nightclub performer; and Steve J. Spears' (b. 1951) *The Elocution of Benjamin Franklin* (1976), a one-character tragi-comedy of a middle-aged cross-dresser who gets too close to a student and ends up all but lobotomized. A Gay Theater Company was formed in Sydney in 1979 to present a more balanced picture of the varieties of homosexual experience.

Outside the English-speaking world, homosexuality has not played a pre-eminent part in mainstream drama. Even **Mishima** (1925–1970) did not choose to treat it, although his own sado-masochistic penchants surface in his Kabuki play *The Drawn-Bow Moon* (1969), in which a naked samurai is tortured on stage. In Germany, Martin Sperr's (b. 1941) *Jagdszenen aus Niederbayern* (Hunting Scenes from Lower Bavaria, 1966), showing a young mechanic destroyed by his narrow-minded provincial community, created a stir and was filmed. The German-language theatre, on the whole, seemed to equate homosexuality with violence. The Austrian dramatist Wolfgang Bauer (b. 1941) in *Magic Afternoon* (1968) had two layabouts indulge in kissing to torment a young woman, and in *Change* (1969) a gay art-dealer has his face shoved in broken glass. In Bodo Strauss' *Der Park* (The Park, 1985), Cyprian, the type of the creative artist, is brutally murdered by the black park-attendant he fancies. Rainer **Fassbinder** used his films more than his plays to express his concepts of social and interpersonal exploitation.

Although Parisian audiences flocked to a boulevard farce like *La Cage aux Folles*, a more select public has appreciated the absurdist plays of Argentinian-born Copi: he has played in his own works, such as *Le homosexuel ou La difficulté de s'exprimer* (The Homosexual or The Difficulty of Self-Expression, 1971) and *Le Frigo* (The Fridge, 1983). The Soviet theatre, reflecting its society, has diligently avoided the subject; productions of Williams' *Streetcar* and Ronald Harwood's *The Dresser*, for instance, cut all allusions to homosexuality. In Italy, on the other hand, the fashionable theatre and opera have been dominated by elegant director–designers like Luchino **Visconti** and his disciple Franco Zeffirelli (b. 1923). They were responsible for introducing Williams and Albee to Italy, but their flamboyant wielding of high style was often vitiated by a penchant for garish melodrama and maudlin sentimentality.

The **AIDS** crisis has spawned a number of nonce dramas, modern versions of the problem play, where the message is more important than the medium: Larry Kramer's *The Normal Heart*, William M. Hoffman's *As Is*, Rebecca Ranson's *Warren*, Robert Chesley's *Night Sweat*, and the Theater Rhinoceros' dramatic collage *The AIDS Show* (all 1985). They affected the audiences that sought them out, but when they entered the repertory of regional theatres, subscribers often stayed away, refusing to confront the problem of "others." AIDS also had an impact on the theatre by decimating its ranks, its victims including Ludlam and the director–choreographer Michael Bennett (1943–1987), along with dozens of rank-and-file members of the profession. The glaring gaps left in the performing arts by these deaths reveal how dependent they have been on homosexual talent.

BIBLIOGRAPHY. Stefan Brecht, *Queer Theatre*, Frankfurt am Main: Suhrkamp, 1978; Kaier Curtin, *'We Can Always Call Them Bulgarians': The Emergence of Lesbians and Gay Men on the American Stage*, Boston: Alyson, 1987; Terry Helbing, *Gay Theater Alliance Directory of Gay Plays*, New York: JH Press, 1980.

Laurence Senelick

THEBES

Site of the Mycenean citadel of Cadmus (legendary personification of the Semitic peoples of the East), Thebes was the capital of Boeotia in central **Greece** in classical times.

The Theban cycle, celebrated by Sophocles and other writers, offers several salient erotic themes. Cadmus' descendant Laius, warned by an oracle that his son would slay him, forwent sex with his wife Jocasta. Unaware of the danger and frustrated, she got him drunk, had intercourse with him, and in nine months produced the infant Oedipus, whom he ordered to be exposed. Laius was then exiled to the Peloponnesus. Exclaiming "nature compels me," he then raped Chrysippus, his host's 12-year old son, causing a curse to follow him to his Thebes when he returned. Oedipus, saved by a shepherd, grew to manhood, slew his father whom he did not recognize in distant parts, and came to Thebes. Here he ended the plague, married the widowed Jocasta, and sired children by her to begin a new round of tragedies including the execution of his daughter Antigone by her uncle Creon for burying her rebel brother.

After **Crete** and **Sparta**, from which institutionalized **pederasty** was imported about 600 B.C., Thebes became the place Greeks most often named as the locus for the formal type of pederasty. In **Plato**'s *Laws*, the Athenian declares that in Elis and Boeotia (including Thebes) they practiced pederasty uninhibitedly, each adult male living together with the boy he loved. The greatest pederastic poet, **Pindar**, resided in Thebes. When **Alexander the Great** destroyed the rebel city, he left Pindar's house standing to demonstrate his love of culture. After Sparta and Athens exhausted each other in the great Peloponnesian War, Pelopidas and Epaminondas, in exile in Athens, formed an aristocratic conspiracy to liberate their city.

Bravely surprising the Spartan garrison, they organized the Sacred Band (later copied by the Carthaginians) of 300 pairs of lovers, which defeated Sparta at Leuctra (371 B.C.) and Mantinea (362 B.C.) and liberated Messenia, ending Spartan hegemony. Epaminondas was slain at Mantinea with his second *eromenos* (beloved) bravely falling at his side. During the three-cornered struggle that ensued between a leaderless Thebes, a crippled Sparta, and an Athens that had not fully recovered from the Peloponnesian War, Persians interfered and Macedonians encroached. The Greeks were defeated at Chaeronea in 338 B.C., when the Sacred Band died fighting to the last man, and even Philip of Macedonia, the victor, paid tribute to their valor: "Let no man speak evil of such heroes."

Plutarch, a hereditary Theban noble who held a priesthood at Delphi, recorded the careers of notable pederasts in his *Parallel Lives of Famous Greeks and Romans*, and his *Dialogues on Love* debated the relative merits of women and boys.

The ancient city of Thebes possessed two **gymnasia**, one dedicated to Heracles, the other to Iolaus, often regarded in classic times as his *eromenos*. At the latter place pairs of male lovers were accustomed to pledge their troth. About three miles outside the city lay the Kabeirion, the shrine of a mystery cult revolving around the god Kabeiros and his Pais ("boy"); here modern archeologists have found votive offerings depicting a man and a boy, who is often portrayed holding an animal—a traditional courtship gift.

BIBLIOGRAPHY. Nancy H. Demand, *Thebes in the Fifth Century*, Boston: Routledge & Kegan Paul, 1982.

William A. Percy

THEOCRITUS (CA. 301–CA. 260 B.C.)

Hellenistic philologist and poet. A native of Syracuse, he sojourned in southern Italy and Cos, but having failed to win the patronage of Hiero of Syracuse, he finally won that of Ptolemy II, the founder of the Museum and Library that together with his munificent patronage made **Alexandria** the intellectual center of the **Hellenistic monarchies**. In the famous controversy about the Argonauts, he sided with Callimachus against Apollonius of Rhodes, both of whom resided in Alexandria and sang of pederasty.

Though set in **Sicily**, his bucolic poems were written after he moved to the east, perhaps while he tarried on Cos. He composed his mimes mostly in Alexandria. Like most other Hellenistic poets, he preferred short, polished, erudite, contrived poems. He often chose exotic or at least novel themes and made fresh observations and descriptions. Besides pastoral heterosexual love, he dramatized the love of Heracles for Hylas. Eight of his thirty *Idylls*, the authorship of two of which is uncertain, treat boy love exclusively.

Theocritus used two archaic terms: for lover *eispnelas* (inspirer), employed in Alcman, and for beloved the non-Dorian Thessalian *aites*, (inspired), employed by Alcman to mean "pretty girl" in the feminine. The idyll on Hylas (XIII), Heracles' beloved, gave Theocritus an opportunity to express his personal feelings on boy-love. It is not just mortals, but the immortals as well, who suffer the pangs of love. Heracles is determined to educate the curly-haired boy with whom he is enamoured, to make a brave and renowned man of him, and to bring him up as a father would his son.

In Idyll XXIX Theocritus gives advice to a boy that follows strictly the lines earlier drawn by **Theognis**: the youth is urged to be faithful to his lover, not to play the coquette or exploit his admirer in a venal manner. Youth is fleeting, but with manhood love will yield to a solid and enduring friendship. Idyll XXX depicts a man who has reached the age that disqualifies him for conquests in love, but cannot suppress the passion that he feels for a boy who, while not particualrly handsome, has undeniable personal charm. This piece may well contain genuine autobiographical elements.

The two idylls in which shepherds and goatherds compete in song about their pederastic loves differ: in VII it is poets disguised as shepherds who display their rival skill, in V the speech belongs to genuine rustics, direct and even slightly coarse. Idyll VIII, which may not belong to Theocritus, presents two youths at the very onset of puberty, one in love with a boy, the other with a girl. This poem therefore treats homosexual love between early adolescent agemates, which in the eyes of at least some Greeks was perfectly legitimate. Inspired by the poetic tradition of male love begun by **Ibycus**, Anacreon, and **Pindar**, Theocritus' work proves that the old motifs and values of *paiderasteia* remained alive, at least in literature, into the Hellenistic era.

BIBLIOGRAPHY. Félix Buffière, *Eros adolescent; la pédérastie dans la Grèce antique*, Paris: Les Belles Lettres, 1980; Hans Licht, *Sexual Life in Ancient Greece*, London: Routledge & Kegan Paul, 1932.

William A. Percy

THEOGNIS
(FL. CA. 544–541 B.C.)

Greek elegiac poet. Many of the 1,390 lines, often cited in later works and inscribed on vases, attributed to him are but slightly altered versions of verses by Tyrtaeus, **Solon**, and other early poets, along with repetitions that seem to come from a different hand. In addition, references to people and events in the *Theognidea* extend from 580 to 490, and the surviving verses differ from those cited by the tenth-century Greek lexicon of Suda. Consequently, the extant works seem to be a highly popular Athenian collection made in the fifth century to be sung at **symposia**, and it is difficult to tell which ones originated with Theognis himself.

The gnomology (collection of maxims) addressed to Cyrnus, the poet's beloved boy who appears in many of the poems, may be genuine. With a clear aristocratic bias, Theognis berated the boy, whom he was trying to improve, for flirtations and infidelities. Full of advice on friendship, loyalty, and other conduct befitting a gentleman, Theognis is often taken as the model for the supposed old-fashioned one-to-one erotic relationship used as the basis for *paideia* (instruction). Theognis' collection of maxims, of which the last 158 deal exclusively with boy-love, served in antiquity as a manual of ethical conduct. The poet could not fail to "fawn on" the boy so long as the boy's cheek was beardless. Others, however, find his constant carping and complaints, his reproaches to ungrateful or self-interested boys, distasteful, especially in comparison with the free love advocated by his contemporaries **Ibycus** and Anacreon. Called by some the father of gnomic poetry, Theognis (whom Sir Kenneth Dover unconvincingly dubs the most important early pederastic poet), taught ethics and statecraft in a context of male love, and otherwise emphasized the intellectual and moral formation of the youth as well. His verse thus reflected the role of pederasty in the golden age of Hellenic civilization. In elegies that he composed to be sung accompanied by the flute at symposia, he claimed (probably an interpolation after the fact) that his verse had given Cyrnus immortality, and that youths at symposia would always sing of him: "Woe is me! I love a smooth-skinned lad who exposes me to all my friends, nor am I loath; I will bear with many things that are sore against my liking, and make it no secret; for 'tis no unhandsome lad I am seen to be taken with."

BIBLIOGRAPHY. Kenneth Dover, *Greek Homosexuality*, Cambridge, MA: Harvard University Press, 1978; Thomas J. Figueira and Gregory Nagy, eds., *Theognis of Megara: Poetry and Polis*, Baltimore: Johns Hopkins University Press, 1985.

William A. Percy

THIRD SEX

The notion that homosexuals constitute a third sex, **intermediate** between the poles of the heterosexual male and the heterosexual female, became popular in the nineteenth century. Yet it has some interesting forerunners and analogues. In the myth recounted by Aristophanes in **Plato**'s *Symposium*, the androgynous double beings are termed the "third race," the irony being that these are presented as the archetypes of heterosexual persons who in their present sundered state are always seeking to reunite with their lost half of the opposite sex. Somewhat more to the point is a usage that may have been influential: according to his biographer in the *Scriptores Historiae Augustae*, the Emperor Alexander Severus (reigned A.D. 222–235) spoke slightingly of eunuchs as the *tertium genus hominum* third class of men). The idea is modeled on Latin grammar which recognizes three genders: masculine, feminine, neuter. There is also a grammatical category called *epicene*, for a noun capable of designating either sex; from this technical usage derives the sexual meaning of that word. A satirical attack on the court of the effeminate **Henri III**, *L'Île des Hermaphrodites* (1605), states that in the language of that imaginary country only the common gender (epicene) is known.

Historical forerunners notwithstanding, the use of the concept of the third sex to designate homosexuals seems to have first taken hold in nineteenth-century France. While for Théophile Gautier in *Mademoiselle de Maupin* (1836) the expression "troisième sexe à part" refers to a woman with the qualities of a man (but not a lesbian), in *Splendeur et misère des courtisanes* (1847), Balzac equates "le troisième sexe" with the slang term "tante"—homosexual.

The German equivalent, *drittes Geschlecht*, was introduced by the homosexual reformer K. H. **Ulrichs** (*Vindex*, 1864). At the turn of the century the notion enjoyed a great vogue in Germany, owing in part to the fact that it accorded well with the *Zwischenstufen* (**intermediate**) theories of Magnus **Hirschfeld** and his circle, who amassed data ostensibly showing that homosexual subjects on many indices fell halfway between the normal man and the normal woman. Hirschfeld himself wrote a book on the gay subculture of Wilhelmine Berlin under the title *Berlins drittes Geschlecht*, and the Committee prepared for mass distribution a pamphlet *Was soll das Volk vom dritten Geschlecht wissen?* (What Should the People Know About the Third Sex?). However, a considerable number of homosexual men and women deviate from the norm for their gender solely in their sexual orientation, so that even sympathizers of Hirschfeld dismissed the label as untenable. Although the name *The Third Sex* was conferred on the American release of a 1957 West German film about homosexuality, the expression is now relatively uncommon and enjoys no scientific credence.

While the theory under discussion is now obsolete, in other realms of discourse the overarching conceptual process of enlarging an original binary opposition into a trichotomy may be a valid procedure. Anthropologists, such as Claude Lévi-Strauss, have observed the transformation of dichotomies into trichotomies in the mythology and social organization of tribal societies. In European civilization, the **Anglican** church has sometimes claimed to occupy a third position between the poles of Roman Catholicism and Protestantism. The democratic socialism of **Sweden** has similarly been extolled as a "middle way" between capitalism and communism. In other instances the third element is not an intermediate wedged in the interstice between an original pair, but the last in a series (e.g., Moscow as the "third Rome"; old age as the "third age"). In today's political language the case of the Third World is ambivalent; it may be regarded as intermediate between the other two worlds (neutralism) or set apart from them by reason of its dependent and colonial status—in which case the trichotomy virtually collapses into a dichotomy. The notion was clearly suggested by the analogy with the Third Estate which at the end of the Old Regime was demanding its share of the political power previously monopolized by the clergy and the nobility.

The French philologist Georges Dumézil has argued that tripartition is an archetypal component of the original institutions and religious ideas of the **Indo-European** peoples, who think in terms of the three functions of sovereignty, power, and fecundity. However this may be, the examples cited support the view that formations in terms of threeness are characteristic of human institutions—or of the cultural interpretation of biological givens—but rarely of the biological world itself. Thus our bodies have either one organ (the heart, the nose) or two (eyes, kidneys, arms); never three. So the "third sex" was in the last analysis a social more than a biological reality.

BIBLIOGRAPHY. Claude Courouve, *Vocabulaire de l'homosexualité masculine*, Paris: Payot, 1985, pp. 212–16.

Wayne R. Dynes

TIBULLUS, ALBIUS (50–17 B.C.)

Latin elegiac poet. Apart from his own writings, a poor anonymous biography and references in **Horace** and Ovid furnish the only data on Tibullus' life. In the tradition of poetic lovers that the Latins borrowed from the Greeks, he complained of poverty and failed to gain Maecenas' patronage. Only the first two of the four books ascribed to Tibullus are actually his. Book One celebrates impartially his love for his mistress Delia and for his boyfriend Marathus. Book Two contains poems to another mistress, Nemesis. Occasional pieces in the two books honor his patron Massalla. The third book contains six brief poems by Sulpicia and poems about her

that are perhaps by Tibullus himself. Quintilian termed Tibullus, who combined deceptive simplicity with refinement, the "most terse and elegant" of Latin elegists.

A frequent subject of Tibullus is the *puer delicatus*, the boy who, in the Hellenic tradition, would be young, handsome, and even girlish, that is to say, with none of the repellent coarseness of the adult male. But the Roman counterpart, or those of the **Hellenistic monarchies**, is cruel, unfaithful, and mercenary, closer to the Alexandrian or modern hustler or kept boy than to the classical *eromenos*. Marathus, Tibullus' love, conforms to type: endowed with beautiful hair and a fair complexion, somewhat femininely preoccupied with his physical appearance and the use of cosmetics. He torments his lovers, lies to them, and is unfaithful to them. At one point Tibullus considers terminating the unhappy affair with its psychologically sado-masochistic overtones. Yet Marathus himself, when he falls in love and is repaid in the same coin, is reduced to childish whining and tearful bewilderment. In all these respects Roman pederasty as depicted by Tibullus, like that of **Alexandria**, came nearer than did the Hellenic antecedents to certain modern unedifying variants of the homoerotic liaison.

BIBLIOGRAPHY. P. Murgatroyd, "Tibullus and the Puer Delicatus," *Acta Classica*, 20 (1977), 105–19; Amy Richlin, *The Garden of Priapus: Sexuality and Aggression in Roman Humor*, New Haven: Yale University Press, 1983.

William A. Percy

TILDEN, WILLIAM T., II (1893–1953)

American tennis player. Also known as Big Bill and Gentleman Bill Tilden, he was voted the most outstanding athlete of the first half of the twentieth century by the National Sports Writers Association, ahead of such notables as Babe Ruth, Jack Dempsey, and Johnny

Weissmuller. He was the first American to win at Wimbleton and during the 1920s he remained undefeated in any major match for seven years. He revolutionized the game of tennis and some of his writing on the subject (*The Art of Tennis*) is still considered to be authoritative. Tilden was known as a theatrical tennis player and was very popular with spectators.

He had a great interest in the arts and wrote a novel, *Glory's Net*, many short stories, a silent film, *Hands of Hope*, and an autobiography, *My Story*. He had an intense interest in the theatre and made frequent unsuccessful attempts at acting, often producing his own shows, starring himself.

He was well known for living a lavish life, driving expensive cars, staying in elegant hotels and socializing with the rich and the famous—he was a good friend of Charlie Chaplin. He often traveled with an entourage of handsome teenaged male tennis protégés. When his homosexuality became better known, he was ostracized from the tennis world and was banned from the most prestigious tennis courts. Eventually, he was convicted of contributing to the delinquency of a minor and sent to jail in 1947. Although it was clear that the young man with whom he was caught having sex had no objection to the sexual relations, the court decided to make an example of the famous tennis player. He served six months of a one-year sentence. Tilden died of a heart attack, impoverished, in relative obscurity six years later.

BIBLIOGRAPHY. Frank Deford, *Big Bill Tilden: The Triumphs and the Tragedy*, New York: Simon and Schuster, 1975; Arthur Voss, *Tilden and Tennis in the Twenties*, Troy, NY: Whitson, 1985.
Brian Pronger

TOILET SEX

Most men who patronize public toilets view them as repellent places that are to be utilized and left as quickly as possible. Yet **urination** requires the taking out of the penis and lingering is sometimes a legitimate aspect of answering the call of nature (or can be made to appear so), so that it is not surprising that sexual activities might occur there. A common pattern is for one man to stand for a time at a urinal and show his erect penis; another will then touch it, an implicit contract is accepted—usually wordlessly—and the sexual act is expeditiously completed. Others prefer the somewhat more private toilet stalls, though here it may be somewhat harder to lure others to join in the action. Some of the more commonly used places have the institution of the "watch queen," who through a cough or some other clear signal will indicate the approaching presence of outsiders who may be offended.

The notion, found in some popular books on sex, that gay men are inveterate cruisers of toilets is an overstatement; many homosexuals report a pronounced distaste for undertaking any sexual activity in such places. In fact, Laud Humphreys' classic monograph showed that the overwhelming majority of the sexual customers of the Illinois toilet he studied were bisexuals leading outwardly "normal" heterosexual lives. Such men may be reluctant to frequent gay bars or saunas, but do not regard public toilets as gay-identified social space. No equivalent lesbian practice is known.

Toilets that are known for their sexual activities are described colloquially as "tea rooms." In England the practice of visiting these establishments is termed "cottaging." Some are found on university campuses, in train and bus stations, and at highway rest stops. Appropriate **graffiti** may signal the possibility of sexual activity, so that someone visiting during an off hour may be alerted to return. Such graffiti may also alert isolated homosexuals to the existence of others, previously unsuspected. Occasionally, overcrowding may cause legitimate complaints on the part of straight patrons, but often a single scandalized visitor will demand police action. Regrettably, many toilet visitors, some caught by enticement methods initiated by members of the police force, have had their careers ruined through being detected in the process of "tea-room trade." Insignificant as the offense may have been, the publicity attending the arrest and eventual trial, and the inclusion of the offender's name in centralized files of "known sex deviates," were enough to stigmatize the individual for life. Sometimes the authorities attempt to discourage sex in toilets by removing the stall doors or modifying the structures architecturally so that privacy will be reduced.

A special adaptation of toilets for sexual purposes is often found in the form of "glory holes," openings surreptitiously drilled or carved into the partitions separating the stalls. These serve for the insertion of the erect penis which is then fellated by the occupant of the other booth. This practice combines anonymity, a sense of concentration on the affected organ, and an element of danger that goes even beyond the usual one of employing the public john for sexual purposes. The problem of being unpleasantly surprised was obviated in the glory-hole clubs, commercial establishments that enjoyed some popularity in the late 1970s. With the rising awareness of the need for safe sex, these clubs have largely faded away. Not so, however, the do-it-yourself glory holes in public toilets: despite an often relentless campaign by custodians to close these apertures, they mysteriously keep reappearing.

BIBLIOGRAPHY. Edward W. Delph, *The Silent Community: Public Homosexual Encounters*, Beverly Hills, CA: Sage, 1978; Laud Humphreys, *Tearoom Trade: Impersonal Sex in Public Places*, Chicago: Aldine, 1970.

Ward Houser

TRADE

As a term of gay slang, this word is the modern parallel of ancient Greek, Latin, and Old Norse terms for a male who remains strictly in the **active** role of penetrator, and who usually considers himself heterosexual or bisexual, an attitude which also perpetuates archaic concepts under which only the receiver or *pathic* was considered to be departing from gender norms of appropriate sexual behavior. The modern slang usage probably derives from the association with young male **prostitutes**, engaged in "the sex trade," who are only available in the penetrator role. Trade is generally a term which is not self-applied, but only used by the receptive partner or by uninvolved homosexuals.

The prevalence of trade behavior is usually underestimated since its adherents seldom write books, join organizations, or fill out survey questionnaires. Nevertheless, it may well be that, from a global perspective that includes **Mediterranean**, **shamanistic**, **pederastic**, and Asian patterns, there are more "trade" men than reciprocating homosexuals, and even in advanced western societies this may be the case for members of the **working class**, where the sense that only the passive partner is homosexual is best preserved. Certainly there are extensive areas of sexual encounter outside prostitution in which trade behavior is not only common in western industrial societies, but expected by the receptive partner: cruising military men, **seafarers**, truck drivers, hitchhikers, teenagers, patrons of **toilets** frequented by the general public, frequenters of interstate highway rest areas, those involved in interracial sex, and men in jail or **prison**.

The trade pattern seems to serve as an intermediate stage of **coming out** often enough to have engendered the widespread homosexual saying "Today's trade is tomorrow's competition," but it would be a mistake to draw too broad a conclusion from this saying, which may also reflect the tendency which causes some homosexuals to label anyone and everyone a **queen**. It is not a saying with much currency among those homosexuals who prefer trade for various reasons and who are perhaps more knowledgeable about their patterns. Those who are familiar with scenes in which **"situational"** trade homosexuality can be observed over a longer period of time (prisons, **military** areas, boarding schools) do not see much evidence to support the validity of the saying; if anything, they would report that "today's trade is tomorrow's married heterosexual."

"Rough trade" is a term denoting a potentially dangerous or ruffian male, virtually always self-defined as heterosexual, and who often demonstrates feelings of guilt or remorse after ejaculation which can erupt into violence directed at his partner. Nevertheless, there are not a few homosexuals who find rough trade particularly appealing. Many professional male prostitutes are termed "rough trade" because of their image as "tough guys" even though their actual potential for violence is low, a few highly publicized exceptions notwithstanding.

Research on homosexuality in this century has tended to avoid **role** analysis and focused instead on self-defined homosexuals rather than occasional participants. Clearly, the trade phenomenon needs a great deal more research before investigators can contemplate closing the books on the phenomenon of same-sex relations.

Stephen Donaldson

TRAGEDY
See **Theatre and Drama.**

TRANSSEXUALISM

Transsexualism is the wish for change of sex. This longing may be defined as a gender **identity** disorder characterized by the subject's intense desire for transformation by hormonal or surgical means, or both, into the gender opposite his original one at birth. This insistence is grounded in complete identification with the **gender** role of the opposite sex. The transsexual is thus the ultimate form of what has come to be known as the gender **dysphoria** syndrome.

Such individuals seek to deny and reverse their original biological gender and cross over into the role of the opposite gender. Transsexuals emulate the characteristics of the opposite gender in behavior, dress, attitude, and sexual orientation, and aspire to attain the anatomical structure of the genitalia of the opposite sex. The request for the so-called sex-change operation becomes the obsessive goal of the transsexual's life and brings him to the door of the physician, but in their request for sex reassignment surgery (SRS) they present themselves to the surgeon, not the psychiatrist. They reject the implication that psychiatric referral is required, since they do not conceive their dilemma in psychiatric terms but as a consequence of having been born into the wrong body. In a sense, transsexualism may be considered iatrogenic, in that advances in surgical technique and hormonal therapy now permit the realization of longings for sexual metamorphosis that once belonged to the realm of **mythology** and fairy tales.

History. This fact became known to the public after the famous Jorgensen case in 1952, in which the reporting endocrinologist received letters from hundreds of individuals requesting SRS. A former sergeant in the American army was transformed from a male into an externally functioning female by a Danish plastic surgeon, Paul Fogh-Andersen, in Copenhagen, and Christine Jorgensen, as the individual was subsequently named, made headlines throughout the world. Controversy and criticism erupted almost at once and have continued to the present day, as some psychiatrists branded the whole procedure as medical malpractice.

However sensationalized the case may have been, it called public attention to the fact that surgical relief was available to the sufferer from gender **dysphoria**, and thousands of such individuals came forward to demand the sex change operation. Many of these individuals were referred to Harry Benjamin (1885–1987), who promoted the term *trans-*

sexualism in an article published in the *International Journal of Sexology* in 1953, and continued to provide evaluation, hormone treatment, and referral to medical centers in the United States who would perform SRS. He culminated his years of research and therapy with gender dysphoric patients with the publication of a landmark monograph on the subject, *The Transsexual Phenomenon* (1966), and to pursue his work the Harry Benjamin Gender Dysphoria Association was founded. Between 1969 and 1985 nine international gender dysphoria symposia were held, at which some 150 investigators from a variety of disciplines met to share their findings. Apparently the term transsexual, in its modern meaning, was introduced by the popular editor David O. Cauldwell in 1950.

Psychological Aspects. The relationship between homosexuality and gender dysphoria, particularly in the extreme form of transsexualism, requires clarification. Most homosexuals are satisfied with their sexual orientation and lifestyle, and like normal heterosexuals they have no wish to lose their genitalia. For both male and female homosexuals their genitalia are a source of intense pleasure. However, there are some whose primary homosexuality is so unacceptable to their egos that they cannot bear this sexual orientation. The transsexual frequently states his strong aversion to homosexuality and resents such an identification. Such a self-stigmatized, ego-alien, homosexually oriented gender dysphoric subject sees sex reassignment as the way out of his dilemma. SRS is more ego-integral to such an individual, and the surgeon treating him, than is homosexuality. Some 30–35 percent of those requesting SRS fall into this category.

By contrast, there are also gender dysphoric individuals who demonstrate a fixed and consistent cross-gender identification. Such patients establish themselves as primary transsexuals and successfully pass the "real life" test of cross-gender

living and hormonal therapy for one to two years. Some are actively engaged in psychotherapy before and after this trial period, but all undergo an evaluation process by a professional in the mental health field. Only then is it appropriate to recommend the patient to an experienced surgeon for SRS. Even after this careful screening process, some 10–15 percent of operated patients are thought to have an unsatisfactory outcome from SRS. Most of these probably had an unsatisfactory surgical reconstruction or were improperly selected. Interestingly enough, none of the female transsexuals who were rejected as candidates renounced their gender dysphoria or their pursuit of SRS; they are a more homogeneous diagnostic group than their male counterparts and generally better candidates for SRS.

Medical Aspects. The surgical procedure involves the removal of the penis, scrotum, and testicles, and the creation of a functional neovagina. A successful psychological outcome is largely dependent upon a good functional result, which includes the ability to engage in sexual intercourse without pain or discomfort. The breast enlargement secondary to estrogen therapy is usually not sufficient to preclude breast augmentation mammoplasty, while other forms of plastic surgery are occasionally requested to improve the feminine appearance.

For female-to-male transsexuals the surgical techniques are not so well developed. It is easy enough to remove the breasts by mastectomy, while in the genital area total hysterectomy, salpingo-oophorectomy, and vaginectomy may be performed initially. The creation of an artificial penis is a very complicated and multistaged procedure, which may not allow for functioning that includes penetration. The difficulties inherent in the surgical construction of a penis have not yet been overcome.

Conclusion. Transsexualism remains an object of controversy within the segment of the medical profession that is concerned with the problem. Some clinics now uniformly refer the patient to **psychotherapy** in the belief that the desire for change of sex is intrinsically pathological, while others maintain that SRS is the treatment of choice for carefully evaluated, genuine, primary transsexuals. The broader dimensions of the problem lead into the question of gender identity and the manner in which it is defined by a particular society and experienced by the individual suffering from gender dysphoria.

See also **Hermaphrodite**.

BIBLIOGRAPHY. Harry Benjamin, *The Transsexual Phenomenon*, New York: The Julian Press, 1966; Anne Bolin, "Transsexualism and the Limits of Traditional Analysis," *American Behavioral Scientist*, 31 (1987), 41–65; Ira B. Pauly and Milton T. Edgerton, "The Gender Identity Movement: A Growing Surgical–Psychiatric Liaison," *Archives of Sexual Behavior*, 15 (1986), 315–29.

Warren Johansson

TRANSVESTISM (CROSS-DRESSING)

Most human societies recognize a basic polarity in **clothing** that is deemed appropriate for men and women. In some tribal cultures the distinction takes the form of the material used for the garments: animal products for men, plant fibers for women. Modern industrial societies have adopted a paradigm stemming from the early Middle Ages in Europe in which men wear trousers while women wear dresses. These distinctions are not always rigidly applied so that, after initial disapproval, the adoption of some types of trousers by women in contemporary society has been taken as a matter of course. As a cultural symbol transvestism, sometimes termed cross-dressing, becomes effective only when it is recognized that a norm is being transgressed. In our society, male transvestites are more "marked" than female, and thus more likely to encounter censure.

Psychosocial Aspects. A popular opinion identifies transvestism with homosexual **orientation**. This perception reflects the **stereotype** that homosexuals are driven to adopt the conduct and sensibilities of the opposite sex (**"inversion"**). Yet modern sociological studies have determined that many—perhaps even a majority—of men who engage in cross-dressing are heterosexual. There are married men who insist on wearing female undergarments. Other men join clubs where they can dress in full drag, basking in the company and approval of like-minded fellows. Both forms are relatively private, contrasting with the public display of the more flamboyant drag queen. Although the dynamic of heterosexual transvestism is not yet fully understood, it surely reflects in part a fetishistic attachment to the garments characteristically worn by women, whom the cross-dresser idolizes.

Transvestism, especially when found among male homosexuals (drag queens), is often confused with **transsexualism** or change of sex. Of course many preoperative transsexuals adopt women's dress as a way of gradually acculturating themselves to the identity they are to assume. Yet most homosexual transvestites have no desire to change their sex: the cross-dressing is an end in itself. Not all transvestites strive to achieve a perfect mimicry of the attire of the opposite sex. Some don only some components of the other **gender's** garments and make up, in modes that range from gentle mockery to the harsh parody of gender **roles** known as "gender fuck." In the view of some feminists, male transvestism stems from hatred of women, but most men who engage in full transvestism would affirm that they admire women, and that they are trying to bring forth the woman within themselves. Drag queens, who stand at the opposite end of the spectrum from leather adepts and the macho **clones**, have also evoked some hostility from non-cross-dressing gay men.

Terminology. The word transvestism (which became the standard term in contrast with Havelock **Ellis**'s preference for "eonism") was introduced by the German sex researcher Magnus **Hirschfeld** in 1910. Until then investigators of sexual deviation had classified the transvestites who came under their observation as homosexuals. Among his 7000 homosexual subjects Hirschfeld found 19 who had the urge to cross-dress while remaining heterosexually oriented, and on this basis he concluded that transvestism is a separate condition distinct from homosexuality.

Perhaps because it is sometimes confused with transsexualism and because of its clinical sound, the term transvestism is rejected by some in favor of "crossdressing." The latter term was first proposed by Edward Carpenter in 1911.

Historical Development. Among some tribal peoples, their exists an intermediate gender category filled by men who dress as women. These transvestite men do women's work, and sometimes have priestly and medical powers. They often, though not invariably, engage in homosexual activity with "full men." Among the peoples of eastern Siberia these individuals are known as **shamans**, in North America as **berdaches**, and in the Polynesian cultures of the **Pacific** as *mahu.*

In ancient Athens the festival of the Cotyttia was celebrated by men in women's clothing; in its later form it was characterized by homosexual orgies. Other cross-dressing festivals were celebrated at Argos, Sparta, and other places. Greek **mythology** knows figures who change their sex, and similar traditions are found in India and Africa. During the Roman empire men were sometimes forced to wear women's clothing as a form of humiliation. Before their martyrdom in 303 the soldier–saints Sergius and Bacchus were required to don women's clothing by the emperor. The purpose of this punishment seems to have been as a reprisal for their perceived violation of the requirements of military valor, and not for homosexuality, as one modern scholar has claimed.

The adoption of Christianity introduced an element of religious disapproval of transvestism, as seen in Deuteronomy 22:5: "The woman shall not wear that which pertaineth to a man, neither shall a man put on a woman's garment; for all that do so are an abomination unto the Lord thy God." Despite this prohibition medieval men and women still continued to cross-dress, though such activities tended to be restricted into such zones of licence as **Mardi Gras** or **Carnival**, when the "world was turned upside down." Over the centuries women travelers have often donned men's clothing for convenience and protection. Thus Sts. Pelagia and Marina assumed men's clothing, and even entered monasteries.

In the **theatre** throughout early modern Europe women's parts were taken by boys. In the seventeenth and eighteenth century the lavish clothing styles of the upper class seem to have stimulated desire for unusual clothing, so that men, not necessarily homosexual, could affect women's clothing as "fancy dress." The French nobleman François Timoléon de Choisy (1644–1724) began dressing in female attire as a boy; in adult life, though heterosexual, he often appeared at parties as a woman. The diplomat Charles d'Eon de Beaumont (1728–1810) found dressing as a woman an asset to his career as a spy. In North America Edward Hyde, Lord Cornbury, who was governor of New York and New Jersey from 1702 to 1708, was a heterosexual transvestite.

From eighteenth-century England come a number of reports of women who cross-dressed as men, in most instances to practice trades or enter the army. Henry Fielding's *The Female Husband* (1746) is a fictionalized account of the case of Mary Hamilton, who was convicted of fraud for posing as a man and subsequently marrying a woman. In the nineteenth century several women cross-dressed in order to become physicians. The woman known as

James Barry (1795–1865), not apparently a lesbian, rose to become senior Inspector-General of the British Army Medical Department. As these examples and other instances suggest, care is needed in assessing the sexual orientation of such individuals, who should not be assumed to be homosexual or lesbian without further evidence.

During the nineteenth and twentieth centuries cross-dressers have taken their cue from popular entertainment, including vaudeville, pantomime, nightclub entertainers, and television "impressionists." At certain points particular types of transvestism may engage the public's attention—as the "mannish lesbian" of the 1920s—and the publicity thus engendered may be picked up by gay men and lesbians and incorporated into their sense of self-presentation. That is to say, some gay people take up cross-dressing because that is the way they assume "they are supposed to be."

At its best, transvestism is a form of ludic behavior that causes society to take a fresh look at gender conventions. In the 1980s, when a whole branch of inquiry known as "gender studies," has emerged, the role of transvestism has been evaluated in new perspectives that point to a more complex understanding of the phenomenon.

BIBLIOGRAPHY. Peter Ackroyd, *Dressing Up: Transvestism and Drag: The History of an Obsession*, New York: Simon and Schuster, 1979; Vern L. Bullough, "Transvestism in the Middle Ages: A Sociological Analysis," *American Journal of Sociology*, 79 (1974), 1381–94; Rudolf M. Decker and Lotte C. van de Pol, *The Tradition of Female Transvestism in Early Modern Europe*, New York: St. Martin's Press, 1989; Havelock Ellis, *Studies in the Psychology of Sex*, vol. III, part 2, New York: Random House, 1936, pp. 1–110; Deborah Heller Feinbloom, *Transvestites and Transsexuals*, New York: Dell, 1976; Magnus Hirschfeld, *Die Transvestiten*, Berlin: Alfred Pulvermacher, 1910; Julia Wheelwright, *Amazons and Military Maids: Women Who Dressed as Men in the Pursuit of Life, Liberty and Happiness*, London: Pandora, 1988; Annie Woodhouse, *Fantastic Women: Sex, Gender, and Transvestism*, New Brunswick, NJ: Rutgers University Press, 1989.

Wayne R. Dynes

TRANSVESTISM, THEATRICAL

The androgynous **shaman** or **berdache** who, in primitive cultures, serves an important function as intermediary with the numinous, is considered by some scholars to be sublimated, in civilized societies, into the actor. The shape-changing powers of the shaman include sexual alternation as "celestial spouse," and it has been suggested that fear of this magic resides in the lingering prejudice against the "drag queen." The intermediate between shaman and drag queen was the performer: the German term *Schwuchtel* ("queen," "fairy") originally meant a player of comic dame roles, and the cultural historian Gisela Bleibtreu-Ehrenburg links it with the Latin *vetula*, a frivolous music maker. Among the Taosug people of the South Philippines of the **Pacific**, most musicians are *bantut* or homosexuals, expected to take the female role in courtship repartee; this association of performance and gender reversal implies a shamanistic origin, and confirms the close link between **effeminate** behavior and a special caste of performers.

Historical Origins. The origins of theatre in religious cults meant that women were barred from performance, a prohibition sustained by social sanctions against their public exhibition in general. Therefore, in Europe, before the seventeenth century, and in Asia, before the twentieth, female impersonation was the standard way to portray women on stage, and was considered far more normal than females playing females. The Greek theatre, devoted to the cross-dressing god **Dionysus**, was virtually transvestite by definition. Modern feminist theory argues that this usurpation of the female role by men was an act of suppression, which allowed a patriarchal society to transmit a false image of Woman. However, the Russian classicist Vyacheslav Ivanov, as far back as 1912, considered that the exclusion of the ecstatic maenad from the stage, by diminishing energy, enabled the necessary shift from rite to performance. (It has also been noted that, later, the entrance of women on the French stage under Henri IV and the English stage under Charles II signaled a descent in drama from the epic mode to the domestic or social mode.)

The **Roman** theatre accepted the convention, and scandal arose only when an emperor lost caste by becoming a performer. **Suetonius** tells us that **Nero** enacted the incestuous sister in the mime-drama *Macaris and Canace*, giving birth on stage to a baby that was then flung to the hounds; according to Aelius Lampridius, **Heliogabalus** played Venus in *The Judgment of Paris* with his naked body depilated.

In the Oriental theatre, the transvestite actor, as Roland **Barthes** has said, "does not copy woman but signifies her .... Femininity is presented to be read, not to be seen." Most Southeast Asian dance and drama forms kept the sexes apart in performance, allowing a certain amount of cross-sexual casting; what was to be impersonated had as much to do with aesthetic distinctions between coarseness and refinement as with physical or social gender definitions, so that women often played elegant young princes and men played abusive old women. In Bali, the powerful witch Rangda was always impersonated by a man, because only a man's strength could present and contain her dangerous and religiously empowered magic. These categories have become somewhat blurred in our time, with the admission of women into hitherto closed spheres of activity. By the 1920s, women had taken over the **Indonesian** dance opera *Aria*, but audiences still prefer all males in the operatic

form *Anja*. Similarly, boys dance their own versions of the highly feminine seduction dances, inciting male audiences to caress them after the performance. In popular Javanese drama *ludruk*, the transvestite, who off the stage may be a male prostitute, is an important figure, related to the **androgynous** priesthood of the past. He classifies himself as a woman, presenting not a realistic but a stylized portrait.

China. As early as A.D. 661, **Chinese** actors were segregated into exclusively male or female companies. Ch'en Wei oung's love poems to a boy actor in the seventeenth century are well known. The *tan* or female impersonator of Chinese opera, instituted ostensibly for moral reasons in the reign of Chi'en Lung (1735–1796), received a seven- to ten-year training and had to be an exceptionally graceful dancer, adept at manipulating his long sleeves. The *emploi* is sub-divided into *ching i* or *cheng tan* (virtuous woman); *hua tan* (seductive woman); *lao tan* (old woman), the most realistic; and *wu tan* (military woman). The great Mei Lan-fang (He Ming, 1894–1961), voted the most popular actor in China in 1924, combined virtuous and seductive elements in his portrayals; although he married and fathered a family, in his youth Mei had been the lover of powerful warlords. The clapper operas featuring *tan* had been, from their inception by Wei Ch'ang-cheng in the 1780s, considered by some a danger to public morals; but the first serious ban was imposed in 1963, instigated in part by Mao Tse-tung's wife Chiang Ching. When the Cultural Revolution ended, the *tan* returned, but no more were to be trained. A curious footnote is the liaison between the French diplomat Bernard Boursicot and the opera dancer Shi Pei Pu, in 1964, which produced a child; in 1983, it was discovered that the dancer was a male spy and the diplomat had been truly hoodwinked in their darkened bedroom. As *M. Butterfly* (1988), this incident was wrought into a successful Broadway play.

Japan. In **Japanese** No drama, although all the actors are male, sexual differences are not stressed, the same voice being used whether the role is masculine or feminine. In Kabuki, however, the *onnagata* (female impersonator) or *oyama* (literally, chief courtesan) is an extremely important line of business, with its sharply defined conventions. Originally, Kabuki was played by female prostitutes who often burlesqued men, particularly foreigners; in 1629 women were banned from the stage for reasons of morality. They were soon replaced by boys between eleven and fifteen (*wakashu*) who dressed like courtesans and were particularly beloved for their bangs; they acted out homosexual love affairs or methods of purchasing prostitutes. The increase in sexual relations between the boys and their admirers led to a new ban in 1652, and mature men with shaven foreheads had to take over the female roles. Although this brought about a more refined art, it did not alter the ambience: in the 1680–90s, 80 to 90 percent of the *onnagata* sprang from the ranks of catamites at the *iroko* or sex-boy teahouses. Despite the formalized grace and abstract femininity of the *onnagata*, an inherent characteristic of Kabuki has remained, as Donald Shively points out, "the peculiar eroticism with its homosexual overtones."

The *Ayamegusa* of Yoshizawa Ayame (1673–1729), the standard handbook, insisted that female impersonators behave as women in daily life, and blush if their wives are mentioned. Even a modern, married actor, Tomoemon, has declared, "One must *be* the woman, or else it is merely disguise." This helped maintain the homosexual tradition; boys in training often had relations with one another, while the actors, although lowest on the social scale, were much in demand as lovers (Minanojo, in particular, was the pederasts' *beau idéal*). Women sought to imitate the ideal of femininity they incarnated, and the beauties depicted in classical woodcuts are often *onnagata*. A dramatic genre known as *hengemaro* or the costume-change piece was created around 1697 to showcase their skills and perhaps nourish the clothing-fetishism that is a feature of Japanese culture. Lewdness in love scenes intensified between 1800 and 1840. With the Westernization of Japan, *onnagata* played in Ibsen and other modern dramas, but after World War II actors stopped being exclusive and played both male and female roles in Kabuki, the great exception being Nakamura Utaemon VI (b. 1917). Bando Tamasaburo (b. 1950) is one of the great cultural heroes of modern Japan; well-known as a homosexual who has had affairs with his leading men, he has extended his repertory to Lady Macbeth and Desdemona.

In 1914, a railway magnate founded the Takarazuka Revue Company outside Osaka to attract tourists; soon four troupes, made up entirely of unmarried girls, were performing in repertoire and touring the Pacific. Fifty girls are accepted annually after examinations in diction, singing, Japanese and western dancing, and then subjected to rigorous training; if they marry, they must leave the troupe. Their shows include both Western musicals and traditional folk plays, and their audiences are over 70 percent female; the *otokoyaku* or male impersonator is the star and idol of schoolgirls, who avidly read the fan magazines. The Takarazuka's popularity gave rise to the all-female Shochiku Revue, which resembles a lavish Las Vegas lounge act. Although the Takarazuka prides itself on its purity, in 1988 two of its graduates were involved in a failed love-suicide pact.

Transvestism in the West. Men dressing as women, particularly obstreperous women, was a tradition of saturnalia, Feasts of Fools, and medieval New Year's celebrations, and came to be used in political protest, allowing them to abnegate masculine responsibility and invest themselves with feminine instinct. Cross-dressing is a common accompaniment of carnival time, when norms are turned upside down; men giving birth was enacted at some Hindu festivals, and even Arlecchino in the late *commedia dell' arte* was shown birthing and breast feeding his infant.

But **Christianity**, from its inception, could not countenance such letting-off steam (John Chrysostom condemned cross-dressing in his Easter sermon of A.D. 399), and Western civilization has remained distrustful. By the nineteenth century most large European and American cities had enacted laws making cross-dressing a misdemeanor.

Early English Theatre Gender confusion drama was brought to England from Italy. One of the earliest and most intriguing examples was John Lyly's *Galathea* (1585), in which two girls disguised as boys fall in love with one another, and Venus promises to transform one into a male, to implement their romance. This was complicated by the fact that both girls were played by boys. Just as the Catholic church attacked unruly carnivals and **mardi gras** celebrations, **Protestant** clerics and Puritans censured the "sodomitical" custom of the boy-player on the Elizabethan and Jacobean stage. William Prynne in *Histriomastix* (1633) condemned the practice as "an inducement to sodomy." Boy companies dominated the English theatre until 1580; tradition has it that Portia was created by James Bryston, Lady Macbeth by Robert Goffe, Rosalind by Joseph Taylor, Juliet by Richard Robinson, Ophelia by Ned Alleyn, and Desdemona by Nathaniel Field, who was coached by Ben Jonson. Edward Kynaston (1640?–1706) was the last of the line, playing well into the Restoration when Pepys noted in his diary (1659): "Kynaston as Olympia made the loveliest lady that I ever saw in my life." At the same time in France, Louis XIV had no qualms about appearing in court masques as a bacchante (1651) and the goddess Ceres (1661).

The tradition of the boy actor had arisen in schools, and enjoyed a resurgence in the nineteenth century. The Hasty Pudding Club at Harvard (founded 1844), the Princeton Triangle Club, and the Mask and Wig in Philadelphia still thrive, even though the gender assumptions that inform them no longer obtain. Cambridge had organized an all-male dramatic society in 1855, Oxford in 1879; when **Cambridge**'s Footlights company tried to insert women into its comic revues, a storm of protest forced them to revert to their original practice.

Comedy. Women were members of *commedia dell'arte* troupes from the 16th century, but the comic characters occasionally donned petticoats to the delight of audiences, and this travesty aspect (already present in Aristophanes) grew more important as actresses gained popularity. If beauty and sex appeal were to be projected from the stage by a real woman, the post-menopausal woman could as easily be played by a comic actor; parts like Mme. Pernelle in Molière's *Tartuffe* and the nanny Yeremeevna in Fonvizin's *The Minor* were conceived as male roles, and Nestroy's mid-nineteenth-century farces contain several of these "dame" parts. The theatre historians Mander and Mitchenson have even suggested that "to **camp**" derives from Lord Campley, who disguises himself as a lady's maid in Richard Steele's *The Funeral* (1701). The comic dame had become a fixture of English pantomime by the Regency period, and the great music-hall comedian Dan Leno was responsible for the dame elbowing out Clown as the chief comic performer in panto, opening the way for George Robey, George Graves and others to flourish. Some performers like George Lacy and Rex Jamieson ("Mrs. Shufflewick," 1928–1984) played nothing but dames. A similar tradition was upheld in American popular plays by Neil Burgess (1846–1910) as Widow Bedotte, Gilbert Sarony (d. 1910) as the Giddy Gusher, the Russell Brothers as clumsy Irish maids in vaudeville, George K. Fortescue (1846?–1914) as a flirtatious fat girl in several burlesques, and George W. Monroe (d. 1932) as an Irish biddy in a number of musical comedies. In France, Offenbach's operetta *Mesdames de la Halle* (1858) created three roles of market-women to be sung by men.

The Circus. In the circus cross-dressing was a means of enhancing the seeming danger of stunts: the Franconis in an equestrian version of *Madame Angot* were allegedly the first to do so in the Napoleonic period. The American equestrian Ella Zoyara (Omar Kingsley, 1840–1879) and the English trapezist Lulu (El Niño Farini, b. 1855) were celebrated Victorian examples. Kingsley's personal sexuality is questionable. There is no question about Emil Mario Vacano (1840–1892), Austria's most important and prolific writer on the circus, who had appeared as an equestrienne under the names Miss Corinna and Signora Sanguineta, and was the lover of Count Emmerich Stadion (1839–1900). The Texan aerialist Barbette (Vander Clyde, 1904–1973), who performed a species of striptease on trapeze, ending his act with a dewigging, became the toast of Paris, and was taken up by Jean **Cocteau**.

Such performers were said to be "in drag," a term from thieves' cant that compared the train of a gown to the drag or brake on a coach, and entered the theatrical parlance from homosexual slang around 1870. "Dragging up" provides the central plot device in Brandon Thomas' *Charley's Aunt* (1892), William Douglas Home's sex-change play *Aunt Edwina* (1959), and Simon Gray's *Wise Child* (1968). The German equivalents were Theodor Körner's *Vetter aus Bremen* and *Die Gouvernante* (both 1834). A comedy which created a scandal in New York in 1896 was *A Florida Enchantment* by Archibald Clavering Gunter, in which a magic seed turns a young woman (played by a woman) into a man and a man (played by a man) into a woman; what shocked was the woman's masculine amorous propensities displayed while under the influence of the seed.

Female Transvestism. For unlike female impersonation in the theatre, women dressing as men had little sanction from ancient religion or folk traditions; it has usually been condemned as a wanton assumption of male prerogative. But when women first came on the Western stage, costuming them in men's garb was simply a means to show off their limbs and provide freedom of movement. This was certainly the case during the Restoration, when Pepys remarked of an actress in knee-breeches "she had the best legs that ever I saw, and I was well pleased by it." Between 1660 and 1700, eighty-nine plays presented opportunities for women in men's clothes. Nell Gwyn, Moll Davis, and others took advantage of these "breeches roles," but few could, like Anne Bracegirdle, give a convincing portrayal of a male. Often the part travestied was that of a young rake—Sir Harry Wildair in *The Constant Couple* and Macheath in *The Beggar's Opera*—the pseudo-lesbian overtones of the plot's situation providing a minor thrill.

After the French Revolution, there was a passing fad for historic dramas about women who went to war as men, usually to aid their husbands or lovers. These dramas included Pixérécourt's *Charles le Téméraire, ou le Siège de Nancy* (1814), Duperche's *Jeanne Hachette, ou l'Héroïne de Beauvais* (1822) and a few about Joan of Arc; Mlle. Bourgeois who specialized in such roles was praised for her "masculine energy." The leading English "breeches" actresses of the early nineteenth century, Mme. Vestris and Mrs. Keeley were, on the other hand, noted for their delicacy, and made an impression less mannish than boyish. It was said of Vestris in her best part, in *Giovanni in London, or The Libertine Reclaimed* (1817), "that the number of male hearts she caused to ache, during her charming performance of the character . . . would far exceed all the female tender ones Byron boasts that Don Juan caused to break during the whole of his career."

The first "principal boys" in English pantomime were slender women, but became more ample in flesh throughout the Victorian period, no real effort made to pretend they were men. Jennie Hill on the music halls and Jennie Lee as Jo in various adaptations of *Bleak House*, Vernet in Paris and Josephine Dora and Hansi Niese in Vienna, represented the proletarian waif, a pathetic or cocky adolescent, not a mature male. But the Viennese folk-singer Josefine Schmeer always wore men's clothes off-stage as well. *Peter Pan* (1904), incarnated from its premiere by a series of outstanding actresses including Pauline Chase, Maude Adams, and Mary Martin, benefitted in the National Theatre revival of 1981 from being played by a young man.

Another aspect of male impersonation is the assumption of Shakespearean men's roles by actresses. It was long a practice to cast women as children and fairies. More ambitious was the usurpation of leading parts, with Kitty Clive alleged to be the first female Hamlet. The powerful American actress Charlotte Cushman (1816–1876) played Romeo to her sister's Juliet and later aspired to Cardinal Wolsey; her Romeo was viewed as "a living, breathing, animated, ardent human being," distinct from most ranting Montagus. Women have undertaken Falstaff and Shylock on occasion, but Hamlet has proven to be irresistible. The most distinguished female Dane was Sarah Bernhardt, who, according to Mounet-Sully, lacked only the buttons to her fly; but, according to Max Beerbohm, came off *très grande dame*. (Sarah had a penchant for male roles, also playing Lorenzaccio and L'Aiglon.) In our time, Dame Judith Anderson and Frances de la Tour have tried the experiment, but it has proven unacceptable to contemporary audiences.

Glamour Drag. A new development arose in nineteenth-century variety with the glamorous female impersonator and the "butch" male impersonator. The former might be a comedian who was dressed and made up to resemble a woman of taste, beauty, and chic. Glamour drag

had originated in the minstrel show, where the "wench" role was usually invested in a good-looking youth. The foremost "wenches" like Francis Leon (Patrick Francis Glassey, b. ca. 1840) and Eugene (D'Ameli, 1836–1870) maintained elaborate wardrobes and were regarded as models. The first white glamour drag performer appears to be Ernest Byne, who, as Ernest Boulton (b. 1848), had featured in a sensational trial for soliciting while dressed in women's clothing.

Male impersonation was first introduced on the American variety stage by the Englishwoman Annie Hindle (b. ca. 1847) and her imitator Ella Wesner (1841–1917), both lesbians, in the guise of "fast" young men, swaggering, cigar-smoking, and coarse. They performed in the English music-hall as well, but there a toned-down portrayal aimed at a more genteel audience was affected by Bessie Bonehill (d. 1902). With her mezzo-soprano voice, she blended the coarse-grained fast man with the principal boy into a type that could be admired for its lack of vulgarity. Her example was matched by the celebrated Vesta Tilley (Matilda Alice Powles, 1864–1952), whose soprano voice never really fooled any listener; her epicene young-men-about-town were ideal types for the 1890s, sexually ambiguous without being threatening. Even so, at the Royal Command Performance of 1912, Queen Mary turned her back on Tilley's act.

These minstrel and music-hall traditions lasted longest in black American vaudeville, where the performers' private lives often matched their impersonations. Female impersonators included Lawrence A. Chenault (b. 1877), who played "Golden Hair Nell," and Andrew Tribble (d. 1935), who created "Ophelia Snow." The best-known male impersonator in **Harlem** was Gladys Bentley, aka Gladys Ferguson and Bobbie Minton (1907–1960), alleged to have had an affair with Bessie Smith; later in life, she married and publicly repented her lesbian past.

Musical Comedy. Critics objected when glamour drag entered musical comedy, but succumbed to the success of Julian Eltinge (William Dalton, 1882–1941). The large-boned baritone usually selected vehicles that allowed him quick wardrobe as well as sex-changes; this "ambisextrous comedian," as Percy Hammond called him, wore costumes that rivaled those of female fashion-plates. Better liked by female than by male audiences, Eltinge worked at a butch image, regularly picking fights with insulters and announcing his coming marriage. But his sexual preferences remain a mystery, despite rumors of an affair with a sports writer.

Bert Savoy (Everett Mackenzie, 1888–1923) introduced an outrageous red-haired caricature, garish and brassy, gossiping about her absent girlfriend Margie and launching such catch-phrases as "You mussst come over" and "You don't know the half of it, dearie." His arch camping, performed with his effeminate partner Jay Brennan, influenced Mae West. Francis Renault (Anthony Oriema, d. 1956), billed as "The Slave of Fashion" and "Camofleur," sang in a clear soprano and appeared in Broadway revue; Karyl Norman (George Podezzi, 1897–1947), "The Creole Fashion-plate," switched from baritone to soprano voice, alternating sexes in his act.

Modern Male Impersonators. With the radical changes in dress and manners that followed World War I, the male impersonator became a relic, although the tradition persisted in Ella Shields ("Burlington Bertie from Bow") and Hettie King. Ironically, contemporary feminist theatre groups have revived the type for political reasons, as in Eve Merriam's revue *The Club* (1976), Timberlake Wertenbaker's *New Anatomies* (ICA Theatre, 1981), and German ensembles like Brühwarm. The economic necessity of wearing male dress was the motive force of Simone Benmussa's *The Singular Life of Albert Nobbs*, whose heroine must live as a waiter, both masculine and subservient, and of Manfred Karge's *Man to Man* (1987), in which a widow adopts her husband's identity to keep his job as a crane operator.

In a work like Caryl Churchill's *Cloud Nine* (1979), sexual cross-casting is an important aspect of the play's inquiry into gender roles. Lily Tomlin, in her one-woman show, has created a male lounge singer, Tommy Velour, plausible even to the hair on his chest.

Postwar Revues. During World War II, all-male drag revues were popular in the armed services and, in the postwar U.K., survived as *Soldiers in Skirts* and *Forces Showboats.* Despite the military titles, these were havens for homosexual transvestites, and, perhaps in reaction to wartime austerity, perhaps in nostalgia for a wartime stag atmosphere, the postwar period burgeoned with clubs and revues specializing in glamour drag. In fact it had been the rise of the nightclub in the 1920s which gave female impersonation its reputation as a primarily homosexual art-form.

In the United States, the Jewel Box revue, founded in Miami in 1938 by Danny Brown and Doc Brenner, enjoyed an eight-year run in the postwar period and launched a number of major talents before folding in 1973; its "male" m.c. was the black female cross-dresser Storme De-Larverie. Similar enterprises include Finocchio's in San Francisco, Club 82 in New York, My-Oh-My in New Orleans and the Ha Ha Club in Hollywood, Florida; in Paris, Chez Madame Arthur and Le Carrousel; in West Berlin, Chez Nous and Chez Romy Haag; and in Havana, the MonMartre Club. In London, licensing laws forced professional drag into after-hours clubs and amateur drag into local pubs, just as local interference by the Catholic Church and witch-hunting town councils legislated many of the smaller American clubs out of existence. Club transvestites were often eager to be taken for women: a Parisian star, the Bardot clone Coccinelle (Jacques-Charles

Dufresnoy), pioneered with a sex-change operation and legal maneuvers to be accepted as a woman.

Many gay bars or pubs provided at least a token stage, and the female impersonator became almost exclusively what Esther Newton calls "performing homosexuals and homosexual performers," a relatively young, overt member of a distinct subculture. But the show-business ambience could often neutralize the sexuality for a mixed or heterosexual audience. One of the most successful means of "passing" with such a public is to give impressions of female super-stars, usually including such gay icons as Mae West, Bette Davis, Tallulah Bankhead, and Judy Garland. T. C. Jones (1920–1971), a veteran of the Jewel Box, was introduced to a general public in *New Faces of 1956* and toured his own revue.

Craig Russell (b. 1948) has been both the most widely known and the most versatile in this crowded trade, although Charles Pierce's impersonations make up in vitriol what they lack in accuracy. Many of these performers disdain the appellation "impersonator": Pierce and Lynn Carter (1925–1985) preferred to be known as "impressionists," Jim Bailey as a "singer-illusionist," Russell as a "character actor," and Jimmy James (James Johnson, b. 1961) insists that his heavily researched replication of Marilyn Monroe is a kind of possession. (More original and unnerving is the Dead Marilyn, created by former Cockette Peter Stack, aka Stakula.)

The mid-60s to 70s saw a resurgence of female impersonation as an article of theatrical faith. Danny La Rue's (Daniel Carroll, b. 1928) club in Hanover Square (1964–70) was a resort of fashion, and he became a major star of popular entertainment; despite a homosexual lifestyle well known within the show biz community, he still promotes an aggressively "normal" image. Drag mimes, lip-syncing to tapes, became ubiquitous and reached an elegant apotheosis in Paris' La Grande Eugène. But the "radical drag

queens" Bloolips (founded in London in 1970) sent up this forced glamor and other clichés of variety entertainment to make wide-sweeping political statements about social misconceptions of gender.

"Gender-fuck" and Glitter Rock. More anarchic uses of "gender-fuck" resulted from the emergence of gay liberation from the West Coast hippy scene. The Cockettes and the Angels of Light of San Francisco were among the first to use campy pastiches of popular culture for radical ends; the Cycle Sluts and, later, the street-theatre group, the Sisters of Perpetual Indulgence, parodied traditional drag by mixing the macho of beards, leather, and hairy chests with their spangles, false eyelashes, and net-stockings. Despite the flaunted faggotry of these groups, the outrageousness appealed to heterosexual rock musicians as a new means of assault; the extreme makeups and outfits were adopted by Alice Cooper, the New York Dolls, and Kiss, among others, a school which came to be known as "glitter rock" and "gender-bending." English society, with its own more delicate tradition, gave rise to David Bowie, who presented an androgynous allure. This approach reached a logical terminus in Boy George, whose early publicity touted him as asexual or tamely bisexual.

Drama. Although **Goethe** preferred to see a young man as Goldoni's *Locandiera* (The Mistress of the Inn), for fear lest a woman be as forward as the role demanded, female impersonation did not return to serious drama for a long time. The Russian actor Boris Glagolin (1878–1948) did attempt to play Joan of Arc in St. Petersburg. But in modern times cross-dressing became a serious aesthetic principle in the interpretation of classic texts with both the Lindsay Kemp company and the Glasgow Citizens Theatre. Kemp (b. 1940?), an original dancer and mime, won an international reputation with *Flowers*, an homage to Jean **Genet** and his versions of *Salome* and *A Midsummer Night's Dream*, amalgams of camp sensibility with oneiric imagery. (One Kemp follower who went off on his own was Michael Matou [1947–1987], the Australian dancer and designer, who founded the Sideshow Burlesco in Sydney in 1979.) The Citizens Theatre, under the leadership of Giles Havergal, Robert David Macdonald and Philip Prowse, cast men as Cleopatra, Lady Macbeth, Marguerite Gautier (in *Camino Real*), and so forth, to stress the irreality of gender identification and the conventionality of the theatre form; they were the first to introduce a male Lady Bracknell, an innovation which has since become endemic. Less adventurous was the Royal Shakespeare Company's all-male *As You Like It*, since it cautiously avoided casting adolescents in the leading parts.

Dame Comedy. Before the war, dame comedy had been sophisticated by Douglas Byng (1893–1988), who performed in London supper clubs, cabarets and in revue. Comedy persisted in clowns like Pudgy Roberts who appeared in glamour drag revues, in the all-male Ballets Trockadero de Monte Carlo (founded 1974) and the Trockadero Gloxinia Ballet, and their operatic equivalent the Gran Scena Opera Co., founded by Ira Siff in 1982, with men singing the soprano roles. Formidable dames carry on: Barry Humphries as Dame Edna Everage and piano-entertainers Hinge & Brackett (George Logan and Patrick Fyffe). In the 1980s, "alternative drag performance" could be seen at clubs and pubs in Britain: standard glamour drag was trashed by such as Ivan the Terrible and The Joan Collins Fan Club (Julian Clary and his dog Fanny), who combined self-abuse with attacks on audience expectation.

Drag has also become a component of contemporary performance art, as in John Epperson's *Ballet of the Dolls* (La MaMa, New York, 1988), a confrontation of pulp fiction with the clichés of romantic ballet. This trend has its roots in the "Ridiculous Theatre" movements of the 1970s, which launched Charles Ludlam,

and the Andy **Warhol** Factory which housed Jackie Curtis and Holly Woodlawn. The 300-lb. underground film star Divine (Glen Milstead, d. 1988) was featured in a number of off-off-Broadway plays, most memorably as the prison matron in Tom Eyen's *Women Behind Bars*. A leading exponent is Ethyl (né Roy) Eichelberger (b. 1945), whose one-man *Tempest* and *Jocasta, or Boy-Crazy* are in both the minstrel-vaudeville tradition and the shamanistic current (he sports a tattoo to assert his masculinity whatever his attire). Gender confusion is also the main theme of Los Angeles comedian John Fleck (b. 1953) (*I Got the He-Be She-Be's*, 1986; *Psycho Opera*, 1987).

Breeches in Opera. In early baroque **opera**, a favorite plot was the legend of **Achilles** disguising himself as a maiden on the island of Scyros to avoid involvement in the Trojan war; in this equivocal disguise he was wooed by the king and wooed the princess. The subject was treated seriously by thirty-two operas between 1663 and 1837, and comically by John Gay (*Achilles*, 1732) and Thomas Arne (*Achilles in Petticoats*, 1793), and survived as dramatic material as late as Robert Bridges' *Achilles in Scyros* (1890). Both as a legacy from eighteenth-century castrato singing and for reasons of vocal balance, breeches parts have persisted in opera, and it takes little time for an audience to adjust to sopranos impersonating libidinous youths like Cherubino and Octavian. Musical comedy has utilized the male–female disguise gimmick at least from Franz von Suppé's *Fatinitza* (1878), but without adding anything of distinction to it, at least not since Eltinge. Danny LaRue's appearance as Dolly Levi in a West End production of *Hello, Dolly!* coarsened an already coarse creation. *Sugar* by Jule Styne and Bob Merrill (1972) was simply an overblown remake of *Some Like It Hot*, just as *La Cage aux Folles* by Fierstein and Herman tarted up the French farce for the Broadway marketplace.

See also **Castrati; Dance; Music, Popular; Theatre and Drama; Transvestism (Cross-Dressing); Variety, Revue, and Cabaret Entertainment.**

BIBLIOGRAPHY. Roger Baker, *Drag: A History of Female Impersonation*, London: Triton, 1968; Gisela Bleibtreu-Ehrenberg, *Der Weibmann*, Frankfurt am Main: Fischer, 1984; A. Holtmont, *Die Hosenrolle*, Munich: Meyer & Jessen, 1925; Kris Kirk and Ed Heath, *Men in Frocks*, London: Gay Men's Press, 1984; Laurence Senelick, "The Evolution of the Male Impersonator on the 19th Century Popular Stage," *Essays in Theatre*, 1:1 (1982), 31–44.

Laurence Senelick

TRAVEL AND EXPLORATION

In this context, the literature of travel and exploration refers to books written by Europeans or Americans about what came to be known as the "Third World"—Asia, Africa, the islands of the Pacific, and to a certain extent the Americas (as relating to Amerindians). It would not include work in the field of **anthropology.** This literature of travel and exploration (and conquest) begins around the time of Columbus and goes onward until the early twentieth century, when tourism began to make the whole world a replica of the West and nothing was left to be explored.

Travel Literature. During the sixteenth, seventeenth, and eighteenth centuries, it was possible to write about "sodomie" with some frankness. Accordingly, there are numerous candid references to homosexuality in the various writings of travelers which were collected in massive multivolume anthologies by Richard Hakluyt, Samuel Purchas, and John Pinkerton. Purchas (the source of Coleridge's "Kubla Khan") even has a unique reference to the homosexuality of the Emperor Jahangir of **India.** Many other travel books during this period not collected by any later editor also contain data of this kind.

As the eighteenth century drew to a close, a slow tidal wave of puritanism and prudery rolled over the West, and by 1835 it had ceased to be safe to make open references to homosexuality in books intended for general use. Here and there in France and Germany, scholars during the nineteenth century were able to write articles or even books about homosexuality, or to mention it in passing, but in the English-speaking world there was an almost absolute taboo against mentioning such an "unspeakable" subject at all. Travelers therefore either simply did not mention what they saw in foreign lands with regard to homosexual behavior, or else they mentioned it in veiled phrases ("vice against nature," "abominable vice," "unnatural propensities," and similar expressions). This sort of nonsense went on until the veil was rudely lifted by Arminius Vambery and Sir Richard **Burton** in the late nineteenth century, Vambery being a Hungarian traveler who had visited the court of the pederastic Amir of Bukhara in Central Asia, and Burton being the notorious explorer of Asia and Africa who wrote a whole essay on **pederasty,** which provoked howls of "moral" outrage. But the Oscar **Wilde** trials in 1895 put the lid back on until after World War I, and even to a certain extent until after World War II.

Another problem was that the Asians and Africans themselves—and this is a problem faced also by anthropologists—realized that the Western travelers were hostile to homosexuality, and therefore kept it out of their sight as much as possible. The Japanese after the beginnings of modernization in the late nineteenth century are a case in point. One need only look back to the clandestine nature of homosexual society in the United States up until the 1960s to realize how easy it is to hide a flourishing homosexual subculture from the general public, much more so from passing tourists.

The present writer can attest that homosexuality, so widespread in Morocco, remains totally out of the view of tourists who are not looking for it. Nonetheless, there have been some travelers who were allowed to see homosexual behavior going on right in front of them. In the 1950s, Wilfred Thesiger and Gavin Maxwell visited the tribes in the marsh-lands of southern Iraq (since, alas, ravaged by war), where the young boys were all stark naked, and there were dancing-boys who act as **prostitutes**. The Arabs made no secret of this to Thesiger and Maxwell, but whether they would have made a secret of it to other visitors is hard to say. The fact that Maxwell was a pederast may have made a difference.

Homosexual Questers. There is a second aspect of travel, namely the travels of homosexual men (rarely lesbians) in search of some place on earth where the taboos of the Christian West have no validity. As Kipling put it, "Ship me some-wheres east of Suez, where the best is like the worst, Where there ain't no Ten Commandments, and a man can have a thirst." The idea that somewhere "east of Suez" there was a paradise where "a man can have a thirst" for the forbidden is a powerful myth that took over the imagina-tion of many homosexual men. How many explorers were actually, deep in the re-cesses of their minds, looking for this paradise? The wanderlust of many an explorer and traveler doubtlessly had been inspired by cravings that they hardly dare admit even to themselves. The fact that travel and exploration generally involve being in the company of other men, to the total exclusion of women, and requiring the company of friendly local boys as guides and servants, is bound to have a much stronger appeal to homosexual than to heterosexual men. Even in paradises fa-mous for their women of easy virtue, such as Polynesia, it was homosexual men like Herman **Melville** and Charles Warren Stoddard who led the way, and in Bali, an island famous for its bare-breasted women, there was a colony of European homosexu-als in the 1930s (driven out by the Dutch).

Some homosexual (usually ped-erastic) men have practically made a ca-reer out of wandering around the globe in search of exotic boys: Walter B. Harris, Michael Davidson, and Roland Raven-Hart, to name a few. If one was not too adventur-ous, a simple trip to France or Italy (**Ven-ice**, Capri, **Sicily**) would suffice, and there has long flourished a homosexual colony in Tangier, exotic but near to Europe.

In the 1970s there were several Asian nations whose great poverty caused a sharp rise in the prostitution of young boys (and girls), but a public outcry forced the otherwise amoral police to crack down, or pretend to crack down, on the numer-ous tourists who came in just to patronize the local boys. This sort of prostitution was flourishing in Sri Lanka (Ceylon), **Thai-land**, and the **Philippines**, where the town of Pagsanjan turned pederasty into its main industry. As far back as 1903, Gen-eral Hector **Macdonald**, a hero of the British Army, had committed suicide after having sexual relations with boys in Ceylon.

The fondness for travel among modern homosexuals has led to the publi-cation of various "gay guides," the most complete one being the *Spartacus Interna-tional Gay Guide* (Berlin: Bruno Gmünder Verlag, 1989). The idea that "the grass is greener on the other side" has helped to send thousands of homosexual men in search of sexual freedom or gratification in foreign lands. To a certain extent, this is a glorified version of the sexual encounters that the heterosexual businessman has on trips to other cities—he dare not risk expo-sure in his home town, but nobody knows him in the other city, he is anonymous.

Local Attitudes and Foreign Myths. The question of whether the people of Asia and Africa are more liberal about sex remains to be answered. **Islam** is more puritanical than Christianity, but its cus-tomary sexual segregation provokes wide-spread homosexuality, at least of the situa-tional sort that flourishes in boarding schools or prisons if not the "real" sort.

And poverty creates the desperate amorality that breeds prostitution of all kinds. These are not the best bases for a sexual paradise, even if sexual freedom is more widespread under such conditions. But a lot of men don't care. Hence the sexual "Meccas"—how totally unlike the purity of Mecca!—of the East.

In a sense, the sexual bazaars of the East are an artificially created response to the "east of Suez" image that many Westerners are looking for, and the supply is created to meet the demand. Thus, the image creates its own realization. The modern situation is totally unlike the earlier one because the invention of jet airplanes increased the number of tourists to Asia. In the 1930s, a slow boat to Shanghai to taste the vices of the mysterious Orient was no easy matter, but now one can fly to Asia in one day. The availability of sex and the liberalism of sexual attitudes can often be seen in amusing and ironic comparisons made by people who think that "here" it is hard but "there" it is easy. Some Americans think that Rio de Janeiro is a sexual paradise compared to the United States—the sex more available and the attitudes more liberal—while the Brazilians are thinking that their own country is puritanical and that America is the sexual paradise! But the myth keeps provoking people to travel to other countries in search of better sexual hunting grounds. (This myth also applies to the American image of Scandinavia.) Not long ago, East Baltimore was the Pagsanjan of America, but people continue to think in terms of paradises being far away.

Perhaps in the future, when wealthy Asians are common and the AIDS crisis will have been solved, one can expect the United States to be visited by homosexual tourists from Japan in search of the large and virile Western male of the cowboy and detective films they see at home.

See also **Resorts, Gay.**

Stephen Wayne Foster

Tribade

The Greek term for lesbian, *tribas*—from the verb *tribein*, "to rub"—implies that the women so designated derived their sexual pleasure from friction against one another's bodies. Male imagination supplied further embellishments. Friedrich Karl Forberg, in his commentary on classical sexual mores entitled *De figuris Veneris* (1824), asserted that "the tribades . . . are women in whom that part of the genital apparatus which is called the clitoris attains such dimensions that they can use it as a penis, either for fornication or for pedication. . . . In tribades, either by a freak of nature or in consequence of frequent use, it attains immoderate dimensions. The tribade can get it into erection, enter a vulva or anus, enjoy a delicious voluptuousness, and procure if not a complete realization of cohabitation, at least something very close to it, to the woman who takes the passive role." He adds that the term was "also applied to women who in default of a real penis make use of their finger or of a leather contrivance [dildo] which they insert into their vulva and so attain a fictitious titillation." According to some ancient sources, a pet garden snake could also double for the virile member.

The word *tribas* appears comparatively late in Greek, in astrological authors and satirists of the second century of our era, yet its occurrence in the work of the Roman poet **Martial** at the end of the first century shows that it must have existed in vulgar speech, if not in literature, well before that time. Phaedrus (IV, 14) even equates *tribades* with *molles mares* (effeminate males = homosexuals) as individuals exhibiting disharmony between their genitalia and the direction of their sexual desires. The Latin language formed its own word *frictrix* or *fricatrix* from *fricare* "to rub" on the model of the Greek expression. Preserved by the texts of classical authors whose manuscripts survived into the Renaissance, the word *tribade* found its way into the modern languages, for example in Henri Estienne's *Apologie pour Hérodote* (1566), where it remained the usual term for lesbian well into the nineteenth century. The author of the satiric poem entitled *The Toast*, in Latin and in English, described it as giving an account of "the progress of tribadism in England," and Forberg mentions colleges of tribades called "Alexandrian colleges" in late eighteenth-century London.

Beginning in French in the mid-nineteenth century, the term *lesbian* gradually supplanted *tribade* (and *sapphist*) in learned and popular usage, so that today the word occurs but rarely as a deliberate archaism or classical allusion.

BIBLIOGRAPHY. Friedrich Karl Forberg, *Manual of Classical Erotology (De figuris Veneris)*, New York: Grove Press, 1966.

Warren Johansson

TRICK

This slang term for a casual sex partner stems from the expression "turn a trick." The use of the word in cardplaying, where a succession of tricks determines one's final score, has been a continuing influence on the sexual usage, for cards involve cognate elements of competition and winning and losing. The word's popularity reflects the high visibility of the "promiscuous" **lifestyle**, or sexual pluralism, among male homosexuals. The verb "to trick" is often used for "to have sexual intercourse with" or "to make" in the sense of attaining a sexual conquest.

A trick is often called a "number," expressing the concept that each individual partner is just one in a long series stretching back to the first, and to be prolonged indefinitely into the future. A single sexual encounter, unlikely to be repeated, is termed a "one-night stand." In fact, during the pre-AIDS era a substantial number of gay men reported a history of multiple partnering involving thousands of men. This prodigious activity has no counterpart among women (except per-

haps for prostitutes, which is another matter), nor among heterosexual men, for Don Juan types rarely, if ever, attain such records.

TSVETAEVA, MARINA (1892–1941)

Russian poet. The daughter of a professor of art history at the University of Moscow and founder of the first museum of the fine arts in Russia, Marina Tsvetaeva was educated both at home and then in boarding schools in Switzerland and Germany. Her poetic talent was instinctive and precocious; she began to write at the age of six, and the first book of her collected juvenilia, *Evening Album* (1910), earned the notice of some of the most important Russian poets of the day, one of whom, Max Voloshin, introduced her to literary circles. In the spring of 1911, at Voloshin's celebrated home in Koktebel on the Crimean coast, she met her future husband, Sergei Efron, whom she saw as a high-minded and noble man of action. Among her constant heroes were strong and virile characters, men and women with romantic ideals and the will to act on them—Napoleon, Goethe, Rostand, Sarah Bernhardt, Maria Bashkirtseva.

In 1916 the poet Osip Mandelstam fell in love with her and followed her across Russia in an unsuccessful campaign to win her—an event both celebrated in their poetry. In Moscow in 1917, she witnessed the Bolshevik seizure of power. Her husband joined the White army as an officer, while she was stranded in the capital and did not see him for five years. Her sympathies were on "the other side," and she composed at this time a cycle of poems entitled *The Demesne of the Swans*, glorifying the Tsar and the white forces.

With the war at an end, Tsvetaeva decided to emigrate in order to rejoin her husband, and headed for Prague (a Russian émigré center in the interwar years) by way of Berlin. The literary life of the first emigration, as it is now called, was exceptionally active, and Tsvetaeva had many plans of her own. Even though she had left the Soviet Union, the frontier was not yet closed, and her most famous collection, *Mileposts I*, was published there in 1922. For three years the couple resided happily in Prague, then in 1925 she moved to Paris—another émigré center—and lived there for fourteen years, taking an active and welcome part in the cultural life of the Russian community. However, unknown to her, her husband had been converted to communism and was working for the Soviet secret police. Now rejected and ostracized by the other émigrés, Tsvetaeva resolved to return to the Soviet Union in the wake of her husband, but when she arrived there in June 1939, she was even more hopelessly out of place. To boot, her husband was arrested and shot as an enemy of the people—because he knew too much. Evacuated to Elabuga in the Tatar Autonomous Republic, she committed suicide by hanging herself on August 31, 1941.

It was in Paris at the end of the twenties that Tsvetaeva was introduced to Natalie Clifford **Barney** and invited to Barney's celebrated literary salon at 20, rue Jacob. A model for lesbian characters in almost every novel of the first three decades of the century, Barney (1876–1972) kept one of the most elegant salons in Paris, where the Russian poetess, impoverished, shabbily dressed, and unknown to English and French readers, must have cut a strange figure. The nickname Amazon had been given to Barney by her male admirer, Remy de Gourmont, and she appropriated it for the title of her book *Pensées d'une Amazone* (1920), to which Tsvetaeva replied in turn in her essay "Letter to an Amazon," written in November and December of 1932 and revised at the end of 1934. Part essay and part narrative, it sets forth Tsvetaeva's thoughts on lesbian love based on her personal experiences at various moments in her life.

Love between two women is beautiful and rewarding; God is not opposed to it, but Nature rejects it in the interest of perpetuating the species. A typical lesbian affair—between an experienced older women and a younger partner whom she seduces and initiates—runs onto the rocks when the younger woman feels the maternal instinct and abandons the older one to pursue her biological destiny in the embrace of a man who can give her children. The two part company, and the older partner searches vainly for someone to replace her lost love, but the younger one has become indifferent and is unmoved by the news, years later, of her death. This scenario parallels Tsvetaeva's own liaison with Sofia Parnok. The piece is a poetic and often moving prose rhapsody about a dimension of sexual experience which the poetess could not reconcile with the rest of her erotic personality.

BIBLIOGRAPHY. Simon Karlinsky, *Marina Tsvetaeva: The Woman, Her World and Her Poetry*, New York: Cambridge University Press, 1985; S. Poliakova, *Tsvetaeva i Parnok*, Ann Arbor, MI: Ardis, 1982.

Evelyn Gettone

TURING, ALAN (1912–1954)

British scientist. Alan Turing was born into a social rank just between the British commercial classes and the landed gentry; his father served in the Indian Civil Service and Alan spent much of his childhood separated from his parents. He showed an early talent for science, and maintained this interest through his career in the British public school system, where **science** was simply referred to as "Stinks."

He seems to have been a brilliant, awkward boy whose latent genius went unnoticed by all his teachers; he also had no friends until his very last years at Sherborne. Then he fell in love with a fellow science enthusiast, Christopher Morcom: the Platonic friendship was returned, and Alan Turing was for the first time in his life a happy young man. He had dreams of joining Christopher at Trinity, to pursue science together; unfortunately, Christopher Morcom suddenly died (from a much earlier infection with bovine tuberculosis). The effect on the young Turing was shattering.

He went up to Kings College, Cambridge, and embarked on a brilliant mathematical career; his first substantial contribution was his important article on the computable numbers, which contained a description of what is still known as the "Turing machine." He was made a Fellow of Kings at the very young age of twenty-two.

Turing spent two years in America, at Princeton University, and, on his return to Britain, was drafted into British cryptanalysis for the war effort. Turing was already unusual among mathematicians for his interest in machinery; it was not an interest in applied mathematics so much as something which did not really have a name yet—"applied logic." His contribution to the design of code-breaking machines during the war led him deeper and deeper into the field of what would now be called computer programming, except that neither concept existed at the time. He and a colleague named Welshman designed the Bombe machines which were to prove decisive in breaking the main German Enigma ciphers. For his contribution to the Allied victory in World War II Turing was named an Officer of the British Empire (O.B.E.) in 1946.

He also possessed one of the many brilliant minds of his era which independently conceived of the computer—to be precise, of the automatic electronic digital computer with internal program storage (the original "Turing machine" was a predecessor). The earliest inventor of such a device was the eccentric nineteenth-century Charles Babbage, who could not obtain the necessary hardware to implement his ideas. But in the 1940s the idea became feasible, and the "real" inventor of the computer was an international network of mathematicians and engineers which included John von Neumann and Alan Turing, among many others.

In the post-war era, Turing became fascinated with the concept of artificial intelligence, and was a pioneer in exploring this new domain. (The "Turing test" is still a current phrase among computer scientists.) He was elected as a Fellow of the Royal Society in 1951.

A lifelong homosexual, Turing's life took a bad turn when he reported a burglary to the police. The officers were quick to sniff out the possibility of an "offense against morals" which soon preempted the burglary investigation; Turing gladly described what he had done with a young man in his bed, thinking that a commission was currently sitting to "legalize it." He was brought to trial and sentenced to a year's probation under the care of a psychiatrist, who proceeded to administer doses of female hormone to his patient, this being the current "wonder-therapy" which replaced castration as an attempt to kill the sexual instinct. For the entire year, Turing underwent the humiliation of femininization ("I'm growing breasts!" he confided to a friend), but emerged seemingly intact from the public ordeal. He committed suicide in 1954, by eating an apple he had laced with cyanide.

Turing did little or no theorizing about homosexuality, and his life accomplishments had nothing to do with the question. He does stand out as an example of a gay man whose talents were clearly "masculine" in nature. His love of young men was as simple and unpretentious as the rest of his life. If there is an object lesson in his career, it is perhaps this: this harmless English homosexual atheist mathematician made a huge contribution to winning World War II, and his reward was to be hounded into suicide by the forces of British prudery within eight years of that victory.

BIBLIOGRAPHY. Andrew Hodges, *Alan Turing: The Enigma*, New York: Simon and Schuster, 1983.

Geoff Puterbaugh

TURKEY

The history of same-sex love is almost coterminous with the Turkish state. At the Seljuk court of Konya there flourished the great Sufi poet Jelal al-Din **Rumi** (1207–1273), whose life was decisively marked by his passion for the youth Shams al-Din of Tabriz. Not himself ethnic Turkish, Rumi prepared a path for many other figures who were. **Sufism**, which continues to flourish in Turkey, incorporates a tradition of the beautiful youth or Beloved as the channel of Divine Love. The cultivated school of *divan* poetry, which includes such masters as Kadi Burhanettin (1344–1398), Şeyhi (d. ca. 1430), Nedim (1681–1730), and Şeyh Galib (1757–1799), stems from this source, though sometimes inflecting it in secular directions.

Quite early in Turkish history, its rulers discovered the pleasures of sensual boy-love, and Bayezid I (1360–1403) sent his soldiers to comb the conquered areas to find the most delightful boys for his harem. His example caused the practice of taking boys for sexual purposes to spread in the army, among government officials, and through the nobility. During their wars of conquest the Turkish sovereigns did not fail to renew their supply of **slaves**—especially beautiful, highly desired European youths. This levy as much as anything else contributed to European hatred of the Turks.

Mehmed II, who captured Constantinople in 1453 and made it the capital of the Ottoman Empire, is described as a notorious boy-lover. To rouse his troops to assault the city he painted a glowing picture of the booty that awaited them—especially the gentle, beautiful, aristocratic boys, enough for all. The historical accounts of the fall of the city abound in tales of **rape** and atrocity, as the Greek nobles were murdered and their children enslaved, with the 200 most handsome going to the Sultan's harem. At the battle of Mohacs in 1526, the Turkish victory caused the entire Balkan Peninsula to fall under Ottoman rule. The Croatian Bartolomej Durdevic has left an eloquent description of the boys enslaved after such conquests and sold as **catamites** or male **prostitutes**.

The boys chosen for the service of the ruler ranged in age from 8 to 16; they received a geisha-like training to make them both entertainers and skilled bed partners. When the Turkish Empire ceased to expand, the Sultan imposed an infamous "child tax." Every four years the Sultan's agents would visit each village in European Turkey to select the most handsome boys between 7 and 9 for the army corps, the palace pages' school, and the labor corps. European boys were typically not castrated, but feminized in training, manners, and costume "to serve the lusts of lecherous masters." Much has been written on boy-love in the court of Ali Pasha, the Turkish governor of Ioannina in Greece, whose agents roamed the dominion in search of beautiful children, even killing parents who refused their sons to the governor. Ali and his son are said to have engaged in sadomasochistic practices reminiscent of the writings of the Marquis de **Sade**, both torturing the boys and presenting them with gifts.

Even after Mehmed IV (1641–1691) abolished the "child tribute," the supply of boys was maintained by an active slave traffic into the Turkish Empire. In the 1850s Circassian slave dealers supplied large numbers of children—often sold into slavery by their own parents. Again in 1894, large numbers of the handsomest Armenian boys were taken for sexual purposes. Perhaps no city has ever been so famous for its boy **brothels** as Istanbul, where boys of various nationalities were once available as freely as girls. The anonymous English poem *Don Leon* falsely attributed to Byron (1836) tells of "seeking a brothel where . . . The black-eyed boy his trade unblushing plies." To the extent that this tradition survives in modern Turkey, the brothels have preserved the arts cultivated to their peak in the Sultans' harems.

Yet even with their excesses—which were in fact exaggerated by hostile European commentators propagating the stereotype of the "cruel and lustful Turk"—the Ottomans were also capable of man–boy love, and European boys were all the more desirable because of their capacity for affection and erotic response which the more familiar Near Eastern boys were thought to lack. The boy used for sexual purposes could graduate from his master's bed to become the manager of an estate, the steward of a household, even a general, court official or governor if his protector were powerful enough. Since the homoerotic side of Turkish life was omnipresent and inevitable, those who could take advantage of the opportunity thrived and climbed the social ladder.

Modern Turkey has actually suffered from Europeanization in that the Christian attitudes became part of the political mentality of the Republic, with the familiar practice of raiding gay bars, arresting the patrons, and subjecting them to humiliation and even torture. Yet despite this, the Istanbul of today is thought to have nearly half a million homosexuals, who concentrate in the Beyoğlu (Pera) district, especially the Cihangir quarter. A majority must still conceal their homosexuality from their families and colleagues at work. Arslan Yüzgün's study of 223 homosexual men in Istanbul showed that 56.1 percent are both active and passive, 30.9 percent are passive only and 13 percent are active only. On the whole they are more educated than the average of the Turkish population. However, the traditional stigmatization of the passive as opposed to the active homosexual lingers. The active homosexual is esteemed and can even boast of his ways, the passive homosexual is despised and persecuted by the police even in the absence of laws against his behavior.

The Western gay rights **movement** has finally reached Turkey, and in April 1987 the terror tactics employed by the **police** in Istanbul sparked a resistance movement in which eighteen homosexuals sued the police as a group for the first time, submitted a petition to the Attorney General, and later staged a hunger strike in Taksim Square. Thus another segment of the international gay community has achieved the stage of political consciousness that enables it to organize and fight for its human rights.

BIBLIOGRAPHY. Jonathan Drake, "'Le Vice' in Turkey," *International Journal of Greek Love*, 1:2 (1966), 13–27; Nermin Menemcioglu and Fahir Iz, eds., *The Penguin Book of Turkish Verse*, London: Penguin, 1978; Arslan Yüzgün, "The Fact of Homosexuality in Turkey and the Problems Confronting Turkish Homosexuals," *Homosexuality, Which Homosexuality?* Amsterdam: Vrij Universiteit, 1987, 181–91 [summarizes some of the findings of his *Türkiye'de Eşcinsellik (Dün, Bugün)*, Istanbul: Hüür-Yüz Yayincilik, 1986].
Warren Johansson

TWILIGHT MEN

In Kenilworth Bruce's 1933 novel, *Goldie*, the hero joins a prototypical (and fictional) gay rights organization, The Twilight League. This reflects the title of André Tellier's popular homosexual **novel**, *Twilight Men* (1931). It is doubtful whether the term enjoyed much real currency, but images of shadows and of darkness were common in the fiction of the period—and, given the obligatory tragic ending, all too appropriate.

In the nineteenth century the adjective "crepuscular" enjoyed some vogue to designate a declining civilization, because of the allegory of civilization following a quasi-solar course of ascent, zenith, afternoon fullness, and then descent into twilight; hence crepuscular trenches with *fin-de-siècle* and **decadent**. Richard Wagner's 1874 opera, *Die Got-*

terdämmerung (The Twilight of the Gods), was very popular in this period.

Recently, the term "midnight cowboy," from James Leo Herlihy's 1965 book and the subsequent film, has had some currency. (For reasons not altogether clear, much homosexual social life begins only after ten or eleven in the evening.) Presumably real cowboys have to be up too early in the morning to be out until midnight.

TWIN STUDIES

The study of twins is a useful tool for determining if a given trait or condition has a genetic component. Inasmuch as the sophistication of these studies has increased markedly over the past few decades, their value is increasing. Scientists have learned that such studies should be carefully conducted, and they are normally a helpful, if somewhat unexciting, discipline.

Yet peace and quiet did not attend the first attempts to conduct twin studies in homosexual behavior. Early research (Kallmann) indicated a very high concordance for homosexuality, and these results provoked cries of "Nazi" and "fascist" from the opposite camp, which was convinced that homosexuality was caused by the environment, specifically child-rearing practices. Clearly, ideology was getting entangled with science during these early years (and not for the first time).

So these twin studies must be approached with some care, and one must not automatically expect careful and impartial research in what is still, for many, an essentially contested area. "Concordance" is the degree to which two people share the same trait. John and Peter, not related, may be concordant for blue eyes, if they both have blue eyes. It is easy to determine concordance for eye color. But homosexual behavior is a more complex phenomenon. It may have several distinct subtypes (the effeminate, the

pederast, the loving comrade, and so on). People may also lie about the facts, for obvious reasons.

Despite these problems, it is difficult to read the twin literature on homosexuality without some surprise. "Fraternal" twins come from two sperm and two eggs, and are therefore no more closely related than any other siblings, while "identical" twins come from one sperm and one egg (the egg dividing after fertilization). Recent research has shown that these "identical" twins may not be complete twins in their gene complements (due to unknown factors in the egg-splitting process). One would expect no concordance at all for either fraternal or identical twins, if the strong environmentalist argument were to hold.

But that is not the case. There is no (or very little) concordance for fraternal twins. For identical twins, the concordance rate is approximately eighty or ninety percent, or even higher. This evidence would seem to suggest that people are simply born homosexual, just as they are born with green or blue eyes.

Yet the fact that these people seem to be born with a genetic predisposition to homosexuality carries no necessary implication that all homosexuality results from genetic factors. This may ultimately prove to be the case, but the twin studies do not prove it in and of themselves. In addition, a high concordance rate for homosexuality among identical twins does not mean that such twins are more (or less) likely to be homosexual than anyone else. Finally, there is no evidence at all in the twin studies which indicates that a particular subtype (for example, the effeminate homosexual) is genetically dominant at the expense of other homosexual subtypes.

The twin evidence presents some problems for future research. First, the acid test is the case of identical twins raised apart. There are not yet enough such twin-pairs in the literature. (It would also seem mandatory to obtain more longitudinal data on twin pairs.) Second, there is no clear idea of how this genetic component interacts with the surrounding environment to produce the fairly wide spectrum of human social behavior recorded by anthropology and history. Third, much larger twin studies need to be performed: the total periodical literature covers under a hundred pairs. Fourth, lesbianism and male homosexuality may not be the same sort of thing at all, if early research (Eckert et al.) holds up.

BIBLIOGRAPHY. E. D. Eckert, T. J. Bouchard, J. Bohlen, and L. L. Heston, "Homosexuality in Monozygotic Twins Reared Apart," *British Journal of Psychiatry*, 148 (1986), 421–25; Franz J. Kallmann, "Comparative Twin Study on the Genetic Aspects of Male Homosexuality," *Journal of Nervous and Mental Disease*, 115, (1952), 283–98; Geoff Puterbaugh, "Born Gay? Hand Preference and Sex Preference," *Cabirion*, 10 (1984), 12–18.

Geoff Puterbaugh

TYPOLOGY OF HOMOSEXUALITY

A valuable conceptual tool in seeking to understand a wide-ranging phenomenon or related group of phenomena which show both commonality and diversity, typology is the arrangement or classification of the elements under study so as to highlight both points of similarity and points of difference. Typology traces its roots back to the biologist's taxonomy, or classification of species, a practice which stems ultimately from Aristotle and his school.

In 1922 the great sociologist Max Weber applied the notion of "ideal types" to social behavior. These types were characterized as hypothetical constructs made up of the salient features or elements of a social phenomenon, or generalized concept, in order to facilitate comparison and classification of what is found in operation. Psychology, linguistics, anthropology, the history of science, comparative religion, and other disciplines have since made considerable use of such tools, often called "models" or "paradigms."

Once a typology has been constructed, it becomes an aid in the interpretation of a variety of concrete phenomena, but it can be misused to distort reality, as the features selected to compose them may acquire a distorted importance or concreteness, leading to the neglect of other factors. Hence typologies must be continually subjected to reexamination as new data become available, and revised as the understanding of the phenomena becomes more sophisticated.

Typologies are most helpful in preventing the ascription of traits in one subgroup of the phenomena under study to other subgroups where they may not belong, and in underlining points of commonality which may disclose historical influences or causal factors that otherwise might not have suggested themselves to the investigator.

In natural science, the term "paradigm" has been used since Thomas S. Kuhn's widely read book *The Structure of Scientific Revolutions* (1962) to designate the prevailing system of understanding phenomena which guides scientific theorization and experimentation, and which is held to be the most useful way of explaining the universe, or a part of it, until that paradigm is eventually overthrown by new data and replaced by a newer paradigm. As Kuhn has pointed out, paradigms may function without the conscious adhesion of those who employ them, and in the broadest sense they often form part of the unvoiced inner structure of human existence.

Popular Paradigms and Homosexuality. A somewhat different use of typologies may refer to the models or conceptual schemes held up to groups of people or the public at large in order to assimilate difficult or strange phenomena. When these models substantially guide the concepts and behaviors of the people most involved with them, they take on a normative reality which goes far beyond the theoretical utility of the academic model. Thus, it is one thing for the anthropologist to ascribe monogamous marriage to tribe A and polygamous marriage to tribe B; it is another if the only model of marriage known to the members of tribe B is the polygamous one, so that they react in horror to any suggestion of monogamy.

In the field of homosexuality, such popularly adopted typologies or paradigms have become extraordinarily powerful, though seldom of universal application. One of the great issues remaining in the study of homosexuality is how such popular paradigms are adopted by a culture and how they are lost or overthrown. A puzzling historical example is the paradigm shift in **England** and other industrializing Western countries which occurred from the seventeenth to the nineteenth centuries, such that male homosexual relations came to be seen as usually involving two adults rather than an adult and a boy. A current example is the emergence in countries like **Japan** and **Thailand** and in much of **Latin America** of a new paradigm (mutual **androphilia** or relationships between two adults, both male-identified) to compete with traditional paradigms such as **pederasty** and the model of "normal" males pairing with **effeminate** surrogate females.

Earlier Attempts to Create Scientific Paradigms of Homosexual Behavior and Relationships. In classical antiquity a major division was drawn emphasizing an **active–passive contrast** in sexual behavior, with the active (penetrating) partners considered "manly" and the passive (penetrated) role reserved for boys, slaves, foreigners, those vanquished in battle, and so forth. Beyond this simple dichotomy, little thought was given to typology.

Those, like K. H. **Ulrichs** and K. M. **Kertbeny**, who initiated serious comparative scholarship on homosexuality in the nineteenth century tended to view all homosexual behavior in essentially monolithic terms. They were largely unaware of the degree to which same-sex activity in other times and climes differed from that with which they were familiar. This ten-

dency to assimilate all homosexual conduct to a single model has survived into the present day in what is sometimes called "naive essentialism," evident in the tendency to speak of ancient personalities such as Plato and Alexander the Great, or even mythical figures such as Hylas and Ganymede, as "gay," thus (in this instance) obscuring the difference between ancient pederasty and modern mutual androphilia.

An advance occurred with the more detailed research published by many scholars in the *Jahrbuch für sexuelle Zwischenstufen* (1899–1923) under the editorship of Magnus **Hirschfeld**. In his own comprehensive work *Die Homosexualität des Mannes und des Weibes* (1914), Hirschfeld outlined a typology based on the age of the love object of the homosexual subject: **pedophiles**, who are attracted to pre-pubic children; **ephebophiles**, whose love object is from 14 to 21 (in current usage, from 17 to 21); androphiles, who prefer those from maturity to the beginning of old age; and gerontophiles, who like older people. Equivalent terms for lesbian relationships given by Hirschfeld were korophile, parthenophile, gynecophile, and graophile.

In addition to these schemes, which reflect object choice, Hirschfeld drew up a typology of homosexual acts which distinguished four major categories: manual, oral, intracrural, and anal.

Hirschfeld's older contemporary Richard von **Krafft-Ebing** advanced a typology based on the time of life of homosexual activity, thereby emphasizing adolescent experimentation, "temporary" (**situational**) homosexuality, and late-blooming homosexuality; this latter concept relates to the notion of "**latent homosexuality.**"

In 1913 Hans **Blüher**, who was influenced by Sigmund **Freud**, distinguished three basic types: the "heroic-male" form, characterized by individuals who are markedly masculine and not outwardly distinguishable from heterosexuals (and may in fact be **bisexual**); the type of the effeminate invert; and latent inversion, in which the longing for one's own sex is unconscious, rising to the surface only on particular occasions or not at all.

In the 1940s, Alfred **Kinsey** and his associates developed a sevenfold scale of sexual **orientation**, but this was not a true typology since there were no clear criteria dividing, say, those in group II from those in group III. In fact, Kinsey viewed this fluidity as an advantage since he opposed what he regarded as overrigid classifications.

Toward a Contemporary Typology. None of these writers sought to develop a more global typology which might encompass the full range of cultures and time periods, in part because they had no access to or were not inclined to deal with ethnological and other data regarding societies apart from their own. As **gay studies** began to expand horizons, however, the need for more comprehensive typologies which included a wider range of popular paradigms became evident.

One of the major flaws of earlier typologies was their tendency to concentrate on a single linear axis, producing two-dimensional structures. Inevitably, these schemes left out major lines of differentiation and similarity. More sophisticated new typologies might be drawn on three or even more axes, making them difficult to state simply in words (though sometimes more easily in diagrams), but probably more realistic. One must, of course, stop somewhere, or one ends up with the 687,375 types posited by the Dutch writer L.S.A.M. von **Römer** in 1904. (Most of these are theoretical, von Römer admitted, with only a tenth of them really viable. But even restricting oneself to male homosexuality as such, one would have more than 11,000 types.)

For their part, anthropologists have ascertained, during the first half of the twentieth century, that there are some 3,000 living cultures. The rapid progress of acculturation will probably prevent anthropologists from learning the native organization of homosexuality in the majority of them. Records of the past, however, permit one to add data from many cultures that are now dead, but are sufficiently known for their systems of sexual organization to be catalogued. If there truly were 11,000 same-sex types available for distribution, each culture could have one of its very own—a conclusion no doubt pleasing to the **social constructionists**, who believe that cultural differentiation inevitably produces differentiation of the forms of homosexual behavior. John J. Winkler has claimed that "almost any imaginable configuration of pleasure can be institutionalized as conventional and perceived by its participants as natural." Empirical research has not borne out this universal–polymorphous hypothesis, for there are only a handful of basic types. The conclusion is inescapable: since cultures are legion but sexual arrangements are few, there can be no one-to-one correlation of culture and sexual-orientation typing.

As Stephen O. Murray notes, "There is diversity, intraculturally as well as cross-culturally, but there is not unlimited variation in social organization and categorization of sexuality. Despite pervasive intracultural variability which is highlighted by [the] anthropological tradition of seeking exotic variance, relatively few of the imaginable mappings of cognitive space are recurrently used by diverse cultures." (*Social Theory, Homosexual Realities*, New York, 1984, p. 45).

Why such a limited repertory of types? Although progress in this realm is probably linked to the still-unsolved riddle of the biological and constitutional underpinnings of homosexual behavior, some conclusions may be offered.

A Triaxial Typology. Keeping in mind the wealth of data now available, and the necessity for clear and simple principles governing the definition of ideal types or paradigms, can one construct a useful typology of transcultural and transhistorical homosexual relationships?

Yes, but only along multiple axes. One of these needs to acknowledge that there is more than one gender, and moreover that homosexuality does not always exist in strict isolation from heterosexuality. At one end of the "gender axis" both partners are exclusively male homosexual. Moving toward the middle, at least one of the males also relates heterosexually, then both also relate heterosexually. At the other end of the gender axis one finds two exclusively homosexual/lesbian females, with intervening positions for one or both of the females also to relate heterosexually. In the middle, so to speak, one could place an exclusively heterosexual relationship, but with that position one is no longer concerned. Drawn out, the gender axis might look like this:

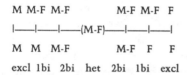

```
M  M-F  M-F        M-F  M-F  F
|——|——|——(M-F)——|——|——|
M  M   M-F         M-F   F   F
excl 1bi 2bi  het  2bi 1bi excl
```

A second dimension, the "**role** axis," can account for the major division between relationships which are role-oriented (generally along active–passive, penetrator–penetratee lines of sexual activity) and those which are significantly sexually reciprocal (with the partners exchanging sexual roles frequently if not customarily). The role axis would have gender-differentiated relationships at one end, followed by age-graded relationships; at the other (reciprocal) end is mutual androphilia. In between but still on the role-oriented side are to be found most forms of situational homosexuality; near the middle and tending to straddle the line are adolescent sexual experimentation (which can be mutual or one-sided) and ephebophilia (which shows many role characteristics but can be sexually reciprocal).

A third dimension, the "time axis," needs to be added to show the major division between those homosexual relationships which are necessarily temporary, or time-limited, and those which have at least the potential for relative permanence. On this axis one finds gender-differentiated and androphile relationships at the "permanent" end; situational and adolescent experimentation at the "temporary" end (some might add one-night stands and anonymous encounters here), with ephebophilia and age-differentiated relationships also on the "temporary" side. A graph combining these two axes looks like this:

Role-oriented

T	Age-differentiated	Gender-	P
e	Situational	differentiated	e
m	Ephebophilia		r
p			m
o	__ Adolescent ____		a
r	experimentation		n
a		Mutual	e
r		Androphilia	n
y			t

Reciprocal

Features of the Types Noted. Some basic features of these paradigms merit notice, bearing in mind that variations of a relatively minor nature can easily be found.

In the age-differentiated type, as seen in ancient **Greek** and in **Islamic** pederasty, **Spartan** korophilia, **pedophilia**, Japanese **Samurai**, the apprentices of the **Middle Ages**, and perhaps the initiatory homosexuality of tribal Melanesia, the older partner has something, namely adulthood and the knowledge that goes with it, that the younger is seeking to acquire. Accordingly, there is a sense of passage of power from the one to the other, aptly symbolized by the fact that the older is the penetrator and the younger the receiver. This state of inferiority that the protégé finds himself in is, however, only temporary, since he will pass to adulthood and penetrator status. The modern term "intergenerational sex" is misleading, since in many societies only a difference of a half or a third of a generation is typically found. The adult in this relationship may often relate to opposite-sex adults or children as well.

The **gender**-differentiated type is seen among the **berdache** of the North American Indians, the **shamans** of Siberia, the *mahu* of the South **Pacific**, the **butch-fem** lesbian pair, the **Indian** hajira, the homosexual **transvestite**, the Thai *katoey*, the **kadesh** sacred prostitutes, the *argr* of medieval **Scandinavia**, and the "straight **trade**" who goes with "**queens**," and can be found in many **Mediterranean**-derived cultures today. In these cultures the penetrated partner in male relationships relinquishes his male **identity** and the prerogatives of manhood for various compensations, which range from relative freedom of dress and manners to the magical powers of shamans. It is not necessary that the passive partner be reclassified as a full woman, though this sometimes occurs; he may be termed "not man" or some approximation to "third sex." What is important is that he is not considered to be of the same gender as his partner. Berdachehood means lifelong commitment to the role; it is not a career stage, as occurs in the age-differentiated type. The other, penetrating partner is in the gender-differentiated model considered to be a normal or typical male who might as easily bond with a female. Female counterparts found in the **Amazon** type relinquish feminine identity and sometimes become warriors, perhaps marrying a "true" female. The "masculine" partner in a male relationship or "fem" partner in a lesbian one will usually relate to the opposite sex also, though the "changed gender" partner does not, leaving two spaces open on the gender axis.

In both of the above models, the gender- and age-differentiated, two distinct roles are assumed, with virtually no overlap or reciprocity; the two partners are also viewed as distinctly unequal, if complementarily so.

Mutual androphilia, the third major type, is relatively recent, found as a widespread model only in the industrialized societies of Western Europe and North America in the nineteenth and twentieth centuries (though it was probably a marginal practice in many earlier complex societies). In mutual androphilia both partners are adults and neither relinquishes his manhood or her womanhood. Sexual reciprocation and sexual role reversal are generally honored if not universally practiced, and in theory the partners are equal. However, the relationship is only *relatively* egalitarian, since other differentials, such as those of race or **class**, may play a part.

Adolescent sexual experimentation usually does not lead to an adult homosexual relationship. It may be either reciprocal, especially in the form of mutual **masturbation**, or it may be role-oriented, depending on the power relationship pre-existing between the **youths** concerned; generally the horny adolescent male seems to prefer to maintain a dominant role but may accept reciprocation if he is unable to persuade or coerce his partner into a submissive role. The teen-age girl, however, seems more willing to reciprocate in experimental play.

Ephebophilia shows characteristics that relate it in some respects to age-differentiated relationships, such as age difference itself, social role differences, and transfer of knowledge, while in other respects it reveals marked contrasts. The ephebe concerned, rather than being penetrated, may take the "male" role as "trade," considering his older partner to be "less than male," or there may be reciprocity as in androphilia.

Perhaps the most amorphous type in this schema is **situational**, a category which frequently shows some overlap with the gender-differentiated because the heterosexually identified participants apply the heterosexual paradigm known to them to the previously unfamiliar homosexual experience. In situations such as **prison** life, this is particularly marked. Because situational homosexuality usually takes place where access to the opposite sex is denied (on shipboard, in army camps and barracks, harems, and boarding schools), there may be no actualized relationship to the opposite sex, though heterosexual feelings are often expressed. Male **slaves** and prisoners of war as well as victims of **rape** and those subjected to sexual forms of enforcing dominance find the role orientation to be emphasized; these victims commonly relate to the opposite sex as much as their penetrators. Still other instances of situational homosexuality involve initiations and rituals, usually emphasizing both role and transience.

Male **prostitution** should not be seen as a unitary phenomenon, but it is occasionally situational (in which cases it is usually role-oriented and highly transient), and in the case of transvestites is clearly gender-differentiated. Most commonly it seems to follow the ephebophilic model.

Conclusion. The triaxial schema presented above seeks to accommodate the current state of knowledge, but doubtless it will be subject to criticism—no typology being able to account for the great diversity of human sexuality—and, as knowledge deepens, will eventually be revised. Nevertheless, it should be helpful in making clear not only the diversity of paradigms encountered in any comprehensive study of homosexuality, but also the limited number of lines or axes of difference which serve as the main features delimiting one model from another.

Stephen Donaldson and
Wayne R. Dynes

ULRICHS, KARL HEINRICH (1825–1895)

German scholar. An early theorist and activist for the legal and social rights of homosexual persons, Ulrichs has been called "the grandfather of gay liberation."

Born in Aurich, Hanover, on August 28, 1825, to a pious middle-class family—his father was a civil architect and his mother's family included several Lutheran ministers—Ulrichs studied law at the universities of Göttingen and Berlin (1844–47) and became a junior attorney in the civil service of the Kingdom of Hanover. But as early as 1854, under circumstances not entirely clear, he voluntarily left state service and afterwards earned his living by writing and related activities: he was for several years a free-lance journalist and private secretary of a representative to the German Confederation in Frankfurt am Main.

During his stay in Frankfurt, Ulrichs built on current advances in embryology to develop a theory of homosexuality that he presented in a series of five booklets (1864–65) entitled *Forschungen über das Rätsel der mannmännlichen Liebe* (Researches Into the Riddle of Love Between Men); the series was later extended to twelve booklets, the last appearing in 1879. Assuming that a love drive that was directed toward a man must be feminine, Ulrichs summed up his theory in the Latin phase *anima muliebris virili corpore inclusa* (a female soul trapped in a male body) and he coined the term "Urning" (**uranian**) for such a person. The theory also applied *mutatis mutandis* to women who love other women.

This so-called **third-sex** theory furnished a scientific explanation for same-sex love drives that showed them to be natural and inborn. It followed that Urnings are neither criminal nor sick. Encouraged by his conclusions, Ulrichs began to intervene in criminal cases and sought to organize Urnings to promote their own welfare. Already in 1865, he drafted a set of bylaws for an "Urning Union" and by the next year he was planning to publish a periodical for Urnings. (He finally realized this plan in 1870, but lack of support allowed only one issue.) This activity was interrupted, however, by the Prussian invasion and annexation of Hanover in 1866. Ulrichs spoke out publicly there against this action and was twice imprisoned.

Exiled from Hanover on his release from prison in 1867, Ulrichs went to Munich to resume his earlier fight. At the meeting of the Congress of German Jurists on August 28, 1867 he pleaded for a resolution urging repeal of all anti-homosexual laws. He was shouted down, but the occasion was historic, for it marked the first time that a self-proclaimed homosexual had publicly spoken out for homosexual rights.

Further efforts by Ulrichs also had little effect; indeed, with the unification of **Germany** following the Franco–Prussian war of 1870–71, the harsh Prussian anti-homosexual law was extended to all parts of the county. In despair, Ulrichs migrated to Italy in 1880, to spend his last years in Aquila, where he edited a Latin periodical. He died there on July 14, 1895.

Although Ulrichs gained little support for his theory, he did contribute to the growing perception in the nineteenth century of the homosexual as a distinct type of person, more frequent in the population than had been thought. (His early estimate that one man in five hundred is homosexual appears low today, but was at first thought to be absurdly high.) But he did not foresee that the Urning would then not be accepted as a natural person, but would be diagnosed by psychiatry as a sick individual. Ironically, it was Richard von **Krafft-Ebing**, author of the perennial best-seller *Psychopathia Sexualis*, who, while acknowledging that it was Ulrichs' writings that had interested him in the study of homosexuality, went on to lead the movement to treat the condition as a pathology or degeneration. (Krafft-Ebing's views may be seen as a sort of secularization of the degeneration theory based on religious grounds that had been proposed in 1857 by Bénédict-Auguste Morel.) This was the prevailing opinion at the turn of the century, when Magnus **Hirschfeld** revived Ulrichs' theory and developed it into his own concept of "intermediate types." Ulrichs, however, will probably be best remembered for his courageous fight against the legal, religious, and social condemnation of homosexuality.

BIBLIOGRAPHY. Hubert Kennedy, *Ulrichs: Life and Works of Karl Heinrich Ulrichs, Pioneer of the Modern Gay Movement*, Boston: Alyson Publications, 1987.

Hubert Kennedy

UNISEXUAL

This word had its origins in the French terminology of botany, where it was introduced in the form *unisexuel* in 1794 to denote plants and flowers having only the organs of one sex (stamens or pistils), as opposed to those which were *bisexuel*, having the organs of both sexes. The linguistic innovation was the outcome of a controversy within botany that ended with the definitive finding that the reproduction of plants is sexual and that

they were not invested with asexual innocence, as earlier investigators had believed—hence the innuendo lurking in the expression "the birds, the bees, and the flowers."

The relevance of these terms to human sexual orientation stems from a development of the third decade of the nineteenth century, which saw the beginning of a semantic renovation of the whole field. In 1869 Károly Mária **Kertbeny** published a pamphlet introducing the adjectives *homosexual*, *doppelsexual*, and *normalsexual*. Kertbeny, who was a professional translator, rejected Karl Heinrich **Ulrichs'** contemporary baroque coinages of the **uranian** family. Instead, he seems to have used the Latin–French botanical terms as models for his own neologisms. While his coinages might have been forgotten, they were noticed by Gustav Jaeger (d. 1917) and used in a chapter of the second edition of his *Entdeckung der Seele* (Discovery of the Soul) in 1880, where he casually introduced the word *Heterosexualität* in the meaning "sexual intercourse with members of the opposite sex."

The French *bisexuel* subsequently took on the secondary meaning of "sexually attracted to members of both sexes," thus shifting from the anatomical sphere to the psychological. All three terms then constituted the triptych *homosexual; bisexual; heterosexual* which fit perfectly into the international Greek–Latin nomenclature of science, though in point of fact the word *homosexual* was introduced to the general public as a journalistic term at the time of the Harden-Eulenburg affair in Germany (1907–08). In French and English the terms were first used from 1893 onward by such authors as Emile Laurent, Marc-André Raffalovich, and Havelock **Ellis**.

Yet Raffalovich entitled his book of 1896 *Uranisme et unisexualité*, combining Ulrichs' German coinage with the older French one, which the semantic shift of *bisexuel* now gave the meaning "sexual attraction to members of one [and the same] sex" or "sexual activity between members of one sex." Although *unisexual/unisexuel* figures sporadically in English and French texts from the first half of the twentieth century, it could not in the long run maintain itself in competition with *homosexual*, and gradually disappeared from use. To determine its exact meaning in a given work, one must analyze the context.

Thus at the outset of the homosexual emancipation movement in the 1860s, two sets of terms were proposed: Ulrichs' Greek-German coinages from classical mythology and Kertbeny's reworking of the Latin–French ones, inspired by the language of botany. Neither set, it should be noted, was of medical origin; the notion that *homosexual* is a medical term is false and unhistorical. That *homosexual* ultimately prevailed is owing, more than anything else, to the extent to which Latin words (and new coinages using Latin roots) have become part of the abstract and scientific vocabulary of the modern languages, in Germanic and Slavic as much as in Romance.

Warren Johansson

UNITED KINGDOM
See **England; Ireland.**

UNITED STATES OF AMERICA

The United States is a republic of nearly 250 million people spanning the continent of North America, but with considerable cultural influence over much of the globe. The homosexual history of what is now the United States presents several distinct features, including: the transplantation and adaptation of European ideas and patterns of behavior; the life ways of the frontier; the persistence of varied Amerindian patterns; the gradual and irregular weakening, with numerous counteroffensives, of the hold of Christian norms over common public mores; the transition from Victorian taboos of silence

to mass-media exposure; and the emergence of the modern homosexual movement, followed by its spread throughout the industrialized non-Communist world.

American Diversity. One abiding characteristic of the United States is that it is an amalgam of very diverse ethnic heritages. Groups outside of the **Protestant** northern European tradition (which has dominated the educated middle class and hence the public and official discussion) have often retained more than traces of the sexual attitudes and practices prevalent in their original homelands, making generalizations risky. Aspects of the **Mediterranean** concept of homosexuality persist among working-class Americans whose ethnic heritage goes back to that area; **blacks** have retained their own distinctive cultural attitudes; Irish Catholics still display their propensity toward homophobic ambivalence; and new waves of sophisticated **Asian** immigrants are bringing their more relaxed perspectives along with them.

All generalizations about the United States must also be qualified not only with respect to chronology but also with respect to regional variations which were quite pronounced until very recently. From the first settlements by Europeans on the eastern seaboard of what is now the United States in the later sixteenth century to the rise to global power status in the twentieth, growth and diversification have been phenomenal. In the 1970s and 80s the number of known primary sources for the earlier history of homosexuality increased considerably, but the evidence is still so scattered that broad conclusions must be inferred from minimal evidence. In due course many of the assertions presented below will inevitably be modified; some may be completely discarded.

The Colonial Period. Before the arrival of Europeans (starting with the Spanish in Florida in 1565), the area which is now the United States was peopled by **Indians** and Eskimos, many of whose tribes had homosexual traditions of their own: the **berdache**, for instance. These traditions, however, had little if any influence on the behavior of the European immigrants who established themselves, mostly under British rule after 1607, by displacing the Indians along the Atlantic coastline; they survive in rudimentary form only in scattered reservations.

The British colonies from Maine to Georgia were sparsely populated and largely isolated from each other and from **England**. The economy was almost entirely agricultural, and subject to devastation from crop failure and in many places to counterattack from native Americans (Indians). Education was rudimentary. In these colonies, children were of great value—useful from a very early age as agricultural workers. The colonists stressed procreational sexual behavior and family arrangements which were likely to lead to that end.

Old Testament and **New Testament** passages describing non-procreational sex as sinful were emphasized by religious authorities, especially in New England where rigid Calvinism was originally paramount. Because these ideas served both secular and clerical goals, they were enshrined in colonial laws. In some cases literal Biblical language entered directly into the early **sodomy** laws. Erotic conduct between males was only one of a series of non-procreative behaviors that were punished. Masturbation and sex with prostitutes received almost equal condemnation. With the possible exception of a New Haven statute of 1655, sexual relations between women do not appear in the statutes.

Generalizations about the enforcement of these laws are difficult. From 1607 to 1740, the colonies provide only nineteen recorded prosecutions (an average of about one case every seven years). There were only four certain executions during that period (with three possible others), despite the death penalty's being mandated by all the statutes. (**Capital** punishment was required for a wide range of crimes in this period, as in England.) The situation about which there are the most data, that of Nicholas Sension of Windsor, Connecticut (tried for sodomy in 1677), reveals a lifetime of attempted homosexual seductions, but Sension was convicted only of attempted sodomy and given a sentence which was a type of probation. Unless the informal social controls (mores) were far more efficient than twentieth-century evidence could lead us to suspect, there was a great deal of same-sex erotic behavior which went unnoticed and certainly unpunished.

Toward the end of the seventeenth century (and earlier in the southern colonies), the legal term **buggery** began to replace the term **sodomy** in the statutes, and gradually Biblical language yielded to more precise descriptions of the prohibited behavior. Pennsylvania under the Quakers led by William Penn remains an exception unique in the Western world at that time: in its "Great Law" of 1682, it reduced the penalty on a first offense for sodomy to six months hard labor and a second offense was punished by life imprisonment. Various southern colonies eliminated the death penalty later in the colonial period.

Little evidence has come to light beyond the legal documents, but it is clear that there was no concept of the "homosexual" or of a sexual **orientation** such as we have today. Homosexual behavior was viewed as a sinful activity into which anyone might fall. Just how the participants perceived their own activities is impossible to know. Only one detailed personal document survives from this entire period plus some hints in the trial records in the legal prosecutions. While it is evident that the colonists had quite clear **gender** roles (differentiation between appropriate male and female activities) which led to considerable male bonding, there is no indication that deep affection between males overlapped with sexual activity. There is not a single known record of the profession of erotic desire along with affection of one male for another.

Britain was not the only colonial power to establish itself in the area which eventually became the United States. The French briefly colonized the Mississippi River valley, leaving a lasting imprint on **New Orleans** characterized by a much more tolerant attitude toward homosexuality than that brought in by the British. The Spanish occupied Florida, Texas, California, and the Southwest, bringing with them a tradition of **macho** masculinity and the Mediterranean style of homosexuality, which has had lasting influence, though more through immigration from other areas once colonized by Spain than by direct residue from the Spanish rule of what is now continental United States territory; Puerto Rico, a Caribbean island whose Spanish-speaking inhabitants have American citizenship, is a clear exception. The Dutch and Swedes also had American colonies for a brief time, but seem to have left no trace on the sexual mores of the areas they settled (New York and Delaware, respectively).

The Early Republic. The American revolution (1775–83), which brought independence to the former British colonies, can be seen as part of the **Enlightenment**, but the influences of the eighteenth-century Age of Reason do not seem to extend to changes in laws about sexual behavior beyond the modification of the death penalties for sodomy which occurred earlier. Thomas Jefferson, a religious freethinker, worked on the reform of the Virginia Criminal Code in 1777–79 and suggested that sodomy along with rape and polygamy be punished by castration rather than by death. Jefferson's ringing endorsement of "liberty, and the pursuit of happiness" in the Declaration of Independence underscored an American ethic which would in time overthrow religious regulation in favor of individual sexual self-expression. In general, however, there is little to indicate that American independence significantly altered homosexual behavior or attitudes toward it.

By the beginning of the nineteenth century, the area east of the Appalachian mountains was viewed as "settled," with the frontier in the areas to the west. However, the eastern seaboard was still sparsely populated, and the largest cities still had less than 50,000 persons. The economy remained agricultural so that the social need for population growth remained undiminished. But if a person had violated the social norms of city life or wanted to, there remained a vast frontier to which one could escape and in which one could be free from most social controls in an anarchist (and in the deep frontier, all-male) setting. In the states south of Pennsylvania, chattel **slavery** still existed. Piracy was common in coastal waters.

It has been suggested by various writers that the isolation of the frontier with its dominant population of males; the inequality of blacks who were owned as property by white masters; and the all-male environment without conventional laws on **pirate** ships were all **situations** in which homosexual behavior thrived. Each of these situations is based on a sound logic, but none as yet commands adequate documentation.

New England (the northern part of the country) in particular had a strong **seafaring** tradition, and surviving sea shanties from the nineteenth century document an amiable familiarity with homosexual practices among the sailors; such tolerant attitudes could not have been too radically at odds with the prevalent opinions among the uneducated New England males from whom the seamen were drawn.

A fascinating letter by Louis Dwight written in Boston in 1826 describes a two-year tour of **prisons** along the entire eastern coast in which he complains that boys in prison are forced to be the sexual partners—whom he labels prostitutes—of older convicts in almost every prison he visited. This one document indicates that males were not averse to looking for same-sex partners if females were not available, but a prison sample is hardly the best evidence of the norms of the general population, though like the case of the New England sailors it could not have been too violently opposed to them.

Social disapprobation of homosexual behavior was strong enough to force those who engaged in it to keep their activities a deep secret. Lesbian relationships were not prosecuted and documentation about them is even scarcer than about same-sex activities among males.

Victorian America. By the time of the American Civil War (1861–65), the United States had expanded its borders to the Pacific coast. A large influx from Ireland in the 1840s along with general immigration from all of northern Europe fostered a distinctive American culture no longer so close to its English roots. While still tiny by present standards, the main eastern settlements were more cities than towns. The agriculture-based economy now had a significant layer of commercial and industrial admixture, especially in the North. **Class** distinctions were becoming clearer. While there had always been rich and poor, social mobility seems to have slowed considerably by mid-century. Religion remained a dominant force in American life, its influence felt especially in the two decades before the Civil War with moral campaigns against slavery and alcohol.

But one aspect of life in which Americans resembled their English cousins was in the place of sexuality in public society. The term Victorian applies to much of the United States as well as to England. The discussion of genital sex and bodily functioning came to be considered inappropriate for polite discourse (or for the young even in school). Proper women were supposed to blush at the slightest allusion to sexuality; references to sex in earlier literature were commonly bowdlerized. As in England, Victorianism may not have extended its reach very far into the **working class** or the earthy frontier.

Prostitution flourished from at least the Civil War onward, and between 1880 and 1924 vast waves of immigration from southern Europe inundated the country with workers to whom Victorianism was alien.

As the religious justifications for these antisexual attitudes lost strength, medical "science" leaped in to provide the basis for the idea that unconventional sexual activity was harmful.

There have been some elaborate theses that the suppression of sexuality in general, and that of homosexuality in particular, were part of the economic control of the dominant class. Such constructs have no documentary support and are inappropriate to a society in which there was still nothing representing a hereditary aristocracy and in which both vertical social mobility or lateral geographical mobility to the western frontier were still possible. Criminal records reveal minimal prosecution of homosexuality. Society seemed to regard it as a dangerous nuisance, but those who wished to practice in private should have been able to find reasonable opportunity for doing so. It is conceivable that a relationship in which sex and love were combined would have been possible in isolated rural areas, still characterizing much of the country and the entire frontier zone.

The Coming of the Twentieth Century. In the last decades of the nineteenth century, a slightly more focused picture begins to emerge of homosexuality in the United States. In the decades between the Civil War and the end of World War I (1918), Victorian morality was dominant in the middle class, but it gradually eroded. The exception to the general picture is the remaining frontier, the Great Plains and Rocky Mountain areas which have been glamorized as the Wild West. Here again one finds a society dominated by males with little rule of law, but unlike the similar places in the earlier periods there are slight documentary evidences of eroticized same sex behaviors among the cowboys. By the end of the century, the frontier was in the last stages of vanishing as settlers filled the once-open spaces.

By the end of the century, criminal subcultures of various types were developing in the larger eastern cities, and there are some descriptions of homosexual meeting places. (Because sodomy and prostitution were against the law, arrests were made and descriptions of these places are found in some police or court records.)

In the background is the medical literature which began to be prominent in the 1880s. The idea of sin (and to some extent even of criminality) yielded to pathology so that sexual **inversion** came increasingly to be seen as a type of mental disorder. It is at this time that the desire for an erotic relationship with a same-sex partner (homosexuality), cross-dressing (**transvestism**), and **gender** confusion (transsexuality) meld into a single concept in which the desire for either contact with a same-sex partner or to cross-dress overlaps with confusion about gender. The influence of German authors who developed **homosexuality** as a concept was felt directly or indirectly in much of the American medical literature of this period, though with some time lag. The medical literature is a hodge-podge displaying varying degrees of revulsion and warped curiosity. All the doctors seemed agreed that the men should be changed if possible (although not everyone tried to do so), and the attempts range from surgical procedures such as castration to weird dietary measures. Medical writers took note of lesbianism, though confusing it with aggressiveness in women.

The first accounts of homosexually oriented individuals show how ideas from medical literature trickled into general knowledge. According to these accounts homosexual meeting places seem to have been filled with men who believed themselves to be women or who at least wanted to cross-dress. While it seems likely that there were more traditionally masculine men who engaged in homosexual behavior, they avoided these places or identification with the men in them. One can only guess that the life of most homosexually oriented men back East was lonely and lacked fulfillment: many must have heeded Horace Greeley's widely cited advice to "go West, young man, go West."

One glimpse of American homosexuality along the East Coast in mid-century is provided by the poems and correspondence of Walt **Whitman**, who thought of himself as robust and manly and was attracted to equally virile **ephebic** youths. His short poem "A Glimpse Through an Interstice Caught" may be a rendering of a bar congenial to such relationships; other poems contain descriptions of **cruising** in the urban landscape and romantic relationships with traveling companions. Whitman, too, seems often to associate the freedom to express homoerotic sentiment with the freedom to travel west.

Toward the end of the century Whitman's writings began to achieve international recognition, having a notable catalytic effect on the English homosexual theorists Edward **Carpenter** and John Addington **Symonds**. Such American poets as Fitz-Green Halleck, George **Santayana**, and Bayard Taylor followed more cautiously. This period also saw the embryonic beginnings of the American gay **novel**, including the work of such figures as Alfred J. Cohen ("Chester Allan Dale"), E. I. Prime-**Stevenson** ("Xavier Mayne"), and Charles Warren Stoddard. Hampered by censorship, the **theatre** lagged behind, and the few gay and lesbian characters that managed to find their way onto the stage were generally enveloped in a haze of ambiguity, if not outright homophobia.

The Interwar Period. More information is available for the period following World War I (1917–18). But while the 1920s were a decade of great change in the sexual habits of heterosexuals, the changes in homosexual behavior are much less revolutionary. This decade was the heyday of the Hollywood silent **film**, and there is some evidence that homosexuality was openly practiced by some of the wilder set of movie stars at this time. Kenneth Anger has noted some of the stories about Ramon Novarro and Rudolph Valentino and the lesbian affairs of Alla Nazimova. Fiction hints tantalizingly at homosexuality in some sophisticated artistic circles in the eastern United States. (American expatriates in **Paris** and on the Riviera included some who were mainly homosexually inclined.) But these are special circumstances and do not reflect the average American's life.

The attempt to present a frank description of lesbianism in Edouard Bourdet's *The Captive*, resulted in a highly publicized closing of the play by the New York police in 1927. Novels dealing centrally with male homosexuality were published in the interwar period, but most seem to have had a limited readership, while the works of Djuna **Barnes** and Gale Wilhelm about lesbianism reached near respectability.

The most important point about the broader period from the Civil War until after World War II is that the data render only sociology or social history and not history in its traditional sense. There is no political history to speak of because there was no community organizing, and there is no intellectual history such as one finds in Europe because the writing by homosexuals lacked intrinsic intellectual interest.

Only one scandal which involved homosexuality in the Navy received newspaper coverage. In the summer of 1921 a subcommittee of the Senate Naval Affairs Committee released a report about a vice squad used in 1919 at the Newport, Rhode Island, Naval Training Station to entrap "perverts." Franklin D. Roosevelt had been the Assistant Secretary of the Navy at the time and claimed that he stopped the illegal methods as soon as he was aware of them. The records of

the investigation, however, provide a vivid and lively picture of abundant homosexuality around the naval base during World War I and shortly thereafter.

Some conclusions that can be drawn from this "snapshot" are that the concept of homosexual orientation was still not widely known among working-class men, that oral sex was more popular among sailors than anal sex, that effeminate homosexuals had a well-organized private social network, that homosexual prostitution was flourishing, and that homosexuals were able to mingle with and "pick up" apparently heterosexual sailors ("**trade**") more or less openly in public spaces where the sailors gathered, and with little or no harassment, until a single violently homophobic Navy official succeeded in getting a lethargic bureaucracy to authorize the investigation. The investigator seems to have had no difficulty recruiting heterosexual men to entrap the homosexuals by engaging in sex with them; these agents were not embarrassed at having performed "male role" insertive sex and did not consider such behavior to be homosexual—the "Mediterranean" concept of homosexuality. One can question how representative this Newport scene was, and certainly maritime traditions regarding homosexuality had a major effect on Newport, but it remains true that the sailors were drawn from all over the country and generally were not career seamen.

Most of the history is social history, but reconstructing it from the available sources is no simple matter. There are, for instance, the letters of the literary critic F. O. **Matthiessen**, who had a long-term homosexual relationship with a painter lasting through the twenties (when he was a young man) and then through the thirties and forties. Not enough comparative material exists to demonstrate this to be representative, even for an upper-middle-class Eastern intellectual. It is unlikely to have been the story of the poor working-class male anywhere, or even of a person in a similar class in the south or west. Individuals with literary aspirations, such as Gertrude **Stein** and Natalie **Barney**, tended to emigrate—though the Great Depression brought some of them back.

One begins to get more memoirs from the thirties. The best of these, such as those of Samuel Steward and Donald Vining, provide a picture of changing self-understanding in several parts of the country. A young man or woman on discovering his or her attractions to same sex partners in the twenties or thirties was probably horrified by the idea. The more educated the person the more likely she or he was to turn to the medical/psychiatric literature for help and guidance. Yet perusing that literature often led to depression or even **suicide** rather than comfort. If he was lucky, the person found someone of similar background with similar impulses, but achieving such a happy outcome was difficult, as everyone disguised his feelings.

A homosexual **subculture** flourished in some of the major cities, but it was frequented by criminal classes and those who were quite "depraved" and unconcerned by their social status—often cross-dressing or acting as if they were confused about their gender. Many were repelled by this atmosphere and declined to look for a sex partner or a friend in such places. Such relationships as did exist often reflected traditional male and female roles; both gay men and women seemed to believe that one partner had to be the male and the other the female. But almost no one lived openly in such a relationship. The partners had separate residences; they certainly would not reveal the nature of their relationship to family or employers. Probably most homosexuals entered a traditional marriage and did their best to perform with an opposite sex partner. Only a very few—obviously seen as cranks—had any idea of what we would call liberation. Henry **Gerber's** attempt to organize in **Chicago** (1924–25) is known but full documentation is unavailable. Even the

organizing during and immediately after World War II was very limited—mainly to **Los Angeles** and **New York**—and certainly clandestine.

During the interwar period, male homosexual meeting places (mainly **bars**) could be found in the nation's largest cities. However such establishments were illegal and operated only with the connivance of the **police**; they were almost always owned by organized crime. Located in hidden places, they were subject to raids and closings and relatively few gay-identified people dared to visit them. It was still relatively uncommon to socialize at private (secret) parties.

World War II and After. The war (1941–45) brought enormous changes in the lives of American homosexuals, and the period after 1945 is the first for which something resembling traditional history can be constructed. For many men in combat the war proved liberating. Men who fear death have less reason to follow restrictive moral codes which limit their pleasure; why worry about what the neighbors think if you and they may be dead tomorrow? Amid a general loosening of sexual codes, the military staged drag shows and soldiers crowded gay bars in nearby cities. In the early years of the war, when manpower was scarce, the armed forces made no attempt to harass homosexuals in the service, but by early 1943 the Navy (followed by the Army), acting on recommendations from **psychiatrists**, began to establish policies to screen out male homosexuals and lesbians from induction and to discharge those already in service; wartime needs however led to irregular enforcement of these exclusionary policies.

Geographical mobility increased enormously in the late 1940s. Adult children often moved away from their parents to their own residence—sometimes in a different town. This made them feel freer to act on their homosexual desires. Bars became more common and could be found in almost all medium- and large-sized cities and occasional rural areas. Some **bathhouses** which provided a locale for sexual relations were allowed to remain open by the police. These semi-public places were still dangerous but marginally more acceptable.

In 1948 the American public was shocked by the publication of the first report by Alfred **Kinsey** and his associates, on the sexual behavior of the American male. Based on interviews with thousands of white men from all walks of life, the Kinsey Report astonished Americans with the news that more than one-third of American males had experienced a homosexual orgasm and that at least a twentieth of them were predominantly homosexual. In 1953 a companion volume on female sexuality proved similarly revealing. The Kinsey Reports occasioned the first national discussion of homosexuality as such, and proved to be the irremovable foot in the door of the Victorian taboo. Kinsey furthermore made homosexuality into a respectable subject of scientific inquiry in the United States, which had lagged behind Europe in this respect.

In 1950 the **Mattachine Society** began in Los Angeles as the first homosexual political organization, inaugurating the modern homophile **movement**, mainly as the brain child of Henry Hay, a Communist who was later expelled from the Party because of his homophile **activism**. A few years later, when Americans were beginning to be frightened by a new Red Scare, the Mattachine moved away from its left-wing and separatist origins and Hay quit the group.

Somewhat later, W. Dorr Legg began the Knights of the Clock and, with the collaboration of Don Slater and others, began to publish a monthly entitled *ONE*. In New York there was some organizing in the late 1940s including the Veteran's Benevolent Society, but records are scarce. Mattachine chapters spread to various cities in the early 1950s, including New York, and had mixed results.

Progress for homosexuals was limited in the fifties largely because of the Red Scare and its main protagonist, Senator Joseph R. **McCarthy** of Wisconsin. With great publicity at the opening of the **television** age the senator linked Communism with homosexuality, starting in February 1950, and certainly frightened homosexually-oriented men in American government. Just how great an influence his ideas had on local police enforcement is difficult to gauge, though the decade left behind a reputation for severe repression and harassment at all levels. The Federal Bureau of Investigation mounted a campaign to ferret out homosexuals in **government**, and the association of homosexuality with security risk remained in federal policy through the next four decades.

The 1950s were the period of ascendancy of **Freudian concepts**. American psychoanalysts believed that homosexuality was caused by dominance of the mother and that it could be "cured" by **psychoanalytic** therapy. The **medical theories** gained extraordinary currency even among homosexually-oriented men and women.

Journalistic exposés such as Laird and Mortimer's "Confidentials" and Jess Stearn's *The Sixth Man* painted a lurid picture of neurotic homosexuals doomed to a lonely, unfulfilled life. Various scandals involving homosexuals were reported in newspapers that had previously avoided even mentioning the word. The "Boys of Boise" (Idaho) scandal in 1956 even became the subject of a popular book by John Gerassi (a decade later), but the exploitation had the unwanted effect of making it more ordinary to discuss "sexual **deviation**." In literary circles, the "**Beat Generation**" developed a much more relaxed attitude toward homoeroticism, led by gay poet Allen Ginsberg and bisexual writer Jack **Kerouac**.

The Sixties. In many areas of American social and cultural history the sixties were a time of rapid change. Restrictions on premarital sex were drastically reduced, leading to more sexual experimentation. Increasing prosperity fostered a general sense of hedonism, supplanting the dutiful ethos (the so-called "Protestant ethic") of the previous decade. Movements for civil rights for blacks and (later) for women led to similar liberationist yearnings in lesbian and gay circles by the end of the decade. Psychoanalytic ideas were challenged in various ways. The cultural curtains of silence began to be pierced with occasional references to homosexuality in fiction, drama, and film. From 1963 on, underground art forms such as those associated with Andy **Warhol** began to tackle the subject directly.

During the decade police tolerance of gay meeting places slowly increased; patrons were less often arrested. In the largest cities, bars began to differentiate into distinct types of clientele by age, styles of dress, social class, and (in rare cases) by **sadomasochism** and fetishes. Gay organizations which had been largely dormant in the 1950s started to grow again on the two coasts (especially in **San Francisco**, on its way to becoming the "gay capital" of the country) and expand to new areas of the country. Illinois became the first state to make sodomy legal, in 1961; others followed toward the end of the decade. The first public demonstrations, sponsored by east coast homophile groups under the leadership of Barbara Gittings and Franklin Kameny, were held in Philadelphia and Washington. In 1966 the first gay **student** group, the Student Homophile League, was started at Columbia University in New York City. The latter half of the decade witnessed annual meetings of a growing national (plus **Canada**) coalition of almost all the often-conflicting gay and lesbian groups, the North American Conference of Homophile Organizations (NACHO, 1966–70). However, while the people involved were seminal thinkers and energetic strategists whose influence would reverberate through the next decade, their numbers were small and their activity received little public notice.

As a result, what they achieved is often unfairly overlooked by the uninformed who think that 1969 marked the beginning of gay political organizing.

Stonewall and the Soaring Seventies. In June 1969, the police attempted to arrest some patrons at the **Stonewall** Inn on Christopher Street in New York's Greenwich Village. The bar violated the then-accepted rules of conduct by allowing men to dance together. Some of the patrons, the most effeminate, resisted arrest; outside, sympathetic "street people" started a riot which lasted for several days. As a symbol of the gay rights movement in the United States (though not of its beginning, as is popularly held), the anniversary of the riots is celebrated annually across the nation by marches and other commemorative activity. A considered historical retrospective on the Stonewall event would see it as the catalyst for the gay **liberation** phase of that movement. The riots were followed in New York by the organization of the Gay Liberation Front (GLF) with a leftist orientation paralleling that of other liberation groups of the late sixties. It was replaced in prominence by the end of the year by the single-issue Gay Activists Alliance (GAA), a militant group which remained dominant in New York for several years and, like the GLF, was copied by similar gay groups all around the United States and even in Europe.

By the middle of the seventies the burgeoning gay rights movement was achieving considerable public notice. It expanded beyond the youthful and more "radical" types who formed groups all over the country immediately after Stonewall. In New York City, Howard Brown, a leading physician who had served as a City Commissioner, publicly announced his homosexuality. A few months later, he helped found the National Gay Task Force (NGTF). By the middle of the decade two openly gay state legislators had been elected, Allan Spear in Minnesota and Elaine Noble in Massachusetts. Gay political clubs were formed in several of the larger cities and a gay presence in the Democratic Party, one of the two major American political parties, had become regularized. Larger cities also began to sprout gay community centers, while many more specialized gay organizations began to form, including professional and occupational groups as well as a myriad of social and hobby-oriented groups. A small but vocal **bisexual** movement emerged. Nearly half the states had abolished their sodomy laws, often through court rather than legislative decision, though progress in that area slowed toward the end of the decade. Some fifty cities (and in 1982 one state, Wisconsin) passed homosexual civil rights **laws** protecting citizens against **discrimination** on the basis of sexual orientation in housing, jobs, and public accommodations. Gay-oriented social services agencies serving the gay **aging** population and **youth** began in the early eighties mainly in New York, Los Angeles, San Francisco, and Chicago.

An indicator of the success and acceptance of these organizations was their receipt of tax funds. Legal Defense Funds modeled on those of older civil rights groups developed on both coasts. These groups litigated test cases involving all aspects of lesbian and gay life with fervor and some notable successes. All these shifts on the political scene changed the lives of many homosexually-oriented men and women. Sexual meeting places such as bars remained open but became more acceptable places to visit—and many were more social in atmosphere. Publication of information appeared in many forms, distributed from newsstands, vending machines, and bookstores. Gay-oriented publications proliferated, and publishing houses were started to provide an ever-increasing number of books on gay themes. A few colleges offered courses about homosexuality. Gay men and women often rejected the traditional "double life" and revealed their homosexuality to families, employers, and friends.

A change in psychiatric classification (formalized by vote of the American Psychiatric Association in 1973 following a decade of work by movement activists) added to a more accepting climate for homosexuals, though the inevitable backlash developed with occasional outbursts by vehement homophobes based in the evangelical Protestant Christian movement (Anita Bryant and Jerry Falwell), the Roman Catholic Church (John Cardinal O'Connor of New York), or the political right wing still frightened many. The inevitable political conflicts which resulted produced a spotty record of victories and defeats, with some major cities repealing their gay rights laws while others adopted them for the first time.

In the cultural arena, the seventies marked a full-scale breakthrough, with homosexuality becoming a common topic in nearly all the arts and major works being aimed specifically at a homosexual audience.

Gays were **coming out** in droves, clustering in social and residential gay **ghettos** where the sense of gay **identity** was continually reinforced, not least by gay businesses. **Homophobia** became unfashionable in sophisticated heterosexual circles, and police harassment had virtually disappeared. An observer at the end of the seventies could easily conclude that the complete liberation of homosexuality was, if not at hand, at least in sight and perhaps inevitable.

Sexual mores, too, loosened up in the course of the decade (extending a trend of the sixties), as **impersonal sex** became widely acceptable and the closed, exclusive lover relationship was attacked as claustrophobic and out-of-date. For much of the gay population, promiscuity was no longer a dirty word. Mass sexual activity flourished in "back-room" bars and outdoor "meat racks," often accompanied by the use of **drugs** like marijuana, "poppers," and cocaine. "The wages of sin are penicillin," seemed to sum up the attitude toward venereal disease.

The Eighties. Progress toward homosexual acceptance as well as the solidification of the internal structures of the gay community in the early 1980s ran into an unforeseen obstacle: the outbreak of a viral infection and associated fatal disease, **AIDS**, which was first noticed by the press and public in the United States as a disease afflicting homosexual men. At first the media ignored the disease, but by 1983 the number of persons with AIDS constituted a major crisis, and by mid-decade it was clear that the gay male communities of major cities, especially New York and San Francisco, were being decimated. In the years before the HIV virus was identified, various theories were put forth, many of them labeling homosexual behavior as a cause. Bigots seized upon the illness as God's wrath upon homosexuals, and some right-wingers called for what amounted to concentration camps.

Even after identification of the virus and considerable efforts at public education, led by Surgeon-General of the United States Everett Koop, there was much unfocused and unwarranted fear of homosexuals in general, and the hysteria which seized many as a result of massive coverage by the media led them to distrust the government's assurances that casual association could not spread the virus. Incidents of homophobic violence and general discrimination increased markedly.

While most of the public discussion remained general and implied that any type of sexuality could spread AIDS, a small but significant part of the mass media began to discuss the differences in transmission risk between such practices as unprotected anal intercourse (high) and fellatio (low or non-existent), thereby describing specific homosexual practices to the mass public for the first time; discussion of homosexuality had to be incorporated in public school curricula.

Gay men responded to the health crisis by altering their sexual behavior; monogamy returned to favor, and condoms became *de rigueur* as a part of "**safe sex.**" Nevertheless, the toll was fearsome, both physically and psychically, and as the energy of gay communities was increasingly devoted to meeting the emergency, political activism unrelated to AIDS waned, and the community infrastructure itself began to atrophy, with bars and baths closing, cruising becoming rare, bisexuals considered anathema by women and going back underground, young heterosexuals stopping their experimentation, the **prostitution** and **pornography** scenes withering, gay studies programs being dropped, and countless numbers scurrying back into the closets from which they had so recently emerged, or resolutely locking themselves in and nailing the door shut.

By contrast, it also increased the determination of some homosexuals to work publicly on efforts to combat the crisis, and made many heterosexuals more aware of and sympathetic toward gay men. Though the crisis slowed political progress, it did not stop it. By the end of the decade two Massachusetts Democratic members of the federal House of Representatives (Barney Frank and Gerry Studds) had identified themselves publicly as homosexuals, and approximately fifty open homosexuals held local and state government offices across the nation, among them a few Republicans. Gay culture in the form of novels, plays, and films flourished more than before, and gay people showed that, despite the worst crisis anyone could imagine, they were here to stay as a visible and significant element of American society.

While AIDS decimated the gay male community, it left lesbians essentially unaffected. Many lesbians gave unstintingly to the efforts to meet the AIDS crisis, but one net effect of the crisis was to differentiate further the situations and interests of male and female homosexuals in America. Males operated in an atmosphere of defensive retrenchment, a return to more conservative sexual mores, fear of the future, and nostalgia for the glorious free-wheeling days of the recent past; lesbians concentrated on developing feminist thought and practice.

Ever since the sixties, America has been an exporter of gay culture and ideas, as movements initiated in the United States rapidly spread abroad, first to Europe and then to Japan and the Third World. This process continued in the eighties, as American homosexuals pioneered in the struggle against AIDS, and other nations where the epidemic was just taking hold looked to the American experience for guidance.

BIBLIOGRAPHY. John D'Emilio, *Sexual Politics, Sexual Communities: The Making of a Homosexual Minority in the United States, 1940–1970*, Chicago: University of Chicago Press, 1983; John D'Emilio and Estelle B. Freedman, *Intimate Matters, A History of Sexuality in America*, New York: Harper & Row, 1988; Lillian Faderman, *Surpassing the Love of Men*, New York: William Morrow, 1981; Laud Humphreys, *Out of the Closets: The Sociology of Homosexual Liberation*, Englewood Cliffs, NJ: Prentice-Hall, 1972; Jonathan Ned Katz, *Gay American History: Lesbians and Gay Men in the U.S.A.*, New York: Thomas W. Crowell, 1976; idem, *Gay/ Lesbian Almanac: A New Documentary*, New York: Harper & Row, 1983; James B. Levin, *The Gay Novel: The Male Homosexual Image in America*, New York: Irvington Press, 1983; idem, *Reflections on the American Homosexual Rights Movement*, New York: Gay Academic Union, 1983; Neil Miller, *In Search of Gay America: Women and Men in a Time of Change*, New York: Atlantic Monthly Press, 1989; [Edward Sagarin] Donald Webster Cory, *The Homosexual in America*, New York: Greenberg, 1951.

James B. Levin

UNNATURAL
See **Nature and the Unnatural.**

URANIANISM
This term for homosexuality is found in some writings of the late nineteenth and early twentieth century. Though the word and its related forms are now obsolete, their history is of considerable cultural interest.

Origins. The concept of *Uranismus* was introduced by the polymath Karl Heinrich **Ulrichs** (1825–1895) in the first of a series of pamphlets, *Vindex*, published in January 1864. There he wrote: "It is a fact that among human beings there are individuals with a male physique, but who feel sexual love for males and sexual horror for females—horror of physical sexual contact with women. These individuals I henceforth designate as 'Urnings,' whereas I call 'Dionings' those individuals who are usually called 'men'—those whose physique is male and who feel sexual love for females and sexual horror for males. The Urnings' love I henceforth call uranian or male love, the Dionings' I call dionian." These expressions, he added, were fashioned from the names of the Greek divinities Uranus and Dione, with reference to **Plato's** *Symposium* (180D), which asserts that there are two goddesses named Aphrodite: "The elder one, having no mother, who is called the heavenly Aphrodite—she is the daughter of Uranus; the younger, who is the daughter of Zeus and Dione—her we call common; and the Love who is her fellow-worker is rightly named common (*pandemos*), as the other Love is called heavenly (*uranios*)." As a classical scholar, Ulrichs naturally thought of one of his favorite Greek texts, but he gave the words a Germanic dress with the termination *-ing*, an old suffix denoting members of a clan. He maintained that contrary to popular belief, there were congenital Urnings, "a particular class of individuals in whom alongside a male physique a female sexual drive is inborn, a particular subspecies of males in whom male love is inborn."

With this doctrine—that the love of male for male is innate—went the assertion that for Urnings their own form of sexual expression was natural and that they should not be forced into the Procrustean bed meant for Dionings (whom one would now call heterosexuals). In later works he employed the terms Urninde and Dioninde for the female counterparts of the Urning and Dioning, and the compound Uranodioning for the bisexual, while the "pseudo-homosexual" he labeled Uraniaster. As the abstract forms he used the nouns Uranismus and Urningtum.

Subsequent Development. Thus by the middle of the 1860s Ulrichs had already arrived at the concepts later to be expressed as homosexual, heterosexual, and bisexual, even if the terms that he invented never achieved general use. The crystallization of the concepts therefore preceded that of the linguistic designations. Yet Ulrichs' terminology did not entirely die: it gradually made its way into the Romance languages and into English, where for a time it competed with other designations for the homosexual. In 1896, for example, Marc André Raffalovich entitled his book *Uranisme et unisexualité;* and in 1908 Edward Irenaeus Prime-**Stevenson** ("Xavier Mayne") employed the terms *Uranian* and *Uraniad* (for the Lesbian) extensively in his 641-page volume *The Intersexes,* but even he already had to qualify the exclusive homosexual as a "complete Uranian" because of the ambivalence attaching to the expressions, which could denote anyone who obtained overt sexual gratification from a member of the same sex.

Also, in a circle of English writers whose main interest was in the adolescent boy (**pederasts** in the classical sense), the term was much used, if only because its novelty and euphoniousness recommended it to the small public, virtually an in-group, which they addressed, and its literal meaning "heavenly" gave it a cachet of the noble and sublime. These were not, in the main, homosexuals attracted to other adult men, but pederasts; their appropriation of the term was another chapter in the history of the separation, if not the conflict, between the boy-lover and the modern homosexual. The mention of Ulrichs' coinage by John Addington **Symonds** (1891) and Havelock **Ellis** (1897)

had placed the word at their disposal. So when Timothy d'Arch Smith wrote his *Love in Earnest* (London: Routledge & Kegan Paul, 1970), he gave it the subtitle *Some Notes on the Lives and Writings of English "Uranian" Poets from 1889 to 1930.* If these were minor literary figures at best, they formed a rather cohesive group with a well-expressed philosophy, and their activity was the first stage in the still controversial effort to rehabilitate the *paiderasteia* of the ancients in the eyes of the modern world. The American art connoisseur Edward Perry **Warren**, under the pseudonym of Arthur Lyon Raile, published in 1928–30 a three-volume work entitled *The Defence of Uranian Love.* Its burden was that corporeal and spiritual love, ordinarily regarded as fit only for man and woman, can exist between man and boy, and that the boy-lover should look to ancient Greece for "the severe beauty, the exacting ideal" of maleness.

In the Romance languages (as in Italian) the terms *uranismo* and *uranista* are recorded in the dictionaries, but for practical purposes they have long gone out of fashion and serve only as recherché synonyms for "homosexual." Apart from "Xavier Mayne," virtually no later writer attempted to use *Dionian* and the other derivatives that Ulrichs coined from Dione, and the word is quite unknown to the heterosexuals whom it designated. However, the German author's usage proves that the threefold division *homosexual; bisexual; heterosexual* existed in his conceptual scheme, even if the linguistic innovations of others later gained acceptance in the international nomenclature of the subject.

Warren Johansson

URINATION, EROTIC

Urination, visibly originating from and aimed by the male sexual organ or from an area in close proximity to the female sexual organ, and directed onto or into the body of the partner, has long played a role as an ancillary erotic activity among a considerable minority of homosexuals, both on its own and in the context of **sadomasochistic** play. In common speech, this eroticized activity is generally referred to as "golden showers" or "water sports."

Fresh urine is a sterile solution of at least 95 percent water into which are dissolved waste products such as urea, uric acid, and mineral salts, as well as traces of other metabolic by-products. It is formed in the kidneys and retained in the bladder until ejected under high pressure through the urethra, at which time it ranges in color from clear amber to colorless, depending on the extent of dilution, and matches the internal body temperature. Until contaminated by airborne bacteria, fresh urine remains odorless. According to United States Surgeon-General Everett Koop, urine is not a vehicle for transmission of the AIDS virus.

Symbolic and Historical Aspects. Urine appears to be invested with emotional significance in the social behavior of other predator species, in the pre-sexual behavior of children, and in the mythology of primitive peoples. Havelock **Ellis**, in his *Studies in the Psychology of Sex*, even suggested that its "perpetually renewed fountain of salt water continues to bear witness to the marine environment which once surrounded our remote ancestors and is still needed to bathe and vitalize the cells in our own bodies."

Cats and other territorial hunters (a category to which human beings adhered for almost all of our evolutionary history) use the scent of their urine to mark out their territory (property) and warn off competitors. Human practitioners of "water sports" often report analogous feelings accompanying this activity: the body urinated upon is "theirs."

Ellis noted that urination "is one of the most frequent channels by which the sexual impulse first manifests itself in young boys and girls," most commonly in the age range of 10 to 12, calling it "clearly the instinctive manifestation of an erotic symbolism." Isidor Sadger, one of **Freud**'s disciples, observed that children like to show their love by urinating on a beloved person, seldom on a disliked one.

Among primitives, urine has been found to be invested with magical properties, sometimes considered a fertilizing agent, occasionally used in initiation ceremonies (as in the Papuan Gulf, where the chief stands over the youth and urinates into his mouth, which makes the youth eligible as a warrior), religious rituals (as holy water) and ceremonies, and in magical potions. Among the Hottentots and the Namaqua, both bride and groom were urinated on as part of the wedding ceremony. Among the Hindus, cow urine is still drunk in sacred rituals.

Urine also has a long tradition of medical use, both as a disinfectant in external use and as a stimulant when ingested. The ancient Romans used it for washing clothes and cleaning teeth.

Erotic Urination. Ellis, in attempting to explain why urination has become eroticized, suggested that the "excretory centers . . . take on some charm from the irradiating center of sex which they enclose," and noted that the power of love canceled the feeling of disgust associated with excretion as a result of childhood toilet training. "It is also desirable because of intimately sexual associations in the act itself, as a symbolical detumescence, a simulacrum of the sexual act, and one which proceeds from the sexual focus itself." Ellis vehemently rejected Richard von **Krafft-Ebing**'s opinion that urinary eroticism was due to "latent masochism," calling it "quite untenable" for the majority of cases.

"The impulse to bestow a symbolic value on the act of urination in a beloved person is not extremely uncommon . . . when existing in only a slight degree, it must be regarded as within the normal limits of variation of sexual emotion," Ellis summarized.

The feelings described by participants in "golden showers" vary considerably. Physically, the giver experiences the relaxation which accompanies the release of the bladder sphincter, while the receiver experiences something like a warm shower, if his body is urinated on. The taste is either slightly acid, or absent, depending on the amount of dilution. Veteran practitioners will often drink large quantities of beer or other diuretics (coffee, soft drinks) in order to increase the amount and frequency and to remove the taste. The previous consumption of asparagus is usually avoided, as it leaves a marked taste in urine. When urination is performed with the penis inside the mouth, both partners experience intimacy and the sensual stimulation of the warmth of the other's body. For both parties, the visual aspect is often highly stimulating, the position of standing urinator and supine recipient being common. (Watching a partner urinate is sometimes erotic even to those who refrain from actual physical contact with the urine.)

Psychologically, the urinator often reports "a real feeling of power and domination"; psychoanalyst Karen Horney reported "phantasies of omnipotence ... associated with the male jet of urine." The recipient usually has corresponding feelings of submission. In sadomasochistic relationships, elements of humiliation may be added, but this element is not necessarily present in non-S/M "water sports." Both parties, but especially the recipient who swallows urine, report heightened feelings of intimacy related to the incorporation of the products of one body into the other. A sense of intimacy may also be related to the feeling of marking or being marked as possession reported above.

While the frequency of erotic urination can only be guessed at in general circles, a survey (reported by Larry Townsend) of over twelve hundred participants in the leather/sadomasochistic gay-male population indicated it was "one of the most popular activities" there, with 31 percent showing "strong," 27 percent showing "moderate," and 19 percent showing "light" interest in it. A smaller sampling of nearly 300 participants divided into "sadists" and "masochists" found that of the former, 70 percent enjoyed giving "golden showers," 80 percent enjoyed urinating into the mouth, and 85 percent enjoyed urinating into the anus. Corresponding figures for the "masochists" were 80, 70 and 60 percent, indicating a diminishing consensus as the urinary target proceeded from body to mouth to anus.

BIBLIOGRAPHY. Havelock Ellis, *Studies in the Psychology of Sex*, vol. 3, New York: The Modern Library, 1936; Larry Townsend, *The Leatherman's Handbook*, New York: The Olympia Press, 1972; idem, *The Leatherman's Handbook II*, New York: Modernismo Publications, 1983.

Stephen Donaldson

USSR
See **Russia and USSR.**

USURY
The odd medieval association of homosexuality and usury is attested by the use of Old French *bougre* to mean "usurer, one who lends money at an excessive rate of interest." In the *Inferno* (11:50) Dante links the two vices toponymically as "Soddoma e Caorsa" (Cahors is a French city in Guienne, then noted as a center of usury). The linkage probably also accounts for Sir Edward Coke's strange claim in the seventeenth century that the Lombards had introduced sodomy into England; in his time it was accepted that the vice was particularly rife in Italy and the Lombards had been the bankers of late medieval London, forming the first Italian colony there.

The medieval association rests upon a Scholastic analysis of money as intrinsically sterile, so that while a cow and a bull produce offspring, gold and silver do not. In the fourteenth century,

Nicole Oresme declared that "it is monstrous and unnatural that an unfruitful thing should bear, that a thing specifically sterile, such as money, should bear fruit and multiply of itself," while Martin Luther declared more concisely, "pecunia est res sterilis" (money is a sterile thing).

A possibly related and much earlier idea depends on the metaphor of coining. Writing about A.D. 30, the Jewish thinker **Philo** of Alexandria called for the death penalty for "the man-woman who debases the sterling coin of nature." The association of sodomy and false coining recurs in the *Basilikon Doron* of King **James** I. A folk recollection of this thought-complex may survive in the expression "queer as a three-dollar bill." The implication of André **Gide**'s *Les Faux-Monnayeurs* (The Counterfeiters, 1926) is more subtle; the schoolboys' effort to produce and circulate counterfeit money seems to symbolize the acquisition of society's false values.

Wayne R. Dynes

UTOPIANISM

Beliefs in a blissful state of social harmony and fulfillment take several forms. Depending on the theorist, such a condition may be detected in the past, may exist now in some other land, or may be expected in the future.

Basic Features. The literary tradition of Utopia (Greek: "no place") began in the Renaissance, with examples by Sir Thomas More (1516), Sir Francis **Bacon** (1627), and Tommaso Campanella (1627). Insofar as sex is discussed at all in the ideal societies, it takes the form of exclusive heterosexual monogamy or even of elaborate schemes for eugenic mating in which procreation remains the focus of concern. Only after the rise of the romantic movement did Charles **Fourier** project his phalansteries, which provided for both lesbian and male homosexuality—but only under strict supervision. Until some of the "intentional communities" of the

mid-twentieth century, Fourier's example remained an exception. Even H. G. Wells' vision of utopia entailed severe restrictions on the sexual activity of women. Although it is often denied, elements of the utopian tradition passed into **Marxism**, where they helped to contribute to the prescriptive heterosexuality enjoined in all countries that have adopted the Marxist–Leninist ideology. Virtually no utopian design allows or even contemplates the promiscuity and free choice of acts and partners in which some advocates of **sexual liberty** would like society to acquiesce; instead utopian thinking endorses the need of society to direct the sexual energy of its members toward the ends desired by the planners. In this regard sexual liberty is simply the logical corollary of laissez-faire in economic life; it fundamentally contradicts the ideal of a planned, goal-oriented social order.

The utopian genre has engendered a countercurrent: the dystopian novel. In Evgeny Zamyatin's novel *We* (written 1920), an insightful forecast of the coming Stalinist tyranny, the consequences of sexual overregulation are clearly shown as one of the integral features of a totalitarian future state. In George Orwell's *1984* (1948), which is in some respects an imitation of Zamyatin's novel, puritanism is enforced by the "Women's Anti-Sex League."

Homosexual Aspects. For generations many male homosexuals have cherished the belief that ancient **Greece** was a paradise for those with homosexual desires. This is part of a larger pattern of idealizing Greek civilization or **Hellenism**. The sexual version of this trend collapses the differences between the various periods of Greek history and the local variations of the Greek states, as well as ignoring the restrictive and normative character of Greek *paiderasteia*, which gave no place of honor to two adult men who were lovers. Another popular locus is **Islam**, but this idealization presents its own problems. In similar fashion, many feminists today believe in a pre- or protohistoric matriarchal society that accorded women places of honor and power. Despite much speculation factual support for matriarchy has not been forthcoming. Textual and archeological evidence is ambiguous at best, and anthropologists—despite much searching and wishful thinking—have failed to document living tribes that are matriarchal in the true sense of the word whose customs might have been survivals of a prehistoric past.

What are the functions of such projections into the past? They are not, it should be acknowledged, necessarily untrue in every respect, and study of past patterns may provide models for attempts to transform one's own society. The problem arises when one assumes that such transformations may be easily secured, or may be accomplished without modifying the source of inspiration to accommodate it to present conditions, which are vastly different from those of ancient civilizations. For others, the privileged historical epoch is a dreamland, and contemplation of it serves to compensate for discontents in one's present life. But in more active individuals this motivation may lead to fruitful historical research.

Then there are projections that reach not across time, but across space. Since the eighteenth century, many male homosexuals have believed that sexual freedom is to be found by **traveling** to the Mediterranean, especially Italy, Greece, and the Arab countries. Today one has the phenomenon of sexual tourism in impoverished countries of the Third World. While some of these countries may indeed have freer sexual mores, in others the easy availability of commercialized sex reflects the economics of the tourist resort and the peculiar status of the foreigner as an "exotic" sexual partner. In other words, the country may be a sexual paradise only for rich foreigners who can leave whenever they wish, without having to suffer the ostracism that might happen to their native counterparts. Such aspirations are not limited to Third World countries. Many American homosexuals believe that Amsterdam or **Berlin** are the places to go, while residents of those cities may have the same impression about **New York** and **San Francisco**. Conditions change quickly, and this type of utopia (the earthly paradise) may merge with the first (the golden age), so that it is, say, San Francisco in the 1970s (before the AIDS crisis) that is viewed with longing .

Sexual utopias that involve the future are sometimes found in **science fiction**. For example, it is possible to imagine a society in which there are more than two genders, or only one. In other projections, sex changes are so simple that they can be completed in fifteen minutes. Bizarre though they may seem, such speculations are interesting as an indication of present aspirations.

The realist urges a stern avoidance of utopian fantasies, and they should not be taken literally. Since the Renaissance, however, with More, Bacon, Campanella, and their successors, utopian writings have served to showcase designs for social change. In an era of rapid technological advance, it is worth pondering how different social arrangements might operate. Such anticipation may be able to affect the outcome.

BIBLIOGRAPHY. Frank E. Manuel and Fritzie P. Manuel, *Utopian Thought in the Western World*, Cambridge, MA: Harvard University Press, 1979.

Wayne R. Dynes

VARCHI, BENEDETTO (1503–1565)

Florentine writer and historian. Born in Montevarchi, he is known today above all for his *Storia di Firenze* (a history of Florence in the period 1527–38). Contemporaries appreciated his poetic and philosophical works; thus the court lady and author Tullia d'Aragona (1508–1556) made him the interlocutor in her *Dialogo dell'infinità dell'amore* (1547). Today his Petrarchan and neo-Platonic poetry wearies through repetition of the same images, aggravated by a certain overproduction which led to his writing hundreds of sonnets. Varchi also wrote plays, such as *La suocera* (The Mother in Law, ca. 1557–60), literary commentaries, and works on the Italian language, such as *Ercolano* (ca. 1560–65).

Varchi's activity is notable for his outspoken defense, which continued until the last years of his life when he encountered much opposition, of the neo-Platonic idea of Socratic (that is homoerotic) love, as it had been set forth theoretically by Marsilio **Ficino**.

Varchi's defense of homosexual love was particularly explicit, and he took little trouble to disguise his same-sex raptures. His sonnets of Socratic love are replete with open declarations of love, while his Latin compositions amount to real confessions, to the point that his poetic work was denounced as "scandalous" by Scipione Ammirato (1531–1601) in his *Opuscoli* (published in 1637).

Varchi witnessed the last phase of the descending trajectory of the vogue of Socratic love. His contemporaries were wary of sonnets "inspired by chaste affection," such as those he wrote for the young Giulio della Stufa. From one letter written by this adolescent we know that his father expressly forbade him to see Varchi. Also several poets, among them Antonio Francesco Grazzini (1503–1584) and Alfonso de' Pazzi (1509–1555), filled Florence with sonnets that took aim at their rival's homosexual tastes.

Benedetto Varchi is probably the most significant figure in a generation of **Renaissance** homosexuals who knew how to devise an instrument of affirmation and defense from neo-Platonic sources. It was in reaction to this boldness that contemporary society found it necessary to heterosexualize the very concept of "Platonic love," purging it of the homoerotic features that Ficino had preserved.

Particularly audacious, if read with Renaissance eyes, is the conclusion of "Sopra la pittura e la scultura" (On Painting and Sculpture; 1546), in which Varchi provides an extensive commentary on two love sonnets of **Michelangelo** addressed to Tommaso de' Cavalieri. Varchi praises at length "all his aspects which are full of Socratic love and Platonic concepts," that is to say the compositions of love for boys. It is significant that Michelangelo appreciated the text, which had been sent to him, and thanked the author.

Varchi's "bad reputation" stems in part from an obscure sexual scandal of which we still know little or nothing (it is discussed by Manacorda). As the sonnets targeting him show, however, the main problem arose from his excessive advocacy of a very audacious concept of Socratic love. When society reached the point of identifying this love with sodomy pure and simple, the situation of Varchi as its advocate became indefensible. It was probably as a result of this development that in the last years of his life he decided to seek protection in the church, becoming a priest.

Nonetheless, as late as 1564, in pronouncing the oration at the funeral of Michelangelo, the impenitent writer could not bring himself to omit (however brief and prudent the mention) of the bonds that linked the great sculptor to Gherardo Perini and Tommaso de' Cavalieri.

One year later Varchi followed Michelangelo. His death ended a cycle of homosexual intellectuals that had started with Marsilio Ficino and closed with the imposition of the new rigid climate of the Counterreformation.

BIBLIOGRAPHY. Giovanni Dall'Orto, "Socratic Love as a Disguise for Same-sex Love," *Journal of Homosexuality*, 16 (1988), 33–64; Guido Manacorda, "Benedetto Varchi: l'uomo, il poeta, il critico," *Annali della R. Scuola normale di Pisa*, 17:2 (1903); Luigi Tonelli, *L'amore nella poesia e nel pensiero del Rinascimento*, Florence: Sansoni, 1933.
Giovanni Dall'Orto

VARIANT

This term, used both as adjective and as noun, enjoyed a limited currency in the 1940s and 1950s as a synonym of **homophile**. It probably owed its origin to the wish to avoid the unfortunate connotations which such terms as **pervert** and **deviate** had acquired by contamination from the older moralizing vocabulary, so that the latter designations were completely unacceptable to the gay community and its sympathizers. Two works that featured the word in their titles were George William Henry's *Sex Variants* (New York, 1941), a collection of risqué sexual biographies of homosexual men and women assembled by his collaborator Alfred A. Gross, and Jeannette Foster's classic study *Sex Variant Women in Literature* (New York, 1956).

While the term could have been applied to the whole range of departures from conventional sex expression, in prac-

tice it was limited to the homosexual, the underlying notion being that homosexuality is a part of the spectrum of normal sexual activity, not some willful or depraved aberration. Hence the usage was an effort to locate homosexual expression in the domain of the biological rather than of the pathological—to guard against the "medicalization" of the subject. In her **bibliographies** Barbara Grier drew a distinction between overt lesbianism and "variant" behavior in which the homosexual expression is latent or even denied. Perhaps because of its blandness and ambiguity, the term largely faded from the literature of the 1960s and later as a positive "gay consciousness" emerged.
Warren Johansson

VARIETY, REVUE, AND CABARET ENTERTAINMENT

Forthright presentation of homosexuality in popular entertainment was not uncommon so long as the deviant was depicted as an outrageous freak: a mincing effeminate in the case of men, a tough bull-dyke in the case of women.

Earlier History. At the beginning of the twentieth century French topical revues teemed with such caricatures; one presented a tableau of an ephebe crowning Count **Adelswärd Fersen** with roses. In *La Revue de Cluny* and *Je veux du nu, na!* (both 1908), Prussian officers were boldly lampooned as "queers" in the wake of the **Eulenburg** scandal. In the 1920s, the American vaudevillian Elsie Janis was startled to find that the Parisian revue in which she starred contained a lesbian sketch and a tableau of **Henri III** tatting with his minions. After World War I, the comedian O'dett brought homosexual gags into the French music hall and the clown Rhum played a "fairy" in his circus routine *La Cabine miraculeuse*. But a sharp dividing line between life and art had always been maintained. At the Chat Noir cabaret, Maurice Donnay's shadowplay

Ailleurs (Elsewhere, 1889) was hailed as a masterpiece, one of its episodes featuring entwined lesbians and a caricatured androgyne. Yet when **Colette** Willy performed at the Folies Bergère in a sketch, "Le Rêve d'Egypte" ("The Dream of Egypt," 1907), in which her sapphic lover, the Marquise de Belbeuf (d. 1944), portrayed a male painter infatuated with his model, the reaction was hissing and scandal.

In the United States, the trade journal *Burlesque* announced hopefully in 1916, "The days of the ... sissy ... are over. They have all been worked to death." This did not prevent their persistence in smart revue, and a generation later one could find Bert Lahr and Ray Bolger camping it up in a parody of *Design for Living* in *Life Begins at 8:40* (by D. Freedman, 1934). Fannie Brice, one of the great headliners of the Ziegfeld Follies, made no secret that her trusted aide and adviser was the maidenly Roger Davis.

Most nightclubs catering to a specialized clientele provided some sort of performance: the writer Katherine **Mansfield** was seen in a one-woman show à la Ruth Draper in a London lesbian club in 1913. Homosexual cabarets in Weimar Berlin were regular tourist attractions. The Eldorado-Diele featured such attractions as the ball-walker Luziana (billed as "Mann oder Frau?," "Man or Woman?"); the Alexander-Palast gave Saturday shows starring the best variety performers of the city, including Mieke the female impersonator. But the outstanding and outspoken gay comedian, Wilhelm Bendow (1884–1950), was beloved by straight and gay audiences alike. In the guise of a scatterbrained "fairy," he insinuated pungent innuendo, blasting politicians and society fads. His fans included the Nazis who allowed him to go on performing until 1943 when the war went sour for them, and he was banned for too much frankness.

Greenwich Village in New York also provided tourist attractions: "during the twenties and thirties, there were many nightclubs in the area which featured homosexuals on public exhibition, either as part of the show or as paid sitters or mixers in the crowd. ... These deviates drew such crowds that many paid homosexuals were only acting that way for a fee" (Leo Klein, *You Are Not Alone*, 1959). Wartime travel restrictions, military and, later, municipal police interference curtailed this type of freak-show. Black clubs in **Harlem**, tolerated by the authorities as peripheral folk-culture, remained open in advertising the predilections of the performers: Bessie Smith, Gladys Bentley, "Moms" **Mabley**, Ada "Bricktop" Smith, and others.

After World War II. Post-war revues emphasized glamour drag and the impersonation of female superstars, making an appeal to audiences of either sexual persuasion. But the increase of homosexual consciousness gave rise to comedians such as Michael Greer and Wayland Flowers with his ventriloquial Egeria, Madame; their jokes could best be appreciated by an in-crowd. In England, popular comedy has always displayed a broad streak of camp much appreciated by the mass public, which manages to segregate it mentally from its condemnation of real-life sexuality: comedians like Frankie Howerd, Kenneth Williams, and Larry Grayson have exploited this, particularly through *double-entendre*.

Glamour drag made a comeback in the 1970s with La Grande Eugène in Paris, Dzi Croquettes in Rio de Janeiro, and even Zou at the Blue Angel in New York. With gay liberation, "alternative cabaret" became more vocal and evident. In England, Bloolips continued to use outrageous drag, self-aware camp, and outworn variety conventions to make political statements. Three-man operations like the Terry Towel Show and The Insinuendos played in pubs and clubs throughout London, to mixed audiences, with great success in the late 1980s. The West German equivalent was the three

Tornados (Gunther Tews, Holger Klotzbach, and Arnulf Rating), founded in 1977.

The first gay revues in the United States were flashy commercial enterprises like Fred Silver's *In Gay Company* (1975). But more extreme drag groups like Hot Peaches and "gender-bender" concepts heralded more politically satirical enterprises. Typical is the five-man United Fruit Company, which arose in 1985: its targets included AIDS, gentrification, U.S. interference in Central America, and TV commercials. San Francisco fostered Gay Comedy Nights at the community arts center, the Valencia Rose, from 1981 to 1985; performers who cut their teeth there later constituted *Can't Keep a Straight Face*, a three-man/three-woman revue which resembles traditional cabaret in its reliance on sketches and in its satirical point. In other cities as well, the emergence of the gay audience from underground and its merging with a "with-it" public has encouraged more elaborate entertainments than mere microphone jockeys; for example, Boston's Club Cabaret has begun to sponsor regular musical revues (*The Ten Percent Revue*, 1987; *Disappearing Act*, 1988).

Lesbian Performers. British lesbian comics have often managed to walk the knife-edge between radical statement and commercial success: Karen Parker and Debby Klein were cited as one of the three top cabaret acts in England in 1987. Siren Theatre Company created a parodic Western, *Hotel Destiny* (1988), which simultaneously spoofed stereotypical film roles and illusions of personality. American lesbian performance in the mid-1980s has centered around the WOW cafe in Manhattan's East Village. In a parody of talk-show formats, Alina Troyana would appear both as the outrageously "femme" Carmelita Tropicana and the "butch" Julio Iglesia to send up traditional gender identities within the lesbian community. Peggy Shaw and Lois Weaver of the Split Britches Company comprise a doubles act

that shifts between these roles. While some stand-up comics, such as Terry Baum, graphically and hilariously depict lesbian sexuality, others, such as Kate Clinton, who began performing at feminist conferences and musical events, have had to tailor their material to more mixed audiences when they moved to comedy clubs. Achieving split focus has not proved a problem for Lily Tomlin, using material by Jane Wagner; having begun as a mainstream comedian, she has become bolder and franker as her particular constituency has grown more conspicuous.

Laurence Senelick

VASE PAINTING, GREEK

Introduced during the Neolithic period of prehistory, ceramic pots were the all-purpose containers of the ancient world. They were used for eating and drinking as well as for long-term storage. In order to increase their value, or make the wares inside more attractive, many vases, especially those intended for the upper classes, bore incised or painted decoration.

In **Greece** during the Mycenean period in the second millennium, figural decorations appeared on vases, though none is erotic as far as present knowledge goes. In the succeeding "dark age," vase painting became austerely geometrical, with schematic animals and human figures appearing only occasionally. A wave of Near Eastern influence enriched this meagre repertoire, heralding the emergence of the full-blown black-figure style featuring an elaborate iconography of mythological and everyday-life scenes. Leading potters and painters, especially at Athens, began to sign their work as a mark of pride. About 530 B.C. a fundamental change occurred in the technique of Greek vase painting, with red figures in reserve against a black ground, a field reversal of the contrast that had been the hallmark of the black-figure mode. Iconographical conventions continued, however, basically unchanged.

In the early sixth century, scenes began to appear in which an older bearded male (the *erastes*) courts a younger man (the *eromenos*). In some instances, the intention is signaled by unmistakeable body language: the older man extends one hand in entreaty to the youth's chin, while the other touches his genitals. In other examples the older man brings a gift, such as a live hare or a rooster. These presents suggest a relationship of older hunting customs with **pederasty**. There are also banqueting scenes (**symposia**) in which older and younger men recline together on couches. In the 1970s Italian scholars published a monumental fresco of this type found at Paestum, a discovery that suggests that many of the scenes known at present only from vase paintings had their counterparts in large-scale works.

In a few instances copulation occurs, though usually intercrurally—that is to say, the older man inserts his erect member between the thighs of the younger. From these scenes Sir Kenneth Dover inferred that anal copulation was rare—a conclusion contradicted by literary evidence. What probably accounts for the discrepancy is that the limited conventions of the artistic language of Greek vase painting permitted only a limited range of depiction, so that one cannot expect the vases to document the full spectrum of ancient sexual conduct.

There are also mythological depictions bearing on homosexuality, the most frequent being those of Zeus' courtship and abduction of the Phrygian youth **Ganymede**. In some pieces, the mythological scene is the doublet of one of daily life, suggesting that the homoerotic inclinations of the gods were regarded as warrants for human conduct.

Homoerotic interests were not limited to a small clientele of purchasers, but were evidently prevalent among the painters and the potters themselves, who often adorned the vases with inscriptions indicating that "So-and-so is beautiful." These *kalos* inscriptions, which occur even when the imagery of vase is not otherwise homoerotic, have parallels in **graffiti**, as seen on the island of Thera. Sometimes they are accompanied on the vases by "pinups," portraits of the beloved youths. Studies of the chronology of the kalos inscriptions indicates that they were allocated among a restricted number of supremely admired sex objects, who were evidently members of the *jeunesse dorée*; each individual reigned only a few years, yielding to other favorites as his beauty faded.

Study of the male images, which are frequently nude, shows something of the changing fashions in male beauty over the generations. In the sixth century the youths were relatively husky, but as time passed they became more lithe and elegant, possessing what would now be called a swimmer's body. By the fourth century an almost androgynous ideal prevailed.

Interest in shapely male bodies persisted through Greek art until the end, in sculpture as well as in painting, but popularity of overtly homoerotic scenes began to taper off in the later part of the fifth century B.C. The reasons for this decline are not entirely understood, but it appears to reflect overall changes in the iconography of vase painting, which became relatively impoverished.

While painted pottery is known from many cultures, no body of homoerotic imagery comparable to that of ancient Greece has as yet been identified. This seeming dearth may reflect in part prudery in publishing and exhibiting relevant pieces, rather than any complete absence. Until recently most homoerotic Greek vases were kept locked in museum storerooms, and photographic reproductions, when published at all, were likely to be cropped or altered. Pre-Columbian Peru had a lively production of erotic ceramics in which explicit scenes of copulation are presented sculpturally; a few of the surviving pieces (some were deliberately destroyed after finding) are homosexual.

See also **Beauty Contests**.

BIBLIOGRAPHY. Sir Kenneth Dover, *Greek Homosexuality*, Cambridge, MA: Harvard University Press, 1978; Gundel Koch-Harnack, *Knabenliebe und Tiergeschenke*, Berlin: Mann, 1983; H. Alan Shapiro, "Courtship Scenes in Attic Vase Painting," *American Journal of Archaeology*, 85 (1981), 133–43.

Wayne R. Dynes

VENEREAL DISEASE
See **Sexually Transmitted Diseases.**

VENICE

This northern Italian city, which stands on a series of islands in a lagoon of the upper Adriatic, is world-famous for its wealth of artistic monuments and for its unique and picturesque urban fabric, punctuated by innumerable canals and bridges.

History. Founded in the middle of the fifth century by refugees from a mainland then ravaged by barbarian invaders, the city remained in Byzantine hands, growing as a commercial center and increasing in autonomy, until independence was achieved in 697. In the ninth century Venice's particular political profile began to emerge: a republic that was at first democratic, then from 1197 on oligarchic. The merchant families who monopolized power (and the title of *nobili*) made sure that Venice's policy was directed to the increase and safeguarding of commerce. Expansion in the East and the securing of trading posts there were favored by the Crusades, especially the Fourth (1204), which the republic succeeded in manipulating to its own advantage to create an empire.

Defeating its maritime rival Genoa in 1378, Venice expanded its domain in the hinterland. The fall of Constantinople to the Turks in 1453 and the discovery of America in 1492 ultimately doomed the city to gradual decline as new trade routes opened on the oceans. Yet the strength of the republic remained impressive: although locked in a seemingly endless conflict with the Turks, sixteenth- and seventeenth-century Venice was nonetheless able to conduct a foreign policy that was independent of the great European powers and of the papacy. The descending curve, which was relieved by festive ceremonial and renewed artistic vitality, ended in 1797 with loss of independence. Conquered by Napoleon, the city was ceded to **Austria**, which kept it until 1866, when Venice joined the new Kingdom of **Italy**.

In the nineteenth and twentieth centuries industrialization occurred in the coastal centers of Marghera and Mestre, which are administratively part of Venice. The city on the lagoon, having lost much of its own population, today lives mainly on the receipts from tourism.

Homosexuality in the Renaissance: Research Parameters. Among the various city-states of **Renaissance** Italy Venice has gained particular attention on the part of historians for its evidence of older patterns of homosexual behavior. The reason for this interest resides not so much in any special quality of homosexual behavior in the republic as in a particular political situation.

A thousand years of political stability, and the city's freedom from invasion and sacking, permitted it to accumulate one of the fullest historical archives in the Western world. These archives have preserved trial records, sentences, and texts of laws against sodomy from the fifteenth century onwards. The accessibility of this material has made it a precious resource for research—the city's tangled and peculiar political structure notwithstanding.

The Administrative Framework. Never having been part of the Holy Roman Empire, Venice never accepted the political forms and legislation in force on the mainland. Venice tended to shun an organic code of laws. In practice it often occurred that two courts were called in, so that differences had to be decided pragmatically, case by case. For these reasons, Venetian antisodomy legislation cannot be studied through one or more laws of a nonexistent code, but through a myriad of *parti* (decrees) promulgated from time to time to deal with particular transgressions. This legal situation recalls that of the English **common law.**

Until the fifteenth century the chief Venetian magistrature responsible for the repression of homosexual behavior was that of the "Signori di Notte" (the Lords of the Night), who had the responsibility of patrolling and overseeing the city. In 1407, however, the Lords were guilty of excess of zeal: in a big operation they arrested 35 sodomites, 14 of whom belonged to noble families of the city. For this reason, the Council of Ten, a body responsible for the security of the state, stepped in, checking the authority of the Signori di Notte so as to block the proceedings. Henceforth almost all sodomy trials were handled by the Consiglio dei Dieci, which also promulgated the decrees concerning the repression of homosexual behavior.

After the Council of Trent (1545–66) Venice also had to accept—not without long resistance and open defiance of the pope—the papal **Inquisition**; it was received, however, only with serious limitations on its jurisdiction. As regards sodomy the Inquisition was competent only for clergy, laity remaining within the jurisdiction of the secular courts. Thus no more than twenty trial records of this sort are preserved among the Inquisition papers.

With the Austrian conquest, Venice received first the penal code of Lombardy-Venetia, and then the Austro-Hungarian code, both of which criminalized sodomy. Annexation to the Kingdom of Italy in 1866 effectively abrogated the sodomy laws.

Social Realities. Recent studies in the Venetian archives (especially those of Ruggiero, Labalme, and Pavan) have brought to light the existence of a flourishing sodomite **subculture** in the Adriatic city, provided with meeting places (minutely listed in the decrees based on careful surveillance) and marked by a certain degree of reciprocal knowledge among the participants. Among the places noted that must be watched were the shops of barbers (who often served as pimps), the establishments of pastry makers, unbuilt land on the edge of the city, and the porches of certain churches.

The pattern of relationships that emerges from the trial records is—like that of **Florence** and other historic Italian cities—**pederastic** in character: that of an adult (who plays the role of insertor) and an adolescent (the insertee). Money almost always played a decisive role in effecting the connection. In general the sodomy trial records reveal a high number of cases of violent assault, which received the death sentence, because these were more likely to be denounced by the victims or their relatives.

The many group trials (for example those of 1407, 1422, 1460, 1464, 1474, 1537, and 1547) show how it was possible, starting with a single arrested person, to find other guilty parties; this was also done through young hustlers who sold their favors to several clients. Yet the traumatic experience of 1407 made sure that no dragnet on a similar scale was attempted afterwards, at least as far as we know. This reflects the usual state of affairs in large cities where the "vice squad" knows the extent of clandestine sexual activity but is also aware that it must not compromise the holders of wealth and power.

Toward the middle of the sixteenth century the trial records also bear witness to taverns in which, with the acquiescence of the proprietor, sodomites could conclude their arrangements in peace and tranquility. The apparent resemblance between this practice and that of the English **molly houses** of the eighteenth century has not been studied, and must be considered not proven. In a trial of 1537, however, we find the use of a feminine name (*Ninfa*, "nymph") for one of the accused, foreshadowing the use of feminine names later in the molly houses of **London**. This period also sees the emergence of more or less organized male **prostitution**, using barbers, tavern keepers, and procuresses as go-betweens.

The attitude of the Venetian Republic toward homosexual behavior was always severely unfavorable, so that in the middle of the fifteenth century there was discussion as to whether to pass—as had been done in other Italian states—from the penalty of burning at the stake to that of hanging or decapitation followed by burning—scarcely humane alternatives. Yet it was probably this severity of punishment that discouraged the people from systematic denunciations of sodomy. When an accusation would lead almost certainly to the condemnation of the culprit to death it was difficult for a friend, a relative, or even an acquaintance to denounce an "unnatural act" of which he had knowledge. Thus the trial records show a number of cases in which people warned their associates or helped them to flee.

To this understandable reticence there must be added, from the fifteenth to the eighteenth century, subterranean currents of **libertine** thought, for the principal center of this philosophical trend was at the University of Padua, in Venetian territory. The tolerance found among the general population, especially among the educated, explains how it was possible to publish in 1652, probably in Venice itself, Antonio Rocco's almost legendary defense of pederasty, *L'Alcibiade fanciullo a scola*.

Later Developments. For the period after the sixteenth century, which has thus far attracted little attention from scholars, there is much to be learned. The persistence or rebirth of a libertine attitude—one tolerant of homosexual acts—is nonetheless witnessed by such documents as the jovial erotic poems written in Venetian dialect by Giorgio Baffo (1694–1768), which treat homosexual relations with the same unbridled joy as heterosexual ones, and the memoirs of one of the most famous Venetians of the eighteenth century, Giacomo (Jacques) Casanova (1725–1798).

After the fall of the Republic Venice became an obligatory stop on the grand tour of the romantic homosexuals of northern Europe in the nineteenth century; here the outstanding names are Count **Platen**, John Addington **Symonds** (who tells in his memoirs of his affair with a Venetian gondolier), and Frederick **Rolfe**, who styled himself "Baron Corvo." It was not an accident that Thomas **Mann** chose Venice as the locale for his novella of the homosexual passion of a middle-aged man, *Death in Venice*.

Until World War II Venice was one of the favored spots of international homosexual tourism, especially in autumn—to the point that such birds of passage (and others mingling with them) were termed *settembrini*, "those who arrive in September." The tolerance of the city's inhabitants made of it a kind of "zone of liberty" for well-healed homosexual visitors.

With the progressive depopulation of the city (from the end of the war to the present the urban nucleus declined from 200,000 to 90,000 inhabitants) and the "clearance" of proletarians to the mainland (Marghera and Mestre) to make room for the mass tourist industry, the city's role as a magnet for the elite gay traveler has declined.

There remain some notable relics of the past which have been given new life by the revival of the Venetian carnival, which is celebrated throughout the world. There is also the voice of the living poet Mario Stefani (b. 1938), who sings both of Venice and of homosexual love. Still these points cannot disguise the fact that today the city stands apart from the main currents of Italian gay life and from those of international gay tourism.

BIBLIOGRAPHY. Patricia H. Labalme, "Sodomy and Venetian Justice in the Renaissance," *Tijdschrift voor Rechtsgeschiedenis*, 52 (1984), 217–54; Gabriele Martini, *Il "vitio nefando"* nella Venezia del seicento: Aspetti sociali e repressione di giustizia, Rome: Jouvence, 1988; Elisabeth Pavan, "Police des moeurs, société et politique à Venise à la fin du moyen âge," Revue Historique, 264 (1981), 241–88; William Ruggiero, The Boundaries of Eros, New York: Oxford University Press, 1985.

Giovanni Dall'Orto

VERGIL (70–19 B.C.)

Greatest Latin poet. Descended from an equestrian family from Mantua, Publius Vergilius Maro was a propagandist in the employ of the Emperor Augustus' pederastic and possibly pathic minister of culture Maecenas, to whose circle he introduced the bisexual lyric poet **Horace**. Vergil created the *Aeneid* as a Latin epic to correspond, the first half to the *Odyssey*, the second half to the *Iliad* of **Homer**, tracing the descent of the Romans from the Trojan hero Aeneas and the fusion of Trojans and Latins into a single commonwealth. The epic, which embodied the high ideals and heroic destiny of the Romans, became the basic text for the education of their upper-class boys. His poem avoided homoeroticism—except for the heroic lovers Nisus and Euryalus.

Influenced by **Catullus** and the Hellenistic poets, Vergil studied Epicurean philosophy at Naples. As a young man he composed *Eclogues* partly taken from the *Pastorals* by **Theocritus**. His *Georgics* were in some ways inspired by Hesiod, but actually more by Callimachus and other Alexandrians. Under the first **Roman emperors** the rush to imitate the cosmopolitanism of **Alexandria** and the **Hellenistic monarchies** helped make pederasty less unacceptable. Of weak constitution, unlike most Roman aristocrats who while teenagers married girls of 12 or 13 as arranged by their respective *patresfamilias*, Vergil was one of the few distinguished Romans never to marry. A biography composed in late antiquity described him unambiguously as a boy-lover. He sang of pederasty in the *Second Eclogue*, which treats the unrequited love of the slave Corydon for their master's favorite, the shepherd Alexis. The old claim that he was merely parroting Hellenistic pederastic themes, which he did, sometimes closely, sometimes freely, to court favor with his patron Maecenas, is no longer believed to "explain away" his subject matter. Though all his bucolic verses have Greek characters and are often set in **Sicily**, Vergil infused Italian elements and personal touches into them.

Christians, who claimed with the Emperor Constantine at Nicaea in 325 that Vergil's fourth and sixth *Eclogues*, celebrating the birth of a son for Augustus, really was divinely inspired to foretell the birth of **Jesus**, have long striven to deny that he actually praised, much less practiced pederasty, hence the concoction of the literary convention that he only followed Greek models or the tale that he so wrote to please Maecenas. His description of the love of Corydon for Alexis furnished the title of André **Gide**'s defense of homosexuality (1924). So if the pederastic theme occupied a minor place in his writing, Vergil remains one of the great homosexual figures of world literature, whose epic poem commemorated the historical destiny of Rome.

BIBLIOGRAPHY. Jasper Griffin, "Augustan Poetry and the Life of Luxury," Journal of Roman Studies, 66 (1976), 87–105; idem, Latin Poets and Roman Life, London: Duckworth, 1986; Saara Lilja, Homosexuality in Republican and Augustan Rome (Commentationes Humanarum Litterarum Societatis Scientiarum Fennicae, 74 [1982]).

William A. Percy

VERLAINE, PAUL (1844–1896)

French symbolist poet. Born in Metz, he published his first book of verse, *Poèmes saturniens*, in 1866. It belonged to the Parnassian reaction to Romanticism, embodying the virtues of classical order and clarity. A few of the poems, however, revealed that he was more suited to a suggestive style than one with the classical rules and the 12-syllable alexandrine. He also employed *vers impair*, with an odd number of syllables, together with unusual verse forms. His subsequent volumes of verse continued this trend toward a distinctive style, transposing into verbal music the make-believe atmosphere and moonlit settings of the eighteenth-century painters popularized by the brothers Goncourt.

In the fall of 1871, although he had been married for some eighteen months, he fell under the spell of the personality of the 17-year-old Arthur **Rimbaud**. The two of them tried to live as lovers in accordance with a new moral code, or rather amoral code, in which a different world was to be created through a different kind of poetry. But the relationship between the two poets was a tortured one and ended in a violent quarrel in Brussels in July 1873 when Verlaine shot Rimbaud in the wrist. Sentenced to two years' imprisonment during which he found the hoped-for reconciliation with his wife impossible, he returned to the Catholic faith in which he had been raised, still trying for years afterward to lead a new life. However, caught between the aspirations of religious faith and the temptations of the flesh, he yielded to the latter.

At one of his teaching posts, the Collège de Notre-Dame at Bethel, he formed a deep homosexual attachment for one of his pupils, Lucien Létinois, who accompanied him when he returned to Paris in July; the two lived near each other for a time until the youth died of typhoid in April 1883. The loss caused Verlaine an emotional shock even more intense than is suggested by the poignancy of the poems in *Amour* composed in his memory. His mother bought the Létinois' farm at Coulomnes, and here he lived for two years, drinking at local taverns, and carrying on questionable affairs with vagabonds and boys imported from Paris, so that his scandalous way of life caused the local people to despise him. The death of his mother in January 1886 left him penniless, and the last years of his life were spent half in the hospital, half as a destitute man of letters on the street. He died in January 1896 at the age of fifty-one.

Explicit homosexuality is a minor theme in Verlaine's work, notably in two collections of verse, *Les Amies* and *Hombres*. The first was a slender volume of six lesbian sonnets entirely in feminine rimes (violating the classical rule that masculine and feminine rimes must alternate), published by Poulet-Malassis in Brussels, where erotic literature had taken refuge to escape the repressive regime of the Second Empire. In it Verlaine veiled his own homoerotic impulses behind scenes of lesbian love. For the modern reader, the tender and playful "girl-friends" radiate a lascivious charm but can scarcely be called obscene. For these sonnets the poet borrowed the vocabulary of Baudelaire, especially the "femmes damnées" of *Les Fleurs du mal*. Evident also is the influence of the Parnassian poets with their chiseled verses on classical themes, particularly in "Sappho." But in his candid portrayal of supple, young, passionate female bodies bathed in a delicate atmosphere, Verlaine was in his day striking out into new territory.

Two of the poems in *Hombres* ("Men") were written by Verlaine and Rimbaud in 1871–72 as contributions to the *Album Zutique*, a kind of guest book kept by the physician Antoine Cros, who invited a group of poets to meet and recite their facetious verses. Two more were composed in 1887 and 1889, the remainder in 1891 when Verlaine was a patient at the Hôpital Broussais. The collection appeared only after the poet's death, published clandestinely in Paris by Messein in late 1903 or early 1904.

Together with a set of poems on heterosexual themes entitled *Femmes*, the verses form a *Trilogie érotique* that has circulated since 1910 for the most part in expensive, quite rare editions often illustrated by well-known artists, but has been excluded from official editions of the complete works. The poems reflect Verlaine's long history of homosexual attachments and casual encounters, beginning in his teens and reaching its high points in the love affairs with Rimbaud and Lucien Létinois. The rural lads of "Mille e Tre" may have been inspired by his sexual escapades at Coulomnes, while "In This Café" hearkens back to to the two bohemian lovers masturbating in public in symbolic defiance of one of society's most stringent taboos. The pieces have their flaws: the sonnets of *Les Amies* are slightly cloying, and a certain repetitiousness (the bane of **pornographic** literature) afflicts *Hombres*. Nevertheless, in his poems Verlaine created a strange and compulsive beauty by embracing the whole range of sexuality with a hearty candor that is all the more exceptional since it belongs to a time when the morbid and the effete were deliberately cultivated. The homoerotic poems, though sexually explicit and sometimes obscene in language, transcend pornography and achieve true literary status.

In another poem, "Ces passions," first published in *La Cravache* of February 2, 1889, and then included in *Parallèlement*, is Verlaine's boldest exaltation of homosexual love, whose daring contrasts all the more with the regularity of the versification and the faultless composition. At the same time, in the third line of certain stanzas the poet inserts ponderous verses with long words meant to suggest the solemnity of the rites of male bonding which they celebrate, while heterosexual unions are dismissed as trifles, "erotic needs," diversions of couples who dare not go beyond the norm.

Verlaine's 1883 sonnet "Langueur," on the fall of the Roman Empire, was credited with launching the **Decadent** movement. However this may be, his name remains unalterably linked with fin-de-siècle aestheticism. The musical quality that characterizes his best pieces largely disappeared from his poetry and other writings in the last decade of his life, but the totality of his work, so imbued with the unique phonic quality of the French language as to be untranslatable, ranks him with the great masters of French poetry.

BIBLIOGRAPHY. Joanna Richardson, *Verlaine*, New York: Viking Press, 1971; Philip Stephan, *Paul Verlaine and the Decadence 1882–1890*, Manchester: Manchester University Press, 1974.

Warren Johansson

VIAU, THÉOPHILE DE (1590–1626)

French poet and libertine thinker. Théophile de Viau was the most talented poet of his generation, which belonged to the first half of the reign of Louis XIII. His militant atheism and stormy, unconventional existence made him the idol of the youth, but his own passion was for Jacques Vallée des Barreaux, nine years his junior, strikingly handsome and intelligent, and gifted with a poetic talent all his own. The master and the disciple went everywhere together, and when they were separated, they exchanged letters that bear witness to a genuine love.

Allowed to return to Paris in March 1620 after less than a year of exile, Théophile was associated with a scandalous publication, a particularly obscene collection of poems entitled *Le Parnasse satyrique*. that appeared in November 1622 and was followed by a decree of Parlement in July 1623 ordering his arrest. The poet fled Paris, but a month later was in absentia sentenced to death by burning at the stake. On the frontier of Picardy Théophile was arrested and brought in captivity to Paris, where an undercover agent of the Jesuits named Louis Sageot denounced him for divine lèse-majesté and sodomy—which in those days were one and the same crime. There followed two years of imprisonment under conditions of suffering and outright torture that nearly broke his spirit, but worst of all was the infidelity of

Des Barreaux, who wrote him a letter urging him to die with joy to purify his soul. However, the wind turned in favor of the accused, and his friends did everything in their power to obtain clemency, which was accorded by a decree of the court in September 1625, which annulled the previous death sentence and merely condemned him to perpetual banishment with confiscation of his goods—in effect an acquittal. There was even a reunion with Des Barreaux. But the poet's health had been fatally undermined by his captivity, and he died the following year.

Théophile's poetry appeals to readers even now because of the poet's intense self-awareness and his ability to give personal expression to common human experience. In the course of the seventeenth century there were ninety-three editions of his poetry, compared with sixteen of Malherbe's. His verses remain scattered in various collections, and some of the attributions are incorrect or at least questionable. In the poems a spirit of male camaraderie prevails in the attitude of the speaker to his male reader/listener. A tone of fraternal intimacy excludes women except as the butt of humor. The homosexual theme is far more positive than in the classical authors whom Théophile read and imitated, just as he assimilated the traditions of the medieval low literature of the wandering scholars. The mood of the poems is an affectionate and gentle humor, or else intimate and endearing love. The major theme is sexuality, but the author can also bemoan the indignities of the patron–poet relationship, indulge in social and political commentary, and reveal his consciousness of the fragility of human life and happiness. One of his poems amasses the names of celebrated homosexuals of past and present, ending with **James I** of England and his favorite the Duke of Buckingham—which suggests that a certain kind of apologetic line had already begun to take shape in the **libertine** subculture of the Renaissance. Singer of love, of pleasure, of liberty,

Théophile de Viau is the spiritual forebear of later generations of poets of the European gay counterculture.

BIBLIOGRAPHY. Claire Lynn Gaudiani, *The Cabaret Poetry of Théophile de Viau: Texts and Traditions*, Tübingen: Günter Narr Verlag, 1981; Maurice Lever, *Les bûchers de Sodome*, Paris: Fayard, 1985.

Warren Johansson

VICTIMLESS CRIMES

The concept of "crimes without victims" has played a major role in the legal and sociological debates of the 1960s and later, when the first serious efforts were mounted to urge repeal of the archaic laws against homosexual acts. It was especially promoted by the work of the American sociologist Edwin M. Schur, *Crimes Without Victims: Deviant Behavior and Public Policy* (1965), which addressed the issues of abortion, homosexuality, and drug addiction.

Basic Features of the Concept. Crimes without victims are the willing exchange by adults of strongly demanded but legally proscribed goods or services, or the commission of acts proscribed by law in which no third party is directly harmed or involved. A characteristic feature of such laws is that since no third party is harmed, there is no one who has an immediate interest in complaining to the police and presenting evidence against the culprits. Also, such offenses typically have a low visibility; they are committed as far from public view as the participants can manage, and it is only as a result of prearranged police surveillance or even entrapment that the crimes can be detected at all.

Schur's argument starts from the premise that "criminal laws do not always effectively curb the behavior they proscribe," but that "laws which are highly ineffective from the standpoint of sheer deterrence" may yet "have pronounced impact. . . . Indeed, it is precisely the criminal laws which fail to deter which may be of greatest interest to the sociologist." The author goes on to say that the "types of deviance examined in this book illustrate a type of unenforceable law that has also created some special interest" because the attempt to repress such behavior by criminal law "seems particularly likely to create secondary deviance and to set the stage for police corruption and demoralization."

In the section on homosexuality Schur concludes that "neither present policy nor a stiffer enforcement of that policy can significantly curb homosexual behavior," and echoes the Wolfenden Committee's proposals for "partial legalization of homosexuality." The most evident results of the laws are the heightening of the homosexual's vulnerability to blackmail and other forms of police corruption and repressive enforcement procedures; the secondary results are the alienation of the homosexual from society and the discrimination inflicted upon him, as well as the demoralizing and humiliating behavior in which he must engage.

Historical Precedents. All this had been said earlier, though never exactly in the language quoted. It was, strictly speaking, never asserted that homosexual behavior harmed anyone engaging in it, but rather—as the critics of victimless crime largely overlook—that the behavior in question was an offense ("**abomination**" in the language of the **Old Testament**) to the deity, and that any community tolerating such practices in its midst would be the object of divine wrath and retribution. The Lutheran jurist Benedict Carpzov (1595–1666) even declared in his treatise on the criminal law of the Kingdom of Saxony that "Often for the crime of a single individual God punishes an entire nation." Early medieval criminal law knew a distinction between *tortious* and *sacral* offenses; the former were crimes in which the wronged party, or his kinsmen and supporters, had the task of bringing the charge before the courts, the latter infringed the divinely ordained laws of the community. Only when centuries of Chris-

tian moral teaching had made **sodomy** a wrongful and heinous act were laws prescribing the death penalty for "unnatural vice" placed on the statute books of every European country. There they remained until the eighteenth century, when they began to disappear as the **Enlightenment** critique of the penal legislation of the Old Regime rejected them as relics of medieval superstition and barbarism.

Resistance to the Concept. In the English-speaking world the influence of the Enlightenment in this area of the law was severely limited by the fact that the right of the state to punish "immorality" in general, and sexual immorality in particular, went virtually unquestioned. Indeed there was a tacit agreement that the state had a duty to punish such behavior in the interest of society. Only with the rise of public criticism of the existing statutes has there come an erosion of consensus as to the validity or purpose of the law. Those who continue to defend the criminalization of homosexual behavior argue that the criminal law keeps homosexuality in hiding where it belongs. In this view the demonstrations and propaganda of gay liberation groups encourage teenagers to experiment with homosexual activity and drift into homosexual **lifestyles**. The undisguised homosexual **subculture** of the large metropolitan cities spawns prostitution and gay bars and meeting places that further all types of sexual deviance. Then too, homosexuality leads to the moral decay of the family that would ultimately destroy the very fabric of society. Finally, homosexuals are mentally ill and in need of psychiatric treatment, and decent, law-abiding members of society need to be protected from them. Such is the neo-traditionalist response.

Social Policy Questions. The concept of "victimless crimes" poses more sharply than any other the question: To what extent should the criminal law be an instrument of social policy? Even if the behavior in question harms no one else directly, there may be larger interests of society that need to be protected or furthered by criminal legislation, and in the eyes of conservatives the upholding of moral standards is one of those vital interests. The underlying assumption of Christian sexual morality is that erotic pleasure experienced outside the bounds of Christian marriage is immoral and wrongful, and in Christian countries the state should have the task of punishing such behavior by criminal sanctions. Where freedom of conscience and separation of state and church are formalized in the Constitution, as they have been in the United States since 1791, no rational ground can be offered for imposing such a moral standard on the entire community, indeed such an attempt violates the liberty and **privacy** of the individual citizen. On the other hand, a law that punishes an individual who knowingly infects another with a sexually transmitted disease falls wholly outside the category of "victimless crime," since the infected party is clearly the victim, and society has an undeniable interest in preventing the spread of syphilis and gonorrhea, not to speak of **AIDS**, which is frequently fatal to those who contract it by sexual intercourse.

Conclusion. The application of the notion of "victimless crime" to homosexual behavior is essentially a restatement of the Enlightenment argument against the laws that prescribed the death penalty for sodomy: namely, that the crime infringes the rights of no other human being, and that in punishing private consensual behavior between adults the state is overstepping its duty to protect the life, liberty, and property of its citizens, while offenses against religion and morality, belonging as they do to the sphere of private conscience, are matters for religious confession and atonement. But given the diffusion of the concept in contemporary sociology, future debates on public policy in regard to homosexuality are likely to see extensive use of the term "crimes without victims."

BIBLIOGRAPHY. Robert M. Rich, *Crimes Without Victims: Deviance and the Criminal Law*, Washington, DC: University Press of America, 1978; Edwin M. Schur, *Crimes Without Victims: Deviant Behavior and Public Policy*, Englewood Cliffs, NJ: Prentice-Hall, 1965; Edwin M. Schur and Hugo Adam Bedau, *Victimless Crimes: Two Sides of a Controversy*, Englewood Cliffs, NJ: Prentice-Hall, 1974.

Warren Johansson

VIDEO

The video-art movement, which emerged in the 1970s, uses tape to produce audio-visual works with their own aesthetic, which is sometimes abstract, sometimes more naturalistic in the manner of *cinema verité*. Museums and galleries of contemporary art have given some attention to video, but have slighted gay and lesbian examples.

One exception to this neglect was a presentation of thirteen video tapes at New York's New Museum of Contemporary Art under the title "Homo Video: Where We Are in the 1980s" from December 1986 to February 1987. The videos shown were heavily influenced by the television documentary model, presenting images and information relevant to **AIDS** and to problems of discrimination, with considerable political awareness, though none of them were conventional documentaries with the standard voice-over narrative. In nearly all cases, these reflected attempts to make videos accessible to a mass audience, or capable of being aired over broadcast television, rather than to present idiosyncratic "pure art" videos.

There was also at least one regularly scheduled cable program featuring gay videos, Rick X's "The Closet Case Show," which had a long run in a weekly format during the mid-eighties in New York City. This show included less didactic videos, such as the 30-minute parody "How to Seduce a Preppy," and may have been more representative of a wider cross-section of gay video as then practiced than the New Museum selection, which was intended to point new directions.

See also **Television**.

William Olander

VIOLENCE

The relationship between violence and homosexuality, both fundamental to social relations, but with quite different historical and cultural forms, is a very complex one. Most of the research has suffered from a lack of general perspective. The most relevant topics are male initiation, persecution and social repression of homosexuality, rape, queer-bashing, homosexual murder, internalization of negative social norms by homosexuals, the esthetization of cruelty by homosexual artists, and homosexual sadomasochism.

Initiation and Male Rape. The initiation of youths into adult styles of masculinity has a long history in which homosexual behavior, sometimes **rape**, plays a prominent role. The anthropologist Gilbert Herdt has documented rituals of manhood in Melanesia where the oral or anal transmission of semen, and so homosexual behavior, is central. These rituals are at the same time cruel: the entry into the world of adult males is a liminal, traumatic experience for the initiates. The enforced submission seems to enhance the youngsters' loyalty to adult males and their affective participation in the latters' secrets. These initiations are an extreme form of such rituals, which exist in other cultures as well. Chinese **pirates** of the eighteenth century used anal rape to initiate captives into their new career as outlaws. The hazing and ragging in boarding schools, in student fraternities, and in sports are modern survivals of these initiations where violence and homosexual penetration occasionally occur.

Male rape in jails, especially in America, seems to be fundamental for the

prison hierarchy, which wardens often tolerate because of its functionality in maintaining order in prison. Donald Tucker published in *Male Rape* an insightful essay on his experiences with involuntary homosexual behavior in jails. The sociologists Wayne Wooden and Jay Parker have written a book on prison sexuality that has much to say on the same topic.

In the myths of **Egypt** and the history of Assyria, and in the armies of ancient **Rome** rape of males served as an official form of punishment. The Turks raped Greeks and Armenians whom they captured. During the 1980s the Panamanian authorities used male rape as a form of punishment for political dissent.

Rape of males "in the community" and by gangs is far more common than usually supposed, but according to researchers both the assailant and the victim are usually heterosexual, and the motivation seems to be the acting out of a superior power position on the part of the aggressor and the humiliation of the victim.

Murder. A special case of violence with regard to homosexuality is that of homosexual lust **murderers**. It seems that especially in places and times where emancipation and discrimination against homosexuality are much discussed and youth move freely, cases of homosexual serial murder happen as expressions of the strained relations of homosexuals with heterosexuals: Germany in the twenties (Haarmann), the United States in the seventies (Corll, Gacy).

Anti-gay Violence. The most common type of violence homosexual men and lesbian women encounter is the violence connected with legal and social **discrimination** against homosexuality. At a very general level, many of them experience psychical and physical violence when **coming out**—from their families, peers, instructors, and colleagues. As the degree of hostility toward homosexuality differs strongly according to historic periods and to national, ethnic, and social backgrounds, the level of violence also varies. The same applies to harassment by queer-bashers, which also seems to have become a rather typical reaction against homosexuals and homosexual emancipation in western countries, as in the assault on Magnus **Hirschfeld** in Vienna in 1921. In a "tolerant" country such as the Netherlands, reportedly half the homosexuals have experienced violence from queer-bashers. Because of the legally sanctioned oppression of homosexuals, which prevailed in many countries until recent times, the level of unofficial harassment in former periods is not well documented, but seems to have been less widespread than nowadays. A special case of violence against homosexuals is the murder of older gay men by boys and younger men in situations of prostitution (J. J. **Winckelmann**, Gustav Gründgens, Marc Blitzstein, Pier Paolo **Pasolini**).

Violence against homosexuals from law-enforcement and **police** authorities is still common in many countries such as Great Britain and the United States, as well as in Eastern Europe and the Third World. In Western Europe, from the Middle Ages until the eighteenth century and in England until the nineteenth, **capital** punishment for sodomy was carried out with some frequency, though mostly in a haphazard way. Several hundred executions have been documented by historians, and several thousand were probably executed, though one can merely speculate on the number of cases of "lynch justice" in which the victim was secretly killed to avoid scandalizing the community. The **Inquisition** more systematically attempted to terrorize potential offenders by parading the few at autos-da-fé to burn them. Thousands more fled prosecution as **exiles and émigrés**. Official violence was most vehement under **Nazism** in Germany (1933–1945), when many thousands of homosexuals died in concentration camps; this aspect of the **holocaust** has been all too often obscured. The legal prosecution of homosexual behavior, in itself the out-come of Christian condemnation of nonprocreative sexuality since the Middle Ages, served to rationalize the social oppression of homosexuality which **nationalism** with its measures toward conformity reinvigorated.

Internalization of Violence. External repression has been internalized by its many victims. In the early modern period, most sodomites did not dare oppose the condemnation of sodomy, and some, often after torture or out of fear, even cooperated with the authorities to prosecute their partners. With the individualization and psychologization of sexual preferences, which can be attested since the eighteenth century, confusion about sexual and gender roles and fear of being contaminated by "wrong" sexual predilections led men to extreme resolutions such as **suicide**. Heinrich von **Kleist**, the German writer, is the first known case of suicide because of individualized homosexuality. Spectacular examples were the Dutch law reformer J. E. Reuvens and the English political leader Lord Castlereagh, both of whom committed suicide, in 1816 and 1822 respectively, after having been **blackmailed** for alleged homosexual relations with unlikely partners. This phenomenon probably peaked in Nazi Germany. Recent sociological literature attests that homosexual men and lesbian women are much more prone to attempt or commit suicide than their heterosexual counterparts. For a long time this way of death provided a common ending for gay and lesbian **novels**.

Literary Treatment. Many homosexual writers transformed violence with regard to homosexual behavior into an esthetics of cruelty. The Marquis de **Sade** was the first to develop an esthetics and philosophy of violence and sodomy. Many others followed suit: in the orbit of the **decadent** movement (**Rimbaud** and **Verlaine**, **Lautréamont**, **Wilde**, **Couperus**); later **Proust** and authors with a surrealist background (**Crevel**, **Jahnn**, Arnold Bronnen); in the postwar era it became a general trend: **Genet**, Tournier, Guyotat, Reve, Bowles, Purdy, Burroughs, **Warhol**, **Pasolini**, **Fassbinder**, **Fichte**. Could their esthetics be understood as a transposition of the feeling of "living dangerously" which was widely shared by homosexuals in those times? In the post-**Stonewall** generation comparable esthetics of cruelty and male love make a new breakthrough, as in the work of such writers as Tony Duvert, Hervé Guibert, Dennis Cooper, and Josef Winkler.

One of the refined forms of violence which have become more visible since the sixties, gay **sadomasochism**, shows that many desire a semblance of cruelty in a situation of mutual consent. This has given birth to a new and innovative variation within gay and lesbian culture.

Conclusions. The widespread connection between male homosexuality and various forms of violence requires some explanation; unfortunately because little has been provided or seriously studied, one is left with speculative suggestions. The comparative dearth of violence in lesbian relationships suggests that there may be a factor of maleness—the absence of the inhibiting influence of females—in the frequency with which violence is associated with male homosexuality. Reported instances of violence among lesbian couples, however, reveal that this may not be the whole story.

The perceived casting off of general social inhibitions against the expression of homosexuality since the **Stonewall Rebellion** (1969) may also carry with it a partial discarding of general social inhibitions against violence. Once the taboo is broken in one area, it may be hard to reimpose it in another. Both homosexuality and violent aggression are secretive, condemned, and suppressed. According to neuroscientists, both are intimately connected with physiological processes, arising in the same areas of the brain (the ancient "reptilian brain"). What cannot be dealt with openly and verbally becomes relegated to the furtive and the physical, whether in favor or opposition.

Because so many cultures associate homosexuality with a deficiency of masculinity, equating aggressive sexuality and aggressive violence with masculinity, there may be an interplay at work which calls forth the latter to confront the perceived failings of the former. In such phenomena as queer-bashing, male rape, and police violence, aggressive violence seems to be used as a kind of shield to ward off the contaminating, tabooed homosexuality, as if its mere presence constituted such a threat to one's male self-image that the other reservoir of maleness, violence, must be summoned to stanch the wound, as in **Nazism** and **Fascism**.

Research on the connection between homosexuality and violence is much needed. If violence (symbolic, attenuated, or expressed without restraints) is indeed fundamental in social relations, the gay and lesbian communities should not ignore it, but find constructive social, perhaps ritual, forms of expressing it. The theatre of cruelty, as Antonin Artaud imagined it, sadomasochism, contact sports, and erotic play-violence offer possibilities for experimentation. Perhaps violence, too, will have to come out of the closet.

BIBLIOGRAPHY. Gilbert Herdt, *Guardians of the Flutes: Idioms of Masculinity*, New York: McGraw-Hill, 1981; Kerry Lobel, *Naming the Violence: Speaking Out About Lesbian Battering*, Seattle: Seal Press, 1986; Brian Miller and Laud Humphreys, "Lifestyles and Violence; Homosexual Victims of Assault and Murder," *Qualitative Sociology*, 3 (1980), 169–85; Eric E. Rofes, *Lesbians, Gay Men and Suicide*, San Francisco: Grey Fox Press, 1983; Anthony Scacco, ed., *Male Rape*, New York: AMS Press, 1982; Larry Townsend, *The Leatherman's Handbook II*, New York: Modemismo Publications, 1983; Wayne S. Wooden and Jay Parker, *Men Behind Bars: Sexual Exploitation in Prison*, New York: Plenum Press, 1982.

Gert Hekma

VISCONTI, LUCHINO (1906–1976)

Italian director of films, theatre, and opera. On his father's side Visconti was descended from ancient Milanese nobility, while his mother inherited great wealth from her industrialist father. The belle époque luxury of his homelife and performances in the family's private theatre were to be utilized in his later directing career. When Visconti was nine his parents were divorced, a step brought on in part by his father's "hobby" of having affairs with young men.

In his twenties, Visconti lived the life of a playboy, his only passion being horses. This interest, however, led him to Paris which he found stimulating both for its intellectual circles and for its sexual freedom. In 1934 he had his first serious affair with a man, the anti-Nazi German photographer Horst Horst. This liaison awakened his interest in film, and he served for a time as an assistant to the great director Jean Renoir. Visconti was also influenced by the poetic cinema of Jean Cocteau, who lived openly with his leading actor, Jean Marais.

Visconti's first major feature, *Ossessione* (1942), which was based on the novel *The Postman Always Rings Twice* by James M. Cain, heralded the neo-realist school of Italian cinema. During the war years in Rome Visconti took an active part in the resistance, which led to his joining the Italian Communist Party. Although the party used him as one of its leading intellectuals, major Communist leaders stayed clear of any direct contact with Visconti because of his homosexuality. In the 1940s and 1950s he directed many foreign plays, which had the effect of a revelation in an Italy that had been culturally isolated by twenty years of fascist dictatorship. He also began to direct operas at Milan's La Scala, which had fascinated him from the age of seven when the house was under the control of Arturo Toscanini. In the view of some critics, the melodrama and artificiality of grand opera spilled over into his films, and not to their advantage.

Visconti made one more major neo-realist film, *La Terra Trema* (1948), a story of Sicilian fishermen in which he used untrained local actors. He first achieved major international acclaim, however, with *Rocco and His Brothers* (1960), a story of the disintegration of a southern Italian family which had settled in Milan. Visconti thus took his place beside Federico Fellini and his former collaborator, Michelangelo Antonioni, as a standard bearer of the Italian "new wave." Four years later he released *The Leopard*, a loving creation of Giuseppe di Lampedusa's novel of the life of a Sicilian aristocrat. During this period Visconti was intimate with Helmut Berger, a handsome but green young German, whom he groomed as a major actor. In *The Damned* (1969), a recreation of the "Night of the Long Knives" in which Hitler's agents murdered Captain Ernst **Röhm** and his homosexual associates, Berger made a striking appearance in a transvestite parody of Marlene Dietrich. *Death in Venice* (1971) starred Dirk Bogarde in an almost spectral rendering of one of Visconti's favorite works, the Thomas **Mann** novella of the same name, while *Ludwig* (1973), in which Berger returned, portrayed the mad homosexual king of Bavaria, **Ludwig II**.

With this trio of great films that openly treated homosexuality, Visconti found a place in the select company of such major contemporary directors as Pier Paolo **Pasolini**, Rainer Werner **Fassbinder**, John Schlesinger, and Franco Zeffirelli, who not only have been openly gay, but insisted on treating the orientation honestly in their films. At the same time, his loving evocations of European aristocratic life before 1914, the world of **Proust** and Mann, Mahler and Klimt, made him a link to the manners and sentiments of a vanished world—that of the belle époque.

BIBLIOGRAPHY. Alain Sanzio and Paul-Louis Thirard, *Luchino Visconti cinéaste*, Paris: Persona, 1984; Gaia

Servadio, *Visconti: A Biography*, New York: Franklin Watts, 1983.

Wayne R. Dynes

VISUAL ART
See **Art, Visual**; **Photography.**

VIVIEN, RENÉE (1877–1909)

Anglo-French poet and novelist. Born in London of an English father and an American mother as Pauline Mary Tarn, Vivien was taken to Paris when she was one year old. There she mainly educated herself by reading French books. Her first love was a neighbor, Violet Silleto, whom she was later to recall in her writings. After her mother removed her again to London, Vivien finally achieved her independence, which was cushioned by a substantial inheritance.

In 1899 she met Natalie Clifford **Barney** in Paris and began a relationship that is chronicled in *Une femme m'apparut* (1904). Although both women had achieved success in their writings in the French language, Barney recognized that Vivien had a real vocation, while her own works were more adjuncts to her opulent life and public persona. It is a mark of Vivien's seriousness that in the last ten years of her life she wrote nine volumes of poetry, two novels, and two books of short stories. Her first poems were published under the name of R. Vivien, and critics who had hailed the "young man's" passionate poetry to women were dismayed when Vivien went public with her real identity as a woman. In fact her work became increasingly gynecocentric, addressing women as a group apart from men.

The relationship with Barney was a stormy one. Both women had affairs with others, Vivien with the colorful Baroness Hélène de Zuylen de Nyevelt, who also wrote novels. Vivien and Barney visited the island of Lesbos together; the impressions gained here in Vivien's company were probably responsible for Barney's founding of her Academy of Women many years later. Vivien's work was always concerned with death and in her last years she gradually starved herself to death, a victim of anorexia, which was not recognized as a disease at the time. In the 1970s her work was revived by both French- and English-speaking feminists and lesbians, and today it forms part of what appears almost as a golden age of lesbian creativity in Paris in the early decades of the twentieth century.

BIBLIOGRAPHY. Karla Jay, *The Amazon and the Page: Natalie Clifford Barney and Renée Vivien*, Bloomington: Indiana University Press, 1988.

Evelyn Gettone

VOGEL, BRUNO (1895–1987)

German writer. The details of Bruno Vogel's biography are obscure; the little that is known comes mainly from an autobiographical sketch by the author himself and conversations that he had with Wolfgang U. Schutte and Manfred Herzer and others in the last years of his life. Vogel belongs to the comparatively few authors, at least in the German-speaking world, whose treatment of homosexuality is not only explicit and overt, but also clearly positive. Moreover, in Vogel this stance melds with his socialist–anarchist politics. After his first volume of stories, *Es lebe der Krieg!* (1924), antimilitarist and gay themes ran to some extent parallel in *Ein Gulasch* (1928). Vogel gained a reputation with his short novel *Alf*, first published in 1929 and reprinted in 1977 in its third edition, in which a critique of the horrors of war combines with a critique of a society that will not grant young men the appropriate form of friendship, tenderness, and sexuality: Alf becomes a victim of the war, because as a victim of incomprehension and of his own confusion in regard to the impossibility of his feelings he has sought out the war as a volunteer.

In *Alf*, Vogel makes one of the protagonists, Alf's young friend Felix, express an almost uncritically positive judgment on psychoanalysis, which is celebrated as "something enormous and grand" because it unmasks the sexual morality propagated by state and church.

In the interwar period Vogel was close to the **Scientific-Humanitarian Committee** (he was briefly an officer) and a member of Hirschfeld's Institute for Sexual Science. He left Germany in 1931, and via Switzerland, Paris, and Norway he reached South Africa in 1937. There he did exactly what Felix praised his deceased friend for having done at the end of the novel: he fought against "baseness and stupidity," this time against apartheid. So in the early 1950s it was time to turn his back on South Africa. He settled in London, where—not even noticed by the Exile-PEN club residing there—he led a hand-to-mouth existence. In 1987 his work *Ein junger Rebell—Erzählungen und Skizzen aus der Weimarer Republik* was published in East Germany.

BIBLIOGRAPHY. "Bruno Vogel und 'Alf': Manfred Herzer spricht mit einem deutschen Dichter in London," *Revolt Mann*, 11 (1987), 6ff.; Friedheim Krey, "Alf: Eine Skizze: Begegnung mit Bruno Vogel," *Emanzipation*, 5 (1977), 17ff.; Wolfgang U. Schutte, "Bekanntschaft mit Bruno Vogel," *Die Weltbühne* (East Berlin), August 25, 1987.

Marita Keilson-Lauritz

VOLTAIRE, FRANÇOIS-MARIE AROUET, KNOWN AS (1694–1778)

French philosopher, dramatist, essayist, and critic.

Life. Born in Paris as the son of a well-to-do notary, Voltaire, as he came to be known from the very beginning of the French Enlightenment, was educated by the Jesuits of the Collège de Clermont, then became a member of the libertine society of the Temple and devoted himself to the study of jurisprudence. Some disrespectful verses directed at the Regent, Philippe d'Orléans, and a quarrel with the Chevalier de Rohan-Chabot led to his imprisonment (1716–18, 1726), followed by exile in England. In a country whose language and literature were still little known on the continent, Voltaire was influenced by the empiricism of Locke, Newtonian physics, and English deism, which had virtually replaced Christianity among the educated classes. Upon his return to France in 1729, Voltaire criticized the literature of the day in *Le Temple du goût* (1732), polemicized against the notion of divine goodness (*Epitre à Uranie*), and without authorization published the *Lettres philosophiques* (1734), to which he added the *Remarques sur les "Pensées" de Pascal*. This criticism of the regime in France led to criminal proceedings which he escaped by taking refuge on the estate of the Marquise du Châtelet in Lorraine (1734–49). Here he composed most of the fifty comedies and tragedies that founded his literary reputation, and in 1746 he was named historiographer of the king and a member of the French Academy.

On the death of Madame du Châtelet, Voltaire accepted the invitation of **Frederick** II of Prussia, with whom he had corresponded since 1736, to reside at the court of Potsdam. Here he pursued his literary, historical, and philosophical work, but quarrels with Maupertuis, president of the Berlin Academy, and with Frederick himself made him seek refuge in Geneva, where he began his collaboration on the *Encyclopédie* of Diderot and d'Alembert (1755). But his writings scandalized the Calvinist theologians of Geneva as much as they had the Catholics. In 1759, while writing the novel *Candide*, directed in part against the optimism of Leibniz and Pope, Voltaire found his definitive retreat at Ferney (1760–78). During this period, the intellectual and political elites of European society maintained close relations with Voltaire, whose influence grew steadily thanks to his many writings, for which—because of the risks which their challenge to the established order entailed—he employed 160 different pseudonyms. In addition to the many thousands of letters from Voltaire to his numerous correspondents, among them the "enlightened despots" of the late eighteenth century, he wrote satires, philosophical tales, and pamphlets against political, clerical, and legal abuses. In the Paris that had received him in triumph for the performance of his last tragedy, *Irène*, Voltaire died on May 30, 1778. Refused burial by the hatred of the Catholic clergy, his body was transported to the Abbey of Scellières, near Troyes. The French Revolution, recognizing in him one of its immortal predecessors, thirteen years later gave him the honors of the Pantheon.

Outlook. Voltaire's attitude toward homosexuality was complex and nuanced by the vicissitudes of his lifetime. There is no evidence that he ever had any homosexual experiences, even in adolescence; his judgment of the homosexuals whom he encountered during his long career was colored mainly by his estimate of their character and by their conduct in his regard. The ambivalence of his attitude may be gauged from the fact that his slogan *"Ecrasez l'infâme!,"* aimed at the Church and its penumbra of influence under the Old Regime, employed the very word which in the dossiers of the French police designated those given to "unnatural vice," *les infâmes*. His hatred of the Catholic Church and of the superstition and intolerance which it had fostered was countered by his firm rejection of atheism, so that by leaving the sphere of private morality to the church he therefore allowed the intolerance of homosexuality on ascetic grounds—and with it the social ostracism of homosexuals—to be perpetuated for two full centuries after the legal sanctions had been stricken from the books. But he is rightly remembered as one of the foremost enemies of the Church, as one whose eloquent voice sounded the call for toleration in the spirit of the Enlightenment.

Works. In 1714 Voltaire wrote a poem entitled *L'Anti-Giton* for the purpose of persuading his friend, the Marquis de Courcillon, to "sacrifice to the true love." If the Marquis was a "heretic in the flesh," he was a brave soldier without the slightest trace of effeminacy; wounded twice at the battle of Malplaquet, he endured the amputation of his leg from the thigh downward while laughing and joking with those around him. The "philosophical sin" did not seem hateful to Voltaire if "it has taken the features of a handsome marquis." On the other hand, the long established notion of homosexuality as a moral failing of the Catholic clergy fueled his hatred, in later life, for the clerical foes whom he despised as sodomites: the ex-Jesuit Desfontaines, the Abbe Larcher and the Reverend Father Polycarpe, a barefoot Carmelite. Their vice then struck him as a consequence of clerical celibacy, and friend of toleration that Voltaire was, he became fanatical in his opposition to it.

Voltaire's friendship with Frederick the Great was decidedly influenced by the feelings of both in regard to homosexuality. It began with a correspondence in which each flattered the other, comparing him to the great thinkers of Greece and Rome. Then after visiting Frederick at Potsdam in 1740 and observing him on his home turf, Voltaire began to write to him in explicitly sexual terms in addition to the usual courtly language, but Frederick was never able to overcome the affection which Voltaire cherished for Emilie du Châtelet, his mistress—and therefore was bitterly jealous of her. Both men acted manipulatively, Voltaire more so, because he hoped that by obtaining from Frederick information that he could relay to French intelligence he could ingratiate himself with Louis XV, while Frederick did everything in his power to lure Voltaire to his court. When he did settle in Potsdam, the authoritarian, militaristic, and unobtrusively homoerotic atmosphere proved not to his liking. Moreover, when Voltaire left Prussia, he took with him a copy of a tiny, privately printed edition of Frederick's poems in French, including *Le Palladion*, with its defense of homosexuality. Alarmed by the potential for harm which disclosure of the book might bring, Frederick attempted to retrieve it by having the Prussian resident in Frankfurt am Main stop Voltaire and search his luggage as he passed through that city. The incident developed into a comic-opera affair before it ended. Voltaire retaliated by publishing anonymously a little book entitled *The Private Life of the King of Prussia*, in which with his inimitable wit he exposed the erotic side of Frederick's personality.

The *Dictionnaire philosophique portatif* (1764), the fruit of twelve years of reflection and a by-product of his work on the *Encyclopédie*, was an alphabetically arranged series of essays in free thought aimed at the beliefs and superstitions of Christianity. It included an article entitled "Amour nommé Socratique" (So-called Socratic Love), which shows Voltaire inclined to skepticism in regard to the supposed toleration which the ancients accorded to the "vice." He begins by asking: "How is it that a vice destructive of the human race if it became universal, that an infamous crime against nature is nevertheless so natural? It appears to be the last degree of premeditated corruption, yet it is ordinarily the lot of those who have not yet had the time to be corrupted." Later he explains that "often a young boy by the freshness of his looks, by the glow of his skin color, and by the softness of his eyes for two or three years resembles a beautiful girl; if he is loved, it is because nature has made the mistake" of bestowing feminine beauty on a youth. Nowhere in the article did Voltaire mention the Judeo-Christian origins of the taboo on homosexual expression, yet in a footnote added in 1769 he alluded to how narrowly the Abbé Desfontaines had escaped burning at the stake, and said that Deschaufours was executed in his place, but only because the word *bougre* in the *Etablissements de Saint Louis* had been misinterpreted as "sodomite" and not as "heretic," the meaning which it had in the fifteenth century.

At this time Voltaire took up the campaign for reform of the criminal law that had been launched by Cesare **Beccaria** with the publication of *Dei delitti e delle pene* (1764). His own contribution to theory was not great, and the essential ideas did not come from him. Rather he supported and vigorously publicized Beccaria's principles, and used all his polemic talent to call the attention of European society to the features of the existing law and practice that had become intolerable. Only with the French Revolution of 1789 did arguments of the two reformers triumph, because they had convinced the vast majority of the people that revision of the criminal law was an urgent issue. The principle that offenses against religion and morality, when they do not harm third parties or the interests of society, do not belong within the purview of the criminal law, has been a backbone of the demand for legal toleration of homosexual expression.

So Voltaire as a heterosexual may have been personally ambivalent toward homosexuality in others, and not inclined to promote sympathy for it, but his lifetime struggle against superstition and cruelty and his pleas for toleration created a climate of opinion in which the forces of reason could continue the campaign for the abolition of laws and beliefs sanctioned by religious authority and tradition.

BIBLIOGRAPHY. Susan W. Henderson, "Frederick the Great of Prussia: A Homophile Perspective," *Gai Saber*, 1 (1977), 46–54; Marcello T. Maestro, *Voltaire and Beccaria as Reformers of Criminal Law*, New York: Columbia University Press, 1942; Roger Peyrefitte, *Voltaire, sa jeunesse et son temps*, 2 vols., Paris: Albin Michel, 1985; Ernest Raynaud, "Voltaire et les fiches de police," *Mercure de France*, 199 (November 1, 1927), 536–56.

Warren Johansson

W

WADDELL, TOM
(1937–1987)

American founder of the **Gay Games**. A decathlete on the 1968 United States Olympic team who placed sixth at the Mexico City Olympics, he was a medical doctor.

As a child, Tom studied ballet but decided to pursue **athletics** instead. When he went to university he discontinued athletic training to devote himself to his medical studies. Drafted into the army, opposed to the war in Vietnam, Waddell managed to avoid going to war and began training for the 1968 Olympics with other military athletes. For a thirty-year-old man to undertake training for an event as demanding as the decathlon is an impressive feat. Moreover, he trained for only three months; it was normal to train for four years. Having a socialist background and strong feelings about racism, he associated himself with the U.S. Olympic team's "black caucus," an action which brought threats of court-martial.

With Sarah Lewenstein, he co-parented a child, Jessica Lewenstein.

In 1980, he proposed the idea of the Gay Games and with others, founded the San Francisco Arts and Athletics, the administrative body for the 1982 and 1986 Games. He had a vision of using the Gay Games to build an "exemplary community" based upon equality and universal participation. He saw the Gay Games as the symbol of equality and inclusiveness which should be taken as the example for all athletic competition.

Four weeks before the 1986 Gay Games he was diagnosed as having pneumocystis carinii pneumonia, an opportunistic infection arising as the result of **AIDS**.

Nevertheless, he competed at the Games in Track and Field and won a gold medal for throwing the javelin. He died of an AIDS-related disease in July 1987.

BIBLIOGRAPHY Ron Bluestein, "'Papa Games' in Profile—Dr. Tom Waddell," *Advocate*, 462 (Dec. 23, 1986), 28–31, 112–13; Roy M. Coe, *A Sense of Pride: the Story of Gay Games II*, San Francisco: Pride Publications, 1986; Nancy Faber, "Tom Waddell," *People Weekly*, 6:15 (Oct. 11, 1976), 51–53; Mike Messner, "Gay Athletes and the Gay Games: an Interview with Tom Waddell," *M: Gentle Men for Gender Justice*, 13 (1984), 22ff.

Brian Pronger

WARHOL, ANDY
(1930–1987)

American artist, filmmaker, and cultural entrepreneur. Andrew Warhola, Jr., was born into a working-class family of Ruthenian origin in Forest City, Pennsylvania, on December 6, 1930. He claimed to have been born two years earlier, on August 6, 1928. Although this falsehood was probably originally created so that he could attend college on money from his father's insurance policy, he clung to a bio-chronology that—unlike most such fibbing which is done for reasons of vanity—made him seem older than he actually was. This personal "disinformation" is part of his life project of forging a surrogate persona that would mediate between his real life, which was often surprisingly banal, and his creative works.

After studying art at the Carnegie Institute of Technology in Pittsburgh, he moved to **New York City** and adopted the name Andy Warhol. Making a living in commercial **art**, he also practiced his own work in the blotted line technique, which fascinated him because of its impersonal print-like quality. Warhol became friendly with two other artists who shared both his sexual orientation and his general outlook on art: Jasper Johns and Robert Rauschenberg. All three were to participate, though in different ways, in the spectacular launching of Pop Art. As his contribution, Warhol created the multiple Campbell's Soup cans and Brillo boxes that made him first a notorious iconoclast and then a representative figure. The aesthetic of these works based on mass-production features goes back to Marcel Duchamp, whose career had intrigued Warhol since his student days.

As Warhol became well known, he attracted an entourage that mixed various social types: all seemed welcome at his vast loft, sometimes known as the Factory since some of his associates were engaged in making collective works at his direction. In the 1960s the artist used the profits from his successful career as a painter and print maker, to produce a series of **films**. Such movies as *Blow Job* (1963) and *My Hustler* (1965) were crudely made but, presented as art, helped to expand the boundaries of the permissible in a cinema still hobbled by the restrictive standards of the Hays Office. More revealing, perhaps, of Warhol's own feelings is the S/M film *Vinyl* (1965), with Gerard Malanga, and the notorious *Chelsea Girls* (1966), in which "superstar" Ondine (Robert Olivio) delivers a notable soliloquy. As the sixties turned into the seventies Warhol, in collaboration with Paul Morrissey, attempted more ambitious films. Characteristically, these revolved around the beautiful but empty figure of the actor Joe Dallessandro, and they served to foster the then-current questioning of role models and sexual **stereotypes**.

Not only was Warhol reshaping two art forms, but he had become a celebrity. His activity was virtually synonymous with the Downtown scene in Manhattan with its **drug** use, sexual freedom, and cultural **anarchism**. At the same time the rapturous reception accorded even his most casual and mediocre productions signaled a change in the art world. The tone for the heroic days of **modernism** in the United States had been set by the high seriousness of such critics as Clement Greenberg and Harold Rosenberg, who had been identified with Abstract Expressionism. The new art scene of the sixties, however, saw the entrance of masses of enthusiastic, green recruits, few of whom bothered to undertake the arduous program of self-education that earlier critics and dealers had considered mandatory. Moreover, as contemporary art became popular, the inevitable simplifications and "hype" of journalism were fed back into the art world itself. Increasingly the new trends were promulgated with the imprint of the "glitterati" rather than of serious intellectuals. Continuing to abound, creative personalities nonetheless began to believe their own press releases.

The great years of Warhol as the incarnation of the sixties zeitgeist were cut short when Valerie Solanas, a disturbed feminist, shot the artist on June 5, 1968. Gravely wounded, Warhol never entirely recovered from the effects of the attack. After this setback he became more selective in his choice of friends, and gravitated to the world of the wealthy and fashionable. This milieu was chronicled in a chic periodical, *Interview*, produced under his auspices. The practice of assigning the execution of his works to assistants became more and more common. At the same time his paintings and prints enjoyed a great vogue in Europe as well as the United States, a status seemingly ratified by the huge retrospective exhibition of his work mounted by New York's Museum of Modern Art in 1989.

The most notable feature of Warhol's works is their blankness and absence of affect. Although he purloined his iconography from the world of mass consumption, it is impossible to tell whether Warhol is celebrating or condemning this aspect of capitalism—probably both and neither.

Warhol's characteristic distancing has several possible sources. Some figures of the nineteenth-century French avant-garde, notably the novelist Gustave **Flaubert**, had championed an ideal of *impassibilité*, of inscrutable detachment, before the motifs they evoked. This standpoint was bequeathed to the artist Marcel Duchamp, who linked it with the world of industrial production. It is also possible that Warhol learned from the playwright Bertolt Brecht, whose ideas were becoming better known in the United States in the late fifties. The German writer emphasized the *Verfremdungseffekt*, or alienation principle, as a distancing device in the theatre. Brecht derived the kernel of this procedure from the "estrangement" (*ostranenie*) of the Russian formalist critics. Finally, it is even possible that pop versions of Eastern religions commending extinction of personality played a role in the mix.

Although Warhol liked to say that he preferred sex on the screen or in the pages of a book to the real thing, he made no secret of his sexual orientation, which added to his glamor. His gayness was not simply a matter of personal inclination but interfaced with a large social circle in New York City, which also included, to be sure, sympathetic straight people. Having come of age in the repressive years immediately after World War II, Warhol would have been very much aware of the need to don a mask to conceal one's true nature from the world. His enduring project of self-fashioning and his artistic blankness are probably best regarded as pearls formed around the irritants internalized during America's most vocally homophobic era. Ironically, the very qualities of his art which the mainstream idolized stemmed from the harsh impact on a sensitive adolescent of a society which proclaimed that it had no room for nonconformity. In this respect his career recalls that of Jean **Genet**,

who also purveyed to the public an image of what it had compelled him to become.

BIBLIOGRAPHY. Victor Bockris, *The Life and Death of Andy Warhol*, New York: Bantam, 1989; Pat Hackett, ed., *The Andy Warhol Diaries*, New York: Warner Books, 1989; Stephen Koch, *Stargazer: Andy Warhol's World and His Films*, New York: Praeger, 1973; Patrick S. Smith, *Andy Warhol's Art and Films*, Ann Arbor, MI: UMI Press, 1986.
Wayne R. Dynes

WARNER, SYLVIA TOWNSEND (1893–1978)

English novelist, short-story writer, and poet. Born in Middlesex, the daughter of a school teacher, Townsend was, like many women intellectuals of her day, educated privately. Her early interests were musical, and she served as an editor of a ten-volume collection of Tudor church music. In the thirties she adopted **Marxism** and became active in left-wing politics and propaganda. She volunteered for service in Spain during the Civil War.

Warner began her career as a poet with *The Espalier* (1925), which was followed by two other volumes in 1928 and 1931 respectively. Subsequently she concentrated on fiction, producing novels that draw upon her interest in the supernatural to produce a world that hovers on the border of reality and fantasy. In 1967 she produced a biography of T. H. White (1906–1964), the author of the novels that became the basis for the musical *Camelot*, who was probably gay.

In 1930 Sylvia Townsend Warner met and fell in love with Valentine Ackland. Making their home among a small group of writers and painters in Dorset, the couple lived together until Ackland's death of cancer in 1969. The daughter of wealthy and dominating parents, Valentine Ackland was twenty four when she met Warner, and had had a number of affairs with both men and women. The younger woman's continuing infidelities were a source of anguish to Warner. Ackland also had a problem with alcoholism, and it is probably only her lover's faith in her that allowed her to continue to write poetry, some of which expresses her erotic involvement with Warner. She followed Warner in the British Communist Party, and the two cherished the belief that the Soviet Union incarnated the freedom, democracy, and justice that they were seeking. Fortunately, their writing on these themes is relieved by descriptions of events and evocations of nature. In the 1940s their political commitment faded, and they became dejected by the drab reality of Britain's welfare state—especially its failure to free women from their economic dependence on men. Although Warner and Ackland were not feminists in the contemporary sense, their durable relationship is a positive example of two women's success in braving the odds.

BIBLIOGRAPHY. Valentine Ackland, *For Sylvia: An Honest Account*, New York: W. W. Norton, 1985; William Maxwell, ed., *The Letters of Sylvia Townsend Warner*, New York: Viking Press, 1982; Wendy Mulford, *This Narrow Place: Sylvia Townsend Warner and Valentine Ackland: Life, Letters and Politics, 1930–1951*, London: Pandora, 1988.
Evelyn Gettone

WARREN, EDWARD PERRY (1860–1928)

American art connoisseur and poet. The great love of his life was an Englishman named John Marshall, whom he met in 1884. Under the pseudonym of Arthur Lyon Raile, he wrote a number of books dealing with **pederasty**. These include *Itamos* (1903), *The Wild Rose* (1909), and an expanded edition of the latter (1928), these being volumes of poetry; *A Tale of Pausanian Love* (1927), a novel; and *The Defence of Uranian Love* (1928–30), an apology for pederasty in three volumes. Under his birth name he also wrote a short story, "The Prince Who Did Not Exist" (1900).

The dominant theme of his writings is the transference of the morals of ancient **Greece** to Oxford University. His refusal to return to America was based on a rejection of democracy, feminism, and Christianity, which he saw as being hostile to the restoration of his pederastic ideals, which were based firmly on the writings of **Plato** and other Greek idealists. He considered the primary task of the pederast to be the formation of the boy's character, not the gratification of lust. The relationship was only to be justified by the character-building aspect of it. There was no room in his philosophy of love for the effeminacy and equality that play so large a role in modern homosexual liberationist theories, and women (lesbian or otherwise) hardly existed as far as he was concerned. His idealism is also out of step with the frank sensuality of today's boy-love movement.

From 1885 to 1910 Perry presented many classical objects to Boston's Museum of Fine Arts. Among these was a notable group of vases with homoerotic scenes; those pieces did not go on public exhibition until 1964.

BIBLIOGRAPHY. Timothy d'Arch Smith, *Love in Earnest*, London: Routledge & Kegan Paul, 1970.
Stephen Wayne Foster

WASHINGTON, D.C.

Incorporated in 1802, the new capital of the United States suffered a setback when it was burned by the British a decade later. Washington grew very slowly until the Civil War, when the city was dignified by Walt **Whitman**'s sojourn. In a notebook the poet laconically records having slept with a soldier on October 9, 1863, an act that others, unknown to us, must often have consummated during the turmoil of wartime. Yet it is not until the "gay nineties" that one can obtain a real glimpse of the Capital's homosexual **subculture**. Lafayette Square, opposite the

White House, was already a favorite **cruising** spot. According to one account, the **black gay** community affirmed itself in an annual ball which many male government employees attended in drag. Some Washington **prostitutes** were reported to have been fond of lesbian activities in their free time.

In the ensuing years the flow of elected and other governmental officials from all parts of the country brought many closeted homosexuals to the city. Massachusetts Senator David I. Walsh was forced to retire after being linked in the 1940s to a male house of prostitution in New York, while the escapades of Sumner Welles, Under Secretary of State, came to the attention of President Franklin D. Roosevelt. An undercurrent of gossip regarding FBI chief J. Edgar Hoover has resisted substantiation to this day. In 1950, however, the accusations of Senator Joseph R. **McCarthy** led to an investigation by a Senate subcommittee of "Employment of Homosexuals and Other Sex Perverts in **Government**." Unlike an earlier subcommittee which concluded by a 4–3 majority that McCarthy had perpetrated "a fraud and a hoax" on the Senate, in this instance the Democratic majority capitulated to the Republican charges against the Harry S. Truman Administration. The report unanimously called for more punitive laws and screening procedures designed to "ferret out sex perverts" on the ground that they were particularly liable to blackmail by Soviet agents even in agencies that had nothing remotely to do with national security. In other words, Magnus **Hirschfeld's** argument that the sodomy laws encouraged the practice of **blackmail** was now turned against homosexuals for political advantage. Although the report referred to government in general, it was the federal District of Columbia (coterminous with the city of Washington) that was the focus of the investigation and recommendations, which were duly enacted into law three years later when the Dwight D. Eisenhower Administra-

tion took office and commenced another purge of "security risks." **Police** surveillance increased, and in the early 1950s arrests by the vice squad topped 1000 annually. In the same time national attention focused on Washington's sins as a result of the spread of muckraking popular journalism, including Jack Lait and Lee Mortimer's gossipy book *Washington Confidential* (1951).

Then in 1954 Senator Lester Hunt, a conservative Democrat from Wyoming, committed **suicide** under mysterious circumstances. It later was revealed that his son had been compromised when the Washington police raided a gathering of homosexuals, and that two Republican Senators had threatened to make this fact known to his constituents should he run for a second term. In a politically distorted form this incident inspired the novel and motion picture *Advise and Consent* in which the culprit is a left-leaning member of the Senate—conveniently reversing the fact that the blackmailers belonged to the Republican Party.

In the 1960s Franklin E. Kameny, a discharged homosexual government employee who fearlessly defended others wrongfully fired, achieved prominence as head of the **Mattachine Society** of Washington. Kameny gained national prominence in the homophile **movement**, organizing the first public demonstrations by homosexuals (at the White House) in 1965. The radical upsurge of the late 1960s brought a gay **liberation** movement to Washington, and there was visible homosexual participation in the mass demonstrations of April–May 1971 calling for an end of the war in Vietnam. Dupont Circle, a center of radical activity in that period, also attracted the gay subculture, and has remained a focus of community life with the Lambda Rising bookstore as a national outlet for gay literature. The Washington gay newspaper, *The Blade*, is considered one of the major papers in the country. Appropriately, the capital is the headquarters of the National Gay and Lesbian Task

Force. The preponderance of black citizens in the District of Columbia has fostered the rise of a vibrant local black gay culture and a favorable local political climate.

Sodomy statutes enacted by the federal Congress for the District of Columbia were repealed in 1981 by the City Council, but the same year Congress overrode the repeal ordinance, leaving sodomy still criminal.

Washington does, however, have one of the strongest **gay rights** laws in the nation, adopted in October 1973 as one of the first such. The Human Rights Law, of which it is part, is enforced by a 15-member commission. At the end of the eighties, four of the commissioners were openly gay or lesbian.

In 1979 and again in 1987 Washington was the scene of national marches for gay rights that attracted myriads of activists and supporters from all parts of the country, showing that in the decade since 1969 the movement had grown from a score of semi-clandestine organizations hiding in the bohemian quarters of the large cities to a phenomenon as vast and variegated as the fabric of American life itself.

Ward Houser

WEIRAUCH, ANNA ELISABET (1887–1970)

German prose writer and playwright. After an eight-year stint (1906–14) as an actress with Max Reinhardt's famous ensemble in **Berlin**, Weirauch discovered her true calling as an author. She began with attempts at dramas but soon turned to prose, and in 1919, the first year of her long career, she published four novels and three novellas. One of these was the first volume of a trilogy entitled *Der Skorpion* (1919, 1921, 1931), which is the work for which Weirauch is remembered today.

This three-volume *Entwicklungsroman* (novel of personal develop-ment) presents the story of Mette Rudloff as she learns and grows from the various loves she experiences for other females. The first volume portrays her from childhood through her early twenties. Although Olga, the woman she loves, does bend to social opprobria and commits **suicide**, Mette refuses to succumb to the prejudice and hostility heaped upon her. She pursues her own path toward happiness, no matter how difficult it proves. Over the course of the next two volumes, Mette learns about the lesbian and homosexual **subcultures**, has several love affairs, and builds her own character so that, at the conclusion, she stands confident in the validity of her choices and at the same time hopeful and able to build a long-lasting relationship with another woman.

The first edition of the initial volume quickly sold out. Readers, especially lesbian readers, praised the sympathetic—and convincing—depiction of lesbian characters which they found here. They begged Weirauch to tell more of Mette's story, a request she then granted twice over. The novels have been translated into several languages. In English alone, they have had seven editions in various forms.

No other of her 64 prose works approached the success of *Der Skorpion*. Her long and successful career, however, was based on her ability to tell a story which the public wanted to hear and which it could easily digest.

A complicated and private person, Weirauch shared her life for almost six decades with another woman.

BIBLIOGRAPHY. Jeannette H. Foster, *Sex Variant Women in Literature*, new ed., Tallahassee: Naiad Press, 1985, pp. 229–34; James W. Jones, "The 'Third Sex' in German Literature from the Turn of the Century to 1933," Ph.D. Dissertation, University of Wisconsin 1986, pp. 630–48; Claudia Schoppmann, *Der Roman "Der Skorpion" von Anna Elisabet Weirauch*, Hamburg: Frühlings Erwachen, 1986.

James W. Jones

WHITE, ANDREW DICKSON (1832–1918)

American university president, historian of ideas, and diplomat. Educated at Yale in the famous "class of 1853," he early conceived the ideal of a university on the European model, with a scientific spirit and a breadth of learning in contrast to the narrow denominational instruction that had been the rule in the American college of the antebellum period. Together with Senator Ezra Cornell of Ithaca, New York, he drew up the charter of a new university that marked a major step toward the secularization and modernization of American higher education. Cornell University, founded in 1865, was novel in that it placed the natural sciences and engineering and the modern languages and their literatures on a par with the classics, and that its board of trustees was never to have a majority of any religious denomination; it was in all respects a modern institution comparable to those that already existed in Europe. White became President of the new university when it opened its doors in 1868.

In 1892 President Harrison appointed him American minister to St. Petersburg, where the minor rank and scanty means of the American legation prevented him from achieving anything of note at the corrupt court of Alexander III. But there he worked on his two-volume *History of the Warfare of Science with Theology in Christendom*, which he completed after his resignation in 1894. Published two years later, the work contained two chapters in which he exposed the story of the destruction of **Sodom** and the pillar of salt into which Lot's wife had been transformed as a geographical legend inspired by the peculiarly barren and salinized terrain on the shores of the Dead Sea. Relying on the investigations of the French geologist Edouard Lartet published in the five-volume work of the Duc de Luynes, *Voyage d'exploration à la mer Morte, à Petra et sur la rive gauche du Jourdain* (1871–75), he explained that the site of these legends had been submerged by the Dead Sea in prehistoric time, and that the fall of the water level exposed the surfaces whose sterility and desolation had been ascribed to an act of divine retribution for the depravity of the former inhabitants. Ignored as the work has been by the official scholarship of the divinity schools, it remains his legacy to critical scholarship on homosexuality.

Named Ambassador to Germany by President McKinley in 1897, he succeeded within a few months after his arrival in Berlin in winning the confidence of the homosexual Emperor Wilhelm II, whose favorite, the later Prince Philipp zu **Eulenburg**, was the center of a gay clique that influenced German foreign policy. He succeeded in keeping Germany neutral during the War of 1898, when the expanding American presence in the Western Pacific threatened to clash with German interests in the region.

BIBLIOGRAPHY. Wolf von Schierbrand, "Ambassador White's Work," *North American Review*, 175 (1902), 632–41; Roland Hugins, "Andrew D. White—Neutral," *Open Court*, 33 (1919), 428–31.
Warren Johansson

WHITMAN, WALT (1819–1892)

American poet and prose writer. Often acclaimed as America's greatest poet, Whitman, of working-class background, was self-taught, but as a printer, school teacher, journalist, and editor he contributed fiction and verse in the worst modes of the day to the best literary journals. There is no evidence of his genius until he suddenly began to write scraps of what was to become *Leaves of Grass* in his notebooks.

The earliest of these are full of philosophical or religious speculations in prose and poetry; those after 1857 are full of names of men he had met in his strolls through Brooklyn and Manhattan, and after

1862 the names of wounded soldiers he met in the military hospitals around **Washington**. These (at least the civilians) seem to be compulsive. The names are rarely repeated, and little information is given: where they met, the man's occupation, place of origin and any peculiarity of appearance or behavior. Aside from the fact that all the names are of **working-class** men, the lists are less informative than a telephone book. The soldier lists are frequently more detailed memoranda.

Life and Works. Probably in June 1847, he had a mystical experience in which he and his soul lay on the grass and his soul "plunged . . . [its] tongue to my bare-stript heart." This experience, whether actual or invented, richly erotic like so many mystical experiences, was the discovery of his true Self which freed his tongue. It has in fact been argued that *Leaves* is an inverted mystical experience. This work, which encompassed his complete poetic opus, was first published in 1855 with twelve poems ("Song of Myself" being rather lengthy); the second edition (1857) had thirty-two, the third (1860) 156, and so on through various printings and editions until 1881. Beginning in 1860, Whitman not only added poems (including the homoerotic **"Calamus"** collection), but dropped them, changed them, and rearranged the order. He has often been criticized for making changes, but he clearly did not do so for purposes of concealment.

Whitman went to Washington in December 1862, to look for his brother, who had been reported wounded, and stayed there for ten years as a volunteer visitor in the military hospitals and supported himself as a government clerk. In 1865 he met and fell in love with a young streetcar conductor, Peter Doyle. His affection was returned, at least emotionally, and the two remained intimate for a number of years, even after Whitman's stroke of 1873 forced his removal to the protection of his brother in Camden, New Jersey. They almost lost touch, but twelve years after Whitman's death (1892) Doyle remembered him as a beloved guide and counselor and confessed that in moments of depression he comforted himself by lying down wrapped in Whitman's old overcoat. In the late 1870s Whitman had a very intense relationship with an eighteen-year-old boy, Harry Stafford, on whose father's farm Whitman took curative mud baths. (It is worth noting that he became a friend of the whole Stafford family.) There were also a number of brief affairs with similarly half-educated, lonely young men. His relationship with Horace Traubel, his secretary and "Boswell" in the last years of his life, was probably of a somewhat different character, for Traubel was older and better educated while Whitman was aging and very ill.

Erotic Nature. It is impossible to determine the nature of Whitman's homosexuality. Some naive critics thought that he was merely talking about the brotherhood of man; others, naive in a different direction, have thought that he was bedding every man mentioned in his notebooks. Oral report from Edward **Carpenter** to Gavin Arthur to Allen Ginsberg stands or falls on the reliability of Gavin Arthur, which is unproved. It seems likely that, beyond the embraces and kisses, he had some experience before his 1873 stroke of man-to-man genital sex, possibly also experience with women. The notebooks and letters give evidence that Whitman had some sort of intimate relationship with two women, one probably an actress, the other a French "artiste," ostensibly an entertainer. Passages in the "Children of Adam" poems (which are heterosexual) seem as "sincere" as any in "Calamus." In his more programmatic poems, Whitman was always careful to say "he and she," "him and her." Women are permitted to have sexual lives, and he sympathizes with a prostitute, but they are generally thought of and idealized as perfect mothers for the new race of Americans.

It was his explicitness about male–female sex that shocked his early readers. Only a few homosexuals in England and some readers in Germany caught what is now obvious to any reader who can admit what he sees on the page. The second and third sections of "Song of Myself" are homosexual in their imagery, as is the subsequent discussion of the body and soul, which climaxes in the intercourse between body and soul in the fifth section. One might also cite the tremendous sweep of eroticism from section 24 to the climax of fulfillment in male intercourse in section 29. Another 1855 poem of interest is "The Sleepers," with its surrealistic imagery.

In contrast to the philosophical and psychological passages of "Song of Myself" and the passionate sexuality without a referent in "Children of Adam," "Calamus" reveals not only Whitman's mastery of the short lyric as against the longer ode or rhapsody (an underappreciated aspect of his art after 1860), but also differ in their obviously personal nature. The object has never been identified, and the poems lack the physicality of the passages referred to above, yet they convey poignantly many of the experiences of being a lover. In "Out of the Cradle Endlessly Rocking" (also 1860), the loss of a lover is imaged through the disappearance of the female of a pair of nesting mocking birds. Again one suspects a personal involvement.

Whitman's poetry changed after the Civil War. He himself considered the 1860 edition to be final and expected that later poems would form a new, more spiritual, book. For various reasons Whitman did not attempt a new book, but wove his new poems into a loose autobiographical cycle centering on the Civil War. Homosexuality appears (actually as early as 1856) as "**adhesiveness**," a term taken from phrenology and meaning for Whitman not only friendship but the capacity for "manly love" as a governing principle of society. He was not merely the poet of an idealized Jacksonian democracy nor of a new political structure, but of a culture bound together by love and religious faith in which each person could fulfill his or her own sexual nature. Representative statements are in "I hear it was charged against me" (1860), "Democratic Vistas" (1871), and in the Preface to "Two Rivulets" (1876).

Whitman, who was disappointed at his contemporary reception, would have been gratified by his reputation in the twentieth century, which is too widespread to more than mention. He is *the* democratic poet and a progenitor of the development of poetry beyond traditional metrical practice in the United States and foreign countries. A remarkable number of modern poets have paid him tribute in prose or verse, among the most notable being Ezra Pound, Pablo Neruda, Federico García **Lorca**, Fernando **Pessoa**, and Allen Ginsberg.

BIBLIOGRAPHY. Gay Wilson Allen, *The Solitary Singer*, Chicago: University of Chicago Press, 1985; M. Jimmie Killingsworth, *Whitman's Poetry of the Body: Sexuality, Politics, and the Text*, Chapel Hill: University of North Carolina Press, 1989; Robert K. Martin, *The Homosexual Tradition in American Poetry*, Austin: University of Texas Press, 1981; Jim Perlman, Ed Folson, and Don Campion, eds., *Walt Whitman. The Measure of His Song*, Minneapolis: The Holy Cow Press, 1981; Charley Shively, ed., *Calamus Lovers: Walt Whitman's Working Class Camerados*, San Francisco: Gay Sunshine Press, 1987; idem, *Drum Beats: Walt Whitman's Civil War Boy Lovers*, San Francisco: Gay Sunshine Press, 1989.

Edward F. Grier

WILDE, OSCAR F. O. W. (1856–1900)

Irish wit, poet, dramatist, novelist, writer of fairy tales, and convicted criminal. His wealthy and eminent parents sent him to Trinity College and to Oxford, where he began to be notorious for his effeminate pose as an aesthete under the influence of Walter **Pater**. This pose culminated in his trip to America and his identification with the effeminate poet in

Gilbert and Sullivan's 1881 operetta *Patience*. However, it appears that he was not yet homosexual, and he married Constance Lloyd, by whom he had two sons, one of whom died in World War I and the other of whom became a writer under the name of Vyvyan Holland.

Introduced to homosexual practices by Robert Ross, Wilde was soon sneaking out of the house to have relations with male **prostitutes**, usually **ephebic** teenagers. He fell in love with a young Scottish aristocrat, Lord Alfred **Douglas**, known as "Bosie," who was beautiful but full of character faults.

Meanwhile, Wilde had been dazzling the literary world with one masterpiece after another, such as *The Happy Prince*, *The Picture of Dorian Gray*, and *The Importance of Being Earnest*. He had become wealthy and famous, and everybody from the Prince of Wales on down went to see his plays.

Success went to his head and he provoked scandal with the overtones of vice in *Dorian Gray* and by consorting openly with Lord Alfred Douglas, who was also patronizing young male prostitutes. Wilde and Douglas introduced André **Gide** to pederasty in Algeria.

The ax finally fell in 1895 when the Marquess of Queensberry, Douglas's father, accused Wilde publicly of being homosexual (or more precisely: "posing as a somdomite [sic]"). Although the aspersion was well founded, Wilde was pushed by Douglas into a suit for libel, which backfired. There were three trials in all. The lawyers quoted passages from *Dorian Gray*, from Douglas' poems in *The Chameleon*, and from some love-letters that Wilde had sent to Douglas, which had been stolen. *The Chameleon* was a literary review that also included a short story attributed to Wilde, "The Priest and the Acolyte," with a pederastic theme. Wilde held out against all of this damaging material until he finally blundered into saying that he had never kissed a certain boy because he was ugly. This was the turning point, and Wilde was convicted of having sexual relations with several male prostitutes and sentenced to two years at hard labor. His marriage fell apart, his sons were removed from him, his house and belongings were auctioned off, many of his friends deserted him, and he contracted an ear infection in **prison** that eventually killed him three years after he was released.

While in prison, he wrote two final masterpieces, "The Ballad of Reading Gaol" and *De Profundis*, the latter being a long letter addressed to Douglas and blaming him for everything that had gone wrong. Wilde hobnobbed with Douglas in France and Italy after leaving prison, but he died in poverty in Paris at the age of 44.

Once he was safely dead, his writings earned for him the stature of a classic, and the horror evoked by his name gradually faded—though we have an account by Beverley Nichols (a man) of the destruction of a copy of *Dorian Gray* by his outraged father when Nichols, as a teenager, was caught reading it (*Father Figure*, 1972).

By now, thousands of books and articles have been written about Wilde and his sexual life, and he is probably the most famous homosexual in history as a homosexual (rather than as a writer or whatever). Scholars have often tried to deny or overlook the homosexuality of many famous men and women, but Wilde's conviction forever assured him of fame—or infamy—for his sexuality, and his life has overshadowed his writings, as he knew it would ("I put my talent into my writings and my genius into my life."). *De Profundis* was eventually made available in its complete form, and a large volume of Wilde's correspondence was published. To a certain extent, the letters take the place of the autobiography that Wilde never wrote. After Wilde died, Douglas converted to heterosexuality, writing several books about his relationship with Wilde.

Frank Harris produced a memoir about Wilde that is full of errors (or lies), and this unfortunately has been taken as a source by several biographers. It was Harris who invented the famous episode of the hordes of homosexuals running over to France as soon as Wilde was convicted. The publication of the Wilde letters automatically makes more recent biographies more accurate, and Ellmann's is a tour de force.

Wilde has been claimed as the author of "The Priest and the Acolyte" (a German translation gives his name as author) and of the pornographic novel *Teleny*, but these attributions are wrong. There is little actual homosexuality in Wilde's writings, mostly in *De Profundis* and *The Portrait of Mr. W. H.*, a novella about Shakespeare. There are some other letters, some poems, and some parts of *Dorian Gray* that reflect Wilde's homosexuality, but not much. It was Douglas rather than Wilde who coined the famous phrase "The Love that dare not speak its name," although Wilde ably defended himself, and was even applauded, when he was asked about this phrase during one of his trials. The one great mystery about him that remains to be solved is why he did not flee to France when he had every chance to do so on the eve of his arrest.

Oscar Wilde was the first famous homosexual to be pilloried by the mass press. On the Continent the ordeal to which he was subjected was widely interpreted as a sign of English hypocrisy and moral backwardness. Yet America tended to follow Britain in its condemnation. In the long run, a certain compensation (though not for Wilde himself) may be detected in the fact that, in the wake of the enormous publicity of the case, in English-speaking countries it became somewhat easier than before to speak of homosexuality, however negatively.

As a thinker Wilde was less subtle than Paul Valéry, less radical than Friedrich Nietzsche, less persevering than his friend André **Gide**. Yet his books are still read, *The Importance of Being Earnest* often reappears in the theatre, and Wilde continues to rank as an incomparable wit. Gay people honor him as a martyr.

BIBLIOGRAPHY. Rupert Croft-Cooke, *Bosie*, London: W. H. Allen, 1963; Richard Ellmann, *Oscar Wilde*, New York: Knopf, 1987; Rupert Hart-Davis, ed., *The Letters of Oscar Wilde*, London: Rupert Hart-Davis, 1962; idem, *More Letters of Oscar Wilde*, New York: Oxford University Press, 1985; H. Montgomery Hyde, *Oscar Wilde*, New York: Farrar, Straus & Giroux, 1975.

Stephen Wayne Foster

WILLIAM III (1650–1702)

Stadhouder of the Netherlands and king of England. The son of William II, stadhouder of the United Netherlands, and Mary, the oldest daughter of Charles I of England, he was born at the Hague after his father's death. A revolution precipitated by Louis XIV's invasion of the Netherlands (1672) caused to him to be made stadhouder for life. In 1664 William Bentinck (1649–1709) joined the Prince's household as a page and instantly endeared himself to his master. In a year the page became a courtier and a key figure in the household. It was, however, ten years later that Bentinck gave the most striking proof of his devotion to the Prince. On April 3, 1675, William fell ill to smallpox, the disease that had killed his father and mother. For 16 days he hovered between life and death, while Bentinck cared lovingly for him. It was only twenty years later that the Venetian ambassador in London learned the full story. When the Prince of Orange was in danger of dying from smallpox, the doctors believed that the violent progress of the disease could be stopped only if "a young man of the same age, lying in bed with the Prince, exposed himself to the dangerous contagion of his illness." Bentinck volunteered his services at once, and the warmth of his body made the Prince sweat so heavily that the smallpox broke out. The Prince recovered, but Bentinck, after contact with the "dangerous fluids," fell ill himself.

William's marriage in 1677 to the English princess Mary, the Protestant daughter of the later James II, was followed in February 1678 by Bentinck's to Mary's lady-in-waiting Anne Villiers. Long in touch with the English opposition to Mary's Roman Catholic father, William let his **Protestant** sympathies be known in England. After secret negotiations, he crossed the Channel (1688) with an army of 15,000, was joined by most of the leading men in England, and took the throne of James II, whom he allowed to go into exile in France. Effected without bloodshed, the so-called Glorious Revolution was the decisive victory in the long struggle between Parliament and the crown, since William had to accept the Bill of Rights (1689) and to give Parliament control of finances and the army.

William's policies did not, however, endear him to his English subjects, and none of his Dutch courtiers was especially popular, but easily the most hated man at court was Bentinck, created Earl of Portland at the coronation. Soon after William's landing, the English realized how much he depended on the advice of this unbending foreigner, who was nicknamed "the Wooden Man." The English peers resented Portland's high-handed manner and the jealousy with which he guarded the king, who did nothing without his approval, while in turn William's lavish generosity soon made him one of the wealthiest men in the country, Groom of the Stole, Treasurer of the Privy Purse, and more. The only Englishman who could compete for William's friendship was Henry Sidney, created Earl of Rodney at the coronation, and loyal to his sovereign even against his own interests; he was tall, handsome, and honest, but a mediocrity who made promises he did not keep and a drunkard as well. William's lack of interest in women, who "missed the homage due to their sex," was another cause of his unpopularity in England. After the death of Queen Mary (1694), who had remained childless during seventeen years of mar-

riage, he took no new wife. When he lay on his deathbed, Bentinck was the last to bid him farewell; "for the last time," he murmured, holding the favorite's hand to his heart.

William III was the most European figure that the House of Orange has produced; for some thirty years he was one of the makers of European history. As protagonist of the Glorious Revolution in England, he was the first king to rule with the consent of Parliament, and by choosing men of Whig persuasion as his ministers, he began (1696) the system of a responsible cabinet. His homosexuality—of which rumors circulated among the high nobility—enabled him to form a lasting bond with his favorite, William Bentinck, who not only saved his life but served him loyally to the end of his reign.

BIBLIOGRAPHY. Henriette Elisabeth Heimans, *Het Karakter van Willem III Koning-Stadhouder: Proeve eener Psychographie*, Amsterdam: H. J. Paris, 1925; Henry and Barbara van der Zee, *William and Mary*, New York: Alfred A. Knopf, 1973.

Warren Johansson

WILLIAMS, TENNESSEE (THOMAS LANIER) (1911–1983)

Major American playwright and a significant fiction writer and poet. Born in Mississippi—the setting, along with **New Orleans** and St. Louis, of many of his most important plays—Williams has been considered to be a Southern writer, but his influence, as the leading proponent of post-World War II psychological realism, has been international.

A prolific writer, Williams produced about seventy plays, including some one-acts, revisions, and works apparently lost and not yet published, as well as three novels, six volumes of short stories, two of poetry, and one of memoirs. Awarded both a Group Theatre and a Rockefeller grant in 1939, he had his first major professional production in 1944, *The Glass Menagerie*, which was followed by a string of critical and popular successes for the next two decades: *A Streetcar Named Desire* (1947), *The Rose Tattoo* (1951), *Summer and Smoke* (1952), *Cat on a Hot Tin Roof* (1955), *Orpheus Descending* (1957), *Sweet Bird of Youth* (1959), and *Night of the Iguana* (1961). From the mid-1960s until his death, Williams' plays met with less success and many critics found his later works derivative, repetitious, and often self-indulgent. But if his last, more experimental and autobiographical phase was less successful than his early canon, the plays are not dramatic failures: *Confessional* and *Out Cry* (1971), *Small Craft Warnings* (1972), *Eccentricities of a Nightingale* (1976), *Vieux Carré* (1977), *Crève Coeur* (1978), and *Clothes for a Summer Hotel* (1980).

Williams stated that he "slept through the sixties" and that both his personal and his professional life shifted in 1963 with the death of his lover of fourteen years, Frank Merlo; in 1969, he was briefly committed to a mental institution, and he later admitted a serious alcohol and chemical dependency during this period. With the publication of his sexually explicit *Memoirs* in 1975, the homosexual themes only implicit in his early drama became central to his work, and his biography began to eclipse his art as he gained an increasing celebrity status as an artistic renegade. Early accused of employing the "**Albertine** Stratagem" by disguising gay males as women in such works as *Summer and Smoke* and being excessively coy about homosexuality in such plays as *Cat on a Hot Tin Roof*, he was, in many of his last works, direct in presenting openly gay characters and themes.

This autobiographical tendency was always most explicit in his fiction. A story such as "One Arm" (1948) is much more direct in its treatment of homosexuality than the plays of the period, and his handling of sexuality became increasingly explicit as he moved from *The Knightly Quest* (1966) to *Moise and the World of*

Reason (1975). His two collections of poetry, *In the Winter of Cities* (1956) and *Androgyne, Mon Amour* (1977), are lyrical explorations of homoeroticism, echoing many of the themes of his plays.

Whether women or gay men, Williams' protagonists are always sensitive people, artists of life on the perimeter of contemporary society, battling against brutal forces which seek to crush and destroy them. Isolated and damaged by the larger world, his characters inhabit poetic and subjective worlds, yearning for a more delicate and civilized past but maintaining a noble stance in the face of seemingly inevitable annihilation. His canon is a testament to the strength and dignity of the isolated individual in a mechanistic world.

BIBLIOGRAPHY. Catherine M. Arnott, ed., *Tennessee Williams on File*, New York: Methuen, 1985; Felicia Hardison Londre, *Tennessee Williams*, New York: Ungar, 1979; Donald Spoto, *The Kindness of Strangers: The Life of Tennessee Williams*, Boston: Little Brown, 1985; Jac Tharpe, ed., *Tennessee Williams: A Tribute*, Jackson: University of Mississippi Press, 1977.

Rodney Simard

WINCKELMANN, JOHANN JOACHIM (1717–1768)

German archeologist, art historian, and prose writer. Born the son of a shoemaker in Brandenburg, Winckelmann's diligence at Latin school and at the universities of Halle and Jena laid the foundation for his later scholarly achievements. After laboring for several years as a village pastor and schoolmaster, in 1748 he obtained a post as librarian to Count Heinrich von Bunau near Dresden, giving him indirect access to the court of Augustus III, who had made the city one of the leading centers of Central European culture. Then in 1754 he transferred to the service of Cardinal Passionei in Dresden itself. Here he began to study actual art masterpieces which he had previously known only from engravings, and this immersion, catalyzing the knowledge that he had gained through many years of insightful reading of Greek literature, brought forth his first statement of artistic theory. Winckelmann's pamphlet *Gedanken über die Nachahmung der griechischen Werke in der Mahlerei und Bildhauer-Kunst* (Thoughts Concerning the Imitation of Greek Works of Painting and Sculpture; 1755) contained the talismanic formula that was to reverberate through his own work and that of subsequent interpreters of Greek art: "noble simplicity and tranquil grandeur."

In order to settle in Rome, where he could examine the vast collections of ancient art that had been assembled there, Winckelmann converted to Roman Catholicism. Securing the support of Cardinal Albani, Winckelmann made the eternal city his base for the rest of his life. After publishing a number of technical volumes on archeology and antiquities, Winckelmann brought out his magnum opus, *Geschichte der Kunst des Alterthums* (The History of Art of Antiquity), at the end of 1763. In this work the archeologist proposed two major innovations: he isolated Greek art from such competitors as Egyptian and Etruscan art, viewing it as sui generis; and he established an overarching developmental sequence of stages for Greek art, wherein the achievements of each individual artist could be seen as responding to governing principles. By implication, Winckelmann argued that the central characteristics of Greek art had an absolute and transcendental value, and hence were valid for his own (and every) epoch.

In 1768 he traveled north to Germany and Austria, where he was received with signal honors by the empress Maria Theresa at the Viennese court. On the return trip south Winckelmann found himself in Trieste with time on his hands while waiting for a boat. In his inn he struck up an acquaintance with an adventurer, one Arcangeli, who seems to have shared his homosexual tastes. Unfortunately, his sleazy companion became covetous of Winckelmann's wealth, and stabbed him to death on June 8, 1768. Although a police report exists, the exact relation between the scholar and the adventurer will probably never be known.

Winckelmann held that handsome young men, particularly those of aristocratic birth, were particularly capable of receiving his teachings of beauty and scholarship. While he never visited Greece, he was certain that the country had brought forth a superior human type, which the artists had simply refined. His appreciation of Greek beauty is grounded in his exaltation of the ephebe, the male adolescent, as the ideal reconciliation of the male and female principles. Accordingly Winckelmann's aesthetic reflects a criterion of **androgyny**, and this feature recurs in the work of the many neo-Classic artists who adhered to his ideas down to the end of the nineteenth century.

Winckelmann was fortunate to live in a time in which contemporary art was discarding the decorative paradigms of the rococo, and he was privileged to guide it into new channels, those of neo-Classicism. Although he enjoyed a European reputation (his most important works were translated into French almost immediately after their appearance), his profoundest influence was in Germany, where his following was not confined to those involved in art and archeology but struck chords in everyone seriously interested in culture. This broad influence was made possible by his German style, which was both limpid and eloquent. His general approach, which has been aptly termed aesthetic paganism, was grounded in his homosexual appreciation of the beauty of the ephebe, but he knew how to confine himself to the results of his perceptions without risking offending his readers by proclaiming too openly their source. Perhaps it would not go too far to compare his role in discovering and conveying transcendental aesthetic values to the priestly function of the primordial **shaman**, whose homoerotic orientation gave him special insights.

More concretely Winckelmann called upon German philology to focus its attention on the whole spectrum of the heritage of ancient **Greece**; his **Hellenism** helped to lay the foundations for a century of supremacy of German classical scholarship. He also had a salutary effect on the discipline of art history, which for a long time afterwards was virtually a German monopoly. He showed that the history of art need not restrict itself to connoisseurship or the biographical study of great masters, but could instead aspire to lay bare the governing laws which made art works what they were and not otherwise. Moreover, he held that art has a history in the most meaningful sense, a history that only a clear concept of organic development could explain. Thus, while Friedrich Nietzsche and others were to show a century after his death that his insights into the specific character of Greek art were incomplete, in that they overstated the elements of tranquility and equipoise, the ideals of scholarly dedication for which Winckelmann stood have remained of lasting significance.

BIBLIOGRAPHY. Wolfgang Leppmann, *Winckelmann*, New York: Knopf, 1970; Denis M. Sweet, "The Personal, the Political, and the Aesthetic: Johann Joachim Winckelmann's German Enlightenment Life," *Journal of Homosexuality*, 16:1/2 (1988), 147–62.

Wayne R. Dynes

WITCHCRAFT

Witchcraft is the form of sorcery allegedly practiced in Western Europe between the thirteenth and eighteenth centuries. Sorcery itself is universal, found in almost every period and every human culture as a set of magical beliefs and practices intended to manipulate the phenomena of nature for the benefit of the sorcerer or his client. Most sorcery is operative, that is to say, the practitioner has the capacity, through spells and paraphernalia, to compel occult forces to do his will. The medieval notion of witchcraft, however, was contractual: the witch had to elicit the patronage of a demon by making a pact with him. As contemporary legends and documents attest, this contractual relationship parallels the feudal bond between liege and lord.

Witchcraft and Christianity. **Christian** theology, taking **Old Testament** texts and **New Testament** stories of demonic possession as its point of departure, transformed the earlier notion of the sorcerer into that of the witch or wizard as the agent of Satan and accomplice of his infernal legions. It further made a logical connection between witchcraft proper and **heresy**, namely any belief obstinately held contrary to the orthodox teaching of the church.

The witchcraft delusion that obsessed European society from 1450 to 1700—hence from the end of the **Middle Ages** until the onset of the **Enlightenment**—is a major problem for the historian that has not yet been fully resolved. Many theories have been advanced to explain the reasons for the phenomenon and the real background, if any, of the belief system cherished by the witch hunters. Earlier investigators often were animated by a **Protestant** or anti-clerical bias that led them to place the blame solely on the Roman Catholic church and Catholic theologians. It is true that Pope Innocent VIII on December 5, 1484 issued the bull *Summis desiderantes*, confirming the support of the papacy for inquisitorial proceedings against presumed witches, and this text became a preface to the *Malleus maleficarum* (Witches' Hammer) published by two Dominican inquisitors in 1487 and reissued in 29 editions, 16 of them in German, down to 1669. The *Malleus* was far more influential in that it colorfully detailed the diabolical orgies of the witches and convinced a credulous public that a plot of cosmic dimensions hatched by Satan himself threatened the very foundations of Christian society.

Part of the problem posed by the witchcraft delusion is that an exotic belief system derived from the Bible and St. **Augustine** was superimposed upon the actual practice of sorcery in all the variants that the racial and ethnic diversity of late medieval Europe, and the particularism of its folk culture, had inherited from pagan, pre-Christian times. Every province had its own customs and superstitions, its enchanted springs and haunted dwellings, its survivals of Celtic or Scandinavian or Slavic lore.

Sexual Aspects. Perverse sexuality played a major role in the fantasies associated with the witchcraft delusion, but contrary to what has been alleged in some recent publications, homosexual relations between human beings and demons, or simply between human participants in witchcraft, do not figure prominently in the sources. The bisexuality and androgyny of demons and the preoccupation with change of sex suggest a psychological substratum of homoeroticism, but comparatively few homosexual acts are reported in the literature of witchcraft.

When **sodomy** does appear in the accounts of sexual union with the Devil, it is heterosexual sodomy (*peccatum contra naturam ratione modi*) that is usually meant, most often anal intercourse or the *osculum infame*, the kiss applied to Satan's posterior. One account of a witches' sabbat, it is true, mentions a gathering held atop Mount Tonale, in the Italian Tyrol, at which handsome youths were provided for the sexual pleasures of the all-male gathering.

There are several reasons for the absence of homosexual relations from the dossiers of witchcraft. The first is that the starting point for the belief system was the passage in Genesis 6:1–4, further developed in I Enoch and the Testaments of the Twelve Patriarchs, according to which the "sons of God," identified in later legend as fallen angels, took wives of the "daughters of men" and had offspring by them, the "men of renown." Hence the whole fantasy of sexual intercourse between demons and human beings was rooted in a heterosexual and demonically procreative context, not a homosexual one. The second is that over the entire span of the witchcraft delusion women outnumbered men by at least three to one as objects of prosecution; in New England, for example, 80 percent of the accused were women. For the male theologians and witch hunters who promoted the delusion, the carnal aspect of woman was the heterosexual one—her power to entice and ensnare men. Lesbianism was then, as later, invisible to the male unconscious, hence it could play no role in the paranoid fantasies entertained by the authorities of church and state. The third is that the crimes blamed upon the witches had no homosexual content, but more often took the form of causing crop failures or other misfortunes that provoked the wrath of peasant communities.

In the treatise of Jean Bodin *De la Démonomanie des sorciers* (1580) there is a comparison between witchcraft and sodomy: "If one avers that one should not dwell upon the confession of something against nature, as some say, [then] the sodomitic buggers should not be punished who confess the sin against nature. But if one wishes to say 'against nature' for something impossible, that is false, for what is impossible by nature is not [truly] impossible, inasmuch as all the actions of intelligence and the workings of God that one often sees, go against the course of nature." In other words, the belief that sodomites had been empowered by the devil to commit "unnatural" acts matched the preposterous claim that witches could ride through the air on broomsticks and perform similar "impossible" feats because of their covenant with Satan.

Modern Revivals. In the 1970s the emerging gay movement overlapped with certain phases of neo-paganism, including a revived interest in witchcraft understood as part of the archaic "nature religion" that has been supplanted by Christianity. Some lesbians took part in the revival of Wicca, or the Craft, which emphasized the spiritual and thaumaturgic power of the feminine as it had been embodied in the traditional healing art of the witch, and also emancipation from the oppressively patriarchal aspects of the **Judeo-Christian** tradition. In like manner, the gay-male Radical Faeries, who held their first gathering in 1979, stressed the distinctive insights of the personality that is neither male nor female, yet partakes of both and throughout human history has played a role as mediator between the divine and the human. The cultivation of a gay spirituality as a dimension of contemporary neo-paganism has for some held the promise of a release from the constricting taboos of Judaism and Christianity and a rediscovery of the enduring values of the homosexual experience in the religious sphere.

Some Comparisons. The witchcraft delusion, as it has been analyzed by historians in modern times, does offer several lessons of paramount importance for the understanding of the attitude toward homosexuality in Christian Europe—a mentality that has far outlasted the belief in witches and their pact with Satan. The first is that the religious mind scorns true motivation and causality, preferring magical influences, even where empirical investigation can find none. This is the attitude that sees in **AIDS** divine retribution for "immorality," and rejoices in the "death of the wicked."

A second crucial point is that witchcraft began like sodomy as a sacral offense but was transferred in time to the secular courts, for the reason that **capital** crimes came increasingly to be the domain of the state rather than the church. The ecclesiastical courts were denied the right to impose the death penalty, but convicted offenders were relaxed to the secular authorities who had no qualms about inflicting it—on witches or sodomites.

A third consideration is that in trials for witchcraft it was most often the prosecutors and the witnesses for the prosecution, not the defendants, who were mentally ill, were in the grip of paranoid beliefs grounded in a magical understanding of the origins of the misfortunes which had befallen the community. The analogy to this in the case of homosexual sodomy is that while the acts committed by the defendants were harmless and even pleasurable, the prosecutors imagined them a source of potential divine retribution that would overtake the whole of society if the "unnatural" acts were left unpunished.

A fourth issue is that in many trials for witchcraft the principal witnesses were children who later were proven to have made the charges without foundation or out of sheer malice. This historical precedent is relevant to the problem of the uncorroborated testimony of children in cases of child abuse, particularly of homosexual **pedophilia**. Both the prosecution and the defense in such cases are often bedeviled by the suggestibility and unreliability of children as witnesses who, because lacking the adult's clear perception of the dividing line between truth and fiction, can be manipulated in a variety of ways scarcely conducive to ascertaining guilt or innocence. It is just this element of immaturity in the child's character that is used to deny minors the right to give valid consent to sexual acts, even when psychological willingness is present, just as civil law withholds many rights from the child simply because it is said to have not yet reached the age at which the majority of normal individuals are capable of exercising such empowerment.

A fifth consideration is that even at the height of the witchcraft delusion there were observers who fulfilled Rudyard Kipling's condition "if you can keep your head when all about you/ are losing theirs and . . . make allowance for their doubting too." That is to say, even in a still medieval society there were educated men who saw through the whole belief system that obsessed their contemporaries, and to the best of their power sought to calm the ignorant and superstitious masses whom fanatics had goaded into paroxysms of irrational fury. A subtle interaction between the authorities in church and state who manipulated the credulity of the uneducated, and the folk upon whose superstitious fears and anxieties they played, maintained the belief in witchcraft. The analogy with modern right-wing demagogues who exploit the lingering **homophobia** of those who are still in the grip of traditional attitudes is self-evident.

Conclusion. The witchcraft delusion has vanished from European society, apart from a few provincial backwaters where it occasionally inspires acts of violence against persons suspected of being witches. In such cases the police naturally proceed against the superstition-ridden perpetrators of the violence, not against the victims. But what the author of this article has termed the sodomy delusion held sway until the middle of the twentieth century, and has only in the last two decades begun to recede. "Moral panics" provoked by an unsophisticated community's discovery of a homosexual underworld in its midst persisted into the not distant past, and in such cases the police acted to enforce superstition and intolerance, while the victims suffered public humiliation and imprisonment, if not worse. Sporadic **violence** against homosexuals is often sanctioned by the mores of the heterosexual society, a form of intimidation that has been exacerbated by the epidemic of AIDS with the irrational fear of the "bearers of contagion" that it inspires. In the politics of conservative and clerical parties fear and aversion in regard to homosexuality still play a baleful role, giving them a hold over segments of the electorate whom they cannot win by more rational appeals. The record of the struggle against the witchcraft delusion may afford valuable lessons for planning the future campaigns of the gay liberation **movement**, and for analyzing the psychological and social processes that—even at the close of the twentieth century—keep such false notions alive in the face of the empirical evidence that contradicts them.

The history of the witchcraft delusion in Western Europe is a dark chapter in the annals of civilization, but the success achieved by reformers in purging the collective mind of the paranoid beliefs with which Christian theology had infected it must give heart to all those who even now struggle for the same goal in regard to homosexuality.

BIBLIOGRAPHY. Nachman Ben-Yehuda, *Deviance and Moral Boundaries: Witchcraft, the Occult, Science Fiction, Deviant Sciences and Scientists,* Chicago: University of Chicago Press, 1985; Mircea Eliade, *Occultism, Witchcraft, and Cultural Fashions: Essays in Comparative Religions,* Chicago: University of Chicago Press, 1976; Robert Muchembled, *Sorcières, justice et société aux 16e et 17e siècles,* Paris: Imago, 1987; Luciano Parinetto, *Streghe e politica: dal Rinascimento italiano a Montaigne, da Bodin a Naudé,* Milan: Istituto propaganda libraria, 1983; Rossell Hope Robbins, *The Encyclopedia of Witchcraft and Demonology,* New York: Crown, 1959; Keith Thomas, *Religion and the Decline of Magic,* New York: Scribner's, 1971.

Warren Johansson

WITTGENSTEIN, LUDWIG (1889–1951)

Austrian-British philosopher. The son of a millionaire industrialist in Vienna, Wittgenstein came to England at nineteen with the intention of studying aeronautics at the University of Manchester. Finding his bent more theoretical, he transferred to **Cambridge** University, where he immersed himself in logic courses taught by Bertrand Russell. In November 1912, at the behest of his fellow student John Maynard **Keynes**, Wittgenstein was elected to the elite secret society known as the Apostles. At that time the group was closely knit and suffused with homoerotic atmosphere. Always prickly, Wittgenstein proved a difficult member and soon stopped attending meetings.

Having joined the Austrian army after the outbreak of World War I, he was captured by the Italians. From his prisoner-of-war camp he succeeded in mailing to Bertrand Russell the manuscript of his *Tractatus Logico-Positivus*. After its publication in 1921, this austere and condensed treatise, which suggested that most branches of traditional **philosophy** were nonsense, was to have a catalytic effect on the emerging logical-positivist trend in philosophy. Except for one article, the *Tractatus* was the only work published by Wittgenstein during his lifetime.

After the war Wittgenstein gave up philosophy, teaching elementary school in a number of Austrian villages. In 1929, however, he returned to Cambridge where he was given a research fellowship. His classes, which were often painful exercises in self-criticism, attracted a small, but devoted following. Much of the material from these lectures went into his manuscripts, which were only published after his death. Although Wittgenstein was appointed professor in 1939, he chose to spend the war as a humble medical orderly—a career decision recalling that of Walt **Whitman** eighty years before. After the war he returned to being a professor at Cambridge, but said that he found it torture. Following a trip to the United States, he died of cancer in 1951.

After his death, his associates undertook the difficult job of seeing that his manuscripts reached publication. The most important of these, the *Philosophical Investigations* (1953), contained major revisions of his earlier thinking, concentrating on questions of language and the nature of philosophy itself. During the third quarter of the twentieth century, Wittgenstein was probably the most influential philosopher in the English-speaking world, and his ideas existed in a fruitful tension with the school of analytic philosophy. This acclaim did not prevent his teacher Bertrand Russell from denouncing his later works as "mental beds"—invitations to shirk the problems that Russell

still regarded as important. As Wittgenstein's reputation slowly faded in England and America in the late seventies and eighties—in part owing to the reception of French contemporary thought—it gained influence in central Europe.

Some of Wittgenstein's renown derives from his reputation as one almost ascetically devoted to pure thought and exempt from any sensuality. When, in the first edition (1973) of his biography, William Warren Bartley, III, first broached the subject of the philosopher's homosexuality, the Wittgenstein establishment reacted with vengeful anger. Although his literary heirs reputedly had in their possession a coded diary containing references to homosexual encounters, they denied any sexual unorthodoxy, and sought to vilify Bartley. Their motives are hard to assess: Wittgenstein was certainly no flaming queen, and those who did not have access to the documents probably did have difficulty in conceiving him as a homosexual, a role for which they had only stereotypical models. Others may have foreseen that the philosopher's sexuality, if openly discussed, would be used by philosophical enemies to tarnish his reputation—as has happened.

The facts appear to be as follows. In his student days in Vienna Wittgenstein became accustomed to cruise in the Prater, a large public park next to the inner city. Here he met youths of the "rough trade" type which remained his preference. Later he was to continue this activity in England. However, he also had long-term affairs with men of his own class, notably with Francis Skinner. Wittgenstein was always uncomfortable with his homosexuality, which accounts for his concealing it from his close friends.

No close relationship seems to link Wittgenstein's sexual orientation and his iconoclastic philosophy. That is to say, he might have reached similar conclusions had he been heterosexual. Nonetheless, his homosexuality—or rather his insistence on remaining in the closet—

contributed to the aura of oracular strangeness which helped to make the author of highly abstruse and technical papers into virtually a household name—at least in academic circles.

BIBLIOGRAPHY. William Warren Bartley, III, *Wittgenstein*, 2nd ed., La Salle, IL: Open Court, 1985.

Wayne R. Dynes

WITTMAN, CARL (1943–1986)

Gay and radical activist. A "red-diaper" baby, Wittman was born in New Jersey and attended Swarthmore College. As a campus leader, he spent summers in Tennessee supporting black civil rights, wrote for the student paper and organized student support for anti-segregation demonstrations in Chester, Pennsylvania, and Cambridge, Maryland.

The Swarthmore Political Action Committee provided a model for the Students for a Democratic Society (SDS). Joining the national council in 1963, Wittman played a prominent role in SDS until his departure in 1966. In September, 1963, SDS established ERAP (Economic and Action Research Project) based on his paper, "Students and Economic Action," which was further elaborated with Tom Hayden in "An Interracial Movement of the Poor?" They called for non-hierarchical organizing: "We are people and we work with people." Wittman joined the Newark SDS project and recalled that "Tom Hayden confidently announced that there was to be no homosexuality or marijuana in our community organizing project, and then proceeded to borrow my room to bed down with his latest woman, leaving me stunned and terrified." ("Us and the New Left," *Fag Rag*, 22/23 [Fall 1978], 22).

While listed as a speaker for the SDS affiliated Radical Education Project during 1967, Wittman went to the west coast where he settled into a mixed San Francisco commune of Resistance (an anti-war group), enjoyed the psychedelic revolution and raised money hustling. During 1968 he organized war resistance events in British Columbia, Oregon, and Washington State.

Although closeted about his love for other men, Carl had begun an active homosexual life at fourteen. "Kids can take care of themselves," he wrote, "and are sexual beings way earlier than we'd like to admit. Those of us who began cruising in early adolescence know this, and we were doing the cruising, not being debauched by dirty old men." Wittman came out in an anti-war magazine ("Waves of Resistance," *Liberation*, 13 [November, 1968], 29–33), where he held that resisting heterosexuality was related to resisting war.

Wittman was part of a gay contingent at a San Francisco demonstration in May 1969 against the States Steamship Line, a Vietnam war supply carrier. His essay, "Refugees from Amerika: A Gay Manifesto," was written after the Steamship demonstration but before **Stonewall** (June 27, 1969) and was first published late in 1969. Providing an ideology for radical gay males and widely reprinted by gay and left movement groups, the Manifesto never became dogma: "the gay **liberation** movement is in its polymorphous, unbureaucratic, anarchistic form," Wittman wrote gleefully in 1970.

In 1969, Wittman acquired land in Wolf Creek, Oregon, with his lover Stevens McClave, who committed suicide in 1974. Between 1973 and Wittman's death he and Allan Troxler were lovers. In Autumn 1974 the first issue of the periodical *RFD* appeared with a cover by Allan and an article by Carl. *RFD* promised "to build some sense of community among rural gay people."

In 1981, Wittman moved to Durham, North Carolina, where he worked in the Durham Food Co-op, was a leader in Citizens for a Safer East Durham, which closed the Armageddon Chemical plant, and helped write *Durham's Convention*

Center: In Whose Interest! while co-director of the North Carolina Public Interest Research Group in 1981–82. Carl was one of the founders of the Durham Lesbian and Gay Health Project and was active in **AIDS** work. He died on January 22, 1986, after he rejected hospital AIDS treatment and chose to die in dignity among friends at home. In choosing the time of his death, he demonstrated his 1963 principle that people must be "confident that they have some control over the decisions which affect their lives."

Charley Shively

WOLFENDEN REPORT

The *Report of the Departmental Committee on Homosexual Offenses and Prostitution*, published on September 3, 1957 by the British government, is known as the Wolfenden Report after the Chairman of the Committee, Sir John Wolfenden (1906–1985), at that time Vice Chancellor of Reading University. This *Report* was destined to have momentous and far-reaching effects.

Creation of the Report. In the wake of several scandalous court cases in which homosexuality had been featured, the British Parliament on August 24, 1954 appointed a committee of 15 men and women whose task it was "to consider . . . the law and practice relating to homosexual offenses and the treatment of persons convicted of such offenses by the courts" along with the laws relevant to prostitution and solicitation. The committee met on 62 days of which 32 were devoted to the oral interrogation of witnesses. All the sessions were private, not only to avoid sensationalizing of the deliberations on the part of the media, but also because "only in genuinely private session" could the witnesses "giving evidence on these delicate and controversial matters" speak "with the full frankness" which the subject demanded. The proposals with respect to homosexuality were for the time a radical innovation: of the 13 members of the Committee who had served during the

full three years, 12 recommended that homosexual behavior between consenting adults in private should no longer be a criminal offense. The *Report* did not explicitly define "consent" and "in private," leaving these words to be interpreted as they would be in the case of heterosexual conduct; it suggested that the age of **consent** be twenty-one; and it tried to relieve from the threat of prosecution the victim of **blackmail** whose homosexual activity had been revealed to the police.

For the **common law** countries of the English-speaking world, the *Wolfenden Report* meant a break with a legal tradition that had gone virtually unchallenged since the enactment of 25 Henry VIII c. 6 in 1533. It urged that homosexual behavior cease to be criminal, that the religious sanctions against it were not grounds for bringing it to the attention of secular courts, and that there "must remain a realm of private morality and immorality which is, in brief and crude terms, not the law's business." The signers of the document recognized that "to reverse a long-standing tradition is a serious matter and not to be suggested lightly." But the task entrusted to the Committee was to "state what we regard as just and equitable law," and that consideration of the question should not be unduly influenced by "the present law, much of which derives from traditions whose origins are obscure." This last remark evidently reflected the work of the Anglican cleric Derrick Sherwin **Bailey**, who had put forward arguments intended to exculpate the Christian Church of responsibility for the legal intolerance of homosexuality, preferring instead to place the onus on pagan, pre-Christian beliefs and laws.

Moreover, and against the testimony of nearly all the **psychiatric** and **psychoanalytic** witnesses, the Committee found that "homosexuality cannot legitimately be regarded as a disease, because in many cases it is the only symptom and is compatible with full mental health in other respects," echoing what Iwan **Bloch** had written in 1907 in *The Sexual Life of Our Time*. This finding provoked an outcry in the psychiatric press, but it anticipated the later decision of the American Psychiatric Association—under pressure from gay **activists**—to drop homosexuality from its classification of mental illnesses. But in turn the judgment of the Committee closed the door on the notion that exclusively homosexual individuals are in any way less responsible for their actions in the eyes of the law.

The choice of twenty-one as the age of **consent** was motivated by considerations which the *Report* itself laid open to question. Some of the witnesses had urged an age of consent as low as seventeen or even sixteen, but the Committee deemed a boy of sixteen "incapable of forming a mature judgment about actions of a kind which might have the effect of setting him apart from the rest of society." It had encountered "several cases in which young men have been induced by means of gifts of money or hospitality to indulge in homosexual behavior with older men," and to fix the age of consent at eighteen would lay young men "open to attentions and pressures of an undesirable kind from which the adoption of the later age would help to protect them, and from which they ought, in view of their special vulnerability, to be protected." The practical implication of this recommendation was that the boy in his late teens, at the peak of his physical vitality and sexual attractiveness, ought to be placed off limits because older males might seek him out as a sexual partner. Such a high age of consent had been unknown even in Victorian times, when most law codes set the age of sexual responsibility for heterosexual activity somewhere between nine and fourteen, but it reinforced a trend to reform the law in favor of adult homosexuals having relations with other adult homosexuals and at the expense of **pederasts**, who would now be threatened with even more severe sanctions.

Results. The publication of the *Report* provoked a storm of debate, all the more as the immemorial taboo on public discussion of homosexuality had now been breached for once and for all. As John Wolfenden himself remarked, the subject "filled the front pages of Wednesday's evening papers, with VICE in inch-high capitals as the main headline." Despite attacks from the conservative sectors of the press, a writer in the *New Statesman* summarized the situation by saying that the liberal wing of the Establishment was solidly behind the recommendations of the *Report*, and that it was only a matter of time before they became law.

This prophecy proved correct: not Great Britain alone, but other English-speaking countries felt the impact of the Wolfenden Report as well. In 1961 the American Bar Association approved the draft of a Model Penal Code from which homosexual offenses between consenting adults were omitted, and the State of Illinois broke the ice as the first American jurisdiction to adopt the new principle. In Canada also the words of the *Report* were heeded, and in 1969 Parliament repealed the section of the Penal Code that made homosexual activity a crime. In England itself the Earl of Arran, inspired by zeal to remove what he regarded as a shameful injustice to a persecuted minority, had in 1965 persuaded the House of Lords—which is not subject to the control of the electorate—to initiate legislation for the same purpose. Eighteen months later, on the initiative of Leo Abse, the House of Commons followed suit, so that in the summer of 1967 the Sexual Offences Act became law in England and Wales—though not (at that date) in Scotland and Northern Ireland, where Protestant fundamentalism worked to stymie repeal of the laws against "immorality." At the behest of various high officers, the British **military** remained exempt from the reform.

With its limitations and with views that now strike many readers as old-fashioned and conservative, the Wolfenden Report was a landmark in the struggle for the legal toleration of homosexuality in common law countries. Its arguments, grounded in a **liberal** tradition that harked back to John Stuart Mill, solidly underpinned the impetus to law reform that made possible the **gay liberation** movement which was to blossom in the 1970s and later throughout the English-speaking world.

BIBLIOGRAPHY. Baron Wolfenden of Westcott, *Turning Points: The Memoirs of Lord Wolfenden*, London: The Bodley Head, 1976; Sir John Wolfenden, et al., *Report of the Committee on Homosexual Offences and Prostitution*, London: H. M. Stationery Office, 1957.

Warren Johansson

WOMEN'S NAMES FOR MALE HOMOSEXUALS

The use of the name Molly for an effeminate homosexual goes back to the early eighteenth century in London where the **molly houses** (male brothels and places of assignation) became notorious. The related form Mary Ann (Molly is a familiar form of the name Mary) seems to belong mainly to nineteenth-century England. Other women's names chosen to refer to gay men have been Cissy (or Sissy), Gussie (Australian), Jessie (British), Margery, Nance/Nancy (common especially after World War I), Nellie, Nola (rare), and Pansy (intersecting with **flower** terminology). While this list could be extended almost indefinitely, these seem to have been the most common names in the English-speaking world. In America in the 1950s, the word nellie (or nelly) was a general adjective meaning "obviously **effeminate**" (the antonym of "butch"), while Mary was often used in the vocative to address any fellow homosexual ("Well, Mary . . .").

Parallels occur in other languages, e.g., Spanish *maricón* and *mariquita* (from María), Portuguese *Adelaida*, and Italian *checca* (from Francesca). In the Flemish-speaking part of Belgium the word *janet* (from French Jeannette) is a generic term for homosexual.

It is a little-known fact that **etymological** analysis shows that a number of key slang terms (common nouns and adjectives) for gay men stem from previous use as pejorative appellations for women. Thus before being applied to homosexuals, **faggot** meant "a slatternly women," while **gay** referred to "a fallen woman; prostitute." The modern **slang** word queen derives from a conflation of standard English *queen*, "consort of a king monarch,"and the obsolete *quean*, "prostitute."

The ultimate grounding of all these acts of naming is the widespread acceptance of the idea of **inversion**—that male homosexuals have feminine qualities, while lesbians have masculine ones. Evidence is much slighter for a lesbian counterpart for these procedures of "transnaming." In Radclyffe **Hall's** *The Well of Loneliness* (1928), however, the heroine is called Stephen.

A question that has received little attention is why a few male names are taken by gay people to be stereotypically suitable for themselves. Until recently at least, Bruce was so regarded in the United States. In Germany Detlev (Detlef) has the same reputation; in France Emile. It may be that these names are a subset of a larger category of given names, such as Algernon and Clarence, considered **sissy**.

Some **campy** coteries have affected the feminine pronouns *she* and *her* for gay men. When these appellations are extended to straight men, the implication is that their heterosexuality is tainted and may soon crumble. Ultimately, there lurks the covert suggestion that all men are gay. Since those who are engaged in this verbal guerrilla war are usually admirers of the **macho** type they would appear to be cutting the ground out from under their feet. In such coteries male names of group members are regularly changed to female ones, e.g., Charles becomes Charlotte, and Don, Donna. These habits seem to be fading.

Wayne R. Dynes

WOOLF, VIRGINIA (1882–1942)

English novelist and essayist. The daughter of Sir Leslie Stephen, a prominent Victorian intellectual, Virginia Woolf was educated largely through reading books in the family library. Unlike her brothers, she did not go to university, and this perceived slight was later to sustain her feminist critique of discrimination against women. In 1912 she married Leonard Woolf, a brilliant Cambridge graduate who had served as a judge in Ceylon, and her sister Vanessa married the art critic Clive Bell. The two couples were major figures in the **Bloomsbury** group, which also included such male homosexual writers as E. M. **Forster**, John Maynard **Keynes**, and Lytton **Strachey**. Through much of her life Virginia suffered from severe spells of mental depression, and it was partly to provide work therapy that she and Leonard founded the Hogarth Press in 1917. At this time she also became a regular reviewer for the *Times Literary Supplement*, a task which brought her knowledge of a wide range of modern literature and laid the foundations for her later more substantial essays.

Virginia Woolf remained a virgin until her marriage, and found the idea of sex with a man repellent. At the time of their engagement she warned Leonard of this aversion, and their sexual relations seem to have been rare. Before marriage Virginia Stephen was closely attached to her sister Vanessa—loving her almost to the point of "thought-incest"—and was deeply involved platonically with Madge Vaughan, a daughter of John Addington **Symonds**, and Violet Dickinson, to whom she wrote an enormous number of letters. Throughout her life, Woolf was to draw emotional sustenance from her intense relations with other women.

Her first novel, *The Voyage Out* (1915), concerns the trip of a young Englishwoman to South America, followed by her engagement and death there. While this novel was conventional in form,

Jacob's Room (1922) joined the mainstream of innovative modernism through its poetic impressionism and indirection of narrative development. After this work, which marks her real beginning as a literary artist, Woolf secured her place in modernism by a series of carefully wrought books. *Mrs. Dalloway* (1925) blends interior monologue with the sights and sounds of a single day in central London. *To the Lighthouse* (1927) explores the tensions of the male–female dyad in the form of a holiday trip of Mr. and Mrs. Ramsey. Its fantastic form notwithstanding, *Orlando* (1928) is of great personal significance, tracing the biography of the hero–heroine through four centuries of male and female existence. This book is a tribute to, and portrait of, her lover Vita **Sackville-West**, whom she had met in 1922. Woolf's most ambitious novel is probably *The Waves* (1931) which presents the contrasting personalities of six characters through a series of "recitatives" in which their inner consciousness is revealed. Shortly after completing her last book, *Between the Acts* (1941), she suffered a final bout of mental illness and drowned herself in a river near her country home.

The posthumous publication of Virginia Woolf's *Letters* and *Diaries* have revealed some unattractive aspects of her personality: she was xenophobic and snobbish, sometimes given to expressions of personal malice, as well as **anti-Semitic** and **homophobic** asides. Yet she participated wholeheartedly in the Bloomsbury ethic of individual fulfillment and social enlightenment. Her use of stream-of-consciousness techniques, and other sophisticated literary devices, places her very near the front rank—if not within it—of **modernist** writers in English.

With the general decline of the Bloomsbury ethos in the middle decades of the century, Woolf's reputation seemed to fade. In the 1970s, however, feminist critics hailed her as a major champion of their cause. There is no doubt that *A Room of One's Own* (1929), and its sequel, *Three*

Guineas (1938), are powerful pleas for women's creative independence. Yet her own feminism was fluid and variable, and thus not easily accommodated to present-minded uses. Throughout her life she struggled valiantly against mental illness, succeeding in building up an imposing corpus of writings while expressing her own emotional feelings in her deep relationships with women.

BIBLIOGRAPHY. Quentin Bell, *Virginia Woolf*, New York: Harcourt Brace Jovanovich, 1972; Louise DeSalvo, *Virginia Woolf: The Impact of Childhood Sexual Abuse on Her Life and Work*, Boston: Beacon, 1989; Lyndall Gordon, *Virginia Woolf: A Writer's Life*, London: Oxford University Press, 1984; Herbert Marder, *Feminism and Art: A Study of Virginia Woolf*, Chicago: University of Chicago Press, 1968; S. M. Squier, *Virginia Woolf and London: The Sexual Politics of the City*, Durham: North Carolina University Press, 1985.

Evelyn Gettone

WORKING CLASS, EROTICIZATION OF

For at least several generations, upper-class Englishmen have sought sexual companionship among the working **class**, including the enlisted men of the **military** (the availability at a fee of Guardsmen for these purposes has become legendary). While this practice, which Timothy d'Arch Smith termed the "Prince and Pauper Syndrome" after Mark Twain's 1882 novel, is hardly limited to England, it is there that it has been most documented, particularly in literature.

E. M. **Forster**, whose novel *Maurice* celebrates the aspiration for a permanent version of such a relationship, remarked: "I want to love a strong young man of the lower classes, and be loved and even hurt by him." (1938). Oscar **Wilde** described his own forays, which tended to involve the criminal underworld, in the striking image of "feasting with panthers." In a more idealizing fashion, John Addington **Symonds** wrote in 1893, "The blending of social strata in masculine love seems to me one of its most pronounced, and socially hopeful, features. Where it appears, it abolishes class distinctions, and opens by a simple operation the cataract-blinded eyes to their futilities." One of the reasons why Walt **Whitman** had such an impact on English homosexuals of this period was that his praise of democracy was (mis)understood in large part as a veiled plea for such prince-and-pauper liaisons. In France, the leftist writer Daniel Guérin justified his innumerable one-night stands with blue-collar workers as a device for achieving collective revolutionary solidarity.

The psychological roots of the aristocracy's attraction to the working class have not been systematically examined, but are undoubtedly related to a sense that the upper class (in particular its intellectuals) has lost some of its masculine vitality, has become "effete," refined, sophisticated, removed from the exercise of physical power, while the (young) males of the lower class are more robust, earthy, grounded, more in touch with their sexuality, more physically aggressive, in short, more **macho**. For economic reasons alone, the ranks of male **prostitutes** tend to be filled from the underclass, and these are more readily available than the sons of the higher classes. There are suggestions of a streak of masochism connected with guilt derived from perceived inequities of class standing. Perhaps it is as much the attraction of opposites, the tension of distance temporarily resolved in the intimacy of sex. The homosexual aristocrat often appears to enjoy a reversal of usual power relationships, giving the working-class male the upper hand in the bedroom, yet paradoxically retaining a firm control over the general relationship. Indeed, the disparity in financial power between the two parties serves to strengthen the aristocrat's sense of overall security (the poor male being too dependent on the largesse of the rich one). At the same time the coarse machismo of the aggressive, disorderly, non-law-abiding working-class male (and especially of the prostitutes, small-time criminals, and members of the armed forces who are most likely to be involved in such relationships) provides the spice of perceived danger to heighten sexual tension.

For the working-class male, there is in addition to financial incentives also the satisfaction of at least temporary domination—in a sphere which is a critical part of his self-imagery—of the otherwise loftily superior aristocrat, and moreover the adventure of obtaining glimpses of an otherwise fabled but unobtainable lifestyle. Psychologically, there is often, on the part of working-class men who remain in what they see as the "male" role, a sense of contempt for the "weak" aristocrat, which serves as compensation for the socially-propagated sense of inferiority of the class as a whole, and feelings of conquest which support a sense of masculinity and therefore help justify participation in homosexual acts.

In America there is a related phenomenon between members of the vast middle class and the working class, and to some extent between layers of the middle class itself. This motif is seen most prominently in the eroticization of such working-class occupations as construction worker, truck driver, cowboy, farmhand, enlisted serviceman, stock clerk, as reflected in gay-oriented art, **pornography**, and the like. It is also a factor in many if not most interracial relationships. An ironic twist to this theme has been the simulation of working-class play roles by members of the educated upper middle class when they dress for social encounters in gay bars; blue-collar work **clothes** are perceived as sexy, whereas tailored business suits are not.

There is some debate as to the extent of sexual democratization in the homosexual **subculture**. Observers have little doubt that non-commercial sexual liaisons cross class lines far more frequently than in heterosexual circles, and that an attractive young son of the work-

ing class can parlay his looks into upward mobility in a way known to the heterosexual culture only for a select few females. On the other hand, there is a question as to how many of these cross-class connections lead to long-lasting relationships; in the long run non-sexual affinities and differences may prove more powerful than the sexual stimulus of an interclass encounter. Even short-term relationships, however, provide exposure to differing class mores and economic situations, and it is at least arguable that these links have led to more political support for the working class among middle-class homosexuals than would otherwise be expected.

These class-crossing associations may be said to be part of a larger phenomenon whereby opposites attract. The parallel—and overlap—with interracial relations has been noted above. Other phenomena that may be psychologically related are intergenerational eroticism and the sexual pursuit of simpletons sometimes termed morophilia.

See also **Fiedler Thesis**.

Stephen Donaldson

WYNEKEN, GUSTAV (1875–1964)

German educator and pedagogical theorist. Born in Stade near Hamburg as the son of a Lutheran minister, Wyneken endured unpleasant experiences at the Ilfeld Boarding School that were one source of his impetus for educational reform. Through Hermann Lietz (1868–1919), the founder of the first Country Home School at Ilsenburg in 1898, he made contact with the educational reform movement. But after some years at Ilsenburg, Wyneken and a group of adherents, among them Paul Geheeb, split off in 1906 to form the Wickersdorfer Freie Schulgemeinde (Wickersdorf Free School Community). Located near the village of Wickersdorf in the Thuringian Forest, the school with its 140 pupils was an example of the pedagogical island: a nascent society of adolescents detached from the larger adult society around them, but possessing a *Jugendkultur* (youth culture) of its own that could be the nucleus of a future social order different from the existing one. But in contrast with the Wandervogelbewegung (the German equivalent of the Boy Scout movement) and the Country Home School Movement, the Wickersdorf community was not nationalist or pietistic in its ideology. It professed an international outlook, since Wyneken taught that the nation does not exist for itself alone, but as part of the higher division of labor within the world community; that if the nation possesses a specific genetic, historical, and cultural heritage, these have meaning only insofar as they outstandingly or uniquely fit it to perform certain of the eternal tasks of mankind as a whole. He rejected as a thing of the past the narrow, chauvinistic education that taught the pupil to hate and despise foreign nations and their cultures.

In the life of the school *Kameradschaften* (comradeships) between teacher and pupil served to institutionalize the pedagogical eros. It was a freely chosen relationship that entailed fidelity, veneration and love. The teacher-leader and pupil-friend addressed each other in the familiar *Du* form and on a first-name basis. The older friend bore in every respect the responsibility for the pupils under his charge. But though these bonds were an integral part of the school's functioning now and then they gave rise to tension and rivalry, in part because the attachments were exclusive and emotionally demanding and could lead to intense possessiveness and an unwillingness to accept the transitory character of the union.

In the fall of 1920 Wyneken became the center of a scandal inside the Wickersdorf School Community. Some of his fellow teachers accused him of having committed homosexual acts with boys in his friendship circle, and even of twice having embraced pupils while nude. Wyneken had to resign as leader of the school to avert possible closing by the government, though a committee of inquiry appointed by the school itself concluded that his conduct did not imply homosexual relations. But a libel suit filed against a teacher named Kurt Hoffmann backfired when the public prosecutor in nearby Rudolstadt brought charges against Wyneken for violating Paragraph 174, Section 1 of the Penal Code (indecent acts with minors), and in the trial that took place behind closed doors on August 30, 1921 he was found guilty and sentenced to one year in prison. Wyneken appealed his conviction and defended his conduct in a book entitled *Eros* (1921), in which he dissociated his behavior from modern homosexuality and likened it to the pedagogical eros of Greek antiquity, to a "new **Hellenism**."

A great controversy ensued in which the main wing of the homophile movement which championed the theories of Magnus **Hirschfeld** was at odds with those who defended *paiderasteia* as superior to modern homosexuality, while those who sought to classify homosexual relationships with minors as pathological denounced Wyneken for "attempting to rationalize homosexuality"—an accusation he rejected. A *roman à clef* about the affair was even written by Erich Ebermeyer under the title *Kampf um Odilienberg* (Struggle for Odilienberg). Even though Wyneken championed a concept of pedagogical eros in which the sensual element was overtly denied, the fate of his experiment was noted by other champions of "free schools," in Germany and elsewhere, who thereafter tried to exclude every scintilla of erotic content from their institutions.

BIBLIOGRAPHY. Thijs Maasen, *De pedagogische eros in het geding*, Utrecht: Homostudies, 1988.

Warren Johansson

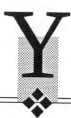

YOURCENAR, MARGUERITE (PSEUDONYM OF MARGUERITE DE CRAYENCOUR; 1903–1987)

Outstanding Belgian-born woman of letters, writing in French. A novelist, short story writer, essayist, poet, playwright, and translator, in 1980 she became the first woman elected to the French Academy. Long a United States resident, in 1982 she was named to the American Academy of Arts and Letters.

Although not an extremely prolific writer, Yourcenar published books beginning in 1921. As her output was on a consistently high level, she built up a reputation for being an author's author. Well versed in the world of classical antiquity, she was seen as a writer dealing with the universal issues of life and death in a detached, but hardly indifferent light. Translation of many of her works into English helped her win the broader audience she always deserved. Extremely reticent about her private life, Yourcenar was working at the time of her death on her autobiography *The Labyrinth of the World*, of which the first two volumes (about her mother's and father's families) have been published.

Throughout her career, Yourcenar showed much interest in male homosexual behavior. She wrote a significant essay on the poet Constantine **Cavafy** and the book *Mishima, or the Vision of the Void*. Her most important pre-World War II fictional works, the two short novels *Alexis* (1929) and *Coup de Grâce* (1937), inspired by André **Gide**'s use of the first-person form, deal with homosexual feeling without direct statement of the theme. In the two major novels of her later years, *The Memoirs of* **Hadrian** (1951) and *The Abyss* (1968), homosexuality is treated in broader social contexts, the **Roman empire** and sixteenth-century Europe, respectively. Yourcenar admired Rainer Maria Rilke and Thomas **Mann**. She translated novels by Henry **James** and Virginia **Woolf** into French. Her fictional works were collected in 1982 in a Pléiade edition, signaling literary canonization.

BIBLIOGRAPHY. Mathieu Galey, *With Open Eyes: Conversations with Marguerite Yourcenar*, Boston: Beacon, 1984; Pierre L. Horn, *Marguerite Yourcenar*, Boston: Twayne, 1985.

Peter G. Christensen

YOUTH

Perhaps the most forgotten, invisible **minority** in the modern industrial world is gay and lesbian teen-age youth. This condition is changing as an increasing number of young people are exploring and expressing sexual identities beyond the heterosexual ones traditionally recognized by society and its agents. Teens are faced, however, with both a hostile and an unbelieving world; they are told "You can't be a homosexual—I won't allow it," which amounts to saying "Society won't allow it."

Historical Patterns. The conceptualization of adolescence as a stage between childhood and adulthood is relatively recent, along with many current beliefs regarding the sexuality of teenagers. Today's parental and pedagogical concern over the development of a homosexual **identity** by teen-agers could not have arisen when the concept of homosexual identity had not taken root—

a situation that persists in much of the Third World today.

Through much of the world, and during much of Western history, the socially significant role of male youth in cultural patterns of homosexuality is and was as the junior partner in **pederasty**. In cultures which viewed pederasty as an accepted part of life, involvement with adult men was not held to have any lasting effect on the sexuality of the boy concerned; he would be sexually involved with an adult male while a teen-ager, then as an adult would marry and father children, while possibly taking a boy himself during the interval between those two stages. In ancient **Greece**, for example, it was considered acceptable for a citizen boy to take a receptive, "feminine" role in sex with another male, but once he reached full manhood he was limited to the aggressive "masculine" role.

In a few cultures, all boys were expected to gather some homosexual experience, and it might even be required for the ritual transition to manhood, as with some Melanesian tribes in the **Pacific** cultural sphere.

Basic Features of the Current Situation. In contrast to many other cultures, Western industrial societies remain permeated with negative attitudes regarding teen-age homosexuality. Yet it is not clear what effect these negative views have on the youth discovering his or her homosexuality. From their later vantage point, few adults can pinpoint exactly when they first became aware of their sexual **orientation**; it seems more of a process than an event, perhaps reflecting the amorphous nature of sexual orientation itself. Accordingly, homosexuality may be present before the ability to reflect and **label** sexual feelings and attractions emerges. This sequence was particularly true in the past, before the concept of homosexuality was widely presented in media accessible to young people, and when youngsters could be very active sexually with others of their sex without ever considering their behav-

ior "homosexual" or themselves "gay" or "lesbian." Even today, one of the characteristic features of homosexual involvement on the part of teen-agers is the lack of information accompanying these activities. Thus, a boy may be experienced with **oral** sex and never suspect the existence of **anal** sex, think that only **transvestites** are homosexuals, that he is the only person in his town who has erotic attraction to other males, that all boys engage in sex with each other, that **"faggots"** are despised but are not connected to anything sexual, and so forth.

In retrospect, many gay and lesbian youths report that they have always felt different and isolated from others without understanding why, but they knew that somehow the difference was important. One gay youth replied, "I always felt different, like I didn't fit in. I thought it was because I read and cared about art."

There is little agreement among investigators as to discrete variables that accurately predict a young person's ultimate sexual orientation or why he or she may feel different from other youths, though the existence of many such variables has been a source of speculation with varying degrees of supporting research evidence. Professionals, parents, and peers often make inferences about an adolescent's sexuality based on certain "suspicious" gender-atypical behaviors, dress, and mannerisms. The prevalence of childhood and adolescent gender-atypical behavior has been documented by a number of investigators; some posit **gender** nonconformity as a causative agent in the development of homosexuality, though this may beg the question: what causes the gender nonconformity? Researchers have suggested that at some level, the child and family know from an early point that the child is sexually "different." This knowledge ultimately affects the child and the family. By incorporating external values, the child learns that homosexuality is wrong, sick, and certainly, undesirable.

By adolescence, the youth with a homosexual identity has learned that she or he is among the most despised members of society and is thus faced with a number of decisions at a time when one may be least able to make the right choices. Should he play it safe and pass as heterosexual, aware of his own deception and of living a lie? Should she compartmentalize her life, separating her sexual self from all other activities and relationships? The answers have usually been provided, theoretically, in various **coming out** models that trace the step-by-step process, usually beginning in adolescence.

Young teens often escape condemnation and criticism for homosexual behavior (although not gender-atypical behavior) because the supposed psychodynamics of their sexuality, according to many psychologists, "allows" a phase of homosexual behavior in early adolescence. Teen-agers are expected to have these developmental detours and to outgrow them with a move to heterosexuality. To some, homosexual adolescents simply do not exist because adulthood must first be attained before a sexual orientation is set.

Explanations for Extent of Homosexual Behavior. Great effort, primarily anecdotal and clinical in nature, has been targeted at explaining the relatively high frequency of homosexual activity among teen-agers. Some argue that sexual experimentation and exploration with same-sex peers occur because their bodies and reactions are more familiar and therefore less threatening than those of their other-sex counterparts; others postulate that reassurance is gained from mutual comparison of size, shape, and sensations associated with changing bodies and sex organs; still others view these "transient homosexual activities" as the product of typical adolescent crushes, hero-worshipping, and intimate same-sex **friendships** (which does not explain why these crushes and so forth arise). More to the point may be the difficulties attendant upon *heterosexual* activity in the early teens, which range from surveillance/chaperoning through lack of privacy to the dangers of pregnancy and the fear (for a girl) of "ruining her reputation." One can even speak of an atmosphere of anti-sexuality (in a heterosexual context) enveloping the early teen-ager, who has just become aware of his or her sexuality and is experiencing a strong sexual drive for the first time. Even in North America, where the sexes are less segregated during the teen years than in most of the world, it is difficult for a young teen-age boy to initiate heterosexual intercourse successfully, whereas opportunities for homosexual experimentation are common, if not as frequently exploited. In more restricted societies, where heterosexual intercourse is virtually impossible for an unmarried teen-ager (with the exception of recourse to prostitutes, which few can afford), homosexuality provides his or her only sexual outlet.

Because only some of the teenagers who have homoerotic impulses ever become gay or lesbian adults, scholarly writers consistently refer to homosexual activities during this period as an aspect of a normal phase leading to adult heterosexual development; there need be no anxiety that they are the harbingers of lifelong homosexuality. Although soothing to concerned and frightened parents, this view may be potentially a source of self-denial if not great anxiety to the youth who is developing a homosexual identity which does not fit these expectations and which is not experienced as a temporary "phase" but rather as a comprehensive and stable sexual orientation tied to the sense of self. Historically and geographically, of course, any sense of self-identity as "homosexual" is culturally conditioned, raising serious questions which relate to but go far beyond this discussion.

Definition and Self-Definition. An additional difficulty is in defining the gay or lesbian youth to himself or herself. This is not an easy issue because at no other time in the course of life is an individual more likely to experience cross-orientation sexual contact or **bisexuality** and less likely to define the self as a homosexual individual. The problem is one of distinguishing homosexual identity, orientation, and homosexual behavior. Sexual behavior and sexual orientation may be independent for a given youth as she or he engages in many forms of sexual activity, with partners varying in age, sex, and other personal variables, regardless of self-labeled or self-professed sexual identity. Although it is likely that the three will be correlated, this may be more of a future than a present reality.

Some lesbian and gay youths live as homosexual virgins and, (as first documented in America by Alfred **Kinsey**) some "straight" youths have engaged in extensive and prolonged homosexual behavior. Youths who will later define themselves as "gay" are more likely than others to engage in homosexual behavior as teens and to do so for a longer period of time, but they are also frequent partakers of heterosexual behavior as well.

Awareness of same-sex attraction and arousal for youth usually begins during early adolescence, shortly after pubertal onset, with homosexual experiences delayed anywhere from moments to decades later. Labeling oneself as "homosexual," however, occurs later, during young adulthood in most studies of males and some several years later in studies of lesbians. The delay is usually attributed to antihomosexual discrimination and its effects on the developing adolescent, but it might also relate to the adolescent's lack of involvement in the gay **subculture** with its emphasis on self-definition along orientational lines.

The Question of Prevalence. Given the complexity of whether one defines homosexuality by reference to behavior or self-label and the fact that many youths experience a diversity of sexual behaviors and an emerging sexual identity over a period of several years, a process which may not be completed until young adulthood, it is difficult to assess the prevalence of homosexual orientation among youth. Some studies are promising in their attempts to describe the incidence and prevalence of both homosexual activity and identity during adolescence, as well as the relationship between the two, but they are limited by their retrospective nature. Only a few empirical studies have been conducted with gay and lesbian youths as the research participants.

The paucity of research on gay and lesbian youth is both prevalent and appalling. Among the contributing factors are the hesitancy of social scientists to confront the stigmatic, legal, and moral issues involved with studying gay and lesbian minors; the invisibility of gay and lesbian youths to themselves, thus compounding the difficulty of finding them as research participants; and the view of those who define homosexually behaving adolescents as individuals temporarily detained from their destination as heterosexual adults. Given these problems, social scientists either ignore gay and lesbian youth or they rely on adult retrospective data-gathering techniques that make particular and often debatable assumptions concerning the accuracy of recall data. Many studies are limited to gay and lesbian adults; these ignore homosexually active teen-agers who do not grow up to become gay-defined adults.

Similarities and Differences with the General Youth Population. In very important ways gay and lesbian youth are similar to other youth, despite the frequently cited and belabored differences that have been the primary mainstay of social scientists bent on gay-versus-straight dichotomies. If indeed it proves to be the case that sexual orientation produces minimal differences in developmental processes, then there is a need for studies of the homosexual population that focus on generic patterns within a homosexual context to see how these patterns are affected by that context. With this effort social scientists would increase the likelihood of learning about normal development in all its manifestations among gay and lesbian youth.

Coming Out. For those who come to consider their homosexuality inevitable and true to their sense of self and who decide to contradict their previous social and assumed sexual identity, there are few sources of assistance. Gay and lesbian organizations have shied away from dealing with them, perhaps because they fear the issue is too controversial (capable of being perceived as a disguised attempt to "**recruit**" young people) and complex (the social, legal, and economic status of dependent youth), or because they lack the personnel, knowledge, and funds to offer support.

Personnel in youth service agencies, schools, youth organizations such as the Boy Scouts and Girl Scouts, and religious youth groups have also been notably reluctant to provide support for self-identified lesbian and gay youth. In New York City the Board of Education has provided an alternative school environment where identified gay and lesbian teen-agers can escape harassment (the Harvey Milk School), but this is a notable exception to a general refusal to address these questions. If anything, adult gay men and lesbians, who might be able to provide constructive role models and sympathetic **counseling**, are systematically excluded from positions that would make them accessible to minors.

Lesbian and gay youths often consider the restrictions which society places on adults' sexual interactions with minors, such as statutory rape (age of **consent**) and child molestation laws, to be infringements on their own rights and a denial of their own sexuality. They complain that adults are inhibited from showing any affection to youths or from supporting them in their struggles against oppression.

Ritch C. Savin-Williams

The London Survey. The most difficult area for "coming out" youths is parents. A survey of over 400 gay and lesbian teen-age Londoners conducted in 1983 by the London Gay Teenage Group found that, of the 250 teens who had come out to parents, in just over half the cases, parents' initial reaction was either "good," "reasonable," or "indifferent." Over a third of the youths reported negative reactions, with the remainder mixed.

Most (61 percent) of the young lesbians, but a quarter of the gay boys in the survey reported that their first sexual experience was heterosexual. The girls reported their first homosexual experience came on the average at age 16 or 17 (with 32 percent at 15 or under), while 62 percent of the boys reported their first homosexual experience at 15 or under. For the boys, their first homosexual experience was very likely with someone older: half of the boys' first partners were 20 or older; for girls it was 43 percent.

At school, youths found that sex education materials rarely provided any useful information about homosexuality. The London survey indicated that homosexuality was four times more likely to be brought up in Religion class than in Sex Education. Only 5 percent of the London youths said they had found any helpful information on homosexuality in their school library.

Somewhat more than half the survey respondents were known to someone in secondary (high) school as homosexual, and almost all of these reported problems as a result. Boys in particular experienced verbal abuse (25 percent) and beatings (16 percent), girls pressure to conform (15 percent) and ostracism (10 percent); both sexes reported isolation (25 percent) and teasing (13 percent). A little over half of these youths reported they knew someone else in school who was gay.

Youths were more likely to be known as homosexual while in college, with 68 percent reporting such knowledge; two-thirds of these knew another gay **student**. Female college students reported more of a sense of isolation (34 percent) than males did (20 percent).

The first person told about the teen's sexuality was usually (55 percent) a friend, followed by siblings (8 percent), mothers (7.5 percent), and lovers (6 percent). The next step in breaking out of the isolation is often to make contact with another homosexual; only 16 percent found this among their friends, with a quarter going to a gay pub or club and 18 percent through a telephone switchboard or the London Gay Teenage Group itself.

Asked to comment on the gay social scene, the London teens tended to criticize the gay pubs and clubs for being too expensive, with too much pressure to drink, and keeping hours too late for them (especially for those still living with parents). In London it is legal for an unaccompanied 16 year old to enter a pub, and the drinking age is 18.

Well over half of the London respondents reported having or having had "a long term homosexual lover"; two-thirds said they were happy with their sex lives, while a third of the unhappy respondents wanted a lover and another third of the unhappiest wanted more of it. Just under 40 percent of the boys reported having had homosexual sex with strangers in public **toilets** or outdoor **cruising** areas, often the only means known or accessible to them for meeting sexual partners.

Depression is often a problem for young homosexuals: 19 percent of the London respondents said they had attempted **suicide** because they were lesbian or gay. Trouble with **police** over homosexuality was reported by 21 percent of the boys and 9 percent of the girls, usually in the form of general harassment.

Runaways, Castaways, and Prostitutes. Self-identified gay and lesbian teenagers may undergo considerable harassment without being able to make use of adult defensive strategies such as finding a more hospitable work environment, moving to a large city or a heavily gay neighborhood, finding emotional support in gay social environments (often bars which do not admit minors), having gay roommates or lovers, and the like. For this reason, some gay and lesbian youth run away from home in hopes of finding a less hostile environment in the big city. Still others (11 percent of the London survey) are driven out of their homes by family members unable to deal with homosexuality or cross-gender behavior. While many of these youths eventually return home, having solidified their sense of sexual orientation in the meantime, others become drifters in the big cities. Some of these are able to find jobs or lovers to take them in, but many become involved in **prostitution**, a trade where youth is much in demand by **ephebophiles** (those interested in the older teens) and "puberphiles" (men interested in boys emerging from puberty) and constitutes nearly all of the supply.

For some gay-identified boys, street hustling seems an attractive endeavor, offering both sexual satisfaction and ready cash as well as entree to many new social worlds. For others, it is simply an occupation for which they are qualified and from which they are not barred by their youth. The lesbian-identified girl, on the other hand, may view prostitution as a distasteful if unavoidable means of earning a living.

Prostitution is also a home town scene of homosexual involvement for many teen-age boys. For some, it is the only means they know or trust for making contact with sexual partners, gay bars being unknown or off-limits owing to age restrictions, and peers ruled out because of fear of exposure.

Many male prostitutes are boys who do not identify themselves as gay, and this activity is justified and rationalized, especially among the sons of the working- and under-class, as an economic rather than an erotic endeavor. This also makes it attractive to boys who are unsure of their sexual orientation but would like to experience sex with other males, and therefore sometimes becomes a route that eventually leads to a homosexual or bisexual identification.

Organizational Responses. At the 1969 annual convention of the North American Conference of Homophile Organizations (NACHO), the NACHO Youth Committee, under Stephen Donaldson's chairmanship, issued a report denouncing the coalition's member organizations for discriminating against youth, maintaining high minimum age limits for membership, and ignoring issues of strong concern to youth such as age-of-consent laws and prostitution. At that time, only a few of the member groups in the homophile **movement** would have anything to do with minors: the Student Homophile League, Vanguard (a San Francisco organization of young male street prostitutes), and the Council on Religion and the Homosexual; the convention majority rejected the report.

With the explosion of gay liberation in the 1970s, gay and lesbian groups became somewhat more open to youths, student groups proliferated, and increasing numbers of cities developed independent youth groups. Groups primarily for youth below college age are still, however, comparatively few; only a few high schools are known to have recognized gay groups. Organizations of this sort have often suffered from lack of support by the adult gay and lesbian communities.

Stephen Donaldson

BIBLIOGRAPHY. Peggie Autin, et al., eds., *Growing Up Gay*, Ann Arbor, MI: Youth Liberation Press, 1976; Mervin Glasser, "Homosexuality in Adolescence," *British Journal of Medical Psychology*, 50 (1977), 217–25; Gilbert Herdt, ed., *Gay and Lesbian Youth*, Binghamton, NY: Haworth Press, 1989; A. Damien Martin, "Learning to Hide: The Socialization of the Gay Adolescent," *Adolescent Psychiatry*, 10 (1982), 52–65; Edward Paolella, "Resources for and about Lesbian and Gay Youth: An Annotated Survey," *Reference Services Review*, 12:2 (1984), 72–94; Thomas Roesler and Robert W. Deisher, "Youthful Male Homosexuality: Homosexual Experience and the Process of Developing Homosexual Identity in Males Aged 16 to 22 Years," *Journal of the American Medical Association*, 219 (1972), 1018–23; Ritch C. Savin-Williams, *Gay and Lesbian Youth: Expressions of Identity*, Washington, DC: Hemisphere, 1990; Lorraine Trenchard and Hugh Warren, *Something to Tell You . . . The Experiences and Needs of Young Lesbians and Gay Men in London*, London: London Gay Teenagers Group, 1984; R. R. Troiden, "Becoming Homosexual: A Model of Gay Identity Acquisition," *Psychiatry*, 42 (1979), 362–73.

ZENO OF CITIUM (335–263 B.C.)

Founder of **Stoic** philosophy, born at Citium on Cyprus, probably of Phoenician ancestry. In 313 he went to Athens to attend the Platonic Academy, but converted to Cynicism, in which vein he wrote his earliest treatises.

He taught in the *Stoa Poikile* (Painted Porch) at the foot of the Acropolis in Athens, where he drew many listeners. When Antigonus Gonatas, king of Macedonia, invited him to his court in Pella, he dispatched a disciple instead of going in person, breaking **Plato's** and **Aristotle's** tradition of serving tyrants. Zeno's complete philosophical system borrowed physics from Heraclitus and Aristotelian logic from Antisthenes and Diodorus the Megaran, but it was his ethics, according to which virtue is the only good and vice or moral weakness the only real evil, that comforted many during the wars and tyrannies of the successors of **Alexander the Great**, the late Roman Republic, and the Empire. A protégé of the Scipios, Paenatius of Rhodes (ca. 150 B.C.), introduced Stoic **philosophy** to **Rome** and harmonized it with the *mos maiorum* to make it the favorite philosophy of Romans until the third century when **Neo-Platonism** replaced it.

Antigonus of Carystus named Zeno as having been an exclusive boy-lover with no interest in women. Ethically Zeno regarded the choice of sexual object, whether male or female, as a purely personal matter. No objective criteria, he opined, can be adduced for preferring either homosexuality or heterosexuality. What is important is the management of one's life in accordance with enlightened self-interest. Zeno was also one of the first Greek philosophers to end his life by **suicide** when he believed that his usefulness was at an end, an example emulated by such followers as Cato the Younger and Seneca the Younger, the most famous Roman adherents except for the Emperor Marcus Aurelius, himself also an expounder of Stoicism.

BIBLIOGRAPHY. J. M. Rist, *Stoic Philosophy*, Cambridge: Cambridge University Press, 1969.

William A. Percy

ZOROASTRIANISM

The most important indigenous religion of ancient **Iran**, Zoroastrianism bears on the history of homosexuality because of its crucial influence on this aspect of **Judaism** and its sacred writings, as well as on the folk angelology and demonology of the intertestamental period and later centuries. The religion of Zoroaster survives today among the small Parsi community in India.

Although it reached its apogee during the Achaemenid Period (ca. 550–330 B.C.), the roots of Zoroastrianism extend much further back into Persian religious traditions relating to nature worship and good and evil spirits, and beyond these to Aryan (**Indo-European**) mythology with its division of celestial beings into two warring classes. This ancient dualism appeared in Greek mythology as the gods versus the titans, and in Indian tradition as the gods (*devas*) versus the demons (*asuras*), but in Persia the labels were reversed, so that the Aryan asuras became the good *ahuras* and the devas became the evil *daevas*. The prophet Zoroaster (from a

Greek version of Zarathustra), believed to have lived about 630–550 B.C., refined the ancient faith into a belief in seven good spirits and seven evil spirits, perpetually at war. Zoroaster said that Ahura Mazda, the chief of the good spirits, would triumph in the end.

The war between good and evil that is being waged in the universe has its counterpart within each individual. Zoroastrians were encouraged to seek piety by leading pure lives and doing good works. This would lead to a victory of good over evil in their personal lives and in the world. This worldview, which can be seen emerging in the sixth century B.C., exerted tremendous influence on Judaism, especially the later Essenes, the Greek and Roman Stoics, the early Christian gnostics, the **Manichaeans**, and the Mithraists, a hero cult which competed with early Christianity. The emphasis on sexual purity in early **Christianity** may well stem ultimately from this Iranian influence.

Shortly after Zoroaster, the Achaemenid family under Cyrus the Great (d. 529 B.C.) established the Persian Empire, which conquered most of western Asia, including Judea, homeland of the Jews. Darius I (d. 486 B.C.), the first Persian ruler certain to have been a Zoroastrian, placed Jews in positions of power and encouraged the restoration of their destroyed main temple and the adoption of a statute book to govern their reorganized community. This included the Holiness Code of Leviticus 12:26; it is here that the death penalty for certain forms of homosexuality appears for the first time (20:13).

The Persian influence can be seen if we compare Leviticus 18:22 and 20:13 with the following passage from the Zoroastrian *Zend Avesta*: "Who is the man who is a Daeva? . . . Ahura Mazda answered: 'The man that lies with mankind as man lies with womankind, or as a woman lies with mankind, is the man that is a Daeva; this one . . . is a female paramour of the Daevas, that is a she-Daeva.'" (Vendidad, Fargard VIII, V:31–32). Noteworthy here is the equal guilt of both parties, unusual for the ancient world, and the ascription of femininity to the guilty. The same chapter proscribes 800 stripes for involuntary emission of semen. Elsewhere in Zoroastrian tradition permission is given for the killing of a homosexual man caught in the act (Commentary on Fargard VIII, VIII:74). Leviticus 20:13 similarly rules: "If a man also lie with mankind, as he lieth with a woman, both of them have committed an abomination: they shall surely be put to death; their blood shall be upon them." The Levitical laws, like the comparable Zoroastrian rules, are cultic—certain behaviors are condemned because they pollute the cult. They may never have been intended to condemn anything other than cohabitation of males with male cultic prostitutes, who were sacred functionaries of the old religions that preceded Zoroastrianism and Judaism.

The major contribution of Zoroastrianism to Western religion, however, was its extreme emphasis on moral dualism, the irreconcilable and never-ending conflict between Good and Evil. This dualism has had incalculable effects, painting any deviation from what is termed Good as something abhorrently Evil, thus giving rise to the notion that sodomites were "in league with the Devil" and had to be combatted with every available means.

BIBLIOGRAPHY. Vern Bullough, *Sexual Variance in Society and History*, New York: John Wiley, 1976; Edward Westermarck, *The Origin and Development of the Moral Ideas*, vol. II, London: Macmillan, 1906–08.

Tom Horner

Index

B oldfaced page numbers indicate an article on the topic.

An attempt has been made to include as many *thematic* entries as possible. Some of them, such as "research problems," are designed to stimulate future scholarship; others, such as "homosexuality, mandatory," seek to throw some light into little-known but interesting corners. For this reason, browsing through the Index may prove rewarding to a wide variety of users.

Titles of books, poems, short stories, plays, and films generally do not appear, but the names of their authors, directors, stars, and the like will be found. The most significant periodicals have been entered, but others omitted. Names in run-on series (e.g., Tom, Dick, and Harry) have been omitted. Scholars' names have been entered if found in the text, but not from the bibliographies or article signatures. Page numbers flow together (e.g., 88-92) even across articles, and a single page number may cover references in more than one article on the same page. The extent of this Index and its inherent complexity have precluded absolute uniformity of criteria and standards for listing. Subheadings do not appear under entries; if some of the resulting long strings of page numbers seem formidable, at least they will reward patient researchers with aspects of the subject at hand which they might otherwise never have encountered.

17, 949, 959, 986-88, 982-83, 997, 1006-07, 1063, 1167, 1207, 1237-38, 1417-18

Judaism, Sephardic: **644-48**, 740

Judeo-Christian tradition: 5-6, 197-98, 221-25, 227-31, 296-99, 432, 435, **648-49**, 728, 897, 915-17, 928, 954-59, 1228-30; see also Abrahamic religions, Judaism, Christianity

Julius Caesar—see Caesar, Julius

Julius II, pope: 241, 943-44

Julius III, pope: 241, 944

Jung, Carl Gustav: 57, 434, 531, **649-51**, 1075

Justinian, Byzantine emperor: 181, 197, 683, 685, 810, 870, 987, 1015, 1119, 1232

Juvenal: 348, **651-52**, 1104, 1123

juveniles—see boys, girls, youth, children (pre-pubic)

Juventius: 206

Kabbala: 581, 645, 656

kabuki: 635, 1291, 1316

Kabul (Afghanistan): 18

kadesh: 191, 486, 533, 541, 646, **653-56**, 682, 916, 1054, 1172, 1276, 1336

Kadesh Barnea (Palestine): 436, **654-56**

Kahlo, Frida: 82

Kainis (Kaineus): 531

Kainz, Joseph: 753, 1295

Kaliardá: **656-57**

Kallman, Chester: 91-92, 320

Kallmann, Franz J.: 459, 1331

Kamasutra: 586

Kameny, Franklin E.: 487, 840-43, 1255-56, 1349, 1385

Kampmann, Christian: **657**

Kamran, king of Afghanistan: 18

Kang Xi (K'ang Hsi): 217

Kansas City (Missouri): 843-44

Kant, Immanuel: 725, 914, 990

Kantorowicz, Ernst: 330, 381, **657-58**

Kaposi's Sarcoma: 30, 98

Kapparah, Rabbi Bar: 313

Karachi (Pakistan): 176

Kardiner, Abraham: 66

Karlinsky, Simon: 1295

Karsch-Haack, Ferdinand: 65, 629

kat(h)oey: 1289, 1336

Katte, Lt. Hans Hermann von: 428

Katz, Jonathan Ned: 1302

Kautilya: 589

Kawaguchi, E.: 171

Kawabata Yasunari: 636

Kazantzakis, Nikos: 281

Kelley, Leo P.: 1165

Kelly, Raymond: 937

Kemp, Lindsay: 1321

Kempf, Edward J.: 941-43, 1267

Kenna, Peter: 1302

Kennedy, Liz: 177

Kenya: 24, 305

Kepner, Jim: vii, 735

kept boys: 741, 1054-58

Kerouac, Jack: 117, **658-59**, 1348

Kertbeny, Károly Mária: 4, 267, 373, 411, 532, 548, 555, 629, **659-60**, 676, 1072, 1340

Key West (Florida): 469, 1109

Keynes, John Maynard, lord: 140, 153, 188, 340, 490, 417, **660-62**, 901, 1398

Khartoum (Sudan): 485

Khatib, Ibn al-: 489

Khayyam, Omar: 515, 612, 1006

khlysty: 1135, 1137

Khomeini, ayatollah: 198, 619, 878

Khronas, Yiorghos: 503

kin selection theory: 1216-17

King, Billie Jean: 88

King, Martin Luther: 1061

King James Version: 631

kings—see royalty

Kinks, The: 860

Kinsey, Alfred C.: 459, 510, 534, 559, 570, 584-86, 609, **662-66**, 1216, 1334

Kinsey Institute for Sex Research: 662-66, 734

Kinsey Reports: 74, 129, 144, 146, 149, 238, 253, 264, 329, 346, 361, 584-86, 662, 664-66, 685, 709, 777, 881, 1348, 1412

Kinsey scale: 584-86

Kinsman, Gary: 1087

Kipling, Rudyard: 1397

Kirkup, James: 1008

Kirkwood, James, Jr.: 865

Kirsch, John: 1217

Kitchen, Dennis: 251

Residencia de Estudiantes (Madrid): 1240
resorts: 159, 469, 1056, **1107-09**, 1196, 1242
Rettilbeini, Rognvaldr: 688
Reuvens, J. E.: 1374
Reve, Gerard: 272, 905
Revolution, French: 424, 703, 1141, 1380
Rex: 1027
Reynolds, Burt: 403
Rhadamanthus: 280
Rhode Island (USA): 1346
Rhodes, Cecil: 363, 877
Rhum (clown): 1360
rhyming slang: 1203
Ribeiro, Domingos Firminio: 163
ricchione: 794-96
Rice, Anne: 1027, 1145
Rich, Adrienne: 1010
Rich, Penelope: 109
Richard I, king of England: 355, **1109-10**, 1285
Richard of Devizes: 155, 355, 741, 812
Richardson, Frank M.: 874
Richardson, Samuel: 440
Richelieu, cardinal: 156, 423, 748
Richmond, Len: 63
Richter, Sviatoslav: 1138
Rigby, captain: 355
Rimbaud, Arthur: 155, 164, 425, 503, 1010, **1110**, 1368
rimming: 48, 930, 1189, 1286
Rinuccini, Ottavio: 933
Rio de Janeiro (Brazil): 164, 846, 1325
Ríos, Fernando de los: 1240
Ritsos, Yiannis: 503
ritual: 591, 597, 888, 937-38, 960-61, 1040, 1337, 1354, 1410; see also initiations
Rivas Cherif, Cipriano: 102
Roback, Abraham: 368
Roberts, Pudgy: 1321
Robertson, Pat: 1068
Robigalia: 1122
Robinson, Tom: 861, 1087
Rocco, Antonio: 34, 211, 343, 733
Rocco, Pat: 405
Rochester, John Wilmot, earl of: 355, 733, 1007, **1111**, 1293
rock (& roll) music: 118, 859-61, 1087-88
Rocke, Michael: 409

rococo: 910-11
Rode, Léon de: 124
Roditi, Edouard: 921
Rodman, James: 1217
Rodwell, Craig: 901, 1253
Rofes, Eric E.: 1265
Rogers, Adrian: 1062
Rogers, Carl R.: 267-68
Röhm, Ernst: 391, 404, 446, 547, 656, 882, **1111-12**, 1376
role models: 386, 709, 712-15, 814
role, sexual and gender: 9-11, 49, 57-58, 149-50, 177-79, 231-32, 235-38, 274-77, 333, 336-37, 347-49, 361-63, 376-78, 461-64, 494, 503, 594, 618-19, 674, 678-79, 710, 796-98, 814, 882, 884, 929-31, 940-41, 1036-40, 1085-86, 1096, **1112-15**, 1121-22, 1156-58, 1163-67, 1219, 1221, 1226, 1248-49, 1269, 1312, 1335, 1365, 1410
Rolfe, Frederick ("Baron Corvo"): 406, 1008, **1115-16**, 1366
Rolling Stones, The: 859-60
Romains, Hippolyte: 251
Roman Catholicism—see Catholic Church
Roman emperors: 67-68, 139, 180-81, 337, 378, 486, 514, 531, 884, 1005, **1116-19**, 1275, 1281
Romania: 126
Romanina, La: 802-03
Romans: 499, 533, 879, 897
Romanticism: 179-80, 212-13, 301, 446
Rome, ancient: 9-10, 67-68, 79, 82, 113, 139, 180, 185, 202, 206, 209, 231-32, 291, 300, 302-03, 308, 319, 348, 362, 363-64, 371-73, 377-78, 419-20, 444, 488, 491, 514, 519-20, 523, 562-63, 683, 752, 770-71, 807, 826, 870, 883-84, 902, 929, 954-55, 958, 965-66, 978-79, 1002-03, 1006, 1036, 1055, 1086, 1094, **1116-24**, 1195, 1206, 1275-76, 1280, 1291, 1307, 1313, 1315, 1354, 1367, 1373
Rome, medieval and modern: 43, 164, 165, 188, 199, 204, 225, 325, 379-80, 402, 943-44, 951-53
Rome, Peter de: 1026
Römer, L. S. A. M. von: 272, 457-58, 629, 891, **1126-27**, 1335